YEARBOOK OF EUROPEAN LAW

Editorial Statement

The *Yearbook of European Law* seeks to promote the dissemination of ideas and provide a forum for legal discourse in the wider area of European law. It is committed to the highest academic standards and to providing informative and critical analysis of topical issues accessible to all those interested in legal studies. It reflects diverse theoretical approaches towards the study of law. The *Yearbook* publishes contributions in the following broad areas: the law of the European Union, the European Convention for the Protection of Human Rights, related aspects of international law, and comparative laws of Europe.

Contributions for publication in the articles section should be sent to the following address:

Professor Takis Tridimas
Co-editor
Yearbook of European Law
Centre for Commercial Law Studies
Queen Mary College, University of London
13–14 Charterhouse Square
London
EC1M 6AX

Tel.: ++44(0)20 7882 6056
Fax: ++44(0)20 7882 5791
Email: t.tridimas@qmul.ac.uk

YEARBOOK OF
EUROPEAN LAW

24

2005

EDITORS

P. EECKHOUT
Professor of European Law
King's College London

T. TRIDIMAS
Sir John Lubbock Professor of Banking Law
Queen Mary College, University of London

BOOK REVIEW EDITOR

G. DE BÚRCA

OXFORD
UNIVERSITY PRESS

OXFORD
UNIVERSITY PRESS

Great Clarendon Street, Oxford OX2 6DP

Oxford University Press is a department of the University of Oxford.
It furthers the University's objective of excellence in research, scholarship,
and education by publishing worldwide in

Oxford New York

Auckland Cape Town Dar es Salaam Hong Kong Karachi
Kuala Lumpur Madrid Melbourne Mexico City Nairobi
New Delhi Shanghai Taipei Toronto

With offices in

Argentina Austria Brazil Chile Czech Republic France Greece
Guatemala Hungary Italy Japan Poland Portugal Singapore
South Korea Switzerland Thailand Turkey Ukraine Vietnam

British Library Cataloguing in Publication Data
Data available

Library of Congress Cataloging in Publication Data
Data available

Typeset by Newgen Imaging Systems (P) Ltd., Chennai, India
Printed in Great Britain
on acid-free paper by
Biddles Ltd., King's Lynn

ISBN 0–19–928537–3   978–0–19–928537–2

1 3 5 7 9 10 8 6 4 2

Editorial Committee

Contents

SURVEYS

REVIEWS OF BOOKS

Abbreviations

AC	Appeal Cases
AETR	Accord européen relatif au travail des équipages des véhicules effectuant des transport, internationaux par route (also ERTA)
AJCL	*American Journal of Comparative law*
All ER	All England Law Reports
AöR	*Archiv des öffentlichen Rechts*
Art.	Article
BVerfG	Bundesverfassungsgericht
BYIL	*British Yearbook of International Law*
CA	Court of Appeal
CAP	Common Agricultural Policy
CBI	Confederation of British Industry
CDE	*Cahiers de droit europeen*
CEN	European Committee for (technical) Standardization
CENELEC	European Committee for Electro-technical Standardization
CFI	Court of First Instance of the European Communities
CFiLR	*Corporate and Financial Law Review*
CFSP	Common Foreign and Security Policy
CLJ	*Cambridge Law Journal*
CLP	*Current Legal Problems*
CM/Cmnd	Command Paper
CML Rev.	*Common Market Law Review*
CMLR	Common Market Law Reports
DÖV	*Die Öffentliche Verwaltung*
DVBl.	*Deutsches Verwaltungsblatt*
ECB	European Central Bank
ECHR	European Convention on Human Rights
ECJ	European Court of Justice
ECLR	*European Competition Law Review*
ECHR	European Convention on Human Rights
ECrtHR	European Court of Human Rights
ECR	European Court Reports
ECSC	European Coal and Steel Community
EEA	European Environmental Agency
EFSA	European Food and Safety Authority

EIPA	European Institute of Public Administration
EFTA	European Free Trade Area
EJML	*European Journal of Migration and Law*
EL Rev.	*European Law Review*
ELJ	*European Law Journal*
EMU	*European Monetary Union*
EPL	*European Public Law*
ERPL	*European Review of Private Law*
ERTA	European agreement concerning the work of crews of vehicles engaged in international road transport (also AETR)
ESCB	European System of Central Banks
EU	European Union
EuGRZ	*Europäische Grundrechte-Zeitschrift*
EUI	European University Institute
Eu LR	European Law Reports
EuR	*Europarecht*
Euratom	European Atomic Energy Community
EuZW	*Europäische Zeitschrift für Wirtschaftsrecht*
GATS	General Agreement on Trade and Services
GATT	General Agreement on Tariffs and Trade
GG	Grundgesetz
GYIL	*German Yearbook of International law*
Harv LR	*Harvard Law Review*
HC	House of Commons
HL	House of Lords
IANL	Immigration Asylum and Nationality Law
ICLQ	*International and Comparative Law Quarterly*
IGC	Intergovernmental Conference
ILM	International Legal Materials
ILO	International Labour Organization
JBL	*Journal of Business law*
JCMS	*Journal of Common Market Studies*
JEPP	*Journal of European Public Policy*
JZ	*Juristenzeitung*
KB	King's Bench
LIEI	*Legal Issues of European/Economic Integration*
Lloyd's Rep	Lloyd's Law Reports
LQR	*Law Quarterly Review*

MEP   Member of the European Parliament
MJ   *Maastricht Journal of European and Comparative Law*
MLR   *Modern Law Review*

n.   footnote
NJW   *Neue Juristische Wochenschrift*

OECD   Organization for Economic Co-operation and Development
OFT   Office of Fair Trading
OJLS   *Oxford Journal of Legal Studies*
OLAF   European Anti-fraud Office
OSCE   Organization for Security and Co-operation in Europe

PL   *Public Law*

QB   Queen's Bench Division of the High Court
QMV   qualified majority voting

RIDC   *Revue Internationale de droit comparé*
RIDPC   *Rivista Italiana di Diritto Pubblico Comunitario*
RMCUE   *Revue du Marché commun et de l'Union européenne*
RMUE   *Revue du marche unique européen*
RTDE   *Revue trimestrielle de droit européen*

SEA   Single European Act
SLT   *Scots Law Times*

TEC   Treaty establishing the European Community
TEPSA   Trans European Policy Studies Association
TRIPS   Agreement on Trade-Related Intellectual
                 Property Rights

UCLA Law Rev.   *University of California at Los Angeles (Law Review)*
UN   United Nations Organization
UNTS   United Nations Treaty Series

WLR   Weekly Law Reports
WTO   World Trade Organization

YEL   *Yearbook of European Law*
YLJ   *Yale Law Journal*

ZaöRV   *Zeitschrift für ausländisches öffentliches Recht und Völkerrecht*

From Bit Part to Starring Role? The Court of Justice and Europe's Constitutional Treaty

*Anthony Arnull**

I. Background

The Court of Justice played something of a bit part in the proceedings of the Convention on the Future of Europe, inaugurated on 28 February 2002. None of the eleven Working Groups set up by the Convention was concerned specifically with the Court. It was not until late 2002, by which time most of the Working Groups had already reported, that the Praesidium (or steering group) was persuaded of the need to consider the implications for the Court of some of the proposals being made and of the desirability of giving both the Court and the Court of First Instance (CFI) a formal opportunity to express their views. Accordingly, a so-called 'Discussion Circle' on the Court was set up. It met for the first time on 17 February 2003 and held three further meetings before presenting its final report on 25 March 2003.[1] It published a supplementary report, on judicial control in the context of the Common Foreign and Security Policy (CFSP), on 16 April 2003.[2] Little over two months later, on 20 June 2003, Parts I and II of the draft Treaty establishing a Constitution for Europe were submitted to the European Council in Thessaloniki along with interim texts of Parts III and IV.[3]

The low profile of the Court in the deliberations of the Convention was attributable mainly to the recasting of the provisions on the Community's judicial architecture effected by the Treaty of Nice, which entered into force while the Convention was sitting.[4] The provisions on the Union Courts agreed at Nice were

---

* Professor of European Law and Director of the Institute of European Law, University of Birmingham. This article is based on a lecture given at King's College London on 24 November 2004 under the title 'Is Europe to have a Constitutional Court?'. The text was completed on 20 January 2005. It builds on an earlier article by the author on the effect of the draft Constitutional Treaty on the Court of Justice: see 'A Constitutional Court for Europe?' (2004) 6 CYELS 1.

[1] CONV 636/03.   [2] CONV 689/1/03 REV 1.

[3] The complete text of the draft Treaty was submitted to the President of the European Council on 18 July 2003: see CONV 850/03; [2003] OJ C169/1. It was accompanied by a report from the Presidency of the Convention which contains a useful overview of its proceedings: see CONV 851/03.

[4] The Treaty of Nice was signed on 26 February 2001. It entered into force on 1 February 2003.

incorporated largely unchanged in the draft Constitutional Treaty[5] and in the Constitutional Treaty itself, which was signed by the Member States in Rome on 29 October 2004.[6] The Treaty's effect on the Court of Justice would therefore be less dramatic than its effect on other institutions and bodies. Be that as it may, the Court has been described as 'one of the big "winners" in the Constitutional Treaty'.[7]

The purpose of this article is to examine the potential impact of the Constitutional Treaty on the Court and to consider what its place would be in the Union's new constitutional dispensation. The main focus will be on whether the Court emerges from the Treaty as a nascent constitutional court for Europe. To set the scene, it is first necessary to say something about the present position of the Court and its likely evolution under the regime agreed at Nice.

While there can be no doubt that the Court of Justice is not at present a specialised constitutional court of the type found in some Member States, it has been endowed by the Treaties with certain constitutional functions and has developed through its case law many principles of a constitutional character.[8] Among the existing constitutional functions of the Court of Justice might be included: (a) the power to rule on disputes between the other institutions over the scope of their respective powers; and (b) drawing the boundary between the competences of the Member States and those of the Community. Constitutional principles developed by the Court of Justice through its case law include direct effect, primacy and the principle of State liability as well as certain general principles of law, notably the principle of respect for fundamental rights and the right to effective judicial protection. The Court of Justice has even described the EC Treaty as 'the constitutional charter of a Community based on the rule of law'.[9]

As has been pointed out,[10] 'while certain heads of jurisdiction are more obviously constitutional in character than others, constitutional issues can arise is almost any type of proceedings before the Court, and the label "constitutional" is not particularly helpful in analysing the Court's various heads of jurisdiction.'

---

[5] See generally T. Tridimas, 'The European Court of Justice and the Draft Constitution: A Supreme Court for the Union?' in T. Tridimas and P. Nebbia (eds), *EU Law for the Twenty-First Century: Re-Thinking the New Legal Order, Volume I* (Oxford, Hart Publishing, 2004) ch 7; House of Lords EU Committee, 'The Future Role of the European Court of Justice' (Session 2003–04, 6th Report, HL 47).

[6] See [2004] OJ C310.

[7] See D. Chalmers, 'The Dynamics of Judicial Authority and the Constitutional Treaty' in J. Weiler and C. Eisgruber (eds), *Altneuland: The EU Constitution in a Contextual Perspective* (Jean Monnet Working Paper 5/04, http://www.jeanmonnetprogram.org/papers/04/040501.html) 1.

[8] See F.G. Jacobs, 'Is the Court of Justice of the European Communities a Constitutional Court?' in D. Curtin, and D. O'Keeffe (eds), *Constitutional Adjudication in European Community and National Law* (Butterworths, Ireland, 1992) ch 4.

[9] Opinion 1/91 on the creation of the European Economic Area [1991] ECR I-6079, para. 21. See also Case 294/83 *Les Verts v Parliament* [1986] ECR 1339, para 23. Interestingly, S. Finer, V. Bogdanor and B. Rudden, *Comparing Constitutions* (Oxford, Clarendon Press, 1995) contains, alongside the Constitutions of the USA, France, Germany and the Russian Federation, extracts from the TEU and the EC Treaty (plus the European Convention on Human Rights).

[10] Jacobs, above n 8 at 31.

That has proved inconvenient in settling on the right division of functions between the Court of Justice and the CFI.

At present, the CFI deals with all direct actions brought by natural and legal persons and, since 1 June 2004, with a limited category of direct actions brought by Member States.[11] At Nice,[12] the Treaty was amended to make it possible for the CFI to be given a preliminary rulings jurisdiction.[13] However, references affecting the 'unity or consistency of Community law' would be 'subject to review' by the Court of Justice if not referred on to the Court of Justice by the CFI on their arrival in Luxembourg.[14] In addition, the Council was given the power to attach to the CFI[15] a new type of tribunal known as judicial panels[16] 'to hear and determine at first instance certain classes of action or proceeding brought in specific areas'.[17] In November 2004, the Council reached agreement on the establishment of the first such panel. To be called the European Union Civil Service Tribunal,[18] it will exercise jurisdiction at first instance in staff cases in place of the CFI. There will be a right of appeal on points of law to the CFI, whose own decisions will in turn 'exceptionally be subject to review by the Court of Justice . . . where there is a serious risk of the unity or consistency of Community law being affected'.[19] The Treaty of Nice also made provision for challenges to decisions of the CFI to be subjected by the Court to a filtering (or leave) mechanism.[20]

The judicial architecture envisaged at Nice is therefore now beginning to take shape. Over time, this process is likely to consolidate the constitutional nature of the

[11] See Dec. 2004/407 of 26 April 2004, amending Arts 51 and 54 of the Protocol on the Statute of the Court of Justice, [2004] OJ L132/5.
[12] See generally P. Eeckhout, 'The European Courts after Nice' in M. Andenas and J. Usher (eds), *The Treaty of Nice and Beyond* (Oxford, Hart Publishing, 2003) ch 11; L. Gormley, 'The Judicial Architecture of the European Union after Nice' in A. Arnull and D. Wincott (eds), *Accountability and Legitimacy in the European Union* (Oxford, OUP, 2002) ch 8; A. Johnston, 'Judicial Reform and the Treaty of Nice' (2001) 38 CML Rev 499; A. Dashwood and A. Johnston (eds), *The Future of the Judicial System of the European Union* (Oxford, Hart Publishing, 2001); A. Arnull, 'Modernising the Community Courts' (2000) 3 CYELS 37; C. Turner and R. Muñoz, 'Revising the Judicial Architecture of the European Union' (1999–2000) 19 YEL 1.   [13] See Art 225(3) EC.
[14] See Art 62 of the Court of Justice Statute.   [15] See Art 220 EC.
[16] Referred to in the Constitutional Treaty as 'specialised courts': see Art I-29(1).
[17] Art 225a EC.
[18] See Dec. 2004/752 of 2 November 2004 establishing the European Union Civil Service Tribunal, [2004] OJ L333/7. cf COM(2003) 828 final, proposing the establishment of a judicial panel (to be called the 'Community Patent Court') to exercise jurisdiction at first instance in disputes relating to the proposed Community patent. The latter proposal was accompanied by a proposal for a decision conferring on the Union Courts and the judicial panels jurisdiction in disputes relating to the Community patent: see COM(2003) 827 final. The proposed decision would be based on Art 229a EC, which requires unanimity in the Council and adoption by the Member States in accordance with their respective constitutional requirements. Art III-364 substitutes the ordinary legislative procedure (ie co-decision) for unanimity and abolishes the requirement for adoption by the Member States.
[19] Art 225(2) EC.
[20] See Art 225(1), (2) and (3), which each stipulate that appeal or review is only permissible 'under the conditions and within the limits laid down by the Statute'.

Court's work. The CFI is conceived as evolving into a court of general jurisdiction—indeed, the Constitutional Treaty calls it the General Court—dealing not only with direct actions brought by natural and legal persons but also with some direct actions brought by institutions and Member States and routine preliminary rulings as well as appeals from judicial panels. The work of the Court of Justice will increasingly comprise mainly the cases which are most likely to raise constitutional questions in the broad sense[21]: (i) the most important direct actions brought by Member States and institutions; (ii) the most important cases referred by national courts; (iii) appeals from decisions of the CFI which the Court of Justice will itself have selected on the basis of criteria which are likely to include the difficulty and importance of the case; (iv) applications for review of CFI decisions where the unity or consistency of Union law is in issue; and (v) applications for opinions on the compatibility with the Treaty of proposed international agreements.

It is against that background that the effect of the Constitutional Treaty on the Court of Justice falls to be considered. In what follows, two categories of provision are singled out for discussion. They concern:

(a) the question of who would have jurisdiction to police the scope of the Constitutional Treaty; and

(b) prospective changes to the jurisdiction of the Court.

The article concludes with an attempt to assess whether the Constitutional Treaty would turn the Court of Justice into a fully-fledged constitutional court.

II. Policing the Scope of the Constitutional Treaty

A. Article I-6: Primacy

One of the provisions of the Constitutional Treaty which has attracted the most attention is Article I-6, which provides: 'The Constitution, and law adopted by the Union's institutions in exercising competences conferred on it, shall have primacy over the law of the Member States.' A declaration by the Member States notes that Article I-6 'reflects existing case law of the Court of Justice of the European Communities and the Court of First Instance'. That case law, beginning in 1964 with *Costa v ENEL*,[22] establishes that, where there is a conflict between a national rule and a European rule, precedence must be accorded to the latter. The status of the conflicting rule of national law is irrelevant: even a provision of a Member State's constitution must give way.[23]

---

[21] cf COM(2003) 660 final, 3–4.

[22] Case 6/64 [1964] ECR 585. See also Case 106/77 *Amministrazione delle Finanze dello Stato v Simmenthal* [1978] ECR 629; Joined Cases C–10/97 to C–22/97 *Ministero delle Finanze v IN. CO. GE. '90 and Others* [1998] ECR I-6307.

[23] See Case 11/70 *Internationale Handelsgesellschaft v Einfuhr- und Vorratsstelle Getreide* [1970] ECR 1125; Case 100/77 *Commission v Italy* [1978] ECR 879; Case C–285/98 *Kreil* [2000] ECR I-69.

Because the opening words of Article I-6 distinguish between the Union Constitution and law adopted by the Union's institutions, the provision arguably does not make it clear that 'the law of the Member States' embraces constitutional norms as well as legislation.[24] It has been contrasted[25] with the 'crystal clear' provisions of the second paragraph of Article VI of the US Constitution, which makes that Constitution, and Laws and Treaties made by the United States, 'the supreme Law of the Land . . . any Thing in the Constitution or Laws of any State to the contrary notwithstanding'. Nonetheless, there is little doubt, given the existing case law[26] and the declaration referred to above, that the Court of Justice would interpret Article I-6 as applying to national constitutional norms as well as to legislation. Otherwise, a Member State would be able to shield itself unilaterally from the requirements of Union law by means of an appropriate amendment to its constitution.

It is true that, by virtue of Article I-5(1), the Union would be required to 'respect the national identities of the Member States, inherent in their fundamental structures, political and constitutional . . . '. It has been suggested that this 'can plausibly be read to authorize domestic courts to set aside secondary EU law when it disrespects national constitutional identities *as a matter of EU Law*'.[27] As we shall see, Article I-5(1) has been accorded significance by national courts when considering the compatibility of the Constitutional Treaty with their domestic constitutions. It undoubtedly constitutes an important guide to the relationship the Treaty is intended to establish and preserve between the Union and the Member States. It is therefore relevant to the interpretation of the Treaty and to the interpretation and validity of Union acts (matters on which, as explained below, the Court of Justice would remain the ultimate arbiter). But in the last resort Article I-5(1) is unlikely to affect the capacity of valid provisions of Union law, properly interpreted, to take precedence over conflicting norms contained in domestic constitutions.

B. The Question of *Kompetenz-Kompetenz*

Article I-6 confers primacy on law adopted by the institutions of the Union only where they are 'exercising competences conferred on it'. It therefore fans the flames of a debate which ignited with the (in)famous Maastricht decision of the German

---

[24] See T. Tridimas, House of Lords EU Committee, 'The Future Role of the European Court of Justice' (Session 2003–04, 6th Report, HL 47), Minutes of Evidence, 102.

[25] See M. Kumm and V. Ferreres Comella, 'The Future of Constitutional Conflict in the European Union: Constitutional Supremacy after the Constitutional Treaty' in J. Weiler and C. Eisgruber (eds), *Altneuland: The EU Constitution in a Contextual Perspective* (Jean Monnet Working Paper 5/04, http://www.jeanmonnetprogram.org/papers/04/040501.html) 9.

[26] The effect of which would be preserved by Art IV-438(4).

[27] Kumm and Ferreres Comella, above n 25 at 10. See also J. Dutheil de la Rochère and A. Iliopoulou, House of Lords EU Committee, 'The Future Role of the European Court of Justice' (Session 2003–04, 6th Report, HL 47), Minutes of Evidence, 73.

Federal Constitutional Court of 12 October 1993.[28] The issue is whether ultimate authority to resolve disputes over the limits of the competences conferred on the Union lies with the Court of Justice or the supreme courts of the Member States. To use the German shorthand, the question is who has *Kompetenz-Kompetenz*, that is, competence to decide on the extent of a competence.

In the Maastricht decision, which involved a challenge to Germany's ability to ratify the Treaty on European Union (TEU), the Federal Constitutional Court held that there would be an infringement of the German Constitution if the act by which Community law became applicable in Germany did not establish with sufficient certainty: (a) the powers that were being transferred; and (b) what they were to be used for. What was essential was that the rights and duties flowing from Germany's membership should be defined in the Treaties so that the legislature could give effect to them with sufficient certainty. The Court found that the TEU satisfied those requirements. Like the Community Treaties, the TEU was based on the principle of conferred powers and the Union would not be competent to determine its own competences. The Member States remained the Masters of the Treaties and their further development.

However, in the course of dismissing the applicant's complaint, the Court engaged in some judicial sabre-rattling, declaring that, if the European institutions adopted an exorbitant interpretation of their powers under the Treaty, the resultant legislation would not be legally binding in Germany and the domestic authorities would not be permitted to apply it. The Federal Constitutional Court would therefore review legal instruments adopted by the European institutions to make sure they were acting within the limits of their powers.[29]

The decision of the Federal Constitutional Court[30] was followed some years later by the Danish Supreme Court,[31] but it involved an element of judicial sleight of

---

[28] The decision is reported in English as *Brunner v European Union Treaty* [1994] 1 CMLR 57. See M. Herdegen, 'Maastricht and the German Constitutional Court: Constitutional Restraints for an Ever Closer Union' (1994) 31 CML Rev 235; U. Everling, 'The Maastricht Judgment of the German Federal Constitutional Court and its Significance for the Development of the European Union' (1994) 14 YEL 1; J. Kokott, 'Report on Germany' in A.-M. Slaughter, A.S. Sweet and J. Weiler (eds), *The European Courts and National Courts: Doctrine and Jurisprudence* (Oxford, Hart Publishing, 1997) 77.

[29] See para 49 of the judgment.

[30] The decision gave rise to a large body of literature exploring some of the deeper themes running through it, such as the origins and character of the Community legal order, the nature of sovereignty and Statehood, the meaning of democracy and citizenship. See eg J. Weiler, 'Does Europe Need a Constitution? Reflections on Demos, Telos and the German Maastricht Decision' (1995) 1 ELJ 219; N. MacCormick, 'The Maastricht-Urteil: Sovereignty Now' (1995) 1 ELJ 259; J. Weiler, and U. Haltern, 'Constitutional or International? The Foundations of the Community Legal Order and the Question of Judicial *Kompetenz-Kompetenz*' in A.-M. Slaughter, A.S. Sweet and J. Weiler (eds), *The European Courts and National Courts: Doctrine and Jurisprudence* (Oxford, Hart Publishing, 1997) 331; M. Kumm, 'Who is the Final Arbiter of Constitutionality in Europe? Three Conceptions of the Relationship between the German Federal Constitutional Court and the European Court of Justice' (1999) 36 CML Rev 351.

[31] See *Carlsen and Others v Prime Minister Rasmussen* [1999] 3 CMLR 854; K. Høegh, 'The Danish Maastricht Judgment' (1999) 24 EL Rev 80. For the UK position, see *Thoburn and Others v Sunderland City Council and Others* ('Metric Martyrs') [2002] 1 CMLR 50 (QBD);

hand. In particular, it failed: (a) to acknowledge the requirements of the EC Treaty; or (b) to explore the legal consequences if a Community act were declared inapplicable in Germany. Under the EC Treaty, the question whether a Community institution has acted within the limits of its powers can be raised in a variety of ways, all of which leave the ultimate decision to the Court of Justice.

Most obviously, a direct action for the annulment of the contested act could be brought before the Union Courts on the ground of lack of competence, a ground explicitly mentioned in the second paragraph of Article 230 EC.[32] The jurisdiction of the Union Courts under that Article is exclusive.[33] Alternatively, the validity of a Community act may be raised indirectly in proceedings before a national court. If the national court needs to decide the issue in order to give judgment and takes the view that the contested act might be invalid, it must make a reference to the Court of Justice under Article 234 EC.[34] The ruling of the Court of Justice is binding on the referring court. If the Court of Justice finds the act valid, other national courts may not treat it as invalid without making a further reference to the Court of Justice.[35] The legality of a Community act may also be challenged in a claim against the Community for damages under the second paragraph of Article 288 EC, over which the Union Courts again have exclusive jurisdiction.[36]

The reason the Treaty gives the Court of Justice the last word on the validity of Community acts is not hard to find: it is to ensure that Community law applies uniformly throughout the Member States. Indeed, the larger the Union gets, the greater the risk of legal fragmentation. The threat to uniformity would be particularly great if each national supreme court were entitled to judge the validity of Community acts against its own constitutional standards, for the contents of national constitutions vary and may even be inconsistent with each other.[37] That is one of the reasons why the Court of Justice rejected the idea that national constitutional norms could provide a yardstick for judging the validity of Community acts.

In practice, the Federal Constitutional Court could therefore only be asked to review the *vires* of a Community act if the Court of Justice had either: (a) not been asked to rule on the act's validity; or (b) had rejected a challenge to its validity. If the Federal Constitutional Court were to find the contested act *ultra vires*

McWhirter and Gouriet v Secretary of State for Foreign and Commonwealth Affairs [2003] EWCA Civ 384 (5 March 2003) (CA).

[32] See also Art 35(6) TEU.

[33] See Case 314/85 *Foto-Frost v Hauptzollamt Lübeck-Ost* [1987] ECR 4199, para. 17.

[34] See *Foto-Frost v Hauptzollamt Lübeck-Ost, ibid*, para 20. National courts of last resort are in any event bound to refer by the third paragraph of Art 234 EC.

[35] See Case C–465/93 *Atlanta Fruchthandelsgesellschaft I* [1995] ECR I-3761; D. Anderson and M. Demetriou, *References to the European Court* (2nd edn, London, Sweet & Maxwell, 2002) 334–5.

[36] See Arts 235 and 240 EC.

[37] See J. Weiler, and U. Haltern, 'Constitutional or International? The Foundations of the Community Legal Order and the Question of Judicial *Kompetenz-Kompetenz*' in A.-M. Slaughter, A.S. Sweet and J. Weiler (eds), *The European Courts and National Courts: Doctrine and Jurisprudence* (Oxford, Hart Publishing, 1997) 331, 357–8.

(and therefore inapplicable in Germany) in either situation, it would be placing Germany in breach of its Treaty obligations. The outcome would mean that Germany had not complied with its obligation to secure within its territory the full effect of an act intended by virtue of Community law to be binding on it. If the validity of the act had not previously been the subject of a ruling by the Court of Justice and the Federal Constitutional Court did not refer the question to the Court of Justice itself, it would be in breach of its own obligations under Article 234. If, on the other hand, a ruling upholding the validity of the act had previously been made by the Court of Justice, the Federal Constitutional Court's failure to respect that ruling or to make a further reference would equally be incompatible with the Treaty.

These breaches might give rise to infringement proceedings by the Commission against Germany under Article 226 EC.[38] Recent case law[39] makes it clear that the decisions of national courts, particularly supreme courts, may be relevant to the question whether a Member State has complied with its Treaty obligations. In the absence of a procedural irregularity by the Commission, the Court of Justice would therefore be likely to find Germany in breach of the Treaty.[40] Germany would in that event be obliged by Article 228(1) EC to take the measures necessary to comply with the ruling of the Court of Justice. If it failed to do so sufficiently promptly, the Commission would be at liberty to ask the Court to impose a lump sum or penalty payment on it under Article 228(2).[41] What of an individual litigant who sought to rely before the German courts on a Community act which had been found to be *ultra vires* and inapplicable in Germany by the Federal Constitutional Court? If his action were dismissed on that basis, he might be entitled to claim damages from the German State in the German courts on the basis that he had suffered loss through the State's failure to comply with the Treaty. The Court of Justice has held[42] that a Member State is obliged to make good damage caused to an individual by an infringement of Community law stemming from a decision of a supreme national court.

---

[38] Or by another Member State under Art 227 EC. Other Member States might even retaliate unilaterally on the basis of some concept of reciprocity, although this would itself be unlawful: see eg Case C–5/94 *The Queen v MAFF, Ex p Hedley Lomas* [1996] ECR I-2553, para 20.

[39] Case C–129/00 *Commission v Italy*, judgment of 9 December 2003.

[40] Member States cannot challenge the validity of directives or decisions addressed to them as a defence in infringement proceedings: Case C–52/00 *Commission v France* [2002] ECR I-3827, para 28. The position may differ in the case of regulations: see para 191 of the Opinion of AG Jacobs in Case C–11/00 *Commission v European Central Bank* [2003] ECR I-7147.

[41] If Germany refused to pay any financial penalty imposed on it, it would be committing a further breach of the Treaty: see U. Everling, 'The Maastricht Judgment of the German Federal Constitutional Court and its Significance for the Development of the European Union' (1994) 14 YEL 1, 15. The Constitutional Treaty would streamline the sanctions procedure: see section III A below.

[42] See Case C–224/01 *Köbler v Austria*, judgment of 30 September 2003. See H. Toner, 'Thinking the Unthinkable? State Liability for Judicial Acts after *Factortame III*' (1997) 17 YEL 165; G. Anagnostaras, 'The Principle of State Liability for Judicial Breaches: The Impact of European Community Law' (2001) 7 EPL 281.

Of course, the primary concern of the Federal Constitutional Court in the Maastricht case was with the terms of the German Constitution and the extent to which it permitted the transfer of powers to a supra-national entity such as the (proposed) European Union. The interpretation of national constitutions naturally falls within the exclusive jurisdiction of the competent national courts. Since the national systems exist alongside the Union legal order, the *potential* for conflict seems unavoidable, at least in the absence of major institutional changes going beyond anything envisaged by the Constitutional Treaty. Even if a new body were set up to deal with such conflicts, as is sometimes proposed,[43] there could be no guarantee that national constitutional courts would accept its decisions any more readily than those of the Court of Justice.

Against that background, the requirements of the EC Treaty and the legal (if not political) consequences that might ensue if the Federal Constitutional Court exercised the power of review it claimed to enjoy might at the very least have been considered relevant to the question of the effect of the German Constitution. After all, the Federal Constitutional Court acknowledged the 'openness of the Constitution to integration' and rejected 'a conception of democracy that would make every democratic state incapable of any integration going beyond the principle of unanimity'[44]. Like qualified majority voting, under which the wishes of individual Member States may sometimes be overridden, the exclusive jurisdiction of the Court of Justice to rule on the validity of Community acts is an essential element of the so-called Community method. This is not inconsistent with the idea of the Member States as the Masters of the Treaties, since in the last resort they can amend the Treaties to reverse the effect of decisions of the Court of Justice they find unacceptable and have in the past sought to do so.[45]

Perhaps the Federal Constitutional Court did not envisage ever exercising the review power it arrogated to itself and merely intended to encourage the Court of Justice to devote more attention to the precise scope of the powers enjoyed by the Community institutions under the Treaties.[46] Indeed, the Federal Constitutional Court spoke in the Maastricht decision of its 'relationship of cooperation'

---

[43] cf J. Weiler, U. Haltern and F. Mayer, 'European Democracy and its Critique' (1995) 18(3) West European Politics 4, 38; C. Schmid, 'From Pont d'Avignon to Ponte Vecchio: the Resolution of Constitutional Conflicts between the European Union and the Member States through Principles of Public International Law' (1998) 18 YEL 415, 467–70.

[44] See para 37 of the judgment.

[45] See eg the Protocol concerning the application of the provision of the Irish Constitution on the right to life of the unborn annexed to each of the Union Treaties at Maastricht; the so-called *Barber* Protocol concerning Art 141 EC annexed to the EC Treaty at Maastricht; the Protocol concerning the acquisition of property in Denmark annexed to the EC Treaty at Maastricht; Art 141(4) EC on affirmative action, introduced by the Treaty of Amsterdam.

[46] J. Weiler, U. Haltern and F. Mayer, 'European Democracy and its Critique' (1995) 18(3) West European Politics 4, 37, draw an analogy with the notorious Cold War policy of mutually assured destruction (MAD). cf Schmid, C. 'All Bark and No Bite: Notes on the Federal Constitutional Court's "Banana Decision" ' (2001) 7 ELJ 95, 106.

with the Court of Justice.[47] If this was the Court's intention, there are grounds for considering its decision, like its predecessors on the protection of fundamental rights,[48] a resounding success.

There is mounting evidence that the Court of Justice now takes more seriously its responsibility for policing the limits of the Community's powers.[49] The Federal Constitutional Court has responded in kind, adopting a less confrontational posture in its more recent case law.[50] The Member States have been content to acquiesce in the current situation,[51] which MacCormick has described as one of 'constitutional pluralism'.[52] Avoiding conflict, he maintains:

is a matter for circumspection and for political as much as legal judgment. The ECJ ought not to reach its interpretative judgments without regard to their potential impact on national constitutions. National courts ought not to interpret laws or constitutions without regard to the resolution of their compatriots to take full part in European Union and European Community.[53]

Both the national courts and the Court of Justice should, he adds, pay due regard to the obligations owed by the Member States to each other under international law.[54] If all the courts involved play their parts conscientiously, the result may be to promote 'constructive negotiation over constitutional conflicts'.[55] This offers the prospect of strengthening the Union by ensuring that the national constitutional courts accommodate the fundamental principles of its legal order while at the same time anchoring the case law of the Court of Justice firmly in national

[47] Above n 28 at paras 13 and 23.
[48] See *Internationale Handelsgesellschaft* ('Solange I'), judgment of 29 May 1974 [1974] 2 CMLR 540; *Wünsche* ('Solange II'), judgment of 22 October 1986 [1987] 3 CMLR 225.
[49] See eg Opinion 1/94 on the competence of the EC to conclude the WTO Agreement [1994] ECR I-5267; Opinion 2/94 on Community accession to the ECHR [1996] ECR I-1759; Case C-376/98 *Germany v Parliament and Council* ('Tobacco Advertising') [2000] ECR I-8419.
[50] For later developments, see U. Everling, 'The Maastricht Judgment of the German Federal Constitutional Court and its Significance for the Development of the European Union' (1994) 14 YEL 1, 15–18; U. Everling, 'Will Europe Slip on Bananas? The Bananas Judgment of the Court of Justice and National Courts' (1996) 33 CML Rev 401; N. Reich, 'Judge-Made 'Europe à la Carte': Some Remarks on Recent Conflicts between European and German Constitutional Law Provoked by the Banana Litigation' (1996) 7 EJIL 103; C. Schmid, 'All Bark and No Bite: Notes on the Federal Constitutional Court's "Banana Decision" ' (2001) 7 ELJ 95; J. Schwarze, 'Judicial Review in EC law—Some Reflections on the Origins and the Actual Legal Situation' (2002) 51 ICLQ 17.
[51] See Kumm and Ferreres Comella, above n 25 at 8.
[52] See N. MacCormick, *Questioning Sovereignty* (Oxford, OUP, 1999) ch 7. K. Alter, continuing the Cold War analogy, uses the term 'détente': see House of Lords EU Committee, 'The Future Role of the European Court of Justice' (Session 2003–04, 6th Report, HL 47), Minutes of Evidence, 53.
[53] MacCormick, ibid., 119–120. See also N. MacCormick, 'The Maastricht-Urteil: Sovereignty Now' (1995) 1 ELJ 259, 265. cf Case C-285/98 *Kreil* [2000] ECR I-69, where the ruling of the Court of Justice led to an amendment to the German Constitution. See M. Trybus, 'Sisters in Arms: European Community Law and Sex Equality in the Armed Forces' (2003) ELJ 631, 653.
[54] MacCormick, *Questioning Sovereignty* (Oxford, OUP, 1999) 120. cf Arts 26, 27 and 46 of the Vienna Convention on the Law of Treaties.
[55] Kumm and Ferreres Comella, above n 25 at 26. See also G. Beck, 'The problem of *Kompetenz-Kompetenz*: a conflict between right and right in which there is no *praetor*' (2005) 30 EL Rev 42.

constitutional values. Recent case law, in which restrictions on freedom of movement were found to be justified on the basis of values enshrined in national constitutions,[56] provides strong evidence of the Court's continuing willingness to contribute to that process.

C. The Effect of the Constitutional Treaty

Would the position change under the Constitutional Treaty? In strictly legal terms, the answer is clearly 'no'. The jurisdiction of the Court of Justice under the Constitutional Treaty would in all essential respects remain unchanged—national courts would continue to be prevented from unilaterally declaring Union acts invalid; the Court of Justice would retain the last word on the extent of the powers conferred on the Union.[57] Would the national courts accept this more readily than in the past? The answer to that question must of necessity be highly speculative, but there are perhaps some grounds for thinking that they might.

One is that the provisions on competences in Title III of Part I of the Constitutional Treaty, particularly the emphasis on the principles of conferral and subsidiarity,[58] would be likely to encourage the Court of Justice to build on its recent case law by examining closely the scope of the legal bases contained in Part III.

More generally, the Constitutional Treaty contains a number of provisions which should serve to underline that the roots of the Union lie in the common values and constitutional traditions of the Member States.[59] In cases involving fundamental rights enshrined in national constitutions, national courts may be reassured by Article II-112(4) of the Charter of Fundamental Rights, which provides: 'Insofar as this Charter recognises fundamental rights as they result from the constitutional traditions common to the Member States, those rights shall be interpreted in harmony with those traditions.' While that provision appears to have been intended merely to codify the current approach of the Court of Justice,[60] it may help to assuage fears among national judges that the Court does not in practice accord sufficient weight to national constitutional traditions. Its effect is reinforced by Article II-113, according to which the Charter of Fundamental Rights may not be interpreted as reducing the level of protection for fundamental rights afforded within their respective fields of

---

[56] See Case C–112/00 *Schmidberger* [2003] 2 CMLR 34 (goods: freedom of expression and freedom of assembly); Case C–36/02 *Omega v Bonn Police Authority*, judgment of 14 October 2004 (services: human dignity).

[57] cf K. Lenaerts and D. Gerard, 'The Structure of the Union According to the Constitution for Europe: The Emperor is Getting Dressed' (2004) 29 EL Rev 289, 301–303.

[58] See Art I-11.   [59] See eg Arts I-2 and I-5.

[60] See Declaration No. 12, Explanations Relating to the Charter of Fundamental Rights, [2004] OJ C310/424, 458; Final Report of Working Group II on 'Incorporation of the Charter/Accession to the ECHR', CONV 354/02, pp 7–8.

application by, *inter alia*, the Member States' constitutions. These features of the Constitutional Treaty were mentioned by the Spanish Constitutional Court in its declaration of 13 December 2004 that the Treaty was compatible with the Spanish Constitution.[61] The Treaty provisions referred by the Spanish Government to the Constitutional Court included Article I-6. The Court pointed out that, in the last resort, the supremacy of its national constitution could be preserved by Spain's withdrawal from the Union under the procedure laid down in Article I-60. That is perhaps the ultimate guarantee of national sovereignty.

It has also been argued that restraint on the part of the national courts might be reinforced in States where ratification of the Constitutional Treaty involves an amendment to the national constitution which itself accords primacy to Union law or where the mere act of ratification is seen as an act of the national constituent power, a real possibility where ratification has been approved by referendum.[62] Much will depend on national circumstances. The declaration of the Spanish Constitutional Court, given in advance of the Spanish referendum on the Treaty, has already been mentioned. A rather different line was taken by the French Conseil Constitutionnel in its decision of 19 November 2004.[63]

The Conseil ruled that France could not ratify the Constitutional Treaty without amending its Constitution. However, the Conseil expressly excluded Article I-6 of the Constitutional Treaty from the list of provisions it considered inconsistent with the French Constitution. The Conseil argued that Article I-5 made it clear that the Treaty had no effect on the existence of the French Constitution and its place at the apex of the internal legal order. The provisions of the Treaty, and in particular the juxtaposition of Articles I-5 and I-6, showed that it did not alter the nature of the Union or the scope of the primacy principle as it resulted, in accordance with the Conseil's previous case law, from the French Constitution itself.[64] In other words, no amendment to the French Constitution was needed because it already gave effect to the primacy principle, the scope of which was unaffected by the Treaty.

The difficulty with that view is that the case law of the Conseil denies primacy to provisions of Community law which are inconsistent with express and specific

---

[61] BOE Suplemento No. 3, 4 January 2005. There were three dissenting opinions. See Santamaria Dacal and Donnat, 'Ratification du traité instituant une Constitution pour l'Europe en Espagne', Fondation Robert Schuman, Le supplément de la Lettre No. 195, http://www.robert-schuman.org/supplement/sup195.htm. The assistance of Nieves La Casta with the Spanish Constitutional Court's declaration is gratefully acknowledged.

[62] Kumm and Ferreres Comella, above n 25 at 14–15.

[63] Decision No. 2004–505 DC of 19 November 2004, Journal Officiel, 24 November 2004, p 19885; available at http://www.conseil-constitutionnel.fr/. See Cahiers du Conseil Constitutionnel No. 18, available at the same website; Levade, 'Le cadre constitutionnel du débat de révision de la Constitution', Fondation Robert Schuman, Le supplément de la Lettre No. 191, 6 December 2004, http://www.robert-schuman.org/supplement/sup191.htm.   [64] See Art 88–1.

provisions of the French Constitution.[65] In its decision of 19 November 2004, the Conseil interpreted Article I-6 of the Constitutional Treaty as consistent with that case law, but that view is impossible to reconcile with the case law of the Court of Justice. The decision of the Conseil seemed to represent an attempt to wrest ownership of the Constitutional Treaty away from the Court of Justice. Its effect was to reinforce the role of the Conseil as guardian of the French Constitution. Were Article I-6 to come before the Court of Justice, it would have to rule on it in the knowledge that, if it disagreed with the Conseil, it would be going beyond the constitutional basis on which the Treaty was ratified by France. That might make it especially difficult for the ordinary French courts, bound by the decisions of the Conseil by virtue of Article 62 of the French Constitution,[66] to follow inconsistent case law of the Court of Justice. Since the French Constitution was to be amended anyway, the Conseil might have said that only the Court of Justice would be able to give authoritative interpretations of the Treaty and that its exclusive authority to do so should be expressly acknowledged.

Once the French Constitution has been amended and the Treaty ratified, it is possible that the French courts would regard themselves as authorised to give effect to it in accordance with the case law of the Court of Justice. Some national courts, it has been argued, might take the view that the express primacy provision, having been inserted by 'electorally accountable constitutional legislators', enjoys greater legitimacy and authority than the case law it reflects. This, it is said, might make some national judges (even) less willing to disapply EU law on national constitutional grounds.[67]

That argument raises the question whether the reverse would be true if the Constitutional Treaty failed to enter into force. Might that make some national courts more willing to review the validity of Union acts for themselves? Even if the primacy provision could be identified as one of the reasons for the failure of the Constitutional Treaty, it should not have that effect. Member States who acceded after the primacy doctrine was enunciated by the Court of Justice (19 of the 25) gave that doctrine the stamp of democratic legitimacy when they ratified their respective accession Treaties, sometimes following national referendums. Even the original six Member States (none of which held referendums on the original Treaties) have since ratified a succession of Treaties, notably the Single European Act, which took the primacy doctrine for granted.[68] So the failure of the Constitutional Treaty ought not to affect the present position in this respect. However, it must be conceded that national courts which are prepared to disregard

---

[65] See eg Decision No. 2004–498 DC of 29 July 2004. cf the decision of the Conseil d'Etat of 3 December 2001, *Syndicat National de l'Industrie Pharmaceutique and Others.*

[66] See J. Bell, *French Constitutional Law* (Oxford, Clarendon Press, 1992) 48–53.

[67] See Kumm and Ferreres Comella, above n 25 at 7, 8, 16–18. A similar argument might be made about Art IV-438(4), preserving the case law of the Court of Justice.

[68] See N. MacCormick, *Questioning Sovereignty* (Oxford, OUP, 1999) 112.

their Treaty obligations might be emboldened by the rejection of the Constitutional Treaty after a referendum campaign in which the primacy provision played a prominent role.

III. The Jurisdiction of the Union Courts

The Constitutional Treaty would introduce a number of significant changes to the jurisdiction of the Court of Justice. Broadly speaking, amendments to the provisions on annulment and preliminary rulings could consolidate the constitutional role already played by the Court. However, there is evidence in the Treaty of continuing misgivings about the extent to which the Court should be allowed to review the actions of the Member States and the institutions in which they are represented. Those misgivings are apparent in: (i) the simplified procedure for imposing sanctions on delinquent Member States; (ii) the new standing rules applicable in annulment actions; and, above all, (iii) the continued restrictions on the Court's jurisdiction over the CFSP, which will continue to mark one of the outer limits of the so-called Community method.[69]

A. Infringement Proceedings

In order to give Member States an added incentive to comply with their Treaty obligations, it was decided at Maastricht that the Court of Justice should have a power to fine a State which did not eliminate a breach of the Treaty sufficiently promptly after a judgment against it. The procedure, initiated by the Commission, is elaborate, involving two administrative stages followed by an application by the Commission to the Court.

The Constitutional Treaty would streamline it in two ways. First, where the State concerned had already been found by the Court to be in breach of its obligations, one of the administrative stages of the procedure (the issuing of a reasoned opinion) would be omitted.[70] Secondly, the Commission would be able to ask the Court to impose a financial penalty in its initial application to the Court in cases of alleged failure to implement a European framework law (what we now call a directive).[71] In the latter case, the relevant provision is oddly worded, referring to a Member State's failure to fulfil 'its obligation to notify measures transposing a European framework law'. A mere failure to notify national implementing

---

[69] cf Art I-1(1): '. . . The Union shall coordinate the policies by which the Member States aim to achieve these objectives, and shall exercise *on a Community basis* the competences they confer on it' (emphasis added). The draft Constitutional Treaty spoke of the Union exercising its competences 'in the Community way': see Art I-1(1).   [70] See Art III-362(2).
[71] See Art III-362(3).

measures would evidently not justify the imposition of a penalty if the framework law had actually been implemented. The text should refer simply to failure *to transpose* a European framework law.

The decision of the Member States to single out this particular species of infringement reflects governments' traditional wariness of judicial oversight. If the concern were purely with ensuring compliance, it would have been more effective to give the Commission a general right to ask in its initial application for a penalty to be imposed. That wariness is also evident in a limit introduced by the Member States on the amount of the sanction the Court may apply. Where a sanction is requested by the Commission in its initial application, the Court may not impose one which exceeds the amount specified by the Commission.[72] That limit did not appear in the draft Constitutional Treaty[73] and will not apply where the Commission makes a separate application requesting a sanction.[74] The latter procedure would be available to the Commission if a sanction initially imposed on a Member State for failure to transpose a European framework law proved inadequate. It seems odd to impose a limit in the one case but not in the other. The distinction can only be explained by reluctance on the part of the Member States to subject themselves to more intense scrutiny by the Court.

B. Annulment Proceedings

(i) Who can be challenged?

The Constitutional Treaty enlarges the class of bodies whose acts would be subject to review by the Court. It would be possible for annulment proceedings to be brought against acts intended to produce legal effects vis-à-vis third parties adopted by: (a) the European Council; and (b) agencies set up by legislation to implement specific Union policies. In the case of the European Council, this change is an unavoidable corollary[75] of the elevation of the European Council to the status of an institution[76] with formal decision-making powers of its own.[77] It would make the position of the European Council the same in this respect as that of the European Parliament.[78] In the case of Union agencies, the change is consistent with Article II-111(1), according to which the Charter of Fundamental Rights is 'addressed to the institutions, bodies, offices and agencies of the Union . . .'. In

---

[72] See the comments of AG Geelhoed in his second Opinion in Case C–304/02 *Commission v France* (pending).   [73] See Art III-267(3).

[74] See Art III-362(2).

[75] The change was not included in the draft Constitution but results from a suggestion put forward by the Working Party of Legal Experts: see CIG 50/03, 210. cf Case C–253/94 P *Roujansky v Council* [1995] ECR I-7.   [76] See Art I-19(1).

[77] See Art I-35(1).

[78] cf Art 230 EC, para 1; Case 294/83 *Les Verts v Parliament* [1986] ECR 1339.

order to preserve a degree of flexibility in the way judicial review of Union agencies is provided, Article III-365(5) provides that legislation creating Union bodies, offices and agencies 'may lay down specific conditions and arrangements concerning actions brought by natural or legal persons against acts of these bodies, offices or agencies intended to produce legal effects in relation to them'. The Union Courts can be expected to ensure that the degree to which such acts are subject to judicial oversight is not thereby reduced.

(ii) Who can challenge?

The Constitutional Treaty would modify the standing rules currently laid down in Article 230 EC, thereby enlarging the capacity of individuals to bring annulment proceedings before the Union Courts.[79] The effect of the existing rules, as interpreted by the Court of Justice, is that individuals may only seek the annulment of Community acts which are not addressed to them where they can establish direct and individual concern. Two cases decided in 2002, while the Convention on the Future of Europe was sitting, underlined the capacity of the latter concept in particular to deprive individuals of effective judicial protection of their rights.

In *UPA*,[80] the applicant sought the annulment of a regulation withdrawing a benefit it had previously enjoyed. In *Jégo-Quéré* v. *Commission*,[81] the applicant sought the annulment of a regulation imposing a prohibition which affected its activities. On the basis of the existing case law, both applications were inadmissible—the applicants were affected by the contested measures only in their objective capacities as traders carrying on particular activities. Moreover, because those measures did not require national implementation, it seemed impossible to contest them in the national courts for want of a national peg on which to hang a challenge.

To avoid depriving the applicants of their right to effective judicial protection, Advocate General Jacobs in *UPA* proposed, and the CFI in *Jégo-Quéré*[82] applied, new, more relaxed, tests of individual concern which would have permitted the applicants to proceed. However, in both cases the Court of Justice reaffirmed the existing case law. Reform of the system currently in force, it said in *UPA*, would require an amendment to the Treaty. Article III-365(4) of the Constitutional Treaty accordingly provides:

Any natural or legal person may . . . institute proceedings against an act addressed to that person or which is of direct and individual concern to him or her, *and against a regulatory act which is of direct concern to him or her and does not entail implementing measures* (emphasis added).

---

[79] The Constitutional Treaty would also enable the Committee of the Regions to bring annulment proceedings for the purpose of protecting its prerogatives: see Art III-365(3).
[80] Case C–50/00 P *Unión de Pequeños Agricultores v Council* [2002] 3 CMLR 1.
[81] Case C–263/02, judgment of 1 April 2004.
[82] Case T–177/01 [2002] ECR II-2365.

There was some discussion in the Convention of whether there should be a further relaxation of the standing rules in cases involving alleged violations of fundamental rights.[83] The idea of distinguishing fundamental rights cases from others was, however, wisely rejected.[84] Genuine fundamental rights cases nearly always raise other issues as well. In any event, it is often possible to dress a case up in terms of a fundamental rights violation. This seems to have been the experience of Germany, where alleged violations of fundamental rights may be brought directly before the Federal Constitutional Court. An additional difficulty would be to define the relationship between any special procedure for alleged violations of fundamental rights and the normal action for annulment. That difficulty would be especially acute if, unlike other direct actions brought by natural and legal persons, a special procedure were to bypass the CFI and go directly to the Court of Justice.

Be that as it may, there remain a number of problems with Article III-365(4). Although Part I of the Constitutional Treaty contains an elaborate hierarchy of acts, oddly the crucial term 'regulatory act' is nowhere defined. However, the *travaux préparatoires* (likely to be treated as persuasive by the Union Courts) indicate that it is intended to refer to any act other than a legislative act.[85] Legislative acts may only be adopted by the European Parliament and the Council acting jointly under the so-called ordinary legislative procedure (that is, co-decision) or by either institution 'with the participation of' the other under special legislative procedures.[86]

Article III-365(4) could therefore cause a sea change in the approach of the Union Courts. The absence hitherto of a hierarchy of norms has prevented the Courts from treating the legislative or regulatory character of an act as relevant to

---

[83] cf the Court's report on the application of the TEU published in May 1995 as part of the preparations for the 1996 IGC, in 'The Proceedings of the Court of Justice and Court of First Instance of the European Communities' (22–26 May 1995, No. 15/95); P. Alston and J. Weiler, *The European Union and Human Rights: Final Project Report on an Agenda for the Year 2000* (Florence, European University Institute, 1998), para 181.

[84] See the views expressed by AG Jacobs to the House of Lords EU Committee, 'The Future Status of the EU Charter of Fundamental Rights' (Session 2002–03, 6th Report, HL Paper 48), Minutes of Evidence, 30; the evidence of Judge Skouris of the Court of Justice to Working Group II of the Convention, Working Document 19, 4–5; the views of the then President of the Court of Justice, CONV 572/03, 5; L. Gormley, 'Judicial Review in EC and EU Law—Some Architectural Malfunctions and Design Improvements?' (2001) 4 CYELS 167, 187–18.

[85] See the final report of the Discussion Circle on the Court of Justice, CONV 636/03, para 22: 'A majority of those members who wanted the fourth paragraph of Article 230 to be amended would prefer the option mentioning "an act of general application". However, some members felt that it would be more appropriate to choose the words "a regulatory act", enabling a distinction to be established between legislative acts and regulatory acts, adopting, as the President of the Court had suggested, a restrictive approach to proceedings by private individuals against legislative acts (where the condition "of direct and individual concern" still applies) and a more open approach as regards proceedings against regulatory acts.' The term 'non-legislative act' could not be used in Art III-365(4) because that is just one of the categories of act identified in the hierarchy which are not legislative: see Arts I-34 to I-37. The term 'regulatory' is also employed in Art III-315(6), but in relation to national provisions.   [86] Art I-34.

the question of standing under Article 230 EC.[87] The effect on the workload of the Courts will be potentially severe, as '[t]he vast majority of EC law-making takes the form of executive [i.e. regulatory] as opposed to (normative) legislative mea-sures.'[88] Particularly affected would be the Commission, whose acts would always be regulatory under the Constitutional Treaty, so it would no longer be necessary for an individual to show individual concern in order to challenge them. This would be especially significant in actions for the annulment of European regula-tions[89] adopted by the Commission in the form of what we now call regulations.[90]

Legislative acts would remain immune from challenge by natural and legal persons unless, as now, they could establish direct and individual concern. This reflects the laws of those Member States which make it more difficult for individuals to challenge legislative measures than other types of measure.[91] Be that as it may, the difficulty confronting an individual wishing to challenge a legislative act which is of direct concern to him without the need for implementation would be likely to lead to continuing pressure for relaxation of the test for indivi-dual concern, particularly where fundamental rights were alleged to have been violated.

It might also make it difficult for a clear distinction to be maintained between legislative and regulatory acts. This emerges clearly if *UPA* is compared with *Jégo-Quéré*. The regulation concerned in the latter case, which was adopted by the Commission to conserve fish stocks, would have been a regulatory act had the Constitutional Treaty been in force. However, the Council regulation at issue in *UPA*, which reformed the common organization of the olive oil market, would probably have been legislative, with the result that the less stringent standing test applicable to regulatory acts would not have applied to it. It is doubtful whether such a fine distinction should produce such a radical effect on the availability of judicial remedies.[92]

The reference to direct concern without the need for implementing measures is also problematic. The Court said in *Les Verts v Parliament*[93] that a measure would be of direct concern to an applicant where it constituted 'a complete set of rules which are sufficient in themselves and which require no implementing provisions'.

---

[87] See A. Ward, '*Locus standi* under Article 230(4) of the EC Treaty: crafting a coherent test for a "wobbly polity" ' (2003) 22 YEL 45.   [88] ibid 56.

[89] Sub-para 4 of Art. I-33(1) provides: 'A European regulation shall be a non-legislative act of general application for the implementation of legislative acts and of certain provisions of the Constitution. It may either be binding in its entirety and directly applicable in all Member States, or be binding, as to the result to be achieved, upon each Member State to which it is addressed, but shall leave to the national authorities the choice of form and methods.'

[90] See eg Joined Cases 789 and 790/79 *Calpak v Commission* [1980] ECR 1949; *Jégo-Quéré*, above n 81; Case C–142/00 P *Commission v Nederlandse Antillen* [2004] 2 CMLR 41; Case C–258/02 P *Bactria v Commission* [2004] 2 CMLR 42.   [91] See AG Jacobs in *UPA* [2002] 3 CMLR 1, 32.

[92] See J. Usher, 'Direct and Individual Concern—An Effective Remedy or a Conventional Solution?' (2003) 28 EL Rev 575, 599. cf Ward, above n 87.

[93] Case 294/83 [1986] ECR 1339, para 31.

However, the case law also establishes that a measure which requires implementation may still be of direct concern to an applicant if: (a) the implementing authority has no discretion[94]; or (b) it is substantially certain how the authority would exercise any discretion conferred on it.[95] Would this remain the case where a regulatory act was challenged?

According to the final report of the Discussion Circle on the Court:

The addition of the words 'without entailing implementing measures' aims to ensure that the extension of a private individual's right to institute proceedings would apply only to those (problematical) cases where the individual concerned must first infringe the law before he can have access to a court. This wording enables private individuals to contest before the Court (CFI) an act containing, for example, a prohibition, but no implementing measure, as the individual concerned can apply for its annulment if he can demonstrate that he is directly concerned by the regulatory act in question.[96]

This implies that the special test laid down in the Constitutional Treaty for regulatory acts is intended to apply only where no alternative remedy is available to applicants in the national courts. Such a remedy would exist where implementing provisions had to be adopted by a Member State, even if it had no, or only limited, discretion in the matter. In order to challenge European regulations adopted in the form of what we now call directives,[97] it would therefore remain necessary for an individual to establish direct and individual concern.

If the Constitutional Treaty enters into force, it therefore seems unlikely to put an end to arguments over standing. There will be several new elements in the equation. In the case of legislative acts, the enhanced democratic legitimacy which the Constitutional Treaty seeks to confer on them will encourage restraint. However, two factors will militate in favour of intervention: first, the need to police the reinforced principles of conferral and subsidiarity[98]; secondly, the incorporated Charter of Fundamental Rights. Would the Court's approach be affected by the enhanced status of Article 47 (renumbered II-107) of the Charter, which enshrines the right to an effective remedy and to a fair trial?

The authors of the Constitutional Treaty have tried to ensure that the answer to that question is 'no'. An updated version of the 'explanations' intended to provide guidance on the interpretation of the Charter[99] says of Article II-107 that it is not:

[i]ntended to change the system of judicial review laid down by the Treaties, and particularly the rules relating to admissibility for direct actions before the Court of Justice of the European Union. The European Convention [i.e. the Convention on the Future of Europe] has considered the Union's system of judicial review including the rules on

---

[94] See eg Case 113/77 *NTN Toyo Bearing Company v Council* [1979] ECR 1185.
[95] See eg Case 11/82 *Piraiki-Patraiki v Commission* [1985] ECR 207.
[96] See CONV 636/03, para 21. *Jégo-Quéré* was a 'problematical case' of the type alluded to by the Discussion Circle.   [97] See sub-para 4 of Art I-33(1), quoted above.
[98] See Art I-11.   [99] See Declaration No. 12, above n 60 at 450.

admissibility, and confirmed them while amending them as to certain aspects, as reflected . . . in particular in Article III-365(4).

According to Article II-112(7), the explanations 'shall be given due regard by the courts of the Union and of the Member States'. However, the explanations themselves acknowledge in an opening statement that they do not 'as such have the status of law',[100] so there is some doubt about the weight likely to be accorded by the Union Courts to the statement quoted above. Indeed, in its report on the draft Constitutional Treaty, the House of Lords EU Committee questioned the extent to which the explanations would 'withstand the development of case law by the ECJ'.[101] If the Committee proved correct, the ability of the Union Courts to contribute through effective judicial review to the Union's accountability and legitimacy would be immeasurably enhanced.[102]

C. Preliminary Rulings

Under the present Treaties, the classic preliminary rulings procedure applies in an attenuated form in two areas: (i) Title IV of Part Three of the EC Treaty on visas, asylum, immigration and other policies related to the free movement of persons; and (ii) the third pillar, Title VI of the TEU on police and judicial co-operation in criminal matters. Under the first area, the right to refer is confined to top national courts.[103] Under the second area, Member States may choose whether to give their national courts a right to refer. If they do, that right may be limited to top national courts or extended to all national courts.[104]

The Constitutional Treaty merges these two areas into a single set of provisions on the so-called area of freedom, security and justice,[105] all of which would be subject to the classic preliminary rulings procedure. The only remnant of the previous regime would be Article III-377, which limits the Court's jurisdiction over national police operations and national measures concerned with 'the maintenance of law and order and the safeguarding of internal security'. That provision seems designed to weaken judicial scrutiny and poses a potential threat to the uniform application of Union law. Moreover, unlike its precursors in the EC and EU Treaties,[106] it is not confined to the preliminary rulings procedure. However, it is concerned with the validity or proportionality of *national* rather than Union measures. The Court only reviews national measures in infringement proceedings. Preliminary rulings set out in abstract terms the requirements of the Treaty, leaving to the referring court the

---

[100] See Declaration No. 12, above n 60 at 424.
[101] See 'The Future of Europe—The Convention's Draft Constitutional Treaty' (Session 2002–03, 41st Report, HL Paper 169), para 257.
[102] See K. Lenaerts and T. Corthaut, 'Judicial Review as a Contribution to the Development of European Constitutionalism' (2003) 22 YEL 1.   [103] Art 68 EC.
[104] See Art 35 TEU.   [105] See Arts I-3, I-14 and I-42 and Arts III-257 to III-277.
[106] Arts 68(2) EC and Art 35(5) TEU.

task of applying them to the facts of the case. The practical significance of Article III-377 may therefore be limited.[107]

One of the reasons for the present limits on the jurisdiction of the Court in these areas was a desire to shield it from the large volume of litigation they generate at the national level. Removal of the shield, and the volume of legislation envisaged by the Hague Programme agreed by the European Council in November 2004, would confront the Court with a large additional class of references, many of which would raise questions of fundamental rights and be likely to arouse strong feelings in the States from which they originated. Moreover, the Court would be expected to prioritise some of these cases. The Constitutional Treaty will require the Court to 'act with the minimum of delay' where a reference by a national court concerns 'a person in custody'.[108] In agreeing the Hague Programme, the European Council invited the Commission to bring forward a proposal, after consulting the Court, for an amendment to the Statute enabling all references concerning the area of freedom, security and justice to be dealt with speedily when the Constitutional Treaty entered into force.[109] These developments could have a major effect on the overall focus of the case law and the way in which the Court is perceived by the general public.[110]

D. The Common Foreign and Security Policy

If what is now the third pillar would largely be brought within the jurisdiction of the Court, the same cannot be said of the second pillar. The failure of the Member States in that context to involve the Court fully is unsatisfactory in principle and is likely to give rise to practical problems. The Court would have jurisdiction to review the legality of restrictive measures against individuals adopted pursuant to the CFSP under Article III-322. It would also have the power to determine the compatibility with the Constitutional Treaty of agreements with third States or international organisations envisaged pursuant to the CFSP.[111] In addition, Articles I-16 and III-308 would be subject to review by the Court. However, most of the provisions of the Constitutional Treaty on the CFSP would be excluded from the jurisdiction of the Court by Article III-376. Some of these provisions merit further consideration.

Article I-16 appears in Title II of Part I, which concerns the Union's competences. It describes the Union's competence in relation to the CFSP and, in its second paragraph, imposes certain obligations on the Member States. The Court of Justice

---

[107] But see the critical comments of the House of Lords EU Committee on the corresponding provision in the draft Constitutional Treaty, Art III-283: 'The Future Role of the European Court of Justice' (Session 2003–04, 6th Report, HL 47) 36–38. [108] See Art. III-369, para 4.

[109] Presidency Conclusions, Annex I, point 3.1; cf Art 104a of the Court's Rules of Procedure.

[110] See Chalmers, above n 7 at 15–17.

[111] See Arts III-303, 323 and 325(11). The latter provision corresponds to Art. 300(6) EC. The Constitutional Treaty reflects the view of most members of the Discussion Circle: see CONV 689/1/03 REV 1, 2 and 3.

might well consider at least some of those obligations justiciable. However, it is not entirely clear whether the Court is really intended to have jurisdiction over that paragraph, since it overlaps to a considerable extent with Article III-294(2). The latter provision is excluded from the jurisdiction of the Court of Justice and gives to the Council of Ministers and the Union Minister for Foreign Affairs[112] the task of ensuring that the principles it lays down are respected. Unlike Article I-16(2), however, Article III-294(2) does not require Member States to comply with 'the Union's action in this area'.[113] Is the Court intended to have the power to review compliance by Member States with that requirement? Presumably the answer to that question is 'yes', for otherwise the apparently deliberate exclusion of Article I-16 from Article III-376 would be undermined.

Article III-308 would prevent the provisions on the CFSP from being used to interfere with other competences enjoyed by the Union under the Constitutional Treaty and *vice versa*.[114] Its purpose is to stop a power or a process applicable in one field from being used to take steps which ought properly to be regarded as falling within a different field. The article is an application of the principle of conferral, the fundamental nature of which explains the grant to the Court of Justice of jurisdiction to apply it.

The limited jurisdiction of the Court of Justice over the CFSP becomes particularly problematic in the context of Article I-6, the primacy provision. The existing doctrine of primacy does not extend to the second or third pillars. The abolition of the pillar structure by the Constitutional Treaty would make the doctrine of primacy potentially applicable across the entire range of the Union's activities. As we have seen, matters currently falling under the third pillar would for the most part be brought within the scope of the classic powers of the Union Courts. Because this is not the case with most of the provisions on the CFSP, it is unclear to what extent a national court would in that context be able to ask the Court of Justice for guidance on the effect of Article I-6 (which would itself be within the jurisdiction of the Court). If national courts are left to their own devices, there will inevitably be divergence between Member States.

Article III-376 therefore looks like a rather unhappy compromise. The Union's growing ambitions in the field of foreign policy, particularly the increasing scale of its military operations,[115] make it almost inevitable that its actions will be subjected to legal challenge. The court best placed to hear such challenges is the Court of Justice. The Constitutional Treaty should therefore have enabled the Court to scrutinise the application of all its provisions on the CFSP.[116] This would have

---

[112] See Art I-28.

[113] The draft Constitutional Treaty referred to 'the acts adopted by the Union in this area': see Art I-15(2).

[114] It is a refinement of Art 47 TEU, which the Court applied in Case C–170/96 *Commission v Council* ('Airport Transit Visas') [1998] ECR I-2763.

[115] See eg Council Dec. 2004/803/CFSP of 25 November 2004 on the launching of the European Union military operation in Bosnia and Herzegovina, [2004] OJ L353/21.

[116] As proposed by some members of the Discussion Circle: see CONV 689/1/03 REV 1, 2.

meant giving it jurisdiction to ensure that the Member States, the Union institutions (including the European Council) and the Union Minister for Foreign Affairs respected the Constitutional Treaty and that individuals had a remedy where it was breached in this field, particularly in cases of alleged violations of fundamental rights.

Foreign policy matters are not excluded from review by the Strasbourg Court. This means that steps taken by the Member States under the CFSP may be challenged there. Moreover, in the absence of special arrangements, Union acts concerning the CFSP would be open to challenge in Strasbourg after the envisaged accession of the Union to the European Convention on Human Rights.[117] Indeed, there is a risk that the Strasbourg Court might review such acts even before accession.[118] If the Strasbourg Court were called upon to exercise its jurisdiction in the absence of prior review in Luxembourg, important features of the Union system might be overlooked or misunderstood. Enlarging the jurisdiction of the Court of Justice over the CFSP would be unlikely to lead it to take an unduly interventionist approach. As Advocate General Jacobs has observed extrajudicially, 'in matters of policy the [Union] Courts exercise a limited jurisdiction, the standard of review allowing the political institutions the appropriate margin'.[119]

IV. A Constitutional Court?

As the French Constitutional Council acknowledged in its decision of 19 November 2004,[120] the title of the Constitutional Treaty cannot conceal that it is in essence an international treaty.[121] Like the Treaties of Amsterdam and Nice, it was agreed, not by a pan-European constituent power, but by the governments of the Member States in accordance with the procedure laid down in Article 48 TEU. It is therefore dependent for its entry into force on ratification by all the

---

[117] See Art I-9(2).

[118] See *Matthews v United Kingdom* (1999) 28 EHRR 361.

[119] House of Lords EU Committee, 'The Future Status of the EU Charter of Fundamental Rights' (Session 2002–03, 6th Report, HL Paper 48), Minutes of Evidence, 29. See also P. Craig, House of Lords EU Committee, 'The Future Role of the European Court of Justice' (Session 2003–04, 6th Report, HL 47), Minutes of Evidence, 11–12. For an example of the Court's approach, see Case C–491/01 *R v Secretary of State, Ex P British American Tobacco* [2002] ECR I-11453, para 123.

[120] Above n 63 at paras 9 and 10.

[121] See P. Eleftheraidis, 'Constitution or Treaty?' (The Federal Trust, Online Paper 12/04, http://www.fedtrust.co.uk/); Beck, above n 55 at 46–49; J. Kokott and A. Rüth, 'The European Convention and its Draft Treaty Establishing a Constitution for Europe: Appropriate Answers to the Laeken Questions?' (2003) 40 CML Rev 1315, 1319–1321. cf K. Lenaerts and D. Gerard, 'The Structure of the Union According to the Constitution for Europe: The Emperor is Getting Dressed' (2004) 29 EL Rev 289, 293, 297–8; A. Albi and P. Van Elsuwege, 'The EU Constitution, National Constitutions and Sovereignty: An Assessment of a "European Constitutional Order" ' (2004) 29 EL Rev 741, 747–55.

Member States in accordance with their own constitutional requirements.[122] Even if it enters into force, it will only be possible to amend it if all the Member States agree.[123] As the Spanish Constitutional Court emphasised in its declaration of 13 December 2004,[124] Member States which wish to do so will be expressly permitted to withdraw from the Union.[125]

The symbolic and political importance of the involvement of the Convention on the Future of Europe in the preparation of the Constitutional Treaty has no bearing on its legal status, for Article 48 TEU makes no reference to conventions.[126] The Convention on the Future of Europe was an elaborate but essentially informal body set up by the European Council at Laeken in December 2001 '[i]n order to pave the way for the next Intergovernmental Conference as broadly and openly as possible'.[127] Its claim to legitimacy was tarnished by doubts about its representativeness and working methods[128] and its failure to connect with the general public. The true nature of the role entrusted to the Court of Justice depends, not on the title of the new Treaty or the fact that it usually styles itself a Constitution,[129] but on the Treaty's pith and marrow.

In general terms, the Court of Justice's role under the Constitutional Treaty seems likely to remain much the same as its role under the present Treaties. Its main functions would still be to ensure that the institutions act within the limits of their powers and that the Member States comply with their obligations and to offer guidance to national courts on the interpretation and application of the Constitutional Treaty. However, the need for the Court of Justice to focus more sharply on constitutional questions may grow as a result of three features of the Constitutional Treaty[130]: (i) the more detailed provisions on the competences of the Union, underlining the importance of the principles of conferral, subsidiarity and proportionality; (ii) the attempt to equip the Union with a hierarchy of legal instruments matching policies to appropriate acts and procedures; and,

---

[122] The first Member State to ratify the Constitutional Treaty was Lithuania, which did so following a parliamentary vote on 11 November 2004.   [123] See Arts IV-443–5.

[124] Above n 61.   [125] See Art I-60.

[126] The ordinary revision procedure laid down in the Constitutional Treaty provides for a Convention to be formally convened: see Art IV-443(2).

[127] Laeken Declaration on the Future of the European Union (Annex I to the Presidency Conclusions, Laeken, 14 and 15 December 2001). The European Council described the text of the draft Constitutional Treaty as 'a good basis for starting in the Intergovernmental Conference': Presidency Conclusions, Thessaloniki, 19 and 20 June 2003.

[128] See Annex III ('Alternative Report: The Europe of Democracies') to the report from the Convention Presidency, CONV 851/03; G. Stuart, 'The Making of Europe's Constitution' (London, Fabian Society, 2003). For a brief response to some of Stuart's points, see N. MacCormick, 'A Union of its Own Kind: Reflections on the Proposed Constitution of the European Union' (Edinburgh, 2004) 3–6.

[129] It is described as a Constitution in Pts I-III, but Pt IV (General and Final Provisions) calls it a Treaty.

[130] cf P. Craig, House of Lords EU Committee, 'The Future Role of the European Court of Justice' (Session 2003–04, 6th Report, HL 47), Minutes of Evidence, 1.

(iii) the incorporation in Part II of the Constitutional Treaty of the Union's Charter of Fundamental Rights,[131] which seems likely to increase the frequency with which fundamental rights are invoked to challenge the activities of the Union and those of the Member States when implementing Union law. Reconciling these features may prove challenging, especially in annulment actions and cases concerning the area of freedom, security and justice.

There is evidence in the provisions of the Constitutional Treaty on infringement proceedings, annulment and the CFSP of the traditional reluctance of governments to subject their actions to judicial scrutiny. Nonetheless, that evidence consists merely of provisions which do not extend the Court's jurisdiction as far as might have been thought desirable. The Member States made no attempt in the Constitutional Treaty to reduce the Court's powers and even went as far as to endorse its existing case law,[132] a resounding vote of confidence. Whether the Court ultimately assumes the mantle of a genuine constitutional court will depend in large measure on the way in which other institutions (particularly the Council) exercise their post-Nice powers concerning the judicial architecture of the Union.[133] The foundations have now been laid.

---

[131] See A. Arnull, 'From Charter to Constitution and Beyond: Fundamental Rights in the New European Union' [2003] PL 774.   [132] See Art IV-438(4).
[133] See Arts 223, 224, 225, 225a, 229a and 245 EC and the corresponding provisions of the Constitutional Treaty, Arts III-355, III-356, III-358, III-359, III-364 and III-381 respectively.

'Scrupulous but Dynamic'—the Freedom of Expression and the Principle of Proportionality under European Community Law

*Yutaka Arai-Takahashi**

I. Introduction

This article explores the ways in which the proportionality appraisal has been carried out by the European Community judicature (ECJ and CFI) under EU law in cases involving freedom of expression. The primary purpose of this article is to obtain an insight into the *modus operandi* of the Community judicial organs in adjudicating issues of fundamental rights by reference to the notion of proportionality. The article consists of five main sections. The first two sections deal with preliminary examinations, briefly discussing the meaning of the principle of proportionality developed as a general principle of EC law and the scope of application of fundamental rights in the context of EU law. In the third section, examinations turn to three areas in which the notion of proportionality is instrumental in elucidating the Community judicature's distinct methodology in relation to freedom of expression: (a) advertisement as form of commercial expression; (b) access to documents or information held by the Council or Commission, and (c) the freedom of expression exercised by the staff members of the Community. Finally, the article furnishes theoretical appraisals of the standard of review applied by the Community judicature in comparison with the standard employed by the Strasbourg Court in the jurisprudence of the European Convention on Human Rights (ECHR). The scope of this comparative assessment is confined, though, to the extent that it aims to provide explanations as to distinct features of the proportionality appraisal under Community law.

The protection of a large and indefinite category of fundamental rights forms a general principle of EC law and binds both the Community legislature and the Member States implementing EC legislation. Yet, the narrow parameters

* Senior Lecturer in International Law and International Human Rights Law, Kent Law School, University of Kent: and Brussels School of International Studies, Belgium. The author is grateful to Prof. G. J. H. Van Hoof and Dr H. Schepel for their helpful comments on earlier drafts.

of appraisal can be defended in that the jurisprudence relating to those three areas stands out in view not merely of its quantity of cases, but also of the depth of proportionality review conducted by the Advocates-General and the Community courts. Further, the case law relating to the freedom of expression under Article 10 ECHR has generated innovative, albeit inchoate, interpretive techniques, such as the less restrictive alternative test and the chilling effect doctrine, as part of intense scrutiny. This will facilitate the comparative survey of methodologies employed by the Court of Human Rights and the Community judicature.

II. The Principle of Proportionality as a General Principle of EC Law

A. Evolution of Proportionality under EC Law

It is uncontested that it is the German concept of proportionality comprised of three specific tests that has provided the foundational basis of the principle of proportionality under EC law.[1] However, once transposed into Community law, the principle of proportionality has acquired an autonomous legal force as a general principle of EC law. It can override acts of the Community legislature and hence ranks higher than secondary legislation (or even basic Treaties) in the hierarchy of the sources of Community law,[2] and which has been tailored to suit needs of Community law. As noted by Tridimas,[3] the first implicit reliance on the notion of proportionality as a ground of review of Community measures can be found in *Fédéchar v. High Authority* in 1956, in which the Court ruled that 'reaction by the

---

[1] T.C. Hartley, *The Foundations of European Community Law* (5th edn, Oxford: OUP, 2003), 151–53; Lord Hoffmann, "The Influence of the European Principle of Proportionality upon UK Law", in E. Ellis (ed), *The Principle of Proportionality in the Laws of Europe* (Oxford: Hart, 1999) 107–115.

For assessment of the principle of proportionality under EC law, see G. de Búrca, 'The Principle of Proportionality and its Application in EC Law' (1993) 13 YBEL 105; 'Proportionality and Subsidiarity as General Principles of Law' in: U. Bernitz and J. Nergelius (eds.), *General Principles of European Community Law*, (London: Kluwer, 2000), Ch. 3.1., pp. 95–112; N. Emiliou, *The Principle of Proportionality in European Law—A Comparative Study*, (London: Kluwer, 1996), Chs. 4 and 5, pp. 115–194; J. Schwarze, *European Administrative Law* (Office for Official Publications of the European Communities/Sweet & Maxwell, 1992); T. Tridimas, "The Principle of Proportionality in Community Law: From the Rule of Law to Market Integration", (1996) 31 *The Irish Jurist* 83; *The General Principles of EC Law*, (Oxford: Oxford Univ. Press, 1999), hereinafter, Tridimas (1999a), Ch. 3; and "Proportionality in European Community Law: Searching for the Appropriate Standard of Scrutiny", in E. Ellis (ed.), *The Principle of Proportionality in the Laws of Europe*, (Oxford: Hart, 1999), at 65–84, hereinafter, Tridimas (1999b).

[2] A.G. Toth, "Human Rights as General Principles of Law, in the Past and in the Future", Bernitz and Nergelius (eds.), *supra* n. 1, at 76. Referring to *Les Verts* and *Chernobyl* cases, Toth observes that general principles of Community law may occupy a higher place than even the basic Treaties, in that the Court has invoked these principles to supplement and amend them: *Id.*, at 78; Case 294/83, *Les Verts v. Parliament* [1986] ECR 1339; and Case C-70/88, *Parliament v. Council (Chernobyl)*, [1990] ECR I-2041.   [3] Tridimas (1999a), *supra* n. 1, at 93.

High Authority to illegal action must be in proportion to the scale of that action',
treating this notion as 'a generally-accepted rule of law'.[4] It was, however, in the
Internationale Handelsgesellschaft case relating to agriculture, that the principle of
proportionality was explicitly invoked as a ground of review.[5] With respect to
national measures, since *Van Duyn*,[6] it is established that in order for national
measures to benefit from derogations from the 'fundamental' freedoms, they must
satisfy the principle of proportionality. The increased reliance on proportionality
by the Community judicature can be explained partly by the expansion of proportionality from the context of administrative measures to that of policy measures.[7]
Further, since *Cassis de Dijon*,[8] the notion of proportionality may be viewed as
substituting that of discrimination as a central guiding principle under Article 28
(ex Article 30), with comparable developments occurring in areas of free movement of services and persons.[9] Challenges against Community acts or measures
on the basis of the principle of proportionality can be instituted either by Member
States or individuals.[10]

Tridimas argues that the principle of proportionality fulfils three primary
functions: first, a ground of reviewing Community measures; secondly, a ground
of scrutinising national measures touching on one of the Community-law freedoms; and thirdly, a tool for regulating the exercise by the Community of its
legislative competence under Article 5(3) (ex Article 3b(3)) of the Treaty.[11] As
regards the second function, it is established in the case law that general principles
of EC law can apply to national implementing measures, with Member States

[4] Case 8/55, *Fédération Charbonnière Belgique v. High Authority*, [1954–6] ECR 292 at 299. See
also Case 15/57, *Hauts Fourneaux de Chasse v. High Authority*, [1957–8] ECR 211 at 228 (The Court
held that the High Authority is not allowed to "act so harshly that those interests [the special interests
of those concerned] are compromised very much more than can reasonably be expected and [that] the
High Authority is bound to act with all the circumspection and care required to balance and assess the
various, often conflicting, interests involved and to avoid harmful consequences in so far as, within
reason, the nature of the decision to be taken permits"); and Case 19/61, *Mannesmann AG v. High
Authority*, [1962] ECR 357, at 370 (The Court held that "[t]he High Authority . . . has . . . a duty to
take account of [the fact] that the aims pursued may be attained under the most favourable conditions and with the smallest possible sacrifices by the undertakings affected", referring to this as the
"principle of justice").

[5] Case 11/70, *Internationale Handelsgesellschaft v. Einfuhr-und Vorratsstelle Getreide*, [1970] ECR
1125, para. 16 (and the opinion of Dutheillet de Lamothe AG, at 1146) (deposits system accompanying import and export licences). See also Case 25/70, *Einfuhr-und Vorratsstelle für Getreide und
Futtermittel v. Koester, Berodt and Co.*, [1970] ECR 1161, paras. 20–36; Case 26/70, *Einfuhr-und
Vorratsstelle für Getreide und Futtermittel v. Guenther Henck*, [1970] ECR 1183, para. 7.

[6] Case 41/74, *Van Duyn v. Home Office*, [1974] ECR 1337, paras. 13 and 18.

[7] Tridimas (1999a), *supra* n. 1, at 94.

[8] Case 120/78, *Rewe-Zentrale AG v. Bundesmonopolverwaltung für Branntwein*, ("*Cassis de Dijon*")
[1979] ECR 649.

[9] See, *inter alia*, Case C-76/90, *Säger v. Société Dennemeyer & Co. Ltd*, [1991] ECR I-4221, paras.
17 and 20; Case C-415/93, *Union Royale Belge des Sociétés de Football Association and Others v.
Bosman and Others*, [1995] ECR I-4921. See also Tridimas (1999a), *supra* n. 1, at 94.

[10] See, for instance, Case 116/82, *Commission v. Germany*, [1986] ECR 2519; and Case 37/83,
Rewe-Zentrale v. Landwirtschaftskammer Rheinland, [1984] ECR 1229.

[11] Tridimas (1999a), *supra* n. 1, at 90.

deemed as agents of the Community.[12] In preliminary reference proceedings under Article 234 (ex Article 177), national courts may request the Court to provide guidance as to compatibility of national measures with Community law by reference to the principle of proportionality.[13] That principle can constrain the discretion of Community institutions when they enact legislation potentially affecting fundamental rights of individual persons. This function helps verify whether restrictions imposed by Community legislation on fundamental rights are justifiable,[14] ensuring that acts of the Community legislators do not curb on an individual citizen's autonomy more than necessary to achieve a legitimate public end. When Community legislation designed to give effect to one of the fundamental rights in a democracy conflicts with exercise of another fundamental right, a Member State implementing such legislation is given a scope of discretion in evaluating the balance between the two countervailing rights, but national discretion must be exercised within the bounds of proportionality. In that sense, the notion of proportionality serves to reconcile two competing rights of individual citizens where there is no hierarchy between those rights.[15]

In relation to the third function, the principle of proportionality, if employed by national courts in fields lacking Community harmonisation, serves to draw a line between areas requiring uniform application of Community law and areas where autonomy of Member States should be preserved.[16] This function is closely associated with that of subsidiarity.[17] Yet, as Advocate General Léger acknowledged in the *United Kingdom v. Council* relating to the Working Time Directive,[18] the operational sphere of these two principles differs: the former comes to the fore

---

[12] The first such recognition was seen in Case 230/78, *Eridania v. Minister for Agriculture and Forestry*, [1979] ECR 2749, para. 31 ("general principles of Community law . . . are binding on all authorities entrusted with the implementation of Community provisions"). See also, Joined Cases 205–215/82, *Deutsche Milchkontor v. Germany*, [1983] ECR 2633, para. 17; Joined Cases 201 and 202/85, *Martin Klensch and Others v. Secrétaire d'État à l'Agriculture et à la Viticulture*, [1986] ECR 3477, paras. 9–10.

[13] See, for instance, Case 215/87, *Heinz Schumacher v. Hauptzollamt Frankfurt am Main-Ost*, [1989] ECR 617, paras. 11, 21–22; Case C-347/89, *Freistaat Bayern v. Eurim-Pharm GmbH*, [1991] ECR I-1747; and Case C-384/93, *Alpine Investments BV*, [1995] ECR I-1141, paras. 13, 40, 45, 51 and 55.

[14] Case C-159/90, *Society for the Protection of Unborn Children Ireland ("Grogan")*, [1991] ECR I-4685, para. 35, *per* van Gerven AG; Case C-376/98, *Germany v. European Parliament and Council*, *per* Fennelly AG; and Case C-74/99, *The Queen v. Secretary of State for Health and Others, ex parte Imperial Tobacco Ltd and Others*, [2000] ECR I-8599, para. 148.

[15] See, for instance, *Lindqvist v. Sweden*, which concerned Community acts designed to enhance the protection of privacy of individual persons in relation to data processing: Case C-101/01, *Lindqvist v. Sweden*, paras. 84–90 (not yet reported).   [16] Tridimas (1999b), at 79–80.

[17] For assessment of the principle of subsidiarity, see N. Bernard, "The Future of European Economic Law in the Light of the Principle of Subsidiarity", (1996) 33 CML Rev 633; N. Emiliou, "Subsidiarity: An Effective Barrier Against the 'Enterprises of Ambition'?", (1992) 17 EL Rev 383; "Subsidiarity: Panacea or Fig Leaf?", in D.O'Keeffe and P.M. Twomey (eds), *Legal Issues of the Maastricht Treaty* (London: Chancery, 1994), Ch. 5; and J.P. González, "The Principle of Subsidiarity", (1995) 20 EL Rev 355.

[18] Case C-84/94, *United Kingdom v. Council*, (*Organisation of Working Time Directive* case), [1996] ECR I-5755, para. 126, *per* Léger AG.

only after the latter settles issues of Community's competence.[19] Further, as a ground of reviewing Community measures, proportionality should be distinguished from the concept of misuse of powers,[20] which is derived from the concept of *détournement de pouvoir* in French administrative law. To prove that an act is marred by misuse of powers, the applicant must demonstrate that the objective pursued by the institution adopting the act was other than that which it is entitled to seek, or evading a procedure specifically prescribed by the Treaty to handle particular circumstances. This means that unlike proportionality, misuse of powers requires an inquiry into subjective elements, the motive or intention, of the author of the act.[21]

B. Components of Proportionality

The tripartite form of proportionality appraisal, which coincides with the counterpart of German public law,[22] consists of the three tests: firstly, the suitability test, which demands that a measure must be capable of attaining a legitimate objective; secondly, the necessity test or less restrictive alternatives test, which requires the agency to ensure that there must not exist an equally effective measure less burdensome of the individual's freedom; and thirdly, the proportionality *stricto sensu* (in narrow sense), which obliges the agency not to impose on the individual a measure entailing a burden or injury that is excessive in relation to the desired end sought to be achieved.[23] In *BSE*, the Court eloquently explains the three-pronged principle of proportionality:

[T]he principle of proportionality . . . requires that measures adopted by Community institutions do not exceed the limits of what is appropriate and necessary in order to attain the objectives legitimately pursued by the legislation in question; when there is a choice between several appropriate measures recourse must be had to the least onerous, and the disadvantages caused must not be disproportionate to the aims pursued.[24]

---

[19] Tridimas (1999a), *supra* n. 1, at 118–119; and *Id.*, (1999b) *supra* n. 1, at 81.

[20] See, for instance, Case C-156/93, *European Parliament v. Commission*, [1995] ECR I-2019, para. 31. See also Case 6/54, *Netherlands v. High Authority*, [1955] ECR 103, at 116; and Case 15/57, *Compagnie des Hauts Fourneaux de Chasse v. High Authority*, [1958] ECR 211 at 230.

[21] Hartley, *supra* n. 1 at 420; and Tridimas (1999a), *supra* n. 1, at 92. See also Joined Cases C-133, C-300 and C-362/93, *Antonio Crispoltoni v. Fattoria Autonoma Tabacchi and Giuseppe Natale and Antonio Pontillo v. Donatab Srl. (Crispoltoni)*, [1994] ECR I-4863, at 4874, *per* Jacobs AG, and by the Court at paras. 23–29; .

[22] See, G. Nolte, "General Principles of German and European Administrative Law—A Comparison in Historical Perspective", (1994) 57 MLR 191; and M.P. Singh, *German Administrative Law—In Common Law Perspective*, (Berlin: Springer, 1985).

[23] Schwarze, *supra* n. 1, at 854–864. See also, M. Herdegen and S. Richter, "Die Rechtslage in den Europäischen Gemeinschaften", in J.Abr. Frowein (ed.), *Die Kontrolldichte bei der gerichtlichen Überprüfung von Handlungen der Verwaltung*, (Berlin: Springer, 1993), pp. 209–244.

[24] Case C-180/96, *United Kingdom v. Commission* ('BSE'), [1998] ECR I-2265, para. 96. See also, Case C-331/88, *Fedesa and Others ('Fedesa')*, [1990] ECR I-4023, para. 13; and Case C-376/98, *Germany v. European Parliament and Council, per* Fennelly AG; and Case C-74/99, *The Queen v. Secretary of State for Health and Others, Ex p. Imperial Tobacco Ltd and Others*, para. 147.

The suitability test, the first limb of proportionality, is similar to the requirement, developed to assess restrictions on the rights under Articles 8–11 ECHR, that an interfering measure must pursue a legitimate aim.[25] Yet, the standard of review under the suitability test of Community law may be more rigorous[26] than in a considerably lax standard applicable in the limitation clauses of Articles 8–11 ECHR. The reason why the assessment of the suitability test may be intense is that it is perceived as closely linked to appraisal of the less restrictive alternative test,[27] which in turn invites more structured evaluations by the Community judicature than in the context of the Strasbourg Court. Another reason is that the evidentiary standard required for the suitability test may be onerous. In *Germany v. European Parliament and Council*, which concerned the Tobacco Directive, Advocate General Fennelly averred that without 'clear evidence' that restrictions on tobacco advertising is likely to result in changes in consumers' behaviour in the direction of better public health, such restrictions would be flawed in relation to the suitability test.[28] Nevertheless, the stringency of this test does not go so far as to suggest that with the advantage of hindsight, the legality of an act or a measure can be contested on the basis that a certain measure has not attained a desired end in practice.[29]

The survey of the case law discloses that the proportionality appraisal conducted by the ECJ and CFI has focused on the second (necessity) and the third test (proportionality in a narrow sense).[30] The less restrictive alternative test has been frequently invoked under Article 30 (ex Article 36),[31] with the varying

[25] P. Van Dijk and G.J.H. Van Hoof, *Theory and Practice of the European Convention on Human Rights*, (3rd edn, The Hague: Kluwer, 1998), pp. 771–773; and D.J. Harris, M. O'Boyle and C. Warbrick, *Law of the European Convention on Human Rights*, (London: Butterworths, 1995), pp. 289–90.
[26] While the suitability test is generally satisfied without much difficulty, in case the contested Community legislation in itself entails restrictions on fundamental rights, the Community judicature may strictly apply this test, obliging the Community institution to demonstrate linkage between that Community legislation and the objective pursued. See, for instance, Case C-376/98, *Germany v. European Parliament and Council*, [2000] ECR I-8419; and Case C-74/99, *The Queen v. Secretary of State for Health and Others, Ex p. Imperial Tobacco Ltd and Others*, [2000] ECR I-8599, para. 151, *per* Fennelly AG.
[27] See, for instance, Case C-368/89, *Antonio Crispoltoni v. Fattoria autonoma tabacchi di Città di Castello (Crispoltoni I)*, [1991] ECR I-3695 (restrictive fixation of maximum quantities); Tridimas (1999a), *supra* n. 1, at 96.
[28] Opinion of Advocate General Fennelly of 15 June 2000, Case C-376/98, *Germany v. European Parliament and Council*; Case C-74/99, *The Queen v. Secretary of State for Health and Others, Ex p. Imperial Tobacco Ltd and Others*, para. 161.
[29] Case 40/72, *I. Schroeder KG v. Germany*, [1973] ECR 125, para. 14. See also, *Gustave Wuidart and Others* in which the Court stated that: "where the Community legislature is obliged, in connection with the adoption of rules, to assess their future effects, which cannot be accurately foreseen, its assessment is open to criticism only if it appears manifestly incorrect in the light of the information available to it at the time of the adoption of the rules in question"; Joined Cases C-267 to C-285/88, *Gustave Wuidart and Others*, [1990] ECR I-435, para. 14.
[30] See, for instance, Case C-254/98, *Schutzverband gegen unlauteren Wettbewerb v. TK-Heimdienst Sass GmbH*, [2000] ECR I-151, paras. 34–36.
[31] See, *inter alia*, Case 104/75, *Adriaan de Peijper, Managing Director of Centrafarm BV*, [1976] ECR 613, paras. 18 and 31; Case 124/81, *Commission v. United Kingdom* ('UHT milk case'), [1983] ECR 203, para. 16; and Case C-62/90, *Commission v. Germany*, [1992] ECR I-2575, para. 11.

level of intensity of scrutiny,[32] either under the public interest grounds stipulated in this escape clause for free trade or under 'mandatory requirements'.[33] In the absence of harmonisation, a Member State's measure restricting Community freedoms does not necessarily fail the test of proportionality on the ground that a less constrictive measure exists in another Member State.[34] In contrast, even in areas such as economic fields, where lax review tends to gain ascendancy, with judicial deference to the competence of Community legislature, the Court may not abandon its scrupulous review. This may be borne out in the Court's approach to specific protective measures such as temporary suspension of imports and the imposition of levies and (fixed-rate) countervailing charges,[35] with rigorous appraisal focusing on the existence of measures the least burdensome of Community-law freedoms.[36]

In relation to the third limb of proportionality appraisal, the test of proportionality *stricto sensus*, the analysis of the case law involving national measures evinces a tendency of the Court to engage in scrupulous evaluations. The Community judicature has juxtaposed a specific national interest against the Community freedoms and evaluated impeding effects of national measures at length, including the nature, whether direct, indirect or speculative, of those national measures.[37] Appraisal of proportionate effects can be swayed by specific circumstances warranting contested national measures.[38] The intensity of scrutiny in relation to the

[32] Tridimas (1999a), *supra* n. 1 at 137.

[33] See, for instance, Case 788/79, *Criminal proceedings against Herbert Gilli and Paul Andres*, [1980] ECR 2071, para. 6; Case 193/80, *Commission v. Italy*, [1981] ECR 3019, para. 21; Case 261/81, *Walter Rau Lebensmittelwerke v. De Smedt PVBA*, [1982] ECR 3961, para. 12; and Case 178/84, *Commission v. Germany*, [1987] ECR 1227, paras. 2, at 28 and 30. For mandatory requirements, see, for example, Case 120/78, *Rewe-Zentrale AG v. Bundesmonopolverwaltung für Branntwein* (*'Cassis de Dijon'*), [1979] ECR 649.

[34] C-384/93, *Alpine Investments BV v. Minister van Financien*, [1995] ECR I-1141, at point 88, *per* Jacobs AG and para. 51 of the judgment; Case C-3/95, *Reisebüro Broede v. Gerd Sandker*, [1996] ECR I-6511, para. 42.

[35] See, for instance, Case 77/86, *The Queen v. H. M. Commissioners of Customs and Excise, Ex p. The National Dried Fruit Trade Association*, [1988] ECR 757, para. 32; Case C-24/90, *Hauptzollamt Hamburg-Jonas v. Werner Faust Offene Handelsgesellschaft KG*, [1991] ECR I-4905, paras. 12 and 26; Case C-25/90, *Hauptzollamt Hamburg-Jonas v. Wünsche Handelsgesellschaft GmbH & Co. KG* (*Wünsche I*), [1991] ECR I-4939, paras. 13, 20–21 and 27; Case C-295/94, *Hüpeden & Co. KG v. Hauptzollamt Hamburg-Jonas*, [1996] ECR I-3375, paras. 14, 15, 21 and 22; and C-296/94, *Bernhard Pietsch v. Hauptzollamt Hamburg-Waltershof*, [1996] ECR I-3409, paras. 15, 16, 25, 31 and 34.   [36] Tridimas (1999a), *supra* n. at 111.

[37] See, for example, Case C-169/91, *Council of the City of Stoke-on-Trent and Norwich City Council v. B & Q plc.*, [1992] ECR I-6635, para. 15. Note, however, that since *Keck and Mithouard* (Joined Cases C-267 and C-268/91, [1993] ECR I-6097), the central issue discussed in this case, namely, the ban on the Sunday trading, can now be classified as a non-discriminatory selling arrangement that does not fall within the ambit of Article 28 (ex Article 30): *infra* section IV.C.

[38] In this respect, see *Commission v. France*, where the Court introduced what Tridimas refers to as the requirement of equivalence when assessing compatibility of national derogating measures with the requirement of proportionality:

Whilst a Member State is free to require a product which has already received approval in another Member State to undergo a fresh procedure of examination and approval, it is nevertheless under a duty to assist in bringing about a relaxation of the controls existing in intra-Community

third test (and to the first test) can be further heightened when the Court has required the Community legislature to state reasons in decisions, as provided in Article 253 EC, in conjunction with the assessment of burden and standard of proof.[39]

As regards the examinations of the second and third limbs of proportionality, lax review may shift the focus of appraisal from existence of less onerous measures to effects of impeding measures, including their scope, duration, and relative severity weighed against the strength of countervailing public interests.[40] However, in a more stringent review, onus may be shifted to the Community legislature or the Member States to prove that a hindrance to Community freedoms or fundamental rights is both the least burdensome *and* proportionate to a specific public end. Even a measure recognised as the least onerous of Community freedoms or fundamental rights may fail the test of proportionality in a narrow sense.[41]

C. The Sliding Scale of Review

The notion of proportionality is inevitably flexible and open-textured in nature, susceptible to varying degrees of review, with a corresponding degree of discretion left to the Community legislature or national authorities.[42] De Búrca argues that the variation of the standard of proportionality under EC law depends on a complex range of factors, including the nature and weight of the interest or right claimed by the applicant, the nature and weight of the public interest objective pursued by the measure, the (non-representative) nature of the Court as against the decision-making authority in relation to policy choices, and the relative lack of expertise of the Court in evidentiary and procedural processes.[43] To this list may be added such variables as

---

trade . . . [and] is not entitled to prevent the marketing of a product originating in another Member State which provides a level of protection of the health and life of humans equivalent to that which the national rules are intended to ensure or establish. It is therefore contrary to the principle of proportionality for national rules to require such imported products to comply strictly and exactly with the provisions or technical requirements laid down for products manufactured in the Member State in question when those imported products afford users the same level of protection.

Case 188/84, [1986] ECR 419, para. 16. See also Tridimas (1999a), *supra* n. 1 at 143–144.

[39] See, for instance, Case T-105/95, *WWF UK v. Commission*, [1997] ECR II-313, paras. 64–72 and 76.

[40] See, for instance, Case 382/87, *R. Buet and Educational Business Services (EBS) v. Ministère public*, [1989] ECR 1235 (prohibition on canvassing at private homes for sales of educational material based on protection of consumers); Joined Cases C-1/90 and C-176/90, *Aragonesa de Publicidad Exterior SA and Publivia SAE v. Departamento de Sanidad y Seguridad Social de la Generalitat de Cataluna*, [1991] ECR I-4151, paras. 14, 16 and 18; and Case C-384/93, *Alpine Investments BV v. Minister van Financien*, [1995] ECR I-1141, para. 51, paras. 45, 51 and 55.

[41] Note, however, Advocate-General Fennelly's suggestion in *Germany v. European Parliament and Council* that with respect to restrictions on 'less important rights' such as commercial expression, once the tests of effectiveness and of minimal necessary burden in the first and second stages of proportionality analysis are satisfied, such restrictions can be presumed to have met the third limb of proportionality: Case C-376/98, *Germany v. European Parliament and Council*; Case C-74/99, *The Queen v. Secretary of State for Health and Others, Ex p. Imperial Tobacco Ltd and Others*, para. 166, *per* Fennelly AG.   [42] Tridimas (1999a), *supra* n. 1, at 140.

[43] De Búrca (1993), *supra* n. 1, at 111–112.

the adverse effect of a measure, ways in which comparable situations are treated on the basis of the principle of equal treatment, the urgency of the situation, and the technical nature of the subject matter calling for special expertise.[44]

With respect to the assessment of proportionality of national measures, it may be questioned whether there is any hierarchy among the grounds of public interest derogation as embodied in escape clauses, or among the (open-ended) list of mandatory requirements.[45] Article 30 (ex Article 36) EC does not provide hierarchy among the grounds of public interest derogation. Yet, the survey of the case law suggests that the nature and relative merit of public interests, as provided in Article 30 (ex Article 36) EC, are crucial for setting the standard of review and evidentiary standard. Both public health and public security, as expressly embodied in that provision, admit of a margin of discretion based on technical evaluations, diminishing the vigour of the Court's appraisal,[46] albeit national authorities are required to prove genuine relevance of such public interests.[47]

It is suggested that the standard of scrutiny varies along the sliding scale stretching from a considerably deferential stance to a very rigorous approach.[48] De Búrca advances that within the spectrum of judicial self-restraint, there is variation from the approach treating restrictive measures as non-justiciable to refusal to examine justifications for restrictions, to shifting to the challenger the onus of proving disproportionate nature of such measures.[49] On one hand, where the Court is confronted with issues involving civil liberties and personal rights, the Court is not hesitant to assert its broad scope of judicial inquiry even in areas of controversy. On the other, where the Court deals with a collective or general public interest and if the complex interest of the State involving economic policy choices is at stake, the court's approach becomes 'considerably more deferential' in their review.[50] Similarly, even in political context, measures touching on national security or economic policy would be likely to reduce the Court's assertiveness.[51]

There are several salient features characterising lax policy of review. First, the less restrictive alternative (or necessity) test may be deprived much of its potential

---

[44] Tridimas (1999a), *supra* n. 1, at 122–123.

[45] Among mandatory requirements, the protection of consumers has been considered as one of the most prominent public interest grounds since the *Cassis de Dijon* case. See, for instance, C-315/92, *Verband Sozialer Wettbewerb eV v. Clinique Laboratoires SNC et Estée Lauder Cosmetics GmbH.*, [1994] ECR I-317, para. 15.

[46] On this matter, contrast, however, Joined Cases 266 & 267/87, *The Queen v. Royal Pharmaceutical Society of Great Britain, Ex p. Association of Pharmaceutical Importers and others*, [1989] ECR I-1295, para. 22 (public health) on one hand, and Case 72/83, *Campus Oil Limited v. Minister for Industry and Energy and Others*, [1984] ECR 2727, para. 44; and Case C-347/88, *Commission v. Greece*, [1990] ECR I-4747, (application of the less restrictive alternative test to the public security grounds), paras. 58–60 on the other.

[47] See, for instance, Case 174/82, *Sandoz BV*, [1983] ECR 2445, para. 22 (public health).

[48] De Búrca (1993), *supra* n. 1, at 111–112. Her more recent survey demonstrates that the varying standard of review and the factors determinative of the standard remain largely unaltered: *Id.* (2000), *supra* n. 1, at 97–99.　　　　　　　　　　[49] De Búrca (1993), *supra* n. 1, at 111–112.

[50] *Id.*　　　[51] *Id.*

effectiveness.[52] Secondly, the court has invoked the so-called non-substitution principle according to which the Community judicature should not replace the role of the Community legislature, with the result that the court is not receptive to the argument that the same objective can be achieved by a less burdensome means.[53] Thirdly, in relation to measures susceptible to complex policy assessment on the part of the Community legislature, the court's review is reduced to the 'manifestly inappropriate' test, the most marginal review, with deference to expertise of the legislature.[54] In the *Fedesa* case concerning the ban on certain hormones on public health grounds, the Court ruled that 'the legality of a measure . . . can be affected only if the measure is manifestly inappropriate having regard to the objective which the competent institution is seeking to pursue'.[55] Tridimas[56] points out that such a lax approach has been conspicuous with respect to four policy areas: measures controlling production,[57] measures for a common organization of the market,[58]

---

[52] See, for instance, Case 40/72, *Schroeder v. Germany*, [1973] ECR 125, para. 32; Case C-331/88, *The Queen v. Minister of Agriculture, Fisheries and Food and Secretary of State for Health, ex parte: Fedesa and others*, [1990] ECR I-4023 (the prohibition of certain hormones on public health grounds), paras. 14–17; Case C-8/89, *Vincenzo Zardi v. Consorzio agrario provinciale di Ferrara*, [1990] ECR I-2515, para. 13; Joined Cases C-133/93, C-300/93 and C-362/93, *Antonio Crispoltoni v. Fattoria Autonoma Tabacchi and Giuseppe Natale and Antonio Pontillo v. Donatab Srl ('Crispoltoni')* [1994] ECR I-4863, para. 45; Case C-280/93, *Germany v. Council*, [1994] ECR I-4973, paras. 93–94.

[53] See, in particular, *Germany v. Council*, where Germany sought to annul Council Regulation No. 404/93 that established a common organization of the market in bananas. There the Court rejected the argument based on the less restrictive alternative test, holding that it could not 'substitute its assessment for that of the Council as to the appropriateness or otherwise of the measures adopted by the Community legislature if those measures have not been proved to be manifestly inappropriate for achieving the objective pursued': C-280/93, *Germany v. Council*, [1994] ECR I-4973, paras. 93–94.

[54] In *Schraeder*, the Court expressly invoked this test:

. . . in matters concerning the common agricultural policy, the Community legislator has a discretionary power which corresponds to the political responsibilities imposed by Articles 40 and 43 [now Article 34 and 37 respectively]. Consequently, the legality of a measure adopted in that sphere can be affected only if the measure is manifestly inappropriate having regard to the objective which the competent institution intends to pursue . . .

Case 265/87 *Hermann Schraeder HS Kraftfutter GmbH & Co. KG v. Hauptzollamt Gronau*, [1989] ECR 2237, paras 21–22.

[55] Case C-331/88, *The Queen v. Minister of Agriculture, Fisheries and Food and Secretary of State for Health, Ex p. Fedesa and others*, [1990] ECR I-4023, para. 14. See also, Case 265/87 *Hermann Schraeder HS Kraftfutter GmbH & Co. KG v. Hauptzollamt Gronau*, [1989] ECR 2237, paras. 21–22; Case 179/84, *Piercarlo Bozzetti v. Invernizzi SpA and Ministero del Tesoro*, [1985] ECR 2301, para. 30. In other cases, the Court has invoked a comparably lax notion of 'patently unsuited' or 'manifestly unsuitable' to measure the excess in discretionary power exercised by the Community institution: Case 138/78, *Hans-Markus Stölting v. Hauptzollamt Hamburg-Jonas*, [1979] ECR 713, para. 7; and Case 59/83, *SA Biovilac NV v. EEC*, [1984] ECR 4057, para. 17.

[56] Tridimas (1999a), *supra* n. 1, at 72.

[57] See, for instance, Case 265/87 *Hermann Schraeder HS Kraftfutter GmbH & Co. KG v. Hauptzollamt Gronau*, [1989] ECR 2237, para. 23; Joined Cases C-133, C-300 and C-362/93, *Antonio Crispoltoni v. Fattoria Autonoma Tabacchi and Giuseppe Natale and Antonio Pontillo v. Donatab Srl. ('Crispoltoni')*, [1994] ECR I-4863.

[58] See *Germany v. Council ('Banana'* case), where the applicant had to discharge an onerous burden to prove that the measures adopted by the Council were 'manifestly inappropriate' or that the Council carried out a 'manifestly erroneous assessment', C-280/93, [1994] ECR I-4973, para. 94.

prohibitions or restrictions on the use of certain products or substances[59] and monetary compensatory amounts.[60] Similarly, lax review is prevalent where the Community legislator is entrusted with discretion as to social policy choices, with the Court's scrutiny confined to whether the exercise of discretion by the Community institution has been vitiated by 'manifest error' or 'misuse of powers' or whether the institution has 'manifestly exceeded' the bounds of its discretion.[61] The Court's reluctance to intervene with searching review as regards issues of economic and social policies can be explained by deference to the competence of Community legislature considered more apt than the supranational judicial organ to deal with such policy options.[62]

In contrast to circumstances where Community acts or measures are contested, a stringent review is discernible in cases where Member States attempt to benefit from escape clauses to derogate from Community-law freedoms.[63] As noted by Tridimas,[64] challenge against compatibility of national measures with Community freedoms invites an intense scrutiny in relation to issues of indirect discrimination as well.[65] In these circumstances, the Court's audacious and extensive review can be justified to safeguard the economic freedoms under Community law against impeding national measures. Further, though not as intense as in the case of assessing national measures affecting the Community freedoms, the Court

---

[59] See, for example, Case C-331/88, *The Queen v. Minister of Agriculture, Fisheries and Food and Secretary of State for Health, Ex p. Fedesa and others*, [1990] ECR I-4023.

[60] See, for instance, Case 5/73, *Balkan Import-Export v. Hauptzollamt Berlin-Packhof*, [1973] ECR 1091, paras. 19–23; and Case 9/73, *Carl Schlüter v. Hauptzollamt Lörrach*, [1973] ECR 1135, para. 23 ('manifestly out of proportion').

[61] See, for instance, Case C-84/94, *United Kingdom v. Council ('Organization of the Working Time Directive'* case), [1996] ECR I-5755, para. 58.

[62] See, *Germany v. Parliament and Council*, which applied the 'non-substitution' principle, according to which the Court will not substitute its own evaluation for that of the Community legislature except where such evaluation was 'manifestly inappropriate' or where the disadvantages for some of those affected were 'wholly disproportionate' to the advantages: C-233/94, [1997] ECR I-2405, para. 56.

[63] Component elements of the principle of proportionality are inherent in many escape clauses. See, for instance, Article 30 (ex Article 36); Article 120 (1) (ex Article 109i) second paragraph; and Article 134 (ex Article 115), third paragraph.

[64] Tridimas (1999a), *supra* n. 1, at 126.

[65] For proportionality appraisal of indirect discrimination based on nationality, see, for instance, Case C-330/91, *R. v. Inland Revenue, Commissioners, Ex p. Commerzbank*, [1993] ECR I-4017 (freedom of establishment in relation to refund only available to companies resident for tax purposes in national territory); Case C-237/94, *O'Flynn v. Adjudication Officer*, [1996] ECR I-2617 (freedom of movement for persons with respect to a national rule making grant of a funeral payment conditional upon the funeral taking place on national territory).

For the role of proportionality in the context of indirect sex discrimination, see, *inter alia*, Case C-328/91, *Secretary of State for Social Security v. Evelyn Thomas and others*, [1993] ECR I-1247 (discrimination in relation to invalidity benefits); and Case C-278/93, *Edith Freers and Hannelore Speckmann v. Deutsche Bundespost*, [1996] ECR I-1165; and Case C-457/93, *Kuratorium für Dialyse und Nierentransplanation e. V. v. Johanna Lewark*, [1996] ECR I-243 (both cases concerning the national rules limiting compensation for loss of earnings, which arose from attending training courses, to individual working hours at the disadvantage of part-time staff members).

has not hesitated to examine at length administrative measures in the field of agriculture, including forfeiture of deposits and securities.[66]

III. The Protection of Fundamental Rights as a General Principle of EC Law

A. Overview

It is settled case law of the ECJ that fundamental rights form an integral part of the general principles of law, and that the ECJ has drawn inspiration from both the common constitutional traditions of the Member States and international human rights treaties, in particular, the ECHR.[67] That fundamental rights constitute general principles of EC law is evidenced in the preamble to the Single European Act and in Articles 6(2)[68] and 46(d) of the Treaty on the EU. The proposed incorporation of the Charter of the Fundamental Rights and Freedoms,[69] which in itself lacks binding force,[70] into the Constitution would reaffirm the EU's commitment to condemn measures incompatible with the observance of human rights.[71]

B. The Scope of Application

There are mainly three circumstances in which the compatibility with fundamental rights need to be assessed under Community law. First, when adopting Community

---

[66] See, for instance, Case 11/70, *Internationale Handelsgesellschaft mbH v. Einfuhr-und Vorratsstelle Getreide*, [1971] ECR 1125, paras. 14–16; and Case 21/85, *A. Maas & Co. NV v. Bundesanstalt für Landwirtschaftliche Marktordnung*, [1986] ECR 3537, paras. 15 and 28; Case 181/84, *The Queen, Ex p. E. D. & F. Man (Sugar) Ltd v. Intervention Board for Agricultural Produce (IBAP)*, [1985] ECR 2889, paras. 15–29.

[67] See, *inter alia*, Case 4/73, *J. Nold, Kohlen- und Baustoffgrosshandlung v. Commission*, [1974] ECR 491, p. 507; Case C-260/89, *ERT v. DEP & Sotirios Kouvelas*, [1991] ECR I-2925, para. 41; Case C-274/99P *Connolly v. Commission*, [2001] ECR I-1611, para. 37; and *Case C-94/00, Roquette Frère SA v. Directeur général de concurrence, de la consumation et de la répression des fraudes, and Commission*, [2002] ECR I-9011, para. 25.

[68] Article 6(2) of the Treaty on European Union provides that:

The Union shall respect fundamental rights, as guaranteed by the European Convention for the Protection of Human Rights and Fundamental Freedoms signed in Rome on 4 November 1950 and as they result from the constitutional traditions common to the Member States, as general principles of Community law.

[69] For examinations of the legal status of the EU Charter, see, for instance, B. De Witte, "The Legal Status of the Charter: Vital Question or Non-Issue?", (2001) 8 MJ 40.

[70] For cautious reference to the Charter, see, for instance, Case C-353/99P, *Hautala v. Council*, paras. 80–83, *per* Léger AG; Case C-347/03, *Regione Autonoma Friuli-Venezia Giulia and Agenzia Regionale per lo Sviluppo Rurale (ERSA) v. Ministero per le Politiche Agricole e Forestali and Regione Veneto*, paras. 106 and 111, *per* Jacobs AG; Case C-160/03, *Spain v. Eurojust*, para. 35, *per* Poiares Maduro AG.

[71] Case C-260/89, *ERT v. DEP & Sotirios Kouvelas*, [1991] ECR I-2925, para. 41; and Case C-299/95, *Friedrich Kremzow v. Austria*, [1997] ECR I-2629, para. 14.

legislative acts, the Community institutions must verify whether provisions contained in the proposed legislation are compatible with the protection of fundamental rights. Secondly, where Member States are interpreting and implementing EC law, they are required to ensure that such implementation does not infringe fundamental rights derived from the ECHR. In *Wachauf*, the Court stated that since 'the requirements of the protection of fundamental rights in the Community legal order . . . are also binding on the Member States when they implement Community rules . . . the Member States must, as far as possible, apply those rules in accordance with those requirements'.[72] The Member States may be deemed as acting as agents of Community law, and their obligation to act in conformity with fundamental rights extends to circumstances where Community measures do not themselves embody the particular right as such.[73]Thirdly, where derogations from the freedoms of Community law are invoked, derogating measures must abide by the requirement of protecting fundamental rights. Analyzing how fundamental rights as general principles of EC law are employed as benchmarks for assessing the legality of derogation from the freedoms of the Community law[74] deserves of elaborated analyses in the following sub-section. With respect to the second and third scenarios, while the Court is not empowered to evaluate the compatibility with the ECHR of national rules falling outside the ambit of Community law, in case such national rules cover aspects of Community law and a reference for a preliminary ruling is made, it must provide all the criteria for interpretation that would enable national courts to decide the compatibility of national rules with the fundamental rights.[75]

C. Applicability of Fundamental Rights to Derogation Clauses

The four freedoms as embodied in EC Treaty are subject to public interest exceptions expressly enumerated in the relevant derogation clauses, and in case of indistinctly applicable measures against free movement of goods, also to 'overriding requirements relating to the public interest' (mandatory requirements). [76] It is

---

[72] Case 5/88, *Wachauf v. Germany*, [1989] ECR 2609, para. 19.

[73] In this regard, see, for instance, Case 36/75, *Rutili v. Minister for the Interior*, [1975] ECR 1219; and Case 222/84, *Johnston v. Chief Constable of the Royal Ulster Constabulary*, [1986] ECR 1651.

[74] For a case concerning free movement of goods, see, for instance, Case C-62/90, *Commission v. Germany*, [1992] ECR I-2575, para. 23 (the right to respect for private life, in particular, the right to the protection of medical confidentiality). For cases involving the freedom to provide services, see, *inter alia*, Case C-260/89, *ERT v. DEP & Sotirios Kouvelas*, [1991] ECR I-2925, para 43 (freedom of expression); Case C-368/95, *Vereinigte Familiapress Zeitungsverlags-und vertriebs GmbH v. Heinrich Bauer Verlag*, [1997] I-3689, para. 24 (freedom of expression); and Case C-60/00, *Mary Carpenter v. Secretary of State for the Home Department*, [2002] ECR I-6279, para. 40 (right to family life).

[75] Case C-260/89, *ERT v. DEP & Sotirios Kouvelas*, [1991] ECR I-2925, para. 42; Case C-71/02, *Herbert Karner Industrie-Auktionen GmbH v. Troostwijk GesmbH*, para. 74, *per* Alber AG (not yet reported).

[76] Case 120/78, *Rewe-Zentrale AG v. Bundesmonopolverwaltung für Branntwein ('Cassis de Dijon')*, [1979] ECR 649.

established case law that public derogations from the freedoms of Community law, which is invoked by a Member State, must be evaluated in the light of general principles of Community law, in particular, both the principle of proportionality and the protection of fundamental rights. For instance, in *ERT*, which concerned the compatibility of television monopoly with free movement of services under Community law, the Court ruled that freedom of expression in itself constituted the general principle of Community law. According to the Court, derogations from both the freedom of establishment and the free movement of services, which were based on public policy, public security and public health as stipulated in ex Articles 66 and 56 (now Articles 55 and 46), must be subordinated to the requirement that such derogations should satisfy conditions for justifying limitations on freedom of expression.[77]

However, extending obligations to protect fundamental rights in derogation context is not free from controversy. Advocate General Jacobs observed in his article in 2001[78] that once the applicability of a particular derogation is confirmed in principle, there should not be further room for assessing whether the derogation is applied with respect for human rights. In contrast, from his constitutional policy perspective, Eeckhout forcefully argues for the extension of the duty to respect human rights in derogation context, stating that if the EU takes human rights seriously, they would inevitably be pervasive in EU law.[79] He contends that the application not only of express derogation and exceptions but also of the *Cassis de Dijon* 'rule-of-reason'[80] should be contested unless such application complies with fundamental rights.[81] Weiler and Fries, writing prior to the adoption of the EU Charter of Fundamental Rights, proposed a medium line of solution to the extension of the duty to respect fundamental rights in derogation context. They maintained that the standard of human rights review by the Community courts should be more deferential than the 'normal Community standard', with 'maximum leeway' accorded to national policy choices. This means that the courts' role would be confined to the assessment of whether a national measure has abided by 'the basic core' encapsulated in the ECHR, without introducing as benchmarks

---

[77] Case C-260/89, *ERT v. DEP & Sotirios Kouvelas*, [1991] ECR I-2925, paras. 43–45.

[78] F. Jacobs, "Human Rights in the EU: The Role of the Court of Justice", (2001) 26 EL Rev 331, at 336–339. Jacobs' restrictive view in 2001 should be contrasted to his previous view that espoused a wider extent of human rights guarantees. See, for instance, C-168/91, *Christos Konstantinidis v. Stadt Altensteig—Standesamt and Landratsamt Calw—Ordnungsamt*, [1993] ECR I-1218, *per* Jacobs AG.

[79] P. Eeckhout, "The EU Charter of Fundamental Rights and the Federal Question", (2002) 39 CML Rev 945, at 977–978.

[80] This *Cassis* rule of reasoning is developed from the rule of reason in *Dassonville*, according to which absent Community harmonization, a Member State can take reasonable measures to prevent unfair trade practice. The *Cassis* formula enables a Member State to provide mandatory requirements to justify a rule inhibiting a free movement of goods without such a rule being caught by Article 28 (ex Article 30): Case 8/74, *Procureur du Roi v. Dassonville*, [1974] ECR 837; and Case 120/78, *Rewe-Zentrale AG v. Bundesmonopolverwaltung für Branntwein ('Cassis de Dijon' case)*, [1979] ECR 649.

[81] Eeckhout, *supra* n. 79, at 978.

any additional EU law list of fundamental rights.[82] The main rationale for such judicial self-restraint is that in contrast to the agency-type scenario, such as the *Wachauf* situation,[83] where the Member States implement Community legislation, a Member State invoking derogations or exceptions is applying its own policy.[84]

Whatever the degree of applicability of fundamental rights in derogation context, it is clear that the application of the principle of proportionality strengthens the standard of scrutiny of national derogating measures.[85] In case of national rules or practices obstructing both Community-law freedoms and fundamental rights, proportionality appraisal can be further intensified. The most intense form of review may operate with onus on national authorities to prove that the restriction in question must be proportionate to the legitimate public end and the least onerous of intra-Community trade or service so that it does not infringe upon the 'very substance' of the fundamental rights guaranteed.[86]

D. The Protection of Fundamental Rights as Part of Mandatory Requirements

Apart from a common scenario in which fundamental rights form a benchmark against which all derogating measures, including those based on mandatory requirements, need to be measured,[87] the protection of fundamental rights is recognised as part of the mandatory requirements that may justify derogation from free movement of goods.[88] In such circumstances, the courts may not disclose as rigorous a standard of proportionality as in a derogation context.

In *Schmidberger*,[89] the ECJ was asked to decide the balance to be struck between the protection of freedom of expression and freedom of assembly on one

---

[82] J.H.H. Weiler and S.C. Fries, "A Human Rights Policy for the European Community and Union: The Question of Competences", in P. Alston (ed.), *The EU and Human Rights*, (Oxford: OUP, 1999), pp. 161–165.

[83] Case 5/88, *Wachauf v. Germany*, [1989] ECR 2609.

[84] J.H.H. Weiler, *The Constitution of Europe*, (Cambridge: Cambridge Univ. Press, 1999), Ch. 3, at 126.

[85] For assessment of escape clauses, see, P. Oliver, *Free Movement of Goods in the European Community: under Articles 30 to 36 of the Rome Treaty*, (3rd edn, London: Sweet and Maxwell, 1996), Ch. IX.

[86] See, *inter alia*, Case 44/79, *Hauer v. Land Rheinland-Pfalz*, (1979) ECR 3727, para. 5; Case 265/87, *Hermann Schraeder HS Kraftfutter GmbH & Co KG v. Hauptzollamt Gronau*, [1989] ECR 2237, para. 15; Case C-62/90, *Commission v. Germany*, [1992] ECR I-2575, para. 23; and Case C-404/92 P, *X v. Commission*, 5 October 1994, [1994] ECR I-4737, para. 18.

[87] Case C-368/95, *Vereinigte Familiapress Zeitungsverlags-und vertriebs GmbH v. Heinrich Bauer Verlag*, [1997] ECR I-3689, para. 24.

[88] Case C-112/00, *Eugen Schmidberger, Internationale Transporte und Planzüge v. Austria*, (2003) ECR I-5659, paras. 74 and 78.

[89] *Id.* This was the first case where respect for fundamental rights has been invoked to justify restrictions on the right under Article 28: C. Brown, Case Comment, "Case C-112/00, Case C-112/00, *Eugen Schmidberger, Internationale Transporte und Planzüge v. Austria*, Judgment of 12 June 2003, Full Court", (2003) 40 CML Rev 1503.

hand, and the free movement of goods on the other. The peaceful demonstration for environmental and health causes by protesters resulted in the complete closure of the Brenner motorway for 30 hours, preventing a German international transport company from securing the delivery of goods through this major trans-Alpine transport between Italy and Germany. Schmidberger brought proceedings against the Austrian government for damages caused to their business, complaining that the failure by Austrian authorities to restrict the impact of the demonstration resulted in the obstacle to the free movement of goods.[90] The Court's reasoning suggests that when mandatory requirements are premised on one of the foundational rights in democracy, the standard of reviewing limitations on the Community freedom may be transformed into a much less intense form than in other context. The Court's readiness to recognize a 'wide margin of appreciation'[91] notwithstanding available means less onerous of intra-Community trade, such as stricter conditions that could have been imposed on the organizers of the demonstration in relation to its site and duration, can be explained by the greater weight given to the demand of the freedom of expression and freedom of assembly.

Similarly, national derogation measures may be based on the combination of public interest grounds and fundamental rights. Again, given the relative merit of countervailing interests, the standard of scrutiny may not acquire intensity. Yet, national authorities must substantiate the merit of such opposing grounds, as can be seen in the case of *Commission v. Germany*.[92] There, the dispute related to a German law prohibiting private individuals importing for their personal needs medical products available on prescription in Germany, which were prescribed by a doctor and purchased in a pharmacy in another Member State. The German government submitted that the contested ban on such importation was necessary to achieve the objective of protecting health and life of humans as provided in ex Article 36 (now Article 30) EC, referring, as one of the specific reasons, to the impossibility of ensuring the frontier control on imported medicinal products without intruding on importers' personal privacy related to medical confidentiality.[93] While rejecting such argument for lack of evidence,[94] the Court ruled that the exercise of national discretion as to derogating measures[95] had to conform to the requirements derived from fundamental rights, including the right to

---

[90] It is well-established in the case law that Article 28 requires a Member State to discharge positive obligations to abstain from taking action, and that Article 28 captures a scenario in which a Member State fails to adopt adequate measures to prevent obstacles to the free movement of goods, which are created by private individuals on its territory: C-265/95, *Commission v. France*, [1997] ECR I-6959, paras. 30–31; and Case C-112/00, *Eugen Schmidberger, Internationale Transporte und Planzüge v. Austria*, [2003] ECR I-5659, paras. 57–58.

[91] Case C-112/00, *Eugen Schmidberger, Internationale Transporte und Planzüge v. Austria*, [2003] ECR I-5659, paras. 89–93.

[92] Case C-62/90, *Commission v. Germany*, [1992] ECR I-2575.   [93] *Id.*, para. 21.

[94] *Id.*, paras. 25–27. On this matter, the Court found that the German government failed to discharge the burden of establishing evidence demonstrating that such control measures could not be implemented without violating importers' privacy.   [95] *Id.*, para. 10.

privacy.[96] In that case, the flimsy nature both of the right to privacy and public health grounds may justify intense review.

E. The Principle of Proportionality and Freedom of Expression under EC Law

Needless to say, fundamental rights guaranteed as general principles of Community law cover freedom of expression.[97] The approach of the Community judicature is to draw on the jurisprudence of the Strasbourg organs under Article 10 of the ECHR to determine the protective scope of this right under the Community law, with the ECHR described as of 'special significance as a source of inspiration'.[98] The ECJ has consistently held that the freedom of expression and the freedom of assembly are subject to limitations pursuant to public interests, provided that such limitations meet the three-pronged criteria as established in the case law of the ECHR ('prescribed by law' or legal basis test; legitimate aims; and 'necessary in a democratic society').[99] The latitudes ('the margin of appreciation') of national authorities in assessing 'pressing social need' can be constrained by the requirement to adduce reasons 'relevant and sufficient' to warrant interference, with their onus of proof heavier in case of prior restrictions on freedom of expression.[100] The weight of public ends and the nature of activities involved are to be factored into this balancing inquiry.

It appears that the approach pursued by the Court is to synthesize interpretive principles developed by the Strasbourg Court under Article 10(2) ECHR into the general method of assessment devised to examine limitations of free movement of goods under EC law. Yet, when assessing restrictions on freedom of expression, the ECJ is inclined to highlight its own distinct interpretive devices, attempting to shape 'autonomous' judicial reasoning. First, in some instances, the ECJ has incorporated the requirement of non-discrimination as part of

---

[96] *Id.*, para. 23. The Court has recognized that the right to respect for private life ranks among fundamental rights guaranteed by the Community legal order: Case 136/79, *National Panasonic v. Commission*, [1980] ECR 2033, paras. 17–18; C-62/90, *Commission v. Germany*, [1992] ECR I-2575, para. 23; and C-404/92 P, *X v. Commission*, [1994] ECR I-4737, para. 17.

[97] Case C-260/89, *ERT v. DEP & Sotirios Kouvelas*, [1991] ECR I-2925, para. 44; Case C-368/95, *Familiapress v. Bauer Verlag*, [1997] ECR I-3689, para. 25. See also Case C-353/89, *Commission v. Netherlands*, [1991] ECR I-4069, para. 30; and Case C-148/91, *Vereiniging Veronica Omroep Organisatie v. Commissariaat voor de Media*, [1993] ECR I-487, para. 10.

[98] Case C-260/89, *ERT v. DEP & Sotirios Kouvelas*, [1991] ECR I-2925, para. 41; Case C-222/84, *Johnston v. Chief Constable of the RUC*, [1986] ECR 1651, para. 18.

[99] Case C-368/95, *Vereinigte Familiapress Zeitungsverlags- und vertriebs GmbH v. Heinrich Bauer Verlag*, [1997] ECR I –3689, para. 26; Case C-60/00, *Mary Carpenter v. Secretary of State for the Home Department*, [2002] ECR I-6279, para. 42. For the case law in the ECHR, see *Steel and Others, v. United Kingdom*, Judgment of 23 September 1998, para. 101.

[100] See, for instance, *Handyside v. United Kingdom*, Judgment of 7 December 1976, para. 49; *Müller and Others v. Switzerland*, Judgment of 24 May 1988, para 33; *Vogt v. Germany*, Judgment of 26 September 1995, para. 52; *Wille v. Liechtenstein*, Judgment of 28 October 1999, paras. 61–63; *Wingrove v. United Kingdom*, Judgment of 25 November 1996, paras. 58 and 60.

elements of proportionality appraisal.[101] Secondly, the ECJ has asserted that the criteria for lawful interference with freedom of expression are whether, 'the restrictions in fact correspond to objectives of general interest and do not, taking account of the aim of the restrictions, constitute disproportionate and unacceptable interference, impairing the very substance of the rights guaranteed'.[102] De Witte[103] observes that this standard formula combines the criteria employed by the Strasbourg Court (proportionate balance in relation to a public end) with a doctrinal notion derived from German constitutional law (the *Wesensgehaltgarantie* under Article 19(2) of the German *Grundgesetz*).[104] The notion of 'the very substance of the rights', which corresponds to the 'very essence' requirement surfaced in cases concerning Articles 6 and 11 ECHR,[105] requires authorities to demarcate the hard core of protected rights that cannot be abridged in any circumstances. Yet, whether and to what extent the Community judicature has lived up to these interpretative underpinnings needs to be closely examined. The Community courts may hold back its dynamic stance and recognize a 'wide margin of appreciation' of national authorities in determining a fair balance between conflicting interests.[106]

For the purpose of investigating the ways in which proportionality appraisal has been undertaken by the Community judicature, the following examinations

---

[101] In *RTL*, the ECJ is confronted with the question whether some provisions of Directive 89/552/EEC, which, for the purpose of co-ordinating broadcasting activities, set a limit on advertising breaks to protect artistic value of feature and television films, can be compatible with freedom of expression. The fact that limitations on frequency applied to all operators was one of the relevant considerations: Case C-245/01, *RTL Television GmbH v. Niedersächsische Landesmedienanstalt für privaten Rundfunk*, para. 72 (not yet reported).

[102] Case C-62/90, *Commission v. Germany*, [1992] ECR I-2575, para. 23; Case C-404/92 P, *X v. Commission*, [1994] ECR I-4737, para. 18; Case C-112/00, *Eugen Schmidberger, Internationale Transporte und Planzüge v. Austria*, (2003) ECR I-5659, para. 80.

[103] B. de Witte, "The Past and Future Role of the European Court of Justice in the Protection of Human Rights", in: Alston (ed.), *supra* n. 82, Ch. 27, pp. 859–897, at 880. Despite the possibility of limitations both expressly and implicitly recognized in the *Grundgesetz* (German Federal Constitutional Law: GG), no infringement of the essential content (*Wesensgehalt*) of fundamental rights is allowed under Art. 19(2) GG. For assessment of the *Wesensgehalt*, see K. Hesse, *Grundzüge des Verfassungsrecht der Bundesrepublik Deutschland*, (Heidelberg: Müller, 1995), at paras. 332–334.

[104] Note that when ascertaining the right of access to court under Art. 6 ECHR, the Strasbourg Court has established the similar notion, the 'very essence' requirement. See Y. Arai-Takahashi, *The Margin of Appreciation Doctrine and the Principle of Proportionality in the Jurisprudence of the ECHR*, (Antwerp: Intersentia, 2002), pp. 36–37.

[105] For application of this notion with respect to the right of access to court under Art. 6, see, for instance, *Ashingdane v. United Kingdom*, Judgment of 28 May 1985, para. 57; *Lithgow v. United Kingdom*, Judgment of 8 July 1986, , para. 194; *Fayed v. United Kingdom*, Judgment of 21 September 1994, para. 65; *Tolstoy Misoslavsky v. United Kingdom*, Judgment of 13 July 1995, para. 59; *Bellet v. France*, Judgment of 4 December 1995, para. 31; *Stubbings & Others v. United Kingdom*, Judgment of 22 October 1996, para. 48; *Tinnelly & Sons Ltd & Others and McElduff & Others v. United Kingdom*, Judgment of 10 July 1998, para. 72; and *Pérez de Rada Cavanilles v. Spain*, Judgment of 28 October 1998, para. 44.

[106] Case C-112/00, *Eugen Schmidberger, Internationale Transporte und Planzüge v. Austria*, (2003) ECR I-5659, para. 82.

will focus on three areas of case law in which the right to freedom of expression has been allegedly infringed or where this right has been invoked to justify derogations from Community-law freedoms. These areas include advertisement as a form of commercial expression, access to documents or information held by the Council or Commission, and the freedom of expression exercised by the staff members of the Community.

IV. Advertisement as Form of Commercial Expression

A. Overview

It is settled case law of the Strasbourg organs that advertising forms part of commercial expression guaranteed under Article 10 of the ECHR.[107] In *Karner v. Troostwijk*, Advocate General Alber defines commercial expression as 'the dissemination of information, the expression of ideas or the dissemination of images in the course of the promotion of an economic activity and the corresponding right to receive such information'.[108] Advertisement also constitutes part of the freedom of expression within the context of Community law.[109] Restrictions on television advertising can be justified by recourse to 'overriding reasons relating to the general interest' (mandatory requirements), including the protection of consumers against abuses of advertising, maintaining a certain level of programme quality as part of cultural policy,[110] or fostering pluralism in media and cultural diversity.[111] The EC has enacted a number of legislative acts regulating television broadcasting activities and advertising, pursuant to public objectives such as the protection of viewers as consumers and preservation of cultural/linguistic diversity. Regulatory control exerted on broadcasting inevitably raises the question of conflict with the freedom of expression exercised by broadcasting corporations.

---

[107] See, *inter alia, Markt Intern Verlag GmbH and Klaus Beermann v. Germany*, Judgment of 20 November 1989, para. 25 *et seq*; and *Casado Coca v. Spain*, Judgment of 24 February 1994, para. 35 *et seq*.

[108] Case C-71/02, *Herbert Karner Industrie-Auktionen GmbH v. Troostwijk GesmbH*, para. 75, *per* Alber AG.

[109] Cases C-376/98, *Germany v. Parliament and Council*; and C-74/99, *The Queen v. Secretary of State for Health and Others, Ex p. Imperial Tobacco Ltd and Others*, [2000] ECR I-8419, para. 145, *per* Fennelly AG (joined opinion); Case C-71/02, *Herbert Karner Industrie-Auktionen GmbH v. Troostwijk GesmbH*, para. 75, *per* Alber AG.

[110] Case C-288/89, *Collectieve Antennevoorziening Gounda*, [1991] ECR I-4007, para. 27; and Case C-6/98, *Arbeitsgemeinschaft Deutscher Rundfunkanstalten (ARD) v. PRO Sieben Media AG*, [1999] ECR I-7599, para. 50.

[111] Case C-148/91, *Vereniging Veronica Omroep Organisatie v. Commissariaat voor de Media*, [1993] ECR I-487.

B. Advertisement Subject to Rules on Free Movement of Goods or to Rules on Free Movement of Services?

As illustrated in the difference in approach pursued by the Court in *GB-INNO-BM*[112] and *Schindler*,[113] and as acknowledged by Advocate-General Alber in *Karner*, it is difficult to draw in practice the distinction between free movement of goods and issues falling within services.[114] In *Karner*, contrary to Advocate General Alber's opinion, the ECJ ruled that when a national measure related both to the free movement of goods and freedom to provide services, and if one of those freedoms is entirely *secondary* to the other and could be considered in conjunction, the Court would in principle examine the national measure in respect of one only of those two economic freedoms.[115] In that case, since the dissemination of advertising was deemed as a secondary element in relation to the sale of the goods at issue, the Court confined examinations to aspects of free movement of goods, excluding those of free movement of services.

Advertisement that is *not* a *secondary* element in relation to the sale of goods is governed by rules on free movement of services. These rules include the public interest derogations based on public policy, security, and health, as enumerated under Articles 39(3) and 46, and in the case of natural persons as stipulated under Directive 64/221.[116] However, the following survey deals with the case law in which the courts have focused on examinations of the rules on free movement of goods.

C. Advertisement as a Selling Arrangement

It is necessary to engage in preliminary observations as to whether an advertisement is classified as a non-discriminatory 'selling arrangement' in the sense of *Keck and Mithouard*,[117] which is not prohibited under Article 28 EC. If that is the case, this

[112] Case C-362/88, *GB-INNO-BM v. Confédération du Commerce Luxembourgeois Asbl*, [1990] ECR I-667 (application of *Cassis*).
[113] Case C-275/92, *Her Majesty's Customs and Excise v. Schindler*, [1994] ECR I-1039, para. 92 (lotteries considered not as 'goods' under ex Art. 30 (now Art. 28) but as "services" within the meaning of ex Art. 60 (now Art. 50).
[114] Case C-71/02, *Herbert Karner Industrie-Auktionen GmbH v. Troostwijk GesmbH*, paras. 91–92, *per* Alber AG.
[115] Case C-71/02, *Karner v. Troostwijk*, para. 46 (not published yet). See also Case C-275/92, *Her Majesty's Customs and Excise v. Gerhart Schindler and Jörg Schindler*, [1994] ECR I-1039, para. 22; and Case C-390/99, *Canal Satellite Digital v. Administración General del Estado*, [2002] ECR I-607, para. 31.
[116] Directive 64/221([1963–64] OJ Spec. Ed. 117) is designed to 'co-ordinate' national derogations. This Directive will be replaced by derogation clauses of a new Directive on the right of citizens of the EU and their families to freely move and reside within the territory of the Union: COM (2001) 257, [2001] OJ C270/150; press releases, IP/04/319, Brussels, 10 March 2004, available at http://europa.eu.int/rapid/pressReleasesAction.do?reference=IP/04/319&format=HTML&aged=0&language=EN&guiLanguage=en.
[117] Cases C-267 & 268/91, *Criminal Proceedings against Keck and Mithouard*, [1993] ECR I-6097.

will obliterate the need for restrictions on advertisement to be justified under the derogation clause of Article 30 EC, although there remains a question as to compatibility with ECHR rights of national legislation or practice falling under the scope of application of EC law.

The ban or restrictions on advertising must be assessed on the basis of the principle established in *Dassonville*, which sets the scope of application of Article 28. According to this principle, a measure having an effect equivalent to a quantitative restriction on imports should be perceived as a measure capable of hindering, directly or indirectly, actually or potentially, intra-Community trade.[118] The earlier case law suggested that legislation restricting or banning advertising could, though not directly affecting trade, be deemed as restricting its volume (and hence free movement of goods) by affecting marketing opportunities.[119]

However, the ECJ signalled a total departure from that approach in *Keck and Mithouard*, in which the ECJ drew a distinction between product-related and sales-related measures, considering in principle the latter not to infringe Article 28 EC in the sense of *Dassonville*.[120] Yet, for selling arrangements to be exempted from the obligation of Article 28, two requirements must be fulfilled: first, such provisions are applicable to all relevant traders operating within the national territory; and secondly, they affect in the same manner, in law and in fact, the marketing of domestic products and of those from other Member States.[121] Since the shift in judicial policy in *Keck and Mithouard*, the ECJ has, with the exception of *Gourmet International*,[122] consistently held restrictions on advertising connected to the sale of goods to be sales-related rules not captured by the prohibition of Article 28 EC.[123] Such adamant policy has been pursued despite misgivings expressed by some Advocates General.[124] In *Karner v. Troostwijk*, both Advocate

---

[118] Case 8/74, *Procureur du Roi v. Dassonville*, [1974] ECR 837, para. 5; and Joined Cases C-267/91 and C-268/91, *Criminal Proceedings against Keck and Mithouard*, [1993] ECR I-6097, para. 11.

[119] Case 286/81, *Criminal proceedings against Oosthoek's Uitgeversmaatschappij BV*, [1982] ECR 4575; Case C-362/88, *GB-Inno-BM*, [1990] ECR I-667; Joined Cases C-1/90 and C-176/90, *Aragonesa de Publicidad Exterior SA and Publivia SAE v. Departmento de Sanidad and Seguridad Social de la Generalitat de Cataluna*, [1991] ECR I-4151; Case C-126/91, *Schutzverband gegen Unwesen in der Wirtschaft e.V. v. Yves Rocher*, [1993] ECR I-2361.

[120] This means that national provisions restricting or banning selling arrangements are not considered as hindering directly or indirectly, actually or potentially, trade between Member States: Joined Cases C-267/91 and C-268/91, *Criminal Proceedings against Keck and Mithouard*, [1993] ECR I-6097, para. 16 *et seq.*   [121] *Id.*

[122] Case C-405/98 *Konsumentombudsmannen (KO) v. Gourmet International Products AB*, [2001] ECR I-1795. In that case, the ECJ ruled that the restriction on free movement of goods caused by the prohibition on advertising of alcohol beverages was justified on the basis of public health exceptions under Article 36 (now Article 30), with that restriction deemed as proportionate.

[123] Case C-292/92 *Ruth Hünermund v. Landesapothekerkammer Baden-Württemberg* [1993] ECR I-6787; C-412/93 *Société d'Importation Eduard Leclerc-Siplec v. TF1 Publicité SA and M6 Publicité SA*, [1995] ECR I-179; Joined Cases C-34/95 and C-36/95 *Konsumentombudsmannen (KO) v. De Agostini (Svenska) Förlag AB and TV-Shop I Sveringe AB*, [1997] ECR I-3843.

[124] See, for instance, C-412/93 *Société d'Importation Eduard Leclerc-Siplec v. TF1 Publicité SA and M6 Publicité SA* [1995] ECR I-179, at 194, *per* Jacobs AG.

General Alber and the ECJ, after examining the evolution of the relevant case law, concluded that the Austrian law on unfair competition law was a selling arrangement that did not breach Article 28 EC, in relation to the effect of that law which, for the purpose of protecting consumers, proscribed the advertisement that stated that the goods originated from an insolvency estate.[125]

D. Derogations under Article 30 EC and Mandatory Requirements

The sheer number of lawsuits involving the free movement of goods, and the fact that judicial reasoning adduced to ascertain derogations from this freedom has been emulated in the context of other freedoms, warrant close inquiry into how national measures derogating from free movement of goods under Article 30 have been scrutinised. Article 30 justifies restrictions on imports based on public morality, public policy or public security; protection of health and life of humans,[126] animals or plants; protection of national treasures possessing artistic, historic or archaeological value; or protection of industrial and commercial property. Apart from those explicitly mentioned public interest grounds, it is established in the case law that in the absence of harmonization, obstacles to intra-community trade in goods, which can be derived from disparities between national law provisions, may be recognized on condition that such provisions apply to domestic and imported products without distinction and are justified as being necessary to pursue mandatory requirements. Mandatory requirements that the ECJ has recognized for 'saving' indistinctly applicable measures against free movement of goods include the protection of consumers and fair trading,[127] linguistic diversity, protection of environment,[128] protection of fundamental rights[129] and press diversity.[130] While

---

[125] Case C-71/02, *Herbert Karner Industrie-Auktionen GmbH v. Troostwijk GesmbH*, para. 39 *per* Alber AG; (not yet reported). In that case, however, Advocate General Alber stressed that restrictions on advertisement deemed as a selling arrangement remained subjected to proportionality scrutiny in the context of the free movement of services. He concluded that a statement intended to distinguish the advertisement from an auction of assets in an insolvency estate was a measure less stringent than total prohibition but equally effective for consumer protection and fair trading: *Id.*, *per* Alber AG, paras. 99–100.

[126] The Court has stressed that Art 30 (ex Art 36) EC remains applicable for so long as harmonization of national legislation in the field of the manufacture and marketing of proprietary medicinal products has not been fully achieved: Case 215/87, *Schumacher v. Hauptzollamt Frankfurt am Main-Ost*, [1989] ECR 617, paras. 15–17; Case C-347/89, *Freistaat Bayern v. Eurim-Pharm GmbH*, [1991] ECR I-1747, para. 26; and Case C-62/90, *Commission v. Germany*, [1992] ECR I-2575, para. 10.

[127] See, for instance, Joined Cases C-34/95 and C-36/95 *Konsumentombudsmannen (KO) v. De Agostini (Svenska) Förlag AB and TV-Shop I Sveringe AB*, [1997] ECR I-3843, para. 46.

[128] See, for instance, Case C-2/90, *Commission v. Belgium*, [1992] ECR I-4431 (transfrontier shipment of hazardous waste); and Case C-389/96, *Aher-Waggon GmbH v. Germany*, [1998] ECR I-4473 (noise emissions from aircraft).

[129] Case C-112/00, *Eugen Schmidberger, Internationale Transporte und Planzüge v. Austria*, (2003) ECR I-5659, paras. 74 and 78.

[130] Case C-368/95, *Vereinigte Familiapress Zeitungsverlags-und vertriebs GmbH v. Heinrich Bauer Verlag*, [1997] I-3689, para. 26. In order to justify an 'overriding requirement' based on press

distinctly applicable measures must be justified only by way of derogation under Article 30 (ex Article 36), non-discriminatory selling arrangements may be justified by way of mandatory requirements, the list of which is open for new additions based on overriding public interests of non-economic nature.[131]

However, national provisions impeding free movement of goods need to be assessed on the basis of two general principles of Community law: first, the principle of proportionality, in particular its second limb of necessity (the less restrictive alternative test)[132]; and secondly, the protection of fundamental rights.[133] In case the Court makes a reversal in its approach and decides to bring issues of prohibition on advertising into the ambit of Article 28 EC, this would require assessment of whether such restrictions can be justified by reference to public interest derogations under Article 30 EC or to the broader list of mandatory requirements.

E. Proportionality Employed to Assess Restrictions on Advertising

When examining compatibility of public interest derogations or mandatory requirements with freedom of expression, the Community judicature undertakes proportionality appraisal not based on interpretive techniques that the Strasbourg organs have deployed in the context of Article 10(2) ECHR, but on the elements of proportionality and along the line of reasoning established in general context of EC law.[134] In *Karner*, when evaluating the suppression of truthful information concerning the origin of goods in a private auction, Advocate General Alber stated that the application of the less restrictive alternative test must be part of an assessment of restrictions on freedom of expression. He closely examined the efficacy of less stringent means, such as the requirement in the text of the advertisement to clarify that the auction was not held by or on behalf of the insolvency administrator. The interlocutory injunction from the Vienna Commercial Court indicated such a less onerous

---

diversity, the Court cited the ECHR judgment in *Informationsverein Lentia and Others v. Austria*, Judgment of 24 November 1993, but the Strasbourg Court in that case did not deal with the question whether press diversity was a legitimate aim.

[131] C. Barnard, *The Substantive Law of the EU—the Four Freedoms*, (Oxford: Oxford University Press, 2004), at 98 and 109; Oliver, *supra* n. 85, at 247; Tridimas (1999a), *supra* n. 1, at 132–133. For recognition of an open-ended nature of mandatory requirements, see Joined Cases C-34/95 and C-36/95 *Konsumentombudsmannen (KO) v. De Agostini (Svenska) Förlag AB and TV-Shop I Sverige AB*, [1997] ECR I-3843, paras. 45–7.

[132] Case C-313/94, *F.lli Graffione SNC v. Ditta Fransa*, [1996] ECR I-6039, para. 17; Case C-3/99, *Cidrerie Ruwet SA v. Cidre Stassen SA and HP Bulmer Ltd*, [2000] ECR I-8749, para. 50; and Case C-71/02, *Herbert Karner Industrie-Auktionen GmbH v. Troostwijk GesmbH*, para. 70, *per* Alber AG. See also Case C-347/89, *Freistaat Bayern v. Eurim-Pharm GmbH*, [1991] ECR I-1747, para. 27; Case C-62/90, *Commission v. Germany*, 8 April 1992, [1992] ECR I-2575, para. 11.

[133] Case C-71/02, *Herbert Karner Industrie-Auktionen GmbH v. Troostwijk GesmbH*, para. 74, *per* Alber AG.

[134] See, for instance, Case C-71/02, *Herbert Karner Industrie-Auktionen GmbH v. Troostwijk GesmbH*, paras. 79–83 *et seq*, *per* Alber AG.

venue, ordering Troostwijk to state that the auction was not an insolvency auction. In line with this judgment and *Yves Rocher*, where the Court found such clarification to be a less stringent measure capable of achieving the legitimate end of consumer protection,[135] Alber found a necessity test to be breached, and the ban on the advertising not to be justified under Article 30 or by 'overriding reasons in the general interest'.[136] Alber's approach based on the necessity test indicates a much more assiduous approach than that of the Strasbourg Court, which has yet to refine the test of less restrictive alternative beyond a haphazard form applied in a piecemeal manner.[137]

F. Commercial Expression and the Lax Standard of Review

The perusal of the ECHR jurisprudence suggests that the protection of commercial expression is weaker than that of political or artistic expression. It has been often stated that unlike political, journalistic, literary or artistic expression that serves to enhance democratic debate and accountability and to foster tolerance of criticizing orthodoxies, commercial expression pursues a social function limited to the promotion of economic activity. While a proportionality review of encroachments on political expression is set at an intense level, with competent authorities required to establish 'convincing evidence of a pressing social need',[138] the scrutiny of commercial expression is limited to whether national competent authorities acted in a reasonable manner when deciding that such encroachments were necessary for the legitimate objective.[139]

In *Karner*, the ECJ, emulating the relevant case law of the ECHR, ruled that in case the exercise of freedom of expression is *not* considered to be of such nature as to contribute to a 'discussion of public interest' and take place in areas where Member States have a 'margin of appreciation', review should be limited to an examination of reasonableness and proportionality of the interference, taking into account the legitimate goals based on consumer protection and fair

---

[135] Case C-126/91, *Schutzverband gegen Unwesen in der Wirtschaft e.V. v. Yves Rocher GmbH*, [1993] ECR I-2361, paras. 16–18.

[136] Case C-71/02, *Herbert Karner Industrie-Auktionen GmbH v. Troostwijk GesmbH*, paras. 83–86, *per* Alber AG.   [137] See *infra* Section G.

[138] See, among others, *Mathieu-Mohin and Clerfayt v. Belgium*, Judgment of 2 March 1987, para. 47; *Lingens v. Austria*, Judgment of 8 July 1986, paras. 41–42; *Castells v. Spain*, Judgment of 23 April 1992, para. 42; *Piermont v. France*, Judgment of 27 April 1995, para. 76; *Bowman v. United Kingdom*, Judgment of 19 February 1998, para. 42; *Vgt Verein gegen Tierfabriken v. Switzerland*, Judgment of 28 June 2001, paras. 74–79 (political advertising); *Feldek v. Slovakia*, Judgment of 12 July 2001, paras. 81–89. See also, *Ahmet Sadik v. Greek*, Commission's Report of 4 April 1995 (no examinations of merits by the Court for non-exhaustion of domestic remedies: Judgment of 15 November 1996). Likewise, for application of stringent scrutiny in relation to journalistic expression, see, *inter alia, Jersild v. Denmark*, Judgment of 24 September 1994; *Praeger and Oberschlick v. Austria*, Judgment of 26 April 1995, para. 38; and *Perna v. Italy*, Judgment of 25 July 2001, para. 42.

[139] See, for instance, *Markt Intern Verlag GmbH and Klaus Beermann v. Germany*, Judgment of 20 November 1989, paras. 33 and 37; and *Jacubowski v. Germany*, Judgment of 23 June 1994, para. 26.

trading.[140] According to the ECJ, such a limited review would be appropriate in a field that is as 'complex and fluctuating' as advertising.[141] With respect, two criticisms may be levelled against the Court's approach. First, the ECJ has followed the misconceived reasoning of the Strasbourg organs when determining its standard of review. The margin of appreciation should not provide a peg on which to hang the argument for restraining the scope of proportionality scrutiny. On the contrary, the notion of proportionality should serve as a benchmark against which a permissible scope of margin needs to be tightly adjusted.[142] Secondly, reference to the concepts of reasonableness and proportionality fails to grasp the depth of difference in those two concepts.[143] In that case, the Court may be criticised for failing to undertake its own close appraisal of proportionality.

In *Germany v. European Parliament and Council*, which concerned the Tobacco Advertising Directive, Advocate General Fennelly suggested a more stringent scrutiny. He opined that despite complexities involved in assessing effects upon the level of tobacco consumption, of both advertising and the comprehensive ban on such advertising, commercial expression was impervious to such a lax standard of judicial review as that applicable to economic rights (the right to property and the right to pursue profession).[144] The crux of his argument is that even commercial expression is linked to autonomy, dignity and personal development of individuals in liberal democracy,[145] so that the standard of review should be set at the intermediate level between the intense scrutiny of restrictions on political expression and more lax review of interference based on protection of morals.[146] Fennelly's view tallies with Twomey's argument that there is 'mixed' expression or commercial expression combining artistic elements or political messages.[147]

Notwithstanding the Court's lax review in *Karner*, the general tendency of the Community judicature is to apply a more intense standard to issues of advertising than that seen in the case law of commercial expression under Article 10 ECHR.[148] That as in the case of restrictions on advertising, derogations from free

---

[140] Case C-71/02, *Herbert Karner Industrie-Auktionen GmbH v. Troostwijk GesmbH*, para. 51–52.

[141] *Id.* In this regard, the ECJ referred to Case C-245/01, *RTL Television*, para. 73 and judgments of the ECHR: *Markt Intern Verlag GmbH and Klaus Bermann v. Germany*, Judgment of 20 November 1989, para. 33; and *VGT Verein gegen Tierfabriken v. Switzerland*, Judgment of 28 June 2001, paras. 69–70.

[142] Arai-Takahashi, *surpa* n. 104, at 193–195.

[143] De Búrca (2000), *supra* n. 1, at 102–103.

[144] C-376/98, *Germany v. European Parliament and Council*; Case C-74/99, *The Queen v. Secretary of State for Health and Others, Ex p. Imperial Tobacco Ltd and Others*, para. 157, *per* Fennelly AG (joined opinion).   [145] *Id.*, para. 154.

[146] *Id.*, para. 156.

[147] Twomey criticizes the Strasbourg Court for its 'over-zealous' application of the margin of appreciation whenever commercial expression is involved: P.M. Twomey, Freedom of Expression for Commercial Actors, in N.A. Neuwahl and A. Rosas (eds.), *The European Union and Human Rights*, (London: Kluwer, 1995), Ch. 14, pp. 265–280, at pp. 273–275.

[148] In contrast, Fennelly AG proposed that the same rationale as underlies the Strasbourg organs' approach under Art. 10 ECHR should apply in the context of Community law: Case C-376/98, *Germany v. European Parliament and Council*; and Case C-74/99, *The Queen v. Secretary of State for Health and Others, Ex p. Imperial Tobacco Ltd and Others*, para. 154, *per* Fennelly AG (joined opinion).

movement of goods also entail encroachments on a fundamental right seems to prompt the Court to embark on a close proportionality scrutiny of public interest grounds or mandatory requirements.

Establishing that a national derogating measure is proportionate to the public objective is not sufficient. The judicial review engaged by the Court is likely to become more in-depth and stringent, with focus on the existence or not of an equally effective measure less burdensome of both economic freedoms in Community law *and* fundamental rights.[149] In the *Familiapress* case, the Court emphasized the need to search for a measure less restrictive of both intra-Community trade and freedom of expression in relation to the outright ban on the sale of periodicals containing prize competitions, which constituted measures having equivalent effect to quantitative restrictions on intra-Community trade under ex Article 30 EC (now Article 28 EC).[150] With respect to the obstacle to the exercise of the free movement of goods, the intense standard of scrutiny can be evidenced by the Court's recognition of measures less obstructive of free trade, which Belgium and Netherlands submitted, such as blacking-out or removing the page featuring prize competitions in copies destined for Austria, or a statement that Austrians would not qualify for the prize competitions.[151]

With respect to the burden of proof and evidentiary standard as well, the survey of the case law reveals a potential of more rigorous scrutiny by the Community judicature than in the case of commercial expression under Article 10 ECHR. This can be illustrated in the requirement that the Community institutions must prove that the necessity test has been fulfilled, with no less obstructive measure capable of achieving the same legitimate end. In *Germany v. European Parliament and Council*, while imposing on Community institutions the onus of establishing the necessity of comprehensive ban on advertising on tobacco-related product, Advocate General Fennelly proposed a standard of proof less rigorous than that required in case of political expression, obliging the relevant authorities to prove 'reasonable grounds' for choosing the interfering measure in conformity to public interests.[152] Yet, he demanded the Community institutions to adduce coherent evidence that less restrictive measures would not have been equally effective for achieving the legitimate objective of reducing tobacco consumption.

---

[149] See, for instance, Case C-368/95, *Vereinigte Familiapress Zeitungsverlags- und Vertriebs GmbH v. Heinrich Bauer Verlag,* [1997] ECR I-3689, para. 27.   [150] *Id.*, paras. 27–28.
   [151] *Id.*, paras. 32 and 34.
   [152] Case C-376/98, *Germany v. European Parliament and Council*; and Case C-74/99, *The Queen v. Secretary of State for Health and Others, Ex p. Imperial Tobacco Ltd and Others,* para. 159, *per* Fennelly AG (joined opinion). Unfortunately, the ECJ focused on the pleas based on ex Art. 100a (now Art. 95) of the Treaty as an inappropriate legal basis for the contested Directive (Directive 98/43EC) and on the infringement of both ex Art. 57(2) and Art. 66 of the Treaty (now, Art. 47 (2) and 55 respectively), finding it unnecessary to examine the plea based on the breach of proportionality: Case C-376/98, *Federal Republic of Germany v. European Parliament and Council,* [2000] ECR I-8419, paras. 9 and 118.

It must be emphasized that the standard of review employed to assess commercial expression is not so low as the one applicable to assessment of economic policies. When assessing such policies, the Court has even suggested that the proportionality review could be limited to examining 'whether the exercise of such discretion is vitiated by a manifest error or a misuse of powers or whether [the institutions] did not clearly exceed the bounds of [their] discretion'.[153] In case of economic rights such as the right to property and the freedom to pursue a trade or professional activity,[154] the susceptibility of those rights to general policy choice in complex fields has been cited as a justification for lowering the standard of reviewing legislative choices.[155] The lax scrutiny, which relieves the principle of proportionality of its main function to curtail a Member State's exercise of discretion, would be approximated to the English judicial review test of *Wednesbury* unreasonableness.[156] It is submitted that the proportionality appraisal in the Community law context even in the most reticent mode should not be lowered that far.[157] In that sense, it is of much consequence for the Community Court to make effective use of the general rules based on the notions of proportionality and 'the very essence' even in respect of economic rights.[158]

V. Access to Information

A. Background

The Final Act of the Treaty on European Union signed at Maastricht on 7 February 1992 includes a Declaration (No. 17) on the right of access to information,[159]

---

[153] Case C-180/96, *United Kingdom v. Commission* ("*Mad cow disease*" case), [1998] ECR I-2265, para. 60. Case C-376/98, *Germany v. European Parliament and Council*; and Case C-74/99, *The Queen v. Secretary of State for Health and Others, ex parte Imperial Tobacco Ltd and Others*, para. 156, *per* Fennelly AG (joined opinion).

[154] See, for instance, Case C-44/94, *R. v. Minister for Agriculture, Fisheries and Food, Ex p. Fishermen's Organisations and Others*, [1995] ECR I-3115, paras. 57–61.

[155] Case C-180/96, *United Kingdom v. Commission*, [1998] ECR I-2265, para. 60; and Case C-376/98, *Germany v. European Parliament and Council*; Case C-74/99, *The Queen v. Secretary of State for Health and Others, Ex p. Imperial Tobacco Ltd and Others*, para. 156, *per* Fennelly AG (joined opinion).

[156] For assessment of the *Wednesbury* unreasonableness test, see G. de Búrca, "Proportionality and Wednesbury unreasonableness: The Influence of European Legal Concepts on UK Law", (1997) 3 EPL 561; P. Craig, "Unreasonableness and Proportionality in UK Law", in Ellis (ed.), *supra* n. 1, at 85–106; Lord Irvine of Lairg, "Judges and Decision-Makers: The Theory and Practice of Wednesbury Review", (1996) PL 59. Note also, *R. v. Home Secretary, Ex p. Brind*, [1991] 1 AC 696, in which the House of Lords rejected the principle of proportionality as a ground of review.

[157] On the basis of her analysis conducted in previous article (De Búrca, (1997), *Id.*) and of the examination of *R. v. Chief Constable of Sussex, Ex p. International Trader's Ferry Ltd* (1998) 3 WLR 1260, De Búrca argues that 'a loose and impressionistic reasonable test' cannot be equated to 'a structured proportionality test', on the basis that 'the nature of the judicial inquiry is required to be considerably more rigorous and more careful in the case of the latter': De Búrca (2000), *supra* n. 1, at 102–103.

[158] Case 265/87, *Schraeder v. Hauptzollamt Gronau*, [1989] ECR 2237, para. 15 (and the case law cited therein); Joined Cases T-34/96 and T-163/96, *Connolly v. Commission*, [1999] ECR-SC I-A-87 and II-463, para. 111.   [159] [1992] OJ C191/95, Declaration No. 17.

emphasizing the linkage between the transparency of the decision-making process on one hand and the democratic nature of the institutions and the public's confidence in the administration on the other. On 6 December 1993 the Council and Commission adopted a Code of Conduct concerning public access to Council and Commission documents. The Code of Conduct embodies the general principle that the public will have the 'widest possible access to documents'.[160] In order to give effect to the undertaking expressed in the Code of Conduct, the Council adopted Decision 93/731/EC on public access to Council Documents[161] while the Commission adopted, on 8 February 1994, Commission Decision 94/90/ECSC, EC, Euratom on public access to Commission documents.[162] This gradual move to expansive scope of accessibility to documents in Communities has resulted in the insertion of a new article, Article 191a (now Article 255 EC), into the EC Treaty by the Treaty of Amsterdam. Article 255(1) EC reads that, '[a]ny citizen of the Union, and any natural or legal person residing or having its registered office in a Member State, shall have a right of access to European Parliament, Council and Commission documents, subject to the principles and the conditions to be defined in accordance with paragraphs 2 and 3'.[163] In conformity with such a trend, a proposal has been submitted for a regulation of the European Parliament and of the Council regarding public access to European Parliament, Council and Commission documents,[164] the result of which is Regulation 1049/2001 of the European Parliament and of the Council of 30 May 2001 regarding public access to European Parliament, Council and Commission documents.[165]

Probably the most important step in the direction for enhanced status of this principle is the classification of this right as a fundamental right as incorporated into the Charter of Fundamental Rights of the European Union. Article 42 of the Charter provides that, '[a]ny citizen of the Union, and any natural or legal person residing or having its registered office in a Member State, has a right of access to documents of the Institution, bodies and agencies of the Union, in whatever form they are produced'. The explanatory note to Article 42 of the Charter reveals a close link between this provision and Article 255 EC.[166] The consequence of the

---

[160] Case T-14/98, *Hautala v. Council*, [1999] ECR II-2489, para. 81.

[161] [1993] OJ L 340/43. The Council's power to adopt that decision was based on ex Art. 151(3) EC, which reads that, "[t]he Council shall adopt its Rules of Procedure".

[162] [1994] OJ L 46/58. Decision 94/90 was adopted on the basis of Art. 162 of the EC Treaty (now Art. 218 EC).

[163] However, the limited effect of the principle of transparency, as incorporated into the EC Treaty by the Treaty of Amsterdam, is demonstrated in *Petrie v. Commission*, where the Court of First Instance held that Art. 1 and 255 EC have no direct effect and that the latter could not be invoked to interpret pre-Regulation rules: [2001] ECR II-3677, paras. 34–38; S. Peers, "The New Regulation on Access to Documents: A Critical Analysis", (2002) 21 YBEL 385, at 389.

[164] Proposal 2000/C 177 E/10 ([2000] OJ C 177E/70). See also a draft recommendation on public access to official information prepared by the Council of Europe: Draft prepared by the Group of Specialists on Access to Official Information at its 6th Meeting (from 27–29 September 2000); as referred to in Case C-353/99 P, *Hautala v. Council*, Case C-353/99P, para. 62, *per* Léger AG.

[165] [2001] OJ L145/43.   [166] Case C-353/99 P, *Hautala v. Council*, para. 84, *per* Léger AG.

right of access to documents being described as a fundamental right is that Community institutions, including the ECJ, are required to give full effect to this right.[167] The rights set forth in the Charter are not purported to be binding, but the solemnity of its form and the procedure for its adoption requires the Charter to be interpreted as a 'privileged instrument' for identifying fundamental rights in Community law. There is a growing recognition that the Charter, which will be integrated into the EU Constitution, constitutes 'the highest level of reference values' for the protection of fundamental rights as a matter of Community law.[168]

B. General Rules

It is well-established in the case law since *Netherlands v. Council* that Council Decision 93/731 and Commission Decision 94/90 provide more than a measure of internal organization based on Article 151(3) EC and confer upon citizens the *fundamental right* to access to documents.[169] The right to access to documents is construed as including the right to access to information contained therein.[170] The foundational basis of the right of access to documents can be found in the democratic principle underlying the cornerstones of the Community edifice,[171] and in the need to maintain public confidence in the administration of the democratic system.[172] It is considered as part of the broader principle of transparency,[173] which is designed to provide citizens with a greater role in the decision-making process and to ensure propriety, efficiency and responsibility of Community administration *vis-à-vis* citizens, strengthening the principle of democracy and

[167] In response to the Ombudsman's own-initiative inquiry ((616/PUBAC/F/IJH), [1998] OJ C44/9), institutions other than the Commission, Council and Parliament covered by Regulation 1049/2001, such as the Court of Auditors and ECB, have adopted rules on access to documents, but the ECJ fails to ensue.

[168] Case C-353/99 P, *Hautala v. Council*, paras. 80–83, *per* Léger AG.

[169] See Case C-58/94, *Netherlands v. Council*, [1996] ECR I-2169, paras. 34–37 (access to Council documents based on Decision 93/731); and Case T-105/95, *WWF UK v. Commission*, [1997] ECR II-313, para. 55 (access to Commission documents based on Commission Decision 94/90). For analysis of the right of access to documents, see D. Curtin, "Citizens' Fundamental Right of Access to EU Information: An Evolving Digital Passepartout?", (2000) 37 CML Rev 7; D. Curtin and H. Meijers, "Access to European Union Information: An Element of Citizenship and A Neglected Constitutional Right", in Neuwahl and Rosas (eds.), *supra* n. 147, 77; D. Curtin and H. Meijers, "The Principle of Open Government in Schengen and the European Union: Democratic Retrogression?", (1995) CML Rev 391 *et seq.*; P. Dyrberg, "Current Issues in the Debate on Public Access to Documents", (1999) EL Rev 157.

[170] Case T-14/98, *Hautala v. Council*, [1999] ECR II-2489, paras. 87–88 (concerning access to a report of a Council working party on conventional arms exports); Case C-353/99 P, *Hautala v. Council*, para. 94, *per* Léger AG; and Case T-188/98, *Aldo Kuijer v. Council*, [2000] ECR II-1959, para. 54.

[171] Case C-58/94, *Netherlands v. Council*, [1996] ECR I-2169, points 14 & 19, *per* Tesauro AG.

[172] Case C-353/99 P, *Hautala v. Council*, para. 52, *per* Léger AG.

[173] For analysis of the principle of transparency, see Peers (2002), *supra* n. 163; and A. Tomkins, "Transparency and the Emergence of a European Administrative Law" (1999–2000) 19 YBEL 217.

respect for fundamental rights.[174] The right of access to documents held by public authorities is now guaranteed in the domestic legislation of most Member States as a constitutional or legislative principle.[175] In *Svenska Journalistförbundet*, the CFI emphasized that, '[t]he objective of Decision 93/731 is to give effect to the principle of the largest possible access for citizens to information with a view to strengthening the democratic character of the institutions and the trust of the public in the administration'.[176] Further, in *Kuijer II*,[177] for the first time the CFI has recognized a symbiotic linkage between citizen participation and fundamental rights.[178]

A citizen requesting access to any unpublished Commission document can do so without being compelled to give a reason for the request.[179] Any restrictions on this fundamental right call for strict interpretation so as not to defeat the object and purpose of the Decisions.[180] Such effective interpretation has prevented the Commission stretching the meaning of authorship in relation to documents drafted by 'comitology' committees[181] in order to evade the obligation to disclose information.[182] The effective guarantee of the right of access to documents demands that Council Decision 93/731 and Commission Decision 94/90 must be interpreted in conjunction with the duty to state reasons 'clearly and unequivocally' in individual decisions provided in Article 253 (ex Article 190) EC,[183] so

---

[174] Case T-309/97, *Bavarian Lager v. Commission*, [1999] ECR II-3217, para. 36; and Case T-211/00, *Aldo Kujer v. Council*, para. 52. See also G. de Búrca, "The Quest for Legitimacy in the European Union", (1996) 59 MLR 359.

[175] Case C-58/94, *Netherlands v. Council*, [1996] ECR I-2169, para. 34.

[176] Case T-174/95 *Svenska Journalistförbundet v. Council*,[1998] ECR II-2289, para. 66.

[177] T-211/00, *Kuijer (II) v. Council*, [2002] ECR II-485, para. 52.

[178] Peers (2002), *supra* n. 163, at 390.

[179] Case T-174/95, *Svenska Journalistförbundet v. Council*, [1998] ECR II-2289, para. 65, Case T-111/00, *British American Tobacco International (Investments) Ltd v. Commission*, [2001] ECR II-2997, para. 42.

[180] With respect to Council Decision 93/731 on access to Council documents, see Case T-174/95, *Svenska Journalistförbundet v. Council*, [1998] ECR II-2289, para. 110; and Case T-211/00, *Kuijer v. Council*,[2002] ECR II-485, para. 55. In relation to Commission Decision 94/90/ECSC, EC, Euratom, see, for instance, Case T-105/95, *WWF UK v. Commission*, [1997] ECR II-313, para. 56; Case T-309/97, *Bavarian Lager v. Commission*, [1999] ECR II-3217, para. 39; Case T-124/96, *Interportc I*, [1998] ECR II-231, para. 49; Case T-92/98, *Interporc Im- und Export GmbH v. Commission*, [1999] ECR II-3521, para. 38; and Case T-191/99, *David Petrie, Victoria Jane Primhak, David Verzoni and Others v. Commission*, [2001] ECR II-3677, para. 66.

[181] The establishment of 'comitology' committees is based on ex Art. 145 (now Art. 202) EC, which states that the Council may confer on the Commission, in the acts which the Council adopts, powers to implement the rules which the Council lays down, and pursuant to so-called 'comitology decision', Council Decision 87/373/EEC of 13 July 1987 laying down the procedures for the exercise of implementing powers conferred on the Commission ([1987] OJ L197/33).

[182] Case T-188/97, *Rothmans International BV v. Commission*, [1999] ECR II-2463, paras. 55–57 and 61–62 (access to documents drafted by 'comitology' committees).

[183] Case T-105/95, *WWF UK v. Commission*, [1997] ECR II-313, para. 66; and Case T-92/98, *Interporc Im- und Export GmbH v. Commission (Interporc II)*, [1999] ECR II-3521, para. 77. It is well-established that the duty to state reasons in individual decisions pursue the double objective of protecting interests of interested parties by informing them of the reasons for adopting a certain measure and enabling the CFI and ECJ to exercise judicial review of the contested decision: Case C-350/88, *Delacre and Others v. Commission*, [1990] ECR I-395, para. 15; and Case T-85/94, *Branco v. Commission*, [1995] ECR II-45, point 32.

that a document must contain, at least for each category of documents, specific grounds justifying the Community institution's finding that information falls within one of the exceptions provided in the relevant Decisions.[184]

Whether the notion of transparency, or its constituent element, access to documents held by Community institutions, is now viewed as a general principle of Community law remains controversial.[185] The fact that the application of Article 255 is limited to the three institutions (Commission, Council and Parliament) may hamper the claim that this provision has generated the status of a general principle.[186] Broberg[187] argues that while legislative developments, including the recognition of the right of access to documents under Article 42 of the Charter cannot suffice to uphold the general principle status of this right, the evolution of the case-law has led to such recognition.[188] Advocate General Léger takes the view that since the CFI recognized this right on the basis of Declaration No. 17 and the Code of Conduct in *Interporc*, access to documents has formed part of the general principles of Community law.[189] His contention is that the identification of a general principle of EC law does not depend on establishing existence of either constitutional rules common to Member States or rules embodied in international treaties to which the Member States are parties.[190]

C. Exceptions under the Derogation Clauses

Controversy has arisen as to the criteria for ascertaining restrictions on the right of citizens to access documents on the grounds of public interest derogations

---

[184] See, for instance, Case T-105/95, *WWF UK v. Commission*, [1997] ECR II-313, paras. 70–72.

[185] For the view that access to documents constitutes a general principle of EC law, see, *inter alia*, B. Vesterdorf, "Transparency—Not Just a Vogue Word", (1999) Fordham ILJ 902–929, at 927; H. Ragnemalm, "The Community Courts and Openness Within the European Union", (2000) 2 Cambridge YELS, 19–30, at 24. Contrast these with M. O'Neill, "The Right of Access to Community-Held Documentation as a General Principle of EC Law", (1998) EPL 403–432, at 431; and Dyrberg, *supra* n. 170, at 168, n. 23.

[186] M.P. Broberg, "Access to Documents: A General Principle of Community Law", (2002) 27 EL Rev 194–205, at 197; and D. Curtin, "Citizens' Fundamental Right of Access to Information: An Evolving Digital Passepartout?", (2000) 37 CML Rev 7, at 14.

[187] Broberg, *Id.*, at 198 and 203.

[188] In para. 53 of the *JT's Corporation* case, the CFI ruled:

It should be pointed out that the authorship rule may be applied by the Commission when handling a request for access so long as there is no higher rule of law prohibiting it from excluding from the scope of the Code of Conduct documents of which it is not the author. The fact that Decision 94/90 refers to declarations of general policy, namely Declaration No. 17 and the conclusions of several European Councils does nothing to alter that finding, since those declarations do not have the force of a higher rule of law . . .

If this paragraph is read in conjunction with the requirements that the public should be granted the widest possible access to documents and that the authorship rule must be interpreted narrowly, it is possible to argue that the right of access to documents forms a 'higher rule of law' or a general principle of Community law: Broberg, *Id.*, at 203.

[189] Case T-92/98, *Interporc v. Commission*, [1999] ECR II-3521, para. 38.

[190] Case C-353/99 P, *Hautala v. Council*, para. 69, *per* Léger AG.

provided in the Community legislation. Two relevant Decisions, Council Decision 93/731 and Commission Decision 94/90, adopt a two-tier system comprised of mandatory exceptions and discretionary exceptions. Article 4(1) of Council Decision 93/731 states in mandatory terms that:

Access to a Council document shall not be granted where its disclosure could undermine:

—the protection of the public interest (public security, international relations, monetary stability, court proceedings, inspections and investigations),

—the protection of the individual and of privacy,

—the protection of commercial and industrial secrecy,

—the protection of the Community's financial interests,

—the protection of confidentiality as requested by the natural or legal person who supplied any of the information contained in the document or as required by the legislation of the Member State which supplied any of that information.

Further, the Council's access rules introduced in the 2000 Decision amended the 1993 rules and included two new mandatory 'public interest' exceptions based on protection of 'the security and defence of the Union and one or more of its Member States' and 'military and non-military crisis management'.[191] Article 4(2) of Council Decision 93/731 in turn embodies a discretionary exception, providing that, '[a]ccess to a Council document may be refused in order to protect the confidentiality of the Council's proceedings'.

In terms almost identical to Article 4 of Council Decision 93/731, Article 1 of Commission Decision 94/90, which has formally adopted the Code of Conduct,[192] lays down two categories of exceptions to the right of access to Commission documents. The first paragraph of Article 1 of the Commission Decision 94/90 embodies the first category of exceptions in compulsory terms, and these mandatory exceptions purport to guarantee the interests of the third

---

[191] Art. 1(4) of 2000/527, [2000] OJ L212/9. As Peers notes, the Commission did not amend its access rules to include the equivalent exceptions, on the basis that such exceptions would fall within the exceptions based on 'international relations' or 'public security' in its existing rules: Peers (2002), *supra* n. 163, at 397, n. 63.

[192] The Code of Conduct states that:

The institutions will refuse access to any document where disclosure could undermine:

—the protection of the public interest (public security, international relations, monetary stability, court proceedings, inspections and investigations),

—the protection of the individual and of privacy,

—the protection of commercial and industrial secrecy,

—the protection of the Community's financial interests,

—the protection of confidentiality as requested by the natural or legal persons that supplied the information or as required by the legislation of the Member State that supplied the information.

They may also refuse access in order to protect the institution's interest in the confidentiality of its proceedings.

parties or of the general public.[193] The second category of exceptions, framed in enabling terms in the second paragraph of that provision, embodies the 'institutional confidentiality' relating to the internal deliberations of the institution and involves only the interests of that institution.[194]

Three observations may be made as regards the Court's approach to these categories of exceptions. First, the Commission and the Council can invoke jointly an exception from each category to refuse access to its documents,[195] or combination of two or more mandatory exceptions.[196] Secondly, it is necessary to make inquiry into whether the five categories of public interest exceptions are exhaustive. In *Carlsen*, the CFI even ruled that the five categories were not exhaustive, and that other matters such as 'the maintenance of legal certainty and stability of Community law' and the ability of the Council 'to obtain independent legal advice' could be included as public interest exceptions.[197] However, the fact that the relevant paragraph does not include the wording, 'in particular', which indicates open-ended nature of a list,[198] suggests that the list is exhaustive.[199] Thirdly, the CFI in the earlier case law held that the Commission was 'obliged to refuse' access to documents falling under any one of the mandatory exceptions laid down in Article 1(1) of Commission Decision 94/90, once the relevant circumstances were shown to exist.[200] This statement is perilously misleading in that it suggests denying a possibility of circumscribing the scope of those exceptions in search for effective guarantee of the right of access to documents. Though this statement has occasionally resurfaced,[201] the subsequent case law has shifted its focus to analyzing whether, and if so under what circumstances, access to part of documents not covered by those mandatory exceptions can be justified, in particular by reference to the principle of proportionality.

---

[193] Case T-105/95, *WWF UK v. Commission*, [1997] ECR II-313, para. 60; and Case T-111/00, *British American Tobacco International (Investments) Ltd v. Commission*, [2001] ECR II-2997, para. 35.

[194] Case T-105/95, *WWF UK v. Commission*, [1997] ECR II-313, para. 60; and Case T-111/00, *British American Tobacco International (Investments) Ltd v. Commission*, [2001] ECR II-2997, para. 35.

[195] Case T-105/95, *WWF UK v. Commission*, [1997] ECR II-313, para. 61; Case T-174/95, *Svenska Journalistförbundet v. Council*, [1998] ECR II-2289, para. 114.

[196] Case T-20/99, *Denkavit Nederland BV v. Commission*, [2000] ECR II-3011, para. 41 (protection of the public interest relating to inspections and investigations, and protection of commercial secrecy).

[197] Case T-610/97 R, *Carlsen v. Council*, [1998] ECR II-485, para. 47; and Peers (2002), *supra* n. 163, at 397.

[198] On this matter, see Case C-97/96, *Daihatsu Deutschland*, [1997] ECR I-6843, para. 21 (as to a non-exhaustive list of ex-Art. 54(3)).

[199] Peers (2002), *supra* n. 163, at 398.

[200] See, for instance, Case T-194/94, *John Carvel and Guardian Newspapers v. Council*, [1995] ECR II-2765, para. 64; Case T-105/95, *WWF UK v. Commission*, [1997] ECR II-313, para. 58; Case T-204/99, *Mattila v. Council and Commission*, [2001] ECR II-2265.

[201] See, for instance, *Olli Mattila v. Council*, [2001] ECR II-2265, para. 62.

D. The Proportionality Appraisal under the Derogation Clauses

(i) Overview

The CFI has at times stated that determining whether releasing a document to the public would undermine public or other interests under the derogation clauses falls within the responsibilities conferred on the Council and Commission by the Community Treaties. Such an argument, however specious it may be, would risk minimizing judicial scrutiny, confining it to verifying whether the procedural rules have been complied with, the decision properly reasoned and the facts accurately stated, and whether there has been a manifest error of assessment of the facts or a misuse of powers.[202] However, quite contrary to this deferential rhetoric, a closer look at the case law discloses an eagerness of the Community judicature to apply a heightened standard of scrutiny.

An audacious approach can be confirmed in two respects. First, the Community judicial organs have emphasized that exceptions to the access rule laid down in the Community legislation must be construed and applied strictly[203] so as not to undermine the 'effectiveness' of the general rule.[204] Secondly, akin to the case law concerning derogations from Community-law freedoms,[205] restrictions on the right of access to information need to be evaluated on the basis of the principle of proportionality.[206] With respect to the 'institutional confidentiality' exception, this must be subordinated to stringent scrutiny based on the third limb of proportionality, with the institution required to balance its interest in confidentiality of documents and an applicant's interest in access.[207] Further, the second

---

[202] Case T-14/98, *Hautala v. Council*, [1999] ECR II-2489, para. 72; Case T-211/00, *Kuijer v. Council*, para. 53.

[203] See, for instance, Joined Cases C-174/98 P and C-189/98 P, *Netherlands and Van der Wal v. Commission*, [2000] ECR I-1, para. 27; Case T-20/99, *Denkavit Nederland v. Commission*, [2000] ECR II-3011, para. 45; and Case T-111/00, *British American Tobacco International (Investments) Ltd v. Commission*, [2001] ECR II-2997, para. 40.

[204] Case T-105/95, *WWF UK v. Commission*, [1997] ECR II-313, para. 56; Case T-14/98, *Hautala v. Council*, para. 84, [1999] ECR II-2489; and Case C-353/99 P, *Hautala v. Council*, para. 25. See also cases concerning Council Decision 93/731: Case T-174/95, *Svenska Journalistförbundet v. Council*, [1998] ECR II-2289, para. 110; and Case T-211/00, *Aldo Kuijer v. Council*, [2002] ECR II-485, para. 55.

[205] See, for instance, Case 222/84, *Johnston v. Chief Constable of the Royal Ulster Constabulary*, [1986] ECR 1651, para. 38.

[206] Case T-14/98, *Hautala v. Council*, para. 85; and Case T-211/00, *Aldo Kuijer v. Council*, [2002] ECR II-485, para. 57. The proportionality appraisal depends on the importance assigned to public interests, including the right to a fair trial and the right to privacy. See, for instance, Joined Cases C-174/98 P and C-189/98 P; *Netherlands and Van der Wal v. Commission*.

[207] See, for instance, Case T-111/00, *British American Tobacco International (Investments) Ltd v. Commission*, [2001] ECR II-2997, paras. 51–57. For application of proportionality to 'institutional confidentiality' in general, see Case T-194/94, *Carvel and Guardian Newspapers v. Council*, [1995] ECR II-2765, paras. 63–67; Case T-105/95, *WWF UK v. Commission*, [1997] ECR II-313, paras. 58–59; and T-204/99, *Mattila v. Commission and Council*, [2001] ECR II-2265 para. 107.

and third limbs of proportionality enjoin the Community institution to examine the possibility of partial access to documents. The institution must verify whether administrative burden entailed in removing confidential passages would outweigh a citizen's right of access to documents.[208] In *Hautala*, the ECJ rejected the argument, which the Council and Spanish government put forward, that mandatory exceptions based on the public interest relating to international relations would exempt the Council from contemplating partial disclosure of information.[209] A rigorous stance can be borne out by the Court's assertion that a refusal to grant partial access would be 'manifestly disproportionate', even for the purpose of ensuring confidentiality of items of information covered by public interest exceptions.[210]

(ii) The Mandatory Exceptions and the Proportionality Appraisal

For the Council or Commission merely to invoke mandatory exceptions to the right of access to documents is hardly sufficient to justify obstruction to the right of access to documents. Impediments to access to documents based even on confidentiality of information on (pending or possible) EC or national proceedings may invite a heightened scrutiny. With specific regard to the protection of confidentiality relating to the possible opening of an infringement procedure under Article 226 (ex Article 169) EC, the right of access to documents must prevail even if disclosure of documents in proceedings before the Community judicature might be prejudicial to the Commission.[211]

Maintaining confidentiality of information in the file of pending proceedings is essential to ensure not only the procedural autonomy of national and Community courts but also the right to a fair trial of individual persons in the proceedings, including the right to adequate defence and the right to a fair hearing by an independent tribunal.[212] The ECJ has recognized the right to a fair trial as the 'general principle of Community law', which is inspired by Article 6 ECHR.[213]

Notwithstanding such concern to maintain judicial authority and due process in proceedings, the case law of the Community judicature suggests a rigorous scrutiny, which underpins the policy objective of greater access to information. Such assertive policy may be discerned in three respects. First, the Court has required the Community institutions to carry out all necessary steps to ascertain the opinion of national courts, determining whether or not to disclose information. In *Netherlands*

---

[208] Case T-14/98, *Hautala v. Council*, [1999] ECR II-2489, paras. 85–87; Case C-353/99 P, *Council v. Hautala*, [2001] ECR I-9565, paras. 27–31.

[209] Case C-353/99 P, *Council v. Hautala*, [2001] ECR I-9565, para. 27.   [210] *Id.*, para. 29.

[211] Case T-92/98, *Interporc Im- und Export GmbH v. Commission*, [1999] ECR II-3521, para. 42.

[212] That the right to a fair trial encompasses the right to an independent tribunal is fully established in the case-law of Art. 6 ECHR: *De Wilde, Ooms and Versyp v. Belgium (Vagrancy* Cases), Judgment of 18 June 1971, para. 78.

[213] Case C-185/95 P, *Baustahlgewebe v. Commission*, [1998] ECR I-8417, paras. 20–21; and Joined Cases C-174/98 P and C-189/98 P, *Netherlands and Van der Wal v. Commission*, [2000] ECR I-1, para. 17.

and Van der Wal v. Commission, contrary to the CFI which ruled that in view of the importance of the right to an independent tribunal, the courts hearing a dispute were the only body that could grant access to the documents in the relevant proceedings,[214] both Advocate General Cosmas[215] and the ECJ[216] obliged the Community institutions to consult national courts to seek disclosure of the greater part of documents in accordance with the principle of 'the widest public access possible' as provided in Decision 94/90. Secondly, the ECJ has engaged in thorough examinations of the justifications for confidentiality of information. Such examinations may rely on the Commission's co-operation with national courts pursuant to Articles 85 and 86 EC, according to which national courts can seek advice of the Commission to determine whether to suspend proceedings or to adopt interim measures.[217] In *Netherlands and Van der Wal*, such a scrupulous assessment resulted in the ECJ's finding against the Commission on the ground that documents supplied by the Commission to national courts were those that it already possessed, and based on its earlier documents or its general views independent of the data connected to pending national proceedings.[218]

Thirdly, an audacious stance may be glanced through the suggestion that the institution would have to bear a high evidentiary standard to justify refusal to disclose information. In *WWF UK*, the CFI stressed that the Commission is not obliged in all cases to furnish 'imperative reasons' warranting the application of the public interest exception and to risk jeopardizing the 'essential function' of the exception.[219] Yet, in *Hautala*, Advocate General Léger required the Council or Commission to demonstrate, by reference to specific categories of documents, why it considered that the documents were related to a possible infringement procedure.[220] Along the case law relating to assessment of limitations on fundamental rights,[221] he justified heightened evidentiary standard by recourse to the notions of proportionality and 'very substance' of the rights guaranteed.[222]

---

[214] Case T-83/96, *Van der Wal v. Commission*, [1998] ECR II-545, paras. 47–51.

[215] Joined Cases C-174/98 P and C-189/98 P, *Netherlands and Van der Wal v. Commission*, paras. 78, 81 and 92, *per* Cosmas AG.

[216] Joined Cases C-174/98 P and C-189/98 P, *Netherlands and Van der Wal v. Commission*, [2000] ECR I-1, para. 27. According to the ECJ, the Commission can refuse disclosure only if the national court in question objects to it: *Id.*, paras. 28 and 32–33.   [217] *Id.*, paras. 17–29.

[218] *Id.*, para. 24.

[219] Case T-105/95, *WWF UK v. Commission*, [1997] ECR II-313, para. 65; and Case T-204/99, *Olli Mattila v. Council*, [2001] ECR II-2265, para. 87; Case T-309/97, *The Bavarian Lager Company Ltd v. Commission*, [1999] ECR II-3217, para. 46. See also, Case T-105/95, *WWF UK v. Commission*, [1997] ECR II-313, para. 63; and Case C-191/95, *Commission v. Germany*, [1998] ECR I-5449, para. 44.

[220] Case T-105/95, *WWF UK v. Commission*, [1997] ECR II-313, para. 64; and Case T-191/99, *David Petrie, Victoria Jane Primhak, David Verzoni and Others v. Commission*, [2001] ECR II-3677, para. 79.

[221] See, *inter alia*, Case 4/73, *Nold v. Commission*, [1974] ECR 491; Case 44/79, *Hauer v. Land Rheinland-Pfalz*, [1979] ECR 3727, paras. 23 and 32; Case C-62/90, *Commission v. Germany*, [1992] ECR I-2575, para. 23; Case C-404/92 P, *X v. Commission*, [1994] ECR I-4737, paras. 17–18; Case C-84/95, *Bosphorus*, [1996] ECR I-3953, para. 21; and Case C-293/97, *The Queen v. Minister of Agriculture, Fisheries and Food, Ex p. Standley and Others*, [1999] ECR I-2603, paras. 54–58.

[222] Case C-353/99 P, *Hautala v. Council*, [2001] ECR I-9565, para. 106, *per* Léger Ag.

(iii) The Voluntary Exceptions and the Proportionality Appraisal

With respect to voluntary exceptions provided in Article 4(2) of Council Decision 93/731 or in Article 1(2) of Commission Decision 94/90, both the ECJ and CFI have held that the Council or Commission enjoys a 'margin of discretion' in assessing applicability of such exceptions. The CFI has alluded even to the non-substitution principle, stating that, 'the Court [CFI] must, without substituting its own assessment for that of the Commission, ascertain whether the Commission has indeed struck a balance between the interests at stake without overstepping the boundaries of its power of assessment'.[223] For all such deferential rhetoric, the Court's consistent policy has been to evaluate scrupulously whether the institution has duly discharged obligations to state reasons for refusing access to documents. The exercise of discretion must be strictly constrained by the requirement that a 'genuine balance' be struck between the interest of the citizen in obtaining access to the documents and any interest of the institution in maintaining the confidentiality of its deliberations.[224]

E. Partial Access and Proportionality

Although the Court has recognized that in the absence of specific Community legislation, it is left to the institution to determine conditions for dealing with requests for access to documents,[225] the perusal of the case law suggests that it has intensified the standard of scrutinizing the possibility of securing partial access. Apart from requiring the institution to provide reasons for denying disclosure of information,[226] the Community judicature is ready to engage in close assessment of each of the three limbs of proportionality.

With respect to the test of less restrictive alternatives (the test of necessity), the Court has examined whether the Community institutions could have pursued the possibility of granting partial access to documents, expunging confidential part and disclosing only the part of the documents not covered by the public interest derogations. Refusal to consider such possibility as a measure less injurious of a

---

[223] Case T-111/00, *British American Tobacco International (Investments) Ltd v. Commission*, [2001] ECR II-2997, para. 41.

[224] With respect to the discretionary exceptions under Art. 4(2) of Council Decision 93/731/EC, see, for instance, Case T-194/94, *Carvel and Guardian Newspapers v. Council*, [1995] ECR II-2765, paras. 64–65; and Case T-174/95, *Svenska Journalistförbundet v. Council*, [1998] ECR II-2289, para. 113. In relation to the voluntary exceptions under Art. 1(2) of Commission Decision 94/90, see Case T-105/95, *WWF UK v. Commission*, [1997] ECR II-313, para. 59; and Case T-111/00, *British American Tobacco International (Investments) Ltd v. Commission*, [2001] ECR II-2997, para. 40.

[225] Case C-58/94, *Netherlands v. Council*, [1996] ECR I-2169, paras. 37–38.

[226] This requirement is embodied in Art. 253 (ex Art. 190) of EC Treaty.

citizen's right[227] will infringe this test,[228] amounting to a 'manifestly disproportionate' decision[229] or 'a manifest error of assessment' in serious breach of the Decision on access to documents.[230]

In relation to the third limb of proportionality, the judicial organs have demanded that the relevant Community institutions must duly weigh the interest in public access to fragmentary parts against the interests of good administration. The latter interest may be adversely affected by the burden of blanking out confidential passages covered by public interest derogations.[231] It must be verified whether the administrative burden of removing confidential part will be so onerous as to exceed the limits of what may be deemed as reasonable.[232] The survey of the case law reveals three indications of rigorous appraisal of proportionality in a narrow sense. First, the Court's reasoning suggests that even when access to part of documents is recognized as the least injurious of the citizens' right, this partial access still needs to be examined on the basis of the test of a proportionate balance.[233] Secondly, the duty to state reasons in individual decisions provided in Article 253 has reinforced the standard of review.[234] Omission to provide *specific* reasons why disclosure of documents (and specific categories of information therein) would harm public interest or the institution's interest will be viewed as failure to undertake a 'genuine balance' of interests at stake.[235] Thirdly, as Advocate General Léger suggested in *Hautala*, a stringent evidentiary standard may apply to the task of ascertaining the third test, so that a derogation from the right of partial access to documents can be recognized only where the institution has provided convincing evidence that the administrative burden would exceed the bounds of what can reasonably be required.[236]

---

[227] Case C-353/99 P, *Council v. Hautala*, [2001] ECR I-9565, para. 29; and Case T-14/98, *Hautala v. Council*, [1999] ECR II-2489, para. 85.

[228] Case C-353/99 P, *Hautala v. Council*, [2001] ECR I-9565, para. 29; paras. 115–116, *per* Léger AG; and Case T-14/98, *Hautala v. Council*, [1999] ECR II-2489, para. 77 and 85.

[229] Case C-353/99 P, *Hautala v. Council*, [2001] ECR I-9565, para. 29.

[230] See, for instance, Case T-211/00, *Aldo Kuijer v. Council*, [2002] ECR II-485, paras. 68–69.

[231] See, for instance, Case T-14/98, *Hautala v. Council*, [1999] ECR II-2489, para. 86.

[232] Case C-353/99 P, *Hautala v. Council*, [2001] ECR I-9565, para. 30; Case T-211/00, *Aldo Kuijer v. Council*, [2002] ECR II-485, paras. 57 and 71.

[233] For instance, in *Mattila*, the CFI implicitly recognized that the impossibility of separating documents at issue and removing component parts from them provided a ground for concluding that notwithstanding a failure by the Council to grant partial access to the documents at issue, the principle of proportionality was not infringed: Case T-204/99, *Olli Mattila v. Council*, [2001] ECR II-2265, paras. 73–74.

[234] Under Regulation No. 1049/2001 on Access to Documents, Art. 9(4) reiterates the requirement that the institutions must provide reasons to refuse access to sensitive documents 'in a manner which does not harm the interests protected in Article 4'.

[235] Case T-105/95, *WWF UK v. Commission*, [1997] ECR II-313, paras. 64–72 and 76 (discretionary exception based on the institution's interest in the confidentiality of its proceedings).

[236] Case C-353/99 P, *Hautala v. Council*, [2001] ECR I-9565, paras. 120–121, *per* Léger AG. On this matter, he referred to a case dealing with a different issue: Case 104/75, *De Peijper*, [1976] ECR 613, para. 18.

F. Evidentiary Standard and the Duty to State Reasons

When describing a condition for invoking mandatory requirements (disclosure 'could undermine' one of the listed public or other interests), both Article 4(1) of Council Decision 93/731 and Article 1(1) of Commission Decision 94/90 use present conditional, 'could'. The Council and the Commission are obliged to evaluate whether, on the basis of the information available to them, disclosure is 'likely' to undermine one of public interest grounds enumerated in those derogation clauses.[237] The searching review by the Community judicature can be confirmed in two respects: (a) burden of proof and high evidentiary standard shifted to the Community institution; and (b) the duty imposed on the institution to specify reasons for refusing disclosure of information even relating to national security.

First, the standard of proportionality review by the Community judicial organs is intensified by their decision to impose on the Community institutions (Council and Commission) a weighty evidentiary standard to justify refusing access to documents.[238] The ECJ and CFI have required the institution to provide an analysis of factors specifically relating to the context or the content of information,[239] as well as the nature and detail of the information contained in the documents.[240] The Community judicial organs have not hesitated to examine at length the content and context of documents by their own motion. They have also closely examined whether otherwise sensitive information, such as information concerning Commission's inspection on compatibility with Community law of a Member State's practice or information containing identities of Member States' delegates, has already become public knowledge or lost importance by the time request for access was made.[241] In *Kuijer II*, which concerned mandatory exceptions based on public interests relating to international relations, the CFI required the Council to demonstrate that, 'the risk of the

---

[237] For public access to Council documents, see Case T-174/95, *Svenska Journalistförbundet v. Council*, [1998] ECR II-2289, para. 112; and Case T-211/00, *Aldo Kuijer v. Council*, [2000] ECR II-485, para. 56.

For public access to Commission documents, see Case T-105/95, *WWF UK v. Commission*, [1997] ECR II-313, para. 42; Joined Cases C-174/98 P and C-189/98 P, *Netherlands and Van der Wal v. Commission*, para. 43, *per* Cosmas AG.

[238] To invoke merely that documents relating to deliberations of the institution contain information on positions taken by representatives of the Member States would fail to abide by the obligation to balance the interests at stake: Case T-194/94, *Carvel and Guardian Newspapers v. Council*, [1995] ECR II-2765, paras. 72–73 (access to Council documents); Case T-111/00, *British American Tobacco International (Investments) Ltd v. Commission*, [2001] ECR II-2997, para. 52.

[239] Case T-211/00, *Kuijer v. Council*, [2002] ECR II-485, para. 61.

[240] Case T-204/99, *Olli Mattila v. Council*, [2001] ECR II-2265, para. 64. See also Case T-123/99, *JT's Corporation Ltd v. Commission*, [2000] ECR II-3269, paras. 46–48.

[241] Case T-111/00, *British American Tobacco International (Investments) Ltd v. Commission*, [2001] ECR II-2997, para. 56. For *a contrario* case based on continuous inspections, see Case T-20/99, *Denkavit Nederland BV v. Commission*, [2000] ECR II-3011, para. 48.

public interest being undermined must . . . be reasonably foreseeable and not purely hypothetical'.[242] The CFI concluded that absent Council's analysis of factors *specific* to the contents or the context of each report, which suggested a danger to a public interest, the mere fact that documents contained negative statements about political situation in a third country, did not suffice to justify restrictions on access to documents.[243] The Council was found to have breached the principle of proportionality and erred in law when refusing the applicant's request for the information on the list of contact persons to which access was permitted in certain Member States.[244]

Secondly the Community judicial organs are not reluctant to constrain the Community institution's exercise of discretion in determining undefined and ambiguous terms included in mandatory exceptions, such as the public interests relating to public security.[245] They have strictly construed the duty to state reasons in individual decisions provided in Article 253 and obliged the institution to establish a specific causal relationship between the disclosure of information and the danger to public security.[246] Absence of such proof required by the duty to state reasons may upset the balance within the meaning of the third limb of proportionality appraisal.[247]

G. Regulation No. 1049/2001 on Access to Documents

Regulation No. 1049/2001[248] was adopted on 31 May 2001[249] with two additional-related texts: a joint Declaration of the European Parliament, Council and Commission on the access to document rules of other EU institutions, agencies, or bodies[250]; and two Statements by the Commission and certain Member

---

[242] Case T-211/00, *Kuijer v. Council (Kuijer II)*, [2002] ECR II-485, para. 56. See also *Interporc I*, in which the CFI stated that, '[t]he use of the form "could" means that before deciding on a request for access to documents the Commission must consider, for each document requested, whether in the light of the information in its possession disclosure is in fact likely to undermine one of the interests protected under the first category of exceptions': Case T-124/96, *Interporc Im-und Export GmbH v. Commission*, [1998] ECR II-231, para. 52. See also Case T-174/95, *Svenska Journalistförbundet v. Council*, [1998] ECR II-2289, para. 112.

[243] Case T-211/00, *Kuijer v. Council ('Kuijer II')*, [2002] ECR II-485, paras. 60–61.

[244] *Id.*, para. 74.

[245] The concept of public security, which is not susceptible to a single and specific meaning, has been construed to cover both the internal security of a Member State and its external security (Case C-70/94, *Werner v. Germany*, [1995] ECR I-3189, para. 25), interruption of supplies of essential commodities such as petroleum products (Case 72/83, *Campus Oil v. Minister for Industry and Energy*, [1984] ECR 2727, para. 34); and disclosure of information that could obstruct the attempt to prevent criminal activities (Case T-174/95, *Svenska Journalistförbundet v. Council*, [1998] ECR II-2289, para. 121).

[246] Case T-174/95, *Svenska Journalistförbundet v. Council*, [1998] ECR II-2289, paras. 122–123.

[247] *Id.*, paras. 126–127.

[248] For appraisal of this Regulation, see Peers (2002), *supra* n. 163.

[249] Regulation No. 1049/2001 was adopted one month after the deadline set by Art. 255(2) EC (which was inserted as a result of the Treaty of Amsterdam): Peers, *Id.*, at 387.

[250] [2001] OJ L173/5.

States relating to the application of the Regulation to documents on infringement proceedings.[251]

Article 4 of Regulation No. 1049/2001 embodies three categories of exceptions in its paragraphs 1–3, with supplementary rules provided in paragraphs 4–7. The first category of exceptions further consists of two sub-categories, one based on the public interest and the other based on the protection of privacy and the 'integrity of the individual'. Article 4(1)(a) provides that the institutions 'shall' refuse access where it 'would undermine' the protection of 'public security', 'defence and military matters', 'international relations', or 'the financial, monetary or economic policy of the Community or a Member State'. In the second limb within this division, Article 4(1)(b) stipulates that the institutions 'shall' refuse disclosure if it 'would undermine' the protection of 'privacy and the integrity of the individual, in particular in accordance with Community legislation regarding the protection of personal data'.[252]

Article 4(2) sets out the second category of exceptions, requiring the institutions to refuse disclosure if it 'would undermine' the protection of 'commercial interests of a natural or legal person, including intellectual property', 'court proceedings and legal advice', and 'the purpose of inspections, investigations and audits'. Unlike the first category, this exception does not apply in case there is an 'overriding public interest in disclosure'. Finally, Article 4(3) embodies the third category of exception, which is subject to a higher threshold of application. The institutions are obliged to refuse access to a 'document, drawn up by an institution for internal use or received by an institution, which relates to a matter where the decision has not been taken by the institution'. Applicability of this exception depends on whether its disclosure 'would seriously undermine' the institution's decision-making process, and whether there is no overriding public interest' in disclosure.

In relation to Articles 4(1)(b) and 4(2), the institutions must show that release 'would', rather than 'could', undermine the relevant interest, with the change in the wording indicative of a more stringent standard than in the pre-Regulation rules. The confidentiality of information concerning Council's proceedings and Commission's deliberations under Article 4(2) of Council Decision 93/731 and Article 1(2) of Commission Decision 94/90 respectively is now incorporated as an 'internal use' exception, which is a mandatory exception but susceptible to a considerably stringent test (the 'would seriously undermine' test) and to the requirement of an 'overriding public interest' in disclosure.[253]

---

[251] Statements 47/01 and 48/01, in Monthly Summary of Council Acts, May 2001 (Council Doc. 10571/01, 4 July 2001); Peers (2002), *supra* n. 163, at 385.

[252] The distinction between public and private interests under Art. 4(1) of the Regulation is relevant only to the maximum period of exceptions under Art. 4(7), which allows continuous application of exceptions beyond 30 years to all the documents falling within privacy or commercial interests, while reserving such possibility only to 'sensitive documents' relating to public interest.

[253] Peers (2002), *supra* n. 163, at 397.

Susceptibility to a balancing exercise may be diminished under Article 4(6) of the Regulation No. 1049/2001, which incorporates the established case law on partial access rules.[254] As Peers notes, the new Regulation applies the partial access rules to all circumstances,[255] departing from the previous rules under which there was an exception to partial release in case an administrative burden was considered to outweigh the private person's interest.[256]

H. Access to Documents under Article 10 ECHR?

Article 10(1) of the ECHR provides that the right of freedom of expression shall include 'freedom . . . to receive . . . information and ideas . . .'. However, in *Guerra*, the Strasbourg Court explicitly rejected the claim that Article 10 encompasses a positive obligation on national authorities to disclose relevant information to the public.[257] The phrases, 'freedom . . . to receive . . . information' is construed as prohibiting State authorities from interfering with the exchange of information and ideas among the citizens but *not* including the right to access to documents held by public authorities.[258] In contrast, Judge Palm and other minority judges attempted to limit applicability of such dictum to particular circumstances of that case, leaving the scope of a State's 'positive obligation to make available information to the public and to disseminate such information which by its nature could not otherwise come to the knowledge of the public'.[259] With respect, it is submitted that Judge Palm's view that reserves the positive duty under Article 10 should be the correct interpretation. The Strasbourg organs have introduced the technique of evolutive interpretation that regards the Convention as a 'living instrument', allowing a change in the meaning of some key ECHR provisions and the departure from the precedent.[260] Yet, the Strasbourg organs'

---

[254] See, *inter alia*, Case T-14/98, *Hautala v. Council*, [1999] ECR II-2489, paras. 76–89; Case T-123/99, *JT Corporation v. Commission*, [2000] ECR II-3269, para. 44; and Case T-304/99, *Mattila v. Commission and Council*, [2001] ECR II-2265, para. 67. See also Case C-353/99 P, *Hautala v. Council*, [2001] ECR I-9565, paras. 21–32, confirming the CFI's judgment.

[255] Peers (2002), *supra* n. 163, at 409.

[256] Case T-14/98, *Hautala v. Council*, [1999] ECR II-2489, para. 86, upheld in the appeal; Case C-353/99 P, *Hautala v. Council*, [2001] ECR I-9565, para. 30.

[257] *Guerra and Others v. Italy*, Judgment of 19 February 1998. Compare, however, O'Neill, *supra* n. 185, at 403 *et seq.*

[258] The Strasbourg Court's approach to *Guerra* differs from Art. 19 of the International Covenant on Civil and Political Rights (ICCPR), which expressly provides the 'right to seek information and ideas', though controversy remains as to whether Art. 19 of the ICCPR obliges the Member States to furnish requested information. See, for instance, *Communication No. 633/1995, Robert W. Gauthier v. Canada*, Human Rights Committee's views of 7 April 1999, A/54/40, Vol. II (1999), Annex XI, sect. L, p. 93–110.

[259] See *Guerra and Others v. Italy*, Judgment of 19 February 1998, Concurring Opinion of Judge Palmer, joined by Judges Bernhardt, Russo, Macdonald, Makarczyk, and Van Dijk.

[260] For assessment of evolutive interpretation, see E. Kastanas, *Unité et Diversité: notions autonomes et marge d'appréciation des Etats dans la jurisprudence de la Cour européenne des droits de l'homme*, (Brussels: Bruylant, 1996); and P. Mahoney, "Judicial Activism and Judicial Self-Restraint in the European Court of Human Rights: Two Sides of the Same Coin", (1990) 11 HRLJ 57.

approach may be deemed as reticent and incremental as compared to an audacious approach followed by the Luxembourg counterpart. More creative and policy-oriented judicial reasoning has underpinned the Community judicature's decision-making, as evidenced in the enunciation that both Council Decision 93/731 and Commission Decision 94/90 should be understood as providing a fundamental right of access to documents, going beyond a framework of internal organisation under Article 151(3) EC.[261]

VI. Freedom of Expression Exercised by Staff Members

A. Overview

The democratic foundation of the Communities means that all staff members of the Community institutions enjoy fundamental rights, including freedom of expression.[262] That freedom of expression is one of the fundamental rights most closely linked to democratic pillars requires Community legislation imposing limitations on that freedom to be interpreted restrictively.[263] The duty of allegiance to the Communities imposed on officials in the Staff Regulations must not be construed in a manner that conflicts with freedom of expression.[264] An official's public dissent or criticism of the employing institution cannot in itself be considered liable to prejudice the interests of the Communities.[265] Further, an official's comments on staff reports drawn by his/her superiors do not breach the duty of allegiance unless s/he uses profoundly insulting language or disrespect.[266]

B. Limitations and Proportionality Appraisal

Issues of the extent to which staff members enjoy freedom of expression have frequently arisen in relation to Articles 12 and 17 of the Regulations and Rules applicable to officials and other servants of the European Communities ('the Staff

---

[261] See, for instance, Case C-58/94, *Netherlands, v. Council*, [1996] ECR I-2169, paras. 34–37.

[262] C-100/88, *Oyowe and Traore v. Commission*, [1989] ECR 4285, para. 16; Case T-183/96, *E v. Economic and Social Committee*, [1998] ECR-SC IA-67; II-159 para. 41; Joined Cases T-34/96 and T-163/96, *Connolly v. Commission*, [1999] ECR-SC I-A-87 and II-463, para. 148.

[263] Case C-340/00P, *Cwik v. Commission*, [2001] ECR I-10269, para. 18.

[264] C-100/88, *Oyowe and Traore v. Commission*, [1989] ECR 4385, para. 16; and Case C-150/98 P, *Economic and Social Committee of the European Communities v. E.*, Judgment of 16 December 1999, [1999] ECR I-8877, para. 13.

[265] Case C-274/99 P, *Connolly v. Commission*, [2001] ECR I-1611, para. 43 *in fine*; Case T-82/99, *Cwik v. Commission*, [2000] ECR-SC I-A-155 and II-713, paras. 57–58 and 60; Case C-340/00 P, *Cwik v. Commission*, [2001] ECR I-10269, para. 22.

[266] Case C-150/98 P, *Economic and Social Committee of the European Communities v. E.*, [1999] ECR I-8877, para. 15.

Regulations'). Article 12 of the Staff Regulations provides:

An official shall abstain from any action and, in particular, any public expression of opinion which may reflect on his position.

. . .

An official wishing to engage in an outside activity, whether gainful or not, or to carry out any assignment outside the Communities must obtain permission from the appointing authority. Permission shall be refused if the activity or assignments is such as to impair the official's independence or to be detrimental to the work of the Communities.

Article 17(2) stipulates:

An official shall not, whether alone or together with others, publish or cause to be published without the permission of the appointing authority, any matter dealing with the work of the Communities. Permission shall be refused only where the proposed publication is liable to prejudice the interests of the Communities.

It must be questioned whether the requirement that staff members must obtain permission prior to publication is an unlawful censorship impinging on the freedom of expression or a preventive measure proportionate to the legitimate end based on the duty of loyalty and the Community's good administration and reputation. The Community judicial organs have taken the view that Articles 12 and 17 of the Staff Regulations do not constitute a bar to the freedom of expression of officials, and the limitations imposed by this provision are 'reasonable' and 'not . . . disproportionate'.[267] They have emphasized that the assessment of restrictions on freedom of expression exercised by officials depends on the two-pronged tests devised to ascertain encroachments on fundamental rights in general: first, whether restrictions correspond to 'objectives of general public interest pursued by the Community'; and secondly, whether or not such restrictions amount to a 'disproportionate and intolerable interference which infringes upon the very substance of the rights protected'.[268]

C. Burden of Proof

Refusal to permit publication of the text by staff members would give rise to a manifest error of assessment unless the Community authorities discharge an onerous burden to prove, on the basis of 'specific, objective factors', that such publication is 'liable to cause serious harm', or entails 'a real risk of causing serious

---

[267] For Art. 12 of the Staff Regulations, see Case T-183/96, *E v. Economic and Social Committee*, [1998] ECR-SC IA-67; II-159, para. 41. For Art. 17 of the Staff Regulations, see Joined Cases T-34/96 and T-163/96, *Connolly v. Commission*, [1999] ECR-SC I-A-87 and II-463, para. 151.

[268] Joined Cases T-34/96 and T-163/96, *Connolly v. Commission*, [1999] ECR-SC I-A-87 and II-463, para. 148. See also Case 265/87, *Hermann Schraeder HS Kraftfutter GmbH & Co. KG v. Hauptzollamt Gronau*, [1989] ECR 2237, para. 15; Case C-404/92 P, *X v. Commission*, [1994] ECR I-4737, para. 18; and Case T-176/94, *K v. Commission*, [1995] ECR-SC I-A-203, II-621, para. 33.

prejudice' to the interests of the Communities.[269] Prior to determining whether to grant permission to publish aspects of Community activities, the relevant Community authorities must examine any detrimental impact of the intended publication, taking into account differing factors. These include the sensitive nature of the publication, the author's position in the hierarchy,[270] the nature of the intended publication (personal view or possibility of being mistaken as an official view), the readership to which the publication is addressed (a small circle of experts or the public at large), and the public knowledge of the content of the publication (whether or not it is already disseminated by other means).[271]

D. Brief Comparison with Civil Servants' Right to Freedom of Expression under Article 10 ECHR

In relation to staff cases, the Community judicature closely observes how the notion of proportionality has enabled the Strasbourg organs to cater to the need to weigh in balance civil servants' rights to freedom of expression and their 'duties and responsibilities' in the meaning of Article 10(2) ECHR.[272] In the earlier case law, the Strasbourg organs exhibited hesitancy to challenge national disciplinary decisions that encroached on civil servants' freedom of expression.[273] Nevertheless, in the more recent cases,[274] they have applied a more stringent standard of review than in other areas, such as cases involving the protection of morals, approximating their scrutiny to the ECJ's proportionality appraisal in general. As forcefully contended by Advocate General Ruiz-Jarabo Colomer in the *Cwik* case, it remains, however, possible that the Community system can provide *even* higher standards of fundamental rights than the ECHR system, which is confined to the framework based on 'the lowest common denominator'.[275] In that case, Advocate-General Ruiz-Jarabo Colomer went so far as to suggest that in order to justify the prohibition of publications of a text, the Community institution must establish at least a 'definite risk of serious harm' by reference to factors that were

---

[269] Case C-274/99 P, *Connolly v. Commission*, [2001] ECR I-1611, para. 53; and Case C-340/00P, *Cwik v. Commission*, [2001] ECR I-10269, paras. 18, 23 and 28.

[270] In the context of the ECHR, see *Wille v. Liechtenstein*, Judgment of 28 October 1999, para. 63; Opinion of the European Commission of Human Rights in its Report of 11 May 1984 in *Glasenapp v. Germany*, para. 124.

[271] C-274/99 P, *Connolly v. Commission*, [2001] ECR I-1611 para. 45; Case T-82/99, *Cwik v. Commission*, [2000] ECR-SC I-A-155 and II-713, paras. 66–69; and C-340/00P, *Cwik v. Commission*, [2001] ECR I-10269, paras. 26 and 28.

[272] See, for instance, Case C-274/99 P, *Connolly v. Commission*, [2001] ECR I-1611 para. 49. For the case law under the ECHR, see *Vogt v. Germany*, Judgment of 26 September 1995; *Ahmed and Others v. UK*, Judgment of 2 September 1998, para. 56; and *Wille v. Liechtenstein*, Judgment of 28 October 1999, para. 62.

[273] See, for instance, *Glasenapp v. Germany*, Judgment of 28 August 1986; and *Kosiek v. Germany*, Judgment of 28 August 1986.

[274] See, for instance, *Vogt v. Germany*, Judgment of 26 September 1995.

[275] Case C-340/00, P *Cwik v. Commission*, [2001] ECR I-10269, para. 29, *per* Ruiz-Jarabo Colomer AG.

'equally definite and sufficiently objective in nature'.[276] The proposal to apply such a heightened standard can be contrasted to the approach followed in the jurisprudence of the Strasbourg Court.[277]

VII. The Principle of Proportionality under the Jurisprudence of the ECHR

A. The Elements of Proportionality under the ECHR

The principle of proportionality is one of the cardinal, interpretive principles developed by the European Court of Human Rights in its jurisprudence. While express reliance on this principle is frequent, there remain unsettled issues as to its content, criteria for its application, the standard of review associated with it, as well as its status under the ECHR. The Strasbourg organs (the European Court of Human Rights and the ex European Commission of Human Rights) have not elaborated the elements of proportionality in the way as has been developed in the EC law. The jurisprudence of the Strasbourg organs[278] suggests a general balance model that requires Member States to strike a 'fair balance' between rights of individual applicants and common public interests.[279] The fair balance test that, while still lacking clarity and being susceptible to exercise of discretion, has become pervasive in the Strasbourg Court's adjudicative discourse, especially in determining the scope of positive obligations on Member States under the Convention.[280] Essential to the intrinsic role of proportionality in bolstering effective guarantee of the rights of individuals is the requirement that a reasonable relationship must be attained between the means employed and the public end to be sought. This requirement finds a counterpart in the third element of proportionality in EC law and German administrative law. Such protective role is nevertheless contingent on whether the Court is ready to factor into this equation such elements as severity and duration of the intruding measure, as well as special circumstances of individuals (gender, age, health, disability, etc).

---

[276] *Id.* paras. 27 and 31–32, *per* Ruiz-Jarabo Colomer AG.

[277] See, for instance, *Worm v. Austria*, which concerned limits of permissible comments likely to prejudice, intentionally or not, the pending criminal proceedings or to undermine the confidence of the public in the administration of criminal justice. The application of a more lax standard, such as that based on an abstract risk of harm, led the Strasbourg Court to endorse prior restraint on publications: judgment of 29 August 1997.

[278] For examination of the principle of proportionality under the European Convention, see Arai-Takahashi, *supra* n. 104; M. Eissen, "The Principle of Proportionality in the Case-law of the European Court of Human Rights", in Macdonald, Petzold and Matscher (eds.), *supra* n. 1, Ch. 7; and J. McBride, "Proportionality and the European Convention on Human Rights", in Ellis (ed.), *supra* n. 1, 23.   [279] *Soering v. UK*, Judgment of 7 July 1989, para. 89.

[280] A. Mowbray, *The Development of Positive Obligations under the European Convention on Human Rights by the European Court of Human Rights*, (Oxford: Hart, 2004), pp. 175 and 186–187.

A close appraisal of the case law demonstrates that though sporadic and unelaborated, a cluster of interpretive devices (or principles) have been carefully teased out of foundational values of the Convention. The creation of such distinct principles suggests that the Strasbourg Court is conscious of its quintessentially 'constitutionalizing' decision-making process, delineating the relationship or the hierarchy among the rights, and the institutional division of labour between European and national judicial bodies or non-judicial ones.[281] First, the Strasbourg organs have applied an 'evolutive' or 'dynamic' interpretation, according to which changing social attitudes are adduced to warrant departure from precedent in interpreting the scope of Convention rights.[282] Evolutive construction is a method fully anchored in the case law, and while serving to enhance the Convention rights, it is instrumental in overriding the precedent in polemic issues such as treatment of children born out of wedlock,[283] homosexuals,[284] and transsexuals.[285] However, a caveat must be entered that the Strasbourg organs' reliance on this method remains incremental and selective, and much more reticent than the robustly teleological approach followed by the ECJ under EC law.[286] Secondly, in some instances, the Strasbourg organs have demanded that national authorities should adopt a measure less burdensome of an individual person's rights and capable of achieving the same legitimate objective with equal effectiveness.[287] This so-called less restrictive alternative test or doctrine corresponds to the

---

[281] Greer endorses the view that the ECHR's constitution can be discerned in the foundational values and principles, and that constitutional questions are seen in the application of interpretive principles: S. Greer, "Constitutionalizing Adjudication under the European Convention on Human Rights", (2003) 12 OJLS 405, at 407.

[282] First recourse to evolutive construction was seen in *Tyrer v. United Kingdom*, which related to judicial corporal punishment under Art. 3 ECHR. The Court held that, ". . . the Convention is a living instrument which . . . must be interpreted in the light of present-day conditions": Judgment of 25 April 1978, para. 31.

[283] See, for instance, *Marckx v. Belgium*, Judgment of 13 June 1979; and *Johnston and Others v. Ireland*, Judgment of 18 December 1986.

[284] See, for example, *Dudgeon v. United Kingdom*, Judgment of 22 October 1981; *Norris v. Ireland*, Judgment of 26 October 1988; *Modinos v. Cyprus*, Judgment of 22 April 1993 (cases concerning criminalization of private homosexual conduct); *Lustig-Prean and Beckett v. United Kingdom*, Judgment of 27 September 1999; and *Smith and Grady v. United Kingdom*, Judgment of 27 September 1999 (cases concerning homosexuals in the army). See also cases concerning difference in age of consent between homosexuals and heterosexuals: *S.L. v. Austria*, Judgment of 9 January 2003; *L. and V. v. Austria*, Judgment of 9 January 2003; *B.B. v. United Kingdom*, Judgment of 10 February 2004; and *Sutherland v. United Kingdom*, Application No. 25186/94, Commission's Report of 1 July 1997 (unpublished).

[285] *Christine Goodwin v. United Kingdom*, Judgment of 11 July 2002; *I. v. United Kingdom*, Judgment of 11 July 2002; and *Sheffield and Horsham v. United Kingdom*, Commission's Report of 21 January 1997 (overturned in the Court's judgment of 30 July 1998). Compare these with Case C-13/94, *P v. S. & Cornwall County Council*, [1996] ECR I-2143.

[286] As regards application of evolutive interpretation under EC law, see, for instance, Case 283/81, *Srl CILFIT and Lanificio di Gavardo SpA v. Ministry of Health*, [1982] ECR 3415, para. 20. For assessment of this method, see J. Bengoetxea, *The Legal Reasoning of the European Court of Justice—Towards a European Jurisprudence*, (Oxford: Clarendon, 1993), pp. 251–262.

[287] In *Goodwin v. United Kingdom*, the Strasbourg Court found that an order requiring a journalist to disclose his source of information about a company's financial affairs was not supported by 'sufficient reasons' on the ground that an injunction against publication of the information was effective in

test of necessity, the second element of the Luxembourg Court's tripartite inquiry. Thirdly, with respect to the freedom of expression, the application of the chilling effect doctrine has set the fulcrum of the balancing inquiry closer to the rights.[288] Emergence of both the less restrictive alternative doctrine and the chilling effect doctrine, albeit in need of much articulation and refinement, can be perceived as the maturation of the Strasbourg Court's proportionality inquiry. It can also be viewed as reinforcing what Greer describes as the 'priority to rights' principle within the ECHR's overall 'constitutional' framework.[289]

Compounding the analysis of the principle of proportionality in the ECHR context is its interplay with other interpretive principles. In particular, potential effectiveness of this principle in shielding individual persons' rights against unjustified encroachments by State authorities is hampered by the Court indulgently applying the doctrine of margin of appreciation[290] in an uneven and unstructured manner.[291] The application of this doctrine, albeit finding no express legal basis in the Convention, is pervasive, providing national authorities with a variable scope of discretion in assessing appropriate standards of the Convention. The margin of appreciation can be regarded as the presumption of compatibility with the Convention's obligations ('*conventionnalité*'), which is nevertheless rebuttable.[292] However, the application of this doctrine raises three serious problems relating to proportionality appraisal. First, the lax review associated with this doctrine can furnish the Strasbourg Court with 'auto-justification' for detracting from its supervisory responsibility. This problem is compounded by the failure of the Strasbourg organs to articulate coherent criteria for determining the standard of

---

obstructing dissemination of confidential information by the press: Judgment of 27 March 1996, para. 42. See also *Castells v. Spain*, Judgment of 23 April 1992; *Piermont v. France*, Judgment of 27 April 1995; *Incal v. Turkey*, Judgment of 9 June 1998, para. 54; *Ceylan v. Turkey*, Judgment of 8 July 1999, para. 34; *Arslan v. Turkey*, Judgment of 8 July 1999, paras. 46–50; and *Baskaya and Okçuoglu v. Turkey*, Judgment of 8 July 1999, paras. 62–67; and *Ahmet v. Sadik v. Greece*, Commission's Report of 4 April 1995, para. 51. In contrast, for cases refusing to apply this test, see, *inter alia, Mellacher and Others v. Austria*, Judgment of 19 December 1989, para. 53; *Tre Traktörer AB v. Sweden*, Judgment of 7 July 1989, para. 62; and *Murphy v. Ireland*, Judgment of 10 July 2003, paras. 76–82 (lax review of sufficient reasons and the rejection of the less limitative alternative suggested by the applicant).

[288] See, *inter alia, Castells v. Spain*, Judgment of 23 April 1992, para. 46; and *Goodwin v. United Kingdom*, Judgment of 27 March 1996, para. 39.   [289] Greer, *supra* n. 281, at 415.

[290] For examination of this doctrine, see, for instance, Arai-Takahashi , *supra* n. 104; and E. Benvenisti, "Margin of Appreciation, Consensus and Universal Standards", (1999) NYUJInt'lLPol 843; *Kastanas, supra* n. 260; and P. Mahoney, "Marvellous Richness of Diversity or Invidious Cultural Relativism?", (1998) 19 HRLJ, the special issue, *The Doctrine of the Margin of Appreciation under the European Convention on Human Rights: Its Legitimacy in Theory and Application in Practice*, 1.

[291] Arai-Takahashi, *supra* n. 104, at 233–234. Lester warns that the margin of appreciation doctrine 'will become a source of pernicious "variable geometry" of human rights,[which] erod[es] the "*acquis*" of existing jurisprudence and giving undue deference to local conditions, traditions, and practices': Lord Lester of Herne Hill, "The European Convention on Human Rights in the New Architecture of Europe: General Report", *Proceedings of the 8th International Colloquy on the European Convention on Human Rights* (Strasbourg: Council of Europe, 1995), pp. 227, at 236–7.

[292] McBride, *supra* n. 278, at 29.

review within the variable range. Secondly, the application of this doctrine may result in the onus of proof on applicants challenging interference or omission by national authorities.[293] Thirdly, the Strasbourg Court has too often sought refuge in that doctrine to side-step 'constitutional' questions, such as the priority or the hierarchy among conflicting rights, and the balance between the rights and collective goods.[294]

Matscher argues that the principle of proportionality should be perceived as 'corrective and restrictive of the margin of appreciation doctrine',[295] with the two concepts operating on the opposite sides of the same coin. However, the relationship between the two elusive principles can find more coherent explanations within a broader 'constitutional' framework. Greer discerns three 'constitutional' principles in the jurisprudence of the ECHR: the 'rights' principle; the 'democracy' principle; and the 'priority to rights' principle. According to his classification, whilst the principle of proportionality is a secondary principle adhering to the 'priority' principle, the margin of appreciation doctrine lends itself to the 'democracy' principle. It is what he calls the 'priority to rights' principle, which embraces the notion of proportionality, that should be given the primary role so that the ECHR's constitutional structure, barely inferable from the application of interpretive principles, can be 'more deliberately articulated and more consistently applied'.[296]

B. Freedom of Expression and the Standard of Review under the ECHR

The foundational importance ascribed to freedom of expression in democracy has enabled this freedom to be classified as one of the 'privileged rights' among those rights guaranteed under the ECHR, susceptible to a more exacting review than in other contexts, in particular than in cases concerning the right to property. Interpretive techniques associated with stringent scrutiny such as the chilling-effect doctrine,[297] and the less restrictive alternative doctrine may become more visible than in the case law dealing with other provisions of the ECHR, albeit the application of such techniques is confined mainly to cases involving political expression.

Within the ample catalogues of case law on freedom of expression, the nature of expression has further introduced the 'hierarchy' into forms of expression. While

---

[293] *Id.*   [294] Greer, *supra* n. 281, at 432–433.
[295] F. Matscher, "Methods of Interpretation of the Convention", in: R.St J. Macdonald, F. Matscher nd H. Petzold (eds.), *The European System for the Protection of Human Rights* (Dordrecht: Martinus Nijhoff, 1993), pp. 63, at 79.   [296] Greer, *supra* n. 281, at 408.
[297] See, for instance, *Lingens v. Austria*, Judgment of 8 July 1986, paras. 44 and 47; *Barfod v. Denmark*, Judgment of 22 February 1989, para. 29; *Goodwin v. UK*, Judgment of 27 March 1996, paras. 39, and 42–46; *Bladet Tromsø and Stensaas v. Norway*, Judgment of 20 May 1999, paras. 64 *et seq*; and *Nikula v. Finland*, Judgment of 21 March 2002, para. 54. See also, *Glasenapp v. Germany*, Commission's Report of 11 May 1984, para. 111.

the Strasbourg Court has displayed readiness to recognise greater merits of political expression and artistic expression than countervailing interests, whether overriding public interests or rights of other individual persons, its approach to restrictions on commercial expression tends to be much less rigorous, with considerable deference to discretion of national authorities. Restrained stance in areas of commercial expression can be confirmed in three respects: (1) the absence of stringent appraisal based on assertive techniques such as the less restrictive alternative test and the chilling-effect doctrine; (2) the evasion of in-depth analysis of specific facts of the case; and (3) the onus of proof placed on those challenging impediments to commercial expression. Apart from such general outlook, the standard of review is contingent on the nature and strength of overriding public interests. Public interests based on the protection of morals[298] and national security[299] are susceptible to a broad margin of appreciation, with the Strasbourg Court receptive to justificatory grounds pleaded by a defendant State without scrupulously weighing the evidence of such grounds.

VIII. Conclusion

The foregoing survey reveals that when confronted with issues involving fundamental rights, the Community judicature has often attempted to transpose and adjust judicial techniques established by the Strasbourg organs to the EC law context. Convergence of judicial policy in the application of proportionality is discernible in cases relating to staff members' freedom of expression under EC law, and to a lesser extent, in cases concerning advertisement as part of commercial expression.

Yet, two salient features must be noted. First, even if many ECHR interpretive techniques relating to the principle of proportionality have been introduced into EC law, once they are incorporated, they are hammered out to the mould of Community law. Secondly, in many cases, the ECJ's assertive policy has applied teleological, activism-oriented interpretive principles of its own to the assessment of fundamental rights under EC law. In relation to the right of access to documents, the right that has yet to be recognised under Article 10 ECHR, the Community judicature's decision-making policy is remarkably assertive, with the standard of proportionality review exhibiting intense scrutiny. For instance, it has been discussed that even in context of mandatory exceptions provided in Council

---

[298] See, for instance, *Handyside v. United Kingdom*, Judgment of 7 December 1976, para. 48; and *Müller and Others v. Switzerland*, Judgment of 24 May 1988, paras. 32, 35–36. See also, *Otto-Preminger-Institut v. Austria*, Judgment of 20 September 1994; and *Wingrove v. United Kingdom*, Judgment of 25 November 1996.

[299] See, *inter alia, Klass and Others v. Germany*, Judgment of 6 September 1978; *Leander v. Sweden*, Judgment of 26 March 1987; and No. 15404/89, *Purcell and Others v. Ireland*, Decision of 16 April 1991, 70 DR 262.

Decision 93/731 and Commission Decision 94/90, they have shown readiness to require the Community institutions to examine the possibility of partial access and to state reasons for non-disclosure.

Overall, the survey suggests that the standard of proportionality review applied by the Community judicature is more intense than that applied by the Strasbourg Court under the ECHR.[300] This difference in the standard of review can be attributed to different foundations of the two European judicial orders. The assertiveness of both the ECJ and CFI can be explained by their prudent but determined policy drive to act as a guardian of European integration.[301] Since its outset, Community law has constantly evolved along the path to an ever more harmonized common market regime. Application of an intense standard of review can be deemed as essential to weed out obstructions to integration process erected by national measures. On this matter, the ECJ's approach to general principles of EC law[302] marks an added dimension of the Community judicature's confidence in its creative, dynamic and robust role,[303] albeit within the bounds of the conferred powers of the Community as stated in Article 5 (ex Article 3b) EC. General principles of Community law encompass a range of administrative and constitutional legal principles and serve to fill gaps most saliently in the protection of human rights and State liability of damage.[304] While recourse to general principles can be justified to avoid a *déni de justice*,[305] the legal basis of such unwritten rules that occupy a high status in the hierarchy of sources of Community law remains elusive.[306] The fact that the general principles of law have been developed without expressly referring to Article 38 (1) of the Statute of the International Court of Justice demonstrates the

[300] S. Hall, "The European Convention on Human Rights and Public Policy Exceptions to the Free Movement of Workers under the EEC Treaty", (1991) 16 EL Rev 466.

[301] This view remains unchanged notwithstanding that as evidenced in the ECJ's opinion rejecting the possibility of the Community's accession to the ECHR (Opinion 2/94 on Accession by the Community to the ECHR, [1996] ECR I-1759), the Community judicature is more reticent in its approach to integration, than the most ardently pro-integrationist Commission.

[302] Apart from the protection of fundamental rights and the principle of proportionality as general principles of Community law, it is well-known that the Court has distilled and elevated into general principles some administrative law principles, including legal certainty and protection of legitimate expectations.

[303] In *Brasserie du Pêcheur and Factortame*, the ECJ's classic formula typifies its creative method of interpretation:

Since the Treaty contains no provision expressly and specifically governing the consequences of breaches of Community law by Member States, it is for the Court, in pursuance of the task conferred on it by Article 164 [now Art 220] of the Treaty ensuring that in the interpretation and application of the Treaty the law is observed, to rule on such a question in accordance with generally accepted methods of interpretation, in particular by reference to the fundamental principles of the Community legal system and, where necessary, general principles common to the legal systems of the Member States.'

Case C-46 [1996] ECR I-1029, Case C-48/93, ECR I-1144, para. 27.

[304] Toth, *supra* n. 2, at 76–77.

[305] M. Herdegen, "The Origins and Development of the General Principles of Community Law", in Bernitz and Nergelius (eds.), *supra* n. 1, 3 at 5.

[306] Toth suggests that part of its basis may be natural law: Toth, *supra* n. 2, at 77–78.

Community judicature's determination to create "a new legal order of international law",[307] or an autonomous and self-contained legal order.[308]

In contrast, the ECHR has been adopted under an international, rather than supra-national, treaty framework characterised by reticent policy underpinnings. First, the ECHR system has pursued a modest agenda to harmonise standards of human rights around a minimum standard of guarantees or the "common minimum denominator" among a wide range of Member States, without pretensions of building a uniform human rights regime.[309] The first consideration may be reinforced after the expansion of the Council of Europe to former communist countries, including some constituent republics of the former USSR still struggling to fend off legacies of repressive regimes. Secondly, the Strasbourg organs have flirted with the doctrine of *quatrième instance* to justify not overtaking the primary role of national organs in safeguarding fundamental rights. According to this, the primary responsibility of safeguarding fundamental rights remains assigned to Member States' constitutional laws and judicial bodies. Underlying this principle is the question of legitimacy and democratic accountability, with the national authorities deemed as better placed to evaluate needs of their citizens.[310] Thirdly, closely connected to the doctrine of *quatrième instance* is the principle of non-substitution that requires the Strasbourg judicial organs not to substitute their views for the national courts' fact-finding and evidence they have garnered. This principle is premised on considerations of judicial economy.[311] The second and third principles are reminiscent of the principle of subsidiarity under Community law. However, in the realm of EC law, the principal rationale for developing the notion of subsidiarity is different. The concern among some Member States that the audacious approaches of the Community legislature (notably the Commission) would encroach on their sovereign prerogatives has provided a policy incentive to the introduction of this notion as a constitutional safety valve. Fourthly, the Strasbourg Court has yet to make express endorsement of 'general principles' of the ECHR, akin to those developed under the Community law, with its scope of creativity in unfolding 'constitutional' principles appearing to be constrained within the narrow parameters of sources of international law as recognised in Article 38(1) of the Statute of the ICJ. It is submitted that failure by the Strasbourg Court fully to engage in such constitutional discourse may account for the ambiguous status of the notion of proportionality under the ECHR.

---

307 Case 26/62, *Van Gend en Loos*, [1963] ECR 1 at p. 12.

308 Herdegen, *supra* n. 305, at 6. It may be argued that the ECJ's approaches to general principles of law have been inspired by the *Conseil d'Etat's* application of *principes géneraux*. *Id.*

309 Judge Evrigenis stated that, '[t]he Convention is not an instrument of uniform law . . . leaving States free . . . to select the legal ways and means of protecting them [rights] . . . harmonis[ing] the law of Contracting States around a minimum standard of protection': D. Evrigenis, 'Recent Case-law of the European Court of Human Rights on Articles 8 and 10 of the European Convention on Human Rights', (1982) 3 HRLJ 121, at 137–138.

310 Arai-Takahashi, *supra* n. 104, at 239–40.   311 *Id.*

The divergence in standard of proportionality review applied by the two European judicial organs risks leading to the dislocation of the standard of fundamental rights. Such a risk, actual or potential, is highly problematic if proportionality is conceived, as it is, to import the overarching principles of justice and fairness to the decision-making process and to ensure the greater safeguard of individual citizens' autonomy and fundamental rights.[312] This would exacerbate the familiar problem of the two separate European judicial organs under the EU and the Council of Europe yielding conflicting decisions and findings on the scope of protection of fundamental rights.[313]

The elaborate and structured manner of intense proportionality scrutiny revealed in the jurisprudence of EU law highlights the need of the Strasbourg Court to make an adjustment of its deferential policy to the review generally applied by the ECJ/CFI. This would enable the ECHR fully to live up not only to its law-making treaty character[314] but also to its designation as the 'constitutional instrument of European public order in the field of human rights'.[315] It is desirable that in lieu of the Community courts lowering their standard of review, a converged but intense standard of scrutiny should be established between the two judicial systems whenever fundamental rights are involved. The cross-fertilisation of increasing judicial co-operation between these systems will facilitate the task of building a desired common platform of judicial review in Europe with a view to achieving enhanced safeguarding of the individual's rights.

---

[312] Schwarze, *supra* n. 1, at 679.

[313] Lenaerts and Smijter argue that the Charter of Fundamental Rights fails to resolve the three main problems relating to protection of fundamental rights in the EU: (1) the gaps in the jurisdiction of the Community judicature; (2) the possible divergence between the case of the Strasbourg Court and the Community counterpart with respect to rights guaranteed in the ECHR; (3) and absence of supervision by the Strasbourg Court over acts of the institutions of the Union in relation to their compatibility with the ECHR: K. Lenaerts and E. de Smijter, "The Charter and the Role of the European Courts", (2001) 8 MJ 49. For the ECJ case law at odds with the rulings of the Strasbourg Court, compare, for instance, Cases 46/87 and 227/88, *Hoechst AG v. Commission*, [1989] ECR 2859 and *Niemietz v. Germany*, Judgment of 16 December 1992, (the right to privacy of the business premises under Article 8 ECHR rejected by the former but upheld in the latter); and Case 374/87, *Orkem v. Commission*; and *Funke v. France*, Judgment of 25 February 1993, (right to remain silent under Article 6 (1) ECHR rejected in the former but upheld in the latter).

[314] No. 788/60, *Austria v. Italy*, (1961) 4 *Yearbook of the European Convention on Human Rights* 116, at 138; *Loizidou v. Turkey* (Preliminary Objections), Judgment of 23 March 1995, para. 93. See also, A. Drzemczewski, "The *Sui Generis* Nature of the European Convention on Human Rights", (1980) 29 ICLQ 54.

[315] Nos. 15299/89, 15300/89 and 15318/89, *Chrysostomos, Papachrysostomou and Loizidou v. Turkey*, Decision of 34 March 1991, 68 DR 216 at 242.

Constitutionalizing Europe at its Source: The 'European Clauses' in the National Constitutions: Evolution and Typology*

*Monica Claes***

I. Introduction

There is currently much debate on the exact nature of the Treaty establishing a Constitution for Europe: is it a veritable Constitution, or rather a Treaty; is it a Constitution masquerading as a Treaty or *vice versa*; a Treaty masquerading as a Constitution?[1] There is probably some truth in most of these propositions: it is a document, negotiated, signed and (possibly) ratified in the form of a classic international Treaty; but it contains characteristics of a Constitution, constituting a polity, proclaiming its common fundamental values, and dividing powers between the Member States and the European Union ('Union'), distributing powers among the various Union institutions, and delimiting the powers of both the Member States and the Union *vis-à-vis* the European citizens, and including a catalogue of fundamental rights. However, the distinction with the previous situation, of founding Treaties which were, be it only by the Court of Justice,[2] several national courts and European lawyers[3] named a 'constitutional charter', seems to

---

* This article was presented at the Conference on *The National Constitutional Reflection of European Union Constitutional Reform* held in Madrid at the Universidad Carlos III, 5–7 September 2004. It does not take account of the constitutional amendments introduced afterwards, at the occasion of the ratification of the Constitutional Treaty. I would like to thank the participants to the conference for their useful comments. The conference papers were published in M. Cartabia, B. De Witte and P. Pérez Tremps (eds), *Constitucion Europea y Constituciones Nacionales*, (Valencia: Tirant lo Blanch), 2005.

** Senior Lecturer in European Law, University of Tilburg.

[1] See for instance: J.H.H. Weiler: 'A Constitution for Europe? Some Hard Choices', *Journal of Common Market Studies* n° 40, 2002, 563–80; P. Elefteriadis: 'Treaty of Constitution?'.

[2] Most famously in Case 294/83 *Les Verts v European Parliament* [1986] ECR 1339 and Opinion 1/91 *on the EEA Agreement* [1991] ECR I-6079.

[3] Examples include J.H.H. Weiler: *The Constitution of Europe. 'Do the new clothes have an emperor?' and other essays on European integration*, (Cambridge University Press, Cambridge

be one of degree rather than of substance. Formally legally speaking, nothing much appears to be changing, except that the previous situation is now officially and formally sanctioned and made public: it is no longer a well kept secret shared by lawyers that Europe is to have a Constitution. This may well be the most 'constitutional' element of the Constitutional Treaty in the making, namely its explicit *recognition* as a Constitution.[4]

Now, the constitutional nature of the Treaty establishing a Constitution for Europe and its constitutional legitimacy depends on several elements, such as the manner which it is adopted,[5] its name, its character as the highest law of the land, which is now expressly stated in Article I-6.[6] It further depends on its content, including of course the catalogue of fundamental rights, norms regulating the delimitation of powers between the EU and its Member States and the division of powers between the European institutions—classic requisites of a Constitution—and finally on the manner in which it will develop and transform into constitutional law as interpreted by the Union institutions, including the Court of Justice, and the Member States. Yet, in the discussion of the constitutional nature of the Treaty, the issue of the relationship with national Constitutions is crucial. Indeed, whatever the nature of the Treaty establishing a Constitution for Europe, it does not make *tabula rasa* of national Constitutions. The document may claim to be the constitutional document constitutionalizing the European Union, each of the Member States making up the EU already have their own national Constitutions claiming ultimate authority. The latter remain in existence, and will continue to be perceived, in most Member States, as the country's highest norm, as the foundational document and the source of all powers. The State's membership of the European Union derives from it, at least from a national perspective,[7] and so does, in most cases, the effect of European law in

---

1999); J. Gerkrath: *L'émergence d'un droit constitutionnel pour l'Europe*, Éditions de l'Université de Bruxelles, (Brussels 1997); G.F. Mancini: "The Making of a Constitution for Europe", [1989] CMLR 595.

[4] The hint to H.L.A. Hart's 'rule of recognition' is intentional.

[5] A European-wide referendum, or national referendums on the same day, for instance, could have marked a 'We the People' moment.

[6] Art. I-6 reads: 'The Constitution and law adopted by the institutions of the Union in exercising competences conferred on it shall have primacy over the law of the Member States'. Formally legally speaking, nothing much is changing: the provision merely codifies what was already in the existing treaties as interpreted by the ECJ. Nevertheless, the explicit statement of the principle of primacy in the Treaty does make a difference.

[7] From a European and international law perspective that is not so: membership derives from the Treaties ratified by that State, and ratification accordingly is the alpha, while national constitutional provisions do not matter a great deal. Can it even be said that even from a national perspective, the constitutional provisions may, in practical reality and in some Member States, be of limited importance? Several Member States (Belgium and Portugal are the most obvious examples) have joined the Communities or Union without a constitutional authorisation, and membership was even considered unconstitutional, but that did not prevent the State's active participation in European integration or the effectiveness of the law deriving from the Treaties in the domestic legal order. In other Member States as well, there have been doubts as to whether the constitutional provisions put forward as supplying the constitutional foundation of membership, and the procedure followed to

the national legal order. And most likely, the general conviction in many Member States will be, either politically or legally or both, that the State remains an independent and sovereign State which can withdraw from the Union. This point is very often stressed and marked as an important step forward in the European Constitution, that it sanctions the right to withdraw.[8] Now, given that the national Constitutions are still widely viewed as the original source of EU powers, and as the ultimate foundation of the EU, constitutional legitimacy of the EU and its Constitution will derive both from the EU Constitutional document and from the national Constitutions. Could it even be argued that the constitutional nature of the European Constitution will depend *more* on the national Constitutions than on any element contained in the Constitutional Treaty itself? If that is the case, the historic moment made up by the establishment of the Constitution for Europe, must be accompanied by a national effort to constitutionalise Europe and to complete the European constitutional moment with a national one.

In any event, the new emphasis on the constitutional nature of the Treaty, intensifies the issue of the relationship between European and national constitutional documents. If the Treaty is now explicitly recognised as a Constitution, the relationship between both Constitutions, at the European and the national level, and between their constitutional claims of ultimate authority comes more to the fore. In a multi-level constitutional system or *Verfassungsverbund,*[9] in a *Constitution composée*, where the exercise of public power at both the national and European level is limited by constitutional documents at both levels, what is the relationship between the constitutional documents at the national and European level? As this relationship can be viewed from different angles, from the national perspectives, the European perspective,[10] and looking at it from the outside, there will be many possible answers to these questions. This article aims at the national perspective, and intends to provide an overview of the different types of national constitutional Europe provisions, and their evolution. A few words of caution must precede the discussion. First, the focus will, for practical reasons, be on constitutional texts: The intention is merely to give an overview of the constitutional provisions.

---

transfer powers to the EC or EU, were really sufficient, but that does not alter the participation of the State in decision-making or in accepting and applying the law deriving from the EC/EU.

[8] Art. I-60 (1) states that 'Any Member State may decide to withdraw from the Union in accordance with its own constitutional requirements'.

[9] A discussion of the notion of multi-level constitutionalism and similar concepts can be found, among others, in I. Pernice: 'Multi-level Constitutionalism and the Treaty of Amsterdam: Constitution-Making Revisited?', Common Market Law Review, n° 36, 1999, pp. 703 ss.; I. Pernice and F. Mayer, 'De la Constitution composée de l'Europe', *Revue trimestrielle de droit européen*, n° 36, 2000, pp. 623 ss.; N. Walker, 'The Idea of Constitutional Pluralism', *Modern Law Review*, n° 65, 2002, pp. 317 ss.

[10] For a discussion of the European perspective concerning the relation between the national constitutional laws and the European legal order from the European law perspective, see J. Wouters, "National Constitutions and the European Union", *Legal Issues of Economic Integration*, 2000, 25.

Second, the analysis will be restricted to the 15 'old' Member States.[11] Third, this means that the discussion still covers 15 Constitutional texts, with an unavoidable danger of over-simplification and inaccuracy. Finally, the article is 'old fashioned' in the sense that it focuses on prevailing constitutional provisions and the way in which they have been applied in the past. It does not, at least not in a systematic manner, approach the question as to what the national constitutional reaction should be if the proposed Treaty is indeed to be regarded as something else, a true European Constitution.[12]

Now, national constitutional provisions may serve various *purposes* in the context of European integration. A first objective is the mere issue of membership: is it at all possible, for the State, to become a member of the European Communities and/or of the European Union? Is it at all constitutional for the State to participate? This question will most often be considered in terms of sovereignty issues, either external sovereignty (sovereignty of the State, or its independence in relation to other States) or internal sovereignty (in the form of national or popular sovereignty) or both, and is mostly dealt with in the form of a *transfer of powers* or enabling provision.[13] Second, and closely linked to the previous issue and most often included in the same provisions, several Constitutions pose *substantive or procedural conditions* to the State's participation in European integration, and state constitutional limits to European integration or at least to the State's participation therein. Third, only a few Constitutions contain provisions on the manner in which national representatives or delegates in the European institutions are to be appointed. The previous categories are all '*allez*-provisions': they concern the transfer or passing on of power and competence to the EU. Another set of categories could be typified as '*retour*-provisions': they concern the national constitutional response to what comes back from the EU. One of these matters concerns the *effectiveness* of the Treaties and the law deriving from them in the domestic legal order, and their *force and rank* in relation to national law including the Constitution itself. Can the law deriving from the Treaties be effective in the national legal order in the way prescribed by the Treaties as interpreted by the Court of Justice, including its direct effect and primacy? These questions relate to the normative effect of European law in the national legal order. Next, some national Constitutions contain provisions concerning the national division of competences in the area of European decision-making, either as between

---

[11] For a discussion of the Europe provisions in the Constitutions of the 10 new Member States, see A. Albi, ''Europe Articles' in the Constitutions of Central and Eastern European Countries', 42 CMLR, 2005, pp. 399–423.

[12] Some of these questions have been addressed in the reports for the XXth FIDE Congress held in London in 2002, available on www.fide2002.org.

[13] The notion 'transfer of powers provision' is used here in its widest sense of all types of provisions allowing for membership. There are several variations: some Constitutions speak of a transfer, delegation or attribution of competences or sovereign rights to an international organisation/ or the EC and/or EU, while others allow for a limitation of sovereignty. The former has been referred to as the Belgo-German model, while the latter is the Franco-Italian model, see B. De Witte, 'Sovereignty and European Integration: The Weight of Legal Tradition', *Maastricht Journal*, n° 2, 1995, p. 145, at p. 152.

government and parliament, often in the form of a duty to give information, or as between the central State and the federated entities in a federal State. In addition, provision may also be made for special procedures applying when European law is implemented. These clauses accordingly relate to the *consequences* of EU membership for the internal division of powers. Finally, sometimes *specific constitutional provisions* are found to contradict the Treaties or the law deriving from them, and may need re-adjustment. A recurring example is a constitutional provision securing the exclusive right to issue the national currency. Each of these types of provisions will be considered in turn.

II. Transfer of Powers Provisions

A. The General Picture

Most of the 25 current Member States' Constitutions contain a transfer or powers provision of some form—general or specified, including special procedural requirements or not, and whether or not including any substantive conditions—and have joined on the basis of these provisions. The origin of these provisions dates back to the post-war period, when provisions allowing, in some form or other, for the participation of the State in international organisations and for the transfer of competences or the limitation of sovereignty to that effect, were first inserted in the new Constitutions of *France* (S. 15 of the Preamble to the 1946 Constitution),[14] *Italy* (Art. 11 of the 1948 Constitution)[15] and *Germany* (Art. 24(1) of the 1949 Basic Law).[16] The aim of these provisions was to allow for the participation in forms of international co-operation, mostly in order to promote peace and prevent war, without the need to perform constitutional amendment. This type of provisions has become exemplar, and many other to be Member States followed suit and amended their Constitutions to include a similar provision (the *Netherlands* (Art.62 in 1953, now numbered 92),[17] *Luxembourg* (Art. 49*bis*, 1956),[18] and *Denmark* (S. 20, 1953)).[19] They have in all cases served as the basis for initial accession and membership. Only a few countries have joined the

---

[14] S. 15: 'Sous réserve de réciprocité, la France consent aux limitations de souveraineté nécessaires à l'organisation et à la défense de la paix'.

[15] Art. 11: 'L'Italia ripudia la guerra come strumento di offesa alla libertà degli altri popoli e come mezzo di risoluzione delle controversie internazionali; consente, in condizioni di parità con gli altri Stati, alle limitazioni di sovranità necessarie ad un ordinamento che assicuri la pace e la giustizia fra le Nazioni; promuove e favorisce le organizzazioni internazionali rivolte a tale scopo'.

[16] Art. 24(1): 'The Federation may by a law transfer sovereign powers ("Hoheitsrechte") to international organizations'.

[17] 'Legislative, executive, and judicial powers may be conferred on international institutions by or pursuant to a treaty, subject, where necessary, to the provisions of Article 91(3)'.

[18] Art. 49bis: 'The exercise of the powers reserved by the Constitution to the legislature, executive, and judiciary may be temporarily vested by treaty in institutions governed by international law'.

[19] S. 20: '(1) Powers vested in the authorities of the Realm under this Constitution Act may, to such extent as shall be provided by Statute, be delegated to international authorities set up by mutual

Communities in the absence of any transfer of powers provision, notably *Belgium* and *Portugal*, but both mended that 'defect' afterwards, ie some years into membership and participation in the pooling of sovereignty.[20]

Since then, there has been an evolution from general 'old-fashioned' transfer of powers provisions authorising membership typically of 'international organisations' to more specific Europe provisions, referring explicitly to the EC and/or EU, and often including also substantive conditions for membership and prescribing a special procedure for the ratification of further transfers. The Treaty of Maastricht and the debate surrounding it, the constitutional crisis if you will, seems to constitute the turning point: from that time onwards, many Member States have taken their own Constitution more seriously, or *vice versa*, have taken Europe more seriously in their national Constitutions. Also, *Sweden* and *Austria*, joining after the entry into force of the Treaty of Maastricht, did not consider their general transfer of powers provisions sufficient to carry the massive transfer involved in accession and made the necessary constitutional arrangements before joining. Nevertheless, this is merely a trend, with some Member States standing out both ways: *Ireland* seems to have taken the new approach from the moment it joined in 1972, while countries like the *Netherlands, Belgium* and *Italy*,[21] in differing degrees, still do it the old fashioned way, basing membership on general transfer of powers provisions, and ratifying Treaty amendments and new transfers with ordinary Acts adopted by simple majority. Before looking into these aspects in more detail, the preceding question as to the reason *why* a transfer of powers provision is at all necessary will shortly be considered. Then the evolution from the 1950s until today will be considered, marking the evolution in the types of provisions.

agreement with other states for the promotion of international rules of law and co-operation. (2) For the passing of a Bill dealing with the above a majority of five-sixths of the Members of the Parliament shall be required. If this majority is not obtained, whereas the majority required for the passing of ordinary Bills is obtained, and if the Government maintains it, the Bill shall be submitted to the Electorate for approval or rejection in accordance with the rules for Referenda laid down in Section 42'.

[20] Belgium: art. 25 bis (1970), now numbered art. 34: 'L'exercice de pouvoirs déterminés peut être attribué par un traité ou par une loi à des institutions de droit international public'; and Portugal: art. 7(5) (1989): 'Portugal is pledged to the reinforcement of the European identity and to the strengthening of the commitment of the States of Europe to democracy, peace, economic progress and justice in the relations between their peoples' and art. 7(6) (1992): 'Provided that there is reciprocity, Portugal may enter into agreements for the joint exercise of the powers necessary to establish the European Union, in ways that have due regard for the principle of subsidiarity and the objective of economic and social cohesion', see R.M. Moura Ramos: 'The Adaptation of the Portuguese Constitutional Order to Community Law', in A.E. Kellermann et al., *EU Enlargement: The Constitutional Impact at EU and National Level*, (The Hague, T.M.C. Asser Press, 2001), pp. 131–139.

[21] The Italian Constitution has been amended in 2001 to include EU-provisions in the chapter on regionalization. The first sentence of Art. 117 reads: 'Legislative power shall be exercised by the State and by the Regions in accordance with the Constitution and within the limits set by European Union law and international obligations'. The provision was not intended to introduce a general primacy clause, and the place of the provision in the chapter on regionalization would point in a different direction, but the text seems to be stating unequivocally that acts also adopted by the central State organs are subject to European law, and there seems to be no reason why the provision would not be justiciable. The question

B. Why a Transfer of Powers Provision?

Now, why is it apparently considered an essential constitutional requirement that the transfer of powers to outside bodies or institutions is explicitly provided for in the Constitution? Why is membership considered to be on shaky constitutional grounds in the absence of such a provision? It has to do mainly with the principle of sovereignty in most of its appearances[22]: *sovereignty of the State* (the external element of sovereignty, the independence of the State under international law), *sovereignty of the Nation and /or of the people* (which hold ultimate authority and from which all powers derive; if they are to be exercised in a manner different from what has been decided in the Constitution, there must be explicit constitutional provision for it). Linked to the latter meaning of sovereignty, membership interferes with the separation of powers as laid down in the Constitution, both as between the various State organs at a central level in the applicable variation of the *Trias*, as between the central State and the federated and decentralized entities and other bodies. Accordingly, and given the central place of the principles of sovereignty, independence and separation of powers in most Constitutions, it is considered indispensable to explicitly authorize the transfer of powers or limitations of sovereignty to international organizations or outside bodies. Without such authorization, prior constitutional revision would be required before such treaty could be entered into.[23] Of course, these provisions remain purely national, and do not carry effects on the international plane. The fact that *Belgium* and *Portugal* joined in the absence on constitutional provisions authorising a transfer of powers, and even if, as was stated in both countries at the time, accession was unconstitutional, that does not change anything at the international and European level. Ratification, from that perspective, is the alpha, and national constitutional provisions are strictly speaking irrelevant. Yet, from the national perspective, they are considered indispensable.

Even in the Member State with probably the weakest sovereignty tradition, the *Netherlands*, membership is based on a transfer of powers provision.[24] From the *travaux préparatoires*, it appears that the provision was adopted with a view to participation in European integration, more particularly EDC and EPC, both of which failed in the end. The constitutional amendment in 1953 was not considered

---

of course remains as to which court, constitutional or ordinary, would have ultimate authority! However, the mere transfer of additional powers to the EU at the time of a treaty amendment is still done under the old Art. 11, by way of an ordinary Act of parliament adopted by simple majority.

[22] See for a comparative insight in the notion of sovereignty in the context of EU membership N. Walker (ed): *Sovereignty in Transition*, (Oxford, Hart Publishing, 2003).

[23] See also B. De Witte: "Constitutional Aspects of European Union Membership in the Original Six Member States: Model Solutions for the Applicant Countries?", in A.E. Kellermann *et al.*, *EU Enlargement: The Constitutional Impact at EU and National Level*, (The Hague, T.M.C. Asser Press, 2001), pp. 65–79, at p. 68.

[24] B. De Witte: 'Do Not Mention the Word: Sovereignty in Two Europhile Countries: Belgium and The Netherlands', in N. Walker (ed.), *Sovereignty in Transition*, (Oxford, Hart Publishing, 2003), p. 351.

essential, as a transfer of powers was generally not considered contrary to the Constitution. However, in order to remove all possible doubts, and because the creation of supranational organizations was expected to spread, the provision was adopted, highly influenced by the examples of the neighbouring States. It was not, however, phrased in terms of sovereignty, an unusual, 'mystic and therefore dangerous word'.[25] But the general feeling was, as stated by van Panhuys, that 'taking into account that every international obligation limits the sovereignty of States, article 67, from a legal point of view, is not so sweeping as it might seem at first sight'.[26]

Nevertheless, there are limits as to the nature and extent of the transfer which these provisions can authorize. In most Member States, they do not allow for wholesale transfers, and there are limits to what can be achieved under them in terms of the extent to which they can be deviated from the Constitution. It is widely accepted that any transfer implies some form of deviation from the Constitution, in the sense that the treaties entail a derogation from the constitutional allocation of State powers. Yet, and this is assumed in most Member States even if it is not always specifically enshrined in the constitutional texts, some transfers are so wide that they cannot be covered by the general transfer of powers provision, and require constitutional amendment. This is the central issue, for instance in the Danish debate, where until now it has been decided that Section 20 does offer sufficient authorization for the transfer involved in the Treaties, and no constitutional amendment has been effected so far. At the other extreme, when Austria joined the EU, it was assumed that accession involved a *Gesamtänderung* of the Constitution and required an overall constitutional revision.

In many Member States, the general understanding is that a transfer cannot result in derogation from the core principles of the Constitution. Once the Treaty has entered into force, this is the judge-made theory of the *controlimiti*, which will be discussed shortly. In other Member States, these limits are stated explicitly in the text of the Constitution, as conditions imposed on the conferral of powers. In many States, a treaty diverging from the constitutional provisions can be ratified only after prior amendment of the Constitution. This has been done several times in the framework of European integration, for instance in *France* at the occasion of the Treaties of Maastricht and Amsterdam, and in *Spain* for the Treaty of Maastricht, all following a judgment of a constitutional court. In the *Netherlands*, however, it *is* possible to derogate from other constitutional provisions by a treaty whereby powers are transferred.[27] The Constitution merely prescribes a special procedure for transfers deviating from the Constitution, requiring approval of at least two thirds of the votes in both Chambers.[28] But both in the case of the

---

[25] So H.F. Van Panhuys: 'The Netherlands Constitution and International Law', *American Journal of International Law*, n° 47, 1963, p. 537, at p. 552.   [26] ibid.

[27] Even though it is not clear whether this includes all other provisions including, for instance, the fundamental rights.

[28] See on this procedure, L. Besselink: 'Becoming a Party to Treaties Which Diverge From the Constitution', *European Public Law* n° 9, pp. 471–479; J.W.A. Fleuren: 'Verdragen die afwijken van

Netherlands and in *France* and *Spain*, the difficulty is to decide whether a particular treaty deviates from the Constitution to such extent that it cannot be covered by the transfer of powers provision. In the *Netherlands*, the decision is taken by the government and both Chambers of Parliament, but on imprecise grounds, and none of the European Treaties has thus far been considered to require prior amendment. In *France*, it is the *Conseil constitutionnel* who decides when seized, and it does so on the basis of the criterion of the 'conditions essentielles de la souveraineté nationale'.[29] In contrast, the *Belgian* transfer provision contained in Article 34 seems to have been interpreted so broadly as to allow for any deviation of constitutional provisions. In *Orfinger*, the *Conseil* held that "cet article ne détermine nullement les pouvoirs qui peuvent attribués et ne les limite donc nullement".[30] If that is indeed the case, this means that the Belgian Parliaments can, with an ordinary Act adopted by simple majority, allow a transfer of powers which may result in any derogation from the Constitution ensuing from that transfer.

C. From General Transfer of Powers to More Specific Europe Provisions: a Touch of Legal History

(i) The Foundational Period

When the founding treaties were first concluded, none of the six Member States amended its Constitution to constitutionalize membership of the European Communities and to specifically provide for the constitutional modifications that would follow from such membership either directly or indirectly. What is more, not all of the original national Constitutions even allowed for the transfer of sovereign powers or competences or for a limitation of sovereignty, implicated in accession. Belgian membership of the Communities was probably unconstitutional until the 1970 constitutional amendment which introduced a transfer of powers provision. In the other Member States, the transfer was based on the general transfer of powers or limitation of sovereignty provisions in the Constitution, whether or not these were adopted with membership of an international organization like the EC in mind.[31] Remarkably also, in five of the original six Member States the treaties were approved by an ordinary statute, requiring a simple majority. This

---

de Nederlandse Grondwet', in D. Breillat, C.A.J.M. Kortmann and J.W.A. Fleuren, *Van de constitutie afwijkende verdragen*, (Deventer, Kluwer, 2002), pp. 43–78.

[29] In addition, an inconsistency between a treaty and a specific provision of the Constitution may also require constitutional amendment.

[30] And further: 'si l'on peut, comme l'a fait la section de législation du Conseil d'État, souhaiter que le texte constitutionnel soit adapté aux exigences du droit européen, une telle adaptation ne saurait conditionner l'application de ce droit, qui s'impose même en son absence', *Conseil d'État*, decision of 5 November 1996, *Journal des tribunaux*, 1997, p. 253; English version in A. Oppenheimer: *The Relationship Between European Community Law and National Law: The Cases*. Vol. 2, (Cambridge, Cambridge University Press, 2003), p. 155.

[31] German (art. 24(1) GG), Italy (art. 11); the Netherlands (art. 67, now art. 92); Luxembourg (art. 49*bis*); France (paragraph 15 of the Preamble to the 1946 Constitution).

was even so in the Netherlands where the Constitution explicitly provided for a special procedure to be followed when a transfer of powers would deviate from to the Constitution (art. 92, under the procedure as provided in art. 91(3)). Only in *Luxembourg* was ratification approved by a two-thirds majority in Parliament, as required by art. 49*bis* of the Constitution.

It was only at the occasion of the Treaty of Maastricht that these original transfer of powers provisions have, in two of the original six Member States, *Germany* and *France*, been adapted to the developing nature of the Communities and the establishment of the Union, while the other four still stick to the old way. In addition, general transfer of powers provisions have also been considered insufficient in the Member States acceding after the Treaty of Maastricht had entered into force.

But the trend began in *Ireland*. It was the Irish Constitution which was the first one to mention the EC explicitly.[32] In the absence of a transfer of powers provision, and given specific provisions of the Constitution which pointed against the constitutionality of membership,[33] a specific constitutional authorization was introduced by way of referendum, the normal procedure for constitutional amendment.[34] The Third Amendment specifically authorized Ireland to join the EC, and provided constitutional immunity to European and Irish law necessitated by membership.[35] Of the other two States acceding in 1973, the *United Kingdom* stands out for obvious reasons: with no written Constitution to amend, but a seemingly insurmountable barrier made up by the principle of the sovereignty of parliament, the United Kingdom acceded under the European Communities Act 1972. The aim of the Act was to give effect to the law deriving from the Treaties and to reinforce this with a strong rule of construction, requiring other statutes to be read accordingly, and requiring the courts to apply the principles laid down by the Court of Justice.[36] These provisions have appeared

[32] The United Kingdom is for the time being left out of the comparison because of its special features.

[33] Most notably the provisions on independence, sovereignty and separation of powers: Article 5 of the 1937 Irish Constitution, Bunreacht na hÉireann, reads: 'Ireland is a sovereign, independent, democratic State'; Article 6: '1. All powers of government, legislative, executive and judicial, derive, under God, from the people, whose right it is to designate the rulers of the State and, in final appeal, to decide all questions of national policy, according to the requirements of the common good. 2. These powers of government are exercisable only by or on the authority of the organs of State established by this Constitution.' Art. 15.2.1 reads: 'The sole and exclusive power of making laws for the State is hereby vested in the Oireachtas: no other legislative authority has power to make laws for the State.'

[34] As provided in Art. 46–47 of the Constitution.

[35] Art. 29.4.3°: 'The State may become a member of the European Coal and Steel Community (established by Treaty signed at Paris on the 18th day of April, 1951), the European Economic Community (established by Treaty signed at Rome on the 25th day of March, 1957) and the European Atomic Energy Community (established by Treaty signed at Rome on the 25th day of March, 1957). No provision of this Constitution invalidates laws enacted, acts done or measures adopted by the State which are necessitated by the obligations of membership of the Communities, or prevents laws enacted, acts done or measures adopted by the European Communities or by institutions thereof, or by bodies competent under the Treaties establishing the Communities, from having the force of law in the State'.

[36] For a summary of the EC Act and its effects, see A. Dashwood: 'The British way: Cohabiting with Community Law', in A.E. Kellermann et al. (eds), *EU Enlargement: The Constitutional Impact*

successful to convince the courts to give effect to Community law with priority over conflicting rules of national law.[37] But they were not drafted as 'transfer of powers' provisions and certainly not as transfer of *sovereign* rights or limitation of *sovereignty* provisions, which would have been wholly irreconcilable with the prevailing principle of parliamentary sovereignty. *Danish* accession took place on the basis of Section 20 of the Danish Constitution, which had been inserted in 1953 with a view specifically to allow Denmark to participate in supranational organizations.[38] Any such transfer is enacted through an Act adopted by a five-sixth majority, or if this qualified majority cannot be obtained, the Bill adopted by simple majority must be approved in a decisive referendum. It can then be rejected by a majority of voters, constituting not less than 30 per cent of the population entitled to vote. There was much debate at the time of accession as to whether Section 20 did indeed provide sufficient basis for a transfer of the kind involved in participation in the Communities.

A private individual in 1972 attempted to block accession on the basis of Section 20 of the Constitution, seeking a declaration from the courts that the procedure followed for accession was unconstitutional. In his opinion, accession required Denmark to *surrender* sovereignty, and accordingly necessitated a specified constitutional amendment under Section 88 of the Constitution. The courts declared the case inadmissible for lack of interest on the part of the applicants bringing the case and because the Bill had not yet been adopted.[39] But the issue of whether membership was constitutional under Section 20 or rather a constitutional amendment was called for would continue to linger on and would re-appear at the occasion of the Treaty of Maastricht.[40]

The next accessions of *Greece, Spain* and *Portugal* again took place on grounds of 'old-fashioned', general and/or confusing transfer of powers provisions (in the case of *Spain*, art. 93, and *Greece*, art. 8(2) and/or (3)), or in the absence of any clear constitutional authorization (in the case of *Portugal*). Nevertheless, both in *Spain* and *Greece*, accession was authorised by a special Act, an organic law in

---

at EU and National Level, (The Hague, T. M. C. Asser Press, 2001), pp. 81–87; P.P. Craig: 'Britain in the European Union', in J. Jowell and D. Oliver (eds), *The Changing Constitution,* 4th edn, 2000), pp. 61–88; for an early discussion of the EC Act, see J.D.B. Mitchell, S.A. Kuipers and B. Gall: 'Constitutional Aspects of the Treaty and Legislation relating to British Membership', [1972] CMLR 134.

[37] See the landmark decision in *House of Lords,* decision of 11 October 1990, *R v Secretary of State for Transport, Ex P Factortame Ltd and Others,* [1990] 3 CMLR 375; published also in A. Oppenheimer: *The Relationship Between European Community Law and National Law: The Cases.* Volume 1, (Cambridge, Cambridge University Press, 1994), p. 882.

[38] H. Koch, 'The Danish Constitutional Order', in A.E. Kellermann et al. (eds), *EU Enlargement: The Constitutional Impact at EU and National Level,* (The Hague, T. M. C. Asser Press, 2001), p. 109, at p. 109–110.

[39] *østre Landsret,* decision of 19 June 1972, *Grønborg v Prime Minister,* UfR 1972, 903 H; [1972] CMLR 516; *Højesteret,* decision of 27 September 1972, *Grønborg v Prime Minister,* [1972] CMLR 516, both reprinted in A. Oppenheimer, *The Relationship Between European Community Law and National Law: The Cases,* (Cambridge, Cambridge University Press, 1994), at 268.

[40] This will be discussed further *below.*

Spain, and in *Greece* an act adopted by a three-fifth majority in Parliament, even if it was not entirely clear whether this was constitutionally required. At the occasion of the *Greek* constitutional amendment of 1975, two transfer of powers provisions had been included in article 28 (2) and (3) of the Constitution, with a view to clearing the constitutional path for accession to the European Communities, and furnishing the basis in domestic law for accession to the EC.[41] What is striking when compared to transfer of powers provisions in other Constitutions is that the Greek provision contains both versions, the transfer of powers version (after the German example) and the Italian-style limitation of sovereignty version, but both paragraphs prescribe different procedural requirements and substantive conditions. First, they require different parliamentary majorities: a transfer of powers requires the approval by a three-fifths majority of the members of Parliament (para 2), while a limitation of the exercise of national sovereignty can be achieved by the approval of a majority of its members (para 3). Second, while the procedural requirements of paragraph 2 are more stringent, paragraph 3 contains explicit substantive *conditions* to limitations of sovereignty, which indicate the limits within which limitations may be consented to, relating in particular to fundamental rights and democracy. When Greece actually applied for membership, the legal discussion centred on the question as to which one of both paragraphs, or both together, was applicable: did accession imply a transfer of powers, a limitation of the exercise of sovereignty, or both? The Government, when submitting the Bill in Parliament, stated that in its view an absolute majority of its members would suffice, but that it would consent, by way of an exceptional concession not creating a precedent, to the application of the stricter requirement of a three-fifths majority as required by paragraph 2.[42] In practical effect, the issue became moot since the bill obtained a comfortable majority passing the three-fifths requirement, but the legal issue as to which paragraph applied continued. It has now become the majority opinion, among Greek lawyers, that

---

[41] Art. 28 provides: '1. The generally recognized rules of international law, as well as international conventions as of the time they are ratified by statute and become operative according to their respective conditions, shall be an integral part of domestic Greek law and shall prevail over any contrary provision of the law. The rules of international law and of international conventions shall be applicable to aliens only under the condition of reciprocity.

2. Authorities provided by the Constitution may by treaty or agreement be vested in agencies of international organizations, when this serves an important national interest and promotes cooperation with other States. A majority of three-fifths of the total number of Members of Parliament shall be necessary to vote the law ratifying the treaty or agreement.

3. Greece shall freely proceed by law passed by an absolute majority of the total number of Members of Parliament to limit the exercise of national sovereignty, insofar as this is dictated by an important national interest, does not infringe upon the rights of man and the foundations of democratic government and is effected on the basis of the principles of equality and under the condition of reciprocity'.

[42] See D. Evrigenis, 'Legal and Constitutional Implications of Greek Accession to the European Communities', *Common Market Law Review* n° 17, 1980, p. 157, at p. 161. However, given that the Acts approving the consecutive treaties have always obtained more than the three-fifths majority, the issue has not been resolved definitively.

both paragraphs apply simultaneously in the context of Greek participation in the European Union, and hence that both the substantive conditions of paragraph 3 and the procedural requirements of paragraph 2 must be complied with.[43] The Greek Constitution may thus have been the first one to explicitly establish substantive constitutional conditions to the participation in the European Communities!

The 1978 *Spanish* Constitution was drafted with a possible membership of the Communities in mind and taking account of the constitutional experiences of the existing Member States. Nevertheless, the Constitution does not expressly mention the EC or the EU. Article 93 of the Constitution, ie the general transfer of powers provision, formed the constitutional basis for accession.[44] The 1976 *Portuguese* Constitution did not envisage accession to supra-national organizations. It was adapted to imminent accession in 1982, when several provisions incompatible with membership were abrogated, and article 8(3) was inserted with a view to allowing the automatic integration of secondary legislation adopted by international organisations in the Portuguese legal order, without however including the authorisation for a transfer of powers.[45] The occasion of the 1989 constitutional amendment was seized to insert a general provision in art. 7(5) providing that 'Portugal is pledged to the reinforcement of the European identity and to the strengthening of the commitment of the States of Europe to democracy, peace, economic progress and justice in the relations between their peoples'. Yet, it was only in 1992, at the occasion of the constitutional amendment set-off by the ratification of the Treaty of Maastricht, that a real transfer of powers provision was inserted, custom made for the EU as had become the *modus operandi* by then, and including also substantive conditions for participation in the EU.[46]

By way of conclusion, it can be said that with the exception of *Ireland*, all Member States joined on grounds of a general transfer of powers provision and

---

[43] So J. Iliopoulos-Strangas, 'Le droit de l'Union européenne et les Constitutions nationales. Rapport hellénique', (XXth FIDE Congress, London, 2002), at pp. 23–26, available on www.fide2002.org.

[44] Art. 93 reads: 'By means of an organic law, authorization may be established for the conclusion of treaties which attribute to an international organization or institution the exercise of competences derived from the Constitution. It is the responsibility of the Parliament or the Government, depending on the cases, to guarantee compliance with these treaties and the resolutions emanating from the international or supranational organizations who have been entitled by this cession'.

[45] 'Legislation emanating from the competent bodies of international organisations to which Portugal is a party is directly in force in the internal order, as long as such is found expressly established in the respective constitutive treaties', translation taken from R.M. Moura Ramos: 'The Adaptation of the Portuguese Constitutional Order to Community Law', in A.E. Kellermann et al. (eds), *EU Enlargement: The Constitutional Impact at EU and National Level*, (The Hague, T.M.C. Asser Press, 2001), pp. 131–139, at 132. The reference to 'expressly' provided for direct effect obviously begged the question of the direct effect of other types of Community law, and the constitutional revision undertaken in 1989 removed the word 'expressly' from the provision.

[46] Art. 7(6) reads: 'Provided that there is reciprocity, Portugal may enter into agreements for the joint exercise of the powers necessary to establish the European Union, in ways that have due regard for the principle of subsidiarity and the objective of economic and social cohesion', translation taken from R.M. Moura Ramos, *op.cit.*, at p. 133.

only *Portugal* amended its Constitution before accession. There were no custom made Europe provisions. Yet, there was already a trend towards procedural conditions for accession: while among the six founding States only the *Luxembourg* Constitution required a two-thirds majority, *Denmark, Ireland, Greece* and *Spain* all joined following special procedures, and an ordinary act adopted by simple majority in Parliament did no longer suffice to authorize accession.

(ii)   The Single European Act: Constitutional Standstill

The *Single European Act* was by all but one Member States' approved and ratified on the basis of the general existing provisions. Only in *Ireland* did it give rise to constitutional amendment, after a court case brought by a private individual, Mr Crotty, who challenged the constitutionality of Ireland's participation in the Single European Act. The Irish courts held that the Third Amendment could indeed not serve as the basis for ratification.[47] Accordingly, the Constitution was amended by the Tenth Amendment adopted by referendum. After *Crotty*, major Treaty reforms implying further transfers must be preceded by a referendum to introduce the necessary arrangements in the Constitution.[48]

It is remarkable that none of the other Member States used the occasion of the Treaty amendment to set the constitutional record straight. Indeed, in constitutional terms much had happened since the ratification of the founding treaties. First, the Court of Justice had 'constitutionalised' the Treaties[49]: it had transformed them from classic international treaties as they may have seemed at the time, into the constitutional charter of a special legal order, deriving from an autonomous source, for the benefit of which the Member States had limited their sovereignty or transferred powers to a Community which now had real powers of its own. It was now beyond any doubt that the law deriving from the Treaties was to be applied in the domestic legal order with precedence over conflicting provisions of national law, and even constitutional provisions could not be opposed to it. The constitutionality of the Treaties and of secondary legislation could not be questioned.

The national constitutional immobility is particularly striking in those Member States where the courts, in some cases constitutional courts, had struggled with constitutional issues surrounding membership under the founding treaties. Indeed, the *Italian* and *German* constitutional courts and the *Danish* courts had been confronted with actions challenging the constitutionality of the

---

[47] *Irish Supreme Court*, decision of 18 February and 9 April 1987, *Crotty v An Taoiseach* [1987] ILRM 400; [1987] IR 713; A. Oppenheimer: *The Cases*, Vol. 1, p. 594.

[48] See G. Hogan: 'The Nice Treaty and the Irish Constitution', *European Public Law* n° 7, 2001, pp. 565–573.

[49] Landmark cases include: Case 26/62 *Van Gend en Loos* [1963] ECR 1; Case 6/64 *Costa v ENEL* [1964] ECR 585; Case 11/70 *Internationale Handelsgesellschaft* [1970] ECR 1125; Case 106/77 *Simmenthal* [1978] ECR 585; Case 294/83 *Les Verts v European Parliament* [1986] ECR 1759; See on the constitutionalisation process: J.H.H. Weiler: *The Constitution of Europe. 'Do the new clothes have an emperor?' and other essays on European integration*, (Cambridge, Cambridge University Press) 1999.

State's membership. It was argued before them that the constitutional transfer of powers provisions and the procedure by an ordinary Act of Parliament could not suffice to support a transfer of powers or limitation of sovereignty of the kind effectuated by the European Community Treaties. Both the *Italian* and the *German* constitutional court declared that the constitutional provisions as they stood did suffice and that the State could join the Communities on grounds of an ordinary statute and that membership was constitutional, but in all instances, the discomfort of the constitutional courts was obvious.[50]

Furthermore, it had become clear in the case law of several constitutional courts that under the prevailing constitutional provisions, membership could not have the full consequences as required by the Court of Justice. More particularly, it had not appeared possible for those courts to accept the unconditional and absolute primacy of Community law over the national Constitution, at least not over its core principles. This theory of the constitutional *controlimiti* was first developed in the case law of the *Corte costituzionale*[51] and later followed by the *Bundesverfassungsgericht.*[52] In essence, the position is as follows: while article 11 of the Italian Constitution and article 24 of the German Constitution provide for the transfer of powers to the European Communities or allow for the limitation of sovereignty in their favour by a treaty approved by an ordinary statute, these provisions do not allow for the absolute primacy of the Treaties and the law deriving from them. They must be read in the context of the entire Constitution taken as a whole, which determines the limits of the possible transfer or limitation. While some deviation from constitutional provisions may be accepted as a consequence of membership, there are certain core principles of the Constitution which cannot be touched upon, such as the unalienable rights of man or constitutional fundamental rights, or the fundamental principles of the constitutional order. Accordingly, Community law cannot take precedence over these core principles. This theory has become famous mostly as the *Solange* case law, or as the theory of *controlimiti.*[53]

---

[50] *Bundesverfassungsgericht*, decision of 5 July 1967, *EEC Treaty Constitutionality Case*, BVerfGE 22, 134 and decision of 18 October 1967, *EEC Regulations Constitutionality Case*, BVerfGE 22, 293, Oppenheimer, *The Cases*, Vol. 1, at p. 410; *Corte costituzionale*, decision n. 16/64 of 24 February 1964, *Costa v ENEL*, 1 CMLRev., 1963–1964, 363; decision n. 98/65 of 16 December 1965, *San Michele*, [1967] CMLR 160; reference to the Danish cases see fn. *39 above*. See on these cases M. Claes: *The National Courts' Mandate in the European Constitution*, (Oxford, Hart Publishing, 2005) (forthcoming).

[51] *Corte costituzionale*, decision n. 183/73 of 27 December 1973, *Frontini*, 18 Giru. Cost. I 2401; 2 [1974] CMLR 372; A. Oppenheimer: *The Cases*, Vol.1, 1994, at p. 629; later confirmed, in this respect, in *Corte costituzionale*, decision n. 170/84 of 8 June 1984,*Granital*, Giur. Cost. I 1098; 21 CMLRev., 1984, 756; A. Oppenheimer: *The Cases*, Vol. 1, 1994, at p. 642.

[52] *Bundesverfassungsgericht*, decision of 29 May 1974, *Internationale Handelsgesellschaft (Solange I)*, BVerfGE 37, 271; 2 [1974] CMLR 540; A. Oppenheimer, *The Cases*, Vol.1, 1994, at p. 415.

[53] See on the theory of *controlimiti* the contribution by A. Celotto and T. Groppi: "Diritto UE e diritto nazionale: primauté vs controlimiti", in M. Cartabia, B. De Witte and P. Pérez Tremps (eds), *Constitución Europea y Constituciones Nacionales*, (Valencia: Tirant lo Blanch), 2005, p. 287. To be sure, the notion of *controlimiti* referred to here are only the material *controlimiti*, and not the procedural requirements applying at the time of ratification.

It is important to note, however, that as interpreted by these courts, the *controlimiti* were provisional, or transitory, and could accordingly disappear. Once engraved in stone, written into the text of the Constitution, they become much more difficult to eliminate. Especially in the German case, the *Bundesverfassungsgericht* made it clear from the beginning that the reservations were temporary and could disappear as soon as the Communities would provide sufficient guarantees of their own in the area of fundamental rights protection. The Court demonstrated its approval of the fundamental rights policy of the Court of Justice and despite the absence of a full-fledged fundamental rights catalogue in *Solange II*.[54] Yet, other concerns relating to Community law came to the fore gradually. The *Bundesfinanzhof* and several commentators had objected to the activist case law of the Court of Justice. The *Bundesfinanzhof* did not want to accept the position of the Court of Justice concerning the direct effect of Directives. In its view, the Court of Justice had developed Community law beyond what had been agreed by the Member States in the Treaties. In *Kloppenburg*,[55] the *Bundesverfassungsgericht* held that the Court of Justice had not done so and had not gone beyond the limits of the judicial function: it was entitled to develop the law, as any other court, and in the case of direct effect of Directives, there could be no objection from the viewpoint of the Act approving the EEC Treaty or article 24 of the Constitution to the method of judicial development of the law used by the Court of Justice. Yet, the decision also contained the warning that the European Communities and its Court of Justice could not extend the jurisdiction of the Communities limitlessly in this way: the Community was not a sovereign State with *Kompetenz Kompetenz*. In *Kloppenburg*, it was the *Bundesfinanzhof* which lost face, and it was held to have infringed the right to a lawful judge by its refusal to send a question for preliminary ruling to the Court of Justice. But the concern from a constitutional law perspective for the creeping extension of Community powers by the use of the then article 235 of the EC Treaty, the implied powers theory of the Court of Justice and its *effet utile* case law would continue to build up. Furthermore, the concern for fundamental rights protection had, despite the decision in *Solange II*, not faded completely. These issues would be central in the *Maastricht Urteil*.

(iii)   Maastricht: The Constitutional Turning Point

The Treaty of Maastricht and the national and European constitutional crisis surrounding it constituted the turning point, but not in all Member States. In four out of six original Member States, the same (unprincipled) approach to

---

[54] *Bundesverfassungsgericht*, decision of 22 October 1986, *Wünsche Handelsgesellschaft (Solange II)*, BVerfGE 73, 339, Oppenheimer: *The Cases*, Vol.1, 1994, p. 461. It must however be emphasised that the BVerfG never completely gave up jurisdiction to step in. It merely promised not to exercise it except in exceptional cases under srtict conditions.

[55] *Bundesverfassungsgericht*, decision of 8 April 1987, *Kloppenburg*, BVerfGE 75, 223; [1988] 3 CMLR 1; Oppenheimer: *The Cases*, Vol.1, 1994, p. 497.

European integration was followed at the occasion of the Treaty of Maastricht, and those of Amsterdam and Nice for that matter: *Belgium*, the *Netherlands, Italy, Luxembourg*. In the *Netherlands*, there was some discussion as to whether the special procedure provided in the Constitution for transfers which were contrary to the Constitution must be followed in the case of the Treaty of Maastricht, requiring a two-thirds majority in Parliament. However, both government and Parliament maintained that the situation did not materialize, as did the majority of academia, and the Treaty was approved and ratification authorized by way of an ordinary statute.[56] No constitutional amendments were performed. In *Belgium*, it was stated by the Council of State acting in its advisory capacity that the Treaty of Maastricht contained provisions contrary to the Belgian Constitution, more particularly on the right to vote, but the Prime Minister stated that given the fact that the Treaty would in any case prevail over the Constitution (*quod non!*), there was no need for prior amendment. The Treaty was approved by way of an ordinary statute under article 34 and the constitutional amendment was effectuated only well after ratification, in 1998.[57] This left the *Cour d'arbitrage* in a very awkward position, when the constitutionality of the Act approving the Treaty of Maastricht was challenged for breach of article 8 of the Constitution, restricting the right to vote to Belgian nationals. The conflict was manifest, and had been pointed out before, but a declaration of unconstitutionality could hardly be said to be a workable outcome: a decision of a constitutional court declaring a treaty unconstitutional does not carry any direct effects on the international scene, where the Treaty remains in force; in the internal field, it would be very difficult for such court to have its decision enforced; and if enforced, it could only contribute to the international liability of the State. The *Cour d'arbitrage* found a way out of the dilemma by declaring the action inadmissible for lack of standing.[58]

In *Italy* there was some debate on whether article 11 could supply constitutional support to some of the far-reaching provisions of the Maastricht Treaty, particularly in the monetary field, but as in the Netherlands, these views were ignored, and the Treaty was approved by ordinary statute under article 11, without any further constitutional amendment.[59]

---

[56] A.W. Heringa: 'De verdragen van Maastricht in strijd met de Grondwet', *Nederlands Juristenblad*, 1992, pp. 749–752; see on the procedure in general L. Besselink: 'Becoming a Party to Treaties Which Diverge From the Constitution', *European Public Law* n° 9, pp. 471–479; J.W.A. Fleuren: 'Verdragen die afwijken van de Nederlandse Grondwet', in D. Breillat, C.A.J.M. Kortmann and J.W.A. Fleuren, *Van de constitutie afwijkende verdragen*, (Deventer, Kluwer, 2002), pp. 43–78.

[57] F. Delpérée, 'La Belgique et l'Europe', *Revue française de droit constitutionnel*, 1992, p. 643. The same course of action was followed in Luxembourg, see B. De Witte: 'Constitutional Aspects of European Union Membership in the Original Six Member States: Model Solutions for the Applicant Countries?', in A.E. Kellermann et al. (eds), *EU Enlargement: The Constitutional Impact at EU and National Level*, (The Hague, T.M.C. Asser Press, 2001), pp. 65–79, at p. 72.

[58] *Cour d'arbitrage*, decision n. 76/94 of 18 October 1994, *Treaty of Maastricht*, available on www.arbitrage.be.

[59] See B. De Witte: 'Constitutional Aspects of European Union Membership in the Original Six Member States: Model Solutions for the Applicant Countries?', in A.E. Kellermann et al. (eds),

Also in *Denmark* was the Treaty of Maastricht approved for ratification on grounds of the classic transfer of powers provision under section 20 of the Constitution, by way of a referendum.[60] Yet, once approved, the Act authorising ratification of the Treaty of Maastricht under section 20 was again challenged, and this time the courts did allow the case. The *Højesteret* held that the Treaty of Maastricht implied a transfer of powers within a range of common and essential areas of life and therefore of its own was of far-reaching importance to the Danish people as a whole, and the applicants did not have to show any further concrete and direct individual concern.[61] The applicants contended that Section 20 of the Constitution could not provide a sufficient constitutional basis for Danish ratification of the Treaty of Maastricht, as it only allowed for transfers 'to a specified extent', while the Treaty lacked sufficient precision and allowed for further expansion under Article 308 EC (then article 235 of the EC Treaty) and the case law of the Court of Justice. Secondly, they argued that the delegation of sovereignty was on such a scale and such nature that it was inconsistent with the Constitution's premise of a democratic form of government. In its final decision on the merits, the *Højesteret* rejected these claims, while conceding that constitutional issues may arise later. However, given the supervision of the Danish government in cases where decisions are adopted under article 308 EC, the control of the Court of Justice and ultimately of the Danish courts, the Treaty could be ratified under the procedure provided in section 20, without the need for constitutional amendment.[62]

In other Member States, the text of the Constitution *was* amended in order to allow for ratification. This was the case in *Germany, France, Ireland, Spain* and *Portugal.* In *Germany*, ratification was preceded by the introduction of a new Europe provision in article 23 of the Constitution, confirming to some extent the *Solange* case law of the *Bundesverfassungsgericht*. There was wide agreement that article 24 did no longer suffice as the ground for participation in the European

---

EU Enlargement: The Constitutional Impact at EU and National Level, (The Hague, T. M. C. Asser Press, 2001), pp. 65–79, at p. 72–73.

[60] As is sufficiently known, the first referendum resulted in a no-vote, the second referendum on the Treaty including the Edinburgh Agreement approved the Treaty for ratification. Strictly speaking, there was no formal need for a second referendum, as five-sixth of the Danish *Folketing* had already given its approval. Yet, it was thought politically desirable to again submit it to the people. As with the Accession Treaty, private individuals had tried to prevent accession before the courts, arguing that a constitutional amendment was called for. Once again, the challenges were declared inadmissible.

[61] *Højesteret*, decision of 12 August 1996, *Treaty of Maastricht (admissibility)*, UfR 1996, 302, commented in J. Svennigsen, 'The Danish Supreme Court Puts the Maastricht Treaty on Trial', 4 *Maastricht Journal*, 1997, 101.

[62] For a further discussion of the case, see M. Claes, *The National Courts Mandate in the European Constitution*, (Oxford, Hart Publishing, forthcoming), Chapter II.5.2; K. Høegh, 'The Danish Maastricht Judgment', [1999] EL Rev 80; H. Rasmussen, 'Confrontation or Peaceful Co-existence? On the Danish Supreme Court's Maastricht Ratification Judgment', in *Judicial Review in European Union Law. Liber Amicorum in Honour of Lord Slynn of Hadley*, Vol I, D. O'Keeffe and A. Bavasso (eds), (The Hague, Kluwer Law International, 2000), 377; P. Biering, 'The Application of EU Law in Denmark: 1986 to 2000'; [2000] 37 CMLRev. 925.

Union, and a new veritable Europe provision was inserted in article 23 as part of the so-called *'Maastricht-Novelle'.*[63] The provision serves several purposes. First, it is an *'Integrationsklausel'*, obliging Germany to participate in the project of European integration. Yet, membership is no longer unconditional: the provision prescribes specifications with which the European Union must comply for German participation to be constitutional (*'Struktursicherungsklausel'*). These conditions are framed in vague and open terms, and will require further interpretation as European integration goes along. The absolute limits of German participation in the European construct are contained in the reference, in article 23, to the *Ewigkeitsklausel* of article 79: the core of the German constitutional identity is untouchable, and unalterable: the division of the Federation into *Länder*, their participation on principle in the legislative process, the principles laid down in articles 1 (human dignity) and 20 (the basic institutional principles, such as democracy, social federal State, popular sovereignty, rule of law, and *'streitbare Demokratie'*)[64] cannot be amended. This function of article 23 as prescribing the absolute limit of further integration is referred to as its role of *'Bestandssicherungsklausel'*.

As for the procedure to be followed, the second sentence of article 23(1) states that *Hoheitsrechte* may be transferred by a law with the consent of the *Bundesrat*, without prescribing a special majority. However, where the Treaty or subsequent treaties revising it were to amend or supplement the Basic Law, or make such amendments or supplements possible, a two-thirds majority in both *Bundestag* and *Bundesrat* is required. It could of course be argued, that any transfer of sovereign rights implies a constitutional amendment, and it is not entirely clear which

---

[63] Note that the constitutional amendment was not, as in France for instance, the consequence of the decision of the *Bundesverfassungsgericht*: despite the not so European friendly tone of the judgment, the Court did reject the claim that the proposed Treaty was unconstitutional: it could be ratified. The constitutional amendment preceded that decision of the *Bundesverfassungsgericht*. Art. 23 reads: '(1) With a view to establishing a united Europe, the Federal Republic of Germany shall participate in the development of the European Union that is committed to democratic, social, and federal principles, to the rule of law, and to the principle of subsidiarity, and that guarantees a level of protection of basic rights essentially comparable to that afforded by this Basic Law. To this end the Federation may transfer sovereign powers (*'Hoheitsrechte'*) by a law with the consent of the *Bundesrat*. The establishment of the European Union, as well as changes in its treaty foundations and comparable regulations that amend or supplement this Basic Law, or make such amendments or supplements possible, shall be subject to paragraphs (2) and (3) of Article 79.

The remainder of the provision deals with the relations between the German organs in the context of EU decision-making and will be discussed further below. On Art. 23, see for instance M. Nettesheim: 'EU-Recht und nationales Verfassungsrecht. Deutscher Bericht für die XX. FIDE-Tagung 2002', available on www.fide2002.org.

[64] Art. [Basic institutional principles; defence of the constitutional order] : (1) The Federal Republic of Germany is a democratic and social federal state.

(2) All state authority is derived from the people. It shall be exercised by the people through elections and other votes and through specific legislative, executive, and judicial bodies.

(3) The legislature shall be bound by the constitutional order, the executive and the judiciary by law and justice.

(4) All Germans shall have the right to resist any person seeking to abolish this constitutional order, if no other remedy is available.

treaty amendments will and which will not require a special majority. In addition to stating conditions for German participation and thus constitutionalizing explicitly the *Solange* case law of the *Bundesverfassungsgericht*, the provision also deals with the internal division of powers and responsibilities in the area of European decision-making, both as between parliament and the government and between the *Bund* and *Länder*.

In *France* it was the *Conseil constitutionnel* which, when inquired about the constitutionality of the proposed Treaty of Maastricht, held that certain provisions of the Treaty did conflict with specific provisions contained in the Constitution, or with the 'conditions essentielles de l'excercice de la souveraineté nationale'. As a consequence, a new Title on the European Communities and the European Union was inserted.[65] Article 88-1 served to underpin French membership of the Communities and the European Union and give it a stronger constitutional basis. The provision has recently been interpreted by the *Conseil constitutionnel* as implying a constitutional obligation to transpose Community Directives, 'à laquelle il ne pourrait être fait obstacle qu'en raison d'une disposition expresse contraire de la Constitution'.[66] The provision has thus also served to grant (limited) constitutional immunity to Community law. Article 88-2 allowed for participation in the European Monetary Union (EMU) and free movement of persons, ie the areas where the *Conseil constitutionnel* had found an incompatibility with the Constitution. Article 88-3 served to make the necessary arrangements to allow for the right to vote and stand as a candidate for European citizens. Finally, article 88-4 intended to increase the control functions of the French Parliament in European decision-making. These provisions are rather restrictive and concern only those elements that had been declared unconstitutional by the *Conseil constitutionnel*. Rather than to change individual provisions in the Constitution, they introduce a parallel title in the Constitution, while leaving the existing provisions intact.

---

[65] Amendments introduced by the *loi constitutionnelle* n. 92–554 of 25 June 1992: Article 88-1: 'La République participe aux Communautés européennes et à l'Union européenne, constituées d'États qui ont choisi librement, en vertu des traités qui les ont instituées, d'exercer en commun certaines de leurs compétences.

Article 88-2: Sous réserve de réciprocité et selon les modalités prévues par le traité sur l'Union européenne signé le 7 février 1992, la France consent aux transferts de compétences nécessaires à l'établissement de l'union économique et monétaire européenne ainsi qu'a la détermination des règles relatives au franchissement des frontières extérieures des États membres de la Communauté européenne.

Article 88-3: 'Sous réserve de réciprocité et selon les modalités prévues par le Traité sur l'Union européenne signé le 7 février 1992, le droit de vote et d'éligibilité aux élections municipales peut être accordé aux seuls citoyens de l'Union résidant en France. Ces citoyens ne peuvent exercer les fonctions de maire ou d'adjoint ni participer à la désignation des électeurs sénatoriaux et à l'élection des sénateurs. Une loi organique votée dans les mêmes termes par les deux assemblées détermine les conditions d'application du présent article.

Article 88-4: Le gouvernement soumet à l'Assemblée nationale et au Sénat, dès leur transmission au Conseil des Communautés, les propositions d'actes communautaires comportant des dispositions de nature législative.

Pendant les sessions ou en dehors d'elles, des résolutions peuvent être votées dans le cadre du présent article, selon des modalités déterminées par le règlement de chaque assemblée.

[66] *Conseil constitutionnel*, decision n. 2004-496 DC of 10 June 2004, *Loi pour la confiance dans l'économie numérique*, available on www.conseil-constitutionnel.fr.

The *Irish* Constitution was amended by the usual referendum, adding a specific authorization to ratify the Treaty of Maastricht and extending the constitutional immunity to EU law. Also, in *Spain* and *Portugal* the Constitution was amended in view of ratification of the Treaty of Maastricht. The *Spanish* Constitution was, following the decision of the *Tribunal constitucional*,[67] amended to provide for the right to stand as a candidate in municipal elections.[68] It was accordingly a most limited amendment, and does not even mention the EU, or EC law. It merely intended to eliminate the direct conflict with a constitutional provision. Finally, the *Portuguese* constitutional amendment was intended to constitutionalize the European Union,[69] to delete inconsistencies and to increase the powers of the parliament in the context of EU decision-making.

Why then did the Treaty of Maastricht constitute a turning point? First, Maastricht *did* comprise a quantum leap in European integration. It was the final confirmation that Europe was indeed more than an ordinary international organization, more than a common market, that it touched upon all aspects of daily life and could affect fundamental rights even in areas where it had been considered unthinkable before.[70] But the Treaty did more and established a new European Union, and powers were transferred or at least arrangements were made to co-operate in areas touching upon the core activities of the State: defence, foreign affairs, justice and home affairs, but also in the context of EC law, in the area of economic and monetary union; it even included citizenship. Secondly, decisions of the constitutional courts in Germany (though after constitutional amendment), France and Spain (indicating the constitutional provisions requiring amendment) demonstrated the constitutional implications of the Treaties. While the French and Spanish decisions seemed concerned mainly with this Treaty and 'short term issues', especially the German *Maastricht Urteil* did lay the finger on elements of European integration which were, to say the least, questionable from a constitutional point of view, European or national, concerning the most fundamental constitutional principles common to Western democracies: the rule of law, the principle of democracy, fundamental rights protection. Thirdly, there may have been a spill-over from the Member States which joined later: The

---

[67] *Tribunal Constitucional*, decision n. 1236/92 of 1 July 1992, *Treaty of Maastricht*, [1994] 3 CMLR 101; A. Oppenheimer: *The Cases*, Vol.1, 1994, p. 712.

[68] Article 13: 'Only Spaniards shall have the rights recognized in section 23, except in cases which may be established by treaty or by law concerning the right to vote and the right to be elected in municipal elections, and subject to the principle of reciprocity'. (This text includes the first constitutional reform adopted on 27 August 1992, it just added the words 'and the right to be elected' to the paragraph).

[69] Art. 7(6): 'Provided that there is reciprocity, Portugal may enter into agreements for the joint exercise of the powers necessary to establish the European Union, in ways that have due regard for the principle of subsidiarity and the objective of economic and social cohesion'. In addition, Art. 15(5) allowed for the right to vote and stand as a candidate in European elections. The exclusive right of the Bank of Portugal to issue currency and define the main goals of the finance and monetary system was eliminated, and finally, the powers of the Portuguese Parliament in EU decision making were reinforced. This point is developed further below.

[70] So for instance in Case C–159/90 *SPUC v Grogan* [1991] ECR I-4685.

original treaties had been approved by an ordinary statute adopted by simple majority in five of the founding six, and only in *Luxembourg* by a qualified majority. But the accession of *Denmark* required a referendum since the five-sixth majority in parliament had not been reached, while the *Irish* accession had required a full-fledged constitutional amendment by referendum. In *Greece*, the accession was approved by a qualified majority of three-fifths in Parliament, mainly for political reasons. *Spain* joined on grounds of an organic Act adopted by an absolute majority of all members, under the general transfer of powers provision. These events had not lead the old Member States to change their old habits in the case of the Single European Act, but they may have contributed to increasing constitutional awareness when Maastricht was to be ratified. Finally, a likely factor may also have been the awareness that popular support had dropped, that the necessary legitimacy was lacking as exemplified by the popular response to the IGC and the Treaty it came up with and the dramatic outcomes of the referendums.

(iv)   Sweden, Finland and Austria: The Classic Transfer of Powers Provisions do not Suffice

The three Member States which joined the EU after the Treaty of Maastricht had entered into force did not consider their general transfer of powers provisions sufficient. In two of the three Member States acceding after the ratification of the Maastricht Treaty, *Sweden* and *Austria*, were the available general transfer of powers provisions considered too slim for the massive transfer implicated in membership. *Austria* conducted a total revision of the Constitution (*Gesämtänderung*) and adopted a special Constitutional Act facilitating accession. In *Sweden*, the transfer of powers provision was completed with a special Europe provision.[71] The *Finnish* Constitution did not include a general or specific transfer of powers provision, and none was inserted at the time of accession, but accession was achieved by way of an exceptive enactment.[72]

In *Finland*,[73] membership is not constitutionally founded on a transfer of powers provision, but rather on an exceptive enactment, which is considered to make a hole in the Constitution, which must hence be read in context. The Constitution prevailing at the time contained no provision on the transfer of competences or sovereignty to international organisations; such transfer was even considered contrary to articles 1 and 2 of the Constitution, declaring Finland's sovereignty and the division of powers. It was also generally agreed that the Accession Treaty deviated fundamentally from the Constitution. The

---

[71] See below.   [72] See further below.
[73] See on the constitutional implications of Finnish membership, T. Ojanen: 'The Impact of EU Membership on Finnish Constitutional Law', *European Public Law* n° 10, 2004, pp. 531–564; P. Aalto: 'Accession of Finland to the European Union: First Remarks', *European Law Review* n° 20, 1995, pp. 618–628; N. Jääskinen, 'The Application of Community Law in Finland: 1995–1998', *Common Market Law Review* n° 36, 1999, pp. 407–441.

Constitutional Law Committee of the Finnish Parliament conducted a prior revision of the constitutional implications of accession. And yet, a revision of the Constitution was not considered necessary,[74] because of the institution of exceptive enactment or *leges fugitivae*, which allow for indirect derogation from the Constitution without full-fledged constitutional amendment, but following the same procedure. Such exceptive enactments were explicitly provided for by article 95 of the old Constitution Act. If such a proposal relates to the approval of an international treaty, the procedure is simpler than the usual constitutional amendment, since the proposal can be passed immediately without the need to await the next general elections, if the required two-thirds majority in parliament is attained.[75] Accordingly, the Treaty of Accession was incorporated into Finnish law by two-thirds majority through an exceptive enactment, without changing the actual wording of the Constitution. A new Constitution was adopted in 2000, containing several provisions relating to participation in the EU, but there is no general Europe provision of the Franco-German type, and membership is still considered to be based on the same exceptive enactment.

Since 1981, article 9(2) of the *Austrian Bundes-Verfassungsgesetz* provides that 'Legislation or a treaty requiring sanction in accordance with Article 50 (1) can transfer specific federal competencies to intergovernmental organisations and their authorities and can within the framework of international law regulate the activity of foreign states' agents inside Austria as well as the activity of Austrian agents abroad'.[76] The provision was limited to the transfer of *federal* powers, which could be accomplished by an ordinary statute. The exact interpretation of the provision was still being discussed when Austria applied for membership, but it was consented that it would not suffice to constitutionalise accession to the EU. EU-membership would bring about a fundamental change to several fundamental principles of the Austrian Constitution, at least those of democracy, separation of powers and the rule of law.[77] Accession was consequently considered to require a *Gesamtänderung* of the *Bundes-Verfassungsgesetz* in accordance with article 44 (3) of the B-VG.[78]

[74] Amendment of the Constitution required two consecutive votes in parliament, with a general election in-between and a two-thirds majority in the second vote. The urgent procedure required that the Bill be declared urgent by a five-sixth majority and then approved by the current parliament by two-thirds majority, see P. Aalto, *op. cit.*, at p. 620.

[75] As provided by art. 69(1) of the old Constitution Act.

[76] The provision was inspired by art. 20(1) of the Danish Constitution, article 49*bis* of the Luxembourg Constitution and article 24(1) of the German Basic Law, so H. Schäffer, 'Österreichischer Landesbericht', in J. Schwarze (ed), *The Birth of a European Constitutional Order. The Interaction of National and European Constitutional Law*, Nomos Verlagsgesellschaft, Baden-Baden, 2001, p. 339, at p. 350; on the Austrian case. See also H. F. Koeck, 'EU Law and National Constitutions—the Austrian Case', available on www.fide2002.org.

[77] S. Griller: 'EU Membership and Constitutional Transformation in Accession Countries. The Example of Austria, Finland and Sweden (1995)', paper presented at the VIth IACL Congress in Chile, 2003, available on www.iaclworldcongress.org/english/program.shtml, at p. 3.

[78] Article 44 (3) reads: 'Any total revision of the Federal Constitution shall upon conclusion of the procedure pursuant to Article 42 but before its authentication by the Federal President be submitted to a referendum by the entire nation, whereas any partial revision requires this only if one third of the members of the House of Representatives or the Senate so demands'.

Such total revision, the first one since the adoption of the Constitution in 1920, requires a two-thirds majority vote in parliament and the original designation of the provision as a constitutional law, and the submission to a referendum. In order to facilitate accession, the Constitution Act on Austria's Accession to the EU was adopted, the so-called EU-Accession Act.[79] The Act authorised the competent organs to conclude the accession Treaty as agreed upon on 12 April 1994, with the approval of the Austrian people, and with the approval of the *Nationalrat* and the *Bundesrat*.[80]

Since the authorisation was limited to the specified Accession Treaty, it could not support any further transfers negotiated during future IGC's. As a consequence, the Amsterdam and Nice Treaties and the 2003 Enlargement Treaty were all approved and ratified on the basis of a special Constitutional Act. These later amendments were not treated as total revisions, but like the original EU-Accesssion Act, they did require a qualified approval by the Austrian Parliament.[81] In addition, a new chapter was introduced in the first part of the *Bundes-Verfassungsgesetz*, "On the European Union", dealing specifically with the modalities for participation of Austrian organs in EU-decision making, and to arrange the internal division of powers in EU matters, including the duty imposed on the government to inform parliament and the duty to inform the *Länder* of any proposals which touch upon their interests and competences.[82]

Also, in *Sweden* the constitutional transfer of powers provision was considered insufficient to allow for the transfer required by accession to the EU. Delegation of decision-making power to international organizations is made possible though article 10:5 of the Swedish Instrument of Government. The provision came into existence in 1965 in order to make an association with the EC possible, and to allow for the transfer to international organizations for peaceful

[79] The EU-Accession Act is a constitutional act, which has not been incorporated in the *Bundes-Verfassungsgesetz* itself. The Austrian Constitution consists of the *Bundes-Verfassungsgesetz* properly speaking, and so-called *Bundesverfassungsgesetze* (note that the hyphen is missing). All that is required for a law to be considered constitutional is that it has been designated as a constitutional act and that a special procedure was followed to adopt it.

[80] This is the text of the entire Law: Bundesverfassungsgesetz über den Beitritt Österreichs zur Europäischen Union: Auf Grund des Ergebnisses der Volksabstimmung wird kundgemacht:
Artikel I Mit der Zustimmung des Bundesvolkes zu diesem Bundesverfassungsgesetz werden die bundesverfassungsgesetzlich zuständigen Organe ermächtigt, den Staatsvertrag über den Beitritt Österreichs zur Europäischen Union entsprechend dem am 12. April 1994 von der Beitrittskonferenz festgelegten Verhandlungsergebnis abzuschließen.
Artikel II Der Staatsvertrag über den Beitritt Österreichs zur Europäischen Union darf nur mit Genehmigung des Nationalrates und der Zustimmung des Bundesrates hiezu abgeschlossen werden. Diese Beschlüsse bedürfen jeweils der Anwesenheit von mindestens der Hälfte der Mitglieder und einer Mehrheit von zwei Dritteln der abgegebenen Stimmen.
Artikel III Mit der Vollziehung dieses Bundesverfassungsgesetzes ist die Bundesregierung betraut.

[81] Approval by the *Nationalrat* and the *Bundesrat* requiring the presence of at least half of the respective members and a two thirds majority in favour. The Treaty of Amsterdam did require prior constitutional amendment also. It was not considered to affect the constitutional order fundamentally, so there was no need for a referendum, but it did affect the Constitution in the area of security policy. Hence, a constitutional amendment was performed of art. 27f.　　　[82] Arts. 23a-23f.

co-operation.[83] It was revised in 1985 to define the conditions for delegation: delegation was possible only to a limited extent, and was excluded concerning fundamental laws or statutes limiting fundamental rights. When Parliament decided that Sweden would apply for membership in 1990, it was agreed that the Constitution did not permit the delegation needed.[84] Since 1995, the Instrument of Government differentiated between transfers of powers to the EC and other transfers of powers. [85] Powers could be ceded to the EC provided that the EC gave equal protection to human rights as under the Constitution and in the ECHR. The provision was inspired by the position of the German *Bundesverfassungsgericht* in its *Maastricht Urteil*, and worded in terms of 'so long as'. That was the only condition: there were no explicit requirements as to the type or scope of the powers that could be transferred. However, it was assumed that the transfer cannot be such that the fundamental characteristics of the Swedish form of government would no longer apply.[86] A procedural requirement was also inserted: delegation to the EC requires the approval of three-fourths of those present and voting in the *Riksdag*. Alternatively, the accession Treaty could be approved in the manner prescribed by the Constitution for constitutional amendment.[87]

The constitutional provision, introduced in 1994, allowed for the delegation of powers to the EC, rather than the newly established EU. The idea was that the second and third pillar were restricted to purely intergovernmental co-operation, and that the EU did not possess any decision-making powers of its own. It was not considered necessary to allow delegation of decision-making powers to the EU.[88] At the occasion of the Amsterdam Treaty, that stance was doubted, but in view of the cumbersome procedure of constitutional amendment, article 10:5 was not amended, and the Treaty was approved under it. It was only in 2002 that the constitutional amendment was accomplished.[89] The beneficiary of a transfer of

---

[83] See U. Bernitz: 'Swedish Report', in J. Schwarze (ed), *The Birth of a European Constitutional Order. The Interaction of National and European Constitutional Law*, (Nomos Verlagsgesellschaft, Baden-Baden 2001), p. 389, at pp. 418–419.   [84] ibid. at p. 419.

[85] The Europe provision in art. 10:5 read until 1 January 2003: 'The *Riksdag* may entrust a right of decision making to the European Communities so long as these provide protection for rights and freedoms corresponding to the protection provided under this Instrument of Government and the ECHR. The *Riksdag* authorises such delegation in a decision which has the support of at least three fourths of those present and voting. The *Riskdag* may also take such a decision in the manner prescribed for the adoption if a fundamental law', translation taken from S. Griller: *op. cit.*, at pp. 31–32, see also his comments on the translation.

[86] So G. Schäder and M. Melin, 'The Swedish National Report', XXth FIDE Congress, London 2002, available on www.fide2002.org, at pp. 4–5.

[87] So G. Schäder and M. Melin, ibid. Constitutional amendment requires two successive decisions in identical wording by the *Riksdag* with a general election in between. In addition, a proposal may be put before a referendum if one third of the *Riksdag* so decides. The referendum is then held simultaneously with the general election.   [88] U. Bernitz: 'Swedish Report', *op. cit.*, at p. 431.

[89] Article 10:5 of the Instrument of Government now reads: 'The *Riksdag* may transfer a right of decision-making which does not affect the principles of the form of government within the framework of European Union cooperation. Such transfer presupposes that protection for rights and freedoms in

powers was changed from 'the EC' to read 'within the framework of European Union co-operation'. At the same time an additional condition for transfers of rights was inserted to the effect that such transfer may not relate to competences affecting 'the principles of the form of government'. A further modification provided that the *Riksdag* may approve an agreement within the framework of such co-operation even if the agreement does not exist in final form, so as to enable the *Riksdag* to influence the so-called framework decisions.[90]

It is striking that each of these new Member States considered that accession to the EU required prior constitutional amendment, and deemed the general transfer of powers provision insufficient to supply the required constitutional foundation for membership, while many of the old Member States' membership is still based on these old-fashioned provisions to date. These new Member States do realise what they are getting into, and they have the opportunity to draw lessons from the experiences of the existing Member States, also of their constitutional courts. It is a fact, for instance, that the Swedish constitutional provision was inspired directly by the Maastricht decision of the German Constitutional Court. In contrast, the old Member States have adapted to the constitutional realities of

the field of cooperation to which the transfer relates corresponds to that afforded under this Instrument of Government and the European Convention for the Protection of Human Rights and Fundamental Freedoms. The *Riksdag* approves such transfer by means of a decision in which at least three fourths of those voting concur. The *Riksdag's* decision may also be taken in accordance with the procedure prescribed for the enactment of fundamental law. Transfer cannot be approved until after the *Riksdag* has approved the agreement under Article 2.

A right of decision-making which is directly based on the present Instrument of Government and which purports at the laying down of provisions, the use of assets of the State or the conclusion or denunciation of an international agreement or obligation, may in other cases be transferred, to a limited extent, to an international organisation for peaceful cooperation of which Sweden is a member, or is about to become a member, or to an international court of law. No right of decision-making relating to matters concerning the enactment, amendment or abrogation of fundamental law, the *Riksdag* Act or a law on elections for the *Riksdag*, or relating to the restriction of any of the rights and freedoms referred to in Chapter 2 may be thus transferred. The provisions laid down for the enactment of fundamental law apply in respect of a decision relating to such transfer. If time does not permit a decision in accordance with these provisions, the *Riksdag* may approve transfer by means of a decision in which at least five sixths of those voting and at least three fourths of members concur.

If it has been laid down in law that an international agreement shall have validity as Swedish law, the *Riksdag* may prescribe, by means of a decision taken in accordance with the procedure laid down in paragraph two, that also any future amendment of the agreement binding upon the Realm shall apply within the Realm. Such a decision shall relate only to a future amendment of limited extent.

Any judicial or administrative function not directly based on this Instrument of Government may be transferred, in a case other than a case under paragraph one, to another state, international organisation, or foreign or international institution or community by means of a decision of the *Riksdag*. The *Riksdag* may also in law authorise the Government or other public authority to approve such transfer of functions in particular cases. Where the function concerned involves the exercise of public authority, *Riksdag* approval shall take the form of a decision in which at least three fourths of those voting concur. The *Riksdag's* decision in the matter of such transfer may also be taken in accordance with the procedure prescribed for the enactment of fundamental law.'

[90] The other modifications concerning the relations between parliament and government in European affairs will be considered further below.

membership even though their constitutional texts may seem at times inadequate. Yet, this has not prevented these States to participate in European integration and in decision-making at the European level. They have become so accustomed on the basis of their 'old fashioned' Constitutions, that it is now argued that there is no need for constitutional amendment: if it ain't broken . . . .

D. 'The Addressee: International Organizations, or this EU'

None of the original constitutional provisions mentioned the EC or Europe explicitly: they typically referred to 'international organizations', often specifically indicating the aim of peaceful co-operation with other nations. Gradually, more and more Constitutions have been amended to include the EC, EC/EU or Europe explicitly. Such customized 'transfer to the EU' provisions can be found for instance in the Constitutions of *Germany* (art. 23, since 1992), *France* (art. 88–1, since 1992), *Sweden* (art. 10.5, since 2002), *Portugal* (art. 7.5, since 1989 and 7.6. since 1992), while *Finnish* membership is based on a custom-made exceptive enactment designed for EU membership, and *Austrian* accession on a special constitutional act mentioning each of the European Treaties specifically, while articles 23a to 23f regulate the election and nomination of Austrian members of the European institutions and provides for the internal effects of membership on the relations between the Austrian constitutional organs. The *Irish* Constitution is even more specific and refers to each of the founding treaties and the major Treaty amendments specifically, each time allowing for the ratification of the relevant Treaty.

In other Member States, the transfer provisions are still to 'international organizations' without specifying the EU. Some of these Constitutions do not make any reference the EU and membership at all. The *Netherlands* Constitution, for instance, does not mention Dutch membership or the EU at all to the extent even that were an alien to land in the Netherlands and pick up the Dutch Constitution, he may well miss the fact that the Netherlands have been a member of the EC and EU from the 1950s onwards! The same is true for *Luxembourg, Denmark*, and *Spain*. In other Member States, membership is equally founded on the old provision, while the EU does figure in other parts of the Constitution, such as in *Italy*[91] and *Belgium*.[92] In *Greece*, the Constitution was clarified in 2001, by way of the introduction of an interpretative clause stating that 'Article 28 constitutes the foundation for the participation of the Country in the European integration process'. So while EU membership remains to be based on the general transfer and limitation provision of article 28, it is spelled out that the provision operates also as a Europe provision.

[91] See art. 117, discussed more in detail further below.
[92] See arts. 8(3) on EU citizens' right to vote or art. 168 on involvement of parliament in the amendment of the Treaties.

III. Procedure for The Approval of a Transfer

A. Constitutional Provisions on Transfer of Powers

It may seem remarkable that originally, most Member States did not provide for a special procedure for Parliament to approve transfer of powers to international organizations in general or to the EU specifically, and several still do not until this day. At the time of their ratification the founding Treaties were, in terms of the procedure followed for their conclusion and ratification, treated as ordinary international treaties. This probably has to do with the fact that it was not realised at the time what huge impact these Treaties would have, and how far integration could go, deviating even from the constitutional provisions. It may not have been clear, and it was definitely not made explicit, that the Treaties and the law stemming from them were considered to take precedence over national law, including the Constitutions. It may not have been realised that Member States *really* lost sovereign control over those powers transferred in a novel way. After all, every international obligation restricts the sovereign exercise of constitutional powers in some way. When the impact of the transfers, their real effects had become clear, only *Germany* changed the constitutional procedural conditions for further transfers, to require a qualified majority of two-thirds both in the *Bundestag* and *Bundesrat*, but restricted to the establishment of the European Union, as well as changes in its treaty foundations and comparable regulations *that amend or supplement the Basic Law, or make such amendments or supplements possible.*[93] In those cases, the *Ewigkeitsklausel* of article 79(3) equally applies.[94]

In *France, Belgium, Italy,* and *Portugal,* and for obvious reasons in the *United Kingdom,* no special procedure is constitutionally prescribed for the approval of treaties involving a transfer of powers, and an ordinary Act of Parliament adopted by simple majority will be sufficient. In *Belgium,* approval of the parliaments of the federated entities is also required where the Treaties concern matters falling within the competence and jurisdiction of those entities.[95] This implies that a Treaty may have to be ratified by six different parliaments, as was the case also for the Treaties of Nice and Amsterdam for instance.[96] In the *Netherlands,* none of the

[93] See on the provision for instance M. Nettesheim: 'EU-Recht und nationales Verfassungsrecht. Deutscher Bericht für die XX. FIDE-Tagung 2002', available on www.fide2002.org.

[94] The relevant part of art. 23 reads: 'The establishment of the European Union, as well as changes in its treaty foundations and comparable regulations that amend or supplement this Basic Law, or make such amendments or supplements possible, shall be subject to paragraphs (2) and (3) of Article 79'. Art. 79: '(2) Any such law [amending or supplementing the Basic Law] shall be carried by two thirds of the Members of the Bundestag and two thirds of the votes of the Bundesrat. (3) Amendments to this Basic Law affecting the division of the Federation into Länder, their participation on principle in the legislative process, or the principles laid down in Articles 1 and 20 shall be inadmissible'.

[95] As provided by art. 167 (2) and (3) of the Constitution.

[96] Chamber and Senate at the federal level, Councils of the French-speaking and of the German-speaking communities, and Councils of the three regions (Flemish, Walloon and Brussels Capital regions).

European Treaties has been approved under the special procedure for 'unconstitutional treaties' and a simple majority was considered sufficient.[97]

Nevertheless, there seems to be a trend to make transfers subject to more stringent procedures, requiring a qualified majority in Parliament, perhaps even a referendum. Most of the Member States acceding after 1958 did so on grounds of more stringent procedures, and their Constitutions require more than an ordinary Act for the approval of (certain) amendments of the Treaties. Treaties by which powers are transferred to international organizations or the EU are not treated as any other treaty, but require a special procedure to be followed. The *Danish* Constitution, for instance, requires a five-sixth majority in Parliament for the approval of transfer of powers treaties, or failing that, a positive outcome in a binding referendum.[98] The *Greek* Constitution seems to require a three-fifth majority in its article 28.[99] Article 93 of the *Spanish* Constitution requires the adoption of an organic law.[100]

The *Austrian* Constitution distinguishes between 'ordinary' transfer treaties and those with the effect of constitutional amendment. The former category requires approval by a majority of votes in the *Nationalrat*,[101] while the latter requires a two-thirds majority in the *Nationalrat* with at least half of the members present,[102] or where it results in a fundamental change of the constitutional order, by way of referendum. Austria joined the EU upon having conducted first, a total revision of the Constitution by way of referendum, and the subsequent approval of the Accession Treaty by a qualified majority in the *Nationalrat*. The Treaty of Amsterdam did require a constitutional amendment, but not a total revision of the Constitution, while the Nice Treaty was approved by an enabling Act.[103] The *Swedish* Constitution now provides in its Article 10:5 that: 'The *Riksdag* approves such transfer by means of a decision in which at least three fourths of those voting concur. The *Riksdag's* decision may also be taken in accordance with the procedure prescribed for the enactment of fundamental law. Transfer cannot be approved until after the *Riksdag* has approved the agreement under [the provisions dealing with the approval of treaties]'. The *Finnish* Constitution, on the other hand, does not provide for a special procedure for transfer of powers treaties: it doesn't even foresee that category. Treaties, including the European treaties in the absence of any special provisions, require approval by an ordinary act adopted by a majority of

---

[97] Even if in practical effect a two-thirds majority was attained.

[98] The accession to the EC, the SEA, the Treaties of Maastricht (twice) and Amsterdam were approved by referendum as was EMU membership in 2000; the Treaty of Nice was approved by parliament.

[99] It is not entirely clear whether the European Treaties require this special majority, see above.

[100] Adopted by absolute majority in Congress and simple majority in the Senate (art. 81).

[101] And approval by the *Bundesrat* if the relevant treaty settles matters within the exclusive sphere of competence of the *Länder*, arts. 50 and 42 of the Constitution.

[102] And approval by the *Bundesrat* if the relevant treaty settles matters within the exclusive sphere of competence of the *Länder*, arts. 50 and 44 of the Constitution.

[103] So H. Köck: 'EU Law and National Constitutions. The Austrian Case', paper presented at the XXth FIDE Congress, London, 2002, available on www.fide2002.org, at p. 15.

the votes cast. However, if the proposal concerns the Constitution, the decision is to be made by at least two-thirds of the votes cast.[104]

Ireland is the only Member State which amends its Constitution each time the Treaty is formally amended. This is not explicitly provided for in the Constitution, but follows from the Supreme Court judgment in *Crotty*, and has developed into constitutional convention. The *Irish* Constitution was amended by referendum for each major Treaty modification.[105]

B. Does a Transfer of Powers Imply a Derogation from the Constitution?

Membership entails exceptions to the constitutional provisions and/or modifications thereof. Given the primacy of Community law, and the obligations imposed on the Member States, constitutional provisions can no longer be invoked as against Community law, not even before the national courts, and including also constitutional fundamental rights. Moreover, these provisions cannot be invoked either before the Court of Justice, which may develop Community law in a manner which appears to conflict with the Constitution. Finally, specific provisions of the Constitution may be affected by the Treaties, such as the provision in many Constitutions that the right to vote is restricted to nationals, or a provision concerning minting or the Central Bank. It will be clear, even if not uncontested, that the national Constitution does not remain unaffected by membership, and from the moment of accession onwards, the Constitution must be read in context of membership. The effects of participation in the EU with direct repercussions on constitutional provisions and principles include the following: several powers which traditionally belong to the exclusive competence of the State organs are now shared with European institutions, other States, or removed entirely, such as issuing money, adopting legislation, decision-making in the field of foreign affairs and even defence; a large portion of a Member State's legislation derives from the EU institutions, even in core fields of State sovereignty; the law deriving from the EU, especially EC law is to have effect in the national legal order, with precedence over conflicting provisions of national (constitutional) law; democratic legitimacy is affected in several ways, by the transfer to the Union and the internal power shift from parliaments to governments; fundamental rights may be protected differently.

As mentioned before, the transfer of powers provisions have as their main purpose to constitutionalize a transfer of powers, or to make it at all constitutional for the State to participate in a pooling of sovereign powers which originally

---

[104] Art. 94 (1) and (2) of the Constitution.

[105] So far, in the context of participation in the EU, referendums have been held on accession (1972), the SEA (1987), the Treaties of Maastricht (1992), Amsterdam (1998) and Nice (twice, in 2001 and 2002). Referendum is the procedure prescribed to amend the Constitution.

belong to the State. A crucial question[106] will then be whether the transfer of powers can be considered to effectuate constitutional amendment on its own, ie whether the other provisions of the Constitution must cede for the law deriving from the treaties as approved, from the transfer,[107] or rather, vice versa, whether the transfer of powers provision itself must be read in context, and is thus limited by the remainder of the Constitution, or by its core principles.[108] The issue is reflected in the procedural requirements for the approval of the (European) treaties, but there is a striking variation in approach. Some national Constitutions, in particular the *French* and *Spanish*, provide a special procedure before the Constitutional Court to detect inconsistencies between the Constitution and a proposed Treaty, and state that the Treaty cannot be ratified before the inconsistency is eliminated, by constitutional amendment. This has happened in the case of the Treaties of Maastricht (in *Spain* and *France*) and Amsterdam (*France*). However, also in States where the Constitution does not make special provision for the case of unconstitutional treaties, the presumption is that inconsistencies are to be removed, and that an unconstitutional treaty should not be entered into. This is the case, for instance, for *Belgium*, even if the practice at the time of the Treaty of Maastricht was different,[109] or in *Denmark*. In these countries, the amendment of the Constitution and the ratification of the treaty necessitating amendment are separate issues. Once the Constitution is amended and the inconsistencies are removed, the treaty can safely be approved following the usual procedures, with ordinary statute or special majority, as provided.

Other Constitutions provide for a special procedure to be followed for the ratification of unconstitutional treaties in general, or for transfer of powers treaties which affect the Constitution. The *Netherlands* Constitution provides for a special procedure for unconstitutional treaties in general, requiring approval by two-thirds of both Houses of Parliament. This means that the unconstitutional treaty does not require a prior constitutional amendment. It can enter into force, and will have priority over the Constitution.[110] In other countries, the Europe provision increases the constitutional requirement for approval of treaties which

---

[106] This will be considered further in section VI on the relationship between EU law and constitutional law.

[107] As seems to be the case in the *Orfinger* decision of the Belgian *Conseil d'État*, and as may be the opinion of the *Cour d'arbitrage*, as indicated extra-judicially by the president of the *Cour d'arbitrage* in M. Melchior and P. Vandernoot: 'Controle de constitutionnalité et droit communautaire dérivé', *Revue belge de droit constitutionnel*, 1998, p. 7. It must be stressed that the assumption in the *Orfinger* decision was that the Treaty was constitutional when ratified, but that it had become unconstitutional by the interpretation of it by the ECJ. This was considered less of a problem than the case of an unconstitutional treaty. For a discussion of this case, see M. Class, *The National Courts' Mandate in the European Constitution*, (Oxford, Hart Publishing, 2005) (forthcoming).

[108] As seems to be the case in Italy ever since *Frontini* and *Granital*; as was the case in Germany under *Solange* even before the Constitution explicitly stated conditions to membership which may operate as exceptions to the primacy of EU law; see fn 51 and 52 *supra* above and accompanying text.

[109] See fn. 1998 and accompanying text.

[110] As follows from arts. 120 and 94 of the Constitution; see G. Hogan: 'The Nice Treaty and the Irish Constitution', *European Public Law* n° 7, 2003, pp. 565–573.

diverge from the Constitution or affect its operation. That is the case, for instance, in *Germany* (art. 23), *Sweden* (art. 10:5) and *Finland* (art. 94), and in *Austria*, which even differentiates between 'simple' constitutional amendments and overall revisions of the Constitution (arts. 50 and 44 of the Constitution).

As mentioned before, *Ireland* stands out in this respect, since it regards each Treaty amendment as implying a constitutional amendment, and hence the procedure for such modification must be followed: the proposal for an amendment of the Constitution must be initiated in *Dáil Éireann* as a Bill, and upon having been passed by both Houses of the *Oireachtas*, be submitted by Referendum to the decision of the people.[111] The procedure was first followed for accession, and later, as a result of the *Crotty* judgment, also for the Single European Act, and the Treaties of Maastricht, Amsterdam and Nice. According to *Crotty*, a constitutional amendment is required each time the amending Treaty 'alters the essential scope or objectives of the existing organisation', without, however, stating that every amendment is unconstitutional, and requires constitutional amendment: some treaty amendments are protected by the 'necessitated' clause in the constitutional immunity provision of article 29 of the Constitution.[112] Nevertheless, it may now have become constitutional convention to ratify by constitutional amendment.

C. Referendums on European Matters

Referendums have thus been held in many Member States on European issues, but for various constitutional reasons and with different purposes. First, referendums have been held in several Member States to decide on accession itself. These referendums, especially where they were not formally required on formal constitutional grounds, serve to legitimate the giant step into membership of a Union in which sovereign powers deriving from the people are pooled. There is a widespread feeling, at least in the Member States joining later, that the people should themselves make such fundamental decision on their polity. Accession referendums have been held in all 10 new Member States (the 2004 group); in *Finland, Austria, Sweden, Norway* and *Switzerland* (where they failed, precluding accession), in *Ireland* and *Denmark*. In the *United Kingdom*, a referendum was held on continued membership of the EEC in 1975. Secondly, referendums have been held in the course of the constitutional ratification process of Treaty amendments, as is the case in *Denmark*, where a referendum must be held to ratify a transfer of powers treaty, if the required four-fifths majority in the *Riksdag* is not attained. Thirdly, referendums have also been organized in the course of the ratification process, on grounds of a voluntary decision of the government to submit it to the people. This has been the case, for instance, for the Treaty of Maastricht in *France*, where the President has the right to call a referendum. Finally, the *Irish* referendums are, as mentioned before, constitutionally required, since (most) Treaty

---

[111] Art. 46 of the Constitution.   [112] This provision is discussed further below.

ratifications require constitutional amendment, and accordingly, must be put before the people in a referendum.

In some countries, referendums are not provided for in the Constitution, or are even unconstitutional. Holding a referendum may thus itself require prior amendment of the Constitution.[113] Whether or not a referendum will be organized in the course of the ratification of the Constitutional Treaty is not entirely clear in all Member States, and the issue will not be further pursued here.

D. Ratification 'In Accordance with the Constitutional Requirements': the practice

Now, the *practice* of ratification has not always followed the formal constitutional requirements, or at the very least, the latter have at times been interpreted with some creativity, either to facilitate or speed up the process and possible to avoid challenging referendums, or vice versa, to let the people participate in 'constitutional' decisions and as a result, give the treaties increased legitimacy. In the *Netherlands*, for instance, while the Constitution does provide for a special procedure to be followed when a Treaty is considered to deviate from the Constitution, the more lenient procedure has always been followed, with government and parliament simply denying that the Treaties did in fact deviate. In many other countries, the opposite has happened, and a more stringent procedure was followed than that constitutionally provided for the transfer of powers under the Constitution. In *Greece*, for instance, there was much discussion as to whether accession must be approved by a simple or a qualified majority, and the government opted for the qualified majority for political reasons, and to furnish the accession with maximum legitimacy. In *Denmark*, the Government had announced that a referendum would be organised whether or not the required five-sixth majority in Parliament would be attained, and several referendums preceding accession were probably not formally required under the Constitution. In *Finland* a consultative referendum was organized for political reasons and to increase legitimacy of accession, but not because of a constitutional requirement.

Constitutional practice does not always follow the constitutional texts. Political expediency and practicability, a (perceived) need for speediness, or an attempt to prevent political blockage over the European Treaties, have helped to decide how the treaties had to be ratified in accordance with the constitutional requirements in practical effect. The picture emerging is not always elegant: necessary constitutional amendments that are postponed until a more convenient time (eg Belgium both in 1951–1958 and 1992); special majorities which are omitted, or simply an inconsistent handling of subsequent treaties with no clear reason. This also goes to show how the application of the rules at times involves preferences, for

---

[113] For information of the constitutional provisions concerning referendums, and for the discussion of a referendum on the European Constitution, and a regular update, see www.european-referendum.org.

instance to decide whether or not a particular treaty affects the constitution to such extent that it requires a special majority; or whether or not a treaty goes beyond what is authorized by a particular provision in the Constitution.

IV. Substantive Constitutional Conditions on Participation in the European Union

Several national Constitutions contain explicit conditions on membership, relating most often to the protection of fundamental rights, the principle of democracy and the limits of the transferred powers.

These conditions were first made explicit in the case law of the *Corte costituzionale* and the *Bundesverfassungsgericht* (and later also, other constitutional courts), and then formalized in the texts of several Constitutions. Explicit constitutional conditions can now be found, for instance, in *Germany* (art. 23, democratic, social, and federal principles, the rule of law, and the principle of subsidiarity, and the level of protection of basic rights...); in *Denmark* (art. 20, 'to such extent as shall be provided by Statute', interpreted by the *Højesteret* as conditioning participation, in terms of *Kompetenz Kompetenz*, and fundamental rights); in *Greece* (art. 28(3) the rights of man and the foundations of democratic government and is effected on the basis of the principles of equality and under the condition of reciprocity); in *Portugal* (art. 7.5. democracy, peace, economic progress and justice in the relations between their peoples, and art. 7.6. the principle of subsidiarity and the objective of economic and social cohesion); in *Sweden* (art. 10:5 fundamental rights under the Instrument of Government and the ECHR, and the principles of the form of government); and in *Finland* (art. 94(3) democratic foundations of the Constitution).

Several Constitutions do not contain any *explicit* conditions, such as Constitutions of the *Netherlands, Belgium, France, Italy,*[114] *Ireland, Spain* and *Austria.* Some of these even provide for the unconditional primacy of EU law (*Ireland*, art. 29.4.10) or treaty law in general (*Netherlands*, arts. 94 and 120) over the Constitution, implying that once entered into force, the treaties and the law deriving from them apply unconditionally. However, even where constitutional conditions and reservations are not made explicit in the constitutional texts, participation is mostly not perceived as unconditional, and substantive conditions are presumed. Especially in Member States where there is a constitutional court or a court having jurisdiction upholding the Constitution as the State's highest norm, such a court may show a tendency to also uphold it against EU law, and if

---

[114] The *French* and *Italian* Constitutions do for instance contain eternity clauses, prohibiting certain constitutional amendments, in particular concerning the republican form of government (art. 89 of the and French Constitution and art. 139 of the Italian Constitution). But there are no (separate) limits as to the powers that can be transferred or the conditions which an international organization has to comply with.

necessary, to make the effectiveness of EU law in the national legal order conditional upon its compliance with fundamental constitutional values. That is the case, for example, in *Italy*, where it is the *Corte costituzionale* which has read *controlimiti* in the *principi inviolabili* of the Constitution. In contrast to the German case, the case law of the *Corte costituzionale* has not been codified in the constitutional texts, and the *controlimiti* remain unwritten. But it is even true in *Ireland*, and despite the explicit constitutional immunity supplied to EU law by article 29.4 of the Constitution. After all, Walsh J stated in *SPUC v Grogan*, 'It cannot be one of the objectives of the European Communities that a Member State should be obliged to set at nought the constitutional guarantees for the protection within the State of a fundamental human right'.[115]

I will not discuss the issue here whether the constitutional provisions, textual or not, also mark the outer limits of European integration and whether these have been reached with the Constitutional Treaty. Yet, a few comments on the functions and effects of these provisions are in place. First and foremost, these provisions serve as guidelines or rather as *instructions* to those responsible at the national level to negotiate the Treaty, to Parliament (or the people!) when approving it for ratification. Secondly, these instructions are also directed to the national institutions and organs co-operating in the coming into existence and implementation of EU law. Finally, and only in ultimate analysis, they may serve as standards for review by national courts, as *controlimiti* against the incoming tide of EU law. This use of these provisions is obviously not in accordance with the basic principles of EU law, its primacy, the duty of loyal co-operation, the exclusive jurisdiction of the ECJ to rule on the validity of European law. Nevertheless, the presence of these *controlimiti* in the constitutional texts or in constitutional law as developed by the courts may well be the price to be paid for the loyal acceptance of European law in the bulk of cases, and for the participation and loyalty of the Member State, and may well increase the Union's legitimacy on the whole.

The downside of these provisions may be that if their symbolic function of constitutional guarantee is all that they amount to, if they are nothing more than a mere lip-service to the fundamental principles, these substantive conditions may appear to be deceptive and achieve the opposite of what they intend: once in force, the treaties and the law deriving from them are cut loose from the national Constitutions with its conditions, which are checked at the time of ratification, but then *carte blanche* is given as the constitutional test was passed. It is indeed especially at the time of ratification, and even more so during the negotiation of Treaty revisions, that these conditions must be taken into consideration, but also in the process of decision-making in which national institutions and organs participate. In addition, it must be clear that these substantive conditions are never typically national, they are not unique and exclusive to one Member State: all express concern for general fundamental principles, which (should) apply with

---

[115] Irish High Court, decision of 11 October 1989, *SPUC v Grogan* [1989] IR 753.

equal force, be it not always exactly in the same manner, to the European level. In a system of multi-level or intertwined constitutionalism, these principles will have to be taken into account also at European level.

V. National Participation in European Institutions

Only a few Constitutions contain provisions concerning the participation of nationals or national organs in the European institutions. The *Austrian* and *Portuguese* Constitutions are most elaborate in this respect. Article 23 of the Austrian Constitution states rules concerning the election of Austrian MEPs and incompatibilities, and on the nomination of the Austrian members of the European institutions, including the Commission.[116] The *Portuguese* Constitution includes similar provisions.[117]

More Member States' Constitutions include provisions concerning the right to vote and to stand as a candidate in European elections and/or municipal elections for European citizens.[118] The main reason is that the existing provisions reserved this right for nationals and were accordingly in direct conflict with the provisions of the Treaty of Maastricht.

VI. The Incoming Tide: The Effect of EU law in the Domestic Legal Order and Its Relation with Constitutional Law

In many Member States, the effect of EU law in the domestic legal order derives from a provision in the Constitution.[119] This is not true for all States: in *Belgium* and *Luxembourg* for instance, the precedence of international treaties in general is based on the very nature of treaty law, independent of a constitutional provision, which, in the *Belgian* case, applies *a fortiori* for Community law.[120] This position reflects the statement of the Court of Justice in *Costa v ENEL* that: 'The law stemming from the Treaty, an independent source of law, could not because of its special and original nature, be overridden by domestic legal provisions, however framed, without being deprived of its character as Community law and without the legal

---

[116] Arts. 23a-23c.

[117] Art. 164 p.: Parliament elects the Portuguese members of the European institutions, except for the Commissioner.

[118] *Spain* (art. 13(2)), *France* (art. 88–3), *Belgium* (art. 8), *Portugal* (art. 15), and *Germany* (art. 28(1)(3).

[119] See on this issue M. Claes: *The National Courts' Mandate in the European Constitution*, (Oxford: Hart Publishing, 2005) (forthcoming).

[120] *Cour de cassation*, decision of 27 May 1971, *Fromagerie Franco-suisse le Ski, Journal des tribunaux*, 1971, p. 460; [1972] CMLR 330; A. Oppenheimer: *The Cases*, 1994, Vol. 1, p. 245. As for the relationship between EU law and Belgian constitutional law, see below.

basis of the Community itself being called into question'.[121] Nevertheless, and despite the fact that the Court of Justice has demonstrated that it is possible to conceive the primacy of Community law independently of national constitutional provisions, and irrespective of the traditional stance on the effect of international treaties, it has not prohibited the national courts to find the basis for primacy of Community law in the national Constitution or the national legal order, as long as the same result is achieved. In some Member States it has been a provision explicitly giving effect and precedence to international treaties in general (such as arts. 55 of the *French* Constitution[122] and arts. 94 and 120 of the *Dutch* Constitution),[123] in others it was a transfer of powers provision (as in the case of art. 11 of the *Italian* Constitution, and arts. 24, now 23, of the *German* Basic Law). These provisions serve (also) to open up the national legal order for European law, allowing for a bridge over which European law can march in (Germany), or authorizing a retreat from certain areas in which national law is no longer operative (Italy). Yet, the Italian and German provisions are part of the Constitution and must, according to the constitutional courts, be read in the light of the Constitution as a whole. Consequently, they have also allowed the constitutional courts to make exceptions to the primacy of Community law, where it conflicts with core principles of the Constitution. Accordingly, some constitutional provisions must cede to European law, but that is not the case for these core principles. In *Belgium*, the transfer of powers provision of article 34 operates in the opposite direction. The stance adopted by the *Cour de cassation* in *Le Ski* has not been embraced unconditionally by the *Cour d'arbitrage*, which condones the primacy only of those treaties which pass the constitutionality test. Unconstitutional treaty provisions must cede. Nevertheless, there are signs that article 34 may be used as the device to make an exception for European law. It has been stated already by the *Conseil d'État*[124] that article 34 authorizes the transfer of powers to international organizations unconditionally, and that it allows for exceptions to be made to the Constitution.

---

[121] Case 6/64 *Costa v ENEL* [1964] ECR 1141.

[122] However, in view of the recent decision of the *Conseil constitutionnel*, the precedence of EU law before the French Constitution, at least parts of it, must now be considered to be based on art. 88–1, see *Conseil constitutionnel*, decision n. 2004-499 DC of 29 July 2004, *Loi relative à la protection des personnes physiques à l'égard des traitements de données à caractère personnel et modifiant la loi No 78-17 du 6 janvier 1978 relative à l'informatique, aux fichiers et aux libertés*, available on www. conseil-constitutionnel.fr.

[123] Note that many scholars in the Netherlands are of the opinion that the effect and precedence of Community law derives from the very nature of Community itself, as espoused by the ECJ in *Van Gend en Loos* and *Costa v ENEL*, and that art. 94 is irrelevant in this respect. There are no clear statements on principle of the Dutch courts on the issue. In my view, however, the basis for the primacy of EU law is to be found in art. 94, be it that it must be read in the light of the case law of the ECJ. This was, after all, the position of the drafters of the Constitution in 1983. This position may also be confirmed by the decision of the Hoge Raad in *Waterpakt, Hoge Raad*, decision of 21 March 2003, *Waterpakt v Staat der Nederlanden*, NJ 2003/691, annotated by T. Koopmans; AB 2004/39, annotated by Ch. Backes. available on www.rechtspraak.nl.

[124] *Conseil d'État*, decision of 5 November 1996, *Orfinger v Belgian State, Journal des tribunaux*, 1997, p. 254; A. Oppenheimer, *The Cases*, Vol. 2, pp. 162–167.

Accordingly, European law takes precedence even over conflicting provisions in the Constitution. Writing extra-judicially, the President of the *Cour d'arbitrage* has indicated that the *Cour* may also take recourse to the same provision when confronted with a conflict between Community law and the Constitution.[125]

Not many Constitutions expressly provide for the direct effect and primacy *of EU law* specifically. The Italian Constitution has been amended in 2001 to include EU-provisions in the chapter on regionalisation. The first sentence of Article 117 reads: 'Legislative power shall be exercised by the State and by the Regions in accordance with the Constitution and within the limits set by European Union law and international obligations'. The provision was not intended to introduce a general primacy clause, and the place of the provision in the chapter on regionalisation would point in a different direction, but the text seems to be stating unequivocally that European law also has priority over acts adopted by the central State organs (but not over the Constitution). The *Irish* Constitution does contain such an unequivocal primacy clause, and even affords constitutional immunity to EC, EU and Irish law necessitated by membership.[126] Article 8(3) of the *Portuguese* Constitution appears to comprise a *renvoi* to the case law of the Court of Justice, and accordingly, may also allow for the primacy of EU law before the Portuguese Constitution.[127] In order to rule out any ambiguity, and in view of ratification of the Constitutional Treaty containing a primacy provision in its article I-6, the Portuguese Constitution has already been modified to include a primacy provision, with *controlimiti*.[128]

Explicit constitutional provision for the primacy of European law *even before the Constitution* itself is thus provided in the *Irish* (unconditional) and *Portuguese*

[125] M. Melchior and P. Vandernoot: 'Controle de constitutionnalité et droit communautaire dérivé', *Revue belge de droit constitutionnel*, 1998, p. 7.

[126] Article 29.4.10: 'No provision of this Constitution invalidates laws enacted, acts done or measures adopted by the State which are necessitated by the obligations of membership of the European Union or of the Communities, or prevents laws enacted, acts done or measures adopted by the European Union or by the Communities or by institutions thereof, or by bodies competent under the Treaties establishing the Communities, from having the force of law in the State'. Ordinary primacy', ie the precedence of EU law before ordinary Acts of Parliament results from the EC Act.

[127] Article 8 [International law]:

1. The rules and principles of general or customary international law are an integral part of Portuguese law.

2. Rules provided for in international conventions that have been duly ratified or approved, shall apply in national law, following their official publication, so long as they remain internationally binding with respect to the Portuguese State.

3. Rules made by the competent organs of international organizations to which Portugal belongs apply directly in national law to the extent that the constitutive treaty provides.

[128] Constitutional amendment of April 2004: Article 8 (4) (international law): 'As disposições dos tratados que regem a União Europeia e as normas emanadas das suas instituições, no exercício das respectivas competências, são aplicáveis na ordem interna, nos termos definidos pelo direito da União, com respeito pelos princípios fundamentais do Estado de direito democrático': 'The provisions of the treaties of the European Union and the provisions adopted by its institutions are applicable in the domestic order in the ways and terms defined by the law of the Union, with respect for the fundamental principles of the rule of law and democracy'. In addition, the European transfer of powers clause was amended to state substantive conditions of democracy and rule of law (art. 7(6)).

Constitution (under condition of democracy and rule of law), and in the *Dutch* Constitution where it applies to all international treaties. Nevertheless, until this day, *controlimiti* continue to exist in most other Member States, in the text of the Constitution and/or in the case law of the (constitutional) courts. The incorporation of a general primacy provision in the Constitutional Treaty does not in itself, and of its own, supply a watertight warranty against such national *controlimiti* being invoked. National provisions of the *Irish* and *Portuguese* type constitute the true revolution to sanction primacy of EU law even over conflicting constitutional norms, offering the maximum harmony between the European and national ositions, without however guaranteeing absolute primacy in all cases.

VII. The National Constitutional Response: Provisions Concerning the National Separation of Powers in EU Matters

Membership of the EU and participation in EU decision-making has important effects on the national separation of powers. Indeed, international relations are, in most States, the province of the government. Transfer of powers to the EU will have as an effect that legislative powers are removed from the national or federal parliaments, and put in the hands of the European institutions where the balance of powers is different. If EU law is treated as an element of 'ordinary' international relations under the Constitution, this implies a power shift from the legislative branch to the Executive: it is governments which are represented in the Council, for instance, and co-operate in the legislative function at the European level, and foreign affairs is traditionally the province of governments, with more limited control than in other areas. A transfer of powers to the European institutions thus not only implies that powers are removed from the State, but also that they are removed from the democratically-elected bodies and put in the hands of institutions which are not directly democratically-legitimated and there are growing concerns over accountability and transparency. This element of the European democratic deficit, combined with the (perceived) restricted powers of the European Parliament and the specific nature of the European Parliament not representing national interests and positions, and lacking real partisan politics, has increasingly lead to the adoption of constitutional provisions, with the aim of increasing the national democratic legitimacy of EU decision-making or at least control of the State's participation therein. These provisions seem crucial given the dual democratic legitimacy of the EU.

One type of constitutional provisions concerns the duty of the government to inform parliament, so as to allow it to co-operate in the definition of the national position, to influence the outcome of the European decision-making process, and to hold the government accountable for its actions at European level. That is the case in *France* (art. 88–4);[129] in *Germany* (art. 23(1) and (2));[130] in *Portugal* (art. 161(n); art. 163(f) and art. 197(i));[131] in *Sweden* (art. 10.6–7);[132] in *Austria* (art. 23ᵉ);[133] and

---

[129] Art. 88–4: 'The Government shall lay before the National Assembly and the Senate any drafts of or proposals for acts of the European Communities or the European Union containing provisions which are matters for statute as soon as they have been transmitted to the Council of the European Union. It may also lay before them other drafts of or proposals for acts or any document issuing from a European Union institution.

In the manner laid down by the rules of procedure of each assembly, resolutions may be passed, even if Parliament is not in session, on the drafts, proposals or documents referred to in the preceding paragraph'.

[130] (2) The *Bundestag* and, through the *Bundesrat*, the *Länder* shall participate in matters concerning the European Union. The Federal Government shall keep the *Bundestag* and the *Bundesrat* informed, comprehensively and at the earliest possible time.

(3) Before participating in legislative acts of the European Union, the Federal Government shall provide the *Bundestag* with an opportunity to state its position. The Federal Government shall take the position of the *Bundestag* into account during the negotiations. Details shall be regulated by a law.

[131] Article 161 [Political and legislative powers of the Assembly]: The Assembly of the Republic has the following powers: n. To give its opinion, as provided by law, on matters that are pending decision within the organs of the European Union and that have a bearing on their exclusive legislative powers;

Article 163 [Powers in relation to others organs]: The Assembly of the Republic has the following powers in relation to other organs: f. To monitor and to evaluate, in accordance with the law, the participation of Portugal in the process for implementing the European Union;

Art. 197 [Political powers of the government]: In performing its political functions, the Government has the following powers: i. To submit to the Assembly of the Republic, at appropriate times, information concerning the process for implementing the European Union, in accordance with Article 161 (n) and Article 163 (f).

[132] Art. 10:6.: The Government shall keep the *Riksdag* continuously informed and confer with bodies appointed by the *Riksdag* concerning developments within the framework of European Union cooperation. More detailed rules concerning the obligation to inform and consult are laid down in the *Riksdag* Act.

The Government shall keep the Advisory Council on Foreign Affairs continuously informed of those matters relating to foreign relations which may be of significance for the Realm, and shall confer with the Council concerning these matters as necessary. In all foreign policy matters of major significance, the Government shall confer with the Council, if possible, before making its decision.

Art. 7. The Advisory Council on Foreign Affairs consists of the Speaker and nine other members elected by the *Riksdag* from among its members. More detailed rules concerning the composition of the Council are laid down in the *Riksdag* Act.

The Advisory Council on Foreign Affairs is convened by the Government. The Government is obliged to convene the Council if at least four members of the Council request consultations on a particular matter. Meetings of the Council are presided over by the Head of State or, in his absence, by the Prime Minister.

A member of the Advisory Council on Foreign Affairs and any person otherwise associated with the Council shall exercise caution in communicating to others matters which have come to his knowledge in this capacity. The person presiding over a meeting of the Council may rule that a duty of confidentiality shall apply unconditionally.

[133] Artikel 23e. (1) Das zuständige Mitglied der Bundesregierung hat den Nationalrat und den Bundesrat unverzüglich über alle Vorhaben im Rahmen der Europäischen Union zu unterrichten und ihnen Gelegenheit zur Stellungnahme zu geben.

(2) Liegt dem zuständigen Mitglied der Bundesregierung eine Stellungnahme des Nationalrates zu einem Vorhaben im Rahmen der Europäischen Union vor, das durch Bundesgesetz umzusetzen ist oder das auf die Erlassung eines unmittelbar anwendbaren Rechtsaktes gerichtet ist, der Angelegenheiten betrifft, die bundesgesetzlich zu regeln wären, so ist es bei Verhandlungen und Abstimmungen in der Europäischen Union an diese Stellungnahme gebunden. Es darf davon nur aus zwingenden außen- und integrationspolitischen Gründen abweichen.

in *Finland* (art. 93 (2)).[134] In *Belgium*, information of the Chambers is explicitly required under the Constitution, only in the case of Treaty revisions.[135] In other Member States, where no explicit provision is made to this effect, the usual rules will normally apply, or the duties of the government *vis-à-vis* parliament in the context of the EU are regulated in statutory law,[136] or even in *circulaires*, or by constitutional custom or convention. Nevertheless, the nature of multi-level decision-making in the EU is very different from national decision-making, or the usual mode of decision-making in international organizations and foreign affairs in general. Specific constitutional regulation or adaptation of the constitutional rules to the realities of European decision-making is in place.

A special case concerning the national separation of powers in response to membership concerns the constitutionalization of techniques whereby legislative powers in the area of EU law, especially in the implementation of EU law, are transferred from Parliament to the Government, or where the legislative process is simplified in this context. This is the case for instance in *Ireland*.[137] Article

(3) Wenn das zuständige Mitglied der Bundesregierung von einer Stellungnahme des Nationalrates gemäß Abs. 2 abweichen will, so hat es den Nationalrat neuerlich zu befassen. Soweit der in Vorbereitung befindliche Rechtsakt der Europäischen Union eine Änderung des geltenden Bundesverfassungsrechts bedeuten würde, ist eine Abweichung jedenfalls nur zulässig, wenn ihr der Nationalrat innerhalb angemessener Frist nicht widerspricht.

(4) Wenn der Nationalrat eine Stellungnahme gemäß Abs. 2 abgegeben hat, so hat das zuständige Mitglied der Bundesregierung dem Nationalrat nach der Abstimmung in der Europäischen Union Bericht zu erstatten. Insbesondere hat das zuständige Mitglied der Bundesregierung, wenn es von einer Stellungnahme des Nationalrates abgewichen ist, die Gründe hiefür dem Nationalrat unverzüglich mitzuteilen.

(5) Die Wahrnehmung der Zuständigkeiten des Nationalrates gemäß den Abs. 1 bis 4 obliegt grundsätzlich dessen Hauptausschuß. Die näheren Bestimmungen hiezu werden durch das Bundesgesetz über die Geschäftsordnung des Nationalrates getroffen. Dabei kann insbesondere geregelt werden, inwieweit für die Behandlung von Vorhaben im Rahmen der Europäischen Union anstelle des Hauptausschusses ein eigener ständiger Unterausschuß des Hauptausschusses zuständig ist und die Wahrnehmung der Zuständigkeiten gemäß den Abs. 1 bis 4 dem Nationalrat selbst vorbehalten ist. Für den ständigen Unterausschuß gilt Art. 55 Abs. 2.

(6) Liegt dem zuständigen Mitglied der Bundesregierung eine Stellungnahme des Bundesrates zu einem Vorhaben im Rahmen der Europäischen Union vor, das zwingend durch ein Bundesverfassungsgesetz umzusetzen ist, das nach Art. 44 Abs. 2 der Zustimmung des Bundesrates bedürfte, so ist es bei Verhandlungen und Abstimmungen in der Europäischen Union an diese Stellungnahme gebunden. Es darf davon nur aus zwingenden außen- und integrationspolitischen Gründen abweichen. Die Wahrnehmung der Zuständigkeiten des Bundesrates gemäß Abs. 1 und diesem Absatz wird durch die Geschäftsordnung des Bundesrates näher geregelt.

[134] Art. 93(2): 'The Government is responsible for the national preparation of the decisions to be made in the European Union, and decides on the concomitant Finnish measures, unless the decision requires the approval of the Parliament. The Parliament participates in the national preparation of decisions to be made in the European Union, as provided in this Constitution'.

[135] Art. 168: 'Dès l'ouverture des négociations en vue de toute révision des traités instituant les Communautés européennes et des traités et actes qui les ont modifiés ou complétés, les Chambres en sont informées. Elles ont connaissance du projet de traité avant sa signature'.

[136] For instance in the Act assenting to the Treaties, for a discussion of the (complex and confusing Dutch situation, see L.F.M. Besselink *et al.*: *De Nederlandse grondwet en de Europese Unie*, (Europa Law Publishing, Groningen 2002), pp. 55–91.

[137] See most recently, B. Doherty: 'Land, Milk and Freedom. Implementing Community Law in Ireland', *Irish Journal of European Law*, 2004, pp. 136–170.

29.4.10 of the Constitution provides constitutional immunity, among others, to Irish acts done or measures adopted which are necessitated by membership. The European Communities Act 1972 gave the government wide powers to implement Community obligations, and even amend other Acts which would normally belong to the exclusive jurisdiction of the *Oireachtas*. Challenges that this procedure is unconstitutional have been rejected by the courts.[138] The question of whether a specific procedure deviating from the usual legislative procedure should be inserted in the Constitution is also debated in other countries.[139]

Third, the federal States, *Germany*[140] and *Austria*[141] have made specific arrangements concerning the effects of membership on the separation of powers between the federation and the federated entities.

Finally, several Constitutions make specific provision for the State's participation in decision-making in what is now the second and third pillar, for instance because of the State's neutrality as constitutionally provided; or in order to provide for parliamentary control over these areas, where such control is lacking at the European level. Also participation in Schengen has in several Member States led to constitutional modifications.[142]

---

[138] In the Irish Supreme Court, decision of July 2003, *Maher v Minister for Agriculture* [2001] 2 IR 139, available also on www.bailii.org, the Supreme Court did, however, strike down an individual implementing measure as unconstitutional. Cases on this issue are notoriously difficult under Irish constitutional law as they turn on the question of what is necessitated under membership (and hence enjoys constitutional immunity) and what is not.

[139] For the debate in The Netherlands, see L.F.M. Besselink *et al.*: *De Nederlandse grondwet en de Europese Unie*, (Europa Law Publishing, Groningen 2002), pp.95–157.

[140] Art. 23 (4) The *Bundesrat* shall participate in the decision-making process of the Federation insofar as it would have been competent to do so in a comparable domestic matter, or insofar as the subject falls within the domestic competence of the *Länder*.

(5) Insofar as, in an area within the exclusive competence of the Federation, interests of the *Länder* are affected, and in other matters, insofar as the Federation has legislative power, the Federal Government shall take the position of the *Bundesrat* into account. To the extent that the legislative powers of the *Länder*, the structure of *Land* authorities, or *Land* administrative procedures are primarily affected, the position of the Bundesrat shall be given the greatest possible respect in determining the Federation's position consistent with the responsibility of the Federation for the nation as a whole. In matters that may result in increased expenditures or reduced revenues for the Federation, the consent of the Federal Government shall be required.

(6) When legislative powers exclusive to the *Länder* are primarily affected, the exercise of the rights belonging to the Federal Republic of Germany as a member state of the European Union shall be delegated to a representative of the *Länder* designated by the *Bundesrat*. These rights shall be exercised with the participation and concurrence of the Federal Government; their exercise shall be consistent with the responsibility of the Federation for the nation as a whole.

(7) Details respecting paragraphs (4) through (6) of this Article shall be regulated by a law requiring the consent of the *Bundesrat*.

[141] Art. 23d and 23e.

[142] So for instance *Austria*, art. 23 f; at the occasion of the ratification of the Treaty of Amsterdam, the *Irish* Constitution was amended to adapt to provisions on closer co-operation (flexibility), police and judicial co-operation and free movement, pursuant to which obligations may be entered into by a number of EU Member States of the short of the full membership. The new provision was considered necessary, in order to confer on the State sufficient powers for it to exercise the options or discretions provided by the Treaty of Amsterdam should it so decide. Similar provision was made for the options in the Nice Treaty. See Art. 29.4. 6 ° 'The State may

It would appear that this category of provisions is, in terms of fundamental constitutional principles of democracy, rule of law, accountability and separation of powers, of far greater importance than the transfer of powers provisions. And yet, it appears that these constitutional provisions regulating the effects of the State's participation in the EU are not fully developed in many Member States. For instance, at a time when the national parliaments have found their way into the European Constitution at the European level, it seems misguided not to provide for sound constitutional guarantees at the national level to increase democratic control over national participation in the Council, or to oversee the process of implementation of European law. This is where the real European deficit in national Constitutions, contributing to the constitutional deficit in Europe, is to be found, and much less in the transfer of powers provisions.

VIII. Specific Provisions

In most Member States there does not seem to be a consistent policy of cleaning up the Constitution and adapting it to a changing environment. Many Constitutions contain provisions which must to say the least be read in perspective, others are simply no longer in conformity with the changed realities of membership. That is the case for instance with provisions concerning the right to vote or the exclusive right of issuing currency. The question is, of course, what to do with these provisions: must they, each separately, be adapted as integration goes along? This would, it is submitted, be inconsistent with the required rigidity of Constitutions. Another technique is to make one provision indicating that the Constitution must be read in the light of EU membership. Such blanco *renvoi* may however seem to go too far as it would seem to be putting the national Constitutions on hold as a general rule. But most Member States approach the problem on an *ad hoc* basis, adapting the Constitution from time to time, but not consistently and in a rather disorganised manner. Sometimes the need for amendments is acknowledged, but given the complexity and length of the procedure, the actual amendment is postponed until a later more convenient time, for instance, after a general election or in order to profit from experiences gained.[143]

---

exercise the options or discretions provided by or under Articles 1.11 [police and judicial co-operation in judicial matters, MC], 2.5 [general provision on closer co-operation, MC] and 2.15 [Title IV of ECT: visas, asylum, immigration, MC] [of the Treaty of Amsterdam] and the second and fourth Protocols set out in the said Treaty but any such exercise shall be subject to the prior approval of both Houses of the Oireachtas'.

[143] See Belgium in 1952 and 1992; Portugal at the time of accession; and Sweden.

IX. Conclusion

An overview of the Europe provisions in national Constitutions, though not complete and restricted to the 'old' 15 Member States, does show some trends.

First, most Member States' Constitutions do seem to suffer from a *European deficit*.[144] The way in which European integration is dealt with in the constitutional texts is often disappointing, often inconsistent, at times downright clumsy. The national constitutional aspect of the European Constitution is in many cases underdeveloped. The Constitutions of the *Netherlands, Luxembourg, Spain,* and *Denmark* make no explicit mention of membership of the EU. That is not to say that these Member States are automatically therefore not good members of the Union, and political support for European integration has in three of these countries even been quite high. Furthermore, from the constitutional legal perspective, the texts do make transfer of powers to international organizations possible, and, in the *Dutch* and *Luxembourg* case allowing for the full supremacy of EU law even before the Constitution. But the Constitution leaves no trace of any *sui generis* character of the EU and the law deriving from it, as being different from classic international law. The least that can be said is that these States may not be taking their own Constitution seriously, and that they may not do justice to the functions of a constitutional document, which is, among others, to constitute the polity. To omit the EU and the State's participation in it from the national Constitution can even be considered a devaluation of the national Constitution, and expression of carelessness as regards the supposed most fundamental norm of the polity. It seems that the longer a State participates in European integration, the less extensive the constitutional provisions are on membership and its consequences.[145]

Many other Constitutions do mention Europe, in many different ways, and in different places of the Constitution, either as a separate Chapter in the general provisions of the Constitution, (*Austria*), as a variety of international organizations to which powers are transferred (*Germany, Greece* (through the interpretative clause), and *Portugal*) as or a specific type of international relations (as in the *Irish* Constitution or the *Swedish* Instrument of Government), or as a separate chapter situated close to the provisions just mentioned as in the French Constitution. The *Italian* and *Belgian* Constitution do make mention of

[144] So B. De Witte: 'Constitutional Aspects of European Union Membership in the Original Six Member States: Model Solutions for the Applicant Countries?', in A.E. Kellermann et al., *EU Enlargement: The Constitutional Impact at EU and National Level*, (The Hague, T.M.C. Asser Press, 2001), pp.65–79, at p. 73.
[145] Of course there are other factors, such as constitutional culture—compare for instance the detail of the Portuguese Constitution and the abstract and general nature of its Dutch counterpart; the role of courts and lawyers in the interpretation and development of constitutional law; the political stance on Europe and so forth.

the EU, but they do so in the corpus of the Constitution in less expected places, apparently presuming membership.[146]

There is a trend to replace the old and general transfer of powers provisions with specific Europe provisions. More and more, these contain explicit constitutional conditions and reservations as against the State's participation in the EU. Also, the procedures for further transfers have become more stringent, be it that they are not always applied (after all, the Treaty must be ratified, once agreed, one might cynically argue). These trends may point in the direction of a Constitutionalization of Europe, not by the Court of Justice, or even the national constitutional courts, but by the *pouvoir constituant* itself. This national constitutionalization seems indispensable for a veritable constitutionalization of Europe, and seems crucial to supply the European Constitution with constitutional legitimacy. It would seem that with the adoption of a formal European Constitution at the European level the time has come for a complete rethinking of the national Constitutions' approach to the European Constitution.

---

[146] Art. 117 of the Italian Constitution in the chapter on regionalisation; art. 168 of the Belgian Constitution on the involvement of parliament in the amendment of the EU Treaties—while these are not mentioned before; and art. 117 on the date for European Parliament elections).

The Court Under the Influence of its Advocates General: An Analysis of the Case Law on the Functioning of the Internal Market*

Kamiel Mortelmans

que les conclusions soient conformes ou contraires à la solution adoptée, celle-ci se trouve éclairée et même confortée, que se soit par analogie ou par opposition.'[1]

I. Introduction

In the 1970s and 1980s the Court of Justice played a crucial role in establishing the common and internal market. Since 1993 it has had an important task in ensuring the proper operation of the internal market. As Koopmans observed, this case law is predominantly purpose-oriented. The standards to be developed should contribute to the realization of the market the Treaty intends to establish.[2]

The legal contours of the internal market have been continuously refined, particularly thanks to the attentiveness of economic operators and the willingness of national courts, which continue to refer preliminary questions to the Court. Infringement proceedings brought by the Commission against the Member States under Article 226 EC have also provided further clarifications in this regard.

The evolution of the Court's case law on the internal market has been analyzed in many publications.[3] The role played by the Advocates General in this process has received less attention.[4] Given the number of cases concerning the internal

---

* This article is dedicated to the memory of P. VerLoren van Themaat, former Advocate General and my predecessor as Professor of European and Economic Law at the Europa Institute, University of Utrecht. See, further, section VII.A.

[1] M. Lagrange, Le rôle de L'Avocat général, discours prononcé à l'àudience solennelle de la Cour, 8 October 1964. The text of this speech and those of other member of the Court may be consulted in the Library of the Court of Justice.

[2] T. Koopmans, 'The Theory of Interpretation and the Court of'Justice', in: *Liber Amicorum in Honour of Lord Slynn of Hadley, Volume* 1, (The Hague, 2000), pp. 52, 54.

[3] See, most recently, C. Barnard, 'The substantive law of the EU', *The four freedoms*, (Oxford, 2004).

[4] Exceptions are P. Oliver, assisted by M. Jarvis, *The free movement of goods in the EU*, (4th edn, London, 2003). P. Oliver and W.-H. Roth, 'The Internal Market and the four freedoms', (2004)

market, most Advocates General who have been a member of the Court since the 1970s have had the opportunity to express their views on this subject.

A number of judgments dating from the 1960s were also of vital importance for the establishment of the common market. In *Van Gend en Loos*, the Court, contrary to Advocate General Roemer's Opinion, accorded direct effect to Article 12 EEC (now Article 25 EC).[5] In *Costa/Enel*, the Court held, in line with Advocate General Lagrange's Opinion, that Article 52 EEC (now Article 43 EC) takes precedence above provisions of national law which are incompatible with it.[6]

In both these judgments the emphasis is on the constitutional and procedural aspects. This is not the subject of the present article which, rather, will deal with the views developed by the Advocates General on a number of basic, substantive tenets of the internal market.

The case law on Article 25 EC will not be discussed. The most important judgments on the customs union and tariff barriers date from the 1960s and 1970s. In Opinions presented subsequently Advocates General confirmed this case law.[7]

The theme of the article may be illustrated by the following two examples taken from a number of leading cases.

A. Grundig/Consten and Dassonville

In *Dassonville*,[8] the Court for the first time defined the concept of measure having equivalent effect to a quantitative restriction on imports. The Court described this concept contained in Article 28 EC, as encompassing 'every trading arrangement of the Member States which is capable of hindering directly or indirectly, actually or potentially intra-Community trade'. This *Dassonville* formula from 1974 greatly resembles the description which the Court gave in 1966 in its *Grundig/Consten* judgment[9] to the term 'agreements which may affect trade between the Member States' within the meaning of Article 81 EC. In its judgment the Court stated that it had to be established whether the agreement is capable of constituting a threat, either direct or indirect, actual or potential, to freedom to trade between Member States in a manner which might harm the attainment of the objectives of a single market between States.

CML Rev, p. 407. De Advocaat-Generaal gehoord, *Essays over de totstandkoming van Europees gemeenschapsrecht* (Ed. A. Alvarez), (Antwerp, 1995). In this publication Advocate General Van Gerven's legal secretaries discuss his Opinions and provide an inside perspective.

[5] Case 26/62, *Van Gend en Loos*, (1963) ECR 1. See, on this subject, Brown & Jacobs, *The Court of Justice of the EC*, (by L. Neville Brown and T. Kennedy), (5th edn, London, 2000), p. 71.

[6] Case 6/64, *Costa/Enel*, (1964) ECR 585. See, A. Dashwood, 'The Advocate General in the Court of Justice of the EC', *Legal Studies*, 1982, vol. 2, p. 215.

[7] Thus, in Case C-234/99, *Nygard*, (2002) ECR I-3665, Advocate General Mischo refers to the settled case law on Art. 25 EC since Case 24/68, *Commission v. Italy*, (1969) ECR 193.

[8] Case 8/74, *Dassonville*, (1974) ECR 837.

[9] Joined Cases 56/64 and 58/64, *Grundig/Consten*, (1966) ECR 299. See on this topic P. VerLoren van Themaat, 'Some Opinions of Gordon Slynn as Advocate General', in: *Liber Amicorum in Honour of Lord Slynn of Hadley, Volume I*, (The Hague, 2000), p. 13. Advocate General Van Gerven, Opinion in C-145/88, *Torfaen*, (1989) ECR 3851, pt. 21.

The Judge-Rapporteur in *Grundig/Consten* was Trabucchi. Trabucchi was also the Advocate General in *Dassonville*. It might quite simply be concluded from this that the Advocate General in *Dassonville* suggested to the Court to apply the *Grundig/Consten* formula to define the concept of measures having equivalent effect in Article 28 EC. This is not, however, apparent from Trabucchi's Opinion. He does reject the thesis that the prohibition of Article 28 EC only applies to measures which distinguish between national products and imported products and the United Kingdom's view that Article 28 does not apply to potential restrictions of intra-Community trade.

The influence of the Advocate General on the *Dassonville* case law was, at least on paper, more limited than one might have expected.

B. Torfaen, Hünermund and Keck

In *Keck*,[10] the Court introduced the distinction between product requirements and selling arrangements. Advocate General Van Gerven, who had also presented Opinions in the precursors to this judgment, such as the *Torfaen* Case,[11] had the opportunity to present his views twice in the *Keck* case. In both of his Opinions and in line with his earlier approach in the Sunday closing cases, like *Torfaen*, he applied an open market-oriented test. The Court adopted a different approach by taking a rule oriented criterion as the dividing line.[12]

In *Keck* (24 November 1993) the Court did not follow its Advocate General, but it did follow Advocate General Tesauro who, after Van Gerven had presented his second Opinion in *Keck* (28 April 1993), in his Opinion in *Hünermund* (27 October 1993) expressly applied the distinction between product requirements and selling arrangements, which he in part had derived from legal literature.[13] I will return to the *Keck* saga later (section V.A.(ii)).

C. Plan of Discussion

Both examples demonstrate that the interaction between the Court and its Advocates General may assume different forms. In this article this interaction will be described systematically in respect of a vital aspect of Community law, the internal market. The discussion will be conducted along the following lines.

First, the role of the Advocate General in the development of Community law *in general* will be considered (section II). This will be followed by a discussion of criteria which may be used to gauge the influence of Advocates General on the Court's case

---

[10] Joined Cases C-267/91 and C-268/91, *Keck*, (1993) ECR I-6097.

[11] Advocate General Van Gerven, Opinion in C-145/88, *Torfaen*, (1989) ECR 3851.

[12] See W. Van Gerven, 'Constitutional aspects of the European Court's case-law on Articles 30 and 36 EC as compared with the U.S. dormant commerce clause', in: *Mélanges en hommage à Michel Waelbroeck, Volume I*, (Brussels, 1999), p. 1633.

[13] Opinion in Case C-292/92, *Hünermund*, (1993) ECR I-6787, pt. 11. See on this subject p. Oliver, *supra* n. 4, p.123.

law (section III). Both analyses are based on and elaborate upon contributions by other authors on this subject and where appropriate these will be up-dated.

Next, the influence of the Advocates General on the case law relating to the internal market will be discussed. On the basis of the analysis in section III two criteria will be applied to gauge their influence: a quantitative criterion (section IV) and a qualitative analysis of the four core issues which serve as a point of reference (section V). These core issues are the aspects which are considered in most cases on free movement: the applicability of the prohibition (internal situation, *Keck*), the qualification of the restriction (is it discriminatory or is it neutral in its application?), the applicability of an exception (Treaty exceptions and case law based exceptions) and the proportionality of the restriction. In this context attention will also be given to the relationship between the prohibitions (primary Community law) and secondary Community law.[14]

The combination of the quantitative and qualitative analysis make it possible to arrive at a balanced judgment on the influence exerted by the Advocates General on the Court's case law (section VI). Finally, in the final two sections VII and VIII a number of concluding remarks will be made on the Advocate General's role in respect of the functioning of the internal market.

The way in which the Court and its Advocates General accord horizontal direct effect to the Treaty provisions will not be discussed in this article.[15] Unlike the points of reference used in this article, the emphasis there is not in substantive Community law.

II. The Role of the Advocate General in the Development of the Court's Case Law in General

The role of the Advocates General in the development of Community law is discussed most frequently by the Advocates General themselves and their legal secretaries in articles and farewell addresses.[16] This would be an attractive research topic for a sociologist of law. The older articles mostly discuss the function of the Advocate General in the Community judicial system and its *sui generis* character as compared with the function in national legal systems.[17] More recent contributions, in addition, provide insight in the light of existing practice, into the role the various Advocates General have played in the course of time.

---

[14] See on this topic, Kamiel Mortelmans, 'The relationship between the Treaty rules and Community measures for the establishment and functioning of the internal market: towards a concordance rule?', (2002) CML Rev 1303.

[15] For this topic, I refer to Oliver and Roth, *supra* n. 4, p. 407.

[16] In the footnotes I refer to Advocates General Lagrange, Fennelly, Darmon, Jacobs, Van Gerven, VerLoren van Themaat, Mischo, Lenz, Ruiz-Jarabo Colomer and to the legal secretaries Barav, Oliver, Dashwood, Tridimas, Wouters, Roeges, Gori, Barents, López Escudero and Temmink. I myself was a legal secretary in the Cabinet of President J. Mertens de Wilmars.

[17] eg, A. Barav, *Le commissaire du gouvernement près le Conseil d'État français et l'avocat général près de la Cour de justice des CE, Revue internationale de droit comparé* (1974), p. 809.

One advantage of this obviously is that insiders know what they are talking about. One disadvantage is that now and then it would appear that their articles do not have the character of an *opinio pro curia* but of an *oratio pro domo*. The illustrations they use relatively often are drawn from their own Opinions.

In its Order in *Emesa* the Court elaborates on the function of the Advocate General. The Court makes its considerations in the light of the European Court of Human Rights' judgment in the *Vermeulen* case.[18] The Court points out that there is no hierarchical relationship between the Advocates General and that they cannot be compared with public prosecutors. Nor are they subject to any authority, in contrast to the manner in which the administration of justice is organized in certain Member States. They are not entrusted with the defence of any particular interest in the exercise of their duties. The Court adds that the Opinion of the Advocate General does not form part of the proceedings between the parties. The presentation of the Opinion rather opens the stage of deliberation by the Court. It is not therefore an opinion addressed to the judges or to the parties which stems from an authority outside the Court or which derives its authority from that of a public prosecutor's department. Rather, it constitutes the individual reasoned opinion, expressed in open court, of a Member of the Court of Justice itself.[19]

The role of the Advocate General was at issue once again in *Kaba II*.[20] In this case the question was raised as to whether parties were permitted to react to alleged errors of fact in Advocate General La Pergola's Opinion in *Kaba I*.[21] The Court side-stepped this question, but Advocate General Ruiz-Jarabo Colomer discusses the problem in depth in his Opinion in *Kaba II*. He based his analysis on the judgment of the European Court of Human Rights in the *Kress*[22] case, which had been given in the meantime, and arrived at the same conclusion as the Court in its Order in *Emesa*. In this latter case, Ruiz-Jarabo Colomer had not presented a formal Opinion, though he had been heard by the Court. The *Kaba* case thus enabled him to present his views on the subject in second instance publicly.

According to Article 222 EC, the Court is assisted by Advocates General. Each 'large' Member State (France, Germany, the United Kingdom, Italy and Spain) has a permanent Advocate General; the 'smaller' Member States provide an Advocate General in rotation (at present the Netherlands, Austria and Portugal have an Advocate General). The number of Advocates General (eight) was not increased on the accession of 10 new Member States on 1 May 2004.[23]

---

[18] ECHR, Judgment of 22 January 1996, Reports, 1996 I, p. 224. See T. Tridimas, 'The role of the Advocate General in the development of Community Law: Some Reflections', (1997) CML Rev., p. 1380.

[19] Case C-17/98, *Emesa*, Order of 4 February 2000, (2000) ECR I-667, pts. 12 and 14. See further, F. Benoît-Rohmer, (2001) CDE p. 403 and R. Lawson, (2000) CML Rev., 983. See also ECHR, Decision as to the applicability of 13 January 2005, *Emesa*.

[20] Case C-466/00, *Kaba II*, (2003) ECR I-2219.

[21] Case C-356/98, *Kaba I*, (2000) ECR I-2623.

[22] ECHR, Judgment of 7 June 2001. See F. Benoît-Rohmer, (2001) RTDE p. 727.

[23] Joint Declaration on the Court of Justice of the European Communities, OJ [2003] L236/971.

In accordance with Article 222 of the EC Treaty, the Advocate General's duty is to make, in open court, acting with complete impartiality and independence, reasoned submissions on cases brought before the Court of Justice. This general task may be subdivided into a number of specific duties. Tridimas, formal legal secretary to Advocate General Jacobs, identifies four such specific duties.[24] These duties are also referred to in other publications, but the authors concerned do not deal with these as systematically as Tridimas.[25]

Preparing a case (see section II.A) and suggesting a solution (section II.B) are the classical duties which all Advocates General fulfil. In placing the case in context and indicating new avenues (section II.C) the Advocate General assumes a more creative role, possibly contributing to the further development of the law.

Referring to Leijten (a former Advocate General at the Supreme Court of the Netherlands), Van Gerven distinguishes between a supporting task of the Advocate General and a task which is aimed at shaping the law.[26] The supportive task involves preparing the case and proposing a solution (sections II.A and II.B). The more creative task of shaping the law involves placing the case in a broader context and/or proposing new ways to deal with the legal problem at hand (sections II.C and II.D).

Identifying these different aspects of the function of the Advocate General makes it possible to analyze this function in a more balanced manner, without being restricted to the more basic question as to whether or not the Opinion is followed by the Court. The final sections of this article will deal with the dynamic process of exerting influence and being followed.

A. Preparing the Case

In allocating a case to an Advocate General, formerly by the President of the Court[27] and now by the First Advocate General, as a rule no regard is had to specializations, rather the aim is to ensure a balanced workload between the Advocates General.[28] Certain circumstances (such as linguistic knowledge or knowledge of the national legal system involved) may contribute to a case being assigned to one Advocate General in particular.[29] It may be inferred from the allocation of cases in

---

[24] Tridimas, *supra* n. 18, p. 1358.

[25] S. Hackspiel in: Von der Groeben and Schwarze (Hrsg.), Kommentar zum Vertrag über die Europäische Unon und zur Grundung der Europäische Gemeinschaft, 6. Auflage, Baden-Baden, 2003, Artikel 222, p. 339; F. Jacobs, 'Advocates General and Judges in the European Court of Justice: some personal reflections', in : *Liber Amicorum in Honour of Lord Slynn of Hadley, Volume I*, (The Hague, 2000), p. 17, does not simply enumerate, but his analysis of the task of the Advocate General tallies well with Tridimas' analysis.

[26] L. Roeges, De genese van een conclusie in: De Advocaat-Generaal gehoord, *supra* n. 4, p. 12.

[27] See Article 10 Rules of Procedure of the Court of Justice, amendment of 12 September 1979, [1979] OJ L238.   [28] Brown & Jacobs, *supra* n. 5, p. 65; Hackspiel, *supra* n. 25, p. 338.

[29] D. Ruiz-Jarabo Colomer and M. Lopéz Escudero, 'L'institution de l'avocat général à la Cour de Justice des CE' in *Mélanges en hommage à Fernand Schockweiler*, (Baden-Baden, 1999), p. 529.

practice that in a given period one Advocate General may present Opinions in associated cases. On example is Advocate General Jacobs who dealt with various cases in the field of intellectual property law.[30] However, in this same period other Advocates General also dealt with cases in this same field.[31]

If various Advocates General deal with associated cases in given period, taken together their Opinions can cover quite a bit of ground. The cases *Torfaen*[32] and *Keck*[33] (Advocate General Van Gerven), *Hünermund*[34] (Advocate General Tesauro) and *Greek Baby Milk*[35] (Advocate General Lenz), which were mentioned above, illustrate this point.

This 'balanced opinion approach' cannot always be followed as it depends on the existence of certain arbitrary circumstances, such as the simultaneous reference to the Court of a number of cases on similar problems. Now and then this does occur, as was the case with a series of preliminary references on gambling (*Läärä, Zenatti, Gambelli*) which came to the Court in the same period. Various Advocates General were given the opportunity to discuss this subject, which given the large number of submissions made by the Member States is experienced as being rather sensitive, in relation to the internal market.[36]

The Advocate General assists the Court in preparing a case. The Advocate General himself is assisted by his legal secretaries. Brown & Jacobs observe that in some respects the relationship of the Advocate General with his legal secretaries may be closer than that of the judges with theirs, since the judges will be able to discuss among themselves, while the Advocate General is on his own.[37] The way in which this 'internal situation' works in practice may be inferred from the experiences published by Advocate General Van Gerven's legal secretaries.[38] At any rate, given the differences in the socio-legal cultures of the Member States and the personalities of those concerned, the *cabinet* of every Advocate General will operate in its own particular way.

After the written observations have been analyzed, the Advocate General will be able to influence the direction the case is to take by consulting with Judge-Rapporteur before he submits his preliminary report on the case to the

---

[30] eg, cases on the Trade Mark Directive, such as Joined Cases C-427, 428 & 436/93, *Bristol Myers Squibb*, (1996) ECR I-3457; Case C-251/95, *Puma*, (1997) ECR I-6191 and Case C-355/96, *Silhouette*, (1998) ECR I-4799.

[31] Advocate General Gulmann presented an Opinion on the Trade Mark Directive in Case C-443/99, *Merck*, (2002) I-3703.   [32] *Torfaen, supra* n. 11.

[33] *Keck, supra* n. 10.   [34] *Hünermund, supra* n. 13.

[35] Case 391/92, *Commission v. Greece*, (1995) ECR I-1621.

[36] Case C-124/97, *Läärä*, (1999) ECR I-6067 (Advocate General La Pergola), Case C-68/98, *Zenatti*, (1999) ECR I-7289 (Advocate General Fennelly) and Case C-243/01, *Gambelli*, (2003) ECR I-13031 (Advocate General Alber).   [37] Brown & Jacobs, *supra* n. 5, p. 68.

[38] *De Advocaat-Generaal gehoord, supra* n. 4. See, too, H. Temmink, 'De referendaris bij het Hof van Justitie van de EG', in: *Magistraten zonder grenzen. De invloed van het Europese recht op de Nederlandse rechtspleging*, (Nijmegen, 2002), p. 51.

general administrative meeting of the Court.[39] In addition, during the preparation of the oral hearing and the oral hearing itself, the Advocate General can contribute to the clarification of the case by putting specific questions to the parties to the proceedings and intervening parties. Together with the Judge-Rapporteur the Advocate General is the guardian of the procedure.[40] This aspect of the Advocate General remains, to the extent that he does not refer to it in his Opinion, undisclosed to the outside world.

According to Advocate General Lenz, the Advocates General and the Court are engaged in a 'Wettbewerb um die beste Lösung'[41] (a competition for reaching the best solution.). This may be so, but it should be pointed out that the Court does occupy a dominant position on the relevant market!

Finally, now the report for the hearing since the beginning of the 1990s is no longer published together with the Court's judgment, the Advocate General can provide information to the outside world on the background to the case and the submissions of parties. A good example of this background information being provided in a transparent manner is Advocate General Stix-Hackl's Opinion in *Carpenter*.[42]

B. Proposing a Solution

In every case in which he presents an Opinion the Advocate General makes a proposal for the resolution of the case. The Advocate General's Opinion provides the judges other than the Judge-Rapporteur a single coherent picture of the complexities of case.[43] The Judge-Rapporteur also has this task, but as Advocate General Mischo dryly observes, the analyses of the Judge-Rapporteur are 'couvertes par le sécret du déliberé'.[44]

In preliminary reference procedures the Advocate General provides an answer to the questions submitted by the national court and in direct actions he will recommend the Court to decide in favour of one of the parties. Comparing the Advocate General's Opinion with the ruling given by the Court or with the answers it provides to preliminary questions makes it possible to gauge—superficially—whether or not the Advocate General has been 'followed'. In a number of cases the answers offered by the Advocate General are more comprehensive than those provided by the Court, as the Advocate General usually deals with all aspects of the case (admissibility and substance) and answers all the preliminary questions referred by the

---

[39] Brown & Jacobs, *supra* n. 5, p. 66; Hackspiel, *supra* n. 25, p. 339.
[40] Jacobs, *supra* n. 25, p. 21.
[41] C.O. Lenz, 'Das Amt des Generalanwalts am Europäischen Gerichtshof', in: *Festschrift für Ulrich Everling, Volume 1*, (Baden-Baden, 1995), p. 725.
[42] Case C-60/00, *Carpenter*, (2002) ECR I-6279.
[43] Brown & Jacobs, *supra* n. XL 5, p. 69; Jacobs, *supra* n. 25, p. 21.
[44] Address by M. Mischo, First Advocate General at the audience solennelle of 6 October 2003.

national court. Thus, in *Deutsche Post*, the Court confined itself to answering the questions on the competition rules and did not, in view of these answers, go on to deal with the questions relating to the freedom of movement. Advocate General La Pergola did discuss these latter aspects.[45]

The reverse situation hardly occurs. If an Advocate General were to be reticent in dealing with certain aspects of a case, he would probably limit his influence. Advocates General do not engage in this type of self-mutilation (however, see section IV.B, *in fine*). If an Advocate General considers an application to be inadmissible or a preliminary question to be irrelevant, he nevertheless usually will deal with the other aspects of the case as subsidiary points. One example is Advocate General Saggio's Opinion in *Guimont*. He took the view that it was unnecessary to provide an interpretation of Article 28 EC in this case, as the underlying facts constituted an internal situation. Nevertheless, he did provide an answer to the question on Article 28 EC in case the Court did not share his opinion as to the internal situation character of the case; his answer tallied with the Court's ruling in this case.[46] This example illustrates that it may sometimes be rather difficult to determine whether or not the Court has followed its Advocate General!

The Advocate General does not know beforehand how the Court will react to his Opinion. Advocate General VerLoren van Themaat, quoted by his colleague Advocate General Darmon put it this way: 'There is a degree of pleasant suspense in their work, in as much as they never know in advance whether their points of view will finally turn out to be concurring opinions or dissenting opinion'.[47]

C. Placing the Case in a Broader Context

Court judgments are often rather concise and do not always provide insight into the underlying facts and legal issues. Furthermore, for some time now, the report for the hearing is no longer published. As a result of these circumstances, reading the Advocate General's Opinion is generally a necessary preliminary exercise to understanding the judgment. As Advocate General Lagrange once put it, the Opinion is a 'décanter' of the case.[48]

The fact that the Advocate General's Opinion is now published before the Court's judgment in the European Court Reports is illustrative of the complementarity of the Opinion and the judgment in this respect.

In many Opinions the Advocates General summarize the submissions of the parties to the proceedings and intervening parties. The Advocate General himself will relate the legal arguments he advances to justify the solution he proposes to

---

[45] Joined Cases C-147/97 and C-148/97, *Deutsche Post*, (2000) ECR I-825.

[46] Case C-448/98, *Guimont*, (2000) ECR I-10663.

[47] M. Darmon, 'The role of the Advocate General at the Court of Justice of the EC', in: *The Role of Courts in Society* (edited by S. Shetreet), (Dordrecht, 1988), p. 432.

[48] Lagrange, *supra* n. 1, p. 3.

existing case law.[49] This is especially useful where the Court is (too) brief in its reasoning. One illustration is provided by the *Cinéthèque* case. Having established that there was a restriction of the freedom to provide goods, the Court simply went on to consider that the restriction could be justified under Community law. The Court does not indicate on which grounds the restriction was justified, nor (evidently) does it deal with the proportionality requirement.[50] Advocate General Slynn, on the other hand, does discuss this topic at some length placing it in the context of the European Convention on Human Rights. The case concerned the freedom of expression.

In recent years the Court frequently refers to its older case law. Nevertheless, the analysis provided by the Advocate General remains useful as he, being unaware of how the Court will approach the case, usually discusses the at times changeable case law extensively. An example of this is Advocate General Tesauro's Opinion in *Hünermund* referred to above.

(i) Opinions and Comparative Law

Legal comparison can be important in determining the proper context in which to consider a case.[51] For many topics which are brought before the Court, there are no precedents in Community law. A thorough comparative study, usually conducted by the Court's documentation department makes it possible to identify 'the general principles common to the laws of the Member States' (cf. Article 288 EC). The Opinions of Advocates General on the non-contractual liability of the Member States for infringements of Community law provide an illustration of this.[52]

As far as the internal market is concerned, legal comparison may fruitfully be undertaken with systems which are characterized by a similar degree of economic integration. In this respect, it is quite obvious to refer to the American commerce clause. To my knowledge, Advocates General have hardly ever undertaken a (systematic) comparison between the provisions on the free movement of goods and the US commerce clause in their Opinions, although it is apparent from their contributions to the academic debate that they were aware of this link.[53] Advocate General Geelhoed did make this comparison in his Opinion in *BAT* as the starting point for his considerations on the power of the Community to adopt Directive 2001/37 (tobacco) on the basis of Article 95 EC.[54]

There are two possible explanations for the lack of comparison with the American situation. First, very little up-to-date research material is available

---

[49] Jacobs, *supra* n. 25, p. 19; Hackspiel, *supra* n. 25, p. 341.
[50] Joined Cases 60 and 61/84, *Cinéthèque*, (1985) ECR 2603, pts. 22–23.
[51] Tridimas, *supra* n. 18, p. 1360.
[52] eg, Joined Cases C-6/90 and C-9/90, *Francovich*, (1991) ECR I-5357.
[53] eg, Van Gerven, *supra* n. 12.
[54] Case C-491/01, *BAT*, (2002) ECR I-11453. Opinion of Advocate General Geelhoed, pt. 108.

which could serve as a basis for an Opinion of an Advocate General.[55] Secondly, it cannot be said that the American legal system is one of the national legal systems referred to in Article 288 as a source of general principles of Community law. The same can be said of the Swiss Internal Market Law of 6 October 1995.[56] In Article 3 of this Law the protection of the health and life of humans is put on the same footing as the protection of the environment (compare section V. C (iii)).

(ii) Opinions and Academic Debate

Some Advocates General analyze cases in which they are presenting an Opinion not only against the backdrop of the existing European and national case law, they also pay regard to academic debate on the issues involved in the cases they are dealing with. As Lord Mackenzie Stuart once observed in a tribute to Maurice Lagrange, it is as if the Advocate General held a professional Chair of Community Law.[57]

Not all Advocates General are so inclined. The Dutch Advocate General Geelhoed, who holds a Chair of Community Law at the University of Utrecht, only refers sparingly to academic writing. By contrast, the Opinions of his university colleague Van Gerven of the Catholic University Leuven were often supported by a large number of references in footnotes. When someone from within the Court remarked on this, Van Gerven answered by quoting a line from Peter Schaffers's play Amadeus. After the première of 'Die Entführung aus dem Serail', Mozart was told by Emperor Joseph II that his opera contained 'too many notes'. Mozart smartly retorted: 'there are just as many notes as are required'.[58]

The answer to this problem lies somewhere in the middle. Where an Advocate General (partially) bases his Opinion on insights which have been developed in academic writing, it is no less than appropriate for them to acknowledge this in their Opinion. Examples of this are provided by the Opinions of Advocates General Tesauro in *Hünermund*[59] and Jacobs in *HAG II*.[60] If an Opinion merely confirms existing case law it would be rather overdone to expect the Advocate General to burden his Opinion with extensive references to academic writing. Otherwise, each Advocate General (and legal secretary) has his own style with, as is also apparent from their academic publications with many or few references in footnotes.

Like some Judges,[61] certain Advocates General participate actively in academic debate. This outlet provides them with the opportunity to defend or expand upon

---

[55] According to Van Gerven, *supra* n. 12, p. 1638–1639, who refers to W-H. Roth, Freier Wahrenverkehr und staatliche Regelungsgewalt in einem Gemeinsamen Markt: Europäische Probleme und Amerikanische Erfahrungen, München 1977 and to K. Lenaerts, Le juge et la constitution aux États-Unis d'Amérique et dans l'ordre juridique européen, Brussels, 1988.

[56] Bundesgesetz über den Binnenmarkt of 6 October 1995, www.admin.ch/ch/d/sr/943_02/

[57] Quotation derived from Brown & Jacobs, *supra* n. 5, p. 67.

[58] A. Alvarez, 'Een lans breken voor een samoerai', in: De Advocaat-Generaal gehoord, *supra* n. 4, p. 10.   [59] *Hünermund, supra* n. 13. Opinion pt. 8.

[60] Case C-10/89, *HAG II*, (1990) ECR I-3711. Opinion, pts. 33 *et seq.*

[61] eg, R. Joliet, *Journal des Tribunaux. Droit Européen*, (1994), p. 145 and in Colum.J.Eur.Law, 1995, p. 436, where he presented an exegesis of the Judgment in *Keck*.

their views or even (cautiously) to react to a judgment of the Court (where they were not followed). Conversely, a publication in a legal periodical permits an Advocate General to express his views on a subject on which he would have wished to have presented an Opinion, but has not had the opportunity to do so.[62] Such a publication may also make it possible to alleviate the evident frustration where it proved impossible—for procedural reasons—not to present an Opinion which was already prepared. Thus, Advocate General Stix-Hackl's Opinion in the *Tibor Balog* Case was not presented as a result of a rather late withdrawal,[63] although the main analysis of the problem at hand was published.[64]

D. New Avenues

In the three aspects of the task of the Advocate General just described the emphasis is on continuity. The Advocate General assists the Court in ensuring a consistent and harmonious development of the law.[65] However, the Advocate General may also assume a more innovative role. This is more the exception than the rule as most cases are rather routine in character. Generally speaking there are two ways in which the Advocate General can innovate. Either he can present a view on an issue which has not yet been addressed in the existing case law or he can reject the existing case law.

(i) Opinions on New Issues

In some cases parties[66] fail to advance certain arguments. The Advocate General is in a position to pick up such arguments and present them *ex officio* to the Court. Sometimes the Court, too, overlooks or ignores an argument.[67] Where the Advocate General has discussed this point it later turns out to be the only source of an authoritative statement on the issue.

An innovative solution may be presented as an (extensive) *obiter dictum*. One example of this is presented by the observations of Advocate General Geelhoed in *Ospelt* on the relationship between EMU and the free movement of capital.[68] Such observations in Opinions usually do not reappear in the Court's judgment, but once they have 'ripened' somewhat they may play a role in later cases.

In other cases the views expressed by the Advocate General on an issue which was not raised in the proceedings may be very much like (free) legal advice. In *Rieser*, questions had been asked on the consequences of a Directive being declared invalid.

---

[62] The documentation on the site of the Court presents direct access to the academic publications of the Advocates General and their legal secretaries.

[63] Case C-264/98, *Tibor Bolag*. See Agence Europe, 30 March 2001.

[64] A. Egger and C. 'Stix-Hackl, 'Sports and Competition Law: a Never Ending Story?', (2002) ECLR, p. 81   [65] Brown & Jacobs, *supra* n. 5, p. 71.

[66] For illustrations, see P. Gori, 'L'avocat général à la Cour de Justice des CE', (1976) CDE p. 386–387.   [67] For illustrations, see Dashwood, *supra* n. 6, p. 214–215.

[68] Case c-452/01, *Ospelt*, (2003) ECR I-9743 Opinion of Advocate General Geelhoed, pts 34 *et seq.*

From the response given by Advocate General Alber it was quite clear that the Directive concerned could not be invoked by the interested party. However, as he was intent on providing the referring court with a useful answer, Advocate General Alber pointed out that the company in the main proceedings could invoke the provisions on freedom to provide services and that the conditions for justifying the restriction involved were not fulfilled.[69] The Court did not address the issue, but here a vigilant market operator could suffice with the Advocate General's Opinion.

(ii) Rejection of Existing Case Law

Innovation incited by the Advocate General is more radical where he rejects the solution the Court has hitherto adopted. Suggesting an alternative to the case law will only have some chance of success if the Opinion is based on excellent reasoning and is therefore strongly convincing. One example of such an Opinion is that presented by Advocate General Jacobs in *HAG II*.[70] The Advocate General's views on the interpretation to be given to the exception on grounds of the protection of intellectual an commercial property in Article 30 EC in respect of a trade mark induced the Court to revise its case law on the scope of this exception.[71]

In the Portugese, French and Belgian *Golden Share* cases, Advocate General Ruiz-Jarabo Colmer defied the Court's case law on the relationship between the right to property and the provisions on free movement, which the Commission had based its case upon.[72] The Court did not follow his Opinion.[73] It did not expressly reject the Opinion, it simply confirmed its existing case law.[74] In the British and Spanish *Golden Share* Cases which followed thereafter, Advocate General Ruiz-Jarabo Colomer maintained his earlier stance.[75] In the Spanish case, the Spanish Government stated explicitly that it shared the views Advocate General Ruiz-Jarabo Colomer had expressed in his Opinion in the earlier *Golden Share* Cases.[76] Again, the Court did not follow Advocate General Ruiz-Jarabo Colomer and referred to its Judgments in the earlier *Golden Share* Cases.

III. To Follow or Not to Follow: General Criteria

Following this general description of the Advocate General's role in the proceedings before the Court, we will now consider the influence the Advocate General

---

[69] Case C-157/02, *Rieser,* (2004) ECR I-1477 Opinion of Advocate General Alber, pts 119 *et seq.*

[70] *HAG II, supra* n. 60. See, on this issue, Tridimas, *supra* n. 18, p. 1367.

[71] Opinion of Advocate General Jacobs in *HAG II, supra* n. 60, pt 67.

[72] Opinion of Advocate General Ruiz-Jarabo Colomer, Opinion, pt. 39.

[73] Case C-367/98, *Commission v. Portugal,* (2002) ECR I-4731; Case C-483/99, *Commission v. France,* (2002) ECR I-4781 and Case C-503/99, *Commission v. Belgium,* (2002) ECR I-4809.

[74] eg Case C-503/99, *supra* n. 73, pt. 43.

[75] Case C 463/00, *Commission v. Spain,* (2003) ECR I-4581 and Case C-98/01, *Commission v. United kingdom,* (2003) ECR I-4641.   [76] Case C-463/00, *supra* n. 75, pt. 41.

has on the development of Community law. The fact that Advocates General do have influence can be inferred from the fact that the deliberations start with the question whether or not the Court intends to follow the Advocate General's Opinion.[77] In their farewell addresses for Advocates General this practice is confirmed by the Presidents of the Court.[78] The following anecdote catches this perfectly: 'One former Judge of the Court, when asked by the Queen of the Netherlands how the judges' deliberation proceeded, replied: Your Majesty, the first question which we ask ourselves is the following: are we going to follow the Opinion of the Advocate General?'[79]

Having 'influence' is a much broader concept than 'being followed', but 'exerting influence' is much more difficult to measure.

In this article, two methods will be used to measure the influence of the Advocates General on the Court's case law. On the one hand, a number of leading cases will be taken in order to determine whether or not the Advocate General was followed. On this basis a statistical survey can be drawn up: the quantitative test (section IV). On the other hand, it will be examined whether the Court follows the Advocate General in respect four core internal market themes (section V). This approach builds upon Tridimas' views.[80]

The rest of this section will look at the criteria which may be used in order to determine whether or not an Advocate General is followed by the Court. There are two possible approaches. First, the direct route, where the Court itself states that it is adopting the views of the Advocate General (section III.A). Secondly, the indirect route, comparing the judgment with the Opinion to establish whether or not the Opinion has been embraced (section III.B).

A. Following the Advocate General: The Direct Route

(i) The Court Refers to the Opinion in its Judgment

In recent years the Court occasionally states explicitly in its judgment that it is following the Opinion of the Advocate General, or that it is adopting (in part) the interpretation suggested by him to arrive at its decision. A recent example of this is provided by the *Loi Evin* case in which the Grand Chamber refers to Advocate General Tizzano's Opinion five times.[81]

The Court does not refer systematically to the Opinion of the Advocate General, which is a good thing. Referring 'has advantages in terms of procedural

[77] Darmon, *supra* n. 47, p. 433. N. Fennelly, 'Reflections of an Irish Advocate General', *Irish Journal of European Law*, (1996), p. 19. Whether this working method in 2005 is still current is not known to me, but I presume it is.
[78] eg, President Lecourt in his farewell address for Roemer, as cited in Fennelly, *supra* n. 77, p. 19.
[79] Fennelly, *supra* n. 77, p. 19.   [80] Tridimas, *supra* note 18, p. 1363.
[81] Case 262/02, *Commission v. France*, (2004) ECR I-6569 pts. 30, 34, 37, 38 and 39.

economy, it must inevitably blur the distinction between the roles of Judge and Advocate General to the detriment of the authority of the Court itself'.[82] This point of view, expressed by Brown & Jacobs, is shared by Advocate General Fennelly.[83]

This cautious approach does not exclude occasional references being made to the Advocate General's Opinion, especially in cases where the Court undeniably has adopted the reasoning set out in the Opinion on an issue which the Advocate General has raised *ex officio*. In such cases, eg *Schmidberger*,[84] it is the Advocate General who has taken an innovative approach: honour must be given where it is due.

The fact that the Court does not refer in its judgment to the Advocate General's Opinion does not mean *a contrario* that it is not following him. In cases in which the Court decides not to follow the Advocate General, it will never—to my knowledge—state this explicitly, but may so indirectly by referring to existing case law.[85] In this way the Court asserts its authority without admonishing the Advocate General. The *Golden Share* cases referred to above provide an illustration of this subtle behaviour.[86]

Sometimes the Advocate General will indicate in a later case on the same issue that the Court did not agree with him. An example of this is provided by the second Opinion of Advocate General Van Gerven in the *Keck* case in which he points out the Court had not followed his Opinion in *Torfaen*.[87] The Advocate General may also remind the Court that it did not follow the Opinion of a colleague in another similar case, as did Advocate General Van Gerven in *Torfaen* on Advocate General Slynn's Opinion in *Cinéthèque*.[88]

(ii) A Judge Providing Information on the Deliberations

Is a judge participating in the deliberations permitted to break the secrecy by indicating that the Court followed its Advocate General in a particular case? A presumably unique instance of this was provided by the former President of the Court Rodríguez Iglesias in the Liber Amicorum for former Advocate General and former Judge Slynn.

In the *Reinheitsgebot* case, Germany defended its purity law for beer, *inter alia*, by stating that it was justified on grounds related to the health of the German beer consumer. 'Since beer is a foodstuff of which large quantities are consumed in Germany, the German Government considers that it is particularly desirable to

---

[82] Brown & Jacobs, *supra* n. 5, p. 70.

[83] In point 21 of Case C-36/92P, *SEP*, (1994) ECR I-1911 'the Court considers: 'For the reasons stated in paragraphs 21 to 42 of the Advocate General's Opinion, the first, second, third, fourth and fifth grounds of appeal must be rejected as unfounded'. On this exaggerated reference to the Advocate General, see Fennelly, *supra* n. 77, p. 16.

[84] Case C-112/00, *Schmidberger*, (2003) ECR I-5659, pt 66.

[85] Fennelly, *supra* n. 77, p. 16.   [86] *supra* n. 73 and 75.   [87] *Torfaen, supra* n. 9, pt. 8.

[88] *Torfaen, supra* n. 9, pt. 16.

prohibit the use of any additive in its manufacture'.[89] The Court rejected this argument pointing out that the additives prohibited by Germany in the preparation of beer were permitted in the preparation of other beverages.[90] This argument was taken from Advocate General Slynn's Opinion.

Rodríguez Iglesias goes on to remark that the Advocate General 'gave a far more graphic explanation'. I will quote the lines to which Rodríguez Iglesias referred: 'It seems to me disproportionate to seek to justify rules which exclude the whole of society from beer other than nationally produced beer because some additives may constitute a risk for a person who drinks in excess of 1000 litres of beer a year or for an alcoholic already suffering from cirrhosis of the liver. Accepting that such persons may need protection there are other ways of achieving it, medical advice as to quantum and self-restraint to name only two.'[91]

Rodríguez Iglesias made this remark to demonstrate that 'the advantage of being an Advocate General is that you can say what you like'.[92] However, Rodríguez Iglesias goes one step further by revealing which answer then Judge Joliet would have preferred to have given to this sloppy German argument:

'[i]t seemed that once Germans crossed the borders of their own country, which they do on a fairly regular basis, their attitude to beer changed since in foreign parts they have no difficulty in calling "beer" the whole variety of beers available to them, (which they like to consume, KM) in rather large quantities. Of course, you will not find this in the Judgment because when Judges have such brilliant ideas, the collegiate body of Judges excludes them from the draft.'[93]

This spirited example indicates the potential of the Advocate General and the restrictions of the Court. Cheers!

B. Following the Advocate General: The Indirect Route

Where the Court is silent on whether or not it follows the Advocate General's Opinion, the outsider is forced to do some research of his own. In that case the Court's considerations and ruling must be compared with the considerations and conclusion of the Advocate General's Opinion. It is not sufficient only to compare the Court's *dictum* with the Advocate General's final conclusion. In order to determine to what extent the Advocate General has been followed by the Court it is necessary to read, interpret and compare the full texts of both the judgment and the Opinion. This exercise will be carried out for a number of cases in under the following heading.

---

[89] Case 178/84, *Commission v. Germany*, (1987) ECR 1223, pt. 39.
[90] Case 178/84, *supra* n. 89, pt. 49.
[91] Case 178/84, *Commission v. Germany*, (1987) ECR 1257.
[92] G.C. Rodrígues Iglesias, Drinks in Luxembourg. Alcoholic Beverages and the Case Law of the European Court of Justice, in: Liber Amicorum in Honour of Lord Slynn of Hadley, Volume I, The Hague, 2000, p. 528.   [93] ibidem.

IV. To Follow or Not to Follow: Quantitative Analysis

It is impossible to examine all cases on the provisions prohibiting non-tariff restrictions within the internal market in order to find an answer to the question whether or not the Court followed the Advocate General. At a rough estimate there are hundreds of cases in this field.

As was mentioned in the introduction, cases concerning procedural issues, such as (horizontal) direct effect, will not be discussed in this article. The quantitative analysis will focus on two subjects of substantive law: the validity of secondary Community law in the light of the Treaty provisions on freedom of movement (section IV.A) and the basic tenets of the provisions on freedom of movement (section IV.B).

A. The Validity of Secondary Law and Provisions on Free Movement

Measuring the Advocate General's influence in cases concerning the relationship between primary and secondary Community law is not that difficult. Two issues should be looked at more closely.

First, there is the question whether a Community act was adopted on the correct legal base. Taking two recent tobacco cases in which this question was raised, it appears that the Advocate General and the Court agreed on the course to be taken. In the first case on tobacco advertising the Court, in line with Advocate General Fennelly's Opinion, decided that the Directive concerned was invalid.[94] In the second tobacco case the Court, in line with Advocate General Geelhoed's Opinion, decided that the Directive concerned was valid.[95]

I will not go into this topic any further as the provision of primary Community law involved is not one of the basic prohibitions, such as Article 28 EC, but the legal base for Community acts, Article 95 EC. This does not alter the fact that there is a clear connection between the two provisions. However, case law is sparse on the matter, so that it is not possible to draw reliable conclusions as to the influence exerted by the Advocate General, or more specifically as to whether or not he has been followed, on this aspect.

Secondly, there is the question as to whether a Community act is compatible with the basic prohibitions which form the basis of the internal market. Here, more case law is available. I selected all cases (known to me) in which the relationship between the basic prohibitions of the internal market and secondary Community law was considered. Next, I looked at the conclusion both the Court and the Advocate General had reached on the validity of the Community act. I did not take account of the reasoning employed by them, although it sometimes varied.

---

[94] Case C-376/98, *Germany v. EP and Council*, (2000) ECR I-8419.
[95] Case C-491/01, *BAT*, (2002) ECR I-11453.

Of course, this delicate subject arises in other cases too, but the research I carried out shows that it is not always tackled in a uniform manner.[96] This may be illustrated by two examples. The first is the *Deposit-Guarantee Scheme* case in which Germany requested the Court, *inter alia*, to annul a provision in Directive 94/19 as being incompatible with the provisions on free movement. Neither the Court nor the Advocate General dealt directly with this point.[97] Secondly, there are cases in which the Court does pick up the validity issue, subsequently to 'deactivate' it. This was the case in *Ruwet*[98] and *Commission v. Italy (grapefruit)*. Both cases were decided in accordance with the Opinions of Advocates General Fennelly and Jacobs respectively.[99]

Where the validity of a Community act is called into question the Advocate General arrives at the conclusion more often than the Court (*Rum, Ravil, Parma*) that it is invalid. In his Opinion in *Cassis de Dijon*, Advocate General Capotorti even raised the question whether in the light of the interpretation given to Article 28 EC in *Dassonville*, certain elements of Directive 70/50, which provided specifications of the concept of measures having equivalent effect, should not be deemed to be invalid.[100] I have not been able to find an Opinion in which the Advocate

Table 1. The validity of Community acts in the light of the basic prohibitions of the internal market

Case	Name	ECR	AG	Decision ECJ	Opinion AG
218/82	Commission v. Council (Rum)	1983, 4063	Rozès	valid	invalid
15/83	Denkavit	1984, 2171	Mancini	valid	valid
37/83	Rewe	1984, 1229	Slynn	valid	valid
240/83	ADBHU	1985, 531	Lenz	valid	valid
41/84	Pinna	1986, 1	Mancini	invalid	invalid
C-284/95	Safety Hi-tech	1998, I-4301	Léger	valid	valid
C-388/95	Belgium v. Spain (Rioja)	2000, I-3123	Saggio	valid	valid
C-114/96	Kieffer	1997, I-3629	Elmer	valid	valid
C-469/00	Ravil	2003, I-5053	Alber	valid	invalid
C-108/01	Parma	2003, I-5121	Alber	valid	invalid

[96] See on this point, Mortelmans, *supra* n. 14, p. 1324.

[97] Case C-233/94, *Germany v. EP and Council*, (1997) ECR I-2405. See further, W-H. Roth, 35 CML Rev., p. 465.

[98] Case C-3/99, *Ruwet*, (2000) ECR I-8749, pt. 23. Advocate General Fennelly did investigate the validity point and reached a positive conclusion, see pt. 29.

[99] Case C-128/89, *Commission v. Italy*, (1990) ECR I-3229. See, in particular, Advocate General Jacobs, Opinion, pt 12. See further Jans, (1992) SEW 209.

[100] Case 120/78, *Rewe*, (1979) ECR 672.

General takes the view that a Community act is not incompatible with primary Community law, but the Court decides that it is.

The outcome of these 'validity cases' may have important consequences for the policies of the Community legislator and for the Commission's executive policy. Perhaps the collegiate character of the Court, which takes decisions after consultation, may explain why it more frequently reaches a conclusion favourable to the Community, than a sole Advocate General, who operates independently and presents his own, personal Opinion.

B. The Interpretation of the Provisions on Free Movement

For the purposes of considering how the Court and the Advocate General deal with the basic tenets of the provisions on free movement (applicability and interpretation of the prohibition and exceptions, proportionality test), a choice had to be made out of the hundreds of cases on this subject. In looking for a selection criterion which would allow a balanced judgment to be made, I decided to use the third edition of Craig and de Búrca's case book.[101] In the chapters devoted to the internal market, these authors have included a large number of excerpts from Court decisions. I analyzed all these cases. They cover the time span from 1974 to 2000, so that the Opinions of many Advocates General could be included. The cases include both preliminary references and direct actions.

The selection consists of many leading cases and some cases which can be regarded as sequels to these cases. The judgments were mainly decided by a Full Court, which is quite logical as one might expect that the decision of the Court to decide the case in plenary session would basically[102] influence the academic's decision to include it in a case book. Nevertheless, a number of judgments of Chambers are also included, such as *Torfaen* and *TK Heimdienst*, which are important for a correct understanding of the pre- and post-*Keck* case law. The list of 47 cases is indeed a selection. Craig and de Búrca refer to many more cases in the relevant chapter, but if they have not cited excerpts of a judgment at length, it will not appear on my list. One salient consequence of using Craig and de Búrca for my selection was that relatively few cases on the free movement of capital were included.[103] For this reason—and also because the cases concerned were fairly recent so that they could not have been included in the third edition of Craig and de Búrca's case book—I added a number of judgments which wholly or in part deal with the free movement of capital: *Bordessa*,[104]

---

[101] P. Craig and G de Búrca, *Eu Law Text, Cases and Materials*, 3rd edn, Oxford, 2003.
[102] A case like *Torfaen, supra* n. 9, is the exception to the rule, but the judgment in this case was overruled by *Keck, supra* n. 10.
[103] Many of these judgments are referred to, but no excerpts were included and that was my selection criterion.
[104] Joined Cases C-358/93 and C-416/93, *Bordessa*, (1995) ECR I-361.

Konle,[105] *Ospelt*,[106] and the *Golden Share* cases against Portugal, Belgium and France.[107]

This selection does not cover all the leading cases relating to the internal market. Some cases, such as *Groenveld*,[108] *Alpine Investments*,[109] and *Bosman*,[110] which Craig and de Búrca mention, but do not reproduce excerpts of, will be discussed in the analysis in the following section V.

For each case I examined whether the Advocate General had been followed on four key issues: the applicability of the basic prohibition; the qualification of the restriction; the indication of the justification; and the proportionality of the national measure. I used three indicators: followed (+); not followed (−); and followed in part (+/−).

As, in their Opinions, Advocates General often present both principal conclusions and alternative conclusions in case the Court does not agree with the principal conclusions, it is possible that although the Court may not adopt the solution favoured by the Advocate General, it may follow his alternative in whole or in part.

This may be illustrated by Advocate General Ruiz-Jarabo Colomer's Opinion in *Smits and Peerbooms*.[111] He takes the primary view that the provisions of medical services-in-kind cannot be considered to services within the meaning of Article 50 EC. As a result, Article 49 EC does not prevent sickness insurance funds from obliging persons insured by them to request prior permission to receive medical services from a professional or an institution with whom or which it has not concluded a health care agreement. The Court, however, took the view that this medical care did qualify as a service within the meaning of Article 50 EC. This is indicated in the schedule as (−) for the aspect applicability of the basic prohibition. If the medical services concerned did fall within the ambit of Article 50 EC, and Advocate General Ruiz Jarabo Colomer had adopted this as an alternative possibility, the permission requirement would amount in practice to a restriction of the freedom to provide services. As this is also the view the Court took, the indicator used in this case for the qualification of the restriction was (+). The Advocate General and the Court agreed that the restriction could be considered as justified in order to maintain the financial stability of the system; this resulted, again, in (+). As to the following issue, the Advocate General considered the measure to be both necessary for and proportionate to the aim pursued. The Court's stance on this point was more subtle, which led to the indicator (+/−).

Most judgments and Opinions follow a certain pattern, which may or may not be due to the (sometimes reformulated) preliminary questions, and which I have used as my point of departure for Table 2. In a number of cases it is not entirely

---

[105] Case C-302/97, *Konle*, (1999) ECR I-3099.   [106] *Ospelt, supra* n. 68.
[107] *Golden Shares, supra* n. 73 and 75.   [108] Case 15/79, *Groenveld*, (1979) ECR 3409.
[109] Case C-384/93, *Alpine Investments*, (1995) ECR I-1141.
[110] Case C-415/93, *Bosman*, (1995) ECR I-4921.
[111] Case C-157/99, *Smits and Peerbooms*, (2001) ECR I-5473.

Table 2. Quantitative analysis of the basic tenets of the internal market

case	name	freedom	ECR	Advocate General	applicability of basic prohibition	qualification of restriction	indication of justification	proportionality
2/74	Reyners	E	1974, 631	Mayras		+	+	+
8/74	Dassonville	G	1974, 837	Trabucchi		+/−		
33/74	van Binsbergen	S	1974, 1294	Mayras		+		
41/74	van Duyn	W	1974, 1337	Mayras				+
67/74	Bonsignore	W	1975, 297	Mayras				+/−
36/75	Rutili	W	1975, 1219	Mayras				+/−
48/75	Royer	W	1976, 497	Mayras				+
118/75	Watson/Belmann	W/S/E	1976, 1185	Trabucchi				+/−
30/77	Bouchereau	W	1977, 1999	Warner				+/−
82/77	van Tiggele	G	1978, 25	Capotorti		+		
120/78	Cassis de Dijon	G	1979, 649	Capotorti		+	+/−	+
149/79	Commission/B (public service)	W	1982, 1845	Mayras/Rozes				
53/81	Levin	W	1982, 1035	Slynn		+	+/−	
249/81	Commission/Ireland (souvenirs)	G	1982, 4005	Capotorti	−	−		
174/82	Sandoz	G	1983, 2445	Mancini		−	+	+
72/83	Campus oil	G	1984, 2727	Slynn		−	+	+/−
207/83	Commission/UK (origin)	G	1985, 1201	Darmon		−	+	+
231/83	Cullet	G	1985, 305	VerLoren van Themaat		+	+	+
267/83	Diatta	W	1985, 567	Darmon			+/−	
61/84	Cinèthéque	G/S	1985, 2605	Slynn		−	+/−	
178/84	Commission/D (Reinheitsgebot)	G	1987, 1227	Slynn		+	+	+
121/85	Conegate	G	1986, 1007	Slynn		+	+	+
63/86	Commission/Italy (housing)	E/S	1988, 29	Cruz Vilaça		+		
263/86	Humbel	S	1988, 5365	Slynn	+			

may be drawn with one 'admissibility issue' which was not examined in this context, the horizontal effect of the basic provisions on the freedom of movement. Reference may be made, for example to, Advocate General Fennelly who in the *Angonese* Case, in view of the rest of his Opinion, did not wish to go into the question as to whether or not Article 39 EC has horizontal direct effect,[114] and Advocate General Lenz who in *Bosman* answered this question in the affirmative.[115] In both cases, the Court decided that Article 39 EC does have horizontal direct effect.

A closer analysis of the Court's judgments on the horizontal effect of the provisions on free movement reveals that there is a dichotomy in the case law.[116] Fennelly's apprehension was as such quite understandable, but, as was observed above (section II.B. Proposing a solution), it is the Advocates General's duty 'to give an Opinion'.

In defining the restriction, the Court and the Advocates General disagree to a lesser extent. Nevertheless, certain *causes célèbres* which will be discussed in the next section, such as *Keck*,[117] *Groenveld*,[118] and *Cassis de Dijon*[119] show that Court and Advocate General may have a difference of opinion on this point.

There is a lot of agreement as to the indication of the grounds of justification. This is not surprising as the applicable exceptions were invoked during the proceedings: in preliminary references by the referring court and intervening Member States and in direct actions by the defending Member State.

As to the application of the proportionality test, the Advocate General is often followed in part. In a number of cases either the Court or the Advocate General leave the application of the proportionality test to the national court. In other cases the dividing line between proportionate and disproportionate is vague. In order to be able to make a proper decision a criterion is required. Advocate General Van Gerven has made some suggestions in that direction (see section V. D.).

A more elaborate interpretation of this data will be presented in section VI, after the discussion of the same topic on the basis the qualitative criterion in section V.

V. To Follow or Not to Follow: Qualitative Analysis of the Basic Tenets

This substantive approach complements the quantitative analysis and makes it possible to draw conclusions in respect of the more creative aspects of the Advocate General's function: placing the case in a broader context (section II.C) and initiating new case law (section II.D).

---

[114] Case C-281/98, *Angonese*, (2000) ECR I-4139.   [115] *Bosman, supra* n. 110.
[116] See Oliver and Roth, *supra* n. 4, p. 422.   [117] *Keck, supra* n. 10.
[118] *Groenveld, supra* n. 108.   [119] Rewe *(Cassis de Dijon), supra* n. 100.

The point of departure of this substantive approach are the basic tenets relating to the provisions on free movement and the evolution of the interpretation given to them through the years. In this way it is possible not just to focus on the most important cases, like *Cassis de Dijon* and *Keck*, but to extend the discussion to the judgments which preceded and succeeded them.

The following basic tenets will be discussed:

- the non-applicability of the basic prohibition: the internal situation and *Keck* (section V.A),
- the qualification of the restriction (do they apply with or without distinction?) (section V.B),
- the identification of the exception (Treaty exceptions or imperative requirements (section V.C),
- the proportionality of the national measures (section V.D).

The convergence between the freedoms[120] will be taken as the point of departure. Notable differences in the case law on the four freedoms will be touched upon where appropriate.

A. The Non-Applicability of the Basic Prohibition

In the course of the years a number of tenets have been developed in respect of situations in which the basic prohibition does not apply. Two will be discussed here: the internal situation and the *Keck* approach. Other techniques, such as the *de minimis* rule proposed by Advocate General Jacobs in *Leclerc*, but not embraced by the Court,[121] and the hypothetical situation approach will not be dealt with.

(i) Internal Situation

In one of the first cases in which this point was raised, the *Knoors* case, the Court decided, in line with Advocate General Reischl's Opinion, that Community citizens who had used their right of free movement, could on returning to their home country to work, invoke the basic provisions on free movement where they encountered restrictions.[122]

In another case in which this topic was raised explicitly, the *Saunders* case, the Court considered that the underlying facts amounted to an internal situation, so that the basic prohibition did not apply.[123] Advocate General Warner, however, reached the conclusion 'that a worker has a right of free movement not only between Member States, but also within his own Member State'.[124]

[120] See Oliver and Roth, *supra* n. 4, p. 439.
[121] Case C-412/93, *Leclerc TF1*, (1995) ECR I-179.
[122] Case 115/78, *Knoors*, (1979) ECR 399.
[123] Case 175/78, *Saunders*, (1979) ECR 1129.
[124] See Dashwood, *supra* n. 6, p. 214.

In *Lancry*, which concerned charges levied within one Member State, the Court essentially followed the same reasoning as Advocate General Warner in *Saunders*. In doing so, the Court distanced itself from the Opinion presented by Advocate General Tesauro who had warned the Court that if inter-regional charges were both brought within the scope of Article 25 EC, this would undermine the settled case law on purely internal situations.[125] In its judgment in *Pistre*, the Court confirmed this broad interpretation of the basic prohibition. The Court did not follow Advocate General Jacobs in this case.[126]

In later case law both the Court and the Advocates General have given considerable attention to the internal situation question. And rightly so, this is a point of principle: can frontiers exist in an internal market which by definition is a market without internal frontiers? The Court and the Advocates General frequently disagreed.[127] I refer to the cases of *Angonese* (Advocate General Fennelly, not followed),[128] *Guimont* (Advocate General Saggio, not followed),[129] *Reisch* (Advocate General Geelhoed, followed),[130] and *Carbonati Apuani* (Advocate General Poiares Maduro, followed in part).[131]

I am inclined to think that the concept of the internal situation is rather flexible.[132] If the Court wants to avoid giving judgment, the internal situation provides a fine reason for declaring the case 'inadmissible'. In *Grogan*, Advocate General Van Gerven had concluded that the Irish prohibition of advertising for abortion clinics situated in the United Kingdom, fell within the scope of the provisions on the freedom to provide services. The Court, however, decided that the situation qualified as an internal situation, presumably to avoid getting engaged in the extremely difficult debate on the freedom of expression and the right to life.[133]

In *Carpenter*, the Court, unlike Advocate General Stix-Hackl, took the view that the passive provision of services by Mr Carpenter in Germany from his home country, the United Kingdom, came within the ambit of the freedom to provide services, presumably because it wanted to recognize Mr Carpenter's rights to free movement no matter what.[134]

---

[125] Joined Cases C-363/93, 407–411/93, *Lancry*, (1994) ECR I-3957. Advocate General Tesauro's Opinion pt. 28.

[126] Joined Cases C-321/94 and C-324/94, *Pistre*, (1997) ECR I-2343.

[127] As was observed explicitly by Advocate General Geelhoed in Joined Cases C-515/99, C-519–524/99, *Reisch*, (2000) ECR I-2157, pt. 87. See, too, Oliver and Roth, *supra* n. 4, p. 430.

[128] *Angonese*, *supra* n. 114.

[129] *Guimont*, *supra* n. 46. See, on this subject Oliver, *supra* n. 4, p. 152.

[130] *Reisch*, *supra* n. 127.

[131] Case C-72/03, *Carbonati Apuani*, (2004) ECR I-8027.

[132] See, too, the critical analysis of G. Davies, *Nationality discrimination in the European Internal Market*, (The Hague, 2003), p. 117.

[133] Case C-159/90, *Grogan*, (1991) ECR I-4685. See, on this matter, W. Wils, Subsidiariteit, onderneming en samenhang (S.O.S). Inhoudelijke grond(s)lagen in de conclusies van AG Van Gerven, in: De Advocaat-Generaal gehoord, *supra* n. 4, p. 43.

[134] *Carpenter*, *supra* n. 42.

(ii) Keck

In the introduction it was observed that Advocate General Tesauro's Opinion in *Hünermund*[135] provided a point of reference for the Court's judgment in *Keck*.[136] Advocate General Van Gerven was not followed by the Court in *Keck*, as was also the case in *Torfaen*. In this case Advocate General Van Gerven introduced a threshold criterion which greatly resembled the criterion which is applied in Article 81(1) EC cases.[137] Looking back at this proposal, one of Advocate General Van Gerven's former legal secretaries opines that this approach was perhaps too ambitious to be applied by national courts.[138]

Following *Keck* a number of Advocates General, including Van Gerven in *'t Heukske*,[139] applied the *Keck* test and further refined it. Other Advocates General disagreed with the Court's solution.

In an infringement case concerning a Greek measure requiring the sale of baby milk through fixed outlets, chemists, Advocate General Lenz considered that there could be no doubt that this measure fell within the scope of the prohibition.[140] However, the Court chose not to follow this, in the words of Advocate General Fennelly's strongly argued Opinion.[141] It applied its freshly decided *Keck* judgment in a formalistic manner and placed the Greek measure outside the scope of Article 28 EC.

In *Leclerc*, which related to rules restricting a type of advertising, Advocate General Jacobs suggested his market access approach.[142] The Court did not follow him as far as Article 28 was concerned. Advocate General Jacobs' point of view was adopted, however, in *Bosman*[143] on free movement of workers and in *Alpine Investments* on freedom to provide services.[144]

In the *TK Heimdienst* case, the Court, taking a different view from Advocate General La Pergola, reconciled the two approaches by giving a restrictive interpretation to the second *Keck* condition, the *de facto* discrimination.[145] In this way the market access approach is taken account of indirectly.[146] This judgment was followed by the Court's judgment in *Gourmet*.[147] In this case Advocate General applied the *Keck* approach and concluded that Article 28 EC was applicable because there was *de facto* discrimination.

---

[135] *Hünermund, supra* n. 13.
[136] *Keck, supra* n. 10. A good survey is given by S. Feiden, Die Bedeutung der "Keck"-Rechtsprechung im System der Grundfreiheiten. Ein Beitrag zur Konvergenz der Freiheiten, Berlin, 2003. [137] *Torfaen, supra* n. 9, pt. 22.
[138] J. Wouters, 'Over schilderwerk, waardenperspectief en het vinden van (rechts) beginselen', in: De Advocaat-Generaal gehoord, *supra* n. 4, p. 60.
[139] Joined Cases C-401/92 and C-402/92, *'t Heukske*, (1994) ECR I-2199.
[140] *Commission v. Greece ('baby milk'), supra* n. 35. [141] Fennelly, *supra* n. 77, p. 16.
[142] *Leclerc, supra* n. 121. [143] *Bosman, supra* n. 110.
[144] *Alpine Investments, supra* n. 109.
[145] Case C-254/98, *Heimdienst Sass*, (2000) ECR I-151.
[146] cf. Oliver, *supra* n. 4, p. 128. [147] Case C-405/98, *Gourmet*, (2001) ECR I-1795.

In *Graf,* Advocate General Fennelly gave a rather refined interpretation of the *Keck* approach.[148]

In the *DocMorris* case, Advocate General Stix-Hackl provided a most extensive analysis of the Court's case law and the Advocates General's Opinions on this subject, and produced an Opinion which, based on the *Keck* approach, also contains elements of the market access approach.[149]

Advocate General Geelhoed gives an in-depth analysis of limited and absolute prohibitions of advertising in the *Douwe Egberts* case.[150] He shows much support for the views expounded by Advocate General Jacobs in *Leclerc*.

On some occasions Advocates General let the opportunity pass unused, as may be illustrated by the Spanish and British *Golden Share* cases. In the case against the United Kingdom, the British Government claimed that in view of the *Keck* case law its measures should be deemed to fall outside the scope of the provisions on the free movement of capital. The Court rejected this argument.[151] Advocate General Ruiz-Jarabo ignored this point, with the exception of an indirect reference to it in a footnote.[152] This is regrettable as this was the first time *Keck* was linked to the free movement of capital.

As Oliver and Roth observe,[153] the Court has not yet achieved sufficient clarity as to the circumstances in which market access is held to be impeded. Neither have the Advocates General!

B. The Qualification of the Restriction

Two subjects will be discussed as they offer most material: first, the genesis of the case law on national measures which apply without distinction (section V.B.(i)) and secondly, the divergent definition of the prohibition in the case of export restrictions (section V.B.(ii)).

(i) Measures which Apply without Distinction

In *Dassonville,*[154] the Court and Advocate General Trabucchi were given the opportunity to give a definition of the concept 'measures having equivalent effect' in Article 28 EC. As was already pointed out (section I), the Court derived its definition from its judgment in *Grundig and Consten,* a case in which Advocate general Trabucchi had been Judge-Rapporteur. Advocate General Trabucchi, however, had not suggested this solution. He had indicated in his Opinion that in

---

[148] Case C-190/98, *Graf,* (2000) ECR I-493. Opinion of Advocate General Fennelly, pt. 18–20. See, further, Oliver and Roth, *supra* n. 4, p. 413.

[149] Case C-322/01, *DocMorris,* (2003) ECR I-14887. Opinion of Advocate General Stix-Hackl, pt. 67. *et seq.*

[150] Case C-239/02, *Douwe Egberts,* (2004) ECR I-7007. Opinion of Advocate General Geelhoed, pt. 71 *et seq.*   [151] *Commission v. United Kingdom ('Golden Share'), supra* n. 75.

[152] (2003) ECR I-4596, n. 10.   [153] Oliver and Roth, *supra* n. 4, p. 414.

[154] *Dassonville, supra* n. 8.

a situation in which national laws diverge (ie a distorsion), national rules which do not discriminate or are protectionist fall within the scope of the prohibition of Article 28 EC.[155]

In *Cassis de Dijon*, Advocate General Capotorti elaborated upon this point, possibly through the pen of his legal secretary Gori, who also worked for Trabucchi. Advocate General Capotorti concluded that the German measure which was at issue and which applied without distinction to national and imported goods fell within the ambit of the prohibition of Article 28 EC, but that the Article 30 EC could be interpreted in such a way, particularly the exception on grounds of public policy, as to include the protection of consumer interests against commercial fraud. Advocate General Capotorti did propose adopting a broad interpretation of the prohibition in Article 28, but he did not come up with the idea of the imperative requirements.[156] For an Advocate General, this apparently was a bridge too far!

Comparing the judgment and the Opinion in *Cassis de Dijon* provides a remarkable illustration of Brown & Jacobs' observation: 'It may also simply be easier for judges collectively to advance further than an individual Advocate General'.[157]

It may be added that the third element of the *Cassis de Dijon* judgment, the mutual recognition rule, was first introduced in the *Van Wesemael* judgment, in line with Advocate General Warner's Opinion.[158]

(ii) Export Restrictions

Although *Dassonville* only related to import restrictions, some years later the same definition that was given in that judgment to determine the scope of the prohibition of Article 28 EC was used in *Bouhelier* which concerned export restrictions within the meaning of Article 29 EC.[159]

Some years after *Bouhelier*, in *Groenveld*, which also concerned export restrictions Advocate General Capotorti confirmed the *Dassonville* formula. A Chamber of three judges of the Court took a different view and defined the scope of Article 29 EC in such a way that it only applies to discriminatory measures.[160] Given the fact that this Chamber of three intended to reverse the case law on this subject and, in doing so, was going against the Opinion of the Advocate General, it would appear to be obvious that *Groenveld* should have been referred to the Full Court, as indeed happened later in *Keck*.

Advocate General Capotorti got a second chance in *Oebel*.[161] He reacted touchily to the way this affair had been dealt with by the Court and persisted in

---

[155] ibid., (1974) ECR 858 and 859.

[156] *Cassis de Dijon, supra* n. 100. See, on this, Oliver, *supra* n. 4, p. 116.

[157] Brown & Jacobs, *supra* n. 5, p. 71.

[158] Joined Cases 110 and 111/78, *Van Wesemael*, (1979) ECR 35.

[159] Case 53/76, *Bouhelier*, (1977) ECR 179.   [160] *Groenveld, supra* n. 108.

[161] Case 155/80, *Oebel*, (1981) ECR 1993.

applying the broad definition to Article 29 EC. The Court, however, confirmed *Groenveld* and once again did not follow the Advocate General.

In *Alpine Investments*, Advocate General Jacobs criticised the restricted approach of the *Groenveld* judgment.[162] As was observed by Oliver,[163] this criticism should be seen in the light of Advocate General Jacobs' attack on the *Keck* formula. To a large extent, the Court followed Jacobs' point of view in the field of the freedom to provide services and later, in *Bosman*, also in respect of the free movement of workers, in line with Advocate General Lenz' Opinion.[164]

Oliver and Roth have made some proposals to align the case law on Articles 29 and 49 EC.[165] Advocates General to whom cases were assigned which related to this topic, like Advocate General Saggio in *Guimont*,[166] unfortunately did not go down the road towards convergence.

C. Indication of the Exception

Three subjects will be discussed under this heading: first, the interpretation of existing exceptions (section V.C.(i)), secondly, invoking new exceptions besides those laid down in the Treaty (section V.C.(ii)) and thirdly, the question whether these exceptions may be invoked in all cases (section V.C.(iii)).

(i) Interpretation of Existing Exceptions

This subject did not present any notable problems, as was also apparent from the Tables 2 and 3 in section IV. The parties concerned usually had invoked one or more exceptions, following which the Court considered, in accordance with the Advocate General, whether the exception was available in the circumstances of the case.

On occasion, one point of discussion was whether the ground for justifying the national measure were not actually economically inspired. In one of the last gambling cases, *Gambelli*,[167] the Court, in line with Advocate General Alber's detailed Opinion, looked through the barrage of exceptions (public policy, public security, combatting fraud, consumer protection) invoked by the other Member States in earlier cases (*Schindler*, *Läära* and *Zenatti*),[168] and unmasked the true interests

---

[162] *Alpine Investments, supra* n. 109.   [163] Oliver, *supra* n. 4, p. 142.

[164] *Bosman, supra* n. 110. Opinion of Advocate General Lenz, pt. 206.

[165] Oliver and Roth, *supra* n. 4, p. 420. See, too, H-W. Roth, Wettbewerb der Mitgliedstaaten oder Wettbewerb der Hersteller? Plädoyer für eine Neubestimmung des Art 34 EWG, (1995) ZHR, p. 78 and P. Oliver, (1999) CML Rev. p. 802.

[166] *Guimont, supra* n. 46. Opinion of Advocate General Saggio, pt. 19.

[167] *Gambelli, supra* n. 36.

[168] Case C-275/92, *Schindler*, (1994) ECR I-1039 (Advocate General Gulmann), Case C-124/97, *Läära*, (1999) ECR I-6067 (Advocate General La Pergola) and Case C-68/98, *Zenatti*, (1999) ECR I-7289 (Advocate General Fennelly).

behind the Italian measure as being economic in character so that they could not be accepted as justification.

In a number of recent cases the Advocate General presented a fresh approach to the existing exceptions. In *Schmidberger*, Advocate General Jacobs considered that the exception relating to the protection of the environment which had been invoked was not applicable in the circumstances of the case, but that the freedom of expression laid down in Article 10 ECHR could provide a ground for justification. The Court adopted this solution proposed by the Advocate General, with an explicit and justified reference to his Opinion.[169] In *Carpenter*, Advocate General Stix-Hackl following a submission made by the British Government applied Article 8 ECHR as ground for justification. She, too, was followed by the Court.[170]

(ii) New Exceptions

A very broad definition of the scope of the prohibitions contained in the basic provisions on the internal market calls for more exceptions than provided for in the Treaty, ie Articles 30, 39 and 46 EC. In the case of Article 57 EC on the free movement of capital there is less need to seek a balance in the same way, as the Member States, in revising the EC Treaty in 1991, added a number of 'imperative requirements' which were relevant to capital movements, such as fiscal controls, to the Treaty.

As was already pointed out (section V.B) in *Cassis de Dijon*, Advocate General Capotorti sought to restore the imbalance caused by the broad definition of Article 28 EC by giving an extensive interpretation to the exception of public policy contained in Article 30 EC.[171] Other Advocates General followed a similar path, like Advocate General Van Gerven in *Fedicine*.[172] He took this approach because the measure involved in this case was discriminatory in character, which meant that it could not be justified on grounds of cultural policy. In the end, the Advocate General reached the conclusion that the proportionality requirement had not been fulfilled. The Court dismissed this point without further ado by observing that cultural policy is not mentioned as a ground for justification in Article 46 EC.

Once it had become clear that the list of imperative requirements named in *Cassis de Dijon* was not exhaustive, the Advocates General accepted various grounds invoked by the Member States if the other conditions for justifying a restriction had been complied with. One illustration of the very many is provided by the *Konle* case in which the objective of town and country planning was accepted by the Court, in accordance with Advocate General La Pergola's Opinion.[173]

---

[169] *Schmidberger, supra* n. 84.
[170] *Carpenter, supra* n. 134. Opinion of Advocate General Stix-Hackl, pt. 25.
[171] *Cassis de Dijon, supra* n. 100.   [172] Case C-17/92, *Fedicine*, (1993) ECR I-2239.
[173] *Konle, supra* n. 105.

(iii) New Exceptions Only Available in Respect of Measures which Apply Without Distinction?

According to the system of the *Cassis de Dijon* judgment, rule of reason exceptions can only be invoked in respect of national measures which apply without distinction to national and imported goods and services. This presents problems particularly for national measures adopted for the protection of the environment. At the time of drafting the EC Treaty this exception was not included as at that time environmental problems were not perceived as being so great that intervention by public authorities was necessary.

In the *Walloon Waste* case, the Court applied an interpretative device to arrive at the conclusion that the national measures at issue were in fact measures which applied without distinction, thus making it possible to apply environmental protection as a ground for justification. Advocate General Jacobs, reasoning along classical lines, had concluded that the environmental protection exception was not available in this case.[174] He was not followed by the Court.

Undoubtedly this crossing of the lines influenced the point of view Advocate General Jacobs defended later in *Dusseldorp*,[175] and *PreussenElektra*,[176] that the imperative requirement, protection of the environment, needs to be given Treaty status and therefore also becomes applicable to measures which do discriminate. The Court did not follow him on this point and perseveres in producing contradictory Judgments in this field.

These judgments do not only concern cases in which the protection of the environment is involved as a ground for justification, but also cases in the field of public health where the exception invoked is the financial stability of the health care system.[177]

D. Proportionality of the National Measure

The two *Hag* cases are a *cause célèbre* in Community law. The reversal of *Hag I*[178] by the Court in *Hag II*,[179] was a direct consequence of Advocate General Jacobs' Opinion in this case.[180] This an example of the Advocate General being 'followed' in its truest sense.

---

[174] Case C-2/90, *Commission v. Belgium*, (1992) ECR I-4431. Opinion of Advocate General Jacobs, pt. 23.

[175] Case C-203/96, *Dusseldorp*, (1998) ECR I-4075. Opinion of Advocate General Jacobs pts. 89–90.

[176] Case C-379/98, *PreussenElektra*, (2001) ECR I-2099. Opinion of Advocate General Jacobs, pts 225–226.

[177] See, on this subject, Oliver and Roth, *supra* n. 4, p. 436. See, e.g., *Smits and Peerbooms, supra* n. 111.   [178] Case 192/73, *Hag I*, (1974) ECR 731.

[179] *Hag II, supra* n. 60.

[180] Fennelly, *supra* n. 77, p. 18; Tridimas, *supra* n. 18, p. 1367; Oliver, *supra* n. 4, p. 350.

In the first years after the common market had been realized in a legal sense (1974–1977), the Court was frequently confronted with the question of how the exception on grounds of public policy should be interpreted in the context of the free movement of persons. Following Opinions of Advocate General Mayras, the Court interpreted this concept restrictively. The *dramatis personae* in these cases were criminals (*Royer*[181]), prostitutes (*Adoui*[182]), drug users (*Bouchereau*[183]), and trade union executives (*Rutili*[184]). In view of the fundamental character of the prohibition of restriction to the free movement of persons, the narrow interpretation of this exception is something like an article of faith for all Advocates General. However, as in all cases involving expressions of faith, the world divides into moderate and orthodox factions.

In a number of cases the Court and the Advocate General disagree about the proportionality issue. This may only concern a technical procedural point that is only relevant in preliminary reference cases. Thus, the Court may choose to leave the application of the proportionality test to the case in hand to the national court, where the Advocate General may already have carried out this exercise. In these circumstances, the Advocate General's Opinion is the only signal the referring court receives from Luxembourg on this point. An illustration of this is provided by the *Torfaen* case, in which Advocate General Van Gerven applies the proportionality test in full, as an alternative point, whereas the Court, after having provided a number of general guidelines, refers this issue back to the national court.[185] Other examples are *Gourmet* (Advocate General Jacobs)[186] and *De Agostini* (Advocate General Jacobs).[187]

In other cases, the disagreement may concern an instrumental issue relating to the degree of public intervention. The requirement of prior authorization is more restrictive than an *ex post facto* inspection or the requirement of a prior declaration. The application of the proportionality test in these cases may lead to a rather detailed examination of both the national measure and the way in which it is applied in practice by the national authorities.

Recent case law on transactions in real estate, eg in *Reisch*[188] and *Ospelt*,[189] shows that Advocate General Geelhoed and the Court have different views on this final element of the internal market check. This subject was also at issue in *Bordessa* (Advocate General Tesauro).[190]

---

[181] Case 45/76, *Royer*, (1976) ECR 497.
[182] Joined Cases 115/81 and 116/81, *Adoui*, (1982) ECR 1665.
[183] Case 30/77, *Bouchereau*, (1977) ECR 1999.
[184] Case 36/75, *Rutili*, (1975) ECR 1219.   [185] *Torfaen, supra* n. 9.
[186] *Gourmet, supra* n. 147.
[187] Joined Cases C-34/95, C-35/95 and C-36/95, *De Agostini*, (1997) ECR I-3843.
[188] *Reisch, supra* n. 127.   [189] *Ospelt, supra* n. 106.   [190] *Bordessa, supra* n. 104.

In some cases a rule of thumb may be useful. In his Opinions in *Gourmetterie van den Burg*,[191] *Grogan*[192] and some Sunday closing cases, such as *Conforama*,[193] Advocate General Van Gerven presented a systematic approach to the proportionality test, in which he distinguishes between the phase of the necessity test and the phase of the proportionality test in the strict sense. As one of Van Gerven's former legal secretaries, Wouters remarks, this test may prove to be a useful instrument for the Court in cases, like *Schindler*[194] in which it only carries out the necessity test and not the proportionality test in the strict sense.[195] As such, Wouters is right, although there are other cases, like *Müller-Fauré*,[196] in which the Court applies the proportionality test in full. One must not forget, as Judge Timmermans once observed in a textbook, that the Court does not write textbooks.[197]

VI. To Follow or Not to Follow

In this section a number of general observations will be made on the basis of the analyses in sections IV and V. These observations will focus on two situations: first, the question whether or not the Court follows the Advocate General (VI.A) and secondly, the question whether or not the Advocates General follow each other (VI.B).

A. The Court does or does not Follow the Advocate General

In his farewell address to the Court, Advocate General Lagrange remarks that it is necessary for the Court and the Advocates General to agree on:

'principes essentiels de nature à orienter définitivement la jurisprudence, notamment quant au droit communautaire tel qu'il se dégage des Traités. Il est certain, en effet, qu'un désaccord fondamental à cet égard avec les avocats généraux aurait, en parlysant leur personnalité, considérablement amoindri l'importance et utilité de leur fonction. Fort heureusement, ce ne fut pas le cas.'[198]

This statement was made in 1964, years before the transitional period for the common market had ended and the first judgment on non-tariff barriers to trade had been given. It may be derived from the quantitative and the qualitative analysis presented in this article that the Court and the Advocates General agree on most major issues. 'Fort heureusement' to use Lagrange's expression.

---

[191] Case 169/89, *Gourmetterie van den Burg*, (1990) ECR I-2143.
[192] *Grogan, supra* n. 133.
[193] Case C-312/89, *Conforama*, (1991) ECR I-997. Opinion of Advocate General Van Gerven, pt. 14.					[194] *Schindler, supra* n. 168.
[195] Wouters, De Advocaat-Generaal gehoord, *supra* n. 4, p. 57.
[196] Case C-385/99, *Müller-Fauré*, (2003) ECR I-4509.
[197] R.H. Lauwaars en C.W.A. Timmermans, *Europees gemeenschapsrecht in kort bestek*, (6th edn, Groningen, 2003), p. 198.					[198] Lagrange, *supra* n. 1, p. 4.

A number of variants emerge from the analysis which make it possible to describe the relationship between the Court and the Advocates General in more systematic terms. These variants confirm the thesis defended above (see section II) that being followed is but one aspect of having influence.

(i) Following in the True Sense

In this case either no case law of the Court exists on the subject-matter or it does, but the Advocate General believes that it should be led in a different direction.

If the Court agrees with the Advocate General in such a situation, this is what we would term being followed in the true sense. An example of this is the *Hag II* judgment.[199] If, on the other hand, the Court disagrees, this is the case of the Advocate General not being followed. An illustration of this is *Keck*.[200] In both these cases the Advocate General played an innovative role (see section II.A).

Where the Advocate General is followed in the true sense, this is usually hailed in academic writing, but there are very few cases which belong to this category, at least in the field of the internal market.

(ii) Following Indirectly

This variant concerns the situation in which in Case A, the Court does not follow the Advocate General who has presented an Opinion in Case A, but the Advocate General who has presented an Opinion in Case B.

An illustration of this situation is provided by Advocate General Tesauro's Opinion in *Hünermund*, which was referred to earlier (section I). In *Keck*, the Court followed Tesauro's Opinion and not the Opinion presented by Advocate General Van Gerven.

This type of following the Advocate General is most exceptional. It presupposes that there is a situation in which an innovation in the case law is imminent, whilst simultaneously other similar cases are ripe for decision and have been assigned to different Advocates General. This type of cross-fertilisation also occurred, albeit less conspicuously, in the electricity cases (Advocate General Cosmas)[201] and in *Franzén* (Advocate General Elmer).[202] Both cases concerned the compatibility of national monopolies with Articles 28 and 31 EC. The Court did not follow either of the Advocates General in these cases (eg on the points relating to Articles 28 and 31 EC).

(iii) Following at a Later Stage

Sometimes the Court does not follow the Advocate General in the case at hand, but later in a different case. This fact may incite the Advocate General, primarily, to

---

[199] *Hag II, supra* n. 60.   [200] *Keck, supra* n. 10.
[201] eg, Case C-157/94, *Commission v. Netherlands*, (1997) ECR I-5699.
[202] Case C-189/95, *Franzén*, (1997) ECR I-5909.

insist on the position he defended in his earlier Opinion, but, in the alternative, to discuss the case in the light of the Court's judgment in the first case. It would seem to me that it must give the Advocate General great satisfaction where the Court decides to adopt the views he expounded earlier in a later case: you see, I was right after all!

A striking example of an Advocate General being proved right at a later stage is Advocate General Slynn's Opinion in *Cinéthèque* on the relationship between the internal market rules and the European Convention of Human Rights. He was not followed in that case. In the later *ERT*[203] case, Advocate General Lenz referred to the Court's judgment in *Cinéthèque*. However, the Court decided to follow the solution proposed by Advocate General Slynn in his *Cinéthèque* Opinion. As it happens, former Advocate General Slynn sat as a judge in the *ERT* case. I will make some remarks on this coming and going of Advocates General in the conclusion (section VII.A).

(iv) Not Following

The Court and a number of Advocates General have different views on a number of significant points relating to the internal market. I would refer to the scope of the internal situation (section V.A.(i)), the *Keck* approach (section V.A.(ii)) and the applicability of imperative, requirements in respect of discriminatory national measures (section V.C.(iii)). Until now the Court has not developed a clear and consistent approach to these topics. It is difficult for an Advocate General to 'follow' a vacillating Court. This is a point of concern both for the Court and the Advocates General.

In my view it is the task of the Advocates General in a situation of such uncertainty in the case law to work constructively towards a solution. This means that the Advocate General must prepare a case carefully, produce a well-reasoned Opinion in which he places the problem in a broader context and, if necessary, indicate a new direction for the case law: the four tasks of the Advocate General (section II).

This positive approach may be illustrated by reference to the Opinions of Advocate General Lenz in *Bosman*[204] and in the *Spanish Strawberry* case.[205] In both of these cases the Advocate General's proposals set the stage for the Court handing down a leading judgment. Taking the *acquis communautaire* as his point of departure, the Advocate General succeeded in both cases in being innovative, expressing his own personal views, though placing them in a broader Community context.

A less positive approach, in my opinion, is the way in which Advocate General Ruiz-Jarabo Colomer dealt with the five *Golden Share* cases[206] and a number of health insurance cases. In both fields he reached the conclusion, presumably following his own personal convictions, that public interests ought to prevail over

---

[203] Case C-260/89, *ERT*, (1991) ECR I-2925.   [204] *Bosman, supra* n. 110.
[205] Case 265/95, *Commission v. France*, (1997) ECR I-6959.
[206] *Golden Share* cases, *supra* n. 73 and 75.

the operation of the market. This question of economic policy is the core of the interpretation given to the prohibitions in the basic provisions of the internal market and the exceptions to these.[207]

I do not object to an Advocate General expressing a personal opinion and that this opinion may be diametrically opposed to the established views of the Court. This is what happened in *Müller-Fauré*[208] and the Portugese, French and Belgian *Golden Share* cases. However, where the Court decides not to follow the Advocate General, I think that when the same question arises in a later case which is assigned to him, this Advocate General at the very least ought to discuss the position adopted by the Court, if only as an alternative point. Advocate General Ruiz-Jarabo Colomer did this in *Smits and Peerbooms*,[209] but he did not in the two subsequent *Golden Share* cases against Spain and the United Kingdom. Be that as it may I do agree with the First Advocate General granting Advocate General Ruiz-Jarabo Colomer a second round in the case against the United Kingdom, so that he had the opportunity to reply to the Court. In order to give a balanced approach, another Advocate General could have given an opinion in the case against Spain. Advocates General are not to be given cases in which their home Member State is directly involved.[210]

Consequently, I do not agree with the *Drei Glocken* case being assigned to Advocate General Mancini. The Court did not follow his Opinion in this case. A case concerning the quality of spaghetti obviously goes to an Italian's culinary heart, which may inhibit the smooth operation of the legal mind. Advocate General Mancini argued forcefully that the Italian measure involved was compatible with Community law as it was justified in the interests of the protection of the consumer. The Court, however, ruled, in accordance with its judgment in *Reinheitsgebot*,[211] that it did not comply with Articles 28 and 30 EC. Mancini, who had visited a Luxembourg supermarket and reported on his findings there in his Opinion and in that context compared the Commission with the sleeping fisherman in Hemingways' 'The Old Man and the Sea',[212] may have been an adviser to the Court in this case, he was not an impartial adviser.

(v) Following in Appearance

In this situation the Court's case law on a certain subject is settled. If the Advocate General merely applies this case law to a new case and the Court does the same, it

---

[207] See on this M. Poiares Maduro, *We the Court: the European Court of Justice and the European Economic Situation: a critical reading of Article 30 of the EC Treaty*, (Oxford, 1998).

[208] *Müller-Fauré, supra* n. 196.

[209] *Smits and Peerbooms, supra* n. 111. Opinion of Advocate General Ruiz-Jarabo Colomer, pt. 50.   [210] Ruiz-Jarabo Colomer and López Escudero, *supra* n. 29, pp. 529–530.

[211] Case 178/84, *Commission v. Germany*, (1987) ECR 1227.

[212] Case 407/85, *Drei Glocken*, (1988) ECR 4233. Opinion of Advocate General Mancini, pt. 14.

cannot be said that the Court is following the Advocate General. It follows him in appearance only. Rather it is the Advocate General who is following the Court! This frequently happens in cases attributed to Chambers of five or three judges where the case law is settled. Here the Advocate General fulfils his classical role of preparing the case (section II.A).

B. Advocates General do or do not Follow Each Other

Sometimes Advocates General disagree among themselves, as is apparent from their divergent views in *Keck*-type cases. I did not research this aspect of Advocates General either following or not following each other systematically, but as a 'by catch' of the main subject of analysis, I can make a few observations on this topic.

Just as the Court never states that it is not going to follow the Advocate General, an Advocate General usually will never state that he is not following his colleague. One exception to this is Advocate General Gulmann's Opinion in *Bostock*.[213] In his Opinion in *Konstantinidis*, Advocate General Jacobs had expressed the view that an employed person or a self-employed person who relies on the free movement of persons in connection with employment or an occupation in another Member State is entitled to assume that, wherever he goes to earn a living in the European Community, he will be treated in accordance with a common code of fundamental values, in particular those laid down in ECHR.[214] In the final footnote to his Opinion in *Bostock*, Advocate General Gulmann cites this statement by Advocate General Jacobs and adds to this 'that the Court did not adopt a view on that suggestion, which in my opinion is, too far reaching'.[215]

The Opinions of the Advocates General gain force where they refer to each other explicitly and follow each other. A fine recent example of this is an Opinion presented by Advocate General Maduro, who makes his mark in the *Carbonati Apuani* case by analysing the various points of view expressed by the Court and the Advocates General on the internal situation and then states his own opinion on the matter.[216]

According to this *esprit de corps* view, in the electricity cases,[217] in which the question was raised as to whether electricity should be considered to be a 'good', Advocate General Cosmas should have referred not only to the Court's judgment in the *Walloon Waste* case, but also to Advocate General Jacobs' Opinion which guided the Court in this case.

---

[213] I have taken this example from Oliver, *supra* n. 4, p. 12.
[214] Case C-168/91, *Konstantinidis*, (1993) ECR I-1198. Opinon of Advocate General Jacobs, pt. 46.
[215] Case C-2/92, *Bostock*, (1994) ECR I-955. Opinion of Advocate General Gulmann, pt. 31.
[216] *Carbonati Apuani*, *supra* n. 131.
[217] *Commission v. Netherlands*, *supra* n. 201. Opinion of Advocate General Cosmas, pt. 12.

VII.　The Role of the Advocate General in the Functioning of the Internal Market

Which general conclusions can be drawn on the role played by the Advocates General in the course of the years in respect of the establishment and the functioning of the internal market? In order to provide an answer to this, the question must be sub-divided into two other questions: have the Advocates General had the opportunity to give their views on the legal aspects of the internal market (section VII.A)? and have they seized this opportunity (section VII.B)?

A.　The Advocate General and the Internal Market

The point of departure of this article was the presumption that all Advocates General have had the opportunity to present Opinions on the realization of the internal market. This presumption may be now be refined.

(i)　All Advocates General are Equal, but Some are More Equal Than Others

All Advocates General were given the opportunity, first by the President of the Court and since 1974 from the First Advocate General, to present Opinions on non-tariff barriers and the establishment of the internal market.

The fact that the five large Member States have a permanent Advocate General at the Court and the other Member States only enjoy this privilege on a rotational basis, means that there is an inbuilt inequality between the five large Member States on the one hand and the smaller Member States and the newly acceded Member States, who have yet to provide an Advocate General, on the other.

Consequently, some Advocates General who have held the position for many years, have been able to make a significant contribution to the development of the case law on the internal market. For the 1970s I would name Advocates General Mayras and Trabucchi, and for the 1980s Advocate General Slynn. Advocate General Jacobs presented a number of innovating Opinions in the 1990s which sometimes were followed (*Hag II*[218]) and sometimes were not followed by the Court (*Walloon Waste*,[219] *Leclerc*[220]).

It is more difficult for Advocates General who have held the position for a shorter period—in most cases they are from the smaller Member States[221]—to

---

[218] *Hag II, supra* n. 60.　　　[219] *Walloon Waste, supra* n. 174.　　　[220] *Leclerc, supra* n. 121.

[221] In his preface to De Advocaat Generaal gehoord, *supra* n. 4, former Judge Kapteyn criticizes this situation. Cf. Ruiz-Jarabo Colomer and López Escudero, *supra* n. 29, p. 529. It is also difficult to reconcile this situation with Art. 223 EC, fourth paragraph ('the retiring Advocates General shall be eligible for reappointment'). See Hackspiel, *supra* n. 25, p. 337.

make their mark.[222] It is the responsibility of the First Advocate General to ensure that sufficient cases on the internal market are attributed to the group of rotating Advocates General to enable them to develop a broad and balanced view on various issues in this field.

Advocate General VerLoren van Themaat, who first as a high official in the European Commission and next as an academic[223] contributed to the genesis of the *Dassonville* case law, did not have much opportunity during his short term as Advocate General to develop his views. Only a few of the cases he dealt with concerned free movement issues (*Cullet*,[224] *Oosthoek*,[225] *Beele*[226]). However, an article which he published in Dutch in 1980[227] and which was later translated into French, has circulated among the Members of the Court and may be regarded as a pseudo-Opinion on this subject.[228]

(ii) Advocates General Who Become Judges and Vice Versa

It is not only the interaction on questions of substance which matters, sometimes personal transfers occur. Three Advocates General (Mancini, Slynn, Gulmann) became judges, whereas two judges (Trabucchi, Capotorti) went in the opposite direction. La Pergola started as a judge, then became an Advocate General and subsequently was re-appointed as a judge.

It is difficult to assess the impact of this coming and going. Most indications may be found in the Opinions of former judges who later became Advocates General, as in the latter function they express their personal views. In comparing *Grundig and Consten* with *Dassonville* (see section I), it appeared that Trabucchi, who was the Judge-Rapporteur in *Grundig*, did not mention the *Dassonville*-formula, which was inspired by *Grundig*, explicitly in his Opinion in *Dassonville*.

Whenever an Advocate General becomes a judge, it would seem obvious that he would defend the views he expressed as an Advocate General during the deliberations of the Court. Whether this is or is not the case belongs to the confidentiality of the deliberation room. As the Advocate General in *Delhaize* Gulmann

---

[222] R. Barents, Procedures en procesvoering voor het Hof van Justitie van de Europese Gemeenschappen en het Gerecht van Eerste Aanleg van de EG, Deventer, 1996, p. 18.

[223] P. VerLoren van Themaat, (1967) SEW, p. 632 and (1970) SEW, p. 258. For a discussion in English of these two articles which were published in Dutch, see, A. Meij and J. Winter, 'Measures having an effect equivalent to quantitative restrictions', (1976) CML Rev p. 79. L.W. Gormley, *Prohibiting Restrictions on Trade within the EEC*, (The Hague, 1985), Ch. 2.

[224] Case 231/83, *Cullet*, (1985) ECR 305.   [225] Case 286/81, *Oosthoek*, (1982) ECR 4575.

[226] Case 6/81, *Beele*, (1982) ECR 707.

[227] P. VerLoren van Themaat, 'De artikelen 30–36 van het EEG/Verdrag', *Rechtsgeleerd Magazijn Themis*, (1980) p. 368.

[228] This text was published later, see P. VerLoren van Themaat, 'La libre circulation des marchandises après l'arrêt Cassis de Dijon', (1982) CDE p. 123. See, too, P. VerLoren van Themaat and L.W. Gormley, 'Prohibiting Restriction of Free Trade within the Community: Articles 30–36 of the EEC Treaty', (1981) *Northwestern Journal of International Law and Business*, p. 577.

considered that Article 29 EC had been breached in that case and the Court followed him on this.[229] In the subsequent case of *Belgium v. Spain* which essentially concerned the same problem, the Court, in accordance with Advocate General Saggio's Opinion, ruled that the Spanish measure concerned was not incompatible with Article 29 EC.[230] Gulmann was the Judge-Rapporteur in this case. I was not present in the deliberation room and do not know if Advocate General Gulmann agreed with Judge Gulmann. Perhaps former Advocate General Gulmann relied on the observation made by Advocate General Saggio: 'It might appear that the Court took a different view in its Judgment in *Delhaize*, a view that is inconsistent with the analysis now proposed, but on closer examination it is clear that the inconsistency is only apparent.'[231]

Judge La Pergola did not sit in *Kaba II*, given the fact that the central question in this case was the allegedly incorrect rendition of the facts in Advocate General La Pergola's Opinion in *Kaba I* (see section II).

B. The Opinions of the Advocates General and the Internal Market

Following Advocate General Van Gerven's analysis, the Advocate General has a supporting task and a task which is aimed at shaping the law (see section II).

Each Advocate General exercises these functions in his own personal manner. In this respect, he depends on the cases which are allocated to him. If he only has to deal with standard cases, the best he can do is to analyze the case in the broader context of similar cases, but he will not be able to innovate. The situation is different for judges. In important cases, which for that reason are dealt with by the Grand Chamber, every judge can express his views.

In theory, it should be easier for an Advocate General to play an innovating role than for the Court. An Advocate General has much more room for manoeuvre than a Chamber of the Court and certainly more than the Full Court.[232] Presumably this is a relevant factor in the validity cases analysed above (see section IV.A).

In practice the situation is different. In explaining the caution of certain Advocates General to propose new solutions, Brown & Jacobs observe: 'It may also simply be easier for the Judges collectively to advance further than an individual Advocate General.'[233] How difficult is it then for an individual Advocate General to deviate from the settled case law?

(i) Regularly Innovative, Often Refining, Sometimes Deviating Opinions

If the leading judgments of the Court are compared with the Opinions of the Advocates General it is striking how innovative the Advocates General have been

---

[229] Case C-47/90, *Delhaize*, (1992) ECR I-3669.
[230] Case C-388/95, *Belgium v. Spain*, (2000) ECR I-3123.
[231] Case C-388/95, *supra* n. 230. Opinion of Advocatea General Saggio, pt. 32.
[232] According to Tridimas, *supra* n. 18, p. 1359.
[233] Brown & Jacobs, *supra* n. 5, p. 71.

in important cases concerning the internal market. I refer to a number of examples drawn from the analysis carried out in section V. In *Dassonville*, Advocate General Trabucchi reached the conclusion that, besides discriminatory measures, national measures which applied without distinction to national and imported goods were caught by the prohibition of Article 28 EC. This point of view was supported by Advocate General Capotorti in *Cassis de Dijon*. In *Torfaen*, Advocate General Van Gerven did present an innovative point of view, but in *Keck* the Court did not follow Van Gerven's Opinion. Instead it adopted the different views presented by Advocate General Tesauro in his innovative Opinion in *Hünermund*. As to the free movement of workers, Advocate General Lenz' Opinion in *Bosman* co-determined the Court's stance on Article 39 EC. The same applies to Advocate General Jacobs' Opinion in *Alpine Investments*. Advocates General also played an important role in respect of applying the ECHR in the context of Community law, like Advocate General Slynn in *Cinéthèque*, Advocate General Jacobs in *Schmidberger* and Advocate General Stix-Hackl in *Carpenter*.

In very many cases, Advocates General, through their meticulous interpretation of the Court's case law and their analysis of legal writing, have contributed to further refining the course taken by the Court. From this point of view the Advocates General were constructive commentators of the Court's judgments. Examples of this are provided by Advocate General Van Gerven's Opinion in *Vlassopoulou*,[234] Advocate General La Pergola's Opinion in *Centros*[235] and Advocate General Ruiz-Jarabo Colomer's Opinion in *Überseering*.[236]

In some cases Advocates General adopted a position which deviated from the position adopted by the Court. I am not referring to cases in which the Advocate General was surprised by the Court, like Advocate General Capotorti in the *Groenveld* Case (section V.B.(ii)). In these cases the Advocate General followed the line set by the Court up to the penultimate case, and then the Court changed its course. The cases I am referring to are those in which the Advocate General deviated from settled case law, thus giving the Court the opportunity to follow the Opinion 'in the true sense'. Examples of this situation are provided by the Opinions of Jacobs in *Hag II* (section V.D), Mancini in *Drei Glocken* (section VI.A), Van Gerven in *Torfaen* (section V.A.(ii)) and Ruiz-Jarabo Colomer in the *Golden Share* cases (section VI.A). The Court only followed its innovating Advocate General in *Hag II*.

(ii) Having Influence and Being Followed: A Dynamic Process

According to Article 222 EC, the Advocate General assists the Court by making reasoned submissions on the cases brought before it. Through this assistance the

---

234 Case C-340/89, *Vlassopoulou*, (1991) ECR I-2357.
235 Case C-212/97, *Centros*, (1999) ECR I-1459.
236 Case C-208/00, *Überseering*, (2002) ECR I-9919.

Advocate General influences the decision ultimately to be taken by the Court. It may then be determined *ex post facto* that the Court followed its Advocate General, either in the true sense or in appearance only. As Advocate General Lagrange put it in the lines quoted at the beginning of this article: 'que les conclusions soient conforme ou contraires à la solution adoptée, celle-ci se trouve éclairée et même confortée, que se soit par analogie ou par opposition.'

The qualitative analysis in section V demonstrates that in many cases the Advocate General's influence is not limited to the case in which he presented an Opinion. It is clear that the judicial process is a dynamic process. What is decisive is not so much the number of Opinions in general and in leading cases in particular which are followed by the Court, but the interaction between the Court and the Advocates General on questions of substance in the course of the years.

VIII. The Influence of the Advocates General on the Internal Market: Is the Mosaic Complete?

Nearly all cases concerning the internal market are brought before the Court of Justice and not the Court of First Instance.[237] Seen from this perspective, it may be said that the Advocate General in a certain sense delivers a first instance judgment.[238] The comparison is not wholly justified as the Advocate General cannot be considered to be a single judge court. He is, according to Article 222 EC, an independent adviser of the Court.

From the analysis in sections IV and V, four short periods emerge during which the Court and the Advocates General worked intensively on the development of the rules on the internal market. The dynamic process analysed in section VII can be illustrated by looking at the work of the Court and the Advocates General in these periods (see section VIII.A). The legal work, the mosaic, is not yet complete. On the contrary the influence of the Court and the Advocates General on the functioning of the internal market can still grow (see section VIII.B).

A. Four Periods of Great Dynamism

(i) 1974–1976

During this period the first interpretation of the prohibitions in the basic provisions on free movement was given (*Dassonville*,[239] *Van Binsbergen*,[240]

---

[237] Exceptions to this are: Case T-69/89, *Magill*, (1991) ECR II-485, Case T-113/96, *Dubois*, (1998) ECR II-125 and Case T-266/97, *VTM* (1999) ECR II-2329. In its judgment in Case T-313/02 of 30 September 2004, *Meca-Medina*, the Court of first Instance refers to the opinion of Advocate General Lenz in *Bosman*, Advocate General Cosmas in *Deliège* and Advocate General Alber in *Lehtonen*, see pt 42.   [238] Brown & Jacobs, *supra* n. 5, p. 20; Dashwood, *supra* n. 6, p. 124.
[239] *Dassonville*, *supra* n. 8.   [240] Case 33/74, *Van Binsbergen*, (1974) ECR 1299.

Reyners[241]) and the important public policy exception was clarified (*Van Duyn*,[242] *Rutili*,[243] *Royer*[244]).

This period came a few years after the completion, legally speaking, of the common market on 31 December 1969. The judgments addressed the issues of the direct effect of the basic provisions on free movement in the Treaty, the broad definition of the prohibition in these basic provisions and the restrictive interpretation of the exceptions. The Court and the Advocates General agreed on the essential points.

(ii) 1978–1979

The second period focused more on the further refinement of the scope of the prohibition in the basic free movement provisions (*Van Wesemael*,[245] *Cassis de Dijon*,[246] *Auer*,[247] *Groenveld*[248]) and to deal with certain 'growing pains'. such as reverse discrimination (*Knoors*[249] and *Peureux*[250]) and the internal situation (*Knoors* and *Saunders*[251]).

In the light of the passiveness of the Council of Ministers, which was paralyzed by the unanimity requirement, and of the attitude of the judges then in office, this period constituted the heyday of judicial activism.

In this period the Court and the Advocates General sometimes agreed (*Cassis de Dijon*, *Knoors*) and sometimes disagreed (*Saunders*, *Groenveld*). It may be inferred from some lines in Advocate General Mayras' Opinion in *Peureux* that he had consulted with Advocates General Reischl (*Knoors*) and Warner (*Auer*) and that they had all arrived at the same conclusion.[252]

(iii) 1993–1995

In the third period, the start of which was hailed by Reich as the November Revolution,[253] the prohibition of Article 28 EC was curtailed (*Keck*, its precursors and successors) and in later case law (*Alpine Investments*, *Bosman* and *Leclerc*) new solutions were explored (market access) in order to define the scope of the prohibition in the basic provisions.

In line with the principle of subsidiarity which was introduced into the EC Treaty by the Treaty of Maastricht, the Court, along with the Advocates General, exercised more restraint in this period. This is a functional interpretation. It may be inferred from the *petite histoire* recounted by those involved,[254] that this was a conscious choice which was supported by the majority of the Court. Advocate General Van Gerven and quite a few of his later colleagues did

---

[241] Case 2/74, *Reyners*, (1974) ECR 631.   [242] Case 41/74, *Van Duyn*, (1974) ECR 1337.
[243] *Rutili*, *supra* n. 184.   [244] *Royer*, *supra* n. 181.   [245] *Van Wesemael*, *supra* n. 158.
[246] *Rewe*, *supra* n. 100.   [247] Case 136/78, *Auer*, (1979) ECR 437.
[248] *Groenveld*, *supra* n. 108.   [249] *Knoors*, *supra* n. 122.
[250] Case 86/78, *Peureux*, (1979) ECR 897.   [251] *Saunders*, *supra* n. 123.
[252] Case 86/78, *Peureux* (1979) ECR 921.
[253] N. Reich, 'The November Revolution of the Court of Justice: Keck, Meng and Audi Revisited', (1994) CML Rev. p. 459.   [254] eg, Joliet, *supra* n. 61.

not and do not agree with this transition. In contrast with the preceding two periods the Court and the Advocates General did not form a closed front during this revolution.

(iv) 2002–2004

At present the Court and the Advocates General are in a fourth period. This period focuses on two groups of people: on the one hand, the 'haves', like *Reisch*[255] and *Ospelt*,[256] who invoke the provisions on freedom of establishment and the free movement of capital; and on the other hand, the 'have nots', like *Akrich*,[257] *Carpenter*,[258] and *Chen*,[259] persons from third countries who through family ties have a bond with the Community.

The first group consists of persons who may be regarded as the classical inhabitants of the internal market, who following the introduction of directly effective provisions on the free movement of capital by the Treaty of Maastricht, invoke these provisions to be able to build a second house or to neutralise the effects of their removal to a Member State with a more moderate fiscal climate. The latter situation is usually at the origin of cases involving Dutch nationals living in Belgium.[260]

The second group consists of new inhabitants of the internal market, who come from third countries, but have a bond with the Community. eg through marriage to a national of a Member State.

Both groups of cases concern the relationship between the provisions on the free movement of persons and the European Convention of Human Rights (right to property, right to family life). The Court and the Advocates General agree as to the general line to be followed. The case law in respect of the 'have nots' is still in a state of continuous development.

B. Unfinished Mosaic

'The legal system can be compared to an unfinished mosaic: every new stone (legislative rule, judicial decision, authoritative opinion) must fit in the existing pattern; but at the same time, it adds to this pattern and develops it'. Koopmans borrowed this metaphor from a conversation he had with his colleague Mancini.[261]

The Advocate General, too, as an impartial adviser[262] contributes to completing this mosaic. He is independent from the Court and the parties to the proceedings, but not from the Treaty.[263]

---

[255] *Reisch, supra* n. 127.   [256] *Ospelt, supra* n. 106.
[257] Case C-109/01, *Akrich*, (2003) ECR I-9607.   [258] *Carpenter, supra* n. 134.
[259] Case 200/02, *Chen*, (2004) ECR I-9925.
[260] eg, Case C-385/00, *De Groot*, (2002) ECR I-11819.   [261] Koopmans, *supra* n. 2, p. 49.
[262] Brown & Jacobs, *supra* n. 5, p. 64; Darmon, *supra* n. 16, p. 433.
[263] Fennelly, *supra* n. 77, p. 14.

From a legal point of view, the internal market has been a fact since 1 January 1993. As it evolves, the case law reveals that not all the stones of the mosaic are in place and even that some stones need replacing or placed elsewhere in the pattern.

The accession of 10 new Member States and the accompanying transitional problems will give rise to new case law. Social developments, particularly those arising from aliens and asylum policy, will present new challenges to the Court.

According to Article 20, final paragraph, of the Statute of the Court, where it considers that a case raises no new point of law, the Court may decide, after having heard the Advocate General, that the case will be determined without a submission by the Advocate General. It is to be expected that this possibility will gradually be used more often in the future so that the Court and the Advocates General can focus their attention on cases which are important from a legal point of view. Advocate General Mischo expressed the view, at his (second) farewell, that this will enhance the position of the Advocates General.[264]

As a result of the influx of many new judges, the Court at present is in a phase of transition. In this situation, the relatively stable group of Advocates General, as representatives of the *acquis jurisprudentiel*,[265] can play a useful role in interpreting the core of the *acquis communautaire*, the basic provisions of the internal market, and where necessary to uphold them and defend them.

---

[264] Address by Mr. Mischo, First Advocate General at the solemn session of 6 October 2003. See *Agence Europe*, 9 October 2003, p. 16.

[265] In the words of Tridimas, *supra* n. 18, p. 1385.

No-One Slips Through the Net? Latest Developments, and Non-Developments, in the European Court of Justice's Jurisprudence on Art. 230(4) EC

Stefan Enchelmaier *

I. Introduction: The Court's Judgments in *Jégo-Quéré* and *Unión de Pequeños Agricultores*

The capacity to bring actions (or *locus standi*) in order to challenge the validity of secondary Community law, accorded to individuals in Art. 230(4) EC,[1] has been the subject of many academic studies.[2] Most commentators are critical of the European Court of Justice's (ECJ's) approach, which they see as too restrictive. The criticism is fairly old, yet the Court for decades seemed unperturbed. This

---

* Dr. jur. (Bonn), LL.M. (Edinburgh), M.A. (Oxon.), Senior Research Fellow, Max-Planck-Institute for Intellectual Property, Competition and Tax Law, Munich. Thanks are due to Katja Ziegler, Andreas von Medem, Derrick Wyatt and Diamond Ashiagbor for their comments on the draft of this chapter. It is dedicated to the memory of the late Dr Sally Ball, Trinity College, Oxford.
1 Previously Art. 173(2), later Art. 173(4) EEC.
2 Without any claim to completeness, the following may be mentioned: Albors-Llorens, *Private Parties in European Community Law*, (OUP 1996); Arnull, 'Private Applicants and the Action for Annulment under Art. 173 of the EC Treaty', (1995) 32 CML Rev 7; Arnull, 'Private Applicants and the Action for Annulment since Codorníu', (2001) 38 CML Rev 7; Cooke, 'Locus standi of private parties under Art. 173(4)', [1997] IJEL 4; Craig, 'Legality, Standing, and Substantive Review in Community Law', (1994) 14 OJLS 507; Daig, 'Zum Klagerecht von Privatpersonen nach Art. 173(2) EWGV, 146 EAGV', in: Aubin *et al.* (eds.), Festschrift für Otto Riese, (Heidelberg, 1964), p. 187; Harding, 'The private interest in challenging Community action', (1980) 5 EL Rev 354; Harlow, 'Towards a Theory of Access to the European Court of Justice', (1992) 12 YEL 213; Lenaerts and Corthant, 'Judicial Review as a Contribution to the Development of Europe an Constitutionalism', (2003) 22 YEL 1; Moitinho De Almeida, 'Le recours en annulation des particuliers (art. 173, 2ème alinéa, du traité CE): nouvelle réflexions sur l'expression "la concernent . . . individuellement"' 'in: Lutter *et al* (eds.)., Festschrift für Ulrich Everling, (Baden-Baden, 1995), p. 849; Neuwahl, 'Article 174 Par. 4 EC: Past, Present, and Possible Future', (1996) 21 ELR 17; Nihoul, 'La recevabilité des recours en annulation introduits par un particulier à l'encontre d'un acte communautaire de portée générale', (1994) 30 Revue Trimestrielle de Droit Européen 171; Ragolle, 'Access to justice for private applicants in the Community legal order: recent (r)evolutions', (2003) 28 ELRev 90; Rasmussen, 'Why is

seems odd, given that the Court has not been shy, particularly during the 1990s, to introduce important innovations into other areas of the law. Notable examples are its jurisprudence on Member States' liability for breaches of Community law (*Francovich* and its progeny),[3] national procedural law (*Factortame II*[4]), and free movement (*Keck*,[5] and *Angonese*[6]). Some of these developments were instigated by voices in the academic literature.[7] Sheer judicial conservatism might, of course, be one explanation for the absence of development in the Court's case law on Art. 230(4). It is, however, worth asking whether the jurisprudence is as problematic as is made out, or whether the ECJ might not have better reasons to 'stick to its guns' than it is often given credit for.

Taking stock is justified for another reason, too: the year 2002 saw two judgments in short sequence, in cases *Jégo-Quéré*[8] and *Unión de Pequeños Agricultores*,[9] which brought new momentum to the debate. These cases, however, appear to point in opposite directions: the first, *Jégo-Quéré*, breaks new ground, whereas the second, *Unión de Pequeños Agricultores*, refuses to do so. This article will analyse the two cases as part of a wider contemplation of the judicial system as established by the Treaty.

II. The Case Law before *Jégo-Quéré* and *Unión de Pequeños Agricultores*

Art. 230(4) provides: 'Any natural or legal person may [. . .] institute proceedings against a decision addressed to that person or against a decision which, although

---

Art. 173 interpreted against private applicants?' (1980) 5 EL Rev 112; Temple Lang, 'Actions for declarations that Community Regulations are invalid: the duties of national courts under Article 10 EC', (2003) 28 EL Rev 102; Usher, 'Direct and individual concern—an effectice remedy or a conventional solution?' (2003) 28 EL Rev 575; Vandersanden, 'Pour un élargissement du droit des particuliers d'agir en annulation contre des actes autres que les décisions qui leur sont addressées', (1995) 31 Cahiers de Droit Européen 535; von Danwitz, 'Die Garantie effektiven Rechtsschutzes im Recht der Europäischen Gemeinschaft', [1993] Neue Juristische Wochenschrift 1108; Waelbroeck, 'Editorial—Le droit au recours juridictionnel effectif du particulier—trois pas en avant, deux pas en arrière', (2002) 38 Cahiers de Droit Européen, p. 3; Waelbroeck and Verheyden, 'Les conditions de recevabilité des recours en annulation des particuliers contre les actes normatifs communautaire', (1995) 31 Cahiers de Droit Européen 399; Ward, 'Judicial Review and the Rights of Private Parties in EC Law', (OUP, 2000). Ward, 'Locus Standi under Article 230(4) of the EC Treaty: Crafting a Coherent Test for a "Wobbly Polity"', (2003) 22 YEL 45. Older references can be found in Rasmussen, *loc. cit.*, p. 113, fn. 6.

   [3] Joined Cases C-6/90 and 9/90, *Francovich and Bonifaci*, [1991] ECR I-5357; C-46/93 and 48/93, *Brasserie de Pêcheur and Factortame*, [1996] ECR I-1029; C-319/96, *Brinkmann Tabakfabriken*, [1998] ECR I-5255; this case has now started to feed back into the jurisprudence on Arts. 235/288(2) EC (non-contractual liability of the Community), on which it was originally modeled: Case C-312/00P, *Commission* v *Camar et al.*, [2002] ECR I-11355, para. 54.

   [4] Case C-213/89, *Factortame* (No. 2), [1990] ECR I-2433, paras. 19–22.

   [5] Joined Cases C-267/91 and 268/91, *Keck and Mithouard*, [1993] ECR I-6079.

   [6] Case-281/98, *Roman Angonese* v *Cassa di Risparmio di Bolzano*, [2000] ECR I-4139.

   [7] Eric White, 'In search of the limits to Art. 30 EEC', [1989] 26 CML Rev 235, and Josephine Steiner, 'Drawing the line: Uses and abuses of Art. 30', [1992] 29 CML Rev 749, for instance, inspired the Court's judgment in *Keck*.

   [8] Case T-177/01, *Jégo-Quéré* v *Commission*, [2002] ECR II-2365.

   [9] Case C-50/00P, *Unión de Pequeños Agricultores* v *Council*, [2002] ECR I-6677.

in the form of a regulation or a decision addressed to another person, is of direct and individual concern to the former.' Two elements of this require clarification: which acts are open to challenge, or more precisely, what is the legal nature of such acts; and the notion of individual and direct concern.

A. The Legal Nature of Acts Open to Challenge

The starting point for any consideration of *locus standi* is the question which acts are open to challenge at all. There seem to be only three alternatives in Art. 230(4). The object of the challenge can be: either a decision addressed to the plaintiff; or a decision in the form of a regulation, but of direct and individual concern to the plaintiff; or a decision addressed to another person, but (again) of direct and individual concern to the plaintiff. In each case, what seems to be required, in substance if not in form, is a decision. The term 'decision' is to be taken, the ECJ held in an early judgment, in its technical meaning as in Art. 249, fourth subparagraph EC. 'Decision' does not encompass any act whatever, simply because it requires the adopting Community institution to make up its mind, and thus to arrive at a 'decision' in everyday parlance.[10]

Nevertheless, the Court subsequently abandoned this limitation of the challengeable acts. What is instead required is that the challenged act be binding, ie capable of granting or denying rights, or imposing obligations.[11] This quality, however, accrues to decisions as much as to regulations,[12] and also to Directives.[13]

For example, the Court accepted early on that even an act *sui generis*, such as a letter withdrawing provisional immunity from fines under Art. 15(6) of Regulation 17/62, is a suitable object of a challenge under Art. 230(4).[14] This is despite the fact that the Regulation, in paras. 1, 2, and 4 of the same Article, employs the technical term 'decision', yet does not classify the 'information' in para. 6 as a decision. The difference makes good procedural sense in the context of Regulation 17/62, as it avoids the publicity requirement according to Art. 19 of that Regulation. The difference can, therefore, not be put down to an oversight, or a mere editing fluke. In the same vein, although acts which mark only a (preparatory) step in the adoption of a decision properly so-called cannot be challenged,[15] they are suitable objects of a challenge if they can be separately enforced,[16] or if they prevent the adoption of a decision that could, in its turn, be

---

[10] Joined Cases 16/62 and 17/62, *Confédération nationale des producteurs de fruit et legumes et al.* v *Council*, [1962] ECR 471, at p. 478, third paragraph.

[11] See, most recently, Joined Cases T-377/00 T-379/00 *et al*, *Philip Morris International et al.* v *Commission*, [2003] ECR II-1, paras. 76–82.   [12] Art. 249, second subpara. EC.

[13] Art. 249, third subpara. EC; Case C-10/95P, *Asocarne* (II), [1995] ECR I-4149, para. 32. The problem of 'direct concern' in connection with Directives will be discussed below at Section II.C.

[14] Joined Cases 8-11/66, *Cimenteries* v *Commission*, [1967] ECR 75.

[15] Case T-212/95, *Officimen* v *Commission*, [1997] ECR II-1161.

[16] Case 46/87, *Hoechst* v *Commission*, [1989] ECR 2859.

challenged.[17] Later, the Court went so far as to accept as a challengeable act an oral statement, made at a press conference, that a merger was not subject to assessment under Regulation 4064/89. This has legal repercussions which should not go without scrutiny; hence an action lay under Art. 230.[18] From these examples, it follows that the substance of the act, more specifically the effects it has on the plaintiff, are crucial for determining whether the act can be challenged under Art. 230(4).[19] The Court's jurisprudence, however, swung wildly throughout the 1970s and 1980s regarding the distinction between regulations and decisions.[20]

According to the Court, the essential characteristic of a decision is the limitation of the persons to whom it is addressed. A regulation, by contrast, being essentially of a legislative nature, is applicable not to a limited number of persons, but to categories of persons viewed abstractly and in their entirety.[21] The distinguishing criterion was (and still is) whether the measure at issue is of general application or not.[22] In some judgments,[23] the Court looked exclusively at the wording of the provisions in issue, and found it abstract.[24] The abstract character of the language alone prevented any further enquiry, especially regarding individual concern. In other judgments, the Court did not spare so much as a thought for the classification of the challenged act, and instead went straight to the question of individual concern. This was then treated in an equally cavalier manner. One can only speculate about the reasons why the Court, in the latter cases, lurched into considering the merits of the action, but would not have any of it in the former group of cases. At any rate, such unpredictability was less than satisfactory.

The Court finally abandoned this lottery in *Codorníu*,[25] its last judgment before the Court of First Instance was given the competence to hear in first instance all actions brought by individuals. The facts of the case have been sufficiently discussed in earlier literature on Art. 230. Crucially, the Court recognised that a measure can be a 'true' Regulation, not merely a decision in disguise, and

---

[17] Case 120/73, *Gebrüder Lorenz*, [1973] ECR 1471.

[18] Case T-3/93, *Air France* v *Commission*, [1995] ECR II-533.

[19] Case 307/81, *Alusuisse Italia SpA* v *Council and Commission*, [1982] ECR 3463, para. 7.

[20] A useful overview can be found in Trevor Hartley, *The foundations European Community law*, (5th edn, OUP 2003), pp. 362, 364–369, and in Albors-Llorens, *loc. cit.* fn. 2, pp. 103–105.

[21] This has been the standard formula ever since Joined Cases 16/92 and 17/62, *Producteurs de Fruits* v *Council*, [1962] ECR 471, p. 478, last para.

[22] Joined Cases 789/79 and 790/79, *Calpak et al.* v *Commission*, [1980] ECR 1949, paras. 8, 9; Case T-13/99, *Pfizer Animal Health* v *Council*, [2002] ECR II-3305, para. 82, with references.

[23] Joined Cases 789/79 and 790/79, *Calpak et al.* v *Commission*, [1980] ECR 1949, paras. 9–13.

[24] To this day, such 'abstractness' is only excluded where the name of the plaintiff appears in the challenged act, Case T-100/94, *Michailidis* v *Commission*, [1998] ECR II-3115, para. 54. Such mention, moreover, automatically confers individual concern, Case 138/79, *Roquette* v *Council*, [1980] ECR 3333, paras. 15–16, and Section II.B.(ii)(b) below.

[25] Case C-309/89, *Codorníu* v *Council*, [1994] ECR I-1853; the same solution was earlier suggested by Daig, *loc. cit.* fn. 2, p. 196, fn. 20. The formal classification as a regulation had already been abandoned as the decisive criterion for *locus standi* in Joined Cases 239/82 and 275/82, *Allied Corporation* v *Commission*, [1984] ECR 1005, para. 11, regarding regulations imposing anti-dumping duties. On this and other 'special cases', see below Section II.B.(i).

can still be of individual concern to the plaintiff.[26] Hence, what alone counts after *Codorníu* is whether a legally binding act, of whatever description, is of individual and direct concern to the individual bringing an action under Art. 230(4) EC.[27] Nevertheless, in a ritualistic fashion, the Court still goes through the question of classification in every case, despite the fact that it is no longer of any legal consequence whatsoever.[28] Such 'legal mantras'[29] are not necessarily harmful, but they obfuscate the reasoning. Worse, they might provide inroads for exactly the kind of manipulation that was overcome in *Codorníu*.

While the jurisprudence now shows the clarity and flexibility one would wish for, the Court has never explained how *Codorníu* tallies with the wording of Art. 230(4), as quoted above.[30] The Court, arguably, reads the three alternatives as mere illustrations of what the first subparagraph of Art. 230 describes, undifferentiated, as 'acts'. The fourth subparagraph can relate to the first in two ways.

It can be read as a *lex specialis* stipulating, for non-privileged applicants, not only the additional requirements of individual and direct concern, but also narrowing the range of acts individuals may challenge. This reading, however, appears too narrow for two reasons. Firstly, Arts. 220 and 230(2), as expressions of the rule of law, mandate a comprehensive control of the legality of all acts that can affect individuals' rights.[31] To allow control only of decisions would create unnecessary gaps in the legal protection enjoyed by individuals. Secondly, Art. 234(b) EC also speaks, without further qualification, of 'acts'. This provision is in some respects (see below at Section II.D.(ii)), the mirror image of Art. 230(4) EC. It enables individuals to raise, in proceedings before national courts, arguments against the validity of an act of Community law which they would raise before the ECJ if they had standing to do so.

Another interpretation of Art. 230(4) is therefore preferable. The provision is *lex specialis* (and to this extent supersedes the first subparagraph) only with regard to the requirements of individual and direct concern, not also with respect to the categories of acts that can be challenged. With regard to these categories, the two provisions are complementary. This is confirmed by another consideration. The term 'acts' in Art. 230(1) excludes recommendations and opinions,[32] and includes acts of the European Parliament only if they are 'intended to produce legal effects vis-à-vis third parties'. These two qualifications encapsulate the requirement that the

---

[26] Paras. 19–22.

[27] Neuwahl, *loc. cit.* fn. 2, p. 23, first para.; Arnull, *loc. cit.* fn. 2, [2001] CML Rev 24, third para.

[28] See most recently Case T-177/01, *Jégo-Quéré* v *Commission*, [2002] ECR II-2365, paras. 23–24, but then 25–36; Case T-13/99, *Pfizer Animal Health SA* v *Council*, [2002] ECR II-3305, paras. 81–84, and Case C–50/00P, *Unión de Pequeños Agricultores*, [2002] ECR I-6677, para. 35, then paras. 36 ff.; Joined Cases T-94/00, T-110/00, T-159/00, *Rica Foods (Free Zone) et al.* v *Commission*, [2002] ECR II-4677, para. 47, then para. 48.

[29] Arnull, *loc. cit.* fn. 2, [2001] CML Rev 21, third para., speaks of 'circuitous reasoning'.

[30] Albors-Llorens, *loc. cit.* fn. 2, p. 105, first para., calls this a 're-drafting of the Treaty by the Court'.

[31] Case 294/83, *Parti écologist 'Les Verts'* v *European Parliament*, [1986] ECR 1339, para. 23, first sentence.   [32] According to Art. 249 EC, fifth subpara., they have no binding force.

'act' be legally binding.[33] Decisions are, by virtue of their definition in Art. 249, legally binding. In the perspective of the Treaty's drafters in 1957, other acts were not envisaged to affect the interests of individuals in any other than an indirect way. Only later it turned out that this was an oversight, creating gaps in the legal protection of individuals which needed to be filled.[34] Examples are the adoption of the Community's budget (Art. 272(7) EC),[35] or the allocation of funds from it to political parties: before the first direct elections to the European Parliament in 1979, they fought no European election campaigns anyway.[36] In this view, Art. 230(4) merely illustrates, for the sake of clarification, some of the acts individuals might typically want to challenge. It is not meant to rule out challenges to other acts.

B. Individual Concern

The first and most important point to emphasize about the notion of 'individual concern' is that it is a term of art. This should come as no surprise, as we have already seen that the Court insists on a technical meaning of the term 'decision'. What is more, the Court held that 'decisions addressed to another *person*'[36a] includes such addressed to Member States.[37] This is legal terminology, not common parlance. Likewise, the meaning of 'individual' deviates from the sense in which the word is employed in everyday usage. Taken in this (colloquial) sense, nobody could be more individualized than the one and only economic operator in a given field whose business is ruined by a Community Regulation. Nevertheless, the Court has consistently held that it is immaterial whether or not the number, or even the identity, of those affected were ascertainable, or even known to the Community institution which adopted the act challenged by the operator.[38]

For this reason, any criticism based on the colloquial understanding of 'individual' fails to do justice by the Court's jurisprudence.[39] It is misguided to criticize the Court for, as it were, missing the point that there is no natural number smaller than one, or that whole factories cannot be built overnight (to take the example of case *Piraiki-Patraiki*[40]). If one wanted to criticize the Court, one would first have to

---

[33] On this requirement, see most recently Case T-113/00, *Du Pont Teijin Films Luxembourg et al.* v *Commission*, [2002] ECR II-3681, para. 47, and Case T-377/00 (above fn. 11), para. 77.

[34] Arnull, *loc. cit.* fn. 2, [2001] CML Rev 24, second para., speaks of 'difficulties which the authors of Art. 230 quite understandably failed to foresee'.

[35] Case 34/86, *Council* v *European Parliament*, [1986] ECR 2155, paras. 5–6.

[36] Case 294/83, *Parti écologist 'Les Verts'* v *European Parliament*, [1986] ECR 1339, paras. 24–25.

[36a] (emphasis added)   [37] Case 25/62, *Plaumann* v *Commission*, [1963] ECR 95.

[38] Case 231/82, *Spijker Kwasten* v *Commission*, [1983] ECR 2559; extensive references to the case law can be found in, Koen Lenaerts and Dirk Arts (ed. Robert Bray), *Procedural law of the European Union*, (London: Sweet & Maxwell, 1999), pts. 2-052–2-054 (p. 52 f.).

[39] An example of this can be found in Daig, *loc. cit.* fn. 2, p. 210, first para.

[40] Case 11/82, *Piraiki-Patraiki* v *Commission*, [1985] ECR 207—in this (misguided) sense, Paul Craig and Gráinne de Búrca, *EU Law—Text, Cases, and Materials*, (3rd edn, OUP, 2003), p. 489, third para., call the test 'economically unrealistic', yet it has nothing to do with economics, see below.

explain why 'individual', of all the terms employed in Art. 230(4), 'individual' should *not* be taken in a technical sense. If, however, the appropriateness of a technical understanding were accepted, any proposal for a definition of 'individual' is, to begin with, as convincing or unconvincing as the Court's. With regard, more specifically, to the question whether the Court's jurisprudence is 'restrictive', it follows that more arguments are needed than simply pleading, in a circular manner, a pre-conceived understanding based on the non-technical usage of the term.[41]

(i) The so-called 'special cases' of individual concern

There are three areas in which the Court has always followed a pattern of establishing individual concern akin to the one it now uses universally.[42] This was in contrast with the Court's earlier, more erratic ways outside the areas now to be discussed. They are competition law, State aids, and anti-dumping.[43] Two reasons, in particular, are discernible for why these areas were treated differently.

Firstly, in the area of competition law, there is no (or no sufficient) redress in the national courts against measures taken by the Community institutions. The enforcement of Community policy in this area is (or rather, since the recent reforms: was) entirely in the hands of the Commission; national authorities became involved only in an auxiliary function.[44]

Secondly, in all three areas, there are extensive provisions for the participation of economic operators, in the procedure leading to the adoption of measures, by (typically) the Commission. The reason why the participation of economic operators is so comprehensively regulated in competition law, State aids, and anti-dumping, is the complexity of the required economic assessment in each of these areas. This makes it imperative to draw on the intimate knowledge companies have of the markets they are active in. The Commission could not possibly hope to replicate this knowledge through its own research efforts, nor even through measures of enquiry on site such as under Arts. 20 and 21 of Regulation 1/2003.[45]

---

[41] Similarly Harding, *loc. cit.* fn. 2, p. 355, second para.: 'Art. 230, taken together with Art. 249, does not, and was probably never intended to, hold out much hope to private plaintiffs in the case of measures not actually addressed to them'. In the same sense already, Daig, *loc. cit.* fn. 2, p. 194, third para.

[42] Compare Case 169/84, *COFAZ* v *Commission*, [1986] ECR 391, para. 23, and Case 26/76, *Metro* v *Commission* (No. 1), [1977] ECR 1875, para. 13 (second subpara.), with Joined Cases T-32/98 and 41/98, *Government of the Netherlands Antilles* v *Commission*, [2000] ECR II-201, para. 51.

[43] In the field of anti-dumping, the Community institutions always acted by means of Regulations in the sense of Art. 249(2) EC. This explains why the focus there was always on individual concern, rather than on the (redundant) classification of the act as a regulation or a decision.

[44] Things are slightly different regarding State aids. There, Member States are ultimately responsible for recovering aid granted in breach of Art. 87 EC. Similarly, in anti-dumping it is for the national customs authorities to collect the anti-dumping duties stipulated by Council and Commission in a regulation, Joined Cases 239/82 and 275/82, *Allied Corp.* v *Commission*, [1984] ECR 1005, para. 15; Case 231/82, *Spijker Kwasten* v *Commission*, [1983] ECR 2559, para. 11. The national implementing measures in these two areas open up a different route for challenging Community acts, discussed below at Section II.D.(ii).

[45] Council Regulation (EC) No. 1/2003 of 16 December 2002 on the implementation of the rules on competition laid down in Arts. 81 and 82 of the Treaty, [2003] OJ L1/1 of 4 January 2003.

Conversely, the companies on whose expertise the Commission has drawn are also the most competent to spot any flaws in the decision or regulation ultimately adopted. It is therefore sensible to allow them to challenge the measure directly.[46]

What is more, the possibility of challenging the act allows operators to enforce their right to participate in the procedure for its adoption. This is independent of whether or not they have actually been allowed to exercise their right to participate.[47] A refusal to hear them, or the termination, without scrutiny, of procedures in the course of which they would have been heard, perverts the rationale for granting rights of participation in the first place. This rationale is, as we have seen, to put as much relevant information as possible at the Community institution's disposal. A refusal of participation, or termination of the procedure before interested operators can participate, cannot, therefore, be allowed to deprive them of the right to challenge the act under Art. 230(4), a right they would otherwise have had. The act adopted can be said to be 'addressed', to borrow the words of the first alternative in Art. 230(4), to those who have (or would have) participated in the procedure. The information and opinions tendered by these operators should, by law, have been on the mind of the institution which adopted the act.[48]

These reflections explain why a complainant according to Art. 3(2)(b) of Regulation 17/62 can challenge a decision in competition matters,[49] as can even someone who has merely reacted to a notice according to Art. 19(3) of the same Regulation.[50] By contrast, a company may not bring a direct challenge after it remained inactive despite its knowledge of ongoing proceedings before the Commission. It will not help if it later protests that the measure adopted by the Comission impairs its economic interests.[51] In the field of State aids, competitors of the recipients of aid, having submitted comments pursuant to Art. 88(2) EC, may challenge the decision, provided their position on the market is significantly affected by the aid in question.[52] Companies may also challenge the Commission's decision not to open a full investigation, if in the course of the procedure under Art. 88(2) EC, they would have been entitled to submit comments.[53] Regarding anti-dumping, finally, undertakings may challenge the regulation if they are identified in

---

[46] Craig and de Búrca, *loc. cit.* fn. 40, p. 516, fourth para.

[47] *Contra* Moitinho de Almeida, *loc. cit.* fn. 2, p. 851, second para., who insists on actual participation as a condition for individual concern. This would, however, lead to the absurd consequence that the adopting Community institution might try to prevent scrutiny of a substantively illegal act by additionally committing procedural irregularities.

[48] Daig, *loc. cit.* fn. 2, p. 191, *sub* a).

[49] Case 26/76, *Metro* v *Commission* (No. 1), [1977] ECR 1875, para. 13.

[50] Case 75/84, *Metro* v *Commission* (No. 2), [1986] ECR 3021, paras. 21–23.

[51] Case T-87/92, *Kruidvat BVBA* v *Commission*, [1996] ECR II-1931, paras. 63, 67–71.

[52] Case 169/84, *COFAZ* v *Commission*, [1986] ECR 391, paras. 24–25. By contrast, any effect on any competitive relationship whatever will not confer individual concern, Joined Cases 10/68 and 18/68, *Eridania* et al. v *Commission*, [1969] ECR 459, para. 7.

[53] Case C-198/91, *Wm. Cook* v *Commission*, [1993] ECR I-2487, para. 23.

the regulation imposing anti-dumping duties; if their prices were used in calculating the dumping margin; if they were heard during the investigation procedure; or finally, if their observations determined the outcome of that procedure.[54] Two cases from the area of anti-dumping seem to deviate from this pattern, and therefore deserve closer scrutiny.

In its judgment in the first case, *Alusuisse*,[55] the Court held that 'the distinction between a regulation and a decision may be based only on the nature of the measure itself and the legal effects which it produces and *not on the procedures for its adoption*'.[56] This statement, however, has to be read in its context. *Alusuisse*, an importer of a substance on which anti-dumping duties had been imposed— provisionally by the Commission, and definitively by the Council—had *not* participated in the procedure for the adoption of the regulations challenged. Instead, the company pleaded[57] that since some (other) companies had participated, it— ie *Alusuisse*—should be allowed to challenge the measure in the European Court of Justice. The Court's denying this does not, therefore, establish that as a matter of principle, the procedure for the adoption of a regulation is immaterial.[58] Instead, the judgment merely says that a measure can be of individual concern to some (those who participated in the procedure for its adoption) but, at the same time, not to others (those who did not so participate). Arguably, the Treaty may be read to consider this disjunction a regular occurrence: there is no indication that actions pending under Art. 230(4) rule out the admissibility of preliminary references being brought under Art. 234(b), and *vice versa*.[59]

The second case deserving special mention is *Extramet*.[60] Before the judgment in this case, the Court had held that importers do not *per se* have standing against anti-dumping regulations.[61] Rather, they too have to fulfil the above conditions. Where these are not fulfilled, importers can seek redress in the national courts.[62] The judgment in *Extramet*, however, granted the largest Community importer of calcium metal, who was also a processor, *locus standi* against an anti-dumping regulation.[63] The regulation would have made purchases from *Extramet's* traditional

---

[54] Case 264/82, *Timex* v *Commisison*, [1985] ECR 849, para. 14; Case 169/84, *COFAZ* v *Commission*, [1986] ECR 391, para. 24. For further examples, see Lenaerts and Arts, *loc. cit.* fn. 38, pts. 7-066–7-072 (pp. 170–177).

[55] Case 307/81, *Alusuisse Italia SpA* v *Council and Commission*, [1982] ECR 3463.

[56] Para. 13, emphasis added.   [57] Para. 12.

[58] This, however, seems to be the interpretation of Advocate General *Jacobs* in his opnion in Case C-358/89, *Extramet* v *Commission*, [1991] ECR I-2501, para. 26. It is respectfully submitted that reading the passage in isolation gives it an unduly wide scope.

[59] See, eg, the substantially identical challenges in Case C-376/98, *Germany* v *European Parliament and Council*, [2000] ECR I-8419 (admissible), and in Joined Cases T-172, 175–177/98, *Salamander et al.* v *EP & Council*, [2000] ECR II-2487 (inadmissible).

[60] Case C-358/89, *Extramet* v *Commission*, [1991] ECR I-2501.

[61] Case 231/82, *Spijker Kwasten* v *Commission*, [1983] ECR 2559, paras. 9–11.

[62] Joined Cases 239/82 and 275/82, *Allied Corporation* v *Commission*, [1984] ECR 1005, paras. 13–14   [63] Para. 17.

suppliers outside the Community significantly more expensive. What is more, the sole producer of calcium metal in the Community, *Péchiney*, had on past occasions refused to supply *Extramet* with calcium of the required purity. For this reason, the company had turned to suppliers outside the Community in the first place.[64] At the same time, *Péchiney* was also a processor. In this capacity, it was *Extramet's* principal competitor.[65]

One may read this judgment at face value, as exceptionally granting standing to somebody who was not involved in the administrative procedure, on condition that they are 'seriously affected'.[66] The problem with such a criterion is, however, its lack of definition. For any company faced with effective competition, a deterioration in its supply situation can entail serious consequences. If the distortion of competition on a market in the Community is such as to warrant the imposition of anti-dumping duties at all, virtually everybody operating on that market will be seriously affected by the regulation.[67] The economic approach to the question of why *Extramet* was 'seriously affected', therefore, needs to be supplemented by another consideration. Arguably, the legal remedies available, or rather, their unavailability, justify a deviation from the established rules of *locus standi*.

It is true that *Extramet* could have challenged, in the French courts, any attempts by the customs authorities to collect the anti-dumping duties.[68] We can only presume (the judgment is not explicit, one way or another) that in the meantime, and despite any possible interim measures, *Extramet* would have become dependent again, or more dependent than before, on supplies by *Péchiney*. This dependence, a consequence of the anti-dumping regulation, could not retroactively be cured by a repayment of the duties paid by *Extramet*, or by the release of any security furnished instead. Proceedings in the national courts, alleging abuse of a dominant position by *Péchiney* were a course of action attempted before by *Extramet*.[69] *Péchiney* could, however, easily undermine such proceedings by supplying just enough to *Extramet* for the latter to stay in business.[70] *Extramet* would, therefore, not have had an effective remedy in the national courts against the deterioration in its situation. This justified granting it direct access to the ECJ, in

---

[64] This last piece of information is not contained in the judgment, but in para. 8 of Advocate General *Jacobs'* opinion.   [65] Para. 6 of the opinion.

[66] Para. 17 of the judgment.

[67] Nonetheless, those who benefit from it will lack standing because a finding of nullity by the ECJ would not improve their factual or legal situation. See on this requirement Case T-183/97, *Micheli v Commission*, [2000] ECR II-287, para. 34; Case T-89/00, *Europe Chemi-Con (Deutschland) v Council*, [2002] ECR II-3651, paras. 34–35, and Case T-398/02, *Linea GIG Srl v Commission*, [2003] ECR II-1139, paras. 45–47. The same considerations apply for the admissibility of an appeal, Case C–50/00P, *Unión de Pequeños Agricultores*, [2002] ECR I-6677, para. 21. Generally on this requirement, see Lenaerts and Arts, *loc. cit.* fn. 38, pts. 7-075–7-080 (pp. 178–181).

[68] Nihoul, *loc. cit.* fn. 2, p. 183, fourth para.   [69] Para. 6 of the judgment.

[70] This follows from Joined Cases 6/73 and 7/73, *Istituto Chemioterapico Italiano SpA and Commercial Solvents Corp. v Commission*, [1974] ECR 223, para. 25.

order to tackle the regulation direct, as the root cause of its problems.[71] At any rate, the *Extramet* case shows that the Court is willing to deviate from established rules of standing where effective judicial protection so requires. In all other, 'normal' cases, participation in the administrative procedure leading to the adoption of the act challenged will confer standing on the plaintiff.

(ii) The 'mainstream' case law: The Plaumann formula

The *Plaumann* formula, named after a judgment of 1963, holds that for a measure to be of individual concern, it 'must concern the applicant by reason of *certain attributes which are peculiar to him*, or by reason of *circumstances in which the applicant is differentiated from all other persons*, and therefore distinguished individually, just as in the case of the person addressed.'[72] This formula is applicable both in the 'special' areas just discussed,[73] and within the scope of all other ('mainstream') subject-matters of Community law. In the specific areas of competition law, State aids, and anti-dumping, however, it was quickly translated into the much more concrete criterion of involvement in the administrative procedure. It took the 'mainstream' case law somewhat longer to arrive at essentially the same position. Even the exceptional decision in *Extramet* has belatedly found its echo in *Jégo-Quéré*.

In a first step, the Court tried to render the *Plaumann* formula operational only in a negative fashion: there is no individual concern if the applicant is affected merely because he carries on an economic (or other[74]) activity which may at any time be practised by any person.[75] For this reason, it is immaterial whether it is possible to determine those concerned by number or even identity, or whether for practical or economic reasons, nobody would take up the same activity in the foreseeable future.[76]

Another attempt by the Court to break down the *Plaumann* formula into easily applicable criteria was to require that the applicant belong to a 'closed group' of persons.[77] Such a group can be defined as a finite number of persons, sharing peculiar attributes which nobody can acquire any more after the coming into force of the act in question.[78]

---

[71] The Court had used such an efficiency argument before, see Case 175/84, *Krohn & Co. Import-Export* v *Commission*, [1986] ECR 753, paras. 27–29.

[72] Case 25/62, *Plaumann* v *Commission*, [1963] ECR 95, p. 107, last para. (emphasis added).

[73] See, as only one example of many, *Extramet* (fn. 60), para. 16.

[74] Case T-219/95R, *Danielson* v *Council*, [1995] ECR II-3051, para. 71: residence on an island affected by the testing of French nuclear devices.

[75] This appears already in the first ever judgment under Art. 230(4) (then Art. 173(2) EEC), even predating *Plaumann*: Joined Cases 16/62 and 17/62, *Producteurs de fruit* v *Council*, [1962] ECR 471, p. 479, fifth para.; most recently in Case T-13/99, *Pfizer Animal Health* v *Council*, [2002] ECR II-3305, para. 89.

[76] Case 11/82, *Piraiki-Patraiki* v *Commission*, [1985] ECR 207, paras. 12–14.

[77] Case 62/70, *Bock* v *Commission*, [1971] ECR 897, para. 10.

[78] Hartley, *Foundations* (fn. 20 above), p. 356, first para. The requirement of a closed group was later broken down into several requirements, and is in itself no longer decisive, see Case C-152/88, *Sofrimport* v *Commission*, [1990] ECR I-2477, paras. 11–12; Case T-298/94, *Roquette Frères* v *Council*,

There is, however, a fundamental problem with both definitions of individual concern, based on purely factual circumstances: no two individuals or companies will ever be in exactly the same situation. They will be active on different national or regional markets, subject to different legal régimes, pursuing different activities, or offering different products to different customers, and so on. All of these factors will, in some way or other, determine whether and to what extent individuals or companies are affected by a given piece of secondary Community law. If, therefore, factual circumstances alone were to determine individual concern, everyone would be 'individually concerned', ie affected in a way in which no-one else is, in every respect, affected.[79] As a consequence, Art. 230(4) EC could not serve as a filter for the admissibility of direct actions; an *actio popularis* would lie to the Court of First Instance. To rule this out, however, is the very function of the provision. Art. 230(4) is not intended to narrow the categories of acts that may be challenged. Rather, it is meant to stipulate the additional requirements of individual and direct concern. An interpretation that would make it lose its only specific feature, and so render the provision superfluous, is hardly convincing.

It is, arguably, for this reason that the Court looked for legal, rather than factual, criteria. As it turns out, such criteria had already been developed in the 'special cases'. It was, therefore, only natural that the Court adopted these criteria for universal application, at least as a starting point. As a result, the current position is that individual concern will be found in three paradigms.

a) First paradigm: lawful participation in the procedure leading to the adoption of the act

This paradigm comes in two guises: either the Community institution has actively to find out (if only by an invitation to submit the relevant information) who would be affected, and how, by a measure whose adoption it contemplates; or the institution is under an obligation to receive, in the framework of a procedure governed by Community law and normally by a certain closing date, information about the circumstances or intentions of economic operators. The typical example of this second case is an application procedure for licences to import agricultural products from third countries into the Community. Metaphorically speaking, in the first case, the institution—practically always the Commission—has to 'ask', in

---

[1996] ECR II-1531, paras. 41–43; Case T-60/96, *Merck & Co et al.* v *Commission*, [1997] ECR II-859, paras. 58, 63. Nonetheless, Albors-Llorens, *loc. cit.* fn. 2, p. 53, third para., still treats it as *one* decisive criterion. On p. 219, second para., however, she points out that belonging to a closed group is merely an 'external indicator' that the applicant *may* be individually concerned.

79 Similarly, Case T-155/02R, *VVG Internationale Handelsgesellschaft et al.* v *Commission*, [2002] ECR II-3239, para. 31; Case C-312/00P, *Commission* v *Camar et al.*, [2002] ECR I-11355, paras. 74, 77. Craig and de Búrca, *loc. cit.* fn. 40, p. 490, fourth para., argue that: 'the test in *Plaumann* is based on the assumption that some people have attributes which distinguish them from others and that they possess these attributes at the time the contested decision is made'. This does not, however, appear to be the current position of the European Court of Justice, and it would not be able to limit the number of those who have standing.

the second, it has to 'listen'. To put it more technically, the applicant must have a right to participate in the procedure leading to the adoption of the measure it wishes to challenge.[80]

Crucially, in both cases the legal basis of the challenged act must put the adopting institution under a specific duty to avail itself of, and/or to act on, information concerning specifically the applicant(s).[81] It is not sufficient for the institution to be under a general duty to take into consideration the peculiarities of a given sector of the economy. An example of such a duty can be found in Art. 33(2)(a) EC regarding agriculture.[82] Individual concern for a plaintiff will, therefore, arise from the combination of specific legal duties on the part of a Community institution regarding the procedure for the adoption of the act, and from the presence of specific factual circumstances on the part of the applicant, to which the duty of the Community institution refers.[83] Put more simply, legal duties *and* matching facts are required. Facts alone are insufficient.[84] This can be illustrated by two pairs of cases based on similar facts. The outcome of each, nonetheless, differed according to the respective legal frameworks.

The first pair are the cases *Sofrimport*[85] and *Unifruit Hellas*.[86] In both cases, the plaintiff companies were fruit importers. Both also had apples in transit from Chile to the Community when regulations were adopted affecting the importation of the apples.

In *Sofrimport*, a Commission regulation imposed a temporary import ban. As a result, Sofrimport might as well have dumped its apples in mid-Atlantic: the Community would not have them (nor any other markets, we may presume), and the domestic Chilean market is much too small to absorb the large quantities of fruit grown for export, let alone at a price reflecting the costs of the wasted transport. In view of these foreseeable economic consequences, the regulation empowering the Commission to impose import bans also stipulated that the Commission find out which importers had apples in transit during the relevant period. For these, special provisions had to be adopted in accordance with the

---

[80] Joined Cases T-32/98 and 41/98, *Government of the Netherlands Antilles* v *Commission*, [2000] ECR II-201, paras. 51–56.

[81] Case T-13/99, *Pfizer Animal Health* v *Council*, [2002] ECR II-3305, para. 101.

[82] Case T-194/95, *Area Cova* v *Council*, [1999] ECR II-2274, paras. 41–45.

[83] Case C-209/94P, *Buralux et al.* v *Council*, [1996] ECR I-615, paras. 30–34. The passage shows, incidentally, that the judgment is not based on a 'pure *Plaumann* approach', as Craig and de Búrca, *loc. cit.* fn. 40, p. 497, third para., argue. Such an approach does not exist (if it ever did), as becomes clear also from para. 56 of the judgment in Case T-585/93, *Greenpeace* v *Council*, [1995] ECR II-2205, reproduced on p. 499 by Craig and de Búrca.

[84] So is a duty alone to take cognizance of facts not notified in time (*Kruidvat*, above fn. 51).

[85] Case C-152/88, *Sofrimport* v *Commission*, [1990] ECR I-2477. Ward, *loc. cit.* fn. 2, p. 225, fourth para., gives up too early when she argues that the case was 'confined to its special facts'.

[86] Case T-489/93, *Unifruit Hellas* v *Commission*, [1994] ECR II-1201. More recently, see Case T-155/02R, *VVG Internationale Handelsgesellschaft et al.* v *Commission*, [2002] ECR II-3239, paras. 36–37.

principle of proportionality, to mitigate the impact of the regulation. Due to this obligation, *and* because *Sofrimport* answered the description of operators whose circumstances the Commission was under a duty to ascertain, *Sofrimport* was deemed to be individually concerned by the regulation.[87]

In *Unifruit Hellas*, by contrast, the regulation in issue merely imposed an import surcharge. Such a measure does not nearly have the catastrophic impact on imports under way to the Community as does a complete ban. Correspondingly, the basic regulation, vesting in the Commission the power to adopt a regulation stipulating the surcharge, did not provide for an enquiry into the effects of the surcharge on the several operators affected by it. Such an investigation is time-consuming and vulnerable to fraud; proportionality did not require it either. Hence, *Unifruit Hellas* was held not to be individually concerned.[88] Instead, the company had to seek redress in the national courts against the national authorities collecting the surcharge.

The second pair of cases consists of the judgments in *Weddel*[89] and *Binderer*.[90] The first case is one of many examples of a would-be importer of agricultural goods produced in third countries applying for an import licence (*in casu*, for beef). The national authorities charged with implementing the Common Agricultural Policy in the Member States were to collect applications for each importer's desired quantity, and forward them to the Commission. The latter would calculate the overall quantity applied for, compare it to the overall quota set by it, and promulgate in a regulation the reduction coefficient if the sum of the applications exceeded the overall quota. Applying this coefficient, the national authorities would then grant import licences for reduced quantities. The Court held that the regulation establishing the coefficient was in reality a 'bundle of decisions' which affected each applicant for a licence individually.[91]

What is striking about the notion of 'individual' concern in this and similar cases is how little the Commission learns, in the course of the procedure for the allocation of import licences, about those who apply for a share in the general

---

[87] Para. 12. See more recently, Case T-13/99, *Pfizer Animal Health* v *Council*, [2002] ECR II-3305, paras. 102, 104; and Joined Cases T-94/00, T-110/00, T-159/00, *Rica Foods (Free Zone) et al.* v *Commission*, [2002] ECR II-4677, paras. 56, 57, 75. The same pattern can already be seen in Case 11/82, *Piraiki-Patraiki* v *Commission*, [1985] ECR 207, paras. 21 and 28: what was decisive there was not the fact that the company had concluded contracts for the delivery of cotton yarn to French customers, but this fact *plus* the duty incumbent on the Commission under Art. 130 of the Act of Accession of Greece to find out which companies had concluded such contracts. The Commission had to make special provisions for these when it adopted a regulation allowing for restrictions of imports of Greek cotton yarn into France, deviating from the principle of free movement of goods. Craig and de Búrca, *loc. cit.* fn. 40, p. 491, last para., argue that Piraiki-Patraiki enjoyed standing because they had entered into contracts before the date of the decision, to be performed while the decision was in force. That this is not the Court's position becomes apparent from paras. 21 and 27 of the judgment, not reproduced by Craig and de Búrca.

[88] *Unifruit Hellas* (above fn. 86), paras. 24–27.

[89] Case C–354/87, *Weddel*, [1990] ECR I-3847; the same principles are already applied in Case 62/70, *Bock* v *Commission*, [1971] ECR 897.

[90] Case 147/83, *Münchener Weinkellerei Herold Binderer* v *Commission*, [1985] ECR 257.

[91] Paras. 20–23.

quota. The applications forwarded to the Commission by the national authorities contain no information about the (would-be) importer. Yet *Weddel* and the other applicants were held to be individually concerned because the Commission was under a duty, in the framework of the procedure for the adoption of this particular measure, as stipulated in secondary Community law, to receive the information, take cognisance of it, and act on it.[92] This determines the result of each individual application. The quantity each company may import follows from a simple multiplication of the quantity applied for with the coefficient set by the Commission.[93]

By contrast, the plaintiff will not be individually concerned where there are no specific procedural provisions of secondary Community law stipulating participation by the applicant. The individual will have no standing, no matter how intimate an insight into his business practices and legal circumstances a Community institution may have gained. A paradigm case in this respect is that of *Binderer*.[94]

Binderer imported wine from the Balkans into Germany. Because the wines were not made in accordance with Community standards, the company could not use the designations provided for in a regulation. These designations are meant to protect the consumer against misleading labelling. Binderer wished to give consumers some indication as to the quality of the imported wines. For this purpose, the company had devised (German) designations for its wines closely resembling the Community classifications, but not identical to them. To ensure the legality of its labelling, Binderer enquired with the Commission whether it could lawfully use the proposed designations. After some deliberation, the Commission replied in the affirmative. Nevertheless, a few months later, it adopted a new regulation on designations for wines. As a consequence, Binderer could no longer use its designations. The company challenged the regulation in the ECJ, but was held not to be individually concerned.[95]

---

[92] This is the only context in which the 'closed group' label may still meaningfully be used, on the understanding that the group is closed for procedural reasons: submission of applications by the plaintiffs, and action taken by the Community institution on these applications, or on licences already granted, as in Joined Cases 106/63 and 107/63, *Alfred Töpfer and Getreide-Import Gesellschaft* v *Commission*, [1965] ECR 405, p. 411, fifth and sixth paras; Case 100/74, *Société CAM SA* v *Commission*, [1975] ECR 1393, para. 15; Case 88/76, *Société pour l'exportation des sucres* v *Commission*, [1977] ECR 709, paras. 10–11; Case 264/81, *Savma* v *Commission*, [1984] ECR 3915, para. 11. *Contra* Albors-Llorens, *loc. cit.* fn. 2, pp. 150–152.

[93] By contrast, there is no individual concern where the Commission's coefficient is not the only factor used by national authorities to establish a reference quantity which, in its turn, serves for the future allocation of quota, Joined Cases T-198/95, T-171/96 *et al.*, *Comafrica et al.* v *Commission*, [2001] ECR II-1975, para. 106. There is also no individual concern where applications for support payments simply mark those persons who will be affected by a separate measure establishing the factors that go into the calculation of the support payments, Case T-482/93, *Weber* v *Commission*, [1996] ECR II-609, paras. 65, 66. In both cases, the applicants have participated in a procedure (by submitting the original application), but it is not the procedure leading specifically to the adoption of the measures they wish to challenge in the ECJ. These measures determine the outcome of the application originally submitted, but they are adopted without the participation of the applicants. Similarly, already Case 45/81, *Alexander Moksel Import-Export* v *Commission*, [1982] ECR 1129, paras. 15–17.

[94] Case 147/83, *Münchener Weinkellerei Herold Binderer* v *Commission*, [1985] ECR 257.

[95] Paras. 12–15.

It is impossible to say whether Binderer's enquiry, and the information thereby gained, prompted the Commission to adopt the new rules. At any rate, there were no specific rules of secondary Community law which said that the Commission had to take any notice of Binderer and its business practices.[96] Thus, despite the fact that the Commission knew a good deal more about Binderer than it ever knew about the thousands of companies which, over the years, applied for import licences, Binderer was not individually concerned in the technical sense. The exchange of information between the company and the Commission, however detailed, was nonetheless purely informal.

The CFI has held likewise in the case of companies which, having heard rumours of plans for the adoption of Community measures that would affect their business, intervened repeatedly with the Commission. Where there are no specific provisions governing the participation of such companies in the procedure leading to the adoption of the measure, they will not be individually concerned.[97] There is, in other words, no way for plaintiffs to confer 'by force' individual concern on themselves.

(b) Second paradigm: the plaintiff's name is mentioned in the act

The second paradigm of individual concern is that the plaintiff is specifically mentioned in the measure without having participated in the procedure for its adoption.[98] These days, this is a rare occurrence. The scope of the Community's procedural law has been considerably extended over the years, and with it individuals' rights to participate.

(c) Third paradigm: certain rights are affected by the act

The bulk of the Court's case law falls under the first paradigm (procedural rights).[99] Cases under the third paradigm have some common features. Nonetheless, the Court has, so far, only hinted at criteria for determining which situations will fall within the third paradigm. The well-developed first paradigm can serve as a point of reference. Without any indication to the contrary, it must be presumed that the

---

[96] It is a separate question whether, at the level of general principles of Community law, and thus of primary Community law, there exists a rule of good administration, in accordance with which the Commission should acknowledge information, complaints, suggestions, etc., it has received, and inform the person how it handled the intervention. Nevertheless, the Commission may prioritise requests even where there are substantial rights for individuals granted by secondary Community law, see Case T-24/90, *Automec Srl.* v *Commission* (No. 2), [1992] ECR II-2223, paras. 79–86, and now Commission Communication to the European Parliament and the European Ombudsman on relations with the complainant in respect of infringements of Community law, COM (2002) 141 final, 2002/C 244/03, [2002] OJ C244/5.

[97] Case T-481/93 and 484/93, *Vereniging van Exporteurs in Levende Varkens* v *Commission*, [1995] ECR II-2941, paras. 54–62.

[98] Case 138/79, *Roquette* v *Council*, [1980] ECR 3333, paras. 15–16.

[99] Craig and de Búrca, *loc. cit.* fn. 40, p. 496, last para., confound the first and the third paradigm into an 'infringement of rights [third paradigm] or breach of duty [first paradigm] approach'. This is understandable on their presumption that mere factual circumstances can confer individual concern.

third is not meant to be less stringent than the first, but merely to cover different situations.

The starting point is the judgment in *Codorníu*. This company, producing bottle-fermented wine in Catalonia, was held to be individually concerned by a Council Regulation reserving the designation 'grand crémant' to producers of sparkling wines in Luxembourg and parts of France. This was despite the fact that Codorníu had not participated in the procedure that led to the adoption of the regulation. The provisions of the regulation made it illegal for Codorníu to continue to use its trademark which it had registered decades earlier, and which contained the words 'grand crémant' now reserved to others.[100]

In later judgments, by contrast, the Court refused an extension of this jurisprudence to companies holding quota allocations for a previous marketing year, which were not subsequently re-allocated (in whole or in part).[101] There was also no individual concern in the case of purely factual advantages, such as market circumstances conducive to the plaintiff's business, or of production aid granted for a limited period.[102] Similarly, patent holders were held not to be individually concerned by the Commission's refusal to allow some Member States' protective measures against parallel imports of patented drugs.[103] The CFI held that the extent of the protection patent holders enjoyed in the common market was determined by the combined effect of Art. 28 and 30 EC. They could not, based on *Codorníu*, demand the extension of a temporary derogation from a fundamental principle of the Treaty.[104]

If one were to distil an abstract formula from this case law, one might say that a plaintiff will be individually concerned by a measure impairing an absolute and definitive right granted to him by Community or Member State law.[105] An 'absolute' right is one which the holder has against everyone, as opposed to rights merely *vis-à-vis* specific persons, ie contractual rights, or rights resulting from torts. We have seen above from the cases of *Sofrimport* and *Piraiki-Patraiki* that contracts entered into, and affected by an act of secondary Community law, are not in themselves enough to render the parties individually concerned. 'Definitive' does not imply that the right must be granted in perpetuity. Instead, it means that the plaintiff cannot be deprived of the right, and any benefits derived from it, at the discretion of a Community or national authority, without being compensated for the value of the right.

---

[100] Case C-309/89, *Codorníu* v *Council*, [1994] ECR I-1853, paras. 19–21.

[101] Case T-158/95, *Eridania* v *Commission*, [1999] ECR II-219, paras. 61–62.

[102] Case T-482/93, *Weber* v *Commission*, [1996] ECR II-609, para. 69.

[103] These drugs had been imported from Spain and Portugal. Price caps in these countries made the drugs much cheaper there than in other Member States. This made parallel trade lucrative. For a while after these two countries' accession to the Community, however, Member States were authorized to limit imports of pharmaceuticals originating in Spain and Portugal.

[104] Case T-60/96, *Merck & Co et al.* v *Commission*, [1997] ECR II-859, paras. 45, 50.

[105] Case T-114/96, *Confiserie du Tech* v *Commission*, [1999] ECR II-913, paras. 33–34; more recently Case T-13/99, *Pfizer Animal Health* v *Council*, [2002] ECR II-3305, para. 98.

In other words, the challenged Community act must affect property rights.[106] These are both absolute, and definitively assigned to their holder. Other rights, even fundamental rights recognized under Community law, are not suitable to confer individual concern.[107] These rights, in particular the right to pursue a trade or professional activity,[108] would not have the capacity to limit direct access to the ECJ in the same way as the first paradigm does. As has been argued above, many if not every business operating on the market affected by a measure in the areas of competition law, State aids, and anti-dumping, will in some way be affected. To accord each of them, in principle, standing for a direct action in the ECJ would render superfluous the limitation established by the first paradigm. This would pervert the wider function of Art. 230(4) EC.

Another limitation can be derived from the judgment in *Codorníu*, further aligning the third paradigm with the first. In the first paradigm, participation of the plaintiff in the procedure leading to the adoption of the challenged act means that the adopting Community institution can be deemed to be aware of the specific circumstances of the plaintiff, and to have adopted the act specifically with these circumstances in mind. In this sense, the act can be said to be 'addressed' to the plaintiff. This, however, requires publicity, at least for the relevant Community institution, of the information it acts on. This quality of 'there to be seen by everyone' does not attach equally to all property rights. It accrues only to those evident from public registers, or in any other way specifically protected by law. This is true of land rights, patents, or, as in *Codorníu*, trademarks, and other intellectual property rights, but not of rights, typically, in chattels. Accordingly, economic operators using generic descriptions also deployed by other operators for their products, and thus not enjoying any proprietary exclusivity,[109] or operators using non-protected designations of geographic origin,[110] were found not to be individually concerned.

One might contemplate one last limitation, namely a 'reduction to zero' of the property right as a condition for individual concern under the third paradigm. The property right (trade mark) affected in *Codorníu* was, if not cancelled, at least

---

[106] Similarly, Moitinho de Almeida, *loc. cit.* fn. 2, p. 864, second para., who explains *Codorníu* as allowing challenges to 'expropriating' measures of Community law. Arnull's objection (*loc. cit.* fn. 2, [2001] CML Rev 42, second para.) that this confuses admissibility and substance is not convincing. For the action to be admissible, it is enough that the plaintiff *might* have the right claimed, and that it *might* be violated. The action is inadmissible where this can obviously be ruled out. It is only for the substantive assessment to ascertain whether this is in fact the case.

[107] *Contra* Albors-Llorens, *loc. cit.* fn. 2, p. 52, second para., who wants to use any individual right under Community law as conferring individual concern. Her examples, however, are drawn from cases in which individual concern derived under the first paradigm, anyway, so that the Court's jurisprudence cannot be cited in evidence for her submission. Unclear Neuwahl, *loc. cit.* fn. 2, p. 28, fourth para.: 'hard core of human rights norms and rules relating to proper administration'.

[108] Case 44/79, *Lieselotte Hauer* v *Land Rheinland-Pfalz*, [1979] ECR 3727, para. 17.

[109] Case T-114/96, *Confiserie du Tech et al.* v *Commission*, [1998] ECR II-913, paras. 32–34; similarly already Case 26/86, *Deutz und Geldermann* v *Council*, [1987] ECR 941, paras. 10–12: non-protected description of sparkling wine as being made in accordance with the '*méthode champénois*'.

[110] Case T-107/97, *Molkerei Großenhain et al.* v *Commission*, [1998] ECR II-3533, paras. 70–71.

devalued to the point of uselessness. To borrow the language of the Court in the fundamental rights case of *Hauer*, 'the very substance of the right' was impaired.[111] To stay with the case just mentioned, Ms Hauer remained the owner of her vineyard, but was not allowed to plant new vines on it. One potential use of the land was ruled out, but the property in the land remained intact. The ECJ points out[112] that the prohibition on new planting could not be regarded as an act depriving the owner of her property, since she remained free to depose of it or to put it to other uses which were not prohibited. Seen in this light, *Codorníu* merely marks the upper extreme. Any legal impairment of property rights or their exercise must suffice.[113] Factual impairments, on the other hand, are not enough, such as (to stay with the example of the vineyard) the scrapping or lowering of subsidies for wine, rendering the cultivation of some vineyards economically unviable.[114] What is required, instead, is an impairment of the rights themselves, not of the economic advantages of holding them.

To sum up the third paradigm, the holders of property rights evidenced in public registers will be individually concerned by Community measures detracting, in law, from the rights or their exercise.

C. Direct concern

The question behind direct concern has been described as one of the causality of the act's affecting the legal position of the individual.[115] More precisely, direct concern will turn on whether the effects of the act of Community law depend on the use of discretion, either by a Community institution (the one adopting the measure, or another), or by a Member State authority applying Community or national law.[116] There may be no discretion for two reasons. It may be that there is no discretion from the outset, because the legal basis in Community law of the act adopted leaves the authority no choice. Also, the discretion may have been exercised at an earlier stage already, and the course later taken was determined at that time. This occurs, typically, when a Member State applies, under Art. 134 EC, for authorization to restrict imports from third countries.[117] The Commission decision authorizing such protective measures is not an order, but a permission which the Member State may or may not make use of. Nonetheless, Member States are

---

[111] Case 44/79, *Lieselotte Hauer* v *Land Rheinland-Pfalz*, [1979] ECR 3727, para. 23.

[112] Para. 19.   [113] Paras. 23, 29.

[114] The Court emphasized in Joined Cases 133–136/85, *Walter Rau Lebensmittelwerke* et al. v *BALM*, [1987] ECR 2289, para. 18 that 'an undertaking cannot claim a vested right to the maintenance of an advantage which it obtained from an organisation of the market which existed at a given time'.

[115] Hartley, *Foundations* (fn. 20 above), p. 355, 369–373; Albors-Llorens, *loc. cit.* fn. 2, p. 73, second para.

[116] Case 113/77, *NTN Toyo Bearing*, [1979] ECR 1185, para. 11; Case T-13/99, *Pfizer Animal Health* v *Council*, [2002] ECR II-3305, para. 86.

[117] Case 62/70, *Bock* v *Commission*, [1971] ECR 897, para. 14.

important to note that Art. 241 provides no independent action against either the first or the second measure.[133] The admissibility of the action as a whole remains governed by Art. 230(4).[134] If the individual prevails with the plea under Art. 241, his success will be limited to the non-application to the instant case of the first measure. The first measure will not be quashed altogether.[135]

This procedural route applies, for instance, in the area of competition law, when the Commission imposes fines on the participants of an illegal cartel.[136] If a company thought that, say, provisions of Regulation 1/2003[137] violated its rights, it would have no standing to attack the new regulation. This is because the legal basis for the regulation, Art. 83(1) EC, does not provide for any third parties' participation in the adoption procedure; no-one's name appears in it; and no rights of the type in issue in *Codorníu* (see above at Section II.B.(ii).(b)) are implicated. The company would, therefore, have to wait for the Commission to address a decision to it, *eg* ordering it to cease and desist from participating in an illegal cartel. This decision would fulfil the criteria of individual and direct concern, and could thus be challenged under Art. 230(4). Before the CFI, the company could argue, as Art. 241 allows, that the underlying regulation on the basis of which the Commission acted is void, for one of the reasons listed in Art. 230(2) EC. If the Court found this to be the case, the decision addressed to the plaintiff company would be quashed. Other decisions based on the same regulation would, however, remain unaffected (see Art. 231(2) EC), unless they too were challenged within the time limit stipulated in Art. 230(5) EC.

(ii) Legal protection in the courts of the Member States, Art. 234(b) EC

If the second measure is taken by a Member State authority, it will be governed by national law. For this reason, the measure has to be challenged in the national courts. Within the framework of the proceedings in these courts, the same mechanism applies as described before. National authorities may, within the scope of Community law, impose obligations on an individual only if there is a legal basis for doing so in Community law.[138] The individual can, therefore, argue that the first measure is void which the second measure purportedly implements. If this is the case, the second measure is illegal because it lacks a legal base.[139] The national

---

[133] Joined Cases 31/62 and 33/62, *Wöhrmann and Lütticke* v *Commission*, [1962] ECR 501, p. 506, last para. f.   [134] Case C-239/99, *Nachi Europe*, [2001] ECR I-1197, paras. 33–36.
[135] Case T-82/96, *ARAP* v *Commission*, [1999] ECR II-1889, paras. 46–49.
[136] The same procedural mechanism applies with regard to Council Regulation (EC) No. 40/94 of 20 December 1993 on the Community Trade Mark, ([1994] OJ L11/1). This regulation is implemented not by the Commission, but by the Office for Harmonization in the Internal Market (trade marks and designs), cf. Arts. 2 and 111 ff. of Regulation 40/94.
[137] Council Regulation (EEC) No. 17/62 governed, until May 2004, the procedures of the Commission when implementing Arts. 81 and 82 EC. It was repealed and replaced by Council Regulation (EC) No. 1/2003 of 16 December 2002, on the implementation of the rules on competition laid down in Articles 81 and 82 of the Treaty, ([2003] OJ L1/1) of 4 January 2003.
[138] Case T-199/99 (fn. 129 above), para. 126.
[139] This is the same general idea as underlies Art. 241 EC, Case C-216/82, *Universität Hamburg* v *Hauptzollamt Hamburg-Kehrwieder*, [1983] ECR 2771, para. 10.

court can either accept or reject this argument. For reasons of legal certainty, the Court held in *Foto Frost* that finding an act of secondary Community law void is the preserve of the ECJ.[140] For this reason, if a national court contemplates accepting the argument it must refer under Art. 234(b) EC the question whether the first measure is indeed void. Contrary to the wording of Art. 234, second para., this applies to any national court, not just those of last instance.

There is only one situation in which a national court must not refer a question concerning the validity of an act of secondary Community law. It arose in the case underlying the Court's judgment in *Textilwerke Deggendorf* (TWD).[141] The eponymous company had received State aid from the German government. The Commission found that the aid had been granted in contravention of Art. 87 EC, and by a decision obliged the German government to recover the money paid to TWD. The company could have challenged the decision under Art. 230(4) EC, not least because its name appears in both the grounds and in the operative part. Instead, TWD waited until the German government did get back to it, reclaiming, by an administrative act, the sums paid. TWD challenged this act in the German administrative court. The company argued that because the Commission's decision misconstrued Art. 87(2)(c) EC and was thus void, the German government's attempt to claw-back the payments made to it was also illegal.

The German court referred a question to this effect to the ECJ. The Court, however, refused to entertain the reference in the interest of legal certainty: plaintiffs must use the quickest of several available procedural alternatives to establish the nullity of acts they object to. Hence, national courts must not refer a question regarding the validity of the first measure, but must instead presume its validity, if the plaintiff could have challenged the first measure under Art. 230(4), but has failed to do so in time.[142] If this is the case, the plaintiff's only grounds on which to challenge the second measure can be faults committed by the national authority in the application of national law. This would keep the dispute in the realm of national law. If, however, the plaintiff alleged a misapplication of the Community act, the national court would have to contemplate a reference concerning the act's interpretation to the ECJ. References on questions of interpretation (rather than validity) cannot be time-barred as the concern for legal certainty underlying *Textilwerke Deggendorf* do not apply (at least not to the same extent). They are unaffected by the judgment.

---

[140] Case 314/85, *Foto Frost* v *Hauptzollamt Lübeck-Ost*, [1987] ECR 4199, para. 17.

[141] Case C-188/92, *Textilwerke Deggendorf* (TWD), [1994] ECR I-833; critical assessment by Derrick Wyatt, 'The relationship between actions for annulment and references on validity after TWD Deggendorf', in Julian Lonbay and Andrea Biondi (eds.), *Remedies for breach of EC law*, (Chichester; John Wiley & Sons, 1997), p. 55, at pp. 61–63.

[142] Paras. 13–18. Where, however, it is not so clear that the plaintiff in the national court could have challenged the Community act in the ECJ direct, a reference will not be barred: Case C-408/95, *Eurotunnel plc. v Seafrance*, [1997] ECR I-6315, para. 29; Case C-239/99, *Nachi Europe*, [2001] ECR I-1197, paras. 37–40.

III. The Two Weak Spots of the System: Acts Not Requiring
Any Implementation, and Recalcitrant National Courts

As we have seen so far, individuals may challenge an act of secondary Community law under Art. 230(4) in the CFI if they are individually and directly concerned. Failing this, they may challenge the act indirectly, through actions against implementing measures. In the latter case, legal protection will be given either by the CFI, or by the courts of the Member States, co-operating with the ECJ in the framework of the preliminary reference procedure according to Art. 234(b).[143]

As far as their legal effects are concerned, indirect challenges are not inferior to a direct challenge. From the point of view of the individual plaintiff, there is only an insignificant difference between Art. 231 EC and Art. 241 EC. Under the former, the 'first' measure is declared void as the consequence of a successful challenge under Art. 230 as 'first' action. Pursuant to the latter, the 'second' measure is quashed, and the 'first' measure is not applied as a consequence of the successful 'second' action.

The same is true regarding Art. 230 as a first action, and Art. 234(b). Strictly speaking, a judgment on a preliminary reference is binding only *inter partes*, *ie* on the national court referring the question, and on the parties to the dispute before that court. Nevertheless, the Court has held that a finding of nullity is sufficient reason for any other court not to apply the provisions found void. In practice, this is indistinguishable from effects *erga omnes*, *ie* binding effect on everybody. This is reinforced by the Court's jurisprudence that renewed references after a finding of nullity may only relate to the consequences of nullity (on a similar question, see Art. 231(2) EC), while the finding of nullity itself is definitive.[144]

The situation is different with regard to the conditions for the respective challenges. Normally, the adverse effects of a generally applicable, and hence legislative rather than administrative, act of secondary Community law will only materialize in the act's application to individual cases.[145] Of necessity, this entails a delay until implementing measures are adopted. The problems this may cause can be mitigated by the ECJ's suspending the application of an act under challenge, or granting interim relief, under Arts. 242 and 243 EC respectively.

---

[143] Daig, *loc. cit.* fn. 2, p. 195 *sub* B explains the unwillingness of the Court to grant direct access more generously by the presumption on the part of the Treaty's drafters that individuals would receive sufficient protection through the indirect means provided for.

[144] Case 66/80, *Interntional Chemical Corporation* v *Amministrazione delle Finanze dello Stato*, [1981] ECR 1191, paras. 11–14. By contrast, the nullity of an act found valid before may be suggested again in subsequent references, by the same, or by third courts, but with different arguments. This is reflected in the Court's cautious wording of the operative parts of judgments under Art. 234(b) in the 'validity'-alternative: 'consideration of Regulation [1234/5678] has not disclosed any factor of such a kind as to affect its validity', see, eg Case C-491/01 (fn. 130 above), operative part, para. 1.

[145] Similarly, Harding, *loc. cit.* fn. 2, p. 358, second para.: 'until that time their interest may be presumed to be insufficient'. In the same sense Daig, *loc. cit.* fn. 2, p. 195, last para.

National courts may do so on the basis of similar principles.[146] Nevertheless, national courts may not suspend national measures implementing Community acts which would be deprived of their effects unless implemented immediately (*ie*, typically, emergency measures).[147] Although there is no jurisprudence on this point by the European Court of Justice, it may be presumed that the same restriction does not apply to Art. 242 (suspension of Community acts by the ECJ). This is because a suspension ordered by the ECJ has effect for the whole of the Community. This does not to the same extent endanger the uniform application of Community law from Member State to Member State, as would measures taken by the national courts.

These differences notwithstanding, in Art. 230(4) (as a 'second' action in the sense of Section II.D(i) above), and in Art. 234(b), the Treaty provides for a complete system for the protection of the rights of individuals against illegal incursions by the Community.[148] This is because implementing measures can only emanate from either a Community institution, or from national authorities; there is no third possibility. Also, the overall number of challenges, brought one way or another, is not reduced by a narrow, nor increased by a wide, interpretation of Art. 230(4). What is affected is merely the way in which they all, ultimately, reach the ECJ.[149] There are, nonetheless, two situations which are not catered for. In these situations, the presumption of a complete system breaks down, and remedial action might be considered.[150]

The first situation arises if an act requires no implementation at all. This is the case with prohibitions stipulated in a regulation, as opposed to a Directive or decision. Such prohibitions occur, with increasing frequency,[151] in the context of the Community's Common Fisheries Policy. Whenever the stocks of a particular fish species are in danger of being over-fished, the Commission stipulates, by means of a regulation, that vessels from designated Member States stop fishing for a certain time. Such prohibitions have immediate effect. They do not require any implementation, ie measures confirming the prohibition with regard to, or applying it to, individual cases. The only way national authorities become involved at all is by punishing those who breach the prohibition. These regulations can be adopted without the participation of quota holders. The denial of participation is justified in light of

---

[146] Case C-465/93, *Atlanta Fruchthandelsgesellschaft mbH* (III), [1995] ECR I-3761, paras. 32, 33. Nihoul, *loc. cit.* fn. 2, p. 188–189, expresses doubts as to whether a reference on validity will necessarily entail more delay than a direct challenge.

[147] Joined Cases C-143/88 and C-92/89, *Zuckerfabrik Süderdithmarschen et al.* v *Hauptzollamt Itzehoe et al.*, [1991] ECR I-415, para. 31.

[148] Case 294/83, *Parti écologiste 'Les Verts'* v *European Parliament*, [1986] ECR 1339, para. 23. Daig, *loc. cit.* fn. 2, p. 196, second para.

[149] Neuwahl, *loc. cit.* fn. 2, p. 30, fourth para., who does, however, see the advantage of indirect actions that national courts would 'act as a filter for manifestly ill-founded claims.' This might also explain why not every action declared inadmissible under Art. 230 bounces back to the Court under Art. 234(b). *Contra* Arnull, *loc. cit.* fn. 2, [2001] CMLRev p. 51, third para.

[150] Daig, *loc. cit.* fn. 2, p. 196, second para.

[151] See, *e.g*, Regulations (EC) No. 2209/2003, [2003] OJ L330/20; No. 2248/2003, L333/41; No. 2255/2003, L333/48; Nos. 2264–2267, 2282/2003, L336/20–23, 94, all within less than a week.

the urgency with which the measures need to be adopted. They only circumscribe their addressees by the flag of their vessels, not by name. The quota are not property rights of their holders. Lastly, the boats are not rendered useless. The individuals' only chance, therefore, to challenge such a regulation is first to incur sanctions, penal or administrative, and then to challenge the legality of those sanctions.[152]

The second situation not catered for in the present system occurs where a national court is not willing to consider the plaintiff's argument that the act of Community law underlying a national implementing measure might be void, or to refer a question to that effect to the ECJ.[153] There can be many reasons for such reluctance. The political significance of the matter, for instance the realization of a large infrastructure project, may be one consideration. The Community measure can go unchallenged altogether if the higher courts in the national judicial hierarchy share the recalcitrance of the lower ones.

Two mechanisms are conceivable for enforcing the obligation to refer. They are the usual mechanisms for policing Member States' obligations under Community law. One is, or rather would be, the one provided for in Art. 226 EC.[154] The notion of the 'Member State' (the defendant in any action under Art. 226) encompasses any body vested with public authority, whether constitutionally independent or not.[155] National courts thus share in the Member States' obligations under Art. 10 EC to fulfil the obligations arising out of the Treaty, and to abstain from any measures that could jeopardise the attainment of its objectives.[156] In practice, however, the Commission (which has unfettered discretion in this regard)[157] has not once brought an action under Art. 226 against a Member State for an alleged failure of its courts to live up to their obligations as Community courts in the Member States.[158] This is despite flagrant breaches of the duty to refer by, for instance, the *Conseil d'Etat*[159] and the *Bundesfinanzhof*.[160] The reason for the Commission's reluctance is

---

[152] In the same sense, Waelbroeck and Verheyden, *loc. cit.* fn. 2, p. 434, pt. 55.

[153] von Danwitz, *loc. cit.* fn. 2, p. 1112, right column, fourth para.; Nihoul, *loc. cit.* fn. 2, p. 192 *sub* C2.

[154] Imelda Maher, '*National courts as Community courts*', [1995] Legal Studies 226, p. 230, second para.; Gert Nicolaysen, *Vertragsverletzung durch mitgliedstaatliche Gerichte?* [1985] Europarecht 368, *passim*; Lenaerts and Arts, *loc. cit.* fn. 38, pts. 2-052-2-054 (p. 52 f.).

[155] Case 102/79, *Commission v Belgium* ('Tractors'), [1980] ECR 1473, paras. 14–15; Case 97/81, *Commission v Netherlands* ('Drinking water'), [1982] ECR 1819, paras. 11–12; Case C-145/97, *Commission v Belgium* ('Furnished accomodation'), [1998] ECR I-2643, paras. 1, 6, 9. For reasons of procedural economy, however, only the central government will (vicariously) be party to the proceedings before the ECJ.

[156] Case 14/83, *von Colson and Kamann v Land Nordrhein-Westfalen*, [1984] ECR 1891, para. 26; more recently, Case C-129/00, *Commission v Italy* ('Overpayments'), [2003] ECR, I-14637, paras. 29–35, 41. More generally, see Temple Lang (above fn. 2), *passim*.

[157] Case 247/87, *Star Fruit v Commission*, [1989] ECR 291, paras. 11–13; Case 48/65, *Lütticke et al. v Commission*, [1966] ECR 19, p. 27, 5th–8th para.

[158] Case T-219/95R, *Danielson v Council*, [1995] ECR II-3051, para. 77.

[159] ie, the highest French administrative court, in *Ministre de l'Interieur v Cohn Bendit*, English translation in [1980] 1 CMLR 543.

[160] ie, the highest German tax court, in *Kloppenburg* discussed below.

not difficult to fathom. The ECJ's sitting in judgment over a national court would not be conducive to the spirit of mutual respect and co-operation between the ECJ and national courts which is the very foundation of the preliminary reference system.

The second mechanism is the corollary of the first, with enforcement entrusted to individuals in the Member States. Under the *Francovich* line of case law,[161] Member States can be held liable for their courts' failure to refer questions on the validity of a Community act to the ECJ. While this was, for a long time, a rather theoretical possibility,[162] the Court has now expressly recognised this application of its jurisprudence.[163] It is true that the judgment in *Köbler* dealt with the failure to refer a reference for the interpretation of Community law, rather than its validity. The reasoning must, however, be the same for the latter paradigm. What remains is the question which rights are violated by the failure to refer a question on validity. Part of the answer is, the same (property) rights as under the third paradigm for individual concern under Art. 230(4) (the *'Codorníu'* paradigm).

These property rights are rather narrowly circumscribed. They would not help those who wanted to challenge, say, a quota allocation. Article 234 EC, itself, imposes obligations on (some) national courts, but does not give rise to corresponding rights on the part of individuals.[164] These limitations do not, however, determine standing in the national courts. They do also not bar any Community or national rights individuals may have when it comes to references.[165] Article 234 may not be the source of these rights, but it may still be the vehicle for their realization.

IV. Participation by National Courts as a Systemic Weakness? Advocate General Jacobs' opinion in *Unión de Pequeños Agricultores*

The most comprehensive reflection by an Advocate General ('AG') concerning the case law on Art. 230(4) EC was offered by AG Jacobs in his opinion in *Unión de Pequeños Agricultores*. It is appropriate to deal with the opinion first not only because

---

[161] Starting with *Francovich*, and developed in *Brasserie de Pêcheur*, fn. 3 above.

[162] Bernhard Wegener, 'Staatshaftung für die Verletzung von Gemeinschaftsrecht durch nationale Gerichte?' [2002] Europarecht 785, *passim*.

[163] Case C-224/01, *Köbler* v *Austria*, [2003] ECR I-10239, paras. 33–36, 51–59. According to para. 122, breach will not be sufficiently serious, however, if a reply to the question cannot be found in the ECJ's case law, and if the reply was not obvious. The misreading by the national court of a judgment by the ECJ will not suffice. This appears a rather lenient application of the requirements, given that initially, the national court had correctly identified, and referred under Art. 234, an ambiguous point of Community law. Then, however, it withdrew its reference because it thought the answer followed from a judgment rendered by the ECJ in the meantime, yet not exactly on the same point, paras. 107–117.

[164] Joined Cases T-377/00 *et al, Philip Morris International et al.* v *Commission*, [2003] ECR II-1, para. 105.   [165] See Section VI below.

of its thoughtfulness but also because this best reflects the sequence of events: the CFI was appraised of the opinion when it delivered judgment in *Jégo-Quéré*, and the ECJ could draw on both when deciding *Unión de Pequeños Agricultores*.

While building largely on ideas first put forward in the opinion in *Extramet*,[166] the opinion in *Unión de Pequeños Agricultores* significantly develops the argument. In it, the AG takes issue with the proposition that the preliminary ruling procedure provides full and effective judicial protection against general Community measures. He develops two theses to this effect, which will be considered in turn. The gist of his critique is most poignantly captured in the first thesis, on wich the remainder of the opinion rests. His critique is followed by the AG's own proposal for a change in the case law, after two alternative proposals have been rejected.

A. 'Proceedings Before National Courts may not Provide Effective Judicial Protection of Individual Applicants'

The first of the AG's arguments to underpin the thesis that proceedings before national courts may not provide effective judicial protection of individual applicants[167] is that national courts may not declare measures of Community law invalid. This is in contrast with their competences when it comes to the interpretation, application, and enforcement of Community law.[168]

This point is uncontroversial. Since *Foto Frost*,[169] the ECJ, for reasons of legal certainty and in the interest of the uniform application of Community law in all Member States, has insisted on its monopoly to declare Community law void. Some Member States' legal systems reserve the right to quash normative acts to constitutional courts, but limit this increased protection to parliamentary statutes.[170] Any other act of general application can, if illegal, be set aside by any court. In the absence of a hierarchy among the various types of secondary Community law,[171] however, this is not a viable option (yet).[172]

---

[166] Case C-358/89, *Extramet* v *Commission*, [1991] ECR I-2501, pp. 2507 ff.
[167] Heading before para. 38 of the opinion.   [168] Para. 41.
[169] Case 314/85, *Foto Frost v Hauptzollamt Lübeck-Ost*, [1987] ECR 4199.
[170] See, eg Art. 100(1) of the German constitution: 'where a court considers that a law on whose validity its ruling depends is unconstitutional, it . . . shall seek a ruling . . . from the Federal Constitutional Court'.
[171] See Case C-136/96, *Scotch Whisky Association*, [1998] ECR I-4571, para. 47: Regulation as *lex specialis* to a Directive.
[172] Declaration No. 16 annexed to the Treaty on European Union 1992 on the hierarchy of Community acts provided that, 'The Conference agrees that the Intergovernmental Conference to be convened in 1996 will examine to what extent it might be possible to review the classification of Community acts with a view to establishing an appropriate hierarchy between the different categories of act.' This has not been done in subsequent intergovernmental conferences. Arts. I-36 and I-37 of the Draft Constitutional Treaty ([2004] OJ C310/1) do not go beyond the principle that delegated legislation must keep within the limits of the enabling act, already *in nuce* contained in Art. 202 EC, see Case C-159/96, *Portugal* v *Commission* ('Chinese Textiles'), [1998] ECR I-7379, paras. 40–45.

Secondly, the AG argued that plaintiffs have no right for national courts to refer a question on the validity of Community law (or, for that matter, any type of question, be it on validity, or on interpretation) to the ECJ.[173] National legal remedies against such refusal, if they are available at all, take time. Also, even if the national court decides to make a reference, it alone determines the content of the question referred.[174]

This, however, is in the nature of the procedure under Art. 234, it is, in the words of the Court, its 'inherent feature.'[175] The national court retains full responsibility for the resolution of the dispute pending before it.[176] The European Court of Justice is a mere adviser in this, if an authoritative one: more than an *amicus curiae*, but less than a court of higher instance.[177] The responsibility of the national court would be obscured if the parties to the proceedings could, 'over the head' of the national court, engage in whatever sort of dialogue with the ECJ. Consequently, the Court has resisted any attempts at this.[178]

The third argument makes a related point. According to the AG, indirect challenges entail significant extra costs and delay. In the meantime, national courts

---

[173] In the same sense, see Case T-377/00 (above fn. 164), para. 105.   [174] Para. 42.

[175] Case 97/85, *Union Deutsche Lebensmittelwerke et al.* v *Commission*, [1987] ECR 2265, para. 12.

[176] This is the starting point whenever the Court assesses the objection that a reference is inadmissible because the case in the national court (allegedly) does not involve Community law etc., see Case C-439/01, *Libor Cipra et al.* v *Bezirkshauptmannschaft Mistelbach*, [2003] ECR I-745, para. 18. This is not to deny that the guidance given by the Court can vary considerably. Even where the guidance given is more a leash than a helping hand, however, the point remains that the judgment enforceable between the parties is rendered by the national court; the point of Community law is only one of several to be considered.

[177] *Contra* Rasmussen, *loc. cit.* fn. 2, p. 114, fourth para., and p. 122, fourth para., who argues that the aim of the ECJ in denying direct access under Art. 230 is to function as a kind of supreme appelate court for the Community, 'or something very like it' (Conclusion, p. 126). Some of his arguments for this have been overtaken by time: for example, since the extension of majority voting in successive Treaty amendments, Member States have challenged Community acts in increasing numbers. Also, the Court has awarded damages (as representative of the long-running 'milk-quota saga', see Case C-104/89, *Mulder* (No. 2), [1992] ECR I-3061), and has decoupled the action under Art. 235 from national remedies (see, eg Joined Cases T-481/93 and 484/93, *Vereniging van Exporteurs in Levende Varkens* v *Commission*, [1995] ECR II-2941, paras. 69–72). On close inspection, the 'appelate court-hypothesis' is based on a superficial similarity: appelate courts determine questions of law alone, only lower courts are also charged with establishing the facts of the case (Rasmussen p. 124). Under Art. 234, the Court's ruling is on an abstract question of law, the factual side of the dispute is for the national court alone (p. 116, fifth para.). Hence in Rasmusen's view, the ECJ seeks to instal itself as an appelate court (p. 125, second and third para.). Crucially, however, the Court is in no position ever to quash a judgment by a national court, and either to refer it back, or itself to decide the case.

[178] Case C-261/95, *Palmisani* [1997] ECR I-4025, para. 31: 'Article 234 of the Treaty instituted a *system of direct cooperation between the Court of Justice and the national courts* by way of a non-contentious procedure which is *completely independent of any initiative by the parties*, who are merely invited to state their case within the legal limits laid down by the national court' (emphasis added); Case C-412/96, *Kainuun Liikene*, [1998] ECR I-5141, paras. 21–24; Case C-435/97 *WWF et al.* v *Autonome Provinz Bozen et al.*, [1999] ECR I-5613, paras. 28–33. The ECJ will, however, be guided by the submissions of the parties where the national court has set out its concerns against the validity of an act of Community only in vague and general terms, see Joined Cases 103/77 and 145/77, *Royal Scholten Honig*, [1978] ECR 2037, paras. 16–17.

may grant interim relief. To some extent, however, they do so at their discretion. In any case, measures adopted by national courts to grant interim relief are limited in their application to the Member State in question. The plaintiff might seek relief in several Member States simultaneously, but uniform decisions would not be guaranteed.[179]

There are indeed practical disadvantages to this indirect method of challenging Community law. Disapplication of an act of Community law in some Member States, but not in others, would distort competition between economic operators in the several States. How one gauges this danger is another matter. On the one hand, and this confirms the AG's position, Member States' courts have only limited scope for granting interim relief against national measures implementing an allegedly void act of Community law. Before they do so, they must consider the cumulative effects of such disapplication by courts in several Member States.[180] This requirement is intended to caution them against granting interim relief lightly. On the other hand, it is by no means a foregone conclusion that the ECJ will grant interim relief, or that it will at least be readier to do so than national courts.[181]

The wider question behind this and the second argument is, however, why the Treaty should provide at all for the involvement of national courts in the adjudication of the legality of Community acts. The AG's critique is so comprehensive that it can be understood to see the participation by national courts in the control of the validity of secondary Community law *in itself* as a weakness of the system. The Court seems to view things differently. Its answer is aptly summarized by a phrase used in an earlier judgment: the national courts are 'the ordinary courts of Community law'.[182] To put it differently, the division of functions between the ECJ and the national courts is rooted in the same considerations that underly the principle of subsidiarity in Art. 5 EC.[183] This provision applies specifically to the legislative competence of the Community. It does not, however, exhaust the principle of subsidiarity. A wider reading is found in the last recital of the preamble to

---

[179] Para. 44.

[180] Case C-465/93, *Atlanta Fruchthandelsgesellschaft mbH* (No. 3), [1995] ECR I-3761, para. 44.

[181] For a recent denial, see Case T-155/02R, *VVG Internationale Handelsgesellschaft et al.* v *Commission*, [2002] ECR II-3239, paras. 17–19. In fact, the Court grants interim relief very rarely.

[182] Case T-219/95R, *Danielson* v *Council*, [1995] ECR II-3051, para. 77; already in Case 283/81, *CILFIT*, [1982] ECR 3415, para. 7, the Court had spoken of 'national courts, in their capacity as courts responsible for the application of Community law'. Similarly, Marco Darmon, *Réflexions sur le recours préjudiciel*, [1995] 31 Cahier de Droit Européen 577, at p. 578, fourth para.: 'Le juge national est le recours légal du particulier. *Juge communautaire du droit commun*, il applique directment la norme communautaire' (emphasis added). See also Maher, *loc. cit.* 154, *passim*.

[183] Stephen Weatherill, *Law and Integration in the European Union*, (OUP, 1995), p. 109, first para.: '[Art. 234] displays the best aspects of subsidiarity'. Further examples in Weatherill & Beaumont, *European Union Law*, (3rd. edn, London, Penguin 1999), p. 559. In the same sense Nihoul, *loc. cit.* fn. 2, p. 194. By contrast, Waelbroeck and Verheyden, *loc. cit.* fn. 2, p. 435, pt. 58, argue that subsidiarity would require the ECJ to allow direct actions to remedy the shortcomings of challenges under Art. 234; similarly Vandersanden, *loc. cit.* fn. 2, p. 549, pt. 32.

the Treaty on European Union. It says that it is in accordance with the principle of subsidiarity if 'decisions are taken as closely as possible to the citizen'. This idea applies in the judicial sphere, too. The involvement of national courts in the adjudication of Community law gives that law a 'local presence', both institutionally and substantively.

Institutionally, it allows citizens to turn to courts in their proximity, where their language is understood by everyone on the bench, without the help of interpreters. In substantive terms, the participation of national courts in assessing the validity of secondary Community law is the flipside of the principles of supremacy and direct effect of Community law. Those courts routinely apply Community law. They use it as a guide to the interpretation of national law. This helps avoid clashes between the legal orders. Incompatibilities would otherwise have to be resolved by Community law's asserting its supremacy. This outcome, if at all avoidable, is in nobody's interest; it is preferable to interpret national law in a way that renders it compatible with Community law. Apart from this, national courts apply Community law without the medium of national law, as a consequence of either the direct applicability, or direct effect, of Community law. Community law is, thus, as much part of the law of the land as is the law created by national legislatures and courts. Member States' courts are called upon to measure national law by the yardstick of Community law which is, in all its binding varieties, higher-ranking than national law of any description.[184]

In the same way, national courts should be the first ports of call for any queries regarding the compatibility of secondary Community law with higher-ranking (typically primary) Community law. This not only acknowledges, in a way conducive to their willingness to co-operate, their central role in the judicial edifice of the Treaty's judicial system. It also makes national courts the one-stop-shop for the legal protection of the individual, thus bringing decisions in matters vital to the individual 'closer to the citizen'. Seen in this way, the system as set up in Arts. 230 and 234 is not defective. Rather, it embodies a balance between efficiency and integration. This balance may be struck differently. Quite a separate question is, however, whether any 'correction' of this balance can be brought about by jurisprudential means, as the AG argued, or whether this requires a Treaty amendment, as the Court held.

Apart from this, counsel to the plaintiff will always try to cast the net of possible grounds of annulment as wide as possible, including irregularities purely under national law. Pleadings based on national law, however, will always be for the national courts alone. No-one currently suggests transferring them to the ECJ, and the Court has always been adamant that questions of national law are for the national courts alone.[185] As soon as the parties, therefore, allege faults under national law, the bifurcation in the legal protection returns. To make

---

[184] Case 11/70, *Internationale Handelsgesellschaft* v *Einfuhr- und Vorratsstelle für Futtermittel*, [1970] ECR 1125, para. 3.   [185] See the text below at fn. 236 and 237.

matters even more complicated, the national court thus seised might want to refer a question on interpretation under Art. 234(a) to the ECJ. The question, for instance, whether the national authorities have correctly exercised their discretion depends on the leeway the underlying Community act grants them in the matter. The ECJ would not want to give judgment on the question before the validity of the act is ascertained. This is advisable not least because the Community act might have to be interpreted restrictively in order to be legal in the first place.[186] As a consequence, however, the national proceedings would be yoked with the necessity to await the outcome of the Court's finding on validity in exactly the same way as is currently the case with a reference on validity under Art. 234(b).

The AG's third argument was that where no implementation of the act of Community law is required, individuals would have to break the law in order to gain access to justice. This is, in the eyes of the AG, not a reasonable proposition (para. 43). This justified criticism is the very idea underlying the CFI's judgment in *Jégo-Quéré*, considered below.[187]

B. 'Proceedings before the Court of First Instance Under Art. 230 are Generally More Appropriate for Determining Issues of Validity than References Under Art. 234'

To underpin the proposition that proceedings before the CFI under Art. 230 are generally more appropriate for determining issues of validity than references under Art. 234, the AG argues firstly that the adopting institution is party to the proceedings throughout.[188] Secondly, the problems of interim relief mentioned before do not occur.[189] Thirdly, direct actions can only be brought within two months, thus speeding legal certainty. By contrast, preliminary references concerning substantially the same question can be brought before the Court long after this.[190]

The first point is correct, if more of a technical nature. Art. 15 of Regulation 1/2003, for instance, provides for a method of creating transparency in the application of Arts. 81 and 82 EC by Member States' courts. It allows the Commission to make, where necessary, representations in national proceedings. This might serve as a model for Art. 234. Problems of interim relief have been discussed above. The problem of legal certainty, addressed by the third argument, arises also in proceedings before the ECJ. It can be dealt with, more or less satisfactorily, by

---

[186] For an example, see Case 29/69, *Erich Stauder* v *Stadt Ulm, Sozialamt*, [1969] ECR 419, where the Court avoids annulling a Community regulation by interpreting it restrictively in the light of the plaintiff's human rights, or Case 15/81, *Schul*, [1982] ECR 1409, paras. 42–43: interpretation of a Directive on VAT in the light of Art. 90 EC.   [187] cf. Section V below.

[188] Paras. 46–47.   [189] Para. 46.   [190] Para. 48.

limiting to the future (*ex nunc*) the temporal effects of judgments;[191] Art. 231(2) EC envisages this possibility for direct actions.

C. Reform Proposals by the Parties to *Unión de Pequeños Agricultores*

Before advancing his own solution, the Advocate-General rebutted the suggestions of, respectively, the plaintiffs and the defendants. *Unión de Pequeños Agricultores* had suggested that, in the absence of sufficient remedies under national law, an individual should be allowed to bring an action in the ECJ. Against this, the AG argued that the interpretation of national law was not the task of the ECJ. Also, standing might, as a consequence of this approach, differ from Member State to Member State.[192] This is undeniable, and it tallies with the long-standing view of the Court that it is not called on to interpret national law. This argument became decisive in the judgment in *Unión de Pequeños Agricultores* to deny the company standing.[193]

Council and Commission, by contrast, had argued that the solution should be sought in an amendment of the rules of national procedural law if those rules made it difficult or impossible for individuals to obtain legal protection. Against this, the AG highlighted the fact that, as a matter of Community law (Art. 234 EC), there would still be no right for individuals to have national courts refer questions to the ECJ. An obligation under national law, however, would be difficult to enforce. Also, the suggestion would entail a far-reaching incursion into the Member States' procedural autonomy.[194]

One might wonder whether Art. 234 must indeed be read in the way suggested by the AG. In *Foto Frost*,[195] the ECJ already substituted 'shall' (as in Art. 234, third para.) for 'may' in Art. 234, second para. The ECJ has, arguably, not yet exhausted the potential of this judgment. Also, an obligation under national law to refer need not be more difficult to enforce than other procedural provisions. At any rate, Member States' procedural autonomy is not absolute. It is limited by the requirements of equivalence and effectiveness,[196] flowing from Art. 10 EC. This provision belongs to the 'principles' of the Community, as indicated by the Treaty's chapter heading. It is the legal basis for national courts' obligation to interpret national law—public or civil, and whenever adopted—so far as possible in a way that ensures its compatibility with Community law.[197] Hence, if a national

---

[191] Joined Cases C-177/99 and C-181/99, *Ampafrance*, [2000] ECR I-7013, paras. 64–69.
[192] Paras. 50–53.   [193] Para. 43 of the judgment.   [194] Paras. 54–58.
[195] Case 314/85, *Foto Frost v Hauptzollamt Lübeck-Ost*, [1987] ECR 4199.
[196] cf. text and references in fn. 237.
[197] Case 14/83, *von Colson*, [1984] ECR 1891; Case 79/83, *Harz*, [1984] ECR 1921; Case C-106/89, *Marleasing*, [1991] ECR I-4135; Case C-443/98, *Unilever Italia v Central Food*, [2000] ECR I-7535; and Case C-287/98, *Linster*, [2000] ECR I-6917.

court fails to do so, this is a failure to construe Member State law correctly. Like other such failures, it is reviewable under national law. Considered this way, it is more a matter of taste whether an express stipulation that failure to refer questions on the validity of Community law must also be reviewable, is really such a far-reaching incursion at all. A similar principle is already recognized, as a matter of national law, in at least one Member State. Arguably, Community law can also be interpreted in this way.[197a]

D. The Advocate General's Own Reform Proposal

The AG's own solution is that 'a person is to be regarded as individually concerned by a Community measure where, by reason of his particular circumstances, the measure has, or is liable to have, a substantial adverse effect on his interests'.[198] He identified several advantages of this proposal: no-one who was directly affected would ever be without legal protection (para. 63). The disadvantages of indirect challenges would be avoided (para. 65). A simple criterion would replace ever more opaque and questionable distinctions in the case law on Art. 230 (paras. 64, 66–71). These advantages are undeniable, yet they might appear less enticing if one were not to subscribe to all aspects of the AG's critique on which they build.

The AG also argued that the proposal would harmonize the interpretation of Art. 230 with that of Arts. 235 and 288(2) EC (action against Community institutions for non-contractual damages). Under this procedure, comparable limitations as under Art. 230 do not apply, despite the fact that the substantive questions are related (para. 72).

It is true that the substantive questions are similar under both proceedings. This is, however, where the similarities end. According to the jurisprudence of the Court, the two actions are, with few exceptions, independent of each other.[199] What is more, a longer time-limit applies to actions under Art. 235 (five years according to Art. 46 of Protocol No. 6 on the Statute of the Court of Justice, annexed to the Treaty) which the AG highlighted as a shortcoming of indirect challenges as compared to direct ones. An assimilation of Arts. 230 and 235 does, therefore, not appear the most obvious solution to the problems besetting the present system of challenging the validity of secondary Community law.

A further advantage of the proposed solution is, according to the AG, that it would bring Community law up-to-date with developments in the laws of the Member States. The latter are all more generous in granting standing (paras. 85–86).

[197a] cf. Section VI below.

[198] (para. 60) In a similar sense earlier Vandersanden, *loc. cit.* fn. 2, p. 548, pt. 29, with a proposal for a reworded Art. 230 on p. 551, pt. 35.

[199] Case T-186/98, *Inpesca* v *Commission*, [2001] ECR II-557; most recently in Case T-180/00, *Astipesca SL* v *Commission*, [2002] ECR II-3985, paras. 139–141, 145, 146. Albors-Llorens, *loc. cit.* fn. 2, p. 208 also emphasises the different purposes of the two actions.

The argument derived from the admissibility of actions in national courts does not, however, seem to be based on a comparison of like with like. Community regulations, at least basic regulations,[200] are the equivalent of parliamentary statutes in a national setting. It is by no means clear that in all Member States, or even in a majority of them, it is possible to challenge such legislation in the courts.[201]

The AG acknowledges that it may be true that access to judicial review of legislation is generally subject to stricter conditions than review of administrative measures. Nevertheless, the laws of the Member States do not in general *exclude* individuals from challenging legislation (allegedly) violating constitutionally enshrined rights or fundamental principles of law (para. 89).

The point would, however, have to be made that it is *as easy* to challenge legislation as any other legally-binding measure. It might be precisely because of the two tiers of courts, Community and national, involved in the review of Community law, that direct access to the ECJ need not be granted as generously as access to the national courts.[202] In the same way, access to constitutional courts in the national setting is sometimes made dependent on prior exhaustion of all remedies in the ordinary courts.[203]

Finally, the suggested interpretation of Art. 230(4) would, the AG argued, adequately transpose the Court's jurisprudence on the principle of effective judicial protetction in national courts of rights derived from Community law (paras. 97–98).

To the extent that there would be no (reasonable) access to national courts at all, this idea has been taken up by the CFI in *Jégo-Quéré*. With regard to situations where there is access to those courts, the AG's argument seems, once again, to view indirect review under Art. 234(b) as merely an inefficient detour to the ECJ, without any intrinsic value. It is not a foregone conclusion that this is the most plausible, let alone the only possible interpretation (see Section IV.A.(i) above).

---

[200] 'Basic' regulations are those which lay down the broad outlines of policy in a given field. They are typically adopted by the Council, alone or jointly with the European Parliament under the co-operation procedure, and authorize the Commission to adopt more specific implementing provisions. The distinction in Art. 202, third indent, EC (mentioned by the AG in para. 90 of his opinion) does not establish a lesser status, with regard to the possibility of judicial review, of such implementing measures, as least not as the Treaty currently stands, see Moitinho de Almeida, *loc. cit.* fn. 2, p. 870, second para.

[201] see Harlow, *loc. cit.* fn. 2, p. 228, third para.; Harding, *loc. cit.* fn. 2, p. 356, second para.; Moitinho de Almeida, *loc. cit.* fn. 2, p. 869, second para. Like the AG, however, Waelbroeck and Verheyden, *loc. cit.* fn. 2, pp. 404–425, and more guarded pp. 436–439: the first passage refers to acts that would have to be characterised as 'bye-laws', whereas the second, more to the point made in the text, is about statutes properly so-called.

[202] Waelbroeck and Verheyden, *loc. cit.* fn. 2, p. 440, pt. 68 (similarly Ward, *loc. cit.* fn. 2, p. 203, third para.) see a contradiction in the Court's insistence that Member States provide effective remedies for rights derived from Community law (see fn. 237), when the Court itself is not wiling to grant such remedies regarding challenges to Community acts. This criticism is, however, also not based on a comparison of like with like: with respect to challenges of Community measures, the functions of national courts and ECJ are complementary, whereas in the national realm, national courts are alone responsible.

[203] For an example, see §90(2) of the *BVerfGG* (Law on the German Federal Constitutional Court).

In all, therefore, the reform proposal is fully convincing only on the basis of the AG's criticism of the existing system—which one may or may not share.

V. The First Weakness and the Development in the Court's Case Law: *Jégo-Quéré*

A.   The Court of First Instance's Judgment of 3 May 2002

In June 2001, the Commission adopted a regulation for the immediate reduction in the fishing of hake. The regulation applied to specific fishing areas, and prescribed a minimum mesh size for fishing nets in order to protect juvenile hake. Also, the regulation only applied to boats over a certain length, fishing for longer than a defined time. *Jégo-Quéré's* boats and fishing effort answered this description, and hake accounted for ca. 2/3 of the company's catches. The company challenged the regulation before the CFI; the Commission raised the objection of inadmissibility. The Court ran through the test of admissibility in the way described above:

The CFI first established that the provisions of the regulation addressed, in abstract terms, an indefinite category of persons and objectively defined situations.[204] The general scope of its provisions did not, however, mean that the regulation could not be of direct and individual concern to *Jégo-Quéré*.[205] The Court had no problem establishing direct concern, as the regulation did not require the application of other rules, and left no discretion in its application.[206] For the assessment of individual concern, the Court took the *Plaumann* formula as its starting point. The mere fact, however, that *Jégo-Quéré* was the only company whose boats were affected, and that its catches were drastically reduced, was not decisive.[207] There was also no specific provision of Community law which obliged the Commission to ascertain, or to take notice of, the circumstances of *Jégo-Quéré* before adopting the regulation.[208] Article 33 EC, or any informal contacts between the Commission and *Jégo-Quéré*, were equally insufficient to establish individual concern.[209] Nor were there circumstances which singled the company out as did those in *Codorníu* or *Extramet*.[210]

The judgment thus merely confirms what has been developed above. So far, there is nothing novel about it. Nonetheless, *Jégo-Quéré* would, for want of an action under Art. 230(4) EC, have had no legal recourse whatsoever. This was because the regulation required no implementation by national authorities against which the company could turn (para. 39). Access to a judge, the Court pointed out, is a fundamental requirement of the rule of law on which the Community is based. Such access is moreover recognized and protected in the

---

[204] Paras. 23–24.   [205] Para. 25 with reference to, *i.a.*, *Extramet* and *Codorníu*.
[206] Para. 26.   [207] Paras. 29–30.   [208] Paras. 32, 36.   [209] Paras. 33–35.
[210] Para. 37.

European Convention for the Protection of Human Rights, and in the Charter of Fundamental Rights of the European Union proclaimed at the Nice summit in December 2000.[211]

There was no alternative redress for *Jégo-Quéré* commensurate with these standards: none under Art. 234 EC, as the company would first have to break the law before it could challenge the validity of the regulation underlying that law; and none under Art. 235/288 EC, either, because damages would not remove the allegedly illegal act, but merely mend, retroactively, its consequences. Also, under the latter procedure, review by the Court is limited to assess whether a sufficiently serious breach of a superior rule of law for the protection of the individual has occurred.[212] Simple illegality is not enough.

As a consequence, whilst the CFI pointed out that these circumstances did not allow it to declare admissible an action which did not meet the requirements of Art. 230(4),[213] under the prevailing circumstances, there was no need to limit standing to those who are singled out in a way similar to the addressee of the measure, as required by the *Plaumann* formula.[214] Rather, in order to provide a complete system for the control of the legality of all Community acts, a person will be considered as individually concerned if a measure of general scope affects the person directly, and if the person's rights are affected in a manner which is both definite and immediate. This would be the case if the person's rights were restricted, or obligations imposed on him. The number and the situation of others who are equally affected is immaterial in this regard.[215] The action was, therefore, declared admissible, and judgment on the substance was reserved.

The judgment might give rise to two misconceptions. The first is that it is of universal application, thus revolutionizing the interpretation of Art. 230(4).[216] The second might be that it is of no significance at all beyond the narrow confines of the case. In order to understand *Jégo-Quéré's* proper place and contribution to the Court's jurisprudence, these misconceptions have to be addressed in turn.

(i) Revolution?

The first misconception of the judgment could be that it throws overboard the Court's entire jurisprudence on individual concern. In this view, the judgment would replace the essentially procedural notion of individual concern with a substantive one. It is true that the regulation in issue in *Jégo-Quéré* was not of individual concern, in the technical sense, to the company. This alone, however, is not decisive. Crucially, the regulation did not require any implementing measures. There was, therefore, no way to the CFI, nor to a national court, other than following a breach of the prohibition stipulated in the regulation. First incurring prosecution (or being subjected to

---

[211] Paras. 41–42.   [212] Paras. 45–47.   [213] Para. 48.   [214] Para. 49.
[215] Paras. 50–51.

[216] This was the first reaction of some lawyers to the judgment, quoted in Financial Times of 4/5 May 2002, and Ragolle (above fn. 2), at p. 90.

any other procedure with a view to the imposition of sanctions) is, however, no longer regarded as reasonable by the Court. This would force the plaintiff to seek his or her rights, as it were, fighting 'with the back against the wall'. In this, the Court takes up, somewhat belatedly,[217] a suggestion made by AG Verloren van Themaat in his opinion in *Binderer*.[218] The AG had argued that the Court should grant immediate access to a plaintiff in cases where a preliminary reference could only arise out of criminal proceedings in a national court.

In this situation, *Jégo-Quéré* will still not allow just anyone, by means of an *actio popularis*, to challenge a regulation (or other measures not requiring implementation). The judgment expressly retains a test of individual concern: the measure must '[affect the plaintiff's] position, in a manner which is both definite and immediate, by restricting his rights or by imposing obligations on him'. This formula contains two elements. It talks, firstly, about the manner in which the plaintiff must be affected, and secondly, about rights restricted and obligations imposed. On close inspection however, the Court translates the first element into the second. The preposition 'by' indicates that a restriction of rights or an imposition of obligations brings about the required definite and immediate change in the plaintiff's legal position.[219] The restriction or imposition will do so in a situation where the regulation does not require any implementing measures.

Seen in this light, the test for individual concern looks very similar to the definition for when a measure is legally binding.[219a] The difference is, however, that for an act of secondary Community law to be legally-binding, it is enough that it restricts the rights of (or imposes obligations on) anyone at all, not necessarily the plaintiff. This is because the requirement of a binding act applies to actions brought by any applicant, even to those brought by the so-called privileged applicants listed in Art. 230(2) EC. These may challenge a measure in order to defend their own rights, or someone else's, or purely in the interest of the legality of Community law. Private (or 'non-privileged') applicants, by contrast, may only pursue their own interest under Art. 230. In other words, they must, under the *Jégo-Quéré* test for individual concern, argue that they come within the personal scope of the measure in issue. That is, they must make the case that it is they (alone, or among others) on whom the regulation imposes obligations, or from whom it takes rights away.

---

[217] In the order in Case 55/86R, *Arposol* v *Commission*, [1986] ECR 1331, para. 19, the President of the Court held that '. . . any penalties imposed by the courts of that Member State will be imposed in accordance with the procedure in force in that state, so that procedural safeguards, rights of appeal, and the *possibility of requesting the European Court of Justice for a preliminary ruling* will be available' (emphasis added). In the actual judgment, however, the Court held that the regulation in issue was not of direct concern anyway ([1988] ECR 13, paras. 11–13).

[218] Case 147/83, *Binderer* (above fn. 94), at p. 262.

[219] This is confirmed by other language versions of the judgment. The French original says '. . . si la disposition en question *affecte, d'une manière certaine et actuelle*, sa situation juridique *en restreignant ses droits ou en lui imposant des obligations*' (emphasis added). The German version reads '. . . wenn diese Bestimmung ihre Rechtsposition *unzweifelhaft und gegenwärtig beeinträchtigt, indem* sie ihre Rechte einschränkt oder ihr Pflichten auferlegt' (emphasis added).

[219a] cf. Section II.A above.

This substantive test of individual concern is, in effect, not so different from the procedural one. The reason why certain parties are granted the right to participate in the procedure is, on the one hand, that they have first-hand knowledge of the market affected, which is valuable to the Community institution adopting the act. On the other hand, and this is often the corollary of the first aspect, these parties will be affected in their legal position by the measure eventually adopted. To put it differently, those who would have to be heard will mostly be the same as those whose legal position is materially affected. *Jégo-Quéré* does not, therefore, in substance deviate much from the existing case law. Rather, it adapts this case law to the situation of an act which is of direct concern to the plaintiff, and which does not require any implementing measures at all, but which is, at the same time, not of individual concern in the usual, technical sense. For such acts, too, *Jégo-Quéré* establishes a filter against attempts to use Art. 230(4) as an *actio popularis*.

(ii) Nothing Happened?

The second misconception might be that *Jégo-Quéré* was, to use a well-worn phrase, 'decided on the facts'. That is to say, it has no wider implications, and will not again come to be applied, except in strictly identical factual circumstances (allowing, of course, for different parties, and maybe a different regulation under challenge). Quite apart from the fact that this assertion can always be made, to argue in this way would ignore the systematic context of the judgment. As we have seen, there was, previously, a gap in the legal protection of those affected by measures of the type in issue in *Jégo-Quéré*. The gap might have appeared tolerable to the Court some 20 years ago in *Arposol*, but this was not good enough any more.

The Court was finally swayed in the other direction by three factors. There is, first, a heightened awareness of fundamental rights. This has found expression recently in the Charter of Fundamental Rights of the European Union, alluded to in *Jégo-Quéré*.[220] This is true despite the fact that the said document is, at present, not legally binding. Secondly, it is more clearly understood that there is no point in having rights if they cannot be enforced. For this reason, Art. 47 of the Charter grants a right to an 'effective' remedy. Thirdly, Community law has, since the 1990s, come under increased scrutiny, both in the legal, and possibly even more in the political sphere. It could not be seen to cover policy areas previously reserved for the Member States, without correspondingly extending adequate legal protection to individuals.

As it turns out, therefore, *Jégo-Quéré* is only a reading of Art. 230(4) EC in the light of the plaintiff's human rights.[221] This is hardly a novel approach. We find this technique already in 1969, in the *Stauder* case.[222] This judgment started the Court's

---

[220] Paras. 41 and 47.

[221] Similarly, the ECJ explained in Case C–312/00P, *Commission v Camar et al.*, [2002] ECR I-11355, para. 78, that its judgment in *UPA* is motivated by the principle of effective legal protection.

[222] Case 29/69, *Erich Stauder v Stadt Ulm, Sozialamt*, [1969] ECR 419. Another prominent example is the Court's jurisprudence on the duty of Member States' courts to interpret national law in the light of Community law, see fn. 197 above.

jurisprudence on human rights as guaranteed under Community law. In *Stauder*, a regulation was read in the light of the human rights of those affected by it. Human rights were, henceforth, recognized as 'rules of law relating to [the] application [of the Treaty]' in the sense of Art. 230(2) EC. The situation in *Jégo-Quéré* is different in that a provision of the Treaty itself, Art. 230(4), is read in the light of human rights. Here is not the place to embark on a discussion whether the Treaty contains rules of different rank, and what rank unwritten rules should be accorded. Rather, *Jégo-Quéré* fits an established interpretative pattern: that of the teleological interpretation of norms of Community law. The purpose of Art. 230(4) is to help individuals assert their rights under Community law. The interpretation of the provision must be guided by this purpose. The technical (procedural) interpretation of the provision, combined with the remedies available for those lacking *locus standi* under Art. 230 as a 'first action',[222a] is capable of ensuring sufficient legal protection for individuals in most cases. Where the traditional interpretation fails to achieve this, it must be replaced with another, suitable one. No more and no less is done in *Jégo-Quéré*. It would, therefore, be too simple to dismiss the judgment as an isolated incident. *Jégo-Quéré* does contain a principle of wider importance.

B. The European Court of Justice' judgment in *Unión de Pequeños Agricultores*—revocation of *Jégo-Quéré*?

Only a few months after the CFI's judgment in *Jégo-Quéré*, the ECJ had the opportunity again to consider the requirement of effective judicial protection under Community law, in its judgment in the case of *Unión de Pequeños Agricultores* (UPA).[223]

UPA was a trade association representing small Spanish agricultural businesses. It had, in the CFI, challenged a regulation which discontinued an aid scheme for olive oil.[224] The CFI held the action inadmissible because the association did not fulfil the usual conditions (see Section II.A–C above) for individual concern. The CFI also rejected UPA's argument that it should be held individually concerned, and thus granted access to the Court, because the route through the Spanish courts would not grant it effective legal protection. UPA appealed against the order of the President of the CFI to the ECJ. In both instances, the association proferred essentially the same arguments why its fundamental right to effective judicial protection was infringed.

Firstly, the regulation did not require any national implementing measures against which those affected could turn. Unión de Pequeños Agricultores' members could not even breach a prohibition and then challenge the validity of any sanctions imposed on them.[225] Secondly, even if they could, the regulation was

---

[222a] cf. Section II.D.(i) above.
[223] Case C–50/00P, *Unión de Pequeños Agricultores* v *Council*, [2002] ECR I-6677.
[224] Case T-173/98, *Unión de Pequeños Agricultores* v *Council*, [1999] ECR II-3357.
[225] Para. 25 of the CFI's order; repeated, as a ground of appeal, in para. 26 of the ECJ's judgment.

only valid for three years; proceedings in the national court, including a reference to the ECJ, would take longer than that.[226] UPA also contended[227] that the Spanish government had refused a request by the region of Andalucia to challenge the regulation, as a privileged applicant under Art. 230(2). The Commission retorted in the appeals proceedings that UPA or its members could apply to the Spanish authorities for payment of the aids received before, and then challenge a refusal or a failure to comply on the part of those authorities.[228]

In response, the ECJ first set out the traditional definition of individual concern.[229] Next, it stressed individuals' entitlement to effective judicial protection, as required by the rule of law.[230] To this end, the Treaty had established a system of judicial protection, providing both for direct, and indirect means of protection.[231] The ECJ went on to say that Member States must enable individuals to obtain protection under Community law in the national courts. This obligation follows from Art. 10 EC.[232] It was not, however, the Court's task, when reviewing the legality of Community measures, to examine in each case whether indeed, national law enabled individuals to be so protected. It would go beyond the jurisdiction of the ECJ to grant access to the Court directly if national law failed to grant adequate protection.[233] This would, effectively, abolish the requirement of individual concern. It could, therefore, not be done by jurisprudential means. Instead, a formal Treaty amendment would be required (paras. 44–45).[234]

The question whether this overrules *Jégo-Quéré*, if implicitly, can be answered in two ways. Firstly, it can be seen as an overruling.[235] On the face of the judgment in *UPA*, the Court is unwilling to attempt any interpretation of its own of national (procedural) law. It will also not be drawn into controversies between the parties on the interpretation of national law.[236] This is in keeping with the ECJ's jurisprudence on Art. 234. The Court has consistently held that the interpretation of national law is exclusively for the courts of the Member States,[237] a task they

---

[226] Para. 30 of the order, not repeated in the proceedings before the ECJ.
[227] Para. 28 of the order.   [228] Para. 31 of the judgment.   [229] Paras. 35–37.
[230] Paras. 38–39.   [231] Para. 40. See Section II.D above.   [232] Paras. 41–42.
[233] Para. 43. The President of the CFI in a later judgment emphasized that this applies even more where the plaintiffs did not deny that there was recourse to the national courts which allowed the Community act to be called into question, Case T-155/02R, *VVG Internationale Handelsgesellschaft et al.* v *Commission*, [2002] ECR II-3239, para. 39.
[234] The same argument was, before *Jégo-Quéré*, used by the CFI in Joined Cases T-172, 175–177./98, *Salamander et al.* v *EP & Council*, [2000] ECR II-2487, paras. 74–75.
[235] Ragolle (above fn. 2), at p. 97 f.
[236] See, most recently, Case C-153/00, *Paul der Weduwe*, [2002] ECR I-11319, paras. 35–39, and Daig, *loc. cit.* fn. 2, p. 197, second para.
[237] See the summary, with references, in Case C–107/98, *Teckal* v *Commune di Viano*, [1999] ECR I-8121, para. 33. This should not be confused with the Court's respect for the 'procedural autonomy of the Member States', limited, however, by the principles of equivalence (or non-discrimination) and effectiveness, cf. most recently Case C-255/00, *Grundig Italiana* v *Ministro delle Finanze* (No. 2), [2002] ECR I-8003, paras. 33–41, and Case C-336/00, *Republik Österreich* v *Martin Huber*, [2002] ECR I-7699, paras. 55–58, 61. The last mentioned jurisprudence only applies once the meaning of national provisions has been established by the referring national court. The ECJ will treat this

must carry out before referring questions to the ECJ.[238] Seen in this light, any arguments about the deficiencies of national procedures are reserved for proceedings under Art. 226. They have no place in the context of Art. 230. To entertain them in this context would 'go beyond [the Court's] jurisdiction when reviewing the legality of *Community* measures'.[239]

Secondly, however, the ECJ's response has to be understood against the backdrop of the underlying dispute, and of the parties' arguments. There is a crucial difference between the regulations in issue in, respectively, *Jégo-Quéré*, and *Unión de Pequeños Agricultores*. The fishing regulation in issue in *Jégo-Quéré* stipulated an absolute prohibition. Member States have lost all residual competences in the area covered by the Common Fisheries Policy.[240] They cannot grant any quota over and above those provided for at the Community level.[241] For this reason, there could not even be a procedure in which the authorities' future course of action would be in issue.[242] Any interference with the system established by the regulation would be impermissible.[243] As a consequence, there would be no other context but criminal proceedings (or some other procedure resulting in sanctions) in which arguments against the regulation's validity could be raised at national level. This remains true even if national law offered some procedure for seeking, beforehand, a declaration from the authorities that they would not prosecute violations of the regulation.[244] It is established in the court's jurisprudence that the exercise of rights under Community law can never, as such, be against public policy and give rise to criminal sanctions.[245] In the same vein, individuals must not be compelled to assert their rights in criminal proceedings, or *vis-à-vis* prosecuting authorities.

The regulation in issue in *Unión de Pequeños Agricultores*, by contrast, abolished subsidies paid by the Community. State aids paid by Member States are, in principle, prohibited by Art. 87(1) EC. This prohibition, however, is subject to the statutory exceptions in the second paragraph, and to the discretionary ones listed in the third. The Commission has laid down guidelines for State aid in the

---

interpretation as a given, Case C-261/95, *Rosalba Palmisani*, [1997] ECR I-4025. Similarly, the Court will not be drawn into any controversies about the factual basis of the dispute in the national court, *Teckal*, para. 30.

[238] Case C-83/91, *Wienand Meilicke* v *ADV-Orga AG*, [1992] ECR I-4871, para. 29

[239] Para. 43 of *UPA*, emphasis added.

[240] Case 804/79, *Commission* v *UK* ('Fish resources'), [1981] ECR 1045, paras. 29–30.

[241] This is the backdrop to the long-running *Factortame* saga, beginning with Case C-246/89, *Commission* v *United Kingdom*, [1991] ECR I-4585.

[242] For an example of such a procedure, see Case C-491/01, *R* v *Secretary of State for Health, Ex p. British American Tobacco (Investments) Ltd. et al.*, [2002] ECR I-11453: judicial review of 'the intention and/or obligation' of the United Kingdom Government to transpose Directive 2001/37/EC (manufacture, presentation, and sale of tobacco products) into national law.

[243] See, for the pre-emptive effect of a common organisation of the market in an agricultural product, Case 16/83, *Criminal proceedings against Karl Prantl*, [1984] ECR 1299, para. 13.

[244] This is why Temple Lang's (above fn. 2) trust in actions for declarations as a panacea for the problems of Art. 230(4) might not be entirely justified.

[245] Case 48/75, *Royer*, [1976] ECR 497, paras. 32, 39, 48.

agriculture sector.[246] The discontinuation of the scheme of Community aid, therefore, did not mean that any national replacement would under any circumstances be illegal. In fact, of the whole Treaty section on state aids, only Art. 88(3) EC stipulates an unconditional prohibition,[247] and it only addresses Member States, anyway. The worst private recipients of illegal aid might have to fear is civil liability towards their competitors.[248] The *economic* consequences for UPA's members of the reduced income may have been grave. Nonetheless, the companies would never have to defend themselves against these consequences 'with their backs against the wall' from a *legal* point of view.

Seen in this light, *Unión de Pequeños Agricultores* does not overrule *Jégo-Quéré*.[249] The more recent judgment establishes that as long as secondary Community law does not stipulate an absolute prohibition, the Court will not enquire further, under Art. 230 EC, as to what procedures are available under national law. Such an enquiry is, if anything, for proceedings under Art. 226. The earlier judgment concerned precisely such an absolute prohibition. The two judgments can, therefore, exist alongside one another.[250]

VI. The Second Weakness, and the Non-development in the Court's Case Law

A. The Obligation to Refer Questions on Validity

We have seen above (at Section II.D.(ii)) that national courts can be under an obligation to refer to the ECJ questions regarding the validity of secondary Community law. This extends to any piece of secondary Community law of whose illegality a national court is convinced (*Foto Frost*)[251] provided, of course, the question is relevant to the outcome of the case before that court.[252] Conversely, it is always open to the national court to refer a question to the ECJ if it wants to reject the allegation of nullity of the first measure.[253]

A reference may also be appropriate where the plaintiff's arguments are not obviously unfounded, and there is no previous jurisprudence by the ECJ on the question. One might go further, however, and ask whether a reference would be

---

[246] [2000] OJ C28/2, with corrigendum in [2000] C232/17.

[247] Case C-332/98, *France* v *Commission*, [2000] ECR I-4833, paras. 31–32; Case C-39/94, *SFEI et al* v *La Poste et al.*, [1996] ECR I-3547, para. 39.

[248] Case C-39/94, *SFEI et al* v *La Poste et al.*, [1996] ECR I-3547, paras. 72–75.

[249] Waelbroeck, *loc. cit.* fn. 2, [2002] CDE 5, last three paras., and p. 6, last para., highlights that the judgment is by no means clear, and does not pre-empt the future interpretation of the notion of individual concern.

[250] For this reason, it appears that AG Jacobs in his opinion in Case C-263/02P, *Commission* v *Jégo-Quéré*, [2004] ECR I-3425, paras. 46–47, gave up the case for a re-interpretation of Art. 230(4) too early. [251] Case 314/85, *Foto Frost* v *Hauptzollamt Lübeck-Ost*, [1987] ECR 4199.

[252] Most recently Case C-318/00, *Bacardi-Martini* v *Newcastle United FC*, [2003] ECR I-905, paras. 44–51. [253] Case C-321/95P, *Greenpeace* v *Commission*, [1998] ECR I-1651, para. 33.

compulsory in these circumstances. An early answer (in the negative) to this question was that to require a reference of a court convinced of the legality of an act of Community law would amount to exaggerated formalism, and would serve no purpose; courts of last instance were under a duty to refer, anyway.[254] Short of a Treaty revision, however, reconsidering the interpretation of Art. 234(b) offers the best hope of remedying the second weakness in the system of legal protection for individuals under Community law.

The purpose of the procedure under Art. 234 is to safeguard the uniform interpretation and application of Community law in the Member States.[255] In the situation where a national court wants to uphold the validity of an act of secondary Community law, there is not the same danger to the uniformity and coherence of Community law as when a national court wanted to 'go it alone' in matters of interpretation, let alone of validity. Thus, if a national court upholds the validity of an act of Community law, the integrity of the Community legal order remains intact. Material justice, however, would suffer if an illegal act were not expunged. This consideration might yet sway the national court to refer the matter, despite its conviction that the Community act is legal, and despite the absence of much of a threat of sanctions if it does not refer.[256] It is a different matter, however, whether considerations of material justice are enough to impose an *obligation* to refer, even if the national court is convinced of the legality of the Community act.

This obligation could flow from two sources. Firstly from national law, interpreted in the light of the requirement, under Community law, to provide effective legal remedies. In this context, Member States are not obliged to create entirely new remedies.[257] They must, however, make any existing remedies available for the protection of rights derived under Community law, even if such remedies would not be applicable to comparable actions based purely on domestic law.[258] Secondly, the obligation could flow directly from Community law, like the obligation under the *Francovich* jurisprudence to make good damage caused as a consequence of breaches of Community law by Member States.

Upholding material justice is one aspect (besides the creation of legal certainty) of the 'observance of the law' which Art. 220(1) EC sets the ECJ as its task. Article 234 is but one, specific emanation of this overarching mission. This provision, therefore, has to be read in the light of Art. 220. As a consequence, there is not a

---

[254] Bebr, '*Examen en validité au titre de l'art. 177 du traité CEE et cohésion juridique de la communauté*', [1975] 11 Cahiers de droit européen 379, at p. 385, Second para.

[255] Case 283/81, *CILFIT*, [1982] ECR 3415, para. 7; Case 314/85, *Foto Frost* v *Hauptzollamt Lübeck-Ost*, [1987] ECR 4199, para. 15.

[256] This is despite the fact that the ECJ has accepted that Member States can be held liable for their courts' failure to refer. On Case C–224/01, see fn. 163.

[257] Case 158/80, *Rewe* v *Hauptzollamt Kiel*, [1981] ECR 1805, para. 44.

[258] Case C-97/91, *Oleifici Borelli* v *Commission*, [1992] ECR I-6313, paras. 13–15.

choice, or a trade-off, between legal certainty and material justice. As soon as one of them becomes relevant, a reference is mandatory. Hence, whenever arguments are raised regarding the illegality of an act of secondary Community law, and these arguments are not obviously spurious or have already been rejected by the ECJ, every national court is under an obligation to refer a question regarding the validity of the act to the ECJ.

Confirmation for this interpretation can be seen in the Court's judgment in *Foto Frost*. In para. 17 of the judgment, the Court held that, 'since Art. 230 gives the Court the exclusive jurisdiction to declare void an act of a Community institution, the coherence of the system requires that *where the validity of a Community act is challenged before a national court*, the power to declare the act invalid must also be reserved the Court of Justice' (emphasis added).[259] The referring German court in *Foto Frost* was convinced of the illegality of the Community regulation whose applicability or otherwise was crucial to the outcome of the action pending before it (para. 11). Nonetheless, the ECJ does not make this conviction a condition for the obligation to refer. Instead, the obligation to refer follows from the 'necessary coherence of the system of legal protection established by the Treaty' (para. 16). This is in keeping with the Court's jurisprudence that the right to an effective remedy before a court of competent jurisdiction is guaranteed in Community law.[260] 'Effective' legal protection requires that no arguments go unheard by a court that could draw legal consequences from them, and help the party raising them to their right. Such protection cannot, however, be achieved if there is no guarantee that the only court which can entertain arguments regarding the invalidity of secondary Community law would become involved in the proceedings at some stage.

It is true that in para. 14 of the judgment in *Foto Frost*, the Court held that, '[national] courts may consider the validity of a Community act and, if they consider that the grounds put forward before them by the parties in support of invalidity are unfounded, they may reject them, concluding that the measure is completely valid. By taking that action they are not calling into question the existence of the Community measure'.[261] This, however, would preclude plaintiffs from having even serious arguments tested in the ECJ, simply because the national court, for whatever reasons, will not endorse them. The deficiencies highlighted by AG Jacobs in his opinion in *Unión de Pequeños Agricultores* would thus

---

[259] Similarly, in Case C-209/94P, *Buralux et al.* v *Council*, [1996] ECR I-615, para. 36, the Court held that, 'it is therefore possible for the appelants to argue, in support of an action cahllenging a refusal given under the contented provision . . . that that provision is unlawful, thereby obliging the national court to rule on all of the claims made in that respect, after a preliminary reference to the European Court of Justice for an assessment of its validity'.

[260] Case T-177/01, *Jégo-Quéré* v *Commission*, [2002] ECR II-2365, para. 41, with further references.

[261] Reiterated, eg, in Case C-27/95, *Woodspring District Council* v *Bakers of Nailsee*, [1997] ECR I-1847, para. 19.

be compounded. By contrast, the advantages, from the point of view of the integration of Community law in the Member States' legal systems, of plaintiffs having to go through the national courts would not fully accrue. Community law would be applied in the Member State, even when it should not be.[262]

The letter of Community law would be observed, but its spirit would not. To paraphrase the last sentence of para. 14 of *Foto Frost*, not to call the existence of a Community measure into questions can be as wrong (if for different reasons) as to do so. National courts would not act as gateways, but as traps for actions that would be heard by the ECJ, were it not for the absence of individual and direct concern on the part of the plaintiff. *Foto Frost* can, therefore, be read to relieve national courts of the duty to refer only where the allegation of illegality is manifestly unfounded, or has already been rebutted by the European Court of Justice.

The Court's judgment in *CILFIT* leads to the same conclusion, but from a different angle. It establishes a quasi-objective test for when, under Art. 234, a national court of last instance[263] may or may not assume that there is a 'question' of Community law for which it should seek clarification from the ECJ. What counts in this respect is not what the court hearing the case subjectively deems so clear that there is no 'question' about it (hence the test is not purely subjective). Rather, it must, in the absence of jurisprudence by the ECJ on the point, imagine itself in the shoes of every other national court, and of the ECJ (this makes the test quasi-objective). It must also heed the peculiarities of Community law, and must be fully aware of the nuances each of the individual official language versions (all of which are equally authentic) may add to the interpretation.[264] At the very least, these daunting requirements should make national courts very suspicious of their own certainties. In reality, they reduce the Court's endorsement of the *acte claire*-doctrine to mere lip-service. While *CILFIT* applies only to courts of last instance, the method prescribed therein of approaching questions of Community law is not limited to specific courts, or to questions of interpretation rather than validity. As under *CILFIT*, so under *Foto Frost*, certainty is hard to come by in the absence of previous jurisprudence by the ECJ.

---

[262] Ward, *loc. cit.* fn. 2, p. 268, second para. (similarly Olivier Dubos, *Les juridictions nationales, juges communautaire*, Paris (Dalloz) 2001, p. 104, first and second para.), concurs that a declaration of validity can be as problematic as one of invalidity; this is because uncertainty would arise from conflicting findings, in this respect, by several national courts. In other words, the first national court before which serious doubts regarding the legality of an act of Community law are raised might as well refer the question, even if it tends towards a finding of validity, because some plaintiff will sooner or later convince another court of the act's invalidity. In these circumstances, referring the question to the ECJ gets it 'out of the system' in the interest of everybody.

[263] According to Case C–99/00, *Criminal proceedings against K.R. Lyckeskog*, [2002] ECR I-4839, paras. 14–19, the duty to refer pertains to the highest courts and those lower courts against whose judgments no further appeal is *possible*, regardless of whether or not a higher court actually accepts the appeal.   [264] Case 283/81, *CILFIT*, [1982] ECR 3415, paras. 17–20.

B. An Individual Right to have Questions on Validity Referred

The position of individuals with regards to references has recently been bolstered, if cautiously, by the ECJ's judgment in *Köbler*.[265] It would be further enhanced if, as a matter of Community law, there were a right for individuals to have national courts' refusals to refer questions of validity reviewed by higher-ranking national courts.

An example of such a right can be seen in the Bundesverfassungsgericht's (German Federal Constitutional Court) judgment in *Kloppenburg*.[266] The Bundesfinanzhof (German Federal Tax Court), in its judgment in an action brought by Ms Kloppenburg, denied the direct effect of certain Community tax provisions. It did so despite the fact that direct effect of the Directive in question had been established by the ECJ.[267] What is more, the court refused to refer its contrary reading of the Community provisions (and indeed its disapproval of the entire doctrine of direct effect) to the ECJ. This judgment was quashed, on a constitutional complaint by Ms Kloppenburg, by the Federal Constitutional Court.

A constitutional complaint is not an appeals procedure. The Federal Constitutional Court will not check judgments for any misapplications or misinterpretations of statutory law. Within the remit of the Federal Constitutional Court come only violations of human rights granted by the German constitution. In the case of the Federal Tax Court's judgment, the court found a violation of Ms Kloppenburg's right under Art. 101(1), second sentence, GG: 'Nobody may be removed from their lawful judge'. The ECJ is the lawful judge, in the sense of this provision, for all questions where serious doubts are raised regarding the interpretation or validity of Community law.

It is established in the jurisprudence of the Federal Constitutional Court that only arbitrary conduct in this respect will violate the human right. 'Arbitrariness' will be present where the national court either does not even see the possibility of refering a question; where it openly goes against the relevant jurisprudence of the ECJ; or where an answer different from the one given by the national court clearly emerges from Community law as interpreted by the ECJ.[268] This qualification has two advantages: firstly, it renders the test of arbitrariness purely objective and legal;

---

[265] Case C-224/01, *Köbler v Austria*, [2003] ECR I-10239. See also above fn. 163.

[266] (1987) 75 BVerfGE 223—*Kloppenburg*, English translation in [1988] 3 CMLR 1. More recently, and with a summary of the case law on this question, see Bundesverfassungsgericht, 1 BvR 1036/99, *R v Germany*, judgment of 9 January 2001, para. 18 (the judgment can be found at http://www.bverfg.de/). In this case, the Bundesverwaltungsgericht (Federal Administrative Court) had sought to deal of its own with an allegation that provisions in Directive 86/457/EEC amounted to indirect sex discrimination in breach of Directive 76/207/EEC. The question how to solve such conflicts had not been discussed by the ECJ yet, so that the Federal Constitutional Court found that the Federal Administrative Court, by trying to solve the problem applying national methodology alone, had breached its obligation to refer.

[267] Case 8/81, *Ursula Becker v Finanzamt Münster Innenstadt*, [1982] ECR 53, para. 49.

[268] Order of the Federal Constitutional Court of 9 Nov 1987 in Case 2 BvR 808/82, [1988] Europarecht 190—*Denkavit*, under 2(b)(bb) and 3(b). See also *R v Germany*, (above fn. 266), paras. 21–24.

nothing turns on the subjective motivations of the judges when they (allegedly) acted arbitrarily, and the facts underlying the dispute need not be re-examined. Secondly, the test merely establishes an outer limit to the discretion of judges as to whether there are serious doubts about the answer from the point of view of Community law. National procedural autonomy remains otherwise unaffected.

To transfer this model to the Community plane seems preferable to a wholesale reform of Art. 230(4) EC.[269] It is only a variant on the right to legal protection, recognized in the legal systems of all Member States. It would seek a solution to the problem of recalcitrant national courts (or rather, courts over-confident of their interpretive capacities) where it originates, namely in the framework of the judicial system of the Member States. It does not add obligations which national courts do not already have, but rather brings out in sharper relief their existing obligations under Art. 234. Finally, properly qualified by the requirement of arbitrariness, it will not lead to a flood of spurious appeals, but merely help correct the relatively few lapses occurring in an otherwise workable system.

VII. Conclusion

The Community system for the protection of individual rights, as interpreted by the ECJ, is better than the criticism of the jurisprudence on Art. 230(4) EC may lead one to believe. What is more, the Court has recently, in its judgment in *Jégo-Quéré*, closed one of the remaining gaps. At the same time, its judgment in *Unión de Pequeños Agricultores* leaves open the way to solutions for the second weakness in the system. The elements of such a solution are already present, partly in Community law, partly in national law. To draw them together would take the Community one step closer to the realization of the rule of law, as envisaged in Art. 220 EC.

VIII. Epilogue

The European Court of Justice has lately quashed the CFI's judgment in *Jégo-Quéré*.[270] The ECJ gave two reasons. Firstly, it was possible for national law to allow individuals to seek from national authorities a measure open to challenge, where a challenge would otherwise require a breach of the provision to which the individual takes exception. It was possible for the laws of the Member States to do likewise in case the individual wanted to challenge a regulation of direct concern to them.[271] Secondly, the interpretation of Art. 230(4) as proposed by the CFI would remove all meaning from the requirement of individual concern as set out in that provision.[272]

---

[269] *Contra* Usher (above fn. 2), at p. 599 f., who is in favour of legislative reform (as in the draft constitution).   [270] Case C-263/02P, *Commission* v *Jégo-Quéré*, [2004] ECR I-3425.
[271] Para. 35.   [272] Para. 38.

As far as the first argument is concerned, it follows from the Court's preceding quotations from *Union de Pequeños Agricultores*, viz. that it was for the Member States to establish a suitable system of legal remedies. The Community courts would not become involved, even where it was obvious that the Member States had failed to establish such a system.[273] This begs the question what remedies are left to the individual in this case, Articles 230 and 234 being out of the picture? The answer, presumably, is to be found in the judgments in *Francovich* and its progeny, and especially, as far as national courts are concerned, in *Köbler*. Nevertheless, it would be flattering to describe the Court's curt (and above all, hypothetical) assertion as a reasoned engagement with the arguments exchanged on four occasions in Luxembourg, not to mention in the numerous articles on the topic. The second reason is not much more convincing. The CFI did give *a* meaning to the requirement. To hold that this is *no* meaning is only understandable on the assumption that the traditional interpretation is all there is to say about 'individual concern'. Why? The two lines of para. 38 contain, in effect, nothing beyond the Court's asserting its authority.

Finally, lest the perfect be the enemy of the good, it should be said that after two years, Art. 230(4) is back where it was[274]—but that the system as a whole is workable. Short of a Treaty amendment,[275] or legislative action by the Member States, the obligation on national courts as proposed above might offer an alternative way of catching the few cases that still slip through the net.

[273] Paras. 29–34 of the judgment in Case C-263/02P, above fn. 270.

[274] Note also the Court's dealing with individual concern based on procedural rights in paras. 44–47.

[275] Or rather, adoption of the July 2003 draft Constitutional Treaty with Art. III-270(4) which drops the requirement of 'individual concern'. On this, see Usher, *loc. cit.* above fn. 1. In the Council's December 2004 draft Art. III-365(4), however, the requirement reappears for most types of legislative act, especially for 'European Laws', as Art. I-33(1) renames Regulations.

Worker Involvement in the *Societas Europaea*: Integrating Company and Labour Law in the European Union?

*Jeff Kenner**

I. Introduction

First mooted as early as the mid-1950s, the European Company or *Societas Europaea* (SE) was launched as a prototype by Professor Pieter Sanders when delivering his inaugural lecture at the Rotterdam School of Economics in 1959.[1] Sanders envisaged the creation of a uniform type of public limited company operating on a supranational plane whilst co-existing with companies created under national laws. The idealized SE construct would reflect a distinctively European approach to the foundational ethos of the transnational corporation and its system of management and control. The *Societas*, the Latin term for a 'simple partnership', is based on the principle that each partner is the agent for the others, and every partner is fully liable for all contractual obligations of the partnership.[2] Under the original SE model the company would be located within the European public realm,[3] able, on the one hand, to take advantage of the freedom offered by the emergent common market and the liberalization of capital movements, and yet bound, on the other hand, to give voice to the interests of shareholders and others with a stake in the enterprise,

* School of Law, University of Nottingham.
[1] See P. Sanders, 'Towards a European Company?' [1960] *Le Droit Européen* 9. Translated into English in P. Sanders, *European Stock Corporation* (Commerce Clearing House, 1969). For discussion of the original proposal see D. Thompson, 'The Project for a Commercial Company of European Type' (1961) 10 I.C.L.Q. 851.

[2] See D. Thompson, 'The Proposal for a European Company,' *European Series No. 13* (London: Chatham House, 1969) p.23. The term was used by Italian merchants in the Middle Ages. See also, the French term '*société*' and the German '*Gesellschaft*', both used to connote a company or partnership.

[3] In the sense that the company would perform public service activities or functions regulated by the State. This approach is based on the continental public law model. For a critique, see C. Harlow, 'Public Service, Market Ideology and Citizenship' in M. Freedland & S. Sciarra (eds.), *Public Services and Citizenship in European Law: Public and Labour Law Perspectives* (Oxford: Clarendon Press, 1998) 49–56 at 50.

including employees.[4] It was a strikingly simple concept that, rather like the European single currency, had an instant appeal for integrationists who understood its transformative potential and recognized that progress towards economic and political union would be hastened by the establishment of a supranational regime of company law based on a commonality of European values.

Although formally initiated in 1970,[5] the SE proposal was not adopted until 2001 after many setbacks and a great deal of repackaging along the way.[6] This article will trace the long journey of the SE from academic pipedream to legislative reality. Its aims will be, firstly, to explain why the idea of the SE has persisted for over 40 years and how it has evolved, and, secondly, to demonstrate that significant changes to the original SE model reflect shifts in patterns of what we would describe today as 'corporate governance'. These issues will be addressed by reference to two interrelating and recurring themes that lie at the heart of the project. First, the SE framework, uniquely at Community-level, links company law and labour law in an integrated fashion by requiring an element of worker involvement in the enterprise as a precondition. Second, at a conceptual level, the SE represents a Community intervention in favour of an idea of regulated capitalism based on the notion that the public corporation is bound to act in accordance with enlightened principles of social responsibility.[7]

In the conclusion I will contend that the pluralistic SE framework that has emerged is best understood as a signifier of a potential convergence of European models of corporate governance and social policy based on striking a better (if not yet fair) balance between the desire of shareholders to maximize the return on their investment, for whom the ability of the management of the company to act in their best interests is essential, and the broader needs of workers and other stakeholders, whose livelihood is dependant on those actions, and who therefore have a legitimate demand for a degree of influence over the company's operations and future direction.

---

[4] Other 'stakeholders' might include bondholders, creditors and communities affected by corporate activity. See I. Lynch-Fannon, *Working Within Two Kinds of Capitalism: Corporate Governance and Employee Stakeholding: US and EC Perspectives* (Oxford: Hart Publishing, 2003) 3.

[5] COM(70) 600 final, 24 June 1970, [1970] OJ C124/1, EC Bull. Supp. 8/70.

[6] Council Regulation 2157/2001 of 8 October 2001 on the Statute for a European Company (SE), [2001] OJ L294/1, and Council Directive 2001/86/EC of 8 October 2001 supplementing the Statute for a European Company with regard to the involvement of employees, [2001] OJ L294/22. For discussion see V. Edwards, 'The European Company—Essential Tool or Eviscerated Dream?' (2003) 40 C.M.L.Rev. 443, P. L. Davies, 'Workers on the Board of the European Company?' (2003) 32 I.L.J. 75, E. Werlauff, 'The SE Company—A New Common European Company from 8 October 2004' [2003] Euro.Bus.L.Rev. 85, and S. Ebert, 'The European Company on the Level Playing Field of the Community' [2003] Euro.Bus.L.Rev. 183.

[7] See especially, C. Schmitthoff, 'Social Responsibility in European Company Law' (1978–1979) 30 Hastings L.J. 1419 at 1422, and J. Hunt, 'The European Union: Promoting a Framework for Corporate Social Responsibility?' in F. Macmillan (ed.), *International Corporate Law Annual: Volume 2, 2002* (Oxford: Hart Publishing, 2003) 123–40.

II.   The Metamorphosis of the European Company (SE): From Uniformity to Flexibility

In 1965, in response to a memorandum from the French Government, the European Commission set up an expert group chaired by Sanders to investigate the viability of introducing the SE. Nearly four years after the publication of Sanders' Report,[8] the Commission proposed a Community Regulation on the Statute for a European Company (SE)[9] on the basis that there was an asymmetry between company laws of a national character and the economic framework of the common market that needed to be developed in the Community. Put at its simplest, the obvious solution was to permit the formation of companies wholly subject to a specific and uniform legal system that would be directly applicable in all Member States.[10] The creation of transnational SEs was preferred to a unification of company law, which would have been extraordinarily complex even for the original six,[11] and presupposed uniform tax laws, a development regarded as too contentious from the earliest days of the Community.[12]

The proposal for the SE chimed with the Community's industrial policy, which sought to strengthen the competitiveness of European companies by offering them instruments and rules facilitating cross-border mergers and co-operation.[13] In an attempt to match the success of American corporations it was envisaged that the formation of SEs would spur competition between efficient companies, help achieve economies of scale within a larger market and lead to specialization in key sectors.[14] The establishment of SEs would also complement the basic freedom of companies to establish their operations, including subsidiaries, throughout the Member States based on the principles of non-discrimination and mutual recognition.[15] It was hoped that companies would seize the opportunity

---

[8] See Thompson n.2 above and P. Storm, 'Statute of a Societas Europaea' (1967) 5 C.M.L.Rev. 265. For a comparison between the 1966 and 1970 drafts, see P. Sanders, 'Structure and Progress of the European Company' in C.M. Schmitthoff (ed.), *The Harmonisation of European Company Law* (London: The United Kingdom National Committee of Comparative Law, 1973) 83–100. See also, S.D. Cheris & E.R. Fischer, 'The European Company: Its Promise and Problems' (1971) 6 Stan.J.Int.Studies 113, J.B. Hood, 'The European Company Proposal' (1973) 22 I.C.L.Q. 434, and A. Swain, 'The Common Market Responds to the 'American Challenge': The Proposal for a European Company' (1972) 45 S.Cal.L.Rev. 1168.

[9] The legal base for the proposal was the general powers provision in Art. 235 EEC (now Art. 308 EC).   [10] COM(70) 600, preamble.

[11] For example, Germany has been particularly resistant to interference with its rules for the incorporation of companies. See H. Halbhuber, 'National Doctrinal Structures and European Company Law' (2001) 38 C.M.L. Rev. 1385.   [12] Thompson n.1 above at 859.

[13] See the Commission's 'Colonna memorandum' of 1970, EC Bull. Supp. 4/70.

[14] Swain n.8 above at 1170.

[15] Arts. 12, 43 and 48 EC. See generally, V. Edwards, *EC Company Law* (Oxford: Clarendon Press, 1999), M. Siems, 'Convergence, Competition, *Centros* and Conflicts of Law: European Company Law in the 21st Century' (2002) 27 E.L.Rev. 47, and J. Wouters, 'European Company Law: *Quo Vadis?*' (2000) 37 C.M.L.Rev. 257.

of a federal form of incorporation that transcended national obstacles to mergers across frontiers.[16] Further, it was envisaged that companies would choose the location of the SE and move capital for positive reasons of an economic, strategic and organisational nature, rather than out of any negative desire to 'race to the bottom'[17] by shifting their operations to Member States with more lax company law regimes and creating a European equivalent of the 'Delaware effect'.[18]

Under the Commission's original proposal the SE would be entirely optional for companies, which might decide to remain subject to one or other system of national law. Moreover, the Statute would apply to mergers between companies incorporated in different Member States, the formation of a holding company by such companies, and joint subsidiaries formed by such companies. Hence, it was a prerequisite that only public companies established in Member States who wished to operate on a transnational basis would be able to transform themselves into an SE.[19] By contrast with Sanders' draft, companies based outside the Community would only be able to participate in an SE indirectly. They would have to establish a subsidiary in a Member State, which would then be able to launch a joint venture with a European company.[20] The SE was intended to be particularly attractive to small and medium-sized companies who had not been able to expand throughout Europe because of restrictive national rules on mergers or the establishment of subsidiaries.

Comprising some 284 articles, the original SE draft sought to offer a complete system of company law to be applied and interpreted uniformly throughout the Community.[21] At the core of the proposal was a requirement for a dual board,

16 See Davies n.6 above at 77.

17 The 'race to the bottom' theory arises in deregulatory federal systems such as the US where States are allowed to unilaterally lower their social standards in order to undercut other States. Business relocate in response and other States respond by lowering their standards in order to compete. In *Ligett* v *Lee* [1933] US 557, Judge Brandeis used the phrase 'race of laxity' in his dissenting opinion to describe the competition between States to reduce regulatory requirements so as to attract business. See B. Hepple, 'New Approaches to International Labour Regulation' (1997) 26 I.L.J. 353 at 355–356.

18 This term is associated with a spiral of corporate deregulation in the United States following the Delaware Corporation Act of 1899. See W.L. Cary, 'Federalism and Corporate Law: Reflections upon Delaware (1974) 83 Yale L.J. 663, C. Barnard, 'Social dumping and the race to the bottom: some lessons for the European Union from Delaware?' (2000) 25 E.L.Rev. 57 at 57–63, and cf. R.K. Winter, 'State Law, Shareholder Protection and the Theory of the Corporation' (1977) 6 Jo. of Legal Studies 251.   19 Sanders n.8 above at 85.

20 Ibid. at 87. Sanders suggested that this restriction was political but would not necessarily make a significant difference in practice.

21 Matters governed by the proposal included access to and formation of the SE, share capital, company organs, accounts, groups of companies and supplementary provisions dealing with dissolution, liquidation or insolvency of the company. An exhaustive list of matters was to be dealt with at general meetings and the rights of shareholders were to be carefully protected. Under Art. 7(1) any matters governed by the Statute but not referred to expressly were subject not to national law but to the uniform interpretation of the Court of Justice. National law would only be invoked where the question of interpretation fell outside the scope of the Statute, Art. 7(2).

executive and supervisory, based closely on the system of company law in West Germany.[22] Although the executive board would be responsible for day-to-day management and leadership of the SE, the supervisory board would exercise a separate controlling function, appointing the members of the executive board and having 'permanent control over the management of the company by the executive board'.[23] Worker involvement would be guaranteed by the fixed composition of the supervisory board that was to include employees' representatives amounting to between one-third and one-half of its members, the remainder being appointed by the general meeting.[24] The governing idea was to lock in co-operation and the exchange of information while enabling employees to have 'some influence' over the undertaking's strategic policies.

The supervisory board would have the power to advise on any matter of importance to the company, either on request or of its own volition,[25] but would have no power to intervene directly in the management of the company.[26] Prior authorization of the supervisory board would be required before, *inter alia*, closure or transfer of an undertaking or substantial parts thereof, substantial curtailment of its activities, substantial organisational changes and establishment or termination of long-term co-operation with other undertakings.[27]

In addition, a separate external body, or 'European Works Council' (EWC), was to be informed and consulted by the executive board about matters concerning the SE as a whole or several of its establishments.[28] The EWC would effectively act as a workers' interface between the executive and supervisory boards. Drawing from the model of co-determination applying to works councils under West German law,[29] the EWC would have co-decision or *Mitbestimmung* on subjects deemed to be in the workers' interest. In effect, the executive board would need to have the formal approval of the EWC at the planning stage before implementing any significant changes in working practices. By opting for co-determination or 'co-operative governance' the Commission was seeking to move away from ideologies associated with confrontation and align the SE with the German social market model of constructive partnership between management and labour.[30]

[22] Variations of the dual board system were also found in the Netherlands and, as an optional model, in France.   [23] Art. 73(1).
[24] Art. 137. However a two-thirds majority of the employees would be able to decide to have no representatives on the supervisory board, Art. 138. Election would be indirect via a works council, Arts. 139–143.   [25] Art. 73(2).
[26] Art. 73(3).   [27] Art. 66.
[28] Art. 119. An exhaustive list of matters upon which information and consultation would be required can be found in Art. 123.
[29] Under the provisions of the Works Constitution Act, 1972 (amended in 2001). For a detailed explanation of the composition, organisation and powers of works councils in Germany, see P. Burbridge, 'Creating High Performance Boardrooms and Workplaces—European Corporate Governance in the Twenty First Century' (2003) 28 E.L.Rev. 642 at 655–56.
[30] For a comprehensive overview, see the 'Briam Report', 'The German Model of Codetermination and Cooperative Governance', *Report from the Commission on Codetermination*, Bertelsmann Foundation and Hans-Böckler Foundation, (eds.) (Güttersloh: Bertelsmann Foundation, 1998).

The 1970 blueprint was hugely ambitious and ultimately unworkable for several reasons. Firstly, by proposing a rigid dual board system with mandatory worker representation, the Commission was seeking to assert a specific manifestation of what Lynch-Fannon has described as the 'European model of capitalism' in which the corporation is regarded as a public actor subject to State regulation designed to advance macro-economic policy and support the welfare of employees and others.[31] In this model the employees are regarded as insiders with a stake in the enterprise.[32] Companies have a social responsibility to give voice to the interests of employees and other stakeholders within their systems of management and control.[33] The main problem at this time arose, not so much from the assertion of these aspirations, which were broadly shared in the European body politic, but from the Commission's rejection of a diversified solution that would take account of the company and labour law traditions of all countries where SEs would actually have establishments and employees.[34] For example, the proposed solution was insufficiently flexible to allow Italy to retain the unitary board alongside an element of worker involvement that might fall short of participation on the board.[35] In the view of the Commission, however, the dual board was becoming increasingly, if not universally, accepted in the Community.

Moreover, the Commission's strategy served to highlight and, to an extent, exaggerate the different philosophical approaches to the role of the company prevailing in continental Europe and the United States. The UK and Ireland, then in an advanced staged of negotiations to enter the Community, were in an especially difficult position because the hallmarks of their systems of company law, like that of the United States, were diversity of ownership and primacy of shareholder interests.[36] Under the classical Anglo-American model[37] the company was regarded as a private actor largely free from State regulation. In a system that maintained a strict separation between management and control, management's duty was to act in the interests of its shareholders. Employees were regarded as outsiders to be kept at arm's length from corporate decision-making.[38] The

---

[31] See Lynch-Fannon n.4 above at 4–5.

[32] See C. Villiers, 'Workers and Transnational Corporate Structures: Some Lessons from the BMW-Rover Case' (2001) 3 *International and Comparative Corporate Law Journal* 271 at 283.

[33] For a critique of 'stakeholding' see P. Ireland, 'Corporate Governance, Stakeholding, and the Company: Towards a Less Degenerate Capitalism?' (1996) 23 Jo. of Law and Society 287.

[34] Sanders n.8 above at 97.

[35] The unitary board was also a feature of the system of the United Kingdom, then a prospective member of the Community.

[36] See J. Armour, S. Deakin & S.J. Konzelmann, 'Shareholder Primacy and the Trajectory of UK Corporate Governance' (2003) 41 B.J.I.R. 531 at 531.

[37] See generally, A.A. Berle & G.C. Means, *The Modern Corporation and Private Property* (New York: Commerce Clearing House Inc. 1932).

[38] See generally, A. Rebérioux, 'European Style of Corporate Governance at the Crossroads: The Role of Worker Involvement' (2002) 240 J.C.M.S. 111.

'countervailing power'[39] of employees, to the extent that it existed at all,[40] was exercised externally, sourced from labour law, collective bargaining and industrial action. Although the first movement for 'corporate social responsibility' was ignited in the US in the early 1970s,[41] there was no widespread support for workers to be on the board of directors[42] and it would be another 30 years before significant steps were taken to federalize American corporate governance in the wake of the destructive collapse of the Enron Corporation.[43] However, the emphasis has remained on accountability to shareholders, and increased transparency, rather than any formal recognition of stakeholder interests beyond the State level.[44]

In seeking to justify its policy preferences the Commission relied on the rather negative terminology of Article 44(2)(g) EC, which requires co-ordination to the necessary extent of 'safeguards . . . for the protection of the interests of members and others . . . by Member States of companies or firms . . . with a view to making such safeguards equivalent throughout the Community'.[45] Although it offers a 'somewhat fuzzy mandate',[46] this clause was interpreted very broadly by the Commission, which converted it into a positive basis for a wide-ranging programme of legislative harmonization of company laws that might be regarded as barriers to cross-border competition.[47] It was envisaged that the proposed draft Fifth Company Law Directive[48] would make the dual board system with

---

[39] See especially, J.K. Galbraith, *American Capitalism: The Concept of Countervailing Power* (White Plains, New York: M.E. Sharpe, 1956), and Lynch-Fannon n.4 above at 15.

[40] Trade union membership in the US has declined to just over 5 per cent of the labour force in 2000 down from one-third in 1955. See Lynch Fannon n.4 above at 55.

[41] See especially, R. Nader, M. Green & J. Seligman, *Taming the Giant Corporation* (New York: Norton, 1976). Discussed by D.M. Branson, 'Corporate Governance 'Reform' and the New Corporate Social Responsibility' (2000-2001) 62 U.Pitt.L.Rev. 605. For advocacy of European-style worker participation in the US, see A. Conard, 'The Supervision of Corporate Management: A Comparison of Developments in the European Community and United States Law' (1984) Mich.L.Rev. 1459.   [42] See Lynch Fannon n.4 above at 49.

[43] The Enron Corporation collapsed into bankruptcy in the US in December 2001 despite having shares quoted at $100 billion just a few weeks earlier. Many of the company's 21,000 employees had invested their retirement plans in the company. It later emerged that some of the directors had artificially inflated the share price and the auditors had fallen short of their duty to oversee the accounts. See Burbridge n.29 above at 644, and generally, K-A. Heeren & O. Rickers, 'Legislative Responses in Times of Financial Crisis—New Deal Securities Legislation, Sarbanes-Oxley Act and Their Impact on Future German and EU Regulation' [2003] Euro.Bus.L.Rev. 595; and D.M. Branson, 'Enron—When All Systems Fail: Creative Destruction or Roadmap to Corporate Governance Reform?' (2003) 48 Villanova L.Rev. 989.

[44] More than half of the States in the US have adopted 'constituency statutes' that permit directors to consider the interests of non-shareholders. See further, M.W. McDaniel, 'Stockholders and Stakeholders' (1991-1992) 21 Stetson L.Rev. 121, K. Van Wezel Stone, 'Employees as Stakeholders Under State Nonshareholder Constituency Statutes' (1991–1992) 21 Stetson L.Rev. 45, and M.A. O'Connor, 'Corporate Malaise—Stakeholder Statutes: Cause or Cure?' (1991–1992) 21 Stetson L.Rev. 3.   [45] Formerly Art. 54(3)(g) EEC.

[46] See Wouters n.15 above at 268–269.

[47] See the 'Berkhouwer Report' 1966 and the Commission's opinion submitted to the Council (document 10/1964–1965). Discussed by Wouters ibid. at 268.

[48] [1972] OJ C131/44. See further, J. Temple Lang, 'The Fifth EEC Directive on the Harmonization of Company Law' (1975) 12 C.M.L. Rev. 155, W. Däubler, 'The Employee

mandatory worker involvement uniform throughout the Community, rendering superfluous any dispute over the constitution of the SE.

Secondly, the scheme for co-determination was opposed by a 'peculiar coalition'[49] featuring not only pan-European employers' organisations, who, not surprisingly, regarded it as over regulatory and an interference with the managerial prerogative, but also many national trade union confederations. For German unions the proposals were a compromise too far, diluting the traditional areas of *Mitbestimmung* while granting workers' representatives only a minority stake in the supervisory board. The SE would threaten co-determination at the national level. For British unions the prospect of a works council was superficially attractive, so long as it was union dominated, but the imported concept of workers' representatives on the board was regarded as a potential threat to the independence of unions in a system based on the separation of managerial and labour functions.[50] The Commission, having chosen a uniform model for the SE, was caught between a rock and a hard place.

In part the explanation for these divergent views is best understood by reference not only to the disparate systems of company laws in the Community, but also in the context of the variety of 'legal families' that have operated in the labour laws of the Member States.[51] Mechanisms for worker representation in the Community have traditionally been divided into dual and single-channel systems,[52] a distinction that has gradually eroded with the onset of Community regulation of the representation function over the last decade.[53] The dual-channel method, developed most markedly in Germany, divides worker involvement into two distinct spheres of operation. The first sphere is the *collective bargaining* function involving independent trade unions representing workers in establishments or industry-wide. This function is normally performed above the level of the work place and may cover whole sectors. Secondly, there is the *information and consultation* function performed by works councils or equivalent bodies elected by the entire work force.[54] The elected bodies have an input at the 'lower level' of corporate

---

Participation Directive—A Realistic Utopia?' (1977) 14 C.M.L. Rev. 17, and J. Welch, 'The Fifth Draft Directive—A False Dawn' (1983) 8 E.L. Rev. 83.

[49] See B. Keller, 'The European company statute: employee involvement—and beyond' (2002) 33 I.R.J. 424 at 426.

[50] For similar reasons the unions later rejected the findings of the *Committee of Inquiry on Industrial Democracy* ('Bullock Report'), Cmnd. 6706 (London: HM Stationary Office, 1977).

[51] See R. Nielsen, 'The Contract of Employment in the Member States of the European Communities and in European Community Law' (1990) 33 G.Y.I.L. 258.

[52] See C. Docksey, 'Employee Information and Consultation Rights in the Member States of the European Communities' (1987) 7 Comp.Lab.Law Jo. 32 at 35.

[53] See especially, P. Davies & C. Kilpatrick, 'UK Worker Representation After Single Channel' (2004) 33 I.L.J. 121.

[54] Docksey n.52 above at 35. This approach is broadly followed in Denmark, France, Belgium and Luxembourg.

decision-making but, as we have seen, the dual-channel approach may also combine information and consultation mechanisms with active worker *participation* at the 'higher level' of the company board, sometimes described as a third channel.[55] By contrast, the single-channel method originally involved worker representation by unions alone, although Community law now requires employers to have mechanisms to consult all workers irrespective of union recognition or membership in undertakings or establishments covered by the Information and Consultation Directive[56] and in cases of collective dismissals or transfers of undertakings within the scope of the relevant directives.[57] The single-channel operates alongside a single board of directors with no worker representation.[58] For example, until quite recently worker involvement in the UK was limited to voluntary recognition of unions by employers who wished to engage in collective bargaining over the terms and conditions of employment.[59] In the traditional single-channel there was no scope for a separate information and consultation function for works councils independent of recognised unions.

Thirdly, by the mid-1970s the collective European mood had changed. Britain, Ireland and Denmark had joined the Community and were instinctively unsympathetic to the superimposition of an unfamiliar system of company law. Even more importantly, the Community had for the first time begun to suffer an economic decline, ushering in a decade of 'Europessimism'.[60] By 1980 the United States and Japan had overtaken the Community both in

---

[55] Davies & Kilpatrick n.53 above at 121. For example, under the German system in companies with more than 2,000 workers the employees have equal rights with shareholders in appointing members of the supervisory board. If the company has between 500 and 2,000 workers the level of employee representation is one-third. There is no employee representation on the board in companies with fewer than 500 workers. The relevant provisions are contained in the Co-determination Act, 1973 and the Works Constitution Act, 1972. Approximately 6 million workers are affected. See Burbridge n.29 at 653.

[56] European Parliament and Council Directive 2002/14/EC, [2002] OJ L80/29. Discussed below at 240–242.

[57] Following the judgment of the Court of Justice in Joined Cases C-382/92 and 383/92, *Commission* v *United Kingdom* [1994] ECR I-2479. See Council Directive 75/129/EEC on the safeguarding of employees' rights in the event of collective redundancies, [1975] OJ L48/29, as amended by Council Directive 92/56/EEC, [1992] OJ L245/3, now consolidated in Council Directive 98/59/EC, [1998] OJ L225/16. Council Directive 77/187/EEC on the safeguarding of employees' rights in the event of transfers of undertakings, businesses or parts of businesses, [1977] OJ L61/26, amended by Council Directive 98/50/EC, [1998] OJ L201/88, now consolidated in European Parliament and Council Directive 2001/23/EC, [2001] OJ L82/16.

[58] In the UK, s.309 of the Companies Act 1985 obliges company directors to consider the interests of employees as well as those of shareholders when performing their functions. However, employees' representatives do not have standing to enforce this duty and it has rarely been invoked in the courts. See Armour *et al* n.36 above at 537. See further, C. Villiers, 'Section 309 of the Companies Act 1985: Is it time for a reappraisal?' in H. Collins, P. Davies & R. Rideout (eds.), *Legal Regulation of the Employment Relation* (London: Kluwer Law International, 2000) 593–614.

[59] See Davies & Kilpatrick n.53 above at 121.

[60] See, for example, *Prospects for the 80s*, Bulletin of the Economic and Social Committee, 10/81. See further, J. Kenner *EU Employment Law* (Oxford: Hart Publishing, 2003) 71–72.

economic output and competitiveness and, where there was once a comfortable certainty of success based on a mix of regulated free trade, strong State sectors, social protection and industrial partnership, there was now incoherence and a policy vacuum. Amongst influential neo-liberal thinkers there was much talk of 'Eurosclerosis' arising from excessive rigidities in the labour market.[61] In this climate the Commission's vision of a uniform SE model appeared outmoded. Instead the momentum was shifting towards deregulation and an accommodation with the apparently more dynamic Anglo-American model of corporate governance.

By the end of the 1970s it was clear that the SE proposal had run into the ground. In 1974 an influential report of the Economic and Social Committee had concluded that it was 'premature' to impose a uniform company structure when the interests of shareholders and employees could be protected under either the single-tier or two-tier system providing that there was an element of employee involvement.[62] The Commission responded by publishing an even more complex and unwieldy proposal in 1975, which, heralding several later dilutions, contained a revised structure for the supervisory board consisting of one-third employees' representatives, one-third shareholders' representatives and one-third of members representing general interests, co-opted by both of these groups.[63] Discussions on the SE proposal were suspended in 1982 by which time the Commission was in full retreat. Indeed a new draft of the Fifth Company Law Directive[64] was a pale shadow of its former self and, while it allowed for either dualist and monist boards with separate managerial and supervisory functions, the element of worker participation was reduced to the extent that a separate and essentially toothless consultative council could be substituted for worker representation on the corporate board. The result was an even messier compromise that provoked opposition from all sides.[65] Ultimately company law, which, in many other aspects, had converged at Community level,[66] had proved to be an inappropriate vehicle for harmonizing systems of industrial relations and labour law that were deeply rooted in national regional, social and economic structures.[67] It was time for a fresh approach.

[61] See J. Grahl & P. Teague, *1992—The Big Market: The Future of the European Community* (London: Lawrence & Wishart, 1990) 20.
[62] Doc. CES 861/73, 22 April 1974.
[63] COM(75) 150 final, 19 March 1975, and Bull. EC Supp. 4/75. See P. Sanders, 'The European Company' (1976) 6 Georgia Jo.Int. & Comp.L. 367.
[64] [1983] OJ C240/2.
[65] See M. Weiss, 'Workers' Participation in the European Union' in P. Davies, A. Lyon-Caen, S. Sciarra & S. Simitis (eds.) *European Community Labour Law: Principles and Perspectives* (Oxford: Clarendon Press, 1996) 213–235 at 220–222.
[66] For an overview, see Wouters n.15 above.
[67] Lord Wedderburn, 'Industrial Relations and the Courts' (1980) 9 I.L.J. 65 at 71. See Welch n.48 above at 84.

III.   The Davignon Report and the Quest for Worker Involvement

(A)   The Rationale for Worker Involvement

In 1989 the Commission published a new proposal for a Statute for a European Company[68] and, after a gestation period of unprecedented length, the SE Regulation and a supplementary employee involvement Directive were adopted on the basis of this proposal in October 2001.[69] The SE was repackaged as part of the drive to complete the internal market and enhance the competitiveness of the European economy. It was intended to appeal to companies operating in several Member States who were seeking to unify their organisational structures and adapt to the increasingly global dimension of their activities. The diversified approach supported by the SE's original protagonists was reinstated. Under the draft regulation companies would be able to choose between boards that were two-tier (management and supervisory) or single-tier (administrative). Whichever method was chosen, a separate but complementary draft Directive offered a flexible 'cafeteria style' set of options for worker involvement from which to choose: representation on the board;[70] a separate body of employees' representatives; a negotiated solution; or a solution according to the specific national models of the participating countries.[71] The final choice would be determined by an agreement between the boards of the companies forming the SE and the representatives of the employees in accordance with the laws and practices of the Member States. In the absence of an agreement the decision would be left to the company boards.[72] Worker participation on the board ceased to be a pre-requisite for the formation of an SE and the external body (or works council) no longer had the formal right of co-decision.[73]

The Community was now pursuing a twin-track approach. On an inside economic track the Treaty's internal market powers would be harnessed to accelerate the pace of company law harmonization without favouring either the Anglo-American

[68] COM(89) 268 final, 25 August 1989, [1989] OJ C263/4, and Bull. EC Supp. 5/89. For later versions see [1991] OJ C138/8 and C176/1. For discussion see Edwards n.6 above at 445–448.

[69] See n.6 above. The legal base for the draft regulation was changed from Art. 308 (now Art. 235) EC, which required unanimity in the Council and only consultation with the European Parliament, to Art. 100a (now Art. 95) EC, which provided for qualified majority voting (QMV) in the Council and was subject to the co-operation procedure between the Council and European Parliament, as set out in Art. 189(b) (now Art. 252) EC. The legal base for the proposed Directive, which contained the worker involvement provisions, was not Art. 100a, which precluded measures relating to the rights and interests of employed persons, but Art. 54 (now 44) EC, on the basis that, under the general regime of company law harmonization, employees' rights were to be safeguarded by measures 'for the protection of the interests of members and others'. The rather shaky foundation of Art. 54 EC also provided for QMV and co-operation.

[70] Between one-third and one-half of the members would be employees' representatives.

[71] See Keller n.49 above at 426.   [72] See Edwards n.6 above at 446.

[73] See Davies n.6 above at 96.

or continental European models[74] and there would be a further push towards freedom of establishment of companies by applying the principles of non-discrimination and mutual recognition backed up by liberalizing rulings from the Court of Justice.[75] On a parallel labour law track the Community launched legislation to require mechanisms for mandatory worker involvement in medium-sized and larger companies competing in the internal market.[76] In this context a more flexible SE proposal, separating out the elements concerning the Statute for the European Company from the requirements for worker involvement, was more attuned to the economic and social realities of European corporate governance in the 1990s.

Despite the Commission's best efforts to make a diversified SE more attractive to governments, businesses and unions alike, no agreement was reached on the issue of worker involvement until the Nice European Council of December 2000. Before turning to the detailed provisions in the next section it is important to address two fundamental questions. First, why has the Community continued to pursue this element of the SE package? Second, why has it been so difficult to reach agreement?

In order to answer these questions we need to consider the motivations behind the Commission's proposals. The Social Action Programme published by the Commission in 1974 called for[77]:

The progressive involvement of workers or their representatives in the life of undertakings in the Community.

The promotion of the involvement of management and labour in the economic and social decisions of the Community.

In practice the second of these objectives has been easier to fulfil than the first because it offers the prospect of influence for employers' and workers' organizations over the Community's decision-making process without challenging the fundamentals of jealously guarded national industrial relations processes and, just as importantly, without interfering in the organization and management of companies. In this way the European 'social partners' have gradually become institutionalized and,

---

[74] Community legislation now regulates the following areas by means of harmonising Directives (see Edwards n.15 above at 1), *inter alia*, companies' disclosure and publicity requirements, the legality of pre-incorporation and *ultra vires* transactions, the nullity of companies, the formation of public companies and alteration of their capital, mergers and divisions of public companies, companies' annual and consolidated accounts, the qualification of company auditors, disclosure by cross-frontier branches of companies, single member companies, admission to Stock Exchange listing, public offers of listed and unlisted securities, acquisitions and disposals of major shareholdings, insider dealing and, most recently, takeovers. Proposals are on the table concerning Directives on cross-border transfers of a company's seat or registered office and the cross-border merger of companies with share capital. For a full listing of the relevant legislation see COM(2003) 284 final, see n.151 below.

[75] In particular Case 79/85 *Segers v Bestuur van de Bedrijfsvereniging voor Bank- en Verzekeringswezen, Groothandel en Vrije Beroepen* [1986] ECR 2375, Case C-212/97 *Centros Ltd v Erhvervs-og Selskabsstyrelsen* [1999] ECR I-1459, and Case C-208/00 *Überseering BV v NCC Nordic Construction* [2002] ECR I-9919. See further n.231 below.

[76] The Treaty base for this legislation is now Art. 137(2) EC.

[77] Bull. EC Supp. 2/74, p.10.

through accretion on the basis of shared objectives, have exerted genuine influence over the construction of Community law across a wide range of social policy fields.[78]

With regard to the first objective, the Commission frankly acknowledged in its 1975 Green Paper on *Employee Participation and Company Structure* that, by engaging in a debate about the role of employees in decision-making within companies, they were raising an 'undeniably controversial and difficult issue'.[79] This was an understatement for there was disagreement over both the rationale for the establishment of structures for worker involvement and the form that such structures should take. For, as the International Labour Organisation (ILO) has noted[80]:

The belief that workers' participation in decisions within undertakings ought to be promoted for some reason does not in itself imply acceptance of a particular method of bringing it about. *The diversity of methods is as great as the diversity of aims.*

Nevertheless, according to the ILO, international solutions to worker involvement are attractive for a combination of ethical, socio-political and economic reasons.[81] The ethical or moral case is the simplest and most broadly acceptable. Worker involvement is a form of 'human rights at the work place'.[82] Paternalistic subjugation of the interests of the worker based on the master's/employer's 'right to command' his servant/employee is no longer acceptable in a post-industrial society.[83] It follows that it is a pre-requisite of the concept of social justice that a worker should receive 'recognition, treatment and attention as a human being rather than a mere statistical unit of production',[84] a concept well founded in international law.[85] The Green Paper noted that decisions taken by or within the enterprise have a substantial effect on the 'sense of dignity and autonomy as human beings' of workers.[86] These ideas were influenced by Kant's writings on individual freedom and dignity under which property cannot be valued more highly than human personality.[87] Workers' involvement at all levels of corporate decision-making is best understood as a form of 'industrial citizenship' where democracy is extended to every level of society.[88]

---

[78] For discussion, see Kenner n.60 above at 246–292.

[79] Bull. EC Supp. 8/75, p.7.

[80] *Workers' Participation in Decisions within Undertakings* (Geneva: ILO, 1981) p.21. Emphasis added.   [81] Ibid. p.9.

[82] Ibid. p.10.

[83] For an insight into the early development of workers' participation see T. Ramm, 'Workers' Participation, the Representation of Labour and Special Labour Courts' in B. Hepple (ed.), *The Making of Labour Law in Europe: A Comparative Study of Nine Countries up to 1945* (London and New York: Mansell, 1987) 242–276.   [84] ILO Report, n.80 above at 10.

[85] Most importantly in the Universal Declaration of Human Rights (1948). Art. 22 declares that: 'Everyone, as a member of society . . . is entitled to realisation . . . of the economic, social and cultural rights indispensable for his dignity and the free development of his personality.'

[86] Green Paper, n.79 above at 9.

[87] See especially, F. Fabricius, 'A Theory of Co-determination' in Schmitthoff, n.8 above, 138–165 at 143–149.   [88] See Burbridge n.29 above at 643.

The socio-political underpinning for worker involvement in undertakings is more controversial. Can political democracy be equated with a form of industrial or corporate suffrage and, if so, how far should the democratic process reach?[89] More pointedly, should 'industrial democracy'[90] begin and end with information and consultation at the workplace or plant-level collective bargaining 'substructure'?[91] Alternatively, can the concept be extended to the board-level 'superstructure' by establishing forms of representative worker participation on the inside track of corporate decision-making? Aware of the controversy over its proposals for the SE and the Fifth Directive, the Commission suggested a broad approach based on recognition of the[92]:

democratic imperative that those who will be substantially affected by decisions made by social and political institutions must be involved in the making of those decisions.

This was an early indication of the Community's rather fudged approach to the issue of participation that was to re-emerge in the 1989 SE proposal and can now be found in the 2001 Directive.

The political dimension was addressed more directly in a separate ILO report that identified two alternative varieties of participation[93]:

Workers' participation is an eminently political issue . . . This is least visible in those countries where workers' participation is looked upon merely as a *management technique* aimed at improving either work organisation at the shop-floor level or employer-employee communications. It is clearest in schemes that aim at redefining the respective roles of owners, managers and workers in the enterprise, and at *radically changing the power relationships* between them.

Over the last 30 years the Community has been most successful when promoting the first, more limited, variety of participation in the form of establishing systems of information and consultation with workers' representatives as a 'management technique', either for the purposes of transnational information and consultation,[94] or to introduce a regulated procedure for national-level worker information and

[89] See ILO Report n.80 above at 11. See also, E. Batstone in 'Industrial Democracy: European Experience,' reports prepared by E. Batstone and P. Davies for the Industrial Democracy Committee (London: HMSO, 1976) pp.10–11.
[90] See S. Webb & B. Webb, *Industrial Democracy* (London: 1898). For a discussion, see O. Kahn-Freund, 'Industrial Democracy' (1977) 6 I.L.J. 77, cf. P. Davies & Lord Wedderburn, 'The Land of Industrial Democracy' (1977) 6 I.L.J. 197.
[91] This terminology is derived from the 'Bullock Report' n.50 above.
[92] Green Paper n.79 above at 9. My emphasis.
[93] See the official report of the Oslo Symposium, 1974: J. Schregle, 'Workers' participation in decisions within undertakings' in *International Labour Review* (Geneva: ILO, Jan.–Feb. 1976) pp.2–3. Emphasis added.
[94] Council Directive 94/45/EC on the establishment of a European Works Council or a procedure in Community-scale undertakings and Community-scale groups of undertakings for the purposes of informing and consulting employees, OJ [1994] L254/64, extended to the UK by Council Directive 97/74/EC, [1998] OJ L 10/22. Originally proposed as the 'Vredeling Directive' on procedures for informing and consulting the employees of undertakings with complex structures,

consultation,[95] or as a basis for communicating with employees' representatives in the event of collective dismissals,[96] or the transfer of an undertaking,[97] and, more generally, for the purposes of consultation and 'balanced participation' on 'all questions relating to safety and health at work'.[98]

The resulting Directives have placed *procedural* obligations on management to inform and consult their employees without affecting the ultimate decision-making prerogative or the diverse structure of companies. These Directives provide a filter for management and unions to be involved in a form of 'joint regulation' of the workplace,[99] an approach that does not undermine the freedom of action of the parties in industrial relations while allowing for a degree of consensus or 'conflictual partnership'.[100] Moreover, while placing a duty on management to inform and consult unions, works councils, or other representatives of employees in good faith, these Directives do not impose a 'duty to bargain' similar to the American model by which unions can compel management to negotiate with them over pay and other conditions of employment.[101] Most significantly, as Villiers has observed,[102] the employees and their representatives remain *outsiders* who are kept at arm's length from the company, unable to participate fully in its strategic decisions.

By contrast, the Community has been much less successful when addressing the second, more radical, variety of participation, which is concerned with redefining 'power relationships' through proposals for worker participation in harmonized company structures. Proponents have argued that there must be genuine worker participation at both plant and board level that transcends the traditional concept of the enterprise as an instrument dedicated to the entrepreneur's interests and leads to co-determination by management and workers' representatives or, more

in particular transnational undertakings, [1980] OJ C297/3. See also, the equally unsuccessful 'Richard Directive', [1983] OJ C217/3.

[95] European Parliament and Council Directive 2002/14/EC, [2002] OJ L80/29. For the Commission's original proposal, see COM(98) 612, [1999] OJ C2/3. Revised by COM(2001) 296, [2001] OJ C240/133.

[96] Art. 2 of Council Directive 75/129/EEC, [1975] OJ L48/29, as amended by Art. 1(2) of Council Directive 92/56/EEC, [1992] OJ L245/3, now consolidated in Art. 2 of Council Directive 98/59/EC, [1998] OJ L225/16.

[97] Art. 6 of Council Directive 77/187/EEC, [1977] OJ L61/26, amended by Art. 1(2) of Council Directive 98/50/EC, [1998] OJ L201/88, now consolidated within Art. 7 of European Parliament and Council Directive 2001/23/EC, [2001] OJ L82/16.

[98] Art. 11 of Council Directive 89/391/EEC, [1989] OJ L183/1. This would appear to go beyond mere consultation and, according to Weiss, provides for a 'stronger degree of influence'. See M. Weiss, 'The European Community's Approach to Workers' Participation' in A. Neal & S. Foyn (eds.), *Developing the Social Dimension in an Enlarged European Union* (Oslo: Scandinavian University Press, 1995) 100–124 at 106.

[99] See generally, A. Flanders, *Management and Unions: the Theory and Reform of Industrial Relations* (London: Faber, 1970).   [100] See Davies & Wedderburn n.90 above at 198.

[101] National Labor Relations Act, 1964, ss. 7, 8(a)(5) and (9)(a). See *Fibreboard Products Corporation* v *NLRB* [1964] 379 US 203. Discussed by R. Rabin, 'Fibreboard and the Termination of Bargaining Unit Work: The Search for Standards in Defining the Scope of the Duty to Bargain' (1971) 71 Columbia L.Rev. 803.   [102] See Villiers n.32 above at 284.

accurately, a better form of control of, or influence over, enterprise policy.[103] Under this pluralistic model workers and their representatives would become *insiders* with a more central place within the decision-making processes of the company.[104]

While procedural measures concerning the *nature* of management information and decision-making communicated to workers have, over time, won acceptance and been incorporated into Community Directives, proposals concerning company structure and the *means* by which influence is exercised at a strategic level have been less successful. Slow progress in the field of company structure can partly be blamed on the prescriptive nature of the proposals and in part, also, on the absence of a consensus around the link between socio-political considerations and the final element, the economic rationale.

Broadly speaking the economic case for worker involvement in decision-making within undertakings can be summarized as: increasing the efficiency of the undertaking through industrial co-operation; improving the quantity and quality of output by creating a sense of identity within the undertaking; adapting useful ideas made by workers; and reducing the capacity for industrial conflict. This is because, *inter alia*, workers may work more productively because they are sharing in decisions that affect them while the process itself may act as a spur to managerial efficiency.[105] These ideas are attractive to management so long as the structures introduced neither profoundly challenge the distribution of economic power nor seriously threaten the managerial prerogative. For unions such notions are double-edged, simultaneously offering the potential of greater influence while creating the danger of assumed responsibility without sufficient power over the ultimate decision. This may lead to a perception of elitism, arguments about accountability and a build up of pressures and conflicts within the operational structures of worker representation.

The difficulties arising from these perceptions might have been overcome in the 1970s and 1980s if the Commission had taken account of national diversity in company structures and industrial relations traditions when drawing up its company law proposals. However, it was the success of separate but parallel labour law Directives concerning information and consultation in the workplace that was to provide the springboard for the eventual adoption of the SE Statute.

(B) The Pathway to the SE

From the mid-1990s a series of events led to a breakthrough in the impasse over the SE. First, the European Works Councils Directive was adopted.[106] This

---

[103] See S. Simitis, 'Workers' Participation in the Enterprise—Transcending Company Law' (1975) 38 M.L.R. 1 at 7–8.   [104] See Villiers n.32 above at 295.

[105] See K. Walker, 'Workers' Participation in Management: Problems, Practice and Prospects' in 1974 *IILS Bulletin* (Geneva: International Institute of Labour Studies) No. 12, 3–35.

[106] Council Directive 94/45/EC on the establishment of a European Works Council or a procedure in Community-scale undertakings and Community-scale groups of undertakings for the

resembles the EWC concept in the original SE proposal in name only. The 1990s model applies to companies operating on a transnational basis within the EU, but it has been stripped bare of any reference to worker/board co-determination or co-decision which one would normally associate with a national or industry-wide works council. Moreover, the EWC Directive was entirely disconnected from the revised SE proposal. The EWC was envisaged as an *external* outlet for transnational information and consultation designed to be acceptable to management precisely because it would not affect the internal structure of companies or the managerial prerogative. However, the introduction of EWCs has, despite their inherent limitations, provided a road map towards the realization of a different kind of SE that fits in with a more flexible approach to worker involvement in the corporate structure.

The EWC Directive only applies to companies with at least 1,000 employees in the EU, including at least 150 in two or more Member States.[107] Under the scheme of the Directive the company is subject to the law of the country in which its 'central management' is located or, in the case of a group of undertakings, the country in which the central management of the 'controlling undertaking' is located.[108] As with the SE, the EWC project was designed to encourage voluntary action and to do so, it allows employees to trigger the establishment of a Special Negotiating Body (SNB)[109] with wide discretion to negotiate an agreement to set up and constitute an EWC suited to the requirements of the undertaking. The SNB route is a flexible approach designed to encourage the establishment of an EWC with the minimum of legal formality. An even stronger incentive was offered to management in the period before the implementation date of 22 September 1996. Prior to this date agreements to set up information and consultation procedures short of formal EWCs were permitted providing such agreements covered the entire work force and provided for transnational information and consultation.[110]

Where the SNB process fails to lead to an agreement, or if management refuses to co-operate with it, the Directive provides for a more rigid fallback mechanism in the annexed Subsidiary Requirements. These provisions operate as a type of 'penalty default',[111] providing the parties with a powerful incentive to negotiate

---

purposes of informing and consulting employees, [1994] OJ L254/64. Extended to the UK by Council Directive 97/74/EC, [1998] OJ L10/22.

[107] Art. 2(c) of Directive 94/45/EC.

[108] Under Art. 3(1) a 'controlling undertaking' means 'an undertaking which can exercise a dominant influence over another undertaking ('the controlled undertaking') by virtue, for example, of ownership, financial participation or the rules which govern it.' Where the controlling undertaking is located outside the EU, it may designate a representative undertaking within one of the covered Member States—Art. 3(6). If no designation is made, the representative undertaking will be deemed to be the central management of the group with the largest number of employees within the covered Member States.

[109] Under Art. 5(1) the SNB will be established at the request of at least 100 employees or their representatives based in two or more Member States.   [110] Art. 13.

[111] See C. Barnard & S. Deakin, 'Reinventing the European corporation? Corporate governance, social policy and the single market' (2002) 33 I.R.J. 484 at 486.

exposed by the Renault saga, had proposed that where the company is in 'serious breach' of its information and consultation obligations under the Directive, and where such decisions would have direct and immediate consequences in terms of substantial change or termination of the employment contract, those decisions 'shall have no legal effect' on the employment contracts of the employees involved. The final text, however, simply refers to 'adequate sanctions' to be applicable in the event of 'infringement' of the Directive by the employer or employees' representatives.[121] Such sanctions are to be 'effective, proportionate and dissuasive'. This is a significant retreat on the issue of penalties. Ultimately, the national courts will determine the adequacy of such sanctions based on the somewhat oblique notion of effectiveness. Unless the penalties imposed are sufficiently high it will be tempting for management, when contemplating major structural changes, to proceed rapidly and simply factor non-compliance with its information and consultation obligations into the overall cost equation.[122]

Third, by the late 1990s, the Community and its expert working groups were prepared to be more pragmatic, now recognizing the virtues of preserving the heterogeneous nature of corporate structure and labour law prevailing in the Member States. In an influential Green Paper on *Partnership for a New Organisation of Work*[123] the Commission sought to redirect the Community's policies towards facilitating a new balance between flexibility and security in the workplace. It aimed to promote the notion of the 'flexible firm' which, on the one hand, would meet the requirements of employers for a workforce with interchangeable skills and adaptable work patterns capable of coping with fluctuations in demand for their goods and services, while, on the other hand, would offer employees greater job satisfaction, higher skills and long-term employability.[124] Central to this vision was the concept of 'partnership'. National and local actors, most importantly the social partners, were encouraged to accept a 'sense of ownership' of changes aimed at modernizing the organization of work and improving levels of employment.[125] The 'Gyllenhammer Report' on the economic and social implications of industrial change[126] concluded that all economic partners—the business community, employees' representatives and public authorities—needed to anticipate and prepare for industrial change on a continuous basis.[127] This would only be possible if there was a high level of trust based on regular, transparent and comprehensive dialogue.[128]

---

[121] Art. 8(2).

[122] As anticipated in C. McGlynn, 'European Works Councils: Towards Democracy?' (1995) 24 I.L.J. 78 at 82.   [123] COM(97) 127.

[124] Ibid. para. 31.

[125] See C. Barnard, *EC Employment Law*, (2nd edn, Oxford: OUP, 2000) 508.

[126] Gyllenhammer led a high level group of experts with a mandate from the European Council. The report published in 1998 is available at: http://europa.eu.int/comm/dg05/soc-dial/gyllenhammer/gyllen-en.pdf.   [127] Ibid. p.9.

[128] Ibid.

These developments provided a fertile backdrop for the resurrection of the SE. In May 1997 the Commission's Group of Experts on European Systems of Worker Involvement, the 'Davignon Group,' published its Final Report.[129] In a key section it noted that[130]:

Globalisation of the economy and the special place of European industry raises fundamental questions regarding the power of the social partners within the company. The type of labour needed by European companies—skilled, mobile, committed, responsible, and capable of using technical innovations and of identifying with the objective of increasing competitiveness and quality—cannot be expected to simply obey the employers' instructions. Workers must be closely and permanently involved in decision-making at all levels of the company.

The authors were offering matching economic and social rationales for worker involvement in company decision-making. Recognizing that the issue of worker involvement had derailed the SE initiative, the Report approached the subject from a new angle. According to the experts, establishing SEs would help complete the internal market programme and facilitate the process of Economic and Monetary Union.[131] Moreover, SEs would be a useful vehicle for companies seeking to internationalize and concentrate their activities in response to globalization. It would help to streamline existing rules concerning taxation and corporate governance.[132]

Davignon suggested that it would be possible to reconcile the hitherto irreconcilable differences between the actors by pursuing a concerted approach to work organization within the company leading to improved industrial relations, increased worker involvement and a likely improvement in product quality, boosting competitiveness within the European economy.[133] Multinational companies would form SEs to perform new tasks or the organization of operations on a European scale. Companies would have the choice of a two-tier management board or a single-tier board of directors. Whilst Davignon proposed mandatory worker involvement, the framework envisaged negotiations between workers' representatives and the company closely following the EWC model. As the formation of SEs would be optional the new company might develop its own system of worker involvement even if this transcended national systems.[134] Long established methods of worker involvement, such as co-determination, would not be threatened because the new rules would only apply to SEs.

Davignon's proposal for a negotiated solution would allow for tailor-made worker involvement to suit each individual SE, be it a holding company, a merger or a joint subsidiary, and the specific conditions of the enterprise or sector within which it would operate. It would have the advantage of empowering the social partners while avoiding the imposition of a single uniform model. As with EWCs

---

[129] Available at: http://europa.eu.int/comm/employment_social/soc-dial/labour/davignon/davi_en.htm.   [130] Para. 19.

[131] Para. 14.   [132] Ibid.   [133] Para. 20.   [134] Para. 40(d).

the procedure would specify the general objectives[135] and allow complete independence to the parties to determine how to achieve them, but provide fallback arrangements if they failed to reach an agreement. However, in a significant shift of emphasis, the authors addressed the issue of any dispute over the nature of the organization of the company itself in the following terms[136]:

Failure to negotiate an agreement on participation in the European Company must not preclude incorporation as a European Company, *since this would have the effect of removing the owners' right to decide the company's legal form and transferring it to the workforce.*

Hence the workforce would be entitled to participation but not control. In their proposals on the minimum procedural requirements for information and consultation in the SE structure at the 'lower level'—the workplace—the experts' recommendations were broadly consistent with the flexible arrangements established under the Directives on EWCs and Information and Consultation. However, having noted that only seven of the EU's then 15 Member States had rules which made provision for participation of workers' representatives in the various company bodies,[137] the experts rejected a diversified solution in which some SEs could be established with participation at the 'upper level'—the company board—and others without.[138] In their view this would create unacceptable discrimination between companies.[139] Because SEs would be optional companies ought to be free to choose the new model in the knowledge that workers' representatives would be members of the management or supervisory board.[140] This would apply whether the board was monistic or dualistic. Workers would comprise one-fifth of the members of the management or supervisory board, with a minimum of two members.[141]

Davignon avoided the use of terms such as co-determination, co-decision or joint regulation, preferring softer sounding participation, but it was envisaged that workers on the board would have full status with equal rights and responsibilities.[142] The sting in Davignon's tail led to frantic last minute negotiations in the EU Council. Whilst a majority in the Council were supportive because of the opportunities SEs offered for economies of scale and competitiveness within the internal market, several Member States still rejected the notion of mandatory worker participation on the board. Finally, at Nice in December 2000 a compromise was reached that would preserve established methods of worker participation such as the German system, but permit opt-outs from mandatory worker participation in the case of SEs formed by a merger and/or where none of the companies involved are based in Member States that have participation rules.

---

[135] Para. 66 suggests an indicative list of matters that might be covered in the negotiations.
[136] Para. 46. Emphasis added.
[137] Keller lists eight countries, six with supervisory boards (Austria, Denmark, Germany, Greece, Netherlands and Portugal) and two (France and Finland) where a supervisory board is an option. See n.49 above at 424.   [138] Para. 76.
[139] Para. 78.   [140] Para. 81.   [141] Para. 83.   [142] Para. 88.

IV.   Analysis of the 2001 SE

In October 2001 the EU Council adopted two interdependent measures: a Regulation on the Statute for a European Company (SE), 2157/2001/EC,[143] and a Directive supplementing the Statute with regard to the involvement of employees, 2001/86/EC.[144] The effective date of the Regulation was 8 October 2004, the same date by which the Directive was due to be implemented into the national legal orders of the Member States.[145] Whereas the choice of a Regulation was intended to provide a uniform legal framework within which companies might opt to form an SE,[146] the use of a Directive allows for greater flexibility when it comes to adapting the employee involvement requirements to be applied to the SE in the legal systems of the Member States. The choice of a Directive also reflected the fact that although the Council was exercising its general powers under Article 308 EC, and therefore acting unanimously,[147] it was seeking to conform to the norms of the social policy *acquis*, which require the use of Directives.[148] Moreover, by opting for a Directive and emphasizing the importance of maintaining a 'great diversity of rules and practices' in the Member States concerning worker involvement,[149] the Community's legislators were seeking to extinguish any latent concerns that may have existed about compliance with the principle of subsidiarity.[150] As the Commission noted in its 2001

---

[143] [2001] OJ L294/1.

[144] [2001] OJ L294/22. Recital 18 of the preamble of the Regulation describes the Directive as an 'indissociable complement' to the Regulation. For background on the negotiations see Edwards n.6 above at 447–450.   [145] Art. 70 of the Regulation. Art. 14 of the Directive.

[146] See Recital 1 of the preamble of the Directive.

[147] Art. 308 EC also denies the European Parliament the right to co-decision. Although the Parliament's Committee on Legal Affairs recommended a challenge of the legal basis before the Court of Justice this was not taken up by the Parliament's President, mindful perhaps of the historic significance of the Council's decision to adopt these measures after such a long period. See Edwards n.6 above at 450.

[148] Directives are the only legislative instruments available to the Community under Art. 137(2)(b) EC, the legal base that is normally used under the social provisions. Art. 308 may also have been used in this instance because there is no clear mandate for legislation to enact employee participation. Hence, while Art. 137(1)(e) concerning measures in the field of information and consultation of workers provides for qualified majority voting and the co-decision procedure in Art. 251 EC, the separately listed Art. 137(1)(g) concerning measures for the 'representation and collective defence of the interests of workers and employers, including co-determination' requires unanimity and the consultation procedure. Neither exactly covers the ground required to enact the SE Directive.

[149] Recital 5 of the preamble of the Directive.

[150] The issue of subsidiarity is formally addressed in Recital 4 of the preamble of the Directive where it is declared that: 'Since the objectives of the proposed action . . . cannot be sufficiently achieved by the Member States, in that the object is to establish a set of rules on employee involvement applicable to the SE, and can therefore, by reason of the scale and impact of the proposed action, be better achieved at Community level, the Community may adopt measures, in accordance with the principle of subsidiarity as set out in Article 5 of the Treaty . . .' Recital 29 of the preamble of the Regulation deploys similar language to explain how that measure complies with the subsidiarity principle.

Communication on *Modernising Company Law and Enhancing Corporate Governance*,[151] this approach exemplifies a trend towards greater political deference to national law, which made the adoption of SE package possible.

Unanimity in the Council was achieved not least because of an emerging consensus about the essential elements of a modernized European regime of corporate governance that combines the broad, inclusive stakeholder philosophy of continental Europe with elements drawn from the more dynamic, reformed Anglo-American system that now places increasing emphasis on accountability to shareholders,[152] especially greater transparency and tighter regulation of directors. In the United Kingdom reform has been driven by soft regulation via codes of practice on such matters as directors' pay, accounting standards and the role of non-executive directors.[153] Many of these ideas have taken root elsewhere in the EU although the European Commission has rejected the idea of a European Corporate Governance Code.[154] The tendency towards reform has accelerated in the United States with the introduction of the Sarbanes-Oxley Act.[155]

The SE approach, an idea simultaneously regarded as outmoded and ahead of its time in the 1970s and 1980s, has been refashioned and spun as an exemplar of best practice in the global corporate environment of the Twenty-first Century.[156] The 2001 SE remains an optional model but, unlike its earlier incarnations, it now provides an inherently malleable tool for a range of companies wishing to operate more freely within the EU providing they can accept that their employees' 'right of involvement'[157] must be addressed as part of the package. Whether there are sufficient incentives to persuade companies to take the plunge remains an open question.

Article 2 of the Regulation envisages four different ways in which an SE may be formed as a public limited-liability company in the Member State in which it establishes its registered office.[158] In each case the formation of the SE is subject to the general requirement that the companies involved must be registered in at least

---

[151]   COM(2003) 284 final, point 1.1.

[152]   That is not to say that convergence is complete. For example, as Burbridge notes at 644, n.29 above, when the British firm Marks & Spencer closed their continental branches in 2001 they had to notify the London Stock Exchange first under UK listing rules but by doing so they violated French regulations requiring prior consultation with works councils.

[153]   See Burbridge n.29 above at 647–653.

[154]   See COM(2003) 284, n.151 above at point 3.1.

[155]   Following the Enron affair, see n.43 above. Senior directors in the US face up to 10 years in prison for falsely certifying accounts, or 20 years in the case of wilful falsification. Auditors are prohibited from holding consultancies or giving advice to firms they audit. See M. Freedland, 'The Sarbanes-Oxley Act: corporate governance, financial reporting and economic crime' (2002) 23 *The Company Lawyer* 384.   [156]   See especially, COM(2003) 284, see n.151 above.

[157]   See Recital 21 of the preamble of the Regulation.

[158]   See Art. 15(1). Art. 4 stipulates that the SE must have subscribed capital of not less than €120,000. The laws of a Member State may specify a higher figure 'for companies carrying on certain types of activity'.

two Member States and subject to their national laws, and have a head office within the Community.[159] The methods of formation are:

1. A merger of two or more public limited-liability companies.[160]

2. The formation of a holding company by two or more public or private limited-liability companies.[161]

3. The formation of a subsidiary by public or private limited-liability companies.[162]

4. A public limited-liability company may be transformed into an SE if it has had, for at least two years, a subsidiary in another Member State.[163]

Although at least two Member States must be involved the possibilities for forming an SE are broader than under earlier drafts. Significantly, 'a Member State may provide' that a company with a head office outside the EU may participate in the formation of an SE providing that the company is formed under the laws of a Member State, has its registered office there, and 'has a real and continuous link with a Member State's economy'.[164] This provision is specifically designed to be compatible with the 'real seat' system operating in several Member States, which requires that the company should have a real link with the State in whose legal system it claims application in order to qualify under its jurisdiction.[165] The compatibility of 'real seat' with the right of establishment has been questioned in the light of a series of rulings from the Court of Justice.[166] In other Member States a company can establish itself simply through an act of incorporation even if its main activities are in other countries. SEs formed by companies originating in the EU will be able to freely transfer their seat notwithstanding the application of the real seat system under the national jurisdiction.[167] Nevertheless, Member States may be able to

---

[159] There is no scope under Art. 2 for a new company, not already existing in a Member State, to be formed as an SE.

[160] For the detailed provisions see Arts. 17–31. There must either be a merger by acquisition or by the formation of a new company in accordance with the provisions of the Third Company Law Directive on Mergers (Council Directive 78/855/EEC, [1978] OJ L295/36). See further, Edwards n.6 above at 452–454.

[161] Arts. 32–34. For an explanation of the procedures to be followed for forming a holding SE, see Edwards n.6 above at 454–455.   [162] Arts. 35–36.

[163] Art. 37.

[164] Art. 2(5). See also, Recital 23 of the preamble. The source for this provision is the 1962 General Programme for the abolition of restrictions on freedom of establishment, OJ Spec. Ed. IX, Resolutions of the Council and of the Representatives of the Member States, 7.

[165] See E. Wymeersch, 'The Transfer of the Company's Seat in European Company Law' (2003) 40 C.M.L.Rev. 661 at 667–668. Member States that apply this principle, in varying degrees of restrictiveness, include Germany, Austria, France, Italy, Belgium and Luxembourg. The German system is generally regarded as the strictest.

[166] See the cases cited at n.75 above. Discussed further at n.231 below. For a critique of the 'real seat' or *Sitztheorie* system in Germany, see Halbhuber n.11 above, cf. W-H. Roth, 'From *Centros* to *Uberseering*: Free Movement of Companies, Private International Law, and Community Law' (2003) 52 I.C.L.Q. 177.   [167] Art. 8.

continue to operate the real seat system by stipulating that companies must locate their head office and registered office in the same place.[168]

In perhaps the most obvious departure from the prescriptive formality of the original proposal each SE shall comprise a general meeting of shareholders and *either* a supervisory organ and management organ (two-tier system) *or* an administrative organ (one-tier system).[169] Moreover, if neither system exists, it is left to the Member State concerned to determine which of them is appropriate.[170] Evidence of the shift of emphasis from the earlier models can be found in the detailed provisions concerning the two-tier system. Whereas originally the supervisory board, containing a proportion of employee members, would have had 'permanent control over the management of the company by the executive board',[171] it must now, whether or not it has employee members, merely 'supervise the work of the management organ' and 'may not itself exercise the power to manage the SE'.[172]

The Regulation is not a direct act of harmonization and many of the detailed provisions[173] are subject to the requirements of national laws of the Member State where the SE has its registered office. It also expressly incorporates rules derived from Community Directives that have entered into force.[174] Hence the formation and structure of the SE can now be viewed as a normalized process of Community convergence rather than a Commission inspired corporate revolution.

Viewed *in toto* the slimmed-down SE Statute contains only 70 articles and, although it deals with the procedure for the formation of SEs in considerable detail, its approach to the rules concerning structure and governance is marked by a lighter touch. For example, there is no reference to the duties of company directors.[175] In the opinion of at least one commentator this is not a sufficient set of rules by which a company can operate, leaving national law to fill the gaps.[176] By contrast with the original proposal there is to be no single uniform federal system of company law operating in parallel with national regimes but rather a loose overall framework within which 25 different national systems of law will determine the precise form, structure and operating rules for SEs.

Once the company or companies concerned decide to form an SE the employee involvement provisions of the Directive are triggered. Registration of the SE and acquisition of its legal personality can only take place when the requirements of

---

[168] Art. 7. See C. Kersting, 'Corporate Choice of Law—A Comparison of the United States and European Systems and a Proposal for a European Directive' (2002–2003) 28 Brook Jo. International L. 1 at 56.

[169] Art. 38. For discussion of the detailed rules in Arts. 38–60, see Edwards n.6 above at 456–458.

[170] Arts. 39(5) and 43(4).   [171] Art. 73(1) of the proposal contained in COM(70) 600.

[172] Art. 40.

[173] Further provisions concern the general meeting (Arts. 52–60), accounts (Arts. 61–62), and winding up, liquidation, insolvency and cessation of payments (Arts. 63–66).

[174] See Edwards n.6 above at 451. Examples include the First Company Law Directive on Publicity (Council Directive 68/151/EEC, OJ Spec. Ed. (I) 41) and the Third Company Law Directive on Mergers (Council Directive 78/855/EEC, [1978] OJ L295/36).

[175] See Davies n.6 above at 77.   [176] Ibid.

the Directive have been satisfied.[177] However, the Directive offers no positive vision of the social aims of employee involvement in the SE. Rather the 'social objectives' have been reduced to an essentially negative function of ensuring that the establishment of an SE 'does not entail the disappearance or reduction of practices of employee involvement existing within the companies participating in the establishment of an SE'.[178] In practice this means that whereas information and consultation procedures would normally be required by the application of existing Directives, board level participation will only apply where a substantial proportion of the workforce is to be constituted from Member States where such requirements form part of national law. Davies[179] offers the example of an SE formed between private sector companies in Britain and Italy. As a base the Directive would require no participation at board level although an agreement to introduce such a system might be reached between management and labour.

Under Article 12(2) of the Regulation, registration of the SE is conditional on one of three requirements having been met. Either:

1) An agreement on employee involvement has been reached between the companies and the Special Negotiating Body (SNB) representing the employees,[180] or;

2) The SNB has decided not to open negotiations or to terminate negotiations already opened, and to rely on the rules on information and consultation of employees in force in the Member States where the SE has employees,[181] or;

3) The period for negotiations has expired without an agreement having been concluded.[182] In which case, Standard Rules on employee involvement will normally apply as a fallback[183] subject to specified exceptions (discussed below).[184]

Therefore, as with the EWC Directive, and drawing from the Davignon proposals, much will depend on the formation of the SNB and its negotiations with the companies involved. The establishment of the SNB guarantees an element of employee involvement, although not necessarily participation, in the SE

---

[177] Art. 12 (2) and (3) of the Regulation. Under Art. 16 the SE acquires legal personality on the date of registration.   [178] Recital 3 of the preamble of the Directive.

[179] Davies n.6 above at 76.   [180] Under Art. 4 of the Directive.

[181] In accordance with Art. 3(6) of the Directive. In this case it will be deemed that there is no agreement. This procedure will not apply in the case of transformation if there is participation in the company to be transformed. Where Art. 3(6) is activated, the EWC Directive, which normally does not apply to an SE under Art. 13(1) of the Directive, will come into play and will govern the procedures for transnational information and consultation in the SE. Although as Davies points out, n.6 above at 81–82, the employee representatives may also decide to opt out of involvement under the EWC Directive—an unlikely double negative.

[182] Under Art. 5 of the Directive the duration of negotiations is up to six months extendible, by joint agreement, to a maximum of one year from the establishment of the SNB.

[183] See Art. 7(1) and the Annex of the Directive. As Barnard & Deakin note, n.111 above at 487, the term 'Standard Rules' is somewhat misleading as these rules only apply in default of an agreement.

[184] Art. 7(2) and (3) of the Directive.

unless the SNB's members decide otherwise. By contrast with the EWC
Directive, however, management is obliged to launch the negotiation process
with the employees' representatives 'as soon as possible after publishing the draft
terms'.[185] The SNB must be proportionately representative of the employees of
all of the companies, concerned subsidiaries and establishments that will form
the SE.[186] In practice the selection process is likely to be very time consuming as
different rules for choosing the employees' representatives will apply in each
country.[187] The Directive urges that both sides on the SNB 'shall negotiate in a
spirit of co-operation with a view to reaching an agreement on arrangements for
the involvement of employees within the SE'.[188] Negotiations can continue for
six months after the establishment of the SNB but may be extended by agreement for a further six months.[189] The SNB can choose its own experts, including union representatives who may be present at the negotiation meetings in an
advisory capacity.[190] In practice, as with the Subsidiary Requirements under the
EWC Directive, the Standard Rules are likely to be regarded as benchmarks for
workers' representatives in the negotiations. At the very least the inclusion of
Standard Rules is a backstop against the possibility of a 'zero option' of
employee involvement.[191]

Although the options of either not opening negotiations or terminating them
might sound unattractive it may be logical for the SNB to follow one of these
courses.[192] For example, in the case of an SE formed by transformation of an existing
company the arrangements for employee involvement must provide for at least
the same level as those that had previously been in place.[193] Alternatively, one of
these options may be pursued in circumstances where additional safeguards apply
if proportions of the workforce in an SE by merger (25 per cent +) or by a joint
holding company or subsidiary (50 per cent +) are faced with a reduction in their
existing rights to participation.[194] Closing down the SNB process would enable the
company or companies involved to establish the SE more speedily and this may be
regarded as beneficial to workers' interests, especially in highly competitive sectors.
However, although the employees may revive the SNB at a later date they will no

---

[185] Art. 3(1).
[186] Art. 3(2). One seat is to be allocated for each Member State where the number of employees
employed there equals 10 per cent or a fraction thereof, of the number of employees of the participating companies in all the Member States taken together.   [187] See Davies n.6 above at 80.
[188] Art. 4(1).   [189] Art. 5.
[190] Art. 3(5). This provision is stronger than Art. 5(4) of the EWC Directive, which states only
that the SNB may be 'assisted' by their chosen experts. Moreover, the costs of the whole process are to
be borne by the participating companies, Art. 3(7).   [191] Keller n.49 above at 429.
[192] Art. 3(6) para. 2 provides that any decision not to open negotiations or to terminate them
requires the votes of two-thirds of SNB members representing at least two-thirds of the employees
from at least two Member States.   [193] Art. 4(4).
[194] Art. 3(4). In this case a two-thirds majority of the SNB will be required, representing at least
two-thirds of the employees, for any reduction in rights to participation, including the votes of
members representing employees employed in at least two Member States.

longer be able to rely on the Standard Rules as a fallback if no agreement is reached with management at the end of the period for negotiation.[195]

In its provisions on 'lower level' information and consultation[196] the SE Directive essentially reinforces the Community regime of proceduralised regulation already in place and applicable to most, if not all, the companies likely to be involved in an SE. The Directive envisages an agreement between the SNB and management to establish a representative body to act as the 'discussion partner' of the competent organ of the SE in connection with the arrangements for information and consultation.[197] In addition there are specified requirements for the content of any agreement that closely follow the list contained in Article 6 of the EWC Directive.[198] Similarly, the Subsidiary Requirements attached to the EWC Directive are largely replicated in an Part 2 of the Standard Rules.[199] Other provisions concerning the protection of employees' rights and compliance are consistent with the requirements of the Information and Consultation Directive.[200] Rather, the novelty of the SE Directive

[195] Art. 3(6) para. 4 provides that the SNB shall be reconvened on the written request of at least 10 per cent of the employees of the SE at the earliest two years after that decision, unless the parties agree to negotiations being reopened sooner. If no agreement is reached 'none of the provisions of the Annex shall apply'.

[196] Under the definition of 'information' in Art. 2(i) the employees' representative body must be informed 'at a time, in a manner and with a content' that allows them to 'undertake an in-depth assessment of the possible impact' of questions which concern the SE and, where appropriate, prepare consultations with the competent organ of the SE. Under Art. 2(j) 'consultation' means 'the establishment of dialogue and exchange of views' between the employees' representative body and the competent organ of the SE 'at a time, in a manner and with a content which allows the employees' representatives, on the basis of the information provided, to express an opinion on measures envisaged by the competent organ which may be taken into account in the decision-making process within the SE'.

[197] Art. 4(2)(b). Alternatively, under Art. 4(2)(f), the parties may decide to establish one or more information and consultation procedure instead of a representative body.

[198] Under Art. 4(2)(a-e) the agreement 'shall specify', *inter alia*, its scope, the composition, number of members and allocation of seats on the representative body, the functions and procedure for information and consultation on that body, the frequency of its meetings, and the financial and material resources to be allocated to it. Para.(h) provides that the agreement shall include its date of entry into force and duration, cases where it should be re-negotiated and the procedure for its renegotiation.

[199] See Davies n.6 above at 82. One area where the Standard Rules are worded more strongly can be found in Part 2(c) which provides that where there are exceptional circumstances affecting the employees' interests to a considerable extent, such as relocations, transfers, closures or collective redundancies, the representative body (or works council) is entitled to information and consultation at the appropriate level and can express an opinion. If management does not act in accordance with that opinion the representative body 'shall have the right to a further meeting with the competent organ of the SE with a view to seeking agreement'.

[200] Under Art. 10 Member States must guarantee protection of the employment rights of employees' representatives involved in negotiating the formation of the SE or serving on its board and, under Art. 11, must take appropriate measures in conformity with Community law 'with a view to preventing the misuse of an SE for the purpose of depriving employees of rights to employee involvement or withholding such rights'. The principle of effectiveness is incorporated into Art. 12, which obliges Member States to ensure that administrative or legal procedures are available to enable the obligations derived from the Directive to be enforced. Art. 8 concerns matters such as, *inter alia*, confidentiality, freedom of speech, and procedures to ensure disclosure of information to the representative body.

can be found in Article 7 and Part 3 of the Standard Rules that, for the first time at
Community-level, provide a framework for 'higher level' worker 'participation', or
'influence'[201] in the company's board.

The procedures to be applied depend on the method by which the SE is formed
and also the worker participation rules in place in the Member States where the
company or companies forming the SE are registered. In the absence of an agreement on participation,[202] Article 7(1) requires that Member States lay down
Standard Rules that satisfy the provisions set out in the Annex, operating as a
default mechanism. If the Standard Rules are applied every employee representative on the board 'shall be a full member with the same rights and obligations as
the members representing the shareholders, including the right to vote'.[203]
However, in a clear departure from the Davignon Report, the Council opted for a
diversified solution that, in essence, preserves the 'acquired rights' of employees to
participate in company decisions where such rights are in existence.[204] In a key
paragraph in the preamble the following declaration is found[205]:

> Employee rights in force before the establishment of SEs should provide the basis for
> employee rights of involvement in the SE (the 'before and after' principle). Consequently,
> that approach should apply not only to the initial establishment of an SE but also to struc-
> tural changes in an existing SE and to companies affected by structural change processes.

This statement, and the provisions that reinforce it, has two immediate consequences. First, as the Standard Rules make clear, if none of the companies concerned
were governed by participation rules prior to registration, the SE 'shall not be
required to establish provisions for employee participation'.[206] The employees in
question have no 'acquired rights' of participation to be transferred to the SE. The
status quo 'before' the formation of the SE is preserved, whatever method is used,[207]
'after' the SE is born unless the SNB and the companies decide otherwise. Second,
where participation rules govern at least one of the participating companies 'before'
the SE is formed, the employees and/or their representatives shall have the right to
elect, appoint, recommend or oppose the appointment of a number of members
of the administrative or supervisory body of the SE 'after' formation 'equal to the

---

[201] Art. 2(k) defines 'participation' as meaning the 'influence' of the employees' representative
body in the affairs of the company by way of 'the right to elect or appoint some of the members of the
company's supervisory or administrative organ', or 'the right to recommend and/or oppose the
appointment of some or all of the members of the company's supervisory or administrative organ'.
[202] Under Art. 4(2)(g), if it is decided to have arrangements for participation, the agreement shall
cover the substance of those arrangements including the number of members in the SE's administrative (single-tier) or supervisory (two-tier) body which the employees will be entitled to elect, appoint,
recommend or oppose, the procedures as to how these members are to be elected, appointed, recommended or opposed by the employees, and their rights.   [203] Part 3(b) of the Annex.
[204] Recital 18 of the preamble.   [205] Ibid.
[206] Part 3 of the Standard Rules, second para.
[207] This will be the case even where an SE is formed by 'transformation' as 'all aspects of employee
participation shall continue to apply to the SE'—Standard Rules, first para. point (a). It follows that if
there are no aspects of employee participation in the company concerned there is no obligation for
such arrangements to be introduced as part of the process of transformation into an SE.

highest proportion in force in the participating companies concerned before the registration of the SE'.[208] By contrast with Davignon's recommendations, there is no minimum level of employee representation but, in order to guarantee the 'acquired rights' of employees, there may be an improvement on the *status quo* for many employees because the base will be the 'highest proportion' of participation under the national systems in place if the Standard Rules are applied. The system deemed to guarantee the 'highest proportion' of employee participation will be 'exported' to employees in other Member States unless an alternative solution is negotiated.[209]

By defining the appropriate level of participation according to the 'highest proportion' of employees participating in or influencing board-level decisions in the Member States involved, the Standard Rules suggest a straightforward arithmetical calculation, without the need for any qualitative assessment of the 'influence' of employees or their representatives on the board.[210] On the one hand, if we confine the calculation simply to the proportion of workers elected or appointed to serve on the board, the high watermark rule appears to preserve co-determination in German companies within the SE framework, although it may make them less attractive suitors for companies based in other Member States.[211] On the other hand, the 'highest proportion' of participation relates not merely to election or appointment to the board but arises also, under the definition of 'participation' in Article 2(k), from the right to recommend and/or oppose the appointment of some or all of its members. This effectively plays off the sophisticated German and Dutch systems of worker participation against each other. As Davies observes, the system in the Netherlands may trump German style co-determination because workers in Dutch companies, who have no direct representation on the board, have influence over the appointment of all board members because they can oppose any appointment in court.[212] If the Standard Rules come into play it will be left to the national court in the State of registration to resolve such a conundrum in the first instance. The possibility of different interpretations of the Standard Rules may encourage the SNB to seek to negotiate a hybrid that more closely reflects the balance of worker participation systems in place in the States where the companies are based.[213] Alternatively, the system in the Member State of registration may be preferred by the SNB even if this might have a less advanced regime for worker participation.[214] Much will depend on the perceived advantages and disadvantages of the SE proposal for the potential workforce of the new company. One factor to be borne in mind is that, after the decision has been made on employee involvement, whether through an agreement

---

[208] Ibid, first para. point (b).   [209] See Davies n.6 above at 87.
[210] Ibid. at 85.   [211] Ibid. at 76.   [212] Ibid. at 86.
[213] Cf. Keller n.49 above at 437. It is entirely up to the SNB to decide how to negotiate 'arrangements for the involvement of employees within the SE'. Subject to the requirements of Art. 7, the more rigid 'higher proportion' rule only comes into play if the Standard Rules come into effect.
[214] Management are free to choose the Member State where the SE is to be registered. This may cause difficulties. For example, an SE involving a German company, whose system of employee involvement may be deemed to be the most advanced, may be registered in another Member State breaking the link between the board and the integral German works council system—see Davies n.6 above at 86.

or otherwise, it remains an option for the shareholders of the companies to decide not to ratify the arrangements,[215] in which case the SE will not be formed.

From the above discussion it is apparent that there is an inherent tension in the Directive between a desire to allow the parties to freely negotiate a system of worker participation most suited to themselves, if they wish to have one at all, and a concern, on the part of the Member States, to preserve national participation rules (or non-participation regimes) as far as possible. The 'highest proportion' of participation rule, left unfettered, has the potential to undermine long established systems of labour law and industrial relations that form an integral part of the complex social tapestry of each nation State. The remainder of Article 7 of the Directive has been specifically designed to mitigate this risk. The provisions of this Article offer a limited escape route from the Standard Rules in certain circumstances, depending on the method of formation of the SE as follows:

1. Where the SE is formed by transformation, the rules of a Member State relating to employee participation will continue to apply.[216] This provision effectively closes the door on any attempt by a company to transform itself into an SE in order to 'escape' from a national participation regime it dislikes even if the SNB is willing to negotiate such a solution.[217]

2. In the case of an SE established by a merger, a Member State may decide not to apply the Standard Rules relating to participation.[218] In practice this will not make any difference if the merger is between companies in Member States where no participation rules exist[219] but, in any other case, an agreement on arrangements for participation must be reached between the SNB and management.[220]

3. In other cases involving a merger, where the Member State has applied the Standard Rules, the 'highest proportion' test will only apply where at least one or more forms of participation cover 25 per cent of the employees concerned.[221] Where coverage is less than 25 per cent the SNB is empowered to invoke the Standard Rules or, if there was more than one form of participation within the various companies, it shall decide which of those forms is to be established.[222] In the absence of an agreement management will have to accept the form of participation chosen by the SNB.[223]

---

[215] Arts. 23(2) and 32(6) of the Regulation.   [216] Art. 7(2)(a).
[217] This is effected by a combination of Art. 3(6), third para. Art. 4(4), and Part 3(a) of the Standard Rules. See further, Davies n.6 above at 92.   [218] Art. 7(3).
[219] Para. 2 of the Standard Rules.   [220] Art. 12(3) of the Regulation.
[221] Art. 7(2)(b). The SNB retains the power to negotiate an alternative form of participation but any reduction in the level of participation from the 'highest proportion' test shall require, under Art. 3(4), the votes of two-thirds of the members of the SNB representing at least two-thirds of the employees, including members representing employees employed in at least two Member States.
[222] Art. 7(2) second para.
[223] In this case Art. 3(4) requires that there must be an absolute majority of the members of the SNB to determine the preferred system even if this involves a reduction of the participation rights of the minority.

4. In the case of an SE formed by setting up a holding company or establishing a subsidiary the procedure is the same as under point 3 above except that the threshold for the Standard Rules to apply is 50 per cent of workers subject to mandatory participation.

In practice these highly complex requirements are likely to reinforce the 'before' and 'after' *status quo* for the majority of workers in companies forming an SE whatever its method of establishment. Member States who are reluctant to import unfamiliar systems of worker participation are shielded, to a certain degree, by the merger opt-out.[224] Other Member States, who wish to block any escape route from participation, have been offered defensive mechanisms.[225] One anticipated consequence of the merger opt-out is for a significant proportion of SEs to be created without any participation arrangements, even if a majority on the SNB desire them. At the other end of the spectrum, where SEs are formed between companies from Member States where some have participation regimes, there is the possibility of workers being transferred from one form of participation to another more advanced system or being involved in participation for the first time. Notwithstanding the limitations imposed by Article 7, the inherent bias of the Directive favours a gradual 'upward convergence' of workers' participation in the EU, coalescing around the relatively advanced German, Dutch and Nordic models, a process that may be accelerated in the enlarged EU.[226]

In order to gain an appreciation of the potential reach of worker involvement within the diverse SE framework we need to look beyond specific examples and the mechanics of calculating which system of participation, if any, will apply in a given case.[227] Despite the element of uncertainty that surrounds the project it is possible to reach some tentative conclusions on the issue of worker involvement. In particular, when an SE is proposed the workers concerned, many of whom will have existing procedural rights under national and Community law, will be empowered to shape the new entity in a fashion that preserves, or indeed advances, industrial relations traditions and cultural identity. At the outset the mandatory involvement of the SNB will instil an indirect element of 'industrial democracy' into the process of forming the SE even if this falls short of a fundamental shift in the power relationship between management and labour in the new company either in the workplace or the boardroom. However, in the absence of a national system of co-determination, the SE framework offers only the prospect of a distant voice for workers through the external channel of information and consultation machinery, which is essentially no more than a discussion forum. Nevertheless, by retaining a preference for workers' participation, and

---

[224] In particular Spain, Portugal, Ireland and the United Kingdom.

[225] See Rebérioux n.38 above at 127.

[226] Several of the countries that joined the EU on 1 May 2004 have adopted, or are likely to introduce, a two-tier board structure with mandatory worker participation.

[227] Davies n.6 above provides some fascinating potential scenarios at 93–94.

insisting upon it in certain situations, the SE may serve as a lens through which an alternative, more pluralistic, vision of the future direction of European corporate governance can be projected. In this vista there will be no place for any imposed solutions of uniform types of company structure and systems of worker participation. Instead, the social partners, acting with a degree of autonomy and benefiting from a dialogic process that encourages reflexive learning, will have the capacity to act as enablers who can find solutions based on a shared understanding that 'social responsibility' starts at the workplace and 'corporate governance' is an inclusive process within which the company's objectives are set and attained.

V. Beyond the SE—Company and Labour Law Intertwined?

(A) Future Prospects for the SE

Resolving the impasse over the SE and creating an idealized framework for European corporate governance has been an immense task, but has it been worth the effort?

For the SE project to succeed companies will have to be motivated to experiment with an untested form of incorporation that no longer offers a uniform set of rules but rather a menu of choices and references to national law. More will be required than simply a new European identity tag. The evidence suggests that companies will be pragmatic, accepting worker involvement, even participation, but only if shareholder value is respected and overall cost benefits can be anticipated.[228] Efficiencies arising from a unified management and a single EU-wide registration were estimated at up to €30 billion per year in the mid-1990s,[229] but any assumed savings would have to be offset against the costs involved in the complex process of formation. Many firms may be enticed by the prospect of transferring their company seat[230] or merging across borders. In practice such advantages may be short lived if the Court of Justice applies stricter scrutiny to national restrictions on free movement,[231] and if future legislative developments follow the SE approach.

---

[228] See Keller n.49 above at 436.

[229] See the findings of the 'Ciampi Report'—*Improving European Competitiveness*, First Report to the President of the Commission and the Heads of State of Government by the Consultative Group on Competitiveness, June 1995 (Brussels: European Communities, 1995).

[230] For analysis see Wymeersch n.165 above at 690–695.

[231] See Case C-212/97 *Centros Ltd v Erhvervs-og Selskabsstyrelsen* [1999] ECR I-1459, where the Court struck-down restrictions imposed under Danish law on a UK firm seeking to set up a branch in Denmark on the basis that such restrictions were incompatible with freedom of establishment. In Case C-208/00 *Überseering BV v NCC Nordic Construction* [2002] ECR I-9919, where the Court ruled against a German law that denied legal capacity to a Dutch firm that had moved its operations to Germany. Such requirements may be lawful if they are proportionate and can justified by a policy imperative in the public interest. However, transfers designed to avoid taxes in the home State may be legitimately rejected by the receiving State: see Case 81/87 *R v H.M. Treasury and Commissioners of Inland Revenue, Ex p. Daily Mail and General Trust plc* [1988] ECR 5483. Discussed by P. Dryberg, 'Full Free Movement of Companies in the European Community at Last' (2003) 28 E.L.Rev. 528, Halbhuber n.11 above, Roth n.166 above, and Wymeersch, ibid.

For example, the latest draft of the Directive on cross-border mergers has been expressly designed to complement the SE.[232] Following the SE Directive, the proposal aims to protect employees' acquired rights to participation in companies created by merger even if such rights do not exist in one of the Member States involved.[233] If adopted, the new measure would supplement the social policy provisions of the Transfers of Undertakings Directive.[234] Likewise, although predatory cross-border activity may increase following the adoption of the Takeover Directive,[235] which is modelled on the UK's system of shareholder primacy,[236] an attempt has been made to intertwine company and labour law by requiring the board of the company planning a takeover to produce a public document stating the effects on employees and allow for a separate opinion to be issued by the employees' representatives.[237] These developments tie in with proposals to eliminate tax obstacles to cross-border corporate activity.[238] In a parallel development the Council has recently approved the Statute for a European Co-operative Society,[239] which also has a supplementary Directive concerning employee involvement.[240] Moreover, the SE concept may be extended to small and medium-sized enterprises with the launch of the 'European Private Company'.[241] Hence, the SE may act as a harbinger for a realignment of company, tax and labour law in the EU within the context of cross-border corporate activity whether or not this takes place within and between companies actually forming or transforming themselves as SEs.

(B) Beyond the SE—Corporate Social Responsibility in Practice?

In a strange way, despite the interminable delay, the belated emergence of the SE has been timely. Coinciding with a widespread desire for a policy response to

---

[232] See COM(2003) 703 final at point 2 of the Explanatory Memorandum. As Edwards notes, n.6 above at 463, the Tenth Company Law Directive would, if adopted, fulfil the same function as forming an SE by merger without any need for incorporation of the merged company as an SE. In some respects the new draft goes further as it would cover not only public limited liability companies but also all other companies with share capital.

[233] Art. 2 of the draft Directive. See point 3.3 of the Explanatory Memorandum.

[234] European Parliament and Council Directive 2001/23/EC, [2001] OJ L82/16, consolidating Council Directive 77/187/EEC, [1977] OJ L61/26 and Council Directive 98/50/EC, [1998] OJ L201/88. See the express references to the labour law Directives in recital 10 of the draft preamble.

[235] European Parliament and Council Directive 2004/25/EC on takeover bids, [2004] OJ L142/12 (Thirteenth Company Law Directive). See F. Wooldridge, 'The Recent Directive on Takeover-Bids' [2004] Euro. Bus. L. Rev. 147.   [236] See Barnard & Deakin n.111 above at 484.

[237] Art. 9 of Directive 2004/25. These provisions have been introduced to satisfy the demands of the European Parliament, which had rejected an earlier version in a tied vote of 273:273 on 4 July 2001. For the same reasons additional clauses are designed to enable the target company to mount a more effective defence.   [238] See COM(2003) 726 final.

[239] Council Regulation 1435/2003/EC, [2003] OJ L207/1. See also, the proposals for a Council Regulation on a statute for a European Association, [1993] OJ C236/1, and for a Council Regulation on a statute for a European Mutual Society, [1993] OJ C236/40.

[240] Council Directive 2003/72/EC, [2003] OJ L207/25.

[241] See COM(2003) 284 final, n.151 above, point 3.5.

recent corporate scandals, especially post-Enron,[242] the SE offers a balanced and flexible framework, or at the very least, a reference point for the reform of company law in the EU. Furthermore, as the European Commission has suggested in its recent Communication on company law, an effective approach 'will help to strengthen shareholders rights and third parties protection'.[243] Hence, the SE may contribute to a process of reconciliation between the stakeholder and shareholder models of corporate governance within the European sphere[244] after a period during which shareholder primacy has become increasingly dominant on both sides of the Atlantic. Moreover, the SE ties in with the drive for corporate social responsibility (CSR), which has the potential to bridge the gap between social policy and corporate governance.[245]

The European Commission's Green Paper on *Promoting a European Framework for Corporate Social Responsibility* defines CSR as 'a concept whereby companies integrate social and environmental concerns in their business operations and in their interaction with stakeholders on a voluntary basis'.[246] In the EU context CSR is not a substitute for regulation but rather a plea for corporate enlightenment, or even, a return to the philanthropic tradition but with embedded social partnership replacing old-style paternalism. The Green Paper presents a business case for CSR by linking the contribution of stakeholders to economic value on the basis that employees are an 'investment not a cost'[247] and a better working environment will lead to a 'more committed and productive workforce'.[248] Companies would be expected to report to shareholders annually on their performance against economic, environmental and social criteria.[249] Corporate restructuring provides the focus for applying the principles of CSR through the process of worker involvement. Building on its earlier document on *Anticipating and Managing Change*,[250] the Commission stressed that taking into account and addressing the social impact of restructuring contributes to its acceptance and to enhance its positive potential. In a key paragraph it noted that restructuring in a socially responsible manner 'means to balance and take into consideration the interests and concerns of all those who are affected by the changes and decisions' by seeking their 'participation' through 'open information and consultation'.[251]

CSR offers an ethical framework from which the dominant Anglo-American view of the firm can be re-evaluated.[252] As the Commission explains in its follow up Communication, the main function of the enterprise is to 'generate profit for its

---

[242] See n.43 above.   [243] COM(2003) 284 final n.151 above. Introduction.
[244] Hunt n.7 above at 136.   [245] Barnard & Deakin n.111 above at 497.
[246] COM(2001) 366 final, point 20. See further, EU Council Resolution of 3 December 2001 on the follow-up to the Green Paper on corporate social responsibility, [2002] OJ C86/3, Commission Communication on *Corporate Social Responsibility: A business contribution to Sustainable Development*, COM(2002) 347 final, and Council Resolution of 6 February 2003 on corporate social responsibility, [2003] OJ C39/3.   [247] COM(2001) 366, ibid. point 12.
[248] Ibid. point 24.   [249] Ibid. point 71.
[250] *Anticipating and managing change: a dynamic approach to the social aspects of corporate restructuring* (Brussels: European Commission, 2002).   [251] COM(2001) 366, point 36.
[252] Hunt n.7 above at 125.

owners and shareholders as well as welfare for society'.[253] The role of the corporation as a public actor with a societal responsibility to its employees and the wider community is implicit.[254] Ideas on the delivery of CSR are to be brought forward by a Multi-Stakeholder Forum, bringing together business, trade unions and civil society, consistent with a more inclusive, participatory 'new governance' agenda.[255] In addition, Member States are expected to integrate CSR into national policies.[256] However, despite the emphasis on giving stakeholders a voice in corporate governance, even the most basic commitments, such as social and environmental reporting, are not legally binding.[257] By contrast, the flexible SE form of incorporation, with its balance of rights and responsibilities between shareholders and stakeholders, offers companies an opportunity to convert vague commitments to CSR into tangible reality.

Viewed in isolation the SE may amount to no more than a curio or a museum piece placed on display even though its practical uses are limited. In a broader sense, however, irrespective of whether the idea takes hold, it signifies the emergence of an essentially pluralistic conception of European corporate governance in which shareholders' rights are strengthened through greater accountability and transparency and employees' views are transmitted through participation and/or constructive dialogue. In parallel, Community labour law acts as a bulwark against bottom down harmonization arising from regulatory and jurisdictional competition. As Villiers explains,[258] pluralistic corporate governance, in its most advanced form, recognises the intrinsic worth of the contribution of workers to the enterprise and grants them a position of influence at least equal to that of their counterpart shareholders. In this model the interest of the shareholders is no longer the sole determinant of the management of the company.[259] Although the revised SE does not create a relationship of equals it recognizes a balance of interests inside the European corporate space. In many Member States, shareholder primacy will continue to drive corporate governance policies, and, more generally, in response to challenges posed by globalization and trade liberalization,[260] the EU has signed up to flexible labour markets and pro-enterprise fiscal policies,[261] but the SE may play a part in anchoring such policies within an overall framework of 'corporate social responsibility'.

[253] COM(2002) 347, point 3.   [254] See further, Lynch-Fannon n.4 above at 102–103.

[255] See especially the Commission's *White Paper on European Governance*, COM(2001) 428 final. Discussed by Hunt n.7 above at 124. See the critique of Allott who asks whether we are witnessing the governmentalizing of the corporation and the corporatizing of government? See P. Allott, 'European Governance and the Re-branding of Democracy' (2002) 27 E.L.Rev. 60 at 61.

[256] See Council Resolution of 6 February 2003 on corporate social responsibility, [2003] OJ C39/3.

[257] See Hunt n.7 above at 139.   [258] See especially Villiers n.32 above at 293.

[259] See Schmitthoff n.7 above at 1421.

[260] For an insightful analysis of the impact of globalization in this context see M. Rhodes & B. van Apeldorn, 'Capital unbound? The transformation of European corporate governance', (1998) 5 Jo. of European Public Policy 406.

[261] Most importantly in the declaration issued in the Presidency Conclusions of the Lisbon European Council of 23–24 March 2000, which laid down the EU's strategic goal: 'to become the most competitive and dynamic knowledge-based economy in the world, capable of sustainable economic growth with more and better jobs and greater social cohesion'.

Civil Society and the Social Dialogue in European Governance

Daniela Obradovic*

I. The concept of Participatory Governance in the Constitution for Europe

The new Constitution for Europe signed by all the member states of the European Union (EU) on 29 October 2004[1] introduces the concept of participatory democracy as an important element of the future EU governance.[2] Article I-47 of the European Constitution stipulates:

The principle of participatory democracy

1. The institutions shall, by appropriate means, give citizens and representative associations the opportunity to make known and publicly exchange their views in all areas of Union action.

2. The institutions shall maintain an open, transparent and regular dialogue with representative associations and civil society.

3. The Commission shall carry out broad consultations with parties concerned in order to ensure that the Union's actions are coherent and transparent.

The inclusion of the principle of participatory democracy in the new Constitution for Europe has attracted considerable public attention. Indeed, the White paper proposals on better involvement and on consulting civil society

---

* Dr Daniela Obradovic, Faculty of Law, University of Amsterdam.

[1] Treaty establishing a constitution for Europe, OJ C 310, 16.12.2004.

[2] The notion of governance is used in a variety of ways. A wide notion defines governance as every form of ordered rule and collective action to achieve policy results, by solely public, democratically legitimized actors (government) and/or private actors (see e.g. Commission of the European Communities (2002) 'Report from the Commission on European Governance', COM(2002) 705, Brussels, 11.12.2002, note 1 at p 8). The more restricted notion defines governance as those governing mechanisms which do not or only minimally take recourse to public authority and sanctions of government, that blur responsibility between the public and the private sector, and that rest on the interaction of a multiplicity of relatively autonomous actors who influence each other (e.g. Joerges, Christian et al (2002) Governance in the European Union and the Commission White paper, European University Institute: EUI working paper Law, no. 2002/8).

drew, by far, more interest than any other theme during the public consultation on this document.[3]

What this concept actually entails? Theoretically, the principle of participatory governance denotes 'the regular and guaranteed presence when making binding decisions of representatives of those collectivities that will be affected by the policy adopted'.[4] It means that those who could be affected by a decision, holders[5], have to be involved in its creation and implementation. As a matter of fact, participatory governance involves only those organizations judged capable of contributing to the governance of the designated task (such as solicitation of indispensable information, contribution towards building of necessary consensus or towards the successful implementation of decisions) should participate. Participatory democracy requires that parties who are effected by legal provisions should be involved in the opinion-forming process at the earliest possible stage and should be given the opportunity to bring their wishes to bear in this process and to put forward their proposals.

Although Article I-47 of the Constitution for Europe as a non-committal provision does not provide clear and operational definition of the notion of participatory democracy, it undoubtedly refers to the structuring of the involvement of so-called civil society in Union law making and the implementation thereof designated at present as the civil dialogue.[6] It stands for a range of patterns for consultation and discussion, such as particular fora or deliberative panels organized by the Commission at which civic organizations affected by certain political project or legislative initiative could express their concerns and opinions.[7] Civil society organizations are the principle structure of society outside of government and public administration, including economic operators not generally considered being non-governmental organisations (NGOs).[8] Both the concept of participatory democracy

---

[3] Commission of the European Communities (2002) 'Report from the Commission on European Governance', COM (2002) 705, Brussels, 11.12.2002, p.4.

[4] Schmitter, Philippe C. (2002) 'Participation in governance arrangements: is there any reason to expect it will achieve "sustainable and innovative policies in a multilevel context"?' in Juergen R. Grote and Bernard Gbikpi, (eds.), Participatory Governance: Political and Societal Implications, (Opladen: Leske + Budrich), pp. 51–70, p. 56.

[5] Different type of holders can be identified: right-holders, space-holders, knowledge-holders; shareholders, stakeholders, interest-holders and status-holders.

[6] The opinion that the concept of participatory democracy as enshrined in the Constitution for Europe denotes the already established practice of the so-called civil dialogue is upheld by the European Social and Economic Committee (European Social and Economic committee (2003) 'Opinion addressed to the 2003 Intergovernmental Conference', CESE 1171/2003, Brussels, 24–25 September 2003, p.2).

[7] There is no clear-cut distinction between the civil dialogue and lobbying for both concern informal exchange of information between interest groups and Union institutions. Institutionalisation and structuring of the civil dialogue through the introduction of particular procedures and the imposition of minimum requirements which should be meet by civic groups in order to qualify them to take part in the consultation initiated by the Commission will in future establish a sort of delimitation line between those two phenomena.

[8] Under the title on the involvement of civil society in EU governance, the White paper indicates business test panels as an example of existing consultation mechanisms (Commission of European Communities (2001) 'European governance: white paper', COM(2001) 428, Brussels, 25.7.2001, p. 15).

and the civil dialogue concern the structures intended to make possible for those affected by decisions, stakeholders, to participate in decision-making process.

The Treaty of European Union that is currently in force does not make any reference to the civil dialogue. The Commission has developed this concept completely outside the Treaty framework. While the EU Treaty in force is silent as to the notion of the civil dialogue, it formalizes the social dialogue, the involvement of European level employers' and employees' associations, so called social partners, in Union decision-making by virtue of Articles 138 and 139 EC. The autonomy of the social dialogue and its distinctiveness as to the concept of the participatory democracy is retained in the Constitution of Europe. It addresses the promotion of the dialogue between the social partners separately from the issue of the principle of participatory democracy in Article I-48.[9]

Although the Constitution formally makes the distinction between the concepts of the civil and social dialogue, it does not provide the clear guidelines as to substantive differences between them. The lack of the operationalization of the notion of participatory democracy contributes towards the bewilderment surrounding two of those concepts. The fact that the definition of the civil society adopted by the Commission in its White Paper of governance includes the social partners additionally blurs the delimitation line between the social and civil dialogue in the Union.[10] Furthermore, since, both the social and civil dialogue are based upon the preposition that citizens affected by decisions should have an equal and effective opportunity to make their interests and concerns known, substantive distinction between those two modes of governance is not easy to established.

The Commission itself has contributed towards insufficient delimitation of boundaries between those concepts by suggesting that 'policy development related to consultation processes could build upon the experience from the social dialogue and should also aim at creating synergies between the European social dialogue and wider civil society consultation mechanism'.[11] It further adds to the confusion by

---

[9] Article I-48 of the Constitution for Europe reads:

The social partners and autonomous social dialogue

The Union recognizes and promotes the role of the social partners at its level, taking into account the diversity of national systems. It shall facilitate dialogue between the social partners, respecting their autonomy. The Tripartite Social Summit for Growth and Employment shall contribute to social dialogue. The concept of the social dialogue is further elaborated in Articles III-211 and III-212 of the Treaty establishing a Constitution for Europe, OJ C 310, 16.12.2004.

[10] Civil society includes the following groups: trade unions and employers' organizations (social partners); organizations representing social and economic players, which are not social partners in the strict sense of the term (for instance, consumer organizations); non-governmental organizations which bring people together in common cause, such as environmental organizations, human rights organizations, charities; professional associations; grass roots organizations; organisations that involve citizens in local and municipal life with a particular contribution from churches and religious communities (Commission of European Communities (2001) 'European governance: white paper', COM(2001) 428, Brussels, 25.7.2001, p. 14). The Commission has adopted the Economic and Social Committee definition of civil society (see Economic and Social Committee (1999) Opinion on the role and contribution of civil society organizations in the building the Europe, OJ C 329/30, 17.11.99).

[11] European Commission (2002) European Governance: Preparatory Work for the White Paper, Luxembourg: Office for Official Publications of the European Communities, p. 75.

claiming that 'there was no single uniform model, which could be applied to the dialogue between the Commission and civil society organisations'.[12]

This article is intended to highlight the distinction between the concepts of the social and civil dialogue in the European Union and to evaluate the impact thereof upon its governance.

II. The Concept of the Civil Dialogue in the European Union

Informal consultation with interest groups has been constant and distinctive feature of the Commission's pre-drafting phase of the European legislation preparation process from the very beginning of European integration.[13] The Commission has contact with around 1500 interest groups. Two-thirds of these represent business, one-fifth citizen interests, with the reminder representing professions, trade unions, and public sector organizations at national and regional level. In addition to these interest groups, an estimated 350 large firms, 200 regions, and 300 or so organizations supplying commercial public affairs services, are active in engaging EU politics.[14]

The Commission consults interest groups when formulating its policies. It carries out those consultations in order to obtain information, data, statistics, knowledge and expertise necessary for discharging its responsibility to initiate law in the European Union. Since its in-house expertise is limited, information provided by private actors helps the Commission to offset the informational advantage of national officials.[15]

The Commission does not only regard consultation of interested parties to be beneficial for the process of legislation drafting because it helps to ensure that its legislative proposals are sound, but it considers itself to be legally bound to do so.[16] The Commission finds that its duty to wide consultation flows from the Protocol No 7 on the application of the principles of subsidiarity and proportionality, annexed to the Amsterdam Treaty which stipulates that 'the Commission should [. . .] consult widely before proposing legislation and, wherever appropriate, publish consultation documents'.

---

[12] Ibid, p. 72.

[13] Sargenet, Jane A. (1985) 'Corporatism and the European Community' in Wyn Grant, (ed.), *The Political Economy of Corporatism*, (London: Macmillan), pp. 229–253, p. 236.

[14] Greenwood, Justine (2003) 'The world of NGOs and interest representation', in *NGOs, Democratisation and the Regulatory State, A Collection of Papers Presented at the Conferences in London and Brussels*, (London: European Policy Forum), pp. 51–64, p. 52.

[15] Christiansen, Thomas *et al* (2003) 'Informal governance in the European Union: an introduction', in Thomas Christiansen and Simona Piattoni, (eds.), *Informal Governance in the European Union*, (Cheltenham: Edward Elgar), pp. 1–22, p. 9.

[16] Commission of the European Communities (2002) 'Communication from the Commission "Towards a reinforced culture of consultation and dialogue—General principles and minimum standards for consultation of interested parties by the Commission"', COM(2002) 704, Brussels, 11.12.2002, p.3.

Consultations of interested parties by the Commission take place on an ad hoc base through different instruments, such as Green and White papers, communications, advisory committees, informal working groups, business test panels, ad hoc and on-line consultations, etc.

In order to be able to gather the widest possible range of information and expertise available, the Commission endorsed the policy of unrestricted access of interest groups to its officials and declined to introduce any system of licensing for groups that it consulted.[17] The Commission did not impose any particular requirement upon interest groups that it engaged in dialogue with, nor it requested them to fulfil some formal conditions in order to be consulted.

This policy of open access should not be confused with the notion of equal access for all. 'Ownership of resources, such as expertise or information, governs access of interest groups to EU institutions, not possession of an opinion worthy of equal consideration'.[18] Interest groups consulted by the Commission are selected on the basis of their ability to solicit substantial policy input. The unrestricted access policy is intended to provide an incentive for specific interest groups to act as a producer of information, as means of assuring the viability of its proposals. Private actors can only stay involved with the Commission if they manage to present fresh information that is relevant to the decision.[19] One means of reducing the costs of information search, when these appear to be excessively high might be to use agents who are specialized in the production of information.

Apart from engaging with interest groups for the purpose of consultation, the Commission also adopted very close relations with non-governmental associations participating in the distribution of EU-aid to third countries.[20]

Until the mid-1990s the Commission did not make any distinction between diffuse interest groups advancing widely held interests such as environmental protection, consumer protection, equal opportunities between man and women, and civil liberties and private interest groups, such as business associations, in its consultation policy deployed it the process of the preparation of legislative proposals.

In the years following the conclusion of the Maastricht Treaty, the Commission has began to advocate structuring and the formalization of the consultation process with non-profit organisations distinguishing its dialogue with them from

[17] Commission of the European Communities (1992) 'Communication from the Commission "An open and structured dialogue between the Commission and special interest groups"', SEC(92) 2272, Brussels, 2. 12. 1992.

[18] Beetham, David and Lord, Christopher (1998) *Legitimacy and the European Union*, (London: Longman), p. 455; Bouwen, Peter (2002) 'Corporate lobbying in the European Union: the logic of access', Journal of European Public Policy, 9(3): 365–390.

[19] Michalowitz, Irina (2004) 'Lobbying as a two-way strategy: interest intermediation or mutual instrumentalisation?' in Andreas Warntjen and Arndt Wonka, (eds.), *Governance in Europe: The Role of Interest Groups*, (Baden-Baden: Nomos), pp. 76–93, p. 81.

[20] European Commission (1997) 'Communication from the Commission on promoting the role of voluntary organisations and foundations in Europe', COM(97) 241, Brussels, 6.6.1997, p. 14.

its contacts with other groups.[21] By that time the Commission has found it increasingly difficult to manage the logistics of ever growing numbers of lobbyists (20.000 of them around three or for every Commission policy-making official)[22] and in particular to reconcile the policy of open access with the principle of equal opportunity. The relationship between the Brussels and interest groups up to the 1990s could be described as being 'clientele', with the Commission selecting a few groups with which it felt comfortable as the appropriate representatives of social interests. Beginning at least with the Sutherland Report in 1992 the European Commission has sought to open its relationship with groups and to make those relationships more transparent. This has been done through creating a series of fora that promote relatively open dialogue on policy issue.[23]

However, whilst the Commission's dialogue with representatives of management and labour organized at European level called the social dialogue has its basis in law, the Commission intention to structure its dialogue with civic interest groups was not legally institutionalized. Although the Commission has over the years developed quite regular consultation with the diffused interest groups, this dialogue lacked formal Treaty recognition and stable structures. Declaration No. 23 attached to the Maastricht Treaty stresses the importance of co-operation between the European Union and charitable associations, foundations and institutions responsible for social welfare establishments and services, but it does not provide legal basis for the formal involvement of those groups in Union law-making. The subsequently adopted Amsterdam Treaty brought no change. Although the Comite des Sages, the expert group set up in 1996 by the Commission to examine the possibility of codification of the civil dialogue by the Treaty provision, was in favour of such an proposal,[24] this was not accepted during the Amsterdam Treaty drafting. Similarly to Masstricht, the Amsterdam negotiations resulted only in the adoption declarations on voluntary services[25] and sport[26] to be attached to the Treaty that recognize the importance of exchange of information and experiences with non-

---

[21] Ibid and the European Commission (2000) 'Commission discussion paper "The Commission and non-governmental organisations: building a stronger partnership"', COM(2000) 11, Brussels, 18.1.2000.

[22] Greenwood, Justin (2002) 'Advocacy, influence and persuasion: has it all been overdone?' in Alex Warleigh and Jenny Fairbrass, (eds.), *Influence and Interests in the European Union: The New Politics of Persuasion and Advocacy*, (London: Europa Publications), pp. 19–34, p. 29.

[23] Peters, Guy (2004) 'Interest groups and European governance: a normative perspective' in Andreas Warntjen and Arndt Wonka, (eds.), *Governance in Europe: The Role of Interest Groups*, (Baden-Baden: Nomos), pp. 57–65, p. 61.

[24] European Commission (1996) Report by the Comite des Sages 'For a Europe of civic and social rights', (Luxembourg: Office for Official Publications of the European Communities), p. 55.

[25] Declaration 38 reads: The Conference recognises the important contribution made by voluntary service activities to developing social solidarity. The Community will encourage the European dimension of voluntary organisations with particular emphasis on the exchange of information and experiences as well as on the participation of the young and the elderly in voluntary work.

[26] Declaration 29 states: The Conference emphasises the social significance of sport, in particular its role in forging identity and bringing people together. The Conference therefore calls on the bodies of the European Union to listen to sports associations when important questions affecting sport are at issue. In this connection, special consideration should be given to the particular characteristics of amateur sport.

profit organizations operating in the field of social services and sport, with particular emphasis on the encouraging European dimension of these associations.

As a matter of fact, the Commission itself renounced its plan of an explicit reference to the civil dialogue being enshrined in the Amsterdam Treaty. It rationalized that by the fear of the bureaucratization.[27] Instead, it opted for more flexible and less rigid and formal mechanisms, such as advisory committee deliberation, debating and discussions at various policy fora, the setting up of new budget lines promoting co-operation with non-profit organisations and publishing of a directory on European non-profit associations in order to enable officials to consult more systematically and as widely as possible.[28]

The conceiving of the European Social Policy Forum in 1996 marked, according to the Commission, the beginning of a civil dialogue in the European Union,[29] although non-profit organizations were first consulted in a systematic manner when preparing the 1993 Green Paper on European social policy.[30] Subsequently, the Commission has kept organizing policy forums in other areas such as environment, trade,[31] development,[32] fisheries, information society, corporate social responsibility,[33] corporate governance,[34] enterprise and industry,[35] education and dialogue with churches.[36]

---

[27] Commission of the European Communities (1997) 'Communication from the Commission on promoting the role of voluntary organisations and foundations in Europe', COM(97) 241, Brussels, 6.6.1997, point 9.8.

[28] European Commission (1996) Directory of Interest Groups, (Luxembourg: Office for Official Publications of the European Communities). For the current version of it see http://europa.eu.int/comm/civil_society/coneccs/index.htm.

[29] Flynn, Padraig (1996) 'Europe requires a civil dialogue and the support of its citizens' in European Commission, A Report on the Forum: Working on European Social Policy', Luxembourg: Office for Official Publications of the European Communities, p. 8. For the Second forum see http://europa.eu.int/comm/dg05/jobs/forum98/en/intro_en.htm.

[30] Commission of the European Communities (1993) 'Green paper: European social policy: opinion for the Union', COM (93) 551, Brussels, 17 November 1993. The establishment civil dialogue with non-profit interest groups has been stipulated in the range of the Commission documents from that period. See for example: Commission of the European Communities (1996) 'Green paper on "Living and working in the information society: peoples first"', COM(96) 386, Brussels, 24.7.1996, p. 8; Commission of the European Communities (1993) Growth, competitiveness, employment: the challenges and ways forward into the 21st century: white paper, Bull. EC, Supplement 6/93; Commission of the European Communities (1994) 'European social policy—a way forward for the Union: a white paper', COM(94) 333, Brussels, 27.7.1994, pp. 44 and 57; Commission of the European Communities (1995) 'Medium-term social action programme 1995–1997', COM(95) 134, point 9.2.1.

[31] For an overview of the current status of the civil dialogue in trade, see http://www.europa.eu.int/comm/trade/csc/dcs_proc.htm.

[32] With the goal of exchanging expertise and opinions on policy priorities, DG Development holds a continuous dialogue with CONCORD, the Confederation of European non-Governmental Organisations (NGO) for Relief and Development (http://europa.eu.int/comm/development/body/theme/ngo/index_en.htm).

[33] European Commission (2003) EU Multi-stakeholder Forum on Corporate Social Responsibility, (Luxembourg: Office for Official Publications of the European Communities); European multistakeholder forum on corporate social responsibility (2004) Final results and recommendations, 29 June 2004, http://www.eiro.eurofound.eu.int/2004/07/feature/eu0407205f.html.

[34] http://europa.eu.int/comm/internal_market/company/ecgforum/index_en.htm.

[35] http://europa.eu.int/comm/enterprise/consultations/index.htm.

[36] http://europa.eu.int/comm/dgs/policy_advisers/activities/dialogue_religions_humanism.

Besides, the regular consultations were held between the Humanitarian Aid Office of the European Commission (ECHO) and more than 160 NGOs and the biggest pan-European environmental NGOs ('Group of Eight') and the Commission.[37] Those fora are conveyed on informal and ad hoc basis and in the absence of legal framework provided by the Treaty or secondary legislation. Exceptionally, the participation of NGOs in work of some formally established committees such as the Consultative Committee for Co-operatives, Mutuals, Associations and Foundations[38] and the agricultural advisory committees has been based upon European law.

Moreover, the Commission supports the involvement of civic groups in European governance through several civic participation programmes. For a number of years this support has been provided under headings in parts A and B of the EU budget. Most of those programmes have been carried out without any legal basis. This led to the temporary suspension of funding.[39] As the consequence, awarding of grants for promoting civil dialogue is formalized by means of a Council Decision on civic participation.[40] In addition to European umbrella organizations such as the Platform of European Social NGOs,[41] those programmes are oriented towards non-governmental organisations, associations and federations working at European level or cross-industry trade unions, including grassroots and local community organizations. Support may also be granted to bodies pursuing an aim of general European interest, including 'think tanks,' and to organizations collaborating with the Commission under the Community Action Programme to combat discrimination.[42]

This approach has been changed after the publishing of the Commission's White paper on governance in 2001 in which it called for the establishment of a stable framework to facilitate a more co-ordinated and structured dialogue with civic associations.[43] The Commission opted for the institutionalization and

[37] Communication of the European Commission (2000) 'Commission discussion paper "The Commission and non-governmental organisations: building a stronger partnership"', COM(2000) 11, Brussels, 18.1.2000, p. 9.

[38] Commission of the European Communities (1998) Decision of 13 March 1998 setting up a Consultative Committee for Co-operatives, Mutuals, Associations and Foundations (CMAF), 98/215/EC, OJ L 80/51, 18.3.98.

[39] C-106/96 *UK v Commission* ERC [1998] I–2729.

[40] Council Decision of 26 January 2004 establishing a Community action programme to promote active European citizenship (civic participation), OJ L30/14, 4.2.2004.

[41] Support for the running costs of the Social Platform provided under the Community Action Programme to promote active European citizenship amounts to 660,000 euros for years 2004 and 2005 (http://europa.eu.int/comm/employment_social/fundamental_rights/civil/civ_en.htm).

[42] Four European umbrella NGO networks representing and defending the rights of people exposed to discrimination—AGE (The European Older People's Platform), ILGA Europe (International Lesbian and Gay Association—Europe), ENAR (European Network Against Racism), and EDF (European Disability Forum)—are being granted a total of three million euros per year towards their running costs up to the end of April 2007 (http://europa.eu.int/comm/employment_ social/fundamental_rights/civil/ civ_en.htm). For an overview of EU funding available to interest groups see European Citizens Action Service, ECAS (2005) A Guide to European Union Funding (Brussels, ECAS).

[43] Commission of European Communities (2001) 'European governance: white paper', COM(2001) 428, Brussels, 25.7.2001, p. 17; European Commission (2002) European Governance: Preparatory Work for the White Paper, Luxembourg: Office for Official Publications of the European Communities, p. 74.

structuring of contact with the civil society by virtue of special provisions enshrined in the Constitution for Europe and adopted the definition of the civil society which includes economic operators not generally considered to make part of civic groups championing widely accepted causes originally regarded by the Commission as participants in the civil dialogue.

The Commission formalized the civil dialogue process through the adoption of general principles and minimum standards for consulting interested parties (hereafter the minimum standards).[44] They have been applicable since January 2003. The minimum standards serves as a framework for structured consultation procedures conveyed with civic interest groups. The Commission claims that those principles should ensure that all parties affected by the proposal can become more involved, and on a more equal footing, in the process of consultation preceding EU legislation formulation. The aim is to ensure that the parties concerned would have an opportunity to express their opinions. According to the Commission the purpose of adopting five minimum standards is to enable the legislator to be sure of the quality, and particularly the equity, of consultations leading up to major political proposals. The move is motivated by three concerns: to systematise and rationalize the wide range of consultation practices and procedures, and to guarantee the feasibility and effectiveness of the operation; to ensure the transparency of consultation from the point of view of the bodies or persons consulted and from the legislator point of view; and to demonstrate accountability vis-à-vis the bodies or players consulted, by making public, as far as possible, the results of the consultation and the lessons.[45] The Commission wants to assure that all parties are properly consulted.

The minimum standards are applied systematically to all major policy initiatives.[46] They should be considered as a tool created by the Commission for the purpose of the operationalization of its new commitment to introduce an impact assessments analysis for its initiatives in all EU policy areas, which is taking into account the economic, social and environmental impact of the proposal concerned.[47] This strategy provides for all its policy proposals to be assessed for their impact upon the widest possible group of potential stakeholders, in order to

---

[44] Commission of the European Communities (2002) 'Communication from the Commission "Towards a reinforced culture of consultation and dialogue—General principles and minimum standards for consultation of interested parties by the Commission"', COM(2002) 704, 11.12.2002. Those standards have been recently supplemented by European Commission (2005) 'Draft Recommendations to Member States regarding a code of conduct for non-profit organisations to promote transparency and accountability best practices: An EU design for implementation of FATF Special Recommendations VIII–non-profit organization', JLS/D2/DB/HSK D(2005) 8208.

[45] Commission of the European Communities (2002) 'Communication from the Commission "European Governance: better lawmaking"', COM(2002) 275, 5.6.2002, p. 3.

[46] The largest number of consultations related up to now include agriculture and fisheries; employment and social policy; external relations; industry; justice and home affairs; transport and energy; the environment; economic policy; the information society and health; and consumer protection (Commission of the European Communities (2004) 'Report on European governance (2003–2004)', SEC(2004) 1153, p.3.

[47] Commission of the European Communities (2002) 'Communication from the Commission on impact assessment', COM(2002) 276, Brussels, 5.6.2002.

ensure that consideration of the impact of measures is not simply restricted to an elite of those who are politically active on them. The first stage of the impact assessment process consists of applying the minimum standards to consultations preceding all the Commission legislative initiatives.

The main innovations generated by the consultation standards are: the definition of a minimum deadline for consultation; the obligation to report on the result; the obligation for an appropriate reaction to comments receive; the establishment of a single access point for all the Commission's public consultations;[48] and the obligation of displaying of the results of public consultation on the Internet.[49] Standards should be applied together with the following general principles: participation, openness, accountability, effectiveness and coherence The Commission claims that it wishes to maintain an inclusive approach and not to create hurdles in order to restrict access to the consultation process. Those standards also should not prevent lobbying.[50] In other words, it does not intend to create new bureaucratic obstacles for the purpose of limiting the number of those that can participate in consultation processes. Indeed, it provides assurance that 'every individual citizen, enterprise or association will continue to be able to provide the Commission with input.'[51] Its intention is to achieve the balance between open and focused, targeted consultation of those with a pertinent interest.

In the Commission's view, these standards should improve the representativity of civil society organizations and structure their debate with the institutions. They are intended to reduce the risk of the policy-makers just listening to one side of the arrangement or of particular groups getting privileged access.[52] However, it does not apply accreditation requested by some NGOs.[53] The Commission is always rejected an official consultative status for NGOs along the lines of existing accreditation systems in the United Nations and Council of Europe. For those reasons the proposals are placed on the Internet for comments.[54] Although this approach has widen the scope of groups consulted, it has eroded traditional bi-lateral discussions between the Commission and certain interest groups.

The idea of drawing up more extensive partnership agreements with a number of organized civil society sectors which would meet more stringent eligibility criteria than those required by the minimum standards was considered but

---

[48] See http://europa.eu.int/yourvoice/consultations/index_en.htm.

[49] At least eight weeks for receiving replies to written consultations or 20 working days' notice for meetings.

[50] Commission of the European Communities (2002) 'Communication from the Commission "Towards a reinforced culture of consultation and dialogue—General principles and minimum standards for consultation of interested parties by the Commission"', COM(2002) 704, Brussels, 11.12.2002, p. 13.   [51] Ibid., p. 11.

[52] Commission of European Communities (2001) 'European governance: white paper', COM(2001) 428, Brussels, 25.7.2002.

[53] See Platform of European Social NGOs 'Political recommendations on civil dialogue with NGOs at European Level, 14 October 1999.

[54] Open web consultations can be viewed at http://europa.eu.int/yourvoice/consultations/index en.htm.

eventually not accepted by the Commission.[55] The aim of introduction of those partnership agreements would be to encourage, on the basis of these agreements, civil society organizations to rationalise their internal structure, give guarantees of openness and representativeness, and to confirm their ability to rely information or to conduct debates within the member states. On the Commission's part, partnership arrangements will entail a commitment for additional consultations. In return, the arrangements will prompt civil society organisations to tighten up their capacity to rely information or lead debated in the member states.[56] This has not been adopted because of opposition of the European Parliament and the concern that there would be de facto establishment of a regime of privileged associations. However, there is an exception to the Commission policy not to enter into special partnership agreements with interest groups. Relations between the Humanitarian Aid Office of the Commission (ECHO) and around 200 non-governmental organisation it co-operates with are governed by Framework Partnership Agreements (FPAs). The purpose of FPAs is to define roles, responsibilities, and legally-binding rights and obligations of ECHO and NGOs it collaborates with in the implementation of humanitarian operations financed by the European Union.[57]

The codification of standards for the conduct of the civil dialogue is accompanied with the establishment of the CONECCS database (Consultation, European Commission and Civil Society), that offers the general public information on the civil society's non-profit organizations established at European level and the committees and other consultative bodies the Commission uses when consulting organized civil society in an informal or structured manner.[58] This database is constructed as a follower of the directory on European non-profit associations published in 1996 by the Commission.[59] CONECCS became fully operational in June 2002. This index of organizations, which was compiled on a voluntary basis, is intended to serve only as an information source and not as an instrument for securing exclusive access to the Commission consultative process. Part of the organized consultative process on the minimum standards. It is not intended to serve as a system for accrediting certain organisations vis-à-vis the Commission. It should provide an overview of advisory committees set by the Commission and a non-exhaustive list of NGOs active at the European level. Not only NGOs, but also private interest organizations such as World Federation of Advertisers, the European Demolition Associations, or the Banking Federation of the European Union are included.

[55] Commission of the European Communities (2002) 'Report from the Commission on European Governance', COM (2002) 705, Brussels, 11.12.2002, p. 11. Commission of the European Communities (2004) 'Report on European Governance' (2003–2004) SEC(2004)1153, 22.9.2004, p. 5.
[56] Commission of European Communities (2001) 'European governance: white paper', COM(2001) 428, Brussels, 25.7.2002, p. 17.
[57] http://europa.eu.int/comm/echo/partners/fpa_ngos_en.htm.
[58] http://europe.eu.int/comm/civil_society/coneccs.   [59] Ibid.

III. The Concept of the Social Dialogue in the European Union

The Commission's intention to standardise the involvement of non-profit associations in EU lawmaking denoted as the civil dialogue was developed in relation to the already established social dialogue between the European level management and labour. Articles 138 and 139 of the Treaty establishing the European Community (EC) endow the associations representing employers and employees at the European level, the so-called social partners, with law-making and law-implementation powers. Namely, the Commission's legislative proposals in social policy are to be the subject of a mandatory two-stage consultation process,[60] with the possibility for the Commission to suspend the legislative process in the social partners and announce their intention to open negotiation. They can enter into intersectoral or sectoral[61] agreements. There is also possibility for the establishment of company level social dialogue on the base of EC legislation within so-called European work councils.[62] At present, approximately 650 European Works Councils were set up in companies operating within the EU.[63]

The opening of negotiations is totally in the hands of the social partners and the negotiation process is based upon principles of autonomy and mutual recognition of the negotiating parties. Should the social partners decide not to negotiate,[64] the EU institutions regain their legislative competence.[65]

[60] The Commission has consulted the social partners 18 times under this procedure (European Commission (2004) Industrial Relations in Europe 2004, Luxembourg: Office for Official Publications of the European Communities, pp. 107–108).

[61] The sectoral social dialogue at European level is established by the Commission decision of 20 May 1998 on the establishment of the sectoral dialogue committee promoting the dialogue between the social partners at European level, OJ L225/27, 12.8.98. It takes place within 30 sectoral committees. See European Commission (2003) The Sectoral Social Dialogue in Europe, Luxembourg: Office for Official Publications of the European Communities; Commission of the European Communities (2004) 'Communication from the Commission: Partnership for change in an enlarged Europe— Enhancing the contribution of European social dialogue', COM(2004) 557, 12.8.2004, Annex 4, and European Commission (2004) Industrial Relations in Europe 2004, Luxembourg: Office for Official Publications of the European Communities, p. 106.

[62] This is established by Council Directive 94/45 of 22 September 1994 on the establishment of a European Works Council or a procedure in Community scale undertakings and Community-scale groups of undertakings for the purposes of informing and consulting employees, OJ L 254/64, 30.9.94, Council Directive 2001/86/EC of 8 October 2001 supplementing the Statute for a European company with regard to the involvement of employees, OJ L 294/22, 10.11.2001; Directive 2002/14/EC of the European Parliament and of the Council of 11 March 2002 establishing a general framework for informing and consulting employees in the European Community, OJ L80/29, 23.3.2002; and Council Directive 2003/72/EC of 22 July 2003 supplementing the Statute for a European co-operative society with regard to the involvement of employee, OJ L207/36, 18.8.2003.

[63] Commission of the European Communities (2004) 'Communication from the Commission: Partnership for change in an enlarged Europe—Enhancing the contribution of European social dialogue', COM(2004) 557, 12.8.2004, p. 8.

[64] The social partner did not succeed to come to an agreement in the cases of European Works Council, burden of proof in sex discrimination, prevention of sexual harassment at work, national information and consultation, temporary work, and data protection at the workplace.

[65] For example, when the social partners decided not to negotiate, the Council adopted, on proposal by the Commission after consulting the European Parliament, Council Directive 94/45/EC of 22 September 1994 on the establishment of a European Works Council, a procedure in Community

If the agreement is concluded, the social partners may choose whether they wish to implement the agreement via collective bargaining or via a Council decision.

To date, the social partners, the European Trade Union Confederations (ETUC), the Union of Industrial Trade Union Confederation (UNICE) and the European Centre of Public Enterprises (CEEP), have concluded five intersectoral framework agreements under this procedure. Three of those were implemented by the Council Directives,[66] and two shall be implemented by the social partners themselves in accordance with national practices and procedures.[67] Sectoral social partners adopted approximately 300 joint texts, of which three agreements implemented by the Council,[68] and three by procedures and practices specific to management and labour.[69] More recently the cross-industry and sectoral social

scale undertakings and Community scale groups of undertakings for the purposes of informing and consulting employees, OJ l 254/64, 30.9.94; Council Directive 97/80/EC of 15 December 1997 on the burden of proof in cases of discrimination based on sex, OJ L 14/6, 20.1.98; Directive 2002/14/EC of the European Parliament and of the Council of 11 March 2002 establishing a general framework for informing and consulting employees in the European Community, OJ L80/29, 23.3.2002. Currently, the Council is considering the Commission's legislative proposal on temporary work (Commission of the European Communities (2002) Proposal for a Directive of the European Parliament and the Council on working conditions for temporary workers, COM(2002) 701).

[66] Directive 96/34/EC on the framework agreement on parental leave concluded by UNICE, CEEP and the ETUC, OJ 1996, L145/4; Directive 97/81/EC concerning the framework agreement on part-time work concluded by UNICE, CEEP and the ETUC, OJ 1998, L14/9; Directive 99/70/EC concerning the framework agreement on fixed-term work concluded by UNICE, CEEP and the ETUC, OJ 1999, L175/43.

[67] Framework agreement on telework concluded by the ETUC, UNICE and CEEP on 16 July 2002, http://europa.eu.int/comm/employment_social/news/2002/jul/telework_en.pdf, and Framework agreement on work-related stress concluded by ETUC, the Council of European Professional and Managerial Staff (EUROCADRES), UNICE, UEAPME and CEEP on 8 October 2004, http://www.etuc.org/IMG/pdf/Accord-cadres_sans_signat.pdf.

[68] Directive 99/63/EC concerning the agreement on the organisation of working time seafarers concluded by the European Community Ship-owners' Associations (ECSA) and the Federation of Transport Workers' Unions in the European Union (FST), OJ L167/33, 2.7.1999; Directive 2000/79/EC concerning the European agreement on the organisation of working time of mobile workers in civil aviation concluded by the Association of European Airlines (AEA), the European Transport Workers' Federation (ETF), the European Cockpit Association (ECA), the European Regions Airline Association (ERA) and the International Air carrier Association (IACA), OJ L302/57, 1.12.2000. The railway sector social partners also requested the implementation of European agreement on certain aspects of the working conditions of mobile workers assigned to interoperable cross-border services. The adoption of a Council Directive concerning agreement on certain aspects of the working conditions of railway mobile workers assigned to interoperable cross-border services of 27 January 2004 is foreseen (European Commission (2004) Industrial Relations in Europe 2004, Luxembourg: Office for Official Publications of the European Communities, p. 98).

[69] Recommendation framework agreement on the improvement of paid employment in agriculture in the member states of the European Union concluded between the Employers' Group of the Agricultural Professional Organisations in the European Union (GEOPA/COPA) and ETUC, the social partners represented in the Joint Committee on Social Problems Affecting Agricultural Workers in the European Union on 24 July 1997 (http://europa.eu.int/comm/employment_social/soc-dial/social/euro_agr/data/en/970724.doc), Recommendatory Framework Agreement in Telecommunication Sector concluded by the Communications International and Eurofedop, the social partners resented on the Telecommunications Joint Committee on 20 November 1997

partners have begun to adopt an increasing number of new generation texts (autonomous agreements, guidelines, code of conduct, policy orientation etc.) with commitments or recommendations directed at their members and which they undertake follow-up themselves.[70]

Up to now negotiations of the social partners operating at different levels (inter-sectoral, sectoral, company) have been conducted in isolation one from the other and there has been little interconnection between those different levels of the social dialogue. As from recent, the Commission has begun to call for more synergy between separate levels of the social dialogue. In its 2004 Communication on the social dialogue, the Commission expressed the possibility of enhancing synergies between the European cross-industry and sectoral levels.[71] For example, in the area of lifelong learning, some sectors (postal services, banking, cleaning industry) have referred to the cross-industry framework of action. Similarly, on the topic of tele-work, social partners in the electricity and local and regional government sectors have adopted joint texts welcoming the cross-industry agreement and calling on their members to implement in their sectors, in accordance with the procedures and practices specific to management and labour by the July 2005 implementation deadline for the cross-industry agreement. Both sectors also undertake to monitor the implementation of the agreement in their sectors in 2005.

The Commission also suggests that the social partners could explore the possible synergies between the European social dialogue and the company level, stating that one example could be a link between the sectoral social dialogue and European Works Councils (EWCs).[72] It maintains that the range of issues being considered within EWCs is expanding beyond the core issues of company performance and employment and is now covering subjects with a strong European dimension, such as health and safety, equal opportunities, training and mobility, corporate social responsibility (CSR) and environmental issues. The Commission believes that in these cases there may be possibilities for synergies between the EU sectoral social dialogue and EWC and suggests that the European social partners could use the opportunity provided by the Commission's recent consultation on the revision of the EWCs Directive[73] to do this. The Commission also suggests that a link between social dialogue and company policies to promote CSR could be explored further.

(http://europa.eu.int/comm/employment_social/soc-dial/social/euro_agr/data/en/971120b.doc); and Agreement of CER-affiliated companies on the European licence for drivers carrying out a cross-border interoperability service of 27 January 2004 (European Commission (2004) Industrial Relations in Europe 2004, Luxembourg: Office for Official Publications of the European Communities, p. 99).

[70] European Commission (2004) Industrial Relations in Europe 2004, (Luxembourg: Office for Official Publications of the European Communities), pp. 100–104.
[71] Commission of the European Communities (2004) 'Communication from the Commission: Partnership for change in an enlarged Europe—Enhancing the contribution of European social dialogue', COM(2004) 557, 12.8.2004, p. 7.   [72] Ibid, p. 8.
[73] See http://europa.eu.int/comm/employment_social/news/2004/apr/ewc_consultation_en.pdf.

The Commission has supported the social partners' effort in various ways, including by providing financial assistance through its social dialogue budget headings. It provides both direct and indirect financial support to the social dialogue. In terms of logistic support, it finances the costs of dialogue meetings directly. There are also three budget headings which provide indirect financial support in the form of grants to social dialogue activities and industrial relations: (1) industrial relations and social dialogue (14, 850, 000 euros in 2004), information and training measures for workers' organisations (14, 200, 000 euros in 2004), and information, consultation and participation of representatives of undertakings (7 million euros in 2004).[74]

The social partners can also apply for grants under the Commission's education and training, and health and safety budget headings. Indeed, numerous sectors have prepared training manuals with the help of such grants.

Furthermore, the current proposal of the new European Social Fund (ESF) regulation would allow at least two per cent of the ESF resources under the 'convergence' objective to be allocated to capacity building and activities jointly undertaken by the social partners, in particular as regards the adaptability of workers and enterprises.[75]

IV. Civil and the Social Dialogue in the Open Method of Co-ordination

Since it has been decided at the Lisbon European Council in 2000 that European regulatory policy-making (lawmaking) should be complemented by persuasive policy co-ordination, named the open method of co-ordination (OMC), both the civil and social dialogue has been extended in this area.

The rudimental form of the OMC was introduced under the Maastricht Treaty in 1993 for the purpose of co-ordinating national macro-economic policies, and was applied in a somewhat different manner to employment policy by the Treaty of Amsterdam. The Lisbon European Council gave boost to the OMC. It is chosen to be one of the key methods for the implementation of EU strategy for improving the European economy-named, the Lisbon strategy.[76]

---

[74] Commission of the European Communities (2004) 'Communication from the Commission: Partnership for change in an enlarged Europe—Enhancing the contribution of European social dialogue', COM(2004) 557, 12.8.2004, Memo/04/211, p. 5.

[75] European Commission (2004) 'Proposal for a Regulation of the European Parliament and of the Council on the European Social Fund', COM(2004) 493, 14.7.2004, Article 5(2).

[76] The Lisbon European Council held in March 2000 set the goal for the EU 'to become the most competitive and dynamic knowledge-based economy in the world, capable of sustainable economic growth with more and better jobs and greater social cohesion'. This strategy is intends to: (1) improve European competitiveness, and (2) develop the European models of social protection, living up to the expectations of economic growth and of social cohesion. Overall, the strategy aims at raising productivity and potential gross domestic product growth. To reach this objective, the Lisbon strategy

The OMC is not designed to produce law at the Union level, it aims to co-ordinate the actions of the member states in a given policy domain and to create conditions for mutual learning that hopefully will introduce some degree of voluntary policy convergence. It helps member states to develop their own policies through the discussion and dissemination of best practices, with the aim of reaching commonly agreed goals. The OMC is realized through the following procedure: the production of guidelines drafted by the Commission and issued by the Council of Ministers to be translated into national policy through national action plans (NAPs), combined with periodic monitoring by the Commission, evaluation and peer review organized as mutual learning process and accompanied by indicators and benchmarking as means of comparing best practices.[77] The OMC is applied as an instrument for the development of budgetary, economic, employment, and social inclusion policy, and a strategy in pension reform, information society, research and innovation, education and training and youth policy.[78]

The OMC represents significant, though informal[79], channel for the participation of non-profit groups and the social partners in EU governance. Indeed, it is intended by the Union institutions to improve transparency and democratic participation.[80] Under the Lisbon strategy participation entails that 'the Union, the member states, the regional and local levels, as well as the social partners and civil society, will be actively involved, using varied forms of partnerships.[81] Namely,

encompasses sound macroeconomic policies, stepping up the process of structural reform of economy and undertaking the measures for attaining high level of employment. This complementary approach leads to the synergy of macroeconomic, structural reform and employment strategies developed separately under so called Cologne, Cardiff and Luxembourg processes respectively (Presidency Conditions of the Lisbon European Council, 23 and 24 March 2003, para 40, and Presidency Conclusions of the Santa Maria Da Feira Summit, 19 and 20 June 2000, paras, 19–39 at, http://ue.eu.int/ueDocs/cms_Data/docs/pressData/annex/81035ADD1.pdf.

[77] Presidency Conclusions. Lisbon European Council, 23 and 24 March 2000, p. 12 (http://ue.eu.int/ueDocs/cms_Data/docs/pressData/annex/81035ADD1.pdf).

[78] The Commission proposed the application of the OMC in the immigration policy (see Commission of the European Community (2001) 'Communication from the Commission to the Council and the European parliament on an open method of co-ordination for the Community immigration policy', COM(2001) 387, Brussels, 11.7.2001, but the Council failed to adopt it. At present, there is a proposal for the application of this method to health and long term care. For an overview of policy areas where the OMC applies and for the bibliography on the subject, see Burca, Gráinne de (2003) 'The constitutional challenge of new governance in the European Union', European Law Review, vol. 28, no. 4, pp. 814–839, p. 824.

[79] The Convention decided against a constitutionalization of the OMC in order to preserve its informal character (European Convention (2003) Final Report of Working Group VI on Economic Governance, CONV 357/02, Brussels: European Convention). Some authors, though, say that actual reason for this is the lack of legitimacy owing to the involvement of a large number of experts in the process (De la Porte, Charoline and Nanz, Patrizia (2004) 'The OMC—a deliberative-democratic mode of governance? The cases of employment and pensions', Journal of European Public Policy, vol. 11, no. 2, pp. 267–288, p. 268; De la Porte, C and Pochet, P. (2002) Building Social Europe Through the Open Method of Co-ordination, Brrussels).

[80] Council of the European Union (2000) The ongoing experience of the open method of co-ordination, Presidency note, No. 9088/00, 13 June, p. 7.

[81] Presidency conclusions, Lisbon European Council, 23–24 March 2000, point 38 (http://ue.eu.int/ueDocs/cms_Data/docs/pressData/annex/81035ADD1.pdf);   and   Presidency

the involvement of both civil and social dialogue participants is proclaimed to be an important component of the OMC.[82]

V. Distinctive Functions of the Civil and Social Dialogue in EU Governance

Although both civil and social dialogues foster the involvement of interest groups in European governance, their roles are considerably different. They occupy dissimilar positions in the Union decision-making process. While the social dialogue has gradually evolved into an independent lawmaking and policy co-ordination procedure with autonomous agenda setting and implementation mechanisms that can replace Union law or the member states national action plans in the OMC case, though in very limited areas, the civil dialogue is confined to a purely consultative function. The most significant distinction between the social and civil dialogue concerns their objectives and tasks. While the social dialogue is envisaged to be an efficient mechanism for day-to-day policy formation, the civil dialogue is seen as a forum in which the strategic problems of European society could be debated.[83] The European social dialogue differs from the civil dialogue as it offers the opportunity of co-determination of European policy by the European social partners. Since the social partners, in contrast to non-profit groups, require considerable responsibilities for the implementation of Union policies and enjoy substantial autonomy in discharging thereof, the role which two of those groups play in EU governance should be strictly distinguished.

A. Lawmaking

One of the most important differences between the social and the civil dialogue concerns their positions in the Union lawmaking process. There is no decision-taking function envisaged for the participants in the civil dialogue. The civil dialogue has never been intended to exceed consultative, advisory function.[84] Contrary to this, the social dialogue is designed to replace Union legislation by

---

conclusion, Brussels European Council of 22 and 23 March 2005, (http://ue.eu.int/ueDocs/cms_Data/docs/pressData/fr/ec/84331.pdf), point 6.

[82] Presidency conclusion, Barcelona European Council, 15 and 16 March 2002, p. 47 (http://ue.eu.int/ueDocs/cms_Data/docs/pressData/en/ec/71025.pdf).

[83] Commission of the European Communities (1994) 'European social policy—a way forward for the Union: a white paper', COM(94) 333, Brussels, 27.7.1994, p.44.

[84] European Commission (1996) 'Progress report on the implementation of the Medium-Term Social Action Programme 1995–97', Social Europe, Supplement 4/96, p. 17; European Commission (2000) 'Commission discussion paper "The Commission and non-governmental organisations: building a stronger partnership"', COM(2000) 11, Brussels, 18.1.2000, point 1.3.3.

so-called private interest governance in the area of work relations.[85] Article 138 EC empowers the European associations of labour and management to regulate the number of work-related issues through the conclusion of agreements and consequently displace the Union institutions from the sphere of lawmaking related to work.

The Commission emphasized in its 1994 White paper on social policy that a clear distinction has to be drawn between the negotiation process established under the social dialogue procedure and the consultation which the European Union must undertake to deal with social problems which cannot be dealt with by collective bargaining.[86] In the Commission's view the main aim of the civil dialogue is not policy formulation, as in the case of the social dialogue, but (a) to ensure that the views of non-profit organizations can be taken into account by policy makers, and (b) to disseminate information from the European level down to the local level.[87] Obviously, the Commission has not provided for any prospect of giving the civil dialogue participants the real decision-making powers. It is confined to the debating arena which provides civil interest groups with an opportunity to be heard by the Commission, and within which they can express their views. Structuring of the civil dialogue through the introduction of the minimum standards for conducting of consultations with interest groups by the Commission has not changed this.[88] While the formalization of civic groups' consultation by the Commission might strengthen the involvement of civil society organizations in the formulation of EU policy measures, no concrete delegation of policy formulation task took place.

B. Co-ordination of policies in the EU (OMC)

Irrespective of the fact that both the civil and social dialogue protagonists have a role to play in the open method of co-ordination, their respective contributions differ substantially. The Union assigns to the social partners much greater responsibilities

[85] Privatization of the legislative process is not specific for the policy area covered by the social dialogue. It is part of a wider phenomenon of distanciation from legislation by State bodies in favour of more flexible arrangements where key actors tend to be private agents rather than public legislators. In the field of the internal market, for instance, with a so-called new approach to technical harmonization, a large chunk of work previously understood to fall within the remit of the Union legislator was transferred to private standardization bodies such as the European Committee for Electrotechnical Standardisation (CENELEC) and the European Telecommunications Standards Institute (Greenwood, J (2003) Interest representation in the European Union, Houndmills: Palgrave, p. 66). In environmental law, the Sixth Environmental Programme places great stocks on voluntary action by private actors as an important mechanism to bring about desired environmental aims (see Decision No 1600/2002/EC of the European parliament and the Council of 22 July 2002 laying down the Sixth Community Environment Action Programme, OJ L 242/1, 10.9.2002, Article 3(5)).

[86] Commission of the European Communities (1994) 'European social policy—a way forward for the Union: a white paper', COM(94) 333, Brussels, 27.7.1994, p. 42.

[87] Commission of the European Communities (1997) 'Communication from the Commission on promoting the role of voluntary organisations and foundations in Europe', COM(97) 241, Brussels, 6.6.1997, point 9.7.

[88] Commission of the European Communities (2002) 'Communication from the Commission "Towards a reinforced culture of consultation and dialogue—General principles and minimum standards for consultation of interested parties by the Commission"', COM(2002) 704, 11.12.2002, p. 10.

in all stages of the OMC, from designing policies to their implementation, than to non-profit organizations. Whilst the social partners are involved in drafting of policies governed by the OMC in an institutionalized manner, non-profit groups play neither a formal, nor decisive role in this process. The entitlements of non-profit groups in this mode of governance are inferior to those granted to the social partners. Although various Union employment policy documents call for the co-operative partnership with non-profit organizations in the execution thereof, they underscore only the role of the social partners as the crucial players in the OMC.[89] Moreover,

---

[89] Commission of the European Communities (1993) Growth, competitiveness and employment: the challenge and ways forward into the 21st century: white paper, Bull. EC, Supplement 6/93; Commission (1996) Action for Employment in Europe—Confidence Pact, Bull. EU Supplement 4/96, points 3.4 and 3.7; Commission of the European Communities (1997) Interim report on the implementation of the territorial pacts for employment, Bull. EU 6-1997, point 1.3.2; European Council (1997) Presidency Conclusions of the Extraordinary European Council meeting on employment, Luxembourg, 20 and 21 November 1997, points 7, 18, 19, 22 and 28 (http://ue.eu.int/ueDocs/cms_Data/docs/pressData/en/ec/00300.htm); Commission of the European Communities (1997) 'Communication from the Commission on promoting the role of voluntary organisations and foundations in Europe', COM(97) 241, Brussels, 6.6.1997, point 6.7; European Council (1997) Resolution of the European Council on growth and employment, Bull. EU 6-1997, point 1.28, para. 1 and 12; Commission of the European Communities (1997) Communication from the Commission 'Modernising and improving social protection in the European Union, COM(97) 102, Brussels, 12.3.1997, p. 18; Commission of the European Communities (1998) 'Communication from the Commission: Modernising the organisation of work: a positive approach to change', COM(98) 592, Brussels, 25.11.1998; Presidency conclusions, Lisbon European Council, 23 and 24 March 2000, htt;//ue.eu.int/ueDocs/cms_ Data/ docs/pressData/en/ec/00100-r1.en0.htm, point 38; Commission of the European Communities (2000) 'Communication from the Commission to the Council, the European Parliament, the Economic and Social Committee and the Committee of the Regions: Social Policy Agenda', COM(2000) 379, Brussels, 28.6.2000, p.14; Commission of the European Communities (2002) 'Communication from the Commission to the Council, the European Parliament, the Economic and Social Committee and the Committee of the regions: taking stock of five years of the European Employment Strategy', COM(2002) 416, Brussels, 17.7.2002, p. 20; Presidency conclusion, Stockholm European Council, 23 and 24 March 2001, point 30 (http://ue.eu.int/ueDocs/cms_Data/docs/pressData/en/ec/00100-r1.%20ann-r1.en1.html); Presidency conclusion, Barcelona European Council, 15 and 16 March 2002, p. 47 (http://ue.eu.int/ueDocs/cms_Data/docs/pressData/en/ec/71025.pdf); European Commission (2002) 'The European social dialogue, a force for innovation and change', COM(2002) 341, Brussels, 26.6.2002, p. 4; all the Council Employment guidelines (see e.g. Council decision of 22 July 2003 on guidelines for the employment policies of the member states, 2003/578/EC, OJ L 197/13, 5.8.2003, point. 22); Commission of the European Communities (2003) 'Communication from the Commission to the Council, the European Parliament, the European Economic and Social Committee and the Committee of the Regions: the Future of the European Employment Strategy (EES): a strategy for full employment and better jobs for all', COM(2003) 6; Conclusions of the Tripartite Social Summit (Dutch Presidency, Commission and European social partners) held on 4 November 2004, http://www.eu2004.nl/default.asp; High level group chaired by Wim Kok (2004) Facing the Challenge: The Lisbon Strategy for Growth and Employment, Luxembourg: Office for Official publications of the European Communities, p. 7; Commission of the European Communities (2004) 'Communication from ·the Commission: Partnership for change in an enlarged Europe—Enhancing the contribution of European social dialogue', COM(2004) 557, 12.8.2004, Memo/04/211, p.1; Commission of the Economic Communities (2005) 'Strategic objectives 2005–2009: Europe 2010: a partnership for European renewal: prosperity, solidarity and security, COM(2005) 12, Brussels, 26.1.2005, pp. 4 and 5; Presidency conclusion, Brussels European Council of 22 and 23 March 2005, http://ue.eu.int/ueDocs/cms_Data/docs/pressData/fr/ec/84331.pdf, points 6 and 9; Commission of the European Communities (2005) 'Commission staff working paper "working together for growth and jobs: next steps in

the member states are reluctant to grant any other actors aside social partners a formal role within the process.[90]

The social partners are assigned quite prominent functions in the OMC processes governing the co-ordination of economic, employment and social inclusion policies.

In the case of the economic policy, the European level social partners are closely involved in the discussion of the draft guidelines produced within the framework of the Macro-economic dialogue introduced by the Cologne European Council of 1999.[91] This procedure aims at improving the interaction of macroeconomic policies and wage developments with a view to support non-inflatory growth and employment. To this end, the European level social partners and the European Central Bank, Council and Commission representatives meet twice a year, in March and May, within the framework of the Economic Policy Committee, for a confidential exchange of views on ways to promote adequate macroeconomic conditions.[92]

Further, similar to the case of the social dialogue, the European level social partners do have the Treaty-based mandate to participate in the European employment strategy (EES) which is also governed by the OMC. The EES anticipates two types of the social partners' participation. The first one concerns their participation at the EU and national levels in the preparation of the guidelines,[93] EU reports and the national action plans[94] drawn on the base of the Councils guidelines. The second relates to their involvement in the implementation of the guidelines and the process of monitoring thereof.

The social partners organized at European level are mandatory consulted within the Article 130 EC Employment Committee which advises the Labour and Social Affair Council and the Commission in the process leading to the formulation of

implementing the revised Lisbon strategy" ', SEC(2005) 622/2, 29.4.2005; Commission of the European Communities (2005) 'Communication from the Commission on the Social Agenda', COM(2005) 33, Brussels, 9.2.2005, p. 7; and Commission of the European Communities (2005) 'Integrated guidelines for growth and jobs', COM(2005) 141, Brussels, 12.4.2005, p. 31.

[90] Porte, Caroline de la and Pochest, Philippe (2005) 'Participation in the open method of co-ordination: the cases of employment and social inclusion' in Jonathan Zeitling and Philippe Pochet, (eds), *The Open Method of Co-ordination in Action: The European Employment and Social Inclusion Strategies*, (Brussels: P.I.E.-Peter Lang), pp. 353–389, p. 367.

[91] Presidency conclusion, Cologne European Council, of 3 and 4 June 1999 (http://ue.eu.int/ueDocs/cms_Data/docs/pressData/en/ec/57886.pdf).

[92] See Article 1(6) of Council Decision 2000/604/EC on the composition and the statutes of the Economic Policy Committee, OJ [2000] L257/28. See also, European Commission, Directorate-general for economic and financial affairs (2002) Co-ordination of economic policies in the EU: a presentation of key features of the main procedures, Euro papers, no. 45, p. 8; and Commission of the European Communities (2002) 'Communication from the Commission on streamlining the annual economic and employment policy co-ordination cycles', COM(2002) 487, points 4 and 18.

[93] These guidelines must be consistent with the broad economic guidelines issued in relation to EMU.

[94] Commission of the European Communities (1998) 'Communication from the Commission: from guidelines to action: the national action plans for employment', COM(1998) 316, p. 4.

the Employment guidelines.[95] The European social partners are also represented on the Social Protection Committee,[96] which is also engaged in the process of the adoption of the employment guidelines. More significantly, the 1997 Luxembourg employment summit instituted the regular annual meetings between the European level social partners[97] and the Employment and Labour Market Steering group that advises the Council,[98] and between the former and the Commission and the Troika[99] for the purpose of deliberating employment guidelines. It has been decided at the Nice European Council for this gathering to take place before each Spring European Council. Since March 2003 this forum has been formalized through the establishment of a Tripartite Social Summit for Growth and Employment.[100] It is intended to meet the need for coherence and synergy between various processes of consultation between the social partners and the EU institutions such as the above-mentioned Cologne macroeconomic dialogue and the Tripartite Social Summit which has been held since 1997 in the context of the Luxembourg process dedicated to the employment issues. The social partners' role in the Lisbon strategy should be further advanced through the establishment of the so-called European Partnership for Change, recommended by the High level group and set up by the Commission on the request of the Brussels March 2004 European Council to carry out the mid-term review of the Lisbon strategy[101] and to incorporateit in the latest Commission's social agenda.[102] The partnership should ensure gather social partners and other stakeholders around the key priorities of growth and employment. The social partners endorsed the idea at the March 2004

[95] For details see Articles 2 and 5(1) of the Council decision of 24 January 2000 establishing the Employment Committee, 2000/98/EC, OJ L 29/21, 4.2.2000.

[96] See Article 2.4. of the Council decision of 29 June 2000 setting up a Social Protection Committee, 2000/436/EC, OJ L 172/26, 12.7.2000. The Treaty of Nice recognizes it in Article 144 EC.

[97] The following European level social partners organizations participate in this process: the Union of Industrial Employers' Confederations of Europe (UNICE); the European Centre of Enterprises with Public Participation and of Enterprises of General Economic Interest (CEEP); the European Association of Craft, Small and Medium-sized Enterprises (UEAPME); the European Trade Union Confederation (ETUC); Eurocadres; and the Confederation europeenne des cadres (CEC).

[98] Commission of European Communities (1998) 'Communication from the Commission "Adapting and promoting the social dialogue at Community level", COM 98 322, 20.5.98, p. 11.

[99] The Troika consists of the representatives of the member state currently holding the Council Presidency, the member state that held it for the proceeding six months and the member state that will hold it for the next six months.

[100] Council Decision of 6 March 2003 establishing a Tripartite Social Summit for Growth and Employment, 2003/174/EC, OJ 70/31, 14.3.2003. This decision repealed the Decision 99/207/EC, OJ L 72/33, 18.3.1999 which considers operation of the Standing Committee on Employment established by Council Decision 70/532/EEC of 14 December 1970, OJ L 273, 17.12.1970.

[101] Commission of the European Communities (2005) 'Strategic objectives 2005–2009: Europe 2010: a partnership for European renewal: prosperity, solidarity and security, COM(2005) 12, Brussels, 26.1.2005, p. 4; High level group chaired by Wim Kok (2004) *Facing the Challenge: The Lisbon Strategy for Growth and Employment*, (Luxembourg: Office for Official Publications of the European Communities), p. 40.

[102] Commission of the European Communities (2005) 'Communication from the Commission on the Social Agenda', COM(2005) 33, Brussels, 9.2.2005, point 1.3.2.

tripartite social summit. The precise tasks of this partnership are not clearly identified. It seems that its main purpose should be the provision of a link and thus a consistency between the national and the European level.[103] The practical consequence of the introduction of this partnership will be more closed involvement in the formulation of the national action programmes.[104]

National social partners also participate in the co-ordination of the social inclusion[105] and vocational education and training[106] policies and in the elaboration of the annual NAPs. However, but the European management and labour organizations have considerably weaker advisory functions within the OMC process in those areas, since their role in the co-ordination of those policies is not stipulated in the Treaty. On the social inclusion issues their opinion is to be sought by the Social Protection Committee, which is under obligation to 'establish appropriate contacts with the social partners' and not to conduct compulsory consultation with them.[107]

The role of non-profit organisations in the OMC is much more modest in comparison to that assumed by the social partners. Their involvement is, with a few exceptions, of an informal nature, and significantly less influential.

Apart from relatively structured involvement of non-profit organisations in the social inclusion strategy, their participation in the OMC governing other policy areas is relatively sporadic and patchy. The Platform of Social NGOs is informally, but regularly, consulted by the Social Protection Committee which actively takes part in the co-ordination of employment and the social inclusion policies. Beside that, national civil society groups participate in the EU initiatives developed under the Lisbon strategy such as: EQUAL (a programme which aims to promote the transnational exchange of good practice on measures to combat discrimination and inequalities in labour market), ADAPT and EMPLOYMENT (the programme which links its local and national strategies to the National Action Plans for Employment (NAPs) aimed at developing innovative ways to deliver labour market and social inclusion policies), and URBAN and LEADER (the programmes aimed at promoting partnership in local employment in urban and rural areas respectively).[108] More recently, the European Youth Forum was called upon

---

[103] High level group chaired by Wim Kok (2004) *Facing the Challenge: The Lisbon Strategy for Growth and Employment*, (Luxembourg: Office for Official Publications of the European Communities), p. 42.

[104] Ibid, p. 40 and Commission of the European Communities (2005) 'Communication from the Commission on the Social Agenda', COM(2005) 33, Brussels, 9.2.2005, point 1.3.2.

[105] Council of the European Union (2004) Joint report by the Commission and the Council on social inclusion, Brussels, 5 March 2004, http://europa.eu.int/comm/employment_social/soc-prot/soc-incl/final_joint_inclusion_report_2003_en.pdf, p. 122; European Foundation for the Improvement of Living and Working Conditions (2004) *Social Inclusion: Role of the Social Partners*, (Luxembourg: Office for Official Publications of the European Communities).

[106] Winterton, Jonathan (2003) *Social Dialogue and Vocational Training in the EU: Analysis of a CEDEFOP Survey*, (Thessaloniki: CEDEFOP).

[107] Council decision of 29 June 2000 setting up a Social Protection Committee, 2000/436/EC, OJ L 172/26, 12.7.2000, Article 1(4).

[108] European Foundation for the Improvement of Living and Working Conditions 2003 Social Inclusion: Local Partnerships with Civil Society, Foundation paper, No. 4, December 2003, pp. 8–9.

by the March 2005 Brussels European Council to be closely involved in the European youth pact which is to be realized within the framework of employment and social inclusion strategies.[109] Further, national civil society associations together with the locally organized social partners are involved in the operationalization of the Territorial employment pacts.[110] They should also assume a role in the partnership for growth and employment to be formed on the recommendation of the High level group which carried out the mid-term evaluation of the Lisbon strategy.[111] In the pensions, OMC national affiliations of the European Anti-Poverty Network (EAPN) are engaged in consultation and deliberation on the production of national action plans,[112] while the European Older People's Platform (AGE) obtained an informal advisory role.[113] Business representatives are consulted within the framework of the information society action plan.[114] The Commission as well organizes the partnership with the self-managed associations with limited profit-making, co-operatives and mutuals which work in the areas of social services, environment, culture, and sport in order to boost job creation in this sector.[115]

C. Implementation of EU policies

The second significant difference between the social and civil dialogue relates to their respective roles in the process of the implementation of Union policies: both based upon EC law and the OMC. While the social dialogue protagonists are considered to be one of the key actors in the implementation of European social legislation and the employment guidelines with the non-negligible degree of autonomy, non-profit associations are not recognized as agents capable of engaging in that process in a manner comparable to that of the social partners. They do not assume any role in implementation of EU policies. NGOs are, though, involved in the execution of humanitarian operations financed by the EU.[116]

---

[109] Presidency conclusion, Brussels European Council of 22 and 23 March 2005, http://ue.eu.int/ueDocs/cms_Data/docs/pressData/fr/ec/84331.pdf, p. 19. [110] Ibid, p. 9.
[111] High level group chaired by Wim Kok (2004) *Facing the Challenge: The Lisbon Strategy for Growth and Employment*, (Luxembourg: Office for Official publications of the European Communities), p. 40.
[112] Council of the European Union (2004) 'Joint report by the Commission and the Council on social inclusion', Brussels, 5 March 2004, http://europa.eu.int/comm/employment_social/soc-prot/soc-incl/final_joint_inclusion_report_2003_en.pdf, p. 121.
[113] Porte, Caroline de la and Nanz, Patrizia (2004) 'The OMC—a deliberative-democratic mode of governance? The case of employment and pensions' Journal of European Public Policy, 11(2); 267–288, p. 281.
[114] Commission of the European Community (2002) 'Communication from the Commission to the Council, the European Parliament, the Economic and Social Committee and the Committee of the Regions: eEurope 2005: an information society for all: An action plan to be presented in view of the Sevilla European Council, 21/22 June 2002', COM(2002) 263, Brussels 28.5.2002, p. 14.
[115] European Commission (2003) The New Actors of Employment—Synthesis of the Pilot Action 'Third System and Employment, Luxembourg: Office for Official Publications of the European Communities.
[116] http://europa.eu.int/comm/echo/partners/fpa_ngos_en.htm.

(i) Implementation of European law

The Treaty makes possible for the member states to delegate the implementation of Directives to the social partner, but the member states remain to guarantee the achievement of the intended result and the timely implementation of the Directive (Article 137(4) EC).[117] The social partners also play a role in the implementation of anti-discrimination Directives adopted under Article 13 EC.[118] In addition, many Directives contain provisions allowing the social partners to adopt rules so as to take account of differences in national situations. In the case of the Working time Directive, collective agreements or agreements between the two sides of industry can be used to set certain standards[119] and to derogate from those standards.[120] In some cases, the social partners are directly requested to arrive through negotiation at responses to the goal set by the Community.[121]

The social partners can also implement their framework agreements reached under Article 138 EC in accordance to their own procedures and practices. This possibility is stipulated in Article 139(2) EC. Two agreements reached by ETUC, UNICE and CEEP are to be implemented in this way: the agreement on telework[122] and the agreement on work-related stress.[123]

Furthermore, the national social partners are involved in the implementation and monitoring of programmes financed under the Structural Funds through the participation in the work of committees set up by member states for that purpose.[124] They also can participate in the work of the European Social Fund and apply for EU assistance granted in the framework of this fund.[125] A proposal

[117] See e.g. Directive 91/533/EC on conditions applicable to the contract of employment, OJ 1991 L 288/32; Directive 92/56/EC on collective redundancies, OJ 1992 L 255/63; and the Directive 93/104/EC concerning certain aspects of the organization of working time, OJ 1993 L307/18.

[118] E.g. Article 13 of Council Directive 2000/78/EC establishing a framework for equal treatment in employment and occupation; OJ 2000 L303/16 and Article 11 of Council Directive 2000/43/EC implementing the principle of equal treatment between persons, irrespective of racial origin, OJ 2000 L180/22.   [119] Article 4.

[120] Article 17. See also Barnard, Catherine (2002) 'The social partners and the governance agenda', European Law Journal, 8(1): 80–101, p. 86.

[121] This is established by Council Directive 94/45 of 22 September 1994 on the establishment of a European Works Council or a procedure in Community scale undertakings and Community-scale groups of undertakings for the purposes of informing and consulting employees, OJ L 254/64, 30.9.94, Article 5.

[122] http://europa.eu.int/comm/employment_social/news/2002/jul/telework_en.pdf.

[123] http://www.etuc.org/IMG/pdf/Accord-cadres_sans_signat.pdf.

[124] Council Regulation (EC) No 1260/1999 of 21 June 1999 laying down general provisions on the Structural Funds, OJ L 161/1, 26.6.1999, Article 8.

[125] See Regulation (EC) No 1784/1999 of the European Parliament and of the Council of 12 July 1999 on the European Social Fund, OJ L 213, 13.8.1999, Article 6. Until now 35 projects had been funded under this scheme. Project promoters include a wide range of organisations: social partners organisations operating at regional, national and European level; vocational training institutions and universities; independent research institutes and foundations as well as private companies; development agencies; and non-governmental organizations. All projects are based on a partnership approach with social partner organizations. They started running in September 2001 and ended in February 2004 (European Commission (2004) *Innovation Through the European Social Fund*, (Luxembourg: Office for Official Publications of the European Communities), p. 9). See also Commission of the European Communities (2001) 'Communication from the Commission to the Council, the European Parliament, the Economic and Social Committee and the Committee of Regions: strengthening the local dimension of the European Employment Strategy', COM(2001) 629, Brussels, 6.11.2001, pp. 11–12.

for the revision of the existing regulation on the European Social Fund (ESF) provides for even greater involvement of the social partners in programming, implementation and monitoring of its activities.[126] For that purpose at least two per cent of the ESF shall be allocated for capacity building and activities jointly undertaken by the social partners.[127] A more modest role is assigned to non-governmental organizations. They are going to be consulted in 'an adequate manner' and gain quite limited access to the ESF funded activities in the domain of social inclusion and equality between women and men.[128] Contrary to this, similar tasks are allocated to the social partners and civic groups in the process of the implementation of the EU cohesion policy.[129]

The social partners are also involved in the work of five European agencies that provide information to the EU institutions in the policy-making process.[130] As a matter of fact, the Commission insists upon their greater involvement in the work of agencies.[131]

(ii) Implementation of the OMC guidelines

The role of the social partners in the implementation of the OMC guidelines, in particular those related to employment, becomes ever more significant. It has been stated in the 2003 Employment Guidelines that their effective implementation requires active participation of social partners at all stages, from designing policies to their implementation.[132] Not only that social partners should be more closely involved in 'drawing up, implementing and following up the appropriate guidelines', but they should shoulder responsibilities.[133] National Social partners

---

[126] European Commission (2004) 'Proposal for a Regulation of the European Parliament and of the Council on the European Social Fund', COM(2004) 493, 14.7.2004, Article 5(2).

[127] Ibid, Article 5(3).

[128] Ibid, Articles 5(2) and 5(4). See also Commission of the European Communities (2001) 'Communication from the Commission to the Council, the European Parliament, the Economic and Social Committee and the Committee of Regions: strengthening the local dimension of the European Employment Strategy', COM(2001) 629, Brussels, 6.11.2001, pp. 11–12.

[129] Commission of the European Communities (2004) 'Proposal for a Council Regulation laying down general provisions on the European Regional Development Fund, the European Social Fund and the Cohesion Fund', COM(2004) 492, 14.7.2004, Article 10.

[130] The European Foundation for the Improvement of Living and Working Conditions, the European Centre for the Development of Vocational Training, the European Agency for Safety and Health at Work (Bilbao), the European Food Safety Authority, and the European Maritime Safety Agency (Smismans, Stijn (2004) *Law, legitimacy, and European Governance: Functional Participation in Social Regulation*, (Oxford: Oxford University Press), p. 253).

[131] Commission of the European Communities (2002) 'Communication from the Commission: the operating framework for the European Regulatory Agencies', COM(2002) 718, Brussels, 11.12.2002, p.9.

[132] Council of the European Union (2003) Council decision of 22 July 2003 on guidelines for the employment policies of the member states, 2003/578/EC, OJ L 197/13, 5.8.2003, point 22.

[133] Presidency conclusions, Lisbon European Council, 23 and 24 March 2000, point 28, htt;//ue.eu.int/ueDocs/cms_Data/docs/pressData/en/ec/00100-r1.en0.htm, and Presidency conclusions, Barcelona European Council, 15 and 16 March 2002, points 29 and 30, http://ue.eu.int/ueDocs/cms_Data/docs/pressData/en/ec/71025.pdf. See also horizontal objective C in Council Decision 2001/63/EC on guidelines for member states' employment policies for the year 2001, OJ 2001 L22/18.

are expected to contribute to the national implementation of the employment guidelines through their autonomous collective bargaining practices (national pacts, industry, enterprise and regional bargaining) *and* their participation in national government or tripartite and bipartite bodies on employment policies. They can also join bodies for assessing the national implementation of the employment guidelines.

It is significant to point out that until recently, only national social partners and not European level peak associations of management and labour were invited to take part in the implementation of Employment Guidelines because those were addressed to the member states.[134] This is to be changed. The 2003 Employment Guidelines call for reinforcing the role of not only national, but also European social partners in the implementation of the EES and request them to report annually on their contribution.[135] This significantly strengthens the position of the social partners in this policy area since previously only the member states have been charged with the task of reporting. Now, the European level social partners are expected to assume similar competences to those of the member states in the process of the implementation of the employment objectives in the EU. The 2004 guidelines clearly indicate not only member states, but also the social partners as the equally liable bearers of responsibilities for achieving the EES objectives and targets.[136]

As from 2001 the social partners are invited to develop their own process of implementing guidelines for which they have the key responsibilities and identify the issue upon which they will negotiate and report regularly on progress as well as the impact of their actions on employment and labour market functioning. This invitation is far more reaching than the classical Commission undertaking that the broader responsibility of the social partners and their contribution to the implementation of the guidelines needs to be recognized in full respect of their autonomy.[137] The social partners are not only charged with considerably more demanding tasks in the OMC implementation process than non-profit groups, but they are even invited to set up their own process of implementation.

The social partners are currently encouraged not only to 'shoulder' the implementation of the employment policy objectives, but to develope their own implementation process by concluding agreements, where appropriate, and

[134] Council decision of 19 January 2001 on guidelines for member states' employment policies for the year 2001, 2001/63/EC, OJ L 22/18, horizontal objective E and the guidelines 13.

[135] Council decision of 22 July 2003 on guidelines for the employment policies of the member states, 2003/578/EC, OJ L 197/13, 5.8.2003, p. 21

[136] Council decision of 4 October 2004 on guidelines for the employment policies of the member states (2004/740/EC, OJ L 326/45 of 29.10.2004, point 3 and Commission of the European Communities (2005) 'Integrated guidelines for growth and jobs', COM(2005) 141, Brussels, 12.4.2005, p. 31.

[137] Commission of the European Communities (2002) 'Communication from the Commission to the Council, the European Parliament, the Economic and social committee and the Committee of the regions: taking stock of five years of the European employment strategy', COM(2002) 416, Brussels, 17.7.2002, p. 20.

designing adequate indicators and benchmarks and supporting statistical databases to measure progress in the actions for which they are responsible within the EES.[138] The first result of this more autonomous role of the social partners in the employment OMC was achieved in March 2002, when the European social partners agreed to a framework for action for the lifelong development of competence and qualifications (lifelong learning),[139] and in 2005 when the framework of actions on gender equality was adopted.[140] Implementation and monitoring of achievements rest exclusively with the social partners. The social partners decided to promote this framework in the member states and issued annually review developments at a national level and reported on the implementation of the action plan.[141] Evaluations of the impact of those frameworks of actions on the companies and workers are due in March 2006 and 2010 respectively. Autonomy of the social partners involvement in the employment OMC is further enhanced by the adoption of their joint work programme 2003–2005 which foresee for broadening of the social partners independent actions in this area.[142]

In contrast to the social partners, non-profit groups require considerably lesser responsibilities within the process of implementation of European OMC guidelines. Apart from being sporadically called upon to contribute towards translating into practice guidelines adopted within the OMC, the civil dialogue participants' contribution to the national action plans intended for their implementation has been very modest.[143] Although some effort has been made to include civil society organizations in the NAP process on social inclusion, the quality of their participation has been regarded to be unsatisfactory by one of the most prominent European level NGO in this area, European Anti-Poverty Network (EAPN).[144] It emphasises that is all countries but Finland there was no consultation by government with NGOs for the selection of the good practice examples.

---

[138] Council decision of 22 July 2003 on guidelines for the employment policies of the member states, 2003/578/EC, OJ L 197/13, 5.8.2003, p. 21; Council decision of 18 February 2002 on guidelines for member states' employment policies for the year 2002, 2002/177/EC, OJ L 60/60, horizontal objective F and the Guidelines 15; Council decision of 19 January 2001 on guidelines for member states' employment policies for the year 2001, 2001/63/EC, OJ L 22/18, horizontal objective E and the guidelines 13.

[139] ETUC, UNICE, CEEP (2002) Framework of actions for the lifelong development of competencies and qualifications of 27 February 2002, http://www.etuc.org/en/dossiers/colbargain/lll.cfm.

[140] ETUC, UNICE, CEEP (2005) Framework of actions on gender equality of 22 March 2005, http://www.unice.org.

[141] Until now three follow-up reports have been produced on lifelong learning. For the latest report see ETUC, UNICE, CEEP (2005) 'Framework of actions for the lifelong development of competencies and qualifications: third follow-up report, http://www.unice.org.

[142] http://europa.eu.int/comm/employment_social/news/2002/dec/prog_de_travail_comm_en.pdf.

[143] Council of the European Union (2004) 'Joint report by the Commission and the Council on social inclusion', Brussels, 5 March 2004, http://europa.eu.int/comm/employment_social/soc-prot/soc-incl/final_joint_inclusion_report_2003_en.pdf, p. 122; Porte, Caroline de la and Nanz, Patrizia (2004) 'The OMC—a deliberative-democratic mode of governance? The case of employment and pensions' Journal of European Public Policy, 11(2); 267–288, p. 283.

[144] EAPN (2003) Report 'National action plans on inclusion 2003–2005—where is the political energy? EAPN's response to the second round of plans', October 2003, www.eapn.org.

##

288   *Daniela Obradovic*

D. Consultation

This sharp distinction between the civil and social dialogues in the process of lawmaking, co-ordination and implementation of Union policies is blurred by the fact that both modes of governance assume very similar consultative functions. Indeed, the social dialogue covers two functions: decision-making (lawmaking, policy co-ordination and implementation) and consultation, while the civil dialogue is confined to an advisory role.[145] Both the social dialogue in its consultative function and the civil dialogue are employed in the pre-drafting stage of the preparation of EU legislative and policy co-ordination documents.[146] That means, that the Commission seeks opinion from both civil and social dialogue sets of groups when it embarks upon drawing up legislative initiatives or the OMC guidelines. Both types of consultation concern the process through which the Commission wishes to trigger input of interested parties on the occasion of the formulation of an EU legislative proposal or a co-ordinative document. Such consultation enables the Commission to gather opinions of interested parties and take into account different views while drafting law initiatives and OMC guidelines. It also intends to assess the impact of any legislation or policy co-ordination objective by carrying out those two types of consultation.[147] They are supposed to help the Commission and the other institutions to arbitrate between competing claims and priorities and to assist in developing a longer-term policy perspective.

Under Article 138 EC the Commission is obliged when submitting social policy proposals, to consult the European social partners twice during the process of drawing-up an act: on the possible direction of Community action and on the content of the envisaged proposal. The civil dialogue also takes place at the phase of the proposal formulation by the Commission.

How does this social dialogue consultation relate to that conducted under the civil dialogue? The relationship between two types of consultations is very complex and bound to generate a lot of confusion. In order to explain this complicated relationship, it is necessary to highlight the similarities and differences between the two forms of consultations.

[145] The European Court of Justice confirmed the distinction between the functions of consultation and negotiation of the civil dialogue by its judgment, Case T-135/96, *Union Européenne de l'Artisanat et des Petites et Moyennes Entreprises (UEAPME) v Council*, [1998] ECR II-2334, considerations 36 and 37.

[146] Commission of the European Communities (2002) 'The European social dialogue, a force for innovation and change', COM(2002)341, Brussels, 26.6.2002, p. 7; Commission of the European Communities (2002) 'Communication from the Commission "Towards a reinforced culture of consultation and dialogue—General principles and minimum standards for consultation of interested parties by the Commission" ', COM(2002) 704, Brussels, 11.12.2002, p. 15.

[147] On the Commission's implementation of impact assessment for all major initiatives as from 2003, see Commission of the European Communities (2002) 'Communication from the Commission on impact assessment', COM(2002) 276, Brussels, 5.6.2002.

*(i) Distinction between the civil and social dialogue consultative
functions*

Irrespective of the fact that both the social and civil dialogue consultations relate
to the same phase of EU decision-making and that the participants in the both
modes are to be determined by the Commission, they significantly differ from
each other. The Commission itself insists upon drawing 'a clear dividing line'
between these two types of consultation.[148]

**a) The social dialogue consultation as an essential
procedural requirement**

Whilst the consultation with the social partners is compulsory and systematic, the
Commission at present is not under obligation to seek opinion of civil dialog
protagonists. Formally, European institutions cannot take an action in the area of
social policy without consulting the social partners, but they can pass laws
without asking for opinion of civil dialogue groups. Failure on the part of the
Commission to seek advise of the social partners on the social policy issues will
amount to a breach of an essential procedural requirement in the same way as
non-consultation of the European Parliament or the Economic and Social
Committee, where envisaged in the Treaty, prompts the infringement of
European law.[149] Such an obligation does not exist in relation to the consultation
of organizations involved in the civil dialogue.[150] Consequently, while the social
partners do enjoy the right to be consulted in the early stage of legislation preparation, the civil groups cannot claim such a right.

While the Commission is under a legally-binding obligation to consult the
social partners before submitting legislative proposals in the area of social policy, it
seeks advice from associations involved in the civil dialogue on its own motion.
The objective of the civil dialogue is not to establish procedural rights, the respect
of which would be subject to judicial control and review.[151]

Consultation of civil society groups does not go beyond a right to be heard and
it does not ensure the Commission's proclamation from its earlier documents that
the organizations of the civil society should receive appropriate feedback on how

[148] Commission of the European Communities (2002) 'The European social dialogue, a force for
innovation and change', COM(2002) 341, Brussels, 26.6.2002, p. 9; Commission of the European
Communities (2002) 'Communication from the Commission "Towards a reinforced culture of consultation and dialogue—General principles and minimum standards for consultation of interested
parties by the Commission"', COM(2002) 704, Brussels, 11.12.2002, p. 10; Commission of the
European Communities (2002) 'Report from the Commission on European Governance',
COM(2002) 705, Brussels, 11.12.2002, p. 10.
[149] In the case of the European Parliament, see Case 139/79 *SA Roquette Freres v Council* [1980]
ECR 3333, at 3360, para 33–6. In the case of the Economic and Social Committee, see Joint Cases
C-281, 283 to 285 and 287/85, *Germany and others v Commission* [1987] ECR 3203, at 3243-4, para
18, and Article 262 EC.
[150] European Commission (2002) *European Governance: Preparatory Work for the White Paper*,
(Luxembourg: Office for Official Publications of the European Communities), p. 73.
[151] Ibid.

their contributions and opinions have affected the eventual policy decision.[152]
A real dialogue implies a right of the organization to receive a reasoned answer to
the suggestions it puts forward, it is manageable only insofar a selection is made
among the organization.[153] The participants in the civil dialogue do not enjoy a
right to receive an answer. The minimum standards do not provide for an effective
follow-up procedure. The obligation of the Commission to react appropriately to
comments received stipulated by the minimum standards does not confer any
right upon parties, which forwarded their opinions during the consultations, to
be informed in which extended their view has been embraced by relevant EU
policy documents. The Commission finds the idea of providing feedback on an
individual basis (feedback statements) not to be compatible with the requirement
of effectiveness of the decision-making process.[154] An association which feels that
the answer offered by the Commission is not satisfactory is not entitled to apply
for a judicial review of the quality of the grounds given in response to objections
made in the course of the consultation procedure. The Commission clearly states
in its minimum standards for conducting consultation with interest groups that
the situation must be avoided in which a Commission proposal could be
challenged in the European Court of Justice on the grounds of alleged lack of
consultation of interested parties. In its view, such an over legalistic approach
would be incompatible with the need for a timely delivery of policy.[155] This
approach risks, in view of some scholars, to remain a purely formal way of
legitimizing decisions that depend on other parameters, if it is not paired with the
possibility to seek a judicial control of the quality of the answers offered to the
objections put forward by the organizations concerned.[156]

b) Criteria for the selection of parties participating in civil and social dialogue consultations

The second distinction between two of those forms of consultation concerns the
process of the selection of parties for participation in a consultation.

The Commission has the autonomous right to seek information and invite
consultation from any sources that it chooses. It is has the competency to select
associations eligible to participate in both the civil and social dialogue. These organizations, however, were not granted a representational monopoly or accreditation,

[152] Communication of the European Commission (2000) Commission discussion paper 'The
Commission and non-governmental organisations: building a stronger partnership', COM(2000)
11, Brussels, 18.1.2000, p. 10.
[153] Schutter, Olivier de (2002) 'Europe in search of its civil society', European Law Journal, 8(2):
198–217, p. 211.
[154] Commission of the European Communities (2002) 'Communication from the Commission
"Towards a reinforced culture of consultation and dialogue—General principles and minimum
standards for consultation of interested parties by the Commission"', COM(2002) 704, Brussels,
11.12.2002, p. 12.   [155] Ibid, p. 10.
[156] Schutter, Olivier de (2002) 'Europe in search of its civil society', European Law Journal, 8(2)
198–217, p. 214.

and in practice the Commission consults (numerous) other organizations as well. Interest groups have not been recognized or licensed by the Commission. Even though it has established procedures for according special status and preferential treatment to particular interest groups, that recognition is not generally limited to one organization per category. So, in practice, the Commission has the unlimited discretion to choose which organizations to consult. As the consequence of that discretion, the Commission formulated the conditions for the participation of groups in both social and civil dialogue consultations.

It is important to emphasize that although in both cases the determination of eligibility of groups to take part in consultation firmly rests with the Commission, the selection criteria differs considerably. Namely, in order to take part in the civil dialogue or in the consultative phase of the social dialogue, interest groups are expected to meet certain requirements imposed by the Commission. However, the civil and social dialogue participants should fulfil two different sets of the conditions in order to secure a place in the same process of pre-proposal consultation. Even though both the social and civil dialogue consultations relate to the situation preceding the formulation of the Commission proposal, they are subject to two distinct sets of eligibility standards. Moreover, since the Commission does not wish to reduce the number of participants in civil dialogue, it does not make access to consultations subject to a prior eligibility check. It examines whether they meet its requirements at the later stage, ie when it assesses the relevance or quality of comments expressed during the consultation. On the other hand, the social dialogue participants are screened before the launch of a consultation.

The question of representativeness. Both the civil and social dialogue participants are required to meet the Commission test of representativeness in order to qualify for the participation in EU consultations.

According to the Commission, the labour and management associations have to satisfy three conditions in order to take part in the consultative stage of the social dialogue. They should: (1) be cross-industry and be organised at European level; (2) consist of organizations which are themselves an integral and recognized part of member states social partners structures and with the capacity to negotiate agreements, and which are representative of all member states as far as possible; and (3) have the appropriate structures to ensure their effective participation in the consultation process.[157] The question of representativness is to be decided on case-by-case basis as the conditions will vary depending on the subject-matter on which the consultation is undertaken.[158] The Commission determines the

---

[157] Commission of the European Communities (1993) 'Communication on the application of the Agreement on social policy', COM(93) 600 of 14.12.1993, para 24; Commission of the European Communities (1998) 'Commission communication "Adapting and promoting the social dialogue at Community level" ', COM(98) 322, Brussels, 20.5.1998, para. 1.2 at pp. 4 and 5.

[158] Commission of the European Communities (1998) 'Commission communication "Adapting and promoting the social dialogue at Community level" ', COM(98) 322, Brussels, 20.5.1998, p. 9.

eligibility of the parties on the basis of representativeness studies that it carries out from time to time.[159] At present, 70 organizations fulfil those criteria.[160] However, the listing of groups meeting the eligibility requirements for participation in the social dialogue consultation does not imply an accreditation system. Consequently, the Commission does not consult only listed, but also all European or national organizations that might be affected by a proposal.[161] Although the Commission is under obligation to consult social partners designated to be representative, it is not prevented from extending its consultation, on its own motion, to other parties, and indeed it does so.

As far as the civil dialogue consultation is concerned, the Commission introduces the criterion of the representativeness for organizations intended to participate in this forum, similarly as in the case of the social dialogue consultations.[162] However, it does not elaborate what representativeness actually means for the purpose of the application thereof as a criterion for assessing the eligibility of groups taking part in the civil dialogue. How this concept relates to the representativeness requirement developed within the social dialogue consultation process is unclear. The Commission claims that the requirements in respect of representativeness vary in accordance with the nature of the responsibilities conferred on the players. They are limited in the event of simple consultation, but more binding where the social partners can lay down rules that become law.[163] Consequently, the criteria of representativeness as applied in context of the social dialogue may be inappropriate in the area of civil dialogue.

The social dialogue representativeness is predominantly determined in terms of membership.[164] This ground is hardly applicable in the case of the assessment of representativeness of the civil dialogue participants. NGOs are almost never representative in terms of membership. Even so, there are some highly organized groups, such as the Young European Federalists, that

[159] The Commission intends to update the existing representiveness studies. The new survey is going to be carried out by the European Industrial Relations Observatory of the Dublin Foundation, (Commission of the European Communities (2004) 'Communication from the Commission: Partnership for change in an enlarged Europe—Enhancing the contribution of European social dialogue', COM(2004) 557, 12.8.2004, p. 9.

[160] Commission of the European Communities (2004) 'Communication from the Commission: Partnership for change in an enlarged Europe—Enhancing the contribution of European social dialogue', COM(2004) 557, 12.8.2004, Annex 5.

[161] Commission of the European Communities (1993) 'Communication on the application of the Agreement on social policy', COM(93) 600 of 14.12.1993, para. 22.

[162] Commission of the European Communities (2002) 'Communication from the Commission 'Towards a reinforced culture of consultation and dialogue—General principles and minimum standards for consultation of interested parties by the Commission', COM(2002) 704, Brussels, 11.12.2002, p. 11.					[163] Ibid, p. 9.

[164] Commission of the European Communities (1993) 'Communication on the application of the Agreement on social policy', COM(93) 600 of 14.12.1993; Case T-135/96, *Union Européenne de l'Artisanat et des Petites et Moyennes Entreprises (UEAPME) v Council*, [1998] ECR II-2334, consideration 85. The representativeness of the social partners measures membership density, both of the candidate organizations themselves and of each of their members.

can claim an impressive membership all over Europe.[165] However, this is an exception to the rule.

Whether or not NGOs are representative cannot be established exclusively in terms of members whom they speak for. The judgement must also take account of the ability of such bodies to put forward constructive proposals and to bring specialist knowledge to the process of democratic opinion-forming and decision-making since the objective of the civil dialogue consultation is to provide a range of views on a particular issue as well as information gathering. Because of this, in the case of the civil dialogue, representativeness should be understood rather in terms of the range of interests that an actor champions, than in terms of membership.

Since the social partners are expected to play an important role in the implementation of EU decisions preceded by the social dialogue consultation, their capacity to contribute towards their effective execution is of considerable significance for the determination of their representativeness. The social partners' capacity to implement agreements or legislation is dependent upon their membership. That is the reason why the Commission takes into consideration the extensiveness of an association membership when it assesses its representativeness. Contrary to this, the civil dialogue protagonists are not significantly involved in the implementation of EU rules resulting from the decision-making processes that encompass consultations with civic groups. Thus, from this prospective, the membership cannot be regarded as a decisive attribute of the representativeness of the civil dialog actors.

On the other hand, it is very difficult to determine exactly who represents a constituency of civil interest groups; they do not have readily identifiable constituencies. In most cases this is impossible because of great variety of organizations in one filed which all have different approaches to a given issue. The NGOs' claim that they represent civil society cannot be easily validated since there are no established rules concerning the operations of the NGOs. Each sets up its own *modus operandi*. How independent are the NGOs from their donors, funding sources? By which mechanisms do the NGOs receive instructions from the constituencies they are supposed to represent? All those questions cannot be answered with a high degree of certainty. Civic groups are designed as organizations for particular causes, rather than of it. While the social partners further the economic interests of their members—effectively to ensure that their members reap some kind of financial benefit as a consequence of their membership, civil groups galvanize public concerns and champion specific causes.

In addition, a NGO is legitimate not so much because it assembles a great number of people but rather because it has picked up an issue deemed important by the citizens and not sufficiently tackled by public institutions. NGOs are a

---

[165] Goehring, Rebekka (2002) 'Interest representation and legitimacy in the European Union: the new quest for civil society formation' in Alex Warleigh and Jenny Fairbrass, (eds), *Influence and Interests in the European Union: The New Politics of Persuasion and Advocacy*, (London: Europa publications), pp. 118–137, p. 123.

group for, not of, a particular cause, and cannot demonstrate themselves to be representative in the same way that a business association can claim to represent a proportion of the total potential membership constituency.[166] A good example might be the group, SOS VIOL, which suppors rape victims. Obviously raped women are not keen on registering together in an association.[167]

NGOs and Social Movement Organizations (SMOs) point out that increasingly civil society expresses fluidly in the type of formations that represent its values and opinions. New organizations often emerge quickly with strong popular support and dissolve or change into different organizations in a short time. Therefore an insistence on calculating membership would exclude an important part of civil society.[168]

The difficulties in the application of the criterion of representativess to the civil dialogue organizations have been recognized by the Commission. It emphasizes that the issue of representativeness at European level should not be used as the only criterion when assessing the relevance or quality of comments. Other factors, such as their track record and ability to contribute substantial policy input to the discussion are equally important. It pledges that not only opinions of European level organizations are going to be taken into consideration, but also of those operating at national, regional and local level. In its view, minority views can also form as essential dimension of open discourse on policies. On the other hand, emphasizes the Commission, it is important for it to consider how representative views are when taking a political decision following a consultation process.[169] Until now the Commission did not clarify what constitutes evidence of represenatativity and whether only opinion of representative organisations should be taken into consultations.

Openness and accountability as additional eligibility requirements for the participation of civic groups in EU consultations. The Commission supplements the representativity requirement with the two additional ones: accountability and transparency. This is understood as meaning that NGOs are able to participate effectively and constructively in the opinion-forming and decision-making process through the provision of appropriate organizational structures and expertise. The introduction

---

[166] Halpin, D. (2001) 'Integrating conceptions of interest groups: towards a conceptual framework of sectional interest group imperatives', paper prepared for ECPR (European Consortium for Political Research) General Conference, University of Kent, 6–8 September 2001, quoted in Greenwood, Justin (2002) 'Advocacy, Influence and Persuasion: Has it All Been Overdone?' in Alex Warleigh and Jenny Fairbrass, (eds), *Influence and Interests in the European Union: The New Politics of Persuasion and Advocacy*, (London: Europa publications), pp. 19–34, p. 28.

[167] Grote, Jacqueline de (2003) NGOs and Standards of Governance in NGOs, Democratisation and the Regulatory State, A collection of Papers Presented at the Conferences in London and Brussels, 2003, (London: European Policy Forum), pp. 91–94, p. 92.

[168] Ruzza, Carlo (2004) *Europe and Civil Society: Movement Coalitions and European Governance*, (Manchester: Manchester University Press), p. 46.

[169] Commission of the European Communities (2002) 'Communication from the Commission "Towards a reinforced culture of consultation and dialogue—General principles and minimum standards for consultation of interested parties by the Commission"', COM(2002) 704, Brussels, 11.11.2002, pp. 11–12.

of two of those criteria reflects the Commission position that with the better involvement comes greater responsibility. Consequently, civil society must itself follow the principle of good governance, including accountability and openness, that governs the conduct of the Union institutions,[170] though, it is not at all obvious why all organizations in civil society need to abide by the same accountability standards as political organizations, when they, as we showed above, do not perform any policy-forming task within the EU.[171]

The application of those criteria are intended to address the credibility concern related to internal governance procedures of NGOs which are commonly regarded to be insufficiently democratic. The main problem seems to be that decision-making in NGOs is left in the hands of key officers, with very little—if any—supporters' input.[172] None of NGOs functions as a supporter-run organization. Decision-making about lobbying or campaigning is heavily centralised, and shaped entirely by the relevant officers and not by supporters. NGOs cannot be held accountable to their own membership.[173] This contributes towards the development of clientlism in NGOs. Supporters input into decision-making is usually minimal.[174] NGOs often undertake activities about which their supporters know and understand very little, and with which they may disagree. Indeed, the recently conducted field work studies show that most NGO supporters do not seek to play an active role in the governance of the organization.[175] Their internal governance is too elitist to allow supporters a role in shaping policies, campaigns and strategies. They do not function as supporters-run associations. Supporters play no formal role in decision-making of any NGO.

The internal governance of European level interest organizations is even more detached from their supporters. Almost all European associations are organized as confederations, ie associations of national associations that do not admit individuals as members.[176] These factors mean that EU interest organizations have a structural remoteness from the grass roots interests they represent.

Irrespective of the fact that the Commission intention to assess the quality of interest groups consultation, contributions, in terms of the compliance of their internal structure with the principle of good governance, can be regarded to be

---

[170] Commission of European Communities (2001) 'European governance: white paper', COM(2001) 428, Brussels, 25.7.2002, p. 15 and 17.

[171] See on this Follesdal, Andreas (2003) 'The political theory of the white paper on governance: hidden and fascinating', European Public Law, 9(1): 73–86, p. 78.

[172] Sudbery, Imogen (2003) 'Bringing the legitimacy gap in the EU: can civil society help to bring the Union closer to its citizens' Collegium, 26: 75–95, p. 94; Warleigh, Alex (2001) 'Europeanizing civil society: NGOs as agents of political socialisation', Journal of Common Market Studies, 39(4): 619–639, p. 623.

[173] Peters, Guy (2004) 'Interest groups and European governance: a normative perspective' in Andreas Warntjen and Arndt Wonka, (eds), *Governance in Europe: The Role of Interest Groups*, (Baden-Baden: Nomos), pp. 57–65, p. 61.

[174] Warleigh, Alex (2001) 'Europeanizing civil society: NGOs as agents of political socialisation', Journal of Common Market Studies, 39(4): 619–639, p. 631.   [175] Ibid, p. 634.

[176] Greenwood, Justine (2003) Interest Representation in the European Union, Houndmills, p. 77.

appropriate in the situation when a great number of NGOs operates in an undemocratic manner, many scholars consider that this Commission action encroaches upon associations' autonomy.[177] Namely, the danger is that civil society becomes subject to the colonizing forces of the EU political and economic systems both in terms of their organizational forms and their rationalities, which undermine the structures and values associated with civil society. European civil society becomes governmentalized, in the sense of altering its organizational forms and its rationalites in order to facilitate its attempts to influence EU governance.[178] This issue is most acute if we bear in mind that all participants in the social dialogue have undergone internal organizational reforms (ETUC 1991, UNICE, 1992; CEEP, 1994)[179] in order to adjust their structures to the social dialogue requirements and improve their abilities to conclude Europe-wide agreements (introduction on the mandate for negotiation,[180] removing requirements for unanimity). Similarly, eligibility and suitability criteria deployed for the selection of NGOs intended to enter into Frameworks Partnership Agreements with the Commission's Humanitarian Aid Office (ECHO) that are applicable to the humanitarian operations sponsored by the EU also impose very strict rules in respect to internal organizations.[181] Those are two years external audit obligations and specific requirements regarding administrative, financial and operational capacity of applying NGOs.

The Commission could try to interfere in the internal structure of civic organizations. It emphazises that it fully respects the independence of outside organizations. On the other hand, for the consultation process to meaningful and credible it is essential to spell out who participates in it. The Commission by frequently emphasising accountability but also 'the need to respect diversity and heterogeneity of the NGO community' and 'the need to take account of the autonomy and independence of NGOs' assumes that the two concepts can be combined.[182] But in many ways the two categories are different and not easily reconcilable.

[177] Warleight, A. (2001) 'Europeanizing Civil Society: NGOs as agents of political socialization', Journal of Common Market Studies, 39(4): 619–39; Schutter, Olivier de (2002) 'Europe in search of its civil society', European Law Journal, 8(2) 198–217, p. 216; Geyer, Robert (2001) 'Can European Union (EU) social NGOs co-operate to promote EU social policy?', Journal of Social Policy, 30(3): 477–493, p. 479.

[178] Amstrong, Kenneth A. (2002) 'Rediscovering civil society: the European Union and the White Paper on Governance', European Law Journal, 8(1): 102–132, p. 109.

[179] Obradovic, Daniela (1995) 'Prospects for corporatist decision-making in the European Union; the social policy agreement' Journal of European Public Policy, 2(2): 159–183, p. 269.

[180] Nevertheless, none of those organizations enjoys a general bargaining mandate, but rather must seek the agreement of their members afresh each time in order to enter negotiations, ie on an issue-by-issue basis. In addition, any agreement concluded through the social dialogue procedure is to be rubber stamped by all national affiliates.

[181] The selection criteria which ECHO applies in order to determine eligibility of organizations intended to enter into this partnership are guided by three EC regulations on humanitarian aid (http://europa.eu.int/comm/echo/partners/selection_en.htm).

[182] Communication of the European Commission (2000) Commission discussion paper 'The Commission and non-governmental organisations: building a stronger partnership', COM(2000) 11, Brussels, 18.1.2000, p.5.

The scope of application. The scope of application of the criteria for taking part in the civil dialogue is not so well delimited as of those employed for licensing the participation in the social dialogue consultation. Whilst the Commission precisely delineates the ambit of use of the consultation standards in the social dialogue, doubts exist as to the exact area of operation of the civil dialogue requirements.

The Commission's eligibility criteria designated for the social dialogue consultation are not applicable to the consultations within advisory committees or in the context of procedures aimed at garnering the views of interested parties, for example, through the adoption of a Green Paper.[183] Apart from seeking advisory opinion from the social partners within the social dialogue on social policy issues, the Commission also carry out consultations in advisory committees established in some areas of social policy. When serving on those committees, the social partners are not required to fulfil the social dialogue eligibility criteria in order to be consulted.

There are six advisory committees that consist exclusively of representatives of the European social partners. They advise the Commission on social security for migrant workers, freedom of movement of workers, the European Social Fund, vocational training, safety, hygiene and protection at work and equal opportunities for women and men.[184] On all the other committees they are involved with, the social partners serve together with representatives of non-profit groups, companies or experts. Except for the one on Equal Opportunities, they are made up of national rather than European level social partners. This means that the position of the social partners is often not co-ordinated with the views expressed in other fora. Yet the Commission has a well-established tradition of consulting tripartite advisory committees at this stage of the policy-making process. As a consequence both procedures currently take place side-by-side, which implies considerable overlap. To a large extent the two procedures consult the same persons, since the European social partners organizations consulted under Article 138 EC contact the relevant experts of their national organizations, but precisely these same experts are often appointed by their national organizations to sit on the advisory committees. Moreover, the two-stage consultation under Article 138 EC is a relatively rapid procedure compared with the advisory committee, the plenary of which meets only twice a year. The opinion of the committee is thus likely to arrive at a time when the Commission has already largely developed its draft on the basis of the social dialogue consultation. Since only the social dialogue consultation is obligatory,[185] one could doubt the relevance of consultations on

---

[183] Commission of the European Communities (2002) 'The European social dialogue, a force for innovation and change', COM(2002)341, Brussels, 26.6.2002, p. 9.

[184] For a comprehensive, overview of the legal basis for the establishment of all these committees', see Franssen, Edith (2002) *Legal Aspects of the European Social Dialogue*, (Antwerp: Intersentia), pp. 50–51, and Council Decision of 22 July 2003 on setting up an Advisory Committee on Safety and Health at Work, OJ 218/1, 13.9.2003.

[185] The absence of a requirement to consult the advisory committee has been confirmed by the European Court of Justice in Case C-84/94 *UK v Council* ('Working Time case') [1996] ECR I-5755, para 41.

legislative proposals that take place in the advisory committees for the EU governance in future.

The civil dialogue minimum standards are applicable to the Internet-based consultations undertaken during the first stage of the Commission impact assessment strategy, deployed when it intends to launch any policy initiative or legislative proposal. They are not applicable to lobbying activities of numerous interest groups. Instructions on effective lobbying of the European Commission can be found in Burson-Marsteller (2003) *A Guide to the Effective Lobbying of the European Commission: Based on a survey of senior commission officials* (Brussels: Burson-Marsteller).

The second area of the employment of the minimum standards concerns work of the Commission's informal advisory committees for organizing an exchange of views with civic associations. While the Commission clearly states that consultation taking place in the committees established by the Treaty or EU legislation fall outside the range of the minimum standards, it indicates that they should be employed to work of its ad hoc committees.[186] At present the Commission runs nearly 700 ad hoc consultation bodies in a wide range of policies.[187] Although set up by the Commission, grounds for their establishment cannot be found in the Treaty or in EU legislation. Their composition, activities and impact remain rather opaque. By their very nature, these forums provide privileged access to the Commission policy-shaping process for a limited number of stakeholder organizations.

However, the scope of the application of the eligibility criteria stipulated in the minimum standards is far less clear than of those developed in the case of the social dialogue consultation. The reasons for the lack of clarity surrounding the use of the civil dialogue participation requirements are as follows: (a) the existence of several types of consultations with interest groups conducted by the Commission prior to the formulation or the adoption of law proposals that run parallel to each other; (b) the engagement of the same groups in different types of consultations taking part in the pre-drafting stage of the EC legislative process; and (c) the fact that some groups participate in a different capacity in variety of the pre-legislation consultations.

The Commission points out that the minimum standards criteria are not deployed in specific consultation frameworks provided in the Treaty (e.g. consultations taking place within the Economic and Social Committee, the Committee of Regions, the Article 138 EC social dialogue consultation, the Article 79 EC transport committee, or the Article 113 EC committee) or in other consultative bodies based upon-EU legislation,[188] consultation required under international

---

[186] Commission of European Communities (2001) European governance: White paper, COM(2001) 428, Brussels, 25.7.2002, p. 17.

[187] European Commission 2002, European governance preparatory work for the white paper, Luxembourg Office for Official Publication of the European Communities, p. 75.

[188] For example, the Social Protection Committee established by the Council decision of 29 June 2000, setting up a Social Protection Committee, 2000/436/EC, OJ L 172/26, 12.7.2000, or the Article 147 EC Advisory Committee for the European Social Fund operating in accordance with Article 49 of the Council Regulation (EC) No 1260/1999 of 21 June 1999 laying down general provisions on the Structural Funds, OJ L 161/1, 26.6.1999.

conventions,[189] the comitology process,[190] consultation of experts,[191] and dialogue with European and national associations of regional and local government in the EU.[192]

The implications of the limitations imposed by the Commission upon the scope of the application of the minimum standards are quite significant for the further development of the civil dialogue in the Union. The most important consequence concerns the fragmentation and proliferation of rules governing consultation of civic groups by the Union institutions. Balkanisation of those rules, and the absence of a holistic and coherent approach of the Commission when it selects its collaborators among interested organizations obscure an already Byzantine matrix of the civil dialogue. The codification of the participation of civic groups in EU governance is not regulated in an encompassing way.

This proliferation and segmentation of standards guiding the civil dialogue reflects the complexity of the concept itself. Namely, the notion of civil dialogue in the Union encompasses the wide range of actors (variety of non-profit interest groups, social partners); relates to various forms of consultative processes (pre-drafting of legislative proposals, such as consultation held in different policy forums; consultation in committees on already formulated Commission proposals, such as the consultation in the European Economic and Social Committee;[193] and spreads out through different modes of EU governance (e.g. lawmaking and

[189] For example, the condition for participation of interested parties, including NGOs, required under Article 8 of the Aarhus convention (Convention on Access to Information, Public Participation in Decision-Making and Access to Justice in Environmental Matters, http://europa.eu.int/comm/environment/aarhus/index.htm) to which the EU is party, are stipulated in Article 2 of the Directive 2003/35/EC of the European parliament and of the Council of 26 May 2003, providing for public participation in respect of the drawing up of certain plans and programmes relating to the environment, and amending with regard to public participation and access to justice, Council Directive 85/337/EEC and 96/61/EC, OJ 2003 L 156/17, 25.6.2003, and in Article 6 of Directive 2001/42/EC of the European parliament and the Council of 27 June 2001 on the assessment of the effects of certain plans and programmes on the environment, OJ 2001 L 197/37, 21.7.2001.

[190] The notion of comitology concerns the system of committees of member state representatives that assist the Commission in the execution of its implementing powers under Article 202 EC. See Council Decision 1999/468/EC of 28 June 1999 laying down the procedures for the exercise of implementing powers conferred on the Commission, OJ 1999, L184/23.

[191] These consultation is to be conducted in accordance with the standards laid down in Commission of the European Communities (2002) 'Communication from the Commission on the collection and use of expertise by the Commission: principles and guidelines: improving the knowledge base for better policies', COM(2002) 713, 11.12.2002.

[192] Commission of the European Communities (2003) 'Ongoing and systematic policy dialogue with local-government associations', COM(2003) 811, 23.11.2003.

[193] The ESC considers that it should play a crucial role in defining and structuring civil dialogue and become a 'meeting place for organized civil society' and an 'essential link' between the European Union and organized civil society, and a forum for civil dialogue. (The European Economic and Social Committee has expressed this opinion on several occasions, most recently in European Economic and Social Committee (2004) 'Final report of the ad hoc group on structured co-operation with civil society organisations and networks' Rapporteur; Mr Bloch-Laine, CESE 1498/2003, Brussels, 17 February 2004, p. 8).

policy co-ordination based upon the OMC). Such extensive and diversified deployment of the civil dialogue concept accounts for the compartmentalization of the EU norms enacted for the purpose of regulation thereof. The lack of an operational definition of the notion of European civil dialogue and its frequent usage in dissimilar contexts of the EU governance contribute towards mushrooming of participation regulations. There is no coherent set of eligibility criteria for the participation of organizations in the civil dialogue as a whole. Each and every segment of this process is subject to a distinctive regime. Not only that, different type of actors taking part in different forms of consultation (for example, social partners consulted under Article 138 EC and non-profit groups participating in the Social Policy Forum) but also the same type of actors delivering opinion in the same phase of the same mode of governance are subject to different eligibility criteria. Indeed, the participation of civil society groups in the variety of consultations preceding the adoption of law proposals is governed by the rules differing from those stipulated by the minimum standards. For example, the Commission consultation with environmental interest groups taking part in the Environmental Policy Forum should be governed by the minimum standards. However, the Commission is going to gathering exploratory opinions of same groups required under the Aarhus arrangements in accordance with entirely different criteria laid down in its documents implementing this international convention.[194]

The situation is even more complicated as a result of the recent entry of the Economic and Social Committee (ESC) into the pre-drafting stage of the EU legislative process. The EC Treaty provides for the ESC to give its opinion after, rather than before, proposals have been transmitted to the legislature.[195] It officially does not participate in the pre-drafting stage of the EU legislative process, but delivers its opinion on the already adopted Commission proposal. Having found that its formal legal position minimizes impact thereof upon EU decision-making,[196] and being of conviction that the Committee should become 'an indispensable intermediary between the EU institutions and organized civil society',[197] the Commission signed the Protocol with the ESC which contains express provision to the effect that the Commission should invite the ESC to issue exploratory opinions and that the Commission would rely on the ESC to deepen its relations with organized civil society.[198] The rationale behind this protocol is to reinforce its function as intermediary between, on the one hand, the EU institutions, and, on the other, organized civil society. This protocol provides for the Commission

---

[194] See above.   [195] Article 257 EC.

[196] Commission of European Communities (2001) European governance: White paper, COM(2001) 428, Brussels, 25.7.2002, p. 15.

[197] The European Economic and Social Committee has expressed this opinion on several occasions, most recently in European Economic and Social Committee (2004) 'Final report of the ad hoc group on structured co-operation with civil society organisations and networks', Rapporteur; Mr Bloch-Laine, CESE 1498/2003, Brussels, 17 February 2004, p. 2.

[198] Protocol governing arrangements for co-operation between the European Commission and the Economic and Social Committee, 24 September 2001, CES 1253/2001.

to consult the Committee on certain issues on an exploratory basis before even beginning to draw up its own proposal, allowing Committee to play a useful consultative role at an earlier stage in the decision-making process. This means that civil associations organized at national level that participate in the ESC work are consulted prior to the drafting of EU law, once in their capacity as the ESC members, and secondly when they can take part in the Internet consultation. At the first occasion their representiveness should be judged against EU rules governing the ESC activities,[199] and in the second situation the minimum standards are applicable.

The additional confusion regarding the application of the minimum standards is imposed by the fact that particular groups take part both in civil and social dialogue in their different capacities. For instance, when the Commission consults the social partners on the social policy issues within the Article 138 EC consultation it applies its social dialogue requirements, and when it seeks their opinion on identical issues within the framework of the European Social Forum the minimum standards are applicable. However, when the social partners are addressed by the Commission in their capacity as members of a variety of committees operating in parallel to the minimum standards and the social dialogue consultations, they are subject to the set of the eligibility criteria which differs both from the minimum standards and the social dialogue requirements.[200]

We can conclude that the application of minimum standards is strictly confined to the pre-drafting stage of a legislative proposal formulation and that they are not intended to govern the participation of interest groups in the civil dialogue as a whole. More precisely, those standards are deployed by the Commission in three situations arising in the pre-legislative consultative process: (1) in the first stage of the Commission's impact assessment analyses of its draft legislative proposals or any initiative it intend to launch;[201] (2) when the Commission evaluates the interest groups contributions delivered in response to its Internet-based consultations; and (3) when the Commission seeks advise of its numerous, informally set up committees. Those criteria shall apply only to consultation taking place outside fora institutionalized by virtue of the Treaty or EU legislation.

The organizations to which those requirements should apply are mainly those listed in the database CONECCS, although the criteria which are to be met by

---

[199] Regulation on ESC.

[200] In principle, the participants on those committees are co-opted from national government committees and national organizations of employers and employees. Three representatives are sent from each member state. Only representatives of trade unions and management serving on the Advisory Committee on Equal Opportunities for Women and Men are not chosen from the national level social partners' organizations, but originate from respective European confederations. For more details, see Smismans, Stijn (2004) *Law, Legitimacy, and European Governance: Functional Participation in Social Regulation*, (Oxford: Oxford University Press), pp. 189–192.

[201] Commission of the European Communities (2002) Communication from the Commission 'Towards a reinforced culture of consultation and dialogue—General principles and minimum standards for consultation of interested parties by the Commission', COM(2002) 704, Brussels, 11.12.2002, p. 15.

organizations seeking to be included in this database differs substantially from those stipulated by the minimum standards. The CONECCS eligibility criteria are as follows: (1) an organization must be a non-profit representative body organized at European level, ie with members in three or more EU countries; (2) be active and have expertise in one or more of the policy areas of the Commission's activity, (3) have some degree of formal or institutional existence and a document that sets out its objective and the way it is to be managed; (4) have authority to speak for its members, (5) operate in an open and accountable manner; and (6) be prepared to provide any reasonable information about itself required by the Commission, either for insertion on the database or in support of its request for inclusion.[202] The main difference between the minimum and CONECCS standards is that whilst only European umbrella organizations can be registered in the afore-mentioned database, both national and EU level associations are entitled to participate in consultations governed by the minimum standards. Similarly, as in the case of the minimum standards, the Commission has reinforced the requirements regarding accountability and openness of organizations and their capacity to provide input to the Commission.

One still not fully explained implication of the introduction of the minimum standards concerns the relation thereof with the 1992 code of conduct guiding the Commission's relations with special interest groups.[203] This code covers the same type of consultations of the Commission with civil society organizations as the minimum standards. However, until now, the Commission remains silent as to how two of those sets of requirements relate to each other.

VI. The Social Dialogue Autonomy in EU Governance

The most striking feature of the social dialogue that distinguishes it firmly from the civil dialogue is its autonomous nature. While the civil dialogue utterly depends upon the Commission initiative, the social dialogue has become quite independent from the Union institutions and has progressed towards an autonomous process for social standards definition.[204] Whereas the civil dialogue can be regarded as by the Commission-induced consultation, the social dialogue developed into an autonomous governance process, running parallel to the Union legislative and policy co-ordination activities.

The autonomy of the social partners in Union decision-making has been significantly increased in the recent years. The Commission takes the view that in recent

[202] http://europa.eu.int/comm/civil_society/coneccs/inscription.cfm?CL=en.
[203] Commission of the European Communities (1992) 'Communication from the Commission "An open and structured dialogue between the Commission and special interest groups" ', SEC(92) 2272, Brussels, 2.12.1992, Annex II: Minimum requirements for a code of conduct between the commission and special interest groups.
[204] For an opposite opinion, see Lo Faro, Antonio (2000) *Regulating Social Europe: Reality and Myth of Collective Bargaining in the EC Legal Order*, (Oxford: Hart Publishing).

years it has been a qualitative shift in the nature of the social dialogue towards greater autonomy.[205] The social partners' joint contribution to the Leaken European Council of 7 December 2001[206] was a critical step towards the opening of an independent European level social dialogue, ie its greater autonomy. In their Leaken declaration, the European inter-sectoral social partners opted for: (1) the creation of their own work programme; and (2) a more independent social dialogue that is strongly bipartite, with voluntary, non-legally binding agreements to be implemented by the social partners themselves.

Their joint work programme for 2003–2005 was adopted in 2002.[207] It gives boost to their autonomous actions in the area of European social and employment policy, ie contributes towards the increase of their independence in the EU governance.

The Commission supports the development towards a more independent and autonomous social dialogue and non-legally binding agreements in the inter-sectoral social dialogue.[208] It called on the European social partners to further develop their autonomous dialogue and to establish joint work programmes, as highlighted in the European Council Laeken declaration and supported by the Barcelona European Council.[209]

A. Autonomy of social partner in EU lawmaking on social matters

In the area of EU social policy where the social dialogue procedure applies, the autonomy of the social partners is guaranteed by virtue of Article 138 EC. The opening of negotiations is totally in the hands of the social partners and the negotiating process is based upon principles of autonomy and mutual recognition of the negotiating parties.[210] Although the social partners under this procedure can

---

[205] The Commission of the European Communities (2004) 'Communication from the Commission: Partnership for change in an enlarged Europe—Enhancing the contribution of European social dialogue', COM(2004) 557, 12.8.2004, p. 5.

[206] http://www.eiro.eurofound.ie./2001/12/feature/eu0112262f.html.

[207] http://europa.eu.int/comm/employment_social/news/2002/dec/prog_de_travail_comm_en.pdf.

[208] The telework agreement was considered by the Commission to be the great success of the social dialogue (see the speech of Ms Diamantopulu, Commissioner for Employment and Social Affairs, EIRO, July 2002, http://www.eiro.eurofound.i.e./2002/07/Feature/EU0207204F.htm).

[209] European Commission (2002) 'The European social dialogue, a force for innovation and change', COM(2002) 341, Brussels, 26.6.2002, p. 4; Commission of the European Communities (2004) 'Communication from the Commission: Partnership for change in an enlarged Europe—Enhancing the contribution of European social dialogue', COM(2004) 557, 12.8.2004, p. 8. The Council has also encouraged the social partners to conclude agreement 'on an independent basis' ('Council resolution of 6 December 1994 on certain aspects for a European Union social policy: a contribution to economic and social convergence in the Union', OJ C 368, 23.12.94, p. 6–10, para I 21.

[210] Commission of the European Communities (1998) 'Commission communication "Adapting and promoting the social dialogue at Community level"', COM (98) 322, p. 14; Case T-135/96, *Union Européenne de l'Artisanat et des Petites et Moyennes Entreprises (UEAPME) v Council*, [1998] ECR II-2334, consideration 79.

independently determine subjects for the negotiations and implement concluded agreements through their national affiliations, until recently, they have always relied upon the Commission for the initiation of issues for negotiations and on the Council for implementation of the social dialogue agreement by European legislative acts. This practice has been discontinued. The social dialogue has in recent years progressed in the direction of ever increasing autonomy and emancipation from control of the EU institutions. The social partners are now acting in a more autonomous manner, both in respect to the initiation and the implementation of European social agreements.

Although the social partners were not required to restrict their negotiation to proposals tabled by the Commission before the adoption of their multi-annual programme,[211] they in the past have never bargained on their own motion.[212] Prior to its adoption UNICE obstructed any European level negotiations not prompted by the Commission and there was no joint social dialogue agenda set up by EU level employers' and employees' associations.[213]

The adoption of their joint multi-annual work programme makes possible for the social partners to develop into agenda setters in the European Union. This programme enables the social partners to gain control of their own independent social dialogue, and no longer merely respond to consultations launched by the Commission under Article 138 EC. In the past, the social partners reacted to the Commission's initiatives, but they have now become more independent in establishing European social standards.[214] The work programme encourages a more autonomous social dialogue, which is not dependent on consultation from the Commission. It marks a significant departure from previous practice, which consisted of deciding on a case-by-case basis whether or not to deal with a specific issue in the social dialogue as incited by the Commission, and thus broadens the scope for autonomous action.[215]

The programme is going to facilitate further development of their agenda-setting capabilities and enable management and labour organisations to become

---

[211] The freedom of the European social partners to negotiate agreements that are not related to European policy proposals has been recognised in Article 12(2) of the 1989 Community Charter on the Fundamental Social Rights of Workers (Social Europe 1/92), the observance of which is guaranteed in Article 136 EC.

[212] UNICE even declared that it would only agree to take up bargaining in the case of the Commission's initiative (see UNICE (1999) Freeing Europe's employment potential: European social policy on the eve of 2000 seen by companies, position paper; and Boockmann, Bernhard (1998) 'Agenda control by interest groups in EU social policy', Journal of Theoretical Politics, 10(2): 215–236, p. 220).

[213] Treu, Tiziano (2001) 'A new phase of European social policy; the EMU and beyond', The international journal of comparative labour law and industrial relations, 17(4): 461–472, p. 466.

[214] European Foundation for the Improvement of Living and Working Conditions (2003) 'Migration and industrial relations' in Industrial Relations Developments in Europe, Joint Foundation/European Commission Report, Luxembourg: Office for Official Publications of the European Communities.

[215] Smismans, Stijn (2004) *Law, legitimacy, and European Governance: Functional Participation in Social Regulation*, (Oxford: Oxford University Press), p. 361.

genuine partners in establishing European social standards. The social partners will become capable of assuming a less reactive role in the social dialogue process. They will be able to undertake their independent course of social action, parallel to that envisaged by the Commission, and consequently to release themselves from its control. Namely, though the Commission cannot directly participate in collective negotiations when those are commenced on its initiative, it still retains some control over this process.[216] Thanks to its obligation to promote the consultation of management and labour at Community level by ensuring balanced support of the parties stated in Article 138(1) EC, the Commission is able to intervene in the social dialogue. It usually uses its task to supply the social partners with a document that constitutes the starting point and basis of their talks and its role to provide technical support, as a convenient tool of intervention.[217] This venue for exercising the Commission supervision over the social dialogue ceases to exist when the social partners become in charge of their joint agenda. Furthermore, when agreements are negotiated on the Commission's initiative, it may decline a request of the social partners to negotiate on a subject, if it deems the social partners insufficiently representative. In practice though, the Commission has never rejected a request of the social partners to suspend the legislative process. Agreements initiated on the basis of the work programme escape this never used, but nevertheless, the real constrains of the Commission.

The social partners' adoption of the work programme does not suspend the Commission's power to take initiatives under Article 138 EC. But, it changes the conditions under which it does so. The Commission has to share its right of initiative in the field of the social policy with that of the social partners. The right balance will have to be struck between the Commission's power of initiative in the social field and the social partners' independence. The strategic behaviour of the Commission, proposing legislation with the indirect aim of inducing the social partners to enter into negotiations, seems less likely in future. Considering the fact that the social partners have so far entered into negotiations on social policy 'in the shadow of the law', the prospects for the conclusion of this type of framework agreement on social policy are not so bright.

The programme of the social partners is neither exhaustive nor exclusive, for it is to be implemented in conjunction with the Social Policy Agenda which defines the Commission's priorities in the social and employment fields for the period 2000–2005.[218] Where questions are not included in their work programme but

[216] For an detailed overview of the Commission in the Articles 138–139 social dialogue procedure see Obradovic, Daniela (2001) 'The impact of the social dialogue procedure on the powers of European Union institutions' in Compston, Hugh and Greenwood, Justine, (eds.), *The Social Partnership in the European Union*, (Houndmils: Palgrave), pp. 71–97, pp. 76–86.

[217] Obradovic, Daniela (2000) 'The impact of the social dialogue procedure on the powers of European Union institutions' in Compston, Hugh and Greenwood, Justin, (eds.), *Social Partnership in the European Union*, (Houndmills: Palgrave), pp.71–97, pp. 81–86.

[218] Commission of the European Communities (2000) 'Communication from the Commission to the Council, the European Parliament, the Economic and Social Committee and the Committee of Region: Social Policy Agenda', COM(2000) 379, 28.6.2000.

in the Social Policy Agenda, the social partners will still react as before. However, where subjects are included both in the social partners' work programme and in the Commission's agenda, the Commission will take account of the social partners' activities in deciding how to proceed.[219] One example is the issue of stress at work included in their work programme on which the social partners, as indicated above, decided to conclude a voluntary agreement,[220] while this matter is also envisaged in the Commission's Community strategy on health and safety at work 2002–2006.[221] The same is true of social responsible enterprise restructuring, where, at the social partners' request, in 2002 the Commission suspended the second stage of consultation to give leeway to the social partners whose work programme includes preparation of joint guidelines.[222] This does not mean that the traditional legislative route will not be used any more.

The first EU level cross-industry negotiations prompted by the social partners current 2003–2005 work programme rather than by the Commission proposal, were successfully concluded on 8 October 2004.[223] The agreement reached deals with work-related stress.

As far as the autonomous implementation of the social dialogue agreements is concerned, the agreement on telework concluded on 16 July 2002 by the ETUC, UNICE, CEEP is the first social dialogue accord to be implemented in accordance with the procedures and practices specific to management and labour in the member states.[224] The telework agreement will be the first agreement ever to be implemented through the voluntary route foreseen in Article 139(2) EC. The accord should be applied within three years of its signature—by 16 July 2005. The above-mentioned agreement on work-related stress is to be implemented in the same way.

Those two agreements make a break with the previous practice of the implementation of the social dialogue agreements by means of a Council Directive. Consequently, the social partners will not be any more subject to the constraints of their autonomy, as in the cases when their agreements were implemented through EC law. If an Article 138 agreement is to be transposed in EU instrument, that can be done only by the Council on the proposal of the Commission.[225] Although

---

[219] European Commission (2004) 'Industrial Relations in Europe 2004', (Luxembourg: Office for Official Publications of the European Communities), p. 73.

[220] European Foundation for the Improvement of Living and Working Conditions, European Industrial Relations Observatory On-line (2002) EU-level developments in 2002, p. 9, http://www.eiro.eurofound.eu.int/.

[221] Commission of the European Communities (2002) 'Communication from the Commission: adapting to change in work and society: a new Community strategy on health and safety at work 2002–2006', COM(2002) 118, Brussels, 11.3.2002.

[222] European Foundation for the Improvement of Living and Working Conditions, European Industrial Relations Observatory On-line (2002) EU-level developments in 2002, p. 9, http://www.eiro.eurofound.eu.int/.

[223] http://www.etuc.org/IMG/pdf/Accord-cadres_sans_signat.pdf.

[224] http://europa.eu.int/comm/employment_social/news/2002/jul/telework_en.pdf.

[225] Commission of the European Communities (1993) 'Communication concerning the application of the Agreement on Social Policy, presented by the Commission to the Council and to the European Parliament', COM(93) 600, Brussels, 14.12.1993, para. 30; and Case T-135/96, *Union*

neither the Council,[226] nor the Commission[227] has the right to amend the agreement submitted by the social partners for implementation via EC law,[228] in making its proposal for a decision by the Council, the Commission resumes control of the procedure. In its capacity as guardian of the Treaties,[229] the Commission has the right to assess the representativeness of the signatory parties, their mandate, the legality of the agreement, ie whether the contents of the agreement are in accordance with Community law, and the effects on small and medium-sized enterprises set out in Article 137(2).[230] The Council, for its part, is required to verify whether the Commission has fulfilled its obligation.[231] In order to respect bargaining autonomy of the social partners neither the Commission nor the

---

Europeenne de l'Artisanat et des Petites et Moyennes Entreprises (UEAPME) v Council, [1998] ECR II-2334, consideration 84. See also Article 139 EC. This is equally possible for agreements initiated by the Commission and those initiated by the social partners themselves (Commission of the European Communities (1998) 'Commission communication: adapting and promoting the social dialogue at Community level', COM (98) 322, Brussels, 20.5.1998, p. 15.

[226] Commission of the European Communities (1993) 'Communication concerning the application of the Agreement on Social Policy, presented by the Commission to the Council and to the European Parliament', COM(93) 600, 14.12.1993, paras. 15, 38 and 42. As a matter of fact the Council decision must be limited to making binding provisions of the agreement concluded between the social partners, so the text of the agreement would not form part of the decision, but would be annexed thereto (Ibid. para. 41). See also, Commission of the European Communities (1996) 'Proposal for a Council directive on the Framework agreement concluded by UNICE, CEEP and ETUC on parental leave, COM (96) 26, Brussels, 31.1.1996 para. 30. The changes made by the Council never concerned the European agreement itself, but only the preceding articles which were added by the Commission.

[227] The Commission has twice proposed the insertion of an amendment, a non-discrimination clause, in the main body of the draft Directive to which the agreement has been annexed, but the Council rejected this alteration in both cases (see Article 2.5 of Commission of the European Communities (1996) 'Proposal for a Council directive on the framework agreement on parental leave concluded by UNICE, CEEP and the ETUC', COM(96) 26, 31.1.1996; and Article 3 of Commission of the European Communities (1997) 'Proposal for a Council directive concerning the framework agreement on part-time work concluded by UNICE, CEEP and the ETUC', COM(97) 392, 23.7.1997).

[228] In view of the Commission they even retain a priority role in the interpretation of the agreements' provisions. According to Clause 4.6 of the Framework agreement on parental leave 'any matter relating to the interpretation of this agreement at European level should, in the first instance, be referred by the Commission to the signatory parties who will give an opinion'. A similar provision is implied in the preambles of the part-time and fixed-work agreements. However, the European Court of Justice has not confirmed this.   [229] See Article 211(1) EC.

[230] Commission of the European Communities (1993) 'Communication concerning the application of the Agreement on Social Policy, presented by the Commission to the Council and to the European Parliament', COM(93) 600, 14.12.1993, para. 39; Commission of the European Communities (1998) 'Commission communication: adapting and promoting the social dialogue at Community level', COM (98) 322, Brussels, 20.5.1998, p. 17; Case T-135/96, *Union Européenne de l'Artisanat et des Petites et Moyennes Entreprises (UEAPME) v Council*, [1998] ECR II-2334, considerations 88 and 89; Commission of the European Communities (1996) 'Proposal for a Council directive on the Framework agreement on parental leave concluded by UNICE, CEEP and the ETUC', COM(96) 26, Brussels 31.1.1996, consideration 9; Commission of the European Communities (1997) 'Proposal for a Council directive concerning the Framework agreement on part-time work concluded by UNICE, CEEP and the ETUC', COM(97) 392, Brussels, 27.7.1997, consideration 12; and Commission of the European Communities (1999) 'Proposal for a Council Directive concerning the Framework agreement on fixed-term work concluded by UNICE, CEEP and the ETUC', COM(99) 203, Brussels, 28.4.1999, consideration 13.   [231] Ibid.

Council is supposed to modify the agreement. The Council can either adopt an agreement or decline to endorse it. Even if the Commission has no formal right of modification, it may still modify an arrangement in an indirect way. The Commission could refuse to submit it to the Council and bring forward its own proposal instead. This proposal could adjust the agreement to the Commission's own preferences. The Commission and Council have to ensure that other interests do not find themselves unduly ignored as a result of the social dialogue process.

This censorship of the Commission and Council relinquishes when the social partners, as in the case of the telework and work-related stress agreements, decide to implement their agreement reached under the Article 138 EC procedure by themselves. In that case, the social partners gain the independence from the Union institutions as to bringing into effect an agreement. But, this autonomy is not unlimited. This route is considered by the Commission to be inappropriate where fundamental rights or important political opinions are at stake, or in situations where the rules must be applied in a uniform fashion in all member states and coverage must be complete. In those cases, preference should be given to implementation by a Council decision. Autonomous agreements, concludes the Commission, are also not appropriate for the revision of previously existing Directives adopted by the Council and European Parliament through the normal legislative procedure.[232] Agreements on topics with a wider social impact, such as pension entitlements or working time, probably also would not be considered to be eligible to be implemented by the social partners themselves.

Moreover, the social dialogue agreements intended to be implemented by social partners do not absolutely escape the Commission control. It is adamant to undertake its own monitoring of those agreements, to assess the extent to which they have contributed to the achievement of the EU objectives, and put forward a proposal for a legislative act should it decide that those accords do not meet the Treaty aims. The Commission may exercise its right of initiative at any point, including during the implementation period, should it conclude that either management or labour is delaying in pursuit of union objectives.[233]

Another important change is that whereas in the past, social dialogue at the European and national levels was rather disconnected, now there is greater interaction between the two, with the European social dialogue having a greater impact than before on national social dialogue. This means that the national social partners now have a greater need to engage at the European level, but also that the impact of the European social dialogue will, in the future, largely depend on the way in which its results are reintegrated at the national level.

---

[232] Commission of the European Communities (2004) 'Communication from the Commission: Partnership for change in an enlarged Europe—Enhancing the contribution of European social dialogue', COM(2004) 557, 12.8.2004, p.10.   [233] Ibid.

B. Autonomy of the social partner in the OMC

Besides gaining greater autonomy within the social dialogue procedure, which applies in the area of European social policy, the social partners are becoming more independent in their actions conducted within the OMC. Their autonomy within the OMC has been enhanced due to the role they have been assigned in the implementation of the Lisbon strategy,[234] and more generally in the synchronization of other national policies through the OMC.

The joint work programme 2003–2005 has been actually adopted by the social partners in order to enable them to adequately and effectively respond to the increase of their responsibilities for the conception and implementation of the European strategy for growth and employment. In this programme, they agreed to report on social partner actions in member states that are relevant for the implementation of the European employment guidelines. The duty to report on the progress achieved in the implementation of employment guidelines originally has been reserved exclusively for the member states.

Their frameworks of action for the development of competence and qualifications and on gender equality are based on that approach.[235] Of those frameworks of action that are not regulatory, the social partners are to implement on their own by making use of the open method of co-ordination machinery.[236] The role of social dialogue in promoting vocational education and training and lifelong learning is likely to be increased through this mode of co-ordination.[237] It is particularly significant that the social partners are producing annual reports on progress in the priority areas identified and that the social dialogue ad hoc group on education and training will undertake an evaluation after three years in March 2006.

---

[234] See the conclusions of the Lisbon, Barcelona, Nice, and Stockholm European Councils. Mr S. Dimas, Commissioner responsible for Employment and Social Affairs, asserts in his address to the Tripartite Social Summit for Growth and Employment held on 25 March 2004 in Brussels, that the success of the Lisbon strategy depends to a very great extent on the social partners' commitment to take action in this area.

[235] European Trade Union Confederation, Union of Industrial and Employers' Confederations of Europe—UNICE/UEAPME, European Centre of Enterprises with Public Participation and of Enterprises of General Economic Interest (2002) 'Framework of actions for the lifelong development of competencies and qualifications', 14 March 2002, http:/www.unice.org, points 26–29; and ETUC, UNICE, CEEP (2005) Framework of actions on gender equality of 22 March 2005, http://www.unice.org, points 30–341.

[236] Commission of the European Communities (2002) 'Communication from the Commission: the European social dialogue, a force for innovation and change', COM(2002) 341, Brussels, 26. 6.2002, p.18.

[237] The position of the social partners should be especially enhanced in relation to the development of curricula and qualifications; the provision of information, advice and guidelines; and evaluating the impact on both companies and workers (Galgoczi, Bela, Celine Lafoucriere and Lars Magnusson (2004) (eds.), *The Enlargement of Social Europe: The Role of the Social Partners in the European Employment Strategy*, (Brussels: ETUI).

C. Limitations of the social dialogue autonomy
in Union lawmaking

Although the increased autonomy of the social dialogue in EU policy-formation and implementation is the crucial factor that distinguishes it from the civil dialogue designed as a framework for conducting the consultations with interest groups by European institutions, the limits of this autonomy should be recognized.

First, the precise status and intended practical impact of the social partners instruments adopted under their joint work programme 2003–2005 is somewhat uncertain. For example, the European level social partners' text of a statement on managing socially responsible enterprise reconstruction falls short of constituting a code of conduct or a set of recommendations but, assuming that it is ratified by the national social partners organisations, it can be expected that trade unions and employee representative bodies, such as European Works Councils will seek to use its contents to promote good practice by companies in the handling of restructuring. However, unions are unlikely to see it as representing a comprehensive response to the challenges posed by restructuring.

As the social dialogue becomes triggered less by the Commission and depends more upon the willingness and capacities of the social partners to recognize joint concerns and make the necessary resources available for formulating and implementing joint policies, the issue of the social partner capability to sincerely engage in negotiation and effectively implement agreements is likely to aggravate the problems concerning willingness of all the parties to participate in the social dialogue, and those relating to implementation and monitoring. A social dialogue agreement independently initiated, adopted as an non-legally-binding instrument to be implemented by the signatories themselves demands closer involvement of the member organizations in terms of mandating European level organizations, overcoming institutional diversity, and a coherent implementation and monitoring agreements. European management and labour has yet to undertake measures in order to curb those obstacles to autonomous social dialogue at EU level.

The newly developed practice of the social partner to initiate the European level negotiation on their own, as in the case of the stress at work agreement, without being stimulated by the Commission's proposal, raises many controversies. Until recently, the main incentive for the engagement of the social partners into negotiations was the fact that the proposals launched by the Commission could have been adopted through the legislation if the social partners fail to reach an agreement. That happened on several occasions.[238] Negotiation on data protection at the workplace even failed after adoption of the programme. In the absence of any economic pressure for both sides of industry to foster the collective bargaining on the EU level,[239] and due to the lack of appropriate power balance between

---

[238] See above.
[239] Fredman, Sandra (1998) 'Social law in the European Union: the impact of the law making process' in Paul Craig, and Carol Harlow, (eds.), *Law making in the European Union*, pp. 386–411, p. 408.

European trade unions and employer organizations,[240] the incentive for the social partners to negotiate was the regulation that would be enacted if bargaining failed. In other words, the ability to pre-empt legislation formulated by the Commission prompted the social partners into negotiations when the incentive for UNICE was to obtain legislation which is more favourable to its interests than would be the case for legislation adopted via traditional channel. However, this negative motivation is rather weak and becomes less and less credible as a basis for the development of negotiating practice at EU level from the employers' perspective since the stream of legislative proposals by the Commission is declining.[241]

If the joint work programme 2003–2005 and not a Commission proposal is to serve as the basis for the initiation of the social dialogue, the treat of legislation ceases to provide the pressure to bargain. Whether the joint work programme can substitute the treat of the adoption of less favourable law as the incentive for conducting the EU social dialogue remains to be seen. This couches approach is even more justifiable if we take into consideration that even the agreements concluded by the social partners within the social dialogue procedure in the shadow of law were modest in substantive terms.[242] Additionally, the collaboration of the social partners on issues occupying the central stage of work relations such as equal opportunities for men and women still need to be developed.[243]

The second problem which cast doubts as to the significance of the increased autonomy of the social dialogue in EU governance concerns the implementation of

[240] Lo Faro, Antonio (2000) *Regulating Social Europe: Reality and Myth of Collective Bargaining in the EC Legal Order*, (Oxford: Hart); Smismans, Stijn (2004) *Law, Legitimacy, and European Governance: Functional Participation in Social Regulation*, (Oxford: Oxford University Press Publishing), pp. 363 and 370, Obradovic, Daniela (2001) 'The impact of the social dialogue procedure on the powers of European Union institutions' in Hugh Compston and Justin Greenwood, (eds.), *Social Partnership in the European Union*, (Hampshire: Palgrave), pp. 71–97, pp. 81–86; Bernard, Nick (2000) 'Legitimising EU law: is the social dialogue the way forward? Some reflections around the UEAPME case', in Jo Shaw, (ed.), *Social Law and Policy in an Evolving European Union*, (Oxford: Hart Publishing), p. 298; Green-Cowles, M (1995) 'Setting the agenda for a new Europe: the ERT and EC 1992', Journal of Common Market Studies, 33, pp. 501–526; Sadholz, W. and Zysman, J. (1989) '1992: recasting the European bargain', World Politics, 42, pp. 95–128; Apeldoorn, van B. (2000) 'Transnational class agency and European governance: the case of the European Round Table of Industrialist', New Political Economy, 5: 167–181; Hoffman, J., Hoffman. R., K irton-Darling, J., and Rampeltshammer, L. (2002) The Europeanisation of Industrial Relations in a Global Perspective: A Literature Review, (Luxembourg: European Foundation for the Improvement of Living and Working Conditions/Office for Official Publications of the European Communities), p. 58.

[241] Falkner, G (2003) 'The interproffesional social dialogue at European level: past and future' in B. Keller and W.-H. Platzer, (eds.), *Industrial Relations and European Integration*, (Aldershot: Ashgate), pp. 11–29, p. 24.

[242] Schmidt, Marlene (1999) 'Representativity –aA claim not satisfied: the social partners' role in the EC law-making procedure for social policy', The International Journal of Comparative Labour Law and Industrial Relations, 15(3): 259–267, pp. 262–262; Greenwood, Justin (2002) 'Advocacy, influence and persuasion: has it all been overdone?' in Alex Warleigh, and Jenny Fairbrass, (eds.), *Influence and Interests in the European Union: The New Politics of Persuasion and Advocacy*, (London: Europa publications), pp. 19–34, p. 28.

[243] European Foundation for the Improvement of Living and Working Conditions (2002) 'Quality of Women's Work and Employment: Tools for Charge, Foundation Paper No 3', (Luxembourg: Office for Official Publications of the European Communities).

The second problem concerns the lack of any power of European peak associations over their affiliates.[251] The signatories of Euro-agreements can deploy only internal rules in order to ensure the compliance of their national members with the provisions of those accords. On the basis of internal rules of procedure, national organizations can be expelled if they do not act in conformity with these internal rules. This could be the case if they do not implement European collective agreements.[252] The internal rules of procedure of most European social partners' organizations do not, however, give any specific rules with regard to the obligations of the national affiliates flowing from the conclusion of the European collective agreements.

Furthermore, not all-national social partners are associated with the European organizations participating in the social dialogue.[253] Arguably this could mean that the agreement might not apply in workplaces where either the employer is not affiliated to the national organization, which is in turn affiliated to UNICE or CEEP, or there is no union which is a member of the national union which is in turn affiliated to the ETUC. Thus, a situation could develop where coverage becomes patchy, particularly in member states characterized by relatively weak trade union density[254] and representation at the work place and patchy collective bargaining coverage.[255] The binding effect of the collective agreement can be extended to all workers and employers by means of a national legislative measure.[256] This means that the agreement will apply to all workers and employers in the whole branch of industry, regardless of whether they are a member of a trade union or employers association. However, in the majority of member states the collective bargaining in principle revolves around the sectoral social partners' level and quite rarely around intersectoral, cross-industry management and labour associations which further complicate the application of erga omnes validity rules. Organizations which are not affiliated to the agreement signatories can oppose agreement. Additionally, problems arise as certain member states do not have procedures to provide for an erga omnes effect of collective agreements, while at the same time, the binding effect of the collective agreements, as far as the hierarchy of legal sources (legislation, work rules, individual agreements, customs, etc.) is concerned, differs considerably from country to country. Not all the member states have developed reliable methods for implementing universally and compulsory intersectoral nationwide collective agreements to the entire body of employers and employees. Namely, the collective bargaining practices vary significantly from the member state to the member state. The enforceability of social

[251] Franssen, Edith (2002) *Legal Aspects of the European Social Dialogue*, (Antwerp: Intersentia), p. 126.
[252] Ibid, p. 179.
[253] Obradovic, Daniela (1995) 'Prospects for corporatist decision-making in the European Union: the social policy agreement' Journal of European Public Policy, 2(2): 261–283, p. 268.
[254] For an overview of trade union density rates and membership composition for the period 1995–2002 in the EU member state see European Commission (2004) *Industrial Relations in Europe 2004*, (Luxembourg: Office for Official Publications of the European Communities), p. 19.
[255] For an overview of collective bargaining coverage in the EU member state, see ibid, p. 31.
[256] For example, in the Netherlands and Belgium, but not in the United Kingdom. For an overview of the practices of legal or administrative extension of collective agreements in the EU member states, see ibid, p. 33.

partners agreements on individual terms and conditions of employment may be extremely uneven in the various countries.[257] Some member states have procedures for extension of agreements to the private sector as a whole, others do not. In some member states, eg Sweden, Denmark and Finland, there is no possibility of extending a collective agreement on non-unionized workers through State practices. Even where member states employ extension procedures for applying national collective agreements erga omnes, these rules differ greatly, particularly with respect to so-called normative clauses of agreements, ie those where, there are no real guarantees that the agreement will be fully and erga omnes implemented through the existing national collective bargaining structures or mechanisms.

D. Limitations of the social dialogue autonomy in the OMC

The increased autonomy of the social partners within the OMC also should not be considered without reservations. Although the social partners are assigned a quite prominent role in the formulation of the EES, the extend to which their opinion is taken into account is not clear. There was, also, little participation by the social partners in the shaping of the guidelines and the NAPs.[258] It has been recognized in the official evaluation of the Employment strategy as well as in studies carried out by independent research institutions and scholars, that the participation of national social partners is a weak point of the strategy, steaming partially from the difficulty that the social partners have in reaching agreements among themselves,[259] though their participation in the EES has improved over the last few years,[260] and some good exemplary practices have been

---

[257] Treu, Tiziano (1996) 'European collective bargaining levels and the competences of the social partners' in Paul Davies *et al.*, (eds.), *European Community Labour Law: Principles and Perspectives: Liber Amicorum Lord Wedderburn of Charlton*, (Oxford, Clarendon Press), pp. 169–187, p. 173.

[258] Mosher, James S. and Trubek, David. M. (2003) 'Alternative approaches to governance in the EU: EU social policy and the European Employment Strategy', Journal of Common Market Studies, 41(1): 63–88, p. 81; European Commission (2002) *Joint Employment Report*, (Luxembourg: Office for Official Publications of the European Communities).

[259] Commission of European Communities (2002) 'Impact evaluations of the European Employment Strategy: technical analysis supporting COM(2002) 416 final of 17.7.2002 ('Taking stock of five years of the EES'), http://europa.eu.int/comm/employment_social/employment_strategy/impact_en.htm, p. 40; Commission of European Communities (20020 'Communication from the Commission "The European social dialogue, a force for innovation and change" ' COM (2002) 341, 26 June 2002, p. 15; European Commission (2004) 'Communication from the Commission to the Council—Draft Joint employment report 2003/2004, COM(2004) 24, p.4; European Association for Territorial Excellence (2002) Contribution by National Social Partners to the Luxembourg Process (http://europa.eu.int/comm/employment_social/news/2003/jan/coporso_en.pdf); Goetschy, J. (2003) 'The European employment strategy and the open method of co-ordination: lessons and perspectives', Transfer, 9(2): 281–301.

[260] Commission of European Communities (2002) 'Impact evaluations of the European Employment Strategy: technical analysis supporting COM(2002) 416 final of 17.7.2002 ('Taking stock of five years of the EES'), http://europa.eu.int/comm/employment_social/employment_strategy/impact_en.htm, p. 241; High level group chaired by Wim Kok (2004) *Facing the Challenge: The Lisbon strategy for Growth and Employment*, (Luxembourg: Office for Official publications of the European Communities) p. 40; Porte, Caroline de la and Pochest, Philippe (2005) 'Participation in the open method of co-ordination: the cases of employment and social inclusion' in

developed.[261] The social partners point out that although they are usually consulted during the preparation of the NAPs, their comments are not equally taken into account in all the member states.[262] The synchronization and streaming of the broad economic policy guidelines (BEPG) and EES did not change significantly ways of involving of social partners.[263]

Current research indicates that the participation of the social partners in the OMC within the European Employment strategy has proven to be uneven, especially among trade unions.[264] These studies suggest that the NAPs have only contributed to a genuine consultation between the social partners and governments in countries with economy-wide agreements (Finland, Ireland, and the Netherlands) or those with experience of tripartite bargaining (Sweden, Austria, Denmark, Luxembourg). Even in those countries where consultation has taken place, the impact of the social partners was still only of limited nature, since governments view the NAPs as documents, which illustrate national policies of the past couched in the language of future policy action. The influence of the social partners is even more limited in the remaining countries, where at best formal and empty forms of consultations take place with the social partners.[265] Moreover, the cross-national survey conducted by the European Foundation for the Improvement of Living and Working Conditions shows that contribution of the social partners to the development of national action plans on employment remains quite insignificant.[266] Further, the social partners themselves acknowledged that ways of involving social partners did not change significantly with the synchronisation and streaming of the Broad Economic Policy Guidelines (BEPG) and the EES. Generally, no direct link can be perceived between social partners' involvement in constructing the MAP employment and drawing up the national reports on implementation of BEPG.[266a]

Jonathan Zeitling and Philippe Pochet, (eds.), *The Open Method of Co-ordination in Action: The European Employment and Social Inclusion Strategies*, (Brussels: P.I.E.-Peter Lang), pp. 353–389, p. 369; ETUC, UNICE/UEAPME, CEEP (2005) 2005 report on social partner actions on employment in member states, 22 March 2005 (http://www.ueapme.org).

[261] Danau, Dominique, Koutsivitou, Anastasia, Tortopidis, Antonios, and Winterton, Jonathan (2000) *Factors for Success: A Compendium of Social Partner Initiatives relating to the Employment Guidelines of the European Employment Strategy*, (Brussels: CEEP, ETUC and UNICE/UEAPME).

[262] ETUC, UNICE/UEAPME, CEEP (2005) 2005 report on social partner actions on employment in member states, 22 March 2005 (http://www.ueapme.org), pp. 14–18.   [263] Ibid.

[264] Porte, Caroline, de la and Pochet, Philippe (2004) 'The European Employment strategy: existing research and remaining questions', Journal of European Social Policy, 14(1): 71–78, p. 74; Commission of the European Communities (2002) 'Communication from the Commission to the Council, the European Parliament, the Economic and Social Committee and the Committee of the Regions: taking stock of five years of the European Employment Strategy', COM(2002) 416, Brussels, 17.7.2002. European Commission (2003) Communication 'The Future of the European Employment Strategy (EES): a strategy for full employment and better jobs for all', COM (2002) 6, 14 January 2003, Brussels.

[265] Arnold, Christine and Pennings, Paul (2004) 'Recent developments in EU level social policy making and corporatist governance' in Andreas Warntjen and Arndt Wonka,. (eds.), *Governance in Europe: The Role of Interest Groups*, (Baden-Baden: Nomos), pp. 113–129, p. 121.

[266] European Foundation for the Improvement of Living and Working Conditions (2004) Social Partners Involvement in the 2003 NAPs, http://www.eiro.eurofound.eu.int/thematicfeatures5.html

[266a] ETUC, UNICE/UEAPME/CEEF (2005) '2005 Report on social partners' actions on employment in member states', 22 March 2005 (http://WWW.uaepme.org), p.17.

The shabbiness of the social partners participation in employment NAPs can be best illustrated by the de la Porte and Pochet finding based on the empirical studies that the involvement of NGOs in the social inclusion OMC, which is regarded as very weak, is better overall than that of social partners in the EES.[267]

The real impact of the social partners texts adopted on their own initiative addressing the Lisbon themes is very limited. One common difficulty is that many of those texts contain imprecise and vogue follow-up provisions. Effective follow-up at national level is, however, only possible if the European social partners' texts include detailed provisions on this.[268]

Furthermore, the Commission finds that there is a lack of commitment to the Employment strategy on the labour side, and a reluctance to become involved on the employers' side, both at the European and national level[269] since there is no convergence, but continuing divergence of the national industrial relations systems in Europe.[270]

One of the possible explanations for the relatively feeble involvement of the social partner in the employment NAPs is that the agenda of the EES side-steps the main issues with which social partners are concerned: the EES is focused on the increasing of the EU employment rate, while social partners are mainly interested in wage policies, although the Wim Kok group has managed to bring the issue on the agenda in the country specific recommendations.[271] Second, the lack of financial resources could be obstacle, although the social partners, as explained above, are entitled to apply to the European Structural Fund for grants for improving their organizational capacities. The lack of institutional rootedness of the EES within the national policy process and of the real benefits for employers' and employees' association also hinders their dedication to participate in the OMC.

---

[267] Porte, Caroline de la and Pochest, Philippe (2005) 'Participation in the open method of co-ordination: the cases of employment and social inclusion' in Jonathan Zeitling and Philippe Pochet, (eds.), *The Open Method of Co-ordination in Action: The European Employment and Social Inclusion Strategies*, (Brussels: P.I.E.-Peter Lang), pp. 353–389, p. 383.

[268] The Commission of the European Communities (2004) 'Communication from the Commission: Partnership for change in an enlarged Europe—Enhancing the contribution of European social dialogue', COM(2004) 557, 12.8.2004, p. 6.

[269] Porte, Caroline de la and Nanz, Patrizia (2004) 'The OMC—a deliberative-democratic mode of governance? The case of employment and pensions' Journal of European Public Policy, 11(2); 267–288, p. 279; Commission of European Communities (2002) 'Impact evaluations of the European Employment Strategy: technical analysis supporting COM(2002) 416 final of 17.7.2002 ('Taking stock of five years of the EES'), http://europa.eu.int/comm/employment_social/employment_strategy/impact_en.htm, p. 41.

[270] Traxler, F. (1995) 'Farewell to labour market associations? Organised versus disorganised decentralisation as a map for industrial relations', in C. Crouch and F. Taxler, (eds.), Organized Industrial Relations: What Future, (Hants: Averbury: Aldershot).

[271] Porte, Caroline de la and Pochest, Philippe (2005) 'Participation in the open method of co-ordination: the cases of employment and social inclusion' in Jonathan Zeitling and Philippe Pochet, (eds.) *The Open Method of Co-ordination in Action: The European Employment and Social Inclusion Strategies*, (Brussels: P.I.E.-Peter Lang), pp. 353–389, p. 369.

VII. Why the Social Partners Enjoy Stronger Position in EU Governance than Civic Groups

It has been shown, that although both the civil and the social dialogue have to play a part in EU governance, the influence of the latter by far supersede the input of the former. This inequality of powers of non-profit, diffuse interest groups on one side and management and labour on the other, evolved within the civil and social dialogue, persists in the OMC. Although both of those groups are guaranteed a place in EU policy creation and implementation, the position of civil groups is appreciably weaker.

Thus, one should ask why the desirability of a greater involvement of non-profit or civic groups in the process of the implementation of the European employment strategy and social policy has been (as shown above) declared in a range of Union documents, but very little has been done towards the operationalization and putting into practice of these pronounced commitments.

The fact that the Commission insists on civil society meeting certain standards raises questions not only as to whether the Commission is consistent in its demands, but also as to whether a civil society which conforms to such demands carries with it the potential associated with the domain of social action.

It is submitted in this article that the social dialogue owns its superiority over the civil dialogue to its unique powers arising from the position of its protagonists in the sphere of production.

Although it can be credibly argued that the institutional structure of the voluntary organizations operating at the European level is inappropriate for the systematic engagement of these associations in the Union policy process,[272] the weakness of their transnational structure cannot be regarded as a reason for explaining the inferior position of the civil dialogue in relation to the social dialogue. The institutional structure of the social dialogue participants, the European labour and business confederations, is also considered to be inadequate for their involvement in Union lawmaking.[273] The Commission itself warns that the social partners have to develop internal structures that would permit them to react to developments at European level. This presupposes a real commitment from their members in providing them with adequate resources and structures.[274] The Commission is, in particular, concerned with the technical capacity of the European social partner

[272] For a short overview of the scholarship claiming that due to lack of technical competence, resources, and negotiating skills 'NGOs are generally unprepared for the EU system', see Ruzza, Carlo (2002) ' "Frame bridging" and the new politics of persuasion, advocacy and influence' in Alex Warleigh, and Jenny Fairbrass, (eds.), *Influence and Interests in the European Union: The New Politics of Persuasion and Advocacy*, (London: Europa Publications), pp. 93–117, p. 95.

[273] Obradovic, D. (1995) 'Prospects for corporatist decision-making in the European Union: the social policy agreement', Journal of European Public Policy 2(2): pp. 261–283.

[274] Commission of the European Communities (1998) 'Commission Communication "Adapting and promoting the social dialogue at Community level" ', COM(98) 322, Brussels, 20.5.1998, p. 8; European Commission (2002) 'The European social dialogue, a force for innovation and change', COM(2002)341, Brussels, 26.6.2002, p. 8.

organizations to engage in the social dialogue.[275] The limitations in the associational capacities of the social partner organizations concerns the lack of resources of European management and labour associations, difficulties with synchronization of sectoral with cross-sectoral interests since European sectoral business associations are not incorporated in UNICE, and low governability of some national social partners structures for the implementation of cross-border co-ordination.[276] The problem which the European non-profit organizations experience in respect of infrastructure, the heterogeneous nature of their members, the problem of representativity, the inability to implement mutual agreements, insufficient transparency in dialogue, etc. are equally applicable to the social partners. For example, although the question of representativeness of civil organizations raises more contraventions than that of the social partners, the latter also experience problems in that domain. Indeed, an obviously difficulty here is that levels of membership, both for trade unions and employers' organizations are, in many member states, low and what is worse, have been significantly declining over the past two decades.[277] The criteria of representativity specified by the Commission are strictly formal. They relate only to the associations' organizational structure and say nothing about whether the agreements adequately address the interests that the agreement affects and supposedly represents. To be representative means 'representing the objective interests of those affected and/or involved'. The view that the three big umbrella organizations UNICE, CEEP, and ETUC represent all categories of employers and employees, seems to be a highly problematic expedient. Not only are many of the national trade unions and employers' associations not included in these organizations,[278] but the decision-making structures within them, based on the majority principle—often excludes or sidelines important and significant minority views.[279] Furthermore, complication arises if one considers that certain groups of employees clearly appear as under-represented within the trade unions. The proportion of trade union members who are atypical workers—part-time workers, fixed-term and temporary workers—is usually considerably lower than their proportion within the workforce. In particular, women workers are under-represented.[280]

Thus, it can be concluded that the social dialogue does not owe its prevalence over the civil dialogue in EU governance to the better organized institutional structure.

[275] The Commission of the European Communities (2004) 'Communication from the Commission: Partnership for change in an enlarged Europe—Enhancing the contribution of European social dialogue', COM(2004) 557, 12.8.2004, p. 3.

[276] Taxler, Franz (1999) 'Wage-setting institutions and European Monetary Union' in Huemer, G. *et al*, (eds.), *The Role of Employer Associations and Labour Unions in the EMU: Institutional Requirements for European Economic Policies*, (Aldershot: Ashgate), pp. 115–135, p. 132.

[277] Visser, J. (1999) 'Societal support for social dialogue. Europe's trade unions and employers' associations' in Huemer, G. *et al*, (eds.), *The Role of Employer Associations and Labour Unions in the EMU: Institutional Requirements for European Economic Policies*, (Aldershot: Ashgate), pp. 85–114, (pp. 89 and 95).

[278] For example, one of the leading French unions, CGT is not member of the ETUC.

[279] Betten. Lamy (1998) 'The democratic deficit of participatory democracy in Community social policy' European Law Review, 23(1): 20–36.

[280] This problem is recognized by the Commission in (Social Europe, 4, 1995).

We argue that the social dialogue derives its distinctiveness as to the civil dialogue from the special powers and responsibilities of its participants in the social-economic sphere within which these two modes of EU governance operate. The main factor which contributes towards the distinction of the roles of the social and civil dialogue in the EU policy process is the wide acceptance on the European level that only strategic actors, such as management and labour representatives should be given a permanent and critical role in lawmaking, policy co-ordination and policy implementation because they are considered to be resourceful partners in the carrying out of Union key economic projects.

In the Commissions' view the attainment of the Lisbon strategy goals depends to a considerable extent on the action taken by the social partners.[281] Social dialogue is considered in the Union, as shown above, to be the driving force behind successful economic and social reforms envisaged in Lisbon.

The other important Union project, the establishment of the Economic and Monetary Union (EMU) cannot either be completed without the involvement of the social partners. The member states recognize the crucial importance of strict budgetary discipline and elimination of excessive general government deficit for the successful completion of Monetary Union.[282] This budgetary discipline should contribute towards the strengthening of the conditions for price stability and non-inflationary economic growth which are the prime aims of the establishment of the EMU. The restriction of considerable increases in wages is an essential element of any economic strategy aimed at pursuing price stability and low inflation. Moreover, monetary policy itself becomes very difficult whenever wage responsiveness significantly varies across countries.[283] Consequently, under EMU, nominal wages should on average progress in a manner that is compatible with the objective of price stability.[284] This cannot be achieved without the social partners' support.[285] In particular, the Council invited the social partners in member states to conclude wage agreements in accordance with four general rules: (i) aggregate nominal wage increases consistent with price stability; (ii) increases

[281] European Commission (2002) 'The European social dialogue, a force for innovation and change', COM(2002) 341, Brussels, 26.6.2002, p. 6; Commission of the European Communities (2004) 'Communication from the Commission: Partnership for change in an enlarged Europe—Enhancing the contribution of European social dialogue', COM(2004) 557, 12.8.2004, Memo/04/211, p.1.

[282] See Article 104 EC. See also European Council (1997) 'Resolution of the European Council on the stability and growth pact', Bull. EU 6–1997, point 1.27.

[283] Taxler, Franz (1999) 'Wage-setting institutions and European Monetary Union' in Huemer, G. *et al*, (eds.), *The Role of Employer Associations and Labour Unions in the EMU: Institutional Requirements for European Economic Policies*, (Aldershot: Ashgate), pp. 115–135, p. 118.

[284] Council Recommendation 98/454/EC of 6 July 1998 on the broad guidelines of the economic policies of the member states and the Community, OJ L200/44, 16.0.1998, point 2. This message has been updated in the subsequent guidelines. See in particular, European Commission (2003) *Employment in Europe 2003*, (Luxembourg: Office for the Official Publications of the European Communities) p. 75 and Commission of the European Communities (2005) 'Integrated guidelines for growth and jobs', COM(2005) 141, Brussels, 12.4.2005, pp. 15–16.

[285] European Commission (2002) *Report of the High Level Group on Industrial Relations and Change in the European Union*, (Luxembourg: Office for Official Publications of the European Communities), p.12.

in real wages which safeguard the profitability of capacity-enhancing and employment-creating investment; (iii) taking better into account differences in productivity levels according to qualifications, skills and geographical areas; and (iv) avoidance of wage imitation effects.[286]

The collaboration with representatives of both sides of the production chain, employers and labour is considered in the Union to be the most suitable way for securing the national budgetary discipline deemed to be a necessary requirement for participation in the EMU and ensuring that a reduction in the government deficit does not contribute to a sharp increase in unemployment. This prompts the Commission to conclude that 'the EMU process and economic convergence have progressively made visible the importance of the role of social partners, not only in influencing the local competitiveness and employment conditions, but also as a major player in the achievement of growth and an employment-friendly overall policy mix in the Euro zone and in the Community'.[287] Thus, the social partners gained privileged access to policy processes in the Union because they are considered to be in control of national working arrangements targeted by EU most pressing undertakings, the Lisbon strategy and the EMU requirements.[288] On the other hand, civic interest groups not involved in economic activity are considered to be helpful but not essential and not the most capable partners in pursuing the abovementioned policy preference. The Commission finds that, within civil society, the social partners have a particular role and influence, which flow from the very nature of the subjects they cover and the interests they represent in connection with the world of work.[289] The capacity of management and labour to conclude collective agreements on particular topics that include commitments, in the view of the Commission, distinguishes them substantially from other interest groups of a diffuse nature.[290] This capacity of policy implementation serves as a ground for the reinforcement of the involvement of the social partners in the decision-making process of the Union, as called for in the White paper on European governance. As the Commission put it, the social

[286] Council Recommendation 98/454/EC of 6 July 1998 on the broad guidelines of the economic policies of the member states and the Community, OJ L200/44, 16.0.1998, point 6.

[287] Commission of the European Communities (1998) 'Commission communication "Adapting and promoting the social dialogue at Community level"', COM (98) 322, 20.5.98, p. 4. See also Council Recommendation 99/570/EC, [1999] OJ L217/34.

[288] Working conditions, definition of wage standards, continuing training, particularly in new technologies organization of work and working time are few examples of specific topics relevant for the Lisbon strategy and the EMU, which the social partners are entitled to deal with.

[289] Commission of the European Communities (2001) 'European governance: white paper', COM(2001) 428, Brussels, 25.7.2001, p. 14.

[290] Commission of the European Communities (1998) 'Commission communication "Adapting and promoting the social dialogue at Community level",' COM(98) 322, Brussels, 20.5.1998, p. 4; European Commission (2002) 'The European social dialogue, a force for innovation and change', COM(2002) 341, Brussels, 26.6.2002, pp. 5 and 7; The Commission of the European Communities (2004) 'Communication from the Commission: Partnership for change in an enlarged Europe— Enhancing the contribution of European social dialogue', COM(2004) 557, 12.8.2004, p. 6. As the Council resolution on certain aspects for a European Union social policy explains, the social partners are 'as a rule closer to social reality and to social problems ([1994] OJ C368/6, II.3). See also, eg recital 9 of the parental leave Directive.

partners are on account of their implementary ability singular, inimitable players in the Union governance.[291] Consequently, the social partners and other interest groups are positioned differently in relation to the accessibility to the Union policy process.

VIII. The Social Dialogue and the Civil Dialogue: The Complementary Approach Developed by the Commission

The structured involvement of interest groups in EU governance revolves around the phenomena of the civil and social dialogues. Against the background of the significantly developed social dialogue and the embedded role of the limited number of private interest groups from production in Union policymaking, the Commission launched the civil dialogue initiative, intended to introduce numerous interest groups organized outside the sphere of production in EU decision-making. Throughout this study it has been established that the social dialogue occupies a more important place in the European policy formation and implementation process than the civil dialogue. The importance of the tasks assigned to the social partners in the EU governance exceeds by far the magnitude of the civil dialogue functions.

However, this inferior position of the civil dialogue in EU decision-making does not imply the existence of the contention between two of those modes of interest intermediation. The Commission considers the civil dialogue as a process complementary not antagonistic to the operation of the social dialogue.[292] A civil dialogue at European level, in the view of the Commission, should take it place alongside the policy dialogue with the national authorities and the social dialogue with the social partners.[293] The civil dialogue should not replace or compete with the social dialogue, but provide an adjunct to it. According to the Commission, the introduction of the civil dialogue is supposed to remedy the situation arising from the selective promotion of only producers' interests underscored by the social dialogue and from the consequent neglect of groups which lie outside the

---

[291] European Commission (2002) 'The European social dialogue, a force for innovation and change', COM(2002) 341, Brussels, 26.6.2002, p. 10.

[292] Commission of the European Communities (1994) 'European social policy—a way forward for the Union: a white paper', COM(94) 333, Brussels, 27.7.1994, p .44; European Commission (1996) Report by the Comite des Sages 'For a Europe of civic and social rights', Luxembourg: Office for Official Publications of the European Communities, p. 17; European Commission (1996) 'Progress report on the implementation of the Medium-term social action programme 1995–97', Social Europe, Supplement 4/96, pp. 1, 10, and 17; Commission of the European Communities (1997) 'Communication from the Commission on promoting the role of voluntary organisations and foundations in Europe', COM(97) 241, Brussels, 6.6.1997, point 9.7; and Commission of the European Communities (1998) 'Social action programme 1998–2000', COM(98) 259, Brussels, 29.4.1998, p. 4.

[293] Commission of the European Communities (1997) 'Communication from the Commission on promoting the role of voluntary organisations and foundations in Europe', COM(97) 241, Brussels, 6.6.1997, point 9.7.

productive centre of society.²⁹⁴ The EU is considered to systematically privileges business interest over other societal interests, thus creating special challenges to them.²⁹⁵ The Commission view that the social dialogue, which pursues the interests of producers, should be supplemented with the civil dialogue, which promotes interests excluded from profit-driven economic activity, and its proclamation for striking a balance between economic and social aspects of Union social policy, should be examined in the light of a widespread concern that there is political distortion in the Union which follows from the promotion of the special interests of management and labour, and lack of balance between economic-related and other societal interests.²⁹⁶ The civil dialogue should promote legitimate interests of non-productive part of the society and counter balance the interest representation of producers.²⁹⁷ It is concerned to correct the perceived bias in existing contributions favouring business and organized interests.²⁹⁸

Conversely, this Commission undertaking about complementarity of the civil and social dialogue and the balancing of interests' role assigned to the civil dialogue is extremely difficult to achieve in practice. For example, although the Commission consulted civil society associations on the issue of lifelong learning, the social partners used their vested position in the employment strategy to conclude the action plan on this matter without taking into consideration opinions expressed by the consulted civic organizations. This action plan which is to be implemented by the social partners by means of the OMC became an integral part of the official Union Employment strategy.

²⁹⁴ Commission of the European Communities (1993) 'Green paper: European social policy: opinions for the Union', COM(93) 551, Brussels, 17 November 1993, p. 72; European Commission (1996) 'A report on the Forum: Working on European Social Policy', Luxembourg: Office for Official Publications of the European Communities, p. 8; Commission of the European Communities (1997) 'Communication from the Commission on promoting the role of voluntary organisations and foundations in Europe', COM(97) 241, Brussels, 6.6.1997, points 7.1 and 7.2.

²⁹⁵ Polack, Markt A. (1997) 'Representing diffuse interests in EC policy-making', Journal of European Public Policy, 4(4): 572–590, p. 573. Whilst the precise number of European interest groups and fora is disputed, no one doubts the overwhelming predominance (80 per cent) of producer interests among the groups having contact with the Commission, (Greenwood, Justin (2003) *Interest Representation in the European Union*, (Houndmills: Palgrave) p. 19).

²⁹⁶ Wolfgang Streeck (1996) 'Neo-voluntarism: a new social policy regime' in Marks *et al.*, (eds.), *Governance in the European Union*, (London: Sage), pp. 64–94; Sonia Mazey and Jeremy Richardson (1997) 'Agenda setting, lobbying and the 1996 IGC' in Geoffrey Edwards and Alfred Pijpers, (eds), *The Politics of European Treaty Reform*, (London: Pinter), pp. 226–248, p. 236; George Vobruba (1995) 'Social policy tomorrow's Euro-corporatist stage', Journal of European social Policy, 5(4): 303–315. Overall the ability of NGOs to influence EU policy output is less that of corporate lobbyists. Balanya, B. *et al* (2000) *Europe Inc: Regional and Global Restructuring and the Rise of Corporate Power*, (London: Pluto). On balance, it has to be noted that there are also scholars who find that diffuse or civic interests are extensively incorporated in Union rulemaking. See eg, Alasdair R. Young and Hellen Wallace (2000) *Regulatory Politics in the Enlarging European Union: Weighing Civic and Producer Interests*, (Manchester: Manchester University Press), p. 28; Marck Pollack (1997) 'Representing diffuse interests in EC policy-making', Journal of European Public Policy, 4(4): 572–590.

²⁹⁷ European Commission (1996) *A Report on the Forum: Working on European Social Policy*, (Luxembourg: Office for Official Publications if the European Community), p. 8.

²⁹⁸ See on this Follesdal, Andreas (2003) 'The political theory of the white paper on governance: hidden and fascinating', European Public Law, 9(1): 73–86, p. 76.

process can improve capabilities of the Union to achieve its purposes in a less costly manner. For example, the involvement of the social partners is requested in an area of the cohesion policy because it is believed that it could reduce the presently high costs of managing of the Structural Fund, one of the main players in this domain.[306] Consequently, the social partners are, in general, accorded significantly formidable role than civil interest groups in EU governance because their ability to contribute towards implementation of European policies.

Can interest groups involved live up to such great expectations? Whether the greater participation of interest groups in the EU policy process can contribute towards the enhancement of legitimacy in the Union is the issue that exceeds the scope of this article. In the literature at present there exists no common opinion on this matter. Whilst some authors argue that organized interests could provide a core contribution to the reduction of the democratic deficit in the EU,[307] others view their stronger involvement as strengthening of the neo-liberal capitalist dominance of the European process.[308] The Commission itself does not advocate that the involvement of interest groups can necessarily increase legitimacy.[309] Although, the participation of civil organizations and the social partners in European policy-making and implementation can be regarded as a good option for securing to comply on the part of targeting groups as well as for obtaining knowledge about policy effects—and thereby a good option for achieving governability—their involvement cannot guarantee considerable improvement of the legitimacy in the Union. It is more intended to improve the effectiveness and efficiency of the EU decision-making, while disregarding the issue of legitimacy. The Commission acknowledges 'that the White Paper's call for the inclusion of more players in the policy process, while necessary, does not by itself lead to increased democratic legitimacy of policies and institutions'[310] It further insists that the better involvement of more players will actually enhance the effectiveness and efficiency of the decision-making system in the Union.[311] Similarly, the

---

[306] European Commission (2004) *New Partnership for Cohesion: Convergence, Competitiveness, Co-operation: Third Report on Economic and Social Cohesion*, (Luxembourg: Office for Official Publications of the European Communities), p. 17.

[307] For an overview of the debate, see Hosli, M.O. *et al.* (2004) 'Contending political-economy perspective on European interest groups' in Warntjen, Andreas and Wonka, Arndt, (eds.), *Governance in Europe: The Role of Interest Groups*, (Baden-Baden: Nomos), pp. 42–56, p. 42.

[308] Holman, O. and van der Pijl, K (2003) 'Structure and process in transnational European business' in A. Cafruny and M. Ryner, (eds.), *A Ruined Fortress? Neoliberal Hegemony and Transformation in Europe*, (Lanham: Rowman and Littlefield); Hosli, M.O. *et al.* (2004) 'Contending political-economy perspective on European interest groups' in Warntjen, Andreas and Wonka, Arndt. (eds.), *Governance in Europe: The Role of Interest Groups*, (Baden-Baden: Nomos), pp. 42–56, p. 46.

[309] Nevertheless, in its latest document on partnership for achieving the Union strategic objectives 2005–2009, the Commission expressly submits that this partnership which is to be developed between national parliaments, public authorities at all levels, social partners, civil society and voices of stakeholders through the community, will help to generate a sense of European identity (Commission of the European Communities (2005) 'Strategic objectives 2005–2009: Europe 2010: a partnership for European renewal: prosperity, solidarity and security, COM(2005) 12, Brussels, 26.1.2005, p. 5).

[310] Commission of the European Communities (2002) 'Report from the Commission on European governance', COM(2002) 705, Brussels, 11.12.2002, p. 28.   [311] Ibid.

White paper assumes that consultations will not institutionalize conflicts, but instead serve to secure effective policy-shaping.³¹²

At present, it hardly can be concluded that the involvement of interest groups in different policy processes in the Union dramatically increases efficiency of EU governance. The effective implementation of policies cannot be always guaranteed by involving civil actors. Indeed, this study demonstrates that there are considerable limitations on the part of the social partners and civil interest groups to contribute decisively towards the efficient conduct of EU policies. The social partners face significant barriers throughout the range of Union policies in the exercise of their autonomous functions, particularly those related to the implementation. As shown above, the engagement of the social partners in the implementation of the social policy agreements and the employment guidelines within the OMC meets considerable challenges.³¹³ Current research suggests that both on the national as well as the European level, the social partners have been, by large, left on the margins of the EES.³¹⁴ The contribution of the civic interest groups to the improvement of effectiveness of EU governance is even more doubtful. The extent to which the opinions of civil organization expressed in consultations carried out by the Commission are incorporated into its legislative proposals is unknown. Simultaneously, the impact of the engagement of civil associations in the various OMC areas has been minimal. Empirical research actually establishes that interest groups have not yet found a well-established place in the OMC.³¹⁵ Moreover, some governments, such as the Danish and Swedish, resist a greater involvement of civil society in the employment OMC since NGOs are perceived as an unpredictable factor in stable, traditional and well-functioning structures of social partnership of labour and management.³¹⁶

---

³¹² Commission of European Communities (2001) 'European governance: white paper', COM(2001) 428, Brussels, 25.7.2002, p. 12.

³¹³ There is also dissatisfaction with the involvement of the social partners in the work of agencies. See Smismans, Stijn (2004) *Law, legitimacy, and European Governance: Functional Participation in Social Regulation*, (Oxford: Oxford University Press), p. 253, p. 291.

³¹⁴ For an overview of the recent studies on this issue, see Arnold, Christine and Pennings, Paul (2004) 'Recent developments in EU level social policy making and corporatist governance' in Warntjen, Andreas and Wonka, Arndt. (eds.), *Governance in Europe: The Role of Interest Groups*, (Baden-Baden: Nomos), pp. 113–129, p. 121.

³¹⁵ For an overview of those empirical studies, see Smismans, Stijn (2004) *Law, legitimacy, and European Governance: Functional Participation in Social Regulation*, (Oxford: Oxford University Press), p. 253, p. 435.

³¹⁶ Porte, Caroline de la and Pochest, Philippe (2005) 'Participation in the open method of co-ordination: the cases of employment and social inclusion' in Jonathan Zeitling and Philippe Pochet, (eds.), *The Open Method of Co-ordination in Action: The European Employment and Social Inclusion Strategies*, (Brussels: P.I.E.-Peter Lang), pp. 353–389, p. 383. Some scholars uphold this view as well. See eg Smismans, Stijn (2004) *Law, legitimacy, and European Governance: Functional Participation in Social Regulation*, (Oxford: Oxford University Press), pp. 431–436.

European Universalism?—The EU and Human Rights Conditionality

Päivi Leino *

I. The EU and Universality

The Vienna World Conference on Human Rights of 1993 is celebrated by the Western world as a confirmation of the universality of human rights. During the Conference, states from all corners of the world gathered together and adopted a Declaration and Programme of Action, in which they declare 'their commitment to the purposes and principles contained in the Charter of the United Nations and the Universal Declaration of Human Rights' (hereafter the UDHR).[1] In the same document, the World Conference reaffirms:

[. . .] the solemn commitment of all States to fulfil their obligations to promote universal respect for, and observance and protection of, all human rights and fundamental freedoms for all in accordance with the Charter of the United Nations, other instruments relating to human rights, and international law. The universal nature of these rights and freedoms is beyond question.[2]

However, the same document also indicates that the universality of human rights referred to is compatible with the 'significance of national and regional particularities and various historical, cultural and religious backgrounds',[3] thus leaving room for differing interpretations.

The approach of the European Union (EU) proved very influential in the World Conference. In fact, the EU position paper, setting out the principles underpinning its own policy, formed the basis for the final conclusions of the Conference.[4]

* Erik Castrén Institute of International Law and Human Rights, University of Helsinki, Finland. I am grateful to Martti Koskenniemi and Marise Cremona for comments, discussions and suggestions. I also thank Martin Björklund, Kari Hakapää, Christophe Hillion, Jan Klabbers, Kati Kulovesi, Susan Marks and Orla Sheehy, for conversations that have greatly contributed to this article. All remaining errors of fact or weaknesses of opinion are, of course, my own responsibility.

[1] The Vienna Declaration and Programme of Action, adopted by the World Conference on Human Rights on 25 June 1993, A/Conf. 157/23, Preamble.   [2] ibid Part I, Para 1.
[3] ibid Part I, Para 5.
[4] The European Union and the External Dimension of Human Rights Policy: From Rome to Maastricht and Beyond, Communication from the Commission to the Council and European Parliament, (Brussels 22.11.1995, COM (95) 567 final, Para 18.)

Therefore, it is no surprise that for the EU, the documents adopted in Vienna 'created an action framework that is a particular source of inspiration'.[5] Even though the formal status of the Declaration is open to different interpretations, the EU has read the framework as placing states, and itself, under positive obligations. In this spirit:

The Community and its Member States undertake to pursue their policy of promoting and safeguarding human rights and fundamental freedoms throughout the world. This is the legitimate duty of the world community and of all States acting individually or collectively. [. . .] The European Community and its Member States seek universal respect for human rights.[6]

For the EU, universality of human rights, as confirmed in Vienna, has justified making both trade and development aid conditional on the implementation of human rights by third states.[7] The relationship between this practice and the principle of universality forms the main object of this study.

Today, the practice of appealing to the 'universal' language is not limited to the EU, but is invoked by several other Western organizations, such as the World Bank and NATO.[8] But when European human rights declarations are explored in more detail, a contradiction emerges: For the Europeans (and for the Americans), human rights derive from their own traditions, but they still constitute truly universal values. This understanding is already visible in the European Convention on Human Rights (ECHR), which combines elegantly the idea of human rights as both European and universal in declaring that the ECHR 'aims at securing the universal and effective recognition and observance of the rights therein declared'. Still, it states that the 'Governments of European Countries' are 'like-minded and have a common heritage of political traditions, ideals, freedom and the rule of law'.[9] This seems to suggest that while the European countries have a common heritage and have adopted a Convention together, their common enterprise has a vision and an aim that are universal in scope. A more recent example of thinking of this kind can be found in the Charter of Fundamental Rights of the Union.[10]

---

[5] Brussels 22.11.1995, COM (95) 567 final, Para 31. See also Report on the Implementation of Measures Intended to Promote Observance of Human Rights and Democratic Principles (For 1994), Brussels 12.07.1995, COM (95)191 final, 17.

[6] Declaration on human rights, adopted by the European Council, [1991] 6 Bull. EC 17. See also Statement on human rights, adopted by the Foreign Ministers meeting in political co-operation in Brussels on 21 July 1986, [1986] 7/8 Bull. EC 100, point 2.4.4. The same vision is continued in The European Union and the External Dimension of Human Rights Policy (n 4 above).

[7] ibid; Communication from the Commission on the inclusion of respect for democratic principles and human rights in agreements between the Community and third countries, Brussels 23 May 1995, COM (95)216 final.

[8] See K Rittich, *Recharacterizing Restructuring. Law, Distribution and Gender in Market Reform* (Kluwer Law International: 2002) 68–70.

[9] Convention for the Protection of Human Rights and Fundamental Freedoms (Rome, 4 November 1950, entered into force on 3 September 1953, CETS No 005) preamble.

[10] According to the Preamble of Charter of Fundamental Rights of the Union, 'conscious of its spiritual and moral heritage, the Union is based on indivisible and universal values'. The Charter was adopted on 7 December 2000 as a political declaration. It is included in the current draft Treaty for an EU Constitution.

But can human rights principles be both universal and shared by all mankind, and still be the defining characteristic of Europe?[11] The idea of human rights as being universal is actually a thoroughly European one.[12] But the problem is this: either human rights are universal and as such belong equally to everyone, which makes it difficult to use them as a distinctive attribute of Europe. Alternatively, Europe is explained as the defender of values that are shared by all, with Europe then charged with a special task to spread those values (because they are not really Europe's, but universal) elsewhere in the world.[13] This understanding is reflected in the draft Constitution of the European Union, which starts by enumerating the 'Union's values'.[14] According to the following Article, the 'Union's aim is to promote peace, its values and the well-being of its peoples'. Later the draft Constitution specifies that this objective has a strong international dimension:

The Union's action on the international scene shall be guided by, and designed to advance in the wider world, the principles which have inspired its own creation, development and enlargement: democracy, the rule of law, the universality and indivisibility of human rights and fundamental freedoms, respect for human dignity, equality and solidarity, and respect for the principles of the United Nations Charter and international law.[15]

This seems to suggest the way in which human rights are believed to function, as Duncan Kennedy has argued, as 'mediators between the domain of pure value judgments and the domain of factual judgments'.[16] Everyone is believed to aspire to rights in the same way, because they are commonly shared. Human rights are thus neither arbitrary nor subjective but automatically require certain measures to be taken in an objective manner.[17] This is also believed to place them outside

[11] See e.g. The European Union and the External Dimension of Human Rights Policy: From Rome to Maastricht and Beyond, Communication from the Commission to the Council and European Parliament, Brussels 22.11.1995, COM (95) 567 final, Para 12 [emphasis added], which argues that the Union has 'gradually come to *define itself* in terms of the promotion of human rights and democratic freedoms' in the 'international environment in which the universal nature of human rights is increasingly emphasized'.

[12] For a discussion of this point, see R J Vincent, *Human Rights and International Relations* (Cambridge University Press: 1986, 1999) 108. For Leben, the relationship between the European and the universal is explained by the concepts being increasingly overlapping. See C Leben, 'Is there a European Approach to Human Rights?' in P Alston *et al.* (eds), *The EU and Human Rights* (Oxford University Press: 1999) 69, 93.

[13] See P Leino, 'Rights, Rules and Democracy in the EU Enlargement Process: Between Universalism and Identity', (2002) 7 Austrian Rev of Intl and Eur L 53, 61.

[14] Art I-2: 'The Union is founded on the values of respect for human dignity, liberty, democracy, equality, the rule of law and respect for human rights, including the rights of persons belonging to minorities. These values are common to the Member States in a society in which pluralism, non-discrimination, tolerance, justice, solidarity and and [sic] equality between women and men prevail.' Provisional consolidated version of the draft Treaty establishing a Constitution for Europe, Brussels, 25 June 2004.

[15] Art III-193, In practice these principles are promoted through building 'partnerships with third countries, and international, regional or global organisations, which share these principles' and promoting 'multilateral solutions to common problems, in particular in the framework of the United Nations'.

[16] See D Kennedy, *A Critique of Adjudication {fin de siècle}* (Harvard University Press 1998) 305–306.

[17] ibid.

politics and existing power structures. However, as Günther has argued, the idea of universal human rights also has a 'long history of misreading, selective interpretation, and wrong application'.[18] Even the universal comes with its own inclusions and exclusions. It thus might be that for the European and the universal to overlap, other regions and their particular preferences are excluded from the scope of the universal, making the asserted universality far less appealing for those who are disqualified from contributing to its essence.

Although human rights conditionality has met opposition from both industrial and developing states, it has been formally accepted by most of the EU's trading partners,[19] and specific human rights clauses have been inserted into all bilateral agreements of a general nature that the Community has negotiated since 1995. Despite continuing opposition, today all agreements with weak states include the so-called essential element clause.[20] However, the picture is different concerning stronger states. For example, with Australia and New Zealand, the EU failed to reach a general co-operation agreement because these countries opposed the insertion of the clause.[21] Consequently, contractual relations with them, like most other industrialized states, exclude human rights. On the other hand, the existence of the clause in an agreement does not necessarily mean that human rights considerations play a crucial role in the relationship. A good example of this is Russia, with whom the EU has negotiated a human rights clause, which, however, is not invoked in practice. The differing approaches implemented in case of strong and weak countries throw a shadow of double standards on the use of the universalist argument: if the clause is based on universality, should it not be applied equally to all?

It thus seems that the relationship between the universal (human rights) and the particular (the EU) is not without problems. This article explores the problems that emerge when the universal is invoked as a basis for human rights conditionality. The article has three main objectives. After a short introduction to how the EU policy has been developed, it presents the EU approach to weak states

[18] K Günther, 'The Legacies of Injustice and Fear: A European Approach to Human Rights and their Effects on Political Culture' in P Alston *et al.* (eds), *The EU and Human Rights* (Oxford University Press: 1999) 117.

[19] As such, this paper is not so much about the formal acceptance and validity of the clause, which is a matter falling under the law of treaties, but rather about its acceptability and legitimacy.

[20] For the purposes of this article, I use the terms 'weak' and 'strong' states. Another possible characterization would have been 'industrialized' and 'developing' states. However, while Russia, for example, is not necessarily an 'industrialized' state comparable to Japan or the US, it is definitely a 'strong' state, for example, in terms of geopolitical and bargaining power. The same applies to Mexico, especially when compared to most 'developing' states. Therefore, the use of terms 'strong' and 'weak' seemed more appropriate.

[21] The term 'bilateral agreements of a general nature' refers to framework agreements that attempt to regulate all areas of co-operation between the parties. The term excludes, in particular, the so-called sectoral agreements that regulate very specific areas of trade or co-operation. The agreements with Australia and New Zealand belong to the latter group. This kind of agreements have not included human rights clauses.

(Section III) and to stronger ones (Section IV) and observes the differences in approach at the stage of implementation (Section V). Secondly, the article has a brief look at the right to development (Section VI) and the debate on cultural relativism (Section VII), which both demonstrate a difference in approach to human rights between 'the West and the rest'. Thirdly, the article considers the universalist claim of the EU in more detail (Section VIII). What kind of universalism is the EU referring to? Or is the language of universality merely the compliment that diplomatic vice pays to human rights virtue?

II. Development of a New Human Rights Policy

Initially, the EU approached human rights and external trade separately.[22] However, this proved difficult, because international trade and aid policies often have a close linkage with human rights issues.[23] The courage with which the Union today speaks of human rights, democracy, the rule of law and good governance is not without connection to the global political transformations of the late 1980s and early 1990s—it is clearly less risky to speak about the 'universal' when there are few competing models. Today, in the Community vision, serious human rights problems are linked with political and institutional instability,[24] with progress with democracy, the rule of law and human rights functioning as a 'prerequisite for stable trade relations and the orderly implementation of trade agreements', and trade conditionality and sanctions serving as a powerful means in the promotion of human rights worldwide.[25]

After Vienna, the European Commission has 'gradually identified the areas of activity that correspond to a positive, practical and constructive approach based on the concepts of exchange, sharing and encouragement'.[26] In practice, this approach is realized both through the mainstreaming of human rights into EU foreign policy and by making human rights considerations an aspect of external trade and development assistance.[27] The EU implements a suspension mechanism included in Community agreements negotiated with third countries, enabling the

---

[22] This was the case for eg, in relation to South Africa's apartheid regime. See P Alston, 'Linking Trade and Human Rights', (1980) 23 German Ybk of Intl L 126, 135–137.

[23] On this, see Alston (n 22 above) 156.

[24] A Rosas, 'Human Rights in the External Trade Policy of the European Union' in *World Trade and the Protection of Human Rights. Human Rights in Face of Global Economic Challenges*, Publications de l'Institut International des Droits de l'Homme (Bruyland: Bruxelles, 2001) 193, 207.

[25] ibid 205.

[26] The European Union and the External Dimension of Human Rights Policy: From Rome to Maastricht and Beyond, Communication from the Commission to the Council and European Parliament, Brussels 22.11.1995, COM (95) 567 final, Para 34.

[27] On human rights as a part of the Union's common foreign and security policy, see eg A Clapham, 'Where is the EU's Common Foreign Policy, and How is it Manifested in Multilateral Fora?' in P Alston *et al.* (eds.), *The EU and Human Rights* (Oxford University Press: 1999) 627.

Community to defer their implementation in cases of breaches of human rights.[28] Considering developing states, human rights figure in the Community's unilateral scheme of generalized tariff preferences (GSP)[29] and in the Community development policy[30] through the Cotonou Convention, which contains a long and rather elaborate human rights clause.[31] Human rights have played a role in the enlargement of the Union eastwards as one of the formal membership criteria and with a human rights clause included in the Europe Agreements in force with these states.[32] In addition, human rights conditionality applies to financial assistance given by the Community,[33] and is closely tied to the use of economic sanctions.[34]

The history of the human rights clause is at least loosely linked to the break-up of Yugoslavia, which brought to the Community's attention its limited possibilities to suspend the application of agreements it had concluded with third states.[35] The matter was also addressed by the European Court of Justice (ECJ) in

[28] Agreements with human rights clauses are in force with the states of Central and Eastern Europe, the developing world including the 78 ACP States, Morocco, Tunisia, South Korea, Nepal, former Soviet Union states, India, Sri Lanka, Israel, Brazil, Venezuela, Colombia, Ecuador, Peru, Bolivia (Andean Pact), Tunisia, Vietnam, Laos, Cambodia, Egypt, Jordan and Lebanon. Cuba became the 79th ACP state in December 2000 but does not yet participate in the partnership agreement.

[29] The GSP system has been created specifically for developing states and justifies more preferential treatment than the Most Favoured Nation principle. See Council Regulation (EC) No 2501/2001 of 10 December 2001 applying a scheme of generalized tariff preferences for the period from 1 January 2002 to 31 December 2004, published in [2001] OJ L 346/1. The Regulation allows, *inter alia*, for special incentive arrangements for the protection of labour rights and provides for temporary withdrawal of the preferential arrangements in case of for eg, slavery or forced labour, violations of the freedom of association or use of child labour. See also Council Regulation (EC) 2007/2000 introducing exceptional trade measures for countries and territories participating in or linked to the European Union's Stabilization and Association Process, [2000] OJ L 240/1.

[30] See EC Treaty (Treaty of Nice), Arts 170 and 181a.

[31] See also the Partnership agreement between the members of the African, Caribbean and Pacific Group of States of the one part, and the European Community and its Member States, of the other part, signed in Cotonou on 23 June 2000, published in [2000] OJ L 317/3. See esp. Art 9 on 'Essential Element and Fundamental Element'.

[32] See the Europe Agreement with Latvia, [1998] OJ L 26/3, Art 2(1). The Europe Agreements with Poland and Hungary do not include a clause, see [1993] OJ L 348/2 and [1993] OJ L 347/2. On human rights, democracy and the rule of law in the EU enlargement process, see P Leino, 'Rights, Rules and Democracy in the EU Enlargement Process: Between Universalism and Identity', (2002) 7 Austrian Rev of Intl and Eur L 53.

[33] See eg Council Regulation (EC, Euratom) No 99/2000) of 29 December 1999 concerning the provision of assistance to the partner States in Eastern Europe and Central Asia, [2000] OJ L12/1 Para 16; Council Regulation (Euratom, EC) 1279/96 of 25 June 1996 concerning the provision of assistance to economic reform and recovery in the New Independent States and Mongolia, [1996] OJ L 165/1; Council Regulation (EC) 1488/96 of 23 July 1996 on financial and technical measures to accompany (MEDA) the reform of economic and social structures in the framework of the Euro-Mediterranean partnership, [1996] OJ L 189/1; Council Regulation (EEC) No 443/92 of 25 February 1992 on financial and technical assistance to, and economic cooperation with, the developing countries in Asia and Latin America, [1992] OJ L52/1.   [34] See Art 301 EC.

[35] The Community also had similar experiences with other countries, like Uganda and Haiti under the Lomé Convention. See K Arts, *Integrating Human Rights into Development Cooperation: The Case of the Lomé Convention* (Kluwer Law International: 2000) esp. 265, 321–327, 346.

a case considering a Council decision to suspend (and later terminate) a preferential trade agreement with a treaty partner that had more or less ceased to exist (Federal Republic of Yugoslavia).[36] While there was no doubt that the Community was 'faced with a neighbouring State in which rules of law and morals were violated left, right and centre',[37] the ECJ underlined that 'the European Community must respect international law in the exercise of its powers'.[38] As the rules concerning the termination and suspension of treaty relations had become customary international law, they were 'binding upon the Community institutions and form part of the Community legal order'.[39]

It was therefore considered important to create a technical arrangement that would link Community agreements with the relevant provisions of the Vienna Convention on the Law of Treaties,[40] and thus enable the EC to suspend its treaty obligations, for example in cases of serious violations of human rights or disruptions of the democratic process.[41] Subsequently, the Council approved in 1995 a standard clause to be included in Community agreements negotiated with third countries, enabling reaction 'immediately in the event of violation of essential aspects of those agreements, particularly human rights'.[42] Under the new practice, human rights and democratic principles are included as an 'essential element' of the agreement:

Relations between the Parties, as well all the provisions of the Agreement itself, shall be based on respect for human rights and democratic principles which guide their domestic and international policies and constitute an essential element of the Agreement.[43]

---

[36] Case C-162/96 *A. Racke GmbH & Co. v Hauptzollamt Mainz*, [1998] ECR I-3655.

[37] See the case annotation to *A. Racke GmbH & Co. v Hauptzollamt Mainz* by J Klabbers in (1999) 36 CML Rev 179, 187.

[38] Case C-162/96 *A. Racke GmbH & Co. v Hauptzollamt Mainz*, [1998] ECR I-3655, Para 45.

[39] ibid Para 46.

[40] Art 60 of the Vienna Convention establishes that a 'material breach' of a treaty requires 'the violation of a provision essential to the accomplishment of the object and purpose of the treaty'. Such a breach of a 'bilateral treaty by one of the parties entitles the other to invoke the breach as a ground for terminating the treaty or suspending its operation in whole or in part'. The Vienna Convention on the Law of Treaties, Vienna, 23 May 1969, in force 27 January 1980, 1155 *United Nations Treaty Series* 331; 8 *Intl Legal Materials* (1969) 679.

[41] See eg B Brandtner and A Rosas, 'Human Rights and the External Relations of the European Community', (1998) 9 Eur J of Intl L 468, 474.

[42] See General Affairs Council Meeting in Brussels, 29 May 1995, Press Release 7481/95 (Presse 152) at 5. Before that the Community had used different variations of the human rights clause, in some cases supplemented by one of two types of interpretative declarations, namely joint or unilateral declarations. According to the Commission, the use of different formulas could be interpreted as discriminatory practice in some part of the world. Communication from the Commission on the Inclusion of Respect for Democratic Principles and Human Rights in Agreements between the Community and Third Countries, Brussels 23 May 1995, COM (95)216 final, 10–11.

[43] See eg Art 2 of the Euro-Mediterranean Agreement establishing an association between the European Communities and their Member States, of the one part, and the Republic of Tunisia, of the other part, published in [1998] OJ L 97/2.

Sometimes the clause includes references to specific human rights documents: in most agreements, much emphasis is placed on the UDHR[44]; in some others, regional documents, like the Helsinki Final Act or the Charter of Paris, are mentioned.[45]

While there have also been doubts about the EU competence to insert clauses from an internal policy perspective,[46] for the Commission, the human rights clauses 'illustrate the importance the Community attaches to human rights'[47] and make these agreements 'recognized among the international community for their originality, particularly in respect of their approach to human rights'.[48] The clause represents a new principle with little roots in the commercial policies of the individual Member States and falls outside the Community's international trade obligations under the GATT.[49] In addition,

[h]uman rights clauses do not statically reflect the present stage of evolution of international law; rather they aim at advancing the evolutionary process and expanding the protection of human rights well beyond that stage. The EC thus assumes a propulsive role as a qualified interpreter of the legal sensitivity of the international community.[50]

In order to employ human rights conditionality for its trade and development policies, the EU has needed a proper document of reference. As a result, it has turned into perhaps the most eager proponent of the universality of the UDHR. This is because it was (and is) not party to any international human rights treaty that could be used as a reference for shared standards; hence the need to refer to

[44] See eg Economic Partnership, Political Coordination and Cooperation Agreement between the European Community and its Member States, of the one part, and the United Mexican States, of the other part, published in [2000] OJ L 276/45, which recognizes the UDHR as the document enumerating the human rights included in the treaty commitment.

[45] See eg Agreement on partnership and cooperation establishing a partnership between the European Communities and their Member States, of the one part, and the Russian Federation, of the other part, published in [1997] OJ L 327/3.

[46] EU lawyers have, however, tended to reply to such concerns in a positive manner. See eg E Cannizzaro, 'The Scope of EU Foreign Power. Is the EU Competent to Conclude Agreements with Third States Including Human Rights Clauses?' in E Cannizzaro (ed), *The European Union as an Actor in International Relations* (Kluwer Law International: 2002) 297; E Fierro, 'Legal Basis and Scope of the Human Rights Clauses in EC Bilateral Agreements: Any Room for Positive Interpretation?', (2001) 7(1) Eur L J 41.

[47] Report on the Implementation of Measures to Promote Observance of Human Rights and Democratic Principles (For 1994), Brussels 12.07.1995, COM (95)191 final, 24–25.

[48] The European Union and the External Dimension of Human Rights Policy: From Rome to Maastricht and Beyond, Communication from the Commission to the Council and European Parliament, Brussels 22.11.1995, COM (95) 567 final, Para 61.

[49] M Cremona, 'Human Rights and Democracy Clauses in the EC's Trade Agreements' in N Emiliou and D O'Keeffe, *The European Union and World Trade Law* (Chichester, John Wiley & Sons: 1996) 62, 75.

[50] E Cannizzaro, 'The Scope of EU Foreign Power. Is the EU Competent to Conclude Agreements with Third States Including Human Rights Clauses?' in E Cannizzaro (ed), *The European Union as an Actor in International Relations* (Kluwer Law International: 2002) 297, 302.

customary law and general principles.[51] Emphasizing the universality of rights has been a necessary instrument for avoiding the charge of neo-colonialism associated with the Union's human rights conditionality. After all, the Community approach is not to be seen 'as imposing conditions, but in the spirit of a joint undertaking to respect and promote universal values'.[52] Instead of being just an EU concern, according to the Commission, human rights constitute 'a subject of shared interest'.[53] While political conditionality is not the only type of conditionality that the EU invokes, the difference between human rights criteria and other conditions, for example relating to environmental standards, is that the latter are often presented with direct reference to the EU's own interest, while human rights are presented as a shared universal objective.[54] It is in this manner that the principle of universality has been crucial for the development of the EU external human rights policy. However, as will be seen in the following sections, it is implemented in varying ways.

III. Development context

The Community has always wanted to have a defined relationship with the developing world, and therefore the original EEC Treaty (Treaty of Rome) included specific rules concerning the overseas countries and territories of the EEC Member States.[55] However, at that time, decolonization was taking place with an increasing speed, and the new independent countries soon fell outside the scope of the EEC Treaty despite the close links they had with their former colonial rulers. A new preferential trade agreement between the EEC and former colonies, the Yaoundé Convention, entered into force in 1964.[56] After the accession of the UK to the Community in 1973, the earlier focus on mainly French-speaking

---

[51] A similar move had been made for the same reasons in the internal sphere through the practice of the ECJ. While the ECJ relied on common constitutional traditions and the European Convention on Fundamental Rights, however flexibly, in the external arena emphasis was placed on the UDHR.

[52] The European Union and the External Dimension of Human Rights Policy: From Rome to Maastricht and Beyond, Communication from the Commission to the Council and European Parliament, Brussels 22.11.1995, COM (95) 567 final, Para 63.   [53] ibid.

[54] See eg Speech/00/77 by M Wallström, European Commissioner for Environment, held at the Polish Parliament on 9 March 2000, in which reference is clearly made to the EU's own agenda and its own standards. In another speech on 'EU-Russia Environmental Challenges', Speech/01/213, the justification for pushing for higher environmental standards in Russia is that because 'environmental pollution recognizes no state boundaries [. . .] what happens here in Russia directly affects the EU Member States'. Speech given in Moscow on 11 May 2001. Both speeches can be found on the European Commission website.

[55] These were included in Part IV of the EEC Treaty on association of the 'Overseas Countries and Territories'.

[56] See G van Benthem van den Bergh, 'The New Convention of Association with African States', (1963–64) 1 CML Rev 156.

African countries proved insufficient, and the first Lomé Convention, signed in 1975, formed an association between the EEC and 46 countries from Africa, the Caribbean and the Pacific—a very mixed group with considerable differences in history, economic and political systems and structures, size, population and development level.[57] Today, in addition to the 79 ACP states that are approached under the Lomé / Cotonou framework, the EU has adopted regional approaches to the Mediterranean countries[58] and to the developing states in Latin America.[59]

However, the relationship between the Community / Union and the developing world has never been quite straightforward. The Yaoundé Convention (in force 1964–1975) was met with accusations of a 'new system of collective colonialism' or a 'new, stronger, and more dangerous form of neo-colonialism'.[60] Following this, the Lomé framework was constructed in an environment that emphasized two objectives: the need to maintain links with former colonies, on the one hand, but criticism concerning protraction of old colonial exploitation, on the other. Discussion was much influenced by the calls for a New International Economic Order and the underlining of sovereignty, with the South underlining its *right* to development. Within the UN, debates surrounding the right to development emphasized economic and social issues and the need to recognize both colonialism and neo-colonialism as gross violations of international law and regarding some forms of development co-operation as entitlements instead of voluntary acts of charity.[61] It was argued that the Lomé Convention should not be examined 'in isolation of the historical experience of the earlier conventions, agreements and other deals with the imperialistic world'.[62] Consequently, the initial Lomé scheme underlined co-operation, partnership and dialogue. Conditionality could have no place in the scheme.[63] The official European view of the framework has traditionally

[57]   The ACP Group was founded in 1975 with the signing of the Georgetown Agreement and only for that purpose. Also concerning human rights, the picture is very mixed: many of the Caribbean and Pacific States have very limited ratification records of the central international human rights instruments. See in more detail, K Arts, *Integrating Human Rights into Development Cooperation: The Case of the Lomé Convention* (Kluwer Law International: 2000) 76–77.

[58]   The relevant agreements with these countries are Association Agreements and include an essential element clause. See eg the Euro-Mediterranean Agreement establishing an association between the European Communities and their Member States of the one part and the Republic of Tunisia, of the other part [1998] OJ L 97/2.

[59]   See Communication from the Commission to the Council and the European Parliament, The European Union and Latin America. The present situation and prospects for closer partnership 1996–2000, COM (95) 495 final. See also Council Regulation (EEC) No 443/92 of 25 February 1992 on financial and technical assistance to, and economic cooperation with, the developing countries in Asia and Latin America [1992] OJ L 052/1–6.

[60]   For a summary of views, see J Odek, 'Lomé IV: Dynamic or static improvement on the previous conventions?—the sub-Saharan Africa perspective', (1994) 27 Comparative and Intl L J of Southern Africa 164, 164.

[61]   See A Lindroos, *The Right to Development*, The Erik Castrén Institute of International Law and Human Rights Research Reports 2/1999, 64–65.

[62]   See D Wadada Nabudere, 'The Lome Convention and the Consolidation of Neo-Imperialism', (1975) 8(1) East Africa L Rev 1, 31.

[63]   P Hilpold, 'EU Development Cooperation at a Crossroads: The Cotonou Agreement of 23 June 2000 and the Principle of Good Governance', (2002) 7 Eur Foreign Affairs Rev 53, 56–57.

underlined its 'political neutrality', relying on the EC as a new civilian power, and the idea of equal binding contracts with the ACP states.[64]

The link between human rights and development is older than that between human rights and trade.[65] Today, Community development co-operation is defined by the EC Treaty as being 'complementary' to the policies pursued by the Member States, and shall specifically 'contribute to the general objective of developing and consolidating democracy and the rule of law, and to that of respecting human rights and fundamental freedoms'.[66] In addition, the Treaty includes a specific article that serves as a legal basis for financial measures with regard to human rights and democracy.[67] Even outside the EU, a corresponding linkage between human rights and aid is today being widely invoked. Conditionality has become a feature of aid; today it is also manifested in trade.[68] The justification proffered is not the self-interest of the donor state, but the 'good of the country', on which conditions are imposed.[69] The EU has traditionally subscribed to the liberal doctrine, finding that the basic obstacles to economic development are caused by problems in the least developing states themselves, especially the ineffectiveness and corruption of their government policies.[70] Generally, this doctrine explains that problems relating to social, economic and political justice and international inequality require first and foremost measures at the national level, especially the proper implementation of international human rights law.[71] Domestic good governance serves as an essential precondition for economic and social development. For the donors, this is, of course, linked to 'value for money' ideas in public spending, especially as human rights criteria increasingly include even the obligation to fight corruption.[72]

Human rights conditionality has always been objected to by the ACP Partners of the Community, though usually without much success. Their resistance to human rights references has especially related to three aspects: opposing the Lomé Convention as a forum, treating the human rights declarations given in that

---

[64] M Lister, *The European Community and the Developing World. The Role of the Lome Convention* (Avebury: 1988) 189.

[65] See eg P Alston, 'Linking Trade and Human Rights', (1980) 23 German Ybk of Intl L 126.

[66] See Art 177 EC.

[67] See Art 181a EC, which can also be used as a legal basis for agreements, which do not fall under development or other specific categories. However, it has not yet been used.

[68] P Nherere, 'Conditionality, human rights and good governance: a dialogue of unequal partners' in K Ginther *et al* (eds), *Sustainable development and good governance* (Dordrecht, Martinus Nijhoff Publishers: 1995) 289, 290.   [69] ibid.

[70] On the liberal doctrine in general, see eg R Gilpin, *The Political Economy of International Relations*, (Princeton University Press: 1987) 267.

[71] A Anghie, 'Time Present and Time Past: Globalization, International Financial Institutions, and the Third World', (2000) 32 New York U J of Intl L and Politics 243, 259. Anghie writes mainly in the context of international financial institutions, but his analysis bears much relevance for the EU actions, as well.

[72] See eg Art. 9 of the Partnership agreement between the members of the African, Caribbean and Pacific Group of States of the one part, and the European Community and its Member States, of the other part, signed in Cotonou on 23 June 2000, [2000] OJ L 317/3.

forum as unequal, and questioning the interpretation of the rights included in the framework.[73] Protecting Western-style human rights and democratic principles has been considered an impossibility, both because protecting them would be expensive and because this would often fall outside the political priorities of the ruling elites.[74] Many former colonies have seen much irony in their old imperial masters suddenly seeking to run a human rights-based foreign policy.[75] For the developing states, human rights have traditionally represented an issue that could threaten their newly-found sovereignty.[76]

When negotiating Lomé II (which came into force in 1980), the EC objective of including a human rights reference to the agreement seemed somewhat odd—after all, at the time the EEC Treaty included no word of human rights. The ACP states pointed out that human rights were more suitable for discussion in the United Nations, and that economics and trade did not really fit into the same framework with human rights.[77] In addition, the ACP states argued that making allocation of aid conditional on observance of basic human rights constituted 'proof on a neo-colonialist attitude on the part of the donor countries'.[78] During the negotiations, the otherwise divided ACP states presented a united front in wishing to keep human rights references out of the agreement, and were successful in doing that.[79]

However, the Community returned to the issue again in the negotiations of Lomé III (which came into force in 1986). At that time, even the ACP states had on their agenda an issue with human rights implications: they wanted the EC to condemn the apartheid regime in South Africa. For them, this was a major question, and excluding apartheid made a human rights clause difficult to accept. In addition, the ACP states underlined the indivisibility of all rights.[80] The outcome of the negotiations avoided the difficult issues, as the agreement only included some general references to human rights.[81] Nevertheless, despite the opposition

[73] M Lister, *The European Community and the Developing World. The Role of the Lome Convention* (Avebury: 1988) 198.
[74] P Hilpold, 'EU Development Cooperation at a Crossroads: The Cotonou Agreement of 23 June 2000 and the Principle of Good Governance', (2002) 7 Eur Foreign Affairs Rev 53, 58.
[75] T King, 'Human Rights in European Foreign Policy: Success or Failure of Post-modern Diplomacy?', (1999) 10 Eur J of Intl L 313, 314.
[76] L Garnick and C Cosgrove Twitchett, 'Human Rights and a Successor to the Lome Convention', (1979) *Intl Relations* 540, 555.
[77] For a summary of arguments used in the context of Lomé II, see A Young-Anawaty, 'Human Rights and the ACP-EEC Lomé II Convention: Business as Usual at the EEC', (1980) 13 New York U J of Intl L and Politics 63, 80.
[78] RJH Smits, 'The Second Lomé Convention. An Assessment with Special Reference to Human Rights' in 1980/2) Legal Issues of Eur Integration 47, 54.
[79] K Arts, *Integrating Human Rights into Development Cooperation: The Case of the Lomé Convention* (Kluwer Law International: 2000) 171; L Garnick and C Cosgrove Twitchett, 'Human Rights and a Successor to the Lome Convention', (1979) *Intl Relations* 540, 555.
[80] Arts (n 78 above) 176–177.
[81] These were placed in Art 4 of the Convention, which provided for support for the promotion of 'the ACP states' social and economic progress and the well-being of their population through the satisfaction of their basic needs, the recognition of the role of women and the enhancement of people's capacities, with respect for their dignity' and in Annex I, which contained a Joint Declaration on Art 4.

by ACP states, human rights conditionality was gradually made a legally binding part of the framework. More specific human rights provisions were incorporated in Article 5 of Lomé IV (in force 1991).[82] However, in practice the Community applied democracy and good governance criteria from the early 1990s in several cases in order to suspend or restrict the implementation of the agreement, and in doing so 'clearly trespassed the legal boundaries of Lomé at the time'.[83]

Between the negotiations for Lomé IV and its mid-term review in 1994 (the Lomé IV-bis, which entered into force in 1998) great political changes had taken place globally. As a result:

[i]t was no surprise that Lomé's human rights provisions were tabled for reconsideration. The European actors were again the ones who publicly and most forcefully proposed change in this area.[84]

The result mostly reflected the increasing emphasis on political conditionality. In the new agreement, Article 5 was widened to cover even democratic principles, the rule of law and good governance. Simultaneously, these were also made particular aims of the agreement.[85] However, little universality and joint understanding was visible in the Commission Communication from 1998, addressed to the Council and the Parliament but written in order to explain to the ACP states how the Community interprets the human rights elements of the fourth Lomé Convention.[86] While the reforms undertaken by the ACP States had been '[m]odulated by a country's history and present circumstances', the Commission now saw it as a task:

[f]or the EU and its ACP partners to find appropriate responses to a multifaceted trend. The EU and the ACP countries will share the burden of this new political responsibility.[87]

This despite the fact that the ACP states have often appeared less enthusiastic about invoking universality of human rights as the main foundation for their relationship with the EU, which has also made them reluctant to make an active contribution to shaping it.[88]

---

[82] Art 5(1) focused on the link between human rights and development, Art 5(2) a commitment to promote human rights; and Art 5(3) established the possibility of direct positive measures to promote human rights at the request of the ACP States.

[83] K Arts, *Integrating Human Rights into Development Cooperation: The Case of the Lomé Convention* (Kluwer Law International: 2000) 339. Arts names the examples of Surinam, Tanzania and Malawi, which took place between December 1990 and 1996.

[84] ibid 180; M Holland, 'Resisting Reform or Risking Revival? Renegotiating the Lomé Convention', in M Green Cowles and M Smith (eds), *The State of the European Union. Risks, Reform, Resistance, and Revival*, Volume 5, (Oxford University Press: 2000) 390, 401–403.

[85] On this, see Arts (n 83 above) 190. However, in Lomé IV-bis, good governance was not mentioned as an 'essential element' of the agreement.

[86] Commission Communication to the Council and Parliament, Democratisation, the rule of law, respect for human rights and good governance: the challenges of the partnership between the European Union and the ACP states, 12 March 1998, COM (98)146. See also the purposes of the Communication at 1. [87] ibid 2.

[88] K Arts, *Integrating Human Rights into Development Cooperation: The Case of the Lomé Convention* (Kluwer Law International: 2000) 213.

Five years later, the 'trend of sharply increased attention for political issues' continued during the negotiations for the Cotonou agreement.[89] The Commission guidelines issued before the launching of the discussions underlined the old ideas of partnership and contractuality.[90] During the negotiations, however, the EU suggested strengthening political conditionality in relation to good governance and corruption. This caused fierce disagreement between the EU and the ACP states.[91] Even stronger controversy related to the EU's wish to include a clause on migration, which ultimately became Article 13 of the agreement. The EU won the battles, and the Commission was happy to declare, '[a] major innovation of the Cotonou Agreement lies in a mutual commitment to good governance'.[92] Others were more sceptical about the mutuality aspect:

The concept, defined in European terms and by European standards, could be incompatible with individual ACP cultures and institutional capacities. Common assumptions and motivations guiding the good governance agenda cannot be presumed. Not only are the standards of good governance Euro-centric, but the EU exercises the unilateral right to suspend any form of development assistance if it concludes that good governance has been breached.[93]

It seemed that 'the EU strongly pushed for its own priorities', which caused both disagreement and disappointment in most of the ACP states.[94] While the relationship was 'formally based on notions of structural cooperation, equality and joint decision-making', the 'human rights and democracy practice [. . .] is in various ways almost exclusively dominated by Community actors'.[95] In general:

[a] rather disturbing element in Community behaviour lies in the sometimes haphazard introduction of new 'essential elements' in development cooperation.[. . .] New items of

---

[89] K Arts, 'ACP-EU Relations in a New Era: The Cotonou Agreement', (2003) 40 CML Rev 95, 102–104. M Holland, 'Resisting Reform or Risking Revival? Renegotiating the Lomé Convention', in M Green Cowles and M Smith (eds), *The State of the European Union. Risks, Reform, Resistance, and Revival*, Volume 5, (Oxford University Press: 2000) 390, 401–403.

[90] See eg Communication from the Commission to the Council and the European Parliament— Guidelines for the negotiation of new cooperation Agreements with the African, Caribbean and Pacific (ACP) states, COM(97) 357 final.

[91] K Arts, 'ACP-EU Relations in a New Era: The Cotonou Agreement', (2003) 40 CML Rev 95, 100; O Elgström, 'Lomé and Post-Lomé: Asymmetric Negotiations and the Impact of Norms' (2000) 5 Eur Foreign Affairs Rev 175, 191.

[92] Communication from the Commission to the Council and the European Parliament. The European Union's Role in Promoting Human Rights and Democratisation in Third Countries. Brussels, 8.5.2001, COM(2001) 252 final, at 24. After Cotonou, good governance is an 'essential element', but not a 'fundamental element' of the agreement, and suspension is made based on a separate article (Art 97), which includes a similar suspension process but is not reciprocal because defines the Community as a 'significant partner in terms of financial support'. Good governance is defined as relating to 'flagrant cases of mismanagement of public funds in ACP countries'. See B Martenczuk, 'From Lomé to Cotonou: The ACP-EC Partnership Agreement in a Legal Perspective', (2000) 5 Eur Foreign Affairs Rev 461, 471–472.

[93] M Holland, 'Resisting Reform or Risking Revival? Renegotiating the Lomé Convention', in M Green Cowles and M Smith (eds), *The State of the European Union. Risks, Reform, Resistance, and Revival*, Volume 5, (Oxford University Press: 2000) 390, 403–404.

[94] K Arts, 'ACP-EU Relations in a New Era: The Cotonou Agreement', (2003) 40 CML Rev 95, 111.

[95] K Arts, *Integrating Human Rights into Development Cooperation: The Case of the Lomé Convention* (Kluwer Law International: 2000) 211; O Elgström, 'Lomé and Post-Lomé: Asymmetric Negotiations and the Impact of Norms' (2000) 5 Eur Foreign Affairs Rev 175.

conditionality are at times tabled without proper indication of their exact meaning and status. EC developing country cooperation partners are sometimes not consulted. It is quite striking that new priority areas and/or conditionalities are usually set unilaterally and are not the outcome of policy/political dialogue.[96]

Even the voluntary acceptance of the provisions of the agreement by the ACP countries could be questioned:

Given the poor state of the economy of a large number of ACP countries, one can question their freedom of action in this respect. The EC often took a take-it-or-leave-it approach: accept the package as a whole, including trade, aid and potential strings attached, or do not take part in Lomé cooperation at all.[97]

Overall, the human rights debate between the EC and ACP has often appeared as a 'dialogue of the deaf'.[98] Through the years, the discussions concerning the position of human rights in the framework have revealed clear differences in both priorities and underlying concepts, and these differences have remained broadly unchanged throughout the years. On the EC side, the emphasis has been on the status of civil and political rights.[99] The ACP states, for their part, have been active on apartheid and the rights of ACP nationals resident in the EC, and have placed much effort on resisting the EC openings.[100] For them, the right to development should form the background and the basis of the discussion. While there is some dialogue between the EU and the ACP, for example in the Joint Assembly,[101] this does not appear to figure very high on the EU agenda, as the non-binding dialogue does not seem to amount to changes in actual EU policies, especially when new Agreements are being negotiated. Through the years, the positions have remained unchanged, with the ACP states objecting to the EU initiatives, but eventually accepting them for economic reasons.

Despite the EU's insistence that its approach is based on universal values, the Lomé framework continues to be challenged. It has been seen as the continuation of dependency and subordination, with the EU taking the place that was earlier held by the colonial powers.[102] The EU has in practice proved to be reluctant to actually turn its general Lomé rhetoric on partnership, joint decision-making and management into concrete measures.[103] As the Community is the party with

---

[96] Arts (n 94 above) 136.   [97] ibid 212, note 1.   [98] ibid 200.

[99] ibid 201.   [100] ibid 285.

[101] See Partnership agreement between the members of the African, Caribbean and Pacific Group of States of the one part, and the European Community and its Member States, of the other part, signed in Cotonou on 23 June 2000, [2000] OJ L 317/3, Art 17.

[102] J Odek, 'Lomé IV: Dynamic or static improvement on the previous conventions?—the sub-Saharan Africa perspective', (1994) 27 Comparative and Intl L J of Southern Africa 164, 197–198.

[103] K Arts, 'Development Cooperation and Human Rights: Turbulent Times for EU Policy' in M Lister (ed), *New Perspectives on European Union Development Cooperation* (Westview Press: 1999) 7, 18. Elgström argues that the partnership idea has actually weakened during the years. See O Elgström, 'Lomé and Post-Lomé: Asymmetric Negotiations and the Impact of Norms' (2000) 5 Eur Foreign Affairs Rev 175. See also M Holland, 'Resisting Reform or Risking Revival? Renegotiating the Lomé Convention', in M Green Cowles and M Smith (eds), *The State of the European Union. Risks, Reform, Resistance, and Revival*, Volume 5, (Oxford University Press: 2000) 390, 401–403.

economic resources, it is unilaterally able to determine the amounts of financial resources available to specific programmes. The ACP partners, for their part, do not have any comparable leverage but are compelled to rely on decisions ultimately made by the EC in reference to its preferences.[104]

> The Community in the end is the donor and in control of resources. At times, despite its formal insistence on equality, it takes its decisions unilaterally or pushes through its own reading of events or concepts.[105]

As a result, the EU-ACP relationship tends to turn into one of neo-colonial dependency or subordination.[106]

This inequality is not only caused by economic realities but also by the complexities within the EU's own decision-making structures. The EU-ACP relationship is more affected by negotiations within the EU than any results in the discussions between the parties.[107] The possibility of the ACP states influencing their relationship with the EU has even in recent years been marginal.[108] EU development policy has been considered non-transparent and the decision-making process too time-consuming,[109] and the problems have persisted despite the repeated revision of the Lomé Convention.[110] The Community has been urged to make real efforts in order to increase consistency, develop clarity in relation to the thresholds it implements, and institute a more genuine dialogue. It should not forget that 'the human rights, democracy and good governance norms involved apply mutually'.[111]

The Lomé framework has also proved painful for the EU because of its incompatibility with the World Trade Organization (WTO) framework, which has made it more crucial to find solutions that are acceptable for the US rather than for the developing states.[112] In the future, the EU plans to approach the ACP

---

[104] See in general, K Arts, *Integrating Human Rights into Development Cooperation: The Case of the Lomé Convention* (Kluwer Law International: 2000) 205.

[105] K Arts, 'Implementing the Right to Development? An Analysis of European Community Development and Human Rights Policies', (1996) Human Rights in Developing Countries Ybk 37, 67–68.

[106] See in general, M Lister, *The European Community and the Developing World. The Role of the Lome Convention* (Avebury: 1988) 208–216.

[107] For this argument, see O Elgström, 'Lomé and Post-Lomé: Asymmetric Negotiations and the Impact of Norms', (2000) 5 Eur Foreign Affairs Rev 175, 176 *et seq.*   [108] ibid.

[109] See eg B Simma *et al.*, 'Human Rights Considerations in the Development Co-operation Activities of the EC' in P Alston *et al.* (eds), *The EU and Human Rights* (Oxford University Press: 1999) 572 esp. at 615–620.

[110] Specific problems include inconsistency and the need for dialogue to work both ways, and for more positive and constructive partnerships with ACP governments. See eg Communication from the Commission to the Council and the European Parliament. The European Union's Role in Promoting Human Rights and Democratisation in Third Countries. Brussels, 8.5.2001, COM (2001) 252 final.

[111] KCJM Arts, 'European Community development cooperation, human rights, democracy and good governance: at odds or at ease with each other?' in K Ginther *et al* (eds), *Sustainable development and good governance* (Dordrecht, Martinus Nijhoff Publishers: 1995) 259, 266.

[112] On the relationship between the Community development policies and the WTO, see eg F Smith, 'Renegotiating Lomé: the impact of the WTO on the EC's development policy after the

states more on a regional basis through using Economic Partnership Agreements. These agreements are WTO-compatible in removing trade barriers progressively and shall enter into force by 2008, as the current trade preferences of the ACPs will expire at the end of 2007. While this allows for greater diversity in approach, for the ACP states this risks breaking the collective ACP solidarity, which until now has been 'perhaps their biggest negotiation strength and thus guaranteed the best results'.[113]

While the EU is a bad donor, it is often the biggest one.[114] Something positive coming out of Lomé despite its spirit of European colonialism is the 'unmatched trade preference in the EC market and development aid' that the ACPs have enjoyed under its provisions.[115] However, in practice, during the 25 years of its existence, the Lomé framework has not necessarily improved the development level of the ACP states,[116] and these countries are largely dependent on the EU.[117] Even among developing states, the ACP states' share of trade has fallen to bottom position.[118] But for the EU, trade with the ACP states is only of marginal importance, especially as its development interests have gradually shifted elsewhere.[119] The EU-ACP relationship is thus clearly characterized by the economic realities and the unequal bargaining power of the parties, which leaves the EU with an overwhelming contribution to the formulation of the relationship.

IV. Strong States

Some years after the introduction of the human rights clause, the EU launched negotiations with Australia with the objective of concluding a comprehensive

---

Bananas conflict', (2000) 25 ELR 247 esp. at 261–263; S Peers, 'Banana Split: WTO Law and Preferential Agreements in the EC Legal Order' (1999) 4(2) Eur Foreign Affairs Rev 195.

[113] K Arts, 'ACP-EU Relations in a New Era: The Cotonou Agreement', 40 CML Rev (2003) 95, 106–107.

[114] Currently the EU provides approximately half of all public aid to developing states and is in many cases their main trading partner. See eg The European Community's Development Policy—Statement by the Council and the Commission, available at http://www.europa.eu.int/comm/development/body/legislation/docs/council_statement.pdf.

[115] JL Roby, 'Lome IV—No 'Fortress Europe", (1990) Brigham Young U L Rev 1781, 1782.

[116] K Arts, 'ACP-EU Relations in a New Era: The Cotonou Agreement', (2003) 40 CML Rev 95, 96.

[117] O Elgström, 'Lomé and Post-Lomé: Asymmetric Negotiations and the Impact of Norms', (2000) 5 *Eur Foreign Affairs Rev* 175, 178.

[118] M Holland, 'Resisting Reform or Risking Revival? Renegotiating the Lomé Convention', in M Green Cowles and M Smith (eds), *The State of the European Union. Risks, Reform, Resistance, and Revival*, Volume 5, (Oxford University Press: 2000) 390, 401.

[119] This is because the preferences that the ACP states have enjoyed have been largely eroded, with new investments being made in the East and Central European States and the Mediterranean. Other more preferential regimes have been created through the European Economic Area, the Europe Agreements, and with the Mediterranean States and some Latin American countries, which has made it usual to have preferential trade agreements. Moreover, as MFN duties have been lowered in general, the preferential margin of the developing states is disappearing.

framework agreement. During the negotiations, it became clear that the new agreement was, as noted by one Australian observer:

[e]ffectively killed, killed by a human rights squabble. Not, it should be stressed, a squabble over the principle of human rights, but rather the means by which the EU was to impose possible sanctions.[120]

Australia opposed the inclusion of a human rights clause into the agreement because it felt that the clause was inappropriate. This was partly because 'Australian and European virtue on human rights issues makes it unnecessary', and partly because Australia felt that there were more appropriate multilateral bodies, such as the United Nations and the International Labour Organisation, for advancing human rights.[121] For Australia, the insertion of a human rights clause was both bad law and unnecessary, because it would make the entire treaty 'hostage to perceived or contrived human rights disputes', and because 'the similarity of Australian and European attitudes towards human rights ensures that the likelihood of conflict is extremely remote'.[122] In addition, in the view of Australia, human rights and trade policy should be kept separate: 'Neither trade liberalisation nor human rights are advanced when the two issues are mixed'.[123] For Australia, it was clear that 'no other industrialised country [. . .] could accept the inclusion of operative human rights provisions of the type proposed by the Community in a framework cooperation agreement', and therefore, the 1995 Council decision had hardly envisaged applying the clause to countries like Australia 'with which the EU and Member States share similar values and approaches'.[124] Instead of the standard framework agreement corresponding to the EU's current treaty practice, Australia wished to gain a broadly similar agreement that the EU had with other OECD countries such as Canada. Such an agreement would better 'take account of Australia's advanced level of development as well as its role in world trade and the substantial contribution it makes to multilateral organisations'.[125]

On the EU side these arguments were strongly rejected. The European Commission Ambassador in Canberra argued that Australia's refusal to sign was 'puzzling', because human rights had underpinned all EU agreements for nearly two years. For him, there was no cause for the EU to bring a case against Australia on human rights. However, the EU could not possibly make an exception for

---

[120] 'Negative may prove positive' by F Brenchley London, published on 7 February 1997 in *Australian Financial Rev* 27.

[121] 'An EU test on rights', published on 31 January 1997 in *Australian Financial Rev* 36.

[122] 'Human Rights' by G Barker, published on 4 February 1997 in *Australian Financial Rev* 13.

[123] 'EU/Australia: Still no Agreement on the 'human rights clause', Agence Europe No 6903, 30 January 1997 at 8; Barker (n 122 above).

[124] Agence Europe, 'Australia explains its attitude on the human rights clause and suggests two alternatives—talks early this week', Brussels, 27 January 1997.

[125] 'Commission proposes new framework agreement with Australia', Commission Press Release Nr DN: IP/96/100, published on 31 January 1996.

Australia because that would 'undermine its position in negotiating contacts with countries that may have genuine human rights problems'.[126] This was a matter of consistency: it would be easier for Australia to explain to its Asian neighbours why it signed the agreement than it would be for the EC to explain why it had granted an exception for Australia from the agreement practice it had followed with numerous countries.[127] It was insufficient for Australia to claim that the clause was unnecessary and inappropriate for the reason that Australia and the EC were totally committed to virtually identical human rights values. After all, if this was true, then the clause should be easy to sign.[128] While Australia was 'blameless' in relation to human rights, dropping the clause would risk being misinterpreted by other countries.[129] The question was not about Australia's commitment to human rights, but about the formulation of this commitment.[130]

The EU view received support from the Australian Senate, which passed a motion calling on the Australian government to agree to the clause, arguing that the country had nothing to fear from a standard human rights clause. Some senators said that as Australia had already signed the UDHR, '[w]hat's so wrong with signing the UN declaration twice?'[131] Moreover, the Australian aborigine representatives campaigned for the inclusion of the clause.[132] However, the Australian government supported the inclusion of a joint human rights commitment in the treaty's political declaration, because, they argued, '[w]e do not have the capacity of being the world's policing authority or the world's conscience on human rights'.[133]

As a result, the parties failed to reach an agreement and adopted a joint declaration instead.[134] Its preamble notes the 'close historical, political, economic and cultural ties' of the parties, and their 'shared commitments to the respect and promotion of human rights, fundamental freedoms, democracy and the rule of law which underpin our internal and international policies'. In the section concerning the 'Common Goals', the parties reaffirm, among other things, their determination to 'support democracy, the rule of law, and respect for human rights and

---

[126] 'Govt "to set aside race act"' by N Field and G Barker, published on 31 January 1997 in *Australian Financial Rev* 4.

[127] 'An EU test on rights', published on 31 January 1997 in *Australian Financial Rev* 36.

[128] ibid.

[129] Agence Europe, 'Sir Leon Brittan reviews various important and sensitive issues (WTO agreement, Australia, Korea and so on)', Brussels, 7 February 1997.

[130] Agence Europe, 'Still no agreement on the "human rights" clause', Brussels, 29 February 1997.

[131] 'Negative may prove positive' by F Brenchley London, published in *Australian Financial Rev* on 7 February 1997 at 27.

[132] See eg Agence Europe, 'Aborigines ask EU not to renounce "human rights" clause in future cooperation agreement', Sydney, 31 January 1997.

[133] Mr Tim Fischer, Australia's Deputy Prime Minister and Trade Minister. Quoted in 'Human Rights' by G Barker, published on 4 February 1997 in *Australian Financial Rev* 13.

[134] Joint Declaration on relations between the European Union and Australia, signed in Luxembourg on 26 June 1997. See [1997] 6 Bull. EU 117–118. The declaration was reviewed in April 2003 and adopted for the next five years.

fundamental freedoms'. The parties express their will to inform and consult each other with the objective to seeking closer cooperation.[135] When explaining the result to the European Parliament, Commissioner Brittan argued that while 'a somewhat old Council decision stipulates that all agreements of this kind must include the clause on human rights', Australia 'considers it is not the kind of a country on which this kind of clause may be imposed'. Thus, the joint declaration should not be seen as a 'failure of EU human rights policy'.[136]

After Australia, New Zealand soon followed. For Commissioner Brittan, New Zealand initially seemed 'far less formal on the question of human rights', making agreement easy to find.[137] However, in the end even New Zealand refused the human rights clause,[138] and only signed a similar kind of a political declaration as Australia had done a few years earlier.[139] Some time later, the EU agreed to some concessions with Mexico, which claimed priority for the principle of non-intervention, and referred to the treatment received by the industrialized states as a reason to challenge the 'universality of the European attitude'.[140] Unlike Chile and Argentina, which had earlier specifically asked for a human rights clause to be included as a token of their commitment to democratic values, Mexico felt that the clause was unnecessary in the case of an 'old democracy'.[141] Mexico also suggested the crossing out of the reference to the UDHR. The clause was finally accepted in the standard form, but a declaration was annexed to the accord.[142] This was met with criticism by many EU Member States who argued that the amendment enabled Mexico to exclude internal policy from the scope of the clause.[143] However, concluding an agreement with Mexico was important for

---

[135] Joint Declaration on relations between the European Union and Australia, signed in Luxembourg on 26 June 1997. According to the Declaration, co-operation shall contribute to the 'the protection and promotion of human rights and fundamental freedoms. In this respect we will consult bilaterally and within the framework of the relevant bodies of the UN, especially the UN Commission on Human Rights, on human rights issues in general and, in particular, on how to advance our shared objectives of promoting human rights internationally'.

[136] Agence Europe, 'Sir Leon Brittan updates before MEPs on relations with China, Australia and other countries—economic cooperation and respect of human rights are linked'[sic], Brussels, 15 April 1997.   [137] ibid.

[138] Agence Europe, 'EU and New Zealand to negotiate a joint declaration', Brussels, 1 February 1999.

[139] Agence Europe, 'Joschka Fischer, Sir Leon Brittan and Don McKinnon to sign joint declaration at Tuesday's ministerial meeting in Strasbourg', Brussels, 30 April 1999.

[140] Agence Europe, 'Free trade unions call upon union to keep human rights clause in future agreement', Brussels, 22 January 1997.

[141] See E Fierro Sedano, *The EU's Approach to Human Rights Conditionality in Practice*, PhD thesis written at the European University Institute, Florence (submitted in December 2001) 316–319.

[142] See Economic Partnership, Political Coordination and Cooperation Agreement between the European Community and its Member States, of the one part, and the United Mexican States, of the other part, published in [2000] OJ L 276/45. The unilateral declaration adopted by Mexico underlines that the Mexican foreign policy is based on 'non-intervention, peaceful dispute settlement, the prohibition on threats or the use of force in international relations, the legal equality of states, international development cooperation and the defence of peace and international security'. See also Fierro Sedano (note 141 above) 319.

[143] See Agence Europe, 'For Mexican government, negotiations on first agreement are over, and Mexico is not responsible for any deadlock', Brussels / Mexico 20 June 1997; Agence Europe,

the EU because of the NAFTA membership of the former: Without an agreement, EU exports would risk losing out to the US.

In relation to most industrialized states, like the US, Canada and Japan, human rights and trade are not linked. With the US and Canada, the relationship is based on 'action plans'. With Canada, the actual framework agreement dates back to 1976 and includes a reference to how the parties had been 'inspired by the common heritage, special affinity and shared aspirations which unite the countries of the European Community and Canada' in concluding the framework agreement for commercial and economic co-operation.[144] The political dimension is included in a joint declaration, adopted in 1990, which is 'bonded by their common heritage and close historical, political, economic and cultural ties' and 'guided by their faith in the values of human dignity, intellectual freedom and civil liberties and in the democratic institutions which have evolved on both sides of the Atlantic over the centuries'.[145]

The EU has no comparable trade agreement with the US, because the parties aim at developing their relationship using the WTO and not bilaterally. However, the EU and the US have adopted a declaration (1990), which emphasizes how they have formed a 'partnership', although in a legally non-binding way, to 'support democracy, the rule of law and respect for human rights and individual liberty, and promote prosperity and social progress world-wide'.[146] The partnership has a strong global aim with a 'responsibility to act jointly to resolve conflicts in troubled areas', thus being 'guided by the firm belief that the strengthening of democratic institutions and respect for human rights are essential to stability, prosperity, and development'.[147] This goal is, however, clearly external in orientation, as between the parties, there remain several important and long-standing differences of view on human rights.[148] The New Transatlantic Agenda specifies

''Adjustments' to human rights clause raise difficulties', Brussels 19 June 1997; Agence Europe, 'Some member states protest the content of the human rights clause agreed by the Commission and Mexico at the conclusion of negotiations of the interim and global agreements', Brussels, 13 June 1997.

[144] Framework Agreement for commercial and economic cooperation between the European Communities and Canada, [1976] OJ L 260/1.

[145] See the Joint Declaration of Canada, the European Community and its Member States of 22 November 1990, [1990] Bull. EC 91–93. See also 12 [1996] Bull. EU 120.

[146] See the Joint Declaration of the United States, the European Community and its Member States of 22 November 1990, [1990] Bull. EC 90–91. In addition, there are various sectoral agreements in force, for example on cooperation in higher education and vocational education and training, and in customs co-operation and co-operation on research and development activities in different areas. The relationship is based on a New Transatlantic Agenda and accompanying EU-US Joint Action Plan of December 1995 and the Transatlantic Economic Partnership created in May 1998. The ultimate goal is to establish a Transatlantic Market Place, a comprehensive free trade area between the EU and the US.

[147] See the Joint EU—US Action Plan, Part I 'Promoting Peace And Stability, Democracy And Development Around the World', Para 2. The document can be found on the Commission website http://www.europa.eu.int/comm/external_relations.

[148] For example, the EU's worldwide work towards the universal abolition and progressively restricted use of the death penalty has not required taking severe measures against the US, even though the US clearly does not comply with the EU's minimum standards. See the Guidelines on EU Policy towards Third Countries on the Death Penalty, adopted in June 1998 by the Council. Reproduced eg in the *European Union Annual Report on Human Rights* 1998–1999, 73.

that the partners are 'determined to reinforce' their 'political and economic partnership as a powerful force for good in the world'.[149]

An analoguous declaration has been adopted with Japan (1991), though there the reference to common traditions has been omitted. Instead, reference is made to 'common attachment to freedom, democracy, the rule of law and human rights', support to be given to 'social systems' based on these values and the need to foster respect for human rights as a major factor in genuine development.[150] Concerning other Asian states, the 1980 agreement with Indonesia, Malaysia, the Philippines, Singapore and Thailand (ASEAN) includes no reference to human rights but emphasizes 'friendly relations and traditional links', commitment to economic growth, social progress, cultural development, and balance in international relations, and the will to 'facilitate their respective human and material resources on the basis of freedom, equality and justice'.[151]

The situation is the same in respect to the 1985 agreement with China, which notes the development of friendly relations between the parties, sees the agreement as a 'new stage into their commercial and economic relations', and desires, 'on the basis of equality and mutual advantage, to intensify and diversify their trade and actively develop economic and technical cooperation in line with their mutual interests'.[152] The approach used for China when concluding new agreements is a sectoral one,[153] which sidesteps the need for a human rights clause. Different from the other major powers, the agreement with Russia (1997) includes a human rights clause.[154] But despite its existence, the clause has not been invoked, for example in the context of the on-going crisis in Chechnya, even if the entry into force of the agreement was slightly delayed due to the re-commencement of hostilities.[155]

---

[149] The New Transatlantic Agenda, Preamble. The document can be found on the Commission website http://www.europa.eu.int/comm/external_relations/.
[150] See the Joint Declaration published at the end of the European Community-Japan summit meeting in the Hague on 18 July 1991, [1991] 7/8 Bull. EC 109–110. In addition, there are various sectoral agreements in force.
[151] Cooperation Agreement between the European Economic Community and Indonesia, Malaysia, the Philippines, Singapore and Thailand—member countries of the Association of the South-East Asian Nations, [1980] OJ L 144/2, Preamble to the Agreement.
[152] Agreement on Trade and Economic Cooperation between the European Economic Community and the People's Republic of China, [1985] OJ L 250/2.
[153] See the Commission website http://europa.eu.int/comm/external_relations/china/intro/index.htm.
[154] Agreement on partnership and co-operation establishing a partnership between the European Communities and their Member States, of one part, and the Russian Federation, of the other part, published in [1997] OJ L 327/3. Art 2 states that: '[r]espect for democratic principles and human rights as defined in particular in the Helsinki Final Act and the Charter of Paris for a new Europe, underpins the internal and external policies of the Parties and constitutes an essential element of partnership and this Agreement'.
[155] See eg C Hillion, 'Partnership and Cooperation Agreements between the European Union and the New Independent States of the ex-Soviet Union', (1998) 3 Eur Foreign Affairs Rev 399, esp. 417–418; H Timmermann, 'Relations Between the EU and Russia: The Agreement on Partnership and Co-operation', (1996) 12(2) J of Communist Studies and Transition Politics 196, esp. 219–221.

The overall picture thus shows that no clauses have been inserted into the legally-binding parts of the agreements that the EU has with industrialized countries or other major powers, which forms an interesting contrast to the policy implemented, for example, in relation to the ACP states and the Central and Eastern European states. The EU has managed to include a human rights clause in all agreements it has negotiated with developing and other weaker states, which all include substantial trade benefits or preferential treatment. On the other hand, the EU has no 'modern' framework agreements with any of the strong Western powers, as the agreements concluded before 1995 have not been updated to cover the clause. The same applies to the Agreement on the European Economic Area between the EEC and six Western European states, which creates an extension of the internal market to the participating states but does not include human rights conditionality.[156] The EU has not insisted on the inclusion of human rights clauses in sectoral agreements,[157] which play a significant role in its contractual relations with industrialized states, and if these agreements are also in the future concluded on the same basis, then countries like the US, Australia and China will not 'be called on to make a legally binding commitment'.[158] The outcome of this is that the Community / Union human rights policies with its main trading partners are based on political declarations.[159] This does not, in any case, mean that these states would be free from human rights problems, such as the death penalty in the US, breaches of political freedoms in China and aboriginal land rights or the refugee question in Australia.[160]

The differing treatment granted to strong and weak countries is something that the European Parliament, for example, has criticized. It has accused the

[156] The EEA agreement was signed in May 1992 and entered into force on 1 January 1994 between the EEC and Austria, Finland, Iceland, Liechtenstein, Norway and Sweden. Switzerland signed the agreement but stayed ultimately outside. Since then, three of the parties have become members of the EU. For more details, see I MacLeod, ID Hendry and S Hyett, *The External Relations of the European Communities* (Oxford University Press: 1996) 377–380.

[157] See A Rosas, 'Economic, Social and Cultural Rights in the External Relations of the European Union' in A Eide *et al* (eds), *Economic, Social and Cultural Rights* (2nd edn, Kluwer Law International: 2001) 479, 486.

[158] A Ward, 'Frameworks for Cooperation between the European Union and Third States: a Viable Matrix for Uniform Human Rights Standards?' (1998) 3 Eur Foreign Affairs Rev 505, 515.

[159] For example, Japan and the U.S. are not only among the EU's major largest export markets, but also major investors in the EU. They count for 4,6% and 17% of exports and 7,4% and 24,2% of imports respectively. The figures are from the Commission external trade website, http://www. europa.eu.int/comm/trade/issues/index_en.htm. But even states like Canada (12th in terms of EU trade) and Australia (20th) are big players in terms of exports, imports and investment. This is especially so when compared with states coming under the Lomé framework. In figures, Australia's total trade with the EU amounts to almost half of the EU's total trade with all 77 ACP States together. Bilateral EU trade with the US in 2002 was approximately 1 billion € a day, which makes the total EU trade with the US about 16 times more than with Australia. The newest comparable figures on the Commission website are from 1998 and show that Australia's exchanges in goods amounted to 21.034 Mio € while total EU-ACP trade amounted to 44.016 Mio €. See http://www.europa.eu.int/ comm/trade/issues/index_en.htm for figures on Australia and http://europa.eu.int/comm/ development/body/cotonou/statistics/stat06_en.htm for the ACP states.

[160] Details can be found from any human rights NGO website, see eg http://www.amnesty.org.

Commission of 'two speed' and '*à la carte*' human rights policy and argued that while the EU has free hands to give priority to geostrategic, political or economic considerations, it should then not claim that its policy is mainly geared to human rights.[161] The Commission reply pointed out that with Mexico, the clause was finally included, and with Australia, it was a question of coherent '*realpolitik*' choices and choosing between a joint declaration and nothing.[162] However, this practice suggests a double standard in the EU human rights policy. Conditionality seems to be mainly included in agreements with small developing states. On the other hand, the practice of declaration may be distinguished as better in line with the multilateral (WTO/GATT) system.[163] However, this does not completely do away with the impression that EU attitudes towards large industrialized states in human rights matters differ significantly from its policies vis-à-vis Old European colonies.

V. Implementation

Not only are the agreements different between 'weak' and 'strong' states, but there is also a difference in their implementation. In relation to industrialized states that have no bilateral agreement with the EU, the Most Favoured Nation (MFN) principle under the GATT is implemented.[164] Because there are no specific preferences to suspend, any sanctions would go against 'normal' non-preferential trade. Because there is no human rights clause in the GATT,[165] escaping the GATT obligations would require a decision to impose sanctions by the UN Security Council, something that makes the suspension of trade relations with an industrialized

---

[161] Agence Europe, 'In the run up to signing joint EU/Australia declaration (Thursday in Luxemburg), several MEPs criticise European 'a la carte' human rights policy', Brussels 24 June 1997.

[162] ibid.

[163] The option implemented for Australia and New Zealand does correspond to the standard route used for industrialized countries, for which a free trade agreement (FTA) is the only WTO compatible alternative. See Art XXIV(5) of the GATT, which establishes the right to deviate from the general MFN principle in order to form a customs union or a free-trade area. Instead of concluding FTAs, the EU deals with these states under the GATT with reference to the MFN principle. Sectoral agreements, on the other hand, never contain a human rights clause, whatever country they are concluded with. There are thus also good reasons for not concluding general trade agreements with industrialised countries, as they would not offer much more than the commitments already contained within the GATT.

[164] The MFN principle forms the cornerstone of the trade liberalization system under the WTO and is included in Art I of the GATT Agreement. It requires that the same trade preferences are, in principle, granted equally to all WTO members.

[165] The closest that the GATT comes to human rights is Art XX, which justifies measures deviating from GATT obligations, eg in the case of protection of public morals or protection of human, animal or plant life or health. There is, however, a debate going on about integrating a human rights dimension into GATT. See eg Gabrielle Marceau, 'WTO Dispute Settlement and Human Rights', published in the Eur J of Intl L Discussion Forum on Trade and Human Rights, available at http://ejil.org/journal/Vol13/no4/art1.html.

country an unlikely event. The agreements with the developing world again offer specific trade preferences, and in revoking them the EU does not need the backing-up of a Security Council resolution in order to circumvent its obligations under the GATT. In addition, the agreements include the essential element clause, which can be used as a basis for the suspension of the agreement.

Other differences in approach between 'weak' and 'strong' states can be observed in relation to whether the human rights clause, if it exists, is actually invoked or not in cases of suspected human rights breaches. Russia is a 'strong state' with which the EU has negotiated a human rights clause. In general, the EU has found that it should not neglect long-term considerations for the development of its relationship with Russia, and thus, for example, a 'short-term problem' like Chechnya should not be allowed to dominate EU policy-making.[166] The 1999 Common Strategy on Russia includes no mention of political conditionality. Its political dimension ('Consolidation of democracy, the rule of law and public institutions in Russia') and economic dimension ('Integration of Russia into a common European economic and social space') are approached as separate areas of action.[167] In February 2004 the Commission adopted a Communication, in which it called for a stricter EU policy on human rights issues such as media freedom and events in Chechnya. In particular, the Commission argued, the fact that the partnership is based on common values implies that Russian practices running counter to European values should be discussed frankly.[168] This does not, however, seem to imply establishing a closer connection between human rights issues and trade. Or, as Russia's acting Foreign Minister Ivanov concluded shortly after the adoption of the Communication, 'the word "sanctions" does not exist at all in a political dialogue between Russia and the EU'.[169] What is then required by means of actual observance under the political principles included in the agreement is 'highly dependent on the way the two Parties interpret them'.[170] The reference to 'common values' should perhaps mainly be seen as signifying the intention of Europeans to 'integrate Russia into the community of Western values', and the confirmation by Russia of the continuation of reforms leading to this objective.[171]

---

[166] See eg Conclusions of General Affairs Council 2239th meeting, 'Relations with Russia', Brussels 24 January 2000; C Hillion, 'Partnership and Cooperation Agreements between the European Union and the New Independent States of the ex-Soviet Union', (1998) 3 Eur Foreign Affairs Rev 399, esp. 417–418.

[167] See the Common Strategy of the European Union of 4 June 1999 on Russia, 1999/414/CSFP.

[168] Communication from the Commission to the Council and the European Parliament on relations with Russia, COM (2004) 106, 9 February 2004.

[169] Quoted in EUobserver, 'No crisis in EU-Russia relations, says Moscow', 26 February 2004. The document can be obtained from http://www.euobserver.com. On this, see also E Fierro Sedano, *The EU's Approach to Human Rights Conditionality in Practice*, PhD thesis written at the European University Institute, Florence (submitted in December 2001) 359–363.

[170] See C Hillion, 'Institutional Aspects of the Partnership between the European Union and the Newly Independent States of the Former Soviet Union: Case Studies of Russia and Ukraine' (2000) 37 CML Rev 1211, 1221.

[171] H Timmermann, 'Relations Between the EU and Russia: The Agreement on Partnership and Co-operation', (1996) 12(2) *J of Communist Studies and Transition Politics* 196, 203.

Concerning China, a 'strong' state without a human rights clause, the EU has chosen to approach its widely-known human rights problems through political dialogue and avoid a direct linkage between human rights and trade.[172] Following this policy line, the 2003 Commission Communication includes no mention of political conditionality.[173] In fact, the Communication recognises that human rights, the rule of law and political reforms are 'sensitive for China'.[174] Therefore:

[d]ialogue and co-operation should continue to constitute the main EU approach to improving the human rights situation in China, although this should not exclude expressing comments and observations in other appropriate fora.[175]

The Council has confirmed that the EU-China dialogue 'is the Union's preferred channel for working to improve the situation in areas of concern to it', even though the Union has now decided to 'step up the dialogue, focus it better and assess it on a continuous basis'.[176] The Council's conclusion is somehow surprising, recalling that it is talking about *dialogue*: 'The European Union urges China to contribute to this exchange too.'[177]

In relation to the developing world, suspension of agreements has become routine especially under the Lomé / Cotonou agreement. Article 96 of the agreement establishes a compulsory consultation procedure, which applies save for cases of 'special urgency'. Under the procedure, the party that considers that the other party has 'failed to fulfil an obligation stemming from respect for human rights, democratic principles and the rule of law' shall supply information of the breach to the other party and invite to the holding of consultations. However, if no solution acceptable to both parties is found, if consultations are refused or if there is a case of special urgency, 'appropriate measures' can be taken. There are, in fact, numerous cases in which the Council has initiated consultations and then decided on measures.[178] For example, concerning Haiti, the Council decided in January 2001 that the consultations held after some irregularities in the electoral process in Haiti had not led:

[t]o progress in finding a satisfactory solution to the issues raised by the Union, which then drafted provisional conclusions expressing regret that its concerns had not been taken into

---

[172] See M Fouwels, 'The European Union's Common Foreign and Security Policy and Human Rights', (1997) 15/3 Netherlands Q of Human Rights 291, 318–321; E Shaver Duquette, 'Human Rights in the European Union: Internal Versus External Objectives', (2001) 34 Cornell Intl L J 363, esp. at 386–392.

[173] Commission Policy Paper for Transmission to the Council and the European Parliament. A Maturing partnership—shared interests and challenges in EU-China relations, Brussels 10 September 2003, COM (2003) 533 final.   [174] ibid 7.

[175] ibid 13.

[176] See the Conclusions of General Affairs Council 2327th Council Meeting, 'EU-China dialogue on human rights', Brussels 22–23 January 2001, Para 6.   [177] ibid Para 7.

[178] Eg for the case of Comoros, see the Monthly Rev on Human Rights and Democratisation of February 2000, issued by the European Commission External Relations DG; for Fiji, see the Monthly Rev for July-August 2000 and October 2000; Haiti, see the Monthly Rev for July-August 2000, September 2000, December 2000 and January-February 2002; for Cote d'Ivoire, see the Monthly Rev for December 2000 and February 2001.

account and envisaging the possibility of appropriate measures as defined in the ACP-EC Agreement.[179]

Following this finding, the Council first terminated the consultations and then decided on not making available certain sums of money, namely a suspension of direct budget aid, and both redirection of certain funds and possibly non-allocation of other resources under the European Development Fund.[180] Similar measures were taken recently, eg in relation to Zimbabwe following the Council's decision to conclude the consultations under Article 96.[181] While many of these measures can certainly be justified from a human rights perspective, the implementation of the suspension process generally places the party hit by negative measures in a weak position, as it is 'completely at the mercy of the other states parties and can only await, or informally lobby for, a lifting of the measures', which is something that fits ill with the ideas of 'equality between partners and security of their relations'.[182] The position of the Union is even stronger in the area of the GSP, because it is a unilateral measure providing more preferential treatment for developing states under the EU's own discretion, something that is in principle also compatible with the GATT rules.[183] The GSP is an especially significant part of development policy towards those states with which the EC does not have a contractual relationship, or only has a very basic agreement. So far, Myanmar is the only GSP case that has actually led to sanctions due to the use of forced labour,[184] but an investigation has been initiated with respect to Belarus.[185]

---

[179] See the Monthly Rev on Human Rights and Democratisation of February 2001, issued by the European Commission External Relations DG, 10.   [180] ibid.

[181] See Council Decision 2002/148/EC of 18 February 2002 concluding consultations with Zimbabwe under Article 96 of the ACP-EC Partnership Agreement, [2002] OJ L 50/64. The decision was renewed through Council Decision 2004/157/EC of 19 February 2004 extending the period of application of the measures in Council Decision 2002/148/EC concluding consultations with Zimbabwe under Article 96 of the ACP-EC Partnership Agreement, [2004] OJ L 50/60.

[182] K Arts, *Integrating Human Rights into Development Cooperation: The Case of the Lomé Convention* (Kluwer Law International: 2000) 193.

[183] On the 'Enabling Clause', the effect of WTO judgments on the GSP system and recent development, see eg R Howse, 'India's WTO Challenge to Drug Enforcement Conditions in the European Community Generalized System of Preferences: A Little Known Case with Major Repercussions for 'Political' Conditionality in US Trade Policy', (2003) 4(2) Chicago J of Intl L 385. The WTO Appellate Body decided in April 2004 in a case relating to additional benefits granted to certain developing states that comply with certain rules combating drug trafficking that the EC GSP arrangement enabling differentiation between different developing states was in principle compatible with WTO rules presuming that the treatment is non-discriminatory and thus ensures identical treatment to all 'similarly-situated' GSP beneficiaries. See *European Communities—Conditions for the Granting of Tariff Preferences to Developing Countries*, Report of the Appellate Body, WT/DS246/AB/R.

[184] Council Regulation (EC) No 552/97 of 24 March 1997 temporarily withdrawing access to generalized tariff preferences from the Union of Myanmar, [1997] OJ L 85/8.

[185] Commission Decision 2004/23/EC of 29 December 2003 providing for the initiation of an investigation pursuant to Article 27(2) of Council Regulation (EC) No 2501/2001 with respect to the violation of freedom of association in Belarus, [2004] OJ L 5/90.

Moreover, at the suspension stage, it has been argued, consistency is often missing: in relation to some ACP countries the policy has been strict while in other serious situations nothing has been done.[186] Other considerations have often overruled human rights concerns. For example, despite serious human rights concerns caused by military government and annulment of free elections, Nigeria remained an important trade partner of the Community, thanks to its oil exports.[187] The European Parliament repeatedly pointed out the ineffectiveness of the EU sanctions and suggested new more effective ones including an oil embargo, which would deprive the military junta of its main source of income.[188] The sanctions adopted by the Council, however, were of a far more limited nature, including restricted visa policies, interruption of sports contacts, and support for human rights resolutions on Nigeria in UN organs.[189] The visa restrictions were further eased in 1998 in order to enable Nigeria to participate in the 1998 Football World Championship, held in France.[190] The European Parliament saw this exception as a lost opportunity to influence the human rights situation and pointed out that the sanctions were continuously manipulated by the oil companies operating in Nigeria.[191] It was only later in that year that development in Nigeria started to go in a positive direction, with General Abubakar starting to implement a transition programme.[192] Therefore, it seems that sometimes weak sanctions are imposed for political or economic reasons and are thus unlikely to work. But there has also been widespread criticism concerning the effectiveness of negative measures in general, as they seldom address the root causes of human rights problems but punish governments and populations for more general failures.[193]

---

[186] K Arts, *Integrating Human Rights into Development Cooperation: The Case of the Lomé Convention* (Kluwer Law International: 2000) 353.   [187] ibid 351–352.

[188] European Parliament resolution on Nigeria, [1996] OJ C 166/200; European Parliament resolution on Nigeria, [1996] OJ C 362/261; European Parliament resolution on Nigeria [1998] OJ C 14/204.

[189] Common position 95/544/CFSP defined by the Council on the basis of Art J.2 of the Treaty on European Union, on Nigeria, [1995] OJ L 309/1.

[190] Council Decision 97/820/CFSP of 28 November 1997 on the implementation of Common Position 95/544 on Nigeria, [1997] OJ L 338/7. K Arts, 'Development Cooperation and Human Rights: Turbulent Times for EU Policy' in M Lister (ed), *New Perspectives on European Union Development Cooperation* (Westview Press: 1999) 7, 18.

[191] European Parliament resolution on Nigeria of 18 December 1997, [1998] OJ C 14/204.

[192] See Common Position 98/614/CFSP of 30 October 1998 defined by the Council on the basis of Art J.2 of the Treaty on European Union concerning Nigeria, [1998] OJ L 293/77; Council Decision 1998/317/CFSP of 17 May 1999 repealing Common Position 98/614/CFSP concerning Nigeria 1999/614/CFSP, [1999] OJ 133/5; Council Common Position 2001/373/CFSP of 14 May 2001 on Nigeria, [2001] OJ L 132/1; ACP-EU Joint Assembly Res on the Situation in Nigeria, [1999] OJ C 271/52.

[193] DJ Marantis, 'Human Rights, Democracy and Development: The European Community Model', (1994) 7 Harvard Human Rights J 1, 12–13. For critical analysis of the effectiveness of sanctions, see eg J Galtung, 'On the Effects of International Economic Sanctions. With Examples from the Case of Rhodesia' (1967) 19(3) *World Politics* 378.

In addition to various political factors affecting EU implementation of the suspension clauses, human rights-related development projects suffer from a lack of staff on the EU side, which shows in insufficient information, evaluation and impact assessment.[194] In auditing that particular part of the development budget, the European Court of Auditors expressed its concern over the situation. In particular:

[. . .] the Court found little evidence that the Commission had effectively assessed the democracy and human rights situation and needs of the beneficiary countries and that it had developed a strategy specifically tailored to the requirements of the country (identifying key problems and proposing solutions).[195]

Moreover, the Court argued, the guidelines and procedures of the Commission were burdensome, and the objectives and results of individual projects were not clearly defined and quantified:

Frequently, project activities were presented as the purpose of the project. In none of the projects examined were the criteria for judging success made explicit, nor were any mechanisms proposed for evaluating this.[196]

In general, objectives were too generally defined; there was a lack of indicators and information, too many small projects, and a general 'lack of management of results, unsatisfactory systems, concentration of operational aspects [. . .] and delays in implementation and disbursements'.[197] Staff resources were limited and 'considerably below operational needs'.[198] However, the Court pointed out, as the objective of democracy and human rights consists a very broad area of definition, it is not difficult to justify just about any intervention—or non-intervention—by reference to that objective.[199]

The emerging pattern shows how attention is focused primarily on the developing world, as:

[s]ome of the Union's most important trading partners, along with regions carrying great trade potential, have been vested with immunity from legally binding human rights clauses when elaborating their trade relations with the Union.[200]

For some, this is evidence of a double standard being used: while the human rights clause offers some human rights potential, its more effective use would require far

---

[194] See eg B Simma *et al.*, 'Human Rights Considerations in the Development Co-operation Activities of the EC' in P Alston *et al.* (eds), *The EU and Human Rights* (Oxford University Press: 1999) 572, esp. 615–620.

[195] Court of Auditors, Special Report No 12/2000 on the management by the Commission of European Union support for the development of human rights and democracy in third countries, together with the Commission's replies, [2000] OJ C 230/01, Para 22.

[196] ibid Paras 30 and 35.   [197] ibid Para 46.   [198] ibid Para 54.

[199] ibid Para 40.

[200] A Ward, 'Frameworks for Cooperation between the European Union and Third States: a Viable Matrix for Uniform Human Rights Standards?' (1998) 3 Eur Foreign Affairs Rev 505, at 506, 515. (Quote at 506).

more contextual approaches and resort to positive measures instead of negative ones.[201] The Australian case shows how much more difficult it is to get an industrialized country to agree to a human rights clause than a developing country: the political (and economic) leverage available for the former is far greater than for the latter.[202] Even if understandable in terms of traditional relationships and political realities, the impression of double standards lingers on. For others, however, the two-track approach is explicable, because if the EU human rights policy is considered an:

exercise in power and not morality, there is no inconsistency in policy application. Rather, the EU exercises its economic power to achieve human rights goals to the extent that it is economically feasible.[203]

More than double standards, these observers would point to a question of practical achievability. Such a realistic approach would be more reactive and flexible than 'the moralistic and aggressive pursuit of human rights that the EU sets forth in its treaties and resolutions'. This entails that with stronger partners, economic considerations rule, while with weaker ones, the EU affords 'to make policy based on morals', demonstrating how the EU 'is prepared to champion human rights causes only as far as its economic might allows'.[204] Moreover, the EU external agreements are always more about trade (or development) than about human rights: they are by definition trade and not human rights agreements.[205] In addition, the differences relating to the application of the GATT also affect the relationships considerably.

Such differences of opinion are a natural aspect of the choices involved in balancing human rights and economic considerations. The point, however, is that having chosen to appeal to standards of human rights and democracy that it emphasizes are universal, the EU (and numerous other Western organizations using the same argumentation) puts itself in a thorny position. If human rights are universal, then there should be no distinction between the treatment of industrialized and developing states. While the human rights clause does not necessarily lose all of its purpose (for example, in relation to highlighting the importance of

---

[201] See M Bulterman, *Human Rights in the Treaty Relation of the European Community. Real Virtues or Virtual Reality?* (Intersentia: 2001); E Fierro Sedano, *The EU's Approach to Human Rights Conditionality in Practice*, PhD thesis written at the European University Institute, Florence (submitted in December 2001) 306, 393–404; F Hoffmeister, *Menschenrechts- und Demokratieklauseln in den vertraglichen Außenbeziehungen der Europäischen Gemeinschaft* (Springer: 1998); PJ Kuyper, 'Trade Sanctions, Security, Human Rights and Commercial Policy' in M Maresceau, *The European Community's Commercial Policy after 1992: The Legal Dimension* (Dordrecht, Martinus Nijhoff Publishers: 1993) 387.					[202] See Fierro Sedano (n 201 above) 298.
[203] E Shaver Duquette, 'Human Rights in the European Union: Internal Versus External Objectives', (2001) 34 Cornell Intl L J 363, 395.					[204] ibid.
[205] See also Case C-268/94 *Portugal v Council*, [1996] ECR I-6177, Paras 23–27. According to the Court, to adopt 'cooperation policy to respect for human rights necessarily entails establishing a certain connection between those matters whereby one of them is made subordinate to the other'. ibid, Para 26.

human rights, spreading the good word and encouraging ratification of UN Conventions) because it is not used against everyone, a concern over its consistent application puts to question the credibility of a policy based on universality. If human rights are universal, then there should be no presumption that EU and Australian values or practices would *a priori* be more compatible than EU and ACP values or practices. If the EU chooses to claim universality, then it must take into consideration that the expectations of objectivity and consistency follow. In this sense, consistency and objectivity in application seem to follow the universalist claim:

[i]nconsistency in policy implementation cannot easily be dismissed as a function of conflicting foreign policy objectives. The universal nature of these principles itself requires that their application be objective and non-selective.[206]

Therefore, if human rights, as expressed in international law, are universal and the human rights clause is fully in accordance with international law, then the clause should be included in all agreements and invoked as a rule.[207] The mere existence of the clause is not enough; it must also be invoked in the same manner.

On the other hand, for human rights to operate on this basis, they should include a clear set of standards that would make it impossible to claim that one state has been treated differently from another—the standards would be the same, because they are universal. For human rights to apply universally there must be universal set of standards. As a result, if the EU invokes universality, it should engage in all battles around the world with equal strength and interest. However, based on EU practice it seems questionable what kind of universalism it is actually referring to. While universalism is strict when invoked against developing states, it allows for flexibility in relation to the EU's major trade partners. Universalism does not seem to affect 'strong' and 'weak' states in the same way. Moreover, as will be seen in the next section, the contradictions between the 'strong' and the 'weak' states and the contradictions inherent to universal human rights also affect the conception and implementation of specific human rights.

VI. Right to Development

Even though the question of the right to development is not formally a part of the EU-ACP discussions, it lurks in the background and also contributes to group-forming between the 'weak' and the 'strong' states. In 1991, the Council and the

---

[206] G Crawford, 'Human Rights and Democracy in EU Development Co-operation: Towards Fair and Equal Treatment', in M Lister (ed), *European Union Development Policy* (London, Macmillan: 1998) 131, 159.

[207] After all, the '[i]nternational community must treat human rights globally in a fair and equal manner, on the same footing, and with the same emphasis.' See the Vienna Declaration and Programme of Action, Part II, Para 3.

Member States adopted a resolution on development and human rights, which underlined the need for positive measures and increased assistance to countries that respect human rights.[208] Faithful to the liberal tradition, the resolution approached human rights and democracy as a precondition for development. In doing so:

[t]he Council in effect claimed a right to supervise the domestic implementation of the right to development. If aid is to be given to promote development, and development can occur only in a democratic society guaranteeing human rights, in order to ensure that individuals are able to realise their right to development the Community must be entitled to take measures to promote democracy and human rights.[209]

The problem with this logic is that the right to development, which initially was a tool used by the developing states to justify increased amounts of development assistance, suddenly turns into a tool for the developed countries that use it to justify far-reaching domestic adjustments by recipient states, which traditionally would have been considered to fall within the domestic jurisdiction of the latter.[210] With the right to development thus quite transformed, the EU has adopted its own reading of it, and then declared itself responsible for supervising its implementation.

Superficially, this may seem to have meant a transformation in the EU's traditional view, which emphasized individual rights over collective ones. By the time of the 1993 Vienna Declaration, the Community had apparently accepted the earlier Third World view. This was reflected in the Declaration:

The World Conference on Human Rights reaffirms the right to development, as established in the Declaration on the Right to Development, as a universal and inalienable right and an integral part of fundamental human rights.[211]

For the Community, this declaration implied that 'for the first time, there is consensus in the international community on the principle of the right to development'.[212] But in many ways, the Vienna Conference also showed that many of the fundamental differences in approach to the right to development between the EU and the developing world had remained unchanged. For example, in Vienna many developing states condemned the linking of

---

[208] [1991] 11 Bull. EC Para 2.3.1, Art 2. 'Positive measures' have been gradually introduced to the EC development co-operation. See especially Council Regulation 975/1999 of 29 April 1999 laying down the requirements for the implementation of development co-operations which contribute to the general objective of developing and consolidating democracy and the rule of law and to that of respecting human rights and fundamental freedoms, [1999] OJ L 120/1.

[209] T King, 'Human Rights in the Development Policy of the European Community: Towards a European World Order?', (1997) XXVIII Netherlands Ybk of Intl L 51, 66–67.   [210] ibid 67.

[211] The Vienna Declaration and Programme of Action, adopted by the World Conference on Human Rights on 25 June 1993, A/Conf. 157/23, Part I, Para 10.

[212] Report on the Implementation of Measures to Promote Observance of Human Rights and Democratic Principles (For 1994), Brussels 12 July 1995, COM (95)191 final at 18 (emphasis omitted).

development co-operation to structural adjustment policies or civil and political rights.[213]

There have always been two discourses on the right to development that do not meet. For developing states, the entitlement to receive aid has been a very central part of this right.[214] The industrialized states, however, do not interpret the right that way and have never accepted a *duty* to provide assistance. Because they are the ones with the resources, development assistance has remained an act of charity on their part. Likewise, the EU has been unwilling to refer to the right to development in any such way that would tie its hands. Instead, the EU wishes to address the right to development as a question that is separate from what it understands as the universal human rights. Instead of being an entitlement to a right, development is merely an objective, and aid remains linked to performance, EU standards and the need of the developing state.[215] The developing states say they need money so that they can develop and then have resources to implement human rights; the EU says they have to implement human rights first because human rights are the precondition for development,[216] and because there is no entitlement to get aid, human rights (among other things) serve as a condition for receiving it.[217] However, as Kennedy has pointed out, there is from a technical point-of-view no consensus on how to bring about 'development'. Thus, political choices between different alternatives need to be made.[218] By seeing assistance as subject to its own discretion, the EU arrogates this choice to itself. As the donor, it can decide.

The EU (EC) has always been reluctant to accept development as a collective right[219] and has avoided addressing its distributive aspects within its own development policy framework.[220] Nonetheless, these policies have always required political choice: while the EU development policy strengthens some elements of this

---

[213] S Marks, 'Nightmare and Noble Dream; The 1993 World Conference on Human Rights', (1994) CLJ 54, 58.

[214] See eg the UN General Assembly resolution of 4 December 2002 on the right to development, A/RES/57/223, Para 15, reaffirming the commitment of developed countries to give 0–7 of their GNP for official development assistance to developing countries.

[215] Especially after the Cotonou agreement, allocation of aid is no longer automatic but based on needs and performance. See K Arts, 'ACP-EU Relations in a New Era: The Cotonou Agreement', (2003) 40 CML Rev 95, 100.

[216] This is actually occasionally contradicted by findings in the field, showing how many of the fastest growing states have actually been dictatorships and not democracies. See S Seppänen, *Good Governance in International Law*, The Erik Castrén Institute Research Reports 13/2003, 24.

[217] On this, see eg K Arts, *Integrating Human Rights into Development Cooperation: The Case of the Lomé Convention* (Kluwer Law International: 2000) 44.

[218] See D Kennedy, 'Laws and Developments' in A Perry and J Hatchard (eds) *Contemplating Complexity: Law and Development in the 21st Century* (Cavendish Publishing: 2003).

[219] T King, 'Human Rights in the Development Policy of the European Community: Towards a European World Order?', (1997) XXVIII Netherlands Ybk of Intl L 51, 65.

[220] K Arts, 'Implementing the Right to Development? An Analysis of European Community Development and Human Rights Policies', (1996) Human Rights in Developing Countries Ybk 37.

right others remain without consideration.²²¹ Instruments like the Common Agricultural Policy (CAP) and the EU development policy work against each other,²²² because in practice, the CAP 'regularly leads to all sorts of undesirable restrictions and distortions of local markets and consumption patterns in ACP and other developing countries'.²²³

Still, it would be wrong to argue that the right to development is irrelevant for EU policies: it has been a central part of the discussion between European states and developing states since the independence of the latter group, even though there has not been any agreement on what it entails in practice. Therefore, referring to the irrelevance of the right also risks appearing dreadfully indifferent: just because the EU does not like the right to development, it can still be a living reality for the developing states.²²⁴ Simultaneously, the right to development is not necessarily a particularly useful tool. Instead, it seems to work in the same way as many of the other aspects of the EU-ACP relationship, and as such is a symbol of fundamental differences rather than common understandings. From the developing states' view, the discussion on development is completely on the wrong track, as their understanding of both the universal set of rights and their contribution to political practice would be quite different. Therefore, in relation to the right to development, the 'universal' seems to allow different, even opposite, readings.

VII. Cultural Relativism

Cultural relativism has generally appeared as the main challenge to universalism in human rights debates, and as such it surfaced especially in the 1993 World Conference on Human Rights. For the EU, the World Conference evidenced worldwide acceptance of the doctrine of universal human rights. For others, however, it embodied failure to regenerate dialogue between Asia and the West, for example, and in fact provoked hardened attitudes on both sides, and increase in scepticism.²²⁵ The

²²¹ K Arts, 'Implementing the Right to Development? An Analysis of European Community Development and Human Rights Policies', (1996) Human Rights in Developing Countries Ybk 37 67–69. Arts mentions the fair distribution of the benefits of development and the fact that both collective rights and social, economic and cultural rights have been left outside Community development priorities.   ²²² ibid 67–68.
²²³ K Arts, 'ACP-EU Relations in a New Era: The Cotonou Agreement', (2003) 40 CML Rev 95, 99.
²²⁴ See eg UN Commission on Human Rights resolution 2002/69 of 25 April 2002 on the right to development, adopted by a recorded vote of 38 votes to none, with 15 abstentions. The resolution stresses, among other things, 'the need for mainstreaming the right to development and underlines that in relation to the international economic, commercial and financial spheres, core principles such as equality, equity, non-discrimination, transparency, accountability, participation and international cooperation, including partnership and commitments, are important for the realization of the right to development'. ibid Para 22.
²²⁵ B Kausikan, 'Asia's Different Standard', (1993) 92 *Foreign Policy* 24, 32.

central problem with universalism was that the:

hard core of rights that are truly universal is smaller than many in the West are wont to pretend. Forty-five years after the Universal Declaration was adopted, many of its 30 articles are still subject to debate over interpretation and application—not just between Asia and the West but within the West itself.[226]

The Western conception of human rights universalism is thus in many parts of the world strongly rejected, often with reference to 'cultural relativism', which can then relate to the identification and substance of rights, to their interpretation or their form of implementation.[227] For relativists, human rights are to a large extent founded on the Western liberal tradition and would require significant adjustment in order to be grafted onto different traditions[228]: 'rights and rules about morality are encoded in and thus depend on cultural context', meaning that the 'world contains an impressive diversity in views about right and wrong that is linked to the diverse underlying cultures'.[229] As a result, at least some or even most cultural variations are 'exempt from legitimate criticism by outsiders'.[230]

The doctrine of cultural relativism has been invoked for notoriously varying objectives, extending from the usage of the notions of liberty and individualism, equality and collectivism and the abuse of capitalism to how the human rights discourse should aim at a more reasonable and balanced approach and recognize interplay between various cultural factors in the construction and constitution of human rights.[231] Some cultural relativists argue that while human rights as such are universally valid, they should be interpreted differently in Western and non-Western environments. This is because the legitimacy and meaning of moral claims is closely attached to a particular cultural tradition, and for the so-called universal rights this context is the Western one deriving from the Enlightenment:

Understood in this light, the human rights idea is at best misguided in its core claim that it embodies universal values—and at worst a blend of moral hubris and cultural imperialism.[232]

Instead, as Vincent has argued, the plurality of cultures in the world should be allowed to produce their own values, resulting in no universal values: 'This, to a

---

[226] ibid 34.

[227] See J Donnelly, 'Cultural Relativism and Universal Human Rights, (1984) 6 Human Rights Q 400, 401.

[228] S Marks, 'Nightmare and Noble Dream; The 1993 World Conference on Human Rights', (1994) CLJ 54, 55.

[229] HJ Steiner and P Alston, *International Human Rights in Context* (2nd edn, Oxford University Press: 2000) 366–367.

[230] See J Donnelly, 'Cultural Relativism and Universal Human Rights, (1984) 6 Human Rights Q 400, 400.

[231] B Ibhawoh, 'Cultural Relativism and Human Rights: Reconsidering the Africanist Discourse', (2991) 19/1 The Netherlands Q of Human Rights 43, 61.

[232] DF Orentlicher, 'Relativism and Religion', in M Ignatieff, *Human Rights as Politics and Idolatry* (introduced and edited by A Gutmann), (Princeton University Press: 2001) 141, 141–142.

cultural relativist, is not a problem. It is a solution.'[233] If there is failure to consider cultural differences:

Universality obtained at the expense of genuine understanding and commitment cheapens and devalues the idea of human rights. Ultimately, such universality is of little normative value in the reconstruction of societies.[234]

Thus, if local standards and constraints are overlooked, then the globalized human rights standards become difficult to realize, and the promotion of a universal view of human rights will do little to ensure their actual realization in the developing world.[235] Therefore,

The myth of the universality of all human rights is harmful if it masks the real gap that exists between Asian and Western perceptions of human rights. The gap will not be bridged if it is denied.[236]

For Mutua, the essential problem with the current human rights corpus is that it continues the 'Eurocentric colonial project', which casts states in superior and subordinate positions and thus undermines the basic claim of universality presented by the human rights movement.[237] For Mutua, 'European' or 'Eurocentric' refer to cultural specificity and historical exclusivity in a discourse in which human rights 'have either been imposed on, or assimilated by, non-European societies'.[238] Because the West can no longer dominate the world through direct imperial rule, it invokes the:

impartial, universalizing language of human rights and seeks to impose its own narrow agenda on a plethora of world cultures that do not actually share the West's conception of individuality, selfhood, agency, or freedom.[239]

For Mutua, while the UDHR has undeniably laid the foundation for the human rights movement, with its ideas being embraced by diverse peoples across the earth, this is only half the story. In embracing the corpus, these people also wish to contribute to it, even reformulate it radically. Therefore, the human rights movement must 'not be closed to the idea of change or believe that it is the "final" answer'.[240]

---

[233] RJ Vincent, *Human Rights and International Relations* (Cambridge University Press: 1986, 1999) 38.

[234] M wa Mutua, 'Politics And Human Rights: An Essential Symbiosis' in M Byers (ed), *The Role of Law in International Politics. Essays in International Relations and International Law* (Oxford University Press: 2000) 149, 161.

[235] M Monshipouri, 'Promoting Universal Human Rights: Dilemmas of Integrating Developing Countries', (2001) 4 Yale Human Rights & Development L J 25, 26.

[236] B Kausikan, 'Asia's Different Standard', (1993) 92 *Foreign Policy* 24, 32.

[237] M Mutua, 'Savages, Victims and Saviors: The Metaphor of Human Rights', (2001) 42(1) Harvard Intl L J 200, 204–205.   [238] ibid note 14.

[239] See M Ignatieff, *Human Rights as Politics and Idolatry* (introduced and edited by A Gutmann), (Princeton University Press: 2001) 61–62.

[240] M wa Mutua, 'Politics And Human Rights: An Essential Symbiosis' in M Byers (ed), *The Role of Law in International Politics. Essays in International Relations and International Law* (Oxford University Press: 2000) 149, 173.

The belief that human rights provide final answers is closely attached to the unwillingness of many human rights activists to admit that their cause is essentially liberal and Western. In claiming that the grounding of rights is universal and as such:

independent of the particular kind of societies in which they are characteristically found, such advocates place themselves in a false position, and, perhaps paradoxically, weaken the credibility of their stand.[241]

Some cultural relativists say that as human rights are a Western concept, they cannot be implemented elsewhere, because human rights are insensitive to cultural differences and thus not valid outside the West.[242] Instead, '[h]uman rights must be sought in the practice of the various cultures making up the world, and not in what amount to the political preferences of but one of them'[sic].[243] This is because '[p]articular moralities have no purchase on objective truth, and can lay no claim to universality',[244] which makes the West 'no more or less special than any other region'.[245] While it might be acceptable for the West to protest against genocide, murder, torture or slavery, as there is a clear consensus on these, it should refrain from objecting to capital punishment, detention without trial, or curbs on press freedoms, because 'it should recognize that it does so in a context where the international law is less definitive and where there is room for further elaboration through debate'.[246]

Economic realities persisting in the developing world also affect the implementation of human rights. However, Monshipouri argues that cultural sensitivity in the face of economic realities is separate from the cultural relativists' argument. For him, referring to cultural relativism as an excuse for lacking political will to implement human rights is far worse than the problems caused by the economic realities pertaining in some countries, which makes them adhere 'less to some global standard of human rights in order to promote overall human rights in socioeconomic realms'.[247] This is not a question of human rights not being valid in different cultural contexts, but a practical problem relating to the difficulties in committing to the full range of human rights in unequal economic circumstances and priorities: 'Such a commitment—if and when it exists—remains unrealistic at best.'[248] The rights and responsibilities implied in the discourse of universal human rights are thus not matched with equal amounts of time and money: 'When moral ends are universal, but means are limited, disappointment is

---

[241] C Brown, 'Universal human rights: a critique' in T Dunne and NJ Wheeler (eds), *Human Rights in Global Politics* (Cambridge University Press: 1999) 103, 104.
[242] See RJ Vincent, *Human Rights and International Relations* (Cambridge University Press: 1986, 1999) 53. [243] ibid.
[244] ibid. [245] B Kausikan, 'Asia's Different Standard', (1993) 92 *Foreign Policy* 24, 39.
[246] ibid.
[247] M Monshipouri, 'Promoting Universal Human Rights: Dilemmas of Integrating Developing Countries', (2001) 4 Yale Human Rights & Development L J 25, 26. [248] ibid 61.

inevitable.'[249] However, arguing that human rights are not for poor countries but only for rich goes against the idea of universality itself, because it implies that the poor people would not be worthy of the same rights as the rich.

But, as Gellner has noted, 'it is conceivable that relativism be true, and yet human universals obtain; and equally, it is possible that relativism be false, and yet no universals obtain'.[250] In other words, it seems unclear where the limits of cultural relativism should be drawn. Does the doctrine presume that absolutely everything is relative, and that we have to accept *all* the values of *all* cultures?[251] Does cultural relativism exclude moral arguments in favour of universality of *every* human right? For Lukes, cultural relativism must be wrong for several reasons. First, he argues, it is never quite clear who is an insider and who is an outsider, because cultural units are not absolutely coherent. Secondly Lukes points out that moral criticism takes place even *within* cultures and is often directed at the practices of one's own society—are these judgments impermissible? Is criticism always wrong? Thirdly, abstaining from criticism in relation to practices of others does not, to him, represent respect, because regarding others to be beyond or beneath criticism is hardly a form of respect. Fourthly, he asks whether relativist critiques are valid across cultures or only in relation to one. Finally, Lukes argues that in aiming to eliminate conflict, relativism actually misconceives the plurality of moralities: 'If each answer is true in its own place, none can clash'.[252] However, there are arguments that are recognized in more than one particular culture or a way of life, such as human rights: The 'principle that human rights must be defended has become one of the commonplaces of our age'—in fact, 'virtually no one *rejects* the principle of defending human rights'.[253] For Lukes, this is a principle that guarantees an 'egalitarian plateau' for solving political conflicts and arguments in a spirit of taking human rights seriously on all sides.[254]

But in addition to not being fully convincing, the doctrine of cultural relativism risks appearing as dreadfully indifferent. After all, if the West has the perception that its own status is good and provides wonderful conditions for life, then why should it not wish all other societies that which it feels is best? There is nothing fundamentally wrong in wishing to make the world a better place (in fact it seems odd even to have to say this)—otherwise the dangers of overlooking the needs of others are great. Therefore, if we cannot simply remain unmoved by what

---

[249] M Ignatieff, *Human Rights as Politics and Idolatry* (introduced and edited by A Gutmann), (Princeton University Press: 2001) 18.

[250] E Gellner, 'Relativism and Universals' in M Hollis and S Lukes (eds) *Rationality and Relativism* (Blackwell: 1982/1988) 181, 184.

[251] Or, as Laqueur has framed the question, 'under what conditions are differences [. . .] tolerated and regarded as compatible with civilization and with civilized conduct. And under what circumstances are they not?' See TW Laqueur, 'The Moral Imagination and Human Rights' in M Ignatieff, *Human Rights as Politics and Idolatry* (introduced and edited by A Gutmann), (Princeton University Press: 2001) 127, 135–136.

[252] S Lukes, *Liberals & Cannibals: the implications of diversity* (Verso: 2003), 8.

[253] ibid 155 [emphasis in original].   [254] ibid 168.

we see as injustice elsewhere—that is, if altruism is not just a fact but has moral power—then absolute relativism must be wrong.

The outcome of this argument, for better or for worse, is the 'civilizing mission', something that Europe has invoked for centuries. Earlier, in the colonial context, the difference was between civilized Europeans and uncivilized non-Europeans, with international law functioning as a tool for the enterprise.[255] For an uncivilized society to progress into a civilized one, the path to follow was the European model.[256] By the late 19th century, all colonial powers invoked versions of the 'civilizing mission' with trade playing an indispensable part, in fact being the mechanism to civilize backward natives.[257] While European international lawyers have traditionally invoked both humanitarian and cultural arguments, they have never questioned Europe's controlling superiority.[258] This has also applied to traditional European international law, which has in many ways claimed 'be "universal", authoritative, and advanced' and characterized the 'non-European world and non-European cultures as "particular" and backward'.[259]

In this kind of thinking, Europe turns into a model, *the* 'civilization'.[260] By the end of 19th century, as Gong has argued:

[t]he international society of European states was evolving into an international society of self-proclaimed "civilized" states. In declaring that its ranks consisted of the world's "civilized" countries, the "civilized" international society proclaimed its universalist aspirations.[261]

The line between a universal standard of civilization, a European standard of civilization and a standard of European civilization was consequently fine, which made the definition and application of the standard difficult.[262] It also proved tricky to 'civilize' and preserve the cultural heritage of another country at the same time.[263] And as Koskenniemi has shown, even if the standards (however imprecise) invoked were European, the non-Europeans could never achieve European

---

[255] A Anghie, 'Time Present and Time Past: Globalization, International Financial Institutions, and the Third World', (2000) 32 New York U J of Intl L and Politics 243, 244; A Anghie, 'Finding the Peripheries: Sovereignty and Colonialism in Nineteenth-Century International Law', (1999) 40(1) Harvard Intl L J 1, esp. at 22–43.

[256] A Anghie, 'Finding the Peripheries: Sovereignty and Colonialism in Nineteenth-Century International Law', (1999) 40(1) Harvard Intl L J 1, 31.   [257] ibid 62–64.

[258] M Koskenniemi, *The Gentle Civilizer of Nations. The Rise and Fall of International Law 1870–1960* (Cambridge University Press: 2002) 127, 130.

[259] A Anghie, 'Time Present and Time Past: Globalization, International Financial Institutions, and the Third World', (2000) 32 New York U J of Intl L and Politics 243, 275.

[260] On Europe as 'civilization', see JGA Pocock, 'Some Europes in Their History' in A Pagden (ed), *The Idea of Europe. From Antiquity to the European Union* (Woodrow Wilson Center Press and Cambridge University Press: 2001) 55, 58–61. Initially, the international society coincided with the Christian one, but then Europe gradually defined itself as 'civilized'. GW Gong, *The Standard of 'Civilization' in International Society* (Oxford, Clarendon Press: 1984) 4–5.

[261] Gong (n 260 above) 4–5. For a definition of 'civilization' reflecting European norms, see ibid., 14–21.   [262] ibid 21.

[263] ibid 22.

status. Because there was no clear standard for measuring civilization, then everything in fact depended on what the Europeans could approve. What the Europeans could approve depended on how hard the non-Europeans tried. As a result, a paradox emerged:

In order to attain equality, the non-European community must accept Europe as its master—but to accept a master was proof that one was not equal.[264]

The problem with the civilizing mission is that the only solutions offered to solve the problems of society are those formulated by the 'civilized'.[265] But even as 'civilized', the outsiders still do not have true knowledge of what is best for others.

Even as they may be no alternative to the 'civilizing mission', its risks are also apparent. One of them is that the claim to universality is always made in a given syntax and through specific cultural conventions. As Butler has found, this entails that for the claim to be understood in new rhetorical and cultural contexts, it must be translated. If no translation is made, then crossing borders presumes a colonial and expansionist logic.[266] Therefore, both relativism and universalism seem to include both positive and negative sides. If the universalists are right, then there is a moral duty to fight indifference. But why should we wish our standards onto others just because we like them? This goes into the heart of the question concerning the relationship between the European and the universal, and the question is today as urgent as ever.

VIII. What is Universalism?

The association of a rhetoric of universality with human rights conditionality achieves—rhetorically—the outcome that the actor exercising conditionality does not appear to impose Western values on other countries, but simply uses its 'influence to bring the practice of other governments more into line with *their own* professed values (which we share)'.[267] For the EU, it would thus seem important to base its human rights policy on the UDHR because of the universalist prestige of the Declaration. Surely, if anything in the world is universal then the Declaration is, so by linking its measures to the UDHR the EU might avoid the claim that it is acting out of 'moral imperialism'.[268] A major part of the

---

[264] M Koskenniemi, *The Gentle Civilizer of Nations. The Rise and Fall of International Law 1870–1960* (Cambridge University Press: 2002) 135–136.

[265] A Anghie, 'Finding the Peripheries: Sovereignty and Colonialism in Nineteenth-Century International Law', (1999) 40(1) Harvard Intl L J 1, 78. The quote originally refers to the actions of the 'civilized' countries in general and not to the EU specifically.

[266] J Butler, 'Restaging the Universal: Hegemony and the Limits of Formalism' in J Butler, E Laclau and S Žižek (eds), *Contingency, Hegemony, Universality. Contemporary Dialogues on the Left* (London and New York, Verso: 2000) 11, 35.

[267] J Donnelly, *Universal Human Rights in Theory and Practice* (Ithaca and London, Cornell University Press: 1989) 234 [emphasis in original].

[268] On the rhetoric of the universality of human rights in general, see Donnelly (n 267 above) 234.

agreements concluded by the EU include a reference to the UDHR, for example in the following way:

Respect for democratic principles and fundamental human rights, proclaimed by the Universal Declaration of Human Rights, underpins the domestic and external policies of both Parties and constitutes an essential element of this Agreement.[269]

Even more generally, the EU has laid great weight on the argument that human rights are 'universal':

The European Council stresses the universal nature of human rights and reiterates the obligation incumbent on all States, in accordance with the United Nations Charter, to develop and encourage respect for human rights and fundamental freedoms for all, regardless of race, gender, language or religion.[270]

It is, however, not clear what the EU means in legal terms when invoking universality as a basis for its human rights policies, because the international law doctrine appears to be quite divided on the status of the UDHR. First, the EU can simply suggest that the UDHR is 'universal'. But what does this mean? To be exact, this statement is different from arguing that the rights in the UDHR have been universally accepted. The latter argument, again, would be countered at least by historical evidence showing how until the late 1950s the United Nations General Assembly, which adopted the UDHR, was much dominated by the West and its doctrine,[271] with very few non-Western countries participating in the discussions leading to the signing of the UDHR. Consequently, the UDHR mainly reflects a Western view of human rights.[272]

---

[269] See the Economic Partnership, Political Coordination and Cooperation Agreement between the European Community and its Member States, of the one part, and the United Mexican States, of the other part, published in [2000] OJ L 276/45, Art 1. Similar references have been used, for eg with the former Yugoslav Republic of Macedonia, Chile, Croatia, Lebanon, Jordan, Bangladesh, the Republic of Korea, Morocco, Slovenia, South Africa, the Palestine Liberation Organization (PLO), Chile, Argentina, Brazil, Paraguay and Uruguay; a reference to the UDHR is included in the preamble to the agreements with the 78 ACP states, Cambodia, Yemen and Lao People's Democratic Republic.

[270] Declaration by the European Council at the Beginning of the Fiftieth Anniversary of the Universal Declaration of Human Rights, Doc No 7121, 15 December 1997, Para 2. See also Declaration of the Council and the Representatives of the Governments of the Member States meeting in the Council on human rights, democracy and development, [1993] 5 Bull. EC 68 point 1.3.41. On the argument relating to universality in general, see eg M Piehowiak, 'What are Human Rights? The Concept of Human Rights and Their Extra-Legal Justification' in R Hanski and M Suksi (eds), *An Introduction the International Protection of Human Rights* (Institute for Human Rights, Åbo: 1997) 3, 5.

[271] A Cassese, 'The General Assembly: Historical Perspective 1945–1990,' in P Alston (ed), *The United Nations and Human Rights. A Critical Appraisal* (Oxford, Clarendon Press: 1992) 25, 29.

[272] ibid 31 [emphasis omitted]. This is visible, among other things, in how the emphasis is on civil and political rights, how no mention is made of the rights of peoples, and how the approach taken to colonized peoples is purely formal and no instructions were given to the Colonial Powers. During the negotiations the Socialist countries were in a minority position, and after strong resistance finally abstained, actually still lacking a clear human rights strategy of their own. The Third World was largely represented by Latin American states with a Western outlook. The rest had neither strength nor authority to stand up to the Western powers. ibid, at 31–32.

The EU statement could also suggest that the rights enumerated in the UDHR are universally valid even though the Declaration is formally a non-binding recommendation.[273] But the EU could also refer to the UDHR as an expression of general international law, which is the interpretation embraced by several EU lawyers.[274] The UDHR is treated as an expression of 'customary international law, or at least general principles of law recognized by civilized nations'.[275] The same argument has been used to claim that the UDHR has become customary international law and as such binding on all states.[276] Sometimes the UDHR is also regarded as the authoritative interpretation of Articles 55 and 56 of the United Nations Charter.[277]

But the assertion that 'human rights are universal' could also entail that only some rights included in the UDHR are universal.[278] This the doctrine of core

---

[273] See eg A Cassese, *International Law* (Oxford University Press: 2001) 358.

[274] For this view, see A Rosas, 'Art 21' in Gudmundur Alfredsson and Eide Asbjorn (eds), *The Universal Declaration of Human Rights* (The Hague, Kluwer Law International: 1999) 431, 447; B Brandtner and A Rosas, 'Human Rights and the External Relations of the European Community: An Analysis of Doctrine and Practice' in (1998) 9 Eur J of Intl L 468, 475; A Rosas, 'Economic, Social and Cultural Rights in the External Relations of the European Union' in A. Eide *et al* (eds), *Economic, Social and Cultural Rights*, (2nd edn, Kluwer Law International: 2001), 479–492 at 485–486; A Rosas, 'Human Rights in the External Trade Policy of the European Union' in *World Trade and the Protection of Human Rights. Human Rights in Face of Global Economic Challenges*, Publications de l'Institut International des Droits de l'Homme (Bruyland: Bruxelles, 2001) 193, 200–202. This is the way in which the UDHR is claimed to stand out 'as the normative foundation of Community action'. See Brandtner and Rosas, ibid 489; A Rosas, 'The Role of the Universal Declaration of Human Rights in the Treaty Relations of the European Union' in P Baehr, C Flinterman and M Senders (eds), *Innovation and Inspiration: Fifty Years of the Universal Declaration of Human Rights* (Amsterdam, Koninklijke Nederlandse Akademie van Wetenschappen: 1999) 201, 206.

[275] For this view, see Brandtner and Rosas (n 269 above) 476 [footnote omitted]. See also E Riedel and M Will, 'Human Rights Clauses in External Agreements of the EC' in P Alston *et al.* (eds), *The EU and Human Rights* (Oxford University Press: 1999) 723, 735; E Fierro Sedano, *The EU's Approach to Human Rights Conditionality in Practice*, PhD thesis written at the European University Institute, Florence (submitted in December 2001), 401–402.

[276] This view was famously stated in the US Court of Appeals judgment in *Filartiga v Pena-Irala*, United States, Court of Appeals, Second Circuit, 30 June 1980 at 882–883; reproduced in 77 Intl L R 169. See also MG Kaladharan Nayar, 'Introduction: Human Rights: The United Nations and United States Foreign Policy', 19 (1978) Harvard Intl L J 813, 817. For critiques, see eg Alain Pellet, "Human rightism" and international law', Gilberto Amado Memorial Lecture delivered on 18 July 2000 (United Nations: 2000) 8; B Simma and P Alston, 'The Sources of Human Rights Law: Custom, Jus Cogens and General Principles', (1992) 12 Australian Ybk of Intl L 82, 107.

[277] However, it seems unclear whether this would cover all rights in the UDHR or just some of them. See Simma and Alston (n 276 above) 100–101; T Meron, *Human Rights and Humanitarian Norms as Customary Law* (Oxford, Clarendon Press: 1989) 83–84. Art 55 states that the United Nations shall promote, among other 'universal respect for, and observance of, human rights and fundamental freedoms for all without distinction as to race, sex, language or religion'. Art 56 places all Members under an obligation to 'take joint and separate action in co-operation with the Organization for the achievement of the purposes set forth in Article 55.'

[278] See Simma and Alston, (n 277 above) 98–100. See also Oscar Schachter, *International Law in Theory and Practice* (Martinus Nijhoff Publishers: Dordrecht, Boston and London, 1991) 337; Meron (n 277 above) 83; Alain Pellet, " 'Human Rightism' and International Law' Gilberto Amado Memorial Lecture delivered on 18 July 2000 (United Nations: 2000), 9.

fundamental rights.[279] The most foundational rights could include, for example, the prohibitions against genocide, torture and slavery.[280] However, such a list of genuinely universal rights:

> will inevitably be rather brief and will certainly constitute an unsatisfactory or inadequate basis on which to achieve many of the goals appropriately sought by the strongest proponents of international human rights law.[281]

Relying on the core rights doctrine, again, is different from saying that the rights in the UDHR are universal, but states disagree about their content; or that the rights in the UDHR are universal, but states disagree about their implementation. The EU statement is thus very general and ambiguous.

The reference to universal human rights as a basis for active external policies is problematic for one fundamental reason: rights are universal only at the level of abstraction. One good example of this abstraction is the 2003 Commission Communication on the EU-Africa dialogue,[282] which argues that the EU and Africa can 'base their relationship on shared objectives and common values'.[283] This shows how the success of the language of rights is closely attached to its indeterminacy, and when some universal concepts can be identified, they are often based on abstract formulations and open-ended provisions.[284] Abstraction is often the explanation behind the general acceptability of rights. Thus, universalism does not necessarily refer to very exact standards but might instead be more about the universal acceptance of the *idea* of human rights or an international human rights *culture*,[285] which both are quite indeterminate concepts. For Brown, while the international protection of human rights has become a 'settled norm' of international society, instead of actual compliance, this verbal assent only entails that states are not likely to admit that they break international standards.[286] Universal acceptance of human rights thus relates more to an understanding that 'certain things simply cannot legitimately be done to human beings', which is more based on theory than actual practice, making it difficult to

---

[279] See K Arts, *Integrating Human Rights into Development Cooperation: The Case of the Lomé Convention* (Kluwer Law International: 2000) 34.

[280] See A D'Amato, *International Law: Process and Prospect* (2nd edn, Irvington New York, Transnational Publishers: 1995) 179–203.

[281] B Simma and P Alston, 'The Sources of Human Rights Law: Custom, Jus Cogens and General Principles', (1992) 12 Australian Ybk of Intl L 82, 100.

[282] Communication from the Commission to the Council. The EU-Africa dialogue, Brussels 23.6.2003, COM (2003) 316 final.

[283] ibid 3. According to the Communication, those values 'can be found in the Treaty of the European Union, the Cotonou Agreement and the Barcelona Process, as well as in the Constitutive Act of the African Union and in the NEPAD manifesto'.

[284] See P Leino, 'A European Approach to Human Rights? Universality Explored', (2002) 4 Nordic J of Intl L 455.

[285] L Henkin, *International Law: Politics and Values* (Dordrecht, Martinus Nijhoff Publishers 1995) 225. [Emphasis added].

[286] C Brown, 'Universal human rights: a critique' in T Dunne and NJ Wheeler (eds), *Human Rights in Global Politics* (Cambridge University Press: 1999) 103, 115 (footnote omitted).

specify the forbidden actions.[287] The main purpose of human rights is then seen in protecting the individual rather than moral, political or cultural conformity.[288] This level of abstraction is something that should, for example, limit the usefulness of human rights arguments as a basis for conditionality.[289] The UDHR has, however, been an acceptable reference document for most states because it is equally abstract and does not alone imply any specific obligations.

There are also various understandings concerning the practical effect of universalism. Even if the rights included in the UDHR were universal, the document remains true to the limitations placed by statehood and in itself contains little by way of legal obligations in relation to human rights.[290] As the President of the General Assembly pointed out after the vote on the UDHR in 1948, the:

> Declaration only marked a first step since it was not a convention by which States would be bound to carry out and give effect to the fundamental human rights; nor would it provide for enforcement; yet it was a step forward in a great evolutionary process.[291]

This remains to be the case even with the newest norms of international human rights law, as Henkin has argued, which penetrate the 'state monolith' but by being simultaneously 'contained within the state system and respectful of its axioms and traditions'. As a result, human rights norms continue to bind states only with their consent and merely at the inter-state level.[292]

This is also true of the Vienna Declaration, which has served as a central reference for the EU human rights policy. The Vienna Declaration relies on the traditional system of states in emphasizing the role of the United Nations and the obligation of all states to ensure respect for all human rights within their own jurisdictions. In particular, the Vienna framework includes no references to states

---

[287] J Donnelly, 'Cultural Relativism and Universal Human Rights, (1984) 6 Human Rights Q 400, 404 (footnote omitted). This does not entail, for example, that genocide or the practice of torture would have disappeared, even from Europe, although their prohibition is claimed to constitute customary international law. This conclusion is, of course, not without problems under international law. After all, according to the International Court of Justice, customary international law consists of both settled practice and a subjective element, ie *opinio juris*. State practice should be 'both extensive and virtually uniform [. . .] and should moreover have occurred in such a way as to show a general recognition that a rule of law or legal obligation is involved'. See *The North Sea Continental Shelf Cases (Federal Republic of Germany v Denmark Federal Republic of Germany v The Netherlands)*, ICJ Reports 1969, 3 *et seq* at Paras 74, 77.

[288] DF Orentlicher, 'Relativism and Religion', in M Ignatieff, *Human Rights as Politics and Idolatry* (introduced and edited by Amy Gutmann), (Princeton University Press: 2001) 141, 143.

[289] On how human rights have been used as a basis for granting membership in the EU, see P Leino, 'Rights, Rules and Democracy in the EU Enlargement Process: Between Universalism and Identity', (2002) 7 Austrian Rev of Intl and Eur L 53.

[290] See L Henkin, *International Law: Politics and Values* (Dordrecht, Martinus Nijhoff Publishers: 1995) 177.

[291] 183rd plenary meeting of the UN General Assembly, Continuation of the discussion on the draft universal declaration of human rights: A report of the Third Committee, 10 December 1948, A / 777 at 934.

[292] L Henkin, *International Law: Politics and Values* (Dordrecht, Martinus Nijhoff Publishers: 1995) 184.

acting unilaterally in defence of human rights,[293] and remains silent on human rights conditionality, be it in relation to trade or development aid. More specifically, there is no mandate given to states to act unilaterally despite human rights being a 'legitimate concern'. The linkage between human rights and trade has also provoked concern in UN human rights organs.[294] Outside the Vienna framework, it appears that:

[n]either the erosion of sovereignty by the human rights concept, nor the duty to cooperate in the promotion of human rights legitimates conditionality under international law.[295]

There are, of course, different kinds of enforcement, stretching from positive and negative conditionality, removing or not giving benefits, to the application of sanctions, just to name a few. However, it seems that in invoking conditionality, the EU steps outside the globally accepted framework, which makes it difficult to refer to any universal acceptance for its acts.

Even if human rights and the UDHR were proved to be universal, it does not automatically follow that some entity (EU) would be entitled to enforce them. The question thus seems to be, under what conditions could the EU 'represent' the universal? On a theoretical level, the EU's strategy aims at connecting the particular (the European, the Western) with the universal (the so-called international customary law on human rights). But as the universal only exists at an abstract

---

[293] The Declaration states that the 'promotion and protection of human rights must be considered as a priority objective of the *United Nations* in accordance with its purposes and principles, in particular the purpose of international cooperation'. It specifies further that it is within 'this framework and these purposes and principles' that 'the promotion and protection of all human rights is a legitimate concern of the international community'. Therefore, it is the '*organs and specialized agencies related to human rights*', which should 'further enhance the coordination of their activities based on the consistent and objective application of international human rights instruments.' The Vienna Declaration and Programme of Action, adopted by the World Conference on Human Rights on 25 June 1993, A/Conf. 157/23, Part I, Para 4 [emphasis added].

[294] See eg 'Question of the realization in all countries of the economic, social and cultural rights contained in the Universal Declaration of Human Rights and in the International Covenant on Economic, Social and Cultural Rights, and study of special problems which the developing countries face in their efforts to achieve these human rights', UN Human Rights Commission, res 5 (XXXV) 1979 Para 5, in which the Commission expresses 'concern that qualitative and human rights conditions are being imposed in bilateral and multilateral trade policies with the intention and effect of perpetuating the existing structure of world trade.' Adopted through a separate vote requested by Canada by 22 votes to 7 with 2 abstentions. See Commission on Human Rights, report on the Thirty-Fifth Session, Economic and Social Council Official Records 1979, Supplement 6, at 29. The resolution was closely linked to a discussion on struggle against colonialism and the right to development, and the draft resolution was initially submitted by Senegal supported by Burundi, Egypt, Morocco, Senegal and Yugoslavia.

[295] P Nherere, 'Conditionality, human rights and good governance: a dialogue of unequal partners' in K Ginther *et al* (eds), *Sustainable development and good governance* (Dordrecht, Martinus Nijhoff Publishers: 1995) 289, 296. Comparisons to the acts of international and regional human rights organs are difficult to sustain: while they do allow for state petitions, it is not left to the complaining state to enforce the rules or determine whether a violation has taken place. When invoking human rights conditionality, 'the donor is assuming the role of prosecutor, judge, jury and executioner'. ibid, 290–291.

level and escapes definition, articulating it in any specific manner is impossible. Moreover, the universal does not have a representative of its own, because there is no actor with an absolutely universal coverage. The universal is thus necessarily represented by a particular.[296] It is in this way that the EU presents itself as the 'representative' of the UDHR and that which is universal—after all, the universal is always rooted in and coloured by some particular content without having an independent substance.[297] However, the universal and the particular can never coincide completely.[298] While the universal escapes exact definition, the particular always comes with more definite contents, the two being closely linked. But the closer the objectives of the particular become of those of the universal, the weaker the links between the original particular aims and the new universal ones become. As a result, the universal turns into an empty and abstract concept without any specific contents.[299]

Once the particular has established itself as the voice of that which is universal, equality between it and the other members of the community is excluded. Decisions are tied to the particular's own preferences that are presented as the criteria determined by universal norms. Because the differing positions do not comply with that which is universally accepted:

every deviating position will appear as irrational, or at least as partially, subjective, historically conditioned, political biasedly[sic], an atavistic residue from religious, ethnic, or other such particular moralities.[300]

In practice, this situation can be observed in the way in which human rights argumentation has been used in historical contexts, with the claim for the 'universal' often tending to reveal a particular policy.[301] In other words, 'the project of constructing universal human rights has been highly exclusionary'.[302]

If this is the case, then the universality of rights just appears to support the supremacy of one group over others, with a 'particular' dressed to look as the 'universal'.[303] In the actual case this would be so if it appeared that the particular (the EU) uses the universal language mainly in order to promote its own objectives.

---

[296] On this, see S Žižek, 'Class Struggle or Postmodernism? Yes, please!' in J Butler, E Laclau and S Žižek (eds), *Contingency, Hegemony, Universality. Contemporary Dialogues on the Left* (London and New York, Verso: 2000) 90, 111.   [297] Generally, see ibid 110.
[298] E Laclau, 'Identity and Hegemony: The Role of Universality in the Constitution of Political Logics', in J Butler, E Laclau and S Žižek (eds), *Contingency, Hegemony, Universality. Contemporary Dialogues on the Left* (London and New York: Verso: 2000) 44, 56.
[299] ibid [Emphasis in original].
[300] M Koskenniemi, 'Legal Universalism: Between Morality and Power in a World of States', in Sinkwan Cheng (ed), *Law, Justice and Power: Between Reason and Will* (Stanford University Press: 2004, 46, 57).
[301] M Koskenniemi, 'Human rights, politics and love', (2001) 4 Mennesker & Rettigheter 33, 41.
[302] See DF Orentlicher, 'Relativism and Religion', in M Ignatieff, *Human Rights as Politics and Idolatry* (introduced and edited by A Gutmann), (Princeton University Press: 2001) 141, 152.
[303] See M Koskenniemi, 'Human rights, politics and love', (2001) 4 Mennesker & Rettigheter 33, 41.

This could suggest that in referring to universality the EU is, in fact, not representing that which is genuinely shared, but a false universal. However, in principle, there is no reason why the EU could not sometimes act as a genuine universal, representing an interest that is universally recognized and accepted. But how to know whether the universal invoked by the EU is genuine or false? Promoting one's own objectives might do little harm, presuming that those objectives are good and compatible with the objectives of others—after all, because the universal does not have a representative of its own, it can only be present through the particular. Therefore, a preference is not necessarily wrong just because it is particular.

In general, the EU's universality argument seems to be based on a rather wishful vision of the status of human rights.[304] This is something that is typical of 'human rightism', which is known for 'a tendency to indulge in wishful thinking and take sketchily emerging trends or, worse still, trends that exist solely in the form of aspirations, as legal facts'.[305] For the EU, this is problematic—after all, its strong status in relation to the non-Western world is closely linked with its success in presenting its own objectives as those that realize the 'common good'.[306] But as Carr has shown, while it is common to see whatever is good for yourself as equally beneficial to others, many 'theories of the public good' often turn to be just another word for a particular interest.[307] In this way:

Theories of social morality are always the product of a dominant group which identifies itself with the community as a whole, and which possesses facilities denied to subordinate groups or individuals for imposing its view of life on the community. Theories of international morality are, for the same reason and in the virtue of the same process, the product of dominant nations or groups of nations.[308]

The same dominant groups also tend to rely on everyone wishing the same things, and that the interest of the world community coincides with their own. Those not respecting this interest are accused of violating both the universal interest and their own.[309] However, the problem between the universal and the particular remains, as:

these supposedly absolute and universal principles were not principles at all, but the unconscious reflexions of national policy based on a particular interpretation of national interest at a particular time.[310]

---

[304] On this problem in respect of the human rights movement more generally, see D Kennedy, 'The International Human Rights Movement: Part of the Problem?' (2001) Eur Human Rights L R 245.

[305] A Pellet, ''Human rightism' and international law', Gilberto Amado Memorial Lecture delivered on 18 July 2000 (United Nations: 2000) esp. 4–5.

[306] See on this more generally, eg E Laclau, 'Identity and Hegemony: The Role of Universality in the Constitution of Political Logics', in J Butler, E Laclau and S Žižek (eds), *Contingency, Hegemony, Universality. Contemporary Dialogues on the Left* (London and New York, Verso: 2000) 44, 50–51.

[307] EH Carr, *The Twenty Years Crisis* 1919–1939 (London, Papermac: 1939/1991) 75.

[308] ibid 79.   [309] ibid 80.

[310] ibid 87. 'But as soon as the attempt is made to apply these supposedly abstract principles to a concrete political situation, they are revealed as the transparent disguises of selfish vested interests.' ibid 87–88.

Ignatieff has argued that very often the international human rights movement
fails to verify that it actually represents those interests that it claims to be defending.[311] With the Western interventions occurring 'ever more frequently but ever
more inconsistently', the legitimacy of the standards used has been repeatedly
questioned.[312] It often turns out that the 'neutral' nature of human rights is anything but neutral, and that a human rights policy is in fact normative in character.

  While there is nothing fundamentally wrong in using the Universal
Declaration as a reference, the problem is that in many cases it cannot alone justify
a specific policy. Because the UDHR is so general, it is not alone capable of being
policy-orienting. The same ambiguity is then transferred to the human rights
clause, because its technical format is simply far too open-ended to imply any substantive conditions.[313] In the context of EU policies, the charm of the UDHR
turns against those states that are at the receiving end. Because the universality of
the Declaration is difficult to grasp in a way that would determine any detailed
and genuinely universally shared standards, it is too easily taken over by anyone
with a strong voice, claiming to speak for the universal. In practice, the ambiguity
of the UDHR results in the EU defining its contents. The situation becomes
thorny for the weaker state when the standards implemented are open to various
possible interpretations, and the process is entirely based on the interests of the
stronger party—after all, as shown earlier, the procedure relating to the usage of
the clause in practice only works one way. Far too often, the:

> actual contents of the universalist arguments are determined by those who implement
> them on ground. If one is not in such a position, universalist arguments are best left
> unused.[314]

The fact that human rights have become mainstream, the increase in the use of
human rights language does not necessarily mean good things for the protection
of human rights.[315] Instead, the language may just provide a universalist smoke-
screen for contested and particular policies.[316] The problem then does not relate
to some rights being clearly not universally shared, but to basing actions on an
agenda that only reflects the interests of the stronger party. It also remains to be

---

[311] M Ignatieff, *Human Rights as Politics and Idolatry* (introduced and edited by A Gutmann),
(Princeton University Press: 2001) 10. Ignatieff refers especially to NGOs, many of which 'espouse the
universalist language of human rights but actually use it to defend highly particularist causes'. ibid 9.

[312] ibid 19–20.

[313] While the open-ended wording of the human rights clause is politically convenient for the
Community, it leaves legal uncertainty both as to the scope and reach of the clauses and to their
mechanisms of interpretation and application. See eg E Fierro Sedano, *The EU's Approach to Human
Rights Conditionality in Practice*, PhD thesis written at the European University Institute, Florence
(submitted in December 2001), 305.

[314] For this argument relating to good governance as a 'universal' principle, S Seppänen, *Good
Governance in International Law*, The Erik Castrén Institute Research Reports 13/2003, 122.

[315] M Koskenniemi, 'The Pull of the Mainstream', (1990) 88 Michigan L Rev 1946, 1962.

[316] See D Kennedy, 'The International Human Rights Movement: Part of the Problem?' (2001)
Eur Human Rights L R 245, 260.

shown that the EU policies actually make the world a better place. But then again, the abstraction relating to human rights also makes measuring success and progress in implementing them difficult. Despite this, it might well be that in many cases the human rights clause does not work except by allowing the EU to claim it is doing something effective. After all, public support is crucial: if public opinion is concerned about human rights violations, then the Community cannot remain indifferent.[317]

In 1997, Agence Europe reported how the EU and the US had given a negative reply to the suggestion made by the Malaysian Prime Minister Mahatir Mohamad to revise the UDHR in order to make it more reflective of the point of view of developing countries. Mohamad argued that the UDHR had been drafted by 'superpowers who did not understand the needs of poor countries'.[318] The proposal gained support, especially by China, Burma, the Philippines and Indonesia, in the meetings between the ASEAN countries. The Indonesian Prime Minister Ali Alatas argued that the UDHR should 'respond to the real situation in the world where there are at least 120 newly independent countries that did not participate in the debates on the 1948 Declaration'.[319] The EU representative at the press conference said that the EU would be 'extremely reluctant' to embark on such a revision, because for the Union, the UDHR represents one of the 'cornerstones of the international legal and political system'.[320] While the EU recognizes that the human rights world conferences have 'revealed that principles as basic as the universality and indivisibility of human rights continue to meet resistance', its focus is on the 'consensus that has emerged from such conferences', which 'provides the basis of increased dialogue and cooperation between the countries concerned'.[321] So far, the EU has appeared generally negative to all meaningful discussion openings by the non-Western states as to the disputed meaning, status, contents or nature of the UDHR.

It is one thing whether the UDHR should be re-written; quite another whether it should be invoked as a reference of standards, if its contents are mainly understood as those reflecting the EU view on human rights. A lack of substantive dialogue does not only relate to the attempts to reconsider the UDHR but appear as a more general feature of the EU policies in relation to weaker states. However, universalism in its absolute form is the opposite of dialogue: when seeking the limits of what is genuinely universal, openness in relation to its exclusions and inclusions should be fundamental. As Žižek has argued, only 'dead' or 'abstract' universality

---

[317] For a general discussion, see K Arts, *Integrating Human Rights into Development Cooperation: The Case of the Lomé Convention* (Kluwer Law International: 2000) 168, 333.

[318] 'European Union and United States against Revision of UN Declaration on Human Rights, Proposed by Malaysia', Kuala Lumpur, Agence Europe 30 July 1997.   [319] ibid.

[320] ibid.

[321] The European Union and the External Dimension of Human Rights Policy: From Rome to Maastricht and Beyond, Communication from the Commission to the Council and European Parliament, Brussels 22.11.1995, COM (95) 567 final, Para 16.

comes with its own fixed inclusions and exclusions; universality that is 'living' and 'concrete' presumes a:

permanent process of the questioning and the renegotiation of its own "official" content. Universality becomes "actual" precisely and only by rendering thematic the exclusions on which it is grounded, by continuously questioning, renegotiating, displacing them, that is, by assuming the gap between its own form and content, by conceiving itself as unaccomplished in its very notion.[322]

In this sense, true universality seems to require openness in relation to its contents. More than a clear set of criteria that could be used as conditions, universality of rights refers to a general direction for government policies, a horizon, and calls for dialogue and inclusion. Dialogue is also a precondition for the emergence of universal values: to the extent that human rights represent an 'emerging consensus', they mainly provide:

an opportunity for a debate on the manner in which the norms that are contained in international declarations and conventions can best be implemented. Such a debate, and the consensus that, it is hoped, may emerge from that debate, are indispensable conditions for arriving at a greater respect for human rights in all parts of the world.[323]

However, genuine universality in its requirement of dialogue is also more complex—after all, intercultural dialogue on rights questions becomes far more complicated if all cultures are allowed to participate as equals instead of one view dominating the discussion.[324]

But then, one must ask, what is the harm of human rights conditionality? Does it have negative effects? The answer is affirmative if it turns out that empty signifiers (such as human rights, democracy and good governance) are mainly used to maintain old arrangements of control. As Laclau argues, very often the existence of open-ended concepts is crucial for a hegemonic relationship—in fact, they are a precondition for its existence. This is because in order to be a success, a hegemonic relationship presumes empty concepts, which make it difficult to evaluate the relationship between the universal and the particular, and thus enable the particular to present itself as the representative of the universal.[325] Likewise, when invoking these open-ended concepts, those claiming to represent universal interests become non-transparent to those that they claim to represent.[326] However, to

---

[322] S Žižek, 'Class Struggle or Postmodernism? Yes, please!' in J Butler, E Laclau and S Žižek (eds), *Contingency, Hegemony, Universality. Contemporary Dialogues on the Left* (London and New York, Verso: 2000), 90–135 at 102. See also J Butler, 'Competing Universalities' in the same volume, 136, 162.

[323] P R. Baehr, *Human Rights. Universality in Practice* (Palgrave Macmillan: 2001) 18.

[324] M Ignatieff, *Human Rights as Politics and Idolatry* (introduced and edited by Amy Gutmann), (Princeton University Press: 2001) 63.

[325] E Laclau, 'Identity and Hegemony: The Role of Universality in the Constitution of Political Logics', in J Butler, E Laclau and S Žižek (eds), *Contingency, Hegemony, Universality. Contemporary Dialogues on the Left* (London and New York, Verso: 2000) 44, 57 [emphasis omitted].

[326] On the conditions of hegemonic relations in general, see ibid 65–66.

some extent, open-endedness also represents at least the possibility of openness and dialogue. Therefore, the paradox here seems to be that while openness is crucial, open-endedness leads to a lack of transparency.

In general, the relationship between the EU and weaker states is characterized by a lack of such dialogue that could actually bring about substantive changes. Most often, what is offered is a package already negotiated on the EU side, which is then offered to the developing states to accept or reject, and very often argumentation about universal human rights appears in the package. However, to the extent a universal concept of 'human rights', exists, finding agreement on its content requires genuine discussion and a fair process, which gives a possibility to speak to all parties concerned. Human rights are no substitute for political debate but require discussion, because their contents are contested.[327] If there is no dialogue, then it must be presumed that weaker voices are excluded from contributing to the universal. The challenge thus is to distinguish between false and genuine universals. This is a matter of politics.

IX. The Politics of Universalism

Due to the ambiguity of the human rights references invoked by the Union, the problems relating to 'inconsistency' and 'double-standards' appear as inescapable parts of EU policies. Even more generally, due to the kind of norms, values and arguments that human rights constitute, total objectivity is in practice impossible to achieve: human rights arguments require case-by-case analysis, which in its turn makes the achievement of absolute uniformity impossible.[328] This is the way in which the EU sets a trap for itself: when claiming that it knows what is best for others (in the common universal interest), it lacks already from a practical point-of-view (in relation to staffing and systematic reporting) the capacity to deliver it. On the reverse side then is the balancing between transparency and intrusion. While from the transparency point-of-view it would be necessary to provide more detailed information about the standards to be implemented, the more detailed the standards get, the more basis there is for arguments on colonialist attitudes—if the EU were to provide more detailed standards, it would simultaneously push deeper and deeper into the national structures of its 'partner'.

Similar kind of balancing takes place between indifference and imperialism. In order to avoid claims relating to the latter, promotion of human rights through dialogue might be preferable, thus emphasizing the importance of a process that

---

[327] For discussion on this, see J Klabbers, 'Redemption Song? Human Rights Versus Community-building in East Timor', 16 (2003) Leiden J of Intl Law 367, 373–376.

[328] For thoughts going in this direction, see M Koskenniemi, 'The Effect of Rights on Political Culture' in P Alston *et al.* (eds), *The EU and Human Rights* (Oxford University Press: 1999) 99, esp. 107–113.

enables both wide participation by all parties and more contextual approaches. This is especially important keeping in mind that the universal should not be fixed into any particularist reading but is by definition a constant invitation to include and embrace different understandings. However, this approach, arguably implemented, for example, towards China and the ASEAN states has emerged as unsatisfactory, with the EU appearing as indifferent towards human rights considerations. At the same time, the absence of clear articulation risks the transparency of the process.

It seems that there is a difference between two kinds of universality. Firstly, there is the EU kind of universality, which in the language it invokes seems to be of a strict and rather aggressive kind and justifies interference and conditionality. If you invoke this kind of universality, then coherence and objectivity would need to be in place. But universality can also stand for willingness to accept differences. This 'universality abides in the purported logic of aspiration, not always in the reality of attainment',[329] referring to the distant objective of the:

[. . .] universality of the collective human aspiration to make power increasingly accountable, governance progressively just, and the state incrementally more ethical.[330]

Following this view, the function of human rights is mainly in empowering individuals with a language they can use against their own governments, with universality mainly referring to an objective, while still giving a rather wide margin of discretion to national governments. With this kind of universality objectivity is less crucial, because it does not claim to fit everyone in the same way but does allow for individual and regional approaches. This universality seems to be more compatible with the wishes of the non-Western world, with the EU version then emerging as its own particularist interpretation, one which appears contested and false.

If the EU were to adopt a more open, dialogue-oriented approach, would its human rights policy then be more defensible? The problem is that such an approach seems to preclude the idea of human rights clauses. Therefore, a shift to a more dialogic human rights policy would mean jettisoning this aspect of EU policy: based on what has been universally accepted, embracing all understandings in the world, it seems difficult to invoke negative conditionality. On the practical level, in some ways the difference between the two types of universalism might be reflected in the difference between positive and negative conditionality. While the EU kind of universality generally implies the use of negative conditionality (such as threats to break off relations and stop aid), dialogue-oriented universality uses positive, incentive measures and dialogue.

However, the most fundamental problem in invoking human rights conditionality relates to the abstraction of human rights, which allows the stronger party to

329 U Baxi, *The Future of Human Rights* (Oxford University Press: 2002) 101.
330 ibid 105 [emphasis omitted].

determine at the implementation stage what is actually aimed at. The human rights clause is like the UDHR which serves as its reference, and which also leaves completely unclear how the rights included in it should be realized in practice. This could be a practical implication of false universality, even though the EU's approach does not automatically mean that it is acting in bad faith. The wider problem relates to the EU's closed reading of human rights, which does not leave breathing space for differing views and perceptions. Instead, the exclusiveness and dominance of its own view is a slippery slope that easily leads it from universalism to imperialism. What is worse is that avoiding this outcome is practically impossible, as the feature is strongly built into the EU's internal methods of functioning. This is because the EU position is already at the opening stage of external negotiations relatively final as a result of lengthy intra-EU negotiations. Therefore, the re-opening of its negotiating position at the stage when external negotiations are launched is a practical impossibility, which makes the EU structurally unable to engage in such dialogue that could actively affect the outcome.

One good example of the contradictions inherent in the discussion of universal human rights is the right to development. After all, the starting point of the developing states was that aid would be seen as an entitlement, given and received in order to realize development. However, in today's development scheme, equality is always excluded. The inequality between the parties is something that has been characteristic of the relationship between Europe and the third world for a long time. In fact, the modern discipline has preserved much of the old colonial framework, as today the 'essential structure of the civilizing mission may be reconstructed in the contemporary vocabulary of human rights, governance, and economic liberalization'.[331] At the same time, the EU's own reading of the right to development, privileging other human rights at its expense, remains impossible to accept for the developing states. For them, and for many others, it remains to be proved that the right to development actually *requires* enforcement of all other human rights, as the basis is for privileging all or some human rights over that particular right seems uncertain. The problem is that human rights are hardly convincing as a language of global justice ('universal', 'good') if the use of that language is simultaneously seen to enable and even justify the exclusion of perhaps the greatest injustices from the negotiating table as 'not relevant' for the discourse.

But while there is no doubt of the need for action and enhanced efforts in order to achieve development, the right itself is a symbol of balancing between rhetoric and reality; universal rights and agnosticism. As both resources and political will are limited, the rhetoric of universal declarations alone will achieve little. If, however, the right to development were a truly universal right, then a lot would need

---

[331] A Anghie, 'Finding the Peripheries: Sovereignty and Colonialism in Nineteenth-Century International Law', (1999) 40(1) Harvard Intl L J 1, 74, 80. On the 'historical continuum to universalize Eurocentrism', see also M Mutua, 'Savages, Victims and Saviors: The Metaphor of Human Rights', (2001) 42(1) Harvard Intl L J 200, esp. 234–235.

to happen: the West would need to treat its wealth on a completely different basis and be prepared to distribute it in terms of more genuine solidarity,[332] so that the developing states would also be able to exercise an economic power equal to the West. In this way, the right to development is an example of universalism in an agnostic world, which endures a lack of resources and lacks a voice that would be genuinely universal. As such, it articulates the agnostic reality of the world, but also shows how quickly universalism turns into paternalism.

The external imposition of human rights, democracy and good governance could well also be counter-productive. This is because a government may lose its democratic legitimacy if it always responds to the wishes of external actors: 'Good governance is accountability to the governed, not to the donors.'[333] Imposing Western human rights norms from the outside also denies the process through which rights have traditionally been gained in Western societies, ie through struggle, and questions whether external bodies are even equipped to administer human rights in the developing states.[334] In more than one way, the human rights movement contributes to the impoverishment of local political discourse, in promising, in Kennedy's words, 'a way of knowing—knowing just and unjust, universal and local, victim and violator, harm and remedy—which it cannot deliver'.[335] This is because '[j]ustice is something which must be made, experienced, articulated, performed each time anew',[336] and also because 'meaningful and lasting changes can only come from within'.[337] Dictating policies from above arises problems of double standards and hypocrisy, and according to Seppänen, a valid question to be asked is why good governance would be best achieved through universal standards of governance. After all:

Universal standards and local democracy—local power—are, by definition, contradictory objectives.[338]

Human rights play a major role in shaping politics. However, this does not imply that conditionality in its current form works; instead, it might be a characteristic of a false universal. But this does not necessarily mean that all international human rights talk is always wrong and brings about bad outcomes. In fact, even

---

[332] For a scheme creating a Global Resources Dividend, aiming at global economic justice, see TW Pogge, *World Poverty and Human Rights. Cosmopolitan Responsibilities and Reforms* (Cambridge, Polity Press: 2002).

[333] P Nherere, 'Conditionality, human rights and good governance: a dialogue of unequal partners' in K Ginther *et al* (eds), *Sustainable development and good governance* (Dordrecht, Martinus Nijhoff Publishers: 1995) 289, 306.

[334] MRR Lister, 'Rebalancing Lomé: Human Rights, South Africa and the Future' in (1991) 25 *J of World Trade* 21, 24.

[335] D Kennedy, 'The International Human Rights Movement: Part of the Problem?' (2001) Eur Human Rights L R 245, 258.   [336] ibid.

[337] P Alston, 'International Trade as an Instrument of Positive Human Rights Policy', (1982) Human Rights Q 155, 169.

[338] S Seppänen, *Good Governance in International Law*, The Erik Castrén Institute Research reports 13/2003, 121.

human rights conditionality might have positive potential if it takes a form that encourages informed but genuine debates at the local level. Conditionality is at its best an invitation. Nevertheless, when attached to universality, it can at its worst turn into an excuse for not having any dialogue at all—after all, if human rights are universal, then politics are not needed. However, human rights must function as a starting point for discussion because both their contents and their contribution to political practice remain contested. Moreover, it is impossible to aim at amending societal and constitutional structures and introduce new ways of thinking in a third state without political debates, which are likely to lead to local variations. Instead of human rights conditionality being used to dictate specific outcomes and establish largely imported norms and institutions, conditionality should take a more process-oriented view with interaction playing a major role. In that case, even the EU external human rights policies might appear less like just another round of good old European universalism.

Protecting Non-economic Interests in the European Community Legal Order: A Sustainable Development?

Emily Reid [*]

I. Introduction

The purpose of this article is to analyze the emergence and development of non-economic objectives in the European Community, with a view to answering some of the questions concerning the extent to which these are now part of the EU legal order. The study focuses initially upon analyzing the evolving dialectical relationship between economic and non-economic interests within the European single market.[1] Thus it assesses the inter-relationship between economic and non-economic interests, with particular emphasis upon the extent to which a *de facto* legal application of sustainable development has developed in the context of the single market. In particular it examines the *means* by which human rights and environmental protection have been balanced with economic liberalization and development. It subsequently examines how complete the protection provided within the EU legal order is for each of the 'dimensions', or 'pillars', of sustainable development,[2] and contrasts the means by which economic and non-economic interests have been balanced in the context of the single market with the availability (or not) of effective means by which to enforce non-economic interests outside that context.[3] Before undertaking either of these analyses, however, the emergence of the principle of 'sustainable development' is traced and its meaning within the EU legal order is explored.

[*] University of Southampton. I would like to thank Malcolm Ross, Yuri Borgmann-Prebil and Nick Hopkins for their comments on earlier versions of this article and Takis Tridimas for comments and related discussions.

[1] This starting point has been chosen not least because it is in the context of the operation of the single market that non-economic interests initially arose as issues of concern within the European Community. It is also, inevitably, in this context that key developments in the protection and recognition of non-economic interests occurred. For the purposes of this article references to European Community (Community) include the European Economic Community.

[2] Economic development, environmental protection and social concerns (or, for these purposes, human rights as discussed below).

[3] It is not the intention of this article to provide a comprehensive account of *all* the issues identified as relevant, nor will it deal with environmental protection and human rights in all respects with

Over the last 30 years the European Community has addressed the dialectic of economic liberalization and non-economic objectives, including the protection of human rights and environmental protection, in an increasingly sophisticated manner. This shift in approach has been incremental, arising from both the jurisprudence of the Court of Justice, and Treaty amendment. Arguably, the practical manifestation of this shift could amount to the *de facto* development and emergence of a legal application of 'sustainable development'.[4] Yet even if this is the case, questions remain as to the extent to which non-economic interests have been integrated into the EU legal order.

Human rights and environmental protection have been selected for present purposes as *exemplars* of the non-economic interests (and subsequently objectives) which have emerged within the EU legal order. There are three reasons why these particular interests have been chosen: firstly, pragmatically, because both human rights and environmental protection have been the subject of considerable case law before the ECJ and although both have evolved at different speeds and in different manners, common threads may be discerned, giving rise to certain conclusions concerning the wider protection of non-economic objectives. Secondly, as non-economic objectives, these two interests represent two of the great causes of the late twentieth and early twenty-first centuries, harnessing institutional and also considerable popular concern in both the European and international contexts. In addition, both environmental and human rights' protection are the subject of current debate as to their relationship with economic liberalization in the context of the World Trade Organisation.[5] Any conclusions which may be drawn from the European context may therefore also be of relevance to the international debate. Thirdly, these two interests (human rights and environmental protection) are tied together, with economic development, into the triangular dialectical relationship articulated in the principle of 'sustainable development'.[6]

---

the same weight. The article does seek however to highlight and explore particular aspects of the development and protection of these interests in the Community legal order, with a view to identifying particular Community achievements, failings and the implications thereof.

[4] Adopting the Brundtland definition of this concept, see text accompanying note 8 below. The principle of sustainable development has been controversial, particularly as regards its content and definition, and this in turn raises questions as to the extent to which it can be enforced, or applied in practice. Developments in the Community context would indicate that it is capable of practical effect, and can be legally applied (and enforced).

[5] See, *inter alia*, Petersmann, 'Human Rights and the Law of the WTO' (2003) 37 JWT 241; Cottier 'Trade and Human Rights: A Relationship to Discover' (2002) 5 JIEL 3; Schoenbaum 'International Trade and Protection of the Environment: the Continuing Search for Reconciliation' (1997) 91 AJIL 268; Cheyne 'Environmental Unilateralism and the WTO/GATT System' 24 Ga. J Int. & Comp. Law 433; and Marceau 'Conflicts of Norms and Conflicts of Jurisdictions: the Relationship between the WTO Agreements and MEAs and other Treaties' (2001) 35 JWT 1081.

[6] That is not to say that environmental protection, and 'human rights' are the only non-economic interests which may be construed within sustainable development, 'social concerns' is certainly capable of wider application than 'human rights', but human rights may be seen as part of the social pillar. See below for further discussion of the place of human rights within sustainable development.

The principle of 'sustainable development' is one means by which the relationship between economic and non-economic interests has been conceptualized in abstract and, representing a perceived relationship between economic development and non-economic interests, it is of fundamental importance to this study.[7] One key question is whether and if so, under what conditions, the abstract concept may be subject to practical application? If 'sustainable development' is found to be present (or influential) in the EU context this would suggest a number of presumptions (albeit as yet uncertain or not fully defined) as to the nature of that dialectic within the EU. It would also indicate that the principle may indeed be given practical effect. In this event further analysis may in turn shed some light upon the *conditions* necessary in order to give effect to sustainable development.

The evolving relationship between economic and non-economic interests, however, can only offer partial protection to non-economic interests. If we are to understand the European Union's present position in relation to the development of non-economic interests *per se* it is necessary to examine also the *extent* of protection for non-economic rights as free standing rights within the EU legal order, independent of economic considerations. In this specific context the elaboration of rights of citizenship, in particular those accruing under Article 18 EC may prove particularly significant. From these two analyses, together, it is possible to reach conclusions concerning the evolution of the European Union and its developing governance.

Although the present focus is upon internal issues, including the implications and significance of the Community's actions for the evolution of the European Union and its developing governance, the experience of the Community is significant for, and potentially helpful to, the international community in its approach to this same question, not least because the European Community has sought to export its internal values in its relations with third states.

II. What is Sustainable Development?

Sustainable development demands that the pursuit of *economic* liberalization and development does not ignore the key non-economic interests of environmental protection and social concerns. This has, inescapably, proved a controversial concept yet some clarity may be found in the articulation of its definition in the Brundtland Report: 'development that meets the needs of the present without compromising the ability of future generations to meet their own needs'.[8] While argument remains as to its content, with some advocating that sustainable development is a purely physical concept,[9] the Brundtland definition clearly

[7] Notwithstanding the controversy concerning its definition.
[8] World Commission on Environment and Development 'Our Common Future', 1983, at p. 43.
[9] See, for example, Wetlesen, 'A global ethic of sustainability?', in Lafferty and Langhelle (eds) *Towards Sustainable Development: On the Goals of Development and the Conditions of Sustainability* (Macmillan, 1999).

encompasses both the physical environmental element, and consideration of humans and their needs. The Brundtland Report in fact emphasizes the importance of these aspects of sustainable development, noting both that humans, their needs and the environment are inherently inter-related,[10] and that the purely physical (environmental) concept of sustainable development is incomplete (as its protection cannot be pursued without consideration of issues such as *access to resources*).[11]

Crucially, sustainable development does not prioritize any single interest over the others, but requires consideration of each in relation to development issues. The international community has embraced the concept of sustainable development, as articulated by the Brundtland report, and in doing so has clearly set down a marker for the handling of the potential conflict between economic liberalization and non-economic priorities. Yet the *principle* of sustainable development itself does not indicate how this potential conflict should be resolved in practice: the question remains therefore as to whether 'sustainable development' can have any real impact upon the approach taken to development, or to achieving a balance between its economic and non-economic elements. Moreover, 'sustainable development' as an abstract concept, lacks definition: what are the environmental and, more complex perhaps, social elements?

A. 'Sustainable Development' in the European Union

While the environmental dimension of sustainable development may be, *prima facie*, fairly straightforward to understand, the social dimension poses different questions. While this *may* be construed narrowly, the European Community has explicitly recognised human rights as 'an integral part of sustainable development' in the Cotonou Convention: 'Respect for all human rights and fundamental freedoms, including respect for fundamental social rights, democracy based on the rule of law and transparent and accountable governance are an integral part of sustainable development.'[12]

'Sustainable development' was introduced into the Community legal order as a guiding principle in the 1990s, and it was in the Community's Fifth Action Programme on the Environment[13] that the Community's approach to sustainable development became explicitly three prong: 'Towards Sustainability is not a programme for the Commission alone, nor one geared towards environmentalists alone. It provides a framework for a new approach to the environment and to economic and social activity and development.'[14] The Community's subsequent

---

[10] *Supra* note 8, at p. xi.   [11] *Supra* note 8, at p. 43.

[12] Partnership Agreement between the members of the African, Caribbean and Pacific Group of States of the one part and the European Community and its Member States of the other part [2000] OJ L317/3, Article 9.

[13] 'Towards Sustainability: A European Community programme of policy and action in relation to the environment and sustainable development.' [1993] OJ C138/5. See Executive Summary paras. 13 & 39.   [14] *Supra* note 13, para. 39.

Sustainable Development Strategy, adopted at the Gothenburg summit in June 2001,[15] recognizes sustainable development as an *overarching principle* of the European Community and provides that economic growth and social cohesion are inter-dependent with environmental cohesion. It consequently requires that all future major legislative proposals include an assessment of economic, environmental and social costs. The Community appears with that to have adopted the Brundtland definition of the concept.[16]

If sustainable development is to be an over-arching principle, this would indeed lend itself in practice to consideration of the social pillar in the terms employed by the Community and ACP states in the Cotonou Convention, particularly within the relatively culturally homogenous European context, where the protection of fundamental rights forms part of the legal order. The Brundtland report itself requires, as a pre-requisite to the fulfilment of everyone's needs, that everyone has 'the opportunity to satisfy their aspirations for a better life'. Such opportunity is not easily separated in practice from the enjoyment of fundamental human rights. Despite this apparent practical reality, there is, as observed by MacCormick:

standing tension between liberty for individuals and equal well-being of individuals. Individual freedom in a market economy can and does result in great inequalities of material well-being. Programmes for equalization of well-being erode or abolish the liberties exercised by citizens in market societies. These liberties are guaranteed under an order of universal 'legal right'—'the rule of law' as we sometimes say. If 'social justice' demands equalization of well-being, is it then an idea incompatible with respect for legal right? . . .[17]

This raises a fundamental question: is it in fact the case that, far from being part of the social dimension, the protection of human rights is indeed, wholly at odds both with it and with the wider objectives of sustainable development? To return to McCormick:

What I understand as the 'social democratic view' is that there must be a middle way. Despite the admitted tensions between liberty and (material) equality, the good society is one which aims to hold them in balance.[18]

Thus, as MacCormick recognizes, the relationship between fundamental rights and social interests is not as straightforward as might be thought; dependent on the vision of social development the two may indeed be in opposition. Yet he perceives the possibility of a 'middle way' and this middle way is consistent with the recognition by the EU in the Cotonou Convention that human rights are a part of

---

[15] COM (2001) 264 final 'A sustainable Europe for a better world: a European strategy for sustainable development'.

[16] This view of sustainable development as an overarching principle is emphasised by the European Economic and Social Committee in its Opinion of 28 April 2004 *Assessing the EU sustainable development strategy—exploratory opinion*, NAT/229, 28 April 2004, CESE 661/2004, at para. 2.2.2 'Sustainable development must be the overarching principle . . .'

[17] MacCormick *Legal Right and Social Democracy* (OUP, 1982), preface.

[18] *Supra* note 17.

sustainable development. This middle way is without doubt a matter of policy choice, human rights protection is not *necessarily* an inherent part of the social dimension of sustainable development, but in the EC context, as expressed in the Cotonou Convention, that choice has been made. In view of both this and the practical impact of economic rights and development upon human rights (and *vice versa*) as experienced in the context of the Community legal order, analysis will proceed on the basis that human rights protection is an element of the social dimension of sustainable development.[19]

The link between environment and human rights has since been even more explicitly made by the inclusion of 'environmental protection' in the European Union's Charter of Fundamental Rights.[20] In its Exploratory Opinion,[21] however, the European Economic and Social Committee (EESC) criticized the Community's sustainable development strategy for its focus on the environmental dimension and for failure to consider either the inter-generational aspect or (global) distributive justice.[22]

III. Unpacking Sustainable Development in the European Union: the Development of Human Rights and Environmental Policy

An examination of the experience and approach of the European Community may shed some light on the balancing of economic and non-economic interests in practice: the application of sustainable development. The evolution of the European Community, from its original focus upon economic integration, to encompassing the recognition and protection of certain non-economic concerns, has been the subject of considerable academic comment.[23] Yet there are certain

---

[19] Further consideration of this very interesting question is beyond the scope of the present article although there can be no doubt that it is a matter worthy of exploration.

[20] Art. 37—although it should be noted that 'environment' is included therein as a 'principle', rather than as a 'right'.   [21] *Supra* note 16.

[22] *Ibidem* at paras. 2.1.3 and 2.1.10 respectively.

[23] It is not the purpose of this article to retell that history, in relation to the development of fundamental rights protection, see, *inter alia*, Mendelson 'The European Court of Justice and Human Rights' YEL (1982) 125; Lawson R 'Confusion and Conflict? Diverging Interpretations of the European Convention on Human Rights in Strasbourg and Luxembourg' in Lawson and de Blois (eds) *The Dynamics of the Protection of Fundamental Rights in Europe: Essays in Honour of Henry G Schermers Vol III* (Martinus Nijhoff, Kluwer, 1994); Dauses, M.: 'The Protection of Fundamental Rights in the Community Legal Order' [1985] 10 ELRev 389; Schermers, H.G., 'The European Communities Bound by Fundamental Human Rights' (1990) 27 CMLRev 249–258; Coppel and O' Neill: 'The European Court of Justice: Taking Rights Seriously?' (1992) 29 CMLRev 669–692; Weiler and Lockhart: ' "Taking Rights Seriously" Seriously: The European Court and its Fundamental Rights Jurisprudence—Part I' (1995) 32 CMLRev 51–95, and Part II (1995) 32 CMLRev 579–627; Jacobs, F: 'Human Rights in the European Union' Emiliou and O'Keefe (eds) *Legal Aspects of Integration in the European Union* (Lkuwer, London, 1997); Witte, Bruno de 'The Role of the ECJ in Human Rights' in Alston *et al* (eds) *The EU and Human Rights*, (OUP, 1999);

key developments which indicate relatively early recognition of the mutual dependency of the achievement of economic and non-economic objectives. These developments occurred both in the Treaty[24] and through Member State co-operation and were both catalysed, and subsequently reinforced, by the case law of the Court of Justice.[25] The Community has been specifically faced with the apparent tension between the pursuit of economic liberalization and the protection of fundamental rights and the environment on numerous occasions since the 1970s,[26] and this has inevitably shaped its development.

A. The Social Dimension: Fundamental Rights

It was originally anticipated that as the Community concerned economic integration, its operation would have no bearing upon fundamental human rights. Consequently there was no reference to these in the Treaty of Rome. The operation of Community law did in fact impact upon the enjoyment of fundamental human rights, however,[27] and the *lacuna* in Treaty provision, in combination with on the one hand the requirement of States (in particular of the Constitutional Courts) that fundamental rights not be infringed, and on the other hand the principle of supremacy of Community law, caused problems for the Court of Justice.[28] Two elements can thus be seen to have combined in the initial development of fundamental rights' protection in the European Community: firstly the unique nature of the Community legal order (supremacy of Community law); and secondly the realization that economic integration could not be pursued in isolation from fundamental rights. These explain the *need* for the development of Community human rights policy. In the *realization* of that development it also appears to have been crucial that a body of human

---

Spielmann D 'Human Rights Case Law in the Strasbourg and Luxembourg Courts: Conflicts, Inconsistencies and Complementarities', in Alston *et al* (eds) *The EU and Human Rights*. Williams 'EU Human Rights Policy and the Convention on the Future of Europe: A Failure of Design' (2003) ELRev. 28(6) 794–81; Hilson 'What's in a Right? The Relationship between Community, Fundamental and Citizenship Rights in EU Law (2004) 29 ELRev 636–651; For discussion of the development of EC Environmental law and Policy, see Scott J. *EC Environmental Law*; (Longman, 1998); Chalmers D 'Inhabitants in the field of European Community Environmental Law' Columbia Journal of European Law (5) 1998–1999, at p. 39 (also Craig and De Burca, *The Evolution of EU Law* (OUP, 1999)); McGillivray and Holder 'Locating EC Environmental Law' YEL (20) 2001; Notaro N 'The New Generation Case Law on Trade and the Environment' (2000) ELRev. 25, 267–491.

[24] Discussed below.
[25] See, *inter alia*, Case 40/64 *Sgarlata and Others* v. *Commission* [1965] ECR 215; Case 29/69 *Stauder* v. *City of Ulm* [1969] ECR 419; Case 11/70 *Internationale Handelsgesellschaft* v. *Einführ und Vorratstelle für Füttermittel und Getreide* [1970] ECR 1125; Case 4/73 *Firma Nold* v. *Commission* [1974] ECR 491; Case 136/79 *National Panasonic (UK) Ltd* v. *Commission* [1980] ECR 2057; Joined Cases 60 & 61/84 *Cinéthèque* v. *Fédération Nationale des Cinémas Français* [1985] ECR 2605; Case 260/86 *Elliniki Radiofonia Tileorassi AE* v. *Dimotiki Etairia Pliroforissis and Sotirios Kouvelas (ERT)* [1992] ECR I-2925. For comment *supra* note 23. [26] *Infra.*
[27] *Supra* note 25.
[28] See *Sgarlata and Internationale Handelsgesellschaft*, *supra* note 25. See also *Frontini* v. *Ministero delle Finanz Giuisprudenza constitutionale* [1974] CMLR 372.

rights existed which was binding upon, and common to, all the Member States of the Community.[29]

The inevitably ensuing question of the *extent* of Community competence in relation to fundamental rights has been far from straightforward, not least because it raised concern among the Member States regarding their sovereignty, and the encroachment of Community law upon national law. The Court's response to this concern can be seen in *Konstantinidis*[30] and *Kremzow*.[31] The Court of Justice has walked something of a tightrope on the issue of fundamental rights: while ensuring that Community law does not *itself* breach the fundamental rights upheld by the Member States, nor *cause* (or require) them to breach their human rights' obligations (including under the European Convention of Human Rights), at the same time the Court could not exceed its jurisdiction and encroach upon matters of national competence, nor could it assert an active Community competence which had not been conferred.[32]

Alongside the developments in the Court of Justice, the Community institutions were not oblivious to the question of the relationship between Community law and human rights, adopting a joint declaration on this subject in 1977.[33] Nor were the Member States themselves totally inactive on this issue. Reference to fundamental rights was introduced in the preamble to the Single European Act (SEA),[34] and this initial reference was built upon in the Treaty of European Union (TEU) and Amsterdam Treaty (ToA). Until the EU Constitution comes into force however, while respect for human rights is now recognized as one of the founding principles of the Union (Article 6 TEU) it is only in respect of 'Development Cooperation'[35] and, post-Nice, 'Economic, Financial and Technical Cooperation with Third Countries',[36] that the Community has competence to pursue human rights protection as an objective. The Council may also determine, and sanction the existence of a serious breach of human rights by a Member State and, post-Nice, may even determine and sanction a 'clear risk of a serious breach'.[37] Under the EU Constitution human rights protection would be explicitly included as a Union objective, which represents a significant development in principle.[38] In addition, the Charter of Fundamental Rights for the European Union would be incorporated as Part II of the Constitution.

B. The Environmental Dimension

As regards environmental protection, as early as 1972 the Heads of State and Government of the then Member States decided, at the Paris Summit, that the

---

[29] These rights being expressed both in the Constitutions of the Member States as well as in international treaties including, notably, the European Convention on Human Rights (ECHR).

[30] Case 1168/91 *Konstantinidis* v. *Stadt Altensteigstandesamt* [1993] ECR I-1191.

[31] Case C-299/95 *Kremzow* v. *Austria* [1997] ECR I-1759.

[32] On the extent of Community competence, or lack of it, see Opinion 2/94 *on Accession by the Community to the ECHR* [1996] ECR I-1759.   [33] [1977] OJ C103/1.

[34] [1987] OJ L169/1.   [35] Art. 177 (2) (ex Art. 130u(2)) EC.   [36] Art. 181a EC.

[37] Art. 7 EU.   [38] [2003] OJ C169/1, Art. I-3.

Community should pursue an environmental policy—holding that this development would not require treaty amendment:

... Economic expansion is not an end in itself: its first aim should be to enable disparities in living conditions to be reduced. ... It should result in an improvement in the quality of life as well as in standards of living. As befits the genius of Europe, particular attention will be given to intangible values and to protecting the environment so that progress may really be put at the service of mankind.[39]

This statement is significant in that it looks rather like an early articulation of what is now Brundtland's 'sustainable development' although here, in the 1972 context, the improvement in living standards and quality of life is very much an anticipated consequence of economic development, rather than an equal objective. Subsequently, the Community adopted the first of six Community Action Programmes.[40] This declared that although the Treaty had not been amended, the task of the Community required action in relation to various environmental issues. The Community task was later amended, in the TEU, to being to achieve: 'sustainable and non-inflationary growth respecting the environment ... the raising of the standard of living and quality of life ...'.[41] Despite developments in the TEU, notably the weight given to the notion of sustainable growth in the Community task, and the development of the duty of environmental integration (that 'environmental protection requirements must be integrated into the definition and implementation of other Community policies'),[42] Macrory and Hessian argue that as a consequence of its lack of definition, the difficulty in reconciling economic and non-economic goals and the questions it leaves concerning competence, the TEU 'tends to compound rather than resolve difficulties inherent in designing a comprehensive and consistent Community policy concerning the environment'.[43]

The ToA consolidated the approach of the TEU, notably in including the promotion of environmental protection and improvement of the quality of the environment as a new Community task.[44] In what represented a significant shift, however, the duty of environmental integration was moved from the Title on the Environment to Art. 6 TEU. This is important because it put the duty squarely within the general provisions of the Union: rather than remaining a sectoral policy it became central to the Community's objectives. Significantly, it was in the ToA that 'sustainable development' was finally explicitly introduced in to the treaties.[45]

---

[39] EC Commission, Sixth General Report (EC Brussels, 1972), see also the Declaration of the Heads of State and Government of 19/20 October 1972 at the Paris Summit about collaboration in environmental policy [1972] EC Bulletin (no 10) 21.

[40] [1973] OJ C112/1; Second [1977] OJ C139/1; Third [1983] OJ C46/1; Fourth [1987] OJ C328/1; Fifth [1993] OJ C138/1; Sixth [2002] OJ L242.   [41] Art. 2 EC.

[42] Art. 130r(2) EC.

[43] Macrory and Hessian, 'Maastricht and the Environmental Policy of the Community: Legal Issues of a New Environmental Policy' in O'Keefe and Twomey (eds) *Legal Issues of the Maastricht Treaty*, (Wiley, Chancery, 1994), p. 151.   [44] Art. 2 EC.

[45] See Preamble and Art. 6 TEU.

It was not defined however and therefore its inclusion was observed by Macrory to remain of greater political than legal significance.[46]

The Treaty of Nice introduced no substantive changes to environmental protection within the Community, although the Charter of Fundamental Rights includes provision relating to the place of environmental protection within the Union.[47] The Draft Constitution for the European Union provides for a high level of environmental protection and includes '[contribution] to the sustainable development of the Earth' among its objectives.[48] The Constitution also recognizes the relationship between environmental protection and human health— reinforcing the relationship between the physical environmental and human elements of 'environmental' protection.

IV. The Application of Sustainable Development

Elements of sustainable development are thus clearly discernible within the Community legal order, and sustainable development itself has been adopted as a Community principle. Yet this raises a question: what does 'sustainable development add to, or require of, the Community legal order'?

The EESC has identified that 'some view sustainable development as requiring that economic, social and environmental aspects are to be addressed on an equal footing. Others maintain that the aim is not to achieve equal treatment, but rather to seek a 'balanced consideration' of economic, social and environmental aspects'.[49] As the EESC observed, the application of either of these approaches requires 'difficult political decisions'. However, these are not necessarily conflicting positions. To treat these pillars equally does not require the same treatment to be guaranteed in every case. But this does highlight the very real question of *how* to apply sustainable development and even whether it *can* be meaningfully applied. The EESC has criticized the continuing abstract nature of the sustainable development strategy in even stronger terms[50]: 'it should be continually underlined that sustainable development implies fundamental changes in how society functions. Citizens must be empowered on the basis of knowledge and training, to make sustainable development a reality and meet the challenges that it poses for the future.'[51]

The approach of the Court of Justice in *Schmidberger*,[52] however, sheds some light on whether (and how) sustainable development may be applied, giving a

---

[46] Macrory 'The Amsterdam Treaty: An Environmental Perspective' in O'Keefe and Twomey (eds) *Legal Issues of the Amsterdam Treaty* (Hart Publishing, 1999).

[47] Art. 37.   [48] Art. 3.

[49] Opinion of the European Economic and Social Committee on 'The Lisbon Strategy and Sustainable Development' [2003] OJ C95/54, at 4.4.

[50] Exploratory Opinion, *supra* note 16, at paras 2.2.7–2.2.12.   [51] *Ibidem* at para. 2.2.12.

[52] Case C-112/00 *Eugen Schmidberger Internationale Transporte und Planzüge* v. *Austria* [2003] ECR I-5659.

clear message concerning the balance to be struck between the pursuit of the single market and the protection of fundamental rights, or, between economic integration (and development) and fundamental rights.

A. The Evolving Dialectical Relationship between Economic and Non-economic Interests in the Single Market

(i) Balancing Fundamental Rights and Free Movement of Goods

In *Internationale Handelsgesellschaft*,[53] while recognizing fundamental rights as an element of the Community legal order for the first time, the Court stated that fundamental rights were secondary to the achievement of economic integration, and could not bring into question the validity of a Community act, as this would question the legal basis of the Community itself.[54]

The Court subsequently gradually established and refined the limits of its competence in relation to fundamental rights protection: in *Wachauf* it held that it will review national implementation of Community law for its compatibility with fundamental rights,[55] and in *ERT* it extended this finding by holding that the Court will also review derogations from Community law for compatibility with fundamental rights.[56] This clear departure from earlier case law[57] was confirmed in *Familiapress*.[58] But this departure, while significant for its extension of the Court's jurisdiction over fundamental rights, does not really tell us anything of the underlying balance between fundamental rights and economic integration, and it is in relation to this question that *Schmidberger*[59] is significant.

The central question in *Schmidberger*[60] was whether an Austrian decision permitting an environmental demonstration, which would close a main trans-European route for 30 hours, could incur state liability through Austria's consequent failure to guarantee free movement of goods. As the Court observed[61] it had been held in *Commission* v. *France*,[62] that it is a breach of Article 28 not only where a Member State itself causes an obstacle to free movement of goods, but also where it 'abstains from adopting the measures required in order to deal with obstacles to the Free Movement of Goods which are not caused by the state'.[63]

The Court held that Austria's permission that the demonstration (and closure of the route) could go ahead, did amount to a 'measure equivalent to a quantitative restriction'. The question at issue was therefore whether this could be justified. Crucially, the Court recognized Austria's argument that permission for

---

[53] *Supra* note 25.
[54] *Ibidem*, at para. 3.   [55] Case 5/88 *Wachauf* v. *Germany* [1989] ECR 2609.
[56] *Supra* note 25.   [57] Including *Cinéthèque, supra* note 25.
[58] Case C-368/95 *Vereinigte Familiapress Zeitungsverlags-und Vertriebs GmbH* v. *Heinrich Bauer Verlag*, [1977] ECR I-3689.   [59] *Supra* note 52.
[60] *Ibidem*.   [61] *Ibidem*, at para. 57.
[62] Case C-265/95 *Commission* v. *France* (*French Farmers*) [1997] ECR I-6959.
[63] *Ibidem*, at para. 30.

the demonstration to go ahead was granted as a consequence of Austria's requirement to respect fundamental rights, notably those of freedom of assembly and
the right to protest. As well as being protected under Austrian law, these rights
are included within the European Convention of Human Rights,[64] and indeed
(now) within the Charter of Fundamental Rights for the European Union.[65]
Thus not only does Austria itself uphold these rights, it is bound to do so under
the ECHR and the EU has declared these rights to be protected within the
European Union.

Advocate General Jacobs rightly observed the significance of this case by distinguishing it from the earlier case law concerning fundamental rights,[66] for in
Schmidberger Austria invoked the necessity to respect fundamental rights as a
justification for a restriction of a fundamental freedom of the treaty (the free
movement of goods).[67]

The Court distinguished this case from the *French Farmers'* case[68] since in that
case the 'objective pursued by the demonstrators was to prevent the movement of
particular products originating in Member States other than the French
Republic',[69] whereas in *Schmidberger* the protestors were protesting on the basis of
a legitimate and genuinely held opinion, and not seeking specifically to impede
the movement of goods. However, the Court found that as the rights of freedom
of assembly and to protest are not absolute (unlike, for example, the right to life),
these rights can be restricted as long as such restriction did not, 'taking account of
the aim of the restrictions, constitute disproportionate interference, impairing the
very substance of the rights guaranteed.'[70]

The Court thereby permitted a proportionate restriction on the enjoyment of
fundamental rights, at the same time, however, it required that any restriction on
free movement of goods must be proportionate.[71] Fundamental rights and free
movement of goods must therefore be balanced against each other, with each
being subject to the other according to circumstances.[72]

---

[64] Deriving from Art. 10, Freedom of Expression; and Art. 11, Freedom of Assembly.

[65] Art. 11, Freedom of Expression; and Art. 12, Freedom of Assembly.

[66] Including notably *Wachauf* and *ERT supra* notes 55 and 25 respectively.

[67] Opinion of AG Jacobs *supra* note 52, at paras. 91–94. Recently, in Case C-71/02 *Herbert Karner Industrie-Auktionen GmbH* v. *Troostwijk GmbH* judgment of 25 March 2004, *nyr*, the Court was asked whether a national measure restricting statements which could be made in advertising con-
stituted a breach of Art. 28. The Court held that there had been no breach of Art. 28. It went on, however, to consider the argument made by Troostwijk, that the restriction constituted a breach of Art. 10 ECHR, and thereby breached Community Law (despite the fact that it had not been asked to consider this matter by the referring court). In the event it held that there was no breach of Art. 10 ECHR as the measure was proportionate to the aim pursued (consumer protection) and of the fact that the right of freedom of expression is not absolute. The Court's own initiative consideration of this question reinforces the significance of fundamental rights within the Community legal order. The application of proportionality is entirely consistent with its status as a fundamental principle of Community law.   [68] *Supra* note 62.

[69] Judgment of the Court, *supra* note 52, at para. 86.   [70] *Ibidem*, at para. 80.

[71] *Ibidem*, at para 82.

[72] This need for a balancing process has subsequently been reinforced in *Karner* v. *Troostwijk supra* note 67.

In one sense this is nothing new, it is well-established that derogations to free movement are subject to the general principle of proportionality.[73] The two-way application of proportionality is, however, a development: not only must the measure invoked to protect the human rights at issue be the least restrictive means vis-à-vis free movement of goods, but in addition, the exercise of market freedoms (free movement of goods) must have the least possible impact upon the affected fundamental rights. Previously the free movement of goods was the rule and any exception to that must be both justified (whether by reference to a mandatory requirement or Article 30) and proportionate.[74] Following *Schmidberger* it is arguable that the basic priority given to free movement is removed, and free movement of goods must also be justified where there is an infringement of fundamental rights. It must be acknowledged, however, that the starting point for the Court's analysis was that there had been a breach of Article 28, and that the question was therefore whether this could be justified. Thus the initial presumption in balancing the competing rights remained that the restriction on free movement must be justified.

This is a far cry from the Court's statement in *International Handelsgesellschaft* that fundamental rights were secondary to economic integration.[75] As has been observed by Stix-Hackl AG, however, the Court gave no indication in *Schmidberger* as to 'how far a restriction on the scope of protection of a *national* fundamental right entails a restriction on the scope of a corresponding Community guarantee'.[76] Stix-Hackl emphasized in her Opinion in *Omega Spielhallen* that protection of fundamental rights should not be viewed as being negotiable, and that therefore the Community fundamental freedoms[77] should not be balanced against 'fundamental rights' *per se* but rather she emphasizes that the particular rights are assessed with regard to their potential for restriction (as the Court observed with regard to the rights at issue in *Schmidberger*),[78] and that the fundamental freedom 'must then be construed as far as possible in such a way as to preclude measures that exceed allowable impingement on the fundamental rights concerned . . .'.[79] The Court itself in its judgment in *Omega Spielhallen* emphasized that the specific circumstances which may give rise to an invocation of an exception to the fundamental freedoms vary from state to state and also according to era,[80] and specifically that there is no pre-requisite of a common conception of a

---

[73] This was applied to environmental protection in Case 240/83 *Procureur de la République* v. *Association de Défence des Bruleurs de l'Huiles Usagées* [1985] ECR 531 and was defined in Case 302/86 *Commission* v. *Denmark (Danish Bottles)* [1988] ECR 4067.

[74] But see *PreussenElektra, infra* note 94.   [75] *Supra* note 25.

[76] Case C-36/02 *Omega Spielhallen-und Automatenaufstellungs-GmbH* v. *Oberbürgermeisterin der Bundesstadt Bonn* Opinion of 18 March 2004 at para. 508 (emphasis added). While *Omega* concerned primarily the relationship between freedom of provision of services and fundamental rights, the handling of that relationship can be seen to share an approach with the relationship between free movement of goods and fundamental rights, with both the Court of Justice and the Advocate General referring to *Schmidberger* in this regard.

[77] Freedom of movement of goods, persons, capital and of provision of services.

[78] See text accompanying notes 70–72 *Supra*.   [79] *Supra* note 76 at para. 53.

[80] Case C-36/02 *Omega Spielhallen-und Automatenaufstellungs-GnbH* v. *Oberburgermeisterin der Bundesstadt Bonn*, judgment of 14 October 2004, at para. 31.

particular right in order that a state may rely on it to justify an exception to the fundamental freedoms.[81] Thus the Court responded to the uncertainty left from *Schmidberger* concerning the potential to uphold national fundamental rights as against Community freedoms, on grounds of public policy. While in those terms not unsurprising, in this judgment the Court reinforced the mutual balancing of the Community economic right as against the fundamental human right.

Stix Hackl Ag appears to go further, however, in suggesting that if a national restrictive measure were found to be based upon a commonly conceived or recognized right it would not be necessary to examine whether that measure is a justified exception to fundamental Treaty freedoms, but rather it should be dealt with according to *Schmidberger*,[82] thus by balancing the competing rights.[83]

The development of a two-way balancing process in *Schmidberger*, further explored by Stix Hackl AG in *Omega*,[84] is entirely consistent with the principle of sustainable development, and constitutes what could be viewed as a practical legal application of that principle. It also indicates that proportionality could prove to be crucial to the application of sustainable development and suggests that, of the two options offered by the European Economic and Social Committee, the most appropriate way to view the content of sustainable development (requiring practical application) is to take the approach of 'consideration of each of the pillars' rather than the alternative mechanistic 'equal treatment' described.[85] It is submitted that full consideration in each case provides for a more sophisticated, holistic approach to equality.

(ii) Environmental Protection and Free Movement of Goods

The approach of the Court in relation to the development of fundamental rights protection can be contrasted with its approach in the context of environmental protection. In 1985 the Court ruled that environmental protection was 'one of the Community's essential objectives'[86] although this was not stated in the Treaty. This appears, *prima facie*, to be a clear example of judicial activism, yet in view of the 1972 Declaration,[87] any other stance would have been in conflict with the expressed intentions of the Member States. The 1985 ruling was also entirely consistent with the Commission's acknowledgment, in 1980, that environmental protection could constitute a limitation upon Article 30 (now Article 28) of the Treaty. This was confirmed by the Court in the *Danish Bottles* case.[88] Thus it was recognized that environmental protection could take precedence over economic objectives, subject to the requirement of proportionality.[89] This early recognition

---

[81] *Ibidem*, at paras. 36–38.   [82] At para. 72.

[83] Notwithstanding that, as stated above, in its reasoning in *Schmidberger* the analytical starting point of the Court was that the breach of free movement required to be justified.

[84] *Supra* note 76 at paras 52–53.   [85] *Supra*, text accompanying note 49.

[86] *Association de Défence de Bruleurs de l'Huiles Usagée, Supra* note 73, at paragraph 13.

[87] *Supra* note 39.   [88] *Supra* note 73.

[89] *Ibidem*, at paras. 6 and 9, see also Case C-389/96 *Aher Waggon* [1998] ECR I-4478; Opinion of AG Colomer in Case C-463/01*Commission* v. *Germany* Opinion of 6 May 2004 at para. 65; and

of environmental protection as a mandatory requirement is in sharp contrast to the recognition of fundamental rights as a mandatory requirement, which would not occur for a further 15 years, until *Schmidberger*.[90]

The Court consolidated the position of environmental protection in 1992 in the *Belgian Waste* case,[91] when it declared that the principle in Article 130r (now Article 174) EC: 'environmental damage should as a priority be rectified at source' could be invoked to limit the free movement of waste for its disposal. This case was particularly significant because the measure in question (a ban on the import of waste for disposal) was arguably distinctly applicable. The Court reasoned, however, that the special nature of waste required that it be disposed of locally, and that therefore the measure was not in fact discriminatory. The Court did not fully explain, however, why the measure, which did after all treat imported waste differently to locally produced waste, was therefore not discriminatory.[92]

Despite the questions raised by the Court's reasoning in *Belgian Waste*, the Member States have not yet clarified the relationship between environmental protection and free movement of goods, notwithstanding the introduction of the duty of environmental integration[93] which requires that the Community must integrate environmental protection into all its activities and policies. The Court, however, was required to revisit the question of the relationship between free trade and environmental protection in *PreussenElektra*.[94]

The measure at issue in *PreussenElektra* was a German scheme supporting the purchase of electricity from *German* renewable energy sources. Since the measure appeared to breach Article 28 the question was, could an *overtly* discriminatory scheme such as this be justified? In *PreussenElektra* the Court did not assess whether the measure was distinctly applicable and simply held that the measure did not breach Article 28.[95] In effect, 'environmental protection' was used to support the compatibility of the measure with Article 28, rather than to justify a derogation.[96] Since the German scheme was not deemed to require a derogation from

---

Judgment of the Court in Case C–463/01 *Commission* v. *Germany* Judgment of 14 December 2004, nyr at paras. 75–78.

[90] *Supra* note 52.   [91] Case C-2/90 *Commission v. Belgium* [1992] ECR I-4431.

[92] It is interesting to assess whether more satisfactory (or complete) reasoning may be found by borrowing from the WTO approach to non-discrimination and 'like products', this question will be returned to below.   [93] Art. 6 EC, see text accompanying note 42 *et suiv*.

[94] Case C-379/98 *PreussenElektra AG v. Schleswag AG* [2001] ECR I-2099.

[95] *Ibidem*.

[96] This could be consistent with Stix-Hackl's Opinion in *Omega Spielhallen* (*Supra* note 76) that rather than viewing the non-economic objective as justifying a breach, the competing objectives should be balanced (without the conceptualisation of a breach). As can be seen from *PreussenElektra* the potential implications of this could be damaging, however Stix-Haxkl invokes proportionality in the balancing process. For further comment on *PreussenElektra*, see Poli, 'National Regulatory Schemes supporting the Use of Electricity Produced from Renewable Energy Sources and the Community Legal Framework' 2002 J.Env.L. 209; Reid 'Squaring the Circle for Tomorrow's World: A Comparative Analysis of the Approaches of the EC and WTO to Balancing Economic and Non-economic Interests in International Trade' in Tridimas and Nebbia *EU Law for the 21st Century: Rethinking the New Legal Order*, (Hart Publishing, 2004).

Article 28, the Court had no need to consider the proportionality of the measure. Had it done so there can be little doubt, as Advocate General Jacobs observed (having refused to follow the approach of the Court in *Belgian Waste*[97]), that even if it were possible to justify a discriminatory measure this one would fail the proportionality test.[98] This is, of course, in sharp contrast to *Schmidberger*,[99] and also the Opinion of Advocate General Stix Hackl in *Omega Spielhallen*,[100] in which proportionality is applied even where competing objectives were at stake. Indeed proportionality *must* be applied unless environmental protection is to be given automatic priority, this is not, however, in the scheme of the Treaty.

The effect of this case is to permit the considerable Community achievements in economic integration to be jeopardised by reference to environmental protection. Such an outcome is unlikely to have been the intention of the Member States, and demonstrates the very real dangers posed by a failure to decide how to balance *prima facie* conflicting objectives. This outcome would be at odds with the fundamental objectives of the Community including, significantly, those pursued through the adoption of the overarching principle of sustainable development. This demonstrates a very real need for the Community to evaluate the implementation of sustainable development. Yet *Schmidberger* and *Omega Spielhallen* demonstrate that the tools are present within the Community to give full effect to the principle (at least in the context of the single market).

B. Balancing Economic Liberalization and National Regulatory Autonomy: Effects and Context—A More Sophisticated Text?

The difficulties encountered by the Court in reconciling environmental protection and the free movement of goods[101] raise the question of whether the Court's approach, which continues to be based largely upon the *effect* of the measure, and in particular whether the measure has a discriminatory effect upon imported goods, is necessarily the most effective one which can be pursued as regards the balance to be found between economic liberalization and national regulatory autonomy. One crucial strength of the Community approach is that it recognizes the potentially indirectly discriminatory effect of national regulatory measures, and the impediment that these can pose to market integration. The focus on catching both 'distinctly' and 'indistinctly' applicable measures should not be lost or weakened, thus there should not be a *departure* from the 'effects' based test. Despite this, it may be asked whether something could be learnt from the approach adopted in the context of the General Agreement on Tariffs and Trade (GATT).

---

[97] *Supra* note 91.
[98] There was a less restrictive means (certification of origin) which could have been applied to promote the use of renewable energy, without automatically favouring German sources.
[99] *Supra* note 52.   [100] *Supra* note 76.
[101] And Free Movement of Services , as in *Omega Spielhallen, Supra* note 76.

(i) The GATT Approach

In the GATT, there is a prohibition of discrimination against 'like products', in particular there is a requirement that imported products are treated no less favourably than domestically produced 'like products'. The definition applied to 'like products' in the GATT context has not been straightforward, yet, as it now appears to be emerging it could offer some guidance to the Community. The focus in the GATT has traditionally been upon the product itself: if the products themselves are 'like' they should be treated in the same way regardless, for example, of their origin or of the means by which they are produced.[102] 'Likeness' itself has traditionally been determined by an examination of the product characteristics including among others, reference to physical properties and end use.[103] That said, there is more recent recognition that considerations such as consumer perception, health and even the environment may be relevant to determining product likeness (or the lack thereof).[104]

(ii) Lessons for the Community?

If such an approach were applied within the Community it may be possible to allow a measure such as that at issue in *Belgian Waste*[105] to stand, on the basis that (consistent with the principle, observed by the Court, that environmental damage be rectified at source) Belgian locally produced waste is not the same as any other state's waste for the purposes of disposal by Belgium. There might be an obligation upon a state to take responsibility for and process its own waste, which would mean that domestically produced waste could legitimately (and convincingly) be distinguished from imported waste. Any measure which distinguished between imported and domestically produced waste would not therefore be discriminating unlawfully against an imported product. This approach, which focuses explicitly on the specific nature of the goods being dealt with (as the Court appeared to do), rather than simply the effect of the measure *per se* could, crucially, offer a more *complete* (and consequently more satisfactory) way for the Court to reason that the measure is not discriminatory.[106]

---

[102] See, *inter alia*, the *Tuna Dolphin* Dispute BISD 40S/155 (DS21/R) (Not adopted). Reproduced in (1991) 30 ILM 1594. The product-process distinction has caused its own problems as regards national regulatory environmental measures.

[103] See Panel Report European Communities—*Measures Affecting Asbestos and Asbestos Containing* Products WT/DS/135/R, 18 September 2000; Appellate Body Report WT/DS/135/AB/R, 12 March 2001.

[104] See *Asbestos ibidem* and *Shrimp Turtle United States—Import Prohibition of Certain Shrimp and Shrimp Products Report of the Appellate Body, AB-1998-4* WT/DS58/R (98-0000) (1998) ILM 121, also available at http://www.wto.org. This development could potentially mitigate against what has been a particularly restrictive rule as regards a state's ability to pursue national policy objectives. For further comment on the product-process distinction/likeness, see Howse and Regan 'The Product/Process Distinction—An Illusory Basis for Disciplining Unilateralism in Trade Policy' EJIl 11 (2000) 249.   [105] *Supra* note 91.

[106] While this appears to be *effectively* the approach applied by the Court in *Belgian Waste*, explicitly adopting this approach would fill crucial gaps in the Court's reasoning, and could therefore avoid inviting the criticism to which *Belgian Waste* has been subject.

This approach is also consistent with the premise that equal treatment means not only treating products that are the same equally, but also that it can require differential treatment for products which are different. At the same time such an approach could not be abused to justify differential treatment between German renewable energy and other renewable energy, simply on grounds of nationality.[107]

The central weakness of the GATT approach, outside contexts such as these, is that the GATT does not recognize the impediment posed to market integration by indistinctly applicable (indirectly discriminatory) measures—the GATT stops at negative integration, whereas the Community has developed a framework of positive integration. In view of this weakness it is imperative that the Community does not abandon an 'effects-based' test, as that would do a disservice to the realization of market integration. Thus what is required is perhaps a more sophisticated application of the test, which is capable of a more complete evaluation of *effects and context*. The evaluation of 'likeness' should complement rather than replace the 'effects-based' test, as long as market integration remains an objective of the Community's economic development.

PreussenElektra[108] effectively demonstrates the need that any adaptation of the test must be supported by, and pursuant to, clearly established Community principles. *Schmidberger*[109] indicates that the Court is capable of weighing up conflicting values and balancing them. Indeed the Court is familiar with performing such balancing acts from the context of the common agricultural policy.[110] What *PreussenElektra* and *Schmidberger* together demonstrate is a change in the values of the European Union, specifically the adoption of a more complete set of values which complement the original economic, market based objectives.[111]

C. The Application of Sustainable Development in the Single Market: Conclusions

The evolving values of the Community emerging in this case law signal that the Community is indeed more than an economic entity, indicating a corresponding evolution in the shape of its governance. Yet *PreussenElektra* also demonstrates

---

[107] Rather closer to home, the Court is familiar with the issue of dealing with 'similar' products from the context of Art. 90(1) and the interpretation of discriminatory taxation rules, see for example Case 21/79 *Commission* v. *Italy* [1980] ECR 1; Case 148/77 *Hansen* v. *Hauptzollamt Flensburg* [1978] ECR 1787. A comparison between these cases and the GATT Report of the Panel *US Taxes on Petroleum and Certain Imported Substances* (*Superfund*) BISD 34th Supp. (1988) 136, 17 June 1987 (L/1675-34S/136), clearly demonstrates the weakness of the GATT approach in isolation, although arguably the *Superfund* dispute is not the most effective exponent of GATT panel reasoning.

[108] *Supra* note 94.   [109] *Supra* note 52.

[110] Case 197/80 *Ludwigshafener Walzmuhle Erling KG* v. *Community* [1981] ECR 3211 at para. 41; Case 203/86 *Spain* v. *Council* [1998] ECR 4563 at para 10; and case 29/77 *Roquette Frères* v. *France* [1977] ECR 1835.

[111] *Supra* notes 94 and 52 respectively. These developments have occurred in the context of free movement of goods, however, corresponding developments have occurred in the context of free movement of persons, specifically with regard to the elaboration of the rights of citizenship, discussed below.

very clearly the problems which can arise in handling these values where they *prima facie* conflict. At the same time, the adoption of the explicitly two-way test of proportionality in *Schmidberger*, reinforced in *Omega* in the context of services, indicates a maturity of application of law which gives effect to the development of these newer values, and also indicates that it is possible to give effect to the principle of sustainable development: balancing economic rights with human rights and (equally feasibly) environmental protection. *Schmidberger* indicates a new level of integration between fundamental rights and economic liberalization, which gives rise to a shift in expectations of the Community, in particular concerning its developing governance. A parallel development can be seen in the context of free movement of persons, in the elaboration of the rights of citizenship, which demonstrates a disconnection between the right of movement and economic activity. The significance of this must not be understated. The evolution apparent in the case law arising in these contexts indicates that the abstract concept of sustainable development may indeed be the subject of direct application.

V. Sustainable Development in the European Community: The Over-arching principle—Keystone or 'False Front'?

It appears from the approach of the Court in the context of the Single Market that the overarching principle of sustainable development which has been adopted by the Community *is* potentially legally applicable. Yet how truly overarching is this principle in the wider Community legal order? In particular, how complete is the commitment to (and protection for) human rights and the environment, or, what is the *content* and *status* of the Community's environmental and human rights policies? In other words, upon what foundation in the Community legal order does the principle of sustainable development rest?

A. The Content and Status of Fundamental Rights in the Community Legal Order

The protection of both human rights and the environment within the Community legal order initially arose, as seen above, as a consequence of the impact of the internal market upon these interests. In the case of environmental protection the initial issue concerned the distortive impact of varying national environmental standards, whereas in relation to human rights it was the realization that there was no absolute dividing line between the operation of Community policy and the fundamental rights upheld by the Member States.

While the debate concerning the development of Community fundamental rights protection has been largely focussed upon questions of Community *competence* (or lack thereof) in this field, one significant weakness in the Community's protection of fundamental rights has been the lack of a coherent definition of which rights are intended to be protected. The lack of clarity as to the content of 'rights' in the Community legal order is to some extent a consequence of the fact that human rights protection, like environmental protection, initially arose as a by-product of the process of economic integration and the achievement of a Single European Market, rather than as a direct result of Community concern for human rights.[112] This lack of clarity as to the content of rights extends also to the question of for whom these rights are to be protected.[113]

This lack of certainty has been exacerbated by the diversity of terms used, particularly by the Court. The ECJ has recognised its role in the protection of 'human',[114] 'moral',[115] 'individual',[116] 'constitutional',[117] 'community'[118] and 'fundamental personal human rights.'[119] Each of the rights referred to by these varied terms has also, however, been defined as a 'fundamental' right. The reason for this is probably largely political, and rooted in the history of the status of rights in the Community. It cannot be explained by the Court's general reluctance to adopt the terminology of other jurisdictions, but probably rather the reverse: the adoption of rights' terminology from other contexts, without the clear establishment of distinctions between rights. This development raises certain questions: namely what is meant by 'fundamental rights'? How 'fundamental' are they? To whom do they apply? Which 'rights' are referred to in any particular instance?

While the Community has, *prima facie*, a more obvious role (and one which was earlier accepted) in relation to economic (and social) rights than civil and political rights, Article 13 now provides for explicit Community competence in relation to the protection of rights to equality and non-discrimination.[120] The nature of rights conferred can also affect (rightly or wrongly) both the manner in which they are applied and who may benefit from them.

The global descriptor of 'fundamental' within the Community context belies the fact that some individuals resident in the Community benefit from 'fundamental' rights not available to others, such as that to free movement. These rights may be dependent upon factors such as Union citizenship (dependent in turn upon nationality of a Member State), whereas other 'fundamental' rights apply to

---

[112] This is not to lose sight of the fact that it arose as a consequence of a genuine concern for human rights in the national legal orders, and as a result of the direct impact of the operation of Community law upon the enjoyment of national rights.

[113] On this question, see Hilson and Williams *supra* note 23.

[114] ERT, *supra* note 25.   [115] *Konstantinidis, supra* note 30.

[116] Judgment of the Court, Case 118/75 *The State* v. *Watson and Belman* [1976] ECR 1207.

[117] Judgment of the Court, Case 44/79 *Hauer* v. *Rheinland-Pfalz* [1979] ECR 3927.

[118] Advocate-General in *Hauer, ibidem.*

[119] Case 149/77 *Defrenne* v. *SABENA (No.3)* [1978] ECR 1380.

[120] This has been acted upon with the adoption of Council Directive 2000/43/EC of 29 June 2000 implementing the principle of equal treatment between persons irrespective of racial or ethnic origin. [2000] OJ L 180/22 and Council Directive 2000/78/EC of 27 November 2000 establishing a general framework for equal treatment in employment and occupation [2000] OJ L 303/16. Under the Constitution, as seen above, the protection of fundamental rights will be included as a Union objective, *supra* note 38.

all residents and workers of the Community, for example the right to equal pay. This raises questions concerning the depth and meaning of the integration of 'fundamental rights' in the Community legal order.

Analysis of the terminology used by the Court allows the development of a more sophisticated means of classification. Thus those rights given by the Treaty to Community nationals/ Union citizens (such as free movement) could be described as 'Citizens' rights'.[121] Rights (such as that to equal pay) which apply to everyone regardless of nationality or citizenship could be described as 'Community rights'. Those recognized in international law as 'human rights' (including for example the right to life) could be so described. Finally, 'fundamental rights' could continue to be used to describe any of these collectively, in the event that the distinction were not significant. However it may be achieved, greater transparency as to the content and meaning of 'fundamental rights' would facilitate improved understanding of the scope, and in turn enhance the status, of 'fundamental rights' in the Community legal order.[122]

B. The Emergence of a Free-standing Right of Citizenship

Notwithstanding the lack of clarity as to the content and status of fundamental rights in the Community legal order, it must be recognized that the drive towards rights of 'Union Citizenship' reflects, in addition to economic concerns, a desire at Union level to give citizens of the Union something more in the way of political, and increasingly, wider 'fundamental' rights. As AG Geelhoed stated in *D'Hoop*: 'those who drafted the Treaty and the Community legislature [together with the EU Charter] have ... [granted] to Community citizens a number of rights not directly related to economic interests'.[123] The Court itself subsequently, stated that, 'citizenship is destined to be the fundamental status of nationals of the Member States, enabling those who find themselves in the same situation to enjoy the same treatment in law, irrespective of their nationality, subject to such exceptions as are expressly provided for'.[124]

Over the last 10 years or so the Court has gradually developed and refined the substantive content of the rights of citizenship. The key issue concerning citizenship is that rights are conferred subject to the limitations and conditions laid down in the Treaty and in secondary legislation, raising the question of the extent to which citizenship rights can be derived directly from Articles 17 and 18.

---

[121] Yet the 'fundamental' rights of citizenship are even more problematic, as recent case law indicates; see Dougan and Spaventa 'Educating Rudy and the Non-English Patient: A Double Bill on residency Rights under Article 18 EC' (2003) ELRev. 699–712, for case-by-case consideration of the implications of this.

[122] Each of these groups of rights is, of course, a constituent of the social pillar of sustainable development.

[123] Case C-224/98 *D'Hoop* v. *Office National de l'Emploi* [2003] ECR I-6191, at para. 28.

[124] Case C-184/99 *Rudy Grzelczyk* v. *Centre Public d'aide sociale d'Ottignies-Louvain-la-Neuve* [2001] ECR I-6193, at para. 31.

In *Martinez Sala*,[125] the Court effectively drew together the relationship between worker status, the right not to be discriminated against on grounds of nationality and the significance of citizenship. Having held that Sala, a Spanish national resident in Germany *had been lawfully resident* there, the Court found that Sala came within the scope of the provisions on citizenship and on that basis had a right pursuant to Article 17(2) not to suffer discrimination (in accordance with Article 12 (ex Article 6) EC), regardless of worker status.[126] Albeit not insignificant in itself, this ruling left unanswered the question concerning what rights of residence or movement citizenship *itself* confers, and therefore of whether there is any 'added value' of citizenship.

The Court addressed this question in *Grzelczyk*,[127] in which it confirmed its ruling in *Sala* and held that this applies in all situations coming within the scope of the Treaty, and that that includes, significantly the exercise of Article 18. Thus, although Article 18 does not itself provide an unconditional right of residence, it can broaden an existing right of residence, thus triggering the Treaty. This is also significant in that as Article 18 now clearly confers rights, subject to limitations, the onus thus can be seen to shift from a necessity to demonstrate that an individual falls within the scope of the rights, to being how and in what circumstances these rights are to be limited: thus inviting the balancing of the limitations with the right itself.

In *Baumbast*,[128] the Court went a step further in addressing the relationship between the provisions on citizenship and the other provisions of the treaty, when it held that Article 18(1) has direct effect:

A citizen of the European Union who no longer enjoys a right of residence as a migrant worker in the host Member State can, as a citizen of the Union, enjoy there a right of residence by direct application of Article 18(1) EC. The exercise of that right is subject to the limitations and conditions referred to in that provision, but the competent authorities and, where necessary, the national courts must ensure that those limitations and conditions are applied in compliance with the general principles of Community law and, in particular, the principle of proportionality.

The direct effect of Article 18(1) is particularly significant for those who are economically inactive and financially dependent, as can be seen in *Trojani*.[129] In the absence of a right of residence accruing as a consequence of worker status, the question was whether someone in Trojani's circumstances[130] could enjoy a right of residence in a host Member State, accruing directly from Article 18. The Court

[125] Case C-85/96 *Martinez Sala*, [1998] ECR I-2691.   [126] *Supra* note 125 at para 63.
[127] *Supra* note 124 at paras 32–33.
[128] Case C-413/99 *Baumbast* v. *R* [2002] ECR I-7091.
[129] Case C-456/02 *Michel Trojani* v. *Centre Public d'aide sociale de Bruxelles* judgment of the Court of 7 September 2004, *nyr*.
[130] Trojani was a French national, with no means of subsistence. He was living temporarily in a Belgian Salvation Army Hostel and carried out various odd jobs within the hostel for 30 hours a week, in return for which he received board, lodging and some pocket money under a personal rehabilitation scheme.

recalled that any limitation imposed upon the enjoyment of Article 18 must be subject to the principle of proportionality.[131] On the basis of Directive 90/364 the Court held that someone in Trojani's position (without resources) did not derive a right of residence from Article 18 EC, and that to deny them a right of residence on that basis would not be disproportionate. However, Trojani had been granted a temporary residence permit, and on that basis was lawfully resident. Consequently, as a citizen, he was entitled to rely on Article 12 to benefit from social assistance granted to nationals in equivalent circumstances.

On the one hand this looks like a straightforward application of the principles elaborated in *Sala*,[132] but it may be significant that the Court held that: 'A citizen of the Union who does not enjoy a right of residence in the host Member State under Articles 39, 43 or 49 EC may, simply as a citizen of the Union, enjoy a right of residence there by direct application of Article 18(1).' Nothwithstanding that the Court recognizes that the exercise of this right may be limited by the principle of proportionality, if the individual is in possession of a residence permit they may rely on Article 12.[133] This judgment very clearly reinforces the practical significance of national decisions (and procedures by which) to recognize residency, since had he not been granted residency Trojani would not have been able to enjoy the rights of citizenship. Having been given residency, although for no reason grounded in Community law, enjoyment of rights of citizenship could not be denied to him. This does represent an expansion from the earlier case law in which lawful residence had been founded upon (prior) economic activity or student status, and in which the individual had not been an economic burden to the host state throughout their period of residence.[134] Thus, through its elaboration over these cases, particularly *Baumbast*, Article 18 can be seen to have been recognized as a free standing right. Prior to *Grzelczyk* compliance with the criteria of the Residency Directive was constitutive of a right of residency, following *Grzelczyk* as confirmed in *Baumbast and Trojani*, non-compliance may justify an exception from that directly effective right, subject (as a derogation from Community law) to general principles of Community law including proportionality and also fundamental rights *per se*.[135]

C. Implications of the Elaboration of Article 18

There can be little doubt, in light of this case law that the Court has developed the right of citizenship beyond the original, market-oriented, provisions of the Treaty, albeit always with reference to the application of proportionality.[136]

---

[131] *Supra* note 129 at para. 34, recalling *Baumbast, supra* note 128 at para. 91.

[132] *Supra* note 125.   [133] *Supra* note 129, at para. 46.

[134] See *Sala, Gryzelczyk, Baumbast, supra* notes 125, 124 and 128 respectively.

[135] On the potential application of fundamental rights and their implications for residency rights, and on the wider implications of the application of proportionality, in particular the individualisation of citizenship rights, see Dougan and Spaventa *supra* note 121 at 711 and 705–6 and 712 respectively.

[136] Alongside the elaboration of the right of citizenship the Court engaged in some rather creative rulings in relation to free movement of persons and provision of services, notably, in the cases of *Carpenter* (Case C–60/00 *Carpenter* v. *Secretary of State for the Home Department*, [2002]

At the same time, however, the 'right' of citizenship as a 'fundamental right' could be misleading, given its lack of universal application it can certainly not be described as a 'human right'. In the face of this blurred distinction of 'fundamental right' we are returned once again to the question of what is meant by 'right'? Yet, while compounding the problems encountered in defining the content and substance of 'rights', on the other hand, 'citizenship' *reinforces* the development of non-economic interests as free standing in the EC legal order: the elaboration of the right of citizenship in recent case law demonstrates unequivocally the development of non-economic rights within the European Community (notwithstanding that the exercise of rights of citizenship is still explicitly tied to intra state movement[137] and the right of residency in the host state, as well as to nationality of a member State). On the other hand, it is apparent from this that the competing interests at stake in the Community are still pulling each other, as well as the Community, in different directions.[138]

The elaboration of the right of citizenship undoubtedly enhances the rights of Community nationals and contributes to the development of a stronger picture of 'rights' within the European Union through, in particular, the enhanced status of non-economic rights. It does not, however, improve the position of non-nationals, or address the discrepancy in their treatment within the Community legal order.

ECR I-6279) and *Hacene Akrich* (Case C–109/01 *Secretary of State for the Home Department* v. *Hacene Akrich* [2003] ECR-I 9607). Both of these cases raised the question of the relationship between the operation of immigration rules and the enjoyment of fundamental rights. Spaventa observes that these cases, 'seem directed at protecting the individual from disproportionate regulations imposed by Member States regardless of an effect, even only potential, on the exercise of intra-Community economic activities'. Spaventa proposes that the legitimacy needed for this may be found in the principle of citizenship. Whether or not it is accepted that citizenship can indeed provide the necessary legitimacy, there can be little doubt that at any rate these cases should be read in parallel to the Court's elaboration of the right of citizenship. Spaventa *'From Gebhard to Carpenter: Towards a (non-)Economic European Constitution'* (2004) 41 CMLRev. 743–773 at 768.

[137] See Eeckhout 'The EU Charter of Fundamental Rights and the Federal Question' 39 CMLRev. (2002) 945; Davies 'Citizenship of the Union . . . Rights for All', (2002) 27 ELRev 121. The response of the UK Government to the proposal that this position may change suggests this is far from accidental. Reverse discrimination, for example, may not yet be challenged on the basis of rights of citizenship.

[138] There can be little doubt, however, that those who gain least are ultimately the group perceived to have least to offer the Community economically, third country nationals. It is particularly important that the Community address the question of which rights it will protect, and for whom, since, all other considerations aside, the status of third country nationals within the Community is inevitably of particular importance to third states. If the Community's human rights policy in relation to third states is to have credibility it must, itself, be seen to be upholding all the rights it seeks to protect in those third states. This is one question which the European Union Charter may answer, particularly in view of the fact that it was one of the issues raised in the development of the Charter. See House of Commons Research Paper 00/32, at p. 15. See also Williams *EU Human Rights Policy: A Study in Irony* (OUP, 2004); Peers ''Social Advantages' and Discrimination in Employment: Case Law Confirmed and Clarified' (1997) ELRev 157; Hoogenboom 'Integration into Society and Free Movement of Non-EC Nationals' http://www.ejil.org/journal/Vol3/No1/art2.html; Weiler 'Thou Shalt Not Oppress a Stranger: On the Judicial Protection of the Human Rights of Non-EC Nationals—A Critique' http://www.ejil.org/journal/Vol3/No1/art4.html; Peers 'Undercutting Integration: Developments in Union Policy on Third Country Nationals' (1997) 22 ELRev 76–84.

Citizenship provides a body of rights to a particular group, Member State nationals, and thereby creates an effective ring around this group; drawing them together, and distinguishing them from others. Therefore citizenship, by reinforcing this common identity, can have the simultaneous effect of reinforcing the exclusion of non-nationals.[139]

In this sense the development of Union citizenship may have negative consequences for the position of third country nationals within the Union. Whether this is problematic is tied up with the vision of human rights protection within the EU; does the EU, in view of its international commitments and actions, wish to be seen to actively disadvantage, or even simply passively reinforce the disadvantage of third country nationals?

There can be little doubt that as the Community seeks to increase its external activities in relation to human rights, its internal application and enforcement of these will become more important, including, potentially, as third states seek to use the protection of human rights as their own tool. With or without such a development, the treatment of third country nationals is a vital part of the general picture of 'human' rights protection that the Community and Union are creating.

D. The Status of Human Rights in the Community Legal Order

Although the Community currently observes existing human rights standards binding upon the Member States it is not, strictly, bound by any set of human rights provisions (for it is a party to none).[140] Because there was no general power for the Community in the field of human rights, there could be no question of contradictory Community objectives.

If a distinction is observed between social rights and more traditional civil and political rights, there was until recently no development of an autonomous set of Community human rights standards, and no objective to develop such standards *per se* for the Community.[141] To maintain this distinction between social rights and civil and political rights it is necessary to recognize the purpose and limitations of social rights protection within the Community, which was originally to level the economic playing field rather than serve any moral or ethical function.

---

[139] It can also, indeed, have the effect of creating different hierarchies of Community citizens, reinforcing differing rights within citizenship, see Dougan and Spaventa, *supra* note 121, at p. 712: 'On the one hand, Union citizenship is overlaying domestic concepts of solidarity with a new Community dimension. On the other hand, this Community dimension in itself remains fragmented according to the individual's personal status—evolving into a hierarchy within which different classes of Union citizens enjoy different categories of rights'.

[140] The Charter, as an autonomous EU human rights document, complicates this analysis. Although formally it is declaratory of existing rights, not all its rights are derived from other sources. Eeckhout observes that this itself is necessary, as otherwise only 'lowest common denominator' rights protection could be developed, 'The Charter of Fundamental Rights and the Federal Question' 39 CMLRev. (2002) 945.

[141] But note the recent enactment of the Race and Equal Treatment Directives *supra* note 120 and the adoption of the Charter.

As seen above, the initial questions which arose in relation to human rights concerned either the incidental effect of Community measures upon the enjoyment of human rights, or the effect that enjoyment of human rights (and resultant state measures) may have upon Community rights, such as the effect of exercise of the right to protest upon the free movement of goods.[142] *Schmidberger*[143] was therefore significant, in that the Court first recognised that fundamental rights can themselves constitute a mandatory requirement and then used the proportionality test to rule on whether the restriction on free movement of goods was justified. As has been seen, the Court applied proportionality in a two-way manner, which constituted a breakthrough in the relationship between fundamental rights and economic interests and this also indicates an enhancement of the status of human rights in the Community legal order.

E. The Content of Environmental Protection in the Community Legal Order

In contrast, conflicting objectives were set head to head as regards the relationship between environmental protection and economic objectives as early as the 1970s, and since then, even before environmental policy or objectives were formally adopted, the Court has demonstrated itself to be willing to give precedence to environmental protection (generally subject, as is usual in the Community legal order, to the requirement of proportionality.[144])

Consideration of environmental protection before the ECJ arose initially as a consequence of, and reaction to, the market distorting effects of national regulatory measures. Member States therefore defined their policies, and the Court permitted measures pursuant to these policies to be justified where they impacted upon the free movement of goods (subject, of course to proportionality). Environmental protection has subsequently become an explicit, active objective (in contrast with the position of human rights protection), yet despite the development and adoption of the Action Programmes[145] Community environmental policy did not develop as a whole, with a clear vision of what it entails, and is still subject to the criticism that it is an incomplete and unsatisfactory concept. McGillivray and Holder observe that the lack of effective definition of 'environment' has curtailed the development of a holistic environmental policy.[146] This indicates that although *prima facie* 'environmental protection' may be self-evident there is a lack of concrete definition except within specific sectoral contexts. Environmental protection remains a broad, unspecific and aspirational concept, and therefore is somewhat vague.[147]

---

[142] See *R* v. *Chief Constable of Sussex, Ex p. International Traders' Ferry* [1999] 2 AC 418, *Commission v. France (French Farmers) supra* note 62.   [143] *Supra* note 52.

[144] Except in the case of *PreussenElektra, supra* note 94.   [145] *Supra* note 40.

[146] McGillivray and Holder 'Locating EC Environmental Law' YEL 20 (2001).

[147] Environmental policy however encompasses any action to achieve the objectives laid down in Art. 174 EC: 'preserving, protecting and improving the quality of the environment; protecting

It is therefore somewhat surprising that whereas human rights developed as a general principle to be upheld, environmental protection much more quickly became a Community objective in itself. Perhaps this simply reflects the direct economic impact of environmental protection. However, whatever the underlying reasons, that environmental policy developed at all was, as with human rights in the Community legal order, a consequence of the existence of national and international standards and values which the Community responded to.

Moreover there are established objectives within the scope of Community environmental policy which lend it shape and direction. The apparent weakness in its lack of 'definition' could prove to be a strength if 'environmental interests' were properly enforceable, as the lack of a static definition permits ongoing evolution of the Community's environmental policy, to respond to both scientific and value based developments. This potential strength is thrown into sharp relief by the experience in relation to fundamental rights. Those rights which can be traced to an established source are protected within the Community, while newer 'recognized' rights, are unenforceable unless they can be traced to an established source.[148] An inflexible approach to definition and establishment may in fact have the effect of limiting the protection afforded to the Community's non-economic interests.

Thus on balance, it can be seen that there is much to be positive about, the Community is balancing economic and non-economic interests in the context of the single market, and the weight given to non-economic interests in the wider context sends a very positive message concerning the evolving priorities and governance of the European Union in the wider context, as well as demonstrating that the principle of sustainable development can be applied in practice. Yet how far does this really go in establishing the importance of these non-economic values for the Union? A very important question remains concerning the extent to which these non-economic interests are *enforceable* in the Community legal order in the absence of economic counter-interests: thus, to what extent are they enforceable *as free standing rights?*

VI. Enforcing non-economic interests in the European Community: an Essential, yet Problematic, Element of Sustainable Development

It is in the context of judicial review that the limits of the Community approach to non-economic interests are most apparent. This can be seen particularly clearly as regards environmental protection. Until 1995, actions for judicial review brought

human health; prudent and rational utilisation of natural resources; promoting measures at international level to deal with regional or worldwide environmental problems.'

[148] See discussion *infra*.

by individuals under Article 230(4) (ex Article 173 (4)) EC concerned exclusively economic interests.[149] This being the case, it is unsurprising that the test for *locus standi*, 'direct and individual concern', developed in a direction which reflected the economic context of its development. It is highly questionable, however, whether the interpretation of the test developed in that context is appropriate where non-economic interests are at stake.

In *Greenpeace*,[150] the Court was provided with an opportunity to consider whether environmental issues should be considered in the light of criteria other than those developed for, and in the context of, economic rights and interests. The Court, however, like the Court of First Instance before it resisted this opportunity and the invitation of Advocate General Cosmas, and simply applied the traditional test for *locus standi*.

The crucial element concerning *locus standi* and universal interests (such as environmental protection) is the requirement of 'individual concern', which has consistently been interpreted as requiring that a party be affected by the measure in a manner which distinguishes them from any other party. Yet this test is clearly very difficult, if not impossible to satisfy as regards a measure which has an effect upon a universal interest.

In *Greenpeace*, Advocate General Cosmas considered the relevant secondary legislation and observed that this clearly creates legally enforceable rights. He qualified this however by stating that: 'if the rights to be vindicated, or the legal interests of the citizen in connection with the environment, go no further than this, then the protection provided by the Community legal order remains incomplete and fragmentary'.[151]

The Court reasoned that as the measure being challenged (a decision to fund the construction of two power stations) did not directly affect the environmental interest at stake, it was entirely appropriate to apply the traditional case law concerning *locus standi*. (The view of the Court was that the environmental interest was affected by the construction of the power stations *per se*, rather than by the decision to fund the construction of the power stations.)

In contrast Cosmas AG had not dismissed the effect upon the environment as being only indirect, and after considerable analysis of existing case law and argument, stated that easing the requirements of individual concern in certain circumstances would be neither inappropriate nor impossible.

Cosmas' willingness, in principle, to consider such an outcome has subsequently found implicit support from both the CFI[152] and Advocate General

---

[149] Environmental issues, in the Community context, have consistently been considered with reference to their effects upon the market.

[150] Case C-321/95P *Greenpeace and Others* v. *Commission*, [1998] ECR I-1651. For further comment on Greenpeace see Torrens '*Locus standi* for Environmental Associations under EC Law—Greenpeace—A Missed Opportunity for the ECJ' RECIEL 8 [1999] 336; Reid 'Judicial Review and the Protection of Non-Commercial Interests in the European Community' (2000) 1 WJCLI.

[151] Opinion of Advocate General Cosmas, *supra* note 150, at para. 60.

[152] Case T-177/01 *Jégo Quéré & Compagnie SA* v. *Commission* [2002] ECR II-2365.

Jacobs.[153] In *Jégo Quéré*, the CFI held that the *right to an effective remedy* (Article 6 ECHR and Article 47 Charter) required that the strict interpretation of Article 230(4) should be reconsidered. Thus the CFI held that an individual should be recognized to have individual concern if the measure affects their legal position, either by imposing restrictions or restricting their rights.[154] Advocate General Jacobs, in *UPA*, proposed that in order to guarantee effective protection of rights the requirement of individual concern should be reinterpreted in order to recognize that a party has individual concern where 'by reason of his particular circumstances, the measure has, or is liable to have, a substantial adverse effect upon his interests'.[155] De Witte had also, earlier, advocated a relaxation of the requirements of Article 230(4) in relation to human rights, advocating the 'adversely affected' test, framed in such a way as to include associations and public interest groups.[156]

Such an interpretation could conceivably have given local residents in *Greenpeace* individual concern. It would not, however, have overcome the hurdle imposed by the ECJ in ruling that there was no direct effect of the decision upon the environment, and no direct concern in relation to the Commission decision.

The Court's approach to the requirement of direct concern in *Greenpeace* contrasts sharply with that it adopted in *Glencore Grain*.[157] Glencore sought to challenge a Commission decision (addressed to the Russian Federation's financial agents VEB) that they would not provide an emergency assistance loan. The loan was to have been in relation to a contract for the supply of wheat between Richco (now trading as Glencore) and Expokhleb (responsible for negotiations on behalf of Russia). As the loan was not made available, the contract could not be performed. The CFI[158] adopted a *Greenpeace* type of approach, holding that the decision did not affect the existence of the contract, and therefore Glencore was not directly affected.[159] The Court of Justice, however, overturned the order of the CFI. Although it too applied the traditional criteria for the establishment of direct concern, to do so the ECJ looked behind the immediate effect to the decision, to its subsidiary practical effects. Because the contract could not, *in fact*, be performed without the Commission funding, the Court held that Glencore must be directly concerned by the Commission's decision.

Had the *Glencore* approach been used in *Greenpeace*, in combination with a revised interpretation of 'individual concern', it would have been *possible* for the

---

[153] Opinion in Case C-50/00 P *Union de Pequeños Agricultores* v. *Council* [2002] ECR I-6677.

[154] The ECJ has, however, rejected this on appeal in Case C-263/02 P *Commission* v. *Jego Quere*, judgment of 1 April 2004, *nyr*.

[155] *Ibidem* at para. 60. In his Opinion in *Jego Quere supra* note 154, Jacobs has however acknowledged and accepted the Court's ruling in *UPA, supra* note 153, *infra*.

[156] De Witte, 'The Past and Future Role of the European Court of Justice in the Protection of Human Rights', in Alston *et al* (eds) *The EU and Human Rights*, (OUP, 1999).

[157] Cases C-403 & 404/96 P *Glencore Grain Ltd* v. *Commission* [1998] ECR I-2405.

[158] Cases T-491/93 *Richco* v. *Commission* [1996] ECR II-1131 and T-509/93 *Richco* v. *Commission* [1996] ECR II-1181.   [159] Paras 51–53 of the CFI's Order.

Court to have granted the local residents, and possibly Greenpeace, standing without having contradicted its earlier jurisprudence.[160] Not having done so, and having subsequently ruled out the possibility of a revised interpretation of 'direct and individual concern' in *UPA*[161] (on the grounds that this would require amendment of the Treaty)[162] the Court has maintained the position whereby the more universal an adverse impact of a measure upon non-economic interests, the less likely it is that any natural or legal person will be able to challenge that measure.

It would have been helpful if the Court had at least considered the argument relating to the special nature of environmental interests, perhaps at least *recognizing the potential* for a wider interpretation of direct and individual concern in a case concerning non-economic interests. This would have been entirely consistent with its own dicta; for example in *Plaumann* itself,[163] that 'the provisions of the Treaty regarding the rights of action of interested parties must not be interpreted restrictively'.

To have taken an approach such as Cosmas,[164] Jacobs,[165] or de Witte[166] have advocated, interpreting Article 173(4) (now Article 230(4)) EC in a broader manner than hitherto, would have recognized the development of non-economic concerns as giving rise to a distinct direct and individual concern, which is not directly comparable with that arising from the infringement of economic interests, but for which, nonetheless, individuals require protection.

The current position however appears to be that although the objective of environmental protection is being mainstreamed, and although the Court is willing to fully consider the protection of environmental interests where brought before it in conflict with economic interests, there is, as yet, relatively little possibility to enforce an environmental interest. This is problematic in itself, but particularly since the EC in 1998 acceded to the *Aarhus* Convention.[167] The Community has recognised that it does not yet satisfy its obligations in relation to access to justice, and has been working on this since April 2002, when it produced a draft proposal for a Directive to facilitate the implementation of the Convention.[168] This was criticized, however, for failing to offer access in a

---

[160] On the basis that the construction of the power stations could not, in fact, have gone ahead in fact without Commission funding. (Although the Court, admittedly, may not have reached this conclusion on the facts, it is perhaps significant that it did not consider the possibility. This is particularly striking in light of the contemporaneous nature of the two judgments and the potentially similar issue).

[161] *Supra* note 153.

[162] The Court has subsequently confirmed this in *Jego Quere, supra* note 154.

[163] Case 25/62 *Plaumann* v. *Commission* [1963] ECR 95.   [164] *Supra* note 150.

[165] *Supra* note 153.   [166] *Supra* note 156.

[167] Convention on Access to Information, Public Participation in Decision Making and Access to Justice on Environmental Matters.

[168] Working Document I; Consultation began on this issue in May 2002. See in particular Second Working Document Access to Justice in Environmental Matters; http://www.europa.eu.int/comm/environment/aarhus/index.htm.

sufficiently broad range of circumstances.[169] It seems, however, that the granting of adequate access will not be straightforward.[170]

A. The Impact of the Charter on the Enforceability of Individual Rights

Matters are further complicated in this regard by the adoption of the Charter of Fundamental Rights, which provides for a right to an effective remedy.[171] This has raised its own questions for the Community as regards the test for *locus standi*, which in turn has raised questions concerning the enjoyment of fundamental rights *per se*. As seen above, the CFI relied upon Article 47 of the Charter to justify a shift away from the narrow test for *locus standi* under Article 230(4) EC in *Jégo Quere*.[172] Yet as seen above the Court of Justice rejected this development in *UPA*[173] and *Jego Quere*.[174]

This clearly indicates the inter-relationship between rights and environmental interest—what is the 'right to an effective remedy' worth? But also, what level of 'interest' does the individual have in environmental protection?[175] What does this tell us about the Community legal order and the protection of both environmental interests and human rights within that legal order?

The Court certainly adopted a more purposive approach in relation to the protection of economic interests in *Glencore*[176] than in relation to environmental

---

[169] Responses of the European Environmental Bureau to the Working Document, 31 May 2002. See also Consultation Paper 'Access to Justice in Environmental Matters' Based on European Commission Directorate General Environment Working Paper, 11 April 2002, Alan Crockford, Sustainable Development Unit, DEFRA; Communication from the Commission to the Parliament...concerning the common position of the Council on the adoption of a Directive...providing for public participation in respect of drawing up certain plans and programmes relating to the environment and amending with regard to public participation and access to justice, Council Directives 85/337/EEC and 96/61EC, SEC/2002/0581 final and subsequent Opinion of the Commission COM 2002/0586 final.

[170] The Community has still not resolved this problem and has recognized that it cannot fulfil its international obligations, or ratify the Convention until it has done so. It has therefore proposed a Regulation on the application of the provisions of the Aarhus Convention on Access to Information, Public Participation in Decision-making and Access to Justice in Environmental Matters to EC institutions and bodies, COM (2003) 0622 final. This proposal provides (in Title IV—Access to Justice in Environmental Matters) for the development of 'internal review' to mitigate against the strict interpretation of *locus standi* in Art. 230(4).   [171] Art. 47.

[172] *Supra* note 152.   [173] *Supra* note 153.

[174] *Supra* note 154. For discussion of the Court's recent case law on *locus standi* see Arnull, 'April Shower for *Jego Quere*' (2004) 29 ELRev. 287–288; Usher, 'Direct and Individual Concern—An Effective Remedy or a Conventional Solution' (2003) 28 ELRev. 575–600; Ragolle 'Access to Justice for Private Applicants in the Community Legal Order: Recent (R)evolutions' (2003) 28 ELRev. 90–101.

[175] This is related to questions concerning the development of a 'right to the environment' which it is not the purpose of this paper to examine. This question is however reinforced by Art. 37 Charter: what is the meaning of the principle of environmental protection?   [176] *Supra* note 157.

interests in *Greenpeace*.[177] Yet the Court did, in *Greenpeace*, leave the door ajar for a future relaxation in its approach. Subsequent events, however, suggest that the adoption of the Charter, and the controversy as to its status, combined with the approach of the Court, has had the paradoxical effect of slamming that door shut, rather than facilitating the enjoyment of rights.[178]

The CFI, Advocates-General and Court of Justice have been left skirting around the Charter, giving it differing degrees of respect. While the CFI[179] and Advocates-General[180] have been willing to refer to the Charter as at least providing guidance of fundamental rights, the Court of Justice has been reluctant to follow suit.

The potential effect of Article 37 (environmental protection) of the Charter is significant, given that it is framed as an interest in, rather than explicitly a right to, environmental protection. In his opinion in *Commission v. Italy*,[181] AG Colomer stated that 'Environmental protection currently occupies a prominent position among Community policies. Furthermore Member States have a crucial responsibility in that area. Community citizens are entitled to demand fulfilment of that

---

[177] *Supra* note 150.

[178] This would be a particularly unfortunate demonstration of the maxim that it is better not to do a job at all than to half do it. But note proposed changes to individual standing in Draft Constitution—whereby the need to show 'individual concern' would be abolished for an individual seeking to challenge a regulatory act which is of direct concern to them, Art. III-266(4). Under Art. I-28(1) Member States would also be required to provide sufficient rights of review to ensure effective legal protection in the field of EU law.

[179] See *inter alia* Case T-112/98 *Mannesmannröhren-Werke* v. *Commission* [2001] ECR II-729, Case T-54/99 *max.mobil Telekommunikation Service* v. *Commission* [2002] ECR II-313; Case T-177/01 *Jégo Quéré v. Commission*, Order of the Court of First Instance, 3 May 2002, *supra* note 152.

[180] See for example AG Geelhoed in Case C-313/99 *Mulligan and Others* v. *Minister of Agriculture and Food, Ireland and the Attorney General*, [2002] ECR I-5719, at para. 28: 'I also note that Article 17 of the Charter of Fundamental Rights of the European Union recognises the principle of respect of the right to property. As Community law currently stands, however, the Charter does not have any binding effect.' Opinion of AG Tizzano in Case C-173/99 *BECTU* v. *Secretary of State for Trade and Industry* [2001] ECR-I 4881; Opinion of AG Mischo (20 September 2001) in Joined Cases C-20/00 and C-64/00 *Booker Aquaculture trading as Marine Harvest McConnell and Hydro Seafood GSP Ltd* v. *the Scottish Ministers*, 29 September 2001, at para. 126, and also in Cases C-122 and 125/99P *D and Sweden v. Council* [2001] ECR I-4319; Opinion of AG Jacobs in Case C-377/98 *Netherlands* v. *European Parliament and Council of the European Union*, [2001] ECR I-7079 at para. 197; Opinion of AG Léger in Case C-353/99 P *Council of the European Union* v. *Heidi Hautala* [2001] ECR I-9565. See for example AG Geelhoed in Case C-313/99 *Mulligan and Others* v. *Minister of Agriculture and Food, Ireland and the Attorney General*, [2002] ECR I-5719, at para. 28: 'I also note that Article 17 of the Charter of Fundamental Rights of the European Union recognises the principle of respect of the right to property. As Community law currently stands, however, the Charter does not have any binding effect.' Opinion of AG Tizzano in Case C-173/99 *BECTU* v. *Secretary of State for Trade and Industry* [2001] ECR-I 4881; Opinion of AG Mischo (20 September 2001) in Joined Cases C-20/00 and C-64/00 *Booker Aquaculture trading as Marine Harvest McConnell and Hydro Seafood GSP Ltd* v. *the Scottish Ministers*, 29 September 2001, at para. 126 and also in Cases C-122 and 125/99P *D and Sweden* v. *Council* [2001] ECR I-4319; Opinion of AG Jacobs in Case C-377/98 *Netherlands* v. *European Parliament and Council of the European Union*, [2001] ECR I-7079 at para. 197; Opinion of AG Léger in Case C-353/99 P *Council of the European Union* v. *Heidi Hautala* [2001] ECR I-9565.

[181] Case C-87/02, *Commission* v. *Italy*, Opinion of 8 January 2004, nyr.

responsibility under Article 37 of the Charter.'[182] On this basis it appears that Article 37 may be used to reinforce the importance of environmental protection, its integration with other policies and that it is ensured in any actions by the Union. It should be noted that this is the only mention of Article 37 before the Court to date, however, this approach is consistent with that of the Advocate General in *GEMO*, who referred to Article 36 (which provides for the Union's respect for access to services of economic interest, for the purpose of promoting 'the social and territorial cohesion of the Union'), as a reflection of the importance of these services. Since Article 36 is also not framed in terms of 'rights', this supports the implication that these provisions may be used to reinforce the respective interests. Yet reinforcement alone cannot either ensure effective protection of the environmental interest or facilitate the enjoyment of corollary rights. It is also worth noting in this context that in the proposed Constitution, environmental competence is shared, rather than supporting, indicating perhaps that environmental protection it is not intended to be a mere corollary objective.[183]

VII. Conclusions

The objective of this article was to analyse the emergence and development of non-economic objectives in the European Union, and to assess the extent to which these are now part of the Community legal order. It is apparent from the evolution of the European Community that economic and non-economic interests are deeply intertwined, and it is becoming increasingly apparent that it is in fact impossible to deal with these separately. The principle of sustainable development clearly exemplifies the inter-relationship between economic development and non-economic interests, yet, since its adoption as an overarching principle of the European Community many questions have been raised, not least concerning the definition and scope of this principle, as well as whether it can, in fact, be meaningfully enforced.

Yet there is some indication in recent case law that the principle of sustainable development is capable of practical legal effect. *Schmidberger*[184] provides a significant baseline for the European Community in the balance between economic liberalization and development and human rights. Through this, and related case law, the European Community provides evidence for the international community that it is possible to resolve the tension between the pursuit of human rights and economic development. In *Schmidberger* there is evidence not just that human rights and economic development *may* be reconciled, but that the Community is capable of giving practical effect to sustainable development, that the Court has the tools with which to do this, and that the Community legal order

---

[182] *Ibidem* at para. 36.
[183] See relationship between content and enforceability of environmental policy and rights in text accompanying notes 144–148.   [184] *Supra* note 52.

is sufficiently mature to permit the Court to carry out the appropriate evaluation of prima facie (or short term) conflicting interests. *PreussenElektra*[185] in contrast demonstrates the necessity that the Community establish a clear mechanism which the Court should apply in order to resolve the tension which may arise between such objectives.

It appears from *Schmidberger* and *PreussenElektra* together that the proportionality test may well be central to the effective resolution of this tension. These cases also exemplify, however, the changing values and evolving nature of the European Community and indeed the European Union.

However, despite the very positive developments regarding the relationship between economic and non-economic development in the Community, or concerning the application of sustainable development within the context of the single market, questions remain within the Community legal order as regards the depth of commitment to non-economic interests, and the content of rights arising pursuant to these interests. Both environmental protection and human rights protection emerged within the Community as a consequence of a consensus as to their general significance or value, despite a lack of uniformity as to their definition (or application).

Cases in relation to fundamental rights tend to involve individuals seeking to invoke their rights against EC law measures, whereas environmental cases tend to concern national regulatory measures being challenged for breaching EC law. Since there is no underlying consensus as to environmental interests *enjoyable by individuals*, there has been no mechanism by which to enforce these before the ECJ, other than in relation to economic interests. In contrast, human rights (by nature enjoyed by individuals) must be observed both in derogation from, and application of, EC law and may be enforced by individuals. The elaboration of rights of citizenship, in particular the direct effect of Article 18 demonstrates unequivocally that there is a commitment to 'free standing' fundamental rights, going beyond the individual's economic rights. Yet this development also poses many questions for the EU as to the subject, scope and nature of fundamental rights protection.

While the adoption by the Member States of the Charter of Fundamental Rights for the European Union is undoubtedly politically significant in terms of the status afforded by it to fundamental rights, and its inclusion within the Constitution will only enhance that, it has not in fact strengthened the *protection* of rights within the Union. This is a direct consequence of the decision not to endow it with binding effect, that positive decision has had the effect of restraining the development of rights within it which are not derived from another source. That decision is, however, entirely consistent with the Member States' traditional position that their rights are to be ensured within the Community legal order, rather than that the Community itself had any active competence in

---

[185] *Supra* note 94.

relation to fundamental rights.[186] Having consistently ensured the protection of fundamental rights where required to by the Member States, and in doing so having reflected the consensus among the Member States as to the common values to be upheld, it would be surprising if the Court were now to extend that to protect rights declared in a context which the Member States have explicitly provided not to be binding. Thus the very assertion by the States of sovereignty over their rights which led the Court to recognize human rights within the Community legal order in the first place, appears to now be having the effect of limiting the protection of rights within that same Community legal order. The Member States have very effectively provided mixed messages in this regard.

There remains therefore something of a lacuna in the *Court's* approach to the protection of non-economic interests, which may not always be conducive to the same treatment as economic interests (this can be seen very clearly in its approach to *locus standi* of natural and legal persons, both in relation to environmental interests[187] and more recently as regards enjoyment of fundamental rights[188]). Equally, there is a lacuna in the *Community's* development of non-economic policies, notably environmental, without providing adequate means of enforcement and enjoyment of the ensuing rights by individuals, or interest-groups.

The new Charter of Fundamental Rights extends the problem already evident in relation to enjoyment of environmental interests to rights more broadly. The implications of this in relation to rights arising under international agreements, as well as the broad socio-economic rights conferred therein could be profound. It has already been suggested that fundamental rights be integrated into Community policy and action in the same way as environmental protection already is. If environmental policy is to be used as a model, the imperative to resolve existing difficulties becomes even stronger.

It is in the interests of both its own citizens, and the credibility of its external policies that the Union address these issues. The incomplete picture of rights protection currently portrayed within the Union, both in relation to access to justice, and to the lack of 'equality' in benefiting from rights, does not enhance the Union's credibility when it seeks to promote these interests externally.

The Community's strategy for sustainable development[189] highlighted the need to develop a global strategy, and the Commission responded to this call in 2002.[190] This external element of Community policy emphasized the need for greater coherence in EU policies and improved governance at all levels.[191] To this end the Community undertakes to ensure consistency in its international actions and to use its international relations (both bilateral and multilateral) to underpin sustainable development, and to support closer co-operation between the World

---

[186] This position would change, as above, under the Constitution.
[187] *Greenpeace, supra* note 150.   [188] *UPA, supra* note 153.   [189] *Supra* note 15.
[190] COM (2002) 82 final 'Towards a global partnership for sustainable development'.
[191] *Ibidem* at 3.

Trade Organization and both international environmental bodies, and the International Labour Organization.

It appears that a recognition of the need to build upon existing international structures, including the ILO and UNEP, to ensure sustainable development is central to the EU's plans, as is recognition of the need to develop global governance to facilitate this. Difficulty may arise, however, in developing global governance, as this would require a common vision of what constitutes good governance, and a political will to achieve that.

As seen above, the Charter adds little to the protection of human rights within the Union—the Court had already made it clear that, within the scope of Community law, it will ensure that human rights obligations are fulfilled. The Charter itself does not add the internal clarity or consistency necessary for the Community to demonstrate that it is itself applying the standards it wishes to impose on other states through its external pursuit of human rights protection, and to some extent the failure to give it binding effect has weakened the potential protection of certain rights, as well as laying the Community open to criticism where rights declared in the Charter are not seen to be adequately protected within the Union.[192]

What is very clear from the nature of the development of both environmental and human rights protection, albeit incomplete, is that effective protection of these interests is dependent upon a common consensus as to both the nature of the interests to be pursued, requiring shared values, and the means by which these are to be protected. In the Community this has been expressed in relation to human rights in the adoption of the Charter, the new legislation under Article 13, and the draft constitution. In relation to the environment there is explicit acknowledgement of the importance of governance in sustainable development and the recognition of the need to address access to justice in environmental matters.

The Community does appear to be directly addressing the question of the balance of non-economic with economic objectives in the context of the single market, and this reflects a consensus as to the significance of these non-economic values. It has not as yet (citizenship notwithstanding) been equally successful in facilitating the enjoyment of non-economic rights and interests conferred outside that context, and there is little doubt that its approach as regards non-economic interests has been a weaker approach than that taken to the enjoyment of economic rights. Ultimately there appears to be an inevitable paradox that as the EU develops a wider set of values, these are most effectively given effect to in the traditional Community context of the single market.

On the other hand there is much to be positive about—the Court has demonstrated a considerable maturity in the Community legal order within the context of the single market. As regards enforcement of non-economic interests, the Member States must take responsibility for the mixed messages given, and half

---

[192] See discussion in relation to Art. 47, accompanying note 171 *et suiv.*

steps they have taken, with the Charter. These, combined with the approach of the Court in this context, have indeed had the effect of eroding progress in the development of non-economic interests. It is now for the Member States to decide whether they want to give full effect to sustainable development within the Community legal order. If the Union wishes to pursue its external agenda with any force or credibility, however, and so carry through its commitment to sustainable development, the outstanding internal questions must be resolved.

Corporate Social Responsibility in the External Relations of the EU

Alexandra Gatto *

I. The Current Debate on Corporate Social Responsibility

A. Introduction

Recent global trends have given business a greater role and stake in human and environmental issues that were previously the sole responsibility of government. The power and influence of business is growing quickly; of the world's 100 largest economies, 50 are now multinational corporations (MNCs) and 25 per cent of the world's economic output is controlled by only 500 industrial corporations.[1] The issues of human rights and the environment are used as key performance indicators for companies in the attempt to meet the challenge of allying economic growth with respect for human dignity.[2] Furthermore, the immediacy of global communications increases the level of scrutiny of corporate behaviour by media, civil society and non-governmental organisations (NGOs). Against this background, companies have realized that good corporate citizenship is central to healthy foundations and have embraced a series of initiatives that have proliferated at national and international level in recent years.

MNCs are characterized by having legal status and profit motive together with the ability to operate across national borders and outside the effective supervision of domestic and international law. They are not created by a single law. Furthermore, there is no universally applicable law that delineates the limits of their activities and the distribution of power. Control of MNCs is arranged in a

* Alexandra Gatto, LL.M College of Europe, Bruges, is Ph.D. candidate at the European University Institute in Florence, Italy with a dissertation on the responsibility of multinational enterprises for the respect of human rights in the European legal framework. The author would like to thank Professor Inge Govaere and Professor Gráinne de Búrca for their comments on draft versions of this article.

[1] Source CSR Europe, November 2000.

[2] *Business and Human Rights—A Progress Report*, Office of the United Nations High Commissioner for Human Rights (OHCHR), January 2002.

manner that defies territorial boundaries. In economic terms, MNCs differ from domestic enterprises in their capacity to locate productive facilities across national borders; in their ability to trade across frontiers with affiliates thus maintaining a competitive advantage over local firms; in their know-how of foreign markets and in their global organization of their managerial structure according to the most suitable line of authority. Consequently, their impact on human rights and development may be regarded as significant than that of domestic firms.[3]

Although the spread of economic globalization has prompted international efforts to develop mechanisms to hold multinational corporations responsible for their conduct, no clear-cut answer is available in international law in order to define the scope and nature of the social obligations of multinational corporations, nor the mechanisms through which they can be enforced.

This situation poses enormous challenges for the European Union (EU) and its Member States. Firstly, the European Union and the Member States are major donors of official aid to developing countries.[4] Secondly, as a trade policy actor, the EU is at the centre of a 'web of bilateral links'.[5] It acts as a gatekeeper, it negotiates access to other markets and it acts as a competitor in the relations between the major blocs of the world economy.[6] Thirdly, EU-based companies have major investments and operations in the developing countries. The role of the EU, however, cannot be limited to that of a major development agency and trade partner. The complex system of relationships with developing countries in all parts of the world and the role it plays in major multilateral organizations, such as the World Trade Organisation (WTO), the International Labour Organisation (ILO) and the Organisation for Economic Co-operation and Development (OECD), makes the EU a key actor in North-South relations.[7]

Against this background, this article addresses the question of how the EU can contribute to the responsible conduct of MNCs domiciled in its Member States when they operate abroad, particularly in developing countries. Among the several options of intervention currently available under EU law,[8] this article will focus only on the opportunities offered by EU external relations for the promotion of Corporate Social Responsibility.

This question represents a small part of the wider issue regarding the accountability of MNCs. As mentioned above, no clear-cut answers are available in international as well as in EU law in order to define the scope and nature of social obligations of MNCs, nor the mechanisms through which they can be

---

[3] P. Muchulinski, *Multinational Enterprises and The Law*, (Oxford, Blackwell, 1995), at 15.

[4] C. Bretherthon, J. Vogler, *The European Union as a Global Actor*, (London—New York, Routledge, 2002), at109.   [5] *Ibidem*, at 59.

[6] *Ibidem*, at 60.   [7] *Ibidem*, at 109

[8] Cf. O. De Schutter, *The liability of multinationals for Human Rights violations in European Law*, in E. Brems, P. Vanden Heede (Eds.) *Bedrijven en Mensenrechten*, (Antwerpen Maklu, 2003), at 45.

enforced.[9] Therefore, this study focuses on mechanisms, rather than substantive norms.[10]

This article is divided into five parts. Following this introductory Part One, Part Two outlines the conceptual framework against which the article's question will be analysed. An overview of the current debate on Corporate Social Responsibility at both international and EU levels is given. In this context, the EU strategy for the promotion of Corporate Social Responsibility at the international level (in particular in developing countries), and the specific challenges it presents are described. Part Three examines how and to what extent the EU is taking action to promote Corporate Social Responsibility through its relations with other international organizations. In particular, the EU's role in the WTO, the collaboration of the EU in promoting OECD Guidelines and its support of ILO promotion of labour standards are examined. In Part Four, the question as to how the EU has been promoting Corporate Social Responsibility in its bilateral relations is adressed. Particular relevance is given to the General System of Preferences (GSP), the Cotonou Agreement and the Association Agreement between the EU and Chile. Part Five draws conclusions on how the above analysis has responded to the question posed by the paper and suggests possible solutions.

B. Regulatory Versus Voluntary Patterns

At the heart of the current debate on the accountability of MNCs is the tension between regulatory and non-regulatory mechanisms of enforcement. The former implies a revision of existing legislation both at national and international levels in order to create new obligations binding on companies. The latter relies on business self-regulatory power by rejecting legally binding obligations. In addition to this, three different levels at which companies can be held accountable are usually distinguished. The responsibility of MNCs can be enforced by setting international obligations directly on companies.[11] Alternatively States, the direct addressees of human rights obligations under international law, can impose indirect obligations on MNCs. In this case, the question arises as to whether these obligations should be enforced in the host State or in the home State of the MNCs.

[9] International Council On Human Rights, *Beyond voluntarism-Human rights and the developing international legal obligations of companies*, February 2002, available at www.ichrp.org; *Cf.* M. K. Addo, *Human Rights Standards And The Responsibility of Transnational Corporations*, (The Hague, Kluwer Law International, 1999).

[10] Although a comprehensive analysis of the issue would include the relations of the EU with a wider range of international organizations, only the OECD, ILO and WTO will be tackled since they have been identified by the EU as privileged *fora* and partners for the promotion of Corporate Social Responsibility.

[11] *Cf.* M. T. Kamminga, 'Holding multinational corporations accountable for Human Rights Abuses: A challenge for the EC', in Ph. Alston, *et al.* (Eds.), *The EU and Human Rights*, (Oxford, Oxford University Press, 1999), at 558; S. Joseph, 'Taming the Leviathans: Multinational Enterprises and Human Rights', (1999) 46 *Netherlands International Law Review*, 171.

The creation of an international framework creating direct obligations to be imposed upon on companies is currently under discussion within all major multilateral organisations. A number of instruments addressed to MNCs are already set in place. The ILO has recently revised the Tripartite Declaration of Principles Concerning Multinational Enterprises and Social Policy. The OECD Guidelines for Multinational Enterprises were updated in 2001. The United Nations have issued the UN Norms for Transnational Corporations.[12] This intense standard-setting activity is indicative of the growing awareness of, and concern for, the conduct of MNCs. However, these instruments do not create legally binding obligations and largely rely on 'soft law'[13] (ILO and OECD) and voluntary initiatives (the UN Norms for Transnational Corporations). Given the inadequacy of the international legal framework in ensuring the accountability of MNCs, soft law procedures may provide a more reasonable approach[14] than the creation of an international agreement binding on MNCs or the exclusive reliance on voluntary initiatives.

The option of holding governments to account for the behaviour of MNCs mainly relies on the horizontal application of human rights law.[15] According to this doctrine a State may be held directly liable not only for the vertical infringements of human rights—that is, by the State against individuals—but also for horizontal infringements that is, by individuals or private bodies against other individuals or private bodies.[16] This theory stems from a broad interpretation of the States' obligation *to protect* human rights.[17]

[12] Sub-Commission on the Promotion and Protection of Human Rights, Fifty-fifth session, Norms on the responsibilities of transnational corporations and other business enterprises with regard to human rights, E/CN.4/Sub.2/2003/12/Rev.2 of 26 August 2003, available at: http://www.unhchr.ch/Huridocda/Huridoca.nsf/TestFrame/64155e7e8141b38cc1256d63002c55e 8?Opendocument. Accessed on 3.11.3003. Cf. C. Hillemans 'UN Norms on the Responsibilities of Transnational Corporations and Other Business Enterprises with regard to Human Rights', (2003) 4 *German Law Journal*.

[13] The expression 'soft law', as opposed to hard law, was developed to describe declarations resolutions, guidelines, principles and other high levels statements by group of states such as the United Nations, the International Labour Organization and the Organization for Economic Development, that are neither strictly binding norms nor ephemeral political declarations. It is recognized that soft law instruments can have some anticipatory effect in shaping new binding international norms and may acquire considerable strength in shaping international conduct. See on this point International Council on Human Rights Policy, *Beyond Voluntarism-Human Rights and the Developing International Legal Obligations of Companies*, February 2002, accessed at http://www.ichrp.org on 3.3. 2002.

[14] On this point see F. Francioni 'International "Soft Law": A Contemporary Assessment', in V. Lowe, M. Fitzmaurice (Eds.) *Fifty Years of the International Court of Justice: Essays in Honour of Sir. Roberts Jennings*, 1996 at 167 175 and 178.

[15] See generally A. Clapham, *Human Rights in the Private Sphere*, (Clarendon Press, Oxford, 1993). This expression is used both by D. Kinley, 'Human rights as legally binding or merely relevant?', in Bottomley S., Kinley D. (Eds.), *Commercial Law and Human Rights*, (Aldershot, Ashgate, 2002), at 40; and in International Council on Human Rights Policy *supra* at 53.

[16] See 'The Maastricht Guidelines on Violations of Economic Social and Cultural Rights', (1998) 81 *Human Rights Quarterly*, at 87, point 18, Acts by Non State Entities.

[17] A precedent can be found in the notion of third party effect *Drittwirkung* developed by German courts, according to which some German constitutional rights affect private legal relationships. Cf. S. R. Ratner, 'Corporations and human rights: a theory of legal responsibility', (2001) 3 *Yale Law Journal* 443 at 471.

This horizontal applicability of human rights has been upheld in general comments by UN expert bodies and decisions of regional human rights courts in Europe and the Americas. The European Court of Human Rights (EcrtHR), for instance, held that the Netherlands' failure to take legal action against a private person who committed sexual assault against a mentally handicapped dependant was in breach of the victim's right to privacy.[18] The right to privacy was also violated by Italy's failure to prevent a company from releasing toxic gases.[19] In *Hatton*,[20] the ECrtHR spelled out that in the specific case of environmental protection, the mere argument of economic interest was not a sufficient justification for the interference with privacy and family life. The Inter-American Court of Human Rights held the government of Honduras responsible for not having prevented and punished a forced disappearance committed by a persons not associated with the State.[21] In the case of *Yanomani- Brazil*,[22] the Inter American Commission, first formulated the basic obligations of the State to protect individuals from harm caused by economic activity on the part of non-State actors. The Commission held that Brazil was responsible for not having taken timely and effective measures to protect the human rights of the Yanomamy indigenous population, violated by the invasion of oil workers in their lands.

This case law suggests that State responsibility can go very far in addressing human rights violations in the private sphere. However, when a Sate is bound by an obligation *to prevent*, it does not mean that the conduct of individuals as such will be imputable to the States.[23] The responsibility of the State arises only in combination with a failure to act by State organs (for example, failure to adopt relevant legislation).[24] According to this interpretation, two cases arise in which a State may be held responsible for the behaviour of an MNC; firstly, when a State responsible under international law fails to exercise the required degree of due diligence with regard to the conduct of MNCs; and secondly in the case of a corporation exercising elements of governmental authority, either as a result of formal delegation by the authorities or when the conduct of such a corporation may be attributable to the State. Relying on State responsibility, however, still

---

[18] *X and Y v. The Netherlands*, 91 Eur. Ct. H.R. (ser a) at 11 (1985). This case as well as the following ones are cited in S. R. Ratner *supra* at 470.

[19] *Guerra v. Italy*, 1998—I Eur. Ct. H.R. 777.

[20] *Hatton and others v. The United Kingdom*, ECHR Application n. 3602/77 available at www.coe.fr. Quoted in N. Jägers., *Corporate Human rights obligations in search of accountability* (Antwerpen-Oxford New York, Intersentia, 2002), at 153.

[21] In this case, however, there was a high possibility that the persons involved were state agents. *Velásquez Rodríguez* case, Inter—Am. CT. H.R. 8 (ser C) No 4 (1998).

[22] *Yanomami v. Brazil* Case 7615, 5.3.1985, Res. No 12/85 IACH, Annual report, 1985.

[23] The notion of an obligation to prevent was defined in Article 23 of the Draft Articles on State Responsibility provisionally adopted by the International Law Commission on first reading (1999).

[24] See, e.g., Eur. Ct. H.R., *A. v. the United Kingdom*, judgment of 23 September 1998, Reports of Judgments and Decisions 1998-VI, § 22 See, e.g., Eur. Ct. H.R., *A. v. the United Kingdom*, judgment of 23 September 1998, Reports of Judgments and Decisions 1998-VI, § 22.

entails the question of the types of abuses the State has a duty to prevent and remedy.[25]

In most cases, the State that is more likely to take effective action in relation to placing international human rights obligations on MNCs is the one where the parent corporation of the MNC is based (home State). Usually, the technical expertise to impose adequate safety standards and a legal system able to cope with the proper attribution of responsibility within complex corporate arrangements are more easily available in the home State. However, difficulties can occur in relation to whether the home State can regulate the operations that an MNC (either the parent or the subsidiaries) conducts abroad. Such regulation is likely to be perceived as an interference in the territorial sovereignty of another State, which is contrary to international law. Nonetheless, the grounds for extraterritorial regulation have been linked to the nationality principle which holds that a State has jurisdiction over its nationals in relation to offences committed by them anywhere in the world.[26] Furthermore, the home State may regulate the activities of a parent and subsidiary of MNCs, where that regulation seeks to uphold the general interest of the international community. Therefore, it can be argued that the home State can lawfully regulate the activities of a subsidiary to the extent that this is consented to by the host State as being in the interest of the international community, waiving suspicion of collusion with foreign policy goals or domestic benefit of the home State.

Several obstacles can hamper the effectiveness of regulation at the level of the State where the multinational is operating (host State). Firstly, host States can sometimes lack the technical expertise necessary to monitor and regulate corporate activities. Secondly, due to the complex structure of MNCs the determination of liability between parent and subsidiaries can be difficult and host States can be ill-equipped to deal with these cases. Finally, MNCs are so large that they can exercise extensive bargaining power over the government of host States[27] which in turn may be lax in enforcing legislation in order to retain the investment of these companies.

In response to growing corporate awareness and increasing consumer pressure, there has been a significant expansion in the number of voluntary codes of conduct which have been adopted in different business sectors. These instruments include codes of conduct, social labels, social auditing and social reporting.

Codes of conducts are commitments by companies to respect fundamental standards, while social labels are addressed to consumers to indicate that the production of the goods concerned has taken place respecting particular standards.

---

[25] Cf. F. Francioni, 'Exporting environmental hazard through multinational enterprises: can the state of origin be held responsible?', in F. Francioni, T. Scovazzi (Eds.) *International Responsibility for Environmental Harm*, (Kluwer Academic Publishers Group, 2003) at 275.

[26] For e.g., at European Union level, the extra territorial criminal legislation on the sexual exploitation of Children, The Joint Action of 24 February 1997 (under Title VI TEU).

[27] See J. Woodroffe, 'Regulating Multinational Corporations in a World of Nation States', in M.K. Addo (Ed.), *supra* at 139; S. Joseph, *supra* at 78.

They may be placed somewhere in the middle between regulatory and voluntary mechanisms. In fact, clearly worded codes can also have a legal significance because they set out the values, ethical standards and expectations of the company concerned, and might be used as evidence in legal proceedings with suppliers, employees and consumers.

At the level of individual company codes, empirical evidence suggests that though their number is growing, policies or codes of conduct specifically covering human rights are still an exception rather than the rule for companies.[28] Generally, the human rights adressed by industry-wide and individual company codes focus on workers' rights—conditions of employment, health safety, freedom of association and non-discrimination—as well as the rights of children, particularly regarding their employment and education. However, there are many other relevant rights guaranteed by international human rights law such as privacy, the rights of indigenous people, freedom of expression, cultural belief and practice, as well as the right to liberty and a fair trial which are overlooked.

However, a number of codes also express clear commitments to implement the Universal Declaration of Human Rights.[29] Most contain at least some specific commitments about the company's conduct towards groups with which it has a direct connection, such as employees, sub-contractors, suppliers and host governments. Many codes require a company's subcontractors to comply with its provisions and may contain detailed descriptions of prohibited corrupt practices and make commitments to protect the environment and consult local communities affected by their operations. Codes of conduct reveal examples of how corporations can improve the way in which they do business.[30]

With regard to international guidelines for MNCs and codes of conduct, they are neither entirely enforceable domestically, nor entirely non-binding internationally. There is a marked tendency on the part of major States in international norm-creating processes to make less than full use of the existing legislative competences of international organizations in connection with the regulation of MNCs' conduct. It follows that at least for some time to come, codes of conduct for MNCs will not be adopted in the form of a multilateral convention or as a normative act of international organizations. This does not preclude the possibility of the substantive content of such codes moving into the domain of 'hard' international law. Although defined as voluntary and not-legally enforceable, guidelines do not operate so as to

---

[28] D. Cassel, *Corporate Initiative: A Second Human Rights Revolution?*, in Fordham International Law Journal, 1996, at 163; for a parallel survey at a European level, see Ph. Spicher, *Les droits de l'homme dans les chartes d'étique économique*, Bern-Fribourg, Commission nationale suisse pour l'Unesco, Institut interdisciplinaire d'étique e des droits de l'homme de l'Université de Fribourg-Centre Info, 1996.

[29] UN, Universal Declaration of Human Rights, GA Resolution. 217 a, (III), UN Doc. A/180 (1948), downloaded at http://www.unhchr.ch/udhr/index.htm, on 13 April 2002.

[30] An assessment of benefits and limitations of code of conducts can be found in D. SPAR, *The Spotlight on the Bottom Line: How Multinational Export Human Rights*, in Foreign Affairs vol. 7, 1988, at 77.

shield MNCs from the enforcement of the substantive content of the Guidelines by legislative or regulatory actions by States which adopted them.

Social labels are words or symbols on products which seek to influence the purchase decision of consumers by providing an assurance about the ethical and social impact of a business process on other stakeholders. These may imply extra costs but also marketing advantages. The hope is that there will be a consumer premium concentrated in particular in niche markets. Certification has increased rapidly: nonetheless it still accounts for only a minority of products. This implies that such schemes have impact mainly in markets that are both discretionary and publicly visible, such as the garment industries. On the other hand, smaller enterprises may find it difficult to absorb the cost of certification and the proliferation of different certification schemes.

The concept of social disclosure is underscored by the notion that a corporation is responsible to the community at large for its actions and is placed in a position similar to that of a provider of a public service that is called to explain and account for its action in light of broad conceptions of the public interest. This has resulted in a wider conception of disclosure than that needed by financiers of the corporation and include disclosure to employees, the use of local value added statements and environmental disclosure. Many of the schemes listed above have associated monitoring and reporting arrangements. Yet, given their specific focus, these may well not capture a company's full social and environmental impacts. A wider initiative in this area is the Global Reporting Initiative.[31]

Broader disclosure is likely to render more effective market mechanisms that steer companies towards responsible conduct. For example, an important requisite for consumer action is access to information about the company activities and their impact. In the absence of appropriate disclosure, consumers or other stakeholders will be unaware of corporate human rights abuses. Unless the information available is sufficiently detailed and reliable, it will be impossible to identify which companies are the most serious offenders and to ensure that pressure from consumers and investors is appropriately targeted. It is now common for companies to disclose information additional to that required by law. The most popular subject is environmental performance. Although disclosure techniques in other areas are less advanced, there is no reason in principle why companies could not be made to report in all areas in which they have a relevant social impact. An alternative approach to formal publication of information is to allow public access to company's records. External reporting might be a promising way of increasing managerial circumspection and activating social pressure. The European Commission adopted a proposal for a Directive about annual accounts.[32] The Directive requires

[31] Commission of the European Communities, Green paper—*Promoting a European framework for corporate social responsibility* (COM(2001) 366 final, 18.7.2001), at 17.

[32] Proposal for a Directive of the European Parliament and of the Council amending Council Directives 78/660/EEC and 83/349/EEC concerning the annual accounts of certain types of companies and consolidated accounts (presented by the Commission), COM/2004/0725 final—COD 2004/0250.

that EU-based listed companies should disclose an annual corporate governance statement as part of their annual report. The Directive states that within their corporate governance statement companies may also provide an analysis of environmental and social aspects necessary to understand their development, performance and position. While not mandating reporting on CSR issues, the Directive recognizes the relevance of environmental and social issues in the context of corporate governance.

The value added statement is a financial device that seeks to show the production contribution made by the company in the course of an accounting period. For instance, local value added statement by the subsidiary of an MNC can show the overall contribution made by it to the economy of the host country. Such a statement may be of particular use to developing countries where the prime users of information about the operations of MNCs' subsidiaries are not investors but the government as principal economic planner, and other groups concerned with the impact of the MNC on national development.[33] Value added statement is common in European firms' annual reports, although there is no common European Directive on this matter. An example of disclosure can be found in the Eco-Management and Audit Scheme (EMAS) ISO 19000 that encourages companies to voluntarily set up an environmental management and audit system.

These voluntary measures are still considered to be inadequate. The main shortcomings are the vagueness of commitments, the lack of monitoring and compliance mechanisms and the absence of compensation schemes for victims of abuses. One of the main criticisms is that self-regulatory regimes are designed to give the appearance of regulation and thereby ward off criticism and the imposition of external regulation. In other words, MNCs' codes of conduct are often seen as public relations exercises. Most codes of conducts use aspirational language or state broad values of the organization: such as business integrity, openness, enriching the community, treating people with dignity and respect or conducting business responsibly.

Another shortcoming of self-regulation lies in its non-binding character. Voluntary schemes can easily be flouted by less scrupulous MNCs. In addition, companies are generally reluctant to open their operations and activities to independent monitoring or verification of these codes. Furthermore, self-regulation and other voluntary approaches have limited impact on the actual performance of companies.[34] In the absence of legislative requirements, many companies do not even meet the minimum standard specified in international human rights law.

Although the impact of self-regulation cannot be overestimated, they represent an initial step by companies in acknowledging their role in addressing human rights

---

[33] M. R. Zubaidur, *The Local Value Added Statement: a Reporting Requirement of Multinationals in Developing Host Countries*, in International Journal of Accounting, vol. 25, 1990, at 88.

[34] See OECD, *Voluntary Approaches For Environmental Policy: an Assessment*, (Paris, OECD, 1999). This report highlighted that to be credible self-regulation must include credible regulatory threats, reliable monitoring and third party participation and penalties for non-compliance.

issues. Codes of conduct may themselves be understood as an evolutionary step along the way to legally binding standards that carry the support of a responsible majority while ensuring censure and accountability of wrongdoing companies.

On the other hand, despite the fact that there are no legal obstacles to imposing direct human rights duties on companies, these attempts have been so far unsuccessful. The main defeats can be seen in the failure of the Multilateral Agreement on Investment (MAI),[35] the failure to introduce personal criminal liability for legal persons in the Rome Statute of the International Criminal Court level (ICC) and at a European level, and the limited application of the European Parliament's Resolution on EU standards for European enterprises operating in developing countries: towards a European Code of Conduct.[36]

Voluntary initiatives are usually understood by the business community as add-ons to legislative requirements. They are often criticized as being vague as to their commitments and lacking in monitoring and compliance mechanisms. However, they represent an initial step by companies in acknowledging their role in adressing human rights issues. Furthermore, voluntary initiatives as well as soft law mechanisms constitute a first step towards the progressive development of legally binding standards since they promote convergence on uniformly agreed standards.[37]

Corporate Social Responsibility can be regarded as a prompt and flexible solution to the present corporate deficit of accountability. However, this does not imply the rejection of mandatory measures. On the contrary, Corporate Social Responsibility is perceived as complementary to regulatory measures as part of an overall strategy to hold MNCs accountable. A wider basis of consensus created by Corporate Social Responsibility measures can be later translated into legal obligations. The development of legal regulation of environmental matters is a good example of this progressive development of social concern into legal obligations. Just as once few would have believed that environmental issues would be mainstreamed into corporate affairs to the extent that they now are, so today we find a wide range of human rights issues in boardroom discussions.

II. Corporate Social Responsibility: A New Item on the EU External Relations Agenda

A. Corporate Social Responsibility in the Context of EU External Relation

Concerns about the conduct of European MNCs in developing countries have gained momentum within the European Union. A strategy for the development

---

[35] M. T. Kamminga, *supra* at 569.

[36] Resolution on EU standards for European enterprises operating in developing countries: towards a European Code of Conduct, adopted by the European Parliament on 15.1.1999, A4-0508/1998, [1999] OJ C104/176, Rapporteur Mr Richard Howitt, Member of the European Parliament (MEP).

[37] Cf. Similarly on soft law mechanisms, F. Francioni, 'International "Soft Law" ', *supra* at 175.

of Corporate Social Responsibility at EU internal and external level has been recently laid down by the European Commission. This purports to use a wide range of external relations tools for the promotion of Corporate Social Responsibility in developing countries.

The positive interrelation between sustainable development and the promotion of human rights, in third countries in the context of EU trade and development co-operation policies,[38] was recognized for the first time in the Communication on the promotion of human rights and democratization.[39] This document contains an express reference to the role of companies, in that European multinationals were called upon to use their influence within developing countries 'to support rather than undermine that country's own effort to achieve sustainable development'.[40]

This approach was further spelt out in the Communication 'Promoting Core Labour Standards and Improving Social Governance in the Context of Globalisation'.[41] It envisaged use of bilateral dialogue with developing countries, development assistance to increase capacity and additional trade incentives under the GSP where countries comply with minimum social standards.[42]

More recently, it has been recognized that the private sector, particularly MNCs can play a key role in poverty reduction. This is currently the central aim of EU development policy, fully in line with the UN Millennium Declaration.[43] In September 2002 the Commission issued a communication on trade and development,[44] which defines the importance of the relationship between trade, development and the integration of developing countries in the world economy. The Communication conceives of several measures aimed at improving the delivery of trade-related assistance in key areas and enhancing co-ordination and coherence within the EU and with international organizations. The overall objective is to help developing countries to acquire the expertise necessary to deal with the challenges of global trade and, by the same token, to improve their institutional regulatory capacity. In this context, the importance of improving the investment climate in developing countries for the business sector has been

---

[38] Cf. O. De Schutter, *supra* at 48.

[39] Communication from the Commission to the Council and the European Parliament: The European Union's role in promoting human rights and democratisation in third countries, COM(2001) 252 final, 8.5.2001.

[40] See 'Promoting human rights and democratisation in third countries', *supra*.

[41] Communication from the Commission to the Council, the European Parliament and the Economic and Social Committee: Promoting core Labour Standards and Improving Social governance in the context of globalisation (COM(2001) 416 final, 18.7.2001). In particular, the basic tenets of the EU approach are set out in para. 3, and further action at the European Union and international level at para. 5.   [42] O. De Schutter, *supra* at 62.

[43] European Multi-stakeholder Forum on Corporate Social Responsibility—Roundtable on the Development Aspects of Corporate Social Responsibility, 7 April 2003.

[44] Communication from the Commission to the Council and the European Parliament—Trade and development—Assisting developing countries to benefit from trade, COM(2002)0513 final, 18.9.2002.

underlined. Training programmes for negotiators and administrators have been established. Technical assistance for sustainability impact assessments review existing mechanisms for co-ordination of Member States and sharing of 'best practices', seen as key tools to achieve the objective set out in the Communication.[45]

The potential of working together with the private sector has been stressed further in the context of two recent communications on health and education.[46] In both cases, the emphasis was placed on the need for new incentives for multinationals and other private companies in the development of public good and to the enhancement of co-operation with private investors to improve their responsibility for health in developing countries. An overall framework for the promotion of stakeholder dialogue through the establishment of *fora* for discussion was also set out.

Probably the most innovative contribution to this debate is to be found in the Communication on Participation of non-state actors in EC Development Policy.[47] The definition of non-State actors includes:

Non-Governmental Organisations/Community Based Organisations and their representative platforms in different sectors, social partners (trade unions, employers associations), private sector associations and business organizations, associations of churches and confessional movements, universities, cultural associations, media.[48]

The significance of this communication lies in the fact that not only does it reiterate[49] the relevance of all components of civil society to contribute to development, but it also sets out the basic elements of their involvement in practice.

B. The Communication on Corporate Social Responsibility

The most comprehensive approach to Corporate Social Responsibility was defined in the recent Communication on Corporate Social Responsibility: A business contribution to Sustainable Development. Starting from the consideration that businesses are confronted with the challenge of working through the voluntary initiatives and national frameworks that can enhance and sustain the positive benefits of business activity for people and the environment and minimize negative impacts, the Commission[50] suggests the creation of a common European strategy for the promotion of Corporate Social Responsibility.

---

[45] Roundtable on the Development Aspects of Corporate Social Responsibility, *supra*.

[46] As reported in Roundtable on the Development Aspects of Corporate Social Responsibility, *supra* note 43.

[47] Communication from the Commission to the Council and the European Parliament, Participation of non state actors in EC Development Policy, COM(2002) 598 final, 07.11.2002.

[48] *Ibidem*.

[49] This view was already expressed in *Towards a global partnership for sustainable development, supra*.

[50] Communication from the Commission concerning Corporate Social Responsibility: A business contribution to Sustainable Development, COM (2002) 347 final, 2.7.2002.

The Commission defines Corporate Social Responsibility as a concept whereby companies decide 'voluntarily to contribute to a better society and a cleaner environment [...] in their business operations and in their interactions with their stakeholders.'[51]

The EU initiative has the advantage of embracing a '*holistic approach*' to Corporate Social Responsibility. It includes principles on human rights, labour standards and the environment, unlike other international initiatives which tend to include only one dimension of corporate responsibility, such as environmental issues.[52]

It is important to note the distinction made by the initiative between internal and external dimensions of Corporate Social Responsibility. Internally it refers to the respect of employment rights and shareholders. Externally it includes respect for human rights and the impact of companies' activities on the community.[53] The external dimension of Corporate Social Responsibility is seen as contributing to sustainable development. This is in line with the broad definition of sustainability recently adopted by the EU, which includes respect for the environment and core labour standards and expressly encourages '*European companies commitment to Corporate Social Responsibility.*'[54]

Despite the potentially deceptive effect of the combination of two concepts,— CSR and sustainable development (whose definition is still open to debate)[55]— linking the overall issue of CSR to sustainable development could enhance the former's impact on EU external relations. In fact, Corporate Social Responsibility dispays two major features of EU external relations: a social component which is usually translated to the external relations field with the promotion of human rights and core labour standards and an environmental component which corresponds to the concept of sustainability at an external level.

Far from being a magic tool, the Communication suggested that Corporate Social Responsibility can be significantly innovative in that responsibility for the attainment of better labour and environmental standards is placed directly on companies rather than States. It follows therefore, that Corporate Social Responsibility can contribute to reducing the potentially negative impact of foreign investment on local communities, the environment and respect for human rights by defining the standard of behaviour of companies.

As far as methods of accountability are concerned, the Communication on Corporate Social Responsibility seems to offer a balanced strategy which integrates all different mechanisms currently available at the international level. However, emphasis was placed on non-binding mechanisms of implementation.

[51] Commission of the European Communities, Green paper—Promoting a European framework for corporate social responsibility, (COM(2001) 366 final, 18.7.2001), at 11.

[52] Cf. United Nations Environment Programme voluntary initiatives.

[53] The Green Paper, *supra* note 51, at 11, para. 8.

[54] Communication from the Commission to the Council, the European Parliament and the Economic and Social Committee, Towards a Global Partnership for Sustainable development, COM (2002) 82, final, 13. 2. 2002, para. 2.

[55] Submission from Friends of the Earth to the Green Paper, *supra*.

According to the Communication on Corporate Social Responsibility, at internal level emphasis was placed on the reliance on non-binding mechanisms. On the contrary, the promotion of Corporate Social Responsibility at external level includes a comprehensive range of external relations law and policy tools. In particular, three levels of action are foreseen: encouraging Corporate Social Responsibility in international *fora*, the engagement and the promotion of Corporate Social Responsibility directly in developing countries and at the level of MNCs.

The EU is presented as a leader in promoting Corporate Social Responsibility in multilateral and global *fora*. In this context, particular relevance is given to the OECD and the ILO and their existing soft law instruments. In particular, the commitment for the promotion of core labour standards, 'considered as a necessary foundation of the present initiative on Corporate Social Responsibility'[56] has been reinforced.[57]

The OECD guidelines are regarded as providing a valuable list of internationally accepted principles, for the regulation of MNCs. Therefore, it is expressly suggested that adherence and compliance with the Guidelines should constitute an integral part not only in EU external relations agreements, but also in access to subsidies for the promotion of international trade.[58]

The co-responsibility of host States in the implementation of CSR has not been overlooked. Great emphasis has been placed on dialogue with civil society in developing countries and capacity building by providing technical assistance. It is recognized that civil society, NGOs and trade unions can play an essential role in raising awareness of fundamental rights and promoting compliance with the Corporate Social Responsibility principles by monitoring corporate practice on the ground.[59] A central role in raising awareness and co-ordination is to be played by EU delegations in third countries, which are called to act as a link '*between and among third country and European stakeholders*'[60].

C. Issues Specific to the Introduction of Corporate Social Responsibility in Developing Countries

Although the strategy depicted above for the promotion of Corporate Social Responsibility is fairly comprehensive, it must be noted that moving the Corporate Social Responsibility debate to developing countries would involve specific challenges.

---

[56] *A business contribution to Sustainable Development, supra*, para. 7.6.
[57] Cf. *Promoting Core Labour Standards, supra*.
[58] *A business contribution to Sustainable Development, supra*.
[59] P. O'Riordan, 'Corporate Social Responsibility and Human Rights a European Commission Prospective', in E. Brems, P. Vanden Heede (Eds.), *supra*.
[60] Cf. *A business contribution to Sustainable Development, supra* at 23.

By linking social and environmental standards with foreign investment and development, Corporate Social Responsibility initiatives have the potential to generate allegations of privatized neo-colonialism and potential obstacles to trade.[61] However, this view is generally endorsed more by governments, which fear an abusive use of (CSR) standards impairing their comparative advantage, than by companies.

One of the most frequent objections made to Corporate Social Responsibility initiatives is that stakeholders in developing countries have perceived their role as the objects of, rather than the active participants in such initiatives.[62] Indeed developing countries, are rarely involved in defining the policies and standards on Corporate Social Responsibility, which are drawn up by international bodies such as the European Union.[63]

In addition, the private sector in developing countries lacks information regarding Corporate Social Responsibility initiatives, particularlly on their potentially beneficial effects on development. This is partially due to the fact that a connection between CSR, poverty reduction and development has not been sufficiently addressed and clarified. Moreover, an understanding of what (CSR) means in a specific developing country context could help in coping with regional and national differences.

Another problem arises in relation to the methods of monitoring compliance with Corporate Social Responsibility principles. Emphasis is placed on 'participatory approach' which defines dialogue between Southern and Northern non state actors as well as South-South as a new key feature of development policy. Growing awareness by the business community can be regarded as a response to the regulatory pressures coming from different groups in society. However, it is also partially due to an increased acknowledgment that 'human rights are good for business'.[64] Self-regulation is perceived for instance as a risk management strategy. While financial factors appear to be the sole determinant in the decision-making of corporations, it is also true that other considerations must be present when corporations interact globally. For example, the political stability in a State is an important issue for global businesses. MNCs tend to demand that certain conditions exist in a State before they are willing to invest. These investment conditions (sometimes called 'democratic governance requirements') can include acceptance of the rule of law, clear and transparent practices by the government and local institutions and international dispute resolutions. They may also include consideration of a government's record in relation to the protection (or lack of protection) of human rights.

---

[61] T. Fox, H. Ward,' Moving the Corporate Citizenship Agenda to the South', in *Words into Action*, International Institute for Environment and Development, 2002, at 57.

[62] *Ibidem* at 58.

[63] *Cf.* T. Fox, H. Ward, B. Howard, *Public Sector Roles in Strengthening Corporate Social Responsibility: a Baseline Study*, The World Bank, 2002, at 32.

[64] C. Avery, *Business and Human Rights in a Time of Change*, in M. T Kamminga, S., Zia-Zarifi (eds.), *Liability of Multinational Corporations under International Law*, (The Hague, Kluwer Law International, 2000).

The above issues need to be taken into account by MNCs because corporate management preventing MNCs from meeting these requirements and from seizing the opportunity of global competition may hamper the possibility for shareholders to increase their profit. Studies have shown, for example, that taking environmental issues into account in MNCs policies made shareholders better off financially by up to 5 per cent.[65] MNCs are concerned about their reputation and engage in human rights protection campaigns primarily because they think that there can be financial benefits in being good global citizens, not least because a good corporate image makes sound economic sense. In addition, shareholders and investors in developed States have been increasingly active in challenging MNCs in relation to some of their activities that could violate human rights, particularly labour rights.[66]

It seems foreseeable that stakeholders and market forces may lead MNCs to take actions consistent with international human rights law. It will be in the interest of an MNC, in a competitive environment, to ensure that its decisions take into account the interest of all stakeholders and the communities within which it operates.

In conclusion, in order for the EU's action to be effective and consistent with key tenets of EU external policy, participation of developing countries in defining Corporate Social Responsibility and in its implementation and monitoring should be ensured. The extent to which this strategy has been put in place and the question as to how these issues have been addressed will be the object of following paragraphs.

III. Corporate Social Responsibility in EU Relations with International Organizations

A. The EU and the Organization for Economic Co-operation and Development

As seen above, the communication on CSR recognized a central role for the collaboration with the Organisation for Economic Co-operation and Development (OECD). Not only is the OECD regarded as a privileged forum for discussion, it is also perceived as offering the best developed international standards for the conduct of MNCs world-wide. In view of the fact that the

[65] S. Felman, (ed.) *Does Improving a Firm's Environmental Management System and Environmental Performance Result in a High Stock Price?*, New York, ICF Kaiser, 1997 cited in S. Rees, *Omissions in the twentieth century-priorities for the twenty first*, in S. Rees, S. Wright (Eds.), *Human Rights, Corporate Responsibility: A Dialogue*, (Annandale, Pluto Press 2000), at 300.

[66] ILO Working Party on The Social Dimension of the Liberalization of International Trade, GB 273/ WP/SDL/1 (Rev. 1), 273rd Session, Geneva 1998, paras 87–93 cited in R. McCorquodale, *Human Rights and Global Business*, in S. Bottomley, D. Kinley (eds.), *Commercial Law and Human Rights*, (Aldershot, Ashgate Publishing, 2002), at 90.

Commission suggested that compliance with the OECD Guidelines for Multinational Enterprises should be an element of future EU external agreements,[67] as well as a possible condition for the access to EU public procurement, an assessment of these guidelines will be suggested below.

In 1979 the OECD adhering countries adopted a Declaration on International Investment and Multinational Enterprises followed with the Guidelines for Multinational Enterprises (hereinafter 'the Guidelines'). The Guidelines represented one of the first international documents which acknowledged not only that MNCs may have a serious impact on national economies, but also that this impact has peculiar features differentiating it from that of other economic actors.[68] However, the original version of the Guidelines was conceived merely as a tool to maximize the benefits of foreign investment and to reduce the risk of conflicting requirements on MNCs by setting internationally agreed standards.[69] Being addressed to countries that were at an advanced stage of development, the original text made no references to economic development considerations. Environmental, human rights and social concerns regarding the impact of MNCs in third countries were clearly overlooked.[70] In addition to this, the Guidelines were perceived as the expression of the interest of the countries which were the principal sources of foreign investment flow and the 'home States' of MNCs.[71] Their impact on MNCs' activities in developing countries was further limited by the fact that the Guidelines could be applied only in the territories of States adhering to the OECD.[72]

As a result of the review of the Guidelines in 2000, the overall development dimension has been strengthened. The reviewed text introduces far-reaching changes that reinforce the economic, social and environmental elements of the Guidelines. They now cover all internationally recognized labour standards including recommendations for the elimination of child labour and forced labour, disclosure of information, bribery, consumer interest, science and technology.[73] The chapter on disclosure and transparency has been updated to reflect the OECD Principles on Corporate Governance and to encourage social and environmental accountability. The section on the environment urges MNCs to improve their environmental performance by adopting better contingency planning for environmental impact and by enhancing their internal environmental

---

[67] See *infra* IV.

[68] The 'guidelines specifically takes into account the problems which can arise because of the international structure of these enterprises' OECD Guidelines for Multinational Enterprises, (OECD, Paris, 1977), Introduction, para. 6   [69] Cf. International Council, *supra* at 66.

[70] Cf. S. Tully, 'The 2000 review of the OECD Guidelines for Multinational Enterprises', (2001) 50 *International and Comparative Law Quarterly*, 394 at 395.

[71] International Council, *supra* at 67.

[72] Members of the OECD: Australia, Austria, Belgium, Canada, Czech Republic, Denmark, Finland, France, Germany, Greece, Hungary, Iceland, Ireland, Italy, Japan, Korea, Luxembourg, Mexico, The Netherlands, New Zealand, Norway, Poland, Portugal, Spain, Slovak Republic, Sweden, Switzerland, Turkey, United Kingdom, and United States.

[73] S. Tully, *supra* at 396.

management.[74] However, for the purpose of this paper, the most relevant change was the introduction of the recommendation that MNCs should respect human rights.[75] This statement is important in two respects: firstly it links Corporate Responsibility to the 'sphere of influence of companies activities'; secondly, it identifies, in the international law obligations of the State, the standards against which MNCs should measure their conduct. The new text takes into account the changes in the global economy and in particular the fact that MNCs increasingly operate in non-OECD Member States, by extending the application of the Guidelines to the world-wide activities of enterprises operating in OECD-adhering countries.[76] This change can contribute to reducing the risk of MNCs applying a double standard by complying with OECD principles in adhering countries while overlooking them elsewhere.

As a result of the review, the Guidelines enforcement mechanism was improved. This mechanism is based on National Contact Points (NCPs) endowed with the tasks of raising awareness of the Guidelines, solving disputes about their interpretation, and conducting enquiries about the behaviour of the companies. Not only Member States, companies and employee organizations but also 'other organizations', such as non-governmental organizations can now ask a National Contact Point for a consultation when a company has violated the Guidelines. In dealing with the initial assessment on the relevance of the complaint, NCPs have to: (i) ensure that the parties are heard, (ii) act as a mediator helping the parties to reach an agreement, and (iii) finally issue a reasoned decision. If the parties do not reach an agreement at national level, the issue can be referred to a higher OECD Committee on International Investment and Multinational Enterprises (CIME).

Although the National Contact Points and the CIME have the features of a quasi-judicial body, they do not deliver decisions which are legally binding on the parties nor do they judge the behaviour of individual companies. By clarifying the meaning of the Guidelines for the future, they perform a sort of educational role[77] for the business community. Decisions cannot even rely on indirect pressure stemming from exposure to public scrutiny, because companies enjoy confidentiality during the procedure, unless they expressly assent to the NCPs releasing the results of the inquiries.[78] Despite the lack of an immediate impact of this procedure on the behaviour of specific companies, it represents the sole international mechanism to directly and exclusively inspect the conduct of MNCs and which allows, to some extent, civil society to express discontentment by filing complaints.

The application of the Guidelines and their effectiveness in promoting Corporate Social Responsibility principles in developing countries raises several

[74] *Non member economies and the OECD Guidelines for multinational enterprises*, (OECD, Paris, 2000); A. Fatouros, 'The OECD Guidelines in a Globalising World', *(1999), DAFFE, IME RD 3*.

[75] Para. II.2 states that: 'Enterprises should respect human rights of those effected by their activities consistent with the host government's obligations and commitments'.

[76] *Non-member Economies supra* at 9.   [77] A. Fatouros, *supra* at 9.

[78] S. Tully, *supra* at 397.

questions in terms of concrete implementation on the ground. The OECD is currently addressing the issue[79] of how the Guidelines can be applied in non-adhering countries. It has been pointed out that the implementation of the Guidelines may represent a challenge for the non-adhering countries in terms of the financial and human resources necessary for setting up NCPs and participating in the periodical examination of each country's investment policy. Another critic refers to the issue of how the interests of developing countries could be taken into due account if they did not take part in the process of drafting or of reviewing the Guidelines.

Despite these shortcomings, the Guidelines, as an instrument of soft law, have the advantage of being flexible and could provide non-adhering countries with an instrument of policy dialogue and for exchange of practices. This is particularly relevant in areas such as the international regulation of foreign investment, in which a consensus among parties proved to be difficult to achieve.[80] The Guidelines and the attached Decision expressly solicit international co-operation between public authorities, in order to facilitate the implementation of socially responsible practices. NCPs can play a relevant role in this respect. Not only have they to respond to enquiries from non-adhering countries as well as from civil society, but they are also required to offer assistance to companies from their own country which may have difficulty in operating in a non-adhering State. In this context, the extension of the geographical scope of the applicability of the Guidelines introduced by the review of 2000 would be welcomed.

To sum up, despite their recent revision, the effectiveness of the OECD Guidelines must not be overestimated. Firstly, the Guidelines have a merely voluntary character.[81] They simply encourage MNCs to raise their standards beyond those enshrined in national laws: they cannot prevail over them in case of conflict.[82] Nonetheless, they bear some force as a public policy declaration since they represent 'the only multilaterally endorsed and comprehensive code that governments are committed to promoting'.[83] They can be used as a checklist of recommendations that both the foreign investor and the host country authorities can use to set up, develop and monitor a healthy and mutually beneficial relationship. Furthermore, the Guidelines can be regarded as an instrument to enhance communication, facilitate dialogue and help in avoiding possible misunderstandings, thus promoting a better integration of the foreign investor into the local environment.

---

[79] See Joint Statement of Priorities for IDB-OECD Co-operation; La mise en oeuvre des Principes directeurs de l'OCDE sur les entreprises multinationales: un enjeu partagé vers une citoyenneté d'entreprise appliquée, Conférence OCDE, Brussels 10 May 2001.

[80] *Non-member Economies, supra* at 12.

[81] *Contra* N. Horn (Ed.), *Legal Problems of Codes of Conduct for Multinational Enterprises*, (Deventer, Kluwer Law International, 1980), at 407; Cf. International Council, *supra* at 68.

[82] See N. Horn, *supra* note 81; *Non member economies and the OECD Guidelines for multinational enterprises*, (OECD, Paris, 2000); Cf. A. Fatouros, *supra* at 7.

[83] International Council, *supra* at 101.

B. The EU and the International Labour Organization

Compared with the OECD Guidelines, the ILO instruments seem to have a wider geographical scope of application by including the great majority of developing countries. Furthermore, the ILO combines direct scrutiny of corporate behaviour with the monitoring of governments' adherence to, and implementation of the Conventions by providing mechanisms addressed directly to MNCs as well as to States. Nonetheless, the ILO supervisory mechanism shows some weaknesses in the fact that it simply leads to interpretations of the Tripartite Declaration and the identity of the companies involved are kept confidential.[84]

Despite the fact that the European Community is not a member of the ILO, and cannot negotiate or conclude ILO Conventions,[85] the promotion of labour standards is regarded by the Community as 'contributing to the improvement of social governance and the promotion of core labour standards, alongside measures involving governments and other public actors'.[86] Therefore, collaboration with the ILO as the privileged forum of discussion on labour rights, and adherence to its legal instruments, are an integral part of the European strategy to promote CSR at international level.

Similar to the OECD Guidelines, the ILO Tripartite Declaration of Principles Concerning Multinational Enterprises and Social Policy of 1977, subsequently amended in 2000,[87] is a non-legally binding instrument addressed to MNCs, governments, employers and employees organizations. The range of issues covered by the declaration goes beyond labour issues strictly defined—such as non-discrimination, security, working conditions, equal pay, health and safety—and also includes respect for the Universal Declaration of Human Rights, and respect of freedoms of expression and association as essential elements of 'sustained progress'.[88] Although ILO Conventions are only binding on States, technical assistance is provided directly to companies for the implementation of, and compliance with, the Tripartite Declaration.

The enforcement mechanisms include regular reporting on the implementation of ratified ILO Conventions[89] as well as a complaint procedure. A complaint

---

[84] H. Bartolomei De La Cruz, *supra*; International Council, *supra* at 102.

[85] J. Sack, 'The European Community's Membership of International Organisations', (1995) *Common Market Law Review*, 1227 at 1239.

[86] 'Promoting Core Labour Standards', *supra*, para 2.1.

[87] Tripartite Declaration of Principles Concerning Multinational Enterprises and Social Policy, ILO, Geneva, November 2000.   [88] *Ibidem* at Art. 8.

[89] Every two to five years, Members present a report on steps taken to implement the conventions that they have ratified. These reports are examined by a Committee of Experts (CEACR), which can identify particular problems and request additional information. Although these reports cover all ILO conventions, an increased number of CEACR observations relate to the implementation of the fundamental ILO conventions. Additional pressure can be exercised by the annual ILO Conference through the tripartite Committee on the Application of Conventions and Recommendations.

See H. Bartolomei De La Cruz, G. Von Potobsky (Eds.), *The International Labour Organisation*, (Boulder, Westview press, 1996), at 93.

can be filed by ILO members as well as by employers' and workers' organizations. This procedure can lead to the establishment of a Commission of Inquiry, including employer and worker delegates and the ILO. Where a country does not comply with the recommendations of an ILO Commission of Inquiry, the ILO Governing body may recommend to the Conference measures to secure compliance with proposals of the Commission of Inquiry.[90]

In addition, the 1998 ILO's Declaration on Fundamental Principles and Rights at Work[91] calls upon all ILO Member States (including those that have not ratified relevant ILO conventions) to respect the core rights of freedom of association and collective bargaining and the prohibitions on forced labour, child labour and discrimination in the workplace. Pursuant to this Declaration, non-ratifying countries are required to present a report each year indicating their progress in promoting the principles of the fundamental Conventions. These submissions are published in an annual review. Employer and worker groups can provide comments on the submissions. A group of experts may also make comments on the national reports. So far, these comments have only been of a general nature. In turn, the ILO Director General presents an annual global report on one of the four principles of core labour standards, covering both countries which have ratified the relevant conventions and those which have not.

C. The EU[92] and World Trade Organization

There are two ways of addressing the issue of the role of the EU in enhancing Corporate Social Responsibility considerations in the World Trade Organisation (WTO).[93] The first and more apparent perspective refers to the EU as an economic actor within the WTO. The second, less explored, option looks at the role of the EC as an applicant before the WTO adjudicating bodies.

[90] In the ILO's 81-year history this procedure was adopted only once on occasion of the failure of Burma/Myanmar to comply with the conclusions of the Commission of Inquiry.
[91] ILO, Declaration on fundamental principles and rights at work, Geneva, June 1998.
[92] In legal terms, it is the European Communities that are parties in the WTO and not the EU. Member States are also parties to the WTO. This arises from the fact that international trade in goods falls within the scope of the European Community Treaty, whereas Member States retain competence, *inter alia*, for international trade in services. However, the term European Union, as referring to the European Communities and the Member States, is preferred here since emphasis is placed on the EU as a political and economic actor on the international scene. Cf. P. Demaret, 'European Integration in Perspective: 1951–2001', Syllabus de Droit Economique Européen, Année Académique 2002–2003, College d' Europe, Bruges, at 6: 'Legally speaking reference to the European Union is appropriate only when the Council acts on the basis of the second and first pillar. In a loose way one may refer to the European Union also in those cases where the European Union and Member States appear together on the international stage'.
[93] It has been argued that the WTO does not currently offer avenues to complain about the failure of States to improve the accountability of MNCs or either to enforce direct obligations on companies. However, it must be recognized that the WTO bears a central role in the current debate on Corporate Social Responsibility. There is a risk, indeed, that through WTO trade liberalization measures and dispute settlement procedures some of the constraints on companies in relation to the respect of human rights and sustainability (core components of CSR), will be reduced.

The main consideration underlying the first option is that the EC has increased its power as a trading bloc over the years. Today, its share reaches the 12 to 13 per cent which makes the EU the only comparable partner to the USA. As a political consequence, it seems that the WTO rounds can only lead to a successful outcome when these two members are in agreement.[94] As one of the two main players in the world trading system, not only does Europe have a 'systemic'[95] interest in the proper functioning of the WTO but it can also play a relevant role in multilateral negotiations.

On the occasion of the latest trade round launched in Doha in 2002, the EU expressed its willingness to place development at the heart of the multilateral trading system. As a follow up to Doha, the UN Conference on Financing Development held in Monterrey, underlined the importance of increasing official development assistance. According to the basic tenets of a sustainable approach to trade liberalization, the improvement of market access and the mobilization of international private and public resources should take into account the specific needs of developing countries

(i) The EU and Negotiations within the WTO

Against this background, the following paragraphs examine the role that the EU is playing in two ongoing negotiations in the context of the WTO which may contribute to the responsible behaviour of MNCs: the forthcoming WTO Investment for Development Framework, and the negotiations of environmental services in WTO/GATS.

The relevance of an international agreement on investments as a tool to promote the responsibility of MNCs was already apparent during the negotiations of the Multilateral Agreement on Investment (MAI).[96] The MAI, which was discussed in the context of the OECD, simply aimed at creating a level-playing field for investors and it did not contain provisions calling upon MNCs to respect labour standards, human rights or environmental standards. Disagreement over, and criticism of, the provisions referring to these matters, led the negotiations to failure. However, the MAI was seen by international and human rights lawyers as an interesting attempt to impose legally binding international obligations directly onto companies, by contributing to the erosion of the argument according to which MNCs cannot be the addressees of the obligations of international public law.[97] Therefore, it was expected that its underlying idea would be embodied in future international agreements on investment, possibly taking into account the lessons learned from the failure of the MAI.

---

[94] R. Senti, 'The Role of the EU as an Economic Actor within the WTO', (2002) 7 *European foreign affairs review*, 111.

[95] This expression is used in M. Shahin, 'Towards defusing fear of globalisation—with universal rules', available at http://europa.eu.int/comm/commissioners/lamy/speeches_articles/dgts05.htm.

[96] The following analysis of the MAI is based on M. T. Kamminga, *supra* at 557.

[97] Cf. International Council, *supra* at 75, M.T. Kamminga *supra* at 558; *Contra* A. Cassese, *International Law in a Divided World*, (Oxford, Clarendon Press 1986), at 103.

Although the negotiations have still not opened, the European Community expressed its support for the establishment of a multilateral framework of rules governing international investment[98] world-wide in the context of the WTO. The latter is regarded as the most suitable multilateral forum for an international agreement on investments. First of all, it could allow both developed and developing countries to express their interests as home or host countries of international investors. Secondly, the bargaining power of developing countries may be reinforced in the context of multilateral negotiations rather than through bilateral relations. Thirdly, reforms on foreign investment at national level would be more credible if backed by compliance with multilateral commitments. Finally, the WTO offers the undeniable advantage of a well-established institutional framework (including the Dispute Settlement Understanding) and of tried and tested basic non-discrimination principles.

The forthcoming Foreign Direct Investment Agreement (FDI), as well as the MAI, simply attempt to establish a balanced framework of rules on foreign direct investment. However, possible benefits for developing countries cannot be excluded. The establishment of a legal framework could contribute to reducing the existing distortions caused by discriminatory practices, legal uncertainty and lack of transparency. As a consequence of creating uniform rules, a FDI would encourage companies to invest abroad. For example, MNCs could perceive it reducing the risk of investing in certain countries where they are not operating. Similarly, new potential investors, such as small and medium enterprises (SMEs) could decide to expand their activities encouraged by improved transparency and legal certainty in investment rules.

Nonetheless, FDI does not necessarily impact positively on economic growth and development.[99] If the future agreement on FDI is to maximize the benefits of foreign investment, CSR policies and mechanisms of implementation should be integrated. This would provide a tool for both developing countries and foreign investors to minimize possible adverse effects of such changes.

In this respect, the EC expressed the view[100] that rules should be formulated in such a way as to respect development policies and remain within the limits set by existing agreements. While reaffirming its commitment to the principle of non-discrimination, the EC recognizes that traditional provisions on special and differential treatment for developing countries may no longer suffice.[101] Therefore, it maintains that it is necessary to integrate the sustainable development dimension

---

[98] This paragraph is based on the information provided by website of the Directorate General Trade of the Commission of the European Communities, http://europa.eu.int/comm/trade/miti/invest/1806ti.htm.

[99] Cf. T. Fox, H. Ward, B. Howard, *Public Sector Roles in Strengthening Corporate Social Responsibility: a Baseline Study*, (The World Bank, 2002), at 20.

[100] Doha Development Agenda—Trade and Investment Submission by the EC and its Member States to the Working Group on Trade and Investment—Concept paper on The Definition of Investment, downloaded at http://europa.eu.int/comm/trade/miti/invest/contrib.htm.

[101] Exploring the issue relating to Trade and Investment Regional-Seminar on new issues, Chile, December 2000, available at http://europa.eu.int/comm/trade/miti/invest/contrib.htm.

within the basic rules themselves. The FDI should also preserve the ability of host countries to regulate the activity of investors (whether foreign or domestic) in their respective territory. In this respect, opinions expressed by civil society in many WTO Member States, including those regarding investors' responsibilities, should duly be taken into account.

In line with the Doha Declaration, which underlined the role of the reduction or elimination of tariff and non-tariff barriers to environmental goods and services in making trade and environment mutually supportive, the EC has made a negotiating proposal to the ongoing GATS negotiations. The proposal purports the reduction or elimination of barriers to trade in environmental services.

The market of environmental services is a relevant sector for several reasons. First of all, water for human use is considered as key to sustainable development; access to water is a priority of the EU environmental policy and a major topic on the international development agenda. Secondly, environmental services are of growing importance in all countries.[102] Thirdly, the liberalization of this sector could contribute to development by increasing diffusion of modern technology and know-how. In fact, trade in capital, goods and services could be a channel for transfer of environmental technology. Finally, environmental services are relevant for European companies which are world leaders in this sector; they have been providing services not only within the EC, but also in a growing number of third countries.

In this context, the EC is faced with the challenge of ensuring the liberalization of the sector, taking into account its related development aspects. The main objective of the EC in the negotiations is to reduce the obstacles to trade in environmental services and the barriers which European companies face in third countries. Consequently, the EC has placed emphasis on the removal of discrimination and restrictions faced by European companies wishing to supply environmental services in developing countries.[103] Since the most important way to access foreign markets will be via commercial establishment in third countries[104] the investment regime as the regulatory framework force in the host country may constitute a hindrance to the establishment of European MNCs in such countries.

Despite the fact that the main objective of the agreement rests on facilitating access to foreign markets, the EC proposal partially refers to CSR concerns by

---

[102] The environmental services market counts for US$ 300 billion and is expected to double by 2010 with an annual growth rate of 8 per cent (Source: Round table on Development Aspects of Corporate Social Responsibility), *supra*.

[103] The EC has proposed a new classification for environmental services (S/CSC/W/25 dated 28 September 1999, attached to the EC's negotiating proposal S/CSS/W/38). This classification comprises services which can undisputedly be classified as 'purely' environmental and where the services are classified according to the environmental media (ie, air, water, solid and hazardous waste, noise, etc.). The EC has included 'water for human use' in its proposal which would cover not only treatment, but also distribution of water. The requests on water distribution clearly exclude any cross-border transportation either by pipeline or by any other means of transport, nor do they seek access to water resources.   [104] In GATS *jargon*, this would be 'mode 3'.

calling for the integration of development aspects in the agreement. It is made clear that the level of development of trading partners should be taken into account. It follows that developing countries, and in particular the least developed ones, are not expected to open their market to foreign competition to the same extent, and at the same pace, as countries which have more sophisticated technology and know-how. The EC intends to support developing countries in this respect, for example, through the provision of technical assistance. Having recognized the character of water as a common good and its relevance to health and environment, the EC proposal underlined that liberalization cannot lead to the privatization of water resources. The role of the private sector is held as complementary to government and civil society. The capability of host governments to regulate water management and allocation among users to choose the more appropriate form of private participation (such as co-operative societies, informal service providers, local and international companies) should not be undermined or reduced as a result of new negotiations.[105]

Moreover, public funding should be raised[106] and the sector should be made more attractive for private investment in order to meet increasing demand for water infrastructure. It follows that priority should be given to creating a stable and transparent business climate capable of attracting private local and foreign investors. A positive step in this direction is the Water Initiative launched by the EU on the occasion of the World Summit on Sustainable Development. The main feature of this initiative is the principle of integrated water resource management in accordance to which all aspects of water service provision, such as its impact on health and environment, must be considered together. The programme also aims at fostering public-private partnerships within developing countries.[107]

In conclusion, the EC stance in the GATS negotiations is that liberalization of trade in water-related services in the context of the WTO, seems to integrate some aspects of CSR. Not only is the negative impact of investment and establishment of European companies in developing countries addressed, but mechanisms are also suggested to reduce this by fostering technological development and taking into account these countries' administrative capacities and regulatory framework.

(ii) The EC as a Plaintiff before the WTO Adjudicating Bodies

One less explored dimension concerns the impact that EC law and the EC as a plaintiff before the WTO adjudicating bodies may have for the introduction of broader human rights concerns, or 'trade related' concerns in WTO jargon. By

---

[105] Cf. Roundtable on the development aspects of Corporate Social Responsibility, *supra*.

[106] The capital demand for water infrastructure investment is estimated to be up to $180 billion annually compared to present investment levels of $70–80 billion annually. Cf. Round table on Development Aspects of Corporate Social Responsibility, *supra*.

[107] T. Fox, H. Ward, B. Howard, *supra* at 25.

drawing a parallel between the EC and the WTO, it has been suggested[108] that economic integration could also be followed at WTO level by the enforcement of social and human rights, as a response to the negative externalities of market integration.[109] Although the difference between the EU and WTO systems should be borne in mind,[110] it is arguable that the EU can exercise a positive influence on WTO dispute settlements by supporting a human rights-based interpretation of cases or simply by exercising its discretion in bringing cases before the WTO adjudicating bodies.

Contrary to the slow political process the WTO judicial process has brought about some milestone judgments concerning unilateral trade measures taken for environmental, health or animal welfare reasons.[111] In particular the Appellate Body's (AB)'s judgments on *Reformulated Gasoline*,[112] *Hormones*,[113] *Shrimps/Turtles*,[114] and *Asbestos*[115] tried to strike a balance between liberalization principles and trade-related concerns of public policies. It has been suggested that the AB may in the future provide several opportunities to introduce human rights concerns into the WTO system.[116]

The WTO's AB applies principles of international law in order to place WTO rules in the context of international or multilateral agreements. Nonetheless, the WTO adjudicating bodies cannot formally interpret, apply or enforce other treaties and customs and cannot examine obligations of this kind that the WTO members may have, unless this is necessary for the interpretation of WTO law or as a factual determination.[117] Since human rights standards are part of the international rule of law considered as a whole, and WTO members are bound simultaneously by all their international rights and obligations, the WTO adjudicating

---

[108] E.U. Petersmann, 'Time for a United Nations "Global Compact" for Integrating Human Rights into the Law of Worldwide Organizations: Lessons from European Integration', (2002) 13 *European Journal of International Law*, 621.

[109] The underlying idea is that 'markets and democracy are both based on organised dialogues about value judgements and are both integrating social rights into market integration law as a means for limiting social market failures', in E.U. Petersmann, *supra* at 623. The development of EC social policy as a means to counterbalance unfair distribution of resources and purchasing power, and inadequate opportunities of all market participants is expressed by M. Poiares Maduro, 'Striking the Elusive Balance Between Economic Freedom and Social Rights in the EU', in Ph. Alston *et al.* (Eds.), *supra* at 459.

[110] P. Holmes, 'The WTO and the EU: Some Constitutional Comparison', in G. De Burca, J. Scott (Eds.), *The EU and WTO*, (Oxford—Portland Oregon, Hart Publishing), at 82.

[111] R. Quick, 'Involving non-state and third country actors in the EU deliberative process: how and why', available at http://europa.eu.int/comm/commissioners/lamy/speeches_articles/ dgts02.htm.

[112] WTO Cases WT/DS2 and WT/DS4.

[113] WTO Cases WT/DS26 (U.S.) and WT/DS48 (Canada).   [114] WTO Case WT/DS58.

[115] WTO Case WT/DS135.

[116] C. Dommen, 'Economic, social and cultural rights and WTO work on intellectual property rights. Current processes and opportunities', UN doc. E/C.12/2000/20 (13 December 2000); Background paper submitted by the WTO Secretariat, UN doc. E/C.12/2000/18 (29 November 2000); E. U. Petersmann, *Time for a United Nations 'Global Compact' for Integrating Human Rights into the Law of Worldwide Organizations: Lessons from European Integration*.

[117] G. Marceau, 'WTO Dispute Settlement and Human Rights', (2002) *13 European Journal of International Law*, at 762.

bodies could ensure respect for human rights through good interpretation and application of the WTO provisions.[118] The fact that the 'WTO relies disproportionately on its dispute settlement system'[119] also militates in this direction.

This argument is particularly relevant for the purpose of this article. In bringing a case before the WTO adjudicating bodies, the EC often gives voice to the interests of European companies.[120] Moreover, Regulation 522/94 has established official procedures to investigate complaints about competitors in other States, and to pursue them through the WTO system if the claims have merit.[121] Therefore, even if WTO deals with disputes between States, the influence that corporations exercise on countries in order to secure their commercial interests through WTO mechanisms[122] cannot be underestimated.

Given the fact that the EC enjoys a discretionary power in bringing the cases before the WTO adjudicating bodies, it can be argued that this choice of cases and arguments could take into account the principles governing EC external policy, namely the promotion of human rights, labour law and sustainable development.

A case of inconsistency in EU action at external level in the WTO context is represented by the Burma/Myanmar case.[123] The EC filed a complaint before the WTO Dispute Settlement Body against the United States, because of the Massachusetts Selective Purchase Law, which aimed to discourage companies from operating in Burma/Myanmar (a country with a high rate of human rights violations) by excluding them from public procurement in Massachusetts. This law, which was held to be in breach of Articles XIII.4(b) and VIII(b), affected a large number of European companies either because Massachusetts deemed that they themselves did business with Burma, or because they had parent or sister companies which did. The EC decided to suspend the WTO Dispute Settlement Proceedings after the Federal District Court in Boston ruled that the law was unconstitutional. The question of inconsistency arises from the fact that at the time of making the complaint the EU renewed and strengthened political and economic sanctions[124] against Burma, including the withdrawal of GSP privileges due to serious and persistent human rights and labour rights violations.

It can be argued that in this matter a consistent approach would have required the EC/EU to examine other possible options: such as not filing a complaint before the WTO or at least calling on European companies to cease their activities in the country. This case also shows that the activity of the EC before the WTO has the potential to affect and drive EU external relations even beyond trade matters.

---

[118] *Ibidem*, at 757.   [119] P. Holmes, *supra* at 75.

[120] Cf. International Council, *supra*.

[121] Council Regulation 522/94 of 7 March 1994, on the streamlining of decision-making procedures for certain Community instruments of commercial defence and amending Regulations (EEC) No 2641/84 and No 2423/88, OJ L 66/10.

[122] For example, it was claimed that the US complaint in the WTO about European subsidies to Caribbean banana exporters was brought in the interest of the US banana producing companies Dole and Chiquita. International Council, *supra* at 111.   [123] WTO Case WT/DS88.

[124] Council Common Position 96/635/CFSP.

It follows from the above that if Corporate Social Responsibility is to be integrated in all EC policies at internal and external level, this cannot be limited to collaborating with intergovernmental organizations that have already taken up this issue. It should also entail a positive commitment to the balance of commercial versus environmental and social concerns in the context of the WTO.

IV. Corporate Social Responsibility in EU Bilateral Relations

Having described the options available to the EU for the promotion of CSR in international *fora* and having assessed the major international soft law instruments for the regulation of the conduct of MNCs, this Part considers how the EU has integrated Corporate Social Responsibility concerns into its relations with third countries. Particular reference is made to the Cotonou Agreement, the Association Agreement between EU and Chile and the Generalized System of Preferences.

A. The Cotonou Agreement

A Corporate Social Responsibility approach seems to have been strenghtened in the recent enforcement of the Cotonou Agreement.[125] This agreement replaces the Lomé Convention,[126] which had provided the structure for trade and co-operation between the EU and the African Caribbean and Pacific Group of States (ACP)[127] since 1975.

The Cotonou Agreement is an example of a 'comprehensive approach' that integrates different policy instruments: trade, development and political dialogue. Social development and the promotion of core labour standards is also part of the overall development strategy of the Agreement. It provides that 'co-operation shall support ACP States' efforts at developing general and sectoral policies and reforms which improve the coverage, quality of and access to basic social infrastructure and services' and that co-operation shall aim at '*inter alia*' 'encouraging the promotion of participatory methods of social dialogue as well as respect of basic social rights'.[127]

---

[125] Partnership Agreement between the members of the African, Caribbean and Pacific Group of States (ACP) of the one part, and the European Community and its Member States, of the other part, signed in Cotonou on 23 June 2000, 2000/483/EC, [[2000] OJ L 317 of 15.12.2000].

[126] The co-operation with the ACP countries started with the signing of the Treaty of Rome in 1957 which made provision for the association of the OCTs (Overseas Countries and Territories) with the EC as it was then. In 1963, the first co-operation agreement was signed under the name of Yaoundé, which was renewed in 1969. Following the accession of the UK in 1973, a new agreement, the Lomé Convention was signed in 1975 (which included certain Commonwealth countries). It was renewed in 1979, 1984 and 1990.

[127] The Cotonou Agreement was signed by 77 States: 48 countries of Sub-Sahara Africa; 15 countries of the Caribbean; and 14 Countries of the Pacific which includes the 6 new Pacific members of Palau, The Federated States of Micronesia, The Republic of the Marshall Islands, Nauru, Niue and the Cook Islands.

Under Article 50 of the Agreement, the Community and the ACP Countries have reiterated their commitment to the ILO Core Labour Standards. This has been translated into undertakings by the parties to co-operate with a view to promoting labour standards through awareness-raising, enforcement and the strengthening of existing national legislation, education and exchange of information. Article 50(3) underlines that, 'labour standards should not be used for trade protectionist purposes'. This reaffirms the fact that the improvement of labour standards is to be regarded as a key component of the concept of Corporate Social Responsibility endorsed by the Community.[128]

In addition to the reinforcement of previous commitments, the new Agreement emphasizes a participatory approach to ensure the involvement of civil society and economic and social players by providing them with information on the ACP-EC Partnership Agreement, in particular within the ACP countries. The measures to achieve this objective include: 'ensuring the consultation of civil society on the economic, social and institutional reforms and policies to be supported by EC, facilitating non-State actors' involvement in the implementation of programmes and projects, providing non-State actors with adequate support for capacity building, encouraging networking and links between ACP and EU actors'.[129]

It seems that the Cotonou Agreement's potential will be improved since the EC plans to insert CSR issues and the promotion of OECD Guidelines into all external trade relations, such as the future EU-ACP Economic Partnership Agreements into the framework of the Cotonou co-operation.[130]

B. The Association Agreement between the EU and Chile

The Association Agreement between the EU and Chile is the first Agreement in which the parties, in accordance with the Communication on Corporate Social Responsibility, called MNCs to respect the OECD Guidelines for Multinational Enterprises. After the successful conclusion of the negotiations, the EU-Chile Association Agreement was initiated on 10 June 2002 in Brussels, subsequently approved by the Commission and finally signed on 18 November, hence allowing the Chilean Congress to start its own adoption procedure.[131]

[128] 'Towards a global partnership for sustainable development', *supra.*
[129] As reported at http://www.delsur.cec.eu.int/en/eu_and_acp_countries/cotonou/the_cotonou_agreement.htm.   [130] Cf. *A business contribution to Sustainable Development.*
[131] The adoption procedure was completed by the Chilean Parliament on 14 January 2003. Some provisions of the Agreement (ie mainly provisions to the trade in goods, to government procurement, to competition and to the dispute settlement mechanism and the chapter on co-operation) have been provisionally applied since 1 February 2003. The provisions on: political dialogue, current payments and capital movements, intellectual property rights, titles of the trade part such as services and the core of the co-operation part, will enter into force after the assent of the European Parliament has been obtained and once the national Parliaments of the EU Member States have ratified the Agreement. While the European Parliament gave its assent at its plenary session of 12 February 2003, National Parliaments must still ratify the Agreement.

The Association Agreement consists of three main chapters: trade, co-operation and political dialogue.[132] By strengthening the economic ties between the EU and Chile, the trade-related provisions of the Association Agreement are expected to contribute to significant economic and commercial benefits.[133] It covers all areas of trade relations between parties, and goes beyond their WTO commitments. The Agreement includes rules on competition, intellectual property and an effective dispute settlement mechanism. For the first time, a fully-fledged free trade agreement in services has been included in the association agreement. This will apply to public procurement markets as well as to the liberalization of investment. Intensified co-operation is foreseen also in several other areas, with the objective of favouring a sustainable economic, social and environmental model.

The political chapter of the Association Agreement aims at strengthening political dialogue between the EU and Chile. It is permeated by a common commitment to the promotion of democratic values. The EU and Chile agreed to put respect for human rights, freedom of the individual and the rule of law at the core of their political co-operation which entails co-ordination of positions and joint initiatives in international *fora*. Political co-operation will also be fostered by the increased participation and consultation of civil society in such matters. Consultation with parliaments and representatives of civil society is seen as a guarantee of accountability and transparency, hence, the exchange of views on co-operation strategies and their implementation is encouraged.

As regards co-operation, the parties declared to pursue the promotion of sustainable economic, social and environmental development. The most innovative aspects have been introduced in this chapter. The Agreement refers to fields such as co-operation on technical regulations, customs procedures, and intellectual property rights which were not included in the 1996 Framework Co-operation Agreement between the EU and Chile.

The commitment of the parties to the integration of Corporate Social Responsibility principles was apparent since the negotiations.[134] They affirmed

---

[132] Art. 2 of the EU-Chile Association Agreement.

[133] '[. . .] we reaffirm our conviction that the trade chapter will promote economic growth and support sustainable development, to the benefit of both the European Union and Chile. Negotiations have delivered the most ambitious and innovative results ever for a bilateral Agreement of this kind by the European Union as well as Chile'. Joint Declaration signed by the President of the European Council, M. José María Aznar, the President of Chile, M. Ricardo Lagos, and the President of the European Commission, M. Romano Prodi, Madrid, May 17 2002. Downloaded on 4 April 2003 at http://europa.eu.int/comm/external_relations/chile/assoc_agr/ma05_02.htm.

[134] The intention of establishing a political and economic Association Agreement between the EU and Chile was initially drawn up in the Framework Co-operation Agreement of 1996. On the basis of this Agreement, the Commission presented Directives for negotiations to the Council in July 1998, which were subsequently formally approved at the General Affairs Council of 13 September 1999. The objective of establishing a political and economic association between Mercosur, Chile and the EU was then strongly reaffirmed on the occasion of the first EU and Latin America and Caribbean Summit, which took place in Rio de Janeiro on 28–29 June 1999. See Meeting of Heads of State and

that: 'The Community and its Member States and Chile jointly remind their multinational enterprises of their recommendation to observe the OECD Guidelines for Multinational Enterprises, wherever they operate.'

The OECD Guidelines for Multinational Enterprises, along with respect for democratic principles, human rights and the rule of law are defined as essential elements of the agreement. The promotion of sustainable economic and social development and the equitable distribution of the benefits of the Association Agreement are held as guiding principles for its implementation.

In order to understand the reasons leading to the inclusion of Corporate Social Responsibility principles in the Agreement, is it important to emphasize that Chile had experience of sustainability issues for quite some time.[135] Environmental quality and sustainability had been promoted at a national level, by setting up structures which in some cases took the form of fully effective regulatory bodies. Against this background, the EU can play a double role in mitigating the negative sustainability consequences of the EU-Chile Agreement. The EU can act as a participant in initiatives which are already under way and as a supporter where new resources are required for research. Moreover, dialogue between stakeholders, at national and local levels, is to be facilitated where a consensus is still to be reached within Chile.

The Sustainable Impact Assessment (SIA)[136] strongly recommended that Corporate Social Responsibility issues should be included as an essential part of the Agreement and its implementation.[137] The commitment of foreign and domestic companies to high levels of environmental and social behaviour was regarded as contributing 'to the efforts of governments and to maximize the benefits of the Agreement, while minimising its negative impacts'.[138] Corporate Social Responsibility initiatives were held to play a major role in supporting the efforts of stakeholders and flanking measures of the parties. The EU-Chile Association Agreement aims at reinforcing the existing growth trends of Chile.

However, in order to maximize the benefit of the agreement for Chile, pre-existing social and environmental issues should be taken into account and eventual additional mitigating measures should be adopted to address underlying

Government from Mercosul, Chile and the EU Joint Communiqué of Rio de Janeiro—28 June 1999—9410/99 (Press 207). Downloaded at: http://europa.eu.int/comm/external_relations/chile/assoc_agr/pol.htm, on 3 April 2003.

[135] 'The sectors where the sustainability impacts have been most noted are those where there is competition for non-marketed resources: fishing and agriculture'. Sustainable Impact Assessment (SIA) of the trade aspects of negotiations for an Association Agreement between the European Communities and Chile (Specific agreement No. 11) Final Report October 2002, at 217. Downloaded at: http://www.planistat.com/sia/report/SA%20nbr1%20final%20Oct%202002.pdf, on 3 April 2003.

[136] A SIA is a process undertaken before and during a trade negotiation which seeks to identify economic, social and environmental impacts of the trade agreement, and should help to integrate sustainability into trade policy by informing negotiators of the possible social, environmental and economic consequences of a trade agreement.

[137] 'CSR issues should therefore constitute an integral part of the implementation of the Agreement' Sustainable Impact Assessment, *supra* at 217.   [138] *Ibidem* at 13.

situations. CSR initiatives can play a major role in furthering this aim by supporting the efforts of stakeholders and mitigating measures of the parties. By committing to reach high levels of environmental and social performance, both foreign
and domestic companies will help support the efforts of governments, and thus
maximize the benefits of the Agreement, while minimizing its negative impacts.
Moreover, dialogue between stakeholders, at national and local levels, will help in
reaching better understandings on respective concerns and objectives.

The commitment to comply with the OECD guidelines was not transposed
into the operative part of Agreement, in the form of 'social clause', but it is
contained in a Joint Declaration. It seems, however, that further developments are
not precluded. A parallel can be traced with the introduction of human rights concerns into the external agreements of the European Union.[139] In the context of EU
relationships with the ACP States, a reference to fundamental rights was initially
contained in the preamble of the Third Lomé Convention.[140] Human rights were
subsequently included in the operative part of the Fourth Convention[141] and
finally considered as an essential element of the agreement in Cotonou.[142]

C. The General System of Preferences (GSP)

The European Community established a GSP in July 1971[143] with the aim of fostering economic development in developing countries through trade. By granting
a preferential tariff system, the GSP attempted to revitalise exports from developing countries and, by the same token, to favour capital accumulation necessary to
improve the process of industrialization in these countries.[144]

The GSP scheme has been reviewed several times. Council Regulation 3281/94
introduced special incentives, in the form of an additional reduction of duties,
which were conferred on countries whose domestic legal provisions complied
with the ILO Conventions on freedom of association,[145] the rights to organize

---

[139] On this development, Cf. K., Arts, *Integrating human rights into development cooperation: the
case of the Lomé Convention*, (The Hague, London, Boston, Kluwer Law International, 2000) at 167;
M. Bulterman, *Human rights in the treaty relations of the European Community : Real virtues or Virtual
reality?*, (Antwerpen-Groningen-Oxford, Intersentia-Hart, 2001) at 151.

[140] Third ACP- EEC Convention of 1984, [1986] OJ L 86/3.

[141] Art. 5 Fourth ACP- EEC Convention, [1991] OJ L 229/1.

[142] Art. 5(1) Fouth ACP- EEC Convention as reviewed in 1995; now Art. 9 in combination with
Art. 96 of the Cotonou Agreement *supra*.

[143] The GSP scheme was initially promoted by UNCTAD, after its creation in 1964, to permit
industrialized countries to grant autonomous and non-reciprocal trade preferences to all developing
countries. The GSP represents an exception to the most-favoured-nation principle and facilitates a
form of positive discrimination in favour of developing countries. The EC could implement its own
GSP only after an 'enabling clause' was agreed on in the framework of the GATT.

[144] G. Tsogas, 'Labour Standards in the General System of Preferences of the European Union and
The United States', (2000) 3 *European Journal of Industrial Relations* 349, at 352; G. Tsogas, 'Labour
standards in international trade agreements: an assessment of the arguments', (1999) 2 *International
Journal of Human Resource Management*, 351.   [145] ILO Convention No.87.

and to bargain collectively[146] and the minimum age of employment.[147] On the other hand, withdrawal of GSP benefits was foreseen in cases of forced labour or use of prison labour. The current regime is laid down in Council Regulation No 2501/2001.[148] The subsequent revisions have resulted in a progressive expansion of the scope of labour rights and ILO conventions and the introduction of environmental standards. These must be implemented by the beneficiary State in its domestic legislation before it may profit from the special incentives. By adding the ILO conventions on forced labour and non-discrimination in respect of employment and occupation, the new regulation brought the special incentive clause in line with the definition of 'fair labour' standards adopted by the ILO.[149]

The new GSP Regulation is aimed at simplifying the GSP regime without undermining the level of its benefits.[150] Some changes have been introduced to the review and consultation process[151] which have partly improved its transparency and participation. The examination for a request of special incentives, in fact made public by the publication of a notice in the Official Journal of the European Communities, was in order to allow all interested parties to submit written observations. Nonetheless, the process remains to be dealt with entirely by the Commission, with a regrettable lack of transparency and democratic control.[152] For a country to be granted preferential treatment, not only must it prove incorporation of the above-mentioned ILO Conventions in domestic legislation, but it also has to demonstrate that effective implementation and monitoring mechanisms are in place.

On the other hand, the new GSP regulation has expanded the cases of violations of core labour standards which may lead to the temporary withdrawal of preferential arrangements provided for in the GSP Community scheme.[153] These cases now include: (i) the use of slavery or forced labour, serious and systematic violation of freedom of association, the right to collective bargaining or the principle of non-discrimination in respect of employment and occupation; (iii) the use of child labour; and (iv) the export of goods made by prison labour. By

---

[146] ILO Convention No. 98.

[147] ILO Convention No.138.

[148] Council Regulation (EC) No 2501/2001 of 10 December, 2001 applying a scheme of generalised tariff preferences for the period from 1 January 2002 to 31 December 2004, OJ L 346/1. Entered into force on 1 January 2002 (Cf. Art. 41).

[149] See Proposal for a Council Regulation applying a scheme of generalised tariff preferences for the period 1 January 2002 to 31 December 2004, COM(2001)293 final, Brussels, 12.6.2001, para. 32 of the Explanatory Memorandum; and the position of the Commission as expressed in the Communication Promoting Core Labour Standards, *supra*; Cf. De Schutter, *supra* at 60.

[150] Previously the provisions relating to these incentives appeared under Title II (Arts 8 to 21) of the Council Regulation (EC) No 2820/98 of 21 December 1998, which entered into force on 1 July 1999 (Council Regulation (EC) No 2820/98 of 21 December 1998, OJ 1998 L 357/1, last amended by Regulation (EC) No 416/2001, OJ 2001 L 60/43); they now appear under Title III (Arts 14 to 20) (labour standards) and 21 to 24 (environmental standards) of Council Regulation (EC) No 2501/2001 *supra*.   [151] O. De Schutter, *supra* at 59.

[152] Cf. G. Tsogas *supra* at 364.

[153] Cf. Art. 26 of Regulation no 2501/2001 and Art. 22 of Regulation no 2820/98, *supra*.

harmonizing labour rights required for preferential treatment with those which give rise to withdrawal of preferences, in the event of breach, not only was the risk of a applying a double standard[154] reduced, but also the concept of labour standards as uniform and universal was reinforced. Despite the latest changes, criticisms of the mechanism remain valid.

By linking additional benefits to the respect of core labour and environmental standards, the GSP special incentive arrangements confirm the EU's decision to use a trade incentive-based approach to development and the rejection of a sanctions-based approach. On the occasion of the recent meeting of the Multi-stakeholder forum on Corporate Social Responsibility, the Commission defined the GSP as 'the ideal instrument to promote corporate social responsibility around the globe'[155] and renewed its commitment to consider all the possible avenues to maintain the full benefits of the GSP system to developing countries in the forthcoming Communication. Moreover, a process of monitoring and evaluation was introduced in the context of the special drugs regime, established to help the Andean and Central American countries to replace drugs cultivation with alternative products. This was intended not only to combat drug production and trafficking, but also to monitor compliance with core labour and environmental standards.

(i) The GSP and the India Case

In the communication *Promoting core labour standards*, the Commission suggested that:

'in the context of a future review of the EC GSP scheme, consideration should be given to enhancing the possibilities to use GSP incentives to promote core labour standards' Furthermore, 'The EC should seek to maximise the impact of special incentives globally by encouraging other industrialised countries to adopt social incentive schemes, similar to that of the EC'.[156]

The remaining scope for further development and enhancement of labour rights by special incentives was recently questioned however, in light of the case brought by India against the EC before the WTO. India's complaint referred to the legitimacy of EC-GSP special incentives. In particular, the special arrangements to combat drug production and trafficking[157] were challenged.[158]

Although the labour rights preferences were not at issue,[159] the outcome of this case is relevant to the overarching question of this article in two regards. Firstly,

---

154 Cf. G. Tsogas *supra* at 363.
155 Roundtable on the Development aspects of Corporate Social Responsibility, *supra*.
156 *Promoting core labour standards, supra* at 17.
157 Art. 10, Regulation 2501/2001 *supra* at 148.   158 *Ibidem*, Art. 25.
159 Initially, India challenged the special incentives for the protection of labour rights, the environment and for combating drug production. Subsequently, India decided to limit the complaint to the special incentives against dugs production and trafficking. Cf. European Communities—conditions for the granting of tariff preferences to developing countries WT/DS246/AB/R, 7 April 2004, point 4.

the compatibility of the GSP special incentives schemes with WTO law is put under discussion. Secondly, the opinion of the WTO Dispute Settlement Body in this case could provide some indications about a similar case involving labour rights incentives.

In March 2002, India requested consultations with the EC regarding its GSP scheme.[160] According to India the EU's GSP special arrangement was not compatible with Article 1 of the GATT and not justified by the 'enabling clause'.[161] The enabling clause suspends the GATT's Most Favoured Nations rule and allows developed country members to give differential and more favourable treatment to developing countries. Preferences are only permitted under the enabling clause 'in order to increase export earnings, to promote industrialization and to accelerate the rates of economic growth of developing countries'.[162] Although the enabling clause gave rise to contrasting interpretation among Member States of the WTO, its language is not considered to require that once a developed nation extends preferential treatment to one developing country, it must then extend such preferential treatment to all developing countries. It is more questionable whether a differentiation among developing countries can be conditioned on their respective compliance with certain non trade related criteria.

India was particularly concerned by two aspects of the EC's GSP scheme. Firstly, the tariff preferences accorded for combating drug production and trafficking are available only to countries selected by the EC. Secondly, the criteria for allowing preferences were established by the EC. India argued that preferential treatment is an exception in so far as it allows discrimination in favour of developing countries. In addition differentiation among developing countries would have constituted discrimination not allowed by the enabling clause.

India's arguments were rejected by the AB's report published on the 7 April 2004, which reversed the conclusions of the WTO panel issued in December 2003.[163] The panel had interpreted the term 'non discriminatory' in the enabling clause[164] to mean that identical tariff preferences under GSP schemes should be provided to all developing countries, without differentiation. Yet, two exceptions were considered admissible: a differentiation in favour of least developed countries and, in case of *a priori* import limitations, for products originating in particularly competitive developing countries.[165] Consequently, the EC's drugs arrangement was found to be discriminatory because its scheme did not provide

---

[160] For a detailed analysis of the special working group report, see S. De La Rosa, *supra*.

[161] Decision on differential and More Favourable Treatment reciprocity and Fuller Participation of developing countries, GATT document L/4903, 28 November 1979, BISD 26S/203.

[162] Request for Consultations by India, WT/DS246/1, 12 March 2002.

[163] European Communities—conditions for the granting of tariff preferences to developing countries, WT/ DS246/R, adopted by the special group on 28 October 2003. Made public on 1 December 2003.   [164] Para. 2(a) footnote 3 of the enabling clause.

[165] Panel report, *supra* para 7.116.

identical tariff preferences to all developing countries and it did not fall in one of the above mentioned exceptions.[166]

Following the EC's appeal on January 2004,[167] the AB[168] overturned the strict interpretation of the enabling clause's term 'non-discriminatory' adopted by the panel. The AB read the enabling clause as authorizing preference-granting countries to respond positively to needs that are not necessarily common or shared by all developing countries. This may entail different treatment of various beneficiary countries.[169] Nonetheless, the criteria according to which a differential treatment is provided should be transparent and objective.

According to the AB, the EC's special drugs arrangement as set out in Regulation No.2501/2001, does not provide mechanisms or objective criteria that would allow other developing countries similarly affected by the drug problem to be included among its beneficiaries. In addition, the Regulation in question does not specify the criteria according to which a country would be removed from the group of beneficiary countries.

As stated above, the decision on this case would have carried important consequences on the use of conditional preferences to tackle social, labour and environmental issues. The importance of this decision is twofold. On one hand, the AB's decision has dispelled concerns on the compatibility of special arrangements provided by developed countries' GSP schemes.[170] On the other hand, the extent to which developed countries may condition the granting of preferences on a developing country's attainment of standards has been clarified. The AB expressly noted that the EC's special incentive arrangements on the protection of labour rights and the environment, in contrast with the drugs arrangement, included detailed provisions describing the procedure and criteria that apply to a country's request to become a beneficiary.[171] Therefore, according to this analysis, it seems that the labour incentives of the EC GSP Regulation could be used as a positive measure for raising social and environmental standards of developing countries. Higher standards in these countries could in turn compel the MNCs that they host to raise their social and environmental performance.

---

[166] *Ibidem* para. 7.177.

[167] Notification of an appeal by the European Communities, WT/DS246/7, 8 January 2004.

[168] European Communities—conditions for the granting of tariff preferences to developing countries WT/DS246/AB/R, 7 April 2004.

[169] *Ibidem* para. 7/162.

[170] Cf. R. Howse, India's WTO Challenge to Drug Enforcement Conditions in the European Community Generalized System of Preferences: A Little Known Case with Major Repercussions for 'Political' Conditionality in US Trade Policy, downloaded at http://faculty.law.umich.edu/rhowse/Drafts_and_Publications/Howse3.pdf, on 19-5-2004.

[171] Title III (Arts 14 to 20 (labour standards) and 21 to 24 (environmental standards)) of Council Regulation (EC) No 2501/2001 of 10 December 2001 applying a scheme of generalized tariff preferences for the period from 1 January 2002 to 31 December 2004, OJ 2001 L 346/1.

V. Conclusion

This article addressed the question of how the EU can contribute to the responsible conduct of MNCs domiciled in its Member States when they operate abroad, particularly, in developing countries. Among the several options of intervention available under EU law, this article has paid special attention to the manner in which the opportunities offered by EU external relations could contribute to this objective.

This final section assesses the effectiveness of the EU strategy for the promotion of Corporate Social Responsibility in developing countries. It suggests a possible way forward in order to extract more responsible conduct from European MNCs operating abroad.

Despite the fact that the responsible conduct of companies is a relatively new item on the EC external relations agenda, its importance has been increasingly and strongly stressed in development and trade policy. As seen in Part Two, the EU defined a strategy for the development of Corporate Social Responsibility at the external level that involves the use of a wide range of external relations tools for the promotion of Corporate Social Responsibility in developing countries. The question to what extent these principles have actually had an impact on subsequent EU measures and actions at international level has been examined in this Part.

From the analysis of EU relations with international organizations as depicted in Part Three, it emerges that the EU prefers to rely on existing soft law instruments and enforcement mechanisms at the ILO and OECD level, instead of developing a specific EU approach to the matter. Despite the fact that these organizations displayed some readiness to address issues specific to the extension of CSR to developing countries, all of these soft law instruments are considered simply as add-ons to national law. Therefore, the core problem regarding the accountability of MNCs, namely the law and forum they should refer to, is not resolved. On the contrary, the reference to and addition of, several instruments may increase confusion in implementation.

Moreover, it stems from the analysis conducted in Part Four that a slow integration of Corporate Social Responsibility issues into EU agreements with third countries is taking place.

Social provisions have been strengthened in the new Cotonou Agreement, paving the way to a possible integration of a Corporate Social Responsibility clause in future revisions of the Agreement.

The General System of Preferences has evolved in a way that reflects the change in the notion of development adopted by the EU. This evolution was influenced by the objective of 'sustainable development', which is not limited to economic growth, but also includes the respect and improvement of environmental standards and fundamental social rights. Alongside the 'general arrangements' aiming at traditional objectives of economic development—with reductions of the duty rates according to the category to which a product belongs, and duty free access for almost all the products originating from the least developed countries— another arrangement providing incentives favouring respect for fundamental social rights and protection of the environment was put in place. The possibility of promoting labour rights through tariff reductions has been recently reaffirmed by the WTO Appellate Body in the India case.

However, the most prominent example for the promotion of Corporate Social Responsibility in the EU's external relations is given by the new Association Agreement between the EU and Chile. Not only was the agreement preceded by an SIA, which identified economic, social and environmental impacts of the trade agreement, but in a Joint Declaration the parties to the agreement called upon MNCs to respect the OECD Guidelines for Multinational Enterprises. Although in the specific case of Chile, the introduction to this commitment has been facilitated by previous experience in the protection of the environment, it seems that such a commitment will be included in external agreements more often.

It is argued that the EU has developed and codified essential features of its relations with developing countries, which could serve as basic tenets for the promotion of Corporate Social Responsibility at an external level. Human rights, democracy, the rule of law, labour rights, and sustainability can be identified as the focus of EU external relations in recent years. The operational method envisages partnership, de-concentration and co-ordination with other mechanisms as its main tools. It is therefore argued that the issue of Corporate Social Responsibility should be dealt with by the EU by making reference to these basic tenets.

An approach consistent with these values and operational methods could more effectively tackle the problems specific to the extension of Corporate Social Responsibility in developing countries.

From the above analysis, it follows that if developing countries are to effectively benefit from the sustainable development and poverty reduction impact of Corporate Social Responsibility, new initiatives are needed to enable public sector bodies in developing countries to become effective players in defining the terms of the current Corporate Social Responsibility debate and its implementation.

It is suggested that a possible option to promote Corporate Social Responsibility in developing countries would be to enhance the scrutiny by local governments and local NGOs of subsidiaries of companies that are based in one of the Member States of the EU and operating in third countries.

Great potential in this respect is offered by the improvement of partnerships both between the public and private sectors in developing countries and between the private sectors of developing countries and EU countries. While the first type of partnership will strengthen the role of developing country governments, the second can contribute to sharing of best practice and the involvement of the local private sector in development.

In the EU framework, partnership is one of the basic tenets of development co-operation policy, such as in the Cotonou Agreement. More recently, the development of partnerships with private sector and civil society has become a key feature of the EU energy initiative. Nonetheless, the potential of public sector and private sector patnerships has not been explored to date. There are only limited examples of the involvement of the private sector in the development of national strategies for sustainable development and poverty reduction[172] especially in developing countries.

One shortcoming that is evident the fact that partnership initiatives require significant effort and resources from NGOs, trade unions and community-based organizations.[173] On the other hand, in many developing countries 'civil society' is not yet fully-fledged, and constraints on workers' rights and freedom of association often undermine, or indeed impede, the functioning of trade unions. Therefore, for partnership to be effective it should go hand in hand with capacity building at national level and co-ordinated action for the strengthening of labour rights.[174] However, it appears that many sectors in least developed countries and emerging markets offer great potential for partnerships provided as companies are willing to engage.[175]

'But effective partnerships must be built on mutual respect and sustainable partnerships can only be built among equals'.[176] This goal could be met by extending knowledge about Corporate Social Responsibility to third countries and by empowering local NGOs sensitive to social and environmental matters to act in partnership with the EU for the promotion of CSR by scrutinizing and reporting on CSR practice. As illustrated above, programmes for awareness and capacity building in developing countries should be integrated into EU development policy.

The EC maintains 127 overseas delegations and 164 States have established permanent diplomatic missions to the Community in return. Their main task is the management of trade and aid relations.[177] A co-ordination role of ILO, OECD and domestic initiatives could be given to the EU delegation in developing countries. The deconcentration process, which started in 2001 and has been extended to all delegations before the end of 2003, will lead to a gradual transfer of resources and responsibilities to the EC delegations. It is expected that this process will help to improve the quality of the participatory approach in EC development

---

[172] T. Fox, H. Ward, B. Howard, *Public Sector Roles in Strengthening Corporate Social Responsibility: a Baseline Study*, (The World Bank, October 2002), at 22.   [173] *Ibidem*, at 24.
[174] See Promoting Core Labour Standards, *supra* at 11.
[175] At international level, a positive example of partnership is offered by the United Nations Industrial Development Organisation (UNIDO) Partnership Programme. The Programme aims at enhancing the quality, competitiveness and efficiency of small and medium enterprises in developing countries, through the creation of multi-party partnerships and co-operation between public and private sector actors. Cf. T. Fox, Round Table Report—Development Agency Roundtable on Corporate Social Responsibility 28–29 January 2002, International Institute for Environment and Development (IIED) at 15.
[176] T. Fox, H. Ward *Moving the Corporate Citizenship Agenda to the South*, in *Words into Action*, International Institute for Environment and Development (IIED), 2002, at 59. Downloaded at www.iied.org on 5 April 2003.   [177] C. Bretehrton, J. Vogler, *supra*.

policy.[178] This should in turn enable a more efficient and prompt intervention capacity.

The proposed reform of the EU external relations service in the context of the Convention on the Future of Europe[179] also militates in this respect. In fact, it is foreseen that by acting as co-ordination points should extend and improve the role of EU delegations.

Secondly, co-operation with other organizations already active in this field should be enhanced at third country level. For instance, the ILO conventions have been signed by a large number of States and they provide for inspection and scrutiny at national level. The OECD guidelines are supported by a monitoring system based on contact points in each State. NCPs could potentially co-ordinate the exchanges of information between NCPs and EU delegations.

Thirdly, the EU, given its special relations with a large number of developing countries through its development policy, can play an essential role in facilitating dialogue and integrating CSR concerns into its bilateral agreements.

The most notable step in this respect is represented by the Association Agreement between the EU and Chile. For the first time, the parties, in accordance with the Communication on Corporate Social Responsibility, called MNCs to respect OECD Guidelines for Multinational Enterprises. Although it is too early to assess what impact this clause may have on the parties and on other agreements currently under negotiation, it can be argued that by strengthening the inclusion of third countries in defining CSR, the allegations of privatized neo-colonialism frequently accompanying EU conditionality are likely to be avoided.

It is clear from the preceding analysis that for the EU to effectively promote Corporate Social Responsibility in its external relations, in particular within trade and development policies, due account should be taken of developing country's perspectives and other specific features. Consequently, the EU strategy for the promotion of Corporate Social Responsibility in developing countries should focus on raising awareness of Corporate Social Responsibility among companies in these countries in order to develop a better engagement of local communities, who should ultimately be the beneficiaries of higher social, environmental and human rights standards.

---

[178] *Participation of non state actors, supra.*
[179] Cf. Art. III-230 of the Daft Treaty Establishing a Constitution for Europe, Adopted by Consensus by the European Convention on 13 June and 10 July 2003. Submitted to the President of the European Council in Rome. OJ C169/3 of 18.7.2003.

A Distinction Without a Difference: Exploring the Boundary Between Goods and Services in the World Trade Organization and the European Union

Fiona Smith* and Lorna Woods**

Introduction

In many legal systems distinctions are made between 'goods' and 'services' with different regimes applying to each of them. Although in some instances goods and services may be subject to similar rules despite these distinct regimes, in other systems they may be accorded different treatment. Indeed, it may be that, given their inherent characteristics, goods and services should be treated differently. In either case, the underlying issue is how we determine where the boundary between goods and services lies. The boundary may be determined by reference to the essential characteristics of the product itself or by external considerations, including economic characteristics, the legal context or even the purposes to which the product may be put.

At the national level, the policy concerns driving the decision to place the boundary between goods and services at a specified point (the boundary decision) may not be problematic because the rationale for the decision can be imposed by the 'state'. A range of factors may influence the classification of the product because they reflect national interests, even though they fall outside those directly related to the inherent characteristics of the product itself. The legitimacy of the state in this context rarely arises. In contrast problems may arise in international regulatory regimes.

International regulatory structures must be perceived as 'legitimate' by those participating in them. As Franck states, 'legitimacy' in this general sense is 'a property of a rule or rule-making institution which itself exerts a pull towards compliance on those addressed normatively.'[1] At a generic level, this

* Lecturer, Department of Laws, University College, London, UK.
** Professor, Department of Law, University of Essex, UK. This article is also published simultaneously in the Columbia Journal of European Law by common agreement of the editors of the respective journals.
    [1] Thomas Franck, The Power of Legitimacy Amongst Nations, 16 (1990).

definition places the emphasis on the acceptability of either the rules them-selves, or the institution making them to those parties who come within the jurisdiction of the rules and/or the organization presiding over them. On this definition, 'legitimacy' is measured vertically,[2] so that it is the perception of those subject to the rules, or in the context of an international organization, its members, that are relevant, rather than the rule structure per se. Zampetti[3] takes this analysis further in the context of international law and measures this acceptability for the purposes of legitimacy using a three stage analysis: states must be willing to cede sovereignty to the extent that this leads them to comply with the rules administered by the relevant organization,[4] even if it were possible to violate those rules[5]; states' willingness to comply then flows from the rules' coherence, which in turn is measured by the extent to which the rules mirror the domestic goals and aspirations of those subject to them.[6] Interpretation of international rules is not only driven by the underlying rationale of the rule drafters, but also by the need to ensure the continued legitimacy of the rules themselves.[7]

In the context of the defining where the boundary lies between trade in goods and services, classification for the purpose of the rules can be made as much on the basis of ensuring the continued legitimacy of the regulatory structure as a whole, as well as prescribing the de facto classification of the product itself. In reality, this means that the boundary may be fluid for borderline products, particularly where these are politically sensitive. In particular, the classification of borderline products as goods rather than services, or vice versa, where this decision is politically driven may undermine the legitimacy of the organization in the sense defined by Franck and Zampetti. At the international level, achiev-ing such legitimacy means that the boundary decision is about more than just placing the product in one category or another. In addition, it becomes a matter of maintaining a single policy imperative within the international regulatory framework which is acceptable to those participating in the regime, to the extent that the boundary decision results in the continued adherence to the rules by those members of the organization.

---

[2] This point is derived from Jackson's analysis of the construction of the exercise of power within the WTO: see John H Jackson, The World Trade Organization: Constitution and Jurisprudence, 102 (1998).

[3] Americo B. Zampetti, *Democratic Legitimacy in the World Trade Organization: The Justice Dimension*, 37 J. World T. 105, 107 (2003).

[4] A. Hurrell, *International Society and the Study of Regimes: A Reflective Approach*, in Regime Theory and International Relations 49–72, 53 (V. Rittberger with the assistance of P. Mayer ed. 1993).

[5] Ibid. 107.

[6] Zampetti draws on the work of Hurrell and defines this shared commonality in terms of the 'justice component' where rules are made on the basis of common moral values: Zampetti above n 3 108. This point is highlighted in the *United States-Measures Affecting the Cross-Border Supply of Gambling and Betting Services* WT/DS285/R, (November 10, 2004), para 6.125.

[7] Legitimacy in this context is as interpreted by Zampetti and Franck. Above ns 1 & 3.

Broader implications follow from the recognition that the boundary decision is fulfilling more than just a pragmatic legal role. In particular, questions arise over who should make the boundary decision in the international context. Disagreements over the classification of products may mean that tension occurs between members, so that the determination of the boundary between goods and services must try to accommodate the policy imperative of the organization whilst simultaneously addressing the concerns of the members.[8] Not addressing such concerns may lead to calls for the decision to be devolved to the members rather than the organization itself. Difficulties can then arise if the organization is called upon to adjudicate the classification of a product and it only resolves the immediate conflict, rather than appreciating that the boundary decision must be resolved in the light of the organization's rule structure. Failure to continue to prioritize the organization's goals can lead to conflicting decision-making, meaning that it is even more difficult to decide which category problematic products fall into, as judicial decisions are sometimes inconsistent. In particular, the exact place where the boundary lies between goods and services in the context of the World Trade Organization (WTO) is unclear. The WTO panel and Appellate Body jurisprudence is ambiguous. As the discussion will show, the distinction has significance at a number of levels: the application of WTO rules to particular products; and the extent to which the WTO can unilaterally modify members' trade liberalization commitments particularly under the General Agreement on Trade in services (GATS).

Is this problem unique to the WTO? A useful comparator is the European Union, another international organization in which questions of competence as to the determination of such a boundary may arise. Considering the European Union has another advantage: the European Court of Justice (ECJ) has wrestled with the distinction between goods and services in its interpretation of the European Union rules on the free movement of goods and free movement of services. Consequently, there is a greater amount of judicial consideration of this issue within the European Union than in the panel and Appellate Body decisions of the WTO. The Court of Justice judgments allow us to see the difficulties and also to assess any solutions that have been developed.

Exploring where the boundary between goods and services lies at a generic level facilitates an understanding of the boundary problems in more detail. Identifying generic issues provides a fixed reference point that can be used to pinpoint factors used by other jurisdictions to differentiate goods from services. This comparison may allow us to identify those decisions, whether within the WTO or the European Union, which are based on the inherent characteristics of goods and services; those which reflect differences in the two legal orders' structures, as well as those which seem to suggest mere inconsistency of approach and those factors

---

[8] Note the vehement disagreement between the United States and Antigua and Barbuda over the scope of the United States' GATS commitments on gambling and other betting services in *United States-Gambling and Betting Services* above n 6, para 5.17.

that appear irrelevant to both the WTO and the European Union's boundary decision.

The discussion is divided into three parts. First, the WTO's categorization of products as goods and/or services is explored. The analysis focuses on the issues arising from the separation of the rules on goods and services into two distinct agreements, the legal effect of this division and the interpretation of the rules themselves within the two regimes. This discussion allows us to consider whether there is a distinction in the WTO between goods and services and its significance, if any. Second, the discussion considers the European Union's approach to the delineation between goods and services; in particular, how products are categorized and the problems which arise to ascertain whether the European Union encounters similar problems to those faced by the WTO or whether the European Union's approach could inform that of the WTO. Finally, the discussion considers the definition of goods and services at a generic level. Article 31(1) of the Vienna Convention on the Law of Treaties (the Vienna Convention)[9] advocates using the 'ordinary meaning' of the treaty's terms having regard to the general context of the term and also the 'object and purpose' of the treaty when interpreting its provisions; an approach endorsed by the Appellate Body for the interpretation of WTO rules.[10] The third section therefore starts by considering the natural language definition of goods and services and then moves on to determine how the economic and broader trade context of both the WTO and European Union affects the definition. This last section in particular aims at trying to find criteria which would assist in defining objectively the boundary between goods and services, serving the interests of legal certainty and, crucially, of reinforcing the legitimacy of the WTO and the European Union and their respective decision-making processes.

I. Determining The Boundary Between Goods and Services in the WTO

A. Background

Prior to the creation of the WTO on 1 January 1995,[11] only trade in goods was covered by the multilateral trade rules found in the General Agreement on

---

[9] Vienna Convention on the Law of Treaties done at Vienna May 23, 1969, 1155 UNTS 331, 8 ILM 679, (1969).

[10] See *United States-Standards for Reformulated and Conventional Gasoline* WT/DS2/AB/R, April, 29, 1996), (Appellate Body Report) 17. Also in its latest formulation, see the panel's interpretation of the Vienna Convention in *United States-Gambling and Betting Services* above n 8 para 6.46–6.53.

[11] Final act embodying the results of the Urugauy round of multilateral trade negotiations, para 3 (April, 15, 1994). On the Uruguay Round see, Terence P. Stewart (ed.), The GATT Uruguay round: A negotiating history 1986–1992, (1993).

Tariffs and Trade (GATT).[12] Originally negotiated in 1947,[13] the GATT liberalized trade through the reduction of tariff barriers and the elimination of other governmental restrictions on the import and export of goods and goods alone.[14] All goods are covered by GATT rules, but the contracting parties[15] listed specific goods subject to tariff barrier reduction commitments in schedules that were annexed to the main agreement. These schedules formed the basis of individual contracting parties' binding commitments to the process of liberalization.[16] During subsequent rounds of multilateral trade talks,[17] the contracting parties committed to reduce further tariffs on goods contained in these schedules.

All the GATT rules revolve around two fundamental non-discrimination provisions: the most favored nation clause (MFN clause)[18] and the national treatment provision.[19] Whereas the MFN clause operates to prevent contracting parties offering more favorable treatment to goods traded by one contracting party over another, the national treatment clause prevents discriminatory treatment of imported products as against 'like' domestically manufactured products once those goods have entered the contracting parties' domestic territory.[20] GATT also contains some exclusions relating to the imposition of trade barriers in limited circumstances, including some non-trade issues,[21] although in the pre-WTO period these non-trade exemptions were interpreted highly restrictively.[22]

[12] Originally the GATT did not enjoy full legal personality as it was only expected to be temporary in nature. This was in contrast to the WTO which enjoys full independent legal personality as an organization. GATT was brought into force using the Protocol of Provisional Application (PPA), as it was envisaged that the International Trade Organization would come into effect and so the GATT could once again form part of the broader structure. The PPA was therefore a temporary measure to allow the implementation of the commercial rules contained in GATT. Protocol of Provisional Application to the General Agreement on Tariffs and Trade, 30 October 1947, To underline the temporary nature of the GATT and the fact it specifically was not an international organization, states who subjected themselves to the rules were referred to as 'contracting parties'. see John H Jackson, The World Trade Organization: Constitution and Jurisprudence, above n 2, 12.

[13] The GATT encompassed Part IV of the ultimately unsuccessful International Trade Organization: see John H. Jackson, World Trade and the Law of GATT (1969).

[14] John H. Jackson, WJ Davey & AO Sykes (eds), Legal Problems of International Economic Relations: Cases, Materials and Text, 343, (4th ed. 2002).

[15] Those states participating in trade liberalization under the auspices of GATT were referred to as 'contracting parties,' rather than members reflecting GATT's lack of independent legal personality and provisional status. Note that customs territories possessing or acquiring 'full autonomy in the conduct of their external commercial relations and other matters provided for' by the GATT could also claim the status of contracting party: see Article XXVI:5(c) GATT.

[16] Article II GATT. See Jackson, Davey & Sykes above n 14, 338. Also *EC-Customs Classification of Certain Computer Equipment*, Appellate Body Report, WT/DS62/AB/R, WT/DS67/AB/R, WT/DS68/AB/R, June 5, 1998).   [17] See Jackson, Davey & Sykes above n 14, 344–49.

[18] Article I GATT.   [19] Article III GATT.   [20] Article III:2 GATT.

[21] Article XX GATT; also see Article XIX which allowed the contracting parties to impose safeguard measures where domestic industries suffered 'serious injury' as a result of excessive importation due to 'unforeseen developments' in trading patterns.

[22] *Restrictions on Imports of Tuna* DS29/R, circulated on 6 June 1994, not adopted.

Trade in services was excluded from the scope of the multilateral trade rules until the addition of the General Agreement on Trade in Services (GATS) to the WTO in 1995. GATS reduces barriers to trade in services in two ways: first, on a general level, through the elimination of restrictions in domestic regulations. In this respect, GATS contains universal rules which cover all trade in services in Parts I and II and then a series of rules in Part III which apply only to the extent that members elect to be bound by them in their GATS schedules. Second, GATS addresses particular service sectors through subject specific annexes.[23]

Normatively, GATS draws heavily on GATT and features many of its rules including the MFN[24] and national treatment provisions,[25] as well as the general exceptions clause[26] in Article XIV.[27] However, GATS also includes a separate market access commitment based heavily on a combination of the wording of the MFN and national treatment rules in Article XVI.[28] Article XVI does not define 'market access' in the abstract. Instead, it requires any member undertaking full liberalization commitments without restrictions in one service sector in their schedule to give MFN treatment to all services and service suppliers in that sector from other members.[29] In addition to the MFN obligation, Article XVI:2 limits the measures a member can take in relation to that service sector. The prohibited measures include imposing quotas on the number of service suppliers,[30] limiting the value of any transaction,[31] the number of service operations or their output,[32] the number of people that can be employed in the sector,[33] adopting measures which restrict the entity through which the service supplier operates[34] and finally, imposing restrictions on the use of foreign capital, shareholding or level of investment used.[35] GATS rules also only affect those sectors which members have agreed to liberalize in their schedules annexed to the main agreement.[36]

---

[23] Eg Annex on Air Transport; Annex on Financial Services, as well as the highly controversial Annex on Basic Communications. Members entered into further negotiations to liberalize the telecommunications sector, which were concluded in 1997, coming into effect in 1998: see Reference Paper on Regulatory Principles 36 ILM 367, (1997); see M Naftel & LJ Spiwak, The Telecoms Trade War, 102–17, (2000).   [24] Article I GATT & II GATS.

[25] Articles III GATT & XVII GATS.   [26] Article XX GATT.

[27] See the extrapolation of the jurisprudence on Article XX GATT into Article XIV GATS by the panel in *United States-Gambling and Betting Services* above n 6, para 6.448.

[28] Article XVI GATS.   [29] Article XVI:1 GATS.

[30] Article XVI:2(a) GATS: note that such limitations can be in the form of numerical quotas, monopolies, exclusive service suppliers or the imposition of an economic needs test.

[31] Article XVI:2(b) GATS.   [32] Article XVI:2(c) GATS.

[33] Article XVI:2(d) GATS.   [34] Article XVI:2(e) GATS.

[35] Article XVI:2(f) GATS. On the scope of Article XVI GATS, see *United States-Gambling and Betting Services* above n 6, para 6.265. The panel sees Article XVI: 1 as a specific manifestation of the MFN commitment in Article II GATS, ibid para 6.265.

[36] Article XX GATS. Note the re-negotiation deadline imposed by the July 2004 agreement: WTO, Draft General Council Decision of July 2004, July 27, 2004, para 1 (d).

B. GATT or GATS? The Structure of the Agreements

On one view, it is obvious that the question whether a boundary exists between trade in goods and services arises in the context of the WTO: the Marrakesh Agreement Establishing the World Trade Organization (the Marrakesh Agreement) states that the WTO should act to ensure the 'implementation, administration and operation, and further the objectives of . . . the Multilateral Trade Agreements'[37] contained in the substantive rules in Annex 1 to the Marrakesh Agreement. This structural arrangement means that the rules on trade in services[38] and intellectual property[39] are added incrementally to those from the original GATT.[40]

Physically separating the rules into distinct parts in Annex 1 on a subject specific basis in this way points to a distinction between trade in goods and trade in services and a boundary beyond which a product ceases to be goods and becomes services. The wording of the rules themselves within GATT and GATS also supports the existence of such a boundary. This occurs in three ways. First, GATS includes a definition of 'trade in services' in Article I:1, which implies a distinction between it and trade in goods and that this is relevant to the application of the rules in some way.[41] Second, GATS distinguish between different types of commitment, which the rules in GATT do not. Finally, the wording of the obligations in the two agreements are drafted differently.

The first of these points was endorsed by the Appellate Body in *Canada-Certain Measures Affecting the Automotive Industry (Canada-Autos)*.[42] In the case, the panel found Canada's import measures on certain motor vehicles violated GATS because they failed to conform to the MFN obligation in Article II. In reaching its conclusion, the panel focused on the measure's effect, but argued that,

---

[37] Article III:1 Marrakesh Agreement.

[38] The General Agreement on Trade (GATS): Annex 1B Marrakesh Agreement.

[39] Agreement on Trade-Related Aspects of Intellectual Property Rights (TRIPS): Annex 1C Marrakesh Agreement.

[40] The original GATT is legally distinct from the General Agreement on Tariffs and Trade 1994, which is contained in Annex 1A Marrakesh Agreement: Article II:4 Marrakesh Agreement. GATT 1947 is annexed to the Marrakesh Agreement and its rules are incorporated into the WTO scheme by virtue of Article I GATT 1994.

[41] Article I: 1 GATS defines trade in a service in terms of its supply, either between members across borders, by the presence of the consumer in another member's territory, the commercial presence of an entity within the member's territory, or by the presence of a natural person within the territory of another member.

[42] WT/DS/139/AB/R & WT/DS/142/AB/R, (May, 31, 2000). Note that in the landmark case on GATS, the panel refused to make any analysis of the scope of the definition of the scope of 'trade in services' under Article II:1 GATS: WTO, *Mexico-Measures Affecting Telecommunications Services, Report of the Panel, (Mexico-Measures Affecting Telecommunications Services)*, WT/DS204/R, April 2, 2004, para 7.39. Emphasis in this case is more on the scope of the commitments made by Mexico in its GATS schedule and the extent to which they comply with the Reference Paper on Basic Telecommunications: *Mexico Telecoms*, ibid. para 3.1. There is no argument by the parties that the products at issue are services at all, instead, it is the classification point within the general designation as services which is at issue: see Mexico argument, ibid, para 4.72–3 & US argument, ibid, para 4.74. Optimistically the panel argues that the definition of 'services' in Article II is 'comprehensive'. ibid. para 7.41.

as the measures in dispute were capable of violating Article II GATS, a separate analysis whether they did in fact concern services at all was unnecessary.[43] On the panel's interpretation, it is the nature of the violation that determines whether GATT or GATS applies, rather than any nebulous distinction between the type of trade involved in the dispute per se. However, on appeal the Appellate Body rejected the panel's interpretation. Whilst accepting that the analysis should centre on the national measure, the Appellate Body stressed the need to show that the measure did in fact concern trade in services first under Article I GATS, before finding a violation of the other substantive provisions. Consequently, it placed the emphasis on the existence of trade in services per se, thereby focusing on the 'ordinary meaning' of the provisions.[44] Importantly, placing emphasis on whether the measure applies to trade in goods or services highlights a distinction between the types of trade and, consequently, as both agreements cover distinct subject matter, the existence of a boundary between GATT and GATS.[45]

Further, GATS rules are divided into 'general obligations and disciplines' in Part II and specific commitments in Part III. Under GATS, the MFN clause is included in the general commitments, meaning it will apply to all trade in services, unless the member has notified an MFN exemption.[46] In contrast, the national treatment and market access rules in Part III GATS only cover specific commitments.

Locating both these rules in Part III means that members need only comply with the national treatment and market access rules to the extent that they have elected to do so in those service sectors specifically listed in their schedules of commitments annexed to the GATS.[47] If members do not include the sector at all, they are presumed to make no commitment in that sector.[48] This structural disparity means that GATS operates in a different way from GATT, as liberalization under GATS occurs on an ad hoc piecemeal basis dependent on the level of commitment made by all members in a service sector.

[43] WT/DS39/R & WT/DS/142/R, (February 11, 2000), paras 10.233–4. This follows the reasoning of the Appellate Body in *European Communities-Regime for the Importation, Sale and Distribution of Bananas (Bananas)* WT/DS27/AB/R, (September 9, 1997), para 221: the Appellate Body argued that there were some measures that would fall under both provisions and so a determination of which category they fell into was unnecessary.

[44] Article 31 Vienna Convention above n 9, advocates looking for the 'ordinary meaning' of a phrase when considering its interpretation. This approach is supported by Article 3:2 of the Understanding on Rules and Procedures Governing the Settlement of Disputes (the DSU) and endorsed by the Appellate Body in *United States-Reformulated Gasoline*, above n 10, 17. See section III of this article for greater analysis of the 'ordinary meaning' of trade in goods and services.

[45] Above n 42, paras 150–1; 167.

[46] MFN exemptions had to be notified at the time GATS came into force: Annex on Article II Exemptions GATS, para 1. Exemptions can be notified after this date, but these are subject to the waiver requirements in Article IX: 3 Marrakesh Agreement, rather than through GATS itself. MFN exemptions are time-limited to 10 years maximum, Annex on Article II Exemptions GATS, para 6.

[47] The panel in *United States-Gambling and Betting Services* interpreted this obligation in the light of what was actually written in the schedule rather than the United States' intention when they drafted it: above n 6, para 6.136.

[48] G Feketekuty, *Improving the Architecture of GATS*, in GATS 2000: New Directions in Services Trade Liberalization, 98, 85–111, (Pierre Sauvé & Robert M Stern eds, 2000).

Crucially for borderline products, this distinction means that a member's obligations differ if the product is classified as goods rather than services, as liberalization commitments are more stringent under GATT. Under GATT, both the MFN and national treatment rules apply in every case so forcing simultaneous liberalization on a member's external and internal trade policies for that product. Making the national treatment obligation dependent on the existence of a specific commitment in the member's schedule in GATS means there could be instances where only one of the fundamental backbones of the multilateral trade rules applies: for example, the MFN clause might apply, but the national treatment obligations do not.[49]

The fact that GATS' core rules are drafted differently from those of GATT raises the question of whether they will be interpreted differently, despite being based on the latter's fundamental principles.[50] This proposition follows from the general exhortation by the Appellate Body to work from the text of the rules themselves looking for the ordinary meaning[51] of the language of the WTO rules.[52] Using this interpretative tool,[53] it is clear that the wording used in the MFN clause in GATT is different from that in GATS: Article II GATS states that members should accord treatment '*no less favorable* to like services or service suppliers' from other members. This wording borrows heavily from Article III:4 GATT, the national treatment provision, rather than Article I GATT containing the MFN clause in relation to trade in goods. In contrast to Article II GATS, Article I GATT states that in relation to 'customs duties and charges of any kind . . . *any advantage, favor, privilege, or immunity granted* by any contracting party to any [goods] originating in or destined for any other country *shall be accorded immediately and unconditionally to the like product* originating in or destined for the territories of all other contracting parties.'[54] Article I appears more specific, placing the emphasis clearly on the rights granted, rather than on a general commitment to achieve equal treatment found in Article II GATS.

In *Bananas*, the panel accepted that the discrepancy in wording required a different interpretation of the obligations. It proceeded therefore on the basis that

[49] It is difficult to perceive a situation where a member would not want an MFN exemption as well as a reservation in their GATS schedule. This is because if the member did not reserve an MFN obligation, then any export concession granted to one member must then be granted unconditionally to all other members. If a member wishes to protect a specific sector, it is desirable for it to retain control over its external trade policy as unilateral concessions could affect the domestic industry's ability to compete in the international market. Likewise, national treatment and market access reservations in the member's schedule allow differential treatment of the imported products once they are within the member's territory, consequently protecting the designated domestic sector from cheaper imports. By retaining both reservations, a member preserves control over both external and internal trade in a specific sector.

[50] Aaditya Mattoo: *MFN and the GATS*, in Regulatory Barriers and the Principle of Non-discrimination in World Trade Law, 51, 55 (Thomas Cottier & Petros C. Mavroidis eds, Partrick Blatter, 2000).   [51] This follows on from the use of Article 31 Vienna Convention.

[52] *Reformulated Gasoline* above n 10, 17.

[53] The ordinary meaning of 'goods' and 'services' is explored in detail in Section II.

[54] Emphasis added: Article I:1 GATT.

the jurisprudence from Article III GATT, rather than that of Article I GATT, should be used to interpret Article II GATS.[55] By adopting this approach, the panel clearly indicated that a measure subject to the MFN obligation in GATS would potentially be treated differently from one that fell within the GATT. On the panel's view, it mattered whether the measure at issue concerned trade in goods or trade in services, as the interpretation of the obligations is different.[56]

The Appellate Body rejected the panel's interpretation,[57] arguing that as Article II GATS was an MFN commitment, it was more appropriate to use the corresponding MFN jurisprudence in GATT as a guide, rather than that on national treatment, despite the difference in wording.[58] The Appellate Body went on to extend Article II GATS' coverage to both de facto and de jure discrimination so that both MFN clauses had the same scope.[59] On its view, the nature of the obligation was crucial, rather than its phraseology.[60] Consequently, it appears from the *Bananas* analysis that the Appellate Body dismissed the importance of the type of trade in order to achieve a homogenous interpretation of the substantive scope of the MFN clause in GATT and GATS.[61]

In *Canada-Autos*, the panel found a violation of Article II:1 GATS[62] by focusing on the question whether the Canadian measure provided less favorable treatment to a 'limited and identifiable group of manufacturers/wholesalers of motor vehicles of some Members'[63] over others, allowing some manufactures/wholesalers to import vehicles duty-free, whereas others were specifically excluded from this exemption.[64] The Appellate Body rejected this approach, arguing that by equating the treatment of wholesalers with that of manufacturers, the panel was applying a 'goods' analysis, rather than one applicable to GATS. It argued that the wording of GATS meant that the effect on both the manufacturers and the wholesalers had to be considered separately and it was not possible to merely extrapolate the analysis from one sector to the other, as would be the case for the MFN analysis in GATT.[65] Although the Appellate Body was very careful to state that this did not mean that the Canadian measure would not adversely affect

---

[55] WT/DS27/R/USA, (May, 22, 1997), para 7.301. This approach mirrors the second element of Article 31(1) Vienna Convention where the term in the treaty must be interpreted in its context within the general overall meaning of the treaty as a whole: see *Mexico-Telecoms* above n 42, para 7.16.

[56] The emphasis here is placed clearly on the 'trade' aspect of the definition. Note the importance of this issue: see generally section III of this article.

[57] WT/DS27/AB/R above n 43, para 231.   [58] Ibid.   [59] Ibid.

[60] This approach follows on from the general considerations in the Vienna Convention on the Law of Treaties, even if it does lead to confusion. Under Article 31(2) it is possible to determine the 'ordinary' meaning of the language used in the treaty by assessing the general context in which the rules operate. Under Article 31(2)(a) any agreement can be considered alongside the original wording to ascertain what the ordinary meaning is. Also, Article 31(4) allows a special meaning to be accorded to the wording used if it is clear that the parties to the treaty intended this to be so: See *Mexico-Telecoms* above n 42, para 7.15 on the use of the Vienna Convention in the context of the GATS.

[61] Note the earlier discussion where it is still necessary to decide whether there is trade in services for the purposes of the application of the GATS per se.   [62] The MFN clause.

[63] Ibid., para 178.   [64] Ibid., para 179.   [65] Ibid., para 181.

wholesale manufacturers,[66] it stated firmly that GATS' rules could not simply be equated to GATT's.[67]

It is interesting to note that in its analysis the panel placed the emphasis on the type of breach of the rules, rather than the classification of the products. In contrast, the Appellate Body's insisted on an assessment of the type of trade affected by the measure first, before analyzing the breach of the substantive rules.

These approaches appear diametrically opposed to those taken by both bodies in their respective decisions in *Bananas*: in *Bananas* the panel reiterated the difference between the two types of trade in contrast to its stance in *Canada-Autos*; whereas the Appellate Body's views in *Bananas* supported a homogenous interpretation of the obligations in GATT and GATS which diminished the importance between the types of trade, unlike its approach in *Canada-Autos*.

One interpretation of this dichotomy is that the panel's analysis in *Canada-Autos* was influenced by the Appellate Body's view in *Bananas* that the scope of the GATT and GATS substantive obligations should be the same as the context of both agreements clearly pointed to a homogenous approach,[68] therefore diminishing the necessity of defining the boundary between the types of trade. Nevertheless, the Appellate Body's analysis supports the existence of a boundary between trade in goods and services which is significant only for deciding which set of rules applies to the measure at the first instance, rather than interpreting the scope of the obligations once the threshold test is met. On this construction, the distinction between trade in goods and trade in services remains, but only at a superficial level dictated by the pragmatic separation of trade into two distinct agreements. However, in *Canada-Autos* the Appellate Body appears to introduce the question of the type of trade back into the interpretation of the substantive rules, most notably, in the scope of the MFN obligation itself, thereby re-emphasizing a boundary between the two agreements that goes beyond merely de facto separation of the rules.[69]

This bifurcated approach is problematic on a number of levels: first, the jurisprudence is unclear whether the classification of a product as goods or services has implications for the application of the GATT and GATS or not. Whilst *Bananas* removes the importance of the categorization of the product from the scope of the MFN clause by homogenizing the GATT and GATS rules, *Canada-Autos* re-introduces it. Perhaps the explanation for the incoherent approach lies in an imperative to encourage adherence to 'new' rules in GATS by preventing members circumventing rules by arguing that trade in goods is involved to bring

---

[66] Ibid., para 183.

[67] Ibid., para 184. Note however, the panel's acceptance of Article XX GATT as an interpretative tool for Article XIV GATS in *United States-Gambling and Betting Services* above n 6, para 6.448. The panel merely imported the GATT jurisprudence without further analysis. This goes against the Appellate Body approach and may be contested on appeal.

[68] See Section III generally.   [69] *Canada-Autos* above n 42, Appellate Body report para 181.

the measure outside the scope of GATS, or vice versa.[70] Although such pragmatism may be necessary politically, it means that wider questions concerning the purpose of both agreements and the significance of the distinction between the types of trade stay unanswered and interpretational difficulties remain.[71]

C. Classification Methodology: how is the boundary drawn?

Both the WTO rules' structure and application as interpreted by the panels and Appellate Body point to a distinction between trade in goods and trade in services. Establishing whether trade in goods or trade in services is implicated is problematic because there is little guidance in the WTO agreements or dispute settlement reports. GATT does not contain a definition of 'goods' in the abstract, but GATS does have a limited definition of 'services'. Article I:2 GATS defines 'trade in services' in terms of a product's mode of supply: either products are traded across borders, where the consumer travels to another member's territory to receive the product, where products are supplied by the 'commercial presence' of the service supplier within the member's territory, or where there is movement of 'natural persons' to another member in order to supply the product.[72] The emphasis is placed on the way in which the product is traded, rather than on its inherent characteristics, thereby concentrating on the economic element or legal nature of the transaction to drive the scope of the definition.[73] This approach follows the general economic context of GATS in paragraph two of its Preamble,[74] which aims to create a 'multilateral framework of principles and rules for trade in services with a view to the expansion of such trade under conditions of transparency and progressive liberalization and as a means of promoting economic growth of all trading partners . . .'It is mirrored in the panel discussion in *Mexico-Measures Affecting Telecommunication Services*.[75]

Rather than discussing the notion of 'services' in the abstract, the panel placed the emphasis on the scope of the member's commitments in its schedule[76]; an

---

[70] This defence was raised by Canada in *Canada-Certain Measures Concerning Periodicals Report of the Panel* WT/DS31/R, March 14, 1997, para 3.3; also WT/DS31/AB/R, June 31, 1997. (*Canada-Periodicals*).

[71] See the difficulties created by the Appellate Body approach in *Canada-Periodicals* where the emphasis was placed on ensuring the measure in question was covered by the rules. Despite emphasizing the distinction between earlier cases and the need to differentiate between the different types of analysis in relation to GATT and GATS rules, the Appellate Body in *Canada-Periodicals* (ibid) and to an extent in *Canada-Autos* (above n 42) argued that it was possible for one type of trade to be implicated, so that was enough to bring the measure within one set of rules. On this view, there is a boundary, but the exact place is blurred: see later discussion of the case.

[72] Article I:2(a)-(d) GATS.

[73] This view is endorsed by the Appellate Body in *Canada-Autos*: above n 42, para 155. The emphasis on trade may change the categorization of the product from goods to services or vice versa, see section III below.

[74] See section III on the significance of 'trade' in a product to determine whether the product falls within GATT and GATS at all.　　　　　　　　　　　[75] Above n 42, paras 7.41–7.43.

[76] *Mexico-Telecommunications* ibid para 7.57.

approach followed by the panel in *United States-Gambling and Betting Services*.[77] The panel in *Mexico-Telecommunications* noted that the definition of 'trade in services' in Article I:2 GATS was 'defined comprehensively'.[78] The difficulty with this view is that it places the emphasis on the method of transfer without specifying the essential characteristics of the product itself, as Article I is silent on these points. This is problematic when viewed against the Appellate Body's approach in *Canada-Autos* when it clearly stated that the inherent economic characteristics of the product were relevant to the scope of the MFN obligation in GATT and GATS, as both agreements covered different subject matter.[79] On this view, the essential characteristics of the product only appear relevant once the substantive obligations are assessed, rather than when the threshold criteria for the application of GATS is considered. This seems strange when it is not clear that the product constitutes services in the first instance.[80]

Relying on the GATS' definition alone to predict where the boundary lies is difficult: first, fitting the product into one mode of supply does not guarantee that it will automatically amount to trade in services. For example, products traded across borders could constitute trade in services in accordance with mode 1, but equally could be trade in goods for GATT, as both envisage physical product transfer in some respect.[81] Second, GATS uses tautologous definitions forcing the emphasis back onto the existence of a 'service' before the rules apply:[82] for example, GATS applies to 'measures affecting *trade in services*'; 'trade in services' is then defined in Article I:2 as the 'supply *of a service*' under one of four modes; 'supply of a service' for this purpose includes 'the production, distribution, marketing, sale and delivery *of a service*'.[83] Even 'services' themselves are defined as 'including *any service in any sector* except *service sectors* in the exercise of governmental authority'.[84] This tautologous approach is perpetuated in the other modes including 'commercial presence' in mode 3, which comprises '(ii) the creation or maintenance of a branch or representative office within the territory of a member *for the purposes of supplying a service*'.[85] Finally, the definition in Article I GATS recognizes

---

[77] Note the panel did not even question whether the measures at issue were services at all, but went firmly on the scope of the panel reference. See Panel report above n 6, para 6.28.

[78] Ibid. para 7.41.   [79] *Canada-Autos* above n 42, para 181.

[80] Section III below assesses a way in which all these criteria fit together.

[81] This issue is not really resolved by *Mexico-Telecommunications* either, see above n 42, para 7.33. The panel in that case was very careful to restrict its analysis to the facts of the case before it and was reluctant to give any general guidance on the scope of the obligations in GATS: see *Mexico-Telecommunications* above n 42, para 7.3. See generally, Guy Karsenty, *Assessing Trade in Services by Mode of Supply* in GATS 2000: New directions in services trade liberalization, 33, 35–40 (Sauvé & Stern above n 48). There are problems with online trading and broadcasting. Note also the difficulty in the European Union context concerning 'retail services': see section III below.

[82] Ascertaining the 'ordinary meaning' of the language used in GATS would seem to indicate the necessity to ascertain what 'services' means in the abstract, especially given the general context of the definition which forces the definition continually back on to the notion of 'services'. See section II below.

[83] Article XXVIII: (b) GATS. Emphasis added.   [84] Article I:3(b) GATS. Emphasis added.

[85] Article XXVIII: (d) GATS. Emphasis added. Note that the European Union approach segregates those issues covered by mode 3 and mode 4 in separate categories outside the scope of its rules on services. See section III below. See generally Lorna Woods, Free Movement of Goods and Services in the European Community (2004).

that there may be distinctions between types of service, though these distinctions (e.g. the distinction between a service which requires an individual to move to perform the service, by contrast to a service which does not) are not expressly addressed in the more detailed GATS rules.

One way to identify the boundary between goods and services could be by reference to scheduling. Classification for scheduling purposes is complex, but similar for GATT and GATS. Both adopt numerical categorization systems, where products are allocated distinct codes, which are then listed in the members' schedule.[86] Once a product fits within a code, it is classed as either goods or services purely based on the code allocated by the relevant nomenclature. Again, different systems are used for GATT and GATS. GATT generally uses the Harmonized Description and Coding System (HS) nomenclature for goods devised by the World Customs Organization.[87] Members are under no obligation to accept the HS code for scheduling purposes but a significant proportion of them rely on it.[88]

GATS also employs a numerical coding system for scheduling purposes. Initially there was considerable disparity between members over the appropriate scheduling methodology,[89] despite the general exhortation that there should be a common method wherever possible.[90] Following the introduction of Guidelines by the Council for Trade in Services in 2001,[91] members now are encouraged to adopt the Services Sectoral Classification List (W/120) used during the negotiations of the Uruguay Round,[92] based on the more comprehensive United Nations' Central Product Classification System (CPC).[93] W/120 comprises a list of generic services,

---

[86] In the context of the General Agreement on Trade in Services (GATS), see Steve Orava, *Commercial Reality (Or Lack Thereof) in the Classification and Definition of Services in the WTO GATS Negotiations*, 8(1), International Trade Law & Regulation, 5 (2002).

[87] The HS code is divided into 97 separate chapter headings according to the physical characteristics of the products concerned. Each chapter is then sub-divided into headings and sub-heading; each individual product carries a six digit code which reflects its own characteristics as well as the chapter, heading and sub heading it comes under. It is this final six digit code which is used in the member's schedule to indicate that the product is subject to the rules o goods in GATT. See the International Convention on the Harmonized Commodity Description and Coding System, June 14, 1983, as amended by Customs Co-operation Council Recommendation June 25, 1999 which entered into force on January 1, 2002. See www.wcoomd.org/ie/En/Topics_Issues/topics_issues.html (last visited December 12, 2003). See GATT panels: *Spain-Tariff Treatment on Unroasted Coffee*, BISD 28s/102, 111 (June 11, 1981); *Canada-Japan-Tariffs on Imports of Spruce, Pine Fir (SPF) Dimension Lumber*, BISD 36S/167, (July 19, 1989). See Jackson, Davey & Sykes above n 14, 394.

[88] 95 per cent of members: see Jackson, Davey & Sykes, ibid.

[89] WTO, *Scheduling of Initial Commitments in Trade in Services: Explanatory Note*, MTN.GNS/W/164, para 16 (September 3, 1993).

[90] ibid, para 1 & *Electronic Commerce and the Role of the WTO* Special Studies (1998) 51.

[91] WTO, *Guidelines for the Scheduling of Specific Commitments under the General Agreement on Trade in Services (GATS)*, S/L/92, para 23 (March 28, 2001).

[92] WTO, *Services Sectoral Classification List, Note by the Secretariat*, MTN.GNS/W/120, (July 10, 1991).

[93] United Nations, *Provisional Central Product Classification*, Statistical Papers M no. 77, version 1.1 UN Doc. ST/ESA/STAT/SER.M/77/Ver.1.1, March 2002. Note the panel's interpretation of the Guidelines in *Mexico- Telecommunications* above n 42, para 7.43.

which are then sub-divided according to the CPC code. This means that once a product is listed under a generic heading in W/120, the interpretation of the individual product coding is that adopted by the CPC code.[94] Like the HS code for goods, the CPC code operates on a multi-level numerical coding system.[95]

In *United States-Gambling and Betting Services*,[96] the United States disputed the assumption that it had GATS commitments on gambling and betting in its schedule. Despite omitting any reference to the CPC in its schedule, the panel still went on to interpret the United States' commitments using the CPC and W/120 as customary rules of treaty interpretation under Article 31.2 Vienna Convention.[97]

Adopting a numerical methodology to determine when a product constitutes trade in goods or services means that the boundary between the two is drawn on a product-by-product basis using criteria centered on the perceived inherent characteristics of the products themselves based on subjective criteria determined by the members. Consequently, there is no single identifying trait that makes products either goods or services, as the decision on which numeric classification to allocate a product is made on an ad hoc basis. Despite these difficulties the panel in *Mexico-Telecommunications*[98] made it clear that it was important to define the relevant service sector, first according to the CPC criteria and then assess the member's scheduling commitment.[99] The panel appeared happy to accept the member's categorization of the measure under the CPC code and did not concentrate their analysis on this issue.[100]

Although this approach may not be problematic for many traditional products, new products may not fit easily into the existing coding systems, with disagreement arising over the correct classification of the product. There is a risk of discrepancies arising in two contexts: either products can be classified differently within the HS or W/120/CPC code; or more radically, they are classified as goods on one view and services on another. This problem is acute for products traded online although more established products, such as those of the communications industry, have also given rise to problems.[101]

Using the classification methodology to determine the point at which trade in a product ceases to be trade in goods, but then constitutes trade in services is problematic: despite the apparent certainty that a numeric classification system

[94] *Electronic Commerce and the WTO* above n 90, 51.
[95] There are five levels: level one is the section heading and has a one digit code, which is in turn sub-divided into four further levels. Level two is the division heading using a two digit code; level three has a three digit code, referred to as the group heading; level four is the class of service with a four digit code and finally, level five is the service sub-class and has a five digit code.
The CPC also includes an explanation of the scope of each level of the Code: http://unstats.un.org/unsd/cr/registry/regest.asp?CI=16&Lg=1. (Last visited December 3, 2003).
[96] Above n 6.   [97] Ibid. para 6.82.   [98] Above n 42, para 7.77.
[99] Ibid. para 7.77.   [100] Ibid. para 7.35.
[101] WTO, *Considerations Concerning the Relationship Between WTO Provisions and the Subjects Listed Under Paragraph 3.1 of the Work Programme*, G/C/W/128, para 2 (November 5, 1998). The various views are discussed at length in the WTO Secretariat's background note, Job No. (02) 38, May 1, 2002, annexed to the second dedicated discussion on e commerce in May 2002: WTO,

478   *Fiona Smith and Lorna Woods*

creates, in reality the boundary between the types of trade is still fluid because it is not until a product is classified that it acquires a designation as 'goods' or 'services'. A decision over the type of trade involved must still be made first before the classification methodology applies and places the product within a specific code.[102] It is only by ascertaining what type of trade is involved that the appropriate coding nomenclature can be applied: either W/120/CPC or the HS code. Whilst this decision potentially affects which WTO rules apply, it is the member who retains a significant element of choice whether to designate the product as goods or services in the first instance as there are no agreed criteria for choosing the most appropriate coding nomenclature, but only which part of the code in which to place the product once the coding nomenclature is selected.[103]

Relying on the classification methodology to place this boundary rather than any workable definition in the WTO rules means that the classification decision is removed from the WTO and firstly placed on to the two external bodies that devised the nomenclature. Both the World Customs Council and the United Nations might classify products using economic criteria broadly defined, but they operate outside the scope of the WTO and may not take the WTO's broader trade liberalization goals into consideration.[104] Potentially, tension could exist between the interpretation of the classification methodology used by the non-WTO bodies driven by those bodies' goals and the views and aims of the WTO.[105]

Second, the boundary decision also lies with members as they make the decision whether to include a product in their GATT and/or GATS schedules in the first instance. If it is possible to classify a product as both goods and services then a member may classify the product based on historical imperatives, rather than on a conscious decision based on the benefits of classifying a product in one category rather than another. Nevertheless, if a member only wants to make a commitment

Second Dedicated Discussion on Electronic Commerce Under the Auspices of the General Council on 6 May 2002, WT/GC/W/475, (June 20, 2002). Note that the WTO has resolved some issues by the classification of some electronic products as 'goods' under the WTO Ministerial Declaration on Trade in Information Technology Products WT/MIN(96)/16, (December 16, 1996). However, it is unclear what criteria were used to determine whether such products are goods or not, as the products covered are merely annexed to the agreement, rather than being identified by any objective description. Note the European Union suggestions that the computer and other related services CPC category should cover 'basic functions used to provide all computer and related services: computer programs . . . data processing and storage'. However, this is not universally accepted by other members: WTO, *Coverage of CPC-84-Computer and Related Services*, TN/S/W/6, para 7 (October 24, 2002); also, WTO, *Work Programme on Electronic Commerce: Classification Issue: Submission by the European Communities*, WT/GC/W/497, para 16 (May 9, 2003).

[102] See *Mexico-Telecommunications* above n 42, para 7.77.

[103] The WTO has retaken control over the classification decision in some instances, but this is only done in dispute settlement proceedings and is seemingly done on an ad hoc basis: see discussion of *Canada-Periodicals* above n 70.

[104] Deciding classification on a product-by-product basis arguably excludes any other criteria in the boundary decision: see the Preamble to the Marrakesh Agreement, para 1.

[105] Note the problematic discussion of classification in *Mexico-Telecommunications* above n 42, where the panel used its own assessment of the scope of the CPC coding based on the 'ordinary meaning' of the language to define the scope of Mexico's GATS commitments: ibid para 7.67.

under one set of rules to benefit from their narrower liberalization commitments then, arguably, the member may classify the product based on its own domestic political considerations, rather than any global criteria initiated by the WTO.[106]

This problem is manifest principally in audiovisual products and products traded on-line. In these sectors, members disagree on the appropriate classification methodology based on their desire to protect such domestic interests. In relation to audiovisual products, many members excluded the sector from their original GATS commitments and the European Union obtained an MFN exemption.[107] Divergent views between the United States and the European Union in particular, originally centered on whether the broadcast content in audiovisual products should be classified as goods or services.[108] This debate arose because the content can be physically transferred by virtue of the disc or videocassette on which it is recorded, or it can be transmitted via other transmission means. Whilst the former could be regarded as goods, the latter is more appropriately classified as services.[109] The United States supported classification of the audiovisual products as goods following on from the historical inclusion of the film sector within GATT,[110] whereas the European Union argued for its classification as services.[111] Disagreement remains between United States and the European Union views especially over European Union quotas on broadcast content, although the debate is currently centered on the correct classification within the CPC and W/120 coding.[112]

In the case of both audiovisual products and those traded online therefore, it can be argued that the extent to which each is covered by the WTO rules is still a

---

[106] Eg the disagreement between the United States and the European Union on the audiovisual sector has its roots in the different classification of the sector as goods by the United States and as services by the European Union. Note that the European Union position is shaped by the European Court of Justice's judgment in Case 155/73 *Sacchi* [1974] E.C.R. 409. Also, see John David Donaldson, *Television Without Frontiers Directive: The Continuing Tension Between Liberal Free Trade and European Cultural Integrity*, 20 Fordham Int'l LJ 90, 110–1 (1996).

[107] European Commission, Communication on the Future of European Regulatory Audiovisual Policy COM(2003) 784 final, 11–12 (2003). See generally Fiona Smith & Lorna M. Woods, *GATS and the Audiovisual Sector*, 9(1) COMMS. L. 1 (2004). It may be possible that the reason for exclusion of these products is because they do not contain a commercial element: see further section II below.

[108] GATT, Report of the Working Party, GATT Doc./L/1741, 2–3 (March 13, 1962). Note that this dilemma was not discussed in *Mexico-Telecommunications* above n 42.

[109] This debate is not new, see the GATT working party set up to discuss the scope of the film exception in Article IV GATT: GATT Working Party on International Trade in Television Programmes, ibid. [110] Article IV GATT.

[111] The United States objected to the use of 'European Quotas' and 'European Independent Works' in the Television Without Frontiers Directive, (89/552/EEC), (October 3, 1989) as amended by Directive 97/36/EC (June 30, 1997).

[112] WTO, *Audiovisual Services, Background Note by the Secretariat*, (June 15, 1998), S/C/W/40, para 30; WTO, *Communication from the United States, Audiovisual Services*, S/CSS/W/21, para 3 (December 18, 2000). It is not possible to conclude that the classification issue has been resolved even though the US is now negotiating concessions in the sector within the GATS framework. This is because the center of the debate has not shifted due to public concessions on the issue by the US, but more as a result of a change in emphasis within the Doha negotiations. Disagreements could therefore re-occur during the course of the GATS negotiations.

matter of debate amongst members. Consequently, it is unclear for participating businesses which rules apply to them, or even, in the case of the audiovisual sector, whether the rules apply at all.[113]

The involvement of both international organizations and members in the classification decision means that the point at which trade in goods is distinguished from trade in services potentially shifts dependent at what level the decision is made. Consequently, there is a potential tension between the motivation behind members' decision over the classification of a product and that of the international organizations. This tension could be alleviated by the intervention of the WTO, clearly delineating the point at which a product is viewed as trade in goods rather than trade in services for the purposes of the rules.[114] As noted, little clear guidance is available[115] and the discussion has already highlighted the Appellate Body's divergent opinions on the distinction between trade in goods and trade in services and whether there is a boundary between GATT and GATS.[116] Further problems from its pragmatic stance are apparent when trying to ascertain where the boundary should be drawn.

D. Is the Product Goods or Services? Classification by the Panels and Appellate Body

In both *Canada-Autos* and *Canada-Periodicals*, the core of Canada's defence was that the disputed product related to trade in services rather than trade in goods.[117] Canada argued that as it had not made any liberalization commitment in its GATS' schedule, the measure automatically fell outside the rules.[118] Canada's construction identifies a clear boundary between the competence of the WTO and the members as the former would only be able to review the impact of a

---

[113] During the GATS negotiations, Canada, Switzerland and the EU argued that audiovisual products are 'fundamental instruments of social communication and contribute to the cultural identity of a society'. Such cultural content meant they could not be regarded as 'commercial' in the trade sense and so should be outside the scope of the trade rules completely. WTO, *Communication from Switzerland: GATS 2000, Audiovisual Services*, S/CSS/W/74, para 6 (May 4, 2001). Ted Madger, 'Made in Canada-An International Instrument on Cultural Diversity' for 'On the Edge: Is the Canadian Model Sustainable?' Weatherhead Center of International Affairs, May 9–10, 2003, 1. See further on this point, section III below.

[114] This has not been resolved by the *Mexico-Telecommunications*, above n 42, as the panel accepted that the measures at issue were in fact services and they only went on to discuss the relevant mode of supply for the purposes of Article I:2 GATS and also the scope of Mexico's commitments in the Reference Paper: ibid, para 7.140.   [115] *Mexico-Telecommunications*: ibid, para 7.3.

[116] Whilst in *Bananas* it diminished the importance of the boundary between trade in goods and services in GATT and GATS, it appeared to depart from this view in *Canada-Autos* and re-emphasize the distinction between the types of trade as well as stressing a fundamental difference between the interpretation of the rules within the two agreements.

[117] This defence was not raised in *Mexico-Telecommunications* above n 42, para 4.71. The United States only argued that the measures at issue could be classified as 'public services' rather than stating they did not relate to services at all: ibid, para 4.8.

[118] *Canada-Periodicals*-report of the panel, above n 70, para 3.33; *Canada-Autos* Appellate Body report above n 70, para 20.

measure if the member chose to undertake liberalization commitments under the agreement at issue.[119] Canada's view was rejected in both cases.

Whereas Canada adopted a retrospective analysis focusing on the nature of the product itself, emphasizing the essential characteristics that placed it within a specific CPC code, the Appellate Body used a forward looking approach, focusing on the effects of the measure in the sector, rather than on whether the product was goods or services in terms of its classification.[120] Although the Appellate Body's construction follows the wording of GATS closely, it does not address GATS' tautologous language, because it assumes that if there is *any* effect in a service sector, then this is enough to bring the measure within the GATS' rules without more comprehensive analysis. In *Canada-Autos*, the Appellate Body discussed whether 'trade in services' was implicated in one paragraph,[121] stating that provided the product was covered by the CPC classification methodology in some way and there was no dispute on whether the service supplier actually was resident in Canada in some way, this was enough to implicate GATS making discussion of the nature of the product itself unnecessary.[122]

The Appellate Body's dismissal of Canada's argument in *Canada-Periodicals* and *Canada-Autos* allows the WTO, rather than the member, to retain competence over the decision where the boundary between the types of trade lies to avoid circumvention of the rules. From both cases, it is clear that the member must present an argument whether the measure affects trade in goods or trade in services in the first instance,[123] but this decision is subject to challenge through the dispute settlement process. By adopting a pragmatic interpretation based on maximum compliance, the Appellate Body gives no definitive guidance on how to draw the boundary. It is clear from the reports that there is a distinction between the types of trade and the interpretation of the rules within GATT and GATS indicating a boundary between the two agreements, but not where it lies.

The classification decision therefore still rests with the members and international organizations at the first instance, unless there is a dispute. Even when there is a dispute, taking the classification decision away from a member in circumstances where it does not wish to make a commitment in a specific service sector undermines its sovereignty over decisions it had not ceded to the WTO.

---

[119] Article 3:2 WTO Understanding on Rules and Procedures Governing the Settlement of Disputes (the DSU) which stresses that the role of the dispute settlement body is merely to 'clarify the existing provisions . . .' and that 'rulings of the DSB cannot add to or diminish the rights and obligations provided in the covered agreements'.

[120] This follows from the panel's determination in *Bananas*; see *Canada-Autos* Appellate Body report above n 42, para 6.710. See further section III below.

[121] *Canada-Autos* Appellate Body report: ibid, para 157.

[122] A similar approach was taken in *Canada-Periodicals*, Appellate Body report p. 20 above n 70.

[123] This follows from the interpretation of Article I:2 GATS in *Canada-Autos*: see above discussion. Note that the GATT/GATS boundary only received limited discussion in *Mexico-Telecommunications* above n 42, and was not discussed at all in *United States-Gambling and Betting Services* above n 6.

Inevitably, tension arises as all participants have conflicting goals, creating uncertainty for businesses and individuals directly affected by the WTO rules.

The analysis indicates that the WTO's attempt to address the boundary between goods and services is problematic. Both the rules and their interpretation in the panel and Appellate Body reports indicate that there are differences between goods and services. However, it seems unclear whether this distinction is predicated on the inherent characteristics of the products themselves or if it is based on the context in which the rules operate; that is the method by which the products is traded, or whether the approach draws on a combination of these two issues.

II. Can we get any Help from the European Union Case Law?

When considering problems in a given arena, a way forward is often found by considering similar questions in comparable bodies. In the case of the WTO, a trading organization, help might be found in the context of one of the regional trading organizations, the longest established of which is the European Union. Certainly, similarities between the underlying rationale of the WTO and that of the European Union can be seen.[124] In its original incorporation, the European Union established by the Treaty of Rome (TEC), had an essentially trade-based purpose.[125]

Even now, after numerous amendments,[126] the central vehicle by which the European Union aims to achieve its objectives is through the establishment (and proper functioning) of a common market.[127] One of the essential elements of the common market is the four freedoms[128] making up the elements of the internal

---

[124] Although since the Maastricht Treaty there has been a distinction between the European Communities and the European Union, only the term European Union will be used in this article in the interests of simplicity. Further, the European Constitution, when ratified, will remove this distinction.

[125] Article 2 TEC.

[126] In addition to the treaties dealing with the various enlargements of the European Community, the main treaties amending the Treaty of Rome are: the Single European Act, the Treaty on European Union (the Maastricht Treaty), the Treaty of Amsterdam, and the Treaty of Nice. Further discussions on the structure of the European Union are currently in progress; a new Constitution has been signed although the ratification process may take some time. The Treaty of Amsterdam renumbered the treaties; the Constitution will amend the numbering further: Amsterdam numbers will be used in this article.

[127] The European Constitution will change this position: the first of the Union's objectives is to promote peace, its values and the well-being of its peoples. As a second objective, Article I-3(2) specifies that the Union is to 'offer its citizens an area of freedom, security and justice without internal frontiers, and an internal market where competition is free and undistorted'.

[128] Article 3c EC. The European Constitution does not refer to the common market, using the term internal market instead. Some commentators have suggested that the terms internal market and common market should have different meanings, for example because Articles 94 and 95 TEC distinguish between the two terms. Jurisprudence of the Court of Justice suggested otherwise and it seems that the Constitution reflects this position. The text of Article 94 has not found its way into the European Constitution.

market.[129] These four freedoms are defined as the free movement of goods,[130] services,[131] people,[132] and capital.[133] Although the European Community Treaty therefore deals with a greater subject matter than the WTO (for example, by dealing with the free movement of capital[134]) it can be seen that there are commonalities between the two. In particular, the TEC distinguishes between goods and services. Consequently there are similarities between the questions which needed to be addressed by the European Union and those with which the WTO has to deal. Three issues arise. First, to what extent has the distinction between goods and services any significance in the context of the European Union? Second, how has the European Union dealt with this matter? Finally, is the difference between goods and services institutionalized within the European Union in the same (or similar) way that it is in the WTO? Our starting point therefore is a brief outline of the institutional structure of the European Union.

A. Structure of the EC Treaty

Although the general objectives of the TEC are identified in Articles 2 and 3, these provisions are very general and are considered to be of interpretative value only.[135] Greater detail is added through subsequent articles which, as they are more precise, constitute the relevant specific legal obligation. Separate provisions deal with each of the four freedoms; thus goods and services are dealt with under different articles. These are however dealt with in the same treaty, albeit within separate titles of the part of the TEC dealing with substantive policies. Services and goods are therefore subject to the same enforcement mechanisms.[136]

There is an additional, structural difference between these two freedoms: whereas a single provision, Article 49, identifies the freedom to provide services, several different articles deal with the free movement of goods.[137] Somewhat

---

129 Article 14(2) EC. This definition is carried over into the European Constitution: Article III-130(2).
130 Articles 23–31 EC.   131 Article 49 EC.
132 This comprises free movement of workers, Article 39 EC, as well as freedom of establishment, Article 43 EC. Often the free movement of services contained in Article 49 EC is dealt with under this heading, although it is listed separately in the 'four freedoms'. The new section in the EC Treaty, Title IV, concerning visas, asylum, immigration and other policies relating to the free movement of people is not usually considered to be part of the 'four freedoms'. They seem to refer specifically to the movement between Member States rather than movement into the European Union by third country nationals. This statement itself is problematic because both the goods provisions and those relating to capital have elements which deal with the flow of goods/capital into the European Union.
133 Articles 56–60 EC. Note also the separate title, Title VII, dealing with economic and monetary policy. Although linked, these latter provisions do not fall within the ambit of free movement of capital.   134 *Ibid.*
135 Case 270/80 *Polydor* v. *Harlequin Record Shops* [1982] ECR 329, para 16.
136 See Article 226 regarding Commission enforcement actions and the rarer Article 227 which allows Member States to bring actions against other Member States. More indirectly, note the preliminary ruling mechanism in Article 234 EC. The new preliminary ruling mechanism does not relate to Articles 28–30 or Article 49 *et seq.*,
137 Although Article 3c EC refers to all four freedoms together, Article 3a EC also refers separately to 'the prohibition, as between Member States, of customs duties in quantitative restrictions on the

confusingly, the provisions dealing with the free movement of goods are dealt with in the same section as that dealing with the creation of a customs union, blurring the two concepts. Thus, Article 23 defines a customs union as covering 'all trade in goods' including 'the prohibition between Member States of customs duties on imports and exports and of all charges having equivalent effect, and the adoption of a common customs tariff in their relations with third countries'.[138] Developing this provision, Article 25 prohibits customs duties and Article 26 gives the Council the power to set the common customs tariff.[139] Despite the fact that the customs union is a broader concept than just trade in goods, effectively it is trade that this section of the Treaty addresses: people, capital and services are not considered here. The EC Treaty also prohibits non-tariff barriers to trade: Article 28 prohibits quantitative restrictions on imports and all measures having equivalent effect (MEQR); Article 29 is the equivalent provision in relation to exports.[140] Article 30 identifies the grounds of derogation in relation to Article 28 and Article 29.

Although these provisions elaborate the aims of the TEC, and have been held to be capable of being relied upon directly in proceedings before national courts,[141] the provisions are still very broad. Because of the framework nature of the TEC, the institutions have been given the power to enact various types of secondary legislation,[142] which will take effect across the European Union.[143] In this there is a difference in the type of action which the two organizations may take, the European Union having legislative powers that the WTO lacks.[144] As regards the internal market, which according to Article 14(2) TEC includes the free

import and export of goods, and of all other measures having equivalent effect.' Services are not separately identified within Article 3.

[138] Note that the European Union would have had to satisfy the requirements of the original Article 24 GATT.

[139] Note that there is also a provision in dealing with a discriminatory taxation: Article 95.

[140] Note that although the phraseology of Article 29 mirrors that of Article 28, Article 28 has been interpreted to apply more restrictively: Case 15/79 *Groenveld* v. *Produktschap voor Vee en Vlees* [1979] ECR 3409.   [141] That is, they are 'directly effective'.

[142] Proposals are put forward to the European Commission, the body which effectively represents the pan-European interest, for agreement by the Council, which is made up of the representatives of the Member States, either on its own or, in an increasing number of cases, in conjunction with the European Parliament. The procedure used in each case depends on which provision of the EC Treaty is used as the basis for Community action—the enabling provision will in each case specify the procedure to be used and in some instances the instrument (for example Regulation or Directive, which have different legal effects) to be used. The European Parliament is directly elected by the populations of the various Member States; as such it has a claim to represent the peoples of the EU rather than the member States themselves. Decision-making within the Union is therefore complex, representing a kaleidoscopic range of interest groups. The role of the European Parliament is often felt to be crucial in giving the Union and its decision-making some form of democratic legitimacy, although whether this is sufficient has been the subject of some debate: See e.g. P. Craig *The Nature of the Community: Integration, Democracy and Legitimacy* in The Evolution of EU Law (P. Craig and G. de Burca eds, 1999).

[143] Article 249 EC.

[144] Community legislation takes direct effect in the legal systems of the Member States. The terms of the WTO treaties will not necessarily have such effect, depending on the terms of each State's constitution. Further, the WTO does not have direct effect within the Union legal order.

movement of both goods and services, harmonizing measures are the most usual form of action.[145] Article 95 is a general provision to be used 'for the achievement of the objectives set out in Article 14'. Nonetheless, certain areas are expressed to fall outside the scope of Article 95: it does not apply to 'fiscal provisions, to those relating to the free movement of persons nor to those relating to the rights and interests of employed persons'.[146] On this basis, Article 95 has tended to deal with matters relating to the functioning of the internal market as regards goods. Specific treaty provisions deal with the issues relating to services, establishment and people. Notably, Article 52 enables the Community to take action to liberalize a specific service; Article 47 provides that Directives may be issued to 'make it easier for persons to take up and pursue activities as self employed persons', again facilitating the freedom to provide services as well as freedom of establishment.

The difference between these provisions is crucial, as they utilize different negotiating procedures. Depending on which procedure is used, the European Parliament will have different levels of involvement and influence; under Articles 95 and 47(2) its consent to a proposal is required, whereas under Article 52(1) the Parliament need only be consulted. Further, in some instances unanimity in the Council will be required, for example under Article 47(2), but in others, such as Article 52(1) and Article 95, it will not be. Thus the categorization of an issue as falling within goods and services, or more precisely as a general internal market matter rather than relating to the freedom of establishment and the freedom to provide services, has significance for the way in which decisions are made. This has particular impact on the freedom of the Member States to maintain their own national position. Where unanimity in the Council is required, each State effectively has a veto. By contrast, where qualified majority voting is required, a State may have an interest in compromise. The Council in general may have to compromise when the European Parliament effectively vetoes a legislative proposal (co-decision procedure).

Some of the difficulties in this area arise because the precise scope of each of the provisions is not clear and there is some potential for overlap. For example, it is not clear what the relationship is between the services harmonization provisions and Article 95 [147]: the recent telecommunications package included a number of harmonizing Directives which were based on Article 95, that is, the internal market provisions, rather than the services provisions.[148] It is not entirely clear

---

[145] These are sometimes referred to as 'positive harmonization' measures, as they replace inconsistent national rules with Community standards which are then implemented in national law; contrast the decisions of the Court of Justice which strike down inconsistent national rules, but do not replace them with a Community standard. The decisions of the Court of Justice in this area are sometimes referred to as negative harmonization.   [146] Article 95(2) TEC.

[147] See comments of the Advocate-General in Joined Cases C-376/98 and C-74/99 *Germany* v. *European Parliament* and *R* v. *Secretary of State for Health, ex parte Imperial Tobacco Ltd* [2000] ECR I-8419, para 63.

[148] Directive 2002/21/EC (Framework Directive); Directive 2002/20/EC (Authorization Directive); Directive 2002/19/EC (Access Directive); Directive 2002/22/EC (Universal Service Directive) and Directive 2002/58/EC; (Data Protection and Electronic Communications Directive). NB previous ONP Directive also based on Article 95.

why telecommunications services should have been dealt with in this way, as they clearly constitute services and it would seem more natural to use the service specific provisions, or indeed other provisions on Trans-European Networks. By contrast, the Television without Frontiers Directive,[149] which concerns the creation of the internal market in television services, was based on Article 47(2) TEC, that is the provisions relating to services. This inconsistency in approach between types of communication service does not seem to be capable of explanation on the characteristics of the services themselves. The decisions may have been influenced by considerations about the respective involvement in the law-making process of the various institutions and the sensitivity to the Television Without Frontiers Directive. Given the extension of the qualified majority voting and co-decision procedures, the significance of this boundary, at least in terms of the respective strength of the political institutions within the European Union, is likely to diminish, though political influences on categorization are unlikely to disappear entirely.

The fact that separate treaty provisions deal with the free movement of goods and services, which is to some extent repeated in the law-making provisions, suggests that a distinction should be made between the two provisions, an assumption which is supported by decisions of the Court of Justice that indicate that the four freedoms are mutually exclusive.[150] Furthermore, the terms of Article 50 state that the provisions relating to services apply to services 'insofar as they are not governed by the provisions relating to the freedom of movement of goods, capital and persons'. This distinction between the freedoms, however, may be of lesser significance now than might hitherto have been thought.

Some commentators have argued that the jurisprudence of the Court of Justice over the last decade has suggested a convergence in approach towards the various freedoms, specifically one which focuses on the need to ensure access to markets throughout the Member States and which borrows authorities from the jurisprudence in relation to one freedom to another.[151] On this basis, the categorization as goods or services is less significant, as the same conclusion is likely to be reached whichever provision is used.

Although there is clearly some merit in this argument, one cannot suggest that there is no difference in the scope between goods and services. In this there are similarities to the questions faced by the WTO about whether the structural distinction reflects a difference in the way goods and services should be (or are) treated. The crucial difference relates to the scope of Article 28 as opposed to Article 49 (and arguably even Article 29). The original scope of Article 28 EC was uncertain. The central question was whether it only operated to catch those

---

[149] Directive 89/552/EEC as amended by Directive 97/36/EC.

[150] Case 74/76 *Iannelli* v. *Meroni* [1977] ECR 557, para 9. See also Case 7/68 *Commission* v. *Italy* (Re Export Tax on Art Treasures) [1968] ECR 428.

[151] Behrens [1992] EUR 145, Barnard, *'Fitting the Remaining Pieces into the Goods and Persons Jigsaw?'* 26(1) E L Rev. 35–39 (2001).

measures that were overtly discriminatory. The cases of *Dassonville*[152] and *Cassis de Dijon*[153] made clear that the scope of Article 28 would not be so limited; it could apply to 'indistinctly applicable' rules which nonetheless might affect trade. The actual test for the application of Article 28 in *Dassonville* was so broad that an actual impact on trade would not be required.[154] This point is illustrated by the infamous *Sunday Trading* cases,[155] where an English rule which prohibited trading on a Sunday, irrespective of the origin of goods, was found to fall within Article 28. In that case, there had been no proof of an actual effect on inter-State trade.

Following much criticism of the 'over -extension' of Article 28, whereby virtually any a rule which had a potential impact on trading goods could fall within Article 28, the Court of Justice limited the scope of Article 28.[156] It sought to distinguish between those indistinctly applicable rules which did have an impact of intra-Community trade and those which did not. This was significant because, as has famously been noted, Article 28 delimits the boundary between legitimate and illegitimate Member State action[157] (ie that which is compatible with the terms of the Treaty and that which is not) and thereby affects the scope of Member State national competence in other fields, such as consumer or environmental protection.[158]

The case in which this change occurred was *Keck*.[159] It concerned French rules prohibiting sales at a loss. Keck, who operated in a border town, argued that the national rule affected his ability to sell imported goods, following the line of reasoning established in the *Sunday Trading* cases. After expressly stating that it was overturning some of its previous decisions (but not identifying which ones), the Court of Justice held that 'selling arrangements', which apply equally in law and in fact, would not fall within the scope of Article 28. 'Selling arrangements' include rules relating to opening hours for example, as in the *Sunday Trading*

---

[152] Case 8/74 *Procureur du Roi* v. *Dassonville et al.* [1974] ECR 837.

[153] Case 120/78 *Rewe* v. *Bundesmonopolverwaltung fur Branntwein (Cassis de Dijon)* [1979] ECR 649.

[154] The *Dassonville* test reads: '[a]ll trading rules enacted by Member States which are capable of hindering, directly or indirectly, actually or potentially, intra-Community trade are to be considered as measures having an effect equivalent to quantitative restrictions.'

[155] Case 145/88 *Torfaen BC* v. *B & Q plc* [1989] ECR 3851.

[156] See eg J. Steiner, *Drawing the Line: Uses and Abuses of Article 30 EEC*, 29 C.M.L.Rev. 749 (1992); Mortelmans *Article 30 of the EEC Treaty and legislation relating to market circumstances: time to consider a new definition?*; 28 C.M.L.Rev (1991); and White *In Search of Limits to Article 30 of the EEC Treaty*, 26 C.L.Rev. 235 (1989) who both suggested that the then Article 30 had been overextended. Contrast L. Gormley *Commentary on Torfaen BC v. B&Q*, 27 C.M.L.Rev. (1990) and W. Wils *The Search for the rule in Article 30 EEC: Much ado about nothing?* (1993) E.L.Rev. 475 who express views in favour of a broad interpretation of Article 28.

[157] W. Wils *The Search for the rule in Article 30 EEC: Much ado about nothing?* ibid.

[158] Note that even when justifying a national measure, a Member State still lies within the scope of Community law. Such areas do not fall outside the scope of the Treaty entirely. In this there is a distinction between the tradability function (section III) and non-trade values in general. For commentary on the ECJ's approach to balancing competing interests, see eg S. Weatherill *Recent case law concerning the free movement of goods: mapping the frontiers of market deregulation*, 36 (1), C. M. L. Rev. 51–85 (1999)

[159] Joined Cases C-267 and 268/91 *Keck and Mithouard* [1993] ECR I-6097.

cases, or advertising. 'Requirements to be met' or 'product requirements,' which are rules relating to the content of a product such as recipe or packaging rules, would continue to fall within Article 28. In adopting this approach, the Court of Justice seems to be distinguishing between those rules which impose an additional burden on imported products and those rules which, although they may affect access to the market, do not impose a specific additional burden on imports. One might also argue that product requirements affect the tangible condition of the goods; selling arrangements do not. Although the precise impact of *Keck* has been the subject of some debate, it is clear that the notion of 'selling arrangement' has limited the field of application of Article 28.[160]

Subsequently, in *Alpine Investments*,[161] which concerned national rules prohibiting cold calling as a mechanism for selling financial services, it was argued that the distinction between 'selling arrangements' and 'product requirements' should also apply in the context of services. The Court of Justice rejected this argument on the facts, but did not specify whether the *Keck* distinction could ever apply to services. Although the precise position is not clear,[162] it is normally accepted that rules concerning 'selling arrangements' in relation to services may fall within Article 49. Although more recent case law might suggest that the Court of Justice is, at least in some circumstances, seeking to limit the application of the selling arrangements argument in the goods context,[163] the seeming exclusion of the *Keck* distinction from the services jurisprudence would suggest that the scope of Article 28 is now narrower than that of Article 49, thereby re-emphasizing the significance within the European Community of making a distinction between goods and services.

It might be suggested that the Court of Justice in characterizing an issue as relating to services rather than to goods, extends the possibility of reviewing national measures for compliance with Community principles. There are parallels here with the approach of the WTO in *Canada-Autos*, when the issue was considered under the goods regime, thus allowing the matter to come within the scope of the WTO.[164] In the context of the European Union, for example, in *de Coster*[165] a tax imposed on satellite dishes was considered to be the provision of transfrontier

---

[160] This discussion does not arise in relation to Article 29 EC concerning exports; Article 29 is triggered only when a two-stage test involving discrimination is satisfied.

[161] Case C-384/93 *Alpine Investments BV* v. *Minister van Financiën* [1995] ECR I-1141.

[162] See eg S. Enchelmeier *The awkward selling of a good idea or a traditionalist interpretation of Keck* 22 Y.E.L. 249–322 (2003); S. Weatherill *After Keck: Some thoughts on how to Clarify the Clarification* 33(5) C.M.L.Rev. 885 (1996). As will be discussed below, the position is more uncertain following Case C-405/98 *Konsumentombudsmannen* v. *Gourmet International Products* [2001] ECR I-1795, discussed also in P. Koutrakos *On Groceries, Alcohol and Olive Oil: more on Free Movement of Goods after Keck* 26(4) E.L.Rev. 391 (2001); A. Kaczorowska '*Gourmet* can his *Keck* and eat it!' 10(4) E.L.J. 479 (2004).

[163] Case C-405/98 *Konsumentombudsmannen* v. *Gourmet International Products AB* [2001] ECR I-1795 but contrast Case C-71/02 *Herbert Karner Industrie-Auktionen GmbH* v. *Troostwijk GmbH*, [2004] 2 CMLR 5.   [164] See section I.

[165] Case C-17/00) *De Coster* v. *College des Bourgmestre et Echevins de Watermael Boitsfort* [2001] ECR I-9445.

television services rather than goods.[166] It was found to be contrary to Article 49; it is questionable whether such a measure would have fallen within the scope of Article 28. *De Coster* and the boundary between the two categories is discussed in the next section. It should, however, be noted that there is another linked question, which will be discussed further below; that is, should the provisions relating to goods and services be applied cumulatively or in the alternative?[167] A cumulative approach could extend the possible scope of review by the European Union of national laws.

B. Definition of Goods

Notwithstanding any questions about why one might wish to distinguish between goods and services within the jurisprudence of the Court of Justice, it is clear that such a distinction has been made. So, how are goods and services defined within the European Union context? As part of this question, a further issue arises: is there a difference between goods (or services) in a general sense, as opposed to their meaning within the TEC? Re-phrased, are there categories of goods and services that fall outside the TEC altogether? Essentially, this is the argument seen in the content of cultural products within the WTO.[168] The investigation starts by looking at the definition of goods, taking into account this question, and then considering that of services, before trying to identify where the boundary between the two categories lies.

The starting point of any analysis must be the TEC. Although it gives some clues as to the scope of 'services', providing a partial definition in Article 50 TEC, it is silent on the meaning of 'goods'. Indeed, despite the centrality of the free movement of goods to the European project, many of the relevant provisions do not refer to 'goods' at all. Instead we see references to 'imports', for example Article 28 EC, and 'exports', Article 29 EC. Confusingly for those used to the terminology in the WTO, the TEC will also refer to 'products'[169] and mean 'goods' to the exclusion of 'services'. Despite the varying terminology, it seems that the Court of Justice has adopted a common approach to the meaning of 'goods' across the various articles.

Arguments about the scope of the goods provisions arose quite early in the Court of Justice's jurisprudence.[170] The question was not whether the items in question, which were art treasures, were goods as an abstract notion but whether they were goods for the purposes of the TEC.[171] The national rule at issue was an Italian law which imposed taxes on the export of objects of historical, ethnographic

---

[166] Contrast discussion on pay television in Section III.
[167] Note approach within WTO is cumulative and not alternative: see *Bananas*, above section I.
[168] See discussion of tradability function below section III.
[169] See eg, Article 32 EC, Article 90 EC.
[170] Case 7/68 *Commission* v. *Italy* [1968] ECR 428.
[171] Contrast the approach of the WTO in *Canada-Periodicals*, above n 70.

or artistic importance. The Commission argued that the imposition of taxes was contrary to the prohibition on customs duties contained in the Treaty. The Italians countered by suggesting that art treasures were not goods for the purposes of the Treaty because of their cultural nature. The Court of Justice rejected this argument, defining goods as products which have a monetary value ascribed to them and as such can then form the basis of a commercial transaction.

The *Art Treasures* case can therefore be seen as significant in two respects: it excludes the notion that items which have a non-trade value lie outside the scope of the TEC[172]; it also provides the definition for goods, which has been used in the context of rules relating to non-tariff barriers as well as customs duties. Central to this definition is that the products must be capable of being the subject matter of trade. In relation to non-trade issues or Member States' concerns of public interest, these are protected within the European Union legal order by specific provisions derogating from the Treaty freedoms. The question whether the Court of Justice maintained the right balance between the free movement of goods and other policy issues has been much debated in academic literature, but a review of this issue lies outside the scope of this article.[173]

Although the *Art Treasures case*,[174] provides a starting point, it does leave some questions unanswered, notably whether items which have no 'value in money' should be considered goods. This issue came before the Court in the *Belgian Waste case*[175] which concerned, amongst other types of waste, waste that was neither reusable nor recyclable. On the facts, if the waste had a value at all, it had a negative value.[176] How would waste be dealt with in the light of the two-pronged test identified in the Italian *Art Treasures* case? The Court of Justice focused on the second element of that test that is the commercial transaction element.[177] According to the Court of Justice:

objects which are shipped across borders for the purposes of commercial transactions are subject to Article [28] et seq. of the Treaty, including non-recyclable waste.[178]

---

[172] Note the comments of Advocate-General La Pegola in Case C-124/97 *Markku Juhani Läärä, Cotswold Microsystems Ltd, Oy Transatlantic Software Ltd* v. *Kihlakunnansyyttäjä (Jyväskylä), Suomen Valtio (Finnish State)* [1999] ECR I-6067 at para 18, which suggest that only lawful transactions are protected by Article 28, which would suggest a contrary view to that which excludes all ethical considerations from the question of whether the Treaty freedoms might apply, as the *Art Treasures* case seems to imply. This seems to be quite an isolated opinion and this argument may be developing too much significance from what is essentially *obiter dicta*. Contrast the discussion about non-trade concerns within the WTO.

[173] In the field of human rights contrast the views of Coppell and O'Neill, *The European Court: Taking Rights Seriously?* 29 C.M.L.Rev 669 (1992) and Weiler and Lockhart *Taking Rights Seriously: The European Court and Its Fundamental Rights Jurisprudence* 32 C.M.L.Rev. 51 and 579 (1995); G. van Calster, *Court Criticizes Restrictions on Free Movement of Waste* 24 E.L.Rev. 170 (1999); Weatherill, S., *Recent case law concerning the Free Movement of Goods: Mapping the Frontiers of Market Deregulation'* 36 C.M.L.Rev. 51 (1999).   [174] Case 7/68 *Commission* v. *Italy*, above n 170.

[175] Case C-2/90 *Commission* v. *Belgium (Walloon Waste)* [1992] ECR I-4431.

[176] In some cases concerning disposal of waste, it has been suggested that the case be dealt with as a matter of services: the ECJ has not yet accepted this argument. On the boundary between goods and services, see further below.   [177] See discussion on commercial capability, section III.

[178] Ibid., para 26.

It seems that the central notion in determining the applicability of the goods provisions is whether there is an object of a type which is likely to be the subject of a commercial transaction, even where the transaction may involve the provision of a service such as the disposal of waste.

In adopting this approach, the Court of Justice seems to be adopting a natural language-based definition based on the ability to trade and to transfer the product. Emphasis is also placed on the tangible nature of the product, implied by the use of the word 'object'.[179] The implicit centrality of tangibility to the definition of goods can be seen in other cases[180] and it should be noted that in many instances where items are self-evidently goods, the Court of Justice does not consider whether there is a commercial transaction in issue in the case. Thus, any items which are not the immediate subject matter of a contract may also benefit from the free movement of goods provisions; this would include, for example, goods taken on holiday and returned to the state of origin, as well as goods bought on holiday. In considering the nature of the commercial transaction, the Court of Justice emphasized to clarify that the commercial transaction in issue need not involve the transfer of ownership.[181] This position is not unproblematic: some cases involving, for example, the long-lease of cars have been held to fall within the services provisions.[182]

C. Services

Articles 49 and 50 identify the scope of the freedom to provide services, both in terms of the nature of the services themselves and as regards those who may benefit from the right. Article 50 states that services for the purposes of the Treaty are those that are provided for remuneration, insofar as they are not governed by the provisions relating to the other treaty freedoms on goods, capital and persons. Article 51 excludes the transport sector from the scope of Article 49. Special provisions applying to this sector are contained in Articles 70–80 TEC, although in some cases Article 49 has also been relevant. A list of examples in Article 50 TEC states that activities of an industrial or commercial character fall within the definition of services, as do the activities of professionals or craftsmen. Thus, although it gives examples, the Treaty does not outline the characteristics of services as a general concept.[183] It seems implicit from this open definition that the precise scope of services is not clear, being defined almost by what they are not.

---

[179] The definition in Oxford English Dictionary includes 'thing placed before eyes or presented to sense, material thing, thing observed with optical instrument or represented in picture', though there are of course alternative meanings not relevant to this context in which 'object' is intangible. Contrast the wording used in the *Art Treasures* case, above n 172 'product', which does not carry the same inescapable meaning in the natural language. See below section III.

[180] See *Sacchi*, above n 106, discussed further below.

[181] Contrast discussion in section III.

[182] Case C-451/99 *Cura Anlagen GmbH* v. *ASL* [2002] ECR I-3193; see further below.

[183] The approach in GATS mirrors this: see Article 1 GATS, above section I.

Certainly, the question of what a service is has never been answered particularly clearly and in some instances the Community institutions have had difficulty identifying the scope of a service in a given case.[184] No sector is excluded in principle from the scope of the EC Treaty, so, it seems that the potential category of services is wide indeed.[185] In principle it seems that no specific category is excluded from the potential ambit of the TEC[186] and it is generally accepted that the morality and desirability, or otherwise, of the provision of a particular service will not affect its categorization for purposes of EU law as a service.[187]

This is similar to the approach adopted in relation to the definition of goods, as illustrated by the *Art Treasures* case and the fact that cultural goods fall within the scope of the Treaty as well as with the approach taken in the context of the WTO. The apparent intention is to adopt the widest possible interpretation of the relevant provisions to ensure the maximum number of national measures come under review, thus increasing the effectiveness of the TEC (or WTO). Further, although the Treaty contains certain derogation provisions on which national rules may be justified, the Court of Justice has developed a further category of justifications which is broader and may be used in relation to non-discriminatory national measures which in principle trigger the application of the free movement provisions. The scope for derogation therefore seems broader under the TEC than under the WTO, which may be why non-trade concerns have been less of an issue in this context. In addition, the Community is supposed to take certain non-trade concerns into account, such as sustainable development, when developing and implementing its policies.[188]

Although the terms of Article 49 cover the situation in which a person travels temporarily to another Member State to provide a service there, the freedom to provide services is broader than this. As the Court of Justice made clear:

. . the freedom to provide services includes the freedom, for recipients of services, to go to another Member State in order to receive a service there, without being obstructed by

---

[184] See Case 352/85 *Bond van Adverteerders* [1988] ECR 2085. One might suggest that there are parallels with the approach of the GATS in this context, but contrast the reasoning in the Telecommunications Report in which the services definition was described as being comprehensive, para 7.41.

[185] In many cases the ECJ does not discuss which of the freedoms are appropriate and in some instances may seem to have come to inconsistent decisions. This point was noted early in the Community's life: see W. Van Gerven, *The Right of Establishment and Free Supply of Services within the Common Market* 3 C.M.L.Rev. 344, 160 (1965–6).

[186] See Case C-159/90 *Society for the Protection of Unborn Children* v. *Grogan* [1991] ECR I-4685 at 4739;, Case C-275/92 *H.M. Customs and Excise* v. *Schindler et al.* [1994] ECR I-1039 at 1089–1090; Case 36/74 *Walrave and Koch* v. *Association Union Cycliste Internationale et al.* [1974] ECR 1405 at 1417; Case C-158/96 *Kohll* v. *Union des Caisses de Maladie* [1998] ECR I-1931; Case 263/86 *Belgian State* v. *René and Marie Thérèse Humbel* [1988] ECR 5365; Case C-415/93; *Union Royale Belge des Societes de Football Association ASBL* v. *Jean-Marc Bosman* [1995] ECR I-4921, [1996] 1 C.M.L.R. 645; and Joined Cases C-51/96 and C-191/97 *Christelle Deliege* v. *Ligue Francophone de Judo et Discplines Associées ASBL et al.* [2000] ECR 1–2549.

[187] See discussion in Case 15/78 *Société Générale Alsacienne de Banque SA* v. *Koestler* [1978] ECR 1971.

[188] Article 6 TEC. See also Articles I-3(3) and III-119 of the European Constitution.

restrictions, even in relation to payments . . . tourists, persons receiving medical treatment and persons travelling for the purpose of education or business are to be regarded as the recipients of services.[189]

Since Article 49 originally envisaged the situation where a service provider is moving to another Member State (and not necessarily from the service provider's State of origin), it will cover the situation in which both service provider and recipients move to a third Member state. A fourth category can be identified: that is, when the services themselves move. In this situation services such as broadcasting, telecommunications and even banking and insurance are considered.

Although these possibilities might be considered analogous to the modes of supply identified by GATS, there is not an exact match and the 'mode of supply' terminology is not used within the European Union. In fact, the Court of Justice rarely considers this issue expressly, although one might suggest that the distinction between services and their modes of supply is implicit within the Community structure. As noted above, there are different treaty bases for harmonizing measures relating to different aspects of service provision. It is arguable that there is a different approach to cases involving the movement of persons (workers, establishment and some services cases), which are influenced by the concept of European citizenship,[190] and those in which the service moves, which do not refer to citizenship.[191]

In the context of goods, it did not matter whether the goods in a particular case were the subject of a commercial contract for the purposes of the EC Treaty. In services, although a parallel approach would seem desirable in principle, there is a crucial difference between the goods provisions and those relating to services. Whilst there is no definition of goods, there is a limited definition of services which specifies that services should be provided 'for remuneration'. This reinforces the economic element of the definition of a service. Does this requirement mean, however, that we are looking for services of that type that are generally provided for remuneration, or for those which are provided for remuneration in a given set of circumstances?

Initially, the question came before the Court of Justice in the context of education. The Advocate General noted that, '[s]tate education, however, like health care, is *largely* financed from State taxes'.[192] It was eventually decided that State education fell outside the scope of Article 49 TEC, so this might be taken as implying that it will be necessary to look at each individual case to determine whether remuneration existed. The Court of Justice did not expressly develop the

---

[189] Case 186/87 *Cowan* v. *French Treasury* [1989] ECR 195, para 16.

[190] Article 18 TEC.

[191] This issue will be unique to the European Union; issues of citizenship do not arise within the context of the WTO.

[192] Case 263/86 *Belgian State* v. *René and Marie Thérèse Humbel* [1988] ECR 5365, 5379 (authors' emphasis).

point. A similar approach was taken in other cases concerning public education. As the Advocate General in *Wirth* argued:

the possibility that a provision of services is involved cannot be ruled out when the tuition or studies are financed entirely or essentially out of contributions from the students . . .[193]

It could be suggested that there was a difference between educational services depending on who provided them and how they were paid for; ie the question whether a situation fell within the definition of 'services' for the purposes of Article 49 would be decided on a case-by-case basis. In *Wirth* the Court of Justice seemed to accept the distinction between private and State-provided education without ruling on the general point about the scope of services.[194]

Other cases concerning tourism take a different view. To determine whether a service falls within Article 49, the approach in these cases suggests the type of service as a general issue should be looked at rather than the individual case.[195] Furthermore, the emphasis on the precise existence of a contract, implicit in the education cases, is weakened in a move towards the 'commercial character' approach we find in the goods jurisprudence. For example, in a number of cases concerning broadcast advertising, the Court of Justice was not concerned with who was paying for the broadcast programming provided it was paid for.[196] This development has the effect of suggesting that an approach based on the *type* of services has now been adopted, rather than looking to see if there is a commercial transaction (one based on remuneration) in a given case. In this regard we can see parallels between the goods and services jurisprudence being developed; certainly a potential distinction has been eradicated.

D. Boundary between goods and services

The Court of Justice has generally taken the view that where the service is the main object of the transaction, the issue falls under Article 49, even though the Treaty specifies that the services provisions are residuary in character. For example, in *Schindler*,[197] which concerned the import of lottery tickets into the United

---

[193] Case C-109/92 *Stephan Max Wirth* v. *Landeshauptstadt Hannover* [1993] ECR I-6447, para 12, 6456.

[194] For another example of another area in which the distinction between economic and non-economic is significant, see the case law on sport: Case C-415/93 *Union Royale Belge des Societes de Football Association ASBL* v. *Jean-Marc Bosman* [1995] ECR I-4921 and Joined Cases C-51/96 and C-191/97 *Christelle Deliege* v. *Ligue Francophone de Judo et Discplines Associées ASBL et al.* [2000] ECR I-2549.

[195] Case 186/87 *Cowan* v. *French Treasury* [1989] ECR 195; and Case C-274/96 *Criminal proceedings against Horst Otto Bickel and Ulrich Franz* [1998] ECR I-7637.

[196] Even within the public sector, which following the education cases might have been thought to lie outside the scope of the Treaty, there have been developments in the field of health care. These cases again operate to blur the boundary between public (funded by taxation system) and private (direct payment, or payment via an- insurance company) provision of a service, thereby removing the significance of the payment mechanism in a specific case: Case 352/85 *Bond van Adverteerders* [1988] ECR 2085.   [197] Case C-275/92 *Schindler* [1994] ECR I-1039.

Kingdom, the tickets were found to be merely instrumental to the provision of the game of chance, a service.[198] Significantly, the tickets had no value in themselves but only as evidence of participation in the game of chance. Similarly, in *van Schaik*,[199] the Court of Justice found the supply of car parts was incidental to the contract for services to repair the car. By contrast, in the case of manufacture of goods, because the process 'leads directly to the manufacture of a physical article', manufacture is viewed as the supply of goods rather than the provision of manufacturing services.[200]

The boundary is not always clear. A number of cases concerning the processing of waste, which might be considered to constitute the provision of a service, have been dealt with as concerning a prohibition on the export of goods.[201] Equally, the Court of Justice has gone to great lengths to emphasize that commercial contracts need not involve the transfer of ownership to trigger the protection of the goods provisions, yet in some leasing cases it has held that what is in issue is a service because what is being supplied is not the object itself but the use of the object.[202] In some of the services cases discussed below, the legal relationship between product and trader is not necessarily considered.[203]

More questions arise where an item is required for the provision of a service: in a Dutch case concerning the acquisition of surgeons' scalpels the Court held that the goods provisions were applicable.[204] In doing so, it was following the approach adopted in the *Dundalk Water* case, in which it was held that:

[t]he fact that a public works contract relates to the provision of services cannot remove a clause in an invitation to tender restricting the materials that may be used from the scope of the prohibitions set out in Article [28].[205]

These cases do not sit easily with cases like *van Schaik*, where the provision of goods was absorbed into the provision of services.[206] *Dundalk Water* may have been the product of its own time; at that stage the goods jurisprudence was broader and better developed than the case law relating to services. Another factor may be the question whether the goods remain separate and have a capital value themselves. For example, in *Schindler* the Court of Justice noted that the only value of the lottery tickets was as evidence of the service, the game of chance. By

---

[198] Approach affirmed in Case C-42/02 *Lindman*, judgment of 13 November 2003.
[199] Case C-55/93 *van Schaik* [1994] ECR I-4837.
[200] Case 18/84 *Commission* v. *France* (Tax Breaks) [1985] ECR 1339.
[201] Case C-209/98 *FFAD* v. *Københavns Kommune* [2000] ECR I-3743.
[202] Case C-294/97 *Eurowings Luftverkehr* [1999] ECR I-7447, para 33, confirmed in Case C-451/99 *Cura Anlagen GmbH* v. *ASL*, judgment of 21 March 2002.
[203] See, for example, *de Coster* where it seemed entirely irrelevant to the discussion as to whether de Coster owned the satellite dish or was merely hiring it, for example from a satellite television service provider.
[204] Cases C-157–160/94 *Commission* v. *Netherlands* [1997] ECR I-5699, paras 15–20 and the Opinion of the Advocate General, para 15.
[205] Case 45/87 *Commission* v. *Ireland* (Dundalk Water) [1988] ECR 4929, para 17.
[206] See also Case C-108/96 *Denis Mac Quen et al; de Coster*.

contrast in *Läärä*,[207] the Court found that gaming machines were goods with a capital value, in addition to being necessary for the provision of gambling services.

The question of the boundary between goods and services in relation to the import of gaming machines arose again in *Anomar*.[208] There were two issues: one related to the distinction between rules relating to the import and distribution of gaming machines as opposed to their operation, the other concerned the issue of whether the two sets of rules were severable. The Court of Justice followed the approach in *Läärä* applied, arguing:

[e]ven though the operation of slot machines is linked to operations to import them, the former activity comes under the provisions of the Treaty relating to the freedom to provide services and the latter under those relating to the free movement of goods.[209]

Confusingly, the Court then added:

[t]he activity of operating gaming machines must, irrespective of whether or not it is separable from activities relating to the manufacture, importation and distribution of such machines, be considered a service within the meaning of the Treaty and, accordingly, it cannot come within the scope of Articles 28 EC and 29 EC relating to the free movement of goods.[210]

Although *Anomar* and *Läärä* may be consistent in identifying the independent existence of gaming machines as key in determining the boundary between goods and services, in the light of cases such as *de Coster* (discussed below), it is hard to discover a consistent rule within the cases applied by the Court of Justice, thus adding an element of uncertainty into the jurisprudence.

Anomar raises another question: that is whether goods and services provisions should be applied cumulatively or in the alternative. A linked issue is whether the goods provisions should be applied, given the wording of Article 50 TEC, in preference to Article 49 TEC. *Anomar* is not clear: on the one hand it suggests that the import of gaming machines is an issue to be dealt with as goods. Looking at the rules as a question relating to imports and therefore goods suggests the possibility of two situations that may be assessed separately: one dealing with imports, the other dealing with the operation of gambling services. One might argue that the existence of different national measures creating separate violations of the TEC justify treating the situations individually, despite the same products being in issue each time. Despite this, the Court of Justice finally dealt with the issue as a question of services and services alone. *Anomar* can be contrasted with the approach taken in *GIP*, where the same national measure was viewed as affecting different markets: the sale of the product subject to the advertising restrictions; and on the provision of advertising services. This judgment would seem either to dilute

207 Case C-124/97 *Läärä and Others* [1999] ECR I-6067.
208 Case C-6/01 *Associação Nacional de Operadores de Máquinas Recreativas (Anomar) and Others* v. *Estado português*, judgment 11 September 2003.   209 *Anomar*, ibid., para 55.
210 *Anomar*, ibid., para 56.

the principle that only one of the four freedoms should apply to a given situation, by constructing different 'situations' based on the same set of facts and national rules; or, blur the distinction between goods and services, at least in this context. The approach seems to be the reverse of that taken in *Anomar* on two levels. In *Anomar*, there were arguably two sets of rules in issue yet the judgment suggests the rules concern services to the exclusion of goods, irrespective of whether the two situations are severable or not. In *GIP*, one set of rules seemed to be capable of being subject to different treaty provisions.

The reasoning in *Anomar* suggests that goods and services be applied in the alternative, and it also appears to reverse the order of preference expressed in the treaty: despite their residual quality, the services provisions are being applied in preference to the goods provisions. This approach may seem unproblematic when services are clearly in issue but when import rules seem to be subsumed under the services provision as here, difficulties arise.

A similar concern could be expressed in relation to *de Coster*. In *de Coster*, the question would be why were the services provisions applicable rather than the goods rules; a separate question is whether there are two separate legal situations, as the Court of Justice created in *GIP* and arguably existed in *Anomar*.

Within the European Union legal order this question has significance which may not translate the WTO, especially in relation to the possible viewing of advertising as a second legal situation subject to the Treaty, as we saw in *GIP*. As noted above, following the *Keck* case, national rules restricting 'selling arrangements' will not necessarily be caught by Article 28; by contrast, national rules affecting advertising services would clearly fall within Article 49.

Initially, at least, the Court of Justice appears to adopt the former approach, as can be seen in cases involving auctioneers,[211] as well as those relating to broadcast advertising.[212] As noted in *GIP*,[213] which concerned restrictions on the advertisement of alcoholic beverages in magazines available at the point of sale, the Court considered both the impact on the goods and on the provision of advertising services of the impugned rules.[214] The extent to which *GIP* can be seen as a rule having general application has been cast into doubt by *Karner*,[215] handed down in 2004. *Karner* concerned a national rule limiting how the advertising of auctions, with particular reference to sales of goods from insolvent estates. This rule was held to be a 'selling arrangement' and therefore fell outside the scope of Article 28. The question was whether Article 49 could be used in relation to the impact on cross border advertising. Although the Court

---

[211] Case C-239/90 *SCP Boscher, Studer et Frometin* v. *SA British Motors Wright and Others* [1991] ECR I-202–3.

[212] Case C-412/93 *Société d'Importation Edouard Leclerc-Siplec* v. *TF 1 Publicité SA and M6 Publicité SA* [1995] ECR I-179; Joined Cases C–34–36/95 *Konsumentombudsmannen* v. *de Agostini and TV Shop* [1997] ECR I-3843.

[213] Case C-405/98 *Konsumentombudsmannen* v. *Gourmet International Products AB*, above n 162.

[214] In Case C-405/98 (*GIP*), above n 162. it was also suggested, by contrast to *Keck*, above n 159, that the rules did fall within Article 28. [215] Also see discussion in *Anomar* above.

of Justice did not exclude the possibility of Article 49 being used in this way it held:

Where a national measure relates to both the free movement of goods and freedom to provide services, the Court will in principle examine it in relation to one only of those two fundamental freedoms if it appears that, in the circumstances of the case, one of them is entirely secondary in relation to the other and may be considered together with it.[216]

This approach has the advantage of treating all goods/services boundary disputes where double application is possible in the same way. As we have seen, however, the Court of Justice has not been consistent in its approach in this area; how will the national courts fare when asked to answer this issue as 'a matter of fact'?

The area in which problems determining the boundary between goods and services has arisen concerns intangible products. It is generally considered that one of the differences between goods and services is that while the latter are intangible, the former are tangible.[217] In respect of some products, especially those relating to the entertainment and information businesses, this distinction may be sometimes hard to apply. In the early case of *Sacchi*, the Court had to determine whether broadcasting should be viewed as falling within the goods or services provisions. It adopted the latter position, a view it has subsequently reaffirmed,[218] arguing that:

trade in material sound recordings and other products used for the diffusion of television signals are subject to the rules relating to the freedom of movement for goods.[219]

Although the point has not been developed, it would appear from this that the Court of Justice focused on the mechanism of transmission to distinguish between the same product (e.g. seeing a film on video or seeing on television) and the product's physical nature. One might suggest, however, that it is consistent with the approach in *Anomar* and *Läärä* because the technical means of transmission has a value independent of the service provided. For example, blank videos and cds have a separate value, even if they have a specific, service-related function.

It is, however, debatable whether the Court of Justice has consistently maintained the distinction between material items and non-material or intangible items. In *de Coster* in which satellite dishes were in issue,[220] the Court did not even consider the question of whether the matter should be viewed as goods. Even if this is justified by reference to the fact that the satellite box is clearly tied in to the provision of a service and has no function outside that,[221] *de Coster* is inconsistent

---

[216] *Karner*, above n 163, para 46. This approach might be seen to be in direct contrast to the approach in *Bananas*.   [217] See section III for a fuller discussion.

[218] See e.g. Case 52/79 *Procureur du Roi* v. *Debauve* [1980] ECR 833. In more recent cases it has often not considered the question of whether goods or services provisions are relevant.

[219] Case 155/78 *Sacchi* [1974] ECR 409, para 7.

[220] Consider also the approach to hire contracts discussed earlier.

[221] Thereby in a position analogous to goods which are incorporated during the provision of a service, as discussed above.

with the wording of *Sacchi* which specifies that items for transmission or reception of signals constitute goods.

Although one might suggest that the lack of analysis in *de Coster* hides a pragmatic desire to ensure that the national measure fell within the TEC, on one view de *Coster* perhaps reflects the better position.[222] The emphasis on the form of a product has been criticized[223]; it may give rise to difficulties with the development of digital products and artificial distinctions between the same products delivered via different mechanisms: for example, do different rules apply to music sold on compact discs as opposed to those downloaded directly from the Internet?[224]

Equally, the Court of Justice is not necessarily consistent in other cases as to whether the material, or tangible, nature of a product is definitive or not in determining whether goods or services rules should apply. It has, indeed, held that electricity should be viewed as goods.[225] The Court did not explain this finding, although the Advocate General suggested, that this approach is 'perhaps justifiable by virtue of its function as an energy source and, therefore, its competition with gas and oil'.[226]

From the discussion it appears that the WTO and the European Union suffer similar problems when determining where the boundary lies between goods and services. Whilst the solution does not lie in comparing both systems' jurisprudence, answers may be found by looking at the problem at a generic level.

III. Distinguishing Between Goods and Services: Defining the Boundary in a General Context

Determining where to place the boundary between goods and services for regulatory purposes is based on the premise that products comprising 'goods' differ fundamentally from those constituting 'services'.[227] Article 3:2 DSU makes it clear that the WTO rules can be interpreted 'in accordance with customary rules of public international law'. The Appellate Body has interpreted this statement to include the treaty interpretation tools in the Vienna Convention on the Law of Treaties (the Vienna Convention).[228] Article 31(1) of the Vienna Convention states that:

A treaty shall be interpreted in good faith in accordance with the ordinary meaning to be given to the terms of the treaty in their context and in the light of its object and purpose.

---

[222] Note in the jurisprudence on intellectual property rights and parallel imports, the ECJ has recognized the special nature of videos and dvds which links to the nature of them as products that can be repeatedly consumed.
[223] March Hunnings, N., *Casenote on Debauve and Coditel* 17 C.M.L.Rev. 560 (1980).
[224] Contrast approach in WTO which deals with this issue at the level of customs code.
[225] Case C-393/92 *Almelo* [1994] ECR I-1471.   [226] Ibid.
[227] In this context, the term 'products' is used to refer to both goods and services. Contrast the approach taken in EC law, discussed in section II.   [228] See above n 9.

This approach places the emphasis firmly on two aspects: first the 'ordinary meaning' of the language used and second, the 'context' in which the language is used.[229] Both the panels[230] and the Appellate Body[231] have interpreted these obligations to require an investigation into both the natural language construction of the wording and then the purpose which the rules are designed to fulfill. The discussion will take these issues in turn.

The Oxford English Dictionary perpetuates a distinction between both products, defining 'goods' as 'saleable commodities; merchandise or wares'.[232] 'Merchandise' is 'the commodities of commerce' or 'goods to be bought or sold',[233] with 'commodities' as 'a thing of use or value; *spec* a thing that is an object of trade'.[234] In contrast, 'services' are 'the sector of the economy that supplies the needs of the consumer but produces no tangible goods'.[235]

Focusing on services' dissimilarity to goods suggests that the starting point for deciding which category the product falls into is whether it constitutes goods, as it is only failure to meet the 'goods' test that pushes the product into the 'services' category.[236] The Oxford English Dictionary approach assumes that the definition of 'goods' is self-evident, deriving from the value of a tangible product measured in monetary terms which then allows that product to be traded. On this view, once tangibility and tradability are established, the product must be goods.

The notion of 'tangibility' refers to the product 'having material form',[237] which allows it to be 'touched; discernible or perceptible by touch'.[238] In essence, to satisfy the first characteristic in the definition from the Oxford English Dictionary, the product must have an inherent physical existence.[239] This idea is also prevalent in the economics literature.[240] Jagdish Bhagwati argues that it is this tangibility which results in different treatment of the product: for example, such products can be stored.[241] As a consequence, the producer can allow a period of time to elapse before the goods are disposed of, so proximity between the

---

[229] Article 31(2) Vienna Convention.

[230] See *Mexico-Telecommunications* above n 42, para 7.16.

[231] The Appellate Body noted in *United States-Reformulated Gasoline* that the WTO rules should not be interpreted in isolation from public international law. *United States-Reformulated Gasoline* above n 10, 17.

[232] The New Shorter Oxford English Dictionary on Historical Principles Volume 1 A-M, 1116 (Lesley Brown ed. in chief, 1993) (The OED).   [233] Ibid., 1744.

[234] Ibid., 452.

[235] The New Oxford English Dictionary on Historical Principles, Volume 2 N-Z, 2788 (Lesley Brown ed. in chief, 1993).

[236] See similarly approach taken by the EC Treaty, discussed above in section II.

[237] See above n 235 3216 (Vol II).   [238] Ibid., 3216.

[239] See also the Oxford English Dictionary definition of 'tangible': 'able to be touched; discernible or perceptible to touch; having material form'. Above n 235 Vol. 2, 3216.

[240] John David Donaldson, *Television Without Frontiers:' The Continuing Tension Between Liberal Free Trade and European Cultural Integrity*, 20 Fordham Int'l. L.J. 90 (1996), 123 & Jagdish Bhagwati, *Economic Perspectives on Trade in Professional Services*, 1. Uni. Chi. Leg. Forum (1986), 45; Robert E. Stern & Bernard Hoekman, *Negotiations in Services*, 10 World Economy 1 (1987), also see generally, Lorna M. Woods, Free Movement of Goods and Services Within the European Community (2004).   [241] Bhagwati, ibid. 45.

manufacturer and the ultimate consumer is not necessary.[242] In contrast 'services' are 'intangible', or 'not able to be touched',[243] generally because they must be consumed immediately on production and cannot be stored in the same way as goods.[244] Consequently, a certain degree of proximity between the service provider and consumer is necessary, increasing the likelihood of interaction between them both, unlike the position regarding goods where disposal of the product can be conducted at arms length.

In addition to showing that a product must have a physical manifestation to be designated 'goods', the dictionary definition suggests that the product also must be 'saleable',[245] a commodity of 'commerce'[246] and, specifically, 'an object of trade'.[247] On this view, the product must also have some inherent economic value indicated by its inclusion in the trade transaction.

Whilst the dictionary definition explicitly refers to a product's 'tradability' in relation to goods only, it is arguable that even products designated as 'services' must exhibit this 'tradability' characteristic[248]: the definition states that the product's supply and consumption takes place within the economy, first emphasizing the product's transfer from the producer to the consumer, even though tracking the physical transfer may not be as straightforward for the movement of services as for goods; and second that that transfer occurs in a commercial context usually for financial gain.[249]

Focusing on both these elements in the 'services' definition mirrors the Oxford English Dictionary's characterization of 'trade' as a transaction where products are bought and sold for profit.[250] For a product to satisfy the 'tradability' characteristic it must be transferred from one party to another (the transfer element)[251] and also be capable of being the subject of a commercial transaction (the commercial capability element).

The dictionary definition assumes that both the transfer and commercial capability elements are self-evident. However, both elements are based on other fundamental assumptions about the nature of the trade transaction, which make it possible to identify a distinct group of products that can be further sub-divided

---

[242] Bhagwati, ibid. 45. Note Bhagwati argues that not all services will require this close physical proximity, for example where a consumer applies for a bank loan via the internet, but that there will still be an on-going relationship between bank and client which may be helped by a closer relationship than occurs via trade in goods. This is a similar analysis to that adopted by the panel in *Mexico-Telecommunications* on the scope of the 'services at issue' in the dispute: above n 42 para 7.22.

[243] OED Vol 1, above n 232, 1386.   [244] Donaldson above n 106, 124.

[245] OED Volume 2 above n 235, 1116.   [246] Ibid. 1744.   [247] Ibid. 452.

[248] In *Mexico-Telecommunications*, the panel placed more emphasis on the mode of supply of the service, ie, the trade method, rather than on the inherent characteristics of the product themselves: above n 42 para 7.33.

[249] OED Vol I above n 232 definition of 'commerce' as 'carry on trade' and 'commercial' as 'interested in financial return rather than artistry; likely to make a profit' p. 451; also definition of 'economy' as 'the management or administration of resources (freq. financial)' p. 783.

[250] OED Vol II above n 235, 3357.

[251] The panel did point to 'ownership' transfer in *Mexico-Telecommunications* although it did not give a detailed explanation on this point: above n 42 para 7.33.

into goods and services. 'Tradability' therefore acts as a further device to filter out those products that cannot be classified as 'goods' or 'services' at all, but are instead *sui generis* and potentially outside any 'trade' regime completely.[252] On this view, 'tangibility' allows a differentiation between goods and services, whereas 'tradability', in this context, makes a distinction between those products which can be classed as goods or services and all other products which do not fall into either the goods or services definition at all.

By including the 'tradability' test, it is possible to exclude products from any regulatory framework which are incapable of transfer in the sense that it is not possible to transfer ownership from the producer to the consumer; for example in the case of national defence policies. In addition, products incapable of being the subject of a commercial transaction can also be excluded. This argument may have important implications, particularly in the WTO, because it recognizes that some products either have no value in the commercial sense, or they have a value which exceeds the price which would be placed on them if they were disposed of pursuant to a 'trade' transaction.[253]

Although the WTO is primarily a trading agreement where products are exchanged for their market value,[254] questions have been raised about the extent to which it should broaden its scope and include non-economic or more specifically, non-trade issues such as environmental concerns, labour rights, cultural concerns and human rights defined broadly.[255] Whilst the academic literature has explored the wider implications of the integration of non-trade concerns into the

---

[252] Note the problems with cultural products which some WTO members argue should fall outside the WTO rules completely: Richard L. Matheny, III, *In the Wake of the Flood: 'Like Products' and Cultural Products After the World Trade Organization's Decision in Canada Certain Measures Concerning Periodicals* 147 U.P.A.L.R. 245 (1998); W. Ming Shao, *Is There No Business Like Show Business? Free Trade and Cultural Protectionism*, 20 Y.J.Int'L.L. 105 (1995).

[253] Contrast the position in the EU, see section II above.

[254] Subject to subsidies and other questionable trade practices: see JH Jackson, WJ Davey & AO Sykes, Legal Problems of International Economic Relations: Cases, Materials and Text above n 14 generally.

[255] This has been an issue for the EU as well, see: Coppell and O'Neill *The European Court: Taking Rights Seriously?* 29 C.M.L.Rev. 669, (1992); and Weiler and Lockhart *Taking Rights Seriously: The European Court and Its Fundamental Rights Jurisprudence* 32 C.M.L.Rev. 51, (1995) and 579; G. van Calster, *Court Criticizes Restrictions on Free Movement of Waste* 24 E.L.Rev (1999). The literature on this area is vast in the WTO context, but the following provide a useful reference to the main issues, see José E. Alvarez (ed.), *Symposium, The Boundaries of the WTO*, 96 A.J.I.L. 1–159 (2002); Ernst-Ulrich Petersmann, *Human Rights and the Law of the World Trade Organization*, 37 Journal of World Trade, 241, (2003); Eleanor M. Fox, *Competition Law and the Millennium Round*, 2 J.Int'l. Econ. L. 665 (1999); Christopher McCrudden & Anne Davies, *A Perspective on Trade and Labor Rights*, 3 J.Int'l.Econ.L. 43 (2000); Thomas Cottier, *Trade and Human Rights: A Relationship to Discover*, 5 J.Int'l.Econ.L. 111 (2002); John H. Jackson, *World Trade Rules and environmental policies: congruence or conflict?* 49 Washington and Lee Law Review 1227, (1992); Ernst-Ulrich Petersmann, International and European Trade and Environmental Law After the Uruguay Round, (1995); Note the classic treatment of the trade and environment nexus in Daniel C. Esty, Greening the Gatt: Trade, Environment and the Future, (1994); Steve Charnowitz, Trade Law and Global Governance (2002); Steve Charnowitz, *The Moral Exception in Trade Policy*, 38 VA.J.Int'l.L. 689 (1998).

WTO scheme,[256] the debate within the WTO itself has been driven by its members' contributions to the multilateral trade negotiations, which initially focused on the pragmatic possibility of incorporating non-trade issues but premised on adapting the existing rules, rather than fundamentally rethinking the entire economic rationale of the treaty.[257]

A shift in the WTO debate means that the classification of products as non-trade issues may move them beyond the competence of the WTO completely, rather than classifying them as goods or services. The problems with cultural products, particularly in the audiovisual sector, are relevant in this context.[258] The European Union argued during the Uruguay Round of multilateral trade discussions that audiovisual products should be classified as trade in services rather than goods. Despite initial objections from the United States to the classification of the sector as involving trade in services,[259] the audiovisual sector is currently subject to discussions within the context of the GATS negotiations. Building on the existing exemption within GATS, the European Union and Canada are now arguing that the cultural content or value of audiovisual means that they have a worth outside the 'commercial' one traditionally within the competence of trade rules.[260] The heart of these members' argument is that the cultural content of such products means that they fall outside the scope of the multilateral trade rules completely.[261] Clearly, the classification decision in this case is taken on the basis of non-economic considerations, which feeds directly into the role that non-trade concerns play in the WTO.

Once a product has been categorized as one that is capable of being the subject of a trade transaction, then the economics literature indicates that the essential

[256] In the context of trade and human rights, see Petersmann, *Human Rights and the Law of the World Trade Organization* above n 255; see questions raised by Jackson in The World Trade Organization: Constitution and Jurisprudence 103 (1998) above n 2; Kent Jones, *The WTO Core Agreement, Non-Trade Issues and Institutional Integrity*, 1 World Trade Review 257, (2002).

[257] Even though some members are in fact looking to insert derogations from the economic rationale underpinning the WTO agreements by advocating the pursuit of non-trade goals in certain agreements: eg WTO, *Agriculture-Japan*, 28 June 1999, WT/GC/W/217.

[258] Note the substantial disagreement between the United States and the European Union during the Uruguay Round about the classification of audiovisual products as trade in goods or trade in services: An EBU document refers to a summary of the United States' initial request: '. . . the United States requests countries to schedule commitments that reflect current levels of market access in areas such as motion picture and home video entertainment production and distribution services, radio and television production services, and sound recording services'. EBU *WTO-Update on GATS Negotiations and Audiovisual Services*, February 18, 2003, available on EBU website: http://www.ebu.ch/ departments/ legal/topical/legal_t_gats_update.php. (last visited 22 January, 2005).

[259] It is not possible to say definitely that the US accepts the EU's interpretation that the audiovisual sector involves trade in goods, merely that they are not pushing the point in the current negotiations: see above n WTO 'US-Audiovisual Services' s/css/w/21 (18 December 2000) Para 10(1).

[260] This is an interesting position for the European Union to adopt, given the Court of Justice's position that all products are either goods or services, so very few fall outside the ambit of the EC treaty at all: see above section II European Communities, *Communication from the Commission to the Council and the European Parliament: Towards an International Instrument on Cultural Diversity*, COM(2003)520, (August 27, 2003) see S/CSS/W/74 & Madger above n 113.

[261] See WTO, *Communication from Switzerland: GATS 2000: Audiovisual Services*, S/CSS/W/74, para 6 (May 4, 2001).

character of the product as either goods or services is inextricably linked to its tangibility.[262] It assumes that because a product is intangible it cannot be stored and therefore production and consumption occur simultaneously. As a consequence, the trade method differs from tangible products because the method must accommodate such instantaneous use.

For tangible products, the emphasis is placed on the product itself because it is possible to track its physical transfer from the producer to the consumer, taking into consideration any storage to accommodate rising prices. In contrast, the focus for intangible products is on the way the product is provided, rather than on the product *per se*: for example, the product provider may be required to move to the place where the consumer is situated, or the consumer to the product provider[263]; alternatively, the supply of the product takes place via an intermediary who is physically present where the consumer is located. Even if physical movement of either the provider or consumer is not necessary, instantaneous consumption still means that the product must be supplied in a manner which accommodates the fact that the product will be consumed in this manner.[264] On this interpretation, separate rules regulating goods and services are necessary on pragmatic grounds solely due to the different ways in which products are traded.

Although we have suggested that tradability fulfils a filter function, we must question whether this is its sole function. In particular, does this concept manifest itself in the same way in respect of goods and services? If not, it may act as a further conceptual tool for determining the boundary between goods and services. The economics literature has suggested that there is a link between tangibility and the mechanisms by which different products may be traded. Can a similar link be found within the legal context? Implicit in the transfer element of 'tradability' is the transfer of products from the producer to the consumer in a way which allows the consumer to enjoy the product freely without interference from the producer. Commonly, what is envisaged is the transfer of property in the product from the producer to the consumer.[265] To fulfill the transfer element therefore, it must be possible for property in the product to move from the producer to the consumer as a prerequisite or concurrent requirement of the product's physical transfer.[266]

---

[262] Television services provided by SKY & TIVO allow the consumer to pause live TV feed and then re-start the programme when they are ready to watch it. Whilst it can be argued that this is an exception to the instantaneous consumption example, in reality the television signal is still transmitted in real time, but the technology records the relevant programme and then the consumer watches the recording and not the live TV *per se*.   [263] Bhagwati above n 240.

[264] Although it might be possible to store an element of the service, for example saving a film on videocassette, this does not change the essential intangibility of the initial product because it is only the manifestation of the service that is stored and not the service *per se*. On this example, it is the film which is stored on the videocassette and not the provision of the film.

[265] Roy Goode, Commercial Law, C 3rd edn, 2004 27.

[266] In certain circumstances, property may be retained by the producer until payment by the consumer. Even here, retention is conditional on payment or other specified condition and once that condition is fulfilled, the property will transfer to the consumer. However, in the English law context

Acquiring property in the product gives the consumer legal rights in relation to it: predominantly, transfer of property is synonymous with the transfer of ownership and the correlative right to immediate possession of the product.[267] Ownership is notoriously difficult to define in the abstract, but nonetheless the concept has implications for the goods/service boundary.[268]

On one level, the notion of property transfer appears inherently bound up with goods not services because the acquisition of ownership from the producer is predicated on the transfer of possession of the product. Such possession entails 'actual holding or having something as one's own,'[269] implying either physical existence of the thing possessed, or the right to exercise control over the product.

In relation to goods, control over the product is self evident through the act of physical possession of the product itself. Although services' intangibility means it is difficult to possess the service *per se*, the consumer still can have physical evidence of the existence of the service or legal evidence of their right to receive it. Physical existence can occur in three ways: first, after the provision of the service demonstrating that it has been received; for example, when a consumer receives a haircut, the receipt of the service is evident as the hair is shorter. Second, physical evidence of the service may be available before it is provided to indicate that the consumer has the right to receive that service. A legal document, such as a contract or receipt, may fulfil this function. A third, more complex situation may arise, for example, pay television where the consumer must subscribe to a package first and obtain a decoder card and box before they are able to access the television signal sent by the broadcaster.

Evidence of provision of services is linked, but essentially different from the question of whether services in themselves are tangible and whether a national measure affecting a product should be viewed within a goods or services regime. For example: should pay television be viewed as services, goods, or a combination of goods and services? The classification depends on whether the emphasis is placed on the physical manifestation of the product or what the buyer thought they were paying for, or on the type of contract they entered into to.[270] Has

---

this is surrounded by controversy and the courts have been reluctant to allow retention of property except in very limited circumstances: see Goode above n 265, 239–241.

[267] Ibid. 29–30.

[268] In English law, the consumer who 'owns' the product is entitled to the 'residue of the legal rights in an asset . . . after specific rights over the asset have been granted to others'. Goode *ibid.* 31–32. The right to these residual rights gives the consumer an absolute interest in the product, unless another consumer can show they have a better right (or title) to that product. On this view, both consumers 'own' the product, but one has a better right to possession than the other. More than one consumer can be entitled to ownership and possession provided they both show that they all have identical title to the products: Goode ibid. 31–32.   [269] OED Vol II above n 235, 2301.

[270] The emphasis seems to have been placed on what the buyer thought they were contracting for in *Mexico-Telecommunications* above n 42, para 7.42. However, this can be contrasted with the Appellate Body's view in *Canada-Autos* where the consumer's determination does not appear to be a relevant issue above n 42, para 181 as the emphasis was placed on the type of breach instead.

ownership passed in the set-top box or is it in the possession of the viewer only for the period the pay television subscription lasts?

In these difficult situations, the key to classification of products as goods or services could lie in the notion of ownership,[271] and more specifically, possession. It has been argued above that a product is capable of forming the subject-matter of a trade transaction when ownership is transferred from the producer to the consumer. Such ownership gives the consumer an immediate right to possession of the product: that is the consumer/purchaser of the product acquires the right to exercise 'control, directly or through another . . . of the asset.'[272] This control manifests itself in different ways dependent on whether the product transferred is goods or services. In the case of goods, control is the right to enjoy the *physical* product itself, whereas in services, it is control over the right to receive the product. This approach would seem to mirror the tangible/intangible distinction. However, in borderline cases, this may not be enough, particularly when it is not clear what the product actually is—at least from the consumer's perspective. To ascertain the answer to this question and consequently to identify whether the product is goods or services, the starting point must be the function of the product, or how it is perceived by the parties to the transaction.

Where the product's function is to form the subject-matter of the transaction, the product will be goods because its possession is enough to transfer ownership from the producer to the consumer: for example, the sale of a chair is clearly goods because the transfer of ownership requires control over the physical possession of a chair. In contrast, the pay television decoder and satellite dish may be goods when purchased independently, but when purchased as part of a contract to acquire access to the relevant television package, are services. This is because their function is to allow control over access to the SKY signal, thereby permitting possession of the television pictures and the transfer of ownership in the service. Both the decoder box and satellite dish have no other function in the contract to purchase access to the signal. On this interpretation, the inherent tangible nature of a product will not necessarily be determinative of its classification as either goods or services if its function is to facilitate control over another product.[273] We can see in this context that a certain amount of relativism may arise in characterizing the regime to apply in a given situation, and that in some circumstances the type of trading transaction rather than the inherent characteristics of the product itself that affect the classification.

Using the definitions in the dictionary and economics literature provides a coherent starting point for distinguishing between goods and services, but problems arise from relying solely on this material. Both definitions assume that the distinction is intuitive, flowing directly from the economic characteristics

---

[271] Note problems experienced by the European Union in this context: see section II above.

[272] Goode above n 265, 47.

[273] This approach is similar to that adopted by the Appellate Body in *Canada-Autos* para 155 discussed above n 42, section I.

inherent in all products. They also assume there is a single economic criterion that places products into one category or another, so all goods of the same type are always placed in the same category. This view is inadequate as we have seen. It also neglects the role of political imperatives which may influence the product's categorization. The issue ceases to be about the product in isolation, but instead moves more to the context in which the classification question arises. Although a product may be defined as goods or services using economic tools, such classification may be based on an understanding of those tools' application arising from historic views that certain products are more correctly classified as goods rather than services. In problematic borderline cases differing interpretations of the same tools can result in conflicting classification because placing the emphasis on a different part of the transaction can lead to different results: specifically, deciding whether a product is goods depends on which characteristic of the product is deemed to be the tangible element. This problem is manifest in the audiovisual sector.

Historically, the United States' argued that television programmes were 'goods' because it is possible for programmes to be recorded on to videocassette thereby giving them a tangible form.[274] In contrast, the EU argued that such products were services.[275] Although both the United States and the European Union were basing their categorization on television programming's tangibility, the United States emphasized the final manifestation of the product on a physical media which has a tangible form, meaning that the product being classified is tangible, whereas the EU placed importance on the transmission element of the product which has an intangible form, meaning that the product is services not goods. Both interpretations make sense in economic terms, so it is not the economic nature of the product alone that drives the boundary distinction, but the political utilization of it.

Second, the approach in the dictionary and economics literature assumes that products are always assessed purely in economic terms to facilitate trade in those products, while it is clear that this will not always be the case. In certain circumstances, political imperatives construct national policies based on the premise that some products' value lies beyond their inherent commercial worth. We have seen that the EU has argued that products supplied in the audiovisual sector should not be valued purely in economic terms because of the role of the media in society and

---

[274] Gatt Working Party on International Trade in Television Programmes, Report of the Working Party, GATT Doc. L/1741, 2–3 (13 March, 1962) also Donaldson above n 106, 110. Note that the United States has not officially resiled from its position that television programmes are goods not services, but it is negotiating concessions within the General Agreement on Services (GATS) regarding this sector which suggests a change in its views: see section I, also, WTO, Communication from the United States, *Audiovisual Services* S/CSS/W/21, para 10(i) (December 18, 2000).

[275] Case 155/73 *Sacchi* [1974] ECR 409, para 7; contrast also Case C-17/00 *De Coster* v. *College des Bourgmestre et Echevins de Watermael Boitsfort* [2001] ECR I-9445. Films were excluded from this definition following on from their historic classification as goods within the General Agreement on Tariffs and Trade (GATT) Article IV: see GATT, Application of GATT to International Trade in Television Programmes, GATT Doc. L/1615 (November 16, 1961).

in forming cultural identity.[276] Members of the WTO in the services negotiations,[277] including the EU[278] and Canada,[279] have also taken this view.[280] In these circumstances, products may be defined as goods if the decision is driven by economic considerations, but as services if broader issues are included because the product is no longer merely 'goods' purely based on its tangibility.

The dictionary definition and economics literature assume that the reason why a distinction is made between goods and services is merely that they are objectively traded differently, so mechanisms must be put in place to accommodate these divergent trading methods: rules have a passive role because their function is only to support the reality of trade. However, this interpretation means that legal rules have no other function.[281] Instead the discussion has shown that the private law relationship between trading parties may affect our analysis and that relevant legal rules may reflect the national political imperatives underlying product classification. Within national jurisdictions, this means that rules may be heavily based on economic criteria to achieve the requisite goal in one jurisdiction, whereas in another, a combination of economic and non-economic criteria may be adopted. Even where two members use similar economic criteria, the emphasis may change dependent on national objectives. Whether a product is goods or services is therefore a question of law, rather than of economics or fact.[282]

Lack of homogeneity between members on the political imperatives driving the product classification decision means that divergent legal regimes exist. This divergence becomes apparent when those rules are subject to scrutiny by an external arbiter like the European Union or the WTO. Re-classification of the product in line with the rules of the external body becomes a question of direct interference with members' national policies, rather than merely being a question of just amending their rules. Reclassification is instead a matter of replacing existing policy imperatives with those of the external organization. If the essential link between the construction of legal rules and political imperatives lies at the heart of the members' classification decision, then the key to resolution is to formulate a coherent policy on classification based on objective criteria which reflects the goals of the organization itself. This way members are able to see a clear

---

[276] European Commission, The Digital Age: European Audio-Visual Policy-Report of the High Level Group (1998).

[277] Discussions on the future of the General Agreement on Trade in services (GATS) commenced 2000 & were endorsed after the fourth WTO Ministerial Meeting held in Doha, Qatar, in November 2001: see WTO, Ministerial Declaration (November 20, 2001), WT/MIN(01)/DEC/1.

[278] European Commission, Towards An International Instrument on Cultural Diversity, COM(2003)520 (August 27, 2003).   [279] See Madger above n 113.

[280] Switzerland particularly noted that audiovisual products were 'fundamental instruments of social communication' which contributed 'to the cultural identity of a society'. WTO, Communication from Switzerland: *GATS 2000, Audiovisual Services*, para 6, (4 May, 2001), S/CSS/W/74.

[281] See material on NTCs: see eg José E. Alvarez (ed.), *Symposium, The Boundaries of the WTO*, 96 AJIL 1-159 (2002).

[282] 'Fact' is used in this context to denote the 'natural language' interpretation of a product.

rationale to interference with their classification decisions, and more specifically, their national policies.

IV. Conclusions

We have seen that there is a difference between goods and services within the WTO centered on the structure of the underlying agreements. The interpretation of the agreements does not clarify where the boundary between goods and services lies, although the decisions of the WTO Appellate Body and the panels in a number of cases suggest that there may be some significance in the distinction, beyond the purely formal, although this too is not clear. Even within the context of the formal ascription to the category of either goods or services, inconsistencies may arise resulting from who makes the decision and on what basis. It should be noted that the WTO is not alone in facing unclear and inconsistent jurisprudence, as the discussion of the European Union illustrates. Against this background, a discussion of the characteristics of goods and services respectively may serve to identify objective criteria for determining the boundary which can be used not only within the context of the WTO, but also within the European Union.

Based on the natural language and economic literature it seems that there are two concepts underpinning the products caught by the WTO: tradability and tangibility. Both these ideas can be seen in the jurisprudence of the WTO and, particularly in the European Union, though they are not necessarily coherently expressed in this way. These concepts are linked by the function of the product; that is the way in which the product is to be used. The function is often defined by the legal relationship, whether contract or regulation. Here we might emphasize the importance of transfer of property as key to the definition of goods; unfortunately such an approach does not tie in with the jurisprudence of the European Court of Justice in particular.

Function in this sense also links to the idea that what we are looking at is not necessarily the product itself but the national rules that may infringe either the WTO agreements or the Treaty of Rome. Such arguments underpin the reasoning in *GIP* within the European Union; again a line of reasoning not consistently elaborated. In looking at the product's function, the definition of goods and services may overturn decisions that would be made purely on the basis of tangibility, as can be seen in the television cases within the European Union and in the arguments of Advocate General Jacobs comparing electricity (intangible) and oil (tangible), both of which were classified as goods. What we seem concerned with is not necessarily the inherent nature of the product itself but the manner in which legal rules relate to it.

So how can the conflicting approaches to defining the boundary between goods and services be resolved? Tradability and tangibility serve as a series of filters, containing both objective and subjective criteria. Tradability first acts to distinguish between products that are bought and sold and which therefore fall within the economic sphere addressed by the rules in bodies such as the WTO and the European Union. In practice, few transactions fall outside the scope of these treaties. Tangibility then constitutes a rebuttable presumption that intangible items are services, whilst tangible items constitute goods. The product's function, in combination with tradability, then acts as the determining factor. To form the subject-matter of a trade transaction, ownership must be transferred from the producer to the consumer. Following the transfer of ownership, the consumer gains possession of the product, such that they are able to exercise control over it. Whether a product is goods or services depends on whether the consumer needs the product per se, or whether they need it to gain access to the product which forms the subject matter of the transaction.

Whilst these criteria form a framework for making decisions, it is clear that in come cases the boundary will remain contested. The benefit, however, of using a consistent framework for analysis is that it allows for greater transparency in the decision-making process, thus minimizing the risk of inconsistencies and arbitrary decisions and thereby supporting the legitimacy of those decisions.

On a broader level, it is clear that if a supra-national body like the WTO or European Union substitutes a different boundary from that drawn by its members, then that institution is interfering directly with the members' national policies. This raises legitimacy questions: specifically, whether the judicial body is competent to intervene in all subject areas without specific acquiescence by the member and whether the institution is competent to make the decision at all. If re-drawing the goods/services boundary is within the competence of the institution, then another question is the decision's acceptability to members. Members are more likely to accept interference with their national policies if the goods/services boundary is re-drawn according to coherent established principles, rather than being merely a rash response which differs in each dispute brought before the judicial body. The ad hoc approach currently taken in the WTO and the European Union may undermine their credibility and lead to a re-consideration of the extent to which both bodies can interfere with national policies.

Surveys

EC Competition Law 2003–2004

Ian S. Forrester, QC, Jacquelyn F. MacLennan, and Assimakis P. Komninos[1]

I. Introduction

EC competition law developments during 2003 and 2004 have been of profound importance. We saw the demise of the venerable Regulation 17/1962, and of the administrative notification system and authorization system for the clearance of doubtful agreements. On 1 May 2004, Regulation 1/2003[2] revolutionized EC competition law enforcement by introducing the system of legal exception in Article 81 and decentralizing enforcement to national competition authorities (NCAs) and national courts. A new Merger Regulation came into force on the same day.[3] Both Regulations were accompanied by implementing Regulations[4] and, perhaps more importantly, by an array of Commission Notices and Guidelines[5] which constitute a substantial restatement of the law and address

[1] The authors practise European law with White & Case in Brussels. Ian Forrester is Visiting Professor in European Law at Glasgow University. Warm thanks are expressed to Katarzyna Czapracka, Javier Prados, and many others at White & Case, who provided precious assistance in gathering and summarizing very extensive materials to produce this article.

[2] OJ [2003] L 1/1.   [3] Regulation 139/2004, OJ [2004] L 24/1.

[4] Regulations 773/2004, OJ [2004] L 123/18 and Regulation 802/2004, OJ [2004] L 133/1 respectively.

[5] In the antitrust field: Commission Notice on cooperation within the Network of Competition Authorities, OJ [2004] C 101/43; Commission Notice on cooperation between the Commission and the courts of the EU Member States in the application of Articles 81 and 82 EC, OJ [2004] C 101/54; Commission Notice on the handling of complaints by the Commission under Articles 81 and 82 of the EC Treaty, OJ [2004] C 101/65; Commission Notice on informal guidance relating to novel questions concerning Articles 81 and 82 of the EC Treaty that arise in individual cases (guidance letters), OJ [2004] C 101/78; Commission Notice—Guidelines on the effect on trade concept contained in Articles 81 and 82 of the Treaty, OJ [2004] C 101/81; Communication from the Commission—Notice—Guidelines on the application of Article 81(3) of the Treaty, OJ [2004] C 101/97. In the merger field: Guidelines on the assessment of horizontal mergers under the Council Regulation on the control of concentrations between undertakings, OJ [2004] C 31/5; Commission Notice on case referral in respect of concentrations, OJ [2005] C 56/2; Commission Notice on restrictions directly related and necessary to concentrations, OJ [2005] C 56/24; Commission Notice on a simplified procedure for treatment of certain concentrations under Council Regulation (EC) No

many technical substantive and procedural law issues which could not be covered in secondary Community legislation. 2004 also saw the entry into force of two new block exemption Regulations (BER), one on technology transfer agreements,[6] accompanied by Guidelines,[7] and the other on agreements in the insurance sector.[8] The Commission was also busy promoting competition in the liberal professions and conducting internal reviews on the application of Article 82 and on private enforcement. These two last topics will certainly dominate future surveys of competition law developments.

Commission enforcement action proved equally bold. 2004 saw the largest ever fine imposed on a single undertaking, Microsoft, in a case that is certain to make history in EC competition law.

II. The New Decentralized Enforcement System and Other Legislative Developments

A. Competition Law in the New Constitution

The Treaty's competition provisions make up the 'economic constitution' of the European Union, and the Court of Justice has recognized their importance on numerous occasions. Thus the Court has stressed the primacy of Article 81 in the Treaty system, since it 'constitutes a fundamental provision which is essential for the accomplishment of the tasks entrusted to the Community and, in particular, for the functioning of the internal market.'[9]

This pre-eminence of the competition rules was tested during the drafting of the new European Constitution. Some initially thought that such provisions had no place in a constitutional text, while others feared that omitting the competition and free movement rules from the text might be construed as a shift away from those classic Community priorities, and thus as a 'devaluation'. The approach finally followed defers to the long-standing constitutional importance of competition law; indeed, there are good reasons to speak of an 'up-grading'. Thus the new Treaty Establishing a Constitution for Europe lists competition law among the guiding principles and objectives of the Union. Article I-3(2) of the Constitution stresses that 'the Union shall offer its citizens an area of freedom,

139/2004, OJ [2005] C 56/32; Best practices on the conduct of EC merger control proceedings, http://europa.eu.int/comm/competition/mergers/legislation/regulation/best_practices.pdf; Best practice Guidelines for divestiture commitments at http://europa.eu.int/comm/competition/mergers/legislation/divestiture_commitments.

  [6] Regulation 772/2004, OJ [2004] L 123/11.
  [7] Commission Notice—Guidelines on the application of Article 81 of the EC Treaty to technology transfer agreements, OJ [2004] C 101/2.
  [8] Regulation 358/2003, OJ [2003] L 53/8.
  [9] Case C-453/99, *Courage Ltd. v. Bernard Crehan*, [2001] ECR I-6297, para. 20; Case C-126/97, *Eco Swiss China Time Ltd. v. Benetton International NV*, [1999] ECR I-3055, para. 36.

security and justice without internal frontiers, and an internal market *where competition is free and undistorted.'*[10]

Including the principle of free competition among the Union's paramount objectives certainly goes further than the equivalent provision of Article 3(1)(g) EC Treaty. First of all, the constitutional nature of competition law is now celebrated in the primary principles of a formal *constitution*. Secondly, the new text constitutes progress because it refers to the principle of free competition positively ('where competition is free and undistorted'), rather than negatively as in the current Treaty ('a system ensuring that competition in the internal market is not distorted'). This objective is to constitute a guiding principle for the interpretation of specific competition provisions and for ensuring consistency between the Union's various policies and activities.[11] A further extremely important innovation of the Constitution is the portrayal of competition policy as the 'fifth freedom' in the chapter on the internal market.[12]

Perhaps less happily, the new Constitution will bring about some terminology and numbering changes. Firstly, it will be necessary to speak of 'EU competition law' rather than 'EC competition law', since the Maastricht three-pillar structure has been abandoned in favour of a unitary structure, the European Union. Secondly, competition law specialists will once again have to acquaint themselves with a new numbering, as the old Articles 85 and 86, now Articles 81 and 82, will become Articles III-161 and III-162 respectively.[13]

During the drafting of the European Constitution, particular attention was given to the 'Lisbon strategy' and the expressed aim of enabling 'the EU to become the most competitive and dynamic knowledge-based economy in the world', which have recently been enshrined as guiding inspirations for EU policies (although so far with only modest success). Indeed, the Commission recently stressed the pre-eminent role of competition policy in Europe in a Communication entitled 'A pro-active Competition Policy for a Competitive Europe'.[14] The Commission sees competition policy as instrumental for the 'Lisbon strategy':

'A competitive and open internal market provides the best guarantee for European companies to increase their efficiency and innovative potential. Vigorous competition is thus a key driver for competitiveness and economic growth.'

The Commission views the new May 2004 EC competition enforcement framework in light of the Lisbon objectives. This is because enterprises will to the maximum possible extent be subject to 'a unified legal framework throughout the European Union'; the competition rules and their enforcement in individual cases

---

[10] Emphasis added. At the time of printing, the future of the Constitution is obscure.
[11] See Commissioner Monti's last official speech, 'A Reformed Competition Policy: Achievements and Challenges for the Future', Center for European Reform, Brussels, 28 October 2004, at http://europa.eu.int/comm/competition/speeches. [12] *Ibid.*
[13] See further Holmes, 'Competition Law and the Constitution for Europe', *Competition Law Insight*, December 2003/January 2004.
[14] COM(2004) 293 final, Brussels, 20.4.2004.

will be based 'on a more economic effects based approach'; and competition enforcement procedures will become 'more transparent, streamlined and simplified without losing their effectiveness'.

B. The New System of Enforcement

(i) *The Fundamentals of the New System: Regulation 1/2003 and Implementing Regulation 773/2004*

Regulation 1/2003 entered into force on 24 January 2003 and became applicable from 1 May 2004.[15] It was hailed by most actors in EC competition enforcement as a breakthrough, since it abolished the Commission's monopoly on granting exemptions under Article 81(3) and placed 'national competition authorities and courts in the driving seat for much competition law enforcement',[16] thus also giving greater legitimacy to EC competition law. The fundamental basis of the new regime is the abolition of the Brussels-centred notification and authorization system and the decentralization of antitrust enforcement to national competition authorities and courts. The Commission's approach to the reform was consistent with seeing it as the 'privatization' of competition policy enforcement, where the burdens of ensuring respect for the Treaty competition rules will fall entirely on companies and their legal advisers, using self-assessment rather than notification.

The shift has been explained in previous surveys in this Yearbook. There were opposing voices, particularly in the Germanic legal world. In the last three or four years, however, it had become common ground that the old system of administrative authorization and notification had had its day, and that a new system was necessary for the 21st century.[17] Notification of usually innocuous agreements brought dubious benefits and was costly.[18] Worse still, the procedures involved were fundamentally misrepresented and misunderstood. Exemptions were in practice almost never available, so notification was rarely used to procure the Commission's blessing, but rather to obtain the higher moral ground in any future dispute between the contracting partners. It had created a reactive enforcement

---

[15] Article 45 of Regulation 1/2003.

[16] Melanie Johnson, Parliamentary Undersecretary of State for competition, consumers and markets, in: Department of Trade and Industry, *Modernisation—A Consultation on the Government's Proposals for Giving Effect to Regulation 1/2003 and for Re-alignment of the Competition Act 1998*, April 2003.

[17] See e.g. Bellamy, 'The Modernisation of EC Antitrust Policy—Some Reflections: Don't Throw the Baby out with the Bath Water', in: Ehlermann & Atanasiu (Eds), *European Competition Law Annual 2000: The Modernisation of EC Antitrust Policy* (Oxford/Portland, 2001), p. 315; Terhechte, 'Gastkommentar: Die Reform des europäischen Kartellrechts—am Ende eines langen Weges?', 15(12) EuZW (2004).

[18] According to the UK Department of Trade and Industry, the cost for UK companies of notifying an agreement to the Commission was between £30,000 and £100,000 in 2002 (Department of Trade and Industry, *op.cit.*, p. 86).

culture.[19] Flagrantly anti-competitive agreements were of course never notified to the Commission. Indeed, the decentralization of the application of the Treaty competition rules and the abolition of the notification system will assist the Commission to focus on detecting and punishing the most serious infringements.

Under the new system the Commission has the power to adopt four kinds of decisions: it may (a) order the termination of infringements (with or without the imposition of fines),[20] (b) order interim measures (a power which was formerly judicially created), (c) accept commitments and make such commitments binding on third parties,[21] and (d) declare that the competition rules do not apply to particular conduct (positive decision). Only the Commission will be competent to take this last type of decision, and only when the Community public interest so requires.[22]

The new Regulation provides for extensive duties of cooperation between the Commission and NCAs and courts. These are further specified in Notices and Guidelines.[23] It should be noted at the outset that the power to grant exemption decisions has not been decentralized to those authorities and courts, since the legal exception system has made the very concept of exemption obsolete.[24] Instead they will be enforcing Article 81 in its totality, using the analysis under Articles 81(1)

---

[19] See Kjølbye, 'The New Commission Guidelines on the Application of Article 81(3): An Economic Approach to Article 81', 25 ECLR 566 (2004), p. 573, admitting that under the old system the Commission used to spend a considerable amount of time checking individual clauses in notified agreements.

[20] The Commission also has the power, when ordering the termination of an infringement, to impose structural remedies on companies.

[21] For examples of this new procedure see case COMP/37.214-*Joint selling of the media rights to the German Bundesliga* (proposed commitments published in OJ [2004] C 229/13); case COMP/39.116-*Coca-Cola* (proposed commitments published on the Commission's website on 19 October 2004); case COMP/38.348-*Repsol CPP SA* (proposed commitments published in OJ [2004] C 258/7); case COMP/38.381-*ALROSA/DBCAG/City and West East* (proposed commitments published in OJ [2005] C 136/32). In the first two cases the Commission adopted formal Decisions rendering legally binding the commitments concerned: Commission Decision of 19 January 2005 (COMP/37.214-*Joint selling of the media rights to the German Bundesliga*), OJ [2005] L 134/46; Commission Decision of 22 June 2005 (COMP/39.116-*Coca-Cola*). In the other cases the Commission intended to proceed to a formal Decision after inviting interested third parties to submit their comments.

[22] Article 10 of Regulation 1/2003. NCAs will not have the competence to take such decisions. The national courts are, of course, not precluded from applying Articles 81 and 82 in full in their jurisdiction, either negatively or positively. [23] See below.

[24] At this point, however, it should be stressed that companies could still notify agreements to national competition authorities, as nothing in Regulation 1/2003 prohibits this (see Gauer, 'Does the Effectiveness of the EU Network of Competition Authorities Require a Certain Degree of Harmonisation of National Procedures and Sanctions?', in: Ehlermann & Atanasiu (Eds.), *European Competition Law Annual 2002: Constructing the EU Network of Competition Authorities* (Oxford/ Portland, 2004), p. 195). Of course, in such cases an NCA will not be able to grant negative clearance or an exemption, but only to state in its decision that there are no grounds for it to act (Article 5 of Regulation 1/2003). However, the prospective amendment of national competition laws which will mirror the Community abolition of the notification and authorization system will lead to the complete disappearance of the notification procedure in the EU. It is interesting to note that in the UK one of the compelling arguments for abolishing the domestic notification system is precisely the likelihood that undertakings from across the EU will seek to notify agreements under UK competition law, in order to attain in the UK a certain degree of the comfort lost under the new EC system. See Department of Trade and Industry, *op.cit*, paras. 3.19–3.20.

and 81(3) in unity. In the era of decentralization, the Commission is not seen as the *primary* enforcer of EC competition law. The NCAs and national courts are now the primary enforcers and fora for antitrust enforcement. The Commission is, however, seen as the *supreme* enforcer, whose intervention is to be expected in the most important cases which affect the Community public interest rather than more local interests or other private interests.

Among the most important provisions of Regulation 1/2003 is Article 3, which obliges the national competition authorities and courts to apply the competition provisions of the Treaty along with their national laws if there is an effect on trade among Member States. This will undoubtedly lead to a 'Communitization' of competition enforcement by those authorities and courts. More importantly, the new provision excludes the application of national competition law to agreements that are not prohibited under Article 81 taken as a whole, or that are covered by a block exemption Regulation. However, unilateral conduct permitted under Article 82 may still be prohibited under stricter national rules on abuse of a dominant position or economic dependence (as is the case, for example, in German, Greek and French law).[25] In addition, under Article 3(3), the application of Community competition law does not preclude the application of provisions of national law which predominantly pursue an objective different from that pursued by Articles 81 and 82. This refers basically to national unfair competition laws.[26]

Regulation 1/2003 does not stop at devolving competition law enforcement. Its rather neglected second part extensively reshapes the Commission's administrative enforcement powers. A quick review of Chapters V to VIII of the new Regulation and of the accompanying implementing Regulation 773/2004 shows that in the new system the Commission will enjoy a much stronger procedural framework for the effective enforcement of the competition rules.

Starting from the Commission's powers of investigation, Article 18 of Regulation 1/2003 simplifies the system of requests for information by no longer requiring a two-step process. The Commission may now choose between a simple request and a formal decision at the outset. Under Regulation 17/1962 the Commission had no power to interview specific employees: Article 19 of the new Regulation gives it the power to interview individuals and companies, with their consent, for the purpose of collecting information relating to the subject-matter of an investigation. This will be a powerful tool, the more so as the Commission may record such interviews.[27] As before, an inspection may include entering business premises, examining books and business records, taking copies and asking for oral explanations, but the new text also provides for the sealing of business premises and books or records, and for asking representatives or members of staff of undertakings for explanations and recording their answers.[28] The former

---

[25] See also Recital 8 *in fine* of the new Regulation.   [26] *Ibid*, Recital 9.
[27] Article 3(3) of Regulation 773/2004. Offering incorrect or misleading information at an interview is not subject to fines or other penalties.   [28] See also Article 4 of Regulation 773/2004.

distinction between voluntary and mandatory investigations is retained. In the case of mandatory investigations, when an undertaking opposes an inspection ordered by a Commission decision, the delicate problem of cooperation with national judicial authorities arises: Article 20 integrates the principles established by the Court of Justice in *Roquette Frères*,[29] and provides that the national courts' purview is limited to checking whether the Commission decision is an authentic one, and whether the coercive measures sought are arbitrary or excessive. Finally, Article 21 for the first time gives the Commission powers to order the inspection of non-business (domestic) premises: documents held in employees' homes will no longer be immune from Commission inspections. The conditions are quite strict, since the violation of Articles 81 and 82 must be 'serious', and 'reasonable suspicion' must exist that books or other records related to the business and to the subject-matter of the inspection are kept on those premises. A reasoned decision is therefore required, along with the prior authorization of a national judicial authority whose purview again covers the authenticity of the Commission decision and whether or not the specific measure is arbitrary or excessive.

With regard to sanctions for procedural infringements, Regulation 1/2003 breaks with Regulation 17/1962, which aimed at prevention rather than at punishment or deterrence, and undoubtedly increases the significance of these sanctions. Fines for procedural infringements may now reach up to 1 per cent of the undertaking's total turnover in the preceding business year.[30] Fines for both substantive and procedural infringements are now to be calculated on the basis of 'total' annual turnover, meaning that it will not be necessary to calculate the turnover only in the relevant product and geographic markets. Periodic penalty payments have also been modified to strengthen deterrence.[31]

Finally, and importantly, the unsatisfactory 'bits and pieces' situation of the previous system, where different procedural rules were applicable to the transport sector, has been remedied. The new implementing Regulation 773/2004, which repeals Regulation 2843/1998,[32] applies to all sectors, including transport.

(ii) The 'Modernization Package'

Regulation 1/2003 does not establish the details of how the new modernized and decentralized enforcement system will operate. The Commission has filled this gap by adopting several Notices covering such topics as how it will handle complaints, the cases in which it will give informal guidance to companies and the criteria for application of Article 81(3). The Notices also aim to regulate cooperation between the Commission and NCAs and national courts.

---

[29] Case C-94/00, *Roquette Frères SA v. Directeur Général de la Concurrence, de la Consommation et de la Répression des Fraudes*, [2002] ECR I-9011.	[30] Article 23 of Regulation 1/2003.
[31] Under Article 24 of Regulation 1/2003, periodic penalty payments of up to 5 per cent of average daily turnover in the preceding business year can now be imposed on undertakings on a daily basis, for both substantive and procedural infringements.	[32] OJ [1998] L 354/22.

a) Cooperation in the European Competition Network

The devolution of competition enforcement has important consequences for public enforcement nationally, as NCAs now have the power and the duty to apply Articles 81 and 82. Regulation 1/2003 does not establish a 'full faith and credit' principle on mutual recognition of decisions taken by national competition authorities, which will be subject to territoriality: an NCA's jurisdiction will be limited to its national territory.

A focal point of decentralization is collaboration between NCAs and the Commission through the European Competition Network (ECN), whose main objectives are to ensure efficient work-sharing between the public enforcers and promote the coherent application of the EC competition rules. While the ECN is ostensibly not to be viewed in hierarchical terms, there is no doubt that the Commission will play a central role in it, befitting its specific competition law enforcement tasks which flow directly from the Treaty (Article 85).[33] The system established by Chapter IV of Regulation 1/2003 and further explained in the Commission Notice on Cooperation within the ECN is not federal, but follows the standard Community law relationship between the supranational and the national. Naturally, therefore, the Commission, a supranational institution, will not have the power to review directly or strike down decisions by national competition authorities; but its dominant role is nevertheless apparent.

Some problems may arise from divergences in the procedural framework applicable to NCAs. Regulation 1/2003 does not contemplate the harmonization of national procedural rules at this stage; they will continue to apply, subject to the Community law principles of equality and effectiveness. However, the fact that NCAs will now increasingly apply the Community competition rules means that their procedural autonomy will also increasingly be called into question. Inconsistency of application is one of the largest challenges of the new regime. This is already leading to further calls for harmonization of national remedies and procedures.

The Cooperation Notice lays down clear allocation criteria, in some detail. The Commission will not be just a clearing house which distributes cases to NCAs. The basic principle is that members of the ECN should endeavour to re-allocate cases to a single well-placed NCA which fulfils the following cumulative conditions: (i) an agreement or practice has substantial direct actual or foreseeable effects on competition in the NCA's territory and is implemented in or originates on that territory, (ii) the NCA is effectively able to bring the entire infringement to an end, and (iii) it can gather the evidence required to prove the infringement, possibly with the assistance of other authorities. In sum, there must be a clear link between the infringement and the territory of a Member State.[34] The Commission will not initiate proceedings when a competition infringement

---

[33] On the Commission's central role, see Case C-344/98, *Masterfoods Ltd. v. HB Ice Cream Ltd.*, [2000] ECR I-11369, para. 46. [34] ECN Cooperation Notice, paras. 7–8.

affects the territories of only two or three Member States; in such cases the NCAs concerned should instead consider working together.[35] The Commission considers it is better placed to act in cases with a wider geographical scope and some particular importance for Community law.[36] Interestingly enough, the Commission believes that the allocation of cases does not involve a decision on its behalf or that of an NCA: rather, the act or failure to act in question is a preliminary step in a Community procedure, and thus not challengeable before the courts.[37] The basic aim is to allocate cases at the outset of proceedings. Problems of allocation should be resolved promptly, normally within two months from the date of the first information sent to the ECN under Article 11 of Regulation 1/2003.[38]

The Notice envisages exchanges of information between NCAs and the Commission (via the ECN intranet) on complaints received and the initiation of proceedings. It also provides for the exchange and use of data, including confidential information, both between NCAs and the Commission and between NCAs. The information exchanged should only be used in evidence for the purposes of applying Articles 81 and 82, and in respect of the subject matter for which it was collected by the transmitting authority. Stricter rules apply to the exchange of information which may be used to impose sanctions on individuals.[39] The Commission and NCAs must also cooperate during various investigations, including Commission requests for information and investigations.

The position of leniency applicants is particularly problematic. The Notice considers it is in the Community interest to grant favourable treatment to undertakings which cooperate with the Commission in the investigation of cartel infringements. However, it admits that in the absence of an EU-wide system of 'fully harmonized leniency programmes', an application for leniency to one authority is not to be considered as an application for leniency to any other authority. A company seeking leniency would therefore have to apply to the Commission and all NCAs with competence to apply Article 81 and possibly being competent to act against the infringement in question. The problem is perhaps less acute with regard to leniency applications to the Commission, which can always relieve the NCAs of their competence by initiating proceedings, but it becomes more serious if applications for leniency are filed with NCAs under national leniency programmes. Multiple national applications for leniency to different NCAs by different companies would represent a very unfortunate scenario. One solution, favoured in the Notice, would be for an applicant to file leniency

[35] ECN Cooperation Notice, paras. 10–13.   [36] *Ibid*, paras. 14–15.

[37] *Ibid*, para. 31. See also Paulis and Gauer, 'La réforme des règles d'application des articles 81 et 82 du Traité', 11 JdT (Eur.) 65 (2003), p. 72. This has yet to be tested before the Community Courts. In any event, it cannot be excluded that an NCA may be obliged by *national* law to take a formal decision subject to review by the national courts, while reallocating a case within the ECN (see L. Idot, *Droit communautaire de la concurrence, Le nouveau système communautaire de mise en œuvre des articles 81 et 82 CE* (Paris/Bruxelles, 2004), p. 66).   [38] Cooperation Notice, para. 18.

[39] See Articles 12 and 28 of Regulation 1/2003 and paras. 26–28 of the Cooperation Notice.

applications with all national authorities simultaneously.[40] The Commission's leniency programme is not yet successful or predictable enough, and the doubts are likely to increase under the new regime.

A related issue is the exchange between ECN members of information submitted voluntarily by an applicant for leniency. The Notice indicates that information will not be shared with the ECN without the leniency applicant's consent, except in cases where the receiving NCA ensures the protection of the leniency applicant.[41] The Commission has received written commitments in this sense from the vast majority of Member States, and has published a list of the NCAs that have signed a declaration to that effect.[42]

The Notice adds little on the cooperation side to the fairly detailed rules in Regulation 1/2003. Among the most important cooperation and consultation mechanisms are the general duty of cooperation,[43] the obligation of NCAs to consult the Commission at the outset of proceedings under EC competition law,[44] and before adopting a prohibition decision, accepting commitments or withdrawing the benefit of a block exemption,[45] the possibility to consult the Commission in all other cases[46] and the use of the Advisory Committee on Restrictive Practices and Dominant Positions to discuss a case pending before an NCA, before the final decision is taken.[47]

Last but not least, under Article 11(6) of Regulation 1/2003, the Commission retains the power to relieve NCAs of their competence by initiating proceedings for the adoption of a decision. The Commission will only rely exceptionally on this provision, which reproduces Article 9(3) of Regulation 17/1962[48]; nevertheless, its mere existence is a very efficient safety valve in the system. The Commission will have two further powers at the stage of judicial review of decisions by NCAs. Firstly, it will have the possibility to initiate proceedings and adopt a decision which a national court reviewing the NCA's decision must respect, pursuant to Article 16(1) of Regulation 1/2003; secondly, it may intervene as *amicus curiae* in the national judicial review proceedings.

---

[40] Cooperation Notice, para. 38.   [41] *Ibid*, paras. 40–41.   [42] *Ibid*, para. 72 and Annex.
[43] Article 11(1) of Regulation 1/2003.   [44] *Ibid*, Article 11(3).
[45] *Ibid*, Article 11(4).   [46] *Ibid*, Article 11(5).   [47] *Ibid*, Article 14(7).
[48] See *Joint Statement of the Council and the Commission on the Functioning of the Network of Competition Authorities*, Doc. 15435/02 ADD 1 of 10 December 2002 at http://register. consilium.eu.int/pdf/en/02/st15/15435-a1en2.pdf, point 21. According to the Joint Statement, the indicative cases where this mechanism is likely to be used are somewhat exceptional: '(a) Network members envisage conflicting decisions in the same case; (b) Network members envisage a decision which is obviously in conflict with consolidated case law; the standards defined in the judgments of the Community courts and in previous decisions and regulations of the Commission should serve as a yardstick; concerning facts, only a significant divergence will trigger an intervention of the Commission; (c) Network member(s) is (are) unduly drawing out proceedings; (d) There is a need to adopt a Commission decision to develop Community competition policy in particular when a similar competition issue arises in several Member States; (e) The national competition authority does not object.' This specific point in the Joint Statement is taken over *verbatim* in para. 54 of the Cooperation Notice.

b) Cooperation with National Courts

Regulation 1/2003 does not stop at making national courts competent to apply the Treaty antitrust rules in full; it also creates an elaborate institutional framework with prudential mechanisms which aim to meet concerns regarding the consistency of decentralized enforcement of EC competition law. While NCAs form part of a network of public enforcers, the situation of national courts is institutionally different. Indeed, their independence of the executive branch means that they could not formally belong to such a network.

The first important means of cooperation, which was already at the disposal of national courts dealing with EC antitrust issues under the previous system of enforcement but is codified and strengthened by Regulation 1/2003, is the possibility for national courts to seek the Commission's assistance. The European Court of Justice has in numerous cases stressed the Commission's duty to assist national courts in this respect, a duty emanating from Article 10 EC Treaty.[49] The 1993 Cooperation Notice contained detailed provisions on this mechanism, although it must be admitted that national courts made little use of the procedures enshrined therein.[50] This may have been due either to national procedural obstacles to such cooperation with the Commission, or to the courts' general reluctance to take that course because of the perceived limited scope of the information that the Commission could give them under the Notice; or, perhaps most likely, to the belief of a national judge that if a delay in the national litigation is necessary to consult an 'outside' body, better to consult the Court of Justice on the question, rather than the Commission. The express provision of Article 15(1) of the new Regulation aims to resolve these problems by establishing a right for national courts to obtain legal or economic information from the Commission or request its opinion on questions relating to the application of the competition rules.

The new Cooperation Notice develops the details of this procedure further, and also provides for deadlines by which the Commission must reply.[51] Thus a national court may request two kinds of assistance from the Commission. It may ask for documents in the Commission's possession, or for information of a procedural nature, basically concerning the status of the proceedings before the

---

[49] See Case C-2/88, *Criminal Proceedings against J.J. Zwartveld et al*, [1990] ECR I-3365, paras. 17–18; Case C-234/89, *Stergios Delimitis v. Henninger Bräu AG*, [1991] ECR I-935, para. 53.

[50] Up to 1998 national courts had referred to the Commission in 15 cases. These applications for assistance came from Belgium (three cases), France (three cases), Germany (three cases), the Netherlands (one case), Spain (three cases), the UK (one case) and, interestingly, one arbitral tribunal having its seat in Spain. The time taken by the Commission to respond varied from some months in most cases to two years in one case. See further Joris, 'Communication relative à la coopération entre la Commission et les juridictions nationales pour l'application des articles 85 et 86: Cas d'application jusqu'à présent', (1998–4) *EC Competition Policy Newsletter* 47, pp. 47–48. In 1999 national courts used the 1993 Notice on cooperation in order to seek the assistance of the Commission in only five cases (see *Commission XXIXth Report on Competition Policy—1999* (Brussels, 2000), pp. 363 *et seq.*). In 2000 national courts applied to the Commission in seven cases (see *Commission XXXth Report on Competition Policy—2000* (Brussels, 2001), pp. 338 *et seq.*).

[51] National Courts Cooperation Notice, paras. 21–30.

Commission. The Notice promises that the Commission will respond to such requests within a month.[52] Alternatively, the court may ask the Commission for its opinion on economic, factual and legal matters. The Commission will aim to do so within four months.[53] The Cooperation Notice appears to grant this second possibility only if other tools (the case law of the Community Courts and Commission Regulations, Decisions, Notices and Guidelines) 'do not offer sufficient guidance'.[54] This limitation, however, is not in line with the Court of Justice's case law on cooperation between national courts and the Commission. According to the principles emanating from Article 10, the time and circumstances of a national court's request for the Commission's assistance are entirely subject to the national court's discretion. In any event, this limitation appears to be really more of a reminder to national courts to ensure the effectiveness of this mechanism by using it prudently, and not to overwhelm the Commission with requests for assistance.

The national court remains free to decide whether or not to refer to the Commission under the terms of Article 15(1), and the opinions or assistance given by the Commission in this context do not bind national courts.[55] Nevertheless, the cooperation procedure has raised concerns regarding due process, since the Commission's opinion will be transmitted without the parties being heard,[56] and the court might follow it slavishly without giving the parties an effective opportunity to contradict it. As the rules stand, the Commission will not be under an obligation to communicate its submissions to the parties, or to base them on the evidence before the court.

The cooperation procedure between the Commission and national courts also raises some important questions regarding the kinds of information which the Commission can transmit to national courts. One issue is protection of professional and business secrets. The Cooperation Notice attempts to reconcile the various conflicting interests by leaving it up to national courts whether to request information covered by professional secrecy. However, it provides for some safeguards: in particular, before transmitting such information, the Commission must ask the national court whether it can offer a guarantee that it will protect confidential information and business secrets. The Commission has opted for this specific kind of 'dialogue' with the national courts based on a combined reading of Articles 10 and 287 EC Treaty.[57]

The Commission may refuse to transmit any kind of information to national courts, in order to 'safeguard the interests of the Community or to avoid any interference with its functioning and independence, in particular by jeopardizing the accomplishment of the tasks entrusted to it.'[58] This is intended to include

---

[52] National Courts Cooperation Notice, para. 22. The one-month period may be excessive in cases of purely procedural information (for example, on whether proceedings are pending before the Commission).

[53] *Ibid*, para. 28. Again this may not be satisfactory, especially in cases of urgency such as preliminary injunctions proceedings.   [54] *Ibid*, para. 27.

[55] *Ibid*, paras. 19 and 29.   [56] *Ibid*, paras. 19 and 30.   [57] *Ibid*, paras. 23–25.

[58] *Ibid*, para. 26.

correspondence between the Commission and NCAs in the framework of the ECN. Whether litigants may request the Commission, through the national court, to disclose written statements and descriptions given by companies under the Leniency Notice, is crucially important. The Commission declares in the Cooperation Notice that it will only disclose such information to national courts with the leniency applicant's consent,[59] as such disclosure would otherwise prejudice the Commission's effective enforcement of Community competition law. Public enforcement by the Commission and the facilitating of detection through immunity from fines should not operate to the detriment of private enforcement and the compensation of cartel victims. The Leniency Notice must therefore not interfere with such civil claims, which in any case are based on the direct effect of Treaty provisions. Nevertheless, there are less onerous ways to pursue these objectives than by disclosing the documents companies have submitted to the Commission under the Leniency Notice, which would frustrate the aim of making detection of hardcore restrictions of competition easier by discouraging companies from taking advantage of it. Private litigants will therefore have to rely solely on discovery in the context of the civil proceedings, or content themselves with non-leniency-related evidence held by the Commission.

Regulation 1/2003 provides for some other procedures and duties of cooperation. Article 15(2) imposes on Member States the duty to forward copies of their national courts' judgments to the Commission. Choosing to impose such a duty on Member States rather than the national courts themselves was very prudent, because courts are not accustomed to such 'administrative' duties, which could only be carried out by their registries.

A further new cooperation mechanism, introduced for the first time in Article 15(3) of the Regulation, is the power of the Commission and NCAs to file *amicus curiae* briefs in national proceedings. This is intended to be used mainly as a precautionary mechanism drawing the court's attention to specific competition law problems. It is possible that this exceptional new instrument could serve the Commission's aim of helping national courts to come to grips with difficult competition issues which require a high degree of consistent application throughout the EU. In this sense such *amicus curiae* briefs complement the preliminary reference procedure of Article 234 EC (although of course, the Commission's opinion, unlike judgments of the Court of Justice, cannot bind a national court).

The Commission and NCAs are not intended to be parties to the proceedings, but rather to act as objective, neutral and independent economic experts. However, their role has raised some due process concerns, mainly from the private

---

[59] National Courts Cooperation Notice, para. 26. See also paras. 32–33 of the Leniency Notice: 'The Commission considers that normally disclosure, at any time, of documents received in the context of this notice would undermine the protection of the purpose of inspections and investigations within the meaning of Article 4(2) of Regulation (EC) No 1049/2001 of the European Parliament and of the Council.'

practice side.[60] It is feared that some judges might follow the Commission's statements in a 'copy-paste' manner, without giving the parties the opportunity to contradict them effectively. In addition, although Article 15(3) of Regulation 1/2003 restricts such intervention by the Commission solely to cases where 'the coherent application of Article 81 or 82 of the Treaty so requires', and the Notice on cooperation states that the Commission will be guided in its submissions only by its duty to defend the public interest, and not by any private interests involved, it will not always be easy for the Commission to avoid taking sides. Moreover, in our view, the water-tight distinction between the public and the private interest in competition cases of which the Commission is so fond is largely fiction. It is therefore difficult, despite the Commission's eagerness to stress in the Cooperation Notice its detachment from the actual litigation,[61] to see how it could avoid being cross-examined by one or other of the parties, especially when the national court gives them this opportunity.[62]

The conditions for the submission of observations by the Commission and by NCAs differ. NCAs are the preferred *amici curiae* and may submit their observations on any issue 'relating to the application of Article 81 or Article 82 of the Treaty'. The Commission, on the other hand, may submit such observations only exceptionally, if 'the coherent application of Article 81 or Article 82 of the Treaty so requires'.[63] The Commission and NCAs will have the power to submit written observations on their own initiative, but their making of oral observations will be subject to the national court's permission.[64]

To enable the Commission and NCAs to make use of the *amicus curiae* system, Article 15(3) of Regulation 1/2003 imposes a duty on national courts to transmit to the Commission and NCAs any documents necessary for the assessment of the case. This constitutes the only direct duty placed on the courts in the context of cooperation under Article 15 of the new Regulation, and it is a duty of an 'administrative' or 'clerical' nature which will be discharged via the courts' registries.[65] This provision must be seen in conjunction with the Article 15(2) duty of Member States to transmit copies of judgments to the Commission. The two provisions are intended to work in a complementary fashion: in other words, the Commission will only use Article 15(3)(b) to request the documents of a case on which it has received a first instance national judgment. This means that in the majority of cases the Commission will intervene only at the stage of appeal, after being alerted accordingly through the mechanisms of paragraphs (2) and (3)(b) of Article 15 of the new Regulation.

---

[60] See e.g. Bellis, 'Les défis de la modernisation du droit européen de la concurrence', 11 JdT (Eur.) 73 (2003), p. 74.   [61] Cooperation Notice, paras. 19 and 29.

[62] This is a very sensitive issue, which may eventually have to be resolved by the Court of Justice through a preliminary reference by a national court before which the Commission has exercised its power of *amicus curiae* intervention.   [63] Article 15(3)(a) of Regulation 1/2003.

[64] Of course, national procedural law may grant wider powers to national competition authorities in this context. This is not prohibited or excluded by Regulation 1/2003.

[65] Cooperation Notice, para. 33.

c) The Handling of Complaints

As one of the key aims of decentralizing EC competition law enforcement is to enable the Commission to focus on combating the most serious competition law infringements, complaints have acquired an even greater importance. Since the NCAs and national courts are able to apply EC competition rules in their entirety, victims of anti-competitive practices must consider which is the best instance before which to raise such grievances. In the Complaints Notice the Commission gives indications for when parties should complain to the Commission or a NCA, and when they should bring their case before a national court. The Notice also outlines who may make a formal complaint and how the Commission will assess and deal with complaints. It distinguishes between formal or privileged complainants, who show a legitimate interest and fulfil certain requirements, and other non-privileged complainants who provide market information, which may be supplied in any form and does not have to comply with the requirements for complaints pursuant to Article 7(2) of Regulation 1/2003.[66] Only the former category of complainants enjoys clearly defined rights during the subsequent proceedings under Regulation 773/2004.

The Commission will prioritize cases that are important from a policy perspective. In all other cases the Commission considers that NCAs[67] and national courts are the more appropriate fora for complainants.

With regard to national courts, the Commission first stresses the advantages of civil litigation. The major difference between the Commission and a national court is that the Commission will not investigate every complaint it receives, whereas a court must deal with every case before it. National courts may grant plaintiffs damages for losses suffered as a result of competition law infringements, and award costs to successful plaintiffs. They may also adjudicate claims pertaining to contractual obligations, and are usually best placed to adopt interim measures. However, these advantages are purely theoretical; in practice, private antitrust enforcement in Europe is still rare if not effectively non-existent, owing to numerous obstacles and disincentives relating to costs, divergences between national substantive and procedural laws, and even cultural idiosyncrasies.[68] Thus, while the Commission's intention to refer complainants back to national courts, remedies and procedures is understandable, the national route will for many not offer a real alternative.

Interestingly, the Notice states that complainants cannot apply to the Commission for interim measures[69]: it is for the Commission alone to take such

---

[66] The Commission has created an internet address for this kind of informant: http://europa. eu.int/dgcomp/info-on-anti-competitivepractices.

[67] In para. 8 of the Complaints Notice the Commission argues that the public enforcers, i.e. itself and NCAs, cannot investigate all complaints, but must set priorities in their treatment of cases. While this accurately reflects the position of the Commission, it may not be a true statement with reference to those NCAs that do not enjoy discretion to prioritize under their national procedural law.

[68] On private enforcement, see below.   [69] Complaints Notice, para. 80.

measures *ex officio*. Indeed, the letter of Article 8(1) of Regulation 1/2003 seems to depart from the *Camera Care*[70] case law, and excludes the protection of private interests as such from the scope of Commission-ordered interim measures. Instead there is only a reference to 'serious and irreparable damage to competition'. Interim measures whose sole aim is to protect the private interest of a complainant or plaintiff can only be adopted by NCAs, if their national law so provides, or by national courts. Of course, an anti-competitive practice which injures a specific person is likely also to harm competition in general, and thus the public interest.[71] However, this new standard reflects the Commission's anxiety to avoid being swamped with interim measures requests.

For NCAs, the Notice refers complainants back to the ECN Notice. Complainants should address an NCA when there is a material link between the alleged infringement and the territory of a Member State. The Commission appeals to complainants to help reduce the potential need to reallocate cases inside the ECN by deciding carefully where to lodge their complaint.[72]

Regulation 1/2003 reserves the right of making a formal complaint to those who can show a 'legitimate interest', and the Complaints Notice gives a non-exhaustive list of such complaints.[73] On the Commission's discretion to prioritize complaints, the Notice essentially codifies the existing case law[74] and stresses the Commission's intention to focus on infringements of importance for the Community public interest. There is one exception for which the Commission enjoys exclusive competence, namely the withdrawal of the benefit of a block exemption with *erga omnes* effect under Article 29 of Regulation 1/2003. In this case the complainant will be entitled to a formal Commission decision.

After receiving a complaint, the Commission will examine it and then gather further information before deciding whether to initiate proceedings. One noteworthy development in the Complaints Notice is the inclusion of recommended deadlines: the Commission will 'endeavour' to inform the complainant within four months whether or not it intends to investigate the case further.[75] If it decides the case does not warrant further investigation, it will give the complainant another opportunity to submit new evidence. The complainant will have at least four weeks to reply and may ask for an extension.[76] If the complainant does not respond, the complaint will be deemed to have been withdrawn.

---

[70] Case 792/79, *Camera Care Ltd. v. Commission*, [1980] ECR 119, para. 19. According to this case the Commission could adopt interim or interlocutory measures in urgent cases to avoid a situation likely to cause either serious and irreparable damage to a complaining party or harm to the public interest.

[71] For critical comments on this restriction of the conditions under which the Commission may grant provisional measures, see Idot, above n. 37, pp. 125–126.

[72] Complaints Notice, para. 24.   [73] *Ibid*, paras. 33 *et seq.*

[74] See e.g. Case T-24/90, *Automec Srl v. Commission (II)*, [1992] ECR II-2223; Case C-119/97, *UFEX (ex SFEI) et al. v. Commission*, [1999] ECR I-1341.   [75] Complaints Notice, para. 61.

[76] *Ibid*, paras. 70–71.

d) Informal Guidance Letters

In essence, the possibility for companies to ask the Commission informally for guidance represents a concession aimed at compensating in part for the loss of legal certainty following the abolition of the notification and prior authorization system. (As we have noted in previous surveys, legal certainty was not offered by the notification system, save as regards immunity from fines.) The new Notice on Informal Guidance promises to issue guidance letters in exceptional circumstances of 'genuine uncertainty' relating to 'novel or unresolved questions for the application of Articles 81 and 82'.[77] However, companies will not have the right to obtain such opinions, and in no circumstances will this informal system reintroduce a notification system by the back door. A guidance letter does not prejudice the Commission's powers as to a subsequent assessment of the same issues, and cannot bind national courts.[78] However, it may be presumed that guidance letters will have persuasive value before a court, so that their legal effects will resemble those of the old comfort letters. It is expected that the long-standing and commendable accessibility of Commission officials to offer informal and non-binding guidance will continue.

According to the Notice, the Commission will issue a guidance letter when five cumulative conditions, three positive and two negative, are satisfied[79]:

- the question cannot be clarified by reference to the existing EC legal framework, the case law, publicly available Notices, Communications or Guidelines, decision-making practice or previous guidance letters;

- it is useful to clarify the question owing to its economic importance from the point of view of consumers, the fact that the practice concerned enjoys widespread 'economic usage in the marketplace' or the scope of the investments involved and whether the transaction affects structural operations, e.g. joint ventures;

- the information provided to the Commission is on its own sufficient to issue a guidance letter;

- the questions involved are not identical or similar to questions before a Community Court in a pending case; and

- the specific practice concerned is not subject to proceedings pending before the Commission, a national competition authority or a national court.

e) Effect on Trade Notice

Community competition law is applicable when an anti-competitive practice has an actual or potential effect on trade between Member States: this is the

---

[77] Notice on Guidance Letters, para. 5. Under the new system the possibility to issue such letters is extended to Article 82 cases.   [78] *Ibid*, paras. 24 and 25.

[79] *Ibid*, para. 9.

jurisdictional boundary between Community and national competition law. The Court of Justice has interpreted this criterion broadly so as to bring as many practices as possible within the scope of Community law.[80] This involved some artificial stretching of concepts, but was consistent with the Treaty's basic aim of ensuring that competition in the internal market is not distorted (Article 3(1)(g)). In the decentralized enforcement system, a narrow interpretation of the effect on inter-State trade would run counter to one of the main aims of the reform as expressed in Article 3 of Regulation 1/2003, which is to involve as many enforcers as possible in EC competition law enforcement. Understandably, therefore, the Notice on the effect on trade between Member States follows the traditional broad interpretation.[81]

The Notice lists the three elements to be addressed when considering whether trade between Member States may be affected. Firstly, the concept of 'trade between Member States' implies that there must be an impact on the flow of goods and services or other forms of economic activity involving at least two Member States. Secondly, the notion 'may affect' implies that it must be possible to foresee with a sufficient degree of probability that the agreement or practice may have an influence (direct or indirect, actual or potential) on the pattern of trade between Member States. Thirdly, the notion of 'effect' incorporates a quantitative criterion, so that it must be of a certain magnitude for EC law to apply.

The Notice tackles the evaluation of effect by making one negative and one positive presumption, both of which are based on fairly low thresholds and thus extend the scope of Community competition law.[82] An agreement will be presumed not to affect inter-State trade appreciably when the aggregate market share of the parties on any relevant market within the Community does not exceed 5 per cent, and the aggregate annual Community turnover of the undertakings concerned in the case of horizontal agreements, or of the supplier in the case of vertical agreements, does not exceed €40 million.[83] It will be presumed that an agreement or practice which by its very nature is capable of affecting trade between Member States, for example because it concerns imports or exports or covers several Member States, does affect inter-State trade appreciably if the parties' annual Community turnover exceeds €40 million or their market share exceeds 5 per cent.[84]

---

[80] Case 56/65, *Société Technique Minière (LTM) v. Maschinenbau Ulm GmbH (MBU)*, [1966] ECR 235; Case 126/80, *Maria Salonia v. Giorgio Poidomani et al.*, [1981] ECR 1563; Case C-41/90 *Klaus Höfner and Fritz Elser v. Macrotron*, [1991] ECR I-1979.

[81] Some commentators go as far as to argue that under the new decentralized enforcement system, the *de minimis* rule is no longer in accordance with the *effet utile* of the Treaty competition rules: see e.g. Viennois, 'Clarification du champ d'application du droit communautaire de la concurrence: Brèves observations sur la communication de la Commission européenne relative à la notion d'affectation du commerce figurant aux articles 81 et 82 du Traité', *Petites Affiches*, 22-9-2004, No. 190, 9, p. 12.

[82] See paras. 52–53 of the Notice.

[83] This rule is referred to as the 'NAAT' ('non-appreciable-affectation-of-trade') rule.

[84] See para. 53 of the Notice. The 5 per cent positive presumption does not apply if the agreement covers only part of a Member State.

f) Article 81(3) Notice

From a substantive law point of view, the Article 81(3) Notice is perhaps the most important of the modernization Notices. Its avowed aim is to present the Courts' case law and the Commission's decisional practice in a user-friendly manner for national judges, but its real ambitions are wider. The Notice represents an important set of guidelines, even a 'restatement', on Article 81, and constitutes the Commission's final important pronouncement in the context of the modernization of Article 81 which began nine years ago with the publication of the Green Paper on vertical restraints.[85] Its wider importance is evident from the divergence between its title and its actual contents: while it purports to deal only with Article 81(3), it in fact sets out the Commission's current views on Article 81 as a whole, in line with the new system of legal exception which has transformed Article 81 into a unitary norm.

The Notice follows the CFI's *Métropole Télévision* judgment, which admitted that Article 81(1) to some extent calls for an economics-based approach, but took the view that the balancing of pro-competitive and anti-competitive effects should only take place under Article 81(3), which is the only provision that can accommodate a 'rule of reason' test.[86] The analytical framework used in the Notice is highly theoretical and based on a much more rigorous economic analysis than the Commission has applied in previous decisions. The tests it sets out under Article 81(1) is more relaxed overall, but it makes up for this by setting out under Article 81(3) a very demanding test which presupposes a complex and costly economic analysis.

The new Notice seems to depart from the Commission's past formalistic approach of considering that almost any agreement which restricted commercial freedom restricted competition under the terms of Article 81(1), meaning that any substantive analysis of the pro-competitive merits of the agreement only took place under Article 81(3). Instead it considers that assessing whether an agreement infringes Article 81(1) requires first and foremost a substantive analysis of the market and the economic impact of specific restrictions, while the guiding principle becomes consumer welfare.[87] After distinguishing between restrictions of competition by object and effect, the Notice stresses that an agreement will be anti-competitive when there are 'negative effects on prices, output, innovation or the variety or quality of goods and services.'[88] These 'negative effects on competition within the relevant market are likely to occur when the parties individually or jointly have or obtain some degree of market power and the agreement contributes to the creation, maintenance or strengthening of that market power or

---

[85] Green Paper on Vertical Restraints in EC Competition Policy, COM(1996) 721 final.

[86] Case T-112/99, *Métropole Télévision (M6) et al. v. Commission*, [2001] ECR II-2459, paras. 72–77.

[87] See para. 13 of the Notice. See further Bourgeois and Bocken, 'Guidelines on the Application of Article 81(3) of the EC Treaty or How to Restrict a Restriction', 32 LIEI 111 (2005), pp. 112–113.

[88] *Ibid*, para. 24.

allows the parties to exploit such market power.'[89] The Notice defines market power as 'the ability to maintain prices above competitive levels for a significant period of time or to maintain output in terms of product quantities, product quality and variety or innovation below competitive levels for a significant period of time'.[90] This definition is welcome because it orients the competition analysis towards a less formalistic approach.

A general point which should be made here is that under the new Notice, Article 81(1) will only apply if there is a 'decrease in consumer surplus', for example, when the agreement leads to price increases.[91] Notwithstanding this shift, the Notice does not render the long-standing dogma of market integration obsolete. Paragraph 13 of the Notice seems to introduce a presumption that agreements prejudicial to market integration will harm consumers, but it remains important that the market integration aim is subsumed into the consumer welfare test.[92]

The substantive analysis guidelines are contained in paragraph 18 of the Notice. To assess whether an agreement falls under Article 81(1), the Commission will ask whether it restricts actual or potential competition that, (a) could have existed without it, or (b) would have existed in the absence of the contractual restraint. The first question is aimed at assessing whether the agreement reduces inter-brand competition. The test is whether the parties could have acted independently to attain the same objective as that attained by the restrictive agreement. If an agreement does not restrict inter-brand competition, it might still be considered to restrict competition if it contains intra-brand restrictions going beyond what is objectively necessary for the existence of an agreement of that type or nature. This is the focus of the second question.

The Notice then provides an analytical framework for each of the four conditions in Article 81(3). With regard to the first condition, i.e., the improvement of production or distribution of goods or promotion of technical or economic progress, the Commission takes the view that any efficiencies must be 'objective'. The parties must substantiate their nature, the link between the agreement and the efficiencies, the likelihood and magnitude of each efficiency, how and when the efficiency gain will be achieved and any cost of achieving the efficiencies.[93] The Guidelines give two examples of efficiencies which will be relevant for this test: (a) cost efficiencies resulting from the development of new production technologies and methods, integration of existing assets or economies of scale and scope; and (b) non-cost-related qualitative efficiencies brought about by, for example, R&D agreements, licence agreements, joint production of new products or specialized distribution agreements.

The Commission then goes on to analyze when there is a fair share for consumers. The concept of a 'fair share' implies that the passing-on of benefits must at

---

[89] See para. 25 of the Notice.   [90] *Ibid.*   [91] *Ibid*, para. 27.
[92] See also Lugard and Hancher, 'Honey, I Shrunk the Article! A Critical Assessment of the Commission's Notice on Article 81(3) of the EC Treaty', 25 ECLR 410 (2004), p. 412.
[93] Para. 51 of the Notice.

least compensate consumers for any negative impact caused by the restriction of competition under Article 81(1). Consumers must not be worse-off following the agreement. Interestingly, the Notice stresses that in general, the condition that consumers must receive a fair share of the benefits implies that the efficiencies which the restrictive agreement generates in a relevant market must be sufficient to outweigh its anti-competitive effects in *that same relevant market*.[94] This might be read as excluding from consideration non-competition concerns and benefits to other classes of consumers or society at large under Article 81(3), although the Commission's past decisions may suggest the opposite.[95]

When assessing the passing-on of efficiencies, the following factors must be considered:

- characteristics and structure of the market: the higher the degree of residual competition, the more likely that undertakings will try to increase their sales by passing on efficiencies;

- nature and magnitude of the efficiency gains: according to economic theory, output and pricing decisions are determined by variable costs, not fixed costs; the Commission will therefore give substantially greater weight to reductions in variable costs;

- elasticity of demand: the higher the increase in demand caused by a reduction in price, the higher the pass-on rate; and

- magnitude of the restriction of competition: weighing the increased market power caused by the restrictive agreement against the resulting efficiencies.

Regarding the indispensability criterion, the new Notice applies a two-fold test: (a) the restrictive agreement itself must be necessary to achieve the efficiencies; in other words, there must be a direct causal link; (b) the individual restrictions of competition flowing from the agreement must also be necessary for achieving the efficiencies. The assessment is made in the actual context in which the agreement operates and must take account of the structure of the market, the economic risks related to the agreement and the incentive facing the parties: the more uncertain the success of the product covered by the agreement, the more necessary a restriction may be to ensure that the efficiencies will materialize.

---

[94] Paras. 43 and 87 of the Notice.
[95] See for example Commission decision 2000/475/EC of 24 January 1999 (*CECED*), OJ [2000] L187/47, where the Commission approved an agreement to stop production with a view to improving the environmental performance of products. The new more restrictive approach of the Article 81(3) Notice does not fit in well with the Guidelines on horizontal agreements (Commission Notice—Guidelines on the Applicability of Article 81 of the EC Treaty to Horizontal Cooperation Agreements, OJ [2001] C 3/2, paras. 192–193), where the Commission takes a positive stance on the use of environmental agreements by stating that 'environmental agreements caught by Article 81(1) may attain economic benefits which, either at individual or aggregate consumer level, outweigh their negative effects on competition.' The reference to 'aggregate consumer level' may be difficult to reconcile with the Commission's 'same market' approach in the new Notice.

The indispensability criterion here is different from the approach followed under the Article 81(1) 'two-questions' test in paragraph 18 of the Notice, which refers to agreements that have already been considered as restricting competition because the parties could have acted independently, or owing to objectively unnecessary intra-brand restrictions. The test here is whether a restrictive agreement under Article 81(1) produces more efficiencies than would be the case in the absence of the agreement or restriction.[96]

The final condition in Article 81(3) requires an analysis of the various sources of competition in the market, the level of competitive constraint they impose on the parties to the agreement and the impact of the agreement on that competitive constraint. The assessment of actual competition should usually not only consider market shares and past competitive behaviour, but involve a more extensive qualitative and quantitative analysis. The analysis of potential competition entails assessing the levels of entry barriers, including the following factors[97]:

- regulatory framework;
- cost of entry, including sunk costs;
- minimum efficient scale;
- competitive strengths of potential entrants;
- likelihood of entry sponsored by large buyers;
- likely response of incumbents to new entry;
- economic outlook for industry; and
- past entry or absence thereof.

The most welcome development in the Article 81(3) Notice is that it distinguishes clearly between elimination of competition and dominance. It thus departs from earlier Commission Notices which equated the two. While the Guidelines on vertical restraints and on horizontal agreements refuse in principle to exempt agreements by dominant undertakings,[98] paragraph 106 of the new Notice repositions the Commission's approach, in line with the recent *Atlantic Container* cases,[99] to make it clear that the application of Article 81(3) to dominant undertakings cannot be excluded.[100]

---

[96] See Kjølbye, *op.cit.* p. 569.   [97] Para. 115 of the Notice.
[98] See Guidelines on Vertical Restraints, para. 135; Guidelines on Horizontal Cooperation Agreements, para. 36.
[99] Case T-395/94, *Atlantic Container Line AB et al. v. Commission*, [2002] ECR II-875, para. 330; Joined Cases T-191/98, T-212/98, T-214/98, *Atlantic Container Line AB et al. v. Commission*, [2003] ECR II-3275, para. 939. These judgments are reviewed in a later section of this survey.
[100] See Kjølbye, *op.cit.*, p. 576; Nicolaides, 'The Balancing Myth: The Economics of Article 81(1) & (3)', 32 LIEI 123 (2005), p. 140; Rousseva, 'Modernizing by Eradicating: How the Commission's New Approach to Article 81 EC Dispenses with the Need to Apply Article 82 EC to Vertical Restraints', 42 CML Rev. 587 (2005), p. 618.

Thus, the new Notice is somewhat complex, and if its main aim is to offer national judges a user-friendly guide to the intricacies of competition law, it may not have succeeded. The text referring to the Article 81(3) conditions sometimes seems restrictive and cumbersome, which may make it hard for companies to self-assess their agreements. By way of example, companies claiming efficiencies should be in a position to effect a rigorous quantitative analysis reminiscent of a dumping questionnaire:

as accurately as reasonably possible calculate or estimate the value of the efficiencies and describe in detail how the amount has been computed. They must also describe the method(s) by which the efficiencies have been or will be achieved. The data submitted must be verifiable so that there can be a sufficient degree of certainty that the efficiencies have materialized or are likely to materialize.[101]

(iii) Enhancement of Private Enforcement

The modernization and decentralization of EC competition law enforcement will have a big impact on the application of the law by civil courts and on private antitrust enforcement, which is expected to grow from a rather under-developed to a more complete and mature system.[102] National courts will no longer play a marginal role; they will soon become full players in the enforcement of the competition rules, albeit in a role complementary to that of the public antitrust authorities, most notably the Commission. Indeed, the Commission considered private antitrust enforcement as part of effective decentralization to be one of the three main objectives of the modernization reforms. It soon became evident, however, that while modernization and the passage to a legal exception system were a necessary condition to promote private action in Europe, they were not sufficient on their own. The legal and institutional framework of civil litigation in the EU is largely governed by national law, and unification or harmonization of the national provisions is a sensitive subject. In addition, laying down mechanisms to encourage a new class of litigation is sure to be controversial.

Notwithstanding these obstacles, the Commission set out to study the problem and then propose appropriate solutions. It focused on actions for damages rather than other civil sanctions such as restitution, injunctions, nullity of a contractual relationship or the inability to invoke unfair competition law as a basis for claims. The Commission found support for its endeavours in the Court of Justice's *Courage* judgment, which made it clear that national courts were under a Community law duty to grant damages to victims of anti-competitive behaviour.[103] During 2003 the Commission commissioned a study on the conditions for

---

[101] Para. 56 of the Notice.

[102] See various authors in Ehlermann & Atanasiu (Eds.), *European Competition Law Annual 2001: Effective Private Enforcement of EC Antitrust Law* (Oxford/Portland, 2003).

[103] See further Komninos, 'New Prospects for Private Enforcement of EC Competition Law: *Courage* v. *Crehan* and the Community Right to Damages', 39 CML Rev. 447 (2002).

claiming damages in the Member States in the case of infringement of the EC competition rules. The results of the study were published on the Commission's website early in 2004.[104] They showed wide discrepancies between Member States' substantive and procedural law frameworks and identified very few final judgments where victims of anti-competitive conduct were actually awarded damages.[105]

The Commission has established an internal working group which is examining the results of the study and is expected to publish a Green Paper in the second half of 2005. The Green Paper will probably propose 'options' to promote actions for damages through Community legislation (either a Regulation or a Directive), or perhaps a soft law instrument. The working group has been examining a number of revolutionary proposals, including the introduction of punitive damages, shifting the burden of proof from the plaintiff to the defendant, elimination of the 'passing-on defence', clarification of the rules on standing to sue and facilitating 'follow-on claims' for damages against companies found guilty of anti-competitive action by the Commission or national competition authorities.

The Green Paper and its aftermath will certainly bring the Community competition enforcement system closer to the US antitrust system, which is predominantly private enforcement-oriented. However, many sociological and psychological obstacles will remain before private enforcement takes off in Europe. The absence of a plaintiffs' bar, the non-existence of Community courts of full jurisdiction (possibly decentralized) that could hear such claims and the idea that EC competition law is still Brussels-based militate against a rapid revolution, although some mobility in the national context can be identified.[106]

C. New Technology Transfer BER and Guidelines

The modernization of the instruments for enforcing Article 81 continued with the adoption of a new Technology Transfer block exemption Regulation and accompanying Guidelines. Its predecessor[107] was the last 'old-style' BER to undergo the Commission's review. The need to modernize the Community competition rules relating to licensing of intellectual property was acknowledged in the 2002 Commission Communication on the implementation of the 'Lisbon strategy'.[108] The Commission's aim was to adopt a 'simpler and possibly wider block exemption for technology licensing agreements, limiting competition

---

[104] See http://europa.eu.int/comm/competition/antitrust/others/private_enforcement/index_en.html. The study consists of a comparative report, a report on economic models for the calculation of damages and 25 national reports.

[105] See Woods, Sinclair and Ashton, 'Private Enforcement of Community Competition Law: Modernisation and the Road Ahead', (2004-2) *EC Competition Policy Newsletter* 31.

[106] See for example the UK 2002 Enterprise Act and the draft seventh amendment of the German Competition Act.   [107] Regulation 240/1996, OJ [1996] L 31/2.

[108] More Research For Europe: Towards 3% of GDP, COM(2002) 499 final, Brussels, 11.9.2002.

policy scrutiny of licensing agreements to situations where it is necessary, and providing greater legal certainty'.[109]

Following a Commission Report of December 2001 and a public debate on the policy on technology licensing in Europe,[110] the Commission released a draft Regulation and draft Guidelines on the application of Article 81 to technology transfer agreements and invited all interested parties to submit comments on these documents.[111] The drafts were criticized as more restrictive than both the US Licensing Guidelines[112] and the 1996 TTBER. Even though the proposed TTBER introduced market share caps, it still had a relatively long list of hardcore restrictions, and classified as illegal many licensing practices that gave rise to hardly any anti-competitive effect. After further consultations, a more liberal approach was adopted in the final version of the Regulation and the Guidelines, which both came into force on 1 May 2004.

The new TTBER abandons the complex and formalistic approach of its predecessors and brings the EU rules on intellectual property licensing closer to those applicable in the US. In particular, the new TTBER embraces the core principles on which the US Licensing Guidelines are based:

- licensing is generally considered pro-competitive[113]; and

- anti-competitive effects are most likely to occur when there is market power, but market power cannot be inferred from the intellectual property rights alone.[114]

The Regulation abandons the classification of standard clauses as black, white and grey. Instead it adopts two relatively short lists of hardcore restrictions, one for agreements between competitors and the other for agreements between non-competitors. The Regulation does not list white clauses and expressly states that non-exempted clauses do not necessarily infringe Article 81(1).[115] The Guidelines themselves make it clear that the Commission will consider agreements containing

---

[109] More Research For Europe: Towards 3% of GDP, COM (2002) 499 final, Brussels, 11.9.2002. p. 15.

[110] All available at http://europa.eu.int/comm/competition/antitrust/technology_transfer/en.pdf.

[111] OJ [2003] C 235/11 and OJ [2003] C 235/17.

[112] US Department of Justice and Federal Trade Commission, Antitrust Guidelines for the Licensing of Intellectual Property, 6.4.1995, available at http://www.usdoj.gov/atr/public/guidelines/ipguide.htm.

[113] See Recital 5 of the new Regulation and paras. 9 and 17 of the new Guidelines. It is explicitly confirmed that intellectual property rights as such do not give rise to competition concerns, and that in fact technology transfer agreements usually improve economic efficiency and are pro-competitive, in particular because they reduce duplication of R&D, strengthen the incentive for the initial R&D and spur incremental innovation by increasing expected returns, facilitate diffusion and generate product market competition.   [114] See Recital 6 of the new Regulation and para. 15 of the Guidelines.

[115] Recital 8 of the new Regulation provides that 'it is not necessary to define agreements that fall within Article 81(1)', and stresses that competitive assessment of the agreement depends on several factors, such as structure and dynamics of the relevant technology market and product markets.

the hardcore restrictions listed in the Regulation as 'restrictive by their very object'.[116]

The new TTBER, like other revised BERs, adopts market share caps: the block exemption will only be applicable to a defined category of technology transfer agreements between competitors if the combined market share of the parties does not exceed 20 per cent in the affected technology and product market. For vertical restraints the market share ceiling is set at 30 per cent. The adoption of market shares may reduce legal certainty, since markets for technology are often very dynamic. The Commission recognizes this problem in paragraph 24 of the Guidelines, where it states that:

outside the safe harbour of the TTBER it must be also taken into account that market share may not be always a good indication of the relative strength of available technologies. In such situation, the Commission will take into account the number of independently controlled technologies available in addition to the technologies controlled by the parties to the agreement that may be a substitute for the licensed technology at a comparable cost to the user.

The US Licensing Guidelines adopt a similar approach.[117]

Obviously, the block exemption applies only to agreements that do not contain the hardcore restrictions listed in the Regulation. The Regulation lists the following hard-core restrictions regarding horizontal agreements:[118] (a) fixing of prices for sales to third parties; (b) output limitations;[119] (c) allocation of markets or customers, except in a number of specified circumstances;[120] and (d) restrictions on the licensee's ability to exploit his own technology. Hardcore restrictions in agreements between non-competitors comprise (a) restrictions on prices, (b) territorial/customer restrictions,[121] and (c) restrictions of sales to end-users via selective distribution systems.

As in other 'new generation' BERs, Article 5 of the new Regulation lists 'excluded restrictions' which are not covered by the block exemption but do not preclude the rest of an agreement from benefiting from the block exemption. They include grant-back clauses,[122] no-challenge clauses and limitations on the

---

[116] See para. 14 of the Guidelines.   [117] See Section 3.2.2 of the US Licensing Guidelines.

[118] Article 4 of the Regulation.

[119] Except for limitations imposed on the licensee in a non-reciprocal agreement. Output limitations are also permitted when imposed on only one of the licensees in a reciprocal agreement.

[120] A licensor may grant exclusive territorial licences restricting active or passive sales by licensees/licensors in territories reserved for the other party, restricting the licensee from making active sales in the exclusive territory of another licensee and obliging the licensee (in a non-reciprocal agreement) to produce the contract goods for a particular customer in order to create an alternative source of supply for that customer. Field-of-use restrictions on licensees in reciprocal licences, and on licensors and/or the licensee in non-reciprocal agreements, are also allowed.

[121] Except for active sales restrictions. A number of specified types of passive sales restrictions are also permitted.

[122] Clauses obliging the licensee to grant an exclusive licence to the licensor or a third party designated by the licensor in respect of its own severable improvements to, or its new applications of, the licensed technology, or to assign rights to improvements or new applications of the licensed technology to the licensor or a third party designated by the licensor.

licensee's ability to exploit its own technology if the parties to the agreement are not competing companies.

The Guidelines recognize that horizontal agreements pose a greater risk to competition than vertical agreements, which are treated more liberally.[123] The restrictions on tying and non-compete obligations are weakened in comparison to the 1996 TTBER. The Guidelines specify that as long as the agreement is within the market-share safe harbour, non-compete obligations and tying are block-exempted.[124] They also recognize that without market power in the tying market, and provided the tie does not cover a certain proportion of the market for the tied product, foreclosure does not occur.[125] Interestingly, the Commission explicitly refers to potential efficiency gains from tying, including enforcing quality standards and achieving technically satisfactory exploitation of the licensed technology.[126] Similarly, it notes that non-compete obligations may have numerous pro-competitive effects, such as promoting the dissemination of technology by reducing the risk of misappropriation of know-how, ensuring that the licensee has an incentive to invest in and exploit the licensed technology effectively, and compensating a licensor who has made client-specific investments in training and tailoring his technology.[127]

The Guidelines follow an economic analysis and adopt effects-based tests for assessing the legality of licensing agreements. The analytical framework is similar to that under paragraph 18 of the Article 81(3) Notice. First, the Guidelines ask whether the agreement restricts actual competition or competition which might have existed had no licence been granted.[128] This test has been recognized as a proper benchmark for evaluating the effects of licensing agreements.[129] A further test is designed to evaluate 'intra-technology' restraints: does the agreement obstruct competition which would have existed in the absence of its alleged restrictions on competition? Any such restrictions will be condemned unless they are objectively necessary.[130] In other words, an agreement will be declared anti-competitive if an alternative agreement could have been made which achieved the same legitimate ends while leading to greater consumer surplus.

The new TTBER is much broader in scope than the 1996 TTBER, since it applies not only to patent and know-how licensing but also to software copyright,

---

[123] See para. 26 of the Guidelines.

[124] *Ibid*, para. 191 with respect to tying and para. 197 with respect to non-compete obligations.

[125] *Ibid*, para. 193.   [126] *Ibid*, paras. 194 and 195.   [127] *Ibid*, paras. 201 to 203.

[128] *Ibid*, para. 12(a).

[129] See e.g. the comments by Carl Shapiro, 'EU Technology Transfer Draft Guidelines: Economic Analysis and Suggestions for Revisions' at http://europa.eu.int/comm/competition/antitrust/technology_transfer_2/.

[130] See para. 12(b) of the Guidelines: 'The question is not whether the parties in their particular situation would have accepted to conclude a less restrictive agreement, but whether given the characteristics of the market a less restrictive agreement would have been concluded by undertakings in a similar setting.' Although the concerns relating to field of use restrictions were eliminated as they were block-exempted under Article 4 of the new Regulation, it is conceivable that application of this test could lead to problematic results.

and the Guidelines suggest that the new rules are also applicable to other types of copyright agreements.[131] The new rules are better grounded in economics, echoing the approach adopted in the US. All in all, the flexibility of the new Regulation and Guidelines will give businesses the opportunity to structure their agreements in the ways that make the most commercial sense. The downside is that the legal certainty given by the 1996 TTBER 'straitjacket' will not be matched by the new 'safe harbours',[132] an effect reinforced by the new self-assessment regime introduced by Regulation 1/2003.

D. Other Legislative and Policy Developments in the Field of Antitrust

(i) New BER for the Insurance Sector

Legislative developments in 2003 and 2004 included a new block exemption Regulation applicable to the insurance sector. Regulation 358/2003 was adopted under *vires* provided for in Regulation 1534/1991.[133] It covers three types of agreements:

- those on joint calculations, tables and studies;
- those on standard policy conditions and models; and
- those that commonly cover certain types of risks.

Market share caps are adopted only with regard to the third category of agreements. The new Regulation again moves away from 'white lists' and adopts an economics-based approach which assesses the impact of agreements on the relevant market. Joint calculations, tables and studies improve the knowledge of risks and facilitate their rating, thus benefiting consumers. Standard policy conditions or standard models and individual clauses also produce efficiencies, but they must not limit the freedom of participating undertakings to offer different policy conditions to their customers. The common coverage of certain risks is acceptable, but may not impose a comprehensive cover for unrelated risks (bundling) to which a significant number of policyholders are not exposed simultaneously. Co-insurance or co-reinsurance groups (pools) are exempted subject to certain conditions. The exemption for 'new' risks is limited to three years[134]; for risks that are not new it applies to co-insurance and co-reinsurance groups having less than 20 per cent and 25 per cent respectively of the relevant market.

---

[131] Paras. 51–52 of the Guidelines.

[132] See e.g. Fine, 'The EU's New Antitrust Rules for Technology Licensing: A Turbulent Harbour for Licensors', 29 ELRev. 766 (2004).   [133] OJ [1991] L 143/1.

[134] Article 7(1) of Regulation 358/2003.

(ii) Legislative Developments in the Transport Sector

Two further legislative developments which deserve mention concern the transport sector. The first is the adoption of Council Regulation 411/2004, which repeals Regulation 3975/1987[135] and extends the applicability of Regulation 1/2003 to the field of air transport between the Community and third countries.[136] Regulation 1/2003 itself brought inland, maritime and air transport within its scope, leaving air transport between the EU and third countries as one of the very few remaining areas not subject to a common procedural framework and to which the new Regulation did not apply. This meant that the Commission lacked the requisite fact-finding tools and powers to enforce the competition rules in this area, and that the specific rights, powers and obligations assigned to national courts and the competition authorities of the Member States by Regulation 1/2003 did not apply to the sector. The same was true for cooperation between the Commission and NCAs. Regulation 411/2004 also makes it possible for the Commission to adopt block exemptions applicable to air transport between the EU and third countries.

The second development is the amendment of block exemption Regulation 823/2000 on liner shipping conferences (consortia)[137] through Regulation 463/2004.[138] The amendments were necessary to align the block exemption with the legal exception system, and basically concern the abolition of the opposition procedure and the deletion of references to notification of consortia in the Regulation.

(iii) The 'Modernization' of Article 82

Though the Commission's on-going internal 'review' of Article 82 is not a legislative development, it would be a serious omission not to refer to it. The aim of this exercise is to review the Commission's administrative practice in Article 82 analysis and inject an economics-based approach into it, as with Article 81. Public statements by Commission officials indicate that the review may not lead to a 'publishable' text, but it is nevertheless widely expected that a new Notice which will be the first informal Commission pronouncement on this highly sensitive area will be issued, at a time when most commentators agree that the enforcement of Article 82 remains largely 'unmodernized'.[139]

The review will have to address some delicate questions, not least being a number of old decisions upheld by the European Courts on theories which are now an embarrassment. These include the sometimes unwarranted finding of dominance in a narrowly defined market; whether some kinds of conduct may be considered abusive *per se*, while others may deserve a laxer treatment under a 'rule of reason'

---

[135] OJ [1987] L 374/1.   [136] OJ [2004] L 68/1.   [137] OJ [2000] L 100/24.
[138] OJ [2004] L 77/23.
[139] For an evocatively-titled article, see Sher, 'The Last of the Steam-powered Trains: Modernising Article 82', 25 ECLR 243 (2004).

approach; and (*passim*) whether the paramount objective is protection of competition or protection of competitors. One important issue which is being increasingly debated is whether dominant undertakings may have an 'objective justification' for protecting their commercial interests, and the limits of their freedom in this context. Another is the taking into account of efficiencies when deciding whether a certain kind of conduct falls under the prohibition of Article 82. The recent turbulence over standardized rebate schemes confirms that efficiencies, especially in the context of pricing, remain a matter of controversy under Article 82.

E. The New Merger Control System

(i) The New Merger Regulation

The Community institutions' activities in the competition field during 2003 and 2004 were not entirely monopolized by the modernization of the rules for enforcing Articles 81 and 82. On 1 May 2004 a new Merger Regulation entered into force, backed up by a new tool-kit for merger control consisting mainly of an implementing Regulation, Guidelines on horizontal mergers, a guide to best practices when notifying mergers and a string of Notices on case referral, ancillary restraints and the simplified procedure. This 'big bang' was accompanied by the administrative reorganization of DG Competition, with an emphasis on merger control.

The new Merger Regulation introduces three main changes, concerning the substantive test, jurisdictional issues and procedural issues.

The substantive test has been changed from the 'creation or strengthening of a dominant position' to the 'Significant Impediment of Effective Competition' or 'SIEC' test.[140] Thus, in future the test for assessing concentrations will no longer be based solely on dominance; instead the emphasis will be on whether a concentration significantly impedes effective competition in the common market or a substantial part of it, 'in particular as a result of the creation or strengthening of a dominant position'. The SIEC formula steers a middle course between the EU's existing Market Dominance (MD) test and the Substantial Lessening of Competition (SLC) adopted by the US, the UK, Ireland and various other jurisdictions. The focus will now be on whether enough competition remains after the merger to provide consumers with sufficient choice.

The Commission contends that the new test clarifies its powers rather than extending them. It will allow the Commission to intervene when there are anti-competitive effects in oligopolistic markets, even if the merged company is not dominant in the usual sense of the word. Indeed, the Commission will be able to act in situations of non-collusive oligopoly or unilateral effects when the merger

---

[140] Article 2(3) of Regulation 139/2004.

impedes competition, even if the merged entity's market share falls below the traditional dominance threshold and the current test for collective dominance would not be fulfilled. The new SIEC formula will allow it to intervene, for example, in a merger between the number two and three players in a concentrated industry where the merged company is not dominant, provided it can be shown that the merger significantly impedes competition. However, under the new test a merger will not be automatically anti-competitive merely because it is found to create or strengthen a dominant position. More qualitative parameters have to be taken into account, and the Commission will be able to clear even a merger which leads to an increase in the market share of a dominant undertaking, as long as effective competition in the market is not impeded.

Among the jurisdictional changes brought about by the new Regulation, special emphasis should be placed on the new '3-plus rule', which enables companies to request that the Commission alone should examine a concentration which would otherwise require notification in three or more Member States.[141] The new Regulation also amends Articles 9 and 22 of the previous Merger Regulation by making it possible for the parties to ask the Commission to refer a concentration for full or partial examination to a national competition authority on the ground that it may 'affect significantly competition in a market within a Member State which presents all the characteristics of a distinct market'.[142]

Interesting procedural reforms introduced by the new Merger Regulation include the revision of the notification timetable to give the Commission more time to examine mergers (and discuss remedies) in complex cases, thus giving the system greater flexibility. Phase I is now 25 working days with a possible extension of 10 days, while Phase II is now 90 days, with a possible extension of up to 35 days.[143] Moreover, a binding merger agreement is no longer required as a precondition for notification: companies need only demonstrate a sufficiently concrete *good faith intention* to conclude an agreement, e.g. through a letter of intent signed by all undertakings concerned, an MoU, an agreement in principle, etc.[144] This will allow the merging parties to notify earlier. Finally, to increase flexibility in the timing of notifications, the requirement to notify a proposed transaction within seven days of the triggering events has been abolished.

In addition, the Commission has increased its powers of investigation in merger cases, to make them similar to those it enjoys in relation to cartel and dominance investigations.[145] It may now impose fines for supplying it with misleading information of up to 1 per cent of the offending company's aggregate turnover,

---

[141] If none of the competition authorities of the competent Member States objects to the referral within 15 working days of receiving the request, the Commission will examine the merger.

[142] Article 9 of Regulation 139/2004.   [143] *Ibid*, Article 10.

[144] In the case of a public bid, it will be sufficient if the undertaking has publicly announced its intention to make such a bid, provided that the intended agreement or bid would result in a concentration with a Community dimension.

[145] However, the Commission is not allowed to search private premises.

with periodic penalty payments of up to 5 per cent of the aggregate average daily turnover, while the maximum fine of 10 per cent for non-compliance with a decision has been extended to apply to failure to notify. Also, when a merger prohibited by the Commission is implemented, the Commission may now take any necessary measures to restore the *status quo ante*; this goes further than the previous restoration of 'effective competition'.

(ii) The New Implementing Regulation

The Commission soon followed the new Merger Regulation by adopting a new implementing Regulation to replace Regulation 447/1998.[146] Regulation 802/2004 deals with procedures for notifications, time-limits and hearings. It provides for three notification forms: a Form CO, a short notification form for the simplified treatment of certain mergers and a Form RS for pre-notification referrals between the Commission and Member States. The main differences between the old and new Implementing Regulations are the following:

- simplified requirements relating to the beginning and end of time-limits, to reflect the fact that time-limits are expressed in working days under the new Merger Regulation;
- consumer associations will be able to be heard in merger investigations when the proposed concentration affects products or services used by final consumers;
- all parties will be allowed to ask questions during the formal oral hearing, and the parties have the possibility of a preparatory meeting with the Commission to facilitate the efficient organization of the formal hearing;
- regarding confidential information, the Commission has new powers to require the parties to identify the confidential aspects of any documents and specify the undertakings in relation to which the information is considered to be confidential.

The most significant change in the new Form CO is that it adds a new third definition of the market, which applies when one or more parties are engaged in business activities in a product market which is a neighbouring market closely related to a product market in which any other party to the concentration is engaged, and any of their individual or combined market shares in either market is 25 per cent or more.[147] Neighbouring markets are defined as markets where the products are complementary to each other or belong to a range of products generally purchased by the same set of customers for the same end use. The aim of this new definition is to enable the Commission to obtain information for assessing the conglomerate effects of a merger.

At least two mild criticisms can be made of the new implementing Regulation. Firstly, it only allows access to the file after notification of the statement of

---

[146] OJ [1998] L 68/1.   [147] Section 3(III)(b) of Annex I to Regulation 802/2004.

objections.[148] The procedural rights of the parties would clearly be enhanced if access was granted at any time during the procedure. Secondly, like its predecessor, the new Regulation does not specify a deadline by which the Commission must inform the parties if a notification is incomplete, but only requires it to do so 'without delay'. The introduction of a specific legal deadline would have increased legal certainty for the parties by removing any chance for arbitrary exercise of discretion when the workload is very heavy.[149]

(iii) The New Horizontal Merger Guidelines

On 16 December 2003 the Commission adopted Guidelines on the control of horizontal mergers[150] which set out the approach to analyzing the likely impact on competition of mergers between competitors or potential competitors. The Guidelines clarify the economic framework in which the Commission will assess the competitive effects of horizontal mergers. In particular, they acknowledge that the assessment of mergers should go beyond market shares to consider other elements, such as buyer power, efficiencies created by the mergers, possible failing firm defences and an economic analysis of the competitive constraints which each merging party currently poses for the other. In other words, the Commission will analyze the parties' specific positions in the given market in greater detail, with an emphasis on the consumer welfare test. The Guidelines state that mergers will only be challenged if they enhance the market power of companies in a way likely to have adverse consequences for consumers, most notably in the form of higher prices, reduced choice or poorer quality of goods.[151] They also explain, however, that a merger may have harmful effects on competition because it eliminates a competitor from the market, thereby removing an important competitive restraint, or because it makes coordination between the remaining firms quite likely.

The Guidelines raise at least two areas of concern. First, it seems probable that more cases will come under Commission scrutiny, as the SIEC test in the new Merger Regulation is likely to lead it to challenge mergers at levels or market shares below the traditional thresholds of single firm dominance. Intervention in the case of non-collusive oligopolies will obviously increase the number of mergers exposed to the possibility of detailed investigation by the Commission. This increase in the Commission's level of discretion as to whether a specific merger qualifies as a non-collusive oligopoly means that companies planning a merger will be subject to greater uncertainty and less predictability. The Guidelines attempt to offer some guidance to overcome this uncertainty by stating that 'evidence of past coordination is important'.[152] However, they do not explain how or in what way the Commission will assess such evidence, i.e. how important the pre-merger situation will be.

---

[148] Article 17(1) of Regulation 802/2004.   [149] *Ibid*, Article 5(3).
[150] OJ [2004] C 31/5.   [151] Para. 8 of the Guidelines.
[152] *Ibid*, para. 43.

Moreover, the Guidelines do not clarify issues such as how mergers will be assessed in practice. In an attempt to offer more certainty when clarifying its approach, the Commission has introduced the Herfindhal-Hirschman Index (HHI)[153] index into its merger control. The Guidelines state that intervention will be unlikely when the HHI test indicates that market concentration is below a certain level: the Commission will probably not intervene if the new entity's market share after the merger is under 25 per cent. It is also unlikely to identify horizontal competition concerns in the following three 'safe harbours':

- a market with a post-merger HHI below 1,000;

- a market with a post-merger HHI between 1,000 and 2,000 and where the 'delta' (i.e. the change in HHI arising from the merger) is less than 250; and

- a market with a post-merger HHI above 2,000 but where the delta is less than 150.[154]

Regarding the latter two safe harbours, it is interesting to note that any merger which reduces the number of players in a specific market from six to five will result in an HHI of over 2,000, and most transactions in such a market will also add 150 HHI points. A merger involving two firms in a market which previously had six equal-sized firms would imply a post-merger HHI over 2,200 with a delta of 556. Thus, a merger which would reduce the market players from six to five would be seen as 'risky', and this can certainly be interpreted as likely to increase the level of Commission intervention.

(iv) The New 'Package' of Notices

a) Notice on Case Referral

The adoption of Regulations 139/2004 and 802/2004 was accompanied by a 'package' of Notices. The first of these Notices aims to provide guidance on the case referral systems under Articles 4(4), 4(5), 9 and 22 of the new Merger Regulation. For the first time the Commission takes a position on these referrals, and the Annexes to the Notice include valuable information on the details of referrals. The Notice describes the rationale underlying the referral system, sets out the criteria which must be fulfilled for referrals to be possible, explains what factors the Commission will take into account to decide whether to make or accept a referral and provides guidance on the referral procedures, in particular the

---

[153] The HHI is calculated by adding the squares of the individual market shares of all the firms in the market (para. 16 of the Guidelines). For example, a market containing five firms with market shares of 40 per cent, 20 per cent, 15 per cent, 15 per cent and 10 per cent respectively has an HHI of 2,550 ($40^2 + 20^2 + 15^2 + 15^2 + 10^2 = 2,550$). The HHI ranges from close to zero in an atomized market (groceries, bars or window cleaners), to 10,000 in the case of a pure monopoly (a traditional public monopoly over utilities or the like).

[154] Para. 20 of the Guidelines. See further Voigt and Schmidt, 'The Commission's Guidelines on Horizontal Mergers: Improvement or Deterioration?', 41 CML Rev. 1583 (2004), p. 1589.

procedure for the parties to request a referral under Articles 4(4) and 4(5) of Regulation 139/2004.

The Notice gives some guiding principles to be followed when deciding on case referrals[155]:

(a) Jurisdiction should only be re-attributed when the other competition authority is 'more appropriate' for dealing with a merger. The Commission points out the particular need to pay attention to the likely locus of any impact on competition resulting from the merger.

(b) Decisions on the referral of cases should respect the 'one-stop-shop' principle. The Commission states that fragmentation of cases through referral should be avoided when possible, and that it would normally be appropriate for a single authority to deal with the whole of a case.

(c) Due account should be taken of legal certainty. The Commission refers in particular to pre-notification referrals, which should be confined to cases where it is relatively straightforward from the outset to establish the scope of the geographic market and/or the existence of a possible competitive impact.

The Notice sets out the legal requirements for pre-notification[156] and post-notification[157] case referrals by the Commission to Member States and *vice versa*. It also contains a section giving details of the referral system, which refers in particular to the important role of NCAs[158] and to the information to be provided by the requesting parties,[159] and clarifies some specific concepts such as 'prior to notifications', 'concentration capable of being reviewed under national competition law' and 'competent Member State'. The last part also refers to Article 9(6) of the Merger Regulation, which provides that when the Commission refers a notified concentration to a Member State, the NCA concerned must deal with the case 'without undue delay'. It would have been useful if the Commission had taken the opportunity given by the Notice to clarify this term, which is likely to cause a high level of uncertainty for the notifying parties as to how long the NCA will take to deal with the case. Finally, the Notice contains flow charts showing how the referral process works under Articles 4(4), 4(5), 9 and 22 of the Merger Regulation.

b) Notice on Ancillary Restraints

The Notice begins by stating that the amendment of the rules governing the assessment of ancillary restraints introduces the principle of self-assessing such restrictions. It refers to the new Regulation 139/2004, which makes it clear that it is up to the undertakings concerned themselves to assess whether and to what

---

[155] Para. 8 of the Notice. [156] Articles 4(4) and 4(5) of Regulation 139/2004.
[157] *Ibid*, Articles 9 and 22.   [158] Paras. 53 *et seq.* of the Notice.
[159] *Ibid*, para. 59.

extent their agreements can be regarded as ancillary to a transaction. The only exception is in cases of specific novel or unresolved issues giving rise to genuine uncertainty, when the Commission should retain a residual function. The Notice clarifies that this will apply to a case involving a category of restriction not covered by the Notice or, exceptionally, not already dealt with in a Commission decision. The parties will have to request the Commission to assess such cases.

The new Notice is not substantively different from the previous Notice, but it has a new structure and its contents are enriched by references to recent case law and practice. The most significant changes are as follows:

- A transitional period of up to five years is considered justifiable for purchase or supply obligations aimed at guaranteeing the quantities previously supplied.[160] The previous Notice only referred to a three-year transitional period in the case of complex industrial products. This reference is deleted in the new Notice.

- Non-competition obligations between the parent company and a joint venture will be considered as directly related and necessary for implementing a JV during the JV's lifetime,[161] instead of a transitional period of five years as in the previous Notice.

c) Notice on the Simplified Procedure

The new Notice on the Simplified Procedure adds a further category of cases which will fall under that procedure to the three categories identified in the previous Notice. This new category concerns cases where a party is acquiring sole control of an undertaking over which it already has joint control.[162] The Notice offers some examples of cases where a merger which satisfies the criteria for assessment under the centralized procedure can be examined under the normal Phase I investigation procedure. They include mergers involving a change from joint control to sole control, mergers where the earlier acquisition of joint control of the joint venture in question was not reviewed by either the Commission or NCAs, and mergers which present an issue of coordination as referred to in Article 2(4) of the Merger Regulation.

The simplified procedure will not be applied in any case where there are referral requests under Articles 9 and 22 of the Merger Regulation. However, it may be applied following a failed Article 4(4) request or a successful Article 4(5) request, i.e. pre-notification.[163] The procedural section of the new Notice is very similar to that in the previous one; the only noteworthy point is the possibility for the Commission to issue short-form decisions even when a full-form notification has been made.[164]

---

[160] Para. 33 of the Notice.   [161] *Ibid*, para. 36.   [162] Para. 5(d) of the Notice.
[163] *Ibid*, para. 13.   [164] *Ibid*, para. 17.

(v) New Best Practices Guidelines

Shortly after publishing the new Merger Regulation, the Commission issued new Best Practices Guidelines which aim at providing guidance on the day-to-day conduct of EC merger control proceedings. The following key points should be noted:

(a) Pre-notification contacts[165]: this section covers the very important (and under-estimated) process of preparation. The Commission encourages pre-notification contacts between the notifying parties and the Commission, preferably at least two weeks before submitting the formal notification, even if the case looks likely to be smooth. One aim of these contacts is to prevent notifications from being found to be incomplete due to insufficient information. However, such contacts are voluntary, and will be treated as confidential and without prejudice to the initiation of a formal investigation of the case. They should be initiated by the submission of a memorandum providing details of the parties, the transaction and the relevant markets.

(b) Information to be provided—preparation of Form CO[166]: the Commission advises the parties to disclose all relevant information fully and frankly during pre-notification discussions, including internal papers. It also encourages them to put forward in the pre-notification stage any evidence that the merger will lead to efficiency gains which they would like the Commission to take into account. The information provided will be discussed in detail during the pre-notification discussions with the Commission.

(c) Completeness of the notification[167]: the Best Practices Guidelines state that if the information submitted in Form CO is not correct (e.g. incorrect contact details), the notification will be considered incomplete. However, in such cases the Commission will allow the parties one or two days for correcting any errors in the final Form CO.

(d) Procedural issues and fact-finding[168]: the Commission invites parties to seek DG COMP's opinion on procedural matters such as jurisdictional questions. When a transaction is to be reviewed in more than one jurisdiction, it will also discuss issues with the notifying parties regarding the timing and coordination of filings in other jurisdictions.

(e) Meetings[169]: the Guidelines offer some explanation of the different kinds of meetings to be held with the Commission. They include 'state of play' meetings with the parties at various points in the investigation procedure: (i) before the expiry of the deadline for submitting commitments in Phase

---

[165] Paras. 5 to 9 of the Guidelines.   [166] *Ibid*, paras. 16 to 19.
[167] *Ibid*, paras. 20 to 23.   [168] *Ibid*, paras. 24 to 28.   [169] *Ibid*, paras. 29 *et seq*.

I, if the merger appears to raise serious doubts; (ii) within two weeks of initiating a Phase II investigation; (iii) before issuing a statement of objections; (iv) following the reply to the statement of objections and the oral hearing; and (v) before the Advisory Committee meets. In addition, the Commission will be able to hold meetings with third parties who have a sufficient interest in the proposed transaction (such third parties may be provided with an edited version of the statement of objections). More innovative are possible 'triangular meetings' between the Commission, the parties and interested third parties, which will take place on a voluntary basis and are not intended to replace the formal oral hearing. They will normally be prepared on the basis of a prior agenda and be chaired by senior DG COMP officials. It would have been easier to achieve the aim of triangular meetings by allowing third parties to request such meetings, but without a power to compel this might be fruitless.

The Guidelines also refer to the role of third parties, remedies, access to the file,[170] confidentiality rules and the right to be heard, and other procedural rights which are covered by other Commission Notices or by the new implementing Regulation.

(vi) Reorganization of DG COMP

As part of the merger control reform package which the Commission implemented during 2004, DG Competition underwent internal reorganization aimed at improving the efficiency of merger control handling. The reorganization responded to the rationalization of staff resources in view of the accession of the ten new Member States and an expected increase in the workload. It can also be seen in part as a consequence of the recent CFI rulings overturning Commission decisions prohibiting certain mergers[171] on the grounds that the Commission's evidence was not sufficiently strong to substantiate their anti-competitive effects.

The main element in the reorganization is the integration of the Merger Task Force ('MTF') into directorates dealing with specific sectors of the economy: (a) energy, water, food and pharmaceuticals, (b) information, communication and media, (c) services, (d) industry, and (e) consumer goods. The reorganization was implemented in two main stages. During the first stage, the MTF was integrated into each of these sectoral directorates. The second stage involved the MTF's total replacement by a coordination unit reporting to a Deputy Director General who oversees consistency of procedure and policy. This means that each

---

[170] Certain key documents will also be released on an *ad hoc* basis following initiation of Phase II proceedings.

[171] Case T-342/99, *Airtours plc. v. Commission*, [2002] ECR II-2585; Case T-5/02, *Tetra Laval BV v. Commission*, [2002] ECR II-4381; and Case T-310/01, *Schneider Electric SA v. Commission*, [2002] ECR II-4071.

unit in each sectoral directorate will deal with any type of case in its allotted industrial sector, i.e. cartels, mergers, and abuses of dominance.

As a more direct attempt to improve its economic approach when assessing concentrations, the Commission has appointed Professor Lars-Hendrik Röller[172] as Chief Economist in DG COMP. He will be supported by a team of some 10 economists who will provide case-handlers with economic and econometric input and conduct a critical examination of the case team's conclusions. He reports directly to the Director General for Competition. Professor Röller is said to have advised the Commission on the prohibited *General Electric/Honeywell* and the approved *GE/Instrumentarium* mergers.[173] The Commission will also set up individual *ad hoc* panels, including officials from other DGs, to offer the case team an independent internal review and test the Commission's conclusions at different stages during the procedure.

It is somewhat disappointing that this thorough reorganization of DG COMP did not include a requirement for different merger investigation teams in Phase I and Phase II. This would have meant that the Phase II team would bring a fresh pair of eyes and perhaps a different perspective to scrutinizing the conclusions reached by the Phase I team.

III. Important Commission Decisions and European Court Judgments

A. The Commission's Decisional Practice

2003 and 2004 were moderately active years from an enforcement point of view. The total number of cases closed in 2003 was 831, comprising 319 antitrust cases and 231 merger cases. In antitrust, 24 cases were closed by formal decision and the backlog of pending cases was further reduced. In the field of merger control, 231 formal decisions were taken during the year, the number of cases requiring in-depth investigation remaining stable. In 2004 the total number of antitrust cases closed amounted to 391 and the number of merger cases to 242. In antitrust, 28 cases were closed by formal decision, and the number of formal decisions taken in the field of merger control increased slightly.

In 2003 and 2004 the number of new cases in all fields decreased significantly, by about a fifth in the antitrust and merger fields. In antitrust, 262 and 158 new

---

[172] Professor Röller is an eminent and internationally renowned economist. He is Professor of Economics at Humboldt University in Berlin, Director of the Institute for Competitiveness and Industrial Change at the *Wissenschaftszentrum Berlin für Sozialforschung* and Programme Director of the Centre for Economic Policy Research in London, and also has academic experience of the United States.

[173] Commission Decision 2004/134/EC of 3 July 2001 (M.2220-*General Electric/Honeywell*), OJ [2004] L 48/1; Commission Decision of 2 September 2003 (M.3083-*GE/Instrumentarium*).

cases were opened in 2003 and 2004 respectively. The drop in 2004 no doubt reflects the introduction of the new decentralized enforcement system and the demise of notifications. In the merger field, 212 cases were opened in 2003 and 249 in 2004. Thus, 2004 was marked by an increase in the number of mergers and acquisitions notified to the Commission compared with 2003. This was the first such increase since 1999. The 249 notifications made in 2004 represent an increase of 17 per cent over the previous year. The number of final decisions also increased slightly, from 231 in 2003 to 242 in 2004. Of the final decisions in 2004, 64 per cent were adopted under the new Regulation which came into force in May that year, and 57 per cent were adopted under the simplified procedure. There was no change compared with 2003 in the number of cases which gave rise to serious doubts as to their effect on competition and hence required an in-depth (Phase II) investigation; eight such investigations were opened in 2004. Six of the seven transactions subject to a Phase II investigation and concluded in 2004 were finally approved and one resulted in a prohibition.

During 2003 the Commission maintained the trend of anti-cartel activity set during the two previous years. The five decisions issued in 2003 involved some 27 individual companies or associations. These cases were *French beef, Sorbates, Electrical and mechanical carbon and graphite products, Organic peroxides* and *Industrial copper tubes*. The fines imposed in these decisions totalled €404 million, bringing the total amount of fines imposed on hardcore cartels since 2001 to more than €3,200 million. The highest fine was imposed on the electrical and mechanical carbon and graphite products cartel (€101 million). In 2004 the Commission adopted another six decisions against horizontal agreements, involving some 30 companies. These cases were *Copper plumbing tubes, Sodium gluconate, French beer, Raw tobacco in Spain, Hard haberdashery—needles* and *Choline chloride*. Fines totalling over €390 million were imposed in these decisions.

2004 also stands out as the year in which the highest ever fine was imposed on a single company. The €497 million fine imposed on Microsoft was even higher than the total of fines imposed in 2003. The previous record fine imposed on a single company (€462 million) was inflicted on Hoffmann-La Roche in 2002 for its participation in the notorious vitamins cartel.

B. The Application of Article 81

(i) The 'Children' of Wouters—Meca-Medina

In the *Meca-Medina* case[174] the CFI was called on to interpret the ECJ's *Wouters* judgment, and decide whether the anti-doping rules which restrict the freedom of action of athletes, and thus their economic activities, are subject to the competition

---

[174] Case T-313/02, *David Meca-Medina and Igor Majcen v. Commission*, judgment of 30 September 2004, not yet reported.

law rules. In *Wouters*, the Court of Justice had held that certain ethical rules of professional associations which are *prima facie* restrictive of competition may nevertheless fall outside the scope of Article 81(1) on non-competition grounds, mainly when they are justified by an important public interest such as ensuring the independence of the legal profession.

Two professional long-distance swimmers, Mr Meca-Medina and Mr Majcen, complained to the Commission that the anti-doping rules of the International Olympic Committee (IOC) were not compatible with EC competition law or the free movement of services. The Commission decided not to act on the complaint. It considered that the IOC's anti-doping rules were designed solely to combat doping effectively and did not seek to restrict competition. Though the rules might restrict athletes' freedom of action, the Commission concluded that they were inherent to the proper conduct of sporting competition, and that the limitations they imposed did not go beyond what was necessary to attain that objective. The complainants appealed against the Commission's rejection of their complaint. They argued in particular that the Commission had wrongly applied the criteria established in *Wouters* by deciding that the limitation of athletes' freedom resulting from the IOC's anti-doping rules was not a restriction of competition within the meaning of Article 81.

The CFI started its analysis by recalling the judicial precedents to the effect that sport is only subject to Community law insofar as it constitutes an economic activity. It concluded that purely sporting regulations are not subject to the Community requirements on freedom of movement for persons and services, or on competition. The Court distinguished the IOC's anti-doping rules from the rules at issue in *Wouters*, which concerned market conduct—the establishment of multidisciplinary partnerships between lawyers and accountants—and applied to the essentially economic activity of providing legal services. By contrast, the anti-doping rules did not concern market conduct but the conduct of sport, and as such had nothing to do with any economic consideration. The Court took the view that the prohibition of doping was part of the essence of sport, as a particular expression of the requirement of fair play. It therefore held that the method of analysis in *Wouters* could not call into question the Commission's conclusion that the IOC anti-doping rules fell outside the scope of Articles 81 and 82, since that conclusion was based ultimately on the finding that the rules were purely sporting rules.

Interestingly, although the CFI could simply have found that the IOC should not be considered as an 'undertaking' when adopting and enforcing its anti-doping rules, it chose to go further by examining the nature of those rules. This may be due to its desire to take part in the wider discussions inspired by the ECJ's judgment in *Wouters*, and perhaps explains why the CFI judgment reads very much as if it were a response to a preliminary reference. Thus the Court devotes time to dealing with the parties' arguments on free movement of persons and services, though this is difficult to reconcile with the judicial review of a Commission decision rejecting a complaint in the competition field. The Court lacks the power to enforce the free movement rules directly for individuals, so its decision to address these arguments in its ruling is noteworthy. It then goes on to point out that while high-level sport has to a large extent become an economic activity, the anti-doping rules do not pursue any economic objective: they aim solely to preserve a purely social objective, the spirit of fair play, and to safeguard the health of athletes by preventing negative physiological effects.[175] The CFI's language is quite similar to that used by the ECJ in *Wouters*, thus supporting commentators who interpreted *Wouters* as something more than a one-off curiosity.[176]

(ii) The Concept of 'Undertaking'

a) Fenin

Although this was an Article 82 case,[177] we have chosen to deal with it here because the meaning of the term 'undertaking' in that provision is the same as in Article 81. The case concerned a creative attempt to use Article 82 to resolve a serious case of failure by the Spanish national health system to pay suppliers for medical goods and equipment. However, its main interest is that it further clarifies the notion of an 'undertaking' for the purposes of EC competition law.

The Spanish association FENIN represents the majority of the undertakings which market the medical goods and equipment used in Spanish hospitals. In December 1997, FENIN complained to the Commission that the 26 bodies or organizations which run the Spanish national health system ('SNS'), including three national ministries, had abused their dominant position in the Spanish market for medical goods and equipment by taking an average of 300 days to pay amounts owed to members of FENIN, compared to much prompter payments to other suppliers. FENIN claimed the SNS's monopoly position enabled it to discriminate against FENIN members, who were unable to apply any commercial pressure to end its abusive behaviour. The Commission rejected the complaint on the ground that the bodies managing the SNS were not acting as undertakings when they did so, including when they purchased medical goods and equipment. Consequently, Article 82 did not apply.

The CFI confirmed previous case law that the Community competition law notion of an undertaking is that of any entity engaged in an economic activity, regardless of its legal status and the way in which it is financed. The Court rejected FENIN's argument that the SNS was made up of undertakings because it purchased large quantities of goods and equipment. It stressed that the characteristic feature of an economic activity consists of offering goods and services on a

---

[175] Para. 44 of the judgment.

[176] See e.g. Forrester, 'Where Law Meets Competition: Is *Wouters* like a *Cassis de Dijon* or a Platypus?', in Ehlermann & Atanasiu (Eds), *European Competition Law Annual 2004: The Relationship between Competition Law and (Liberal) Professions* (Oxford/Portland, forthcoming).

[177] Case T-319/99, *Federación Nacional de Empresas de Instrumentación Científica, Medica, Técnica y Dental (FENIN) v. Commission*, [2003] ECR II-357.

given market, and not the business of purchasing as such.[178] The CFI continued:

'The nature of the purchasing activity must therefore be determined according to whether or not the subsequent use of the purchased goods amounts to an economic activity.

Consequently, an organization which purchases goods—even in great quantity—not for the purpose of offering goods and services as part of an economic activity, but in order to use them in the context of a different activity, such as one of a purely social nature, does not act as an undertaking simply because it is a purchaser in a given market. Whilst an entity may wield very considerable economic power, even giving rise to a monopoly, it nevertheless remains the case that, if the activity for which that entity purchases goods is not an economic activity, it is not acting as an undertaking for the purposes of Community competition law and is therefore not subject to the prohibitions laid down in Articles 81(1) EC and 82 EC.[179]

On this basis, the Court held that the organizations and ministries managing the SNS were not acting as undertakings for the purposes of EC competition law. The SNS fulfilled a social function, operated according to the principle of solidarity (in that it was funded from social security contributions and other State funding) and provided its services free of charge on the basis of universal coverage. It did not offer goods and services in the context of an economic activity. FENIN's challenge was therefore unsuccessful.

FENIN argued—but late in the day—that public health services may be undertakings for the purpose of Articles 81 and 82 insofar as they provide services to private patients. As its original complaint to the Commission had not referred to services to private patients, the CFI could not take the argument into account for the purposes of its judgment. Nevertheless, this possibility raises further questions. Given that purchases by or on behalf of a public health service would be made in exactly the same way, irrespective of whether they were destined for use with private or public patients, would it make sense for a public health service to be subject to competition law only in respect of some purchases, or because of a small minority of its patients? That could lead to substantial differences between Member States, not to mention legal uncertainty for public health services, other organizations in a similar position and suppliers.

b) AOK Bundesverband

The definition of the term 'undertaking' for the purposes of EC competition law resurfaced, and was substantially clarified, in the *AOK Bundesverband* cases, which dealt with the health insurance sector.[180] The principal issue raised in these cases was whether sickness funds are undertakings and as such subject to the Community competition rules.

---

[178] Para. 36 of the judgment.   [179] *Ibid*, paras. 36 and 37.
[180] Cases C-264/01, C-306/01, C-354/01 and C-355/01, *AOK Bundesverband et al. v. Ichthyol-Gesellschaft Cordes et al*, judgment of 16 March 2004, not yet reported.

All employees in Germany must in principle be insured by statutory sickness funds, which are independently managed bodies with a separate legal personality. They are governed by public law principles and financed through contributions from employees, which are calculated according to the income of the person insured and the contribution rate set by each fund. The fund associations are legally obliged to determine the maximum fixed uniform amounts payable by the sickness funds towards the cost of various types of medicines; if they fail to agree, the maximum amounts will be set by the German Ministry of Health. Although the fixed amount is not imposed as the price of the product in question, the pharmaceutical companies' prices vary only very seldom from the maximum reimbursement level. The ECJ was asked to consider requests for a preliminary ruling by two German courts in the context of a number of actions between the funds' associations and pharmaceutical companies. The main legal issue before the Court was whether, for the purposes of applying Article 81, the sickness funds and their associations should be regarded as undertakings or associations of undertakings when they fixed the maximum amounts payable for medicines.

Advocate General Jacobs concluded that the sickness funds were undertakings for the purpose of Article 81. For him, the decisive factor was that there was some degree of competition between them. He pointed out that the sickness funds themselves determined the amount of the contributions they required from insured persons, who were free to choose which fund to join. Consequently the contribution levels varied from fund to fund, which in his opinion was evidence of price competition between the funds. He thought that the fact that the level of benefits provided by the funds was determined by national law did not preclude the possibility that the funds were acting as undertakings for the purpose of application of Article 81, and that their decisions on the prices of medicines could not be treated differently for this purpose. He pointed out that those decisions were ultimately made by a body consisting exclusively of representatives of the funds, and that they were effective without the Ministry of Health's approval. When deciding on prices, the funds had a clear interest as undertakings in setting the fixed amounts at as low a level as possible, so that they could compete with one another in other ways. For this reason, he held that those decisions could not be considered as made by a public body distinct from the sickness funds. The Advocate General therefore concluded that the decisions setting fixed amounts were in principle caught by Article 81(1). However, they were justified under Article 86(2), unless they could be shown to be manifestly disproportionate as a method for ensuring the ability of the sickness funds to provide services of general economic interest in conditions of financial stability.

Unusually, the Court departed from the Advocate General's Opinion and held that the funds were not undertakings, either in their activity of providing statutory health insurance, or when they determined the maximum fixed amounts. The Court commenced its legal analysis by recalling its settled case law on the notion of an undertaking as any entity engaging in an economic activity, regardless of its legal status or how it is financed. In particular, the ECJ recalled its earlier judgments in the social security sector, where it had examined whether a social security body carried out economic activities. In this respect, the crucial question seems to be whether the prevailing element of a social security system is solidarity or competition.

The Court recalled that in *Poucet* and *Pistre*[181] it had stated that some bodies entrusted with the management of statutory health insurance and old age insurance schemes pursue an exclusively social objective, and do not engage in economic activities. This was the case when the sickness funds concerned merely applied the law and could not influence the amount of the contributions, the use of assets or the fixing of the level of benefits. Their activity was based on the principle of national solidarity and was entirely non-profit-making, and the benefits paid were statutory benefits bearing no relation to the amount of the contributions. On the other hand, the Court had considered in the past that other non-profit bodies which managed statutory social security schemes and engaged in activities of a social character were undertakings engaged in an economic activity that competed with private insurance companies. This was because the bodies in question allowed insured persons to opt for the solution which guaranteed a better investment,[182] or because the fund itself determined the amount of the contributions and benefits and operated in accordance with the principle of capitalization.[183]

The ECJ concluded that the German sickness funds had similar characteristics to the bodies at issue in *Poucet*, because they fulfilled an exclusively social function, were founded on the principle of solidarity and were entirely non-profit-making. The crucial factor for the Court was that the funds were compelled by law to offer their members essentially identical obligatory benefits which did not depend on the amount of the contributions paid. The sickness funds were also joined together by law, to ensure equalization between those whose health expenditure was lowest, and those which insured costly risks and whose expenditure connected with those risks was highest. The Court therefore concluded that the sickness funds carried out exclusively social functions rather than economic activities, and could thus not be considered as undertakings for the purpose of Article 81, although it conceded that they competed with one another to some residual degree.

The Court also considered the possibility of the sickness funds' acting as undertakings when the fund associations determined the fixed maximum amounts, and decided that this was not the case because the funds were obliged by law to fix

[181] Cases C-159/91 and C-160/91, *Christian Poucet v. Assurances Générales de France (AGF) and Caisse Mutuelle Régionale du Languedoc-Roussillon (Camulrac) and Daniel Pistre v. Caisse Autonome Nationale de Compensation de l'Assurance Vieillesse des Artisans (Cancava)*, [1993] ECR I-637.

[182] Case C-244/94, *Fédération Française des Sociétés d'Assurance et al. v. Ministère de l'Agriculture et de la Pêche*, [1995] ECR I-4013.

[183] Cases C-67/96, C-115/97 to C-117/97 and C-219/97, *Albany International BV et al. v. Stichting Bedrijfspensioenfonds Textielindustrie et al*, [1999] ECR I-5751.

the maximum amounts and the procedure for determining the amounts was laid down by law. For these reasons the setting of the fixed amounts was linked to the exclusively social function of providing statutory health insurance, and therefore did not constitute an economic activity.

The Court's judgment is a welcome clarification of the rather complicated case law in this evolving area. It certainly provides for a higher degree of immunity for national sickness funds from the Treaty competition rules, even if some residual competition exists between such funds. The case is perhaps indicative of a more general trend by the Court of Justice to view the 'European social model' more favourably, and move away from certain more economic-oriented pronouncements in the past.[184]

(iii) Effect on Trade between Member States

a) British Sugar

British Sugar, the only processor of sugar beet in the UK, had an agreement with Tate & Lyle, which imports almost 100 per cent of the UK market for cane sugar. In October 1998 the Commission decided that a cartel existed between British Sugar, Tate & Lyle and two sugar merchants.[185] The decision was appealed to the CFI, which delivered its judgment in July 2001,[186] and that judgment was further appealed to the ECJ. The ECJ judgment is interesting for its detailed reference to the criterion of effect on trade between Member States.[187]

The appellants were accused of price coordination in the oligopolistic industrial and retail white granulated sugar markets in the UK. British Sugar claimed the CFI had erred in law when assessing the impact of the alleged cartel on trade between Member States. The ECJ adopted a rather broad and liberal interpretation of the inter-State trade effect criterion, and stressed that even if a cartel relates only to the marketing of products in a single Member State, this is not sufficient to exclude the possibility that it might affect trade between Member States.[188] In this case the market was susceptible to imports, and the cartel participants could only protect their market share by preventing those imports. According to the ECJ, the 'effect on Community trade is normally the result of a combination of factors which, taken separately, are not necessarily decisive'.[189] The Court also pointed out that it was undisputed that limiting imports from other Member States was one of the major preoccupations of the two manufacturers.

---

[184] See Krajewski and Farley, 'Limited Competition in National Health Systems and the Application of Competition Law: The *AOK Bundesverband* Case', 29 ELRev. 842 (2004), p. 849.

[185] Commission Decision 1999/210/EC of 14 October 1998 (*British Sugar plc—Tate & Lyle plc—Napier Brown & Company Ltd—James Budgett Sugars Ltd*), OJ [1999] L 76/1.

[186] Cases T-202/98, T-204/98 and T-207/98, *Tate & Lyle plc, British Sugar plc and Napier Brown & Co. Ltd v. Commission*, [2001] ECR II-2035.

[187] Case C-359/01 P, *British Sugar plc v. Commission*, judgment of 29 April 2004, not yet reported.   [188] Para. 28 of the judgment.

[189] *Ibid*, para. 29.

British Sugar, which was a price leader on the market, shared information about its future prices with other participants in the cartel, and discussed retail prices, in particular with Tate & Lyle. The CFI had therefore been correct in finding that the cartel was likely to have affected inter-State trade.

This broad interpretation of the inter-State trade effect criterion goes in the right direction. In an earlier judgment[190] the Court had opted for a narrower interpretation, but *British Sugar* signals a return to conventional wisdom. In the era of decentralization, a narrow interpretation of the criterion would run counter to one of the reform's most prominent aims, to involve as many enforcers as possible in EC competition law enforcement.

(iv) Cartels

There were a number of important developments in the enforcement of the rules against cartels in 2003 and 2004. Several companies opted to seek the benefit of the leniency policy, while the CFI handed down some important judgments which clarified the state of the law, particularly with regard to certain procedural matters.

a) Organic Peroxides
In this decision,[191] a number of undertakings were fined for operating a price-fixing agreement in the market for organic peroxide, a chemical used in the plastic and rubber industries. The Commission found that the cartel had lasted for 29 years, making it the longest-lasting cartel ever discovered. The fines were relatively low because Akzo Nobel, one of the cartel's founders, received full immunity under the leniency programme. The most interesting legal aspect of the decision is that in addition to the participating companies, the Commission also fined AC Treuhand, a Swiss-based consultancy which had acted as a secretary to the cartel and facilitated the implementation of the agreement. The Commission had only once previously[192] taken action against a cartel organizer, but did not follow up this approach in subsequent decisions. The Commission found that AC Treuhand's role in the cartel went much further than that of a secretary: it had played an essential role in organizing and implementing the cartel, and some of the additional tasks it performed had involved a certain degree of discretion and independent decision-making. In particular, it acted independently from the cartel members by undertaking an audit, which was an essential feature of the agreement. It also stored documents for the cartel participants, reimbursed travel

---

[190] Cases C-215/96 and C-216/96, *Carlo Bagnasco et al. v. Banca Popolare di Novara Scarl and Cassa di Risparmio di Genova e Imperia SpA*, [1999] ECR I-135.

[191] Commission Decision of 10 December 2003 (COMP/37.857-*Organic Peroxides*).

[192] Commission Decision 80/1334/EEC of 17 December 1980 (*Italian cast glass*), OJ [1980] L 383/19. The Commission has fined trade associations in a few others decisions; Commission Decision of 19 December 1984 (Wood Pulp), OJ [1985] L85/1 (fine annulled on appeal). Commission Decision of 26 October 1999 (FEG) OJ [2000] L39/1.

expenses to avoid any traces of illegal meetings and provided legal services, including advice on how to avoid detection of the cartel by the antitrust authorities.

The Commission dismissed the argument that AC Treuhand was not an undertaking or an association of undertakings active on the relevant market concerned
and could therefore not have affected the market, pointing out that it was under
no obligation to prove the exact role of 'facilitators' which clearly participate in an
anti-competitive agreement. The Commission also rejected arguments based on
the Swiss law of obligations, arguing that even if that law was applicable, it could
not oblige AC Treuhand to pursue unlawful activities. It therefore fined AC
Treuhand €1,000, an amount which took into account the novelty of the matter.

This decision marks an important policy change, as it indicates that the
Commission may target independent companies which act as facilitators or organizers of cartel arrangements, although the decision seems to suggest that such
companies will only infringe Article 81 if the scope of their services exceeds that of
a 'purely secretarial function'. Companies which offer auditing services that facilitate the implementation of cartel agreements or play a part in concealing evidence
from antitrust authorities are at risk in the future.

b) Amino Acids

This CFI judgment was an appeal from a 2000 Commission decision fining five
companies (Archer Daniels Midland Co. (ADM) (USA), Ajinomoto Co. (Japan),
Kyowa Hakko Kogyo (Japan), Daesang-Sewon (Korea) and Cheil Jedang (Korea))
a total of €110 million for involvement in a worldwide lysine cartel.[193] Lysine is
the principal amino acid used for nutritional purposes in animal feedstuffs. The
Commission found that these companies had fixed lysine prices, agreed on sales
volume quotas and operated an information exchange system to enforce the quotas. This behaviour qualified as a very serious infringement of Article 81. All the
companies except Ajinomoto lodged appeals with the CFI, invoking errors in the
Commission's calculation of the amount of the fines.

The Court slightly reduced the fines imposed on three of the applicants due to
its different view of the existence and degree of certain aggravating and mitigating
factors. More importantly, it made some interesting statements on the appropriate
calculation of fines.[194] The applicants' main arguments were that:

- the increases for aggravating circumstances and reductions for mitigating
  circumstances should be applied to the basic amount of the fine;
- the fines set should be based on the parties' sales of lysine in the EEA and not
  on their respective total worldwide sales;

---

[193] Commission Decision 2001/418/EC of 7 June 2000 (*Amino Acids*), OJ [2001] L 152/24.
[194] Case T-220/00, *Cheil Jedang Corp. v. Commission*, [2003] ECR II-2473; Case T-223/00, *Kyowa
Hakko Kogyo Co. Ltd and Kyowa Hakko Europe GmbH v. Commission*, [2003] ECR II-2553; Case T-
224/00, *Archer Daniels Midland Company and Archer Daniels Midland Ingredients Ltd v. Commission*,
[2003] ECR II-2597; Case T-230/00, *Daesang Corp. v. Commission*, [2003] ECR II-2733.

- the Commission had breached the principles of legitimate expectations and legal certainty by applying the 1998 Fining Guidelines[195] to an investigation that had preceded them; and

- fining them for behaviour for which they had already been sanctioned in the US amounted to double jeopardy.

The Court found that the Commission had incorrectly increased or reduced the fines for aggravating or mitigating circumstances. It interpreted the Guidelines to mean that such increases or reductions must be applied on the basic amount of the fine. In the Court's view, this method would ensure equal treatment of the various undertakings involved in a cartel. Replying to a written question from the Court, the Commission agreed with this interpretation and acknowledged that it had not applied that method consistently in its decision: when setting the fines to be paid by ADM and Ajinomoto, it had applied the reduction to the amount as already increased to reflect aggravating circumstances. The Court therefore adjusted the fines imposed on ADM and Ajinomoto accordingly.

Regarding the Commission's use of the parties' total worldwide turnover to determine the basic amount of the fines, the Court noted that the Guidelines allow the Commission to take either worldwide turnover or turnover on the relevant market as a basis for calculating fines. However, by not taking into account the parties' turnover in the EEA lysine market, the Commission had not assessed the real impact of the offending conduct on competition, and had consequently disregarded the fourth and sixth paragraphs of Section I.A of the Guidelines. The CFI nevertheless concluded that this did not mean the starting amount of the fines was disproportionate, because the Commission's calculation was not based solely on the parties' worldwide turnover.

On the applicants' arguments drawn from the principles of legitimate expectation, legal certainty, and non-retroactivity of criminal sanctions, the CFI held that the Commission could adjust the level of fines at any time to match the needs of Community competition policy, within the limits of Regulation 17 (which was still in force at the time of the proceedings). The Court made it clear that while penalties imposed under Regulation 17 were not criminal in nature, the Commission was nevertheless bound to respect the general principles of Community law, including the principles of the European Convention of Human Rights (ECHR). There was no question of retroactivity in this case, as the applicable legal rules remained those of Regulation 17: the 1998 Fining Guidelines did nothing to change that basic legal regime. Furthermore, the Commission was not bound to mention the possibility of a change in its fining policy in the Statement of Objections, as this would depend on circumstances that had no direct relationship to the particular circumstances of the case. Moreover, the Guidelines were published before the Commission issued the Statement of Objections in the case,

---

[195] Commission Guidelines on the method of setting fines imposed pursuant to Article 15(2) of Regulation No 17 and Article 65(5) of the ECSC Treaty, OJ [1998] C 9/3.

so the parties would only have had a claim if they had been given legitimate expectations that the principles of the Guidelines would not be applied to calculate their fines; but the Commission had not given rise to such expectations. However, the Court pointed out that the applicants were entitled to entertain legitimate expectations, since they had decided to cooperate with the Commission after the Leniency Notice had been published.

Perhaps the most interesting argument raised by the applicants was that the Commission had breached the principle of *non bis in idem*, as it had failed to take account of the fines already imposed on Kyowa and ADM by the US authorities when calculating the starting amount of their fines. Kyowa and ADM argued that natural justice required penalties already imposed on them for the same reasons to be taken into account, even if their conduct in the EEA constituted an offence separate from that for which they had been fined in the US, due to its differing geographical effect.[196] The Court rejected this line of argument. It acknowledged that *non bis in idem* is a general principle of Community law, upheld by the Community Courts. It then recalled the case law to the effect that while concurrent sanctions resulting from two sets of parallel proceedings, at national and Community level, are in principle acceptable because those proceedings pursue different ends, the Commission must, when determining the amount of a fine in such cases, take account of any penalties already imposed under national cartel law on the company in question for the same conduct.[197] The Court reasoned that *a fortiori*, the principle did not preclude concurrent procedures and penalties in the EU and the US, since the two legal systems clearly pursued different ends.

The Court stated that this interpretation was supported by the scope of the principle that a second penalty may not be imposed for the same offence, as laid down in Article 4 of Protocol 7 to the ECHR and applied by the European Court of Human Rights. The wording of Article 4 made it clear that this principle did not preclude someone from being tried or punished more than once in two or more different States for the same conduct.[198] The Court went on to state that Article 50 of the Charter of Fundamental Rights, which provides that no one may be tried or punished again in criminal proceedings for an offence of which he has already been acquitted or convicted within the EU, had no bearing on this conclusion, as the scope of the right under that provision was expressly limited to cases where the first acquittal or conviction was handed down within the EU.[199]

ADM's argument was based on the ECJ's ruling in *Boehringer*, which stated:

'[In] fixing the amount of a fine the Commission must take account of penalties which have already been borne by the same undertaking for the same action, where penalties have

---

[196] The parties relied on the following cases: Case 14/68, *Walt Wilhelm et al. v. Bundeskartellamt*, [1969] ECR 1, para. 11; Case 7/72, *Boehringer Mannheim GmbH v. Commission*, [1972] ECR 1281, paras. 3–5; Case T-149/89, *Sotralentz SA v. Commission*, [1995] ECR II-1127, para. 29.   [197] *Kyowa*, para. 98.

[198] *Ibid*, paras. 101–102.   [199] *Ibid*, paras. 103 and 105.

been imposed for infringements of the cartel law of a Member State and, consequently, have been committed on Community territory. It is only necessary to decide the question whether the Commission may also be under a duty to set a penalty imposed by the authorities of a third state against another penalty if in the case in question the actions of the applicant complained of by the Commission, on the one hand, and by the American authorities, on the other, are identical.'[200]

ADM argued that this judgment showed the Commission had a duty to offset a penalty imposed by the authorities of a third country against any other penalty, when the third country penalty was imposed for the same facts as those alleged against the applicant by the Commission.[201] The CFI rejected this interpretation, arguing that in this passage the ECJ had not decided the actual question of whether the Commission was required to offset a penalty imposed by the authorities of a third country on the basis of the same facts. In the CFI's view, the ECJ's statement merely meant that it regarded the identical nature of the facts as a precondition for the question of offsetting.[202] The CFI further reasoned that even if *Boehringer* were interpreted differently, the applicants would still have to prove that the facts in the two cases were indeed the same. In this case it had not been shown that the US penalty extended beyond the cartel's US effects to encompass the EEA, an extension which would, moreover, clearly have encroached on the Commission's territorial jurisdiction. The Court also pointed out that the fines imposed by the US courts were calculated on the basis of turnover achieved by ADM in the US.[203]

The CFI also disagreed with the applicants' argument that the principle of natural justice required the Commission to take account of the fines imposed in the US. The Court pointed out that the judgments relied on by the applicants were all determined by the particular situation arising from the close interdependence between the national markets of the Member States and the common market, and from the special system for allocating jurisdiction between the Community and the Member States with regard to cartels on EU territory. The circumstances of the case under consideration were obviously different. Thus, the Court concluded that the applicants had not produced valid legal arguments to establish that the Commission had a duty, when it determined the amount of a fine, to take into account penalties already imposed on the same company, in respect of the same conduct, by authorities or courts of a third country.

c) Greek Ferries
This interesting CFI case originated in on-the-spot investigations by the Commission, which resulted in a decision finding that a number of ferry companies operating in Greece had participated in a price cartel, and imposing fines on

---

[200] *Boehringer*, para. 3. [201] *ADM*, para. 77. [202] *Ibid*, paras. 98–100.
[203] *Ibid*, para. 103.

all the undertakings involved.[204] On appeal to the CFI, the most noteworthy legal questions, especially those relating to the responsibility of a principal for an agent's actions, were discussed at length in the *Minoan Lines* case.[205] The judgment also addresses important questions relating to evidence obtained by the Commission on company premises other than those of the company to which the investigation decision was addressed.

The Commission found that Minoan Lines was the ring-leader of the cartel and fined it severely. Minoan had an agency agreement with ETA, which was its exclusive managing agent for all Minoan ships operating on international routes but not its subsidiary. Minoan argued that several of the anti-competitive activities were ETA's own initiatives, not approved by Minoan and sometimes outside the scope of the ETA-Minoan contracts, and that Minoan should not be regarded as responsible for them. The Commission did not accept this argument. Interestingly, it treated ETA as the '*longa manus*' of Minoan, operating as its representative or as an intermediary acting exclusively on its behalf.[206] In other words, the agent acted as a servant, providing the principal with full details of its participation in the anticompetitive agreements. It was even more telling of the relationship between agent and principal that ETA invariably described itself as 'Minoan' or 'Minoan Athens' when representing Minoan Lines.[207] All these elements clearly made this case special, since although there was a formal agency agreement between the two parties, their conduct essentially indicated a single economic entity. The agent's sole business was to represent Minoan Lines.

The CFI dismissed Minoan's appeal, placing particular emphasis on the particularities of the case, especially the fact that in carrying out its work as Minoan Lines' agent and representative of Minoan Lines, ETA was authorized to present itself to the public at large as Minoan. Its identity was practically coterminous with that of Minoan Lines, which had delegated the conduct of its business to ETA. ETA's offices were in fact the real centre of Minoan's commercial activities, and thus the place where its books and business records relating to the activities in question were kept.[208] The Court noted that even the Athens telephone directory contained an entry for Minoan Lines at ETA's address.[209] According to the Court, this was essentially a case of a single economic entity, applied to the principal-agent relationship. In the relationship between the principal and the agent, the parties adopted the same course of conduct in the market.[210]

---

[204] Commission Decision 1999/271/EC of 9 December 1998 (*Greek Ferries*), OJ [1999] L 109/24.

[205] Case T-66/99, *Minoan Lines SA v. Commission*, judgment of 11 December 2003, not yet reported. The other related cases decided on the same day were Case T-56/99, *Marlines SA v. Commission*; Case T-59/99, *Ventouris Group Enterprises SA v. Commission*; Case T-61/99, *Adriatica di Navigazione SpA v. Commission*; and Case T-65/99, *Strintzis Lines Shipping SA v. Commission*.

[206] Paras. 136–137 of the Decision.   [207] Para. 139 of the Decision.

[208] *Minoan Lines*, para. 69.   [209] *Ibid*, para. 86.   [210] *Ibid*, para. 124.

Referring to the pre-existing case law on the applicability of Article 81 EC to agents,[211] the Court stated:

... if an agent works for the benefit of his principal he may in principle be treated as an auxiliary organ forming an integral part of the latter's undertaking, who must carry out his principal's instructions and thus, like a commercial employee, forms an economic unit with this undertaking ... In the case of companies having a vertical relationship, such as a principal and its agent or intermediary, two factors have been taken to be the main parameters for determining whether there is a single economic unit: first, whether the intermediary takes on any economic risk and, secondly, whether the services provided by the intermediary are exclusive. In so far as concerns the assumption of economic risk ... an agent may not be regarded as an auxiliary body forming part of its principal's business where the agreement entered into with the principal confers upon the agent or allows it to perform duties which from an economic point of view are approximately the same as those carried out by an independent dealer, because they provide for the said agent accepting the financial risks of selling or of the performance of the contracts entered into with third parties. In so far as concerns the question whether the services provided by the agent are exclusive, the Court has held that it tends not to suggest economic unity if, at the same time as it conducts business for the account of its principal, an agent undertakes, as an independent dealer, a very considerable amount of business for its own account on the market for the product or service in question.[212]

The Court concluded that in this case ETA did business on the market only in the name and for the account of Minoan Lines; it assumed no financial risks in connection with that business; and the two companies were perceived by third parties and on the market as forming one and the same economic entity, namely Minoan.[213] However, it would be a mistake to conclude from this ruling that agents and principals always constitute a single economic unit and that an agent's conduct can always be attributed to the principal; the rule remains that a single economic unit will not exist as a matter of course unless there is at least a subsidiary-parent relationship. The Court's judgment must certainly be seen in light of the exceptional facts of the case, and the Court took pains to explain this and refer to those facts on numerous occasions.

The Court also undertook a balancing exercise in assessing the legality of the Commission's investigations on ETA's premises. While it made clear that the Commission must respect defence rights and refrain from any arbitrary or disproportionate intervention in the activities of private individuals, it also stressed the importance of preserving the effectiveness of Commission investigations as a necessary tool for making sure that the Community competition rules were respected. The Court concluded that the Commission's investigations on ETA's premises were legal. The investigation decision which Commission officials had presented to ETA staff before beginning investigations satisfied the requirement

---

[211] Reference to Cases 40/73 to 48/73, 50/73, 54/73 to 56/73, 111/73, 113/73 and 114/73, *Coöperatieve Vereniging 'Suiker Unie' UA et al. v. Commission*, [1975] ECR 1663, para. 480.
[212] *Minoan Lines*, paras. 125–128.   [213] *Ibid*, para. 129.

to state the subject-matter and purpose of the investigation. In light of the detailed statement of reasons in the investigation decision, and the nature of their relationship with Minoan, ETA's employees were therefore in a position to assess the extent of their duty to cooperate with the Commission officials in the investigations. Moreover, ETA's defence rights as an entity distinct from Minoan were not called into question, as the investigation had no bearing on any separate business ETA might have had.

The Court dismissed entirely the argument that the Commission had violated Article 189 of the EC Treaty, which provides that a decision 'shall be binding in its entirety upon those to whom it is addressed'. It ruled that Article 189 was irrelevant for this case, as it only enumerated the legislative measures and decisions available to the Community institutions. Even if this provision were taken into account, it would not effect the validity of the Commission's decision, which would be binding in its entirety on both Minoan and ETA as 'its agent and representative'. The Court was of the opinion that the evidence before it clearly indicated that the Commission was entitled to take the view that ETA's premises were in fact used by Minoan to conduct its business. The Commission was also entitled, for the purpose of exercising its investigatory powers, to take account in its reasoning of the fact that it would be more likely to find proof of an infringement by investigating the premises from which the suspected company in fact conducted its business in practice. The Court therefore concluded that the Commission had fully obeyed the law as regards both the investigation authorizations it had granted and the manner in which it subsequently conducted the investigation, and that in doing so it had preserved the defence rights of the companies concerned.

The Court also rejected Minoan's argument that the Greek authorities influenced the tariff rates applicable to the international part of the lines between Greece and Italy, thus restricting Minoan's autonomy in planning and deciding on pricing policy. The Court held that the Greek government's intervention was limited to measures to encourage the shipping companies to keep their tariffs low and keep annual increases in line with inflation. Thus it was clear that the market still offered scope for competition, which could be prevented, restricted or distorted through autonomous conduct by undertakings.

d) Graphite Electrodes
In this case[214] the CFI decided on appeals by seven companies against a decision finding that a worldwide price-fixing and market-sharing cartel between companies from Europe, the US and Japan existed in the graphite electrodes sector, and imposing fines totalling nearly €220 million on its members.[215] The Court

[214] Joined Cases T-236/01, T-239/01, T-244/01 to T-246/01, T-251/01 and T-252/01, *Tokai Carbon Co. Ltd. et al. v. Commission*, judgment of 29 April 2004, not yet reported.
[215] Commission Decision 2002/271/EC of 18 July 2001 (*Graphite electrodes*), OJ [2002] L 100/1.

significantly reduced the fines after finding that the Commission had misapplied certain rules imposed upon it by its own Fining Guidelines. The reduction had the greatest impact on the fines imposed on the four Japanese companies (Tokai Carbon, Nippon Carbon, Showa Denko and SEC Corporation). The CFI agreed that the Commission has wide discretion in setting the amount of a fine, but scrutinized the Commission's application of the Fining Guidelines very carefully, and stressed in particular the importance of the principles of equal treatment and proportionality when setting fines.

The Court's examination of how the Commission had set the starting amount of the fine is particularly interesting. The Commission had divided the members of the cartel into three categories on the basis of their turnover and market shares. In the Court's words:

[a]s regards the division of the members of the cartel into several categories, which had the consequence that a flat-rate starting amount was fixed for all the undertakings in the same category, although such an approach by the Commission ignores the differences in size between undertakings in the same category, it cannot in principle be condemned. The Commission is not required, when determining fines, to ensure, where fines are imposed on a number of undertakings involved in the same infringement, that the final amounts of the fines resulting from its calculations for the undertakings concerned reflect any distinction between the undertakings concerned in terms of their overall turnover.[216]

However, such a division by categories must comply with the principle of equal treatment, which prohibits different treatment of similar situations and the same treatment for different situations, unless this is objectively justified.[217] The Commission must also apply its method of calculation in a manner which is correct, coherent and, in particular, non-discriminatory. Once it has voluntarily chosen to apply such an arithmetical method, it is bound by the rules inherent therein, unless it provides express reasons for not doing so. In this case, the CFI found that the Commission had not consistently followed the categories for the calculation of fines under the Fining Guidelines, but had used its full jurisdiction to create a new category and modify the starting amount of the calculation in respect of some companies.[218]

Another interesting novelty was the CFI's confirmation that undertakings which, in the course of the administrative proceedings, explicitly admit the substantive truth of the facts alleged against them and in return are granted a reduced fine by the Commission, are in principle estopped from disputing those facts before the Court. In this case the CFI partially allowed the Commission's request to withdraw the reduction of fines initially granted to Nippon Carbon and SGL Carbon for not contesting the facts, as those companies had gone on to contest before the CFI the facts which they had previously admitted.[219]

---

[216] *Tokai Carbon*, para. 217.   [217] *Ibid*, para. 219.   [218] *Ibid*, paras. 232–233.
[219] *Ibid*, paras. 112 and 418.

On attenuating circumstances, the Court rejected the argument that a competition compliance programme and an internal enquiry designed to put an end to an infringement should guarantee more lenient treatment, as they did not alter the reality of the infringement. Consequently, the mere fact that in some previous decisions the Commission had taken such measures into consideration as attenuating circumstances did not mean that it was obliged to act similarly in every case.[220] The Court also rejected the argument that this was in essence a crisis cartel. The Commission was not required to regard the poor financial state of a sector as an attenuating circumstance, and the fact that it had done so in earlier cases did not necessarily mean that it must continue to do so.[221] The Court was equally unimpressed by the argument of one applicant that the Commission had failed to consider as an attenuating circumstance the fact that it had concluded civil law settlements in the US and Canada, pointing out that those settlements had no impact on the infringement committed in the EEA.[222] On the other hand, the Court found that UCAR was entitled to a fine reduction for information it had supplied orally to the Commission. This information was recorded in internal memoranda drawn up by Commission officials, but these memoranda were not part of the investigation file because UCAR did not wish the information to be used as evidence in US proceedings. The Commission inferred that the oral information therefore did not constitute valid evidence for the purposes of point D(2) first indent of the then applicable Leniency Notice, and UCAR was not granted a specific reduction in its fine. The CFI, however, stressed that information provided to the Commission need not necessarily be provided in documentary form. In this case the information provided by UCAR had been helpful to the Commission's investigation and for the finding of an infringement.[223]

Finally, as in the *Amino Acids* cartel case,[224] the applicants argued that when setting the amount of a fine, the Commission should take due account of fines already imposed by competition authorities in third countries, particularly the US and Canada. The CFI was not receptive to this argument, and its reasoning in rejecting it mirrors the reasoning in *Amino Acids*. The CFI recognized that *non bis in idem* is a general principle of Community law, also enshrined in Article 4 of Protocol No 7 to the ECHR.[225] While the principle is not directly applicable to the situation of concurrent proceedings at Community and at Member State level, 'a general requirement of natural justice demands that, in determining the amount of a fine, the Commission must take account of any penalties that have already been borne by the undertaking in question in respect of the same conduct where these were imposed for infringement of the law relating to cartels of a Member State and where, consequently, the infringement was committed within the Community'.[226] However, this is not the case with concurrent proceedings

---

[220] *Tokai Carbon*, para. 343.　　[221] *Ibid*, para. 345.　　[222] *Ibid*, para. 348.
[223] *Ibid*, paras. 431–433.　　[224] See above.　　[225] *Tokai Carbon*, para. 130.
[226] *Ibid*, para. 132.

and sanctions in the EU and in third countries, which have different ends and concern different territories.[227] The Court concluded that the Commission, when determining the amount of a fine, is not obliged to take into account penalties already imposed on the same undertakings by authorities or courts in non-Member States in respect of the same conduct.[228]

The Court also rejected the argument that the companies' fines should not be increased for deterrence because they had already been sanctioned on the basis of the same facts by third countries. The Court ruled that the objective of deterrence which the Commission is entitled to pursue when setting fines is to ensure that companies comply with EC competition law when conducting their EU activities. Thus, the deterrent effect of a fine imposed for infringement of the Community competition rules cannot be assessed by reference to whether an undertaking has complied with the competition rules in third countries.[229]

e) Akzo Interim Measures Cases

During inspections in 2003 in the *'heat stabilizers and impact modifiers'* cartel case, the issue of the extent to which companies can claim attorney-client (legal) privilege arose. It led to the rather rare occurrence of a conflict between the Presidents of the CFI and the ECJ, who had to decide at interim measures whether legal privilege could cover communications with in-house counsel.

The case arose from a dawn raid by the Commission and the Office of Fair Trading ('OFT') officials on Akzo and Akcros Chemicals, during which the Commission seized and made copies of numerous documents. A dispute arose between the competition authority officials and representatives of the companies as to whether five documents seized during the raid should benefit from legal privilege. After briefly reviewing the documents, the officials concluded that some of them ('Set A') might be privileged, but others ('Set B') definitely were not. The Set A documents consisted of a short internal memorandum by the general manager, which apparently contained information gathered for the purpose of obtaining external legal advice in connection with the company's existing competition law compliance programme, and a copy of the memorandum with hand-written notes referring to the contact details of an external lawyer. The Set B documents consisted of handwritten notes used by the same general manager to prepare the memorandum, and emails between the general manager and Akzo's 'competition law coordinator', who was Akzo's in-house counsel and an attorney registered with the Dutch bar. After reviewing the documents, the Commission officials decided that none of them were privileged, and therefore placed them in a sealed envelope which they then removed. The Commission subsequently adopted a decision stating its intention to open the envelope containing the documents.

---

[227] *Ibid*, paras. 134 and 139–141. [228] *Ibid*, para. 142. [229] *Ibid*, paras. 146–147.

The President of the CFI ordered the suspension of this decision,[230] saying that the *prima facie* case on the infringement of professional privilege regarding the documents raised very important and complex questions concerning a possible need to extend somewhat the scope of professional privilege as currently defined by the case law (*AM & S*).[231] The first question was whether the scope of professional privilege, which covers communication with an outside lawyer or any document reporting the text or content of such communication, could be extended to documents drawn up for the purpose of consultation with a lawyer. Next, the President noted the issue of whether the protection afforded to correspondence between independent lawyers and their clients could be extended to cover written communications with an in-house lawyer as well. Moreover, it was possible that the Commission had failed to comply with the procedure defined in the *AM & S* case by having examined, even if only summarily, the documents which the applicants claimed were covered by professional privilege. In the President's view, the applicants had demonstrated the need to suspend the implementation of the decision in order to prevent their suffering serious and irreparable harm: *inter alia*, once the Commission was aware of the information in the documents contained in the sealed envelope, this would as such constitute a substantial and irreversible breach of the applicants' right to respect of the confidentiality protecting those documents. Thus the President held that the Commission was not allowed to read the Set A documents. However, with respect to the Set B documents, he found that the condition of urgency was not established, since the Commission had already reviewed them.

On appeal, the President of the ECJ partly reversed the CFI's Order, for lack of urgency with regard to the Set A documents. He held that the mere infringement of professional privilege is not in itself sufficient to show that the condition of urgency is satisfied, since the Commission's reliance on privileged information could be remedied in the main action. Moreover, in his view the harm had been done, as the Commission had already, 'albeit cursorily', reviewed the disputed documents:

[W]hile the mere reading by the Commission of the information in the Set A documents, without that information being used in proceedings for the infringement of the Community competition rules, may possibly be capable of affecting professional privilege, that circumstance is not in itself sufficient to show that the condition of urgency is satisfied in the present case . . . The harm which might possibly result from a more detailed reading of those documents is not sufficient to establish the existence of serious and irreparable harm, since the Commission is prevented from using the information thus obtained.[232]

---

[230] Cases T-125/03 R and T-253/03 R, *Akzo Nobel Chemicals and Akcros Chemicals v. Commission*, Order of 30 October 2003, not yet reported.

[231] Case 155/79, *AM & S Europe Ltd.* v. *Commission*, [1982] ECR 1575. This case established that legal professional privilege covered only correspondence between clients and independent lawyers, but not dealings with in-house lawyers or lawyers of non-Member State bars.

[232] Case C-7/04 P(R), *Commission v. Akzo Nobel Chemicals and Akcros Chemicals*, Order of 27 September 2004, not yet reported, paras. 41–43.

The ECJ President then confirmed the CFI's finding that since the Commission had already read the Set B documents and would not be able to use them if its decision was annulled in the main case, the condition of urgency was not fulfilled. The assessment of the situation would have been different if Akzo had been able to show that the Commission had taken measures on the basis of the information contained in the Set B documents, but Akzo had not been able to demonstrate that this was more than a hypothetical risk.

These two orders have serious implications for undertakings subject to investigation by the Commission. If they refuse to hand documents over to Commission officials, they may be faced with a decision ordering them to do so, and may be liable to high periodic penalty payments if they fail to comply. They may appeal the decision, but the Court will not automatically suspend the daily fines. On the other hand, if the documents are handed over and the Commission has the opportunity to review them, even briefly, it is unlikely that the company will then be able to obtain interim measures. It would appear that a company's best course of action is to refuse, politely but insistently, to hand over the documents demanded. Commission officials lack the power to seize them by force. The Commission can then take a specific decision demanding their disclosure. That decision is judicially reviewable. In the *AM & S* case, the disputed documents were held in the Court's Registry and reviewed by the Advocate General and reporting judge.[233]

The Orders do not discuss the merits of the case, but they may leave a window of hope that the Courts may be willing to acknowledge legal privilege for in-house lawyers. However, until the main case is decided, it will not be possible to rely on the premise that internal competition law advice and correspondence are covered by legal privilege. Great force of will may be necessary to avoid 'cursory' scrutiny of such documents.

(v) Horizontal Agreements

The more interesting cases were Commission decisions.

a) UK and German Network-Sharing Agreements

T-Mobile and mmO2 entered into agreements to share 3rd Generation ('3G') site infrastructure and to roam on their 3G networks in the UK and Germany. The parties had asked the Commission for negative clearance or, alternatively, an exemption of their agreements under Article 81. In April and July 2003 the Commission adopted two individual exemption decisions determining the extent to which mobile telephony operators can cooperate in network-sharing.[234]

---

[233] See Burnside and Crossley, '*AM&S, AKZO* and Beyond: Legal Professional Privilege in the Wake of Modernisation', Paper Presented at the Conference 'Antitrust Reform in Europe: A Year in Practice' (Brussels, 9–11 March 2005).

[234] Commission Decision of 30 April 2003 (COMP/38.370-*Network sharing UK (BT Cellnet + BT 3G + ONE2ONE Personal Communications)*); Commission Decision of 16 July 2003 (COMP/38.369-*Network sharing Germany (T-Mobile Deutschland GmbH + Viag Interkom GmbH & Co)*).

According to the Commission's approach, site-sharing in itself did not raise competition concerns and therefore was not caught by Article 81(1). The cooperation extended only to basic network elements and the parties retained independent control of their core networks. National roaming between licensed network operators, on the other hand, was found to restrict competition at the wholesale level, with potentially harmful effects in downstream retail markets. However, national roaming allowed operators to provide better coverage, quality and transmission rates for their services, as well as roll-out and service provision within a shorter timeframe, thus benefiting consumers and helping the launch of 3G innovative services. In the two decisions, the Commission exempted national roaming in rural areas until 31 December 2008, while national roaming in urban areas would be phased out by 31 December 2008 in accordance with a strict timetable.

b) UEFA Sports Media Rights Cases

In the past few years the Commission has progressively applied the whole set of competition rules contained in Articles 81 and 82 to sport, while also trying to take into account its 'specific nature'. Sport is essentially characterized by the sporting federations' self-regulation, with only its economic aspects subject to EC competition law constraints.[235] The ECJ's famous piece of legal creativity in *Bosman*[236] accelerated the decline of economic inter-dependence between clubs in professional team sports. Its subsequent judgments have been more cautious. In theory, genuine 'sport rules' which are applied in an objective, transparent and non-discriminatory manner are outside the purview of the Treaty competition rules. Thus, in *Meca-Medina* (reported above), the CFI agreed with the Commission that the IOC anti-doping rules do not fall under Articles 81 and 82 because they are pure sporting rules.[237]

Sports events are among the most valuable premium TV content, and the related rights have traditionally been sold jointly by the sports federations. TV rights are now an important source of income for both sporting bodies and TV broadcasters. The Commission has examined the compatibility of joint selling with the competition rules since the 1980s. In three recent cases the Commission had the opportunity to apply Article 81 to joint selling of TV rights in the football sector.[238] These decisions defined the relevant product market narrowly, as the

---

[235] Case 36/74, *B.N.O. Walrave and L.J.N. Koch v. Association Union cycliste internationale, Koninklijke Nederlandsche Wielren Unie et Federación Española Ciclismo*, [1974] ECR 1405, para. 4.

[236] Case C-415/93, *Union Royale Belge des Sociétés de Football Association ASBL v. Jean-Marc Bosman, Royal Club Liégeois SA v. Jean-Marc Bosman and Others and Union des Associations Européennes de Football (UEFA) v. Jean-Marc Bosman*, [1995] ECR I-4921.

[237] See above. Compare, on the other hand, the recent CFI judgment on the FIFA rules on players' agents (Case T-193/02, *Laurent Piau v. Commission*, judgment of 26 January 2005, not yet reported), which held that the introduction of rules for players' agents is an economic activity.

[238] Commission Decision 2003/778/EC of 23 July 2003 (*Joint selling of the commercial rights of the UEFA Champions League*), OJ [2003] L 291/25; case COMP/37.214-*Joint selling of the media rights to the German Bundesliga* (proposed commitments published in OJ [2004] C 229/13); case COMP/38.173-*The Football Association Premier League Limited* (Article 19(3) Notice published in OJ [2004] C 115/3).

market for the acquisition of TV rights of football which is played regularly throughout every year. In the Commission's view these rights were not substitutable with rights concerning other sports events, for instance golf or American football, because of viewers' specific preferences. This gave the holder of the TV rights significant market power, which was further increased by joint selling agreements. According to Commission theory, a joint selling arrangement is in effect a horizontal restriction of competition, which prevents the clubs that originally owned the TV rights to a match from competing in the sale of those rights to the media. This may restrict price competition and limit output, and thus may also restrict competition between media operators and harm consumers. Joint selling agreements are commonly held to fall under Article 81(1). In all the cases examined here, the Commission had to assess whether and under what conditions they might nevertheless be lawful under Article 81(3).

In its *UEFA Champions League* decision, the Commission recognized that in principle a joint selling arrangement has the potential to improve production and distribution, thus benefiting football clubs, broadcasters and viewers, because it creates a single point of sale for the acquisition of a branded league media product. A single point of sale produces efficiencies by reducing transaction costs. Branding creates efficiencies by helping the media products to gain wider recognition and hence distribution. A league product focuses on the league competition as a whole, and not the individual football clubs participating in it. Consumers want to follow the development of the competition as such, rather than the single games of individual clubs. Enabling the creation of league media products seems to be the best way of achieving this. Joint selling of such products may therefore be justified under Article 81(3).

The question, however, was whether the specific conditions of UEFA's selling arrangements were indispensable for achieving the possible efficiencies and consumer benefits. The agreement provided for the sale of all TV rights in one package, on an exclusive basis, for four years, to a single broadcaster per Member State. The decision is written from the viewpoint of the enforcement of the competition rules. It notes that many rights remained unused, no new media rights were exploited and the clubs could not exploit any media rights individually. It could be argued, to the contrary, that when a league insists on negotiating all rights on behalf of a league member collectively, with a view to dividing the royalties among league members according to their needs, this is a pro-competitive arrangement as it promotes the quality of the sporting competition between the otherwise poorer and weaker teams in the league. These arguments are generally unwelcome to the Commission, which has a long record of challenging collective negotiation arrangements for important packages of rights.

No doubt there was a prolonged haggle during which the right-holder was forced to make concessions, as no sale could be effected in the teeth of Commission condemnation. The Commission considered that the arrangements unduly restricted competition in the market for the acquisition of TV broadcasting rights, and could only be exempted subject to certain conditions:

(a) all media rights must be sold by a tender procedure in separate packages for up to three years;

(b) UEFA would lose its exclusive rights to sell any TV rights that had not been sold by a certain cut-off date; and

(c) both UEFA and individual clubs would be able to exploit certain TV rights concurrently.

According to the decision, these conditions aimed to remedy the restrictive effects of the joint selling arrangement by unbundling the media rights and selling them in several individual packages, permitting several media operators to compete for the rights. It is unclear whether the worthiest beneficiaries of the system, the fans and the weaker clubs, will be better off. The decision's terms make it difficult to be sure, but they may be.

The Commission took a similar approach in the case concerning the joint selling agreements of the *German Bundesliga*, the first case in which the new procedure of Article 9 of Regulation 1/2003 on commitment decisions was followed. In addition, the Commission focused on new technological developments, and ensured that not only could all games be broadcast live via the internet and mobile phones, but also that these live packages would be sold separately.

In the *British Premier League* case the Commission went a step further. In a provisional agreement reached in December 2003,[239] the Football Association Premier League (FAPL) undertook to organize separate bids for separate packages. More importantly, from 2007 onwards, the FAPL must ensure that no one buyer is allowed to acquire all live rights packages exclusively. The new requirement to prevent a single buyer was due notably to the fact that in the first public FAPL tender, concerning the period 2004–2007, BSkyB acquired all the rights packages on offer. Following a parallel Commission investigation into that acquisition, BSkyB undertook in the same provisional agreement to offer a number of top Premier League matches each season to another broadcaster.

c) Belgian Architects

This decision[240] must be seen in the wider context of the Commission's increased focus on restrictions of competition in professional services. A 2004 Report by the

---

[239] According to para. 31 of the Article 19(3) Notice, 'once Regulation (EC) No 1/2003 has become applicable, the Commission intends to adopt a decision making the commitments offered by the FAPL legally enforceable and subsequently close the file'.

[240] Commission Decision of 24 June 2004 (COMP/38.549-*Barème d'honoraires de l'Ordre des Architectes belges*).

Commission on the state of competition in the professional services sector[241] concluded that professional services are characterized by a high level of regulation, either by the State or in the form of self-regulation by professional bodies. The Commission acknowledged that some form of regulation might serve the interests of users and professionals, but urged the introduction of more pro-competitive mechanisms, pointing out that the regulations adopted by professional bodies are decisions by associations of undertakings, which may infringe the prohibition in Article 81. The Commission concluded that such regulations should be tested for proportionality: they must be objectively necessary to attain a clearly articulated and legitimate public interest objective, and must be the least competition-restrictive means of achieving that objective. While recognizing that such rules may be justified, the Commission called on the Member States, the professions and their regulatory bodies to eliminate all unnecessary restriction of competition in professional services. A report on progress in liberalizing professional services will be published in 2005.

The *Belgian Architects* decision shows the Commission's commitment to pursuing antitrust infringements by professional bodies. In this decision the Commission found that the scale of minimum fees applied by the Belgian Architects' Association in 1967 violated Article 81(1). The scale set an architect's fees as a percentage of the value of the work realized, and applied to all architectural services provided in Belgium. The Commission agreed that all recommended prices do not automatically infringe Article 81(1). However, the decision setting the minimum fee scale, known as 'Ethical Standard No 2' was a decision by an association of undertakings which could affect trade between Member States and had the objective of restricting competition within the common market. This was because the *ex ante* publication of the fees had the effect of facilitating price collusion between the architects and effectively restricted price competition. In addition, some other acts of the Association and provisions of the Code of Ethics evidenced its intention to restrict competition in prices between its members by drawing up a minimum fee scale. Finally, the Commission considered whether the application of the balancing test established in *Wouters* would lead to a different result, and concluded that this was not the case, as the minimum fee scale was not necessary to ensure the proper practice of the architect's profession. The Commission set the basic fine at €4.5 million, reflecting its conclusion that the setting of minimum fees constituted a serious violation of EC competition law, but reduced it to €100,000 to reflect the fact that in similar cases decided previously, it had imposed symbolic fines.

---

[241] Commission Communication, Report on Competition in Professional Services, COM(2004) 83 final, available at http://europa.eu.int/comm/competition/liberal_professions/final_communication_ en.pdf. The Commission scrutinized in particular lawyers, notaries, accountants, architects, engineers and pharmacists.

(vi) Vertical Agreements

In the field of vertical agreements, the Luxembourg Courts rendered important judgments that further clarified the law on what constitutes an 'agreement' in the sense of Article 81(1).

a) Volkswagen I

On 18 September 2003,[242] the ECJ dismissed the appeal of German car manufacturer Volkswagen (VW) against a CFI ruling[243] that VW must pay a fine of €90 million for restricting sales and preventing consumers from taking advantage of price differences between Member States. The Commission had adopted a decision[244] in which it held that VW had infringed the EU competition rules by entering into agreements with its Italian dealers in order to prohibit or restrict sales to final consumers and final authorized dealers in other Member States. The Commission fined VW ECU 102 million. The setting of the fine at such a high level seemed to be almost capricious. VW appealed, but the CFI rejected virtually all its arguments, although it reduced the fine to €90 million.

VW further appealed the judgment of the CFI on nine grounds, the two main ones being that: (a) a 3 per cent reduction in the bonus of Italian dealers who completed more than 15 per cent of their sales outside their contract territory was not contrary to the competition rules; and (b) the restriction of supplies to the Italian market was a unilateral measure and therefore not a concerted practice prohibited by Article 81(1). The ECJ dismissed the first of these grounds, partly as being inadmissible and partly as unfounded. It thus confirmed the illegality of the 15 per cent rule, which provided that a dealer's quarterly 3 per cent bonus should be calculated by taking into account sales outside the contractual territory, but only up to a maximum of 15 per cent of that dealer's total sales. It has become difficult for manufacturers to find legal ways of giving their dealers and distributors incentives to make local sales rather than to take the easy profits available as free riders into other territories.

The second ground of appeal concerned the question of what constitutes an agreement for the purposes of Article 81(1). VW claimed that its measures imposing supply quotas for the Italian market were adopted unilaterally and therefore did not amount to an agreement under Article 81(1). VW argued that even if the dealership contracts provided for the possibility of limiting supplies to Italian dealers, the reason for restricting supplies, i.e. to hinder parallel exports, was not called for by the contracts, as the dealers remained free to export.

The Court rejected this argument. It recalled its judgments in *Ford* and *BMW*[245] and held that 'a call by a motor vehicle manufacturer to its authorized

---

[242] Case C-338/00 P, *Volkswagen AG v. Commission*, [2003] ECR I-9189.

[243] Case T-62/98 *Volkswagen v. Commission* [2000] ECR II-2707.

[244] Commission Decision 98/273/EC of 28 January 1998 (*VW*), OJ [1998] L 124/60.

[245] Joined Cases 25/84 and 26/84, *Ford v. Commission*, [1985] ECR 2725; Case C-70/93, *Bayerische Motorenwerke v. ALD*, [1995] ECR I-3439.

dealers is not a unilateral act which falls outside the scope of Article 85(1) [now 81(1)] of the Treaty but is an agreement within the meaning of that provision if it forms part of a set of continuous business relations governed by a general agreement drawn up in advance'.[246] The Court found that the imposition of supply quotas (and the 15 per cent rule) were contained in the dealership contracts themselves, and that the supply limitation was imposed with the express aim of reducing parallel exports. By accepting these contracts, the dealers consented to measures which hindered parallel exports. Faced with both restricted supplies and the 15 per cent rule, they had every interest in selling as many cars as possible in their allocated territories. Thus, the intended hindrance of parallel exports also resulted from the business conduct of the Italian dealers.

This ruling is interesting for companies which want to motivate their dealers and distributors to focus on their allocated territories. The problem in this case seemed to be the combination of limited supplies with a bonus system ('you get only 20 cars, and you get the full bonus only if you sell 17 cars within your territory'). On this basis, it might be assumed that a bonus system as an incentive for local sales would not be covered by this case law if it was not coupled with limited supplies. It is not obvious why it would be illegal to link the payment of a bonus to certain sales targets if the distributor had enough quantities for export sales. However, this view was not shared by the Court in its *Opel* judgment.[247]

b) Volkswagen II

On 3 December 2003,[248] the CFI annulled the Commission's decision of 29 June 2001 in which it had fined VW €30.96 million for infringing Article 81(1).[249] VW had instructed its German dealers in 1996 and 1997 to show 'price discipline'. It sent them several circular letters urging them not to sell new VW Passat models considerably below the recommended retail price and not to grant discounts to consumers. VW also called on dealers to report deviations by other dealers from the 'price discipline' to VW. Some dealers were warned individually to stick to the recommended price, and threatened with legal action or termination of their dealer contract if they did not do so. The Commission concluded in its decision that VW's calls to dealers became an integral part of the dealership contract and therefore constituted agreements within the scope of Article 81(1). The Commission claimed it was not necessary, at least in the case of selective distribution systems such as VW's, to examine the behaviour of the dealer following the circular in order to obtain proof of the dealer's acquiescence to the circular. It argued that such acquiescence must be 'regarded as established as a matter of principle, from the mere fact that the dealer has entered into the distribution network'.[250]

---

[246] Para. 60 of the judgment.   [247] See below.
[248] Case T-208/01, *Volkswagen AG v. Commission*, judgment of 3 December 2003, not yet reported.   [249] Commission Decision 2001/711/EC (*Volkswagen*), OJ [2001] L 262/14.
[250] Para. 25 of the judgment.

The CFI disagreed with the Commission's approach, and annulled the decision on the ground that the Commission had not proved the existence of an agreement between the dealers and VW in relation to the price-setting. It held that the Commission was wrong to assert that the signature by the dealers of a lawful dealership agreement automatically implied their tacit acceptance of future unlawful amendments to that agreement. The CFI confirmed that for an agreement within the meaning of Article 81(1) to exist, it is sufficient, but necessary, that 'the undertakings in question should have expressed their joint intention to conduct themselves on the market in a specific way'.[251] A manufacturer who has adopted, apparently unilaterally, a measure which restricts competition, must therefore have received at least the tacit acquiescence of its dealers. The CFI concluded that such acquiescence must be positively established: the Commission could not hold that apparently unilateral conduct on the part of the manufacturer formed the basis of an agreement, if it did not 'establish the existence of an acquiescence by the other partners, express or implied, in the attitude adopted by the manufacturer'.[252] It was not enough to claim, as the Commission did, that a dealer who has signed a dealership agreement which complies with competition law is deemed by signing it to have accepted in advance a later unlawful variation of that contract. In such cases, 'acquiescence in the unlawful contractual variation can occur only after the dealer has become aware of the variation desired by the manufacturer'.[253] As the Commission had not even tried to establish that the German VW dealers stopped giving rebates to German customers as a result of the circulars, a 'concurrence of wills' between Volkswagen and its dealers could not be assumed. The Commission has appealed the decision to the Court of Justice.

The difference from *Volkswagen I* seems to be that no anti-competitive provisions were contained in the dealership contracts themselves. The anti-competitive element, the call to maintain the resale price, resulted from measures outside the contracts. The question was then whether these measures became an integral part of the dealership contracts. The Court held that it cannot be assumed that a dealer who signs a legal contract has thereby consented to all future amendments, legal or otherwise; such consent must be positively established, and the Commission had failed to do this.

c) Bayer/Adalat

On 6 January 2004, the ECJ delivered its long-awaited judgment in the *Bayer/Adalat* case.[254] It upheld the judgment of the CFI[255] and found that there was no agreement between Bayer and its French and Spanish wholesalers aimed at limiting parallel exports.

---

[251] Para 30 of the judgment.   [252] *Ibid*, para 36.   [253] *Ibid*, para 45.
[254] Joined Cases C-2/01 P and C-3/01 P, *Bundesverband der Arzneimittel-Importeure eV and Commission of the European Communities v. Bayer AG*, [2004] ECR I-23.
[255] Case T-41/96, *Bayer AG v. Commission*, [2000] ECR II-3383.

In the 1980s and early 1990s, Bayer pursued a system of limiting supplies of its medicinal product Adalat to certain wholesalers in France and Spain. The quantities delivered were meant to satisfy domestic demand. Bayer's system consisted of refusing or reducing orders from 'notorious' individual wholesalers, with a view to denying to likely exporters supplies they would sell in higher-price countries. Thus the policy was intended to reduce exports, and this intention was known in the marketplace. However, Bayer's standard contractual terms on the basis of which sales were made contained no prohibition on the making of exports. Bayer's behaviour was said to make deliveries conditional on indications that exports were not intended.

While the CFI had used a 'concurrence of wills' as the decisive criterion for the existence of an agreement, the ECJ used a somewhat easier test, namely whether a particular practice can be put into effect without assistance from others. Thus, an agreement for the purposes of Article 81(1) 'cannot be based on what is only the expression of a unilateral policy of one of the contracting parties, *which can be put into effect without the assistance of others*'.[256]

The ECJ rejected the Commission's argument that the CFI had wrongly applied Article 81(1) by requiring, contrary to the *Sandoz* judgment,[257] proof of the wholesalers' intention to align their conduct to the measures adopted by Bayer, even when they formed part of continuous business relations between the parties. The mere concomitant existence of an agreement which is in itself neutral with a measure restricting competition which has been imposed unilaterally does not amount to an agreement prohibited by Article 81. Consequently, the ECJ held that 'the mere fact that a measure adopted by a manufacturer, which has the object or effect of restricting competition, falls within the context of continuous business relations between the manufacturer and its wholesalers is *not sufficient for a finding that such an agreement exists*'.[258]

The difference between the results in *Bayer* and the two *VW* judgments is striking. Why did Bayer triumph, while VW was fined in one case and only won on shaky grounds in the other? First, Bayer did not deal with its resellers on the basis of a long-term supply agreement, but on the basis of general terms and conditions. More importantly, Bayer's quota system was not accompanied by other controversial features such as bonus schemes. Bayer could put the system into effect without any assistance: it simply sold each wholesaler the number of packs it chose. They did not have to consent to their respective allocations, nor was their cooperation required—Bayer did not check the destination of its products. (Indeed, the wholesalers tried to circumvent Bayer's aim of reducing parallel exports.) The wholesalers had no promotional duties and did no more than perform delivery of a regulated substance.

---

[256] Para. 101 of the judgment, emphasis added.
[257] Case C-277/87, *Sandoz Prodotti Farmaceutici v. Commission*, [1990] ECR I-45.
[258] Para. 141 of the judgment, emphasis added.

d) General Motors/Opel

In 2000 the Commission fined Opel Nederland €43 million for having adopted a general strategy aimed at restricting or preventing export sales from the Netherlands.[259] The Commission considered this strategy had been implemented through individual measures adopted by mutual consent with dealers, as part of the practical implementation of their dealership contracts. These measures consisted in particular of:

- limiting supplies on the basis of existing sales targets to dealers who exported vehicles for sale to customers outside the Netherlands;
- excluding sales to foreign end-consumers from dealers' bonus entitlements; and
- instructing dealers not to make export sales to final consumers and Opel dealers in other Member States.

In its judgment of 21 October 2003,[260] the CFI essentially confirmed the Commission decision. However, it held that the Commission had not sufficiently proved either that the restrictive supply measure was communicated to the dealers, or that the dealers agreed to it. Opel's fine was therefore reduced to €35,475,000. Nevertheless, the CFI accepted the Commission's conclusions in respect of the export ban, which it found to have been accepted by at least nine dealers, and the restrictive bonus policy. Notably, the CFI confirmed that the exclusion of export sales from a bonus system is contrary to Article 81(1), as it is likely to inhibit export sales, even if it is aimed at stimulating local sales in the allocated territory. The CFI found that the policy on bonuses was by its very nature likely to inhibit export sales, even without any restriction on supply, and that the measure constituted an agreement with the object of restricting competition. In the Court's words:

This analysis of the purpose of the measure further implies that the applicants' general line of argument to the effect that the exclusion of export sales from the bonus system was justified by the fact that the bonuses were designed to stimulate sales in the Netherlands, is inoperative.[261]

This finding makes it very difficult for a supplier to encourage a reseller to focus on his own particular territory. Creativity will be necessary to achieve a result which motivates a dealer with territorial responsibilities to pursue sales in the assigned territory, as opposed to making sales where prices are higher. Contractual 'best efforts' clauses should always be safe, though maybe not very motivating.

[259] Commission Decision 2001/146/EC of 20 September 2000 (*Opel*), OJ [2001] L 59/1.
[260] Case T-368/00, *General Motors Nederland BV and Opel Nederland BV v. Commission*, [2003] ECR II-4491.   [261] Para. 103 of the judgment.

e) Van den Bergh Foods

In this new round of the 'ice cream wars',[262] the CFI confirmed the Commission's decision[263] finding that HB (a Unilever subsidiary) had infringed Articles 81 and 82 by providing Irish retailers with freezer cabinets on condition that they used them exclusively to stock HB's ice creams. The cabinets remained HB's property and HB also covered their maintenance costs. Exclusivity was limited to the freezer cabinets and the retailers could sell other companies' products if they wished, though this would entail installing another cabinet. The Commission acted after receiving a complaint from Mars, a competitor whose sales were affected after HB had insisted on retailers' compliance with the exclusivity clause.

The Commission found that the distribution agreements containing the exclusivity clause were incompatible with Articles 81 and 82. The Commission's objections targeted the network of exclusive distribution agreements HB had concluded with various Irish retailers, which in the Commission's view produced a market foreclosure effect. HB had a dominant position in the relevant market, defined as the market for impulse ice-cream in Ireland. In particular, 40 per cent of Irish retail outlets had no freezer cabinets for storing 'impulse' ice-cream other than those provided by HB. The network of similar agreements with HB and other retailers affected 83 per cent of the retail outlets. The Commission reasoned that this situation created substantial barriers to entry, as a new supplier would have to begin by persuading retailers to replace their cabinet or install an additional cabinet, which was not likely in many cases (retail shops having limited space).

The CFI confirmed the Commission's finding that the effect of the agreements as a whole was to restrict competition on the market. Taking into account that the freezer cabinets were provided 'free of charge', that HB's ice cream had a very strong position in the Irish market and that retailers were unlikely to replace HB's cabinets with those of its competitors, the Court held that the agreements had an exclusionary effect. It further rejected HB's argument that there was no foreclosure because 60 per cent of retail outlets were not affected by the agreement. The Court pointed out that the network of similar agreements affected 83 per cent of Irish retail outlets, because other suppliers used similar exclusivity clauses to those in HB's contracts. The Court also rejected the argument that there was no foreclosure as retailers were able to terminate the contracts on two months' notice. The Court thought it was more appropriate to take into account the actual duration of these agreements, which as the Commission had found, lasted eight years on average. For these reasons, the exclusivity arrangements constituted a barrier to the entry of new suppliers on the market and the expansion of existing suppliers.

---

[262] Case T-65/98, *Van den Bergh Foods Ltd. v. Commission*, [2003] ECR II-4653.

[263] Commission Decision 98/531/EC of 11 March 1998 (*Van den Bergh Foods Ltd.*), OJ [1998] L 246/1.

The CFI also upheld the Commission's position that the exclusivity clause did not merit an exemption under Article 81(3), as it did not contribute to improving the production or distribution of the goods in question.

With respect to the Commission's finding of an abuse of a dominant position, HB argued that supplying freezer cabinets to retailers did not constitute an Article 82 infringement because, as the Commission had found, it was standard practice in the relevant market. In addition, it did not have the object of restricting competition, and it benefited the retailers. The Court replied to these arguments by recalling that an undertaking enjoying a dominant position on the market may be precluded from actions which are not questionable if undertaken by non-dominant companies. The exclusivity clause in HB's agreement had the effect of preventing the retailers concerned from selling other brands of ice cream and of preventing competitors from gaining access to the market. For these reasons, the CFI confirmed the Commission's finding that HB had abused its dominant position by inducing retailers to obtain supplies exclusively from HB.

f) JCB Service

In this case[264] the CFI considered an appeal from a Commission decision[265] finding that JCB had violated Article 81(1) by engaging in a number of practices restricting parallel trade. The condemned practices included restrictions on passive sales by authorized resellers, restrictions on sources of supply which prevented cross-supplies between distributors, 'vertical price-fixing' and making distributors' remuneration dependent on the geographic destination of sales. JCB was fined nearly €40 million.

The CFI found sufficient evidence to support the Commission's allegations relating to restrictions on passive sales and on sources of supply. However, the Court disagreed with the Commission's finding that JCB had engaged in vertical price-fixing. JCB had exercised an influence over the fixing of retail prices by issuing a list of recommended retail prices for its products, and determining internal invoice prices for its network according to those prices. Relying on its case law relating to selective distribution systems, the CFI reasoned that some limitation in price competition is inherent in any such system. Both recommended prices (as long as their application does not involve a concerted practice) and an adequate profit margin for dealers had been found not to restrict competition. The Court held that this case law could be applied by analogy to a distribution system which was essentially similar to a selective distribution system. Since the evidence showed that the prices were only recommended, and that the commercial pricing freedom of JCB's distributors was not restricted, the Court held that the Commission's finding of vertical price-fixing could not be upheld.

The CFI also rejected the Commission's finding that JCB's service support fee system restricted parallel trade. The Commission had contested a clause obliging

---

[264] Case T-67/01, *JCB Service v. Commission*, judgment of 13 January 2004, not yet reported.
[265] Commission Decision 2002/190/EC of 21 December 2000 (*JCB*), OJ [2002] L 69/1.

distributors who made sales outside their allocated territory to pay the JCB distributors in the destination territories a service support fee, to compensate for expenses incurred in providing service for machines they had not sold. The amount of the fee was to be agreed between the two distributors. If they could not agree, JCB would determine the fee, taking into account the cost of the service carried out and a reasonable profit element. The Court found that JCB's fee reflected the costs and that it did not exercise an undue influence on the negotiations. Furthermore, the Court considered that the existence of clear guidelines on the fee payable by the seller to the distributor in the destination territory prevented unstructured negotiations between distributors and, contrary to the Commission's assertions, actually facilitated out-of-territory sales.

Nor did the Court subscribe to the Commission's view that JCB's system for multiple deal trading support was designed to deter distributors from selling outside their allocated territories by withdrawing financial support if machines were exported. JCB granted discounts to its authorized dealers who sold several machines to a single end-user. The discount was withdrawn if the purchaser was not an end-user. This would be the case if the machines were discovered in the second-hand or hire-purchase markets, or were resold to unauthorized distributors or outside the territory of the distributor in question. The Commission did not question the principles on which the system was based, but it did question the way in which JCB operated the system, accusing it of partitioning markets. The Court reasoned that an arrangement of this type does not in itself entail any anti-competitive effect. However, if it were proved that the arrangement had the effect of limiting markets or of market-sharing, it would constitute a practice prohibited by Article 81(1)(b) and (c). The Court agreed with JCB's argument that the reason for withdrawing financial support under the system was not because the customer was located in another territory, but because the sales had not been made to end-users, and accordingly reduced the fine to €30 million.

The *JCB* judgment shows that the CFI may be increasingly receptive to arguments in favour of the legitimacy of practices and agreements which may affect parallel trade, as long as there is a reasonable business justification for such practices. The judgment is also significant in that the CFI applied the principles developed in case law on selective distribution agreements to 'a hybrid agreement' which was 'very similar to a selective distribution system'.[266] This confirms the Court's increasing flexibility in assessing vertical restraints under Article 81(1).

g) Souris/Topps (Pokémon)

In a Decision adopted on 26 May 2004,[267] the Commission condemned practices by Topps, a group of companies producing collectible stickers and cards popular with young children, to prevent parallel imports from low-price to high-price

---

[266] Para. 132 of the judgment.
[267] Commission Decision of 26 May 2004 (COMP/37.980-*Souris/Topps*).

countries of cards and sweets bearing the image of Pokémon cartoon characters. The Commission found that Topps had entered into a series of agreements and/or concerted practices with several of its distributors, with the objective of preventing such parallel imports. In 2000 the price it invoiced to its distributors was up to 243 per cent higher in Finland than in Portugal, where the price was lowest. According to the Commission, Topps repeatedly asked its distributors to trace back parallel imports and monitor the final destination of products. Those who did not comply were threatened with supply cuts. The Commission considered this a hardcore violation of Article 81, but imposed a somewhat reduced fine (€1,590,000) in view of the short duration of the infringement and its termination by Topps immediately after it had received a warning.

C. The Application of Article 82 EC

(i) Dominance

a) British Airways ('BA')

This judgment,[268] which dealt with fidelity schemes operated by dominant undertakings, is of particular interest as the first case where dominance was found although the undertaking in question held a market share of slightly less than 40 per cent. The Commission found that BA had abused its dominant position by putting in place a performance reward scheme whereby the commission paid to travel agents was calculated on a sliding scale, based on the extent to which a travel agent increased the value of its sale of BA tickets from one year to another.[269]

The Court first dismissed BA's plea that the Commission had erred in defining the relevant market, and confirmed the Commission's finding that the relevant market was the market for air travel agencies services. These services represented an economic activity distinct from the air transport market, in view of the independence of air travel agencies, the specific nature and the extent of the services provided and their essential character as a distribution channel for airlines. According to the Court, 'the services of air travel agencies represent an economic activity for which, at the time of the contested decision, airlines could not substitute another form of distribution of their tickets'.[270] The Court also considered that since airline tickets were distributed at national level, and consequently the airlines normally purchased the services for distributing those tickets on a national basis, the Commission was right to find that the relevant geographic market was the UK market.

BA further contested the Commission's finding of dominance, claiming that its market share had fallen from 47.7 per cent at the beginning of the 1990s to

---

[268] Case T-219/99, *British Airways Ltd. v. Commission*, judgment of 17 December 2003, not yet reported.
[269] Commission Decision 2000/74/EC of 14 July 1999 (*Virgin/British Airways*), OJ [2000] L 30/1.
[270] Para. 100 of the judgment.

39.7 per cent. The fact that an airline accounted for a large proportion of the tickets sold by a travel agency did not mean that it was an obligatory business partner for that agency. In practice, BA argued, every agency needed to offer the tickets of a broad range of airlines, and the agencies had substantial bargaining power, the final choice of agent being a matter for the customer. The Court rejected these arguments, upholding the Commission's findings that the percentages of sales of BA tickets by IATA-accredited travel agents, and a series of related factors such as the sheer size of BA, the range of its air transport services and its network, meant that BA had the capacity to act with an appreciable degree of independence in relation to its competitors, to travel agents and to travellers.

Further aspects of this important judgment are dealt with later in this section.

b) Atlantic Container

In 1994, 15 shipping companies party to an agreement concerning transatlantic liner services between northern Europe and the US, the Trans-Atlantic Agreement ('TAA'), which was challenged by the Commission, entered into a new agreement establishing a liner conference, the Trans-Atlantic Conference Agreement ('TACA') covering the same shipping trade. Two other companies, Hanjin and Hyundai, joined the conference at the end of 1994 and in 1995. The Commission considered that between 1994 and 1996 the TACA parties had committed a series of infringements constituting an abuse of a collective dominant position on the market for containerized liner shipping between northern Europe and the US.[271] The abuse concerned measures seeking to induce potential competitors to join the TACA rather than take part in the transatlantic trade as independent lines.

The judgment[272] concluded that the Commission had not demonstrated that these measures, rather than particular commercial considerations, had induced the only two shipping companies which joined the conference between 1994 and 1996—Hanjin and Hyundai—to become members of the conference. The Court therefore annulled the Commission's decision in so far as it found that the TACA parties had abusively altered the structure of the market, together with the fines imposed.

The lengthy judgment sheds some light on the legal test of collective dominance. According to previous case law, a finding of collective dominance rested on three elements:

(a) that the undertakings concerned were able to adopt a common policy on the relevant market;

(b) that they were able to anticipate one another's behaviour (thus having the strong incentive to align their conduct in the relevant market, particularly

[271] Commission Decision 1999/243/EC of 16 September 1998 (*Trans-Atlantic Conference Agreement*), OJ [1999] L 95/1.
[272] Joined Cases T-191/98 and T-212/98 to T-214/98, *Atlantic Container Line AB and Others v. Commission*, ECR [2003] II-3275.

in such a way as to maximize their joint profits by restricting production with a view to increasing prices)[273]; and

(c) that there was no effective competition between the operators alleged to be members of a dominant oligopoly.[274]

In *Atlantic Container*, the Court clarified the scope of effective competition between undertakings sharing collective dominance. For the purpose of establishing the existence of a collective dominant position, the Court found that the existence of a collective dominant position within the meaning of Article 82 does not preclude competition between the undertakings holding such a position, and does not require the adoption by those undertakings of the same conduct for all aspects of competition on the relevant market.[275]

The Court then examined price competition and non-price competition between the undertakings holding a collective dominant position, in order to determine whether the existence of either precluded the finding of collective dominance. It confirmed Advocate General Fennelly's Opinion in *Cewal II*[276] by stating that the existence of non-price competition between collectively dominant companies, such as competition regarding the quality of the services provided, was not in principle sufficient to negate the existence of a collective dominant position based on links inferred from their common strategy on price-setting, unless the extent and intensity of those alternative forms of competition was such as to preclude reasonable reliance on their common pricing policy as the basis for establishing a single market entity.[277]

(ii) Abuse: Exploitative Abuses

a) Scandlines Sverige/Port of Helsingborg and Sundbusserne/Port of Helsingborg

Scandlines Sverige and Sundbusserne complained to the Commission in 1997 that the port of Helsingborg in southwest Sweden was infringing Article 82 by levying excessive and discriminatory charges for services provided to ferry operators. The complainants alleged that:

(a) the prices actually charged to ferry operators were excessive because they were unfair in themselves when compared to the costs (plus a reasonable profit) of providing the services; this was said to be confirmed by a comparison with the prices charged to ferry operators by the port of Elsinore in Denmark, and also by a comparison with prices charged to non-ferry operators;

---

[273] Case T-102/96, *Gencor v. Commission*, [1999] ECR II-753, para. 276; Case T-342/99, *Airtours plc v. Commission*, [2002] ECR II-2585, para. 60.   [274] *Airtours, op.cit.*, para. 63.

[275] Para. 655 of the judgment.

[276] Opinion of Advocate General Fennelly in Joined Cases C-395/96 P and C-396/96 P, *Compagnie Maritime Belge Transports SA and Others v. Commission (CEWAL II)*, [2000] ECR I-1365.

[277] Para. 714 of the judgment.

(b) the prices charged to ferry operators were discriminatory when compared with those charged to at least certain cargo operators which competed with ferry operators, and thus placed ferry operators at a competitive disadvantage (i.e. they argued that the services provided to the two categories of users were comparable); and

(c) finally, the port charges were excessive and discriminatory because they were not cost-based and the pricing was not transparent.

In its decisions[278] the Commission followed the methodology set out by the Court of Justice in *United Brands*,[279] i.e. 'whether the difference between the costs actually incurred and the price actually charged is excessive', and if so, 'whether a price has been imposed which is either unfair in itself or when compared to competing products'. The Commission tried to assess the costs actually incurred by the port of Helsingborg in providing the services and compare them with the prices actually charged to ferry operators, in order to determine whether the difference between the costs incurred and the prices charged was excessive. The Commission went on to assess whether the prices were unfair when compared to prices charged to other users or by other ports, or whether the prices were unfair in themselves. It found the allegations not proven, but nevertheless offered some guidelines on how the *United Brands* excessive and unfair price test should be calculated.

First, the Commission found that to determine the costs against which the port's prices for ferry services could be compared, in order to establish whether the difference was excessive, only the costs related to ferry operations should be taken into account[280] and examined separately from all other costs related to the port's other activities. In other words, to decide whether a dominant position has been abused through the charging of excessive and unfair prices for certain services or products, only the costs related to those products or services should be taken into account. *United Brands* made it clear that abuse can only be established when the price bears no reasonable relation to the economic value of the product concerned.[281] On this basis, the Commission found that even if it was assumed that the port's profit margin was high (or even 'excessive'), this would not be sufficient to conclude that the prices it charged bore no reasonable relation to the economic value of the services provided.[282]

The Commission then assessed whether the prices charged by the port to the ferry operators were unfair, expressing regret from the outset that the Courts and its own decisional practice provided little guidance on how to determine when a price was to be considered unfair in itself.[283] The complainants claimed that the

[278] Decisions of 23 July 2004 (COMP/36.568-*Scandlines Sverige AB/Port of Helsingborg* and COMP/36.570-*Sundbusserne/Port of Helsingborg*).
[279] Case 27/76, *United Brands Company and United Brands Continentaal BV v. Commission*, [1978] ECR 207, para. 252.   [280] Paras. 137 and 138 of the *Scandlines Sverige* decision.
[281] *United Brands, op.cit.*, para. 250.   [282] Para. 158 of the *Scandlines Sverige* decision.
[283] *Ibid*, para 217.

assessment should be made by calculating the economic value of the product or service provided, following a cost-plus approach. According to this method, the economic value would equal the costs incurred in providing the service or product, plus a reasonable profit which would be a percentage of the production costs. Any price exceeding the economic value thus determined should be deemed unfair.[284]

The Commission conceded that the legitimacy of a price could also be assessed by using a cost-plus framework examining the respective relations between the production costs, the price (or the profit margin) and the economic value of the service. However, in addition to the cost-plus approach, certain other criteria should be taken into account. Firstly, the costs should be calculated taking into account the cost of capital as well as production costs. Secondly, it was of the utmost importance to take into account non-cost related factors such as demand, which increased a product's economic value because customers valued it highly and were therefore willing to pay more for it. This sort of case is likely to arise again and will always be very difficult to predict.

(iii) General Exclusionary Abuses

a) Michelin II and BA

Michelin II[285] and *BA*[286] are now the key cases setting the standards applicable to the pricing behaviour of dominant firms. In both cases the CFI upheld the Commission's findings that the specific price and rebate schemes of the firms concerned violated Article 82. The CFI also reached the rather controversial conclusion that it is generally unlawful for a dominant company to apply fidelity (loyalty)[287] and target[288] rebate schemes, although such practices are not illegal if used by other non-dominant companies.

The Courts have ruled on a number of occasions that quantity rebates which rely on subjective volume targets are incompatible with Article 82.[289] In *Michelin II*, the CFI found that even quantity rebates which apply equally to all customers and have no discriminatory features may pose a competition problem. The Commission found that the famous tyre manufacturer had abused its dominant position on the French market for both new and retreaded replacement tyres for trucks and buses. It gave quantity discounts based on achieving the same amount of Michelin sales as in previous years.[290] The Commission reasoned that these rebates were designed to

---

[284] *United Brands, op.cit*, para. 219.

[285] Case T-203/01, *Manufacture française des pneumatiques Michelin v. Commission*, [2003] ECR II-4071. [286] Case T-219/99, *op.cit.*

[287] Rebates granted to customers who commit to purchase all or most of their requirements from a particular supplier.

[288] Rebates granted to customers on the condition that they achieve a set volume target during a defined period.

[289] See e.g. Case 85/76, *Hoffmann-La Roche & Co. AG v. Commission*, [1979] ECR 461; Case 322/81, *NV Nederlandse Banden-Industrie Michelin v. Commission*, [1983] ECR 3461.

[290] The Commission questioned the lack of certainty involved in the scheme, its relatively long duration and the fact that the rebate was paid at the beginning of the next purchasing cycle (see paras.

tie dealers to the company, which would have serious foreclosure effects on the market. The Court upheld this finding, and ruled that quantity-based rebates may amount to an abuse of a dominant position if they are loyalty-inducing and are not based on a countervailing advantage that is justified by economic reasons. These will be extremely difficult criteria to satisfy. The CFI agreed with the Commission that Michelin's rebate scheme was fidelity-inducing owing to: (a) the large difference between the rebate rates at the bottom of the scale and those at the top, (b) the fact that the rebate increase obtained at each step of the scale applied to the total purchase during the period of reference, and (c) the relatively long reference period (one year).[291] In addition, the Court ruled that it is not necessary for the Commission to show that the rebates in question actually produce anti-competitive effects. It is sufficient to establish that they are capable of having that effect.[292]

The CFI suggested that a quantity rebate system would be compatible with Community law if the rebates were based on the volume of activity brought by the customers and the economies of scale achieved as a result of the additional purchases.[293] However, the Court found that Michelin had not adduced sufficient evidence that the rebates were based on such efficiency justifications: a mere reference to economies of scale in production and distribution costs was too general to explain the rates chosen.[294] Consequently, the company's quantity rebate scheme was found to be illegal. The Court confirmed the Commission's finding that other rebate schemes used by Michelin, the 'Service Bonus' and the 'Michelin Friends Club', were also illegal. Under the Service Bonus scheme, customers could obtain additional rebates in exchange for specific services.[295] Under the Michelin Friends Club scheme, large customers could obtain additional advantages in exchange for specific commitments, such as ensuring that Michelin products constituted a specified share of their sales.

The *BA* judgment came a few months after *Michelin II*. It does not refer to *Michelin II*, but the CFI relies on the same guiding principles for the purposes of establishing the exclusionary effect and thus the abusive character of a fidelity-inducing rebate system. The case resulted from a complaint lodged by Virgin Atlantic against the agreements and incentive schemes established by BA for travel agents. The Commission found that BA infringed Article 82 EC by offering individualized growth incentives to travel agents. Just as in *Michelin II*, the rebates were progressive, based on past sales during previous reference periods, and were calculated on total sales, not just on incremental sales above the target.

218–225 of Commission Decision 2002/405/EC of 20 June 2001 (*PO/Michelin*), OJ [2002] L 143/1).

[291] Para. 95 of the judgment.   [292] *Ibid*, para. 239.

[293] At paras. 58–59 the CFI cites Advocate General Mischo's Opinion in Case C-163/99, *Portugal v. Commission*, [2001] ECR I-2613, to the effect that if increasing the quantity supplied results in lower costs for the supplier, the latter is entitled to pass on that reduction to the customer in the form of a more favourable tariff.   [294] Para. 109 of the judgment.

[295] E.g. returning used Michelin tyres to Michelin or providing marketing information.

On the discriminatory effect of the performance reward scheme, the Court emphasized that the attainment of growth targets by travel agents led to an increase in the commission paid to them on all the tickets sold, and not only on those sold above the target. As a result, different rates of commission could be applied to identical amounts of revenue generated by travel agents. The Court considered that this effect was liable to distort competition between travel agents and place some of them at a competitive disadvantage within the meaning of Article 82.

When looking at the possible existence of exclusionary effects, the Court applied the same test as in *Michelin II*. The Court first considered that the schemes had a fidelity-building effect. Indeed, by reason of their highly progressive nature, with a very noticeable effect on the margin, the commission rates were capable of increasing exponentially when the amount of tickets sold progressed from one reference period to another. For the same reason, the higher the revenues for travel agents from BA tickets in one period, the greater the reduction in commission rates if the number of BA tickets sold decreased in the next period.

On the question of economic justification, the Court recalled that the achievement by travel agents of sales growth targets for BA tickets resulted in the application of a higher rate of commission on all the tickets sold. The Court therefore found that there was no objective relation between the additional remuneration of the travel agents and the profit arising for BA from the sale of additional tickets. The Court further considered that the retrospective application of the increased commission to all BA tickets sold could entail the sale of certain BA tickets at a price disproportionate to the productivity gains obtained from the sale of extra tickets. The Court did not accept BA's argument that airlines had an interest in selling extra seats on their flights rather than leaving them unoccupied, as the advantage arising from a better rate of occupancy could be offset by the increased commission paid to the travel agent on all tickets sold. The Court therefore concluded that the scheme should be considered as essentially tending to reward growth in sales of BA tickets from one period to another, which had the effect of deterring travel agents from offering their services to other airlines in competition with BA.

Again as in *Michelin II*, the Court held that there was no need to show actual anti-competitive effects. It was sufficient if the Commission showed that the abusive conduct tended to restrict competition or was capable of having such an effect. In that regard, the Court considered that since 85 per cent of air tickets were sold through travel agents, BA's abusive conduct could not fail to have the effect of excluding competing airlines. Moreover, the Court noted that when a dominant operator implements a practice that has exclusionary effects, the fact that the hoped-for result is not achieved is not sufficient to prevent the finding of an abuse within the meaning of Article 82.

The Court further dismissed BA's argument that it suffered discrimination because other airlines which held at least as strong a market position as that attributed by the Commission to BA used the same rebate schemes. The CFI responded that the Commission was entitled to concentrate its enforcement efforts against one company.[296] It also noted that BA's main competitors could not have afforded to offer as attractive a discount scheme.

The issues raised in these cases continue to be among the most internationally controversial in competition law. The approach followed by the Commission and the CFI differs dramatically from that adopted in the US, and remains a huge problem for business.[297] The two judgments are likely to prove an embarrassment for the modernizing of competition law in Europe. If 'fidelity-inducing' is an economic crime, dynamism and innovation in commercial relationships are likely to be risky. The Commission's forthcoming Article 82 Guidelines may shed more light on this area and perhaps adopt a more flexible approach.

b) Deutsche Telekom

On 21 May 2003, the Commission adopted a decision imposing a fine of €12.6 million on Deutsche Telekom AG (DT) for abusing its dominant position through unfair prices for the provision of local access to its fixed telecommunications network (the so-called 'local loops', i.e. the physical circuit between the customer's premises and the telecommunications operator's local switch).[298] Using a newly developed weighted approach to prices and costs, the Commission established that DT charged new entrants higher fees for wholesale access to the local loop than the fees DT's subscribers paid for fixed line subscriptions. According to the Commission, this discouraged new companies from entering the market and reduced the choice of suppliers of telecoms services, as well as reducing price competition for consumers.

New entrants need access to the local loops to be able to offer retail services to end-customers, and such access ('local loop unbundling') is imposed on incumbent operators by EU regulatory instruments. In some Member States, including Germany, the EU measures were preceded by national rules. However, the Commission took the view that local loop unbundling in Germany was not developing fast enough. DT offers local loop access at two levels: (a) through retail subscriptions for end-customers (the downstream market for retail access services); and (b) for competitors, unbundled access allowing them direct access to end-users (the upstream market for wholesale local loop access). These two markets are closely linked. The Commission considered that there were no alternatives to DT's local access network and found DT dominant on the market for wholesale access. It also found DT dominant on the market for retail access to the

---

[296] *BA, op.cit.*, para 70.

[297] See e.g. Ratliff, 'Abuse of a Dominant Position and Pricing Practices: A Practitioner's Viewpoint', in: Ehlermann & Atanasiu (Eds.), *European Competition Law Annual 2003, What Is an Abuse of a Dominant Position?* (Oxford/Portland, forthcoming).

[298] Commission Decision 2003/707/EC of 21 May 2003 (*Deutsche Telekom AG*), OJ [2003] L 263/9.

local loop, with an approximately 95 per cent market share, the remaining 5 per cent being divided between a number of its competitors.[299]

The Commission argued that new entrants needed access to the local loop on a wholesale basis and that because of the insufficient spread between DT's local loop access prices and the downstream tariffs for retail subscriptions, new entrants could not compete with DT for end-consumers. The Commission compared DT's wholesale offering with a bundle of different types of its retail offerings (analogue, ISDN and ADSL connections), using a weighted approach, i.e. taking into account the numbers of DT's retail customers for the different types of access at retail level. It found that for the period from 1998 through 2001, DT charged competitors more for unbundled access at the wholesale level than it charged its subscribers for access at the retail level. From 2002 DT's prices for wholesale access were lower than its retail access prices, but the difference was insufficient to cover DT's own downstream product-specific costs for the supply of end-user services.

The decision raises a number of technical and legal issues. When analyzing the tariffs, the Commission focused solely on access charges and disregarded the fact that local access charges formed part of a package of access and call services offered to end-customers by DT. Further, although the Commission took the regulatory uncertainty into account when setting the fine, it disregarded the regulatory straight-jacket imposed on DT because it was possible for DT to increase its retail charges and avoid the margin squeeze. However, this would have led to imposing higher access charges on end-customers (which the Commission argued could have been offset by lower call charges). While DT argued that the Commission must show the margin squeeze's negative effects on the market (e.g. hindering competition or creating barriers to entry), the Commission relied on the ECJ case law in *Hoffmann-La Roche, Tetra-Pak II* and *AKZO*[300] to maintain that proving a margin squeeze existed was sufficient to establish abuse.

The case also gave rise to an examination of the interface between services of general economic interest (SGEI) under Article 86 and Article 82. DT argued that a drastic increase in access charges would run counter to its universal service obligations. The Commission disagreed that universal service qualified as an SGEI, and also took the view that affordable universal service could not justify 'privileged treatment of access charges compared with call charges'.[301]

The DT decision was followed by a settlement concerning a presumed margin squeeze for broadband access in Germany. Following the Commission's

---

[299] This was not solely a German phenomenon. The Commission's Eighth Implementation Report of December 2002 (COM(2002) 695) admitted that two years after the EU regulatory measures on local loop unbundling came into force, only 1 million subscriber lines across Europe had been unbundled, a large majority of them (855,000) in Germany, where unbundling had already become mandatory under national law from 1998.

[300] Case 85/76, *op.cit.*; Case C-62/86, *AKZO Chemie BV v. Commission*, [1991] ECR I-3359; Case C-333/94 P, *Tetra Pak International SA v. Commission*, [1996] ECR I-5951.

[301] Para. 196 of the decision.

investigation, DT agreed, without prejudice to its legal rights concerning an appeal, to offer significant commitments regarding shared access to the local loop.[302] DT decided to abandon charging monthly line-sharing fees temporarily, reduce line-sharing tariffs substantially on a lasting basis and increase broadband (ADSL) retail tariffs. The Commission noted that it would take new entrants six to nine months to roll out their broadband networks.[303]

c) Wanadoo

On 16 July 2003, the Commission adopted a decision against Wanadoo Interactive, a subsidiary of France Télécom, for abusing a dominant position through predatory pricing of ADSL-based internet access services for the general public.[304] In view of the gravity of the abuse and the length of the period over which it was committed, the Commission imposed a fine of €10.35 million.

From the end of 1999 to October 2002, Wanadoo, a 72 per cent owned subsidiary of France Télécom, marketed its ADSL services known as Wanadoo ADSL and eXtense at prices which were below their average costs. Since the mass marketing of Wanadoo's ADSL services only began in March 2001, the Commission considered that the abuse only started then. Community case law has given rise to two separate methods of analyzing whether an undertaking has engaged in predatory pricing, one based on variable costs, and the other on full costs. Until August 2001, the prices Wanadoo charged to consumers were well below average variable costs. When, as in this case, the company concerned is dominant, there is an automatic presumption of predatory pricing, contrary to Article 82. From August 2001 the prices Wanadoo charged were approximately equal to its variable costs, but below its total costs. This qualifies as abusive predatory pricing by a dominant company when it forms part of a plan to eliminate competitors. Wanadoo suffered substantial losses up to the end of 2002 as a result of these practices, which coincided with a company plan to pre-empt the strategic market for high-speed internet access. While Wanadoo was suffering large-scale losses on the relevant service, France Télécom, which at that time held almost 100 per cent of the market for wholesale ADSL services for internet service providers (including Wanadoo), was anticipating considerable profits in the near future on its own wholesale ADSL products. Wanadoo's policy was deliberate, since the company was fully aware of the level of losses it was suffering and the legal risks associated with the launch of its eXtense service. According to internal company documents, the company was still expecting at the beginning of 2002 to continue selling at a loss in 2003 and 2004.

---

[302] In contrast to full local loop unbundling, shared access relates to the data transmission (broadband) part of a local loop so that another operator may offer voice services over the same line.
[303] See Lücking, 'Presumed Margin Squeeze for Broadband Access in Germany: Settlement with Deutsche Telekom', (2004–3) *Competition Policy Newsletter* 11.
[304] Commission Decision of 16 July 2003 (COMP/38.233-*Wanadoo Interactive*).

During the period of the abuse, Wanadoo's share of the market for the supply of high-speed internet access services to the general public in France rose from 46 per cent to 72 per cent, in a market that grew five times in size over the same period. The Commission found that the level of losses required in order to compete with Wanadoo had a dissuasive effect on competitors. At the end of the period during which the abuse was committed, no competitor held more than 10 per cent of the market. Wanadoo's main competitor had seen its market share fall significantly, and in August 2001 one ADSL service provider (Mangoosta) went out of business. The effects of Wanadoo's conduct were not confined to competitors on the ADSL segment, but extended to cable operators offering substitutable high-speed internet access. The abuse came to an end in October 2002, when France Télécom lowered its wholesale prices by more than 30 per cent compared to the previous prices charged.

The Commission's decision marked the end of an investigation initiated in September 2001 on the basis of information obtained as part of the sector enquiry into local loop unbundling. Although the abuse had been discontinued, the Commission felt it important to adopt a decision because of the risk of repetition. The Commission considered that practices designed to capture strategic markets such as the high-speed internet access market called for particular vigilance. The level of the fine (€10.35 million) therefore reflected the gravity of the infringement and its duration (18 months). The Commission commented that this decision, like the earlier *Deutsche Telekom* decision, demonstrated its determination to prevent exclusionary practices by incumbent operators on strategic markets such as the high-speed internet access market. An alternative view of the facts will doubtless emerge in the likely appeals.

(iv) Refusal to Deal and Essential Facilities Cases

a) IMS Health

2004 was an *annus mirabilis* for Article 82 enforcement against refusals to supply by dominant players. Such intervention is especially controversial in cases of compulsory licensing of intellectual property rights (IPR). Indeed, these cases are at the outer limits of antitrust enforcement policy.

Until recently, compulsory licensing of IPR for antitrust purposes was almost unheard of in EC competition law, but in 2004 two very important and controversial cases placed the possibility centre-stage. The ECJ delivered its long-awaited judgment in the first of these cases, *IMS Health*,[305] just days after the Commission had adopted its decision in the second one, *Microsoft*.[306] The *IMS* judgment, which elaborates on the criteria for compulsory licensing of IPR, first dealt with in

---

[305] Case C-418/01, *IMS Health GmbH & Co. OHG v. NDC Health GmbH & Co. KG*, [2004] ECR I-5039.   [306] See below.

Magill,[307] gave rise to controversies both on its own account and because of its potential impact on the *Microsoft* case.[308]

IMS Health provides pharmaceutical companies with data on wholesaler sales to pharmacies. Pharmaceutical companies use this data to measure the effectiveness of their promotional efforts in each town and district. IMS, together with its customers, developed a geographic format for presenting this data which has become the *de facto* industry standard for reporting pharmaceutical data in Germany. This format divides the map of Germany into 1,860 zones or 'bricks' whose borders coincide with postcodes, by reference to which marketing data describing deliveries, prices and volumes in those zones is compiled and analyzed. When significant competitors appeared on the German market, IMS relied on the copyright in its brick structure to prevent them from operating. The competitors denied that IMS enjoyed copyright before the German courts, and also complained to the Commission. NDC was the most prominent complainant. As in *Magill*, the Commission's intervention was requested to moderate the otherwise fatal consequences of a dominant player's successful invocation at an interlocutory stage of a national IP right. The Commission found that there was no possibility for companies wishing to offer pharmaceutical sales data in Germany to employ any convention for ascribing sales data geographically other than the convention used by IMS. For competitors to supply customers with usable marketing data, that data had to describe sales in geographic zones as their customers delineated them. There were no substitutes or alternatives to reporting sales along the same geographic lines as IMS's postcode map. The Commission found that IMS's bringing of copyright infringement actions was an abuse of its dominant position; the litigation was likely to eliminate all competition and the refusal to grant a licence lacked 'objective justification'. It did not address the possibility that IMS might have hijacked an industry standard.

The Commission's interim decision in *IMS*[309] was, as in *Magill*, widely criticized on intellectual property grounds, since it was thought contrary to 'well-established legal principles' and might 'discourage investment in intellectual property'.[310] Again as in *Magill*, the decision in *IMS* was suspended by the President of the Court of First Instance.[311] The decision was justified at the interim measures stage as concerning an essential facility. The Court of Justice's

[307] Case T-69/89, *Radio Telefís Eireann v. Commission*, [1991] ECR II-485, upheld on appeal by the ECJ in cases C–241/91 P and C–242/91 P, *Radio Telefís Eireann (RTE) and Independent Television Publications Ltd (ITP) v. Commission*, [1995] ECR I-743.

[308] The authors were involved in both earlier cases, and are involved in *Microsoft*.

[309] Commission Decision 2002/165/EC of 3 July 2001 (*NDC Health/IMS Health: Interim Measures*), OJ [2002] L 59/18.

[310] See e.g. Temple Lang, 'European Community Competition Policy—How Far Does It Benefit Consumers?', 18 *Boletín Latinoamericano de competencia* 128 (February 2004), available at http://europa.eu.int/comm/competition/international/others, p. 129.

[311] Case T-184/01 R, *IMS Health Inc. v. Commission*, [2001] ECR II-3193.

ruling in *IMS*, in response to questions raised by the German courts, constitutes the most authoritative pronouncement of the European judicature to date on compulsory licensing of IPR. Drawing on *Magill* and *Bronner*,[312] the Court stated or recapitulated a four-prong test under which a dominant undertaking may be ordered to license its IPR:

(a) the product or service which is protected by IPR must be indispensable for carrying on a particular business;
(b) the refusal is such as to exclude all competition on a secondary market;
(c) it prevents the emergence of a new product for which there is a potential consumer demand; and
(d) the refusal is not justified by objective considerations.[313]

The first three conditions are of particular interest. As to indispensability, the Court, relying on *Bronner*, clarified that this requirement would not be satisfied if there were 'products or services which constitute alternative solutions, even if they are less advantageous'. The condition of indispensability would also not be fulfilled unless there were obstacles making it 'impossible or at least unreasonably difficult' for others to create alternatives.[314] The Court added that 'in order to accept the existence of economic obstacles, it must be established, at the very least, that the creation of those products or services is not economically viable for production on a scale comparable to that of the undertaking which controls the existing product or service'.[315]

On the criterion of excluding all competition on a secondary market, the Court clarified that it is sufficient if a potential or hypothetical secondary market can be identified and all competition on that market is excluded. The Court held that it is not necessary that the upstream product can be marketed[316]: the decisive factor is that two different but interconnected stages of production can be identified, and that the upstream product is indispensable 'inasmuch as the upstream product is indispensable for supply of the downstream product'.[317]

With respect to the emergence of a new product, the Court stressed that this requirement will be fulfilled only if refusal to grant a licence prevents the development of the secondary market, to the detriment of consumers. Thus the party requesting the licence must intend to produce new goods or services which are not offered by the owner of the IPR. Duplication of the product already offered by the right-holder is not sufficient to satisfy this criterion.[318] The Court added that there must also be 'unmet consumer demand' for the new product. The Court left it to the national court to decide on this part of the test according to the facts of the case.

These conditions are cumulative, and are likely to be interpreted restrictively and applied with extreme caution. The Court did not touch on the quality of the

---

[312] Case C-7/97, *Oscar Bronner GmbH & Co. KG v. Mediaprint Zeitungs- und Zeitschriftenverlag GmbH & Co. KG and Others*, [1998] ECR I-7791.   [313] Paras. 37–38 of the judgment.
[314] *Ibid*, para. 28.   [315] *Ibid*.   [316] *Ibid*, para. 44.   [317] *Ibid*, para. 45.
[318] *Ibid*, paras. 48–49.

IPR at stake, though some commentators have stressed the low-value nature of the subject-matter protected by the IMS copyright.[319] This point is raised by Microsoft in its case against the Commission.

b) The Microsoft Saga

On 24 March 2004, the Commission adopted a massive decision of over 1,000 paragraphs, in which it found Microsoft guilty of abusing its dominant position for PC Operating Systems and imposed a record fine of €497 million.[320]

The decision found two separate abuses. First, Microsoft was accused of having refused to supply 'interoperability information' to enable competitors to develop their own technology for making operating systems for server computers performing so-called work-group functions. In the Commission's view, Microsoft's conduct was a mere refusal to supply which could be remedied without it being necessary to violate any IPR held by Microsoft, but even if the decision entailed compulsory licensing of IPR, Microsoft's incentive to innovate receded before the need to protect innovation in general. According to the Commission:

[a] detailed examination of the scope of the disclosure at stake leads to the conclusion that, on balance, the possible negative impact of an order to supply on Microsoft's incentives to innovate is outweighed by its positive impact on the level of innovation of the whole industry (including Microsoft). As such, the need to protect Microsoft's incentives to innovate cannot constitute an objective justification that would offset the exceptional circumstances identified.[321]

Indeed, Commission officials spoke of the likelihood that the degree of innovation in the market would increase as a result of the Commission's intervention. Rival server vendors would be able to focus development efforts on innovations in their products, since they would now be able to compete on the merits of these products, without an 'artificial interoperability obstacle'. Furthermore, as rivals' products improved, this would spur Microsoft's own incentives to innovate, as it would 'no longer be able to simply rely on the artificial interoperability advantage to win in the market'.[322]

---

[319] See e.g. Tesauro, 'The Essential Facility Doctrine: Latest Developments in EC Competition Law', in: Hellenic Competition Committee (Ed.), *EU Competition Law and Policy, Developments and Priorities, Athens Conference, April 19th 2002* (Athens, 2002), p. 100: 'This point, in fact, is to do with the very tension existing between antitrust and property rights, in particular intellectual property rights. In its decision the Commission does not explicitly put into question the value of the copyright at stake. However, one of the factual elements which is thoroughly explored by the Commission is the origin of the brick structure. From the evidence collected by the Commission, one has the feeling that the creation of the industry standard is more to do with the contribution and the involvement of the pharmaceutical companies than with a genuine, independent, creative effort entirely coming from the right holder. Thus, these arguments could have been a factor militating in favor of less stringent protection of such a copyright.'

[320] Commission Decision of 24 March 2004 (COMP/32.792-*Microsoft*).

[321] Para. 783 of the decision.

[322] Former Commission official Jürgen Mensching, speaking at the Fourth Sweet & Maxwell Annual Competition Law Review Conference, 22 October 2004.

Secondly, Microsoft was accused of having integrated improved media functionality into its Windows personal computer operating systems without simultaneously offering, at the same price if it so chose, a version of Windows without that media functionality. According to the decision, such conduct constituted illegal tying, prohibited under Article 82(d). There are, however, some interesting novelties that may indicate a shift in the Commission's decisional practice in this area. One such key difference refers to the requirement of foreclosure. As noted in the decision, 'in classical tying cases, the Commission and the Courts considered the foreclosure effect for competing vendors to be demonstrated by the bundling of a separate product'.[323] According to the decision, this was not a 'classical tying case' since users can and do to a certain extent obtain third party media players through the internet, commonly free of charge. However, in this case the ubiquitous distribution of media functionality in Windows would compel content providers to encode their content almost exclusively in Windows Media formats, which in turn would eventually drive all third-party media players out of the market after the market tipped. Thus, the Commission's theory went, all possibilities for consumer choice would be eliminated, thereby 'indirectly' requiring consumers to use the media functionality in Windows (what the decision refers to as 'indirect' tying).[324]

The Commission, as a remedy for the first infringement, ordered Microsoft to draw up a detailed 'specification' describing the communications protocols[325] by which its server operating systems communicate with one another. Microsoft then had to offer the specifications, several thousand pages long, by licence to competitors for use in developing their own products. The information to be delivered to competitors was said by Microsoft to be secret, protected by copyright and covered by patents, and the fruit of years of engineering effort. Critics, on the other hand, claimed that the communications protocols were not truly valuable or innovative, and that the patents or pending patents which covered them might be invalid or might not be issued; or, alternatively, that the licensees might be able to find means of implementing the licensed technology so as to avoid the techniques over which Microsoft held patent protection. As a remedy for the second infringement, Microsoft had to develop a 'fully-functioning' version of Windows which did not support certain media functionality (186 files were removed from the Windows operating system) and offer it to customers in Europe.

Microsoft filed an action for annulment of the decision in June 2004. The main action is ongoing and judgment is not expected until 2006. Microsoft also applied for interim measures, but its application was dismissed on 22 December 2004 on the ground that Microsoft had failed to show it would suffer serious and irreparable

---

[323] Para. 841 of the decision.   [324] *Ibid*, paras. 836 and 842.

[325] According to Article 1(2) of the decision, a protocol is 'a set of rules of interconnection and interaction between various instances of Windows Group Server Operating Systems and Windows Client PC Operating Systems running on different computers in a Windows Work Group Network.'

harm if the decision was implemented immediately.[326] The outcome was largely determined by factual considerations relevant solely to interim measures. However, the Order contains a number of interesting comments on the merits of the case, as it concluded that Microsoft had shown a *prima facie* case that the decision might be considered illegal.

As to the first abuse, Microsoft argued that the decision did not satisfy the strict conditions under which compulsory licensing may be ordered (referring to the *IMS* judgment in particular). Microsoft considered it would suffer serious and irreparable harm from being forced to license its intellectual property to its competitors, thereby revealing valuable and proprietary intellectual property and allowing them to use the results of its R&D. Revealing business secrets was irreversible. Microsoft also argued that it would be deprived of the ability to determine its business policy and restricted in its ability to improve its products. The balance of interests, Microsoft argued, favoured suspension of the decision, given the clear harm it would suffer.

The President held that Microsoft had demonstrated a *prima facie* case, given 'the questions of principle raised by the case and the fact that certain pleas and arguments require a thorough examination'.[327] The questions of principle related 'to the conditions on which the Commission is justified in concluding that a refusal to disclose information constitutes an abuse of a dominant position prohibited by Article 82 EC' and to the conformity of the decision with the Court of Justice's judgment in *IMS*.[328]

Interestingly, the President found that Microsoft had shown that the information protected by the IPR which was to be the subject of a compulsory licence was 'clearly fundamentally different' from the information at issue in *Magill* and *IMS*, due to its value and the fact that it had hitherto been secret rather than widely known.[329] The Court judging the main action would have to determine whether the nature of the protected information should be taken into account in judging the legitimacy of a compulsory licence.

Having found that Microsoft had established a *prima facie* case that the decision may be illegal, the President turned to whether Microsoft had demonstrated that the immediate implementation of the decision would cause it serious and irreparable harm which could not be undone if the decision was annulled in the main action. The President first considered whether the forced disclosure of the information would constitute serious and irreparable harm. He held that it would not, as the harm needed to be serious and irreparable 'over and above the simple breach of the exclusive prerogatives of the holder of the rights in question'.[330] He rejected Microsoft's argument that disclosure of secret information would cause serious harm, because Microsoft had not explained 'what irreparable damage might be caused to it by the simple fact that third parties had knowledge of data

---

[326] Case T-204/01 R, *Microsoft Corporation v. Commission*, Order of 22 December 2004, not yet reported.   [327] Para. 204 of the Order.
[328] *Ibid*, paras. 205–206.   [329] *Ibid*, para. 207.   [330] *Ibid*, para. 251.

disclosed by it, as opposed to the developments resulting from the use of that knowledge'.[331] Contractual protections could be imposed against disclosure. The President also rejected Microsoft's submission that the decision seriously interfered with its commercial freedoms, as Microsoft's policy was not fundamentally changed, since it had already licensed comparable information in the context of US settlement proceedings. Finally, the President found that there would be no irreversible development of market conditions, and that in any event, if the decision were annulled, there would be no obstacles to prevent Microsoft from regaining a significant part of its lost market share.

The President's ruling is predicated on the assumption that a compulsory licence of IPR cannot in itself be considered as serious and irreparable harm. In order to obtain interim measures, it is necessary to show harm over and above the harm inherent in being forced to license such rights. This part of the ruling appears novel. While the Orders in *IMS Health* and *Magill*[332] do consider other factors, neither case gives any indication that it is necessary to show serious and irreparable harm separate from and in addition to the harm caused by the compulsory licence.

Interestingly enough, the Order also contains one element of much wider significance for any company thinking of entering into settlement negotiations with the Commission. The substantive contents of the failed settlement negotiations in the months preceding the March 2004 decision are used to support the President's findings, the President having expressly asked both sides about the negotiations during the hearing. This puts in doubt the conventional assumption that settlement negotiations with the Commission are without prejudice (unlike settlement negotiations between two parties under the national law of most EU Member States). Any company about to enter into settlement negotiations with the Commission would therefore be wise to reflect: if the negotiations fail, would the company be harmed by the disclosure of what was discussed? It may therefore be necessary to consider entering into a formal confidentiality agreement with the Commission's services. A number of wider implications of this ruling will need to be examined. For example, if settlement negotiations with the Commission are not privileged as a matter of EC law, could third parties (in third countries or in the EU) seek discovery in a national court of the letters and draft settlements that were discussed? Would the same principle apply to discussions with national authorities applying EC law?

Regarding the second abuse, i.e. the alleged tie of media functionality in the Windows operating system, Microsoft argued that the decision adopted a flawed legal approach by wrongly considering this as a case of tying, when in fact it was a case of product integration. There is no demand for a computer operating system without the capacity to play video images, just as there is no demand for a car

---

[331] *Ibid*, para. 253.
[332] Case T-184/01 R, *op.cit.* and Joined Cases C-76/89 R, C-77/89 R and C-91/89 R, *op. cit.* respectively. In both cases the CFI suspended the Commission's decision.

without a carburettor or shoes without laces. There may be separate demands for laces, carburettors and media software, but that does not establish that the offering of an entire product involves a tie. The President found, firstly, that Microsoft's arguments raised 'complex issues' which the Court would have to resolve in the main action.[333] Microsoft had demonstrated a *prima facie* case that the decision might be illegal. In particular, Microsoft's argument that the decision had unlawfully applied a speculative theory of tying based on indirect network effects was 'likely to raise one or more important questions of principle which may affect the legality of the Commission's analysis'.[334] The President noted that it raised 'the complex question whether, and if so on what conditions, the Commission may rely on the probability that the market will 'tip' as a ground for imposing a sanction in respect of tying practised by a dominant undertaking, when that conduct is not by nature likely to restrict competition'.[335] The President recalled that abuse is an objective concept.

The President also found that three other arguments raised by Microsoft gave rise to a *prima facie* case:

(a) first, whether the positive effects of the Windows operating system 'design concept' (to which, Microsoft argued, the Commission had not given sufficient weight) could constitute an objective justification;

(b) second, whether the factual premises underlying the Commission's analysis were correct, in particular, whether its analysis of 'indirect network effects' was contradicted by the continued use by content providers of different formats; and

(c) third, whether Microsoft was correct that 'Windows and its media functionality' do not constitute two distinct products, given that for many years Microsoft and other manufacturers had integrated media functionalities in their client PC operating systems.

However, the President found that Microsoft had not proved it would suffer serious and irreparable harm if it were required to offer a version of its Windows operating system without the media player functionality. The President recalled that the principle of freedom to exercise business activities forms part of the general principles of Community law. However, while the decision would interfere with Microsoft's commercial freedom, the interference could not be regarded as irreparable. If Microsoft were successful in the main action, it could apply its basic design concept to all new products launched following the annulment of the decision. In addition, the financial costs of developing the new 'reduced' version of Windows were not serious and irreparable harm. Furthermore, Microsoft had not proved that the decision would reduce the appeal of the Windows platform, so that software developers would choose another platform. The President also found that any harm would be limited because it was unlikely that sales of the

---

[333] Para. 394 of the Order.   [334] *Ibid*, para. 398.   [335] *Ibid*, para. 400.

'reduced' version of Windows would reach significant levels. Finally, the President found that if the decision were annulled, Microsoft could use updating mechanisms to restore the tying of its media player with the operating system.

Perhaps the most interesting part of the President's Order is its discussion of the issues that will have to be decided by the Court in the main action. The President appears to see merit in the idea that a finding of abuse for which a company can be sanctioned under Article 82 cannot be based on a prospective analysis of the risks for competition, which is by definition speculative. He suggests that 'abuse is an objective concept' but that the tying in question is 'not by nature likely to restrict competition'. This raises a 'complex question; whether, and if so on what conditions, the Commission may rely on the probability that the market will 'tip' as a ground for imposing a sanction'. The President also recognizes that the Commission's analysis relating to the existence of indirect network effects may be contradicted by the factual evidence.

c) Advocate General Jacobs's Opinion in Syfait

On 28 October 2004, Advocate General Jacobs delivered his Opinion in another controversial case involving unilateral refusals to supply. The Opinion is equally controversial and groundbreaking. *Syfait* is a preliminary reference by the Hellenic Competition Committee (HCC), which raises interesting questions with regard to the admissibility of the reference. Here, though, we deal only with the substance of the Opinion.[336] The main question in the case is whether a dominant pharmaceutical undertaking is under a duty to supply unlimited quantities to wholesalers, and thus whether the Commission and NCAs and courts may use Article 82 to challenge unilateral policies of pharmaceutical companies which seek to hinder parallel trade.[337] After the judgment in *Bayer/Adalat* (described earlier in this survey) which reviewed the same question under Article 81, the ultimate determination of this case will be decisive for the future of quota systems in the pharmaceutical industry.

In August 2001 the HCC issued an interim decision in which it found that GSK had abused its dominant position by refusing to supply Greek wholesalers with as much product as they requested, and ordered GSK to supply unlimited quantities. The Greek subsidiary of GSK accordingly sold all its stock in a single day. The main question referred to the ECJ was whether the refusal of a dominant undertaking to satisfy the orders of wholesalers fully constitutes an abuse *per se* within the meaning of Article 82, if the refusal is due to the supplier's desire is to limit the wholesalers' export activity and thereby parallel trade.[338]

---

[336] Case C-53/03, *Syfait and Others v. GlaxoSmithKline AEVE and GlaxoSmithKline plc.* In May 2005, before this survey went to print, the Court issued a judgment in which it declined to accept the referral because it considered that the HCC was not a 'court or tribunal' in the sense of Article 234 of the Treaty.

[337] The level of importance is reflected by the fact that the full bench of the ECJ heard the case.

[338] The authors represent GSK before the HCC and the Court of Justice.

Advocate General Jacobs delivered a monumental Opinion, in which he concludes that a refusal by a dominant pharmaceutical company to meet all its customers' orders with the aim of restricting parallel trade does not automatically constitute an abuse of a dominant position.[339] Although a dominant undertaking will on occasion be under an obligation to supply its products or services, it is clear that there are limits on its obligations to supply under Article 82. Thus, according to the Advocate General, a dominant undertaking is not obliged to meet orders which are out of the ordinary, and it is entitled to take such steps as are reasonable in order to defend its commercial interests.[340] A dominant pharmaceutical undertaking which restricts the supply of its products does not necessarily abuse its dominant position within the meaning of Article 82 merely because of its intention thereby to limit parallel trade.[341] More specifically, the Advocate General accepts that while an intention to partition the market could be assumed in this case, that was an inevitable consequence, given the characteristics of the market, of GSK's attempt to protect what it viewed as its legitimate commercial interests by refusing to meet in full the orders it received. The issue of intent should therefore not deflect attention from the essential question of whether such a refusal may be justified in some circumstances.[342]

The Advocate General then examined whether any of the various factors identified by the HCC were of relevance when assessing whether the conduct was capable of objective justification. He concluded that when pharmaceutical undertakings attempt to block parallel trade, they are not thereby seeking to entrench price differentials of their own making, but rather to avoid the consequences which would follow if the very low prices imposed on them in some Member States were generalized throughout the Community.[343] He also noted that the legal and moral obligations imposed on dominant pharmaceutical undertakings to maintain supplies in each Member State cast doubt on the reasonableness and proportionality of requiring them to supply wholesalers in low-price Member States who intend to export the products supplied.[344] Finally, he stressed that it cannot be assumed that parallel trade in fact benefits either the ultimate consumers of pharmaceutical products, or the Member States as the primary purchasers of those products.

The Advocate General concluded that the restriction of supply by a dominant pharmaceutical undertaking in order to limit parallel trade is capable of justification as a reasonable and proportionate measure in defence of its commercial interests.[345] However, he emphasizes that he regards this conclusion as specific to the pharmaceutical industry in its current condition and to the particular type of conduct being examined.[346]

---

[339] The Advocate General does not comment on the questions of market definition and dominance, and confines his Opinion to the issues of abuse under Article 82.

[340] Para. 67 of the Opinion.   [341] *Ibid*, para. 69.   [342] *Ibid*, para. 71.

[343] *Ibid*, para. 84.   [344] *Ibid*, para. 86.   [345] *Ibid*, para. 100.

[346] *Ibid*, para. 101. Indeed, in para. 68 of the Opinion the Advocate General notes that the factors demonstrating that an undertaking's conduct in refusing to supply is abusive are highly dependent on the specific economic and regulatory context in which the case arises.

Predictably, the Opinion has been warmly welcomed by the European pharmaceutical industry as a whole. It is also a wholesome harbinger of a fresh approach to the status of hitherto sacred cows. This is the first judicial pronouncement from Luxembourg to endorse as lawful measures which have the effect of restricting parallel trade. The use of EC competition law to achieve market integration is unparalleled elsewhere in the world, and it has long been used against practices designed to prevent parallel trade. The Commission supports parallel trade as an important tool for building the common market, and the Courts have always in the past been advocates of the virtues of parallel trade. It is therefore interesting that the Advocate General has recognized that the pharmaceutical market is unique, and that normal conditions of competition do not prevail there. Even though the Court finally decided that the case was inadmissible, the Opinion will form part of its jurisprudence, and the value of its arguments as to the substance of the case is not affected.

d) Ferrovie dello Stato

A decision by the Commission against a less controversial refusal to deal also deserves attention. On 28 August 2003, the Commission announced its finding that the Italian State-owned railway company, Ferrovie dello Stato (FS), had infringed Article 82 by refusing to grant access to the Italian railways for the provision of cross-border passenger services.[347] FS controls the train operating company Trenitalia and the railway infrastructure manager RFI. Georg Verkehrsorganisation GmbH (GVG) complained that since 1995 FS had refused to grant it access to the Italian railway infrastructure, enter into negotiations for an international grouping or provide traction. This prevented GVG from providing an international rail passenger service from various points in Germany via Basle to Milan. To provide this service GVG needed access to the Swiss and Italian railway networks, and it obtained the necessary train path in Switzerland in 1996. However, it also had to form an international grouping with an Italian railway undertaking, pursuant to Directive 91/440,[348] and FS was the only Italian train operator equipped to enter into such a grouping. However, FS refused to enter into an international railway grouping with GVG. It also refused to discuss terms for access to the track or to provide traction services.

The Commission found that FS's behaviour with regard to GVG constituted an abuse of its dominant position, since GVG was effectively denied access to the market and that this had deprived rail customers of the benefit of price competition and choice. Following discussions with the Commission, FS reached a settlement whereby it entered into an international grouping agreement with GVG and agreed on the terms of a traction contract with GVG. FS and RFI undertook to

---

[347] Commission Decision of 28 August 2003 (COMP. 37.685-*GVG/FS*).

[348] Council Directive 91/440/EEC of 29 July 1991 on the development of the Community's railways, OJ [1991] L 237/25.

use their best endeavours to provide GVG with train paths. FS also agreed to enter into international railway groupings with any licensed train operator with a viable plan for operating an international rail service into Italy, and undertook to provide traction in relation to such services for a period of five years. Given the comprehensive settlement arrangement reached, the fact that the infringement has come to an end and the novelty of the case,[349] the Commission decided not to fine FS for its breach of Article 82.

D. Article 86 and National Anti-Competitive Measures

(i) Fiammiferi

The most groundbreaking development in this area was the ECJ's *Italian Matches* (*Fiammiferi*) judgment.[350] This preliminary reference ruling deals with questions pertaining to the scope of the State action defence and the obligations of NCAs to apply EC competition law. The latter question is of particular importance given the decentralization of competition law enforcement.

Under the State action defence doctrine, a company charged with an infringement of the EC competition rules may claim that its conduct falls outside the scope of Article 81 or 82 if it is required by national legislation or the national legal framework eliminated any possibility of competitive activity.[351] In this case, the Italian competition authority had found that the Italian law establishing and governing the operation of a consortium of Italian producers of matches, Consorzio Industrie Fiammiferi (CIF) was contrary to Articles 81 and 10. The Italian legislation required or at least facilitated a system of production quotas structured by CIF. CIF was granted a commercial monopoly consisting of the exclusive right to manufacture and sell matches in Italy. The Italian regulation provided for a quota allocation between the member companies. Until 1993 membership of CIF was compulsory.

The Italian competition authority decided that the applicable Italian law created a 'legal shield' for the conduct of CIF and its members that would be otherwise prohibited under the EC competition rules. It concluded, however, that Italian courts and public authorities should disregard the legislative framework because it was contrary to Articles 3(1)(g), 10 and 81(1) of the EC Treaty. This would imply the removal of the 'legal shield'.[352] In any case, after certain amendments to the legislative framework in 1993, participation in CIF was no longer compulsory and the members could withdraw from the framework. Thus, their participation in CIF from 1994 was regarded as an autonomous business decision

---

[349] GVG had been the first and only new entrant railway undertaking to approach FS with a view to forming an international grouping.

[350] Case C-198/01, *CIF Consorzio Industrie Fiammiferi v. Autorità Garante della Concorrenza e del Mercato*, [2003] ECR I-8055.

[351] See to this effect e.g. Cases C-359/95 and C-379/95 P, *Commission and France v. Ladbroke Racing*, [1997] ECR I-6265, para. 33. [352] Para. 22 of the judgment.

for which they could be held liable. In addition, the companies participating in CIF concluded agreements that were restrictive of competition and were not dictated by the Italian legislative framework. The competition authority requested the companies participating in CIF to terminate these infringements and refrain in the future from any similar agreement.

The ECJ gave its ruling following an appeal against the decision by the Italian competition authority and a request for a preliminary ruling from THE TAR Lazio, the Italian administrative court in charge of reviewing the authority's decisions. The Italian court asked the ECJ whether Community law obliges NCAs to disregard national laws that create conditions in which firms may infringe EC competition law. The ECJ confirmed the position of the Italian competition authority. It also referred to Articles 4(1) and 98 of the EC Treaty, introduced by the Treaty of Maastricht, which provide that in the context of national economic policies the Member States must observe the principle of an open market economy with free competition.[353] Articles 81 and 10 require Member States to refrain from introducing measures which may deprive the competition rules of their useful effect by requiring or encouraging anti-competitive conduct, reinforcing the effects of such conduct, or delegating to private traders responsibility for taking key decisions affecting the economic sphere.[354] The Court held that the State action defence has little significance in this regard, because the Member States' obligations under Articles 3(1), 10 and 81 are distinct from those to which companies are subject under Articles 81 and 82.[355] Invoking the principles of supremacy of Community law and effectiveness, the Court held that a national competition authority whose responsibility is to ensure that the EC Treaty rules on competition are observed has a duty to disregard such national legislation.[356]

The Court then assessed the liability of the companies whose anti-competitive conduct was mandated or encouraged by national legislation. It held that their reliance on prior State action which mandated the anti-competitive conduct shielded them 'from all the consequences of an infringement of Articles 81 and 82 and [did] so vis-à-vis both public authorities and other economic operators'.[357] Thus, the companies would not be liable to fines, claims for damages in private litigation or the Article 81(2) civil sanction of nullity. However, once a national competition authority has decided that national law should be disregarded because it violates the EC Treaty and has found an infringement of these rules, the company concerned may no longer raise the state action defence. Once that decision has become binding on the companies concerned, they may be sanctioned if they continue to engage in the prohibited conduct.[358] The companies also remain subject to fines under Articles 81 and 82 if national law merely encourages the anti-competitive conduct. Such a situation should, however, be regarded as a mitigating factor when setting fines.[359]

---

[353] Para. 47 of the judgment.   [354] *Ibid*, paras. 46 and 50.   [355] *Ibid*, para. 51.
[356] *Ibid*, paras. 47–48.   [357] *Ibid*, para. 54.   [358] *Ibid*, para. 55.
[359] *Ibid*, para. 56–57.

This case is likely to be of great constitutional importance for the future. There are many state-condoned, state-encouraged or state-mandated entities in the new Member States, and they are likely to view the *Fiammiferi* judgment with apprehension.

E. Merger Control

Apart from legislative developments and the coming into force of the new Merger Regulation, the practice of the Commission in 2003 and 2004 was equally active, though less dramatic than in previous years.

(i) Pharmacia/Pfizer[360]

Pfizer Inc.'s acquisition of Pharmacia Corporation led to the creation of the world's largest pharmaceutical company in terms of sales and R&D spending. Although the companies' activities were largely complementary, the transaction implied several horizontal overlaps, mainly in human medicines and animal healthcare. Indeed, the Commission considered that Pfizer's strong market position would be strengthened by the addition of certain Pharmacia products.[361] To remove these competition concerns, the companies proposed a number of divestments and offered to discontinue selling some of their products. A particular feature of this case was the cooperation between the Commission and the US Federal Trade Commission under the 1991/1995 bilateral agreement.[362] They cooperated mainly regarding the remedies offered by the parties concerning urinary incontinence and erectile dysfunction products, which applied worldwide.

(ii) Newscorp/Telepiù[363]

After an aborted transaction between Italian pay-TV company Telepiù's parent Vivendi and the Australian company Newscorp, which would have led to Vivendi's acquisition of Newscorp's subsidiary Stream, an inverse operation was notified to the Commission, whereby Newscorp would acquire Telepiù from Vivendi. Telepiù would thereby merge with Stream, Italy's other pay-TV company, a 50/50 joint venture of Newscorp and Telecom Italia. The operation thus resulted in the creation of a quasi-monopoly in the Italian pay-TV market. Telepiù was already in a dominant position, with two-thirds of the Italian pay-TV market, and the merger with Stream would strengthen this position. The finding that pay-TV faces some competition from cable TV led the Commission to

360 Commission Decision of 27 February 2003 (COMP/M.2922-*Pfizer/Pharmacia*).

361 In the human medicines markets for erectile dysfunction, urinary incontinence and C2A anti-hypertensives, and in animal medicines and oral penicillin antibiotics.

362 For a full version of the agreement, see Council and Commission Decision 95/145/EC,ECSC of 10 April 1995 Concerning the Conclusion of the Agreement between the European Communities and the Government of the United States of America Regarding the Application of their Competition Laws, OJ [1995] L 95/45; Corrigendum, OJ [1995] L 131/38.

363 Commission Decision of 2 April 2003 (COMP/M.2876-*Newscorp/Telepiù*).

conclude that the proposed merger would result in a quasi-monopoly rather than a real monopoly.

Although neither Telepiù nor Stream had ever been profitable, the Commission did not accept that the case met the legal requirements for the 'failing firm defence'. (Newscorp argued that Stream would inexorably have to exit the market if the merger was not approved). However, the Commission took into account the chronic financial difficulties faced by both companies. It also looked at the special features of the Italian market and the disruption which Stream's possible exit from the market would cause to Italian pay-TV subscribers. On the basis of reasoning similar to that for the failing firm defence, the Commission considered that authorizing the merger subject to conditions would have more benefits for consumers than the exit of Stream. Thus this case was one of the rare exceptions where a merger to create a virtual monopoly was considered the best available option. However, although the transaction would create a quasi-monopoly, the Commission tried to ensure that the market remained sufficiently open for the entrance of new competition coming mainly from four sources: e.Biscom, a cable operator with some spare capacity, Digital Terrestrial Transmission (DTT) broadcasters, satellite TV channels and, possibly, an alternative fully-fledged satellite platform.

The Commission agreed with the companies a remedy package similar to those imposed in other telecommunications cases. The package included both structural and behavioural commitments by Newscorp which addressed specific concerns regarding:

- future accessibility of premium content;
- Newscorp's position as the gatekeeper for (a) access to the technical satellite platform, i.e. the system controlling conditional access and the provision of the related technical services, and (b) the Conditional Access System (CAS) technology, i.e. the software program allowing set-top boxes to decrypt the encrypted signal; and
- the fact that potential competitors unwilling to use Newscorp's CAS technology would depend on Newscorp's willingness to cooperate for the setting of simulcrypt arrangements.

The measures in the package aimed to, (a) facilitate inter-platform and promote intra-platform competition, (b) ensure access to bottlenecks, and (c) ensure that premium content was available to competitors. As regards the structural remedies, the Commission agreed with Newscorp that it would have to divest Telepiù's digital and analogue terrestrial broadcasting activities and undertake not to enter into any further DTT activities. The Commission also required the Italian Communications Authority to oversee the implementation of these undertakings.

Finally, the Commission abandoned its preliminary concerns created by the minority share that Telecom Italia would hold in the unified satellite pay-TV platform known as Sky Italia. Its concerns were based on the possibility that

Telecom Italia's participation would reduce the level of competition with the combined platform. The Commission was also concerned with a possible strengthening of Telecom Italia's dominant position through its possible vertical combination with Sky Italia's pay-TV rights. However, lack of evidence led the Commission to discontinue this line of attack.

In short, this case represents a departure from previous Commission decisions. Indeed, the Commission had to sanction a merger creating a virtual monopoly in a market where the Commission in previous cases had sought to preserve platform-to-platform competition as the best way to maximize consumer welfare and promote innovation.

(iii) GE/Instrumentarium[364]

In September 2003, the Commission approved under Article 8(2) of the old Merger Regulation the commitments presented for the acquisition of the Finnish firm Instrumentarium, active in anaesthesia and critical care medical systems, by GE Medical Systems, a subsidiary of General Electric specializing in medical diagnostic imaging technology, including patient monitors and related services and products. This four to three merger affected two of the four leading players in Europe in the market for patient monitors, thus confirming the trend in that market towards consolidation. While the transaction did not raise competition concerns regarding anaesthesia products—delivery systems and ventilators—as these were produced only by Instrumentarium, the Commission concluded, after conducting an exhaustive econometric study, that the new company would significantly increase its market power in a number of countries in the market for perioperative patient monitors *vis-à-vis* hospitals by removing a particularly close competitor and exceeding the market-share presumption for single dominance. One of the Commission's main allegations was that while GE's share was below 10 per cent, this figure downplayed its competitive constraint possibilities, as it was deemed to be a particularly close substitute for Instrumentarium.

The Commission's analysis also showed that GE would be able to favour its clinical information system by withholding the interface information that competitors would need to interface with the anaesthesia delivery systems and other relevant equipment sold by the merged company. As regards the horizontal concerns, GE agreed with the Commission to enter into supply agreements with the purchaser for key components, thus enabling the creation of a new viable competitor. The vertical concerns were removed by an innovative remedies package. GE agreed with the Commission that it would provide the necessary interface information to third parties, in order to enable competitors' monitoring equipment and IT systems to interface with the merged entity's operating room equipment (including anaesthesia delivery systems) and avoid foreclosure of that market for competing producers. The Commission also insisted on the inclusion of certain enforcement mechanisms, including the appointment of a trustee to

[364] Commission Decision of 2 September 2003 (COMP/M.3083-*GE/Instrumentarium*).

monitor compliance with the parties' commitments and a 'fast-track' arbitration procedure allowing competitors to appoint an arbitration panel to resolve possible disputes rapidly.

The econometric study conducted by the Commission in this case is particularly interesting, as it confirmed the Commission's expressed intention to take a more economic approach when analysing mergers and resulted in a greater focus on the closeness of competition between the merging parties. The study allowed the Commission to isolate the impact of GE's presence on the discounts offered by Instrumentarium, and *vice versa*. The Commission concluded that neither party had a significant impact on the size of the discount offered by the other. In a further noteworthy development, the Commission provided full access to both its own analysis and an analysis submitted by third parties. Finally, this case offers one more example of the continuing and intense cooperation between the EU and the US competition authorities.

(iv) Air France/KLM[365]

In February 2004, the Commission authorized the first major consolidation of the fragmented European airline industry, which consisted of the acquisition by Air France of the Dutch company KLM and created the world's largest airline in terms of revenue. This was the first time the Commission had decided on a consolidation in the sector involving a change in control (previous consolidations had taken the form of alliances). The Commission considered that the merger would allow the companies to be more profitable by reducing costs, and would benefit consumers by offering them access to new routes and service improvements resulting from the combined networks.

However, the Commission established that the merger would eliminate or significantly reduce competition on 14 routes where the two companies previously competed actively. For the first time in the Commission's assessment of dominance on routes, it took into account the competition aspect of indirect flights or network flights, though only as to long-haul routes. The Commission's main concern arose from the scarcity of take-off and landing rights at highly congested European hub airports. The companies therefore agreed to surrender 47 pairs of slots (i.e. 94 single take-off and landing slots), thus creating the conditions for 31 new return flights to emerge in the affected routes. They also undertook not to increase their offer of flights ('frequency freeze') in order to give operators a fair chance to compete, and to enter into 'intermodal' agreements with land transport companies, which will allow passengers to make the trip one way by train and the other by plane: this is especially significant for the Amsterdam-Paris route, where the high speed train is a real alternative. Finally, the Dutch and French authorities assured the Commission that they would give traffic rights to other carriers wishing to stopover in Amsterdam or Paris, and refrain from regulating prices on long-haul routes.

---

[365] Commission Decision of 11 February 2004 (COMP/M.3280-*Air France/KLM*).

Unlike previous decisions in this sector, the commitments by the parties on slots are for an unlimited duration. The decision specifies that if the slots are misused or underused, they are to be returned to the slot coordinator rather than the parties. In May 2004, Air France's leading competitor at Orly Airport, Easyjet, appealed the clearance of the merger to the ECJ. Easyjet alleged that, (a) the commitments accepted by the Commission to clear the merger were not sufficient to restore effective competition on routes where the parties' services overlapped and in relation to routes where they held a dominant position, and (b) the Commission should have further considered the merger's impact on the parties' position in their home airport hubs in Amsterdam and Paris, as well as the impact of the EU 'open skies' negotiations with other countries on each airline's competitive position. Regulatory changes following these negotiations could make KLM a potential competitor of Air France.

(v) Air Liquide/Messer[366]

In March 2004 the Commission gave conditional Phase I approval to the acquisition by Air Liquide, the world leader in the production and distribution of industrial gases, of Messer, also active in industrial and medical gases and the services associated with them. The markets affected by the transaction were found to be the European tonnage markets for oxygen, nitrogen, hydrogen, carbon monoxide and synthesis gas, the various markets for bulk and cylinders gases in Germany and the European market for electronic speciality gases (ESGs). The Commission considered that the transaction raised competition issues as to, (i) the market for gas supplies to large industrial customers that require either on-site production plants or direct supply pipelines; and (ii) at national level, particularly in Germany, the market for gas supplied in both bulk and cylinders for industrial and medical use.

The significance of this case lies in the fact that once the Commission had identified competition concerns, the notifying parties offered divestitures at a very early stage of the procedure, and that third parties submitted a large quantity of information. Indeed, the first version of the remedies proposed was sent to the Commission four working days after the notification. The Commission was therefore able to test the proposed remedies and request their modification according to the competition issues it identified in the proposed transaction. It was thus able to issue a decision during the first phase of the procedure that sufficient competition will remain in the markets concerned.

(vi) Sony/Bertelsmann[367]

Following a thorough investigation, and after analyzing responses to a Statement of Objections and conducting an oral hearing, the Commission approved the

---

[366] Commission Decision of 15 March 2004 (COMP/M.3314-*Air Liquide/Messer Targets*).
[367] Commission Decision of 19 July 2004 (COMP/M.3333-*Sony/BMG*).

50/50 joint venture between Sony and Bertelsmann (BMG) for recorded music, ('Artist and Repertoire', A&R), comprising the discovery and development of performing artists and the marketing and sale of records. The transaction gave SonyBMG a market share of approximately 25 per cent, equal to its closest competitor, Universal. The Commission considered that the markets affected by the transaction were those for recorded music, licences for online music and online music distribution. However, the Commission also analyzed whether the transaction would result in the coordination of Sony and Bertelsmann's competitive behaviour in the market for music publishing. Post-merger, the companies' music publishing, manufacturing and physical distribution of records would remain separate. The case represented a sort of testing ground for the Commission's application of collective dominance theories after *Airtours*.[368]

The Commission considered that a possibility of collective dominance in the market for recorded music resulted from characteristics such as multi-market contacts due to the vertical integration of the 'Majors', a stable common customer base and the weekly publication of charts, as well as certain structural links such as compilation, licensing and distribution joint ventures and agreements. The Commission first assessed whether collective dominance existed, applying the criteria laid down in the CFI's 2002 judgments overturning its merger decisions. These criteria relate to common understanding between companies on the scope of coordination, for example regarding prices, and to sufficient transparency to monitor each other's price behaviour. The Commission concluded that although the reduction of Majors from five to four would lead to an increase in transparency as the number of bilateral competitive relationships decreased from ten to six, and certain features of the market would facilitate collusion, there was insufficient evidence to conclude that it would create collective dominance in the market for recorded music.

Regarding the wholesale market for licences for online music, a market qualified by the Commission as in its infancy, the Commission considered that given the differences between the major players in terms of prices and rules of usage, there was insufficient evidence to conclude that a reduction in the number of players would lead to coordination of prices and usage conditions between the remaining players, as they were currently in flux due to the developing state of the market; and that there was not enough evidence to rebut that conclusion. The Commission concluded that Sony was unlikely to achieve a single dominant position in the retail market for online music distribution owing to existing competition to the Sony Connect music downloading service, and the merger would not create a collective dominant position. Online music is an emerging market where the structure of prices and usage conditions are in a state of evolution. Reducing the players from five to four would therefore not increase transparency or the

---

[368] Case T-342/99, *Airtours plc. v. Commission*, [2002] ECR II-2585.

prospects for retaliation to such an extent as to make the creation of a collective dominant position likely.

It is interesting to note that the Commission did not focus on pursuing a unilateral effects theory, but on collective dominance concerns. This can be deduced from its press release, which refers to the absence of a leading or dominant player post-merger. The decision approving the merger was appealed to the CFI in December 2004 by Impala, a trade association representing independent music companies.[369] Two further points should be stressed. Firstly, the Commission showed increased awareness of the requisite legal standard to be met in order to conclude on the creation of a collective dominant position, by following the steps and criteria established by the Court in *Airtours*. Secondly, it is again worth noting the Commission's close cooperation with the US authorities, perhaps as an attempt to smooth out previous disagreements in merger cases. Indeed, the US authorities approved the merger just 10 days after the Commission reached the same conclusion.

(vii) Cableuropa

On 3 July 2002, DTS Distribuidora de Televisión Digital SA (Vía Digital), the second pay-TV operator in Spain, and Sogecable SA, Spain's dominant pay-TV operator, notified their intention to merge to the Commission. Sogecable's main areas of business were the operation of terrestrial television (Canal+ analogue) and direct-to-home satellite pay-TV services (Canal Satélite Digital), the production and distribution of films, the acquisition and sale of sports rights and the provision of technology services. The company was controlled by Prisa (Promotora Informaciones SA, the Spanish media group which publishes 'El País' and 'Cinco Días'), and by Canal+ SA. Vía Digital offered TV via satellite in Spain and was controlled by Telefónica through Admira Media. The remaining capital was divided among institutional shareholders, mainly TV operators (Televisa, Canal 9, Direct TV, TVG, TVC, Telemadrid). After the merger Sogecable would continue to be controlled by Prisa and Canal+, while Telefónica would hold a significant participation in the merged entity.

On 12 July 2002, Spain requested the Commission to refer the case to the Spanish competition authorities under Article 9(2)(a) of the old Merger Regulation, on the basis that the proposed merger threatened to create a dominant position impeding competition in distinct markets within Spain.

Following this request, the Commission reviewed the case and confirmed that the proposed transaction would threaten to create or strengthen a dominant position in the Spanish markets for, (a) pay-TV, where the parties were the two largest competitors and had combined market shares of around 80 per cent in terms of number of subscribers, and 80–95 per cent in terms of sales; (b) acquisition of

---

[369] OJ [2005] C 6/46.

exclusive rights for premium films; and (c) acquisition and exploitation of football matches in which Spanish teams participated (this TV content is the main reason why customers decide to subscribe to pay-TV), other sports and sale of TV channels.

Before deciding to refer the case to the Spanish competition authorities, the Commission also investigated the effect of the transaction in several telecommunications markets, such as the provision of internet access services, fixed telephony services or provision of infrastructures, and took into consideration Telefónica's developing activities in pay-TV. Its investigation indicated that the creation of a structural link between the dominant operators in pay-TV (and audiovisual content) and telecommunications in Spain was likely to strengthen Telefónica's dominant position in a number of those markets.

After conducting this investigation, the Commission concluded that given the national scope of the market affected by the transaction, the Spanish authorities were particularly well placed to carry out a thorough investigation of the operation, and decided to refer the case.

In November 2002, Aunacable and Cableuropa appealed the Commission's decision to refer the merger to the Spanish authorities before the CFI. They claimed that, (a) the Commission did not have competence to refer the proposed merger to a Member State as it affected inter-state trade and more than one Member State; and (b) the Commission had infringed Article 9 of the Merger Regulation by failing to observe the obligation to provide reasons for its referral. Aunacable also claimed that the Commission had breached the principle of good administration by abandoning its policy, and had failed to take into account other closely connected cases, and that the Commission was better placed to deal with the case than the Spanish authorities. This was the first appeal of such a decision. In September 2003, the CFI dismissed the appeal and found that the Commission had not committed a manifest error in determining that the proposed merger affected only distinct national markets.[370] The Court concluded that it was reasonable for the Commission to believe that the Spanish authorities would be able to take appropriate measures to maintain effective competition in the relevant markets.

(viii) MCI

In June 2000 the Commission adopted a decision prohibiting a merger between MCI WorldCom (now called MCI) and Sprint. A day earlier both parties had informed the Commission by fax that they were withdrawing their notification and no longer intended to implement the proposed merger in the form presented in the Form CO notification. The Commission considered that this fax did not

---

[370] Joined Cases T-346/02 and T-347/02, *Cableuropa SA and Others v. Commission*, [2003] ECR II-4251.

amount to a 'formal withdrawal of the merger agreement' notified in January 2000. MCI challenged this finding before the CFI.

The Court[371] began by analyzing MCI's standing to bring an action for annulment of the Commission decision since the notified merger had been abandoned, citing previous case law where legal standing was granted to parties which had abandoned a proposed merger subsequent to a prohibition from the Commission. The CFI went on to annul the Commission decision on procedural grounds, analyzing only the first plea brought by MCI, which dealt with the Commission's lack of power to decide on the concentration once the parties had withdrawn from the transaction. According to the CFI, the parties' withdrawal was to be followed by several amendments to the proposed transaction and the Commission had not taken this into account in its decision. The Court also noted that in previous cases the Commission had simply closed the file following a withdrawal notice from the parties. The CFI considered that the notifying parties were entitled to expect their fax would be sufficient to lead to closure of the file, in accordance with the Commission's administrative practice, which had been made public, and in the absence of indications to the contrary by the Commission. As it discussed only the procedural issues and annulled the decision on that basis, the Court did not examine the substance of the case, including the Commission's definition of the market.

(ix) BaByliss

In November 2003 the Commission approved the merger between SEB, one of the largest manufacturers of small electrical household appliances, and Moulinex, another French company which had been a direct competitor of SEB. The decision followed a previous decision in which the Commission, (a) referred to France the examination of the merger's impact on the French market under Article 9 of the Merger Regulation, (b) authorized the operation unconditionally in five Member States, and (c) made its approval in nine other EU countries subject to the granting of licences involving the Moulinex brand for five years in each of those nine countries. This decision was challenged before the CFI by two rival companies, and was annulled with regard to the unconditional authorization in five markets.[372]

Several aspects of the judgment deserve mention. Firstly, the CFI concluded that the Commission had not given sufficient reasons for finding that no problems arose in certain markets, particularly Spain, Italy, Finland, the UK and Ireland. The CFI held that the Commission had not properly looked at the possibility that the merger would give rise to a portfolio effect on the five national markets, even when there was no significant overlap between the merging

---

[371] Case T-310/00, *MCI, Inc. v. Commission*, judgment of 28 September 2004, not yet reported.
[372] Case T-114/02, *BaByliss SA v. Commission*, [2003] ECR II-1279.

companies' product range. In addition, the CFI found that the Commission had not given sufficient evidence to prove its 'range effect' theory, i.e. that any attempt by the parties to engage in anti-competitive practices would be punished on other non-dominated product markets. Of particular interest is the CFI's finding that the Merger Regulation seeks to prohibit the creation or strengthening of a dominant position rather than to prevent the abuse of such a position.

The appellants argued that commitments offered by the parties and accepted by the Commission had been made too late in the procedure, as the parties had submitted revised commitments after the expiry of the time-limits (five weeks after the notification). The Court, however, confirmed that the time-limit laid down by the Merger Regulation was binding only on the notifying parties and not on the Commission, and that the Commission could accept commitments offered outside these time-limits. Also regarding these commitments, the Court pointed out that neither the Merger Regulation nor the Commission's Notice on Remedies[373] include any reference to the sort of remedies that must or may be presented during Phase I or Phase II proceedings.

From the jurisdictional point of view, it is noteworthy that while the Court approved the Commission's decision to refer the merger to the French authorities, it also commented that systematic referrals to Member States when products raised concerns for distinct national markets could damage the 'one-stop-shop' principle for merger control.[374] From a more general perspective, it is interesting that the Court specifically acknowledged the possibility of challenging before the Court a Commission decision referring a merger case to a national competition authority, on the ground that such a decision individually and directly affects the applicant's legal situation. The Court also stated that such a decision deprives the applicant of an assessment of the proposed transaction under the Merger Regulation. This was the first case where a third party was successful on the merits.

Following the judgment, the Commission carried out a new wide-ranging survey of the five countries concerned in order to assess the operation's effect on competition. The survey analysed the position of each competitor in the market, in terms of turnover, product offerings and brand value. The conclusion reached by the Commission from the analysis was that the SEB group would neither hold nor strengthen a dominant position on any of the relevant markets, whether by adding the market shares generated by the operation or through its overall position in the small electrical household appliance sector taken as a whole (portfolio effect).

---

[373] Commission Notice on Remedies Acceptable under Council Regulation (EEC) No. 4064/89 and under Commission Regulation (EC) No. 447/98, OJ [2001] C 68/3.

[374] Para. 355 of the judgment.

(x) Portugal/Commission

The ECJ judgment in *Portugal v. Commission*[375] is important from a procedural perspective. In this case, the first prohibition decision since 2001, the Court addressed the possibility for Member States to take measures to protect national legitimate interests under Article 21(3) of the old Merger Regulation. Article 21(3) empowers the Member States to take measures to protect their national interests other than those protected by the Commission, namely public security, plurality of the media and prudential rules. It further provides:

Any other public interest must be communicated to the Commission by the Member State concerned and shall be recognised by the Commission after an assessment of its compatibility with the general principles and other provisions of Community law before the measures referred to above may be taken. The Commission shall inform the Member State concerned of its decision within one month of that communication.

Article 21(4) of the new Merger Regulation essentially mirrors this provision.

This case arose in connection with a proposed acquisition of Cimpor-Cimentos de Portugal by Secilpar, a Spanish company, and Holderbank. Cimpor, a former State-owned company, was privatized in 1994. When the preliminary announcement of a takeover bid for Cimpor was published, the Portuguese State held 12.7 per cent of Cimpor's shares, while 10 per cent of those shares had special rights attached.

The proposed acquisition was notified to the Commission for approval under the Merger Regulation and to the Portuguese Minister for Finance for authorization to acquire the voting capital of Cimpor. Authorization was refused in Portugal, *inter alia*, because the acquisition was deemed to conflict with the Portuguese government's restructuring plans for the sector and would have involved the withdrawal of Cimpor from the Portuguese capital market. A copy of the Portuguese government's decision was sent to the Commission. The Commission concluded that the Portuguese decisions blocking the acquisition were not in accordance with Article 21 of the Merger Regulation, because the Portuguese government had not given the Commission prior notice of its intention to disallow a concentration. In addition, the Commission found that the reasons the Portuguese government put forward for disapproving the concentration were not compatible with Article 21 of the Merger Regulation.

This decision was appealed by the Portuguese government, which argued that the Commission had no competence to adopt the contested decision in the absence of any communication from the Portuguese government concerning the interests protected by the national measures. The ECJ rejected this plea. The Court reasoned that the Merger Regulation is based on the principle of precise allocation of competences between the national authorities and the

---

[375] Case C-42/01 *Portugal v. Commission*, judgment of 22 June 2004, not yet reported.

Commission.[376] The Court recalled that the Merger Regulation contained provisions which, for reasons of legal certainty and in the interest of companies concerned, were designed to limit the duration of proceedings.[377] Consequently, Article 21(3) must be interpreted to mean the Commission had competence to take a decision that a Member State had acted in contravention of that article, regardless of whether the Member State had provided the Commission with the requisite notification of its action. To hold otherwise, according to the ECJ, would render the article ineffective by giving Member States the possibility of easily circumventing the controls therein.[378]

It will be interesting to see if any of the principles established by the Court in relation to the Merger Regulation and division of competences between the Commission and the NCAs will be adopted in relation to the new modernized antitrust enforcement regime.

2003–2004 STATISTICS

ANTITRUST CASES

	2003	2004	Total
Total number of new cases	474 (262 antitrust and 212 merger cases)	407 (158 antitrust and 249 merger cases)	881
Total number of cases closed	549 (319 antitrust and 230 merger cases)	633 (391 antitrust and 242 merger cases)	1,182
Number of antitrust cases opened (under Articles, 81, 82 and 86)	262	158	420
Antitrust cases closed by informal procedure	295	363	658
Antitrust cases closed by formal decisions	24	28	52
Cases notified	71	21	92
Complaints	94	85	179
Cases opened on Commission's own initiative	97	52	149

---

[376] Para. 50 of the judgment.   [377] *Ibid*, para. 51.   [378] *Ibid*, paras. 52–56.

MERGER CASES

	2003	2004	Total
Number of merger cases notified	212	249	461
Cases withdrawn in Phase I	0	3	3
Cases withdrawn in Phase II	0	2	2
Number of final decisions (Phase I + Phase II)	231	242	473
Number of decisions imposing fines	0	1	1

FINES IMPOSED UNDER ARTICLES 81 AND 82 EC

Date	Product(s)	Amount of fine(€)
April 2003	French beef cartel	16.68 million
May 2003	Yamaha	2.56 million
July 2003	Deutsche Telekom	12.6 million
October 2003	Sorbates cartel	138.4 million
December 2003	Electrical & mechanical carbon and graphite products cartel	101.44 million
December 2003	Organic peroxides cartel	70.53 million
December 2003	Industrial copper tubes cartel	78.73 million
March 2004	Microsoft	497.198 million
April 2004	CEWAL	3.4 million
May 2004	Topps	1.59 million
June 2004	Belgian Architects' Association	100.000
September 2004	Sodium gluconate	19.04 million
September 2004	Copper plumbing tubes cartel	222.3 million
September 2004	French beers cartel	2.5 million
October 2004	Raw tobacco processing cartel	20 million
October 2004	Needle & haberdashery products cartel	60 million
December 2004	Animal feed vitamin cartel	66.3 million

Reviews of Books

The Treaty of Nice and Beyond: Enlargement and Constitutional Reform by Mads Andenas and John Usher (eds.), (Oxford: Hart Publishing, 2003), viii + 440pp. ISBN 1-84113-339-6.

Even as the Treaty of Nice was being negotiated and concluded, the focus had shifted—notwithstanding hurdles to its ratification—to the 'post-Nice process'. This book is a collection of essays assessing the Nice Treaty and the ensuing process of constitutional reform. The contributions are varied in focus and diverse in perspective, coming not alone from academia but also from prominent figures in the judicial and political spheres. Stretching from the ratification period of 2001 to the early days of the Convention on the Future of Europe in 2003—with most pieces having already appeared elsewhere, either as articles in academic journals or as conference presentations and lectures—the collection covers an interesting period in Europe's recent constitutional debate. Furthermore, in light of recent developments—especially the stalled ratification of the constitutional treaty following the French and Dutch referendums—many of the post-Nice questions have been reinvigorated and the issues central to this volume are of renewed interest.

The volume is divided into four sections which deal with the European Constitution, the Treaty of Nice, the European Courts, and the Charter of Fundamental Rights respectively. The 'European Constitution' and European constitutionalism are, according to the editors, 'the book's central theme'. In somewhat unusual sequence, the first section tackles this theme directly. In the opening essay, Peter Oliver delivers a brief sketch of the Convention on the Future of Europe. Although this is one of the contributions which has most obviously dated in the light of subsequent rapid developments in that arena and the resulting political process, it nonetheless offers an interesting exposition of the Convention's early days and the development of its debates, which clearly remain, for the time being at least, of more than merely historical interest and relevance.

In their survey of 'European Law and National Constitutions' from the 2002 FIDE Congress, Dutheuil de la Rochère and Pernice offer a summary of national reports on the various constitutional questions at the heart of this relationship. While this provides an interesting comparative study of national perspectives on these issues, it suffers—if not through fault of the authors—from a lack of comprehensiveness, not only from the existing 15 Member States but especially from the new Member States, with Cyprus alone reporting.

In two separate German perspectives—the first judicial, the second academic—the section continues with a focus on the perennially problematic question of allocating competences between the EU and its Member States. In a short but thoughtful overview, Udo Di Fabio provides some interesting insights into the heart of this problem, urging caution in any aspiration towards a definitive line-drawing of competences. Pernice follows suit with a more comprehensive overview of the central questions. Taking a close look at the main proposals for reform and assessing their merits and demerits, he too asserts that attempts at legal delimitation can only achieve modest success and emphasizes that the nature of these questions is such that political guidelines are warranted for their effective resolution.

In the final essay in this section, Daniel Thym offers thoughts on European constitutional theory and the post-Nice process. Acknowledging the difficulty of tackling such a vast topic in limited space, he focuses first on aspects of European constitutional theory from the differing perspectives of the United Kingdom and German constitutional systems and contends that the real challenge in the EU context is that of democratic constitutionalism. He then analyses how certain aspects of the post-Nice process relate to this concept and challenge, concluding that 'the historical significance of the post-Nice process will ultimately depend on whether it has strengthened the bond between the European Constitution and the constitutional sovereign: the people'.

This general issue arises in various forms and at various stages in this section, also surfacing explicitly in the Dutheuil de la Rochère-Pernice survey where the question of the ratification of any European constitutional agreement by Member States is discussed. Notwithstanding these references, the two-attempt Irish ratification of the Nice Treaty merits merely an occasional allusion in the footnotes. Yet, in any contextual analysis of European constitutionalism, this surely ranks as a central insight of the entire Nice process. Neglected in the collection as a whole, it was obviously a harbinger of the more serious woes which have since beset the ratification of the constitutional treaty.

It is only in the second section that the volume deals with the Treaty of Nice itself. The articles, in the vein of the Treaty itself, focus as much on what was left undone as on what was actually done. John Usher provides an excellent overview of the central institutional reform issues at stake in the Nice and post-Nice debates and in the context of enlargement. Jo Shaw offers an insightful discussion of the provisions on enhanced cooperation which, lingering lifeless since Amsterdam, were adapted at Nice and will undoubtedly come to fore again in the context of continuing constitutional debate and challenge of accommodating Member States in a Europe of 25. Steve Peers follows with an interesting analysis of Nice, written from the perspective of Treaty structure. Haris Kountouros examines the

Treaty's modest changes in the area of social policy, using this to open out onto more general thoughts on the place and orientation of social policy within the EU enterprise as a whole, while Joseph McMahon explores the possible inclusion of new objectives for the Common Agricultural Policy within the Treaties.

The third section, on the European courts, more successfully captures the detail of Nice and its changes. While, as Usher notes, these may have largely bypassed headline writers, they nonetheless provide 'institutional solutions ... with fundamental long-term consequences'. In a series of articles, the debates on reform of the European judicial architecture are effectively relayed. Alongside Piet Eeckhout's general analysis of the Courts after Nice, the collection offers an important lecture by Francis Jacobs, Advocate-General at the ECJ, on the judicial protection of individuals—focusing on the continued gap in judicial remedies as long as the direct and individual concern test is strictly applied by the Court—and an analysis by Arnull of changes to the preliminary rulings procedure. In many cases, while Nice has offered an enabling framework for reform, relatively little has actually changed on the ground: the fact that preliminary rulings remain exclusively the domain of the ECJ, despite provisions providing for the possible extension of the Court of First Instance's jurisdiction, is one of the most obvious examples of this. All the articles point to the unresolved institutional questions and the enduring reform agenda which remain post-Nice. This is especially so in Heffernan's article 'revisiting' the proposal for some sort of European *certiorari* to act as a filter of the burgeoning caseload of the Court of Justice. With little further reform in this area envisaged in the constitutional treaty, it is only a matter of time before continuing concerns of judicial overload and similar matters of practical necessity once again place these issues on the table.

Finally, the Charter of Fundamental Rights is discussed. As a member of the Charter-drafting Convention, and a protagonist in the debate on how the Charter should ultimately be integrated into the constitutional treaty, the views of the British Attorney-General, Lord Goldsmith, are of special interest. After sketching briefly the reasons why a Charter was necessary and desirable, the lecture goes on to touch upon the more interesting question of the Charter's legal status. Asserting that, as proclaimed at Nice, the Charter lacked the 'precision necessary for law', it will be interesting to see to what extent the concerns expressed by Goldsmith—although tempered through changes made at the Convention on the Future of Europe and in the subsequent IGC—will return to the fore as shadows are once again cast over the Charter's legal status with the halting of the constitutional treaty ratification process. A cautionary note is also sounded in Sionaidh Douglas-Scott's analysis of the Charter from a constitutional perspective: she discusses some of the underlying difficulties in EU human rights protection which remain notwithstanding the Charter, as well as specific difficulties raised by the Charter itself on account of its drafting and scope. Yet the influence and importance of the Charter remain, regardless of the specific response to questions of its legal status which may form part of the debates to come. This is clear from Schwarze's 'German perspective' on the Charter where he places the Charter in the context of the development of human rights in the EU more generally and the jurisprudence of the *Bundesverfassungsgericht* particularly. Noting the broad welcome of the Charter—despite concerns regarding, *inter alia*, the horizontal clauses (which have since been addressed, at least partially, in the constitutional treaty)—Schwarze views the Charter as a positive development not alone in its contribution to the actual protection of rights within the EU system but also, just as importantly, as legitimating and symbolizing the EU as a community of values.

As is clear from this brief review, the volume brings together a diverse collection of pieces on the Treaty of Nice itself and the wider constitutional process it helped set in train. While this is undoubtedly its strength, it can also leave a certain resonance of incoherence. Perhaps reflecting its origins in the midst of a rapidly changing constitutional landscape, the collection seems to overstretch itself between the Treaty of Nice, which its title implies to be its core, and the European Constitution and European constitutionalism which it takes to be its central theme. Notwithstanding the obvious continuum and overlap, it lacks any overarching introductory or concluding note to bring the various topics and themes together in a meaningful way. Although collections of this type are by their nature a miscellany of views, the current abundance of literature on European constitutionalism requires a somewhat more tailored focus for such a compilation to be fully successful.

Moreover, while enlargement forms part of the volume's subtitle, this issue is not dealt with in any significant way in the volume. Its presence in the subtitle makes its absence in the main text all the more noticeable. While it forms an important aside in the discussion of issues such as institutional design, nowhere is the question treated thoroughly or independently, nor is there any contribution from the 10 new Member States.

The book seems to suffer somewhat from the difficult twilight zone between Nice and its 'Beyond'. Perhaps caught between a hesitancy (emerging three years after the Nice IGC itself) and a haste (coming before the Convention and IGC completed their work) to publish, this factor seems moreover to have cast its shadow on the volume's editing. Typographical errors stalk almost every page. Poor, inconsistent and sometimes altogether absent referencing also mars the volume, as does the lack of even the most basic index. Despite these flaws, the volume undoubtedly has renewed relevance in the light of the major obstacles before the constitutional treaty and the default return to the Nice status quo. Some of the substantive issues tackled remain very much on the agenda. Equally, indeed perhaps more importantly, the volume is illuminating as a retrospective of a particular, and peculiar, time in European constitutional discourse.

DAVID FENNELLY

Between Competition and Free Movement: The Economic Constitutional Law of the European Community by Julio Baquero Cruz, (Oxford: Hart Publishing, 2002), 176pp. ISBN 1-84113-336-1.

I) Whom does the constitution command? This question, among the oldest of constitutional law, is brought back on the agenda by the blurring of the public/private divide: the mixed economy, state involvement in the economy, privatization and private regulation made it increasingly difficult to define the circle of addressees of competition and free movement norms. This situation is identified by Julio Baquero Cruz as a constitutional gap, '*a lacuna between competition and free movement*'. The division of the economic constitutional law along private/public lines generates the main questions of his PhD thesis, defended at the EUI Florence in 2001, namely whether free movement rules apply in the private sphere and how competition rules relate to State action.

Since the author perceives these questions to be of uniquely constitutional nature, he starts his enquiry by defining an '*operational concept of Constitution*' (Chapter 2), a cornerstone of which shall be the condition that a constitution '*creates a protected sphere of autonomy vis-à-vis public and private powers for the persons living in the polity*'. In emphasizing individual autonomy regardless of the public or private origin of its threats, he most conscientiously departs from the understanding of a constitution as an instrument to solely legitimize and contain public power. Instead, in applying his concept to the Economy (Chapter 3), he rejects in a first step the notion of an 'Economic Constitution' in favor of 'Economic constitutional law', mainly for interpretative reasons: the latter seems to him not only to be a narrower concept because it does not presuppose the ordo-liberal general decision of the economic structure of the state and the ideal of the private law society, but it also allows for non-economic values to be taken into account through argumentations based on the completeness of the constitution. The integrity of the Constitution could thus be safeguarded. In a second stage he argues that the pragmatic stress on economic goals and efficiency hides the fact that the Treaties were and remain means to further the goals of peace and stability, aiming at the creation of a Community of States and peoples. (See in this context Art. I-1 of the Constitutional Treaty: 'Reflecting the will of the Citizens and States of Europe'.) In this view individual autonomy became protected as such by fundamental rights—and, with the notable exception of comitology, democratic legitimacy became a decisive argument against ordoliberal conceptions (Chapter 4). In further elaborating on the link between primacy and direct effect, the author suggests that an essential distinction should be drawn between policies including both directly applicable rules and enabling provisions, namely free movement and competition, and those policies which only entail enabling norms, e.g. industrial and social policy (Chapter 5). Provisions with direct effect are accorded '*constitutional or higher law status*', constituting expressions of the rule of an open market economy with free competition (Articles 4, 98, 105 EC) against which policies like the CAP are but mere exceptions. Consequently, the social element not having a comparable presence to that of the '*neo-liberal economic ethos of the Community*', the author contends that the Treaty is neither economically neutral nor based on a social market economy, but can best be described as a '*corrected market economy*'.

Based on his interpretation of the legal nature, similarity and differences between competition and free movement (Chapter 6), Baquero Cruz then discusses the gaps which have been characterized by Michel Waelbroeck as the '*privatization of the free movement rules*' and the '*publicisation of the competition rules*'. He firmly contrasts a maximalist conception under which both normative areas, having a teleological unity, namely the internal market, should be viewed as parts of a coherent whole, to a minimalist approach according to which the different respective personal scopes of application were deliberate and complementary. Both reasonings, of which he finds equal proof in the case law, are rejected due to the '*confusion of the relationship between competition and free movement*' which does not allow for either position: arguments discussed in this respect are the different notions of affectation of trade and the different material normative scopes on the one hand, and the blurring of the personal scopes of applicability on the other. Moreover, the shifting normative contents of both competition (liberating the competition rules form the goal of market integration) and free movement (the convergence of economic freedoms) do not allow them to be considered as complementary.

The solution with regard to the central gap shall accordingly be found in a principled middle way avoiding formalistic and rigid positions. After summing up the case law of the extension of the personal scope of free movement to private parties as incoherent, Baquero Cruz welcomes the abolition by the ECJ of '*the enigmatic concept of collective private power*' (Chapter 7). For reasons of uniformity of Community Law he strongly rejects references to national delimitations of state and society, legislation and private governance, or the public or private nature of the actor. Instead he proposes that, '*private action may be caught by the Treaty rules on free movement only when it has the capacity to restrict free movement with a protectionist intent or effect. [. . .] In contrast, private behaviour, that lacks this dimension of 'power over individuals' would not be caught*'.

In a similar vein, the author describes in detail (Chapter 8) the development of the jurisprudence on the 'State action doctrine', i.e. the reasoning of the Court under which conditions state measures fall under the material scope of Article 81 or 82 EC, in conjunction with Article 3 g) and 10 EC (require or favor the adoption of agreements or concerted practices or reinforce their effects): He proposes to drop the requirement of a direct link between the anticompetitive conduct on the part of the undertaking and the State action, and to replace this formalism by a new test based on deference to the degree of democratic legitimacy of the author of the measure.

II) Deconstruction of dichotomist ways of legal thinking needs courage: Here we face the work of a learned scholar, a former référendaire at the ECJ, who risks new perspectives in a field few scholars dare to plough. His often inspired line of thinking and surprising insights make this book a perfect read. Despite or maybe because the enquiry is, in the author's own words, 'non-linear', some chapters are a gem: It is rare to read such an articulate account of the question under which circumstances private persons are bound by primary constitutional law. Baquero Cruz does not fall into the terminological fallacy of the notion of 'horizontal direct effect', which stems from the discussion of secondary law, but instead prefers '*private effect*' or '*inclusion*' of private parties among the addressees of free movement rules. However, one would have liked to hear more on the explicit constitutional reasons that can solidly explain why the Treaty commands private, non-governmental actors as well: the jurisprudence of the ECJ does not help, apart from very general statements no rationale is given: To quote but two cases: In the 1976 *Defrenne II* case (Case 43/75, ECR 1976, p. 455), the seminal judgment before the private effect of free movement entered the stage, the only reason given for the sweeping proposition that the principle of equal pay applies even to contracts between individuals was that Article 141 EC '*is mandatory in nature*' and that states have to perform a '*duty to bring about a specific result*'. Still in 2000, in *Angonese* (Case C–281/98, ECR 2000, p. I-4139) the ECJ built on this approach by simply arguing that if Article 141 EC has private effect, Article 39 EC applies 'a fortiori' to private actors. Baquero Cruz proposes a reasoning based on private power and introduces conditions of intent and effect. It would have been interesting to link this chapter closer to his view that protection against all private power is one of the general conditions of an operative constitution. Baquero Cruz should have gone further in this approach, because, for the time being, the notion of 'power' appears to be too vague and its connotations too manifold to be workable in the area of free movement, and it is doubtful if we need intent in this area of law. His unique contribution lies in undermining the link between private power and control through competition law. Thereby the author opens a discussion on the relation between the power to discriminate and private autonomy on constitutional grounds. In this line of thinking some authors have already suggested to develop the notion of 'private governance' (Stephan Wernicke, Die Privatwirkung im Europäischen Gemeinschaftsrecht, Baden-Baden, 2002, p. 254), using the criterion the ECJ hid well when it argued in the Bosman case that Article 39 EC not only applies to the action of public authorities but extends also to rules of any other nature '*aimed at regulating*' economic activity. Regulation can be understood as synonymous with governance. This is why the former Advocate General Van Gerven considered the Bosman judgment as one which 'constitutionalizes' the common market, converting Treaty provisions from legal acts binding the Member States into legal rules governing the relations even between private actors. Yet another way of reasoning would be to argue that the Treaty did not intend to deny constitutional protection against private violation of fundamental freedoms—the classic rights approach (for a comparative American view in the light of the US Supreme Court's state action doctrine: Louis Henkin, The Age of Rights, New York 1999). These discussions show that there is no consensus yet.

Baquero Cruz's critique of the state action doctrine is equally convincing. It is indeed questionable why democratic legitimacy does not play a part in the ECJ's formula according to which a Member State must require or favour collusion contrary to Article 81 EC or delegate to private traders responsibility for taking economic decisions affecting the economic sphere. Again, comparative constitutional law shows its merits in the argumentation of Baquero Cruz when he explains the well known Midcal Test of the US Supreme Cour, requiring 'active supervision' of private power resulting from a policy choice to depart from the market principle. In fact, this notion of 'control' by the state does not only entail the applicability of the state action defence, but conversely may be used to attribute private actors to the state, thus opening a third category between privatisation of free movement and publicisation of competition law, namely those private actors which are bound by primary—or constitutional—law due to state control. This aspect could however not be part of the book because its focus was not organizational. Nevertheless, the private legal form of an actor does not necessarily preclude his categorization as 'public' as interpreted by Community law ('Buy Irish'). This analysis should always be undertaken before subjecting genuine private actors to public obligations. Finally, the fact that the constitutional cornerstone of a discussion of state intervention into the economy, Article 86 EC, is left out of the enquiry is of no harm because Baquero Cruz's constitutional analysis should be read against his recent publication on this norm (in *EU Law and the Welfare State, Collected Courses of the Academy of European Law* (OUP, 2005)).

The merit of Baquero Cruz's analysis lies in tackling a core issue post-privatisation and deregulation: How do we react to the blurring of the public/private divide? If this divide is no longer an essential dichotomy, and this reviewer could not agree more, we are called upon to develop other legal instruments to shape the emerging situation. This book is therefore a major contribution to a debate beyond competition and free movement.

STEPHAN WERNICKE

Culture and European Union Law by Rachael Craufurd Smith (ed.), (Oxford: Oxford University Press, 2004), 414pp. ISBN 0-19-927547-5.

It is common to state that Community law was born and has developed from an economic foundation. Issues other than those with an economic dimension have had difficulty in finding a status in the Community legal order, and have done so sometimes only after a struggle amongst both the Community institutions and the various legal orders. Whereas social values have been introduced at a slow but continuous pace, cultural issues have not achieved sufficient consensus to guarantee their presence in Community law. Now that the European Union is consolidating itself as an entity which is different from the international organisation of the European Economic Community, the attempt to preserve an identity that legitimates it inwardly (in relation to the Member States) and outwardly (in relation to other international actors) is apparent. For this reason, culture has been given an increasingly more prominent position. Although some precedents may be identified, the consolidation of the legal status of culture was brought about by the Treaty of Maastricht, which introduced in the EC Treaty art. 128 (now art. 151) concerning Community action in the cultural field.

The book now under review analyses the various perspectives of culture in EU law, the starting point of which is the development of a Community cultural policy as a result of the abovementioned art. 151 EC (See the general introduction of the editor, Rachael Craufurd Smith, as well as her Chapter 2, 'Community Intervention in the Cultural Field: Continuity or Change?'). Yet the study goes much further, since it shows how culture timidly appeared in previously existing law. This is the case, for instance, of cultural arguments pleaded by parties in cases before the European Court of Justice in order to justify exemptions to the free movement of goods (See Chapter 3, by Niamh Nic Shuibhne, 'Labels, Locals, and the Free Movement of Goods'). This is also the case of languages in the European Union, as canvassed by Bruno de Witte in Chapter 7 ('Language Law of the European Union: Protecting or Eroding Linguistic Diversity'). This justifies the wideness of the project, which has now materialized into a sound, complete and thought-provoking volume, destined to constitute an authoritative pioneer in the field.

No better opening for a book written in English on culture and (implicitly) diversity than a French quotation on the value of culture for the European Union. In it, culture is regarded in two ways—reflecting the contents of art. 151 EC—as the protection of the diversity of cultures in the European Union and as the development of a common European culture. Being such an important feature for a European identity, why should it be necessary to explain the reasons for this book to be published? Indeed, this is the question Rachael Craufurd Smith asks herself, describing the many areas where culture plays a role in Community and European Union Law.

It would be an impossible task to deal with all chapters in depth. Therefore, I will highlight only some of the questions that are brought up, leaving for the future reader of the book the discovery of more profound debates and nuances within each contribution.

A long and thorough introduction by the editor puts forward the general framework of the book, giving some insight into the very notion of culture. Community/EU law has been reluctant so far to provide a definition of culture, something problematic from a legal point of view, due to the fact that it reduces legal certainty. However, the Court of Justice has accepted cultural arguments on several occasions, as mentioned also in other chapters in the book, admitting that even such a broad concept can justify certain restrictions to the free movement rules. Craufurd Smith also echoes the fact that culture is more and more linked to sectors which did not have cultural connotations in the past. This is the case of tourism, for instance. Indeed, and even if this is not the object of a separate contribution in the book, it is interesting to note here that cultural arguments have led public powers to regulate tourism from a wider perspective than before, thus imposing obligations on tourist industries, such as that dealing with the preservation of the environment and national treasures. Finally, culture cannot be detached in many cases from an economic value. The so-called cultural industries, such as those in the media sector, play a decisive role in the Community action on culture. It is worth noting here that this is indeed one of the areas where the Community has decided to intervene more intensively, not least because its economic value is apparent. The latter shows the manifold character of Community intervention on the basis of culture. The direct application of art. 151 EC is only one of the possibilities, as the introduction and the other contributions demonstrate. Yet a rather pessimistic feeling pervades the volume, since there is a feeling that culture does not play the desirable role it should play in the European context. This is visible in Chapter 2, where Rachael Craufurd Smith canvasses the history of culture as a matter for Community/EU law. Single initiatives undertaken by the Community institutions, or by some of their members at different moments have not been accompanied, until very recently, by a general assumption of the need of a common cultural policy.

Chapters 3 to 5 constitute Part II of the book and refer to the relationship between culture and commerce in three realms. First, Niamh Nic Shuibhne explores the presence of cultural arguments in restrictions to the free movement of goods under the terminological umbrella of 'consumer protection'. Dealing mainly, although not only, with product labelling, the author concludes that consumer protection arguments cannot serve on their own to justify a cultural approach to the free movement of goods. It is convincingly argued that the Community should include culture as a key policy in its agenda. Only then will cultural diversity find its place.

The second of the contributions in Part II gives an account of the cultural implications existing in sport, which would justify differences in relation to the application of fundamental freedoms in this area. Stephen Weatherill is sceptical about the consideration of sport as culture in general terms, at least in regard to professional sport. Indeed, he considers that the existing regulation on trade is so far valid for professional sport, and there is no need to incorporate a specific competence of the Community in this field. In order to reach this conclusion, the author critically analyzes the major disputes arisen in this area in EC law, namely the player transfer system in football, with *Bosman* still being the leading case on the subject. Far from considering the subject as a block, Weatherill dissects each element of the transfer system, trying to identify where the economics of sport are really different from economics in other areas. This argument is further developed in another framework: collective selling of rights to broadcast matches. As the author notes, it is interesting to take into consideration the fact that peculiarities that may be attributed to sport have important implications here. Indeed, collective selling arrangements impose limitations and obligations on third parties—the broadcasters—, thus affecting competition. More specific issues, such as the collective selling of rights undertaken by UEFA on behalf of all participating clubs, are also dealt with in this contribution.

Culture is also present in free movement of cultural goods as regards works of art. Andrea Biondi canvasses this issue and presents a rather optimistic panorama. The Community has already faced this question and, as a result of this, Regulation No 3911/92 on export to third countries and Directive 93/7 on the return of cultural objects were adopted. Yet, Member States should give more active attention to it, on the basis mainly of inter-co-operation. Various questions arise in this context. First, there may be doubt as to whether or not works of art are goods in the economic sense. This has been accepted by the ECJ, which has also considered the special nature of cultural goods, even in cases where the artistic value of the piece was not evident. Secondly, Community law on works of art has focused on the protection against their illegal export, an idea which is present in the abovementioned norms. According to Regulation No 3911/92, administrative procedures have been harmonized to a certain extent, in order to control export, although practice does not show that this control takes place as effectively as would be desired. Biondi proposes, following the French model in controlling this type of export, the creation of specialized administrations in each State, which will also have to co-operate with administrations in other Member States, so that the whole system can function adequately. Specialisation is also proposed in judicial disputes concerning art (such is the case, for instance, of questions of property or, more generally, to the legal status of goods). Here, specialized arbitration courts could perhaps provide the best response.

Part III of the book is related to what could be considered the core of cultural policies by (so far national) public powers, since it deals with Media, Language and Education. Here, two notions of culture cohabit. On the one hand, culture is understood, in a narrow sense, as the ensemble of activities related to the preservation and development of the human spirit, including here artistic and intellectual work of agreed value. On the other hand, culture is also conceived in a broader sense, linked to the concept of civilisation. Rachael Craufurd Smith emphasized in the Introduction the lack of a definition of culture in Community law, and the apparent lack of willingness in the Community to adopt such a definition. In Part III, we see how through the intervention in certain sectors (media, language, education) in a concrete manner, the Community could contribute at least by means of practice, to the elaboration of a definition of culture both in the narrow as well as in the broad sense. This is clearly in connection with the, until now, little used art. 151, where both perspectives are to be found. Although both perspectives are present in Part III, the wide, and more ambitious, approach (culture as civilisation/identity) is more specifically the subject of Part IV, to which I will devote some attention later.

Joshua Holmes provides an insight into cultural aspects of television, taking into consideration the more general framework of the audiovisual policy, which is—as is well known—far more reaching than mere television. It is at least curious to note that the book does not provide a specific treatment of film, an area where culture has been strongly pleaded in order to preserve barriers round the European market and also in order to accept national measures fostering this cultural and economic activity. It is clear that one can find references to it in various chapters. However, a specific treatment of the field would have been welcome, especially at a time when cultural arguments have lost weight and where even Community institutions prefer to regulate it on an economic basis. This is also the case of television. Holmes explores whether or not the Community has developed a cultural policy in the audio-visual sector, concluding that this has not been the case. This is surprising, taking into consideration the strong relationship of television and culture in the Member States. Such an approach has also been followed by the Court of Justice. Holmes touches upon a subject which in another context had been dealt with by Niamh Nic Shuibhne in Chapter 2, *i.e.* the possibility for cultural arguments to play a decisive role in exemptions to the free movement rules. As in Chapter 2, we see again how the Court is not willing to accept this kind of argument, maybe leaving other institutions the role of adopting a cultural policy for the EC/EU. Yet, again, a cultural project for Europe is so far not clear.

Language is one of the main features of European culture(s). Indeed, cultural diversity in the European Union starts by acknowledging language diversity, which applies also to language diversity inside each Member State. Language is such an essential part of national cultures, and Member States are so willing to preserve them, that a generous system of official languages was incorporated in the Communities from the very beginning of their existence. The manifold perspectives of language in EU law are canvassed by Bruno de Witte in Chapter 7. Comparative law is an essential tool for legal analysis and particularly in a topic, such as regulation of linguistic diversity, where the EU may learn from the experiences of Member States. In the past half century, norms on linguistic diversity have been adopted, for various reasons, in certain Member States. Some of the causes that justified the adoption of those norms may exist now in the EU and thus their study could be of use for developing Community language law. However, one would have to be pessimistic when regarding the evolution of norms and practices on language use in the Community institutions. Despite the doctrine of equality, accommodations to this doctrine, which are provided for by Regulation 1/58, have been made regularly on grounds of practicality. Further, the Court of First Instance some years ago opened the door for EU agencies to adopt the linguistic regime they consider most appropriate. The thorough and critical analysis undertaken by De Witte concludes with a complaint about the non-existence of a language policy in the EU. Although some actions on language protection/language use and linguistic diversity may be found in the Union, they are single measures that raise doubts as to whether it is not only a means to keep an image without really entering into the problem.

Education and culture go hand in hand. Education is required in order to acquire culture in the narrow sense and education is needed in order to preserve culture in the broader sense. Therefore, the inclusion of Chapter 8 on Education and Culture in EC law seems more than accurate. Education has walked its own path in EC history. Indeed, even in the absence of a particular Community competence on education, several initiatives on education have succeeded, before art. 126 (now art. 149) EC incorporated the legal basis for them. Several issues of interest arise in this field, one of them being the 'use' of education to 'create' responsible and informed citizens in a democratic society. This could of course be applied to EU law, in order to reinforce the concept of citizenship. Another important subject is mobility of educational actors, a question which has been the source of various decisions of the Court of Justice and which is now at the core of the University debate due to the so-called 'Sorbonne Bologna process'. As Lonbay explains in his contribution, this process is mainly undertaken on the basis of the Open Method of Coordination, *i.e.* the EU is not directing it as an independent actor, but is only taking part in a project fostered by Member States acting among themselves.

Part IV derives, as I argued above, from a broad perspective on culture: culture as an element to constitute or reinforce identity. This is the reason why Chapter 9 deals specifically with art. 151 EC and European Identity. The second chapter in this part, Chapter 10, incorporates another dimension to the question, *i.e.* the status of long-term resident third country nationals, a group of people whose integration in the EU will also contribute to the consolidation of an identity in Community law.

Rachael Craufurd Smith focuses in Chapter 9 on art. 151 EC and its potential to forge a common identity in the EU. Due to the specificities of the EU, a political identity in Europe may not depend on common traditions or common features existing in the past. A common identity can be effectively built up, but the perspective should be towards the future: an agreement on common goals and the establishment of symbols that reflect the existence and the strength of this agreement (classical State symbols such as the flag or the anthem) could contribute to this construction. If art. 151 EC can be used as a basis to foster such an identity, various problems arise: what is the European common culture to which the article refers? Is it a culture which is shared by some Member States but not all? Does it only have to do with art treasures or does it possess a more far-reaching content? What exactly is the content of 'culture' mentioned in art. 151? How can the construction of a European identity co-exist with the preservation and protection of the culture and history of the European peoples? After having canvassed these and other questions, the author finishes by warning against an excessive use of art. 151 to foster European integration. Indeed, among other dangers, is precisely the risk that certain European peoples or population groups could feel estranged by a notion of culture developed by the European institutions. Further, the use of culture for the sake of achieving stronger integration could make of the former a mere tool to foster economic aims.

Theodora Kostakopoulou offers a stimulating reflection on 'the others', _i.e._ those who live and work in the Community, but who still lack a political status as European citizens. One of the main problems the author identifies in this area is the fact that the EU relies on national citizenship in order to confer European citizenship. Yet other status, such as 'civil citizenship' or 'denizen ship', should also be considered as a possible way to acquire a better status in the EU. An impulse was provided by the European Council at Nice, although in practice the legal instruments adopted have not modified the previous regulation. A step further could be found in the Commission's proposal on a Council Directive on the Status of Third Country Nationals who are Long-term Residents on 13 March 2001. However, much is still to be done, in order to integrate long-term residents as full members of the political community.

If culture has been used as an argument to impose differential treatment in movements of goods and services inside the Community, its weight in external relations has been almost equivalent. Therefore, Part V deals with culture and the European Union's External Relations, focusing on cultural cooperation and on the specific sector of the audio-visual. Cooperation seems to be a key word in today's public law and public policies both in Member States and in the Community. Cultural cooperation is, in this reviewer's opinion, even more necessary than cooperation in other fields, since culture presents in its very definition an idea of freedom and diversity that could hardly be protected if the different persons and bodies responsible for it did not cooperate. Therefore, cooperation in the international sphere also seems more than desirable. International cultural cooperation has not been subject for a long time to independent treatment, although cultural cooperation clauses were included in various international agreements. This is discussed by Joseph A. McMahon in Chapter 11, where he explores the strategy developed by the Community, in order to establish a coherent framework for all these cooperation clauses. Agreements exist in relation to specific geographical areas, such as ACP countries, Europe and the Mediterranean. As for Asia, cooperation takes place, _inter alia_, in the realm of the Asia-Europe Foundation, which is not a Community body, but to which the Community contributes in its budget. In his conclusion to the chapter, the author argues in favour of the establishment of a single instrument where culture in international agreements is protected. The proposal would be for the Community to observe the UNESCO's activity in this area, extending its effects to international trade and economy.

In Chapter 12, Olaf Weber focuses his discourse on the audio-visual sector, presenting it as an area where trade and culture inevitably conflict. Indeed, as Weber argues, '_[t]his sector has been selected not only because it develops rapidly and thus forms one of the biggest threats to culture in the analysis of Adorno and Horkheimer, but also because it is regarded as an influential mechanism through which culture is both reflected and changed_' (at 356). Free movement of goods and exemptions to it have been studied by other authors in this volume. Yet Weber returns to it and comprehensively analyses their impact on the audio-visual sector, thereby developing Chapter 6, on

European Community Law and the Cultural Aspects of Television. Specific attention is paid to the WTO regime, addressing the problem of DVDs and video cassettes being covered by GATT, whereas television broadcasting is covered by GATS. These differences in concept and in legal basis may lead to different treatment also in the future. Culture and economics should find a balance in international trade and, although the EC has reached better results in this respect than the WTO, there is still much to fight for, as the author indicates in this chapter.

To conclude the book Paul Kearns presents some 'Concluding Observations' in Chapter 13 on Culture and EU Law which, unusually for such conclusions, are relatively independent of the rest of the book. In rather more philosophical terms than the previous chapters, Kearns offers a post-modern explanation of the regulation of culture in today's Europe, presenting various theories on integration through culture. Further, he proposes an analysis of the relationship between culture and the EU from the point of view of autopoietic theory. Different systems, such as law and culture, are autonomous, but law integrates culture in various forms. The way in which this integration is produced and the possibilities to improve it, in order to achieve harmony are explored by Kearns. This author reproduces a trend that can be detected in various chapters, viz., the all-comprehensive concept of culture, on the one hand, and the lack of an EU cultural policy, on the other. Law should integrate culture within its own system. Yet if culture itself does not offer a proper definition of what it is, then the relationship is problematic from the very beginning.

So much for a book which would require a larger comment, both because of the subject and because of the way it is treated. As has been outlined above, the volume is a pioneer, in so far as culture in EU law has not yet been afforded sufficient attention by scholars. Despite the breadth of the topic, the editor has succeeded in identifying key issues which have been dealt with in detail and with a critical eye by the various contributors. Now it is to be hoped that further research on this promising area (for Europe) will be undertaken.

SUSANA DE LA SIERRA

Tutela Cautelar Contencioso-Administrativa y Derecho Europeo: Un Estudio Normativo y Jurisprudencial by Susana de la Sierra (with a foreword by Luis Martín Rebollo), (Cizur Menor: Thomson-Aranzadi, 2004), 419pp ISBN 84-976-7829-X; and *Una metodología para el Derecho Comparado Europeo (Derecho Público Comparado y Derecho Administrativo Europeo)* by Susana de la Sierra (with a foreword by Jacques Ziller), (Madrid: Thomson-Civitas, 2004), 137pp. ISBN 84-470-2219-6.

Not one but two books has been the outcome of the doctoral *Lehrjahre* of Susana de la Sierra, spent at the privileged environment of the European University

Institute in the hills outside Florence, with occasional scholarly excursions to Paris and Berlin. The first is a very complete and rigorous comparative study of the French, German, Spanish and Community approaches to interim measures. The second, which constituted the first chapter of her doctoral thesis, contains a methodological reflexion on European comparative law, in particular with regard to the fields of public and administrative law.

A first remark is in order concerning the language in which these two books have been written and published. It is well-known that English dominates scholarly writings in the law and elsewhere. Nowadays most people in academic circles understand and write English to a variety of degrees and standards. In addition, the Anglo-American approach to law seems to be in general more interesting, critical and useful, and less formalistic, than those adopted in other legal cultures. In this context, the fact that the present author decided to write and publish in Spanish is indeed Quixotic. Little attention is paid to legal writings in that language outside Spain, just as little as to French works outside France, etc. In addition, a truly European legal science is still under construction—work proceeds very slowly and does not always progress. Outside privileged locations such as the EUI, we mainly have national, sometimes quite nationalistic, legal sciences, that at most take a quick look at each other every now and then. But how many German books are there which refer exclusively to German authors? How many French books citing only French texts, even on European law? And so on. And even at the EUI, how much is still due to national legal traditions, what are the burdens we all bring from our national education, how difficult is it to build and practice a truly European approach for European law? .... We have here, however, a book written in Spanish, which is truly European, reading and sounding German in its structure, but Spanish and French for the formalistic analyses (which are also useful). It is therefore to be hoped that these two books will be read and read in Spanish, and that legal scholars will start paying some attention to what is written in languages other than their own and other than in English.

These two books come from the European University Institute. Accordingly, one would expect to find the law-in-context kind of approach to law that was popularized by Joseph Weiler, Francis Snyder and others from the 1980s and which have been the very signature of work done at the Institute, the beginning of a 'Florence school'. The reader may be dissapointed if that is what she or he is looking for. The two books of Susana de la Sierra are classical legal analyses, very close in their method to German doctrine, and no attention is paid, for example, to the economic analysis of interim measures—which is quite sophisticated and may provide tools more rigorous than the flexible criteria generally used by judges. This remark is not meant as a critique: legal work is, it should be said, even though it is obvious, essential for lawyers. To know what the law is, how is it built, what is its structure, what is the valid and applicable case law in a given legal order, etc., are the natural and first tasks of legal scholars, and these constitute their most valuable work in social terms. Besides, without this basic knowledge, contextual or extralegal analysis is generally imprecise and ultimately useless. Some law-in-context work has been of this latter kind, doing the context but not paying much attention to the law. Perhaps, also, law-in-context is not what should necessarily be done in the doctoral *Lehrjahre*. The books under review and other books emergin from the European University Institute in recent years show a change of direction in its law department. Law-in-context no longer seems to be a dogma. Other approaches are also allowed and even fostered. With this change, however, the Institute's law department risks losing its distinctive mark, its school, its tradition. Perhaps it could try to recover it by attempting to build a truly European legal science (which need not be law-in-context), focusing on European law instead of enlarging the disciplines represented in the department, finding a direction in those fields in which its privileged position can give an added value.

In the second book, Susana de la Sierra characterises comparative law both as a method and as a distinct legal discipline. In my view, however, comparative law is only a *tool* in legal analysis, and a risky one. The two main dangers, which the author analyses with great clarity, are the selection of the legal orders to be compared, and that of the level of analysis. The legal orders compared should be more or less similar. Otherwise, the comparison will be mostly negative: 'how different are these legal orders!', we will repeatedly say to ourselves. But we will learn little in terms of possible solutions to common problems that can be extrapolated to the legal orders compared. And that is the main aim of comparative law. If one compares, for example, the European Union and NAFTA, one will probably conclude that there is little that they can learn from each other, because they are too fundamentally different. One would more usefully compare the Union with the United States or Germany, for example, and the NAFTA with MERCOSUR. The second issue is closely related to the number of legal orders taken into account: the more we select, the more superficial out analysis will be, and we run the risk of missing much detail or even of making mistakes. Susana de la Sierra, a born comparative lawyer, has clearly avoided both risks. The legal orders compared are sufficiently homogeneous to make the comparison useful; their number is neither too small nor too big to allow for a precise description of each; her knowledge of each legal system compared is exemplary, and the comparison always inspired.

However, the shorter book not only presents comparative law as a *tool* or, if you will, as a *method*: it also presents it as a legal discipline, and includes a section ('El Derecho público comparado en el contexto europeo: el Derecho administrativo europeo', pp. 84–97) whose main argument is the following: 'European Administrative Law' would be first of all 'a method, whose essential characteristic lies in the comparison of the various European legal orders' (p. 95); secondly, the comparison should be based on 'neutral' concepts, 'from a functional point of view', 'eschwing conceptual aprioris from a specific legal order' (p. 96); finally, the comparison must pay special attention to the phenomenon of legal cross-fertilisation, which would 'indicate the convergence between legal orders that is favoured by those who defend a European Administrative Law as *ius commune europeum*'

(p. 96); all this, to be sure, while fully respecting the 'specificities of each legal order' and of the principle of subsidiarity which is expressly mentioned in this context (pp. 96–97). Here the author enters a difficult territory. Much depends on one's personal preferences, of course, and I would favour a different approach. It is interesting to study phenomena of convergence among European legal orders, and to acknowledge that European Community law has acted as a catalyst in these phenomena. But one must bear in mind that they are voluntary, quite limited and reversible at any time. In addition, the comparison between 25 legal orders becomes more and more difficult, almost impossible—and sometimes pointless—to form the basis of a European Administrative Law. My own impression is that the public and administrative law of the European Union is rather to be found in the law of the Treaty and in secondary legislation based on it, and also in the case law of the Court of Justice of the European Communities: only here may we find, build and organize legal materials which are original and autonomous from national legal traditions, and which are applied by institutions which make them effective in real life. The identification of a European administrative law would require, in addition, its distinction from European constitutional law, a difficult exercise which has not yet been carried out with success—the Treaty establishing a Constitution for Europe being, in this regard, a failure once again.

The first and longer book, devoted to the issue of interim measures in comparative law, which constitutes the main part of Susana de la Sierra's doctoral thesis, is structured in eight chapters. It is impossible to make justice here to the richness of the book, which is a mine of information for those interested in the subject. The first chapter focuses on the nature of interim measures. The author places interim measures among other institutions meant to alleviate the slowness of justice, and defends a distinct concept in order to differentiate it from other such institutions. Chapter 2, on the supranational context and the case law of the Court of Justice of the European Communities, basically analyses leading judgments such as *Factortame* and *Zuckerfabrik*, which in de la Sierra's view establish criteria which are 'excessively vague, although they correspond, generally, with those in place in national legal orders' (p. 35). She denounces the gaps and insufficiencies of the guidance given by the Court to national courts when they have to grant interim measures in the Community law context. Chapter 3 places the whole subject in a constitutional context, seeing—rightly, in my view—interim measures as a dimension of the fundamental right to legal protection, with particular attention to the case law of the European Court of Human Rights (this general perspective would, I believe, tend to reduce the differences between the granting of interim measures in the various branches of the law and the very specificity of the 'administrative interim measures' to which Susana de la Sierra devotes her book). The next chapters are devoted to a comparison of the four legal regimes taken into account. Chapter 4 introduces each of them. Chapter 5 examines the procedural aspects of interim measures, which are of utmost importance. The last three chapters are devoted to an analysis of the substantive conditions for the granting of interim measures: urgency (or *periculum in mora*), *fumus boni juris* and the balancing of interests.

The most interesting chapter of the three is, in my view, that devoted to the concept of 'balancing of interests' ('*ponderación de intereses*'), which, in de la Sierra's opinion, has become the 'centrepiece of administrative interim protection' (p. 368), and which would currently be a sort of third criterion added to those of urgency and *fumus boni juris*. She defends a particular conception of the idea of 'balancing of interests', a notion which she relates to 'proportionality' and considers very useful to deal with the plural and very complex web of interests that characterise contemporary societies and with interim measures cases which, it seems, she views as being always 'hard cases' (p. 327). I have some doubts with regard to one of the interesting ideas contained in this chapter. It seems to me that at least in European Community law, the 'balancing of interests' is a criterion which only comes into play when the other two (urgency and *fumus*) do not allow the judge to reach a solution. It is, therefore, only a subsidiary criterion for particularly hard cases. Most cases on interim measures are indeed quite clear cases, and do not require the court to proceed to balance the interests of the parties: sometimes there is no real urgency, no real danger of an irreparable damage, or else the legal case presented is weak and does not amount to establishing the required *fumus boni juris*. Besides, in this extremely flexible and indeterminate field and also in other fields, one may want to reduce the use and abuse of 'balancing' and 'proportionality', which sometimes stand for justice but sometimes hide enhanced judicial discretion and reduced legal certainty.

JULIO BAQUERO CRUZ

National Remedies Before the Court of Justice: Issues of Harmonisation and Differentiation by Michael Dougan, (Oxford: Hart Publishing, 2004), 424pp. ISBN 1-84113-395-7.

In recent years, Michael Dougan's insightful articles on various European law subjects have been a source of interest and authority. This reviewer was therefore looking forward to the publication of the revised version of his doctoral thesis '*National remedies in front of the Court of Justice—Issues of harmonisation and differentiation*', and the book is certainly no disappointment. With clarity and strength of argument, Dougan examines how the approach to the EC Treaty project's aim has been moving away from an ideal of regulatory uniformity towards one of regulatory differentiation. The treaty project is just as much about dealing with differences as striving for supranational convergence.

In the light of this process, he seeks to define the appropriate role to be performed by the imperative of uniformity in the decentralized enforcement of EC-law through national procedures and remedies. He argues that traditionally, reliance on domestic rules governing judicial protection has been perceived as a threat to the uniformity of the legal order, a point of view that must be reconsidered in light of the legal reality of regulatory differentiation. He suggests that the imperative of uniformity should be seen in a sectoral perspective. In sectors characterized by high substantive harmonization, it might be legitimate to aim towards uniformity of procedures and remedies, but in areas characterized by regulatory differentiation, it would go beyond the Community's legitimate interest in harmonization to provide for uniform remedies and procedures. Dougan uses the sectoral model as a conceptual tool to analyse some parts of the case law on effective judicial protection of the Court of Justice, finding however that this approach does not find full support in the Court's complex case law and that the Court does not seem to have any clear conception of the imperative of uniformity.

Dougan's first chapter, which not only sets out the contents of the principle of effective judicial protection, but at the same time fills in some of the 'black holes' concerning the application of that principle, can usefully be read by students or practitioners seeking more extensive knowledge of the principle, although some of Dougan's findings are unlikely to remain uncontested in future debates. Dougan structures the principle through a *quartet of concepts*; the fundamental right of access to judicial process, the presumption of national competence, the limits on national competence (substantive Treaty rules, the principle of equivalence and effectiveness) and the direct effect of the general principle of law. The fact that Dougan includes substantive Treaty rules as a third limit on the national procedural presumption is helpful in providing a more complete conceptualization of the limits imposed on the national discretion. It is however difficult to separate the intention and the possible implications of presenting the fundamental right of access as a distinct concept, rather than as one of the limits on the procedural presumption, but this might be merely a matter of taste. The principle of effectiveness is described by Dougan as containing *four different 'types' of effectiveness* which promote different values. This is an interesting but contestable approach. His division between the effectiveness of *rights* and the effectiveness of provisions in the *general interest* is very useful, as this highlights the fact that the principle of effective judicial protection is not necessarily only concerned with the protection of rights, which is sometimes argued. Dougan however argues that the Muñoz case demonstrated conclusively that legislation which does not provide individuals with rights can nonetheless have independent effects. This may in fact be too far-reaching an interpretation of the case, considering that Mr Muñoz actually sought to protect an individual economic interest through the proceedings. The remaining two manifestations of effectiveness as understood by Dougan are concerned with guaranteeing the integrity of the EU's judicial structure; *the effectiveness of the 234 proceedings* and *the validity of EU acts*. It might be open to debate to what extent these manifestations of effectiveness have an independent role in limiting national procedural autonomy. The next section sheds light on the scope and the legal basis of the principle of effective judicial protection, an argument which thus far been given too little attention in academic writing. Dougan chooses to see the principle as a *general principle of law* which is binding on national courts through Article 10 in the Treaty. The author then makes a debatable argument that the general principle of effective judicial protection in certain respects is *capable of having direct effect*. He also underlines the very fundamental question of the scope of the principle, clarifying that the direct effect of a substantive norm is not a condition for the applicability of the principle. Also non-directly effective rights, and possibly other legal interests, enjoy effective judicial protection, as long as they are clear enough. Dougan also points to the fact that the principle is applicable in private law relationships and that it can consequently change procedural positions in civil procedure, a field which also have long been disregarded and which calls for further research.

In Chapter 2, Dougan enters a more 'abstract' part of the thesis, and presents what he refers to as the 'integration through law model' and its view of the fact that national procedures and remedies are applied in decentralised enforcement. He refers to this fact as 'the enforcement deficit', a term which this reviewer dislikes. Dougan's 'integration though law' concept, which should not be confused with the meaning given to it by I.A Cappelletti *et al*, intends to denote a perception of the Treaty project as promoting an ever closer Union, where the concomitant function of the Community is to advance and consolidate the process of convergence through uniform rules. Dougan then sets out to give a historical account of the model's perception of uniformity and effectiveness. Initially, both uniformity and effectiveness were seen as economic imperatives; the aim of the Community was to stimulate economic integration and provide a level playing-field with undistorted competition. This had to be done through enacting uniform legislation, otherwise the effectiveness of the common market would be undermined. Dougan continues to explain how the understanding of effectiveness and uniformity subsequently changed with the horizontal expansion of the Community competences. With the inclusion of welfare regulation within Community competences, the effectiveness of rights could be seen as an independent, social imperative. The need for uniformity in the welfare sphere could however still be justified by an economic imperative, given that the same social standards, for e.g. workers, were necessary to provide a level playing field, but the integration-through-law approach could also use the growing importance of the principle of equality and the institution of citizenship to argue that the imperative of uniformity existed as a self-standing social imperative; that a common body of social and economic rights for all citizens was a legitimate goal of the Treaty project. After a rather lengthy account of this development, Dougan concludes that the idea of integration through law actually embraces a myriad of guises and views on uniformity, ranging from a purely economic ideal of a single market to the goal of a federal state. He still finds that one can identify a core argument for all the different appearances which brings them within the 'integration through law' model; all maintain that the success of the Community depends on the promotion of a regulatory code enforced uniformly and effectively.

From the 'integration through law' perspective, the Community's reliance on national procedures and remedies is perceived as a threat to the economic and socio-political objectives of the EU, as they are not uniform and thus undermine the effectiveness of the rules. The problem with the 'enforcement deficit' should, according to the 'integration through law' perspective, be cured by introducing a uniform system of judicial protection, a cure which can be 'administrated' in three ways; either through the process of regulatory competition, through legislative intervention, or through judicial means. In the remainder of the book, Dougan aims at challenging the argument that the creation of uniform rules on procedures and remedies is an appropriate 'cure' or a necessary measure to take. He acknowledges that the 'integration through law' view of unified judicial protection has been criticized in academic discourse. It has for example been noted that the effectiveness of EC law must compete with internal national interests in fairness and budgetary certainty, that the Community's intervention unduly interferes with cultural choices on judicial protection, and others have questioned whether the creation of unified standards can ever in practice create a uniform state of law, as the application of those standards ultimately lies in the hands of national judges. Dougan however finds that none of this critique of the integrationists' view of a unified judicial protection is sufficiently far-reaching. In his view it fails to challenge the very underlying assumptions of 'integration through law' which are no longer a legal reality. The assumption that the Treaty aims at supranational convergence must be reconsidered, as the Community has moved away from the ideal of uniformity, towards a model of regulatory differentiation, which will be further examined in Chapter 3. The role that the imperative of uniformity should have in relation to national rules on judicial protection must therefore be understood in the light of the reconsidered aim of the Treaty project. Dougan's view that all academic discourse fails to challenge the limited importance of the imperative of uniformity is contestable. It might also have been interesting to see an articulation of the relationship between effectiveness and uniformity, and consequently an account of the extent to which the imperative of effectiveness is really an assumption which has been challenged. Regulatory differentiation does, as Dougan well demonstrates, have an impact on the perceived significance of 'uniformity', but as he acknowledges in Chapter 4, not necessarily on the imperative of 'effectiveness'.

In Chapter 3 Dougan provides an overview of the current position of regulation in the EC system and demonstrates that there is a trend towards regulatory differentiation. He gives a full account of the relative competence of the Union and the Member States to enact rules on matters within EU competence and describes the regulatory differentiation as being of two kinds, vertical and horizontal. Vertical differentiation occurs when the Treaty makes provision for the Member States to participate in a substantive policy sector of community competence. He points out that to find out whether the division of competence is exclusive, shared or complementary is not sufficient to determine the respective competence as this classification does not necessarily coincide with the legal framework being uniform or not; an area of shared competence can just as well contain uniform rules, as one of exclusive competence can show signs of differentiation. There is much proof of regulatory differentiation to be found in the Treaty and Dougan describes instances of this e.g. in the use of derogations from Community legislation, the method of minimum harmonization and conceptual renvois. Dougan finds that most sectors of Community competence have elements of regulatory differentiation. It is however important to notice that regulatory differentiation is not itself a homogenous figure, there is a sliding scale of accepted differentiation in different policy fields, and the acceptance seem to have a sectoral dimension where core internal market activities are uniform while more welfare-oriented policies remain in the hands of the Member States. At one extreme there is competition law and state aid laws which Dougan describes as a field of uniform law. At the other extreme there are areas such as the environment, consumer and social policy, which can hardly be described as uniform. After having shown us the extent and varying faces of vertical differentiation, Dougan gives further proof of the trend of differentiation through looking at measures of variable geometry, or *horizontal differentiation* as he calls them. Measures of this kind concern the Member States' ability to choose whether or not to participate in a sector, such as was the case with the social protocol and Schengen. Horizontal differentiation was institutionalized through the Treaty of Amsterdam, and has subsequently been further developed, but Dougan points out that there still are diverging opinions as to whether the changes really increase the potential for its use. In the light of the Treaty's encouragement of regulatory differentiation as he has demonstrated in the chapter, Dougan concludes that the Treaty doesn't seem to entirely support the 'integration through law' approach to uniform and effective legislation. In the next chapter he develops his argument as to the significance which should be attached to the legal reality of differentiation and how it should affect our understanding of the enforcement deficit. A certain discrepancy in the two conceptual models presented by Dougan can be noted. While 'the integration through law' model is mostly prescriptive, the regulatory differentiation model in Chapter 3 is presented rather as being descriptive of the current legal reality. Dougan, however, rebuts the argument that regulatory differentiation is merely a legal reality, and in Chapter 4, he convincingly argues that regulatory differentiation should be taken seriously and should be regarded as a symptom of restructuring the Union and as a cause for constitutional change. The regulatory differentiation is thus not, as argued by the integration through law line, a regrettable anomaly which must be cured through more uniform rules; it is a doctrinal reconsideration and an update of the goal of the Community legal order. Uniformity does not, however, become a redundant goal for this sake, but Dougan underlines that it is more complex than the suggested by the 'integration through law' approach. The legal reality is thus a tension between uniformity and differentiation. The latter can according to Dougan sometimes be criticized for not providing an adequately uniform and integrated legal order. One's view as to how uniformity and differentiation should in practice be balanced against each other might, as the author points out, vary depending on the actor, and he mentions the Commission as an example of an actor which is rather hostile towards differentiation. Next, Dougan looks at the question how the move towards differentiation should affect the understanding of the 'enforcement deficit', arguing that the role traditionally assigned to the imperative of uniformity with regard to national procedures and remedies by the 'integration through law' approach must be reconsidered. A balance must be struck between the need for uniformity and the acceptance of differentiation, making sure that the Community's intervention into national procedures and remedies is not unnecessarily intrusive, at the same time as Community intervention must make sure that the differentiation does not threaten the legitimate interests of the Community legal order. Whether remedial competence should aim at uniformity or negative harmonisation should be understood from a *sectoral perspective*, which Dougan argues permits us to see the Community as a complex entity with varying degrees of integration and differentiation in different policy fields. Remedial competence in a specific sector should mirror the existing substantive competence over a given subject-matter. In a highly centralized sector it might thus be a legitimate interest of the Community to pursue uniformity in the judicial protection rules, but in areas marked by differentiation, a furthering of uniformity of national procedural and remedial rules would go beyond the Union's legitimate interest. The author presents several valid arguments against taking such a sectoral approach, but these do not prevent him from embracing it, at least as a conceptual tool for analyzing the case law of the Court of Justice. He mentions, for example, that it is very difficult to decide how, and at what level of abstraction, a sector should be defined. Even if a sector can be defined, the level of harmonization or differentiation might still be difficult to establish. Having, for example, identified the sector of consumer law, one finds measures that are pre-emptive, and others that only provide for minimum harmonization. Another argument having been advanced against the sectoral model is that it reinforces the neo-liberal economic bias within the Community legal order, an argument that Dougan, however, successfully rebuts. The third difficulty that Dougan identifies with the sectoral approach is the imperative of effectiveness, although it is arguable whether this really amounts to a basis on which to challenge the model. Every Community measure pursues an objective, and even though there is a sectoral model of uniformity and the concern for uniformity might be low in a certain sector because of regulatory differentiation, the imperative of effectiveness will still set a minimum floor below which the judicial protection provided by the national system cannot fall. Dougan explains that the imperative of effectiveness can require different levels of protection in different sectors and that the sectoral approach does not help us to resolve the complex problem of striking a balance between the interest in effectiveness of EC law and the Member States' legitimate aim in ensuring legal certainty, etc. The author concludes that regulatory differentiation does not seem to be very relevant or helpful for understanding of the imperative of effectiveness, but he underlines that the trend away from expansion should be taken into account when the balance between effectiveness and the national interest is made under the effectiveness test, so that the Community's interest in judicial protection should not be over-emphasized. In sum, Dougan thus acknowledges the limits of the sectoral approach, but although he states that it might not be used for as a blueprint for legislation, it can at least be used as a conceptual tool for analysing the Court of Justice's case law, which is done in Chapter 6.

The following chapter, Chapter 5 is dedicated to discerning what role the requirement of uniformity has in reality played in the case law of the Court of Justice and how to best describe judicial procedural and remedial harmonization. Is it pursuing negative or positive harmonization, setting only minimum standards or insisting on uniform rules? Dougan initially points to the somewhat curious fact that, while uniformity might have been a valid aim of the Community at the outset, the initial case law shows great deference to the national remedies and procedures. As the Community's regulatory policies however started moving towards differentiation, the case-law on remedies and procedures however reached its peak with cases such as *Factortame*, *Francovich* and *Emmott*, and during this period the Court seemed to aim at uniformity. Through detailed studies of the case-law relating to the right to reparation and time-limits, Dougan then searches for the Court of Justice's current approach to uniformity and positive harmonization, and it can be assumed that his conclusions would not have been any different, had he chose to study any other type of remedial or procedural rule. As regards the Court's case law on the *right to reparation*, Dougan convincingly shows how this remedy, which is normally perceived as the foremost case of positive harmonization by the Court, can no longer be seen as anything but an area of negative harmonization. He shows this in relation to four crucial aspects of the right to reparation; the understanding of the substantive conditions under which liability can be incurred, what bodies that can incur liability on the state, the character and extent of reparable damage and the procedural conditions for exercising the right to reparation. They are all expressions of negative harmonization, since he finds that there are no really uniform conditions on the availability of liability, and no clear signs as to what are the recoverable heads of damages. The part on the right to reparation not only proves his argument, it also provides a very good account of post-*Francovich* case law, and can be warmly recommended as reading to anyone interested in the subject. It contains many insightful remarks and propositions such as whether there is at all any right to damages or if *Francovich* was only an expression of a right to some kind of reparation. Dougan concludes that with hindsight, *Francovich* was not about providing uniform legal protection, but rather about the legal accountability of the national authorities. Today, the basis for Community intervention concerning the right to reparation can be entirely structured around the traditional

Rewe requirement of effectiveness and it only amounts to negative harmonization. A similar conclusion is reached concerning the case law on *reasonable time-
limits*. While the Court of Justice seemed to aim at achieving positive
harmonization through the *Emmott* case, Dougan demonstrates how subsequent
case law has made clear that *Emmott* was to be understood in the particular circumstances in the case and rather as an expression of the right to seek judicial
redress, of which the claimant in *Emmott* was deprived because of misinforma-
tion. In post-*Emmott* case law, the Court is thus back at negative harmonization
again, exercising a rather low judicial control over what is to be regarded as a reasonable limitation period. Dougan's findings in the chapter thus suggest that the
Court has given up any general ambition, if this has ever existed, to achieve positive harmonization and that it rather imposes negative limits that mostly catch
only blatant lacunae in the national systems. The real difficulty in the case law
thus, which the author also admits, does not seem to be what role to assign to the
principle of uniformity, but rather to understand what influences the Court's
varying understanding of the requirement of effectiveness. He therefore examines whether there is any model which with predictability and clarity might
describe the Member States' discretion under the imperative of effectiveness.
Dougan inquires into three different models all of which have provided certain
guidance to the Court; the principle of proportionality, the centralized standards
of judicial protection for proceedings in front of the Community courts, and
lastly a model which Dougan calls the 'model of indirect intervention'. The latter
propose that the absence of adequate judicial protection in national law should
not be cured by direct review of insufficient rules, but Dougan asserts that case
law suggests that such insufficient protection rather should be cured through
indirect intervention, that is by making the right to reparation via *Francovich*
available to the claimants. The last model is an innovative and interesting one
and it merits attention, especially as it can be debated whether the model really
provides a sufficient level of protection. Dougan finds the basis for the model in
the case law on the availability of interest, but it is uncertain whether the cited
cases really support a move away from direct intervention. Dougan concludes
that, as is so often the case with models, none of the three models fully explains
the contradictory case law on the level of effectiveness required. Ultimately,
Dougan sums up the chapter by stating that the study of case law thus has indicated that the Court of Justice's approach is one of negative harmonization and
differentiation in procedural rules, although not such a minimal harmonization
as was the case in the 1970s and 1980s, as the high water marks from the middle
period remain valid law. The imperative of uniformity thus seems to have had a
very limited importance for the Court's case law on remedies and procedures, an
approach which, according to Dougan's sectoral model, is well suited only for
sectors that are characterized by minimal harmonization. The description of current case law as a general trend towards negative harmonization however fails to
capture the complexity of the Court's case law, in his view.

He therefore in Chapter 6 sets out to explore whether the Court of Justice is sensitive to the proposed sectoral understanding of the requirement of uniformity, and whether there is proof of positive harmonization in sectors characterized by a highly centralized legislative framework. Dougan identifies three areas in which he finds that the Court has consolidated and created Community remedies to apply instead of pre-existing national law, rather than maintaining the negative harmonization approach laid out in Chapter 5. The first area where such positive harmonization is pursued is, the *decentralised challenge of the validity of EC measures*, which is not, as the writer rightly points out, really a sector on its own. However, an unfettered discretion of the national courts in national proceedings concerning EC measures would mean a risk of getting differing judgments as to the validity of Community acts. Uniformity is thus a legitimate concern in these situations. This is why the Court of Justice has imposed centralized standards concerning the limited jurisdiction of national courts to find a Community act invalid, the availability of interim relief and the substantive conditions under which such must be provided, and it has also, for certain cases, imposed a time-limit of two months, equal to that of Art. 230(5), so the dual system of effective judicial protection cannot be abused through the bringing of national proceedings only because the time-limit for ECJ proceedings has run out. Dougan however remarks that there are other questions in relation to the decentralized challenge of validity of Community norms where the Court seems to apply the laissez-faire approach, such as national rules on standing to apply for judicial review. Dougan concludes that one can thus not talk about a truly uniform legal framework for effective judicial protection in this 'sector'. The second sector showing evidence of a harmonized framework of decentralized enforcement is *state aid law*. As opposed to the previous 'sector', here there exists a link between a highly centralized substantive harmonization and a strong remedial intervention by the court, and there is thus proof that the Court is embracing the sectoral approach to uniformity. Enforcement in the area is divided between Commission and the national courts, where the national courts often only put Community decisions into practice and consequently enjoy little discretion. Dougan concludes that although the state aid sector is the one where the Court has gone the farthest, the process of harmonization of procedures and remedies is not complete. The last sector where a trend towards positive harmonization can be recognized, is the decentralized enforcement of *competition law*. Here, the level of judicial intervention has, however, not quite reached the height of that in state aid law. As opposed to state aid law, the competence in competition law between Member States and the Community is often concurrent, and domestic procedural rules have therefore in this area of law been altered because of the special obligation of mutual cooperation. On that basis, the Court has developed standards e.g. on national rules concerning the provision of information and protection of professional secrecy, as well as on written and oral observation before the national courts. Besides these more uniform standards, Dougan observes that in most other aspects concerning the decentralized enforcement of competition law, the Court has adhered to the approach of minimum harmonization under the effectiveness requirement, despite the fact that the sector is uniformly regulated. That competition law might be an area where a greater control of the national procedural and remedial rules was justified was hinted at in *Eco Swiss*. Later, in the *Courage* case, the Court of Justice had the opportunity to reconsider its case law and move towards uniformity, something that which could be furthered justified in the light of the recently increased decentralization of Articles 81 and 82. Dougan provides an extensive account of the *Courage* case and he touches on many of the inevitable question marks in its wake, such as whether it really provides for a Community remedy in damages, how uniform such a remedy really is, what the relation of such a remedy would have to other available remedies, and how far the principle of private liability could extend. He argues that *Courage* can, with difficulty, be confined to the area of competition law, an argument open to discussion. Dougan, however, concludes that it is unlikely that the *Courage* case in subsequent case law will provide for more than minimum harmonization, which he admits remains to be seen in the future case law. In this light he raises the question whether *Courage* really is uniform enough to satisfy the need of uniformity in the area of competition law, and this criticism is also applied to the Court of Justice's overall acceptance of differentiation in the decentralized enforcement of competition law. Minimum harmonization is from the sectoral perspective not adequate here, in his view. Still, the Court seems reluctant to intervene to enhance effectiveness and uniformity.

Dougan concludes the chapter on whether the Court is embracing a sectoral approach to the imperative of uniformity, by stating that his findings suggest that the Court approaches the Community's enforcement deficit without any clear or confident conception of the appropriate role to be performed by the imperative of uniformity, and it shows that its continued attempts to regulate national remedies and procedural rules remain difficult to explain by reference to the sort of sectoral model developed in Chapter 4 alone. However, in the concluding Chapter 7, he adds that it might be premature to draw any such conclusion on the subjective preferences of the Court, as its choice might very well be a result of institutional insecurity and of its position in the system. However, after looking briefly at whether the Court's approach might be a result of the relation between the Court and the legislator, Dougan admits that although this is relevant, it does not provide an entirely convincing explanation as to the Court's approach to the imperative of uniformity. Dougan concludes the study by stating that any understanding the Court's attitude towards the imperative of uniformity is intertwined with the wider and yet unresolved consideration of the Court's self-perception and sense of purpose. One might, Dougan ends; 'ultimately feel pressed towards the conclusion that remedial harmonisation (whether based on the traditional 'integration through law approach or an alternative 'sectoral' model) is a task to which the Court is inherently unsuited'.

Dougan has presented an impressive work which, beyond throwing new conceptual light on intervention of the Community into national procedures and remedies, also provides us with many insightful comments and perceptive analyses of the entire bulk of case law on the principle on effective judicial protection and related areas. In some parts, however, the work might have benefited from being less detailed, in order make the thrust of the argument appear with greater clarity. Although his ultimate conclusion is that the sectoral approach to the imperative of uniformity does not explain the Court's inaccessible case law on the varying degrees of intervention into national procedural autonomy, he makes a major contribution to the conceptual underpinnings of the Court's case law and its view on uniformity, and his work will probably remain central to the study of this area over the coming years. We have certainly not yet, however, seen the end of the debate as to what factors that are to be taken into account when trying to understand the Court's varying degrees of intervention into national remedies and procedures. It remains to be seen whether the web of the Court's case law will ever be properly unravelled. Dougan's contribution is certainly a step in the right direction.

JOHANNA ENGSTROM

Environmental Assessment: The Regulation of Decision Making by Jane Holder, (Oxford: Oxford University Press, 2004), xxv + 371pp (includes detailed bibliography and appendices). ISBN 0-19-826772-X.

This book provides far more than a detailed account of the emergence and development of environmental assessment as a regulatory mechanism (alongside the development of environmental law itself as a discrete discipline). The sheer depth and sophistication of the scholarship presented here, (which draws on literature from a broad range of disciplines) is outstanding. The main aim of the work is to examine the practical effectiveness of environmental assessment—more specifically—the extent to which environmental assessment succeeds in 'introducing standards, rigour, and environmental principle into decision-making which is often obscure and economically motivated' (at vii). A basic question emerges here: Has environmental assessment made a difference? Holder proceeds to reformulate this question in the following terms: How does law deal with and sanction environmental change through environmental assessment? (at 11). This question prompts a detailed scrutiny of the so-called 'greening' or 'ecologization' of governance and regulation. To this end, environmental assessment is selected and deployed as an analytical tool for exploring the complex relationship between law, environmental governance and the regulation of decision-making. While the work draws primarily on environmental assessment law and policy in England and Wales, the analysis is of far broader application and interest. Those seeking a practical step-by-step guide to the intricacies of environmental assessment law are directed to Tromans and Fuller's *Environmental Impact Assessment: Law and Practice* (Butterworths, London, 2003). Since Holder's work was published, Maria Lee has produced a very accessible and thought-provoking book *EU Environmental Law: Challenges, Change and Decision-Making* (Hart Publishing, Oxford, 2005) which also devotes considerable attention to the structure of environmental decision-making, albeit with a stronger emphasis on the relevant legal rules, including the impact of the Aarhus Convention[1] on this area of law and policy. Lee's work provides an interesting complement to Holder's socio-legal approach. A further reference worth noting here is Liam Cashman's thorough and insightful analysis of environmental assessment as an instrument for achieving integration (see 'Environmental Impact Assessment: A Major Instrument in Environmental Integration' in Onida (ed.) *Europe and the Environment: Legal Essays in Honour of Ludwig Krämer* (Europa Law Publishing, Groningen, 2004)).

Holder begins by observing that environmental assessment 'is currently an undertheorized phenomenon' (at 7). Notwithstanding the pivotal role it plays in modern environmental law and policy, and the exceptional amount of complex case law it has generated, core aspects of the environmental assessment process (such as the variety of information that is fed into decision-making and the actual operation of the assessment process itself) have not been the subject of detailed (legal) scrutiny to date. Holder aims to contribute to this scrutiny. Her core finding is that even though environmental assessment is frequently presented as an almost exclusively *procedural* instrument, it has important *substantive* consequences and 'is highly material to the outcome of a decision' (at 8). One particular focus of the inquiry here is how the (formal) involvement of the developer in the environmental assessment process (via the environmental statement), has the potential to influence the outcome in a variety of ways—even to the extent of 'objectifying' environmental information, devaluing lay or 'non-expert' opinions and (potentially) legitimating a particular project. With a view to presenting a detailed picture of environmental assessment in practice, Holder provides a set of illustrative case studies based on a range of legal texts, especially the environmental statement. This innovative approach moves beyond the obvious limitations of an analysis based exclusively on the existing medley of case law (which is accurately described as 'decontextualized accidents of litigation rather than representations of environmental assessment in practice' (at 10)). Two sets of theoretical approaches are deployed to help facilitate the analysis of environmental assessment as a regulatory mechanism—information theories (concerning, for example, the 'use and abuse' of information within the environmental assessment process) and culture theories (embracing, for example, what Ost has described as a

---

[1] *Convention on Access to Information, Public Participation in Decision-Making and Access to Justice in Environmental Matters* (1998).

'new administrative logic'[2] whereby decision makers become (it is claimed) more aware of environmental protection concerns via the environmental assessment process). The theory of 'reflexive' (environmental) law also features heavily throughout the work (see Orts, 'Reflexive Environmental Law' (1995) 89 *Nw UL Rev* 1227). This reviewer found Holder's framework of analysis very useful in that it compels the reader to engage with the central question of the *actual* role of law, and environmental assessment law in particular, in the decision-making process. It also prompts the reader seriously to question the true worth of environmental assessment as a mechanism for delivering less environmentally harmful decisions and, ultimately, the goal of sustainable development.

Turning then to the main body of the work: Chapter 2 tracks the roots, emergence and evolution of environmental assessment in a variety of forms including Strategic Environmental Assessment (SEA) and, more recently, Environmental Sustainability Assessment (ESA). This chapter also explores the relationship between environmental assessment and sustainable development (at 56–60). Holder identifies three main trends in the (ongoing) evolution of environmental assessment as a regulatory mechanism. First, the basic form of environmental assessment has proven to be 'remarkably consistent'. Secondly, the remit of environmental assessment has expanded considerably. In line with the overarching concept of sustainable development, economic and social impacts are increasingly factored into the environmental assessment process. Thirdly, there is a greater emphasis on multiple levels of decision-making as witnessed by the current focus on SEA at European and international level. These trends provide useful indicators from which to chart and measure future developments in this dynamic field.

Chapters 3, 4, 5 and 6 proceed to scrutinize constituent elements of the environmental assessment process in turn—prediction; significance; alternatives; and participation and protest. Chapter 3, on prediction, highlights, *inter alia*, the difficulty involved in attempts to assign a concrete (legal) meaning to the core concepts of 'likelihood' and 'significance' in the context of prediction of 'the likely significant effects' on the environment. The interdisciplinary nature of environmental assessment, and its role in facilitating a more integrated approach to decision-making, is brought into sharp focus (in particular the law/ecology interface). The type and source of information that is fed into the environmental assessment process is examined closely (in particular the information submitted by the developer and the potential for bias here). The role of law in 'objectifying' environmental information is also raised in this context. Chapter 4 is concerned with the concept of 'significance'—which involves an evaluation of potential risks and/or benefits to the environment. The chapter examines a host of important

[2] Ost, 'A Game without Rules? The Ecological Self-Organisation of Firms' in Teubner *et al.* (eds.) *Environmental Law and Ecological Responsibility: The Concept and Practice of Ecological Self-Organisation* (Chichester, Wiley, 1994).

practical questions including, by way of example, the extent to which law moulds the exercise of discretion in decisions concerning whether or not an environmental assessment is required for a particular project in the first instance (screening) and the role of the developer's perception of 'significance' on the eventual outcome. The key requirement of prior consideration of 'alternatives', and the potential of SEA to enhance the level and quality of attention paid to the consideration of alternative options, is teased out in Chapter 5. An interesting and informative case study focusing on the (still relatively new) Internal Impact Assessment procedure developed within the EC Commission is included in this chapter and Holder is careful to note 'the relative lack of opportunity for public participation' in this process (at 183).

Chapter 6, entitled 'Participation and Protest', explores the role and potential of participation rights in the environmental assessment process, with a strong focus on the European Community EIA Directive.[3] Recent amendments to this Directive, inspired by the Aarhus Convention, reflect what Holder describes as 'new governance approaches to participation in environmental decision making' (at 185). While grand claims are regularly made as to the value of participation and deliberation, it is crystal clear from this chapter that the reality is often far from the ideal. The complexity of the information at issue; the lack of opportunity for public involvement in initial screening and scoping exercises; the time constraints governing rights to participate; and the absence of a third party right of appeal are among the many factors identified as (potentially) undermining meaningful participation. This chapter also traces the gradual judicial acceptance that environmental assessment is more than simply an information gathering exercise and notes the influence of the European Court of Justice, in particular the 'profound effects' of the *Kraaijeveld*[4] and *Bozen*[5] rulings, in underpinning a 'rights-based' approach to participation in the British courts.[6]

Chapter 7 opens by acknowledging the practical reality that a difficult balance must be drawn between formal participation requirements on the one hand and effective administrative decision-making on the other. One focus of inquiry in this chapter is the degree to which environmental assessment constrains the decision-maker's discretion: to what extent does procedure influence the substantive outcome? Holder recalls that environmental assessment requires that the decision maker considers a broad range of specified information—in other words the process serves to 'inform' discretion—but the actual *weight* assigned to competing

---

[3] Directive 85/337/EEC on the assessment of the effects of certain public and private projects on the environment [1985] OJ L/175/40 as amended by Directive 97/11/EC [1997] OJ L/73/5. The Directive was again amended in 2003 by Directive 2003/35/EC [2003] OJ L/156/17. Member States were required to implement the requirements of the 2003 Directive by 25 June 2005.

[4] Case C-72/95 *Kraaijeveld* [1996] ECR I-5403.

[5] Case C-435/97 *World Wildlife Fund (WWF) and Others v. Autonome Provinz Bozen and Others* [1999] ECR I-5613.

[6] The high-water mark here is probably Lord Hoffmann's judgment in *Berkeley v. Secretary of State for the Environment* [2001] 2 AC 603 (*Berkeley No. 1*).

interests and values remains largely unaffected. The potential influence of the duty to give reasons, as a restraint on discretion, is also considered here. The chapter further documents the emergence of a more enlightened judicial understanding of the role of participation in helping to shape outcomes (a trend that has been described by Robert McCracken Q.C. as a path from 'Technocratic Paternalism to Participatory Democracy').[7] Holder concludes that environmental assessment *does* have an impact on outcomes—though not necessarily in terms of environmental protection. On the contrary, it is clear from the analysis presented in this chapter that the process may be deployed to bolster or advance development interests, if not to 'legitimate' particular outcomes that favour development interests.

Chapter 8 provides a sharp critique of environmental assessment against the backdrop of modern strategies for environmental governance and regulation. Such strategies lay great emphasis on multi-level decision-making; proceduralization and opportunities for participation. The emergence of reflexive legal mechanisms (and Holder includes environmental assessment in this category) aims to give effect to these elements by facilitating a collective learning process within organizations which, in turn, may well foster greater environmental awareness and a stronger sense of shared responsibility. It is, of course, extremely difficult to translate these noble aims into practice and Holder demonstrates how the crucial role of the developer in the environmental assessment process potentially skews the procedure in favour of development interests. This state of affairs is presented as an example of the 'rematerialization' of environmental assessment. While, in theory, the process embraces a more pluralistic approach to decision-making, in practice it presents a (covert) method of 'developmental advocacy' (at 291). The chapter concludes on a disappointing but realistic note—the potential of environmental assessment as a regulatory mechanism for environmental protection has not, as yet, been realized.

In sum, this is an excellent work. Holder's careful analysis enhances the reader's understanding of environmental assessment as an interdisciplinary, highly complex and far from neutral process. The role of law in shaping and, at times, reinforcing the competing interests and values that are at work within the process, is skilfully drawn out. The answer to the basic question running through the work—has environmental assessment made a difference?—remains somewhat obscure, partly because the law is still, as Holder notes, in a formative stage. One theme that could have been developed is the impact of judicial review on administrative decision-making. To what extent does judicial review secure effective compliance with the requirements of environmental assessment law on the ground? Given that a right of access to formal (judicial) review procedures has now been incorporated into the structure of the environmental assessment process (via Directive 2003/35/EC), it is

---

[7] 'Environmental Impact Assessment: From Technocratic Paternalism to Participatory Democracy?' paper delivered at seminar on the theme *Enforcement and Implementation of EC Environment Law-Past Problems and Future Remedies* at King's College, London, June 2003. See further McCracken, 'EIA and Judicial Review: Some Recent Trends' [2003] *Judicial Review* 31.

appropriate to reflect more deeply on the role and value of judicial review in securing the various aims set for environmental assessment as a regulatory instrument. Halliday's work, *Judicial Review and Compliance with Administrative Law* (Hart Publishing, Oxford, 2004), provides an interesting starting point from which to pursue this line of inquiry. To conclude, there are interesting times ahead for environmental assessment law and policy. The most significant future developments are likely to take place in the courts both at national and EC level. This state of affairs raises the thorny question of the most appropriate division of responsibility between the courts and administrative decision makers (or, as Halliday puts it, the tension between 'judicial control' and 'agency autonomy') in a field where complex questions of law and fact are often highly contested.

ÁINE RYALL

Decisions of International Organizations in the European and Domestic Legal Orders of Selected EU Member States by Nicolaos Lavranos, (Groningen: Europa Law Publishing, 2004), 310pp. ISBN 90-76871-19-1.

This book is the product of a doctoral thesis defended at the University of Maastricht. The objective of the author is to analyze how Community law affects the legal status and application of binding decisions of (certain) international organizations in Germany, the Netherlands and France (p. 7). It breaks down into six chapters. The first is the introduction which commences by identifying the '*classic legal situation*' whereby decisions of international organizations impose certain obligations on states, while the individual state determines how it implements them (p. 3). It is this relationship that is modified by European law. The author articulates the influence of European law in terms of a metaphor; that of a transformer that is placed between the decisions of international organizations and national law that amplifies the voltage of decisions and in certain contexts renders redundant the pre-existing national transformer (pp. 5–6). This is followed by a short overview of some of the existing literature on decisions of international organizations with Lavranos emphasizing the scant attention paid to their legal status and effect in domestic legal orders and the even more limited consideration accorded to the impact that Community membership has on this issue (pp. 7–10).

After seeking to inject some definitional clarity in relation to international organizations and their decisions (pp. 11–14) we move into the first substantive chapter (Chapter 2) which provides an overview of the legal status of international treaties in the three Member States and the Community legal order. This preliminary analysis is fitting because, as Lavranos points out, there is a close legal relationship between decisions of international organizations and their founding treaties (pp. 10 and 17). However, not much more than a page or so is devoted to each Member State for a general consideration of the status of treaties therein (pp. 17–23). The analysis of international treaties within the European legal order is delved into in greater detail (pp. 23–44). Three subsections deal respectively with the various types of international agreements that can be concluded (those concluded solely by the EC or EU, mixed EC or EU agreements and those concluded solely by the Member States); the ECJ's jurisdiction over these agreements; and, finally, the case law on the direct effect of agreements. Emphasis is placed on the crucial role that Community law plays in mediating the legal status and effect of international treaties, even in the case of certain treaties to which the EC is not a party (eg ECHR, GATT 1947, CITES). It is all well-trodden terrain but a couple of comments are in order concerning the third sub-section on the direct effect of agreements.

Firstly, when it comes to dealing with the direct effect of Free Trade Agreements, Cooperation Agreements and Association Agreements (pp. 41–44), it is disappointing that Lavranos is content to essentially do no more than quote various key paragraphs from several ECJ judgments that sum up the law (paras 10–12 of 312/91 *Metalsa*; paras 21–24 of 103/94 *Krid*; para 25 of 87/75 *Bresciani* and paras 60–62 and 65 of 262/96 *Surul*). Secondly, the reasoning in relation to the direct effect of GATT/WTO law leaves much to be desired. The analysis culminates with the following bold statement: 'it can be concluded that there are no convincing reasons for the European courts not to accept a direct effect of WTO law'. (p. 40). This is not the place to go into such reasons, but the reader so interested would do well to turn to Eeckhout's nuanced defence of the *Portugal* (149/96) judgment (5 JIEL 2002, p. 91). This is reproduced in his 2004 OUP monograph on the EU's external relations which is cited at the start of the GATT/WTO law direct effect sub-section. Unfortunately, no attempt is made to engage with Eeckhout's analysis, nor that of any other commentator sceptical of having general review of Community legislation *vis-à-vis* the WTO agreements. Indeed, the aforementioned conclusion is reached with little by way of argumentation. The sub-section is less than four and a half pages long (pp. 36–40), one and a half of which is taken up quoting (in whole) paragraphs 36–45 of *Portugal*, and only two of which move beyond description (pp. 39–40). In these two pages Lavranos addresses what he understands to be the two prongs of *Portugal*. The first is the ECJ's argument: 'that accepting direct effect would limit the ability of the EC legislature to use the—albeit temporary—alternative possibility of negotiating an agreement for compensation with the other party of the dispute…'. And the second is the reciprocity argument, ie that other major trading partners do not accord the agreement direct effect. In relation to the first, Lavranos points out that the alternatives under Article 22 DSU are not within the EC's control; and, consequently, he argues citing para 96 of AG Alber's opinion in 93/02 *Biret*: 'there is not much room for manoeuvre available for the EC executive and legislature that could be limited by granting direct effect to WTO law or more generally by judicial interference or judicial activism of the ECJ'. (p. 39). Moving on to the reciprocity argument, Lavranos states: 'as AG Alber argued, it is difficult to conceive how the negotiation position of the ECJ *vis-à-vis* the other WTO Members could be affected by granting direct effect to WTO law in the Community legal order'. (pp. 39–40, citing para 102 of opinion 93/02). The AG's reasoning is, however, being taken out of context. Those familiar with his opinions in the *Biret* cases will be all too aware that the argument being advanced therein was concerned solely with adopted dispute settlement reports once the compliance period had expired and not with general review of Community legislation *vis-à-vis* the WTO agreements. It is crucial to keep these two issues separate, and Dr Lavranos' reliance on (or hijacking of) the AG opinion in seeking to attack the *Portugal* reasoning in the direct effect writ large context leaves the two conflated and misrepresents the AG's position (admittedly in one sentence at page 40 the fact that AG Alber was making an argument in the context of adopted reports is acknowledged but the AG had already been cited various times in support of the much broader argument).

Chapter 3 (pp. 49–128) brings us to the meat of the research agenda. It is here that the legal status and impact of decisions of international organizations in Germany, the Netherlands, France and the Community legal order commences. The analysis focuses specifically on decisions of regional fisheries organizations; EC-Turkey Association Council decisions; decisions adopted within the framework of MEA's; Security Council resolutions and ICAO decisions. The first subsection, on decisions of regional fisheries organizations, is the shortest of the five (pp. 53–60). The 'total allowable catches' determined by the various fisheries organizations are, as Lavranos documents, usually implemented by EC Council Regulations and applied directly in Germany but implemented via executive regulations in the Netherlands and France (pp. 57–60). Put succinctly, as a result of the Community's exclusive competence domestic law has come to play a minimal role.

In contrast, there is no shortage of domestic activity when it comes to the EC-Turkey Association Council Decisions (pp. 61–76). As far as consideration is devoted to these decisions at the international and European level, the analysis is superficial and the author uses a large part of the few pages that have been so allocated for quoting from several judgments (at pp. 62–65, paras 18–20 & 37–38 of 277/94 *Taflan Met*; paras 17–20 of 355/93 *Eroglu* and paras 97–98 of 262/96 *Sürül*). Not surprisingly Lavranos finds that the ECJ judgments have transformed the situation in the relevant domestic legal orders. Examples are provided of how ECJ interpretations of Decision 1/80 have rather grudgingly been taken on board by the German and Dutch courts (pp. 65–73). In France, apparently the case law has focused on Decision 3/80 and the briefest of consideration is given to how some of this case law has played out (pp. 73–75).

Next in line are the decisions adopted by the Conference of the Parties (COP) or the Meeting of Parties (MOP) to MEA's (pp. 76–93). Some space is accorded to discussion of whether COPs/MOPs can be qualified as organs of international organizations and though less than three pages in length (pp. 79–81) Lavranos still crams in quotations from no less than six different academic contributions. He comes down in favour of a functional approach that acknowledges the capacity of COPs/MOPs to adopt binding decisions even though no formal international organization is established. This leaves a meagre 12 pages for an analysis of implementation of MEAs at the European level, in the respective domestic legal orders and a summary. A few eyebrows are sure to be raised by his assertive conclusion with respect to the *Biotech* case (377/98), for having quoted paragraphs 52–54 he states: 'Thus, provisions of MEA's, including—in my view—binding COPs/MOPs decisions—can be used by the ECJ to review Community law irrespective of whether they have direct effect or not' (p. 83). We of course await further interpretation of the *Biotech* judgment and, in particular, how it can be squared with prior case law on the criteria for compliance review of Community measures *vis-à-vis* international agreements. Lavranos himself does not offer any thoughts in this respect and absent any further clarification from the ECJ the unqualified conclusion he reaches certainly appears hasty.

As for the decisions adopted within the framework of MEA's and their implementation at the European level, this inevitably depends on the particular MEA and a few examples of variation in this respect are provided (pp. 83–84). The survey of domestic implementation indicates that essentially executive regulations are used (pp. 84–92). In summing up Lavranos contends that: 'from the point of view of the EU Member States, there is no difference any longer in terms of the legal status between 'communitarized' COP/MOP decisions and original secondary Community legislation.' (p. 93). The term 'communitarized' in this context seems to denote decisions from a mixed agreement the provisions of which are not within the Member States exclusive competence and accordingly, following the author's reasoning, benefit as of right from supremacy over all domestic law, and can also be directly effective, attributes that are apparently wanting in the absence of the Community law interface. As a matter of form one might thus make the point—and this at least is how the present reviewer understands Lavranos—that the 'legal status' thus enjoyed is tantamount to that of secondary Community legislation. One is however left wondering what purchase this supposedly enhanced legal status—discussed so enthusiastically throughout the book—actually has in the absence of directly effective Community implementing measures or an ECJ ruling telling us that a given provision of a particular COP/MOP decision is directly enforceable. Now Lavranos does acknowledge that the EC law interface is not 'very visible' in the MEA context, but this does not dissuade him from concluding with his voltage metaphor: 'Nonetheless, the "EC law transformer" transforms all those COP/MOP decisions that fall within the competence of the EC from 12 Volt to 220 Volt before they enter the domestic circuit of the Member States' (p. 93). And yet absent empirical support is it not simply misleading to talk of COP/MOP decisions acquiring this super-charged status not least because the same talk of 220 volts is used in the context of Association Council decisions where in contrast the domestic impact has clearly been immense? Lavranos appears to lose sight of the fact that this super-charged status can be much more apparent than real.

The final two types of decision that are considered in Chapter 3, Security Council resolutions and ICAO decisions, belong to organizations to which the EC is not even a party. That said, as Lavranos documents, competence developments have resulted in the EC gaining an increasing role in their implementation. No domestic cases in the relevant member states were found in which 'communitarized' ICAO decisions were at issue so we are left with a discussion of some cases involving 'non-communitarized' ICAO decisions (pp. 118–127). In respect of the Security Council resolutions, the examination of domestic implementation (pp. 100–110) leads the author to conclude that the classic legal relationship of 'Security Council Resolutions—national law' remains intact but that a new legal relationship is created of 'EC law (transformed Security Council resolutions)— national law' (pp. 110–111). In concluding the chapter it is argued that this additional relationship arises when EC law is involved but the EC is not a member of the international organization (p. 128). But this distinction does not have any analytical purchase; after all, can we not simply say that the classic legal relationship only remains intact insofar as we are dealing with Security Council resolutions outside the sphere of economic sanctions, for in that context their implementation is a matter for the domestic legal order, unconstrained by Community law, to determine. Once we are dealing with economic sanctions then the fact that the Community has come to play the central implementing role via the regulations that are adopted under Articles 301 and 60 changes the pre-existing relationship into 'UN Security Resolutions—EC transposition—domestic law'. In this setting whatever domestic implementation and judicial interpretation there is becomes subject, at least in theory, to the ECJ's role as overseer of the obligations that actually flow from the EC regulations as interpreted in the light of the relevant Security Council resolution. This is attested to by the ECJ jurisprudence thus far in relation to what were Article 133 sanctions regulations (84/95 *Bosphorous*; 177/95 *Ebony* and 124/95 *Centro-Com*) and if this does not constitute a modification of the classic legal relationship—in the sanctions context—it is difficult to see what does. Thus, contrary to the conclusions that Lavranos draws, his case studies do not support the proposition that EC membership of an international organization has an impact on how the respective decisions are transformed by EC law; they do, however, certainly support the proposition—emphasized in the conclusion—that the extent of Community competence in a given domain is important.

Chapter 4 considers the reception afforded to WTO dispute settlement reports and ECtHR judgments (pp. 131–187). The WTO section predates the key ruling in 377/02 *Van Parys* of which Lavranos would surely have been very critical as the gist of the sub-section on Community law is that the European courts were bound by the DSB rulings to which the EC is a party and 'were required to interpret the banana and hormones legislation in the light of the relevant WTO [rulings] ... which essentially means they were required to invalidate them as far as they are inconsistent with WTO law' (pp. 142–143). Given the criticism to which the jurisprudence in this domain has been subjected it is obvious that many would agree, but still Lavranos fails to engage with the complexity of the subject. Admittedly five pages follow specifically on direct effect (pp. 143–147), but this amounts to little more than a descriptive account of *Biret* and criticism of the overly formalistic approach adopted by the refusal of the CFI in that string of cases (T-18/99 *Cordis*, T-30/99 *Bocchi*; T-52/99 *T.Port*) to recognize that the amended banana regulation was intended to implement a DSB decision within the meaning of *Nakajima* (a formalistic approach confirmed in *Van Parys* and T-19/01 *Chiquita*). As far as reception in the Member States is concerned (pp. 148–164), Lavranos initially has it that even independently of the restrictive European case law, constitutional hurdles would constrain their domestic invocability: Germany (domestic implementing act requirement stressed at pp. 148 and 154); Netherlands (requirement for them to be 'binding on anyone' pp. 155–57); France (publication requirement—pp. 162–63—and one would assume the reciprocity hurdle in Article 55 of the Constitution would be problematic). Yet then we are also told that the Community jurisprudence has precluded the German courts from giving effect to the Banana rulings and has made it more difficult to invoke DSB decisions in the Netherlands. In short, Lavranos argues that an EC-law-transformed situation plays a role except when the matter lies within Member State exclusive competence.

Moving on to ECtHR judgments (pp. 165–186), and specifically the European level discussion (pp. 169–177), the author first distinguishes three different scenarios that fall within the field of application of Community law: (1) national measures implementing EC law; (2) national measures adopted under an exception contained in the EC Treaty or in ECJ case law; (3) national measures reproducing EC law for external purposes. He notes that case law has not yet determined whether national measures implementing Directives also fall within the field of application of Community law (the terminology of being 'binding on the Member States when they implement Community rules'—5/88 *Wachauf* para 19 and much reiterated since—has always been assumed to include Directives and indeed was so applied in such circumstances by the ECJ in a mid-2003 judgment—20/00 & 64/00 *Booker*). And in summing up, only a few paragraphs after having begun to distinguish the various components of the 'field of application of Community law', Lavranos puzzlingly states: 'the ECJ applies the ECHR, as interpreted by the ECtHR, whenever national measures of the Member States that intend to implement Community law also affect the rights protected by the ECHR' (p. 171). What then of the other scenarios previously mentioned, such as the *ERT* (260/89) variety? And further confusion is thrown in when the paragraph culminates: 'it is also interesting to note that the same limitation is applied to the Charter of Fundamental Rights vis-à-vis the EU institutions and the EU Member States "implementing Union law" '

(p. 171). Which limitation? Lavranos moves from considering the different variants of the 'field of application of Community law', to summarizing in terms of intended to implement Community law, to the Charter applying the same limitation. And for the rest of the chapter the terminology employed is that of the field (or scope) of application of Community law. The controversy concerning whether or not the Charter's terminology of 'implementing Union law' (now Art II:111(1) of the Constitution) incorporates the *ERT* type of application is not even mentioned.

The European law section then considers the interaction between the ECJ and the Strasbourg court. It touches upon the ECJ's application of the EHCR and developments before the ECtHR (e.g. *24833/94 Matthews* and the eventually dissolved *Senator Lines* conflict) and divergent interpretations that have resulted (*46/87* & *227/88 Hoechst* as contrasted with *13710/88 Niemietz* & *37971/97 Colas Est*– *94/00 Roquette Frères* is cited but its significance in vitiating any such divergence is not explored; *374/87 Orkem* contrasted with *A/256-A Funke*; and, with Lavranos in more critical mood, *17/98 Emesa Sugar* contrasted with the string of ECtHR judgments on the breach of Article 6 that results from an inability to respond to Advocate General submissions in domestic litigation). Lavranos concludes that where a measure falls within the field of application of Community law the classic legal situation is thus modified into an EC law transformed legal situation (ECHR—EC law— national law). Yet in the preceding chapter Lavranos argued that where the Community is not a member of the international organization the existing legal relationship remains intact but a new one is created which begs the question as to why this is not also the case with the ECHR or alternatively why, as already mentioned, we cannot simply say that in, *inter alia*, the Security Council implementation context the classic legal relationship is also affected. This is all rather semantic because nothing turns upon the point, nonetheless one would have expected some clarification from Lavranos on this point of conceptual confusion.

The final substantive chapter (Chapter 5) looks at 'decisions' adopted by the EU within the second and third pillars (pp. 191–230). Lavranos argues that the EU qualifies as an international organization when acting within these pillars with the European Council forming the organ that adopts binding decisions. This is followed by sections exploring the legal effect of second and third pillar instruments (including excessive quotation from such instruments). Some controversial propositions are articulated when Lavranos turns to the possible applicability of supremacy and direct effect to the second and third pillar instruments (pp. 211–227). That the ECJ does not even have jurisdiction under the second pillar does not preclude Lavranos getting some mileage out of this issue (pp. 214–217) and, indeed, even asserts that: 'the absence of the jurisdiction of the ECJ makes it unlikely that a possible direct effect of II. pillar decisions is recognised and imposed uniformly on all EU Member States'. (p. 216).

Would any Community lawyer actually agree that 'only unlikely'—or 'very unlikely' as Lavranos also puts it—actually captures the impact that exclusion of jurisdiction has on the possibility of direct effect being recognised and imposed uniformly on all Member States? And then with respect to third pillar decisions—having contrasted the limited jurisdiction under this pillar with that under the first—he concludes: 'sufficient Community law features exist within the III. pillar which justify the assumption that supremacy and direct effect are also applicable to the binding III. pillar decisions' (pp. 220–201). Astonishingly the author considers the European Convention developments to constitute strong support for this proposition; quite the opposite, the developments cited (final reports of working groups and provisions of the Constitutional Treaty) are testimony to the existing differences between third pillar and first pillar instruments and the desire to redress this in the new constitutional settlement. Moreover, earlier in the chapter the express exclusion of direct effect for decisions and framework decisions in 34(2)(b) & (c) was acknowledged (pp. 205–210) making it all the more perplexing that a few pages later he states such a proposition. Logic seems to return in the sub-section that follows (pp. 222–226) for Lavranos reiterates that direct effect has indeed been excluded (at least for the former two instruments) and considers other possible means of bolstering their impact, arguing, *inter alia*, that the 14/83 *Von Colson* and 106/89 *Marleasing* principles should be applicable to framework decisions. Assessing the extent to which any EC law influence can be identified in the context of second and third pillar decisions, Lavranos points, in the case of the former, to the use of second pillar instruments as the first step in the process of Community implementation of Security Council resolutions and the financing of second pillar activity out of the EC budget and, in the case of the latter, the areas that need to be dealt with by measures from both pillars (pp. 227–229). But these examples hardly support the conclusion that both with respect to the second and third pillar 'an "EC law influenced" legal relationship that is to a large extent comparable with the EC law transformed legal relationship can be identified . . .' (p. 230).

Finally, a concluding chapter provides an overview of the results as they pertain to the international, European and national law levels (pp. 233–250). It largely reiterates what has gone before, the core of which being that in those domains within which the Community has competence, Community law plays a crucial mediating role in determining—essentially enhancing—the legal status and effect that international organisation decisions will have in domestic legal orders.

Lavranos has addressed an important research question but his is a disappointing contribution. Some of the shortcomings have already been touched upon and essentially what stands out most is that the analysis, across the board, is somewhat superficial and that conclusions reached by the author remain unsupported by the text. Perhaps part of the problem was that it was clearly

a very large research agenda in that the book addresses different areas of
Community law, domestic law and international law and the interaction
between them, and it is difficult to provide real expertise across such a broad
spectrum. The result in this case is a text that eschews much complexity and
broaches many difficult areas of law in a cursory and somewhat careless fashion.
Carelessness is also an appropriate adjective for the proofreading, a few of the
many blemishes include: 'Advocate General Alber opined in its Opinion'
(p. 53); 'lasted less then three years' (p. 72); 'did not considered it necessary' (p 99);
'what the extend of the competence' (p. 28); 'the ECJ should squash the ruling'
(p. 146); 'would not be free any more to chose' (p. 177); 'states seem to loose
increasingly control' (p. 248). The occasional minor inaccuracy is also apparent:
at p. 31 Lavranos refers to Article 234 as providing that the ECJ has jurisdiction
to interpret the EC Treaty and secondary Community law acts and cites subparagraph (a) of Article 234 when in fact the latter is only concerned with interpretation of the Treaty and it is subparagraph (b) that grants the interpretative
authority in relation to secondary acts; *Roquette Frères* is cited at pp. 182 and
184 in relation to compatibility of AG opinions with Article 6 ECHR when it
should be *Emesa Sugar*; Article 35(2)(a) and (b) TEU referred to at p. 219 when
it should be 35(3)(a) and (b) TEU; Article 228 is referred to twice at p. 242
when it should be Article 288.

MARIO MENDEZ

Directives in EC Law (2ⁿᵈ edn) by Sacha Prechal, (Oxford: Oxford
    University Press, 2005), xxxiv + 349pp (including bibliography). ISBN
    0-19-826832-7.

This much-anticipated second edition of Prechal's well-known work is an ency-
clopaedia of information and analysis of the form and content of European
Directives and of their impact within national legal systems. The complexity and
sheer pace of developments in this field since the first edition appeared in 1995
has been nothing short of phenomenal.[1] This new work builds on the solid
foundations laid in the first edition and charts developments in the intervening
10-year period. References are made to the first edition at a number of points in
footnotes to the main text, directing the reader to more detailed (earlier) analysis
of particular issues. The first edition is therefore far from redundant.

The Introduction opens by noting, *inter alia*, the increased pre-occupation
with *decentralized* enforcement of Community law *via* the national courts and the
role of the European Court of Justice (ECJ) in championing local enforcement.
Prechal identifies four basic lines of development within this complex and

[1] Prechal, *Directives in European Community Law: A Study of Directives and their Enforcement in
National Courts* (Clarendon Press, Oxford, 1995).

sophisticated body of case law: direct effect; consistent interpretation; the emergence of the principle of 'effective judicial protection'; and State liability. An important question is introduced at 10: has the body of rules governing decentralized enforcement advanced to such an extent as to 'become unworkable for the national courts and entirely opaque for the individual?' Notwithstanding the extensive case law from the Community courts and national courts, a number of important practical issues concerning the enforcement of Directives at national level remain unresolved. Prechal addresses most of these provocative issues head-on in the course of the work. She approaches her topic from the point of view of 'the judicial protection of rights which individuals allegedly derive from Community directives' (at 11). To this end, the book is structured around three core themes: the main characteristics of Directives (chapters 2–5); the Directive as an integral component of national legal orders and the implications of this (chapters 6 and 7); and the mechanisms available to the national courts to facilitate enforcement of Directives (ie consistent interpretation, direct effect and State liability which are considered in chapters 8, 9 and 10 respectively).

It is clear from the outset that the work concentrates almost exclusively on the *Community law* dimension. Yet Prechal acknowledges the difficulty and danger inherent in this approach to her selected subject (at 12). An analysis of Community law in this particular field (however searching), if tackled in isolation from the (legal) situation pertaining at national level, risks presenting an incomplete picture of the *real* local impact of Directives. Prechal is aware of this risk and undertakes what she describes as 'minor excursions' into national legal systems to complete her analysis where necessary. It is impossible to do justice to the depth of the scholarship and close scrutiny of the case law presented throughout this work in the limited space available here. Therefore, propose to concentrate on selected themes with a view to giving an overall flavour of the work.

Chapter 4 section 4.4, which is headed 'Administrative compliance', explores the scope of the (seemingly onerous and far-reaching) obligations imposed on national administrative authorities pursuant to Article 249(3) and Article 10 EC. The 'uncompromising' decision of the ECJ in *Costanzo*[2] reflects the 'vital' role of national competent authorities in delivering Community law at local level. However, when attempting to fulfil the obligation to interpret national law in conformity with a Directive, or when the doctrine of direct effect is engaged, these authorities often do not have the benefit of any judicial guidance. This state of affairs entails serious consequences for legal certainty. Even more significantly, the strong Community law obligation, taken to its logical conclusion, creates a situation where national authorities may be required to go beyond the competences and powers that they enjoy under national (constitutional) law. The position of administrative authorities is 'fundamentally different' from that of

---

[2] Case 103/88 *Costanzo* [1989] ECR 1839.

national courts. The courts are empowered to review and, where necessary, set aside national law that is not in conformity with the requirements of a directive and they also have the option of making a preliminary reference to the ECJ pursuant to Article 234 EC. Prechal therefore questions whether the ECJ's 'transplant' of the general obligation to give 'full' effect to Community law from the national courts to administrative authorities 'is fortunate and realistic' (at 72). She suggests that a more balanced approach to the '*Costanzo* obligation' is required. Drawing on *Dorsch Consult*,[3] and recent rulings such as *Kühne*,[4] Prechal calls attention to a 'mitigating' factor that may operate to moderate the general thrust of the '*Costanzo* obligation', that is, the ECJ's regular reference to the sphere of the national authorities' competence or to matters within their jurisdiction (at 69–71). The principle of national procedural autonomy is identified as another potential 'mitigating' factor here. In *Wells*,[5] the ECJ provided welcome guidance on the scope of the obligation falling on national authorities in the particular context of alleged breach of Directive 85/337/EEC on environmental impact assessment (EIA).[6] It is worth setting out the relevant passages from the Court's judgment here (references to case law omitted):

... it is clear from settled case law that under the principle of co-operation in good faith laid down in Article 10 EC the Member States are required to nullify the unlawful consequences of a breach of Community law. Such an obligation is owed, *within the sphere of its competence*, by every organ of the Member State concerned (para. 64, emphasis added).

Thus, it is for the competent authorities of a Member State to take, *within the sphere of their competence*, all the general or particular measures necessary to ensure that [the objectives set down in the EIA directive are fulfilled]. Such particular measures include, *subject to the limits laid down by the principle of procedural autonomy of the Member States*, the revocation or suspension of a consent already granted, in order to carry out an assessment of the environmental effects of the project in question as provided for by Directive 85/337 (para. 65, emphasis added).

It is clear from the extract set out above that the competent authorities' obligation to nullify the unlawful consequences of a breach of Community law is confined to taking measures that are within their sphere of competence and, furthermore, is subject to the limits set by the principle of national procedural autonomy. The Court then went on to rule (at para. 66) that the Member States is required 'to make good any harm caused by the failure to carry out an [EIA]'. Again, however, the detailed procedural rules to be applied here are a matter for the domestic legal order pursuant to the principle of procedural autonomy, provided that the

---

[3] Case C-54/96 *Dorsch Consult* [1997] ECR I-4961.
[4] Case C-453/00 *Kühne* [2004] ECR I-837.   [5] Case C-201/02 *Wells* [2004] ECR I-723.
[6] Directive 85/337/EEC on the assessment of the effects of certain public and private projects on the environment (the EIA Directive) [1985] OJ L/175/40 as amended by Directive 97/11/EC [1997] OJ L/73/5. The Directive was again amended in 2003 by Directive 2003/35/EC [2003] OJ L/156/17.

principle of equivalence and the principle of effectiveness are respected (para. 67). It follows that the obligation of the competent authorities to give full effect to Community law is far from absolute. *Wells* delivers a sensible result. The ruling is strong on effectiveness—the ECJ, as expected, is uncompromising in terms of its mission to see that the EIA directive (an acknowledged cornerstone of EC environmental law and policy) is not undermined by the actions of recalcitrant Member States. Yet, at the same time, the Court is willing to recognize the practical situation at local level and gives the competent authorities some genuine room to manoeuvre (see further Prechal's analysis at 71 and 269–270).

The *Wells* ruling is, of course, of significance for a number of reasons, not least of which is the welcome clarification offered by the ECJ on the thorny question of so-called 'horizontal side effects of direct effect' (at 261) or, to put it another way, 'incidental effects'. In *Wells*, the Court explained that 'mere adverse repercussions on the rights of third parties' does not operate to prevent an individual from invoking the provisions of a Directive against the Member State (at para. 57). It is, however, most difficult in practice to distinguish clinically between 'mere adverse repercussions' on the one hand and (prohibited) 'horizontal effect' involving *direct* interference with a third party's legal position on the other (see 264–266). Prechal concludes that notwithstanding the clarification provided in *Wells*, the question of 'horizontal effects in "triangular situations"' will remain a haphazard matter which is, from the point of view of legal certainty unsatisfactory' (at 266).

Chapters 6 and 7 provide a thorough account of 'Directives as sources of rights' and 'The role of national courts' respectively. There is much food for thought in both chapters. Chapter 6 demonstrates the high degree of complexity and uncertainty that continues to attach to the concept of 'rights' in Community law and, in particular, in the jurisprudence of the ECJ. The difficult, and at times contradictory, case law on national procedures and remedies is the subject of detailed scrutiny in chapter 7 (at 145–170). Prechal also examines the extent to which the ECJ's interventionist case law on national procedures and remedies has 'directly empowered' the national courts to assume 'new powers', on the sole basis of Community law, with a view to discharging the tasks assigned to them by the ECJ (at 170–172). The final section of this chapter, entitled 'Critique and controversy', repays careful reading. Here, Prechal considers the diverse reactions to the Court's *Peterbroeck* and *Van Schijndel* rulings[7] in the (by now extensive) academic literature. She concludes that the ECJ should continue 'to set standards to be met from the point of view of effective judicial protection of individuals' rights and effective enforcement of Community law'. The pursuit of uniformity, is, in her view, 'unrealistic' and does not make sense in light of how the relationship between Community law and national law is structured at present (at 178). This is a sensible view. In practice, the effectiveness of Community law cannot be isolated

---

[7] Case C-312/93 *Peterbroeck* [1995] ECR I-4599 and Joined Cases C-430/93 and C-431/93 *Van Schijndel and Van Veen* [1995] ECR I-4705.

from local legal and administrative culture. Ignoring this reality in the name of uniformity risks aggravating existing tensions between national and Community law at local level and throwing the integration project into further disarray. (See further the interesting critique of the pursuit of a uniform system of remedies and procedures driven by an 'Integration through law' approach presented in Dougan, *National Remedies before the Court of Justice* (Hart Publishing, Oxford, 2004).)

Chapter 9 is devoted to 'direct effect' and, as expected, Prechal is masterful on this difficult topic. This reviewer was very impressed by her earlier contribution— 'Does Direct Effect Still Matter?' (2000) 37 CML Rev. 1047, in particular her suggestion that in light of the confusion that the concept of direct effect has generated, and continues to generate, there is a danger that:

. . . it may serve as a pretext *not* to apply Community law provisions and it still underlines the 'foreign origin' character of Community law, which should, at a certain stage, be over-come (at 1086, emphasis in original).

Chapter 9 of the current work demonstrates that the confusion surrounding the concept of direct effect persists. However, Prechal succeeds in demystifying direct effect by carefully unpacking the various strands to the concept. She is particularly clear on the concept of direct effect as 'invocability' (cf. chapter 6) and in explaining why, in her view, 'review of legality' of national measures 'is merely a form of judicial activity which takes place *within* the concept of direct effect' (at 237, emphasis in original). Having reviewed the relevant case law, Prechal attempts to 'redefine' direct effect in the following terms:

Direct effect is the obligation of a court or another authority to apply the relevant provision of Community law, either as a norm which governs the case or as a standard for legal review. Directly effective provisions are then provisions having the quality to be applied accordingly (at 241, emphasis in original).

This definition neatly captures the basic idea behind the doctrine of direct effect— that the provision in question must be capable of being applied, or made operational, by the national court or competent authority in question. To equate direct effect with the creation of rights is, according to Prechal, far too restrictive an approach to this broad and dynamic concept (See, for example, Case 8/81 *Becker* [1982] ECR 53). Prechal's definition will certainly be of use to those of us who are charged with explaining this cryptic concept to undergraduate students of European law.

Chapter 11 delivers a thought-provoking conclusion. An interesting section on 'discretion' chastises the ECJ for its failure to provide guidance as to how this important concept is to be understood (at 312–313). This final chapter also draws out the implications of the Court's interventionist approach for the separation of powers and the role of the national courts within the particular national constitutional settings. Overall, Prechal concludes that ' "the directive", as an instrument of EC intervention and the concept it embodies, has proved its usefulness' (at 320). Yet basic issues remain unresolved by the ECJ, especially the persistent problem of horizontal direct effect.

In sum, the second edition of Prechal's detailed study is an important contribution to the existing literature on the enforcement of Community law at national level.

ÁINE RYALL

The Limits of Competition Law: Markets and Public Services by Tony Prosser, (Oxford: Oxford University Press, 2005), 288pp. ISBN 0-19-926669-7.

Introduction

It is rare for a legal text to strike at the centre of a political nerve, whilst at the same time concentrating on legal analysis, and without neglecting the impact of relevant political, social or economic arguments on the law. Tony Prosser's book discussing the *Limits of Competition Law: Markets and Public Services*, does exactly that. Prosser, drawing on his experience of many years on the subject of public service regulation and privatization, investigates a seemingly straightforward question of law: 'to what extent should public services (for example public utilities such as telecommunications, energy, public transport and postal services) be subject to ordinary competition law?'. Yet, in doing so, he delves into a subject matter which is highly politically charged,[1] and the implications of which he acknowledges.

The argument (I): the limits of competition law

His book introduces competition law as one regime available to governments for organising the delivery of public services (defined as including public utilities, see above, but also local community services, social services and public health). However, it makes equally clear that competition law is not a value-free regime. Generally speaking, competition law is 'closely linked to the advantages of the market as a means of allocating goods and services'. It is 'the means by which markets are kept open and competitive'.[2] Or, put differently, 'reliance on competition law is the legal expression of, and surrogate for, the creation and maintenance of open markets'[3]—open markets, that is, in public services. Prosser traces the chief justification for competition law's pro-market attitude to the 'promotion of consumer welfare through maximising efficiency',[4] that in turn increases consumer choice. In order to keep markets efficient, competition law holds enterprises, private or state-owned, to account 'for the exercise of economic power ... to consumers and shareholders through the marketplace',[5] preventing them from obtaining any unfairly protected position.

---

[1] See only the Queen's Speech before the UK House of Commons on 17 May 2005, devoting the UK government to 'accelerate modernisation of the public services to promote opportunity and fairness' and 'bring forward legislation in the key areas of public service delivery: education; health; welfare; and crime'.
[2] p. 17.   [3] p. 2.   [4] p. 18.   [5] p. 2.

Prosser's central argument, however, suggests that where competition rules are applied in the context of public services without limitation, they create 'at minimum a tension between the application of competition law to key public services, such as the public utilities, and the principles underlying the distinctive nature of these services'.[6] There are, in other words, clear limits to competition law and its pro-market attitude, when it comes to determine their suitability as an appropriate legal framework for the organization and delivery of public services.

These limits or tensions are exemplified by the fact that, in several European jurisdictions, a specific regime of public service law rather than general competition law has traditionally been responsible for the protection of what Prosser terms 'public service values', such as universal access rights, or quality and continuity guarantees. The latter tradition (which Prosser loosely terms the 'Continental' view), in many ways depicts a counter model to the competition-based model (loosely linked, in turn, to an 'Anglo-Saxon' perspective). It insists on accountability 'to citizens through law and through institutional scrutiny by regulators and government' rather than an economic form of accountability through markets and competition law.[7] Because the protection of public service values takes place through law and regulation rather than by political means (the tax and social benefits system), this 'Continental' approach leads to an extensive body of public service law, 'reflecting both social rights and a concern for social solidarity', that, in cases of conflict, takes priority over ordinary competition law.[8] That body of law is based on 'the idea that the state has duties to ensure equal treatment of citizens irrespective of their economic resources'.[9] Prosser investigates two examples of such public service traditions, those of France's *service public* and Italy's *servizio pubblico*.[10] Their traditional public service law, especially that of France, 'has tended to start from general principles rather than relying on a gradual, pragmatic development of practice'[11]; and, Prosser observes, 'indeed it is at the level of principle that [the French doctrine of] *service public* is at its strongest'.[12]

In marked contrast to such a principled approach, the view depicted by Prosser as the 'Anglo-Saxon' approach, based on the experiences in UK law, takes a pragmatic attitude to the development of public service values, and instead of subjecting these values to systematic codification, tends to rely on ordinary competition law to protect economic values of maximum consumer choice and efficiency. Public interest considerations, accordingly, play a role only through 'limited exceptions to the general [competition] law'.[13] Thus, describing the current situation in the UK, Prosser writes that '[f]or public service, though not for competition law, the British tradition that [public service values] are to be

---

[6] p. 17.   [7] p. 2.   [8] p. 2.   [9] p. 2.
[10] Of course, similar approaches exist in other European countries, eg the German's administrative law on *Daseinsvorsorge*, following Karl Jaspers' ideas taken further by the administrative lawyer Ernst Forsthoff.   [11] p. 94.
[12] p. 113.   [13] p. 27.

implemented through political rather than legal means has been retained. There is, for example, no attempt to codify the special requirements of public service where they may conflict with the values of competition law.'[14] An exception would seem to exist in the form of a 'new public service' law emerging from 'the gradual development of social regulation based on public service concerns ... in newly competitive markets',[15] especially the utilities markets, following the work of recently set up utility regulators. However, Prosser identifies that the safeguards afforded through these regulations for public service values (most importantly, universal service guarantees) are often 'uncoordinated and inconsistent'[16] and subject to 'inefficiencies and inequities'.[17]

The argument (II): convergence amongst EU Member States and the role of EU law

More interesting still than their theoretically opposed starting points, is Prosser's detailed analysis of their more recent evolution, and—it is safe to say—of the gradual convergence of the 'Continental' and 'Anglo-Saxon' systems, following, in large parts, the influence of a dominating European Community law. That dominance can be seen in two ways. First, national competition rules have gradually been assimilated to EC competition law, not least by taking on board the Community's case law. For example, Prosser illustrates how EC competition law initially led the UK legislature to introduce a competition-based test to regulate monopolies and anti-competitive agreements (see the Competition Act 1998), and to abolish its previous regime based on a broader 'public interest' test. In summary, 'UK competition law has now reached the end of a process of change from a regime in which the public interest is built into the basic test used by the competition authorities, and in which the minister has a central role, to one in which the test is wholly competition-based subject to very limited exceptions for public interest considerations, and is applied by independent authorities.'[18] The second evidentiary sign of the Community's dominant role in the process of convergence between the traditionally 'Anglo-Saxon' competition-based view and the 'Continental' arguments in favour of strong public service law can be found in the Community's liberalization programmes.[19] Prosser identifies that, as a consequence of the Community's political drive towards liberal markets, a process of 'marketization'—'the development of competitive markets in the provision of public services'[20]—has resulted in 'a shift to competition law rather than administration or hierarchy as the major organizing principle of a public service'[21] across the borders of Europe's economies. This can be seen more specifically from the attempts to reform the French doctrine of *service public*, beginning in the 1990s,

[14] p. 65.   [15] p. 93.   [16] p. 94.
[17] p. 94, citing Klein, G., *Life Lines: the NCC's Agenda for Affordable Energy, Water and Telephone Services* (London: National Consumer Council), 2003, p. 56.
[18] p. 27; note that the UK Competition Act 1998 is closely modelled on the provisions of Art. 81 and 82 of the EC Treaty.   [19] Described in Chapter 8.
[20] p. 1.   [21] p. 2.

following tensions between the Community's internal market programme and the traditional French doctrine. It has been emphasized that despite its strong foothold in French administrative law, the doctrine of *service public* is 'not necessarily incompatible with a substantial role for liberalized markets'[22] and accordingly would not debar France from liberalizing its public utilities market, in line with Community law and policy; the crucial point being, as Prosser puts it, 'that this doctrine does not require any particular form of organization for the delivery of public services',[23] but instead separates strictly between the doctrine itself, which firmly enshrines public service objectives, and its 'institutional form',[24] which flexibly allows for market methods such as licensing, franchising or contracting out etc. For example, 'despite the wording of the relevant French requirement (national public services 'are to become public property'), it is no longer interpreted as requiring public services to be under public ownership so long as the public authorities ensure that the provision of the services themselves is protected'.[25]

In making apparent the degree of convergence, despite their different starting points, between the Continental and the Anglo-Saxon views, Prosser in my view provokes some of the most interesting questions throughout his book. He makes evident that the protection of public service values, posing the 'limit' to competition law, deserves particular attention, precisely because neither the Continental nor the Anglo-Saxon approach find practical expression in the political and legal realities of today's Europe. In reality there exists, across Europe, 'a complex mixture of competitive markets, competition law, and public service values, each with their own role and importance'[26]; Prosser offers plenty of examples, eg the case of UK broadcasting discussed in his final chapter. Prosser's book details, for example, the extent to which independent regulatory authorities have gained autonomous powers in both Continental systems and in the UK, and a 'combination of general guidance from government and detailed implementation by the specialist regulators'[27] prevails as the preferred regulatory style across borders; and how that style is further promoted by the European Commission's most recent policy documents on 'Services of General Interest'.[28] As these developments are taking place in synchrony, it emerges that the legal protection of public service values is a matter which, throughout Europe's economies, has become rather unsettled and subject to readjustment; equally, that there is a real risk, especially in view of the considerable influence and sophistication developed by the Community's competition rules which Prosser analyses in some detail,[29] that competition law becomes the 'default' regime for the organisation and delivery of public services; that risk makes it, again, 'far more necessary to determine which special considerations may limit the application of competition law fully to public services'.[30]

[22] p. 238.   [23] p. 106.   [24] p. 107.   [25] p. 239.   [26] p. 236.
[27] p. 238.   [28] discussed in Chapter 7.
[29] Chapter 6, but also in the chapters detailing the position in France, Italy and the UK.
[30] p. 27.

It is perhaps unsurprising therefore that a large part of the book is dedicated to Community law and its role in clarifying the convergent 'complexities' amongst European legal systems identified above. That role, it turns out, is rather more ambiguous than a superficial analysis would suggest. Prosser uses especially the final parts of his book to demonstrate how EC law, initially a trigger for liberalization and an economics-driven competition law, has increasingly proven the place where synergies between social rights and free market rights are sought. According to Prosser, EC law has recently developed a 'degree of synthesis of substantive principles' between competition law and public service values.[31] Most importantly, there is now 'a growing body of "hard law" of public service' in EC law.[32] This is most eminent, according to Prosser, in the Court of Justice's case law. He finds that 'the approach of the European courts has changed, from treating public services (or 'services of general interest') as unwelcome impediments to completing the single internal market to seeing them instead as independently valuable expressions of citizenship rights'.[33] Moreover, Prosser stresses that the recognition of services of general economic interest in both Art. 16 of the EC Treaty and also in Art. 36 of the Charter of Fundamental Rights could indicate that they may be afforded some 'form of constitutional status'.[34]

The argument (III): public service is more than market failure

Finally, then, these considerations underline the weight of Prosser's central argument, where clearly, he takes issue with the efficiency arguments put forward by those in favour of a virtually unlimited application of competition law to public services.[35] Such a view would, according to Prosser, create havoc with public service values, most importantly the value of social solidarity and universal access, as it would prioritize the legitimacy of competition law and treat public service law 'as a means of mopping up residual problems' where the competition rules identify a situation of market failure.[36] Instead, the protection of social solidarity and social rights on the one hand, as well as, on the other hand, that of market efficiency and consumer choice, should be recognized individually, each as having a 'distinct value', a 'legitimacy of its own', neither of which should be ignored.[37] 'Public service should not be reduced to a minimum, such as only basic universal service requirements, applicable merely in cases of market failure'.[38]

In a second, quite distinct, argument, Prosser advocates that in the exercise of balancing, in any one case, between the 'market' values of efficiency and consumer choice on the one hand, and 'public service' criteria embedding social and economic rights and social solidarity, on the other, law ought to play a central role. A body of binding 'hard' public service laws, as opposed to political forms of

---

[31] p. 239.   [32] p. 245.   [33] p. 15.   [34] p. 15.
[35] See eg his discussion of the conception of 'efficiency' on pp. 20–24.
[36] p. 244.   [37] p. 244.   [38] p. 244.

control or non-binding 'soft' norms, are, in Prosser's view, necessary to limit the application of the 'hard' competition rules. One reason for this is most apparent. 'In a conflict between the "hard law" of competition and the "soft law" of public service, the latter is unlikely to survive as a source of distinctive values.'[39] It is slightly less obvious why politics should not take over the task of securing public service values, to counter a competition law that may be driven exclusively by the demands of efficiency. This could be done, for example, by 'using the social security and taxation systems to adjust initial distributions and then to leave the market and competition law to operate unhindered'.[40] Prosser's answer to suggestions of this kind is straightforward. First, according to Prosser, 'redistribution on this scale and the adoption of such a strict distinction between types of intervention is highly unlikely'.[41] He points out that '[i]n the UK currently the Government does not even publish the levels of assistance provided in income support to pay for utility bills'.[42] Secondly, he finds a more profound theoretical flaw with such arguments, as they fail to accredit a rather more fully developed account of 'citizenship' than one based on 'market citizenship'. Law, in order to take account of an 'inclusive' form of citizenship, ought not only to confer rights on individuals, but also to acknowledge the value of 'social solidarity' amongst the members of the community that it is supposed to govern. It therefore ought to express, in the form of public service laws, the 'duties of the community to secure such inclusiveness, resting both on a moral sense of equal citizenship and a more prudential goal of minimizing social fragmentation'.[43]

Assessment

It is, as the general editors note, a 'real strength' of Prosser's book 'that the interplay between [public service law and competition law] is examined from a number of different perspectives',[44] namely at European level and throughout various national systems, and also by means of sector-specific case studies (most extensively on public utilities and public broadcasting). In doing so, the book draws together a subject-matter which, in practice, has recently developed considerable coherence, but has never before been systematically explored in as much depth as that provided by Tony Prosser. Moreover, it raises some specific queries that helpfully lay out further routes of research and investigation.

The first of those relates to the suitability of EC law, and EU law generally, to protect social rights in the future. Prosser takes a relatively optimistic view, based on most recent documents adopted by the Council and by the Commission, and on the Court's jurisprudence. Yet he leaves no doubt that the standing and protection of social and economic rights across Europe 'remain[s] more controversial' than 'traditional political and civil rights such as the right to vote and freedom of expression',[45] most noted in the 'limitations on the enforceability' of

---

[39] p. 245.   [40] p. 37.   [41] p. 34.   [42] p. 34.   [43] p. 35.
[44] general editors' preface.   [45] p. 31.

the EU Charter of Fundamental Rights.[46] These limitations are in contrast to the directly enforceable market access rights afforded to corporations that desire to take on the provision of a particular (public) service.

Prosser's account unveils a second, related, and fundamental query, namely whether a European social solidarity model presents a feasible alternative to the current state of affairs, where social solidarity remains philosophically linked to 'the [nation] state as moral unifier standing above the struggles of civil society'.[47] The textual indications for such a development—most noted, in the context of public services, in Art. 16 EC Treaty—are supremely loose ('Member States...shall take care'), their meaning 'contested' and their direct effect 'doubtful'.[48] It is not difficult to see how, without a firm concept of European social solidarity serving as the moral and philosophical pedestal, the abstract language of social 'rights' insufficiently addresses the imbalance between those rights and the market access rights of service providers. For example, Prosser describes the principles underlying public service, particularly in France ('equality', 'neutrality' and 'adaptability'), as 'notoriously difficult and elusive',[49] which allows them to be 'treated flexibly' and leaves them, in practice, as symbolic statements more than values of direct application.[50] The same could be said of a set of social rights, unless it is ensured that relevant authorities, especially those 'independent regulatory authorities' Prosser identifies as emerging as part of a European regulatory 'style', take them on board and are being held accountable for doing so. To some extent, the 'Europeanization' of standards relating to universal access, continuity, transparency, quality and consumer protection, derived in the context of utilities liberalization, could be interpreted as an emergent European social solidarity principle. Thus, Prosser notes, 'the Community has acquired considerable experience in the liberalized but regulated sectors such as electronic communications (formerly telecommunications) and energy. In combination with developing interest in good governance in the Community, this has provided a substantial body of experience which can now be generalized to other areas of services of general interest.'[51] These experiences may have added some flesh to the bones of a European social solidarity principle, in that they allow for a more concrete application and enforcement of social access rights. In particular, they lay stress on the importance of accountability standards that can serve to hold service providers, but also the independent regulators themselves, responsible for their respective decisions. However, in the absence of a more fully developed political citizenship at European level, it is again difficult to see how those standards translate into the full array of the philosophical and moral arguments founding social solidarity in the nation state. Similar to the separation proposed by the French into the substantive elements of the *service public* doctrine (a matter for the state, ie public law), on the one hand, and its formal implementation

---

[46] p. 34; in this context, see his discussion on pp. 31–34. [47] p. 36. [48] p. 33.
[49] p. 97. [50] p. 239. [51] p. 173, footnote omitted.

(a matter, if necessary, for the market, ie economic law), on the other, it would seem that the substantive elements of social solidarity—the moral obligation to look after the weaker (economically, socially, geographically) parts of the community, based on the acceptance that a society is faced with inequalities, and 'we do not come to the market as equals'[52]—is still very much embedded within the nation state. What is in the process of being 'Europeanized', or, put differently, what Member States are increasingly prepared to delegate to the Community level, is the supervision of the methods that practically give expression to the (national) solidarity principle.

A third, more unsettling, query emerges, namely whether the substantive content of the social solidarity principle itself, irrespective of its national or European character, is subject to change, in that it is affected by a conscious political choice to accept 'less' solidarity, in order to move towards 'more' individualism, exemplified by the liberal free market. Taking again the French public service principles as an example, they 'appear outdated through assuming that the state has a much more fundamental and far reaching role in the economy than is now the case in Western economies'.[53] One may conclude from this, as have indicated above, that a European social solidarity principle would be more modern and appropriate, although doubts exist as to its feasibility. Yet an alternative conclusion suggests that the concept of solidarity, quite simply, is so inextricably linked to the nation state, that whilst the political and economic significance of global institutions (most noted the Community) is continuously growing, the philosophy of solidarity is left to dissipate. It is certainly not within the spirit of Tony Prosser's book to conclude on such a pessimistic note. Prosser finds that the Community increasingly concerns itself with the improvements that can be made to public services, in order to make them 'more responsive to social values as those underlying universal service'.[54] In the United Kingdom, a 'new public service law' has taken hold as a consequence of social standards produced by, and imposed on, both regulators and service providers in the privatized utilities sectors, but also in public broadcasting.[55] However, Prosser also speaks a clear and compelling language, which does take seriously the potential threat posed by economic law, and competition law in particular, to the concept of social solidarity. He accentuates his arguments, finally, by reminding again of the need 'to protect the distinctive values of public service within our growing body of economic law'.[56]

Mention should be made finally of an issue closely related in practice to Prosser's investigation of public service law's underlying objective, namely to provide a mechanism ensuring the accountability of public service providers to central and local government, and, eventually, to the general public. Prosser concentrates his analysis at the 'macro-level' of accountability, scrutinizing the means and methods by which governments, regulatory authorities, and increasingly the EU authorities,

---

[52] p. 29.   [53] p. 105.   [54] p. 172.
[55] Discussed in Chapters 4, 8 and 9.   [56] p. 246.

impose substantive obligations on undertakings in the interest of substantive regulatory goals, such as the provision of a universal service. He draws attention to the 'micro level', the organization and governance internally of those firms carrying out the function of a public service provider (and implicitly to the behaviour of their shareholders and employees), only in passing. In one instance, he does so by reference to a 'public service ethic', assessed by criteria such as 'impartiality, accountability, trust, equity, probity and service'.[57] These criteria denote that the obligations traditionally imposed on public servants are culturally grown and distinct from those applicable to ordinary employees approaching customers in the context of a regular business transaction. The existence of such an ethic indicates that the public will traditionally expect, from those who provide public services, a degree of integrity that goes beyond that expected in a mere business relationship. Where private corporations take on the role of public service providers, it lies with the public authorities, but also within the organization of the firm itself, to ensure that these standards are not lowered. In legal terms, then, the regime dealing with issues of corporate governance, comprising both compulsory company law, but also voluntary means of self-regulation and self-assessment of corporate organization, intersects with the regime that sets and enforces public service obligations, to the extent that they both aim at ensuring the firms' compliance with certain culturally embedded public service criteria.

Prosser, for a second time, expressly refers to an issue broadly related to corporate governance when he discusses the drawbacks of using the concept of market efficiency as a justification for the application of competition law to public services. He argues that productive efficiency, whilst it is generally seen as a positive consequence of the market encouraging providers to 'tighten' their production and organization processes and eliminating wasteful bureaucratic inefficiencies, can eventually lead to the 'squeezing of investment in the search for short-term efficiency gains, putting longer-term security of supply at risk'; further, he points out that the 'competitive pressures' amongst firms may prevent 'useful collaboration between enterprises providing public services'.[58]

A fundamental issue underlying both of Prosser's references to the behaviour of public service providers, especially corporate providers, is of course whether corporations in their present form, built on the primary objective of furthering their shareholders' interest, are institutionally suited to take on the responsibility of providing services, especially in subject areas related to the social realm, that are essential to the well-being and well-functioning of a society. The question as to how, and to what extent, they should be involved in providing public services, and how they should be held accountable if they are involved, is a matter to be decided by the government(s), having a choice between competition law and public service law, or a mixture of the two, as Prosser amply illustrates. However, once they are involved, corporate law inevitably becomes relevant, most pertinently

[57] p. 3.   [58] p. 22.

on issues of corporate governance. Given the current trends favouring their increasing involvement, again illustrated thanks to Prosser's thorough account, it would seem that the intersection between, on the one hand, laws pertaining to corporate governance, and on the other hand, laws protecting public service obligations, is growing.

Conclusion

Prosser's basic argument that competition law must not apply without any limitation to public services (such as public utilities, public transport, energy or public broadcasting), because 'there are certain values in the form of social and economic rights that will trump competition law'[59] is unlikely to meet with extensive criticism. For one, there is by now broad agreement amongst EU Member States, supported by the Commission, on a set of public service obligations that would seem to embody those 'values'. Moreover, the EU itself has taken on board from its Members the idea of social solidarity, that 'the state has duties to ensure equal treatment of citizens irrespective of their economic resources', most notably since Art. 16 was introduced into the EC Treaty.[60]

Yet the scope of those limits, and, moreover, what legal regime determines their ambit are issues of considerable controversy indeed. As can be seen from the foregoing, Prosser's account unveils the weaknesses of competition law's 'efficiency' mantra, yet on closer scrutiny, the 'social solidarity' principle or those 'social and economic rights' forming the basis for many public service laws, certainly those following the traditionally 'Continental' approach, are not without flaws either. Most importantly, their role in providing a basis to counter extensive liberalization, following the European programme, has not been convincing. Possibly, that is a consequence of their being 'notoriously difficult and elusive'.[61] Furthermore, it has been seen that the EU's role in developing a (European) social solidarity principle or to strengthen social and economic rights, is full of ambiguity. Prosser's stand on these issues is, in a nutshell, critical but optimistic. One may or may not agree with either of those assessments, yet the author must certainly be credited for having put forward, with much skill and energy, a coherent and compelling argument.

NINA BOEGER

The European Union, A Polity of States and People by Walter van Gerven, (Oxford: Hart Publishing, 2005), 416pp. ISBN 1-84113-529-1.

It is not a novelty to say that scholarly work in the field of law primarily derives its human resources from two main categories of professionals: Professors and practitioners. EU Law is no exception to this observation. However, what is unique in

[59] p. 34.   [60] p. 35.   [61] p. 97.

this legal branch is that EU Law professors and practitioners frequently possess certain characteristics that differentiate them from legal professionals working in other fields of law. As EU law has developed progressively and alongside the transformation of EU juridico-political institutions, law scholars have tradition-ally played a key part in the evolution of substantive law, and have contributed significantly to the emergence of some of the most important cornerstones of EU legal doctrine. Working often with inter-disciplinary tools and through comparative studies, many such scholars have shown great skill in evaluating legal provisions not only in EC law but also comparatively, looking at EU law as an autonomous legal subject that derives many of its traits from the national law of the Member States, yet filters them through the Community system. On the other hand, practitioners within the EU institutions have long shed valuable light on somewhat obscure provisions of primary or secondary EU law and offered pertinent interpretations of what have sometimes appeared as highly technical pieces of legislation. Since the authority of their opinions emanates from an inten-sive and frequently long, legal career within the European institutions, they are often capable of providing assistance in navigating complex European legal issues that call for considerable expertise and experience.

Walter van Gerven belongs to an exclusive category of EU law scholars who combine those two varieties in one person. After serving as Advocate General at the European Court of Justice, he taught EU Law at the Universities of Louvain and Maastricht and published extensively in the field. Benefiting from a dual—practitioner and theorist—point of view, he engages in a fully-fledged comparative analysis of EU constitutionalism with regard to the major legal systems of the world (including France, Germany and the UK) and grants special attention to the American legal paradigm. The latter is explored throughout the book both horizontally (with respect to the organizational scheme adopted on the federal level) and vertically (institutional relations between the national and state governments) and constitutes a tremendously enriching source for drawing comparative conclu-sions. Another significant characteristic of the book is its use of multi-disciplinary sources, especially those of history and political science. Although the book is primarily addressed to lawyers, historical references, usually preceding the substantive legal analysis of the various themes, make the text accessible to a larger public.

The author's language is clear and comprehensible, leaving no room for doubt about his argument. With the declared aim of making his book accessible to a broad public, whenever EU legal terminology appears in the text (however basic for lawyers it may be) Professor van Gerven provides a definition which operates as a conceptual introduction to the subsequent arguments for the general public and as a helpful refresher for lawyers. Interestingly, the numerous references to well-established ECJ and other case law used in the text, while known to the average EU legal scholar, are placed in novel contexts that frequently introduce original ideas and interpretations. The structure followed covers all the basic sub-categories of EU Constitutional Law.

In the first chapter of his book Professor van Gerven provides a comprehensive account of the EU institutional architecture. He refers to a range of key issues such as the Community institutions, pillars of competence, legislative procedures and the role of the Parliament. He then analyses the role of Member States, the importance of the Commission, the role of 'comitology' in the exercise of the Community executive power, the doctrine of separation of powers and the allocations of competences under the third pillar, concluding with the importance of the 'acquis communautaire' and the divided sovereignty doctrine, making constructive cross-references to the US legal paradigm.

The author clearly adheres to the institutional characterization of the EU as an international organization with a unitary character, and not just a Treaty, subscribing overtly to the well-known scholarly analyis by Ige Dekker and Deirdre Curtin. According to this theory, he sees the second and third pillars as parts of the supranational rather than intergovernmental structure of the Union, and argues that from an international relations point of view the Union behaves as one legal person under all the three pillars. However, he raises the issue of the 'statehood' of the Union to argue persuasively that its current status does not enable it to be described as State or Nation State. Alternatively, he suggests the non-legal term 'citizens state' to describe the Union's *physis*. In search of Europe's cultural identity as the cornerstone of European citizenship, van Gerven provides a very interesting historical account of the consecutive layers of civilization that forged modern European identity and that confine the European public space. This identity has consequences for the emphasis placed on certain values that underpin the European edifice and give it its constitutional particularity.

The next three chapters are devoted to the broad question of democracy within the European Union. The author examines the organization of public power under a government, the pursuit of good governance and the subordination of both to the rule of law within the European Union. With regard to the first of these topics, Van Gerven provides a complete list of executive accountability mechanisms, including political responsibility, that exist in different States, to compare it with how members of the European Commission, the Union's executive, and of the administrative agencies are held liable in cases of mismanagement, fraud, corruption or nepotism. Acknowledging the importance of open government and free access to public documents as cornerstones of transparency and control of Community officials, the author also finds that tribunals of inquiry and criminal law proceedings, which are already in use in several Member States, may be (partially) transposable to the Community legal order. Futhermore, he predicts that the prospective emergence of regulatory agencies within the Union will render necessary the extension of effective control mechanisms to these also.

In the following chapter, the author compares the concepts of rule of law and *Rechstaat*, its German—somewhat different—version, to the judicial review doctrine, as guarantor of the respect for human rights and fundamental freedoms. After a thorough description of the relevant systems and institutions in the United

Kingdom and Germany, he turns to the judicial review exercised by the Court of Justice through the mechanisms of the action for annulment (Art. 230 EC), action for damages (Art. 288 EC) and preliminary reference (Art. 234 EC). Here, references to ECJ case law are abundant and shed valuable light on the judicial construction and interpretation of the relevant procedures. In addition, protection of fundamental rights both in the US and the EU occupies a significant part of the chapter with extensive references to the American Constitution, particularly its first, fifth and fourteenth Amendments, to the Charter of Fundamental Rights, pointing out its significance in granting the benefit of certain rights even to non citizens, and to the European Convention of Human Rights. With regard to the relevant case law, the author finds many resemblances between the ECJ judgment in *Hauer* and US Supreme Court's decisions on the protection of fundamental rights under the due process clause.

One of the most interesting parts of the book is that concerning the principle of legal certainty and its components, the attribution of powers to the Community institutions, and the principles of subsidiarity and proportionality. In that part of the book the author provides an in-depth analysis of the interstate commerce clause of the US Constitution and the evolving interpretation the US Supreme Court has given to it during the 19th and 20th centuries, starting from a traditionally expansive interpretation of Congress' powers to regulate even intrastate commerce to the recent restriction on Congress' power to regulate interstate activities illustrated in such contemporary cases as *United States v. Lopez* and *United States v. Morrison*. Van Gerven also finds resemblances between the ECJ judgments in *Dasonville* and *Cassis de Dijon* on the one hand and the US Supreme Court case law with regard to the state 'legitimate interests' limitation on the other, which is imposed on Congress' power to regulate interstate commerce, amongst other things.

Chapter 4 covers the broad notion of 'Good Governance', under the umbrella of which the author explores integrity and ethical behavior, efficiency and effectiveness, equality of citizens and social justice for all. Former Advocate General van Gerven grants special importance to the principle of equality in law, which has been substantively transformed during its judicial itinerary within the Union. Initially conceived as a prohibition of discrimination on grounds of nationality and gender with respect to the internal market freedoms and equal pay respectively, the principle has gradually ecnompassed 'peripheral' market participants, such as tourists, as beneficiaries of social services, and has become a general principle of equal treatment irrespective of nationality or gender. In that respect, the author sees one more resemblance with the equal protection clause laid down in the Fourteenth and Fifth Amendments to the US Constitution. Similarities also exist in the way affirmative action and limits thereupon are construed in both jurisdictions, with the teleological difference that while in the US the principle aims basically in correcting race discrimination in the European Union it has served primarily as a tool against gender discrimination.

One domain of profound difference between the American and the European constitutional systems is, according to the author and others, social security and health care. While one of the main ambitions of the Union as set forth in the Charter of Fundamental Rights is to provide a comprehensive social security system, including health care, for all, the United States social security system seems reserved exclusiviely to those who are no longer capable of taking care of themselves. The author seeks the root of this difference in the different mentality of Americans as compared to Europeans, in that the former possess a strong tradition of independence 'from any history, inhereted status or even community'. This independence, the author goes on, seems to underpin the principle of freedom of choice, which is seen as the reason why Americans do not feel the need for state safety-nets as much as Europeans. However, it is difficult to accept that Americans do not adhere to communities given that the whole socio-cultural model of the United States is based on the co-existence of different ethnic, religious and race communities under the same federal government. If those communities are capable of financially maintaining a plethora of collective activities such as prayer, arts and culture, one sees no reason why they couldn't reasonably abritate local social security systems in a more or less formal way. This mere observation suffices to search US hostility *vis-à-vis* publicly held social security systems in other values such as an increased sense of self-responsibility and lowered expectations from a government which is more seen as a partner rather than a superposing authority.

Transparency and open government are regarded by the author as fields where the influence of national legal provisions of Nordic States and the Netherlands have been of catalytic influence to the EU legislation, in particular insofar as the expansion of free access of documents within the European Union is concerned. Furthermore, the accrued importance of interest groups and political parties in the decision-making process on the EU level has been underscored by the emergence of lobbying groups operating in Brussels, in a way parallel to which the organizations operate in the United States. These latter tend to be part of new modes of governance, whereby the European Union, Member States and NGOs work close to achieve a major political aim. Although the author acknowledges the advantages of this intense co-operartion, he seems sceptical as to the 'govern-mentalization' of private actors and their role in the exercise of public executive powers. His main concern appears to be the risk of losing a significant part of their autonomy in the pursuit of 'citizen' goals. Notwithstanding the potential risks that emanate from a partnership between public and private actors in the public policy sphere, the advantages of this *cohabitation* seem to largely outweigh this drawback: As private actors usually adopt far less bureaucratic structures than public institutions they are more likely to achieve a higher level of efficiency in the pursuit of a public policy. Moreover, their direct contact with the people may be of quintessential importance to a fair and reasonable allocation of public money. Last but not least, they can operate as pools of massive financial contribution of private individuals without the restraints of time and form usually imposed on the State/Community level, offering additionally the moral reward of charity.

The freedom of press as means of public dissemination of opinions is examined both in the European Union and the United States where it is common ground that state legislative restrictions are less likely to be tolerated by the federal constitutional order as no limitations are provided for in the First Amedement. By contrast, Art. 10 (2) of the European Convention of Human Rights subjects the exercise of the freedom of press to a considerable list of compelling interests that can be taken into account whenever Member States are willing to impose legislative limitation to the right.

In the sixth chapter of the book the author offers a detailed account of the new Treaty establishing a Constitution for Europe, including the procedure within the Convention and its material provisions, with special regard to the horizontal and vertical allocaton of powers, legislative procedures and qualified majority voting, the amending procedure and an overview of the new architecture of EU institutions. Unfortunately, in the present stage of the ratification process, it seems highly unlikely that the text in its current form will ever become binding. Contrary to the author's estimation that none of the Member States would take the responsibility of 'turning the constitution-making endeavor into a failure and risk that other Member States leave them behind', the recent French and Dutch *referenda* clearly stood for the exactly opposite proposition. Not only did they demonstrate that the people rose against their own government's pro-Constitution positions but also they seem to drag with them the remaining Member States towards non-ratification. Given this result, apparently not surprising to the political elites of France at least, the relevant provisions of the Treaty of Nice obtain increased importance as fall-back constitutional text.

In the last chapter of the book Professor Walter van Gerven raises the issue of the best form of government for the European Union. After laying down the alternatives existing in both coasts of the Atlantic, ranging from the Presidential system of the United States passing from the mixed French and German regimes to arrive to the British strong parliamentary tradition, he considers Lijphart's 'consensus democracy with a strong executive' to be the most appropriate form of government for the Union. Strong executive meaning an already powerful and polyvalent Commission, consensus democracy largely involves a reform of euro-parties to reinforce their ideological identity so that they adopt solid positions in issues of European interest and European voters exert their European civic rights upon transnational lists through e-voting. As the author accurately observes, the success of the whole enterprise, ie, involving political parties and citizens in the selection of the European government, will depend upon the will of Member State and Community political elites to let the peoples take over the ongoing process of integration with the risk of dramatically slowing down its pace. As van Gerven correctly points out, whatever the pragmatic drawbacks of this shift to the peoples may be, its necessity is politically and constitutionally justified by the need to increase legitimacy in the Union, a demand that, albeit present in several Community documents and scholarly opinions, has never been taken seriously into account by the political elites.

Overall, the book is an extremely helpful comparative instrument that seeks to understand EU constitutionalism in conjuction with the American institutional paradigm taken in its entirety. Written by a leading EU law scholar who served as Advocate General in the ECJ, Law Professor in the Universities of Leuven and Maastricht, and had the opportunity to spend a sabbatical year at Stanford Law School, it offers a substantive insight on European governance in both a juridical and a politico-historical perspective, in its current stage and in its potential future form. Although theoretical divergence may exist sporadically over issues involving a considerable amount of political discretion, one is bound to recognize the completeness of the work, the author's extensive comparative skills including an in-depth understanding of the world's major political systems, the benefits of engaging in original interdisciplinary analyses and the focal interest that the book will present over the next years given the increasing relevance of the issues it covers. In sum, a must-read for all EU lawyers.

DIONYSIOS V. TSIROS

Table of Cases

COURT OF FIRST INSTANCE (ALPHABETICAL ORDER)

COURT OF FIRST INSTANCE (NUMERICAL ORDER)

EUROPEAN COURT OF JUSTICE (ALPHABETICAL ORDER)

EUROPEAN COURT OF JUSTICE (NUMERICAL ORDER)

TABLE OF COMMISSION DECISIONS

TABLE OF COUNCIL DECISIONS

EUROPEAN COURT OF HUMAN RIGHTS

WORLD TRADE ORGANIZATION

TABLE OF NATIONAL CASES

Denmark

France

TABLE OF OPINIONS

Table of Legislation

Index